CRIMINAL LAW

CRIMINAL LAW

Sweet & Maxwell's Textbook Series

4th edition

Alan Reed, M.A., LL.M., Solicitor
Professor of Criminal and Private International Law,
University of Sunderland

and

Ben Fitzpatrick, B.A., P.G.C.L.T.H.E.
Director of Undergraduate Programmes, York Law School,
University of York

Consultant Editor: Peter Seago, O.B.E., J.P., LL.M
Former Head of Law, University of Leeds

SWEET & MAXWELL

THOMSON REUTERS

First edition 1999
Second edition 2002
Third edition 2006
Fourth edition 2009
by Alan Reed, Ben Fitzpatrick and Peter Seago

Published in 2009 by
Sweet & Maxwell Limited of
100 Avenue Road, London NW3 3PF
(http://www.sweetandmaxwell.co.uk)
Typeset by J.P. Price of Chilcompton, Somerset
Printed in Great Britain by
Ashford Colour Press, Gosport, Hants

No natural forests were destroyed to make this product;
only farmed timber was used and replanted

British Library Cataloguing in Publication Data
A CIP catalogue record for this book is available from the British Library

ISBN: 9781847037404

PREFACE

Criminal law, for many students, turns out to be a rather different subject from the one they were expecting. Media representations of the criminal justice process suggest a world of tension-filled policing and courtroom drama, where much of the focus is on the *facts* of a case, on what happened, rather than on the criminal law itself. However, underpinning any discussion, factual or fictitious, of the criminal justice process, is the possibly more mundane question of what behaviour amounts to a criminal offence. Thus, if the question in a television drama is whether a suspect has committed murder, somebody needs to know what, at law, constitutes the offence of murder. It is this question, applied to a variety of different offences, which is the core task of the criminal lawyer.

We will see that every criminal offence is made up of what amounts to a set of ingredients. If any of those ingredients is missing, the offence is not committed. Thus, if you dishonestly take what you believe is somebody else's property, but it is in fact your own, you cannot steal it, because one ingredient of the offence of theft is that the property in question "belongs to another".

In the first part of the book, we will look at how to work in a general way with the ingredients of offences, before moving on to apply the knowledge of general principles to specific offences. We have not tried to cover every principle, or every offence, in the same level of detail, or to the same depth. Instead, we have tried to focus on those issues which dominate traditional criminal law courses, and which raise particular intellectual challenges.

We have tried to make clear that the criminal law can be a rather troublesome subject. It does not always seem to make sense, and, rather than try to rationalise it where to do so would be impossible, we have attempted, where appropriate, to make clear the basis on which we find the law problematic. We have considered various possibilities for reform of the law, and have referred regularly to the vast body of work in this regard undertaken by the Law Commission.

Despite its troublesome nature, we hope that students find the subject stimulating and challenging. Criminal law operates in the area in which the interests of citizens conflict with each other, and where the state claims a legitimate stake in people's behaviour. It is therefore one of many ideal subjects for developing an understanding of how society fits together, and is regulated.

There is no ideal time to write a criminal law textbook, as the subject moves sufficiently quickly to leave one's work at the whim of significant judicial decision, a law reform proposal, or heightened media interest in a particular issue. Major developments since the last edition of which we have taken account include the Fraud Act 2006, Corporate Manslaughter and Corporate Homicide Act 2007, and Serious Crime Act 2007; the House of Lords decisions in *Rahman* (complicity) and *Kennedy (No.2)* (drug administration and unlawful act manslaughter) are evaluated; significant Court of Appeal decisions in relation to the Sexual Offences Act 2003 and consent are explored, notably *Bree, Devonald, Singh (Jheeta), R. v EB* and *Heard*; developments in other areas especially over full and partial defences in *Wilson, Rashford,* and *Wood* are set out; and see also the initiatives in *Carey, Dhaliwal* and *Rafferty* on causation. The radical proposals of the Law Commission on homicide, complicity, attempts and conspiracy, and intoxication are explored in context.

We should like to acknowledge the help we have received from many people in the preparation of this book. Our work has been supported by a team of consummate professionals at Sweet and Maxwell. They have displayed tolerance beyond the call of duty as they have shepherded the text to production.

We welcome feedback and suggestions from our readers. We have tried to state the law, as we understand it, to March 31, 2009.

A.R.
B.F.

TABLE OF CONTENTS

Preface   v
Table of Cases   xv
Table of Statutes   xlix
Table of Statutory Instruments   lvii

1. Introduction   1

What this book is about, and what it is not about   1
The purposes of criminal law   2
Classifying criminal offences and the structure of the courts   4
The significance of proof   7
Who has to prove what? The burden of proof   7
How much proof is needed? The standard of proof   8
Conclusion   9

2. Actus Reus and Mens Rea: The Elements of an Offence   11

Actus Reus   14
The need for voluntary conduct   15
Has the defendant introduced evidence of automatism?   18
What is the cause of the automatism?   20
Evidential and legal burdens   21
Self-induced automatism   22
Criminal liability in the "state of affairs" cases   23
Liability for failing to act   25
In which crimes may liability be incurred for an omission?   27
Who is under a duty to act   29
Medical treatment   34
Conclusion on omissions   36
Causation   36
A substantial cause   39
Take your victim as you find him   40

Supervening events	41
Actus reus: general reading	57
Mens Rea	57
Introduction	57
What can constitute mens rea?	59
Intention	60
Negligence and recklessness	66
Negligence	67
Recklessness	68
Knowledge	74
Coincidence of actus reus and mens rea	75
Transferred malice	79
Mistake as a defence to crime	82
The basic problem	82
Mistake and Lawfulness	84
Mens rea: general reading	86

3. Strict Liability — 89

Who created this genre of crimes?	90
How can crimes of strict liability be identified?	90
The wording of the act	91
Crimes and Quasi crimes	97
Smallness of the penalty	102
Modern principles for strict liability	103
Defences to offences of strict liability	107
Why do we have crimes of strict liability at all?	109
General reading	111

4. Parties to Criminal Offences — 113

Principal and Secondary Offenders	113
Introduction	113
The principal or perpetrator	115
Secondary parties	117
Knowledge of the type of crime	118
Aids, Abets, Counsels or Procures	120
Joint enterprise	127
The nature of joint enterprise	127
Joint enterprise and murder	128
Liability for unforeseen consequences	136
Is there a need to distinguish between joint enterprise and accessoryship liability	144
Hypothetical example	146
Reform	148
The need for an actus reus	149
The commisison of the actus reus	149
No principal offender	150

Previous acquittal of the principal offender 151
Joint trial of principal and secondary parties 151
Victims as parties to an offence 154
Repentance by a secondary party before the crime is committed 155
Reforming the law on complicity and joint enterprise 159
Assistance given after the commission of the crime 160
General reading 161
Vicarious and Corporate Liability 161
Vicarious liability 162
Express statutory vicarious liability 163
Implied vicarious liability 163
The licensee cases 164
Inapplicability of vicarious liability 167
Summary 167
Conclusion 168
Corporate liability 168
General principles 168
Liability of individual 173
Are there any crimes a company cannot commit? 173
A new offence: the Corporate Manslaughter and Corporate Homicide Act 2007 176
Summary 179
General reading 179

5. General Defences
181

The Mentally Abnormal Offender: Insanity and Unfitness to Plead 181
The defences of insanity and diminished responsibility 186
Insanity 186
Diminished responsibility 195
Hospital orders 202
Conclusions 202
The mentally abnormal offender: general reading 206
Intoxication 206
Voluntary intoxication 207
Involuntary intoxication 215
Self-induced automatism and non-harmful drugs 217
Insanity and diminished responsibility produced by intoxication 219
Drinking with intent 220
Proposals for reform 221
Intoxication: general reading 221
Self-defence, Necessity and Duress 221
Self-defence: the use of force in public and private defence 222
Prevention of crime 223
Self-defence and defence of others 224
Defence of property 226
Excessive force 227
Summary 234
General reading 235

Necessity   236
    Necessity and the killing of another   236
    Necessity and medical treatment   238
    Necessity and statutory legislation   242
    Necessity as a general defence   243
General reading   244
Duress   244
    General background   244
    The ambit of the duress defence   246
    The constituents of duress   252
    Duress and the voluntary joining of criminal associations   262
    Duress of circumstances   265
General reading   269
Infancy   270
    Children under 10 years of age   270
    Children 10 years old and above   270
Entrapment   272
    Y's liability   273
    X's liability   273
General reading   274
Superior Orders   274
General reading   275

6. The Inchoate Offences   277

Attempts   278
    General principles   278
    Actus reus   280
    Mens rea   288
    Are all attempted offences crimes of specific intent?   293
    Attempting the impossible   294
    Acts of preparation   298
    General reading   299
Encouragement or Assistance   299
Conspiracy   305
    General overview   305
    The actus reus in conspiracy   307
        Rationale and the requirement of an agreement   307
        The object of the agreement   309
        Parties to the agreement   314
        Acquittal of a co-conspirator   316
    The mental element in conspiracy   317
        Recklessness as to circumstances will not do   317
        Course of conduct   319
        Intention on the part of each conspirator   320
        Active partipation in the course of conduct   322
        Conditional intention   323
    Impossibility   325

Territorial jurisdiction 325
General reading 326

7. Offences Against the Person 329

General Introduction 329
Who can commit an offence against the person? 330
Who can be the victim of an offence against the person? 330
The unborn child 331
When do you cease to be a human being? 332
Unlawful Homicide 334
Murder and Manslaughter 335
The penalty for murder and manslaughter 336
The actus reus of murder and manslaughter 337
The mens rea of murder 338
The killing of a human being 339
Mens rea on the other external elements of murder 340
Reforming the Law of Murder 341
Voluntary and Involuntary Manslaughter 342
Voluntary Manslaughter 342
The nature of provocation 342
Cooling-off period: a gender issue? 345
The role of judge and jury 347
Self-induced provocation 348
The dual test for provocation 349
The objective question 349
Control characteristics: recent developments 352
Reform 357
Provocation: general reading 359
Involuntary Manslaughter 359
Unlawful act manslaughter 360
The act must be unlawful in itself 361
The unlawful act in drug administration 364
The act must not only be unlawful; it must also be dangerous 365
Must the unlawful act be "aimed at" the particular victim? 367
The unlawful and dangerous act must be the cause of death 369
Gross negligence manslaughter 370
Further categories of involuntary manslaughter? 375
The future of involuntary manslaughter 376
Other Unlawful Homicides 377
Suicide 377
Infanticide 378
Causing death by dangerous driving 378
Homicide: general reading 379
Non-Fatal Offences Against the Person 380
The general framework 380
Common assault 381
Assault 381

The actus reus of battery 385
Mens rea of assault and battery 390
Assault occasioning actual bodily harm 390
Occasioning actual bodily harm 391
Actual bodily harm 391
Mens rea 393
The offences under sections 20 and 18 of the Offences Against the Person
    Act 1861 395
Section 20 395
Section 18 401
Miscellaneous notes on offences against the person 403
Alternative verdicts 403
Laser pointers 403
A hierarchy of offences 403
Racially aggravated assaults 403
Consent as a defence to offences against the person 405
To which crimes is consent a defence? 405
The exceptions to the general rule 413
What is consent? 416
Future reforms of the offences against the person and consent .. 418
Reform of non-fatal offences against the person 418
Reform of consent 419
General reading 420
Sexual Offences 420
General 420
Rape 421
Actus Reus 422
Mens rea 431
Assault by penetration 432
Sexual Assault 433
Causing a person to engage in sexual activity without consent .. 434
Sections 5 to 8: Offences against children under 13 435
Child sex offences 437
General reading 438

8. Offences Against Property I 439

Stealing under the Theft Act 1968 439
Theft 441
The actus reus of theft 441
Appropriates 441
Property 457
Belonging to another 461
The mens rea of theft 471
Dishonesty 471
With intention permanently to deprive 476
Conditional intention 481
General reading 482

9. Offences Against Property II

9. Offences Against Property II	**483**
Fraud Under the Fraud Act 2006 and Other Offences Under The Theft Acts	483
Introduction	483
The Fraud Act 2006	485
Fraud	485
Obtaining services dishonestly	490
Ancillary offences under the Act	491
Making Off Without Payment	492
General reading	495
Robbery	496
Summary	499
Burglary	499
Entry	501
As a trespasser	503
A building	505
Part of a building	506
Mens rea	507
Aggravated Burglary	508
Making Unwarranted Demands with Menaces: Blackmail	510
There must be a demand	511
The demand must be accompanied by menaces	511
The demand must be made with a view to gain for the maker or another, or with intent to cause loss to another	513
The demand must be unwarranted	513
Handling	514
The actus reus of handling	515
Stolen goods	515
Handling	518
The mens rea of handling	521
Knowing or believing that the goods were stolen	521
Dishonesty	523
Proof of mens rea	524
Summary on handling	525
Miscellaneous Provisions	526
Offences of temporary deprivation	526
Abstracting electricity	527
Business frauds	527
Advertising rewards	528
Going equipped for stealing	528
Restitution and compensation	528
General reading	528

10. Offences Against Property III

10. Offences Against Property III	**531**
Criminal Damage	531
The basic offence	531

Actus reus   532
Mens rea   534
Aggravated damage   534
Arson   537
Threatening to destroy or damage property (section 2)   537
Possession of anything with intent to damage or destroy property (section 3)   537
The defence of lawful excuse   538
Lawful excuse under section 5   539
Lawful excuse outside of section 5   540
General reading   541

Index   543

TABLE OF CASES

A v DPP [1992] Crim.L.R. 34; [1991] C.O.D. 442 Div Ct 5–099
—— v —— [2003] All E.R. (D) 393 9–029
—— v United Kingdom [1998] 2 F.L.R. 959; [1998] 3 F.C.R. 597; (1999) 27
    E.H.R.R. 611 ECHR 7–073
A (A Juvenile) v Queen [1978] Crim.L.R. 689 CC (Kent) 10–004
A (Children) (Conjoined Twins: Medical Treatment) (No.1), Re [2001] Fam. 147;
    [2001] 2 W.L.R. 480; [2000] 4 All E.R. 961 CA (Civ Div) 5–065, 5–067, 7–004,
                                              7–107
A Hospital v W [2007] EWHC 425 (Fam); [2007] LS Law Medical 273 Fam Div ... 2–030
Abbott v Queen, The [1977] A.C. 755; [1976] 3 W.L.R. 462 PC (Trinidad and
    Tobago) 5–072
Adams v Camfoni [1929] 1 K.B. 95 4–056
— v Queen, The [1995] 1 W.L.R. 52; [1995] B.C.C. 376 PC (New Zealand) 6–036
Airedale NHS Trust v Bland [1993] A.C. 789; [1993] 2 W.L.R. 316 HL 2–025, 2–029,
                                          5–065, 7–005
Albert v Lavin [1982] A.C. 546; [1981] 3 W.L.R. 955; [1981] 3 All E.R. 878 HL 2–084
Allen v Whitehead [1930] 1 K.B. 211 .... 4–054, 4–057
Alphacell Ltd v Woodward [1972] A.C. 824; [1972] 2 W.L.R. 1320 HL 3–006, 3–011,
                                          3–024
Anderton v Ryan [1985] A.C. 560; [1985] 2 W.L.R. 968 HL 6–015, 6–016, 6–017
Andrews v DPP [1937] A.C. 576; (1938) 26 Cr.App.R. 34 HL 7–039, 7–041, 7–048
Attorney General v Able [1984] Q.B. 795; [1983] 3 W.L.R. 845 QBD 6–002, 7–057
Attorney General's Reference (No.1 of 1974), Re [1974] Q.B. 744; [1974] 2 W.L.R.
    891 .... 9–039, 9–051
—— (Nos.1 and 2 of 1979), Re [1980] Q.B. 180; [1979] 3 W.L.R. 577; [1979] 3 All
    E.R. 143 CA (Crim Div) 8–051, 9–029
—— (No.4 of 1980), Re [1981] 1 W.L.R. 705; [1981] 2 All E.R. 617 CA
    (Crim Div) 2–079
—— (No.6 of 1980), Re [1981] Q.B. 715; [1981] 3 W.L.R. 125 CA (Crim Div) 7–101,
                         7–105, 7–106, 7–107, 7–109, 7–112
—— (No.1 of 1982), Re [1983] Q.B. 751; [1983] 3 W.L.R. 72 CA (Crim Div) 6–037,
                                          6–051
—— (No.2 of 1982), Re [1984] Q.B. 624; [1984] 2 W.L.R. 447 CA (Crim Div) 2–006,
                                          8–014
—— (No.1 of 1983), Re [1985] Q.B. 182; [1984] 3 W.L.R. 686 CA (Crim Div) 8–036
—— (No.2 of 1983), Re [1984] Q.B. 456; [1984] 2 W.L.R. 465 CA (Crim Div) 5–049
—— (No.1 of 1985), Re [1986] Q.B. 491; [1986] 2 W.L.R. 733 CA (Crim Div) 8–031,
                                          8–037
—— (No.1 of 1992), Re [1993] 1 W.L.R. 274; [1993] 2 All E.R. 190 CA
    (Crim Div) 6–006
—— (No.2 of 1992), Re [1994] Q.B. 91; [1993] 3 W.L.R. 982 CA (Crim Div) 2–008

Attorney General's Reference (No.3 of 1992), Re [1994] 1 W.L.R. 409; (1994) 98
    Cr.App.R. 383 CA (Crim Div) 6–010, 6–011
—— (No.3 of 1994), Re [1998] A.C. 245; [1997] 3 W.L.R. 421 HL . . 2–081, 7–004, 7–015,
                                             7–037, 7–040, 7–046, 7–047
—— (No.3 of 1998), Re [2000] Q.B. 401; [1999] 3 W.L.R. 1194 CA (Crim Div) 5–006
—— (No.2 of 1999), Re [2000] Q.B. 796; [2000] 3 W.L.R. 195 CA (Crim Div) 4–062,
                                               4–065, 7–049
—— (No.3 of 2003) [2004] EWCA Crim 864 2–025
—— (No.1 of 2004), Re [2004] EWCA Crim 1025; [2004] 1 W.L.R. 2111; [2005] 4
    All E.R. 457 (Note) 7–057
—— (No.3 of 2004) [2005] EWCA Crim 1882; [2006] Crim.L.R. 63 4–023
—— (No.4 of 2004), Re [2005] EWCA Crim 889; [2005] 1 W.L.R. 2810; [2005] 2
    Cr.App.R. 26 CA (Crim Div) 7–097
—— (No.54 of 2007), Re; sub nom R. v Gower [2007] EWCA Crim 1655; [2008] 1
    Cr.App.R.(S.) 62 CA (Crim Div) 7–084
Attorney General for Jersey v Holley [2005] UKPC 23; [2005] 2 A.C. 580; [2005] 3
    W.L.R. 29 PC (Jersey) 5–015, 5–058, 7–032, 7–033, 7–034, 7–035
Attorney General of Hong Kong v Nai–Keung (Daniel Chan) [1987] 1 W.L.R. 1339;
    (1987) 3 B.C.C. 403 PC (Hong Kong) 8–022
—— v Reid [1994] 1 A.C. 324; [1993] 3 W.L.R. 1143 PC (New Zealand) 8–037
—— v Yip Kai–foon [1988] A.C. 642; [1988] 2 W.L.R. 326 PC (Hong Kong) 9–045
Attorney General of Northern Ireland v Gallagher (Patrick) [1963] A.C. 349; [1961] 3
    W.L.R. 619 HL 2–077, 5–041
Attorney General of Northern Ireland's Reference (No.1 of 1975), Re; sub nom
    Reference under s.48A of the Criminal Appeal (Northern Ireland) Act 1968
    (No.1 of 1975) [1977] A.C. 105; [1976] 3 W.L.R. 235 HL 5–046, 5–057, 7–008,
                                                 7–012
Atwal v Massey [1971] 3 All E.R. 881; (1972) 56 Cr.App.R. 6 Div Ct 9–048
B (A Child) v DPP; sub nom B (A Minor) v DPP [2000] 2 A.C. 428; [2000] 2 W.L.R.
    452; [2000] 1 All E.R. 833 HL 3–021, 3–022, 3–023, 3–024, 7–135
B (A Minor) (Wardship: Medical Treatment), Re [1981] 1 W.L.R. 1421; 80 L.G.R.
    107 CA (Civ Div) 2–028
B (A Minor) v DPP. See B (A Child) v DPP
B and S v Leathley [1979] Crim.L.R. 314 CC (Carlisle) 9–027
Barnfather v Islington Education Authority [2003] EWHC 418 (Admin); [2003] 1
    W.L.R. 2318; [2003] E.L.R. 263 Div Ct 3–024, 3–025
Bateman, Re [1925] 2 K.B. 429; (1925) 19 Cr.App.R. 8 KBD 7–048
Beatty v Gillbanks (1882) 9 Q.B.D. 308 5–050
Beckford v Queen, The [1988] A.C. 130; [1987] 3 W.L.R. 611 PC (Jamaica) 2–085,
                      5–032, 5–046, 5–059, 5–087, 7–006, 7–016
Behrens v Bertram Mills Circus Ltd [1957] 2 Q.B. 1; [1957] 2 W.L.R. 404 QBD 7–037
Blackburn v Bowering [1994] 1 W.L.R. 1324; [1994] 3 All E.R. 380 CA (Civ Div) . . 5–047,
                                                 7–093
Blake v Barnard (1840) 9 C. & P. 626 7–066
—— v DPP [1993] Crim.L.R. 587 .... 10–016, 10–017
Blakely and Sutton v DPP [1991] R.T.R. 405; [1991] Crim.L.R. 763 Div Ct . . 4–008, 4–012
Blyth v Birmingham Waterworks Co (1856) 156 E.R. 1047; (1856) 11 Ex. 781 Ct of
    Exch 2–063
Board of Trade v Owen [1957] A.C. 602; [1957] 2 W.L.R. 351 HL 6–051

Bodkin v Adams [1957] Crim.L.R. 365 7–099

Boggeln v Williams [1978] 1 W.L.R. 873; [1978] 2 All E.R. 1061 QBD 8–043

Bolam v Friern Hospital Management Committee [1957] 1 W.L.R. 582; [1957] 2 All
    E.R. 118 QBD 2–028

Bolduc and Bird [1967] S.C.R. 677 Sup Ct Canada 7–113, 7–116, 7–127

Bratty v Attorney General of Northern Ireland [1963] A.C. 386; [1961] 3 W.L.R. 965
    HL 2–007, 2–009, 2–010, 5–007, 5–009, 5–011

Broome v Perkins (1987) 85 Cr.App.R. 321; [1987] R.T.R. 321 Div Ct 2–007

Buckoke v Greater London Council [1971] Ch. 655; [1971] 2 W.L.R. 760 CA (Civ
    Div) 5–064

Burns v Bidder [1967] 2 Q.B. 227; [1966] 3 W.L.R. 99 Div Ct 2–008

Bush v Commonwealth (1880) 78 Ky. 268 2–040

C v Hume [1979] Crim.L.R. 328 4–031

C (A Minor) v DPP [1996] A.C. 1; [1995] 2 W.L.R. 383 HL 5–098, 5–099

—— v Eisenhower. *See* JJC (A Minor) v Eisenhower

CBS Songs Ltd v Amstrad Consumer Electronics Plc [1988] A.C. 1013; [1988] 2
    W.L.R. 1191 HL 6–022

Callow v Tillstone (1900) 64 J.P. 823; 19 Cox C.C. 576 4–003

Carlgarth, The [1927] P. 93 CA 9–026

Carter v Richardson [1974] R.T.R. 314; [1974] Crim.L.R. 190 QBD 4–007, 4–012

Chamberlain v Lindon [1998] 1 W.L.R. 1252; [1998] 2 All E.R. 538 Div Ct 10–017

Chan Kau (alias Chan Kai) v Queen, The [1955] A.C. 206; [1955] 2 W.L.R. 192 PC
    (Hong Kong) 5–045

Chan Man–Sin v Queen, The [1988] 1 W.L.R. 196; [1988] 1 All E.R. 1 PC (Hong
    Kong) 8–022, 8–049

Chan Wing Siu v R. [1985] A.C. 168; [1984] 3 W.L.R. 677 PC (Hong Kong) 4–015,
                                                                    4–018, 4–022

Chase Manhattan Bank NA v Israel–British Bank (London) Ltd [1981] Ch. 105;
    [1980] 2 W.L.R. 202 Ch D 8–031, 8–032, 8–036

Chelsea Yacht & Boat Co Ltd v Pope [2000] 1 W.L.R. 1941; [2001] 2 All E.R. 409
    CA (Civ Div) 8–025

Christian v Queen, The [2006] UKPC 47; [2007] 2 A.C. 400; [2007] 2 W.L.R. 120 PC
    (Pitcairn Islands) 2–082

Churchill (Victor George) (Senior) v Walton [1967] 2 A.C. 224; [1967] 2 W.L.R. 682
    HL 6–043

Chuter v Freeth & Pocock Ltd [1911] 2 K.B. 832 4–060

Cichon v DPP [1994] Crim.L.R. 918; [1995] C.O.D. 5 QBD 5–068

Clarke v Crown Prosecution Service [2007] EWHC 2228 (Admin) 8–011

Clinton (Chief Inspector of RUC) v Cahill [1998] N.I. 200 NICA 8–048

Collins v Wilcock [1984] 1 W.L.R. 1172; [1984] 3 All E.R. 374 Div Ct 7–062, 7–071

Comer v Bloomfield (1971) 55 Cr.App.R. 305; [1971] R.T.R. 49 QBD 6–004

Commissioner of Police of the Metropolis v Charles (Derek Michael) [1977] A.C.
    177; [1976] 3 W.L.R. 431 HL 9–006

—— v Streeter (1980) 71 Cr.App.R. 113 Div Ct 9–039

Coppen v Moore (No.2) [1898] 2 Q.B. 306 .... 4–052, 4–060

Corcoran v Anderton (1980) 71 Cr.App.R. 104; [1980] Crim.L.R. 385 Div Ct 8–005,
                                                                            9–021

Cotterill v Penn [1936] 1 K.B. 53 KBD 3–010

Cox v Riley (1986) 83 Cr.App.R. 54; [1986] Crim.L.R. 460 QBD 10–004

Cresswell v DPP [2006] EWHC 3379 (Admin); (2007) 171 J.P. 233; (2007) 171 J.P.N.
    500 Div Ct 8–027, 10–017
Cundy v Le Coq (1881) 13 Q.B.D. 207 3–009
Data Protection Registrar v Amnesty International (British Section) [1995] Crim.L.R.
    633; [1995] C.O.D. 325 Div Ct 2–072
Davidge v Bunnett [1984] Crim.L.R. 297 Div Ct 8–034
Davies v DPP [1954] A.C. 378; [1954] 2 W.L.R. 343 HL 4–022
—— v Health and Safety Executive [2002] EWCA Crim 2949; [2003] I.C.R. 586;
    [2003] I.R.L.R. 170 CA (Crim Div) 3–024
Defazio v DPP [2007] EWHC 3529 (Admin) 9–038
Director General of Fair Trading v Pioneer Concrete (UK) Ltd [1995] 1 A.C. 456;
    [1994] 3 W.L.R. 1249 HL 4–052, 4–060
DPP v Armstrong (Andrew) [2000] Crim.L.R. 379; (1999) 96(45) L.S.G. 32 QBD . . 6–024
—— v Beard [1920] A.C. 479; (1920) 14 Cr.App.R. 159; 12 A.L.R. 846 HL   5–028, 5–032,
                                                                    7–007, 7–015, 7–038
—— v Bell [1992] Crim.L.R. 176 5–095
—— v Braun (Klaus Armstrong) (1999) 163 J.P. 271; [1999] Crim.L.R. 416
    Div Ct 5–053, 5–054
—— v Camplin. See R. v Camplin (Paul)
—— v Daley (Frederick) [1980] A.C. 237; [1979] 2 W.L.R. 239 PC (Jamaica) 2–037
—— v Fisher (1992) 156 J.P. 93; [1992] R.T.R. 93; [1991] Crim.L.R. 787 Div Ct . . . 3–005
—— v Gohill [2007] EWHC 239 (Admin) 8–044
—— v Gomez (Edwin) [1993] A.C. 442; [1992] 3 W.L.R. 1067 HL . . 8–004, 8–005, 8–008,
            8–009, 8–010, 8–011, 8–012, 8–013, 8–014, 8–015, 8–016, 8–017, 8–018, 8–029,
                                                               8–030, 9–001, 9–021
—— v H. See DPP v Harper
—— v Harper; sub nom DPP v H [1997] 1 W.L.R. 1406; (1997) 161 J.P. 697 QBD   5–014
—— v Harris (Nigel) [1995] 1 Cr.App.R. 170; (1994) 158 J.P. 896 QBD 5–068
—— v Howard [2008] EWHC 608 (Admin) Div Ct 7–097
—— v Huskinson (1988) 152 J.P. 582; (1988) 20 H.L.R. 562; [1988] Crim.L.R. 620
    Div Ct 6–017, 8–033, 8–034
—— v Jones [1990] R.T.R. 34 5–095
—— v K [1997] 1 Cr.App.R. 36; [1997] Crim.L.R. 121 Div Ct 7–120
—— v K (A Minor) [1990] 1 W.L.R. 1067; [1990] 1 All E.R. 331 QBD 7–070, 7–074,
                                                                                  7–095
—— v K and C [1997] 1 Cr.App.R. 36; [1997] Crim.L.R. 121 Div Ct 4–039
—— v Kent and Sussex Contractors Ltd [1944] 1 K.B. 146 4–061
—— v Lavender (Melvyn) [1994] Crim.L.R. 297 Div Ct 8–049
—— v Little. See DPP v Taylor (Keith Richard)
—— v M [2004] EWHC 1453 (Admin); [2004] 1 W.L.R. 2758; [2005] Crim.L.R. 392
    Div Ct 7–097
—— v Majewski [1977] A.C. 443; [1976] 2 W.L.R. 623 HL . . . 5–028, 5–029, 5–030, 5–031,
                                                    5–032, 5–035, 5–036, 5–037, 5–038
—— v Morgan [1976] A.C. 182; [1975] 2 W.L.R. 913 HL 2–084, 4–039, 6–010, 6–011,
                                                                                  7–130
—— v Newbury (Neil) [1977] A.C. 500; [1976] 2 W.L.R. 918 HL 7–040, 7–041, 7–044,
                                                                                  7–046
—— v Nock [1978] A.C. 979; [1978] 3 W.L.R. 57 HL 6–050
—— v Pal [2000] Crim.L.R. 756 Div Ct 7–097

DPP v Ray [1974] A.C. 370; [1973] 3 W.L.R. 359 HL 9–006, 9–016, 9–017
—— v Santana–Bermudez [2003] EWHC 2908 (Admin); (2004) 168 J.P. 373; [2004]
    Crim.L.R. 471 . . . . 2–027, 7–064, 7–070
—— v Shannon (David Charles) [1975] A.C. 717; [1974] 3 W.L.R. 155 HL 6–042
—— v Smith (Jim) [1961] A.C. 290; [1960] 3 W.L.R. 546 HL 2–058, 7–078
—— v Smith [2006] EWHC 94 (Admin); [2006] 1 W.L.R. 1571; [2006] 2 All E.R. 16
    Div Ct 7–079
—— v Stonehouse [1978] A.C. 55; [1977] 3 W.L.R. 143 HL 6–003
—— v Taylor (Keith Richard); sub nom DPP v Little [1992] Q.B. 645; [1992] 2
    W.L.R. 460; [1992] 1 All E.R. 299 QBD 7–061
DPP (Jamaica) v Bailey [1995] 1 Cr.App.R. 257; [1995] Crim.L.R. 313 PC (Jamaica) . . . .
    5–059
DPP for Northern Ireland v Lynch [1975] A.C. 653; [1975] 2 W.L.R. 641 HL 5–071,
                    5–072, 5–075, 5–076, 5–077, 5–078, 5–082
—— v Maxwell [1978] 1 W.L.R. 1350; [1978] 3 All E.R. 1140 HL . . . 4–006, 4–007, 4–013
Dobson v General Accident Fire and Life Assurance Corp [1990] 1 Q.B. 274; [1989]
    3 W.L.R. 1066 CA (Civ Div) 8–008, 8–012, 8–030
Donnelly v Jackman [1970] 1 W.L.R. 562; [1970] 1 All E.R. 987 Div Ct 7–071
Du Cros v Lambourne [1907] 1 K.B. 40 4–011
Eddy v Niman (1981) 73 Cr.App.R. 237; [1981] Crim.L.R. 502 Div Ct 8–005, 8–006,
                                            8–008, 8–010
Edwards (alias David Christopher Murray) v The Queen [1973] A.C. 648; [1972] 3
    W.L.R. 893; [1973] 1 All E.R. 152 PC (Hong Kong) 7–024
Ekbatani v Sweden (A/134) (1991) 13 E.H.R.R. 504 ECHR 5–004
Elliott v C (A Minor) [1983] 1 W.L.R. 939; [1983] 2 All E.R. 1005 Div Ct . . 2–068, 2–072
Environment Agency v Brock Plc [1998] Env. L.R. 607; [1998] 4 P.L.R. 37 Div Ct . . 3–024
Environment Agency (formerly National Rivers Authority) v Empress Car Co
    (Abertillery) Ltd [1999] 2 A.C. 22; [1998] 2 W.L.R. 350 HL . . . 2–032, 2–042, 2–044,
                                                3–006
Evans v Hughes [1972] 1 W.L.R. 1452; [1972] 3 All E.R. 412 QBD 5–050
F (Mental Patient: Sterilisation), Re. *See* F v West Berkshire HA
F v West Berkshire HA; sub nom F (Mental Patient: Sterilisation), Re [1990] 2 A.C.
    1; [1989] 2 W.L.R. 1025 HL 5–065
FJH Wrothwell v Yorkshire Water Authority [1984] Crim.L.R. 43 CA (Civ Div) . . . 3–006
Fagan v Commissioner of Police of the Metropolis [1969] 1 Q.B. 439; [1968] 3
    W.L.R. 1120 Div Ct 2–027, 2–077, 7–064, 7–070, 7–072
Faulkner v Talbot [1981] 1 W.L.R. 1528; [1981] 3 All E.R. 468 Div Ct 7–062
Ferguson v Weaving [1951] 1 K.B. 814; [1951] 1 All E.R. 412 Div Ct 4–003, 4–056
Finnegan v Heywood, 2000 S.C. 444 5–040
Floyd v DPP [2000] Crim.L.R. 411 8–033
Gammon (Hong Kong) Ltd v Attorney General of Hong Kong [1985] A.C. 1; [1984]
    3 W.L.R. 437 PC (Hong Kong) 3–005, 3–012, 3–018, 3–020, 3–024, 3–025, 3–028
Gardner v Akeroyd [1952] Q.B. 743 4–056
Garrett v Arthur Churchill (Glass) [1970] 1 Q.B. 92; [1969] 3 W.L.R. 6 Div Ct 4–013
Germany v Kumar (No.1) [2000] Crim.L.R. 504 QD 8–033
Gillick v West Norfolk and Wisbech AHA [1986] A.C. 112; [1985] 3 W.L.R.
    830 HL 4–009, 5–065
Gray v Barr [1971] 2 Q.B. 554; [1971] 2 W.L.R. 1334; [1971] 2 All E.R. 949 CA (Civ
    Div) 2–007, 7–044

Green v Burnett. *See* James & Son v Smee

Griffiths v Freeman [1970] 1 W.L.R. 659; [1970] 1 All E.R. 1117 Div Ct 9–037

—— v Studebakers Ltd [1924] 1 K.B. 102 4–060

HL Bolton Engineering Co Ltd v TJ Graham & Sons Ltd [1957] 1 Q.B. 159; [1956] 3
     W.L.R. 804 CA 4–061

Hallett Silberman Ltd v Cheshire CC [1993] R.T.R. 32 4–052

Hardman v Chief Constable of Avon and Somerset [1986] Crim.L.R. 330 CC
     (Bristol) 10–004

Harrow LBC v Shah [2000] 1 W.L.R. 83; [1999] 3 All E.R. 302; [1999] 2 Cr.App.R.
     457 QBD 3–025

Haughton v Smith [1975] A.C. 476; [1974] 2 W.L.R. 1 HL . . . 6–014, 6–015, 6–050, 8–050,
                                                                                                                    9–038

Haystead v Chief Constable of Derbyshire [2000] 3 All E.R. 890; [2000] 2 Cr.App.R.
     339 Div Ct 7–061, 7–069

Henshall (John) (Quarries) v Harvey [1965] 2 Q.B. 233; [1965] 2 W.L.R. 758
     Div Ct 4–062

Hibbert v McKiernan [1948] 2 K.B. 142; [1948] 1 All E.R. 860 Div Ct 8–031

Hill v Baxter [1958] 1 Q.B. 277; [1958] 2 W.L.R. 76 QBD 2–006, 3–026, 5–014

Holmes, Re. *See* Holmes v Governor of Brixton Prison

Holmes v Governor of Brixton Prison; sub nom Re Holmes [2004] EWHC 2020
     (Admin); [2005] 1 W.L.R. 1857; [2005] 1 All E.R. 490 . . . . 9–002, 9–007

Howker v Robinson [1973] Q.B. 178; [1972] 3 W.L.R. 234 Div Ct 4–055

Hui Chi–Ming v Queen, The [1992] 1 A.C. 34; [1991] 3 W.L.R. 495 PC (Hong
     Kong) 4–016, 4–017, 4–020, 4–040

Hyam v DPP [1975] A.C. 55; [1974] 2 W.L.R. 607 HL   2–055, 2–080, 2–081, 5–029, 7–015

Invicta Plastics Ltd v Clare [1976] R.T.R. 251; [1976] Crim.L.R. 131 Div Ct 6–022

Iqbal v DPP [2004] EWHC 2567 (Admin); [2004] All E.R. (D) 314 9–038

JBH and JH (Minors) v O–Connell [1981] Crim.L.R. 632 5–099

JJC (A Minor) v Eisenhower; sub nom C (A Minor) v Eisenhower [1984] Q.B. 331;
     [1983] 3 W.L.R. 537 QBD 7–083

Jaggard v Dickinson [1981] Q.B. 527; [1981] 2 W.L.R. 118 Div Ct 5–039, 10–016

James & Son v Smee; sub nom Green v Burnett [1955] 1 Q.B. 78; [1954] 3 W.L.R.
     631 QBD 3–005, 4–052

Johnson v DPP [1994] Crim.L.R. 673 QBD 10–017

—— v —— [2008] EWHC 509 (Admin); (2008) 105(10) L.S.G. 27 Div Ct 7–097

—— v United Kingdom (1999) 27 E.H.R.R. 296; (1998) 40 B.M.L.R. 1 ECHR 5–024

—— v Youden [1950] 1 K.B. 544; [1950] 1 All E.R. 300 Div Ct 4–006

Kaitamaki v Queen, The [1985] A.C. 147; [1984] 3 W.L.R. 137 PC (New
     Zealand) 2–077, 7–120

Kamara v DPP [1974] A.C. 104; [1973] 3 W.L.R. 198 HL 6–029

Kane v HM Advocate. *See* MacAngus (Kevin) v HM Advocate

Kaur v Chief Constable of Hampshire [1981] 1 W.L.R. 578; [1981] 2 All E.R. 430 Div
     Ct 8–010, 8–012

Kay v Butterworth (1945) 173 L.T. 191 2–006

Kenlin v Gardiner [1967] 2 Q.B. 510; [1967] 2 W.L.R. 129 Div Ct 7–071

Kewin v CPS. *See* R. (on the application of Lewin) v Crown Prosecution Service

Kilbride v Lake [1962] N.Z.L.R. 590 . . . . 3–019, 3–026

Knuller (Publishing, Printing and Promotions) Ltd v DPP [1973] A.C. 435; [1972] 3
     W.L.R. 143 HL 6–034

Kokkinakis v Greece (A/260–A) (1994) 17 E.H.R.R. 397 ECHR 7–053
Laskey v United Kingdom (1997) 24 E.H.R.R. 39 ECHR 7–104
Lawrence v Commissioner of Police of the Metropolis [1972] A.C. 626; [1971] 3
    W.L.R. 225 HL 8–006, 8–007, 8–008, 8–009, 8–011, 8–012, 8–017, 8–029, 8–030
Lee Chun Chuen (alias Lee Wing–Cheuk) v Queen, The [1963] A.C. 220; [1962] 3
    W.L.R. 1461 PC (Hong Kong) 7–020
Lennard's Carrying Co Ltd v Asiatic Petroleum Co Ltd [1915] A.C. 705 HL 4–061
Lewis v Lethbridge [1987] Crim.L.R. 59 Div Ct 8–034
Liangsiriprasert v United States [1991] 1 A.C. 225; [1990] 3 W.L.R. 606 PC (Hong
    Kong) 6–051
Lim Chin Aik v R. [1963] A.C. 160; [1963] 2 W.L.R. 42 PC (Singapore) 2–014, 3–009,
                                                                 3–019, 3–026
Linnett v MPC [1946] K.B. 290 4–054
Lister & Co v Stubbs (1890) L.R. 45 Ch. D. 1 CA 8–037
Lloyd v DPP [1992] 1 All E.R. 982; (1992) 156 J.P. 342 QBD 10–004
—— v Johnson (1798) 1 Bos. 8 P. 340 4–001
Low v Blease [1975] Crim.L.R. 513; (1975) 119 S.J. 695 Div Ct 8–021
Luc Thiet Thuan v Queen, The [1997] A.C. 131; [1996] 3 W.L.R. 45 PC (Hong
    Kong) 7–031, 7–032, 7–033
MacAngus (Kevin) v HM Advocate; sub nom Kane v HM Advocate [2009] HCJAC
    8; 2009 S.L.T. 137; 2009 S.C.C.R. 238 2–045
McCrone v Riding [1938] 1 All E.R. 157; (1938) 158 L.T. 253 2–063
Magna Plant v Mitchell [1966] Crim.L.R. 394; 116 N.L.J. 780 Div Ct 4–062
Malnik v DPP [1989] Crim.L.R. 451 Div Ct 5–050
Mancini v DPP [1942] A.C. 1; [1941] 3 All E.R. 272; (1943) 28 Cr.App.R. 65 HL . . 7–020
Martin v State (1944) 31 Ala. App. 334 2–014
Mawji v Queen, The [1957] A.C. 126; [1957] 2 W.L.R. 277 PC (Eastern Africa) 6–040
Meah v Roberts [1977] 1 W.L.R. 1187; [1978] 1 All E.R. 97 Div Ct 3–013
Meli v Queen, The; sub nom Thabo Meli v R. [1954] 1 W.L.R. 228; [1954] 1 All E.R.
     373; (1954) 98 S.J. 77 PC (Basutoland) 2–078, 2–079
Meridian Global Funds Management Asia Ltd v Securities Commission [1995] 2 A.C.
     500; [1995] 3 W.L.R. 413 PC (New Zealand) 4–062, 4–065
Metropolitan Police Commissioner v Caldwell. See R. v Caldwell (James)
Midland Bank Trust Co Ltd v Green (No.3) [1979] Ch. 496; [1979] 2 W.L.R. 594;
    [1979] 2 All E.R. 193 Ch D 6–040
Miller v Ministry of Pensions [1947] 2 All E.R. 372; 63 T.L.R. 474 KBD 1–014
Minor (Stephen Scott) v DPP (1988) 86 Cr.App.R. 378; (1988) 152 J.P. 30 QBD . . . 9–057
Moore v I Bresler Ltd [1944] 2 All E.R. 515 KBD 4–061
Morphitis v Salmon (1990) 154 J.P. 365; [1990] Crim.L.R. 48; (1990) 154 J.P.N. 186
    Div Ct 10–004
Morris, Anderton v Burnside. See R. v Morris (David Alan)
Mousell Bros v LNWR [1917] 2 K.B. 836 . . . . 4–052, 4–060
Moynes v Coopper [1956] 1 Q.B. 439; [1956] 2 W.L.R. 562 Div Ct 8–035
NHS Trust A v M [2001] Fam. 348; [2001] 2 W.L.R. 942 Fam Div 2–030
National Coal Board v Gamble [1959] 1 Q.B. 11; [1958] 3 W.L.R. 434 Div Ct 4–013
National Rivers Authority (Southern Region) v Alfred McAlpine Homes East Ltd
    [1994] 4 All E.R. 286; [1994] Env. L.R. 198 QBD 4–060
National Rivers Authority v Yorkshire Water Services Ltd [1995] 1 A.C. 444; [1994] 3
    W.L.R. 1202 HL 2–032

Neville v Mavroghenis [1984] Crim.L.R. 42 CA (Civ Div) 3–009
Norfolk Constabulary v Seekings and Gould [1986] Crim.L.R. 167 CC (Norwich) . . 9–027
Norris v United States [2008] UKHL 16; [2008] 1 A.C. 920; [2008] 2 W.L.R. 673 HL . . . .
   6–035
Nottingham City Council v Wolverhampton and Dudley Breweries Plc [2003] EWHC
   2847 (Admin); [2004] Q.B. 1274; [2004] 2 W.L.R. 820 4–050
O'Brien v Anderton [1979] R.T.R. 388 6–003
Oxford v Moss (1979) 68 Cr.App.R. 183; [1979] Crim.L.R. 119 QBD 8–023
Palmer (Sigismund) v Queen, The [1971] A.C. 814; [1971] 2 W.L.R. 831 PC
   (Jamaica) 5–054, 5–056, 5–060
Partington v Williams (1976) 62 Cr.App.R. 220; [1977] Crim.L.R. 609 Div Ct 6–015
People v Beardsley (1967) 113 N.W. 1128 2–025
Pepper (Inspector of Taxes) v Hart [1993] A.C. 593; [1992] 3 W.L.R. 1032 HL 8–004
Pharmaceutical Society of Great Britain v Storkwain Ltd [1986] 1 W.L.R. 903; [1986]
   2 All E.R. 635 HL 3–009
Phillips (Glasford) v Queen, The [1969] 2 A.C. 130; [1969] 2 W.L.R. 581 PC
   (Jamaica) 7–020
Pilgram v Rice–Smith [1977] 1 W.L.R. 671; [1977] 2 All E.R. 658 Div C 8–005
Pollard v Chief Constable of West Yorkshire [1999] P.I.Q.R. P219 CA (Civ Div) . . . 5–046
Powell v MacRae [1977] Crim.L.R. 571 Div Ct 8–037
Proudman v Dayman 91941) 67 C.L.R. 536 High Ct of Australia 3–026, 3–028
R. v A [2005] All E.R. (D) 38 . . . . 5–033, 7–112
—— v Abbott (Charles Clement) [1955] 2 Q.B. 497; [1955] 3 W.L.R. 369 CCA 4–035
—— v Abdul–Hussain (Mustafa Shakir) [1999] Crim.L.R. 570 CA (Crim Div) 5–085,
   5–094
—— v Abdullahi (Osmund Mohammed) [2006] EWCA Crim 2060; [2007] 1 W.L.R.
   225; [2007] 1 Cr.App.R. 14 7–136
—— v Abramovitch (Myer) (1912) 7 Cr.App.R. 145 CCA 9–050
—— v Abu Hamza [2006] EWCA Crim 2918; [2007] Q.B. 659 CA (Crim Div) 6–024
—— v Acott (Brian Gordon) [1997] 1 W.L.R. 306; [1997] 1 All E.R. 706 HL 7–023
—— v Adams [1993] Crim.L.R. 72 CA (Crim Div) 8–019
—— v Adenusi (Oladele) [2006] EWCA Crim 1059; (2007) 171 J.P. 169 . . . . ●–050
—— v Adomako (John Asare) [1995] 1 A.C. 171; [1994] 3 W.L.R. 288 HL 2–047, 7–049,
   7–051, 7–052, 7–053, 7–054, 7–110
—— v Ahluwalia (Kiranjit) [1992] 4 All E.R. 889; (1993) 96 Cr.App.R. 133 CA
   (Crim Div) 7–021, 7–022, 7–034
—— v Ahmad (Zafar) (1987) 84 Cr.App.R. 64; (1986) 18 H.L.R. 416 CA (Crim Div) . . . .
   2–022
—— v Aitken (Thomas Adam) [1992] 1 W.L.R. 1006; [1992] 4 All E.R. 541
   CMAC 5–033, 7–112
—— v Ali [1989] Crim.L.R. 736 CA (Crim Div) 7–027
—— v Ali (Liaquat) [2005] EWCA Crim 87; [2006] Q.B. 322; [2006] 2 W.L.R. 316
   CA (Crim Div) 6–044
—— v —— (Mumtaz) (1995) 16 Cr.App.R.(S.) 692; [1995] Crim.L.R. 303 CA (Crim
   Div) 5–091
—— v Allan (George Donald) [1965] 1 Q.B. 130; [1963] 3 W.L.R. 677 CCA 4–009
—— v Allen (Christopher) [1985] A.C. 1029; [1985] 3 W.L.R. 107 HL 9–017
—— v Allsop (Anthony Adward) (1977) 64 Cr.App.R. 29; [1976] Crim.L.R. 738 CA
   (Crim Div) 6–035, 6–036

R. v Altham. *See* R. v Quayle (Barry)

—— v Anderson (Lascelles Fitzalbert) [1966] 2 Q.B. 110; [1966] 2 W.L.R. 1195 CCA.... 4–022, 4–023, 4–025, 4–032

—— v —— (William Ronald) [1986] A.C. 27; [1985] 3 W.L.R. 268 HL 6–046, 6–047, 6–048

—— v Antoine (Pierre Harrison) [2001] 1 A.C. 340; [2000] 2 W.L.R. 703 HL 5–001, 5–002, 5–006, 5–014, 5–015

—— v Arnaot (May) [2008] EWCA Crim 121 5–095

—— v Arnold (Lydon Ewart) [1997] 4 All E.R. 1; [1997] Crim.L.R. 833 CA (Crim Div) 8–033

—— v Arthur (1981) 12 B.M.L.R. 1 2–028

—— v Asbury [1986] Crim.L.R. 258 5–053

—— v Ashton [1992] Crim.L.R. 667 CA (Crim Div) 6–046

—— v Atakpu (Austin) [1994] Q.B. 69; [1993] 3 W.L.R. 812 CA (Crim Div) 8–015, 8–018

—— v Attorney General Ex p. Rockall [2000] 1 W.L.R. 882; [1999] 4 All E.R. 312 QBD 6–030

—— v Austin (Christopher Timothy) [1981] 1 All E.R. 374; (1981) 72 Cr.App.R. 104 CA (Crim Div) 4–038

—— v Ayres (David Edward) [1984] A.C. 447; [1984] 2 W.L.R. 257 HL 6–030, 6–035

—— v Aziz [1993] Crim.L.R. 708 CA (Crim Div) 9–017, 9–018

—— v B; sub nom R. v EB [2006] EWCA Crim 2945; [2007] 1 W.L.R. 1567; [2007] 1 Cr.App.R. 29 7–121

—— v Backshall (David Anthony) [1998] 1 W.L.R. 1506; [1999] 1 Cr.App.R. 35 CA (Crim Div) 5–093

—— v Bailey (1818) Russ & Ry 341 9–024

—— v Bailey (John Graham) [1983] 1 W.L.R. 760; [1983] 2 All E.R. 503 CA (Crim Div) 2–006, 2–012, 5–035, 5–037

—— v Baillie (John Dickie) [1995] 2 Cr.App.R. 31; [1995] Crim.L.R. 739 CA (Crim Div) 7–023

—— v Bainbridge (Alan) [1960] 1 Q.B. 129; [1959] 3 W.L.R. 656 CCA 4–006, 6–031

—— v Baker [1994] Crim.L.R. 444 CA (Crim Div) 4–042

—— v Baker and Ward [1999] 2 Cr.App.R. 335 .... 5–083, 5–086, 5–092

—— v Baker and Wilkins [1997] Crim.L.R. 497 5–082

—— v Ball [1989] Crim.L.R. 730 CA (Crim Div) 7–045

—— v Ball (Michael Anthony) [1983] 1 W.L.R. 801; [1983] 2 All E.R. 1089 CA (Crim Div) 9–050

—— v Bamborough (Arron)1996] Crim.L.R. 744 CA (Crim Div) 4–032

—— v Barnard (Philip Charles) (1980) 70 Cr.App.R. 28; [1980] Crim.L.R. 235 CA (Crim Div) 6–032

—— v Barnes (1991) 155 J.P. 417; [1991] Crim.L.R. 132 CA (Crim Div) 9–048

—— v Barnes (Mark) [2004] EWCA Crim 3246; [2005] 1 W.L.R. 910 CA (Crim Div) 7–110

—— v Barr (Graham) (1989) 88 Cr.App.R. 362 CA (Crim Div) 4–015

—— v Bastian (Stephen) [1958] 1 W.L.R. 413; [1958] 1 All E.R. 568 (Note) CCC .. 5–021

—— v Bayley and Easterbrook [1980] Crim.L.R. 503 CA (Crim Div) 8–051

—— v Becerra and Cooper (1976) 62 Cr.App.R. 212 .... 4–042, 4–043, 4–045

—— v Beckett (1836) 1 M. & Rob. 526 7–083

R. v Belfon (Horace Adrian) [1976] 1 W.L.R. 741; [1976] 3 All E.R. 46 CA (Crim
    Div) 7–093
—— v Bell (David) [1984] 3 All E.R. 842; [1985] R.T.R. 202 CA (Crim Div) 2–068
—— v Benge (1865) 4 F. & F. 504 2–034
—— v Bentham (Peter) [2005] UKHL 18; [2005] 1 W.L.R. 1057; [2005] 2 All E.R. 65 . . . .
    9–030
—— v Berry (John Rodney) (No.3) [1995] 1 W.L.R. 7; [1994] 2 All E.R. 913 CA
    (Crim Div) 3–009
—— v Betty (Carol) (1964) 48 Cr.App.R. 6 CCA 4–024, 4–025
—— v Bevans (Ronald George Henry) (1988) 87 Cr.App.R. 64; [1988] Crim.L.R.
    236 CA (Crim Div) 9–035
—— v Bezzina (Anthony) [1994] 1 W.L.R. 1057; [1994] 3 All E.R. 964 CA (Crim
    Div) 3–018
—— v Bingham [1991] Crim.L.R. 433 CA (Crim Div) 5–010
—— v Bird (Debbie) [1985] 1 W.L.R. 816; [1985] 2 All E.R. 513 CA (Crim Div) . . 5–048
—— v Birmingham and Gloucester Ry (1840) 3 Q.B. 223 4–065
—— v Birtles (1969) 53 Cr.App.R. 469 5–102
—— v Bland (1987) 151 J.P. 857; [1988] Crim.L.R. 41 4–011
—— v Blaue (Robert Konrad) [1975] 1 W.L.R. 1411; [1975] 3 All E.R. 446 CA
    (Crim Div) 2–048, 2–049, 2–050
—— v Bloxham (Albert John) [1983] 1 A.C. 109; [1982] 2 W.L.R. 392 HL 9–044
—— v Bodkin Adams [1957] Crim.L.R. 365 2–028
—— v Bonner (George Andrew) [1970] 1 W.L.R. 838; [1970] 2 All E.R. 97 (Note)
    CA (Crim Div) 8–014
—— v Bonnick (1978) 66 Cr.App.R. 266 CA 5–059
—— v Bonnyman (1942) 28 Cr.App.R. 131 2–025
—— v Booth [1999] Crim.L.R. 144 10–012
—— v Bourne [1938] 3 All E.R. 615 5–065
—— v —— [1964] Crim.L.R. 833 CCA 4–005
—— v Bourne (Sydney Joseph) (1952) 36 Cr.App.R. 125 CCA 4–038
—— v Bowden [1993] Crim.L.R. 380 5–027
—— v Bowell (Paul) [2003] EWCA Crim 3896 2–027
—— v Bowen (Cecil) [1997] 1 W.L.R. 372; [1996] 4 All E.R. 837; [1996] 2 Cr.App.R.
    157 CA (Crim Div) 5–088
—— v Bowles (Lewis) [2004] EWCA Crim 1608; (2004) 148 S.J.L.B. 876 CA (Crim
    Div) 6–004
—— v Boyea (1992) 156 J.P. 505; [1992] Crim.L.R. 574 CA (Crim Div) 7–105, 7–106
—— v Bradish (Liam Christopher) [1990] 1 Q.B. 981; [1990] 2 W.L.R. 223 CA (Crim
    Div) 3–008
—— v Bradley (Ivan) (1980) 70 Cr.App.R. 200; [1980] Crim.L.R. 173 CA (Crim Div) . . . .
    9–050
—— v Brady (Philip) [2006] EWCA Crim 2413; [2007] Crim.L.R. 564 CA (Crim
    Div) 5–031
—— v Brain (1834) 6 C. & P. 349 7–004
—— v Bree (Benjamin) [2007] EWCA Crim 804; [2008] Q.B. 131; [2007] 3 W.L.R.
    600 . . . . 7–124, 7–125, 7–126
—— v Brewster (David Edward) (1980) 71 Cr.App.R. 375; (1980) 2 Cr.App.R.(S.)
    191 CA (Crim Div) 8–033
—— v Briggs [2007] Cr.App.R.(S) 425 4–023

R. v Briggs (Basil Ian) [1977] 1 W.L.R. 605; [1977] 1 All E.R. 475 CA (Crim Div)   2–065
—— v —— (Linda Joan) [2003] EWCA Crim 3662; [2004] 1 Cr.App.R. 34; [2004]
Crim.L.R. 495 CA (Crim Div) 8–005, 8–018
—— v Bristol Magistrates' Court Ex p. E [1999] 1 W.L.R. 390; [1998] 3 All E.R. 798;
[1999] 1 Cr.App.R. 144 Div Ct 10–002
—— v British Steel Plc [1995] 1 W.L.R. 1356; [1995] I.C.R. 586 CA (Crim Div) ... 4–060
—— v Broad [1997] Crim.L.R. 666 CA (Crim Div) 6–045
—— v Brockley (Frank) [1994] B.C.C. 131; [1994] 1 B.C.L.C. 606; (1994) 99
Cr.App.R. 385 CA (Crim Div) 3–012
—— v Brooks (Edward George) (1983) 76 Cr.App.R. 66; (1983) 2 Tr. L.R. 85 CA
(Crim Div) 9–017
—— v Brown [1993] Crim.L.R. 961 CA (Crim Div) 5–016
—— v Brown (Anthony Joseph) [1994] 1 A.C. 212; [1993] 2 W.L.R. 556 HL 2–004,
7–051, 7–071, 7–075, 7–086, 7–100, 7–101, 7–104, 7–106, 7–109
—— v —— (Michael Thomas Ernest) [1970] 1 Q.B. 105; [1969] 3 W.L.R. 370 CA
(Crim Div) 9–043, 9–044, 9–051
—— v —— (Vincent) [1985] Crim.L.R. 212 CA (Crim Div) 9–024, 9–025
—— v Bruzas (John) [1972] Crim.L.R. 367 6–002
—— v Bryce (Craig Brian) [2004] EWCA Crim 1231; [2004] 2 Cr.App.R. 35 4–006,
4–013
—— v Bryson [1985] Crim.L.R. 669 CA (Crim Div) 7–093
—— v Bunn, *The Times*, May 11, 1989 2–050
—— v Burgess (Barry Douglas) [1991] 2 Q.B. 92; [1991] 2 W.L.R. 1206; [1991] 2 All
E.R. 769; (1991) 93 Cr.App.R. 41 CA (Crim Div) 2–006, 2–009, 5–011, 5–012
—— v —— (Lee); sub nom R. v Byram [2008] EWCA Crim 516 2–045
—— v Burley (Donald) [2000] Crim.L.R. 843 CA (Crim Div) 5–095
—— v Burns (James) (1984) 79 Cr.App.R. 173 CA (Crim Div) 6–041
—— v Burstow. *See* R. v Ireland (Robert Matthew)
—— v Byram. *See* R. v Burgess (Lee)
—— v Byrne (Patrick Joseph) [1960] 2 Q.B. 396; [1960] 3 W.L.R. 440 CCA 5–015,
5–016, 5–020
—— v Cahill [1993] Crim.L.R. 142 8–047
—— v Caldwell (James); sub nom Metropolitan Police Commissioner v Caldwell
[1982] A.C. 341; [1981] 2 W.L.R. 509 HL 2–065, 2–067, 2–068, 2–069, 2–070,
2–071, 2–072, 3–010, 5–038, 6–010, 7–074, 10–007, 10–010
—— v Calhaem (Kathleen Nell) [1985] Q.B. 808; [1985] 2 W.L.R. 826 CA (Crim
Div) 4–008
—— v Campbell (1987) 84 Cr.App.R. 225 CA (Crim Div) 5–015
—— v Campbell (Colin Frederick) [1997] 1 Cr.App.R. 199; [1997] Crim.L.R. 227 CA
(Crim Div) 8–037
—— v —— (Tony) (1991) 93 Cr.App.R. 350; [1991] Crim.L.R. 268 CA (Crim Div) .....
6–005, 6–007
—— v Camplin (Paul); sub nom DPP v Camplin [1978] A.C. 705; [1978] 2 W.L.R.
679 HL 7–019, 7–020, 7–026, 7–027, 7–029, 7–031, 7–032
—— v Caresena [1996] Crim.L.R. 667 8–018
—— v Carey (Claire Anne) [2006] EWCA Crim 17; [2006] Crim.L.R. 842 7–045
—— v Cascoe (Handel Barrington) [1970] 2 All E.R. 833; (1970) 54 Cr.App.R. 401
CA (Crim Div) 7–020
—— v Cash (Noel) [1985] Q.B. 801; [1985] 2 W.L.R. 735 CA (Crim Div) 9–045

R. v Cato (Ronald Philip) [1976] 1 W.L.R. 110; [1976] 1 All E.R. 260 CA (Crim Div). . . .
2–034, 7–042, 7–046

—— v Champ (Kathleen Angela) (1981) 73 Cr.App.R. 367; [1982] Crim.L.R. 108
CA (Crim Div) 3–007

—— v Chan–Fook (Mike) [1994] 1 W.L.R. 689; [1994] 2 All E.R. 552 CA (Crim
Div) 7–078, 7–079

—— v Charlson (Stanley) [1955] 1 W.L.R. 317; [1955] 1 All E.R. 859 Assizes
(Chester) 2–007, 2–011, 5–010

—— v Cheshire (David William) [1991] 1 W.L.R. 844; [1991] 3 All E.R. 670 CA
(Crim Div) 2–046, 2–047, 2–048

—— v Chrastny (Charlotte Barbara) (No.1) [1991] 1 W.L.R. 1381; [1992] 1 All E.R.
189 CA (Crim Div) 6–040

—— v Christie (Paul Andrew) (1990–91) 12 Cr.App.R.(S.) 540 CA (Crim Div). . . . 9–034,
9–035

—— v Church (Cyril David) [1966] 1 Q.B. 59; [1965] 2 W.L.R. 1220 CCA . . 2–078, 4–024,
7–044, 7–047

—— v City of Sault Ste Marie (1978) 85 D.L.R. (3d) 161 S Ct of Canada 3–028

—— v Clarence (1888) 22 Q.B.D. 23 . . . . 7–069, 7–084, 7–086, 7–128

—— v Clark (Brian James) [2001] EWCA Crim 884; [2002] 1 Cr.App.R. 14 CA
(Crim Div) 8–048

—— v Clarke (May) [1972] 1 All E.R. 219; (1972) 56 Cr.App.R. 225 CA (Crim
Div) 5–013

—— v Clarkson (David George) [1971] 1 W.L.R. 1402; [1971] 3 All E.R. 344
CMAC 4–010

—— v Clear (Thomas Walter) [1968] 1 Q.B. 670; [1968] 2 W.L.R. 122 CA (Crim
Div) 9–034

—— v Clegg (Lee William)[1995] 1 A.C. 482; [1995] 2 W.L.R. 80 HL 5–056, 5–060,
5–104

—— v Clothier (Julian Robert) [2004] EWCA Crim 2629 7–052

—— v Clouden [1987] Crim.L.R. 56 CA (Crim Div) 9–021

—— v Clowes (Peter) (No.2) [1994] 2 All E.R. 316 CA (Crim Div) 8–031

—— v Coady (Terence Patrick) [1996] Crim.L.R. 518 CA (Crim Div) 8–029, 9–006,
9–015

—— v Coffey [1987] Crim.L.R. 498 CA (crim Div) 8–047

—— v Cogan and Leak. *See* R. v Cogan (John Rodney)

—— v Cogan (John Rodney); sub nom R. v Cogan and Leak [1976] Q.B. 217; [1975]
3 W.L.R. 316 CA (Crim Div) 2–083, 4–005, 4–039, 7–130

—— v Cole [1993] Crim.L.R. 300 . . . . 5–030, 5–036

—— v Coleman (1986) 150 J.P. 175; [1986] Crim.L.R. 56 CA (Crim Div) 9–044

—— v Coles (Lee Henry) [1995] 1 Cr.App.R. 157; [1994] Crim.L.R. 820 CA (Crim
Div) 2–068

—— v Collett (Michael) [1994] 1 W.L.R. 475; [1994] 2 All E.R. 372; [1994]
Crim.L.R. 607 CA (Crim Div) 3–012

—— v Collins (Stephen William George) [1973] Q.B. 100; [1972] 3 W.L.R. 243 CA
(Crim Div) 9–024, 9–026

—— v Collister (Thomas James) (1955) 39 Cr.App.R. 100 CCA 9–033

—— v Concannon [2002] Crim.L.R. 213 3–025

—— v Coney (1881–82) L.R. 8 Q.B.D. 534 QBD 4–010

R. v Congdon (1990) N.L.J. 1221 4–041

R. v Constanza (Gaetano) [1997] 2 Cr.App.R. 492; [1997] Crim.L.R. 576 CA (Crim
Div) 7–067
—— v Conway (Francis Gerald) [1989] Q.B. 290; [1988] 3 W.L.R. 1238 CA (Crim
Div) 5–082, 5–093
—— v Cooke (David) [1997] Crim.L.R. 436 CA (Crim Div) 9–055
—— v Cooper and Schaub [1994] Crim.L.R. 531; (1994) 91(5) L.S.G. 35 7–120
—— v Corbett (Christopher) [1996] Crim.L.R. 594 CA (Crim Div) 2–038
—— v Cort (Peter Laurence) [2003] EWCA Crim 2149; [2004] Q.B. 388; [2003] 3
W.L.R. 1300 7–128
—— v Cory Bros & Co Ltd [1927] 1 K.B. 810 Assizes (Glamorgan) 4–064
—— v Cousins (Robert William) [1982] Q.B. 526; [1982] 2 W.L.R. 621 CA (Crim
Div) 5–046
—— v Cox (Adrian Mark) [1995] 2 Cr.App.R. 513; [1995] Crim.L.R. 741 CA (Crim
Div) 5–015
—— v Craig and Bentley, *The Times*, December 10–13, 1952 . . . . 4–002, 4–045
—— v Cugullere (Sidney) [1961] 1 W.L.R. 858; [1961] 2 All E.R. 343; (1961) 45
Cr.App.R. 108 CCA 9–030
—— v Cullen Unreported (1974) 8–033
—— v Cunningham (Roy) [1957] 2 Q.B. 396; [1957] 3 W.L.R. 76 CCA 2–052, 2–065,
2–066, 2–067, 2–070, 2–071, 2–072, 2–083, 3–010, 4–003, 4–007, 4–012, 5–028,
7–009, 7–015, 7–016, 7–017, 7–074, 7–088, 7–089, 9–026, 10–007, 10–010
—— v Curr (Patrick Vincent) [1968] 2 Q.B. 944; [1967] 2 W.L.R. 595 CA (Crim
Div) 6–023, 6–024
—— v D; sub nom R. Dhaliwal [2006] EWCA Crim 1139; [2006] 2 Cr.App.R. 24 . . 2–050,
7–044, 7–047, 7–078
—— v Dadson (George) (1850)175 E.R. 499; (1850) 3 Car. & K. 148 Assizes 2–002,
2–003, 2–004, 2–053, 2–085, 5–055, 7–016
—— v Dalby (Derek Shaun) [1982] 1 W.L.R. 425; [1982] 1 All E.R. 916; (1982) 74
Cr.App.R. 348 CA (Crim Div) 7–046
—— v Dalloway (1847) 2 Cox C.C. 273 . . . . 2–033, 7–059
—— v Davies (Peter John Brinley) [1975] Q.B. 691; [1975] 2 W.L.R. 586 CA (Crim
Div) 7–020
—— v Davis (1823) Russ & Ry 499 9–024
—— v Davis (Gary) (1989) 88 Cr.App.R. 347; [1988] Crim.L.R. 762 CA (Crim
Div) 8–036
—— v Dawson [1976] Crim.L.R. 692 CA (Crim Div) 7–045, 9–021, 9–022
—— v Day [2001] Crim.L.R. 984 4–024
—— v Dean (Brian) [2002] EWCA Crim 2410 7–052
—— v Dear (Patrick) [1996] Crim.L.R. 595 CA (Crim Div) 2–050
—— v Deller (Charles Avon) (1952) 36 Cr.App.R. 184; (1952) 102 L.J. 679 CCA . . 2–001,
2–002, 2–003, 2–004
—— v Denton (John Thomas) [1981] 1 W.L.R. 1446; [1982] 1 All E.R. 65 CA (Crim
Div) 10–005, 10–016
—— v Devonald (Stephen) [2008] EWCA Crim 527 . . . . 7–126, 7–127, 7–134
—— v Deyemi (Danny) [2007] EWCA Crim 2060; [2008] 1 Cr.App.R. 25; (2008) 172
J.P. 137 CA (Crim Div) 3–023, 3–025
—— v Dhaliwal. *See* R. v D

R. v Dhillon (Kuljit Singh) [1997] 2 Cr.App.R. 104; [1997] Crim.L.R. 286 CA (Crim
    Div) 7–023
—— v Dhillon [1997] Crim.L.R. 295 5–059
—— v Dias (Fernando Augusto) [2001] EWCA Crim 2986; [2002] 2 Cr.App.R. 5;
    [2002] Crim.L.R. 490 CA (Crim Div) 2–043, 2–044, 7–042
—— v Dica (Mohammed) [2004] EWCA Crim 1103; [2004] Q.B. 1257; [2004] 3
    W.L.R. 213 CA (Crim Div) 7–086, 7–099, 7–106, 7–113, 7–121, 7–128
—— v Dickie (Andrew Plummer) [1984] 1 W.L.R. 1031; [1984] 3 All E.R. 173 CA
    (Crim Div) 5–013, 5–014
—— v Dietschmann (Anthony) [2003] UKHL 10; [2003] 1 A.C. 1209; [2003] 2
    W.L.R. 613 . . . . 5–017, 5–018, 5–019
—— v DPP [2007] EWHC 739 (Admin); (2007) 171 J.P. 404; (2007) 171 J.P.N. 738
    Div Ct 9–020
—— v —— Ex p. Kebilene [2000] 2 A.C. 326; [1999] 3 W.L.R. 972 HL 5–015
—— v Dix (Trevor Glyn) (1982) 74 Cr.App.R. 306; [1982] Crim.L.R. 302 CA (Crim
    Div) 5–015
—— v DJ [2007] EWCA Crim 3133 2–034
—— v Donaghy and Marshall [1981] Crim.L.R. 644 CC (Snaresbrook) 9–021
—— v Donovan (John George) [1934] 2 K.B. 498; (1936) 25 Cr.App.R. 1 CCA . . . 7–101,
                                                                                            7–106
—— v Doring (Petra) [2002] EWCA Crim 1695; [2002] B.C.C. 838; [2003] 1
    Cr.App.R. 9 CA (Crim Div) 3–025
—— v Doughty (Stephen Clifford) (1986) 83 Cr.App.R. 319; [1986] Crim.L.R. 625
    CA (Crim Div) 7–020
—— v Doukas (Joseph Davis) [1978] 1 W.L.R. 372; [1978] 1 All E.R. 1061 CA (Crim
    Div) 9–006, 9–057
—— v Downes (1875) 13 Cox C.C. 111 2–018
—— v Downes (Patrick Joseph) (1983) 77 Cr.App.R. 260; (1983) 147 J.P. 729 CA
    (crim Div) 8–047
—— v Drameh [1983] Crim.L.R. 322 Crown Ct 9–015
—— v Drew (Martin Ralph) [2000] 1 Cr.App.R. 91; [1999] Crim.L.R. 581 CA (Crim
    Div) 6–032
—— v Dryden [1995] 4 All E.R. 987 CA (Crim Div) 7–031
—— v Dudley [1989] Crim.L.R. 57 CA (Crim Div) 10–011
—— v Dudley (Thomas); sub nom R. v Dudley and Stephens (1884–85) L.R. 14
    Q.B.D. 273 . . . . 5–063, 5–064, 5–065, 5–076, 7–100
—— v Dudley and Stephens. See R. v Dudley (Thomas)
—— v Duffy [1949] 1 All E.R. 932 CCA 7–019, 7–021
—— v Duffy (Elizabeth Lilian) [1967] 1 Q.B. 63; [1966] 2 W.L.R. 229 CCA 5–047
—— v Duguid (1906) 70 J.P. 294 6–041
—— v Dunbar [1988] Crim.L.R. 693 CA (Crim Div) 4–025
—— v Dunnington (Kevin Vincent) [1984] Q.B. 472; [1984] 2 W.L.R. 125 CA (Crim
    Div) 6–002
—— v Durkin (John) [1973] Q.B. 786; [1973] 2 W.L.R. 741 CA (Crim Div) 9–053
—— v Dyke (Ian James) [2001] EWCA Crim 2184; [2002] 1 Cr.App.R. 30; [2002]
    Crim.L.R. 153 8–034
—— v Dyson [1908] 2 K.B. 454 7–009
—— v Dytham (Philip Thomas) [1979] Q.B. 722; [1979] 3 W.L.R. 467; [1979] 3 All
    E.R. 641; (1979) 69 Cr.App.R. 387 CA (Crim Div) 2–025

R. v EB. *See* R. v B

—— v Eagleton (David Edgar) (1982) 4 Cr.App.R.(S.) 47; [1982] Crim.L.R. 322 CA
(Crim Div) 6–003

—— v Easom (John Arthur) [1971] 2 Q.B. 315; [1971] 3 W.L.R. 82 CA (Crim Div) . . . . .
8–050

—— v Edwards [1991] Crim.L.R. 45 CA (Crim Div) 6–047

—— v Egan (Michael) [1998] 1 Cr.App.R. 121; (1997) 35 B.M.L.R. 103 CA (Crim
Div) 5–001, 5–006, 5–020

—— v Elbekkay [1920] 1 K.B. 340 7–127

—— v El–Faisal (Abdullah Ibrahim) [2004] EWCA Crim 343 CA (Crim Div) 6–024

—— v El–Ghazal [1986] Crim.L.R. 52 CA (Crim Div) 6–031

—— v El–Kurd (Ussama Sammy) [2001] Crim.L.R. 234 CA (Crim Div) 6–045

—— v Ellames (Charles John) [1974] 1 W.L.R. 1391; [1974] 3 All E.R. 130 CA
(Crim Div) 9–013

—— v Elvin [1976] Crim.L.R. 204 CA (Crim Div) 3–019

—— v Emmett (Stephen Roy), *The Times*, October 15, 1999 CA (Crim Div) 7–105

—— v English. *See* R. v Powell (Anthony Glassford)

—— v Enoch (1833) 5 C. & P. 539 7–004

—— v Esop 91836) 7 C. & P. 456 2–082

—— v Evans [1992] Crim.L.R. 559 2–037

—— v Evening Standard Co Ltd Ex p. Attorney General [1954] 1 Q.B. 578; [1954] 2
W.L.R. 861 CA 3–003

—— v Fallon [1994] Crim.L.R. 519 CA (Crim Div) 6–009

—— v Faraj (Shwan) [2007] EWCA Crim 1033; [2007] 2 Cr.App.R. 25; (2007)
104(21) L.S.G. 25 CA (Crim Div) 5–051

—— v Feely (David) [1973] Q.B. 530; [1973] 2 W.L.R. 201 CA (Crim Div)   8–043, 8–044

—— v Fegan [1972] N.I. 80 5–050

—— v Fennell (Peter) [2000] 1 W.L.R. 2011; [2000] 2 Cr.App.R. 318; (2000) 164 J.P.
386; [2000] Crim.L.R. 677 CA (Crim Div) 10–002

—— v Fenton (1830) 1 Lew C.C. 179 7–038

—— v Fernandes (Roland Anthony) [1996] 1 Cr.App.R. 175 CA (Crim Div) 8–048

—— v Finch and Jardine Unreported, 1983 5–049

—— v Finlay (Paul Anthony) [2003] EWCA Crim 3868 CA (Crim Div) 2–044

—— v Firth (Peter Stanley) (1990) 91 Cr.App.R. 217; (1990) 154 J.P. 576 CA (Crim
Div) 2–022

—— v Fisher (1865) L.R. 1 C.C.R. 7 10–004

—— v —— [1987] Crim.L.R. 334 5–053

—— v Fitzgerald [1992] Crim.L.R. 66 . . . . 4–002, 4–035

—— v Flattery (1877) 2 Q.B. 410 7–127

—— v Flynn [1970] Crim.L.R. 118 8–041

—— v Foreman [1991] Crim.L.R. 702 CA (Crim Div) 9–045

—— v Forman and Ford [1988] Crim.L.R. 677 CC 4–011, 4–035

—— v Forrester [1992] Crim.L.R. 792 CA (Crim Div) 9–020

—— v Forsyth (Elizabeth) [1997] 2 Cr.App.R. 299; [1997] Crim.L.R. 581 CA (Crim
Div) 2–074, 9–048, 9–051

—— v Fotheringham (William Bruce) (1989) 88 Cr.App.R. 206; [1988] Crim.L.R.
846 CA (Crim Div) 5–033, 5–034

—— v Fowler (Christopher Guy) (1988) 86 Cr.App.R. 219; [1987] Crim.L.R. 769 CA
(Crim Div) 9–050

R. v Francis [1982] Crim.L.R. 363 CA (Crim Div) 9–030

—— v Francom (Mark Frank) [2001] 1 Cr.App.R. 17; [2000] Crim.L.R. 1018 CA
(Crim Div) 4–010

—— v Franklin (1883) 15 Cox C.C. 163 7–038

—— v Fretwell (1862) 28 J.P. 499 4–013

—— v Fritschy [1985] Crim.L.R. 745 CA (Crim Div) 8–005, 8–010, 8–015

—— v G [2008] UKHL 37; [2009] 1 A.C. 92; [2008] 1 W.L.R. 1379   2–065, 2–069, 2–070,
2–071, 2–072, 3–010, 3–025, 5–038, 6–010, 7–074, 7–131, 7–135, 9–026, 10–007,
10–010

—— v G; sub nom R. v Gemmell and Richards [2002] EWCA Crim 1992; [2003] 3
All E.R. 206; [2003] 1 Cr.App.R. 23 CA (Crim Div) 3–025

—— v Gallasso (Lesley Caroline) (1994) 98 Cr.App.R. 284; [1993] Crim.L.R. 459 CA
(Crim Div) 8–005, 8–013, 8–018

—— v Galvin (Peter Anthony) [1987] Q.B. 862; [1987] 3 W.L.R. 93 CA (Crim
Div) 6–016, 6–017

—— v Gamble [1989] N.I. 268 .... 4–022, 4–023

—— v Gardner (1992) 14 Cr.App.R.(S) 364 7–022

—— v Garwood (Patrick Augustus) [1987] 1 W.L.R. 319; [1987] 1 All E.R. 1032 CA
(Crim Div) 9–034

—— v Geddes (Gary William) (1996) 160 J.P. 697; [1996] Crim.L.R. 894 CA(Crim
Div) 6–007

—— v Gelder, *The Times*, May 24, 1994 CC (Chester) 7–065

—— v Gemmell and Richards. *See* R. v G (2002)

—— v Ghosh (Deb Baran) [1982] Q.B. 1053; [1982] 3 W.L.R. 110 CA (Crim
Div) .. 6–037, 8–017, 8–040, 8–043, 8–044, 8–045, 9–002, 9–007, 9–008, 9–010, 9–011,
9–036, 9–049

—— v Giannetto (Robert Vincent) [1997] 1 Cr.App.R. 1; [1996] Crim.L.R. 722 CA
(Crim Div) 4–002, 4–035

—— v Gibbins and Proctor (1918) 13 Cr.App.R. 134 .... 2–018, 2–019, 2–022

—— v Gibson (1984) 80 Cr.App.R. 24 4–011

—— v Gibson (Richard Norman) [1990] 2 Q.B. 619; [1990] 3 W.L.R. 595; [1991] 1
All E.R. 439 CA (Crim Div) 3–003, 6–034

—— v Gilks (Donald) [1972] 1 W.L.R. 1341; [1972] 3 All E.R. 280; (1972) 56
Cr.App.R. 734 CA (Crim Div) 8–036

—— v Gill (Samuel James)[1963] 1 W.L.R. 841; [1963] 2 All E.R. 688 CCA 5–085

—— v Gilmartin (Anthony) [1983] Q.B. 953; [1983] 2 W.L.R. 547 CA (Crim Div)   9–006

—— v Gilmour (Thomas Robert) [2000] N.I. 367; [2000] 2 Cr.App.R. 407 CA (Crim
Div) (NI) 4–026

—— v Gingell (Stuart Matthew) [2000] 1 Cr.App.R. 88; (1999) 163 J.P. 648 CA
(Crim Div) 9–044

—— v Gittens (Charlesworth Alexander) [1984] Q.B. 698; [1984] 3 W.L.R. 327 CA
(Crim Div) 5–017

—— v Goldman [2001] Crim.L.R. 894 6–024

—— v Goodfellow (Kevin) (1986) 83 Cr.App.R. 23; [1986] Crim.L.R. 468 CA (Crim
Div) 7–046

—— v Goodwin (Phillip) [1996] Crim.L.R. 262 CA (Crim Div) 9–057

—— v Gordon (Michael Ryan) [2004] EWCA Crim 961 4–018

—— v Gore (Lisa Therese) (Deceased) [2007] EWCA Crim 2789; [2008] Crim.L.R.
388 CA (Crim Div) 7–058

R. v Gotts (Benjamin) [1992] 2 A.C. 412; [1992] 2 W.L.R. 284 HL 5–080

—— v Governor of Brixton Prison Ex p. Levin [1997] Q.B. 65; [1997] 1 W.L.R. 51;
[1996] 3 W.L.R. 657; [1996] 4 All E.R. 350 Div Ct 8–016

—— v —— Ex p. Osman (No.1) [1991] 1 W.L.R. 281; [1992] 1 All E.R. 108
Div Ct 8–015

—— v Governor of Pentonville Prison Ex p. Osman (No.1) [1990] 1 W.L.R. 277;
[1989] 3 All E.R. 701 QBD 8–049

—— v Gowans (Paul Robert) [2003] EWCA Crim 3935 2–048

—— v Gower (2007). *See* Attorney General's Reference (No.54 of 2007)

—— v Graham [1996] N.I. 157 CA (NI) 4–044

—— v Graham (Hemamali Krishna) [1997] 1 Cr.App.R. 302; [1997] Crim.L.R.
340 9–055

—— v —— (Paul Anthony) [1982] 1 W.L.R. 294; [1982] 1 All E.R. 801 CA (Crim
Div) 5–087, 5–094

—— v Grainge (Albert Robert Burns) [1974] 1 W.L.R. 619; [1974] 1 All E.R. 928
CA (Crim Div) 9–047

—— v Grant (Heather) [2001] EWCA Crim 2611; [2002] Q.B. 1030; [2002] 2 W.L.R.
1409 5–002

—— v Great North of England Ry (1846) 9 Q.B. 315 4–065

—— v Greatrex and Bates [1999] 1 Cr.App.R. 126 4–023

—— v Greaves, *The Times*, July 11, 1987 CA (Crim Div) 9–045

—— v Green (Barry Roland) [1992] Crim.L.R. 292 CA (Crim Div) 8–045

—— v Gregory (John Paul) (1983) 77 Cr.App.R. 41; [1982] Crim.L.R. 229 CA (Crim
Div) 9–045

—— v Gregory and Mott [1995] Crim.L.R. 507 2–060

—— v Gresham (Lawrence) [2003] EWCA Crim 2070 .... 8–018, 8–036

—— v Griffin [1993] Crim.L.R. 515 CA (Crim Div) 6–005, 6–007

—— v Griffiths (Leslie George) (1974) 60 Cr.App.R. 14 CA (Crim Div) 9–047

—— v Gross (1913) 23 Cox C.C. 455 7–020

—— v Grundy [1977] Crim.L.R. 543 CA (Crim Div) 4–043

—— v Gullefer (Ian John) [1990] 1 W.L.R. 1063; [1990] 3 All E.R. 882 CA (Crim
Div) 6–003, 6–004

—— v H (Karl Anthony) [2005] EWCA Crim 732; [2005] 1 W.L.R. 2005; [2005] 2
All E.R. 859 CA (Crim Div) 1–009, 7–062, 7–133

—— v Haider Unreported, March 22, 1985 9–042

—— v Hale (Robert Angus) (1979) 68 Cr.App.R. 415; [1979] Crim.L.R. 596 CA
(Crim Div) 9–021, 9–022, 9–045

—— v Hall (1848) 1 Den. 381 8–047

—— v Hall (Edward Leonard) (1985) 81 Cr.App.R. 260; [1985] Crim.L.R. 377 CA
(Crim Div) 9–047, 9–048

—— v —— (Geoffrey) [1973] Q.B. 126; [1972] 3 W.L.R. 381 CA (Crim Div) 8–033

—— v Hallam [1995] Crim.L.R. 323 CA (Crim Div) 3–009, 8–001, 8–033

—— v Hallam (James Edward) [1957] 1 Q.B. 569; [1957] 2 W.L.R. 521 CCA 2–074

—— v Halliday (1889) 61 L.T. 701 2–037

—— v Hancock (Reginald Dean) [1986] A.C. 455; [1986] 2 W.L.R. 357 HL 4–020

—— v —— (Stephen Frederick) [1990] 2 Q.B. 242; [1990] 2 W.L.R. 640; (1990) 90
Cr.App.R. 422 CA (Crim Div) 8–031

—— v Hancock and Shankland [1985] 3 W.L.R. 1014; [1986] 1 All E.R. 641 CA
(Crim Div) 2–059

R. v Hardie (Paul Deverall) [1985] 1 W.L.R. 64; [1984] 3 All E.R. 848 CA (Crim Div)....
　　　　　　　　　　　　　　　　　　　　　　　　　　　　2–012, 2–068, 5–038
—— v Harmer (Roy Peter) [2005] EWCA Crim 1; [2005] 2 Cr.App.R. 2; [2005]
　　Crim.L.R. 482 CA (Crim Div) 6–044
—— v Harris (Martin) (1987) 84 Cr.App.R. 75 CA (Crim Div)................. 9–021
—— v Harrison [1996] Crim.L.R. 200 3–008
—— v Harry [1974] Crim.L.R. 32 9–034
—— v Harvey [1999] Crim.L.R. 70 CA 6–046
—— v Harvey (Alfred Alphonsus) (1981) 72 Cr.App.R. 139; [1981] Crim.L.R. 104
　　CA (Crim Div) 9–036
—— v Hasan (Aytach) [2005] UKHL 22; [2005] 2 A.C. 467; [2005] 2 W.L.R. 709;
　　[2005] 4 All E.R. 685 .... 5–071, 5–083, 5–086, 5–087, 5–092
—— v Hatton (Jonathan) [2005] EWCA Crim 2951; [2006] 1 Cr.App.R. 16; [2006]
　　Crim.L.R. 353 5–033,
—— v Hayward (1908) 21 Cox C.C. 692 2–035
—— v Heard (Lee)[2007] EWCA Crim 125; [2008] Q.B. 43; [2007] 3 W.L.R. 475 CA
　　(Crim Div) 5–030, 5–031, 7–133
—— v Heath [2000] Crim.L.R. 109 .... 5–091, 5–092
—— v Hegarty [1994] Crim.L.R. 353 CA (Crim Div) 5–088
—— v Hendy (Jason Geoffrey) [2006] EWCA Crim 819; [2006] 2 Cr.App.R. 33;
　　[2006] M.H.L.R. 244 CA (Crim Div) 5–017
—— v Hennessy (Andrew Michael) [1989] 1 W.L.R. 287; [1989] 2 All E.R. 9 CA
　　(Crim Div) 2–006, 5–010, 5–011
—— v Hennigan (James) [1971] 3 All E.R. 133; (1971) 55 Cr.App.R. 262 CA (Crim
　　Div) 2–034
—— v Hibbert (1865–72) L.R. 1 C.C.R. 184 CCR 3–002
—— v Hicks (Gareth Peter) [2007] EWCA Crim 1500 CA (Crim Div) 7–083
—— v Higgins (1801) 102 E.R. 269; (1801) 2 East 5 Assizes (Leeds) 6–021
—— v Hill (Valerie Mary) (1989) 89 Cr.App.R. 74; [1989] Crim.L.R. 136 CA (Crim
　　Div) 10–017
—— v Hilton (Peter Arnold) [1997] 2 Cr.App.R. 445; (1997) 161 J.P. 459 CA (Crim
　　Div) 8–022
—— v Hinks (Karen Maria) [2001] 2 A.C. 241; [2000] 3 W.L.R. 1590; [2000] 4 All
　　E.R. 833 HL 8–016, 8–017, 8–018, 9–001
—— v Hinton–Smith (David John) [2005] EWCA Crim 2575 7–134
—— v HM Coroner for East Kent Ex p. Spooner (1987) 3 B.C.C. 636; (1989) 88
　　Cr.App.R. 10 QBD 4–064
—— v HM Coroner for Inner London South District Ex p. Douglas–Williams [1999]
　　1 All E.R. 344; (1998) 162 J.P. 751 CA (Civ Div) 7–054
—— v Holbrook (1878) 4 Q.B.D. 42 4–050
—— v Holden [1991] Crim.L.R. 478 CA (Crim Div) 8–041
—— v Holland (1841) 2 Mood. & R. 351 2–049
—— v Hollinshead (Peter Gordon) [1985] 2 W.L.R. 761; [1985] 1 All E.R. 850 CA
　　(Crim Div) 6–048
—— v Hollis [1971] Crim.L.R. 525 CA (Crim Div) 9–023
—— v Home Secertary Ex p. Anderson. See R. (on the application of Anderson) v
　　Secretary of State for the Home Department
—— v Hood (Kenneth) [2003] EWCA Crim 2772; [2004] 1 Cr.App.R.(S.) 73 7–052
—— v Hoof (Mark Anthony) (1981) 72 Cr.App.R. 126; (1980) 2 Cr.App.R.(S.) 299
　　CA (Crim Div) 10–010, 10–012

R. v Hopkins and Kendrick [1997] 2 Cr.App.R. 524; [1997] Crim.L.R. 359 CA (Crim Div) 8–016, 8–035

—— v Horseferry Road Magistrates' Court Ex p. K [1997] Q.B. 23; [1996] 3 W.L.R. 68 QBD 5–014

—— v Howe (1958) 100 C.L.R. 448 .... 5–056, 5–067, 5–072, 5–074, 5–076, 5–080, 5–087, 5–093

—— v Howe (Michael Anthony) [1987] A.C. 417; [1987] 2 W.L.R. 568 HL   4–016, 4–040

—— v Howells (Colin David) [1977] Q.B. 614; [1977] 2 W.L.R. 716 CA (Crim Div) 3–008

—— v Hudson and Taylor [1971] 2 Q.B. 202; [1971] 2 W.L.R. 1047 CA (Crim Div) 5–082, 5–085, 5–086

—— v Huggins (1730) 2 Strange 883 4–050

—— v Hughes (1785) 1 Leach 406 9–025

—— v —— (1860) Bell C.C. 242 4–037

—— v —— [1995] Crim.L.R. 957 CA (Crim Div) 5–055

—— v Humphreys (Emma) [1995] 4 All E.R. 1008; [1996] Crim.L.R. 431 CA (Crim Div) 7–022, 7–031, 7–033

—— v Humphreys and Turner [1965] 3 All E.R. 689 4–037

—— v Hurley and Murray [1967] V.R. 526 .... 5–083, 5–085

—— v Hurst (Marnie Michelle) [1995] 1 Cr.App.R. 82 CA (Crim Div) 5–088

—— v Hussain (Akhtar) [2002] EWCA Crim 6; [2002] 2 Cr.App.R. 26; [2002] Crim.L.R. 407 CA (Crim Div) 6–032

—— v —— (Iftikhar) [1981] 1 W.L.R. 416; [1981] 2 All E.R. 287 CA (Crim Div) .. 3–008

—— v Hussey (1924) 18 Cr.App.R. 160 5–051

—— v Hutchins [1988] Crim.L.R. 379 CA (Crim Div) 5–029

—— v Hyam [1997] Crim.L.R. 439 8–045

—— v Hyde (David Charles) [1991] 1 Q.B. 134; [1990] 3 W.L.R. 1115 ..... 4–015, 4–020

—— v Hysa (Alfred) [2005] EWCA Crim 1791 7–125

—— v Ibrams (James David) (1982) 74 Cr.App.R. 154 CA (Crim Div) 7–021

—— v ICR Haulage Ltd [1944] K.B. 551; (1945) 30 Cr.App.R. 31 CCA 4–061

—— v Inseal [1992] Crim.L.R. 35 CA (Crim Div) 5–018

—— v Ireland (Robert Matthew); sub nom R. v Burstow [1998] A.C. 147; [1997] 3 W.L.R. 534; [1997] 4 All E.R. 225 HL ... 2–064, 7–065, 7–066, 7–067, 7–076, 7–078, 7–084, 7–086, 7–095

—— v Isitt (Douglas Lance) (1978) 67 Cr.App.R. 44; [1978] R.T.R. 211 CA (Crim Div) 2–007

—— v Ismail [1977] Crim.L.R. 557 CA (Crim Div) 9–047

—— v JF Alford Transport Ltd [1997] 2 Cr.App.R. 326; [1999] R.T.R. 51 CA (Crim Div) 4–013

—— v Jackson [1985] R.T.R. 257 5–053

—— v Jackson (Robert Valentine) [2006] EWCA Crim 2380; [2007] 1 W.L.R. 1035; [2007] 1 Cr.App.R. 28 CMAC 3–012

—— v Jackson, Golding and Jackson [1985] Crim.L.R. 442 CA (Crim Div) 6–049

—— v Jakeman (Susan Lesley) (1983) 76 Cr.App.R. 223; [1983] Crim.L.R. 104 CA (Crim Div) 2–077

—— v James (Leslie); sub nom R. v James (Leslie) [2006] EWCA Crim 14; [2006] Q.B. 588; [2006] 2 W.L.R. 887 .... 5–015, 5–058, 7–033

—— v James and Ashford (1985) 82 Cr.App.R. 232 6–022

—— v James and Karimi. See R. v James (Leslie)

R. v Janjua (Nadeem Ahmed) [1999] 1 Cr.App.R. 91; [1998] Crim.L.R. 675 CA
(Crim Div) 7–016
—— v Jeff and Bassett (1967) 51 Cr.App.R. 28 CA (Crim Div)................. 9–007
—— v Jenkins [1983] 1 All E.R. 993 9–029
—— v Jennings [1990] Crim.L.R. 588 CA (Crim Div) 7–041
—— v Jheeta (Harvinder Singh) [2007] EWCA Crim 1699; [2008] 1 W.L.R. 2582;
[2007] 2 Cr.App.R. 34 CA (Crim Div) 7–122, 7–123, 7–126, 7–127
—— v Johnson (Christopher Richard) [1989] 1 W.L.R. 740; [1989] 2 All E.R. 839;
(1989) 89 Cr.App.R. 148 CA (Crim Div) 7–024
—— v —— (Dean) [2007] EWCA Crim 1978; [2008] Crim.L.R. 132; (2007) 104(37)
L.S.G. 35 5–008
—— v Jones, *The Times*, December 18, 1963 5–093
—— v Jones (John) [1976] 1 W.L.R. 672; [1976] 3 All E.R. 54 CA (Crim Div).... 9–026
—— v —— (John McKinsie) (1974) 59 Cr.App.R. 120; [1974] I.C.R. 310 CA (Crim
Div) 6–032
—— v —— (Kenneth Henry) [1990] 1 W.L.R. 1057; [1990] 3 All E.R. 886 CA (Crim
Div) 6–003, 6–004, 6–005, 6–007
—— v —— (Margaret) [2004] EWCA Crim 1981; [2005] Q.B. 259; [2004] 3 W.L.R.
1362 CA (Crim Div) 10–017
—— v —— [2006] UKHL 16; [2007] 1 A.C. 136; [2006] 2 W.L.R. 772 5–046
—— v —— (Terence) (1986) 83 Cr.App.R. 375; [1987] Crim.L.R. 123 7–112
—— v Jordan (James Clinton) (1956) 40 Cr.App.R. 152 CCA 2–046, 2–048
—— v K (Age of Consent: Reasonable Belief) [2001] UKHL 41; [2002] 1 A.C. 462;
[2001] 3 W.L.R. 471; [2001] 3 All E.R. 897 HL 3–021, 3–023, 3–024, 7–135
—— v K (Patrick Joseph) [2004] EWCA Crim 2685; [2005] 1 Cr.App.R. 25 CA
(Crim Div) 6–035
—— v Kanwar (Rena Louise) [1982] 1 W.L.R. 845; [1982] 2 All E.R. 528 CA (Crim
Div) 9–043, 9–044, 9–051
—— v Kell [1985] Crim.L.R. 239 CA (Crim Div) 8–040
—— v Kelly (Anthony Noel) [1999] Q.B. 621; [1999] 2 W.L.R. 384; [1998] 3 All E.R.
741 CA (Crim Div) 8–024, 10–005
—— v —— (Ronnie Peter) (1993) 97 Cr.App.R. 245; [1993] Crim.L.R. 763 CA
(Crim Div) 9–031
—— v Kemp (Albert) [1957] 1 Q.B. 399; [1956] 3 W.L.R. 724 Assizes (Bristol).... 5–010,
5–012
—— v Kennedy (Simon) No.1) [1999] Crim.L.R. 65 .... 2–043, 2–044, 7–042, 7–046
—— v —— (No.2) [2007] UKHL 38; [2008] 1 A.C. 269; [2007] 3 W.L.R. 612 HL   2–039,
2–043, 2–044, 2–045, 7–042, 7–047
—— v Kenning (David Matthew) [2008] EWCA Crim 1534; [2009] Q.B. 221; [2008]
3 W.L.R. 1306 CA (Crim Div) 6–033
—— v Khan (Mohammed Iqbal) [1990] 1 W.L.R. 813; [1990] 2 All E.R. 783 CA
(Crim Div) 5–029, 6–010, 6–011, 6–012, 6–043
—— v Khan and Khan [1998] Crim.L.R. 830 .... 7–043, 7–054
—— v Kimber (David Michael) [1983] 1 W.L.R. 1118; [1983] 3 All E.R. 316 CA
D(Crim Div) 2–084, 7–100
—— v King [1938] 2 All E.R. 662 9–039
—— v Kingston (Barry) [1995] 2 A.C. 355; [1994] 3 W.L.R. 519; [1994] 3 All E.R.
353 HL 2–052, 5–027, 5–035, 5–036, 7–060
—— v Kite and OLL Ltd Unreported, December 8, 1994, Winchester Crown Ct ... 4–065

R. v Klass (Kennedy Francis) [1998] 1 Cr.App.R. 453; (1998) 162 J.P. 105 9–031
—— v Klineberg (Jonathan Simon) [1999] 1 Cr.App.R. 427; [1999] Crim.L.R. 417
 CA (Crim Div) 8–033
—— v Kohn (David James) (1979) 69 Cr.App.R. 395; [1979] Crim.L.R. 675 CA
 (Crim Div) 8–022
—— v Konzani (Feston) [2005] EWCA Crim 706; [2005] 2 Cr.App.R. 14 . . . 7–099, 7–106,
 7–121
—— v Kopsch (1925) 10 Cr.App.R. 50 5–008
—— v Korniak (Anthony John) (1983) 76 Cr.App.R. 145; [1983] Crim.L.R. 109 CA
 (Crim Div) 9–048
—— v Kosh (1964) 44 Cr. 185 (Sask., CA) 4–043
—— v Krause (1902) 66 J.P. 121 6–022
—— v Kromer (Edward Thomas) [2002] EWCA Crim 1278 CA (Crim Div) 7–020
—— v Lamb (Terence Walter) [1967] 2 Q.B. 981; [1967] 3 W.L.R. 888 CA (Crim
 Div) 7–040, 7–050, 7–063
—— v Lambert [1972] Crim.L.R. 422 9–036
—— v Lambert (Steven) [2002] Q.B. 1112; [2001] 2 W.L.R. 211 CA (Crim Div) . . . 2–064,
 5–015
—— v Lambie (Shiralee Ann) [1981] 1 W.L.R. 78; [1981] 1 All E.R. 332 CA (Crim
 Div) 9–006
—— v Landy (Harry) [1981] 1 W.L.R. 355; [1981] 1 All E.R. 1172 CA
 (Crim Div) 6–037, 8–043
—— v Lane and Lane (1986) 82 Cr.App.R. 5 4–035
—— v Langmead (1864) Le. & Ca. 427 9–045
—— v Larkin (Henry) [1943] K.B. 174; [1943] 1 All E.R. 217 CCA 7–038
—— v Larsonneur (Germaine) (1934) 24 Cr.App.R. 74 CCA   2–005, 2–013, 2–014, 3–001
—— v Latham [1965] Crim.L.R. 434; (1965) 109 S.J. 371 CCA 5–003
—— v Latif (Khalid) [1996] 1 W.L.R. 104; [1996] 1 All E.R. 353 HL 2–041, 2–042,
 2–044, 2–077
—— v Latimer (1886) L.R. 17 Q.B.D. 359 CCR 2–080, 2–081
—— v Laverty (Charles) [1970] 3 All E.R. 432; (1970) 54 Cr.App.R. 495 CA (Crim
 Div) 9–006
—— v Lawrence and Pomeroy (1971) 55 Cr.App.R. 64 9–034
—— v Le Brun (John) [1992] Q.B. 61; [1991] 3 W.L.R. 653; [1991] 4 All E.R. 673
 CA (Crim Div) 2–040, 2–078, 2–079
—— v Lees (James Anthony) [2007] EWCA Crim 1640 CA (Crim Div) 9–023
—— v Lesbini (Donald) [1914] 3 K.B. 1116; (1916) 11 Cr.App.R. 7 CCA 7–019
—— v Lewis [1970] Crim.L.R. 647 CA (Crim Div) 2–037, 7–067, 7–084
—— v Lewis (Gareth Edmund) (1988) 87 Cr.App.R. 270; [1988] Crim.L.R. 542 CA
 (Crim Div) 3–008
—— v Lidar [2000] 4 Archbold News 3 CA 7–054
—— v Lightfoot (Richard James) (1993) 97 Cr.App.R. 24; (1993) 157 J.P. 156 CA
 (Crim Div) 2–082
—— v Linekar (Gareth) [1995] Q.B. 250; [1995] 2 W.L.R. 237 CA (Crim Div) 7–127
—— v Lipman (Robert) [1970] 1 Q.B. 152; [1969] 3 W.L.R. 819 CA (Crim Div) . . 2–012,
 5–037
—— v Litchfield [1998] Crim.L.R. 507 7–052
—— v Litholetovs (Mihails) [2002] EWCA Crim 1154 CA (Crim Div) 6–004
—— v Lloyd (Derek William) [1967] 1 Q.B. 175; [1966] 2 W.L.R. 13 CCA 5–020

R. v LLoyd (Sidney Douglas) [1985] Q.B. 829; [1985] 3 W.L.R. 30 CA
(Crim Div) 8–048, 8–049
—— v Lockley (Adrian Neil) [1995] 2 Cr.App.R. 554 CA (Crim Div) 9–021
—— v Loukes (Noel Martyn) [1996] 1 Cr.App.R. 444; [1996] R.T.R. 164; [1996]
Crim.L.R. 341 CA (Crim Div) 4–039
—— v Lovesey and Peterson [1970] 1 Q.B. 352 4–025
—— v Lowe (Robert) [1973] Q.B. 702; [1973] 2 W.L.R. 481; [1973] 1 All E.R. 805
CA (Crim Div) 2–016, 7–049
—— v Lunderbech [1991] Crim.L.R. 784 CA (Crim Div) 6–034
—— v M [2005] Crim.L.R. 479 9–057
—— v M (John) [2003] EWCA Crim 3452; [2004] M.H.L.R. 86 .... 5–001, 5–002
—— v —— (Richard) (A Juvenile); sub nom R. v Marjoram [2000] Crim.L.R. 372   2–038
—— v M (2004). See R. v Montila (Steven William)
—— v MH [2004] WL 137 6–006
—— v McCarthy (Michael Reginald) [1967] 1 Q.B. 68; [1966] 2 W.L.R. 555 CCA .. 5–001
—— v McCullum (Miriam Lavinia) (1973) 57 Cr.App.R. 645; [1973] Crim.L.R. 582
CA (Crim Div) 9–048
—— v McDavitt [1981] Crim.L.R. 843 CA (Crim Div) 9–017
—— v McDonald (Lloyd George) (1980) 70 Cr.App.R. 288; [1980] Crim.L.R. 242
CA (Crim Div) 9–048
—— v McDonnell [1966] 1 Q.B. 233; [1965] 3 W.L.R. 1138 Assizes (Bristol) 6–039
—— v McGrowther (17546) 18 State Tr. 391 5–082
—— v McHugh (1993) 97 Cr.App.R. 335 8–033
—— v McHugh and Tringham (1988) 88 Cr.App.R. 385 8–014
—— v McInnes (Walter) [1971] 1 W.L.R. 1600; [1971] 3 All E.R. 295 CA (Crim Div) ....
5–056, 5–060
—— v McIvor (John Gerard) [1982] 1 W.L.R. 409; [1982] 1 All E.R. 491 CA (Crim
Div) 6–037, 8–043, 8–044
—— v McKechnie (Roy Maurer) (1992) 94 Cr.App.R. 51; [1992] Crim.L.R. 194 ... 2–035
—— v Mackie (Robert) (1973) 57 Cr.App.R. 453; [1973] Crim.L.R. 438 CA (Crim
Div) 2–037
—— v Macklin (1838) 2 Law CC 225 4–014
—— v McKoy (Daniel) [2002] EWCA Crim 1628 2–002
—— v M–Loughlin (1838) 8 C. & P. 635 7–083
—— v McNamara (James) (1988) 87 Cr.App.R. 246; (1988) 152 J.P. 390 CA (Crim
Div) 3–008
—— v McShane (Yolande Tregenna) (1978) 66 Cr.App.R. 97; [1977] Crim.L.R. 737
CA (Crim Div) 6–002, 7–057
—— v Mahmood (Asaf) [1995] R.T.R. 48; [1994] Crim.L.R. 368 4–023
—— v Mainwaring (Paul Rex) (1982) 74 Cr.App.R. 99 CA (Crim Div) 8–034
—— v Malcherek (Richard Tadeusz) [1981] 1 W.L.R. 690; [1981] 2 All E.R. 422 CA
(Crim Div) 2–048, 7–005
—— v Malone (Thomas Patrick)[1998] 2 Cr.App.R. 447; [1998] Crim.L.R. 834 CA
(Crim Div) 7–125
—— v Mandair (Singh Mandair) [1995] 1 A.C. 208; [1994] 2 W.L.R. 700 HL 7–085
—— v Marchant (Thomas John) [2003] EWCA Crim 2099; [2004] 1 W.L.R. 442;
[2004] 1 All E.R. 1187 CA (Crim Div) 2–033
—— v Marjoram. See R. v M (Richard) (A Juvenile)
—— v Marks [1998] Crim.L.R. 676 4–040

R. v Marlow (Michael David) [1998] 1 Cr.App.R.(S.) 273; [1997] Crim.L.R. 897 CA
    (Civ Div) 6–021, 6–022
—— v Marriott (Charles Percival) [1971] 1 W.L.R. 187; [1971] 1 All E.R. 595 CA
    (Crim Div) 3–007
—— v Marsh (William) [1997] 1 Cr.App.R. 67; (1996) 160 J.P. 721; [1997] R.T.R.
    195; [1997] Crim.L.R. 205 CA (Crim Div) 9–053
—— v Marshall (Adrian John) [1998] 2 Cr.App.R. 282; (1998) 162 J.P. 489 CA
    (Crim Div) 8–048
—— v Martin (1881) 8 Q.B.D. 54 .... 7–069, 7–084
—— v Martin (Anthony Edward)[2001] EWCA Crim 2245; [2003] Q.B. 1; [2002] 2
    W.L.R. 1; [2002] 1 Cr.App.R. 27; [2002] Crim.L.R. 136 .... 5–057, 5–058
—— v —— (Colin) [1989] 1 All E.R. 652; (1989) 88 Cr.App.R. 343 CA
    (Crim Div) 5–082, 5–093
—— v —— (David Paul) [2000] 2 Cr.App.R. 42; (2000) 164 J.P. 174; [2000] CA
    (Crim Div) 5–058, 5–087, 5–095
—— v Matheson (1958) 42 Cr.App.R. 145 5–003
—— v Matthews [2003] 2 Cr.App.R. 461 CA 2–027
—— v Matudi (Misawki Kurawku) [2003] EWCA Crim 697; [2003] E.H.L.R. 13 CA
    (Crim Div) 3–024, 3–025
—— v Mavji (Ramniklal Nathoo) [1987] 1 W.L.R. 1388; [1987] 2 All E.R. 758 CA
    (Crim Div) 2–015
—— v Mazo (Ellen) [1997] 2 Cr.App.R. 518; [1996] Crim.L.R. 435 CA (Crim Div) ......
                                                                        8–016, 8–035
—— v Meade and Belt (1823) 1 Lew C.C. 184 7–064
—— v Meech (Arthur James) [1974] Q.B. 549; [1973] 3 W.L.R. 507 CA
    (Crim Div) 8–034
—— v Mellor (Gavin Thomas) [1996] 2 Cr.App.R. 245; [1996] Crim.L.R. 743 CA
    (Crim Div) 2–047
—— v Mercer [2001] All E.R. (D) 187 4–002
—— v Meredith [1973] Crim.L.R. 253 CC (Manchester) 8–029
—— v Merrick (1980) 71 Cr.App.R. 130 6–042
—— v Merrick (David Stephen) [1996] 1 Cr.App.R. 130; [1995] Crim.L.R. 802 CA
    (Crim Div) 10–010, 10–015
—— v Miah [2003] 1 Cr.App.R. 100 9–033
—— v Miah (Alamin) [2004] EWCA Crim 63 4–010
—— v Millard and Vernon [1987] Crim.L.R. 397 .... 6–008, 6–010, 6–011
—— v Miller, *The Times*, May 16, 1972 5–017
—— v Miller (James) [1983] 2 A.C. 161; [1983] 2 W.L.R. 539 HL ... 2–004, 2–022, 2–027,
                                                                    2–077, 7–064, 7–070
—— v —— (Peter) [1954] 2 Q.B. 282; [1954] 2 W.L.R. 138 Assizes (Winchester) .. 7–078
—— v Millward (Sidney Booth) (1994) 158 J.P. 1091; [1994] Crim.L.R. 527 CA
    (Crim Div) 4–012, 4–039
—— v Mir, *Independent*, May 23, 1994 6–043
—— v Misra (Amit) [2004] EWCA Crim 2375; [2005] 1 Cr.App.R. 21; [2005]
    Crim.L.R. 234 7–053
—— v Mitchell (Carl) [2003] EWCA Crim 2188; [2004] R.T.R. 14; [2004] Crim.L.R.
    139 CA (Crim Div) 10–017
—— v —— (Frank) (1999) 163 J.P. 75; [1999] Crim.L.R. 496 CA (Crim Div) 4–044,
                                                                             4–045

R. v Mitchell (Ronald James) [1983] Q.B. 741; [1983] 2 W.L.R. 938; [1983] 2 All E.R.
    427 CA (Crim Div) 2–080, 2–081, 7–046
—— v Mohammed (Faqir) [2005] EWCA Crim 1880 .... 5–015, 5–058, 7–033
—— v Mohan (John Patrick) [1976] Q.B. 1; [1975] 2 W.L.R. 859 CA (Crim Div).. 6–008
—— v Moloney (Alistair Baden) [1985] A.C. 905; [1985] 2 W.L.R. 648 HL   2–055, 2–058,
                                   2–059, 2–061, 4–020, 5–029, 6–008, 7–054
—— v Monaghan [1979] Crim.L.R. 673 CA (Crim Div) 8–006
—— v Montila (Steven William); sub nom R. v M [2004] UKHL 50; [2004] 1 W.L.R.
    3141; [2005] 1 All E.R. 113 6–044
—— v Morhall (Alan Paul) [1996] A.C. 90; [1995] 3 W.L.R. 330 HL   7–028, 7–031, 7–032
—— v Morris (David Alan); sub nom Morris, Anderton v Burnside [1983] Q.B. 587;
    [1983] 2 W.L.R. 768 CA (Crim Div) 8–004, 8–006, 8–007, 8–008, 8–009, 8–010,
                                                         8–014, 8–015
—— v —— (Harold Lyndon) (1984) 79 Cr.App.R. 104; (1985) 149 J.P. 60 CA (Crim
    Div) 9–030
—— v Morrison [2003] All E.R. (D) 281 6–009
—— v Morrison (Lawrence Andrew) (1989) 89 Cr.App.R. 17 CA (Crim Div) 7–092
—— v Moses and Ansbro [1991] Crim.L.R. 617 CA (Crim Div) 6–036
—— v Most (1881) 7 Q.B.D. 244 6–022
—— v Mowatt (Sidney Linton) [1968] 1 Q.B. 421; [1967] 3 W.L.R. 1192 CA (Crim
    Div) 7–088, 7–089, 7–092
—— v Muhamad [2003] EWCA Crim 182 3–024
—— v Mulligan [1990] S.T.C. 200 8–047
—— v Mullins (1843) 3 Cox C.C. 526 5–102
—— v Nash [1999] Crim.L.R. 308 6–003
—— v Navvabi (Hesamadin) [1986] 1 W.L.R. 1311; [1986] 3 All E.R. 102 CA (Crim
    Div) 8–022
—— v Nawaz Unreported, May 13, 1999 4–042
—— v Nedrick (Ransford Delroy) [1986] 1 W.L.R. 1025; [1986] 3 All E.R. 1; (1986)
    83 Cr.App.R. 267 CA (Crim Div) 2–060, 2–061, 6–009
—— v Newell (1980) 71 Cr.App.R. 331 5–059
—— v Ngan (Sui Soi) [1998] 1 Cr.App.R. 331; (1997) 94(33) L.S.G. 27 CA (Crim
    Div) 8–015
—— v Nicholls (1874) 13 Cox C.C. 75 2–026
—— v Nicklin (David John) [1977] 1 W.L.R. 403; [1977] 2 All E.R. 444 CA (Crim
    Div) 9–037
—— v Nkosiyana 1966 (4) S.A. 655 6–021
—— v Notman [1994] Crim.L.R. 518 CA (Crim Div) 2–034
—— v O–Brien (1856) 4 Cox C.C. 398 9–025
—— v O'Connor [1991] Crim.L.R. 135 CA (Crim Div) 5–031, 5–033, 7–016
—— v O'Donnell (Paul Anthony) [1996] 1 Cr.App.R. 286; (1996) 29 B.M.L.R. 65
    CA (Crim Div) 5–003
—— v O'Flaherty (Errol Carlton) [2004] EWCA Crim 526; [2004] 2 Cr.App.R. 20;
    [2004] Crim.L.R. 751 .... 4–023, 4–042, 4–044
—— v Ofori (Noble Julius) (1994) 99 Cr.App.R. 223 CA (Crim Div) 9–038
—— v O'Grady (Patrick Gerald) [1987] Q.B. 995; [1987] 3 W.L.R. 321 CA (Crim
    Div) 5–031, 5–032, 5–033, 5–047, 7–016
—— v O'Hadhmaill [1996] Crim.L.R. 509 CA (Crim Div) 6–049
—— v O'Leary (Michael) (1986) 82 Cr.App.R. 341 CA (Crim Div) 9–031

R. v Olugboja (Stephen) [1982] Q.B. 320; [1981] 3 W.L.R. 585 CA (Crim Div).... 7–121, 7–122

—— v Ortiz (1986) 83 Cr.App.R. 173 .... 5–082, 5–083

—— v Osborne (1919) 84 J.P. 63 6–005

—— v O–Shea [2004] Crim.L.R. 948 6–022

—— v O'Toole (Michael) [1987] Crim.L.R. 759 6–008

—— v Owino (Nimrod) [1996] 2 Cr.App.R. 128; [1995] Crim.L.R. 743 CA (Crim Div) 5–053, 5–054, 5–055, 5–060

—— v P&O European Ferries (Dover) Ltd (1991) 93 Cr.App.R. 72; [1991] Crim.L.R. 695 Central Crim Ct 4–064, 4–065

—— v Pagett (David Keith) (1983) 76 Cr.App.R. 279; [1983] Crim.L.R. 393 CA (Crim Div) 2–033, 2–040

—— v Park (James Chalmers) (1988) 87 Cr.App.R. 164; [1988] Crim.L.R. 238 CA (Crim Div) 9–038, 9–042

—— v Parker [1993] Crim.L.R. 856 CA (Crim Div) 6–043, 10–010

—— v Parker (Daryl Clive) [1977] 1 W.L.R. 600; [1977] 2 All E.R. 37; [1977] Crim.L.R. 102 CA (Crim Div) 2–065

—— v —— (Philip) [1997] Crim.L.R. 760 CA (Crim Div) 8–037

—— v Parkes [1973] Crim.L.R. 358 CC (Sheffield) 9–035

—— v Parmenter (Philip Mark) (No.1) [1991] 2 W.L.R. 408; [1991] 2 All E.R. 225 CA (Crim Div) 7–074, 7–080, 7–088, 7–092, 7–105

—— v Patnaik Unreported, November 5, 2000 CA 6–006

—— v Pearman (Stephen Dennis) (1985) 80 Cr.App.R. 259; [1985] R.T.R. 39 CA (Crim Div) 6–008

—— v Pearson (William) [1992] Crim.L.R. 193 CA (Crim Div) 7–020

—— v Pembliton (Henry) (1872–75) L.R. 2 C.C.R. 119 CCR 2–080, 2–081

—— v Perman (Sam) [1996] 1 Cr.App.R. 24; [1995] Crim.L.R. 736 CA (Crim Div) 4–032, 4–043

—— v Petters and Parfitt [1995] Crim.L.R. 501 4–014

—— v Phekoo (Harold) [1981] 1 W.L.R. 1117; [1981] 3 All E.R. 84 CA (Crim Div) 2–084

—— v Philippou (1989) 89 Cr.App.R. 290 .... 8–014, 8–029

—— v Phillips (Aaron) [2004] EWCA Crim 112 CA (Crim Div) 7–093

—— v Pike [1961] Crim.L.R. 547 CCA 7–054

—— v Pitchley (Abraham Joseph) (1973) 57 Cr.App.R. 30; [1972] Crim.L.R. 705 CA (Crim Div) 9–043

—— v Pitham (Charles Henry) (1977) 65 Cr.App.R. 45; [1977] Crim.L.R. 285 CA (Crim Div) 8–005, 8–049, 9–045

—— v Pitts (1842) Car. & M. 284 2–037

—— v Pittwood (1902) 19 T.L.R. 37 2–026

—— v Pommell (Fitzroy Derek) [1995] 2 Cr.App.R. 607; (1995) 92(27) L.S.G. 32 CA (Crim Div) 5–094

—— v Pordage [1975] Crim.L.R. 575 CA (Crim Div) 5–035

—— v Poulton (1832) 5 C. & P. 329 7–004

—— v Powell (Anthony Glassford); sub nom R. v English [1999] 1 A.C. 1; [1997] 3 W.L.R. 959; [1997] 4 All E.R. 545 HL ... 4–016, 4–019, 4–020, 4–022, 4–023, 4–026, 4–032, 4–033

—— v Preddy (John Crawford) [1996] A.C. 815; [1996] 3 W.L.R. 255; [1996] Crim.L.R. 726 HL 8–015, 8–048, 9–001, 9–051

R. v Prentice [1993] 4 All E.R. 935 7–050

—— v Price, *The Times*, December 22, 1971 5–016

—— v Price (Ronald William) (1990) 90 Cr.App.R. 409; [1990] Crim.L.R. 200 CA
(Crim Div) 8–045

—— v Prince (1875) L.R. 2 C.C.R. 154   2–082, 2–083, 3–001, 3–002, 3–023, 5–028, 6–043

—— v Quadir and Khan Unreported, July 24, 1997, Case No.9602311 6–007

—— v Quayle (Barry); sub nom R. v Altham [2005] EWCA Crim 1415; [2005] 1
W.L.R. 3642; [2006] 1 All E.R. 988 CA (Crim Div) 5–068

—— v Quick (William George) [1973] Q.B. 910; [1973] 3 W.L.R. 26; [1973] 3 All
E.R. 347 CA (Crim Div) 2–012, 5–010

—— v R (Rape: Marital Exemption) [1992] 1 A.C. 599; [1991] 3 W.L.R. 767 HL . . 4–039,
7–120

—— v Rafferty (Andrew Paul) [2007] EWCA Crim 1846; [2008] Crim.L.R. 218 CA
(Crim Div) 2–039, 4–045

—— v Rahman (Islamur) [2008] UKHL 45; [2009] 1 A.C. 129; [2008] 3 W.L.R. 264;
[2008] 4 All E.R. 351 .... 4–019, 4–021, 4–022, 4–023, 4–032, 4–033

—— v Ransford (1874) 13 Cox C.C. 9 6–022

—— v Rashford (Nicholas) [2005] EWCA Crim 3377; [2006] Crim.L.R. 547 5–048

—— v Rashid (Abdul) [1977] 1 W.L.R. 298; [1977] 2 All E.R. 237 CA
(Crim Div) 9–006, 9–057

—— v Reader (1977) 66 Cr.App.R. 33 9–047

—— v Reardon [1999] Crim.L.R. 392 4–013

—— v Redfern (John Michael) (1992) 13 Cr.App.R.(S.) 709; [1993] Crim.L.R. 43
CA (Crim Div) 4–062

—— v Reed (Nicholas) [1982] Crim.L.R. 819 CA (Crim Div) 4–012, 6–049

—— v Reid (Barry) (1976) 62 Cr.App.R. 109; [1976] Crim.L.R. 570 CA
(Crim Div) 4–024, 4–025

—— v —— (John Joseph) [1992] 1 W.L.R. 793; [1992] 3 All E.R. 673 HL . . 2–068, 2–069

—— v Renouf (John William) [1986] 1 W.L.R. 522; [1986] 2 All E.R. 449 CA (Crim
Div) 5–045, 5–050

—— v Richards (Darrell) (No.2) [2002] EWCA Crim 3175 .... 2–043, 2–044

—— v —— (Isabelle Christina) [1974] Q.B. 776; [1973] 3 W.L.R. 888 CA (Crim Div) . . . .
4–040

—— v Richardson (Diane) [1999] Q.B. 444; [1998] 3 W.L.R. 1292; [1999] Crim.L.R.
62 CA (Crim Div) 7–112, 7–113, 7–116

—— v —— (Nigel John) [1999] 1 Cr.App.R. 392; [1999] Crim.L.R. 494 CA (Crim
Div) 5–033

—— v Richens (Andrew Ronald) [1993] 4 All E.R. 877; (1994) 98 Cr.App.R. 43 CA
(Crim Div) 7–021

—— v Rizvi (Zafar) [2003] EWCA Crim 3575 6–044

—— v Roberts (John Joseph) (1984) 78 Cr.App.R. 41; (1984) 148 J.P. 14 CA (Crim
Div) 6–042

—— v —— (Kelvin James) [1993] 1 All E.R. 583; (1993) 96 Cr.App.R. 291 CA
(Crim Div) 4–016, 4–017, 4–018, 4–020

—— v —— (Kenneth Joseph) (1972) 56 Cr.App.R. 95; [1972] Crim.L.R. 27 CA
(Crim Div) 2–037, 2–038, 7–080

—— v —— (William) (1987) 84 Cr.App.R. 117; [1986] Crim.L.R. 188 CA (Crim
Div) 8–045, 9–049

—— v Roberts and George [2997] Crim.L.R. 209 4–039

R. v Robertson (Eric John) [1968] 1 W.L.R. 1767; [1968] 3 All E.R. 557 CA (Crim
    Div) 5–001
—— v Robinson [1977] Crim.L.R. 173 CA (Crim Div) 8–040, 9–020, 9–022
—— v —— Unreported, February 3, 2000 (Case No.9903443Y3) 4–045
—— v Robinson (Harry) [1915] 2 K.B. 342; (1916) 11 Cr.App.R. 124 6–004
—— v Rodger and Rose [1998] 1 Cr.App.R. 143 CA (Crim Div) 5–094
—— v Roffel [1985] V.R. 511 8–014
—— v Rogers Unreported, June 15, 1999 (Case No.99/2314/W4) 5–088
—— v Rogers (Philip) [2007] UKHL 8; [2007] 2 A.C. 62; [2007] 2 W.L.R. 280 HL   7–097
—— v —— (Stephen) [2003] EWCA Crim 945; [2003] 1 W.L.R. 1374; [2003] 2
    Cr.App.R. 10 CA (Crim Div) 2–044, 2–045, 7–042, 7–043
—— v Rook (Adrian) [1993] 1 W.L.R. 1005; [1993] 2 All E.R. 955 CA
    (Crim Div) 4–027, 4–028, 4–043
—— v Rose (Christopher) [2004] EWCA Crim 764 4–006
—— v Rossiter (Ethel Amelia) [1994] 2 All E.R. 752; (1992) 95 Cr.App.R. 326 CA
    (Crim Div) 7–023
—— v Rostron (Terry) [2003] EWCA Crim 2206 . . . . 8–031, 8–040
—— v Rothery (Henry Michael) (1976) 63 Cr.App.R. 231; [1976] R.T.R. 550 CA
    (Crim Div) 8–024
—— v Rowland (Philip) [2003] EWCA Crim 3636; (2004) 148 S.J.L.B. 26 CA (Crim
    Div) 7–030
—— v Rowley (Michael) [1991] 1 W.L.R. 1020; [1991] 4 All E.R. 649 CA (Crim Div) . . . .
    6–002
—— v Ruffell (Stephen David) [2003] EWCA Crim 122; [2003] 2 Cr.App.R.(S.) 53
    CA (Crim Div) 2–026, 7–052
—— v Russell (Raymond) (1985) 81 Cr.App.R. 315; [1985] Crim.L.R. 231 CA (Crim
    Div) 9–030
—— v Ryan (Lee Bernard) (1996) 160 J.P. 610; [1996] Crim.L.R. 320 CA (Crim Div) . . . .
    9–025
—— v S [2005] All E.R. (D) 339 (Mar) 7–057
—— v Saik (Abdulrahman) [2006] UKHL 18; [2007] 1 A.C. 18; [2006] 2 W.L.R. 993
    HL 6–043
—— v St Margaret's Trust Ltd [1958] 1 W.L.R. 522; [1958] 2 All E.R. 289 CCA . .   3–024,
    3–027
—— v St Q [2002] 1 Cr.App.R.(S.) 440 9–036
—— v Sakavickas (Rolandas) [2004] EWCA Crim 2686; [2005] 1 W.L.R. 857; [2005]
    1 Cr.App.R. 36 CA (Crim Div) 6–044
—— v Salisbury [1976] V.R. 452 Supreme Ct of Victoria 7–085, 7–086
—— v Sanders (William John) (1982) 75 Cr.App.R. 84; [1982] Crim.L.R. 695 CA
    (Crim Div) 9–044
—— v Sang (Leonard Anthony) [1980] A.C. 402; [1979] 3 W.L.R. 263 HL 5–100
—— v Sansom (Alec James) [1991] 2 Q.B. 130; [1991] 2 W.L.R. 366 CA (Crim Div) . . . .
    6–051
—— v Satnam and Kewal (1983) 78 Cr.App.R. 149 7–130
—— v Saunders and Archer (1573) 2 Plowd. 473 QB 4–039, 4–042
—— v Savage (Susan) [1992] 1 A.C. 699; [1991] 3 W.L.R. 914 HL . .   7–061, 7–069, 7–078,
    7–080, 7–088, 7–092, 7–105
—— v Scalley [1995] Crim.L.R. 504 2–060
—— v Scarlett (John) [1993] 4 All E.R. 629; (1994) 98 Cr.App.R. 290 CA (Crim
    Div) 5–053, 5–054, 5–055, 5–060, 7–040

R. v Seers (John Samuel) (1984) 79 Cr.App.R. 261; (1985) 149 J.P. 124 CA (Crim Div) 5–016

—— v Senior (1832) 1 Mood. C.C. 346 7–004

—— v Shadbolt (1835) 5 C. & P. 504 7–083

—— v Shadrokh–Cigari (Hamid) [1988] Crim.L.R. 465 CA (Crim Div) 8–031, 8–037

—— v Shama (Abu) [1990] 1 W.L.R. 661; [1990] 2 All E.R. 602 CA (Crim Div) ... 2–022

—— v Sharp (David Bruce) [1987] Q.B. 853; [1987] 3 W.L.R. 1 CA (Crim Div) ... 5–091

—— v Shelton (Peter Alan) (1986) 83 Cr.App.R. 379; (1986) 150 J.P. 380 CA (Crim Div) 9–037

—— v Shepherd (Martin Brian) (1988) 86 Cr.App.R. 47; [1987] Crim.L.R. 686 CA (Crim Div) 5–091

—— v Sheppard (James Martin) [1981] A.C. 394; [1980] 3 W.L.R. 960 HL 3–010

—— v Shivpuri (Pyare) [1987] A.C. 1; [1986] 2 W.L.R. 988 HL 6–016, 6–017, 9–038

—— v Shorrock (Peter Coar) [1994] Q.B. 279; [1993] 3 W.L.R. 698; [1993] 3 All E.R. 917 CA (Crim Div) 3–003

—— v Shuck [1992] Crim.L.R. 209 CA (Crim Div) 8–008

—— v Silverman (Michael John) (1988) 86 Cr.App.R. 213; (1987) 151 J.P. 657 CA (Crim Div) 9–010

—— v Simpson (Calvin) [1983] 1 W.L.R. 1494; [1983] 3 All E.R. 789; (1984) 78 Cr.App.R. 115; (1984) 148 J.P. 33; [1984] Crim.L.R. 39 CA (Crim Div) 9–030

—— v Singh (Gurmit) [1966] 2 Q.B. 53; [1966] 2 W.L.R. 88 Assizes (Leeds) 6–019

—— v —— (Gurphal) [1999] Crim.L.R. 582 CA (Crim Div) 7–051

—— v Siracusa (Francesco) (1990) 90 Cr.App.R. 340; [1989] Crim.L.R. 712 CA (Crim Div) 6–045, 6–048

—— v Skipp [1975] Crim.L.R. 114 CA (Crim Div) 8–005, 8–006, 8–007, 8–008, 8–010

—— v Slack (Martin Andrew) [1989] Q.B. 775; [1989] 3 W.L.R. 513 CA (Crim Div) 4–015

—— v Slater (Darren Terence) [1996] Crim.L.R. 494 CA (Crim Div) 9–038

—— v Slingsby [1995] Crim.L.R. 570 7–106

—— v Sloggett (Sydney Ernest) [1972] 1 Q.B. 430; [1971] 3 W.L.R. 628 CA (Crim Div) 9–037

—— v Small (Adrian Anthony) (1988) 86 Cr.App.R. 170; [1988] R.T.R. 32; [1987] Crim.L.R. 777 CA (Crim Div) 8–046

—— v Smith [1979] Crim.L.R. 251 CC (Birmingham) 2–025

—— v Smith (Morgan James) [2001] 1 A.C. 146; [2000] 3 W.L.R. 654 HL .. 5–015, 7–029, 7–030, 7–031, 7–032, 7–033, 7–034, 7–035, 8–037

—— v —— (Sandie) [1982] Crim.L.R. 531 CA (Crim Div) 5–016

—— v —— (Thomas Joseph) [1959] 2 Q.B. 35; [1959] 2 W.L.R. 623 CMAC 2–046, 2–047, 2–048, 2–049, 2–050

—— v Spencer [1988] Crim.L.R. 707 7–059

—— v Spratt (Robert Michael) [1990] 1 W.L.R. 1073; [1991] 2 All E.R. 210; (1990) 91 Cr.App.R. 362 CA (Crim Div) 2–066, 7–080

—— v Spriggs [1993] Crim.L.R. 622 9–053

—— v Spurge (Frederick Albert) [1961] 2 Q.B. 205; [1961] 3 W.L.R. 23 CCA 2–008

—— v Squire [1990] Crim.L.R. 341 CA (Crim Div) 8–045

—— v Stagg [1978] Crim.L.R. 227 9–048

—— v Steane (Anthony Cedric) [1947] K.B. 997; [1947] 1 All E.R. 813 CCA 2–056

—— v Steer (Dennis) [1988] A.C. 111; [1987] 3 W.L.R. 205; [1987] 2 All E.R. 833 HL 10–008, 10–009

R. v Stephen (Malcolm R) (1984) 79 Cr.App.R. 334; (1985) 149 J.P. 89 CA (Crim
 Div) 2–068
—— v Stephens (1865–66) L.R. 1 Q.B. 702 Ct of QB 3–003, 4–050
—— v Stephenson (Brian Keith) [1979] Q.B. 695; [1979] 3 W.L.R. 193 CA (Crim
 Div) 2–065
—— v Stewart (Benjamin James) [1995] 4 All E.R. 999; [1996] 1 Cr.App.R. 229
 (Note) CA (Crim Div) 7–023
—— v —— (Heather); sub nom R. v Stewart and Schofield [1995] 3 All E.R. 159;
 [1995] 1 Cr.App.R. 441 CA   4–024, 4–025, 4–026, 4–027, 4–028, 4–032, 4–033, 6–026
—— v Stewart and Schofield. See R. v Stewart (Heather)
—— v Stokes [1982] Crim.L.R. 695 9–053
—— v Stone (John Edward); sub R. v Stone and Dobinson [1977] Q.B. 354; [1977] 2
 W.L.R. 169; [1977] 2 All E.R. 341 CA (Crim Div) 2–026, 7–054
—— v Stone and Dobinson. See R. v Stone (John Edward)
—— v Stones (James) [1989] 1 W.L.R. 156; (1989) 89 Cr.App.R. 26 CA (Crim Div) . . . . .
 9–031
—— v Stringer (Neil Bancroft) (1992) 94 Cr.App.R. 13; [1991] Crim.L.R. 639 CA
 (Crim Div) 4–004
—— v Suchedina (Hasnain) [2006] EWCA Crim 2543; [2007] 1 Cr.App.R. 23; [2007]
 Crim.L.R. 301 CA (Crim Div) 6–044
—— v Sullivan (Patrick Joseph) [1984] A.C. 156; [1983] 3 W.L.R. 123 HL . . 2–006, 5–009,
 5–010, 5–012, 5–014
—— v Sullivan and Ballion [2002] Crim.L.R. 758 8–024
—— v Suratan (Darren Anthony) [2004] EWCA Crim 1246 2–048
—— v T [1990] Crim.L.R. 256 CC 2–011
—— v Taaffe (Paul Desmond) [1983] 1 W.L.R. 627; [1983] 2 All E.R. 625 CA (Crim
 Div) 6–018
—— v Tabassum (Naveed) [2000] 2 Cr.App.R. 328; [2000] Lloyd's Rep. Med. 404;
 [2000] Crim.L.R. 686 . . . . 7–113, 7–116, 7–128
—— v Tandy (Linda Mary) [1989] 1 W.L.R. 350; [1989] 1 All E.R. 267 CA (Crim
 Div) 5–017, 5–018, 5–019, 5–040
—— v Taylor (1859) 1 F. & F. 511 6–007
—— v Taylor [1979] Crim.L.R. 649 CA (Crim Div) 9–023
—— v Taylor [1998] Crim.L.R. 582 4–002
—— v Taylor (Robert John) [2001] EWCA Crim 1044; [2002] Crim.L.R. 205 CA
 (Crim Div) 6–044
—— v Thomas (Emrys) (1985) 81 Cr.App.R. 331; [1985] Crim.L.R. 677 7–069
—— v Thomson (1965) 50 Cr.App.R. 1 6–046
—— v Thornton (Sara Elizabeth) (No.1) [1992] 1 All E.R. 306; (1993) 96 Cr.App.R.
 112 CA (Crim Div) 7–021
—— v —— (No.2) [1996] 1 W.L.R. 1174; [1996] 2 All E.R. 1023 CA (Crim Div) . . 7–022,
 7–031, 7–033
—— v Tokeley–Parry [1999] Crim.L.R. 578 9–044
—— v Tolson (1889) 23 Q.B.D. 168 3–023
—— v Tomsett [1985] Crim.L.R. 369 CA (Crim Div) 8–005
—— v Toor (Pritpal Singh) (1987) 85 Cr.App.R. 116; [1987] Crim.L.R. 122 CA
 (Crim Div) 9–048
—— v Tosti and White [1997] Crim.L.R. 746 . . . . 6–005, 6–007
—— v Tracey (1821) 168 E.R. 893 10–004

R. v Tulloch Unreported, February 25, 2000 CA 5–020

—— v Turner (Frank Richard) (No.2) [1971] 1 W.L.R. 901; [1971] 2 All E.R. 441
CA (Crim Div) 8–029

—— v Tyler and International Commercial Co [1891] 2 Q.B. 588 4–065

—— v Tyrrell [1894] 1 Q.B. 710 CCR 4–041, 6–028, 6–041

—— v Uddin (Rejan) [1999] Q.B. 431; [1998] 3 W.L.R. 1000 CA (Crim Div) 4–023

—— v Valderrama–Vega [1985] Crim.L.R. 220 CA (Crim Div) 5–082

—— v Van Dongen (Anthony Gerrard) (Appeal against Conviction [2005] EWCA
Crim 1728; [2005] 2 Cr.App.R. 38; [2005] Crim.L.R. 971 7–024

—— v Velasquez (Campo Elkin) [1996] 1 Cr.App.R. 155 CA (Crim Div) 6–002

—— v Velumyl [1989] Crim.L.R. 299 CA (Crim Div) 8–044

—— v Venna (Henson George) [1976] Q.B. 421; [1975] 3 W.L.R. 737 CA (Crim
Div) 7–074

—— v Vickers (John Willson) [1957] 2 Q.B. 664; [1957] 3 W.L.R. 326 CCA 7–015,
7–017

—— v Vincent (Christopher James) [2001] EWCA Crim 295; [2001] 1 W.L.R. 1172;
[2001] Crim.L.R. 488 CA (Crim Div) 9–016, 9–017

—— v W; sub nom R. v Wilson [2007] EWCA Crim 1251; [2007] 2 Cr.App.R. 31;
[2008] Crim.L.R. 138 5–079

—— v Wacker (Perry)[2002] EWCA Crim 1944; [2003] Q.B. 1207; [2003] 2 W.L.R.
374 CA (Crim Div) 7–051, 7–052

—— v Wain (Peter) [1995] 2 Cr.App.R. 660 CA (Crim Div) 8–034

—— v Wakely, Symonds and Holly [1990] Crim.L.R. 119 4–015

—— v Walker [1962] Crim.L.R. 458; 111 L.J. 344 CCA 6–031

—— v —— [1984] Crim.L.R. 112; (1983) 80 L.S.G. 3238 CA (Crim Div) 6–016

—— v Walker (John Charles) (1990) 90 Cr.App.R. 226; [1990] Crim.L.R. 44 CA
(Crim Div) 2–060, 6–008, 6–009

—— v Walkington (Terence John) [1979] 1 W.L.R. 1169; [1979] 2 All E.R. 716 CA
(Crim Div) 9–028

—— v Waltham (1849) 3 Cox 442 7–083

—— v Wan and Chan [1995] Crim.L.R. 296 4–027

—— v Wang (Cheong) [2005] UKHL 9; [2005] 1 W.L.R. 661; [2005] 1 All E.R.
782 6–003

—— v Warner (Brian William) (1971) 55 Cr.App.R. 93 CA (Crim Div) 8–047

—— v Watson (Clarence Archibald) [1989] 1 W.L.R. 684; [1989] 2 All E.R. 865 CA
(Crim Div) 2–035, 2–038, 7–045, 7–046

—— v Webster (Andrew) [1995] 2 All E.R. 168; [1995] 1 Cr.App.R. 492 CA (Crim
D8iv) 10–009

—— v —— (Peter David) [2006] EWCA Crim 415; [2006] 2 Cr.App.R. 6; [2006]
R.T.R. 19 4–011

—— v Weekes (Stephen) [1999] 2 Cr.App.R. 520; [1999] Crim.L.R. 907 CA (Crim
Div) 5–020

—— v Weller (David Alan) [2003] EWCA Crim 815; [2004] 1 Cr.App.R. 1; [2003]
Crim.L.R. 724 7–030

—— v Wellington [1993] Crim.L.R. 616 CA (Crim Div) 7–020

—— v Wells (Colin John) [2004] EWCA Crim 792 CA (Crim Div) 9–045

—— v Welsh [1974] R.T.R. 478 CA (Crim Div) 8–024

—— v Wheeler (Stephen Godfrey) (1991) 92 Cr.App.R. 279 CA (Crim Div) 9–040

—— v Wheelhouse [1994] Crim.L.R. 756 4–039

R. v Whitchurch (1896) 24 Q.B.D. 420 6–041

—— v White [1911] 2 K.B. 124 2–033

—— v Whitehouse [1941] 1 W.W.R. 112 CA (British Columbia) 4–042, 4–044, 4–045

—— v Whiteley (Nicholas Alan) (1991) 93 Cr.App.R. 25; (1991) 155 J.P. 917 CA
(Crim Div) 10–004

—— v Whiting (Paul Anthony) (1987) 85 Cr.App.R. 78; (1987) 151 J.P. 568 CA
(Crim Div) 9–023

—— v Whybrow (Arthur George) (1951) 35 Cr.App.R. 141; (1951) 95 S.J. 745
CCA 6–008

—— v Widdowson (1985) 82 Cr.App.R. 314 6–004

—— v Willer (Mark Edward) (1986) 83 Cr.App.R. 225; [1987] R.T.R. 22 CA (Crim
Div) 5–093

—— v Williams (Barry Anthony) [1992] 1 W.L.R. 380; [1992] 2 All E.R. 183 CA
(Crim Div) 2–038, 7–047

—— v —— (Gladstone) [1987] 3 All E.R. 411; (1984) 78 Cr.App.R. 276 CA (Crim
Div) 2–085, 5–032, 5–046, 5–051, 5–054, 5–055, 5–087, 7–016, 7–127

—— v —— (Roy) [2001] 1 Cr.App.R. 23; [2001] Crim.L.R. 253 CA (Crim Div) ... 8–022

—— v Williamson (Alan) (1978) 67 Cr.App.R. 35; [1978] Crim.L.R. 229 CA (Crim
Div) 9–030

—— v Willoughby (Keith Calverley) [2004] EWCA Crim 3365; [2005] 1 W.L.R.
1880; [2005] 1 Cr.App.R. 29 CA (Crim Div) 7–052, 7–053

—— v Wilson (2007). *See* R. v W

—— v Wilson (Alan Thomas) [1997] Q.B. 47; [1996] 3 W.L.R. 125; [1996] 2
Cr.App.R. 241 CA (Crim Div) 7–104, 7–105

—— v —— (Clarence George) [1984] A.C. 242; [1983] 3 W.L.R. 686 HL .. 2–021, 7–067,
7–069, 7–085, 7–086

—— v —— (George) [1955] 1 W.L.R. 493; [1955] 1 All E.R. 744 CCA 7–066

—— v Windle (Francis Wilfred) [1952] 2 Q.B. 826; [1952] 2 All E.R. 1 CCA 5–008

—— v Winson [1969] 1 Q.B. 371; [1968] 2 W.L.R. 113 CA (Crim Div) 4–055

—— v Wood (1830) 1 Mood. 278 7–083

—— v Wood (Clive) [2008] EWCA Crim 1305; [2009] 1 W.L.R. 496; [2008] 3 All
E.R. 898 CA (Crim Div) 5–017, 5–018

—— v Woods (Walter) (1982) 74 Cr.App.R. 312; [1982] Crim.L.R. 42 CA (Crim
Div) 5–033

—— v Woollin (Stephen Leslie) [1999] 1 A.C. 82; [1998] 3 W.L.R. 382; [1998] 4 All
E.R. 103; [1999] 1 Cr.App.R. 8 HL 2–060, 2–061, 4–020, 6–009

—— v Wright [2007] All E.R. (D) 267 7–125

R. (on the application of Abbott) v Colchester Magistrates' Court [2001] EWHC
Admin 136; (2001) 165 J.P. 386; [2001] Crim.L.R. 564 Div Ct 10–002

R. (on the application of Anderson) v Secretary of State for the Home Department;
sub nom R. v Home Secertary Ex p. Anderson [2002] UKHL 46; [2003] 1 A.C.
837; [2002] 3 W.L.R. 1800 7–008

R. (on the application of Burke) v General Medical Council [2004] EWHC 1879
(Admin); [2005] Q.B. 424; [2005] 2 W.L.R. 431 2–030

R. (on the application of Grundy & Co Excavations Ltd) v Halton Division
Magistrates' Court [2003] EWHC 272 (Admin); (2003) 167 J.P. 387; [2003] 1
P.L.R. 89 Div Ct 3–024

R. (on the application of H) v Mental Health Review Tribunal for North and East
London Region [2001] EWCA Civ 415; [2002] Q.B. 1; [2001] 3 W.L.R. 512 .. 5–024

R. (on the application of Lewin) v Crown Prosecution Service; sub nom Lewin v CPS
    [2002] EWHC 1049 (Admin) 2–027
R. (on the application of T) v DPP. *See* T v DPP Queen's Bench Division
    (Administrative Court)
Rabey v R. (1980) 54 C.C.C. (2d) 1 2–011
Race Relations Board v Applin [1973] Q.B. 815; [1973] 2 W.L.R. 895 CA (Civ Div) .....
                                                                          6–021
Rance v Mid–Downs HA [1991] 1 Q.B. 587; [1991] 2 W.L.R. 159 QBD 7–004
Read v Coker (1853) 13 C.B. 850 .... 7–066, 7–068
Redhead Freight v Shulman [1989] R.T.R. 1; [1988] Crim.L.R. 696 Div Ct 4–062
Reference under s.48A of the Criminal Appeal (Northern Ireland) Act 1968 (No.1 of
    1975). *See* Attorney General of Northern Ireland's Reference (No.1 of 1975),
    Re
Revill v Newberry [1996] Q.B. 567; [1996] 2 W.L.R. 239 CA (Civ Div) 5–048
Rice v Connolly [1966] 2 Q.B. 414; [1966] 3 W.L.R. 17 Div Ct 9–044
Roberts v Ramsbottom [1980] 1 W.L.R. 823; [1980] 1 All E.R. 7 QBD 2–007
Roe v Kingerlee [1986] Crim.L.R. 735 Div Ct 10–004
Rogers v Arnott [1960] 2 Q.B. 244; [1960] 3 W.L.R. 73 QBD 8–005
Rolle v Queen, The [1965] 1 W.L.R. 1341; [1965] 3 All E.R. 582 PC (Bahamas) ... 7–020
Roper v Taylor–s Central Garages (Exeter) Ltd [1951] 2 T.L.R. 284 2–073
Royall v R. (1991) 65 A.L.J.R. 451 2–037
Ryan and French v DPP (1994) 158 J.P. 485; [1994] Crim.L.R. 457 Div Ct 9–045
Ryan v R. (1967) 121 C.L.R. 205 High Ct Of Australia 2–007
S v DPP [2003] EWHC 2717 4–006
—— v Masilela [1968] (2) S.A. 558 2–079
—— v Robinson 1968 (1) S.A. 666 Supreme Ct of South Africa 7–099
SW v United Kingdom (A/355–B) [1996] 1 F.L.R. 434; (1996) 21 E.H.R.R. 363
    ECHR 7–120
St George's Healthcare NHS Trust v S [1998] 3 W.L.R. 936; [1998] 3 All E.R. 673
    CA (Civ Div) 5–065, 7–072
Scott v Commissioner of Police of the Metropolis [1975] A.C. 819; [1974] 3 W.L.R.
    741 HL 6–029, 6–035
Seaboard Offshore Ltd v Secretary of State for Transport [1994] 1 W.L.R. 541; [1994]
    2 All E.R. 99 HL 4–062
Searle v Randolph [1972] Crim.L.R. 779 Div Ct 3–007, 3–008
Secretary of State for the Home Department v Robb [1995] Fam. 127; [1995] 2
    W.L.R. 722 Fam Div 5–065
Shaw v DPP [1962] A.C. 220; [1961] 2 W.L.R. 897 HL 6–023, 6–024, 6–034
Shaw (Norman) v Queen, The [2001] UKPC 26; [2001] 1 W.L.R. 1519; [2002] 1
    Cr.App.R. 10 PC (Belize) 5–058
Sherras v De Rutzen [1895] 1 Q.B. 918 QBD 3–009, 3–019, 3–026
Smith v Chief Superintendent of Woking Police Station (1983) 76 Cr.App.R. 234;
    [1983] Crim.L.R. 323 QBD 7–067
—— v Desmond [1965] A.C. 960; [1965] 2 W.L.R. 894 HL 9–021
—— v Mellors and Soar [1987] R.T.R. 210 4–035
Sodeman v R. [1936] 2 All E.R. 1138 5–008
Somerset v Hart (1884) 12 Q.B.D. 360 4–054
Sopp v Long [1970] 1 Q.B. 518; [1969] 2 W.L.R. 587 QBD 4–055
Stapleton v R. (1952) 86 C.L.R. 358 5–008

Stevens v Gourley (1859) 141 E.R. 752; (1859) 7 C.B. N.S. 99 CCP   9–027
Sweet v Parsley [1970] A.C. 132; [1969] 2 W.L.R. 470 HL   3–011
T v DPP; sub nom R. (on the application of T) v DPP [2003] EWHC 266 (Admin);
    [2003] Crim.L.R. 622   7–079
Tesco Stores Ltd v Brent LBC [1993] 1 W.L.R. 1037; [1993] 2 All E.R. 718 Div Ct   4–060
Tesco Supermarkets Ltd v Nattrass [1972] A.C. 153; [1971] 2 W.L.R. 1166 HL   3–026,
    4–060, 4–061, 4–062

Thabo Meli v R. See Meli v Queen, The
Thatcher v R. (1987) 39 D.L.R. (4th) 275 Sup Ct of Canada   4–002
Thorne v Motor Trade Association [1937] A.C. 797; (1938) 26 Cr.App.R. 51 HL . . .   9–034
Thornton v Mitchell [1940] 1 All E.R. 339 . . . .   4–038, 4–039, 4–052
Transco Plc v HM Advocate (No.1) 2004 J.C. 29; 2004 S.L.T. 41 HCJ   4–065
Treacy v DPP [1971] A.C. 537; [1971] 2 W.L.R. 112 HL   9–033
Troughton v Metropolitan Police [1987] Crim.L.R. 138 QBD 9–017, 9–018
Tuck v Robson [1970] 1 W.L.R. 741; [1970] 1 All E.R. 1171   4–011
Turberville v Savage (1669) 86 E.R. 684; (1669) 1 Mod. 3 KB   7–066
United States v Holmes (1842) 26 Fed. Cas. 360   5–064
—— v Jennell, 749 F. 2d. 1302 (9th Cir., 1985)   5–090
V and T v United Kingdom (24724/94) [2000] 2 All E.R. 1024 (Note); (2000) 30
    E.H.R.R. 121 ECHR 5–004, 7–008
Vane v Vane; sub nom Vane v Yiannopoullos [1965] A.C. 486; [1964] 3 W.L.R. 1218
    HL 4–050, 4–054
—— v Yiannopoullos. See Vane v Vane
Wai Yu–Tsang v Queen, The [1992] 1 A.C. 269; [1991] 3 W.L.R. 1006 PC (Hong
    Kong) 6–036, 6–037
Wakeman v Farrar [1974] Crim.L.R. 136 Div Ct   8–033
Warner v Commissioner of Police of the Metropolis [1969] 2 A.C. 256; [1968] 2
    W.L.R. 1303 HL 3–007, 3–011, 9–013
Watmore v Jenkins [1962] 2 Q.B. 572; [1962] 3 W.L.R. 463 QBD   3–026
Waverley BC v Fletcher [1996] Q.B. 334; [1995] 3 W.L.R. 772 CA (Civ Div)   8–031
Welham v DPP [1961] A.C. 103; [1960] 2 W.L.R. 669 HL   6–036
Westminster City Council v Croyalgrange Ltd [1986] 1 W.L.R. 674; [1986] 2 All E.R.
    353 HL 2–074, 3–009
Wilcox v Jeffrey [1951] 1 All E.R. 464   4–010
Williams v Phillips (1957) 41 Cr.App.R. 5; (1957) 121 J.P. 163 Div Ct   8–031
Wilson v Pringle [1987] Q.B. 237; [1986] 3 W.L.R. 1 CA (Civil Div)   7–075
Wings v Ellis [1985] A.C. 272; [1984] 3 W.L.R. 965 HL   2–027
Winterwerp v Netherlands (A/33) (1979–80) 2 E.H.R.R. 387 ECHR 5–023, 5–024
Winzar v Chief Constable of Kent, The Times, March 28, 1983 Div Ct   2–014
Woolmington v DPP [1935] A.C. 462; (1936) 25 Cr.App.R. 72 HL   1–012
Yip Chiu–Cheung v Queen, The [1995] 1 A.C. 111; [1994] 3 W.L.R. 514 PC (Hong
    Kong) 5–104, 6–047, 6–048
Yorkshire Traction Co Ltd v Vehicle Inspectorate [2001] EWHC Admin 190; [2001]
    R.T.R. 34   4–013
Z v United Kingdom (29392/95) [2001] 2 F.L.R. 612; [2001] 2 F.C.R. 246; (2002) 34
    E.H.R.R. 3 ECHR   3–025
Z (Local Authority: Duty), Re [2004] EWHC 2817 (Fam); [2005] 1 W.L.R. 959;
    [2005] 3 All E.R. 280 Fam Div   7–057
Zekevic v DPP (Victoria) [1987] 162 C.L.R. 645   5–056

TABLE OF STATUTES

1797 Incitement to Mutiny Act (37
    Geo.3 c.70) 6–024

1803 Malicious Shooting or Stab-
    bing Act (Lord Ellen-
    borough's Act) (43 Geo.3
    c.53) 7–015

1827 Larceny Act (7 & 8 Geo.4
    c.29) 8–004
    s.39 2–002

1839 Metropolitan Police Act (2 &
    3 Vict. c.47)—
    s.44 4–054

1843 Libel Act (6 & 7 Vict. c.96)—
    s.7 4–050

1861 Accessories and Abettors Act
    (24 & 25 Vict. c.94)—
    s.8 . . 4–001, 4–002, 4–005, 4–008
    Malicious Damage Act (24 &
    25 Vict. c.97) 2–067
    s.51 2–080
    Offences Against the Person
    Act (24 & 25 Vict. c.100) . . . .
        2–065, 2–067, 4–023,
        5–038, 5–081, 7–001,
        7–061, 7–084, 7–088,
        7–102, 7–103, 10–009
    s.4 . . . . 6–022, 6–024
    s.9 7–010
    s.16 7–067
    s.18 . . . . 2–019, 2–055, 4–027,
        5–011, 5–029, 5–032,
        5–037, 5–044, 5–080,
        7–001, 7–009, 7–061,
        7–079, 7–081, 7–084,
        7–086, 7–090, 7–092,
        7–093, 7–094, 7–095,
        7–114

    s.20 . . . . 2–021, 2–035, 2–037,
        2–066, 4–027, 5–027,
        5–029, 5–033, 5–037,
        7–001, 7–061, 7–067,
        7–069, 7–079, 7–080,
        7–081, 7–082, 7–083,
        7–084, 7–085, 7–086,
        7–088, 7–089, 7–090,
        7–092, 7–093, 7–094,
        7–097, 7–102, 7–103,
        7–106, 7–110, 7–114,
        9–029
    s.23 . . . . 2–044, 2–045, 2–052,
        2–053, 2–065, 7–041,
        7–042, 7–043, 7–047,
        7–080, 7–089
    s.47 . . . . 2–037, 2–080, 5–053,
        5–082, 7–001, 7–061,
        7–066, 7–076, 7–079,
        7–080, 7–081, 7–085,
        7–089, 7–094, 7–097,
        7–102, 7–103, 7–114
    s.55 3–002
    s.56 . . . . 4–038, 6–041
    s.58 . . . . 5–065, 7–004

1872 Licensing Act (35 & 36 Vict.
    c.94)—
    s.12 2–014
    s.13 3–009
    s.16(1) 3–009
    (2) 3–009

1875 Explosives Act (38 & 39 Vict.
    c.17)—
    s.3(1) 9–030

1883 Explosive Substances Act (46
    & 47 Vict. c.3)—
    s.4 3–009
    Trial of Lunatics Act (46 & 47
    Vict. c.38)—
    s.2 5–006
    (1) 5–006

1911   Official Secrets Act (1 & 2
         Geo.5 c.28)—
         s.2(2) 6–016
1916   Larceny Act (6 & 7 Geo.5
         c.50) 9–022
         s.32 2–001
1921   Licensing Act (11 & 12 Geo.5
         c.42)—
         s.4 4–056
1929   Infant Life (Preservation) Act
         (19 & 20 Geo.5 c.34)—
         s.1 7–004
1933   Children and Young Persons
         Act (23 & 24 Geo.5
         c.12)—
         s.1 3–010
         s.50 5–097
1934   Incitement to Disaffection Act
         (24 & 25 Geo.5 c.56) ... 6–024
1938   Infanticide Act (1 & 2 Geo.6
         c.36) 7–058
1945   Family Allowance Act (8 & 9
         Geo.6 c.41)—
         s.9(b) 6–023
1948   British Nationality Act (11 &
         12 Geo.6 c.56)—
         s.3 7–010
1949   Wireless Telegraphy Act (12,
         13 & 14 Geo.6 c.54)—
         s.1(1) 6–022
1953   Prevention of Crime Act (1 &
         2 Eliz.2 c.14)—
         s.1 7–095
         (4) 9–030
1955   Air Force Act (3 & 4 Eliz.2
         c.19)—
         s.51 3–012
       Food and Drugs Act (4 & 5
         Eliz.2 c.16)—
         s.113 3–026
1956   Sexual Offences Act (4 & 5
         Eliz.2 c.69) 7–118, 7–133
         s.1 7–127
         (3) 7–127
         s.3 7–127
         s.6 4–009
         s.14 3–023
         s.20 3–002

       Copyright Act (4 & 5 Eliz.2
         c.74) 6–022
1957   Homicide Act (5 & 6 Eliz.2
         c.11) 5–015, 5–023, 7–015,
                          7–020, 7–023
         s.1 .. 7–004, 7–007, 7–015, 7–038
         s.2 .. 1–011, 5–002, 5–005, 5–018,
                     5–025, 7–001, 7–018,
                          7–034
         (1) 5–015, 5–018, 5–019
         (4) 4–040
         s.3 .. 7–019, 7–020, 7–023, 7–024,
                     7–026, 7–030, 7–032
         s.4 .... 7–018, 7–057
1960   Indecency with Children Act
         (8 & 9 Eliz.2 c.33)—
         s.1(1) 3–022
1961   Suicide Act (9 & 10 Eliz.2
         c.60) 6–002
         s.1 4–013
         s.2 .... 2–028, 7–057
         (1) 6–002
       Housing Act (9 & 10 Eliz.2
         c.65)—
         s.13(4) 3–009
1963   Betting, Gaming and Lotteries
         Act (c.2)—
         s.53 4–063
1964   Licensing Act (c.26) 4–053
         s.163(1) 4–051
         s.169(1) 4–055
         s.172(1) 4–054
       Criminal Procedure (Insanity)
         Act (c.84) 5–002
         s.1 5–006
         s.4 .... 5–001, 5–002
         (2) 5–002
         (5) 5–001
         s.4A 5–001, 5–002, 5–004,
                          5–006, 5–015
         (2) 5–001, 5–002
         s.5 .... 5–001, 5–003, 5–004
         s.6 5–021
1965   Dangerous Drugs Act (c.15)—
         s.5(6) 3–011
1967   Criminal Law Act (c.53) ... 2–002,
                          4–001, 4–002
         s.3 .. 2–085, 5–045, 5–046, 5–047,
                     5–051, 5–057, 10–017

s.4 .... 4–002, 4–047
    (1A) 4–047
s.5 4–047
s.6 7–085
    (3) 7–094
Criminal Justice Act (c.80)—
  s.4(1) 6–002
  s.5(1) 6–002
  s.8 .. 2–056, 5–027, 5–028, 5–029
1968 Criminal Appeal Act (c.19)—
  s.6 5–003
  s.12 .... 5–006, 5–014
  s.14 5–003
Firearms Act (c.27) 5–094
  s.1(1) 3–008
  s.5(1) 3–008, 3–025
    (b) 3–008
  s.19 3–008
  s.57(1) 9–030
Trade   Descriptions   Act
    (c.29)—
  s.11(2) 4–061
  s.20 4–063
  s.24 4–061
    (1) 3–026
Theft Act (c.60) 1–006, 8–001,
    8–030, 8–046, 9–001,
    9–015, 9–021, 9–022,
    9–024, 9–037, 9–052,
    9–053
  s.1 .. 8–003, 8–011, 8–014, 8–032,
    9–001
    (1) 8–006, 8–009, 8–017
    (2) 8–038, 8–039
  ss.1–6 .... 8–003, 9–020
  s.2 .... 8–026, 8–040, 9–007
    (1) 8–017, 8–039, 8–040,
    9–020
    (a) 8–017, 8–040
    (b) 8–041, 8–041, 9–016
    (2) 8–039, 8–041
    (3) 8–044
  s.3 .... 8–017, 8–018
    (1) 8–004, 8–015, 8–016,
    8–018
    (2) 8–019, 9–040
  s.4 .... 8–020, 8–024, 9–054
    (1) 8–020, 8–021, 8–022,
    8–023, 8–025

    (2) 8–020, 8–025, 8–026
    (a) 8–025
    (b) 8–025
    (c) 8–025
    (3) ... 8–025, 8–026, 10–005
    (4) 8–027, 10–005
  s.5 .. 8–017, 8–028, 8–032, 8–037
    (1) 8–029, 8–031, 8–032,
    8–033, 8–036, 8–037
    (2) 8–031
    (3) 6–017, 8–029, 8–032,
    8–033, 8–034, 8–035
    (4) 8–015, 8–029, 8–031,
    8–032, 8–035, 8–036
  s.6 .. 8–041, 8–044, 8–046, 8–049
    (1) 8–017, 8–047, 8–048
    (2) 8–050
  s.7 8–003
  s.8 .... 9–020, 9–021, 9–022
  s.9 .. 9–024, 9–025, 9–026, 9–027,
    9–030
    (1)(a)   4–007, 4–029, 6–001,
    6–005, 8–051, 9–023,
    9–025, 9–026, 9–028,
    9–029, 9–030, 9–031
    (b) ... 4–029, 4–031, 6–001,
    9–023, 9–024, 9–026,
    9–029, 9–030, 9–031
    (2) 9–023
    (3) 9–023, 9–027
    (4) 9–023
  s.10 .... 9–030, 9–031
  s.11 9–053
  s.12 .... 8–041, 8–049, 9–053
  s.12A 9–053
  s.13 .... 6–022, 9–054
  s.15 .... 2–022, 8–005, 8–011,
    9–001, 9–015, 9–016
  s.15A 9–001
  s.16 9–001
    (2)(a) 9–015
  s.17 9–055
  ss.17–20 9–055
  s.18 9–055
  s.19 9–055
  s.20 9–055
    (2) 9–001
  s.21 .... 9–032, 9–034, 9–035
    (2) 9–033

s.22 . . . . 6–016, 9–037, 9–038
    (1) 9–044
s.23 9–056
s.24 . . . . 9–038, 9–039, 9–051
    (2) 9–040
    (3) 9–039, 9–051
    (4) 9–038
s.24A 9–001, 9–051
s.25 6–019, 9–006, 9–013, 9–057
s.27(3) 9–050, 9–051
    (a) 9–050
    (b) 9–050
s.28 9–058
s.34(2) 9–035
    (b) 9–038
Medicines Act (c.67) 3–009, 7–041
s.58(2)(b) 7–041
s.67 7–041
Transport Act (c.73)—
s.99(5) 4–013

1969 Tattooing of Minors Act (c.24) . . .
                        7–113
1971 Misuse of Drugs Act (c.38) 3–007,
              3–016, 5–015, 5–068,
                        7–042
s.4(1) 7–046
s.5 3–007
    (1) 3–007
s.19 6–021
s.28 . . . . 2–061, 3–007, 3–008,
                  3–016, 3–026
    (2) 5–015
    (3) 5–015
    (b) 2–064, 3–008
Criminal Damage Act (c.48) . . . . .
            2–022, 2–067, 2–071,
            5–051, 8–001, 8–005,
            10–001, 10–012
s.1 . . . . 2–069, 2–080, 10–012,
            10–013, 10–014, 10–017
    (1) 2–027, 2–065, 3–003,
            5–034, 6–043, 10–002,
            10–004, 10–008, 10–012,
                  10–016
    (2) . . . 6–010, 6–043, 10–008,
            10–010, 10–011, 10–012,
                  10–015
    (a) 10–011
    (b) . . . 5–029, 5–038, 10–011

    (3) . . . 2–027, 6–010, 10–003,
            10–010, 10–015
s.2 . . . . . 10–013, 10–015, 10–017
s.3 . . . . 6–005, 6–019, 10–014,
            10–015, 10–017
s.4 10–008
    (2) 10–002
s.5 . . . . 5–051, 5–068, 10–006,
            10–015, 10–016, 10–017,
                  10–018
    (2) . . 5–034, 10–016, 10–017,
                  10–018
    (a) 10–016, 10–017
    (b) 10–017
    (3) 10–016
    (5) 10–015, 10–018
s.10 . . . . 10–004, 10–005
    (1)(a) 8–027
    (2) 10–005
Town and Country Planning
    Act (c.78)—
s.89(5) 3–012
1972 Criminal Justice Act (c.71)—
s.36 4–065
1974 Health and Safety at Work
    etc. Act (c.37) 4–065
s.3(1) 4–060, 4–065
s.37 4–067
1976 Race Relations Act (c.74)—
s.12 6–021
Sexual Offences (Amend-
    ment) Act (c.82) 7–130
s.1 7–120
    (2) 7–130
s.7(2) 6–006
1977 Protection from Eviction Act
    (c.43)—
s.1(3) 2–022
Criminal Law Act (c.45) . . . 4–001,
           6–029, 6–030, 6–033,
           6–035, 6–041, 6–042,
                  6–046
s.1 . . 6–030, 6–032, 6–051, 7–001,
                  8–015
    (1) 6–031, 6–032, 6–045
    (a) 6–032, 6–047
    (b) 6–050
    (2) 6–043, 6–044
    (4) 6–051, 7–001

s.2(2) 6–041
   (a) 6–040
s.5 6–034
   (2) 6–035
   (8) 6–042
   (9) 6–042
s.12 7–067

1978   Theft Act (c.31) 8–001, 9–001,
                          9–015, 9–017
       s.1 .. 9–001, 9–011, 9–015, 9–016
       s.2 9–001
       s.3 .. 6–030, 9–003, 9–015, 9–016,
                                  9–017
          (1) 9–016
          (3) 9–018
          (4) 9–015
       s.4(3) 9–016
       Protection of Children Act
          (c.37)—
       s.1(1) 6–024

1979   Customs and Excise Manage-
          ment Act (c.2) 6–045
       s.170 6–016
          (2) 2–077
          (b) 6–045
       Sale of Goods Act (c.54)—
       ss.17–18 10–012

1980   Magistrates'   Courts   Act
          (c.43)—
       s.44 4–001

1981   Forgery and Counterfeiting
          Act (c.45) 6–051, 7–001,
                                  8–001
       s.1 7–001
       s.2(1) 7–001
       Criminal Attempts Act (c.47) 6–003,
                6–007, 6–013, 6–015,
                6–016, 6–018, 8–050
       s.1(1) 2–001, 2–022, 6–002,
                6–003, 6–008, 6–010
          (2) 6–015, 6–016, 6–017,
                              6–031
          (3) 6–015, 6–031
          (4) 6–002
          (a) 6–002
          (b) 6–002

       (l) 6–002
       s.3 6–002
       s.4(3) 6–003
       s.5 .... 6–031, 6–050
       s.6 6–019
       s.9(1) 5–098

1982   Aviation Security Act (c.36)—
       s.1(1) 5–085

1983   Mental Health Act (c.20) ... 5–022
       s.47 5–001
       s.48 5–001
       s.72 5–024

1984   Telecommunications   Act
          (c.12) 7–066
       Road Traffic Regulation Act
          (c.27) 3–017
       Child Abduction Act (c.37)   6–041
       Video   Recordings   Act
          (c.39)—
       s.11(1) 4–060
          (b) 4–060

1985   Companies Act (c.6)—
       s.458 9–014
       Prosecution of Offences Act
          (c.23)—
       s.10 6–035
       Weights and Measures Act
          (c.72)—
       s.34 3–026

1986   Insolvency Act (c.45) 3–012
       Company   Directors   Dis-
          qualification Act (c.46)   3–012
       Public Order Act (c.64) 7–001
       s.3 7–001
          (1) 7–041

1987   Criminal Justice Act (c.38)—
       s.12 .... 6–030, 6–035

1988   Merchant   Shipping   Act
          (c.12)—
       s.31 4–060
       Criminal Justice Act (c.33)   6–002,
                                  6–044
       s.39   3–003, 6–002, 7–001, 7–061
       s.40 .... 7–062, 7–094
       s.41 .... 7–062, 7–094
       s.93A 6–044

Road Traffic Act (c.52) 2–060, 7–059
  s.1 .. 2–004, 2–008, 2–032, 2–033, 2–063, 4–039, 7–059
  s.2 .. 2–004, 2–032, 2–033, 2–063, 3–017, 7–059
  s.2A 4–039, 7–059
    (1) 7–059
    (2) 7–059
    (3) 7–059
  s.2B 2–063
  s.3 .. 2–063, 2–083, 3–017, 5–028, 7–039, 7–059
  s.3A 7–059
  s.4 .... 3–017, 3–026
  s.5 .. 3–001, 3–017, 3–026, 6–002
  s.6(4) 2–015
  s.7(6) 2–015, 2–024
  s.34 5–068
  s.170 2–024
    (4) 2–015, 2–024
Road Traffic Offenders Act (c.53)—
  s.34(1) 3–001
  s.62(1) 2–013
  s.64(5) 2–013
    (6) 2–013, 2–014

1989 Prevention of Terrorism (Temporary Provisions) Act (c.4)—
  s.18 2–015
  Water Act (c.15) 3–020

1990 Food Safety Act (c.16)—
  s.21 3–026
  Computer Misuse Act (c.18) 10–004
  s.3 10–004
    (6) 10–004

1991 Criminal Procedure (Insanity and Unfitness to Plead) Act (c.25) 5–001, 5–002, 5–003, 5–007, 5–024
  s.2 5–001
  Sch.2 5–003
  Road Traffic Act (c.40) 4–039, 7–059
  s.1 .. 2–004, 2–008, 2–032, 2–033
  s.2 .. 2–063, 2–083, 5–068, 7–039

Criminal Justice Act (c.53) .. 9–027
  s.26 ...... 8–003, 8–011, 9–023
Water Resources Act (c.57)—
  s.85(1) 2–042, 4–060
Dangerous Dogs Act (c.65) 3–018
  s.1(2)(d) 5–068
  s.3 3–018
    (1) 3–018
  s.10(3) 3–018

1992 Aggravated Vehicle-Taking Act (c.11) 9–053

1993 Education Act (c.35)—
  s.293 7–073
Criminal Justice Act (c.36)—
  Pt 1 6–051
  s.2(1) 8–015

1994 Criminal Justice and Public Order Act (c.33) 2–001, 7–120
  s.142 .... 7–120, 7–127
Drug Trafficking Act (c.37) 6–044

1996 Law Reform (Year and a Day Rule) Act (c.19) 2–033, 7–009
Sexual Offences (Conspiracy and Incitement) Act (c.29) 6–051, 7–001
Education Act (c.56) 7–073
  s.444(1) 3–024
  s.548 7–073
Theft (Amendment) Act (c.62) 9–001, 9–051

1997 Protection from Harassment Act (c.40) 7–066
  s.1 7–066
    (1) 2–064
    (2) 2–064
  s.2 7–066
  s.4 7–066
    (1) 2–064
    (4) 2–064
Sex Offenders Act (c.51)—
  Pt II 7–001

1998 School Standards and Framework Act (c.31) 7–073
Crime and Disorder Act (c.37) ... 6–041, 7–097
  s.28(1) 7–097

(a) 7–097
s.29(1) 7–097
(c) 7–093
(3) 7–093
s.34 ...... 4–039, 5–098, 5–099,
7–002
Criminal Justice (Terrorism
and Conspiracy) Act
(c.40) 6–051, 7–001
s.5 .... 6–033, 6–051, 8–015
Human Rights Act (c.42) .. 1–006,
5–015
s.2 1–009
s.6 5–015
1999 Contracts (Rights of Third
Parties) Act (c.31) 8–033
2001 Anti-Terrorism, Crime and
Security Act (c.24) 7–097
2002 Proceeds of Crime Act (c.29) .....
6–044
2003 Sexual Offences Act (c.42) 2–022,
2–084, 3–002, 3–021,
3–023, 4–009, 4–041,
5–031, 6–006, 6–010,
6–011, 6–043, 7–118,
7–120, 7–127, 7–130,
7–131, 7–133, 7–135,
7–136
s.1 .. 2–001, 6–002, 6–010, 7–119,
7–123
(2) 7–131
ss.1–4 7–135
s.2 .... 7–132, 7–133
s.3 .. 3–023, 5–030, 5–031, 5–035,
7–133, 7–136
s.4 .... 7–127, 7–134, 7–136
s.5 .. 3–025, 6–016, 6–018, 6–028,
7–135
ss.5–8 7–135
s.7 7–136
s.8 .... 3–022, 7–136
s.9 .... 4–041, 7–136
s.10 .... 3–022, 7–136
s.11 7–136
s.12 7–136
s.13 .... 7–135, 7–136
s.63 .... 6–007, 9–023

s.74 ...... 7–121, 7–123, 7–124,
7–125, 7–126
s.75 .... 7–123, 7–126, 7–131
(2) 7–123, 7–124
(d) 7–124
s.76 .... 7–113, 7–123, 7–126,
7–128, 7–131
(2) 7–126
(a) 7–127, 7–128
(b) 7–127
s.78 .... 7–132, 7–133
(a) 7–133
(b) 7–133
s.79 .... 7–062, 7–069
(2) 7–120
(8) 7–132
Sch.7 para.1 9–023
Criminal Justice Act (c.44) .. 7–008
s.269 7–008
s.285(1) 9–053
Sch.21 7–008
2004 Domestic Violence, Crime
and Victims Act (c.28) 4–011,
5–001
s.5 .... 4–011, 4–035
s.22 .... 5–001, 5–003
s.24 ...... 5–002, 5–003, 5–023
Human Tissue Act (c.30) ... 8–024
Children Act (c.31)—
s.58 7–073
2006 Fraud Act (c.35) 2–022, 9–001,
9–002, 9–003, 9–006,
9–007, 9–038
s.1 9–004
(3) 9–004
s.2 .. 2–001, 6–030, 8–019, 9–004,
9–008, 9–010, 9–012
(2) 9–005
(3) 9–005
(4) 9–005
(5) 9–007
s.3 .... 9–004, 9–008
s.4 .... 9–004, 9–010
s.5 .. 9–006, 9–008, 9–010, 9–012
(3) 9–006
s.6 .... 9–013, 9–014
(1) 9–013
s.7 .... 9–013, 9–014
s.8 9–014

s.9 9–014
s.11 . . . .   9–011, 9–012
      (1)(a) 9–011
      (2)(b) 9–012
2007 Corporate Manslaughter and
      Corporate Homicide Act
      (c.19) 4–066
      s.1 4–066
            (3) 4–066
            (4)(b) 4–066
      s.2(5) 4–067
      s.3 4–067
      s.4 4–067
      s.5 4–067
      s.6 4–067
      s.7 4–067
      s.8 4–067
      s.9 4–068
      s.10 4–068
      s.17 4–066
      s.18 4–067
      s.19 4–067

Serious Crime Act (c.27) . . . 5–100,
            6–021, 6–024, 6–027
Pt 2   6–001, 6–021, 6–024, 6–028
s.44 . . . .   6–024, 6–025
ss.44–46 6–025
s.45 6–025
s.46 . . . .   6–025, 6–027
s.47 6–025
      (5) 6–026, 6–027
      (a) 6–026, 6–027
      (6) 6–026
s.48 6–027
s.50 6–027
      (3) 6–027
s.51 6–028
s.53 6–028
s.58 6–028
s.59 6–024
Sch.4 6–028
2008 Criminal Justice and Immigra-
      tion Act (c.4)—
      s.76 5–045
Health and Safety (Offences)
      Act (c.20) 4–065

TABLE OF STATUTORY INSTRUMENTS

1920 Aliens Order (SR & O
  1920/448) 2–013
1939 Defence (General) Regu-
  lations (SR & O 1939/927)
  reg.2A 2–056
1951 Motor Vehicles (Construction
  and Use) Regulations (SI
  1951/2101) 4–052
1955 Motor Vehicles (Construction
  and Use) Regulations (SI
  1955/482) 4–013

1981 Traffic Signs Regulations and
  General Directions (SI
  1981/859)
  reg.34 5–068
1996 Products of Animals Origin
  (Import and Export) Regulations (SI 1996/3124)
  reg.21 3–024
  reg.37 3–024

Chapter 1

INTRODUCTION

WHAT THIS BOOK IS ABOUT, AND WHAT IT IS NOT ABOUT

This book is about the substantive criminal law in the jurisdiction of England and Wales. **1–001**
That is to say, it is about the elements which make up criminal offences and defences. For
example, what does one have to do to be guilty of the offence of murder? What
circumstances must exist in order for one to say that they can have a defence of self-
defence? The book looks at the main areas of law covered in undergraduate and analogous
criminal law courses. We begin by considering general principles; what one might view as the
building blocks of criminal liability. These are the ideas and tools that lawyers use when
analysing criminal offences and when deciding whether a given offence has been committed
on given facts. We move on to consider specific offences and defences.

The book is doctrinal in nature. That is to say, it considers the rules of criminal law and
how they apply to particular scenarios. In that sense, we take the view that there is only
really one question in criminal law! That is, "has a particular offence been committed on
given facts?" We do of course go further than that. Criminal law is controversial and it is a
significant part of studying criminal law that one does not accept the law as necessarily
"right". We do subject the law to critical scrutiny and offer our own views on how the law
might be best arranged and reformed.

What this book is not about is the background against which the criminal law operates.
That is to say, we do not consider criminological questions to do with the causes of criminal
behaviour or with the circumstances under which criminal behaviour is more and less likely.
We also do not consider in any detail the procedures through which crimes are detected,
investigated, and, where appropriate, pursued through the courts. It is also not a *principal*
purpose of this book to ask what behaviour should and should not be criminal, although we
inevitably touch on that question in a variety of contexts as we proceed. The mere fact that
we do not consider these issues in this book is absolutely not to suggest that they are not
important. Quite the opposite. You can only really fully understand the criminal law by
knowing about and reflecting on the reasons behind criminal behaviour; on the procedural
rules used for enforcing the law; and on the reasons for designating a particular behaviour as
criminal. However, we have to leave that work to others, and we hope that you will pursue
those questions through your study.

In this introductory chapter we do touch briefly on some aspects of these questions. We will consider:

1. The purposes of criminal law. What is the criminal law for?

2. The classification of criminal offences and the structure of the courts.

3. The importance of proof in criminal law.

THE PURPOSES OF CRIMINAL LAW

1–002 What is the criminal law for? Most people would have a view on this, although it is unlikely that everybody's view would be the same. One of the reasons why criminal law is such a controversial area is that there is often disagreement at this fundamental level. If people are not agreed on what the criminal law is for, it is unrealistic to expect them to agree on what behaviours should and should not be criminal.

You might think that it is impossible to identify a *single* purpose which the criminal law should serve, and we would agree. There are a number of different, sometimes competing, purposes which the criminal law might serve.

The criminal law might be seen as one barometer of social norms. On this view, the criminal law is an expression of society's views of what constitutes acceptable and unacceptable behaviour. However, there may be behaviours which most people would view as unacceptable yet which they might not wish to criminalise. By definition, impoliteness (albeit that it is hard to define!) is frowned upon. Yet we would not use the criminal law to pursue the person who drove sneakily into the newly-vacated parking space for which we had been patiently waiting. Many people would view infidelity in a relationship as wrongful, yet we do not criminalise it. So when does the criminal law get involved? The answer is hard to give with precision. However, the thing to remember is that the criminal law is not primarily used for resolving private disputes. When a criminal case is brought, it is, in the vast majority of cases, brought on behalf of the state. Criminal law is a public matter (you may see criminal law referred to as a branch of *public law*)—the criminal law articulates *social* norms. So, for the criminal law to get involved, the wrongful behaviour would seem to have to be of a level of seriousness to warrant the intervention of the state. To this point, our reasoning is of course incomplete, because we have not given specific criteria which identify that level of seriousness. Indeed, it is probably not possible to identify that level of seriousness with absolute clarity. What we suggest is that you think about the various types of criminal offence that you encounter in your study and in your daily life, and ask yourself how those behaviours demand the intervention of the state.

1–003 Let us consider an example. Everybody would surely agree that there should be a law against murder (although how murder is defined might be a more controversial question). This may all sound rather obvious, but murder is a crime because it is viewed as sufficiently serious and damaging, not merely to the individuals involved, but also *to society*, that it should be prohibited. There are other behaviours, however, where it would be harder to identify universal agreement as to whether the criminal law should be involved. In relatively recent years, there has been controversy regarding the use of criminal law to regulate, for example, abortion, prostitution, and homosexual behaviour.

One question that arises at this point is the extent to which the criminal law should prohibit behaviour that might be considered *immoral*. One view is that the criminal law should correspond with moral values—and this must be at least partially correct. However, we have already suggested that the simple fact that a behaviour is morally wrong is not a sufficient reason for criminalising it. Our position is, broadly speaking, a liberal one. That is to say, people should be at liberty to do as they wish unless there is a strong enough reason for saying that a particular behaviour should not be permitted. In general, there should be as little criminal law as is necessary, and the use of criminal law as a device to regulate human behaviour should be a last resort. Criminal law is, after all, public law, and when it is used, it is being used by the state against the individual citizen. We think that the difficulty with identifying with certainty whether a behaviour is truly immoral makes immorality alone an unsatisfactory criterion for applying the criminal law. So, is there any other factor which helps to determine whether it is appropriate to label a particular behaviour as criminal? In our view, it can be useful to ask whether a behaviour actually causes harm. If so, there is a stronger case for criminalising it. Of course, this requires a closer analysis of what constitutes "harm" than we can provide in this book, but we might, using the example of murder, identify a fairly obvious harm to the victim, but also a less clearly defined, but still significant harm caused to society by the carrying out of a murder. Murder constitutes a clear breach of a clear social rule; a rule which not only recognises the intrinsic moral value of life, but which also enables society to function more smoothly, in the knowledge that there is a rule which says that murder is wrong.

That murder is a crime suggests also that the criminal law has a protective function. Not only does it seek to protect what might loosely be called society at large, but it also protects recognised individual interests. Thus, there are criminal laws against certain forms of interference with the bodily integrity of others, and there are offences relating to interference with property. Where the interference with the person or property is sufficiently serious, the criminal law can intervene.

When the criminal law is breached, a mechanism is available for the pursuing of an **1–004** offender through the courts. If that offender is found guilty of having committed a particular offence then they are sentenced—various forms of sentence are available, depending on the offence in question. An offender may for example be imprisoned; fined; required to compensate the victim of a crime; required to undertake one of a variety of forms of community penalty. The purposes of sentencing are quite complex, and are beyond the scope of this book, but one of the purposes which it is worth noting is the function of punishment. The criminal law identifies behaviours which attract punishment. Indeed, you will sometimes see criminal law referred to as *penal law,* that is, the law which relates to penalties or punishments.

The criminal law seeks to protect relevant social and individual interests not merely after the event, by providing for the punishment of offenders, but also before the event by seeking to deter potential offenders from committing crimes in the first place. By making particular conduct criminal, and by providing for punishment for those engaging in such conduct, the criminal law has a deterrent function. The extent to which the criminal law acts as an effective deterrent is a matter of controversy and complexity. You may have already noticed that to be a deterrent, the law must be known about by those who would engage in the prohibited conduct. It is not clear at all how much of the criminal law is a matter of public knowledge. Furthermore, even if the law is known about, potential offenders must be sufficiently concerned by the likelihood of being caught, and by the severity of the possible punishment, if they are to be deterred from offending behaviour.

Although the criminal law has other purposes, we will conclude our discussion at this point by drawing attention to a final one. We call this *differentiation.* The criminal law, through its identification of offences, differentiates between behaviours which are crimes and those which are not crimes. It also differentiates between crimes of greater and lesser seriousness. We might divide differentiation into two sub-purposes. By identifying behaviour which is criminal and distinguishing it from behaviour which is not criminal, the criminal law allows citizens to regulate their own behaviour with *fair warning* that if they behave in a particular way, they will commit a crime and leave themselves open to the consequences. The principle of *fair warning* is an important aspect of the criminal law in a democratic society. It indicates that the law cannot be made or applied in an arbitrary fashion. Nor can it be applied retrospectively. If "behaviour x" is not criminal when it is carried out, then the simple fact that an offence is subsequently created which prohibits "behaviour x" does not make criminal the original instance of that behaviour. In differentiating crimes of greater and lesser seriousness, the law should adhere to the principle of *fair labelling.* Consider two situations in which person A causes the death of person B. In the first situation, A has deliberately killed B with a knife. In the second situation, A pushed B in the course of an argument. B fell and hit his head on the pavement and was killed. You might think that in both of these situations A has committed some kind of criminal offence. You might also think that in the first situation, A's conduct is more serious than in the second. You might consequently want to be able to label A's behaviour differently in the first situation from in the second. The criminal law responds to this wish by labelling the offence committed in the first scenario "murder"; and in the second "manslaughter".

Of course, differentiation, fair labelling, fair warning, deterrence, punishment, protection and the articulation of social norms are purposes rather than rules. You might find that in different situations, some purposes take priority over others. You might also find that in some situations, one or more purposes are not fulfilled. This is one of the challenges of the subject and it tells us that criminal law is not an absolutely coherent system. We would encourage you, when you are dealing with any particular offence or defence, to ask yourself what purpose or purposes are and are not being served by its existence.

CLASSIFYING CRIMINAL OFFENCES AND THE STRUCTURE OF THE COURTS

1–005   We do not wish to divert ourselves to too great an extent into matters which would best be regarded as matters of legal method or legal system; or constitutional law, but we should briefly note the sources of criminal law—that is to say, the ways in which criminal law is made. The first point to note is that for this purpose, criminal law is no different from other branches of the law of England and Wales. There are two principal sources of criminal law: statutes (or Acts of Parliament), and the common law (sometimes called judge-made law). Statutes are laws created by Parliament and are the supreme form of law—you may have come across the doctrine of Parliamentary Sovereignty. The common law is developed by judges making decisions in cases which are then followed by other judges in later cases. It is important to note that these sources of law are not wholly distinct. Consider a statute governing theft, the Theft Act 1968. That statute defines the offence of theft by reference to the notion of "dishonesty" which is itself only partially defined in the statute. The definition of dishonesty has therefore required development by judges. We will see below that the cases in which the law is developed tend to be appeals rather than trials. It is sometimes said that Parliamentary Sovereignty means that Parliament can make laws as it pleases. You might be wondering at this stage whether that means that Parliament has the power to declare *any* behaviour criminal. Could Parliament for example legislate to make it a criminal offence to have long hair? On one view the answer would be yes. However, another view suggests that Parliament only has authority to create laws which are themselves broadly in line with democratic principles, as Parliament depends on those principles for its own existence. Furthermore, it would be politically unwise for Parliament to legislate in an extreme fashion, as its own legitimacy and credibility would be undermined. Parliament has also enacted the Human Rights Act 1998, which, in simple terms, encourages Parliament to legislate in accordance with the European Convention on Human Rights. Parliament is not obliged to do so. However, should a law be enacted which made it a crime to have long hair, then it would be possible for a court hearing a case on the matter to issue a "declaration of incompatibility", which is a statement that the court considers the law not to measure up to the standards of relevant provisions of the Convention. The "no long hair" law would be likely to violate art.8 (right to privacy and family life) and art.10 (right to freedom of expression) of the Convention. The declaration of incompatibility is, in effect, an invitation to Parliament to revisit the issue. There is also a particular limitation on the *legal* power of Parliament to make laws. The notion of the supremacy of European Community (EC) Law suggests that Parliament can only make laws which are themselves compatible with EC law, although this is not a major issue in criminal law.

The classification of criminal offences is inextricably linked to the structure of the courts, as the type of offence with which we are dealing determines the court in which that offence is tried, and consequently, which courts are involved in any subsequent appeals.

All criminal cases which get to court are considered in the first instance in the magistrates' court. What happens next depends on the type of offence. Criminal offences fall into one of three types:

Summary offences are the least serious offences, typically what one might view as **1–006** "technical" motoring offences, though also including minor assaults and low value criminal damage. These offences are tried in the magistrates' court. In that court, the case is heard by a bench of lay magistrates or a professional magistrate known as a District Judge (Magistrates' Court). The magistrates decide questions of fact—that is to say, what they make of the evidence before them—and questions of law—that is to say, what law is relevant to the case. On the law, magistrates are assisted by a Legal Adviser (formerly known as a court clerk). The sentencing powers of magistrates are limited—the maximum sentence that can be imposed in the magistrates' court is, at the time of writing, six months' imprisonment, although there have been plans to increase that maximum to 12 months, which have not yet been brought into force.

The most serious offences are offences *triable on indictment only*. These offences include murder and rape. The indictment is the document setting out the charge faced by the defendant. These offences are tried in the Crown Court by a judge and jury. Broadly speaking, the jury decide questions of fact, and the judge decides questions of law. Thus, to give an example, the judge in a murder case would decide, by reference to the relevant authorities, what the law on murder was and what a defendant would have to do to commit murder. The judge would then explain this to the jury who would take a view on the evidence they had heard and decide whether what the defendant had done matched the definition of murder provided by the judge.

There is a significant middle category of offences which may be tried in the magistrates' court or in the Crown Court. These are known as offences *triable either way*. They include more serious assaults; higher value criminal damage; dishonesty offences. Where an offence is triable either way, what determines whether it is ultimately tried in the magistrates' court or the Crown Court? The magistrates may decide that the case is too serious for them, and that if the defendant were to be found guilty he or she would merit a sentence in excess of their sentencing powers. In such a case the magistrates would decline to hear the case and it would be tried in the Crown Court. Even if the magistrates are willing to try the case, a defendant in a case of an offence triable either way may elect to have the case tried in the Crown Court. In simple terms, the magistrates may send a case up to the Crown Court irrespective of the defendant's wishes, but they may not retain it against the defendant's wishes.

1–007   You will see in your studies of criminal law that we are not particularly concerned with what goes on in trials. This is because trials ask a very particular question, namely "have the prosecution proved that the defendant committed the offence charged?" Trials are thus principally about the application of law to whichever version of the facts the magistrates or jury believe to be correct. In broad terms, trials do not have any impact on *what the law actually is*.

However, imagine in our example earlier that the judge was explaining the definition of the offence of murder to the jury and the explanation was erroneous. Let us say that the offence was explained in such a way that the jury were invited to convict of murder even if they thought the defendant only intended to frighten, rather than to kill the defendant. This definition is clearly too broad, and any defendant convicted following such a direction would feel aggrieved, as the jury had effectively been given far too much leeway to return a guilty verdict. Such a defendant would appeal and the court to which the appeal was taken would take a view on whether the trial judge had got the law right or wrong. In this case, they would clearly conclude that the trial judge was wrong, because the offence of murder requires either that the defendant intends to kill or to cause grievous bodily harm. In deciding that the trial judge was wrong, the court would explain its view of what the law actually was. It is through these *appellate* decisions that the criminal law develops. In one sense, our use of murder as an example was not ideal, because the law is actually quite well established. However, to take another example, the law on sexual offences was substantially rewritten by a statute in 2003. One element of the new offence of sexual assault is "touching". An appellate court had to decide whether "touching" included the touching of clothing not directly touching the skin. It decided that such conduct did fall within the definition of touching, and that decision now guides future courts on the meaning of "touching" unless and until it is overruled.[1]

We have identified that trials take place in the magistrates court or the Crown Court. If a defendant has been convicted, and they feel that the conviction is wrongful, for example because the trial judge has got the law wrong (imagine, for example, a judge directing a jury, or magistrates deciding that "touching" included being within five metres of somebody), to which court(s) can they appeal?

1–008   Matters are slightly more straightforward where a defendant is convicted in the Crown Court. Such a defendant would appeal to the Court of Appeal (Criminal Division). The type of appeal with which we are principally concerned is the appeal in which it is suggested that the judge or magistrates have got the law wrong. Such appeals are said to be on a point of law. The Court of Appeal may dismiss or allow the defendant's appeal. The prosecution or defendant may appeal against the decision of the Court of Appeal to the House of Lords, but only if either the Court of Appeal or House of Lords gives leave (permission) to appeal, and if the Court of Appeal certifies a point of law of public importance. The House of Lords is currently the most senior court for our purposes, and it only hears criminal appeals based on a point of law of public importance. You can see from that that it has a significant function in clarifying the law. The criminal business of the House of Lords will be taken over by the new Supreme Court in 2009.

[1] See *R v H (Karl Anthony)* [2005] EWCA Crim 732; [2005] 2 Cr.App.R. 9; [2005] Crim.L.R. 735.

Where a defendant is convicted by magistrates he may appeal to the Crown Court for a rehearing of the case (this would not be before a judge and jury but would take place before a judge sitting with magistrates). For our purposes, the most significant appeals are those "by way of case stated". Such an appeal can be by the prosecution or the defence and corresponds, for our purposes, to an appeal on a point of law. These appeals are taken to the Divisional Court of the Queen's Bench Division of the High Court. The prosecution or defendant may appeal against the decision of the Divisional Court to the House of Lords, but only if either the Divisional Court or House of Lords gives leave to appeal, and if the Divisional Court certifies a point of law of public importance.

Thus, for our purposes, the criminal law is shaped by the decisions of the Divisional Court; the Court of Appeal; and the House of Lords, in ascending order of significance. Other courts, such as the Privy Council are of persuasive authority, but are outside the technically binding structure of precedent which applies to the courts of England and Wales. We presume, for the purposes of this book, a modest knowledge of the doctrine of precedent, but it is hopefully clear that decisions of superior courts are binding on those below them. It is also worth drawing attention to the European Court of Human Rights, the relevant decisions of which the courts of England and Wales must "take into account" in accordance with s.2 of the Human Rights Act 1998.

THE SIGNIFICANCE OF PROOF

As we have already stated, the rules of criminal evidence and procedure are beyond the **1–009** principal scope of this book. However, it is worth spending a brief period considering an issue which is integral to the criminal process, and hence of underlying importance to the criminal law: the issue of proof.

Two questions are relevant for our purposes. The first question asks, "Who has to prove what in a criminal trial?" Thus, when a defendant is charged with murder, does the prosecution have to prove that the defendant committed the offence, or does the defendant have to prove that he or she did not? The second question asks, "How much proof does one need to 'win' on a particular issue?". Thus, when the defendant above is charged with murder, how persuaded does the court have to be that he or she did it before a conviction is permitted?

The first of these questions relates to what is known as the *burden of proof*; the second to the *standard of proof*.

Who has to prove what? The burden of proof

The basic rule of criminal evidence is that the prosecution must prove the case against the **1–010** defendant. Thus, if a defendant is charged with murder, the prosecution must prove that all the elements of murder are present—that is, that the defendant unlawfully caused the death of a human being, with the intention to kill or to do grievous bodily harm. The requirement for the prosecution to prove the case reflects what is known as the presumption of innocence. You have probably heard the phrase, "innocent until proven guilty". That is the presumption of innocence. Also, remember that most prosecutions are brought on behalf of the state, which has far more resources than most defendants. Thus, it is only fair that it should be the prosecution which has to prove the case.

In *Woolmington v DPP*, Viscount Sankey L.C. stated:

> "Throughout the web of the English Criminal Law one golden thread is always to be seen, that it is the duty of the prosecution to prove the prisoner's guilt, subject to . . . the defence of insanity and subject also to any statutory exception. . . . No matter what the charge or where the trial, the principle that the prosecution must prove the guilt of the prisoner is part of the common law of England and no attempt to whittle it down can be entertained".[2]

You can see from that quotation how significant the burden of proof is supposed to be. You can also see that there are certain situations where the prosecution does not bear the burden of proof. Suppose that a defendant wants to claim that they are insane, in order to avoid conviction. According to *Woolmington*, this is a situation where it is the defendant who must prove they are insane. Notice also that Viscount Sankey refers to "statutory exceptions" to the burden of proof being on the prosecution. There are many of these throughout the criminal law. To give an example which we will consider in due course, where a defendant is charged with murder and wishes to run the defence of diminished responsibility to try and reduce the offence to manslaughter, s.2 of the Homicide Act 1957 requires the defendant to prove that he was suffering from diminished responsibility.

So the starting point is that the prosecution must prove the elements of the offence against the defendant. What about defences? We know that there are specific exceptions where it is made clear in (or indeed, in some cases, where it can be implied from) a statute that a defendant must prove a defence. However, what about general defences like duress, or self-defence, or defences like provocation (only a defence to murder) which originated at common law? In a criminal case does the prosecution have to *dis*prove these defences as a matter of routine? You can probably already see that if the prosecution did have to do so, a criminal trial would become unwieldy and extremely drawn out. So, for some defences such as the ones just mentioned, the prosecution do indeed have to disprove them, but only if they are a live issue. So, there must be sufficient evidence of the possibility of duress to make it a live issue before the prosecution will be required to disprove it. Such evidence may be raised by the defendant, or it may emerge from the prosecution case, or it may be spotted by the court on its own initiative.

How much proof is needed? The standard of proof

1–011 Once we know who bears the burden of proof on a particular issue, we still have to know how much proof is required for that burden to be discharged. So, how persuasive do the prosecution in a murder case have to be that the defendant committed the prohibited act? The answer is that the prosecution must prove their case *beyond reasonable doubt*. It is not absolutely clear what this means, but you should note that it does not mean "with absolute certainty".

The Judicial Studies Board (the training body for judges) suggests that judges direct juries on the standard of proof in the following terms:

> "How does the prosecution succeed in proving the defendant's guilt? The answer is— by making you sure of it. Nothing less than that will do. If after considering all the evidence you are sure that the defendant is guilty, you must return a verdict of 'Guilty'. If you are not sure, your verdict must be 'Not Guilty'."[3]

[2] [1935] A.C. 462 at 481–482.
[3] See the Judicial Studies Board website at *http://www.jsboard.co.uk*.

In *Miller v Minister of Pensions*, Denning J. stated:

> "If the evidence is so strong against a man as to leave only a remote possibility in his favour which can be dismissed with the sentence 'of course it is possible, but not in the least probable,' the case is proved, but nothing short of that will suffice."[4]

What about situations where the burden of proof is on the defendant (for example, the defence to murder of diminished responsibility)? When a burden of proof is on the defendant, it need never be satisfied beyond reasonable doubt. Rather, the required standard is "the balance of probabilities. This means, effectively, more likely than not. Here is Denning J. again in *Miller v Minister of Pensions*:

> "The . . . degree of cogency . . . required . . . is well settled. It must carry a reasonable degree of probability . . . If the evidence is such that the tribunal can say: 'We think it more probable than not' the burden is discharged, but, if the probabilities are equal, it is not."[5]

CONCLUSION

In this introductory chapter we have tried to set the scene for what follows. We have tried to **1–012** provide a context which makes it easier for you to imagine the offences we are about to discuss being (a) created; and (b) processed through the courts. We have considered what the criminal law is actually for, and in doing so have hopefully raised as many questions as we have provided answers. We have considered the structure of the courts, and, as we have said, you will see as we proceed that the significant courts for our purposes are those which hear appeals. We have also considered the notion of proof, which is integral to an understanding of how criminal law "works" in practice. We hope that mentioning proof at this stage makes it easier to understand any references to the idea which we make later in the book.

We move on now to consider the basic principles of criminal liability. These are also the building blocks from which all criminal offences are metaphorically constructed; and the tools that lawyers use to analyse criminal offences. They are the ideas of actus reus and mens rea.

[4] [1947] 2 All E.R. 372 at 373.
[5] [1947] 2 All E.R. 372 at 374.

Chapter 2

ACTUS REUS AND MENS REA: THE ELEMENTS OF AN OFFENCE

We can start our investigation of criminal liability by reference to the old maxim that a man **2–001** is presumed innocent until proven guilty. This is another way of saying that the burden of proof in a criminal trial is generally upon the prosecution. It is for the prosecution to prove that the accused did what is alleged and not for the accused to prove his innocence. Let us for the moment suppose that D has been charged with rape. He has pleaded "not guilty". This means that everything is in issue; the accused by his plea is admitting nothing. The prosecution will now have to prove his guilt. In a civil case the parties to the action will have exchanged formal documents known as the pleadings. It is quite possible that during the course of this exchange of documents certain matters will be admitted and thus, no longer in issue. For example, in a personal injuries action based on negligence, the parties may, by the time of the trial, have agreed that the defendant was negligent; the only issue remaining is the quantum of damages. Criminal law does not operate in this way. A plea of not guilty means that nothing is admitted.

The prosecutor will, therefore, have to prove that the accused raped the victim. What does this entail? The prosecutor will have to prove that the accused (A): (1) intentionally penetrated the vagina, anus or mouth of another person (B) with the penis; and (2) that B was not consenting to the penetration. The prosecutor must also prove that at the time of the penetration (3) A did not reasonably believe that B was consenting. Whether a belief is reasonable is to be determined having regard to all the circumstances, including any steps A has taken to ascertain whether B consents.[1] The three facts are the elements of the offence of rape which must be proved by the prosecution in order to obtain a conviction. The first two elements relate to what might be described as the external elements of the crime: that is, they are the elements which are not related to the accused's state of mind. Element 3 can be described as the internal or fault element in that it indicates with what state of mind the accused brought about the external elements. The external elements are usually referred to as the actus reus of the offence, literally guilty act. The internal elements are known as the mens rea or guilty mind.[2]

---

[1] Until 1994 only a woman could be the victim of the crime of rape. Following the Criminal Justice and Public Order Act of that year the offence was extended to cover vaginal or anal intercourse with a woman or man. The offence was totally redefined by s.1 of the Sexual Offences Act 2003 to cover penile penetration of the vagina, anus or mouth. See below at para.7–119.

[2] The combination of external and internal elements is usually expressed by the Latin maxim *"actus non facit reum nisi mens sit rea"*, which can be translated as "an act is not criminal in the absence of a guilty mind".

We can say at the outset that in the crime of rape the prosecution bears the burden of establishing each of these elements to the satisfaction of the court. In a criminal case the court will not be satisfied unless the prosecution has established the elements beyond reasonable doubt so that the jury are sure.[3] If the jury are left in reasonable doubt as to any element, the accused is entitled to be acquitted. Thus, if the accused fails to achieve even the slightest penile penetration of the victim's vagina, anus or mouth there can be no conviction for rape. Equally rape is not established where the victim was in fact consenting even though the accused thought she was not. In both of these examples the accused may be guilty of attempted rape[4] but the absence of an element of the offence means that the completed substantive offence is not proved.

Thus we can say that every offence consists of a set of ingredients; failure to establish any required ingredient will mean that the particular offence in question cannot be proved; though there may be other offences available. At one time, in any crime requiring proof that the accused had caused an unlawful homicide it had to be established that the death of the victim had occurred within a year and a day of the harm inflicted by the accused. If death occurred even a minute later than a year and a day the accused could not be convicted of any offence which involved proof of an unlawful killing; there was an irrebuttable presumption that the harm so inflicted was not a cause of the death.[5] Another illustration of the need to establish all elements of the offence is *Deller*.[6] D had sold his car to P representing to P that he was free to sell the car and that it was not subject to encumbrances.[7] D believed that these representations were untrue and that he was not free to sell the car. At his trial, for what today would be fraud by false representation contrary to s.2 of the Fraud Act 2006,[8] it became clear that the document which would have created an encumbrance was ineffective and so his statements to the buyer were, in fact, true. He was clearly dishonest and he had obtained the money for the car, but an essential ingredient of the actus reus was missing; there was no false representation and there could, thus, be no conviction for that offence.[9]

2–002   The reason for the need for the actus reus is that the law does not impose criminal liability simply on the basis of the accused's intention. In every offence the elements will consist of certain conduct of the accused or the production by the accused of a prohibited result. In murder the accused must be proved to have caused the unlawful killing of another human being; in rape the accused must have had sexual connection with a woman or man who did not consent; in theft the accused must be proved to have appropriated property belonging to another.

The reason for the second requirement—of a certain state of mind—is even more obvious. A broad distinction needs to be drawn between persons who deliberately cause harm and those who cause harm unavoidably and accidentally; the former, it may be supposed, are rightly brought within the purview of the criminal law, while the latter are not. In relation to "serious" crimes (sometimes referred to as crimes *mala in se*—wrongful in themselves) this is normally the position. In relation to "minor" crimes, however, (crimes *mala prohibita*—wrongful because prohibited by law) criminal liability is frequently imposed

---

[3] As to burden and standard of proof see above, paras 1–009—1–011.
[4] For attempts, see below, para.6–002.
[5] See below, para.7–009. This rule was an early attempt to overcome the problems of proving that the act of the accused was the cause of the death.
[6] (1952) 36 Cr.App.R. 184.
[7] i.e it was not security for any loan.
[8] This offence at that time was obtaining by false pretences contrary to the Larceny Act 1916 s.32.
[9] He could, today, be guilty of attempted fraud contrary to the Criminal Attempts Act 1981 s.1(1), see below, para.6–004.

even though the accused is not really at fault. These offences are known as offences of strict or absolute liability. We shall examine these crimes, and the policies which are said to justify them, in a later chapter, though some incidental mention of them will be made in this chapter.

Even if the prosecution can establish that the accused has deliberately killed another human being, B, it does not inevitably follow that he will be convicted of murder. The crime of murder requires that the killing should be unlawful.[10] The accused may claim that he killed B because he saw that B was just about to kill C. The law permits the use of reasonable force in self-defence, defence of property and prevention of crime. Once the accused has raised the issue of justification it is for the prosecution to prove that no circumstances of justification existed or that even if they did, the accused had used more force than was reasonably necessary in the circumstances.[11] By raising the defence the accused is challenging the prosecution to prove that the killing was in fact unlawful.

Suppose, however, that D is driving past a bar when he sees P crossing the road ahead of him. He knows that P has been having an affair with his wife and so he deliberately drives his car at P intending to kill him; P is killed instantly. It is later discovered that P is a member of a terrorist gang and was about to throw a bomb into the crowded bar where it would almost certainly have caused death. Should D be treated as a criminal for his murderous intent against P or should he be treated as a hero for saving the customers in the bar? You probably think this is an extremely unlikely situation, but the same problem arose in *Dadson*.[12] D was charged with unlawfully and maliciously shooting at any person with intent to maim, disfigure or disable such person or to do some other grievous bodily harm to such person. He was a police officer whose patrol area included a copse from which there had been a large number of thefts of wood. D saw a person running away from the copse and he shouted to him to stop. When he failed to do so D shot and wounded the suspect. At that time it was considered perfectly lawful for an officer to shoot at an escaping felon to prevent his escape.[13] Stealing wood was a misdemeanour unless the accused had two previous convictions for stealing wood, in which case it became a felony.[14] D had no reason to believe that this suspect had any previous convictions for stealing wood, but as a matter of fact he had, and therefore on this occasion he was an escaping felon. It is quite clear that the prosecution could establish that D had deliberately shot at the suspect with the necessary intent. It was, however, argued that since the suspect was, in fact, an escaping felon, the shooting was not unlawful; in other words the prosecution had failed to prove all the elements of the offence.[15] On the face of it, this seems to be a good argument; it would appear that the killing is not in fact unlawful and therefore, as with *Deller*,[16] the prosecution cannot prove the existence of all elements.

The Court for Crown Cases Reserved, however, upheld his conviction. Pollock C.B. said, **2–003** "The prosecutor (suspect) not having committed felony known to the prisoner at the time when he fired, the latter was not justified in firing at the prosecutor; he was guilty of

---

[10] Unlawfulness is an element to be found in the offences against the person generally and indicates the availability of justification as a defence.

[11] For a more detailed discussion of the burden and standard of proof in criminal cases see paras 1–009—1–011.

[12] (1850) 175 E.R. 499. See generally B. Hogan "The Dadson Principle" [1989] Crim.L.R. 679. This article is strongly in favour of the view that D should not be able to rely on unknown circumstances of justification.

[13] At that time crimes were divided into felonies (the more serious offences) and misdemeanours. This distinction survives in some common law jurisdiction, but was abolished in our jurisdiction by the Criminal Law Act 1967. See further Ch.4, para.4–001.

[14] Larceny Act 1827 s.39.

[15] There is no general agreement as to whether absence of justification is part of the actus reus or mens rea. What is clear, however, is that once the issue of justification is raised, the prosecution will lose the case unless it can prove the absence of justification. See further below para.5–044.

[16] (1952) 36 Cr.App.R. 184. See also, *McKoy, The Times,* July 17, 2002.

shooting at the prisoner with intent to do him grievous bodily harm, and the conviction is right."[17]

How then, if at all, can *Dadson* be distinguished from *Deller*? In *Deller* the prosecution failed to prove that there was a deception; in *Dadson* the prosecution cannot prove that the shooting was unlawful. The answer lies in the nature of the defence of justification. What the court in *Dadson* is saying, is that in certain circumstances the accused will be justified in inflicting grievous bodily harm or even death, but only if he is aware of the circumstances when he does the otherwise prohibited act. If the prosecution can establish that the accused was unaware of the circumstances which would constitute justification the defence fails and the prosecution have established that the act was unlawful. So long as the accused is aware of the facts which justify the shooting he may rely on the defence; it would not matter that he was unaware that the law provided such a justification. Thus, if *Dadson* was aware that the suspect had two previous convictions for theft of wood, he would have been acquitted; it would not have mattered that he did not know that it was legal to shoot escaping felons.

In *Deller* the prosecution had to prove that what the accused had said was false and this they simply could not do.

We shall now examine the elements which go to make up the actus reus and mens rea in more detail.

ACTUS REUS

2–004   Literally, actus means "act" but this would be too restricted a definition. While most crimes are committed by acts of the accused this is not always the case. We shall see that in certain situations the crime can be brought about by the failure of the accused to act. For this reason it is perhaps better to define actus as "conduct" since this is apt to cover both acts and omissions. Even this will not cover every situation since in a very limited number of crimes liability is imposed for what is known as a state of affairs without the requirement of any conduct on the part of the accused.[18]

A crime, however, requires more than conduct: the actus must be reus. If X fires a rifle he is engaged in conduct but to fire a rifle, without more, is not a crime. Suppose, then, that X aims his rifle at Y and deliberately kills him. X has now brought about a consequence which consequence is normally proscribed by the law of murder—*normally* but not always. Whether or not X will be guilty of murder depends upon the circumstances surrounding the killing. X will not be guilty of murder if Y is an enemy in time of war or if X is carrying out the lawful execution of Y or if X is acting in circumstances of self-defence.

Thus we can say of the actus reus of any crime that it comprises a combination of (a) some conduct, (b) a prohibited result and (c) certain surrounding circumstances. Not all crimes require a prohibited result. Rape, for example, requires only conduct and certain surrounding circumstances. The prosecution must prove that the accused intentionally penetrated the vagina, anus or mouth of another person with the penis (conduct), and that the victim was not consenting (surrounding circumstances). Murder on the other hand

---

[17] (1850) 175 E.R. 499 at para.2–002.
[18] See, below, paras 2–013—2–014. Although the terms actus reus and mens rea have become widely used in criminal law, their usage was criticised by Lord Diplock in *Miller* [1983] 2 A.C. 161 at 174. "[I]t would be conducive to clarity of analysis of the ingredients of a crime that is created by statute . . . if we were to avoid bad Latin and instead to think and speak . . . about the conduct of the accused and his state of mind at the time of that conduct, instead of speaking about actus reus and mens rea."

requires all three elements; a killing of a human being (conduct plus result), the killing being unlawful (circumstance).[19]

The traditional view is that criminal liability comprises actus reus plus mens rea.[20] Under this approach defences such as justification are normally included as part of the actus reus. Professor Lanham, however, has argued that a crime comprises three elements, actus reus, mens rea and absence of a valid defence.[21] Under this approach we should say of a person who has killed in self-defence, that the prosecution can establish that the accused has brought about the actus reus of the offence with the necessary mens rea, but that the prosecution have failed to disprove his defence of justification. This approach has the advantage that it serves to emphasise that if an element is classified as a defence element, the accused will bear an evidential burden to make a live issue of the defence, though the prosecution will still bear the burden of proof. Further, it highlights the distinction between cases such as *Dadson* and *Deller*. On the other hand it has the disadvantage that it may not always be clear whether an issue is part of the actus reus or a defence. In rape, for example, it is suggested that lack of consent on the part of the victim is seen as part of the definition of the offence and hence part of the actus reus. On the other hand in the crime of battery[22] the prosecution must prove a non-consensual application of force, but in *Brown*[23] the House of Lords thought consent was a defence element.

1. THE NEED FOR VOLUNTARY CONDUCT

It is part of the prosecution's case to prove that the actus reus was brought about by the voluntary conduct of the accused. Suppose that D was driving home on his motorcycle when he skids on a patch of ice and crashes. He lands on his head and loses consciousness. The next thing that he remembers is passing out in the kitchen of his house. He has driven home, but he has no recollection of doing so. Later he is charged with driving through a red traffic light on this journey home. D may plead that he did not intend to drive though the lights, and nor did he consciously take an unjustified risk of driving through the lights at red. This would be an assertion that he lacked mens rea. Unfortunately for D the offence does not require the police to prove anything more than that D drove through the lights; it is an offence of strict liability which dispenses with the need for mens rea.[24] However the offence does require that the prosecution establish that the defendant was driving the motorcycle at the time it went through the red light and driving requires the conscious exercise of will on the part of the driver. In our example D was not consciously exercising his will over the motorcycle, it was an unconscious or involuntary exercise of will. Once D has introduced sufficient evidence to show that he blacked out, the prosecution will not succeed unless they can prove that when D went through the lights he was "driving" his motorcycle. It is,

2–005

---

[19] The offence of causing death by dangerous driving contrary to s.1 of the Road Traffic Act 1988, as amended by s.1 of the Road Traffic Act 1991, is a "result" crime; the forbidden consequence of death is part of the actus reus. However, the offence of dangerous driving contrary to the Road Traffic Act 1988 s.2 as amended, is a "conduct" crime. In relation to the actus reus it must simply be shown that D was driving dangerously; nothing else need occur.

[20] See, for example Glanville Williams, *Textbook of Criminal Law*, 2nd edn (London: Stevens & Sons, 1983), Ch.2.

[21] [1976] Crim.L.R. 276.

[22] Usually known as common assault. See below, para.7–062.

[23] [1994] 1 A.C. 212, see below, paras 7–102—7–104.

[24] An offence of strict liability is one in which, on at least one element of the actus reus, the prosecution is relieved of the need to prove mens rea. The element in question is often the element at the core of the allegation. Thus it is an offence for a butcher to sell adulterated meat. The prosecution merely have to prove that he consciously sold the piece of meat in question and that it was, in fact, adulterated. The prosecution does not have to show that the butcher knew or ought to have known that the meat was bad. See further Ch.3.

therefore, necessary to remember that there is a distinction between the requirement for voluntary conduct from the need to prove that the accused acted with mens rea. Failure to prove that the accused brought about the actus reus by a conscious exercise of his will always leads to an acquittal[25]; failure to prove that the accused acted intentionally, recklessly or negligently may or may not lead to an acquittal.

Care needs to be taken over the meaning of the word "involuntary" in this context. It is being used to convey the notion that the defendant brought about the actus reus of the offence, but that he did so without any willed muscular control on his part.[26] In our example we would say that the driver was acting automatically or in what is known as a state of automatism. Later we shall encounter the defence of duress where the accused brings about the actus reus of a crime because he is being threatened with death or grievous bodily harm unless he does so. It may be said that his action is involuntary in that his freedom of choice has been overborne, but he is not acting automatically. He intentionally brings about the actus reus of a crime in order to avoid a very unpleasant consequence.

2–006 The main point to remember is that in no case can the defendant be convicted if the actus reus was not brought about by voluntary conduct on his part.[27] Where the assertion is that he brought about the actus reus while unconscious, the court will want to know the cause of the blackout and the accused will be expected to produce evidence, normally medical evidence, in support of his claim. Once there is evidence that the accused was acting automatically, it will generally be for the prosecution to prove beyond reasonable doubt that the accused was not acting automatically when he brought about the actus reus. Not all automatic conduct will be dealt with in this way. Consider the following examples:

(a) A pushes B so that B collides with C and knocks C over. If B is charged with assaulting C, he can claim that there was no voluntary conduct on his part whatsoever and he would be entitled to an absolute acquittal.

(b) D is charged with passing a traffic light which was showing red. He claims that just before he approached the lights he was attacked by several wasps which had flown into the car and as a result he instinctively tried to defend himself and thereby failed to control the car.[28] It is generally accepted that in such a situation D would not at that moment be "driving" the car, and would be treated as being merely behind the wheel. The relevant principles were clearly set out by Lord Goddard C.J. in *Hill v Baxter*: "Suppose a driver had a stroke or an epileptic fit, both instances of . . . Acts of God: he might well be in the driver's seat or even with his hands at the wheel, but in such a state of unconsciousness that he could not be said to be driving. A blow from a stone or an attack by a swarm of bees introduces some conception akin to a novus actus interveniens."[29]

(c) E is about to drive home in his car when he bangs his head on a low ceiling beam. He remembers nothing until he is stopped by the police for careless driving. Medical evidence shows that he could have been driving totally automatically. As

---

[25] It is generally accepted that Parliament does not enact legislation which dispenses with the need for voluntary action on the part of the defendant. But see *Larsonneur* (1933) 24 Cr.App.R. 74, discussed below, para.2–014.

[26] Under the American Model Penal Code an action will be treated as being voluntary where it is the product of the "effort or determination of the actor"; Model Penal Code s.1.13(3).

[27] See, generally, P. Robinson, "Causing the Conditions of One's Own Defence" (1985) 71 Virginia L.R. 1.

[28] An illustration discussed in the case of *Hill v Baxter* [1958] 1 Q.B. 277 at 286.

[29] [1958] 1 Q.B. 277 at 283.

with our example earlier of the defendant jumping the red light, E will be entitled to a complete acquittal[30] on the ground of automatism; he was not "driving" his car. It will be for the prosecution to prove that he was acting consciously.[31]

(d) F is charged with hitting his girlfriend on the head with a video-recorder. He claims that at that moment he was sleepwalking and totally unconscious.[32] In this situation he is clearly claiming to act automatically. However, as we shall see later,[33] when the court investigates the cause of the unconsciousness it will conclude that it has been caused through an internal abnormality of F's sleeping patterns and as such will be held to be a disease of the mind. The result is that if F continues to pursue this line of defence he will be held to have raised the defence of insanity or more precisely insane automatism.[34] As we shall see, the defendants in examples (c) and (d) will both be entitled to be acquitted since they have acted involuntarily. However the courts have drawn a distinction. E cannot be held responsible in any way for his automatic conduct—there is little chance that E will repeat his experience and there is nothing that could be done to prevent it. E is, therefore, entitled to be acquitted unconditionally. F, on the other hand, has a sleep problem which might recur and is probably treatable. By treating his case as one of insane automatism he will be acquitted but on the ground of insanity and the court will have power to ensure he has treatment.

(e) G is charged with assaulting H. G claims that he is a diabetic and that the assault occurred during a hypoglycaemic blackout caused by his failure to eat after taking his insulin. On the face of it this is a case of non-insane automatism.[35] However, there is evidence that on several previous occasions G has failed to eat properly following the insulin injection and that he is aware that on such occasions he is liable to black out and act aggressively. In this situation the court will hold that his recklessness in failing to eat properly coupled with his awareness of the consequences is adequate evidence of recklessness required to establish the mens rea of the assault.[36]

(f) J is charged with assaulting K whom he is alleged to have pushed into some iron railings. J's defence is that he was so drunk he blacked out and fell unconsciously against K. Again this is a case of automatic conduct, but here the cause is self-induced drunkenness. Where this is found to be the case the court will treat the defence as voluntary intoxication and not automatism.[37]

The courts have held that a two stage approach should be adopted in cases where the defence of automatism is raised.[38] First, the court should consider whether or not there is in fact evidence of automatism or whether what is being alleged is something less than fully automatic conduct. Secondly, the court should investigate the aetiology of the automatism; does it arise from a disease of the mind, in which case it is insane automatism, or was it

---

[30] As opposed to one obtained on the grounds of insanity.
[31] Contrast *Kay v Butterworth* (1945) 173 L.T. 191.
[32] These are the facts of *Burgess* (1991) 93 Cr.App.R. 41.
[33] See below, para.5–006.
[34] See below, para.5–011 for a treatment of the rules relating to insanity as a defence.
[35] See below, paras 5–010—5–012 for further treatment of the distinction between insane and non-insane automatism.
[36] See *Bailey* [1983] 2 All E.R. 503, discussed below, para.2–012.
[37] See below, para.5–027 for intoxication as a defence.
[38] See, *Attorney-General's Reference (No.2 of 1992)* (1993) 97 Cr.App.R. 429 at 434.

caused by other factors in which case it is non-insane automatism? This distinction between insane and non-insane automatism is very important. Not only will it determine whether the accused walks entirely free at the end of the case,[39] but it dramatically affects the burden of proof. If the judge rules that the defendant has introduced evidence of non-insane automatism, the prosecution will have the burden of proving beyond reasonable doubt that the accused voluntarily brought about the actus reus of the offence. If, on the other hand, the trial judge rules that the defendant has introduced evidence that the automatism was due to a disease of the mind, if the defendant wants to pursue the defence, then he will bear the burden of proving on a balance of probabilities that he brought about the actus reus in a state of insane automatism. In practice, most defendants change their plea to one of guilty once they become aware that they stand the risk of being found not guilty by reason of insanity.[40]

A. Has the Defendant Introduced Evidence of Automatism?

2–007   Under this two-staged approach, the defendant must introduce some evidence that he was acting automatically. The first question, therefore, is what do we mean by automatic conduct? The classic definition is provided by Lord Denning in *Bratty v Attorney-General for Northern Ireland*[41] where he said:

> "No act is punishable if it is done involuntarily; and an involuntary act in this context—some people now prefer to speak of it as 'automatism'—means an act which is done by the muscles without any control by the mind, such as a spasm, a reflex action or a convulsion; or an act done by a person who is not conscious of what he is doing, such as an act whilst suffering from concussion or whilst sleepwalking."

An interesting decision is that in the case of *Ryan v R.*[42] R had robbed a service station threatening the cashier with a sawn-off rifle; the rifle was loaded and the safety catch was off. He attempted to tie up the cashier with one hand while pointing the rifle at him with the other. Unfortunately, the cashier made a sudden movement and R shot him dead. R said that he had been startled by the sudden movement and had pressed the trigger "involuntarily".[43] The majority in the High Court of Australia took the view that he had voluntarily placed himself in a situation where he might need to make a split-second decision and the fact that he so responded by pulling the trigger did not make that act an involuntary act in the nature of an act done in a convulsion or epileptic seizure. While it is easy to sympathise with the majority it is hard to disagree with Barwick J. in the minority who said that on the defendant's account of events the pulling of the trigger was a reflex action and not one for which, in law, the defendant would be responsible. Ormerod refers to the analogy of a sudden movement of a tennis player in retrieving a difficult shot. There is no doubt that the tennis player's action is a willed muscular movement albeit that the decision to make it is made in a split second. He argues, correctly it is suggested, that D's squeezing of the trigger

---

[39] There is an unqualified acquittal only in cases of non-insane automatism. Where the jury finds insane automatism the accused will be acquitted on the grounds of insanity.

[40] See, e.g. *Sullivan* [1984] A.C. 156 and *Hennessy* [1989] 1 W.L.R. 287. If D is alleged to have murdered P and he pleads diminished responsibility (see below, para.5–015.) then it is open for the prosecution to try to prove that D was insane. In this case D will bear the burden of proving diminished responsibility on a balance of probabilities while the Crown must now prove beyond reasonable doubt that D was insane.

[41] [1963] A.C. 386 at 409.

[42] (1967) 121 C.L.R. 205, High Court of Australia.

[43] See, also *Gray v Barr* [1971] 2 All E.R. 949.

is more akin to an act done in a convulsion or epileptic seizure than it is to that of the tennis player.[44]

Little attention was paid until recently to the phrase in the above quotation by Lord Denning "without any control by the mind". It was generally accepted that any serious loss of willed muscular control would suffice. Thus in *Charlson*[45] the accused was alleged to have hit his son on the head with a mallet and to have thrown him out of a window. He was acquitted on the basis of automatism stemming from a brain tumour. It is extremely unlikely that Charlson exercised absolutely no control over his bodily motions, but it was generally accepted that his muscular control was severely impaired and that amounted to automatism.[46]

A more restricted test was seen in *Broome v Perkins*.[47] The defendant had driven his car for a distance of about six miles but was unable to recall the journey at all. The state of his car revealed that he must have hit other vehicles and he therefore went to the police and was eventually charged with careless driving. He pleaded automatism on the basis that he was a diabetic and his behaviour was consistent with that of low blood sugar. Evidence revealed that during the course of the journey he had collided with small vehicles but had missed larger ones such as lorries. The Divisional Court said that there was no evidence of automatism because to a certain extent he had exercised some degree of conscious control over his vehicle when he reacted to large objects; his driving was not, therefore, totally automatic.

Despite intense criticism of this harsh ruling,[48] it was accepted as an accurate statement of **2–008** law by the Court of Appeal in *Attorney-General's Reference (No.2 of 1992)*.[49] In that case a driver of a heavy goods vehicle driving on a motorway shunted a recovery vehicle which was parked on the hard shoulder into the rear of another vehicle which had broken down and was also on the hard shoulder just ahead of the recovery vehicle. The drivers of the two parked vehicles were standing between their vehicles and were crushed to death. The lorry driver was charged with causing death by reckless driving.[50] The defendant claimed to have been driving in a state known as "driving without awareness". In such a condition the driver's capacity to avoid a collision ceases to exist, but he remains capable of driving his vehicle within the road markings. The driver would be largely unaware of what was happening ahead and largely unaware of steering.

Lord Taylor C.J. concluded[51]: "As the authorities cited above show, the defence of automatism requires that there was a total destruction of voluntary control on the defendant's part. Impaired, reduced or partial control is not enough. Professor Brown[52] accepted that someone 'driving without awareness' within his description, retains some control. He would be able to steer the vehicle and usually to react and return to full awareness when confronted by significant stimuli."[53] There was therefore no evidence of automatism to be left to the jury and the defence fell at the first hurdle.

---

[44] D. Ormerod, *Smith and Hogan Criminal Law*, 12th edn (Oxford: Oxford University Press, 2008), p.56, referring to I.D. Elliott, "Responsibility for Involuntary Acts: *Ryan v The Queen*" (1968) 41 A.L.J. 497.

[45] [1955] 1 W.L.R. 317.

[46] *Charlson* was treated as a case of non-insane automatism, but today it is generally accepted that a brain tumour would constitute a disease of the mind and hence it should have been classified as insane automatism. See below, para.5–010.

[47] (1987) 85 Cr.App.R. 321; see also *Roberts v Ramsbottom* [1980] 1 All E.R. 70 and *Isitt* (1978) 67 Cr.App.R. 440.

[48] See, for example J.C. Smith in his commentary: [1987] Crim.L.R. 271 at 272.

[49] (1993) 97 Cr.App.R. 429. See, also *C* [2007] EWCA Crim 1862.

[50] This offence has now been replaced with causing death by dangerous driving; Road Traffic Act 1988 s.1 as amended by the Road Traffic Act 1991 s.1.

[51] (1993) 97 Cr.App.R. 429 at 434.

[52] An expert witness.

[53] Professor Brown could not explain why the flashing yellow lights of the recovery vehicle had not snapped him out of his condition.

It will be appreciated that automatism is a very narrowly defined concept which involves the total loss of conscious control. It would exist where D loses total control of his vehicle on account of being attacked by a swarm of bees; where X grabs hold of Y's arm and forces Y who is holding a knife to stick it into Z's back; where D drives in an unconscious state having received a blow on the head or where D was sleepwalking at the time he assaulted P. The courts will be alert to ensure that in any case where D alleges that he blacked out, the blackout was indeed total and that he did not exercise any conscious control over his actions.[54]

An analogous situation may occur in which D, despite being fully conscious, nonetheless is deprived of total control of his actions. Suppose, for example, D is driving his car when, through no fault of his own, his power brakes fail and he passes traffic lights at red. He is entitled to be acquitted on the basis of a total lack of control.[55] This point was made by Salmon J. in *Spurge*: "There does not seem to this court to be any real distinction between a man suddenly deprived of all control of a motor car by a sudden affliction of his person and being so deprived by some defect which suddenly manifests itself in the motor car. In both cases the motor car is suddenly out of control of its driver through no fault of his."[56]

B. What is the Cause of the Automatism?

2–009 Only if there is evidence that the accused was acting in a state of automatism should the court proceed to answer the second question of whether we are dealing with insane or non-insane automatism. In Chapter 5 we shall investigate fully the McNaghten Rules for the discovery of insanity.[57] It is clear that the courts have made a significant change to their earlier perception of this distinction. In *Bratty v Attorney-General for Northern Ireland* Lord Denning said that sleepwalking was one of the most obvious examples of automatism, and it is clear that he meant non-insane automatism. Today, however, following the decision of the Court of Appeal in *Burgess*[58] it is equally clear that sleepwalking is to be classed as insane automatism. The reason for this change is easy to perceive. The judges are clearly concerned that they do not release into the community a person whose mental or physical condition poses a threat to others. They have tended to classify as insanity automatic conduct which poses a threat to others, is likely to be repeated and which is capable of being treated. Mental or physical disorders which may affect the working of the mind have these characteristics and by holding such conduct to be insane automatism the courts are enabled to hold the person not guilty while at the same time rendering the defendant subject to such treatment as they think fit.

On the other hand automatic conduct which is caused by, for example, a blow on the head, is not likely to recur, is not treatable and poses no further threat to the community. It is safe therefore to allow the defendant an unfettered acquittal on the basis of non-insane automatism.

[54] The Draft Criminal Code Bill does not impose such a strict requirement that D has a total loss of conscious control. By cl.33 it is provided that D acts automatically when in a condition depriving himself of *effective* control over his acts.
[55] *Burns v Bidder* [1967] 2 Q.B. 227. Note that in this case D could rely on sudden brake failure as a defence to the strict liability offence of failure to accord precedence to a pedestrian on a crossing.
[56] [1961] 2 All E.R. 688 at 690.
[57] See below, para.5–006.
[58] (1991) 93 Cr.App.R. 41; see generally R.D. Mackay "The Sleepwalker is not Insane" (1992) 55 M.L.R. 714.

C. Evidential and Legal Burdens

The trial judge will have to decide whether and on what basis to leave the issue of **2–010** automatism to the jury. Unless the defendant has established some evidence that he was acting in a totally automatic state, there is no issue to be left to the jury. In *Bratty v Attorney-General for Northern Ireland*[59] Lord Denning said that it will rarely be enough for the accused to give evidence on oath that he suffered a blackout. Medical evidence will generally be required. Once the judge is satisfied that there is evidence of automatism, he must decide whether it is non-insane or insane automatism. If he rules that the automatism was caused by a disease of the mind, he must direct the jury that it is for the defendant to satisfy them on a balance of probabilities that he was acting as an insane automaton. If he rules that the automatism was caused by an external factor such as a blow on the head, he must direct the jury that it is for the prosecution to prove beyond reasonable doubt that the accused voluntarily brought about the actus reus and that he did not do so automatically. This is a very hard burden for the prosecution to discharge and is why the courts have ruled that the accused must provide substantial evidence of non-insane automatism before the prosecution needs to rebut it. Suppose D is charged with driving through a red light and pleads that he blacked out just before going through the lights. If all that was required by the accused to discharge the evidential burden was for him to say on oath that he blacked out, leaving the prosecutor to prove beyond reasonable doubt that the accused did not blackout, it would become a very popular defence.[60]

This approach to automatism is not without its problems. In the first place, as we shall see later[61] it leads to unreal distinctions being drawn. A diabetic defendant who pleads automatism on the basis of a blackout may find he has pleaded insane automatism. If he has simply forgotten to take his insulin and as a result suffers a rise in his blood-sugar count resulting in a hyperglycaemic blackout, he will be treated as insane since it is the diabetes which has caused the attack; there are no external factors operating. If on the other hand he takes too much insulin or fails to eat enough he will suffer a hypoglycaemic blackout which will be held to have been caused by the external element, insulin. In this situation he is a non-insane automaton.[62] Burgess was held to be insane since his sleepwalking had been caused by internal bodily activity which had produced an abnormal sleep pattern. Had he managed to find an expert prepared to testify that it was much more likely that a cheese sandwich had caused the sleepwalking episode, he would have been totally acquitted.

Where the accused is acquitted on the basis of non-insane automatism he is entitled to a **2–011** full acquittal. In *R v T*,[63] T was charged with robbery and causing actual bodily harm. The Crown Court[64] accepted that the post-traumatic stress disorder she was suffering as a result of being raped three days before the commission of the alleged offences could amount to a defence of non-insane automatism to the charges. In essence, the dissociative state arising from being raped which resulted in post-traumatic stress was held to be due to an external cause; the post-traumatic stress was held not to amount to a disease of the mind and the defendant was treated as not acting consciously. However, even if you can ignore the fact that despite the stress disorder it was highly unlikely that the loss of self-control was total,[65]

[59] [1963] A.C. 386.
[60] As to burden and standard of proof generally—see above, paras 1–009—1–011.
[61] See below, paras 5–010—5–012.
[62] See, generally Lederman, "Non-insane and Insane Automatism: Reducing the Significance of a Problematic Distinction" (1983) 34 I.C.L.Q. 819. See also, *Poole* [2003] All E.R. (D) 448 where D's loss of consciousness was induced by his failure to take his epilepsy medicine.
[63] [1990] Crim.L.R. 256.
[64] Before Southan J. at Snaresbrook Crown Court.
[65] See above, para.2–006.

how long will it be before the effect of the rape will cease to be an external cause and become an internal one? Consider, for example, D, who is playing football when he receives a blow on the head. He appears to recover, but then punches the referee. Medical evidence shows that D's conduct was probably due to the blow on the head; an external factor which would support non-insane automatism. What, however, would the position be if on the following weekend he punched another referee and again claimed it was due to the blow on the head? At some stage the external factor must become an internal one. *R v T* should be contrasted with *Rabey*[66] in which R was charged with causing a girl, with whom he had become infatuated, actual bodily harm with intent. He claimed that he was suffering from non-insane automatism in the form of a dissociative state caused by the psychological blow of discovering that she held him in low esteem. The Supreme Court of Canada upheld the decision of the Ontario Court of Appeal to allow the prosecutor's appeal against R's acquittal and to order a new trial. The Supreme Court approved the statement by Martin J. that "the ordinary stresses and disappointments of life which are the common lot of mankind do not constitute an external cause . . .".[67] In effect, the court was saying that any dissociative state had been caused by his own psychological or emotional make-up and that is an internal factor. Rape on the other hand is not the common lot of mankind and could have a devastating effect on even the most well-balanced individual; it can properly be treated as an external factor.

As we have seen,[68] according to recent cases where the accused seeks to rely by way of defence on automatic conduct, the court must first consider whether there is evidence that the conduct was totally automatic. If the court holds that the accused was exercising some control the defence of automatism, both sane and insane, fails; there is no need for the court to enquire into the aetiology of the defendant's condition. However, it would appear that there is no reason why the accused could not be found to be insane. Take, for example, the case of *Charlson*[69] where the defendant, under the influence of a brain tumour, hit his son on the head with a mallet and threw him out of the window. That was held to be a case of non-insane automatism. It is thought the reasoning would differ today. In the first place it seems unlikely that Charlson's lack of bodily control was total. If that is the case, automatism both non-insane and insane is ruled out. Nevertheless Charlson would now be considered to have been suffering from a disease of the mind and so long as this resulted in a defect of reason so that he did not appreciate what he was doing, he can be held to be insane.[70]

D. Self-induced Automatism

2–012   Where the automatism has been induced by the voluntary consumption of alcohol or dangerous drugs[71] the automatism will be of no defence to a charge of a basic intent crime.[72] In *Lipman*,[73] L and his girlfriend had been taking the drug LSD. L experienced a hallucination in which he thought he was descending to the centre of the earth and was fending off serpents. When he recovered he discovered that he had rammed several inches

---

[66] (1977) 37 C.C.C. (2d) 461, affirmed (1980) 54 C.C.C. (2d) 1.
[67] (1980) 54 C.C.C. (2d) at 7.
[68] Above, para.2–006.
[69] [1955] 1 W.L.R. 317, discussed above, para.2–007.
[70] See below, paras 5–010—5–012 for further discussion of the defence of insanity.
[71] As to dangerous drugs see *Hardie* [1984] 3 All E.R. 848; below, para.5–038.
[72] A crime of basic intent is one to which intoxication is no defence and in general these are crimes where the mens rea is satisfied by proof of recklessness. See further below, paras 5–028—5–031.
[73] [1970] 1 Q.B. 152.

of bed sheet into his girlfriend's mouth and she had died from suffocation.[74] His conviction for manslaughter was upheld; both manslaughter and the assault upon which it was based[75] are crimes of basic intent and evidence of his drugged state was irrelevant even though he was acting as a complete automaton. Even where the automatism has not been caused by alcohol or drugs, the accused may nonetheless be prevented from relying upon it as a defence. For example, if D is charged with an assault and he pleads non-insane automatism which was caused by his failure to eat properly after an injection of insulin, on the face of it he should be able to rely upon the defence. If, however, this is not the first time that this has happened or if it is clear that he had been expressly warned by his doctor of the consequences of failing to eat properly then it is less clear that he should be allowed to rely upon automatism. If he is charged with a basic intent offence of assault and he is aware that a failure to eat properly might lead to a hypoglycaemic episode during which he could become aggressive, unpredictable and uncontrolled, his awareness that he might become aggressive will suffice as the recklessness needed for the offence. If he is not so aware of the possible consequences, he should be able to rely on the automatism by way of defence.[76] Thus in *Bailey*,[77] B who suffered from diabetes was charged with wounding with intent and unlawful wounding in that he had struck the victim on the head. B claimed to have been acting in a state of non-insane automatism brought about by failure to eat properly after a dose of insulin which had led to hypoglycaemia. The Court of Appeal held that since he was not aware that his failure to eat properly could cause him to become aggressive, he was entitled to rely upon his self-induced automatism not only in relation to wounding with intent which is a specific intent crime, but also to the charge of unlawful wounding which is a crime of basic intent.[78]

If D is aware that he blacks out from time to time, he may nevertheless be entitled to rely upon it as a defence if he is in no way to blame for the blackouts. However, if knowing of this possibility, he drives a car, he will be guilty of dangerous driving from the outset.

E. Criminal Liability in the "State of Affairs" Cases

In the preceding sections we said that whatever the mens rea requirement of a crime, it was **2–013** always incumbent on the prosecution to prove that the actus reus was brought about by a willed muscular movement on the part of the defendant.[79] There is, however, no rule which says that criminal liability cannot be imposed without some voluntary conduct on the part of the accused. Parliament could, for example, legislate that it was a criminal offence to be over six feet tall. In such an unlikely event it would be no defence for the accused to say that he had no control over his height. Of course, you will say that Parliament would never enact such an offence, but it has to be accepted that it is theoretically open to Parliament to do so and, as it happens, there are some offences which appear to impose criminal liability without any proof of a voluntary act on the part of the defendant. These offences are often known as status offences or state of affairs offences.[80]

[74] She had also suffered blows to the head but these were not the cause of death.
[75] For unlawful act manslaughter see below, para.7–038.
[76] It is suggested that it is not sufficient that he ought to have foreseen the fact that he might become aggressive. cf. Lawton L.J. in *Quick* [1973] 3 All E.R. 347 at 386.
[77] [1983] 2 All E.R. 503; see below, para.5–037.
[78] See below, para.5–039, for an analogous approach in intoxication cases.
[79] In practice, the prosecution would not have to deal with this issue unless the defendant had introduced some evidence to show that the actus reus had been brought about automatically. See above, para.2–010.
[80] See, generally P.R. Glazebrook, "Situational Liability" in P.R. Glazebrook (ed.), *Reshaping the Criminal Law* (London: Stephens, 1978), p.108.

Where a constable is of the opinion that a stationary vehicle is committing or has committed a fixed penalty offence,[81] he may fix notice of the fixed penalty to the car.[82] The registration number of the car will enable the police to track down the owner of the car but he may well say that he was not the driver of the car at the time of the offence and what is more he can prove it. It was to avoid such difficulties for the prosecution that Parliament enacted that "it shall be conclusively presumed . . . that [the owner] was the driver at that time[83] . . . that acts or omissions of the driver of the vehicle at that time were his acts or omissions"[84] Thus if the owner's son has parked his car illegally in London, the father will be liable even though at the time he is fast asleep in a hotel in New York. It is, however, a defence for the owner to show that the person driving the car was doing so without his consent.[85] Thus, liability is incurred only if the accused consented to possession of the car. Nonetheless, given actual consent on the owner's part, he can be liable for certain fixed penalty crimes without the need for any voluntary conduct on his part.

It is easy to see the need for such a provision. Without such a provision it would become almost impossible to recover parking fines. More difficult to accept is the ruling in *Larsonneur*[86] where L, a French subject, was convicted on a charge that she "being an alien to whom leave to land in the United Kingdom has been refused was found in the United Kingdom," contrary to the Aliens Order 1920. She had originally arrived legitimately in the United Kingdom bearing a passport containing certain conditions. These conditions were later varied and a condition imposed that she should leave the United Kingdom by a certain date. She left the United Kingdom on that date and sailed to Ireland where she was arrested and sent back to the United Kingdom under police arrest. When the ship docked at Holyhead, after the date on which she had been required to leave the United Kingdom, she was handed over to the custody of the British police and was subsequently charged with the offence cited above. It was argued on her behalf that the offence required that the prosecution should prove not just that she was found here, but also that she had landed without permission. This would require proof of voluntary conduct on her part and "the evidence showed that she had not landed at all, but that she had been landed by a superior force over which she had no control." The Court of Criminal Appeal, however, held that she had been rightly convicted. She was, within the meaning of the order, an alien to whom permission to land had been refused and she had been found in the United Kingdom.

2–014   In the vast majority of cases in which this provision is applied, there will be no concern; the defendant of his own free will, will have entered the country illegally. Equally there can be little objection to the legislation which presumes that the owner of the car was responsible for its illegal parking, particularly since that legislation provides a defence for a situation where the car has been taken without the owner's consent. Objection would undoubtedly be taken had the car been illegally parked by a thief who had stolen the car from the owner's house while the owner was on holiday abroad. This is what is objectionable about *Larsonneur*. The word "found" has been interpreted to cover a situation which has been brought about without any voluntary conduct on the part of the defendant.[87] Of course, her conduct was not involuntary in the sense that she did not have control over her muscular movements when she walked ashore. Nonetheless the judgment implies that she would have been convicted even if she had been physically carried ashore by the police and if that is the

---

[81] For example, illegal parking.
[82] Road Traffic Offenders Act 1988 s.62(1).
[83] This applies even if the owner may be a limited company.
[84] Road Traffic Offenders Act 1988 s.64(5).
[85] Road Traffic Offenders Act 1988 s.64(6).
[86] (1933) 24 Cr.App.R. 74.
[87] See David Lanham, "Larsonneur Revisited" [1976] Crim.L.R. 276, for a defence of *Larsonneur*.

case then she would also commit the offence had she been captured by terrorists in Ireland and physically thrown ashore in the United Kingdom.

Larsonneur is not the only example of such an offence. In *Winzar v Chief Constable of Kent*[88] the defendant had somehow arrived at a hospital where the doctor realised that his only problem was that he was drunk and thereupon ordered him to leave. He was later sighted slumped on a chair in a corridor and the police were summoned to remove him. The police carried him outside and put him in a police car which was parked in the highway. He was later charged with being found drunk in the highway contrary to s.12 of the Licensing Act 1872 and his conviction was upheld by the Divisional Court. Goff L.J. said, "It is enough for the commission of the offence that (1) a person is in a public place or highway, (2) he is drunk, and (3) in those circumstances he is perceived to be there and to be drunk".[89] Surely on this construction of the statute he was "found" by the police in the hospital corridor and carried by them into the highway.

In both *Larsonneur* and *Winzar* the offence was brought about by the act of the police. It is clear that if Parliament passes a statute which creates an absolute offence with no requirement of willed conduct on the part of the defence and makes it clear that there are to be no defences whatsoever, the courts will be bound to enforce that legislation. In s.64(6) of the Road Traffic Offenders Act 1988, we saw an offence which requires no voluntary conduct on the part of the owner of a car. This provision deliberately sets out to make the defendants liable for the acts of others in a justifiable attempt to collect parking fines. Yet even here there is a defence for the defendant who can show that the car was being driven by another without his consent. But *Larsonneur* and *Winzar* are not cases where the defendants were justifiably made liable for the conduct of others; they were offences in which they were made liable for their own conduct when that conduct was controlled by others. Would it not be preferable to construe all statutes creating offences as requiring voluntary conduct on the part of the accused unless either the statute expressly exempted the prosecution from the requirement or at least it could be shown that the accused was at fault in bringing about the state of affairs? Certainly a more logical approach was taken by the Privy Council in *Lim Chin Aik*[90] where it held that D did not commit the offence of remaining in Singapore contrary to an order prohibiting his entry into the republic, when he was ignorant of the prohibition.

We have seen that if D has given his son a general permission to drive his car, D will be liable for a parking ticket incurred by his son, even though he is away on holiday at the time. If, however, D had parked his car in a two-hour parking zone, and was about to drive it away before the time expired when he was arrested by the police on suspicion of theft or kidnapped by terrorists, he will have no defence, and it would not seem to matter whether or not the abduction was lawful.

2. LIABILITY FOR FAILING TO ACT

We have seen[91] that in the general run of cases the prosecution must prove that the accused **2–015** brought about a prohibited result or behaved in an unlawful manner. Thus in murder the accused must have brought about an unlawful killing and this he will normally have done by

---

[88] *The Times,* March 28, 1983.
[89] For a contrasting US authority see *Martin v State* (1944) 31 Ala. App. 334 where it was held to be essential for a conviction of being drunk on a public highway that D had made a voluntary appearance on the highway. His conviction was quashed as police officers had forcibly carried him in a drunken state from his own home to the highway and subsequently arrested him there.
[90] [1963] A.C. 160.
[91] Above, para.1–011.

a positive act such as shooting the victim. Can he, however, be convicted of murder on account of a failure by him to take steps that would have prevented the death in the hope that the victim would die? Certain basic points can be made at the outset:

1. Parliament has expressly created offences of omission in which the accused is liable for failing to do something. For example, it is an offence for a motorist who has been requested to provide a sample of breath for a roadside check to fail to do so without reasonable excuse.[92] Equally, if the roadside test proves positive, it is an offence to fail without reasonable excuse to provide a specimen of his breath for analysis by the Intoximeter at the police station.[93] It is an offence for motorists in certain circumstances to fail to provide information.[94] These offences present no problems of principle and the majority concern fairly minor regulatory offences examples of which include failing to submit a tax return.[95]

2. Many situations which might at first glance appear to be omissions, later on further examination turn out to be positive acts. For instance, it may be thought that a person who is prosecuted and convicted of failing to have a television licence is being prosecuted for an omission. The offence, however, is to operate a television set without having obtained the necessary licence and this is a positive act. The same is true of most licensing offences. In the majority of cases it will not matter whether you class such offences as offences of omission or commission since the statute will make it clear that an offence has been committed. However, as we shall see later, in some situations it will be crucial to draw the distinction.[96]

3. Where the offence involves proof that the defendant caused a prohibited result, it is more difficult to see how the accused could be liable for failing to act. For example, if a small child is drowning in a paddling pool in only two feet of water, in what sense can two persons who watch the child drown be said to have killed the child. What they have done is failed to stop the child drowning. The child brought about its own death by falling into the pool; it is not possible to say that by doing nothing the two observers brought about any acceleration[97] of the child's death. However, the law has found no difficulty in holding defendants guilty of murder or manslaughter for failing to act. As we shall see it does this by imposing on certain individuals a duty to act. If either of the observers had been the parent or guardian of the child he or she would have been under a duty to act and would be liable for failing to act. We would say that the parent had murdered the child and the observer who was a stranger to the child was guilty of no offence. In reality neither observer actually killed the child; the duty on the parent, however, enables the court to hold him or her liable for the death.

---

[92] Road Traffic Act 1988 s.6(4).
[93] Road Traffic Act 1988 s.7(6).
[94] Road Traffic Act 1988 s.170(4). In relation to non-disclosure of information see also Prevention of Terrorism (Temporary Provisions) Act 1989 s.18.
[95] In relation to cheating the revenue see *Mavji* [1987] 1 W.L.R. 1388.
[96] See below, para.4–050.
[97] Since in a way we are all dying, killing can be described as the acceleration of death.

In most criminal prosecutions the prosecutor will be seeking to prove that a prohibited **2–016** situation or result has been brought about by the acts of the accused. However, in certain situations it will be the fact that the accused has failed to act which has led to the prohibited event occurring. For example, if A pushes B under the water and holds him there till he dies, then it is clear that A's actions have caused B's death. On the other hand if A sees B drowning in the swimming pool in a situation in which it would be easy for A to rescue B, but A does nothing, the result will be the same—B will die. However, this time B would die whether A was there or not. Should the law, therefore, hold A liable for B's death? It would be easy to answer yes, and indeed some countries have tried to create such liability in what are often known as easy rescue clauses.[98] Most of us would find the picture of A simply watching B drown to be morally abhorrent. Yet if we take the view that, in principle, A should be liable for his failure to act we would probably cause more problems than the courts would be able to handle. It is one matter to hold a person liable for the death of a child whom he has just watched drown in two feet of water. Such cases would be rare. The water would probably be much deeper, and the currents strong; the observer may be a modest swimmer. How much of a risk can the law expect A to take with his own life in order to rescue (a) his son or (b) a perfect stranger? The answer that he should take such risks as the court deems reasonable in all the circumstances would merely involve the court in a minute examination of all the surrounding circumstances and possibly A's appreciation of them.

A far more modest approach is adopted here. As a general rule there is no liability for failing to act unless such liability is specifically provided for. Where the prosecution seeks to hold a defendant guilty for failing to act it will need to establish two prerequisites: (a) it will have to establish that the offence was one for which liability may be incurred by failing to act,[99] and (b) the prosecution will have to prove, in addition to the normal elements of the actus reus, that D was under a duty to act and that he had failed to discharge that duty.[100]

A. In which Crimes may Liability be Incurred for an Omission?

There is no general statement of principle. Offences have been considered on an ad hoc **2–017** basis as they have appeared before the courts.

(i) Offences Against the Person

Murder and Manslaughter.   There are plenty of authorities to support the assertion that **2–018** murder and manslaughter are both crimes that can be committed by a person who has, with the appropriate mens rea, breached a duty of supporting another. It is true that nearly all the examples concern prosecution for manslaughter,[101] but *Gibbins and Proctor*[102] is clear

---

[98] Note s.2.01(1) and (2) of the American Model Penal Code defines a voluntary omission as being an omission to perform an act of which the defendant is physically capable. Such provisions are frequently known as easy rescue clauses.

[99] There will usually be no difficulty in those offences such as failing to take a breath test, where Parliament has expressly created liability for failing to do something. The Act will make it clear on whom lies a duty to act.

[100] See, generally B. Hogan, "Omissions and the Duty Myth" in *Criminal Law: Essays in honour of J.C. Smith* (1986); A. Ashworth "The Scope of Criminal Liability for Omissions" (1989) 105 L.Q.R. 424 and G. Williams "Criminal Omissions—the Conventional View" (1991) 107 L.Q.R. 86.

[101] It is generally accepted that manslaughter can be committed by omission. However it appears that one form of manslaughter—unlawful act manslaughter—cannot be committed by omission; see *Lowe* [1973] Q.B. 702. This form of manslaughter requires proof that the accused has done an unlawful and dangerous act and the court in *Lowe* held that where the allegation was that the accused had failed to act, the prosecution would have to prove gross negligence manslaughter. As to the various types of manslaughter see below, para.7–007.

[102] (1918) 13 Cr.App.R. 134.

authority that murder may also be committed by omission. In that case both defendants were under a duty to support the child, Nelly—the man because he was the father and the woman with whom he was living because she had accepted money for the child's food from the father and had therefore assumed responsibility for the child. It was held that if the prosecution could establish that they had withheld food from the child with intent to cause her grievous bodily harm, they were both guilty of murder.[103]

Strangely, although the position is clear that a person can be held liable for the two most serious offences against the person by a failure to act, the position in relation to all the other major offences against the person is obscure.

2–019 Wounding and causing G.B.H. with intent. It is probably safe to assume that offences under s.18 of the Offences against the Person Act 1861 can be committed by omission. Since the trial judge in *Gibbins and Proctor* directed the jury in terms of an intention to cause grievous bodily harm as the mens rea for the murder charge, it would be highly illogical had the child not died but had suffered grievous bodily harm, that the couple should have escaped conviction. It would mean that until the child died, Gibbins and Proctor were under no duty to support her; this duty would have arisen only the moment the child died. It is, of course, far less likely that a wound would be perpetrated by omission and although there is no authority on the matter it seems likely that the courts would hold that a wound could be the result of omission.

2–020 Assault and battery. At the other end of the scale it has been often said that assault and battery require commission and that they cannot be brought about by pure omission. Ormerod, however, gives the example of the defendant who digs a hole. If he digs it with the intention that P should fall into it, this is a positive act leading to a battery when P falls into the hole. If he digs it with no intent to cause harm but later remembers that P will be calling round that evening and deliberately leaves it for P to fall into, again this could be said to be a positive act. On the other hand if D's gardener digs the hole, tells D to be careful and D deliberately does nothing in the hope that P will fall into it, we now have a pure omission. There would seem to be no good reason why D should be any less liable for deliberately not telling P about the hole the gardener has dug, than he should be when he has dug the hole himself.[104]

2–021 Wounding and inflicting G.B.H. If it is accepted that assault and battery can be committed by an omission, there would be no logical reason why the offences of unlawful wounding and infliction of grievous bodily harm under s.20 of the Offences Against the Person Act 1861 should be treated differently.[105]

(ii) Offences Against Property

2–022 There is no direct authority as to whether the words destroy or damage are capable of extending liability under the Criminal Damage Act 1971 to omissions. Nonetheless in *Miller*[106] the House of Lords held the defendant to owe a duty to protect property he had

---

[103] In *Downes* (1875) 13 Cox C.C. 111 it was held that a parent could be guilty of manslaughter for failing to obtain medical treatment for their sick child. The parents' refusal to obtain such treatment was motivated by their religious beliefs.

[104] D. Ormerod, *Smith and Hogan Criminal Law* (2008) at p.64. See also J.C. Smith "Liability for Omissions in Criminal Law" (1984) 4 *Legal Studies* 88. No authority exists which asserts that assault necessitates an *act* and Professor Smith is of the opinion that such a requirement is unnecessary.

[105] Until *Clarence Wilson* [1984] A.C. 242 at 260 it was held that the word "inflict" in relation to grievous bodily harm meant it had to be brought about by an assault. In *Clarence Wilson* the House of Lords held that whereas an assault was no longer to be regarded as an essential requirement of inflicting grievous bodily harm, it would normally be present. If an assault requires an act as opposed to an omission, it might cast some doubt on whether inflicting grievous bodily harm can be committed by an omission.

[106] [1983] 2 A.C. 161, see below, para.2–027.

accidentally put at risk from fire. It is suggested that there is no logical reason why in appropriate cases liability should not also be imposed for failing, for example, to put out a fire where there is a duty to look after the premises.[107]

In general, the question of whether a specific offence may be perpetrated by a failure to act will be a matter for the court to determine by interpretation of a word or phrase within a statute. Thus in *Firth*[108] the Court of Appeal held that the word "deceive" in s.15 of the Theft Act 1968[109] could be construed to include liability for omission. In that case a doctor failed to inform the necessary authorities that certain patients were private patients, thereby obtaining N.H.S. services for them.[110] In *Ahmad*,[111] on the other hand, the court held that the phrase "does acts" required a positive act; liability could not be incurred for failing to act. The defendant was a landlord who commenced major structural alterations to the bathroom of a flat but then took no further steps to finish the job. It was held that Ahmad was not guilty of "doing acts calculated to interfere with the peace or comfort of a residential occupier with intent to cause him to give up occupation of the premises" contrary to s.1(3) of the Protection from Eviction Act 1977. The wording of the statute did not impose liability for an omission. The defendant had not done "acts" merely by failing to finish the alterations thereby leaving the premises uninhabitable. In *Speck*,[112] S had sat passively for some five minutes while a six year old child touched his penis through his trousers thereby causing S to have an erection. It was held that his passive behaviour could be construed as an invitation to the child to continue and this was an act of gross indecency.

It seems very clear that in *Gibbins and Proctor*[113] Proctor, at least, intended that Nelly should die. Suppose that the child had been rescued in the nick of time, that she was suffering grievous bodily harm, but that she survived. Could Proctor have been charged with attempted murder? Section 1(1) of the Criminal Attempts Act 1981 requires that the accused "does an act which is more than merely preparatory to the commission of [the offence intended]". It seems likely that the courts would probably decide that this provision too clearly calls for a positive act, and therefore Proctor would not be liable for the attempted murder.[114]

This area of the law is far from satisfactory. It is suggested that there is no convincing reason why all crimes should not be capable of being committed by omission as well as by positive act.

B. Who is Under a Duty to Act?

As we said earlier, where the prosecution allege that the accused has committed an offence **2–023** by failing to act, they must prove first that the crime is one that can be brought about by a failure to act and secondly that the accused was under a duty to act. In this section we shall look at the occasions in which the courts have held that the defendant was under a duty to act.

---

[107] The Criminal Law Code Team was obliged to accept the recommendation of the Criminal Law Revision Committee in their 14th Report that assaults required acts. They concluded that if omissions could not be the basis for assaults, they should not form the basis for crimes of damaging property.

[108] (1989) 91 Cr.App.R. 217.

[109] Obtaining property by deception, since repealed by the Fraud Act 2006.

[110] See, also *Shama* [1990] 2 All E.R. 602.

[111] (1986) 84 Cr.App.R. 64.

[112] [1977] 2 All E.R. 859. This behaviour would now be covered by the Sexual Offences Act 2003.

[113] (1918) 13 Cr.App.R. 134, discussed above, para.2-018.

[114] For attempts see below, para.6–002.

(i) Duty Imposed by Statute

2–024   In many cases the duty and the person upon whom it lies are clearly stated in a statute. Section 170 of the Road Traffic Act 1988 is a typical example. It makes clear that a driver of a motor vehicle involved in certain road traffic accidents is under a duty to stop and, if required to do so by persons having reasonable grounds for so requiring, to provide information. A failure to comply with these requirements is an offence.[115] So we can see exactly the scope of the duty and upon whom it falls. A further example under this legislation is provided by s.7(6) which makes it an offence for a person to fail to provide a specimen of breath for analysis when properly requested so to do.

(ii) Duty Arising from Status

2–025   In the preceding paragraph the scope of the duty was clearly defined by the statute. In the majority of cases the scope of the duty is less clear. Since most of the cases deal with situations in which it is alleged that the failure to act by the accused has led to death of a victim, it would seem that we are dealing with a duty to preserve life.[116] It is clear that parents are under a duty to preserve the life of their children. Thus, in the example of the child drowning in a shallow pool of water, if one of the observers is a parent of the child, he or she will be under a duty to save the child from drowning. Exactly how far the parent would be expected to go in order to save the child's life is not clear. If the child is drowning in a deep, fast flowing river, the law would not expect the parent to risk his or her own life. The parent would be expected to take such steps as are reasonable in the circumstances to preserve the child's life.[117] Is there a corresponding duty on the child to preserve its parents' lives? There is no authority on this point, but it would seem logical for there to be such a duty once the child is over the age of 10 and in a position to act. In *William Smith*[118] it was held that a brother owed no duty of caring for his sisters. The same lack of authority surrounds duties arising out of close relationships in general.[119] However, it may be that a husband and wife are under a duty to preserve the life of the other.[120]

If a duty is based upon a close relationship, there is the question of when such a duty will come to an end. On the assumption that a duty to take care does in fact exist between husband and wife, it is possible that one spouse can release the other in certain circumstances from the duty to care for the other. In *Smith*[121] the wife, who had an aversion to doctors and medical treatment, refused to allow her husband to seek medical assistance on her behalf after she had given birth to a still-born child at home. She then gave permission for her husband to call a doctor, but this was too late and she died. Her husband was charged with manslaughter as medical evidence suggested that her life could have been saved with prompt treatment. Griffiths J. told the jury it was for them:

> "[T]o balance the weight that it is right to give to his wife's wishes to avoid calling a doctor against her capacity to make rational decisions. If she does not appear too ill it

---

[115] s.170(4).

[116] See, D. Ormerod, *Smith and Hogan Criminal Law* (2008), p.66.

[117] See, generally, A. Leavens "A Causation Approach to Criminal Omissions" (1988) 76 Cal. L.R. 547; and G. Mead "Contracting in to Crime: A Theory of Criminal Omissions" (1991) 11 O.J.L.S 147.

[118] (1826) 172 E.R. 203.

[119] In the draft Criminal Code the proposal of the Law Commission is to impose liability upon D if he might have prevented the actus reus. By cl.17(1) it is provided that "a person causes a result . . . when . . . (b) he omits to do an act which might prevent its occurrence and which he is under a duty to do according to the law relating to the offence."

[120] In the well-known US authority of *People v Beardsley* (1967) 113 N.W. 1128, it was held that no duty was owed by D to his lover who voluntarily took morphine in his presence.

[121] [1979] Crim.L.R. 251. See also *Bonnyman* (1942) 28 Cr.App.R. 131.

may be reasonable to abide by her decision. On the other hand, if she appeared desperately ill then whatever she may say it might be right to override."

The implications from the direction in *Smith* is that if the wife was not too ill then it was permissible for her to direct her husband not to call the doctor. The husband would then be released from his duty to care for her. This principle is also supported, albeit obiter, in the important House of Lords decision in *Airedale NHS Trust v Bland*.[122]

In the case of a parent's duty towards a child, it may be that in normal circumstances the duty terminates when the child reaches 18.[123] If this is the case then it would seem that any duty the child had towards the parent should also terminate at that time. All this suggests that there are few clear cut answers. Beyond the parental situation it would probably be more sensible to base duties to act not upon a special relationship, but upon an undertaking by an individual to look after another. This is described in the next section.

The holding of certain offices will create a duty to preserve the lives of others. Thus, the captain of a ship is under a duty to protect the lives of his passengers and crew. Policemen have a general duty to protect the lives of citizens. In *Dytham*[124] a uniformed policeman's failure to intervene to stop a man being kicked to death rendered him liable to a charge of misconduct in a public office. The court cited a passage of *Stephen* where he said:

"Every public officer commits a misdemeanour who wilfully neglects to perform any duty which he is bound either by common law or by statute to perform provided that the discharge of such duty is not attended with greater danger than a man of ordinary firmness and activity may be expected to encounter."[125]

(iii) Voluntary Assumption of a Duty

In *Instan*,[126] D lived with P, her aunt, who paid for the food they consumed. When the aunt **2–026** became bedridden D failed to supply her with any food or to seek assistance. It was held that D had voluntarily assumed the responsibility of looking after her aunt and that her failure to discharge this duty had led to the aunt's death. D was, therefore, rightly convicted of manslaughter.[127] Similarly in *Stone and Dobinson*[128] where a couple assumed the responsibility of caring for an infirm relative, the Court of Appeal held that by the very assumption of that responsibility a corresponding legal duty was imposed upon them to ensure that the duty was satisfied.[129] The cases involve assumption of a duty in respect of a relative, but there is no logical reason why the assumption should not be in respect of a non-relative. If D undertakes to look after his bedridden friend, particularly if this is in return for payment, he should be regarded as under a duty to preserve his friend's life.[130] The guardian of a child can be said to have assumed a duty in respect of the child.

---

[122] [1993] A.C. 789.
[123] If the child is dependent for any reason on its parents, then the duty would presumably continue.
[124] (1979) 69 Cr.App.R. 387. See also, the decision in *Attorney-General's Reference (No.3 of 2003)* [2004] EWCA Crim 864, relating to misconduct in public office and conscious awareness on D's part of the duty imposed.
[125] (1979) 69 Cr.App.R. 387 at 394. Art.145. *Stephen's Digest of the Criminal Law*, 9th edn (London: 1950).
[126] [1893] 1 Q.B. 450.
[127] See, also *Nicholls* (1874) 13 Cox C.C. 75; *Stone and Dobinson* [1977] 2 All E.R. 341.
[128] [1977] 2 All E.R. 341.
[129] The imposition of a duty in this case is confused by the fact that both defendants were of extremely weak intellect and both were psychologically and physically unable to care for the victim.
[130] It has been suggested that it is "proper to sanction breaches of the duty assumed, both because of the potentially dangerous expectations such an assumption excites and also because by taking the responsibility the defendant has thereby chosen to restrict his own freedom of action." W. Wilson, *Criminal Law* (London: Longman, 1998), at pp.82–83.

A duty may be undertaken through contract. In *Pittwood*[131] P was under a contractual obligation to look after a railway level crossing. One of his duties involved ensuring that on the approach of a train the crossing gates were closed to road users. On one occasion he negligently left the gates open to road users which would indicate that it was safe to cross the railway lines. As a result a man was killed when his cart, which was crossing the railway lines, was struck by a train. P argued that he owed no duty to road users who were crossing the lines; his duty was solely to the railway company who employed him.[132] The court, however, held that his contract with the railway company was sufficient to place him under a duty to road users and his grossly negligent breach of this duty rendered him liable for manslaughter. Similar arguments would apply to lollipop traffic controllers and lifeguards appointed by a seaside local authority.

A doctor may be under a duty of care to his patients arising out of contract with a private patient, or with the National Health Service. Several difficult problems have emerged in relation to medical cases and we shall return to this shortly. Drug administration cases have also presented interpretative confusion.[133] In *Ruffell*[134] the Court of Appeal upheld the defendant's conviction of manslaughter. D and V had jointly engaged in drug-taking, a mixture of heroin and cocaine, at D's house. Subsequently, V became ill during the night and V tried to revive him. The next morning the accused left V outside his house where he died from drug intoxication and hypothermia. The trial judge told the jury that they could assume a duty of care was established from the fact that V was a guest in the accused's house, that they were friends, and because D had sought to revive him following the taking of the drugs. This direction on the assumption of a duty of care was endorsed on appeal, but the precise basis on which the duty arose was not clear.

(iv) Supervening Fault

2–027   In some jurisdictions a person who had created a dangerous situation was held to be under a duty to take steps to mitigate the danger. Thus, whereas a stranger who came across a burning house could stand by and admire the spectacle, the person who caused the blaze would be under a duty to have the fire brought under control, and a failure to do this would lead to liability for the damage which resulted. Such a situation arose in *Miller*[135] where M was squatting in a house belonging to another. He had lain down upon a mattress and lit a cigarette. He dropped off to sleep and awoke to find his mattress smouldering. Instead of seeking assistance to put the fire out, he went off in search of another mattress. The house caught fire and £800 of damage was done. M was charged with arson contrary to s.1(1) and (3) of the Criminal Damage Act 1971. The main problem, as perceived by the courts, was that when the accused accidentally set fire to the mattress he did not have the necessary mens rea for an offence under s.1(1), but when he became aware of what he had done, he did nothing to rectify the situation.[136] M was convicted and his appeal was dismissed by the Court of Appeal who treated, as a continuous act of the accused, the whole course of conduct of the accused from the moment at which he fell asleep and dropped the cigarette on to the mattress until the time the damage to the house by fire was complete. On this basis the court held that it was sufficient to constitute the statutory offence of arson if the prosecution could prove:

---

[131] (1902) 19 T.L.R. 37.
[132] He was arguing privity of contract.
[133] See below at paras 2–046—2–048.
[134] [2003] EWCA Crim 122. See below, para.7–053. See also *Evans* [2009] EWCA Crim 650.
[135] [1983] 2 A.C. 161.
[136] In fact it is suggested that the accused could have been convicted for his act in setting fire to the mattress. Section 1(1), as far as this case is concerned, required that the accused recklessly damaged property belonging to another.

(a) that the accused was aware of the danger he had created; and

(b) that during the period defined above, he failed to try to prevent or to minimise the damage which would result from his conduct although it was in his power to do so; and

(c) at the time he failed to take steps to minimise or prevent the danger he was reckless as to whether property would be damaged or destroyed.

This approach is similar to that taken in *Fagan v Metropolitan Police Commissioner*[137] where F had accidentally parked his car on a policeman's foot and had not released the foot when asked to do so. This was another case in which the actus reus and mens rea appeared not to correspond in point of time, but the court held that it sufficed that the accused formed the necessary mens rea for assault at any time during which his wheel was on the policeman's foot.

The House of Lords dismissed Miller's appeal but took a different approach from the Court of Appeal. Lord Diplock said that because he felt it much easier to explain to jurors, he favoured an approach based upon a duty to act which is brought into being by the accused's realisation of the danger he has created. Lord Diplock added, however, that he recommended the use of the word "responsibility" rather than "duty" which is more appropriate in civil law situations. He said that under this approach a suitable direction for the jury would be:

"that the accused is guilty of the offence under s.1(1) of the 1971 Act, if, when he does become aware that the events in question have happened as a result of his own act, he does not try to prevent or reduce the risk of damage by his own efforts or if necessary by sending for help from the fire brigade, and the reason why he does not is either because he has not given any thought to the possibility of there being any such risk or because having recognised that there was some risk involved he has decided not to try to prevent or reduce it."[138]

It is suggested that this approach is of general application to crimes against the person and against property when it has to be proved that the defendant brought about a result with the necessary mens rea. It seems likely that were the facts of *Fagan* to present themselves again the court would no longer take the continuous act approach. It is more likely to conclude that once the accused becomes aware that he has driven on to someone's foot he is under a duty to put matters right. If with the necessary mens rea he fails to do so he is guilty of the offence.

This approach is only needed where there is a problem relating to the coincidence of mens rea and the act which it is alleged led to the prohibited result. Where there is no requirement of mens rea, the approach is unnecessary.[139] Incidence of a duty to act deriving from the *Miller* principle arose more recently in the unusual case of *DPP v Santana-Bermudez*.[140] A female police officer, effecting a lawful search of D, requested that he turn

---

[137] [1969] 1 Q.B. 439.
[138] [1983] 2 A.C. 161 at 179. Lord Diplock asserted that D became under a responsibility to take reasonable steps to counteract the damage to the property at risk: "I see no rational ground for excluding from conduct capable of giving rise to criminal liability, conduct which consists of failing to take measures that lie within one's power to counteract a danger that one has oneself created, if at the time of such conduct one's state of mind is such as constitutes a necessary ingredient of the offence", [1983] 2 A.C. 161 at 176.
[139] See, e.g. *Wings Ltd v Ellis* [1985] A.C. 272.
[140] [2003] EWHC Admin 2908; [2004] Crim.L.R. 471.

out his pockets, suspecting drug possession. V specifically asked D if he was sure that he did not have any "needles or sharps" on his person. A negative response was falsely given. Her finger was pierced by a hypodermic needle upon conducting the search. The Administrative Court determined that D was liable for assault occasioning actual bodily harm. It was expressly held that where someone by act or word or a combination thereof created a danger and thereby exposed another to a reasonably foreseeable risk of injury which materialised, this could amount to the actus reus of assault occasioning actual bodily harm.[141] As in *Miller*, D owed a duty of care to V, and the failure to inform of the "sharps" constituted the actus reus of the offence.

C. Medical Treatment

2–028 It is not suggested that there is a whole new batch of rules to deal with cases involving medical treatment. Nonetheless many of the important cases deal with this issue and it will be useful to discuss them together. The general discretion under which doctors operate was set out in *Bolam v Friern Hospital Management Committee*.[142] The level of duty owed by doctors, surgeons and other health carer professionals is, in many respects, a matter of common sense. Any doctor must act as the reasonable doctor would in that situation. Under the so-called *Bolam* test a doctor will satisfy his duty if he acts in accordance with a practice which a responsible body of medical opinion would recommend. In essence, it will be a defence to liability provided that the doctor's actions are considered adequate by a significant number within the medical profession.

As a general rule a doctor is under a duty to preserve the lives of his patients. This duty might arise from contract or torts, and it can certainly be terminated by a patient. If P, for example, is diagnosed to be suffering from cancer, he may instruct his doctor that he is not willing to undergo an operation, and the doctor would commit an assault if he ignored that request. On the other hand a doctor would be guilty of murder if he injected the patient with a drug to accelerate his death.[143] He would be guilty of aiding and abetting suicide contrary to s.2 of the Suicide Act 1961 if he helped the patient to commit suicide by, for example, pushing some tablets to within the patient's reach.

The legislature has been unwilling to introduce a euthanasia provision which would enable a doctor to terminate a patient's life in certain very restricted situations. However bad the patient's quality of life, the deliberate acceleration of death by a doctor amounts to murder. The courts have tried to mitigate this situation by drawing a distinction between acts and omissions. The courts may be prepared to hold that a doctor was entitled to allow a patient to die because this is a failure to act. In *Arthur's* case[144] the parents of a Downs Syndrome child had indicated they did not want it to live. The doctor thereupon instituted a regime under which it would receive neither food nor treatment. It also appeared that the doctor had administered a drug which the prosecution alleged would suppress the child's desire to

---

[141] See, also, *Matthews* [2003] 2 Cr.App.R. 461 CA. D deliberately pushed V into a river, unaware that V was unable to swim. On attaining that realisation there was a concomitant duty to act under the *Miller* principle; as D failed to act and intended to kill or cause GBH to V there was liability for murder. No duty arose, however, in *Lewin v CPS* [2002] EWHC Crim 1049 where D simply left V, his drunk friend, asleep in his car in the summer heat of Spain, and V died; see *Bowell* [2003] EWCA Crim 3896.

[142] [1957] 1 W.L.R. 582.

[143] Most painkilling drugs may accelerate death. This may produce difficult issues for a prosecutor where death would seem to have been accelerated by the administration of a painkilling drug. Is the doctor liable to be convicted of murder? Possibly the answer is that he should only be liable if the evidence shows that the acceleration of death was the prime motive in administering the drug. See *Bodkin Adams* [1957] Crim.L.R. 365.

[144] (1981) 12 B.M.L.R. 1; see further Gunn and Smith, "Arthur's Case and the Right to Life" [1985] Crim.L.R. 705.

eat. It was held that the withholding of food was an omission and something, in the circumstances, the doctor was entitled to do. On the other hand if the jury found that he had administered a drug to suppress the child's desire to eat, that would be a positive act and Dr Arthur would be guilty of murder.[145] The court, thus, holds that a parent, whose normal duty is to preserve the child's life, may properly take a decision to refuse consent to a medical operation which would prolong its life. As Gunn and Smith say, the case does not provide authority for the proposition that the doctor could have made the decision against the wishes of the parents, nor that the parents could make such a decision without medical advice.

In *Airedale NHS Trust v Bland*,[146] B was one of the victims of the Hillsborough Stadium **2–029** disaster of April 1989 in which many football supporters had been crushed to death. B had not been killed in the incident, but had never recovered consciousness having suffered irreversible brain damage. He was in a persistent vegetative state (PVS), being kept alive by a life support system and fed through a nasogastric drip since he was unable to swallow. The Trust, with the agreement of B's parents, sought a declaration from the High Court that it might discontinue the life sustaining treatment, including the feeding, and also all medical treatment except for that which would allow him to die with the greatest dignity and least distress. The declaration was granted by the High Court and supported by the Court of Appeal. The Official Solicitor appealed to the House of Lords on the grounds that it would constitute murder to discontinue the feeding of the patient.

The case is a classic example of a court attempting to phrase everything in the language of omission as opposed to commission. The action for which permission was sought involved, inter alia, the switching off of the respirator and the withdrawal of the nasogastric tube. Are these acts or can they be seen as omissions? Lord Goff held that the discontinuance of the life support could properly be categorised as an omission. This would be easier to accept if, for example, the system needed re-activating every 12 hours, since then you could, without any degree of artificiality, say that non-reactivation was a failure to renew the life support. Turning off a respirator looks very much like an act. This is made even more difficult to accept by Lord Goff's response to the question of an interloper switching off the machine. This would apparently constitute a positive act because "although the interloper may perform exactly the same *act*[147] as the doctor who discontinues life support, his doing so constitutes interference with the life-prolonging treatment then being administered by the doctor. Accordingly, whereas the doctor, in discontinuing life support, is simply allowing his patient to die of his pre-existing condition, the interloper is actively intervening to stop the doctor from prolonging the patient's life, and such conduct cannot possibly be categorised as an omission."[148]

It is difficult to see how the same action can be seen as both an act and an omission. Nevertheless the House of Lords is prepared to hold the steps that will have to be taken to allow B to die are omissions rather than acts. That being the case the remaining question is whether the doctors should be allowed to let B die.

On admission of B to the hospital the duty on the doctors is to do what is in B's best **2–030** interests. Initially that will involve keeping him alive to assess his physical condition and to decide upon a course of treatment. But there may come a time when it is no longer in his best interests that the treatment should be continued and then it should be discontinued. Lord Goff continued:

---

[145] In fact he was charged with attempted murder and not murder because the prosecution could not establish that the drug actually accelerated the child's death; see also *Re B (A Minor)* [1981] 1 W.L.R. 1421.
[146] [1993] A.C. 789; [1993] 2 W.L.R. 316.
[147] Emphasis supplied.
[148] [1993] A.C. 789 at 866.

". . . the question is not whether it is in the best interests of the patient that he should die. The question is whether it is in the best interests of the patient that his life should be prolonged by the continuance of this form of medical treatment or care.

The correct formulation of the question is of particular importance in a case such as the present where the patient is totally unconscious and where there is no hope whatsoever of any amelioration of his condition. In circumstances such as these, it may be difficult to say that it is in his best interests that the treatment should be ended. But, if the question is asked, as in my opinion it should be, whether it is in his best interests that the treatment which has the effect of artificially prolonging his life should be continued, that question can sensibly be answered to the effect that it is not in his best interests to do so."[149]

It is very hard to see any real distinction between saying that the treatment should be ended or that the treatment should not be continued; both have precisely the same effect. However the former is in the nature of an act while the latter is in the nature of an omission and it is upon this slim distinction that the House felt able to grant the declaration. Of course, even now, the hospital cannot terminate the life of someone like B with a painless and quick injection. The patient must be allowed to starve to death. This is scarcely a satisfactory state of affairs. There is a concomitant obligation imposed on doctors to respect the rights enshrined in ECHR,[150] and as held in *R (Burke) v GMC*[151] it is difficult to countenance how withdrawal of artificial feeding from a sentient patient can be reconciled with the Convention provision.

D. Conclusion on Omissions

2–031   The very sketchy nature of this section and the large areas where there are gaps and uncertainties, go to support the underlying principle that it would be very difficult and possibly impossible to construct a law based upon a general liability to act. Nonetheless the law needs to be made clearer. We need a clear statement as to which crimes can be committed by omission. On the whole it is suggested that the general position should be that all crimes can be committed by a failure to act unless specifically excluded by legislation. Secondly we need a clearer statement of who is under a duty and the extent of that duty. Here it is suggested that the position relating to close family or other social ties needs to be clarified, preferably in a fairly restricted way, the major liability being left to arise out of an assumption of a duty.

3. CAUSATION

2–032   We said earlier[152] that an actus reus generally comprises several elements. These elements take the form of conduct, surrounding circumstances and results. Any given actus reus will contain at least one of these elements. Where the actus reus includes a prohibited result, the prosecution will have to prove that the accused caused the prohibited result by his unlawful

---

[149] [1993] A.C. 789 at 868.
[150] See, e.g. *NHS Trust A v M; NHS Trust B v H* [2001] Fam 348, determining that discontinuance of hydration by artificial means and nutrition from an individual in a persistent vegetative state did not contravene art.2.
[151] [2004] EWHC 1879 (Admin). The case established that it is important to respect the privacy rights of a patient within art.8. See, also, *A Hospital v W* [2007] EWHC 425.
[152] Above, para.2–004.

conduct. The actus reus of common assault and battery do not require proof that the accused caused a result, merely that he acted in a particular way[153]; these are sometimes referred to as conduct crimes. Assault occasioning actual bodily harm requires proof that the accused acted in a certain way, but also that his act caused actual bodily harm; this may be referred to as a result crime. The offence of dangerous driving[154] requires no result, merely proof that the accused was driving dangerously. The offence of causing death by dangerous driving[155] on the other hand requires proof that the accused by his dangerous driving caused the death of another. Murder and manslaughter are both result crimes requiring proof that the accused brought about an unlawful death. Rape is not a result crime; it requires proof simply that the accused acted in a particular way.

Where the crimes require proof that the accused brought about a result, issues of causation may arise.[156] The majority of the cases involving causation tend to centre on the question of causing death and for that reason the topic is frequently covered in the section on homicide. Since, however, the issue is of general relevance, we shall deal with it as part of the actus reus. The issue of causation generally presents few problems. If D is alleged to have killed P by blowing his head off with a shotgun, the trial judge will normally have to invite the jury to decide whether the prosecution have established that D blew P's head off with a shotgun and that he did so with the necessary mens rea. The question of whether this caused P's death will, in a case like this, normally be self-evident. On the other hand problems may arise if D alleges that the death was caused not by his act of stabbing P, but by the grossly negligent treatment given by a doctor at the hospital. In such a case the court will have to decide whether the action of the doctor broke the chain of causation so as to relieve D of liability for the killing. Whatever the answer to that question, D will of course remain liable for the serious injury he inflicted upon P.

It is quite normal for several factors to combine to bring about a given result. It is a question of law for the judge to determine which of these factors or causes can in law be a cause of the result.[157] Suppose that A invites B to dinner. B sets off to catch a bus to A's house, but because the bus driver is two minutes ahead of schedule, B misses the bus and decides to walk. On his way he is run over by C who was driving dangerously. At the hospital B is treated negligently by a surgeon and dies on the operating table. We can say that several factors led to B's death. In the first place, but for A's invitation or the bus driver's bad timing he would not have been run over. C's dangerous driving and the surgeon's negligence are also factors which led to B's death. All of these are what are called factual causes; but for these factors B would not have died.[158] In any case in which the prosecution have to prove that the accused caused a result, they must prove at least that the accused's act was at least a factual cause of the result, or to put it another way, but for the unlawful act of the accused the result would not have occurred. It is for the court to direct the jury as to which of these factual causes is capable in law of amounting to a cause of B's death. In our example the court will find that although without A's invitation to dinner, B would not have ended up in hospital, this is not capable of being a legal cause of the death. The same would be true of the bus driver's poor sense of time.

---

[153] See below, para.7–062.
[154] Road Traffic Act 1988 s.2, as amended by the Road Traffic Act 1991 s.1.
[155] Road Traffic Act 1988 s.1, as amended by the Road Traffic Act 1991 s.1.
[156] In cases of result crimes where strict liability applies (i.e. the prosecution is relieved of the need to prove mens rea, see below, para.3–001) it is possible for causation to be established even though D was unaware of the prohibited result and was not even negligent as to that result; see *National Rivers Authority v Yorkshire Water Services* [1994] 3 W.L.R. 1202; *Environment Agency v Empress Car Co Ltd* [1999] 2 A.C. 22.
[157] See, generally A. Norrie, "A Critique of Criminal Causation" (1991) 54 M.L.R. 685.
[158] A factual cause is sometimes referred to as a sine qua non, meaning something without which the result would not have occurred. Literally "without which, not".

2–033   On the other hand, C's dangerous driving might well be capable in law of amounting to a cause of B's death. If C is charged with causing death by dangerous driving, the first issue for the jury is whether C's dangerous driving was a factual cause of B's death. On the face of it there would appear to be little difficulty in so holding, but caution is needed. In *Dalloway*[159] the accused was charged with the manslaughter of a small child. It was alleged that he had been driving his cart in a grossly negligent manner. He was standing up in the cart and was not holding the reins, which were lying on the horse's back. The child had run across the road only a few yards in front of the cart and had been killed as one of the cart's wheels ran over him. The type of manslaughter relied upon required proof that the accused killed the victim by his grossly negligent conduct[160] Now there is no doubt that D killed the child and it is equally clear that he was driving in a grossly negligent manner. However, this is not enough. In his summing up to the jury Erle J. directed them that if they concluded that had he been holding the reins and by using the reins he could have saved the child then he was guilty of manslaughter. If, however, they thought that he could not have saved the child even had he been holding the reins, they should acquit. In other words in order to convict D of manslaughter, they must be satisfied that it was the bad driving which killed the child. If he would still have killed the child had he been driving properly, manslaughter is not made out. Today D would probably be charged with causing death by dangerous driving.[161] The principles are the same. First the prosecution must establish that D was driving dangerously and secondly that because he was driving dangerously he killed the child. Again D would have to be acquitted if the jury were not sure that had he been driving safely he would not have killed the child. There is, however, one major difference today. Suppose that X is driving at a dangerously high speed when a child steps out from behind a bus and is knocked down and killed by X. It may well be that even the most cautious driver would not have been able to avoid hitting the child and X would have to be acquitted of causing death by dangerous driving or manslaughter. But there is now an offence of dangerous driving[162] and both Dalloway and X are guilty of this offence; this is a conduct crime and not a result crime.[163]

In our example C will probably argue that although he knocked B down because he was driving dangerously, nevertheless the surgeon was the cause of death, because had he operated properly, B would have recovered. C is arguing that the surgeon's incompetence breaks the chain of causation between his dangerous driving and B's death and thereby releases him from liability. It is very tempting here to imagine that all we need to do is to get medical evidence which will show whether B died as a result of being knocked over or because he was killed by the medical treatment. However, it must be remembered that causation is a legal issue and it is for the judge to rule on what can in law amount to a cause

---

[159] (1847) 2 Cox C.C. 273.
[160] See further below, para.7–048.
[161] Contrary to the Road Traffic Act 1988 s.1, as amended by Road Traffic Act 1991 s.1. See *Marchant* [2004] 1 W.L.R. 442 CA the modern variant of *Dalloway*. D was impaled on a metre-long spike protruding from D's agricultural vehicle. The spike was not covered by a guard, however, despite this culpability the collision would have occurred in any event.
[162] Road Traffic Act 1988 s.2, as amended by the Road Traffic Act 1991 s.1.
[163] See, also *White* [1911] 2 K.B. 124; W put poison in his mother's drink. She drank some of the mixture and died. Medical evidence revealed that she died of a heart attack and not from poisoning. Nor did the evidence show that the heart attack was caused by the poison. His act, therefore, in poisoning the drink did not amount to a factual cause of his mother's death. He would, however, be guilty of attempted murder.

of death.[164] Notwithstanding that if the medical evidence shows that with decent medical treatment B would have made a full recovery, it is nonetheless for the court to rule whether, even if this was the case, C should be relieved of liability for B's death.

We said earlier that most of the cases on causation centre on unlawful homicide and here the prosecution have to prove that the accused caused the death of the victim. In most cases this will be straightforward and medical evidence will confirm whether, for example, the accused's stab wound caused the victim's death. However, early lawyers did not have the benefit of modern medical knowledge and, particularly in cases where there was a lengthy period between the attack by the accused and the subsequent death, it might be very hard for the prosecution to prove that it was, in fact, the act of the accused which caused the subsequent death. To provide for such cases the common law developed a rule known as "the year and a day rule". Under this rule, in any case where the prosecution had to establish that the accused had caused an unlawful homicide,[165] if the death occurred later than one year and a day after the last act by the accused alleged to be responsible for the death, it was conclusively presumed that the accused had not killed the victim. As medical knowledge advanced such a rule became unnecessary. Indeed it is quite clear today that it would be possible for an accused to inflict harm upon a victim so that the victim died outside the year and a day period. If D deliberately inflicted P with the AIDS virus in order to kill P, it is quite likely that death will not occur within a year and a day.[166] The rule was, therefore, abolished by the Law Reform (Year and a Day Rule) Act 1996. The Act, however, provides that proceedings against a person for a fatal offence[167] must either be instituted by or with the consent of the Attorney-General, where the injury alleged to have caused the death was sustained three years before the death occurred, or the person has previously been convicted of an offence committed in circumstances alleged to be connected with the death. A simple example of the second situation would be a case where D has been convicted of causing grievous bodily harm with intent to do grievous bodily harm and the victim subsequently dies. D can now be charged with murder, but only if the Attorney-General either gives his consent or institutes the proceedings personally.

A. A Substantial Cause

It is usually said that the accused's act must be a substantial cause of the result. In practice **2–034** this is taken to mean that it must not be so insignificant as to be dismissed by the court on the de minimis principle.[168] For example, in the case of crimes involving proof that the accused killed a human being, the prosecution must prove that the accused's act made a

---

[164] The judge determines the legal principles on causation, but the jury determines whether the causal link between D's conduct and the prohibited consequence is established. The position was set out by Goff L.J. in *Pagett* (1983) 76 Cr.App.R. 279 at 290 considered further below, para.2–040): "it is for the judge to direct the jury . . . in the most simple terms, in accordance with the legal principles which they have to apply. It would then fall to the jury to decide the relevant factual issues which, identified with reference to those legal principles, will lead to the conclusion whether or not the prosecution have established the guilt of the accused of the crime of which he is charged."

[165] Murder and manslaughter were the obvious cases, but it also operated in any crime in which the prosecution had to prove that the accused had killed another.

[166] In the majority of offences the application of the rule simply meant that D was convicted of a lesser offence; for example wounding with intent to do grievous bodily harm. If, however, the original charge was gross negligence manslaughter there was probably no available lesser offence since there are no general non-fatal offences against the person where the mens rea is negligence.

[167] A fatal offence means murder or manslaughter or any other offence of which one of the elements is causing a person's death, or the offence of aiding, abetting, counselling or procuring a person's suicide.

[168] By cl.17(1)(a) of the Draft Criminal Code Bill 1989, it is provided that D's act must make "a more than negligible contribution to the occurrence".

significant contribution to the death.[169] Since in a sense we are all dying, killing involves the acceleration of that process. If D slits the victim's throat so that P will die in three minutes it is clear that D is a substantial cause of P's death. If while P is dying, E pricks him with a pin and causes P to lose a drop of blood, it would be possible to say that E has caused P to die a fraction of a second earlier than he would have died from the slit throat. However, the court would hold this to be so insignificant that it can be ignored. Thus in *Armstrong*[170] the victim, who had already consumed a lethal amount of alcohol, was supplied with heroin by the defendant. There was no evidence that the heroin had in any way accelerated the victim's death; it could not, therefore, be held to be a legal cause of his death.

It must be remembered that for a given result there may be more than one legal cause. If D stabs P so that P is admitted to hospital where he receives very poor treatment, both D and the surgeon may be said to be causes of P's death. A jury assessing D's liability for the killing are not expected to concern themselves with the question of whether D or the surgeon was more to blame. Their task is simply to determine whether D's assault was a substantial cause of P's death. As we shall see, if D's conduct was an operating cause of death when P dies, D will be held liable for the death however negligent the surgeon's performance.[171] The surgeon may well face criminal charges himself, but that is not the concern of the jury trying D for murder. In *Benge*[172] B was employed by a railway company as a foreman platelayer. On the day in question his job was to take up a section of track. On account of his negligence adequate warning was not communicated to the driver of a train and an accident followed. At his trial for manslaughter it was argued that despite his negligence the accident would not have happened had others not been negligent; the driver, for example, was not keeping a proper look out. The court rejected this argument. It is not for the jury to apportion blame. The prosecution have to prove that B's gross negligence was a substantial cause of the death and this they had done. The fact that he was not the sole or even major contributing factor was irrelevant. Of course, the other men who were grossly negligent could also have been prosecuted.

For the moment we can say that when there is more than one alleged cause of the prohibited result, the court must in respect of each determine whether it is a factual cause of the death and, if so, whether it was a substantial operating cause at the time the result occurred. Thus, if D stabbed P, and while he was in hospital a terrorist entered the ward and blew P's head off with a shotgun, only the act of the terrorist can be said to be a substantial operating cause of the death at the moment death occurred.[173] In many ways causation is a matter of common sense; the judge has to direct the jury as to which of the competing causes can amount in law to a cause of the prohibited result. In our opening example of the invitation to dinner, the invitation itself may be a factual cause, but common sense would tell you it is unlikely to be capable of being a legal cause. In the following section we shall have a look at some of the more unusual situations which give rise to issues of causation.

B. Take Your Victim as You Find Him

2–035   If D hits P on the head intending to cause him only slight harm, but P has a thin skull and suffers very serious head injuries, D will be held responsible for the injuries actually caused despite having no way of knowing about P's condition.[174] The offence he will be charged

---

[169] See, e.g. *Hennigan* [1971] 3 All E.R. 133; *Cato* [1976] 1 W.L.R. 110; *Notman* [1994] Crim.L.R. 518.
[170] [1989] Crim.L.R. 149. See, also, *DJ* [2007] EWCA Crim 3133 in which the prosecution failed to prove a causal link between D's conduct (fracture of V's cheekbone) and V's death through a heart attack.
[171] See below, paras 2–046—2–048.
[172] (1865) 4 F. & F. 504.
[173] See further below, para.2–048.
[174] See, for example *Hayward* (1908) 21 Cox C.C. 692; and *Watson* [1989] 2 All E.R. 865.

with will be based upon the injuries actually caused together with his mens rea at the time he hit P. Should P die, D will be charged with manslaughter under what is known as the unlawful act doctrine.[175] He will not be guilty of murder since he does not intend to cause death or grievous bodily harm. If P does not die but suffers grievous bodily harm, D can be held liable for unlawfully and maliciously inflicting grievous bodily harm.[176] Although D intended only some slight harm, this is the mens rea required for the offence of inflicting grievous bodily harm.[177]

In *McKechnie*[178] D injured V who was suffering from a duodenal ulcer. As a result of the wound, the doctors were not able to perform essential surgery on the ulcer and it haemorrhaged, killing V. It was held that D was liable for the death; only if the decision not to operate was an "extraordinary and unusual" one would the chain of causation be broken.

We shall see later that similar problems are raised when the accused alleges that had the victim taken better care of himself following the attack, the injury would have been far less severe.[179]

C. Supervening Events

In this section the cases deal with a situation in which the accused claims that the chain of **2–036** causation which links his unlawful act with the prohibited result has been broken by a subsequent event. This intervening event is usually referred to as a novus actus interveniens which literally means "a new act intervening". Virtually all the cases concern the liability of the accused for an unlawful killing, and the problem for the judge will be whether the intervening factors can be held to relieve the accused of liability for the unlawful killing.

(i) Fright and Flight Cases

The issue before the court in these cases is whether the accused can be held responsible for **2–037** injuries suffered by the victim in trying to avoid violence at the hands of the defendant. In *Roberts*[180] R had given a lift to a girl hitchhiker. The girl alleged that the defendant had made advances to her and had then snatched at her coat to remove it. Fearing what might happen the girl jumped from the moving car and sustained injuries as a result. R was eventually charged with assault occasioning actual bodily harm.[181] To secure a conviction for the offence the prosecution must prove that the defendant caused actual bodily injury. In *Roberts* the accused claimed that the jury should have been directed that they could only convict him if they found that he had foreseen that the girl might leap out of the car as a result of his touching her. The Court of Appeal dismissed this argument. Stephenson L.J. said the proper test is:

> "Was it [i.e. the jump from the car which led to her injuries] the natural result of what the alleged assailant said and did, in the sense that it was something that could reasonably have been foreseen as the consequence of what he was saying or doing? As it was put in one of the old cases, it had got to be shown to be his act, and if, of course, the victim does something so 'daft', in the words of the appellant in this case, or so

---

[175] He has deliberately committed an unlawful and dangerous act, see below, para.7–038.
[176] Contrary to the Offences Against the Person Act 1861 s.20; see below, para.7–082.
[177] See below, para.7–083.
[178] (1992) 94 Cr.App.R. 51.
[179] See below, para.2–049.
[180] (1972) 56 Cr.App.R. 95; see also *DPP v Daley* [1979] 2 W.L.R. 239.
[181] Contrary to the Offences Against the Person Act 1861 s.47; see below, para.7–076.

unexpected, not that this particular assailant did not actually foresee it but that no reasonable man could be expected to foresee it, then it is only in a very remote and unreal sense a consequence of his assault, it is really occasioned by a voluntary act on the part of the victim which could not reasonably be foreseen and which breaks the chain of causation between the assault and the harm or injury."[182]

Thus, in this type of case, if the jury conclude that the victim's conduct was the natural consequence of the assault, the accused can be held liable for the resulting injuries.[183] The test is one of reasonable foreseeability; was the victim's reaction within the range of reasonably foreseeable responses? This was applied in *Mackie*[184] where a child of three fell down the stairs and died in an attempt to escape a thrashing from D, his violent father. D was found guilty of manslaughter; the attempt to escape was viewed as the natural consequence of D's unlawful act.

Of course, the prosecution must prove that the accused has brought about the actus reus of the offence with the necessary mens rea. In *Roberts* the accused had been charged with assault occasioning actual bodily harm.[185] This requires that the prosecution proves that R intentionally applied force to the victim or consciously took an unjustified risk of doing so (the assault) and that this caused actual bodily harm.[186] Therefore, in *Roberts* the prosecutor merely has to prove that R intended to grab hold of her coat and that it was within the range of foreseeable consequences that she would leap from the car. If, however, the girl had suffered grievous bodily harm and the accused had been charged with inflicting grievous bodily harm contrary to s.20 of the Offences Against the Person Act 1861, the prosecution would have to prove that the accused intended or foresaw that the victim would suffer some bodily harm.[187] This would no doubt be easy in a case such as *Halliday*[188] where D's wife had almost jumped from a window when D approached her in a threatening manner. It is less straightforward in cases such as *Lewis* where the husband making threats was on a different side of a locked door.[189] The court does not address the problem of mens rea, concentrating mainly on the issue of whether the wife's reaction was a natural response. It would suffice that the jury were satisfied that L intended to injure his wife with his fists and the harm was actually caused by her jump from the building. But if Roberts had been charged with inflicting grievous bodily harm to the girl hitchhiker it is less easy to conclude that R foresaw his advances would cause any bodily injury.

2–038   In *Williams*[190] the accused was charged with the manslaughter of a victim who had hitched a ride in the accused's car and had leapt from the car thinking he was about to be violently robbed. The Court of Appeal held that in fright and flight cases where a death occurred the jury should be directed first to look at the issue of causation taking into account any relevant

---

[182] (1972) 56 Cr.App.R. 95 at 102.
[183] For other examples of fright and flight see *Pitts* (1842) Car & M. 284; *Evans* [1992] Crim.L.R. 559; *Williams* [1992] 2 All E.R. 183. In *Royall v R* (1991) 65 A.L.J.R. 451 before the High Court of Australia, Mason J. remarked, "[G]enerally speaking an act done by a person in the interests of self-protection, in the face of violence or threats of violence on the part of another, which results in the death of the first person, does not negative the causal connection between the violence or threats of violence and the death, the intervening act of the deceased does not break the chain of causation."
[184] (1973) 57 Cr.App.R. 453.
[185] See below, para.7–076.
[186] Any non-consensual touching will constitute an assault (more correctly this is a battery); there is no requirement of mens rea in relation to the actual bodily harm which is caused by the battery.
[187] See below, at paras 7–082—7–084; there is no requirement that the prosecutor must prove the accused intended or foresaw grievous bodily harm.
[188] (1889) 61 L.T. 701.
[189] [1970] Crim.L.R. 647.
[190] [1992] 2 All E.R. 183.

characteristics of the victim and the fact that in the agony of the moment the victim might do the wrong thing. Then the jury should be directed as to the requirements, in this case, of unlawful act manslaughter.[191] Although judges would probably be advised in the light of *Williams* to direct the jury in this two step approach, it is suggested that all the court is saying is that the jury must be made aware of all the ingredients of the offence charged.

The reference to "relevant characteristics" is also not without its difficulties. Stuart-Smith L.J. probably had in mind characteristics such as age and sex, which are likely to affect an ordinary person's reaction.[192] Such characteristics would be obvious to the defendant. What of less normal characteristics? In *Corbett*[193] C was charged with the manslaughter of B, a mentally handicapped person of 26 who suffered from bouts of mental illness and who had problems with high alcohol consumption. It was alleged that on one occasion after a bout of heavy drinking the two men argued and C began to attack B. B ran off and fell into a gutter where he was run over by a passing car. The trial judge directed the jury that they should consider whether what B had done was something that might be expected as a reaction of somebody in that state. It is clear in this case that C was aware of B's characteristics, but should they be taken into account if they are unknown to the accused? If the girl in *Roberts* had, unbeknown to R, suffered from a mental illness which made her unduly timid and likely to overreact, should the jury be asked to consider whether the reaction was within the range of reasonable foreseeability for someone with this illness or for someone of normal mental capacity? Perhaps the answer should be that the characteristic should only be taken into account if it is one the accused was aware of, or at least ought to have been aware of.[194] If, for example, the accused knows that the victim is daft and likely to jump from the car at the slightest provocation, he should be judged on that basis.

(ii) Subsequent Events

Suppose that D hits P on the head and leaves him unconscious on a mainline railway line. P is subsequently killed when he is run over by a train. The answer to this type of case is straightforward. If the subsequent occurrence is reasonably foreseeable, then D will be liable for the subsequent death. In our example, D would clearly be held responsible for P's death; the arrival of a train was obviously foreseeable. Equally if D knocked P unconscious and left him on a beach where the tide was coming in, D would be held responsible for P's death by drowning. If, however, D had pulled P to what was generally accepted as beyond the reach of the sea, he would not be liable for D's death if the beach were struck by a freak tidal wave which swept P out to sea.   **2–039**

An interesting recent case in this regard is *Rafferty*.[195] D and his co-defendants subjected P to a violent attack on a beach. At one point, D approached and elbowed P in the back to keep him down. D then stole P's ATM cash dispenser card and decamped from the scene for around forty minutes in an attempt to obtain cash. During this period the other parties

---

[191] See below, para.7–038 for unlawful act manslaughter. It is suggested that the approach suggested by Stuart-Smith L.J. in *Williams* is overcomplicated. The test for causation would be whether the act of the accused in jumping out of the car was within the range of reasonably foreseeable reactions to the threats. The test for unlawful act manslaughter would be whether the unlawful act of the accused was such that all reasonable and sober persons would inevitably recognise that it might subject the other to the risk of some harm albeit not serious harm. With the greatest of respect these two tests are virtually the same. Both ask whether harm is within the range of reasonable foreseeability. The trial judge needs only to leave the manslaughter test slightly modified to make it clear that the harm which is reasonably foreseeable is harm which is caused by the victim jumping from the car.

[192] This would be in line with the test for provocation, see below, para.7–019.

[193] [1996] Crim.L.R. 594; see also *Marjoram* [2000] Crim.L.R. 372 (objective test applies to whether a reasonable person could have forseen V's attempt to escape as a possible consequence of D's assault).

[194] See, *Watson* [1989] 2 All E.R. 865, discussed below, para.7–045.

[195] [2007] EWCA Crim 1846; [2008] Crim.L.R. 218.

in this unlawful enterprise continued their violent attack on P, stripped him, then drowned him. It was held that the drowning was of a fundamentally different nature from the other harm inflicted on P;[196] the drowning was uncontemplated and as such being outwith the scope of the planned event consequently broke the causal connection for D's homicide liability.[197] It is a "fundamental" principle of criminal law that a free, informed and deliberate act breaks the chain of causation.[198] In *Rafferty* their Lordships articulated the classic statement of principle set out by Professor Glanville Williams:

> "If D murderously attacks a victim and leaves him for dead, when in fact he is not dead or even fatally injured, and if X then comes alone and, acting quite independently from D, dispatches the victim, the killing will be X's act, not D's and D would be completely innocent of it. The analysis is not changed if D was aware of the possibility or even probability of X's intervention, provided that he was not acting in complicity with X."[199]

(iii) Conduct by Third Parties

2–040 If D punches P in the face rendering him unconscious and then leaves P lying in the street, it is quite likely that a third party will try to render help to P. If in doing so he makes P's condition much worse, it is suggested that D's liability for any subsequent injuries will depend upon the test of whether such injuries were reasonably foreseeable. It is quite foreseeable that a third party will try to render assistance by possibly putting him in a car to drive him to the hospital. If, this action aggravates the injuries inflicted by D so that P dies, D will be held liable for the death. If, on the other hand, the third party tries to roll P all the way to the hospital, then this is perhaps not reasonably foreseeable.[200] In an American case, *Bush v Commonwealth*,[201] V was injured by D as a result of which he went into hospital. While in hospital he was infected with scarlet fever by his surgeon. It was held that the scarlet fever was not the causal consequence of the initial wound; it was not a natural consequence of D's unlawful act.

In *Pagett*[202] P had kidnapped a girl. He held her in front of him as a shield and then fired shots at armed police officers who instinctively returned fire, killing the girl. He was charged with her manslaughter but argued that the police actions constituted a novus actus—a break in the chain of causation. Basing himself on the fright and flight cases, Goff L.J. said:

> "There can, we consider, be no doubt that a reasonable act performed for the purpose of self-preservation, being of course itself an act caused by the accused's own act, does not operate as a novus actus interveniens. . . . Furthermore, in our judgment, if a reasonable act of self-defence against the act of the accused causes the death of a third party, we can see no reason in principle why the act of self-defence, being an involuntary act caused by the act of the accused, should relieve the accused from criminal responsibility for the death of the third party."[203]

2–041 It is very easy to begin to share out blame for the girl's death between the accused and the police. It should, however, be remembered that the court is concerned to deal only with the charge against Pagett that he killed her unlawfully. The court said it would normally be a

---

[196] See below para.4–014 for discussion of joint enterprise principles.
[197] [2007] EWCA Crim 1846 at [50] per Hooper L.J.
[198] See *R v Kennedy (No.2)* [2007] UKHL 38; [2007] 4 All E.R. 1083 at 1088 per Lord Bingham.
[199] See G. Williams, "Finis for Novus Actus" [1989] C.L.J. 391 at 396.
[200] See, *Le Brun* [1991] 4 All E.R. 673, discussed below, paras 2–078—2–079.
[201] (1880) 78 Ky 268.
[202] (1983) 76 Cr.App.R. 279.
[203] (1983) 76 Cr.App.R. 279 at 289.

sufficient direction to a jury that "the accused's act need not be the sole cause, or even the main cause, of the victim's death, it being enough that his acts contributed significantly to that result".[204] Had the police officers been able to weigh up the situation calmly and had they decided to shoot Pagett it would not have been possible to say that Pagett killed the girl. On the actual facts, however, Pagett caused the police to react instinctively in self-defence and it is, therefore, quite legitimate to say that he caused her death. The same result would follow had Pagett's action caused the police to shoot an innocent bystander.[205]

There is a statement by Goff L.J. that the conduct of the police in a case like this should be reasonable in all the circumstances. Is this right? Suppose that it is later decided that the action of the officers in that split second was unreasonable, should P be relieved of liability? It is suggested that P should not be exculpated. It may be that the police should face criminal charges, but it still remains the case that P caused them to fire instinctively at the girl.[206]

In essence, the "free deliberate and informed" intervention of a third party has been determined to exculpate and relieve D of liability.[207] This received the support of the Court of Appeal in *Pagett,* and subsequently in *Latif*[208] the House of Lords gave it a ringing endorsement. Interestingly, the issue of causation was not recognised as such until it reached the House of Lords. The case involved the importation of heroin worth £3.2 million. British customs officers in Pakistan, acting upon information received from a paid informer, intercepted heroin which D intended to import into England and brought it here where D took delivery. In fact, he took possession of a quantity of Horlicks, which had been got up to look like drugs. The House of Lords accepted that D could not be held liable for "being concerned" in a fraudulent evasion of the prohibition on importation, because his acts had not caused the evasion; the importation had been "effected" by the free, deliberate and informed act of the officers who had not acted in concert with D. The defendant could not be held responsible for an event which he had not caused. Lord Steyn gave the leading speech, adopted by each of the other members of the House:

> "The general principle is that the free, deliberate and informed intervention of a second person, who intends to exploit the situation created by the first, but is not acting in concert with him, is held to relieve the first actor of criminal responsibility (see H.L.A. Hart and T. Honoré, *Causation in the Law* (2nd edn, 1985) pp.326ff; Blackstone *Criminal Practice* (1995) pp.13–15, para.A1.27–1.29). For example, if a thief had stolen the heroin after Shahzad delivered it to Honi, and imported it into the United Kingdom, the chain of causation would have been broken. The general principle must also be applicable to the role of the customs officers in this case. They acted in full knowledge of the content of the packages. They did not act in concert with Shahzad. They acted deliberately for their own purposes whatever those might have been. In my view consistency and legal principle do not permit us to create an exception to the general principle of causation to take care of the particular problem thrown up by this case."[209]

---

[204] (1983) 76 Cr.App.R. 279 at 290.

[205] The same result can be achieved by the use of the felony murder rule; see below, para.7–015.

[206] It was reported in *The Times,* December 4, 1990 that the High Court awarded the victim's mother £8,155 damages against the force for its failures during the siege and castigated the force for suppressing a secret senior officer's report.

[207] See H.L.A. Hart and T. Honoré, *Causation in the Law* 2nd edn, (Oxford: Oxford University Press, 1985) p.326.

[208] [1996] 1 W.L.R. 104.

[209] [1996] 1 W.L.R. 104, 115, per Lord Steyn; but their Lordships nonetheless dismissed the appeal because the facts revealed that the defendants were guilty of an attempt. Given the particular charge, and the facts of the case, the defendants were rightly convicted.

2–042 The important case of *Environment Agency v Empress Car Co (Abertillery) Ltd*[210] fits uneasily with the general principle of voluntariness expressed in *Latif*. The decision in *Empress* is perhaps best explained in terms of public policy concerns over the control of pollution but unfortunately their Lordships appeared to confuse culpability and specific interpretation of legislation, with causation. Empress was convicted of causing polluting matter to enter controlled waters, contrary to s.85(1) of the Water Resources Act 1991. Their conviction was upheld by the House of Lords. They owned a yard which drained straight into a river, and kept a tank of diesel in this yard. Apparently, the arrangement of the tank was wholly inadequate to prevent diesel from spilling into the yard, and then draining into the river. The overflow pipe had no lock on the tap, and there was no proper "bund" around the tank, to prevent spillages and overflow from spreading into the yard. There was an ever-present risk of diesel leaking into the river, by accident or by negligence. As it turned out, an unknown saboteur deliberately opened the top on the overflow pipe, so a whole tank of diesel drained into the river. Empress was found to have caused this result.

The outcome in *Empress* was that a deliberate intervening act does not break the chain of causation unless it is extraordinary. The rationale articulated was that the company should be responsible for a result which they did not cause simply because the act of vandalism by which it was effected was not so extraordinary as to be unforeseeable. However, on the general principle expressed in *Latif*, the saboteur's act should have broken the chain of causation. It seems, thus, that causation is a variable concept. For some crimes there is a duty imposed on certain individuals to guard against certain harms, to the extent even of taking reasonable precautions to prevent others from causing such harm. Furthermore, if another individual does cause this exact harm because of D's failure in their duty to prevent it, the impact is that it does not break the chain of causation because it falls within the circumstances envisaged.

(iv) Drug Administration and Joint Responsibility

2–043 In tandem with the confusing perspective adopted in *Empress*, there co-exists the problematic issue of foreseeability and the supply of drugs. Over the last decade our appellate courts in evaluating causation in this regard have shown the fluctuating vagaries of uncertainty akin to the heroine in a Doestoevsky novel. The House of Lords in *Kennedy (No.2)*[211] has restored orthodoxy in asserting that an independent act by a fully-informed actor breaks the chain of causation. A defendant who supplies heroin to V for self-injection will not be guilty of unlawful act manslaughter if V is a fully-informed adult who autonomously decides to inject himself, and subsequently dies from the injection of heroin. The "free and voluntary" self-administration of the drug is effected by V, an act to which "choice" applies, and it is insufficient for culpability that D facilitated or contributed to this administration.[212]

The pathway to this conclusion has been tortuous, albeit legally significant for causation principles. The case of *Kennedy (No.1)*[213] had sent our law down a cul-de-sac. D supplied V with a heroin-filled syringe. V paid him and injected it and subsequently died. D was convicted of manslaughter. It was felt that by preparing the syringe, rather than just providing the drugs, D was unlawfully assisting or encouraging D to inject himself, an act which the court seemed to think was a crime. The essence of the decision of the Court of Appeal seems to have been that the judge had correctly directed the jury that preparing the

---

[210] [1999] 2 A.C. 22.
[211] [2007] UKHL 38; [2007] 4 All E.R. 1083.
[212] [2007] UKHL 38; [2007] 4 All E.R. 1083 at 1091 per Lord Bingham.
[213] [1999] Crim.L.R. 65; see also below para.7–047.

mixture, and handing it to the victim for immediate injection, was capable of amounting to a significant cause of death. Considerable emphasis was placed upon the fact that D's supply of the syringe amounted to encouragement to V to inject himself, and thus D was jointly responsible for the act. Assisting or encouraging another to commit an offence is a specific crime, and D is liable in such a scenario as a secondary party, but V himself committed no crime. V could lawfully kill himself; there is no crime of self-manslaughter. V's self-injection of the heroin was the immediate cause of death. In truth, as in *Empress*, D's conduct merely provided the backdrop to the "free, deliberate and informed" intervention of a third party, i.e. V himself.

Subsequently, in *Dias*[214] a differently constituted Court of Appeal, in light of criticism of the *Kennedy (No.1)* decision, adopted a different perspective, without actually overruling the earlier precedent. D's conviction was quashed, despite the fact that he also admitted to having prepared a syringe and given it to the deceased. It was determined that the act of injecting oneself with a controlled drug is not a crime.[215] Hence, the defendant in *Kennedy (No.1)* could not have been convicted as a secondary party by virtue of the fact that he had assisted and encouraged the deceased to inject himself:

> "There is the offence of possession of such a drug, and that offence was committed by V, the deceased. We have considered, therefore, whether that renders the act of injection unlawful for these purposes, but we find it difficult to see that it can do so. The causative act (the act causing death) was essentially the injection of the heroin rather than the possession of it . . . Such possession amounted to an offence, but the act of injecting was not itself part of the offence. It was merely made possible by the unlawful possession of the heroin . . .
>
> As there is no offence of self-manslaughter, it is difficult to see how the appellant could be guilty of that offence as a secondary party because of his encouragement or assistance to V over the injection of the drug."[216]

The Court of Appeal in *Dias* asserted that, in cases where D is accused of manslaughter because he supplied V with drugs, a conviction can only be upheld if the issue of causation is left to the jury to decide. This formed a mark of separation between *Kennedy (No.1)* and *Dias*; in the former the issue of causation had been left to jury consideration, but not in the latter. Of course, the court in *Dias* was mindful of the inconsistency effected by the *Kennedy (No.1)* rationale, and left it open to future days to decide that D caused V's death even if V injected himself. However, the judicial reasoning shows evident support for the proposition that a voluntary act of injection should relieve D of liability.

More opaqueness followed in *Rogers*,[217] the next case in this sequence. D provided the **2–044** drugs for V, and had physically assisted V by holding a belt around his arm as a tourniquet while V injected himself.[218] V collapsed with cardiac arrest and died eight days later. Their Lordships adopted a novel and idiosyncratic view that D had, in effect, engaged as a principal offender in relation to the drug injection.[219] Apparently, the purpose and impact of the tourniquet was to raise a vein in which the deceased could insert the syringe.

[214] [2001] EWCA Crim 2986; (2001) 165 J.P. 1010.
[215] See also, *Richards* [2002] EWCA Crim 3175.
[216] [2001] EWCA Crim 2986 at [21]–[24]. This rationale in *Dias,* self-injection embodied as the causative act not being unlawful, was followed by the Court of Appeal in *Richards* [2002] EWCA Crim 3175.
[217] [2003] 2 Cr.App.R. 10; [2003] EWCA 945; [2003] Crim.L.R. 555. See, generally, R. Heaton, "Dealing in Death" [2003] Crim.L.R. 497; and T.H. Jones, "Causation, Homicide and the Supply of Drugs (2006) 26 *Legal Studies* 139.
[218] See, generally, A. Reed, "Involuntary Manslaughter and Assisting Drug-Abuse Injection" (2003) 67 J.C.L. 431.
[219] For discussion of principal offenders and mode of participation see below at para.4–003.

Accordingly, by applying and holding the tourniquet, D was "playing a part in the mechanics of the injection which caused death". Hence it was immaterial whether V was committing a criminal offence: a supposed point of departure from *Dias*. In *Rogers*, the appellate court concluded that an individual who "actively participated" in the injection process committed the actus reus, and could have no answer to, an offence under s.23 of the Offences Against the Person Act 1861 of administering a noxious thing (heroin),[220] or a charge of manslaughter if death resulted.[221] However, it needs highlighting that a principal offender is any person who by his own conduct *directly brings about the actus reus of the crime*.[222] Is this apposite to the appellant in *Rogers*? Certainly any crime may have more than one principal offender and s.23 is no exception. He certainly facilitated the self-administration by V. The act causing death, however, was the self-injection of the needle thereby "administering" the noxious substance. This final act was committed voluntarily and independently by V, and in line with *Dias*, it is submitted that no offence is committed by D.

A further level of confusion was added at appellate level in *Kennedy (No.2)* before rationalisation was subsequently restored by the House of Lords.[223] The Criminal Cases Review Commission referred the case of *Kennedy (No.1)* back to the Court of Appeal. It will be recalled that D had done no more than supply the heroin-filled syringe which V self-injected. Their Lordships reviewed the line of cases following on from the first appeal, and upheld the conviction despite the conflicting views expressed in *Dias* and *Richards*. There was an acknowledgement that there had been an error in *Kennedy (No.1)* in predicating liability of a drug supplier on principles of accessoryship. Furthermore, the doctrine enunciated in *Empress*[224] was regarded as constrained in nature, restricted to regulatory pollution offences of strict liability. New revolutionary ideals now applied, based undoubtedly on public policy concerns related to drug administration. The actions of D and V were viewed in *Kennedy (No.2)* as "one combined operation". When the heroin was handed to V for immediate injection, it could be considered that D and V were engaged in the one activity of administering the heroin.[225] Thus, D was responsible for "*taking the action in concert*"[226] with V to inject himself with the syringe of heroin which had been made ready for immediate use. On this basis, the combined presumption of *acting in concert and joint responsibility*, the Lord Chief Justice determined that the unlawful act contrary to s.23 of the Offences Against the Person Act 1861 (unlawfully and maliciously administering a noxious substance) was causative of V's death. Hence no break in the chain of causation apparently occurred through V's voluntary act of self-injection.

Confusion reigned supreme. The Court of Appeal in *Kennedy (No.2)* appear to have created a new category of mode of participation for drug administration—*acting in concert together*. This raised the difficult conundrum of "acting together" in relation to which

---

[220] s.23 provides: "Whosoever shall unlawfully and maliciously administer to or cause to be administered to or taken by any other person any poison or other destructive or noxious thing, so as thereby to endanger the life of such person, or so as thereby to inflict upon such person any grievous bodily harm, shall be guilty of [an offence] . . . and shall be liable . . . [to a maximum penalty of 10 years' imprisonment].

[221] Subsequently, in *Finlay* [2003] EWCA Crim 3868 D's conviction for unlawful act manslaughter was upheld when he had done no more than prepare the syringe and hand it to V who self-injected with heroin. Liability, following *Rogers*, was predicated on the concept of joint principalship. Buxton L.J. asserted in *Finlay* at [14]: "*Rogers* is thus clear authority for saying that if a 'helper' is in fact a joint principal with the deceased, then he can be guilty of an offence under s.23 even though the deceased is not guilty of an offence by self-administration."

[222] See below at paras 4–002—4–003.

[223] [2005] EWCA Crim 685.

[224] See above at para.2–042.

[225] [2005] EWCA Crim 685 at [43] it is stated: "If Kennedy either caused the deceased to administer the drug or was acting jointly with the deceased in administering the drug, Kennedy would be acting in concert with the deceased and there would be no breach in the chain of causation".

[226] Terminology derived from *Latif* [1996] 1 W.L.R. 104 at 115 per Lord Steyn; see above at para.2–041.

specific offence? V does not commit the s.23 offence as he does not have an intention to administer a noxious thing to another person or recklessness thereto; moreover, no offence exists of self-manslaughter. Joint principalship appears wholly inapposite—without V's voluntary self-injection there is no administration and no death. Further problems are engendered if the acting in concert principle is extended beyond drug administration to other categories of participatory conduct.[227] Consider a scenario where D2 hands D1, a knife, the stabbing occurs virtually simultaneously with no interval, and V dies. Are the participants "acting in concert together" over the killing, or as previously understood, is D2 an accessory to V's murder? How "immediate" must assistance be for joint responsibility?

The House of Lords has recently settled the current uncertainty by expressly acknowledging that a free, deliberate and knowing act of a third party can break the chain of causation even where that conduct is not only foreseeable but foreseen. Assistance of drug-abuse injection may take a variety of forms encompassing: acquiring the illegal substances; preparation of the syringe; holding a belt as a tourniquet; or actually injecting the substance directly. It is the actual administration of the needle which ought to represent a point of demarcation. The other acts merely provide a backdrop for the independent and voluntary act of V which, on established causation principles, should constitute an intervening act exculpating D. A point finally reconciled at the highest level.

The House of Lords in *Kennedy (No.2),*[228] the unanimous six-page judgment provided by **2–045** Lord Bingham, have effectively applied legitimate principles on causation, novus actus interveniens, and voluntary behaviour by a non-coerced actor. The victim's independent act operates as a bulwark against liability for unlawful act manslaughter in this scenario. The previous decade of inconsistent and illogical appellate precedents, highlighted above, have been swept away from our judicial landscape as an unfortunate aberration. Lord Bingham cogently stated that:

> "It also follows that there is no legal sense in which the appellant can be said to have been a principal jointly with the deceased or to have been acting in concert. The finding that the deceased freely and voluntarily administered the injection to himself, knowing what it was, is fatal to any contention that the appellant caused the heroin to be administered to the deceased or taken by him . . . [T]he appellant supplied the heroin and prepared the syringe. But the deceased had a choice whether to inject himself or not. He chose to do so, knowing what he was doing. It was his act."[229]

The House of Lords were clear to affirm in *Kennedy (No.2)* that the decision has no impact or relevance to drug administration cases and liability for gross negligence manslaughter.[230] However, it operates as a cathartic reaffirmation of doctrine in relation to autonomy, voluntariness and informed capacity. A by-product, as Lord Bingham articulates, is an adoption of earlier classic statements on causation by Professor Glanville Williams:

---

[227] See below at para.4–003 for discussion.
[228] [2007] UKHL 38; [2007] 4 All E.R. 1083.
[229] [2007] UKHL 38; [2007] 4 All E.R. 1083 at 1090.
[230] For consideration of gross negligence manslaughter see below at para.7–048. See, generally, D Ormerod, "Case Comment on *R v Kennedy (No.2)*" [2008] Crim.L.R. 222 at 225. Professor Ormerod cogently states that a D may still be inculpated for gross negligence manslaughter in the context of drug administration: "That offence will not apply where D has merely supplied the drugs to V. The free informed choice by V to self-inject will break the chain of causation: one of the elements of the offence of gross negligence manslaughter. It may, however be applicable where having supplied the drugs, and after V has self-administered, D realises that V is having difficulty breathing or that the dose may have been too strong and that V is in danger. In those cases D is, arguably, under a duty to V and if he fails to fulfil that (it being sufficient perhaps to call the emergency services) he is at risk of conviction if V dies and a jury finds his conduct "grossly" negligent; and see M. Nkrumah, "*R v Kennedy* Revisited" (2008) 72 J.C.L. 117.

"I may suggest reasons to you for doing something; I may urge you to do it, tell you it will pay you to do it, tell you it is your duty to do it. My efforts may perhaps make it very much more likely that you will do it. But they do not cause you to do it, in the sense in which one causes a kettle of water to boil by putting it on the stove. Your volitional act is regarded (within the doctrine of responsibility) as setting a new "chain of causation" going, irrespective of what has happened before."[231]

Their Lordships in *Kennedy (No.2)* went further in explicitly overruling the earlier decision in *Rogers* where D was convicted, as seen, on the predicate of active participation in the injection process as he held the tourniquet whilst V self-injected. D will only be liable where he is "administering the drug", and on this essential matter Lord Bingham stated:

"the crucial question is not whether the defendant facilitated or contributed to the administration of the noxious thing but whether he went further and administered it."[232]

Although Lord Bingham concluded that it was possible to "imagine factual scenarios"[233] in which two individuals could properly be regarded as acting together to administer an injection, nonetheless it is difficult to countenance any examples beyond the facts in *Rogers* other than the explicit injection by the defendant. Interestingly, however, the recent case of *Byram*[234] addressing convictions attained pre-*Kennedy (No.2)* raised the spectre of non-automatic acquittals where D "assisted" V by finding a vein and putting the tip of the syringe against the vein. It remains for later days to see if novel situations arise whereby D is inculpated for manslaughter in this arena.[235]

Further grist to the mill has been added in this regard by the recent Scottish High Court of Justiciary decision in *Michael Kane v H.M. Advocate*,[236] controversially rejecting the House of Lords perspective adduced in *Kennedy (No.2)* and establishing the possibility of culpability of the supplier of a self-administered drug for culpable homicide predicated upon reckless conduct. Their Lordships focusing upon issues of immediacy and directness of the ingestion, allied to foreseeability of action (the victim's conduct) determined that Scots law in appropriate cases might properly attribute responsibility for ingestion and so for death to the reckless offender.[237] Reliance was placed on the doctrinal template adopted in some states in America, and specifically on extant law prevalent in South Africa, to establish that a deliberate decision by the victim of the reckless conduct to ingest the drug would not necessarily break the chain of causation.

(v) Medical Cases

2–046   One area in which the problem of subsequent action by a third party has to be assessed is medical treatment of the victim. The general problem in this series of cases is that the defendant has committed an offence of violence against a victim which has necessitated the

---

[231] G. Williams, "Finis for Novus Actus?" (1989) 48 C.L.J. 391 at 392.
[232] [2007] 4 All E.R. 1083 at 1091.
[233] [2007] 4 All E.R. 1083 at 1092. Interestingly, Lord Hoffmann's comments in *Empress Car* on legitimate causation principles were treated as sui generis, and limited to the factual pattern therein vis-à-vis pollution and enforcement of strict liability. Lord Bingham asserted at 1089: "[T]he reasoning in that case cannot be applied to the wholly different context of causing a noxious thing to be administered to or taken by another person contrary to s.23 of the 1861 Act".
[234] [2008] EWCA Crim 516; and see, generally, D. Hughes, "Case Comment on *R v Byram*" (2008) 72 J.C.L. 353.
[235] See, generally, L. Cherkassky, "Kennedy and Unlawful Act Manslaughter: An Unorthodox Application of the Doctrine of Causation" (2008) 72 J.C.L. 387.
[236] *The Times,* February 6, 2009.
[237] See T.H. Jones, "Causation, Homicide and the Supply of Drugs" (2006) 26 *Legal Studies* 139. Reliance was placed by the High Court of Justiciary on the critique provided therein on effective causation principles.

hospitalisation of the victim. While in hospital the victim receives poor treatment and dies. Charged with an unlawful homicide offence, the initial assailant will argue that the hospital, and not he, caused the victim's death by poor treatment.[238] There is a temptation to think it is all or nothing; that either the accused is to blame or the doctor is to blame. It is crucial to remember that a prohibited result can have more than one legal cause. The question for the jury in the trial of the accused is whether in law his act can be held to be a substantial and operating cause of death. If the doctor's treatment was grossly negligent, he could well be charged with manslaughter, but that does not necessarily mean that the accused is relieved of liability for the death. It is perfectly possible for the court to hold that both caused the victim's death.

Until the decision of the Court of Appeal in *Cheshire*,[239] guidance was to be found in the cases of *Jordan*[240] and *Smith*.[241] In *Jordan*, J had stabbed the victim causing serious injuries. The victim's treatment in hospital was initially successful. His wounds had virtually healed when a series of appalling blunders[242] led to his death from pneumonia. J was convicted of murder and he appealed to the Court of Criminal Appeal. On his appeal the court heard evidence from two medical experts who said that death had been caused not by the stab wound, but by the abnormal medical treatment. The Court of Criminal Appeal accepted this conclusion and allowed his appeal. The decision can be criticised on the basis that the court seemed to treat the issue of causation as being a medical and not a legal one. Even if the medical evidence shows that the victim would not have died but for abnormal treatment, it is still open for the court as a matter of law to hold that an accused in such a case takes the risk that the victim may receive abnormal treatment and that such treatment will not absolve the defendant from liability for the subsequent death. In *Jordan* the court seems simply to have accepted the conclusion of the medical witnesses that, in medicine, the cause of death was the abnormal treatment. The treatment was variously described as being "palpably wrong" and "not normal".

The decision caused concern in medical circles. It was feared that if the treatment received in hospital was in any way below the standard which should be expected, the chain of causation between the initial assailant and the eventual death would be broken. The Court of Criminal Appeal had another chance to look at the principles involved in *Smith*. During a barrack room brawl S stabbed the victim, puncturing his lung. The victim was then carried to the Medical Officers' tent, being dropped twice on the way. The Medical Officer was swamped with work and as a result failed to appreciate the seriousness of the victim's condition. He prescribed totally inadequate treatment and Smith died two hours after the initial stabbing. Evidence showed that despite the serious nature of the injuries, proper treatment would have given him a reasonable chance of survival and his chances would have been as high as 75 per cent had blood transfusion facilities been available. There is a very clear distinction between this case and *Jordan*. If you were to ask, from what did the victim in *Smith* die, the answer would be "from the stab wound", which, unlike the wounds in *Jordan*, was still a substantial and operating case at the time of death. Lord Parker C.J. said:

"Only if it can be said that the original wounding is merely the setting in which another cause operates can it be said that the death does not result from the wound. Putting it

---

[238] See, generally J.E. Stannard, "Medical Treatment and the Chain of Causation" (1993) 57 J.C.L. 88.
[239] [1991] 3 All E.R. 670.
[240] (1956) 40 Cr.App.R. 152.
[241] [1959] 2 Q.B. 35.
[242] He was given a drug he was known to be allergic to and he was given large quantities of fluid despite contrary instructions on his medical notes.

another way, only if the second cause is so overwhelming as to make the original wound merely part of the history can it be said that the death does not flow from the wound."[243]

Of *Jordan* Lord Parker C.J. said, "The court is satisfied that *Jordan's* case was a very particular case depending upon its exact facts."[244] This form of words is often used to indicate that such facts are unlikely to arise again and that the case should not be regarded as a useful precedent. Where the wound is still life threatening the accused can expect to remain liable for the subsequent death. The accused will only have a chance of claiming that the chain of causation is broken, where the court forms the view that the injuries he caused merely explain why he was in hospital where the real cause of death occurred. In other words the chain will be broken only, and not always then, when the court can equate the initial wounding with our hypothetical illustration of the invitation to dinner which caused the victim to be at that place where he was run over by the man driving dangerously.

2–047   In *Cheshire*[245] C shot and seriously injured the victim. At a point when the wounds were no longer regarded as life threatening, the victim suffered breathing difficulties. A standard tracheotomy was performed and a breathing tube was inserted into his windpipe. No one noticed that the scar tissue around the tube was tightening and eventually he was killed by suffocation. Is this a case more like *Jordan* or *Smith*? On the face of it, it would seem to more closely resemble *Jordan* in that the initial injury was no longer regarded as life threatening. Death according to one medical witness was due to negligent, but not grossly negligent, treatment in the hospital.

On appeal against conviction Beldam L.J. said that there was a tendency in these cases to try to quantify the blame, but this would normally be of little use. The question for the jury is whether the accused caused the deceased's death; they were unlikely to get much help from discussions about recklessness or gross negligence. "A momentary lapse of concentration may lead to more serious consequences than a glaring neglect of duty."[246] Beldam L.J. concluded:

> "Even though negligence in the treatment of the victim was the immediate cause of his death, the jury should not regard it as excluding the responsibility of the accused unless the negligent treatment was so independent of his acts, and in itself so potent in causing his death, that they regard the contribution made by his acts as insignificant. It is not the function of the jury to evaluate competing causes or to choose which is dominant provided that they are satisfied that the accused's acts can fairly be said to have made a significant contribution to the victim's death."[247]

The direction is hardly a model of clarity. What is a juror to make of the phrases "so independent of his acts" or "and in itself so potent in causing death"? It would appear to mean that where a defendant necessitates medical treatment for his victim, he will take the risk of the victim dying from negligent treatment even where the initial wound itself has ceased to be life threatening, unless the treatment is very bad; probably grossly negligent.

2–048   The Court of Appeal held that the gunshot wound had directly led to the rare medical complication which had not been spotted by the hospital staff and hence the wounding was at least one cause of the victim's death if not the only cause and this was enough.

---

[243] [1959] 2 Q.B. 35 at 43.
[244] [1959] 2 Q.B. 35 at 43.
[245] [1991] 3 All E.R. 670.
[246] See, a similar example in *Adomako* below, para.7–049.
[247] [1991] 3 All E.R. 670 at 677. See also *Mellor* [1996] 2 Cr.App.R. 245; [1996] Crim.L.R. 743.

So where does this leave us? Perhaps we can make the following observations:

(1) Causation is a matter of law for the judge to leave to the jury. It is, of course, highly important to hear medical evidence and that includes evidence of what, in the opinion of the expert witness, caused the death of the victim. Nevertheless, at the end of the day, the courts could take the stance that an accused who puts his victim in hospital takes the risk that the treatment he will receive will be grossly negligent or even reckless.

(2) In cases such as *Smith* and *Blaue*,[248] where the wound inflicted by the accused is still a substantial and operating cause, the accused will remain liable for the death even though the doctors were grossly negligent or even reckless. Suppose, for example, the doctor in *Smith* had refused to treat him at all on the grounds that he was one minute late for his coffee break, it is submitted that Smith would remain liable for the death of the victim. The doctor, of course, could also be prosecuted.

If, however, an act occurred in *Smith* which rendered Smith's act for the time being non-operating, he might escape liability. If, for example, while the victim lay waiting attention, another patient blew his head off with a shotgun it would be possible to say that at the moment of death, there was only one operating cause and that was the gunshot. In these extreme circumstances, Smith's act has become part of the history. On the other hand again, if the gunshot wound did not kill the victim instantly, then it is likely that both Smith and the gunman would be liable.

(3) Where the initial wound is no longer life-threatening, as in *Cheshire* and *Jordan*, the accused may still be held accountable for the death which is brought about by the poor treatment by hospital staff. The test here is now that in *Cheshire*, which involves determining whether the treatment is so independent of the accused's acts and so potent in itself in causing his death. Thus, in *Cheshire*, the accused was held responsible for the breathing difficulties which led to the negligent (but not grossly negligent) supervision of the breathing tube. *Jordan* can be defended on the basis that the treatment in that case was held to be palpably wrong and was probably grossly negligent.

It is suggested that Ormerod[249] is on the right lines when he suggests that the test should be one of reasonable foresight; was the treatment or its administration so extraordinary as to be unforeseeable?

(4) Where the accused causes P to be treated in hospital for a minor non-life-threatening injury and the anaesthetist by a negligent oversight causes P to die it is suggested that the position is controlled by the test in *Cheshire*. If, for example, D punches P on the nose making it necessary for P to undergo surgery with a general anaesthetic, D must take the risks associated with anaesthesia. Only if the treatment is grossly negligent will D escape liability for P's death on the operating table.

(5) Where the doctors take the view, having applied the standard tests, that the victim will never recover and therefore switch off the life support systems, the accused who caused the injury will not be allowed to say that the sole cause of death is the doctors' action in switching off the machine.[250]

---

[248] [1975] 3 All E.R. 446, discussed below, para.2–049. Difficulties may, of course arise where medical evidence is in conflict presenting a dilemma for the jury; see, e.g. *Gowans* [2003] EWCA Crim 3935 where the initial victim also contracted fatal septicaemia in hospital. Careful jury direction is needed cf. *Suratan* [2004] EWCA Crim 1246.

[249] Ormerod, *Smith and Hogan Criminal Law* pp.86–87.

[250] *Malcherek and Steel* [1981] 1 W.L.R. 690.

(vi) Conduct by the Victim

2–049 We saw earlier that the accused must take the victim's physical condition as he finds it.[251] We must now ask whether this applies to the victim's psychological make-up. Can you be taken to assume the risk when you injure another that the victim may not seek medical treatment or may even do things which makes the initial wound even more serious, and possibly fatal? Is the victim under a duty to take steps to minimise the harm caused to him by the accused?

In *Holland*,[252] during a heated argument, H injured the finger of his victim. The surgeon recommended that the finger should be amputated, but the victim refused and two weeks later died of lockjaw. It was held that H was responsible for the victim's death. In a situation like this it is not open to the accused to say that he should be relieved of liability because the victim could have taken greater care of himself.

Now *Holland* is an old case and the victim was probably aware that as many died in hospital from the treatment and lack of hygiene as died from the reason for their being in hospital. Under such circumstances it was probably not unreasonable for the victim to have refused treatment. Does it, therefore, follow that if the victim's refusal to undergo treatment is unreasonable H would be liable only for the injury to the finger and not for the subsequent death? Can we say that in today's world a refusal to undergo hospital treatment would be unreasonable. This might seem tempting, but such an approach is rejected by the approval given to *Holland* by the Court of Appeal in *Blaue*.[253] B had stabbed a woman several times and one of the wounds had penetrated her lung. The hospital prescribed a blood transfusion, but the victim, being a Jehovah's Witness, refused. As a result the victim died. It was accepted that she had been fully warned that she would die without a transfusion and the prosecution also accepted that she would not, in fact, have died had she received a transfusion. B was convicted of her manslaughter and appealed on the ground that he should not be held responsible for a death caused by the victim's refusal to undergo treatment which almost certainly would have saved her life.

Should we say that the maxim "take your victim as you find him" applies to both his psychological as well as physical characteristics? Is it right that B should be liable for a death the victim could have avoided? Lawton L.J. was clear about one matter: "The physical cause of death in this case was the bleeding into the pleural cavity arising from the penetration of the lung. This had not been brought about by any decision made by the deceased girl but by the stab wound." B tried to argue that the court should hold that the chain of causation is broken if the victim's response to the accused's act is unreasonable or daft. This argument was rejected; it would introduce too much uncertainty into the law. In the first place, against whose standards is the conduct of the victim to be judged? Lawton L.J concluded:

> "It has long been the policy of the law that those who use violence on other people must take their victims as they find them. This in our judgment means the whole man, not just the physical man. It does not lie in the mouth of the assailant to say that his victim's religious beliefs which inhibited him from accepting certain kinds of treatment were unreasonable. The question for decision is what caused her death. The answer is the stab wound. The fact that the victim refused to stop this end coming about did not break the causal connection between the act and death."[254]

---

[251] Above, para.2–035.
[252] (1841) 2 Mood & R. 351.
[253] [1975] 3 All E.R. 446.
[254] [1975] 3 All E.R. 446 at 450.

On the facts of *Blaue*, the Court of Appeal almost certainly reached the correct decision. The initial wound was extremely serious and it was this wound which killed her[255] In some respects this case is like *Smith*.[256] Death followed fairly soon after the initial stabbing and in both cases the stab wound was the operating cause of death and in many ways her refusal to allow a blood transfusion is irrelevant. It would have been different had her wounds almost healed when an accident in the hospital caused the wounds to open requiring a blood transfusion.

It does appear, however, that the Court of Appeal supports adherence to the rule that you take your victim as you find him, and that includes his psychological make-up. But how much further does the rule go? Would the court have reached the same conclusion had Blaue's victim indicated that she wanted no blood transfusion because she wanted to die and she wanted Blaue to be prosecuted for her death? Would the courts treat *Holland* in the same way as in 1841? The clear indication from *Blaue* is that they would. The initial injury in *Holland* was far less severe and unlikely to be life threatening in itself. Is it right that the accused should be held liable for a death caused by the victim's refusal to seek relatively simple medical treatment? Again it would seem totally wrong that in a case like *Holland* the accused could be made liable for the death of the victim, if that victim had deliberately set about to aggravate his finger wound. What is the position of a rapist whose victim commits suicide?

In *Dear*[257] D was charged with the murder of V. It was alleged by the prosecution that D's **2–050** 12½-year-old daughter had complained that V had sexually assaulted her, whereupon D took a Stanley knife and slashed V repeatedly. V died two days later. D claimed that there had been a break in the chain of causation because V had committed suicide following the attack, either by deliberately re-opening the wounds which had healed, or by failing to staunch the flow of blood from wounds which had reopened of their own accord. The Court of Appeal had held that the trial judge had directed the jury correctly by telling them that the real question was whether the injuries inflicted by D were an operating and significant cause of the death. Rose L.J. said:

> "It would not be helpful to juries if the law required them to decide causation in a case such as the present by embarking on an analysis of whether a victim had treated himself with mere negligence or gross neglect, the latter breaking but the former not breaking the chain of causation between the defendant's unlawful act and the victim's death."

Following cases such as *Blaue* and *Smith*, if the jury conclude that the injuries inflicted by the defendant were still a significant and operating cause at the time of death, then it is irrelevant that there are other causes also operating. It is enough that D was *a* cause. In *Dear*, V's death was caused by bleeding from the artery which D had caused and so the jury were entitled to find that D's conduct made an operative and significant contribution to the death despite the presence of other operating factors. If, however, the wounds had healed, the position might be different; the suicide might break the chain of causation. The Court of Appeal holds that if V had committed suicide because of D's attack on him, then the chain of causation would not be broken. On the other hand if V had committed suicide because of

[255] It was a substantial and operating cause; see above, para.2–046.
[256] [1959] 2 Q.B. 35, discussed above, para.2–046.
[257] [1996] Crim.L.R. 595.

his shame at what he had done to D's daughter then the chain would have been broken; it would no longer be possible to say that V would not have committed suicide but for D's attack on him.

An interesting recent case in this regard, albeit inconclusive in terms of defining relevant principles, is that of *Dhaliwal*[258] V, in an abusive marriage, took her own life after suffering psychological trauma and subsequent to a final act of violence against her. The Court of Appeal intimated that the assault operated as the immediate trigger (the final straw) which precipitated V's suicide. The suggestion herein is that the final unlawful act may be conjoined together with the earlier abuse to establish a cause. In essence, unlawful violence on an individual with a "fragile and vulnerable personality" which was proved to be a material cause of death (even if the result of suicide) would at least arguably be capable of amounting to manslaughter. In one sense *Dhaliwal* is similar to *Blaue* and *Dear* in that V consciously took a decision which ended her life. However, in *Blaue* and *Dear* it proved self-evident that the initial wounds inflicted by D were a continuing and substantial cause of death. It is far harder to countenance that the "unlawful act" in *Dhaliwal* is a material cause of death. Does the deliberate act of V in taking her life constitute a *novus actus interveniens*? Professor Card has cogently asserted:

> "An act done to commit suicide would clearly seem to be deliberate and informed, but (depending on the degree of trauma suffered by the victim) it could be found not to be voluntary in certain cases; if so the chain of causation would not be broken."[259]

In neither *Blaue* nor *Dear* does the court adopt a test of reasonable foresight. In *Blaue* the court rejected a suggestion that unreasonable conduct by the victim should break the chain of causation; probably rightly so since this would have introduced all sorts of difficult questions as "reasonable by whose standards?" A test of reasonable foresight, however, would not introduce such problems. The jury would simply be asked whether the victim's reaction was within the foreseeable range of responses. Such a test is adopted in the fright and flight line of cases,[260] and it is hard to reconcile those cases with the present line of authority represented by *Blaue*. In both lines of authority the issue for the jury is whether or not something done by the victim breaks the chain of causation; it seems absurd to have two separate tests. If we take the question of the rapist whose victim commits suicide, we can say that under the *Blaue* test the rapist can be said to have caused the death of his victim, because she would not have killed herself had she not been raped. Applying the test of reasonable foresight, the question would be whether suicide was within the foreseeable range of responses which might be expected from a person in this situation and the answer is far less clear.[261]

---

[258] [2006] 2 Cr.App.R. 24; see, generally, J. Horder and L. McGowan, "Manslaughter by Causing Another's Suicide" [2006] Crim.L.R. 1035; and L. Cherkassky, "Kennedy and Unlawful Act Manslaughter: An Unorthodox Application of the Doctrine of Causation" (2008) 72 J.C.L. 387.

[259] See R. Card, *Card, Cross and Jones: Criminal Law*, 18th edn (Oxford: Oxford University Press, 2008) p.71.

[260] See above, para.2–035.

[261] See, *Bunn, The Times*, May 11, 1989; which illustrates the problems of proof the prosecution may encounter in this type of case. See also commentary by J.C. Smith on *Dear* [1996] Crim.L.R. 596. He cites a case in which an elderly man had committed suicide because he had been tricked by cowboy builders into paying £4,000 for minor building works. The coroner held that the builders had unlawfully killed the victim. This would certainly be the result of applying the test in *Blaue*, but would it satisfy the reasonable foresight test of the fright and flight cases? Even if it satisfied a causation test would it meet the requirement of the *Church* test for unlawful act manslaughter? Was it (obtaining property by deception (now fraud)) an act such as all sober and reasonable people would inevitably recognise must subject the other person to, at least, the risk of some harm resulting therefrom, albeit not serious harm?

ACTUS REUS: GENERAL READING

Ashworth, A., "The Scope of Criminal Liability for Omissions" (1989) 105 L.Q.R. 424.   **2–051**

Cherkassky, L., "*Kennedy* and Unlawful Act Manslaughter: An Unorthodox Application of the Doctrine of Causation" (2008) 72 J.C.L 387.

Gunn, M.J and Smith, J.C., "Arthur's Case and the Right to Life" [1985] Crim.L.R. 705.

Heaton, R., "Principals? No Principles!" [2004] Crim.L.R. 463.

Hogan, B., "Omissions and the Duty Myth" in *Criminal Law: Essays in Honour of J.C. Smith* (1986).

Jones, T.H., "Causation, Homicide And The Supply of Drugs" (2006) 26 *Legal Studies* 139.

Leavens, A., "A Causation Approach to Criminal Omissions" (1988) 76 *California Law Review* 547.

Mackay, R.D., and Mitchell, B., "Sleepwalking, Automatism and Insanity" [2006] Crim.L.R. 901.

Mead, G., "Contracting into Crime: A Theory of Criminal Omissions" (1991) 11 O.J.L.S. 147.

Moore, M., "Causation and the Excuses" (1985) 73 *California Law Review* 1091.

Norrie, A., "A Critique of Criminal Causation" (1991) 54 M.L.R. 685.

Ormerod, D., and Forston, R., "Drug Suppliers as Manslaughterers (Again) [2005] Crim.L.R. 819.

Reed, A., "Involuntary Manslaughter And Assisting Drug Abuse Injection" (2003) 67 J.C.L. 431.

Robinson, P., "Causing the Conditions of One's Own Defence" (1985) 71 *Virginia Law Review* 1.

Smith, J.C., "Liability for Omissions in Criminal Law" (1984) 4 *Legal Studies* 88.

Stannard, J.E., "Medical Treatment and the Chain of Causation" (1993) 57 J.C.L. 88.

Williams, G., "Criminal Omissions—The Conventional View" (1991) 107 L.Q.R. 86.

MENS REA

1. INTRODUCTION

So far we have considered the external elements of the offence which constitute the actus **2–052** reus of a criminal charge. It would be possible to, and indeed it has been suggested that we should,[262] convict people solely on the basis that they have brought about the prohibited actus reus, and that all questions of culpability should be relevant only to sentence. This is not, however, the common law approach to criminal liability. In the vast majority of crimes liability rests upon the prosecution being able to prove culpability in the sense that at the time the accused brought about the actus reus he did so with a certain state of mind; the mens rea. Translated literally, mens rea means guilty mind, but this is misleading and too imprecise as a yardstick of liability. We should make it clear from the outset exactly what we are or are not looking for.

We use the word "culpability" which in everyday use connotes moral blameworthiness, and it is true that in the majority of crimes the establishment of the necessary mens rea will in itself establish moral blame, but not necessarily so. In *Kingston*[263] the Court of Appeal

---

[262] See, Barbara Wootton, *Crime and the Criminal Law* (Hamlyn Lectures No.15) 1963.
[263] [1994] 3 All E.R. 353; see below para.5–035.

suggested that "an accused person may be entitled to be acquitted if there is a possibility that, although his act was intentional, the intent arose out of circumstances for which he bears no blame". The House of Lords rejected any such principle. If the prosecution can prove that the accused brought about the actus reus of an offence with the necessary state of mind, it is entitled to a conviction despite the fact that society would attach no moral blame to what the accused has done. We use the word culpability, therefore, to mean the state of mind required by the definition of the offence.

This is further illustrated by the case of *Cunningham*.[264] Here a building, which had originally been one house, was converted into two. The cellar was divided by a wall of loose stone rubble. C's prospective mother-in-law, W, occupied one house and C was to move into the other after his marriage. C wrenched the gas meter off the wall in his cellar in order to steal money from it. His action fractured the gas pipe and gas seeped through the rubble and partially asphyxiated W. He was charged with unlawfully and maliciously administering a noxious substance to W contrary to s.23 of the Offences Against the Person Act 1861. The trial judge directed the jury that "malicious" meant "wicked—something which he (Cunningham) has no business to do and perfectly well knows it". On this basis C undoubtedly had a guilty mind. He knew he was up to no good and there was no doubt that he had committed the crime of theft and possibly burglary into the bargain. Nonetheless the Court of Criminal Appeal held this to be a misdirection. The word "maliciously" in the definition of the offence indicated that the prosecution must prove that the accused brought about the prohibited act with a certain state of mind. Byrne J. held that this state of mind had been accurately defined by Professor Kenny when he wrote:

> "In any statutory definition of a crime, malice must be taken . . . as requiring either (1) an actual intention to do the particular kind of harm that in fact was done; or (2) recklessness as to whether such harm should occur or not (i.e., the accused has foreseen that the particular kind of harm might be done and yet has gone on to take the risk of it)."[265]

In the context of *Cunningham*, the prosecution would, therefore, have to establish at least that C caused the gassing of W and that at the time he did so he either intended to administer this noxious substance to her or that he at least deliberately took an unjustified risk that what he was doing might lead to his neighbour being gassed. Once this is proved, it is irrelevant that, for example, W was the most detested person in the town and that no one would have held C to be morally blameworthy.

It is also worth stating at this point that mens rea should not be confused with motive. This can be illustrated by a simple example. If D kills his grandfather in order to obtain an inheritance he will be charged with murder. The prosecution will have to prove that he intended to kill[266] his grandfather. The prosecution do not have to prove why he killed his grandfather; motive is not an element of the crime of murder. Of course, in practice, establishment of motive will assist the prosecution to establish the intent to kill.

2–053 We have seen that the actus reus of most crimes consists in a series of elements or ingredients. In the majority of crimes the prosecution will have to establish some degree of mens rea on each element. We have seen already two states of mind which constitute mens rea, namely intention and recklessness, and in the more serious offences you will expect to find a requirement to establish *at least* recklessness on each element of the actus reus.

---

[264] [1957] 2 Q.B. 396.
[265] [1957] 2 Q.B. 396 at 399.
[266] Or, cause grievous bodily harm, though this would be unlikely if he wishes to inherit following his grandfather's death.

In the offence of murder. The actus reus of the offence requires the prosecution to prove that D unlawfully killed a human being. We have seen that the prosecution must prove that the accused either intended to kill or seriously injure a human being. Suppose D was drinking in a public house when he sees X take out a knife and act as if he were about to stab Y with it. D, thereupon, hits X over the head with a bar stool, and kills him. It may well be that we can prove that D intended to kill or seriously injure X, though he will say that he did so to protect Y. As part of the actus reus the Crown must prove that the killing was unlawful. A killing in self-defence or defence of another would be justified if reasonable force was used to prevent X from stabbing Y.[267] Suppose, however, X was merely demonstrating to Y how he would act a certain scene from a play, then there would, in fact, be no justification for D's action. The killing would be unlawful. However, again we must remember that each element of the actus reus is likely to require mens rea. In murder the prosecution will have to prove not only that the killing was unlawful, but also that D knew it to be unlawful or was at least reckless as to this.[268] If D genuinely believed that X was about to stab Y, the prosecution will not be able to establish the required mens rea.

Thus, at least in the more serious offences, the prosecution must prove some state of mind of D pertaining to each element of the actus reus. In practice, the prosecution will have to prove the mens rea on certain parts of the actus reus only if the accused has made a live issue of that aspect. Thus, in murder, the prosecution will always have to prove that the accused intended to kill or seriously injure a human being. If there is no evidence to suggest that the killing was not unlawful, the accused having based his defence upon the killing being accidental, the issue of justification will not be left to the jury.[269]

2. WHAT CAN CONSTITUTE MENS REA?

We have already seen that mens rea may take the form of intention or recklessness. Where **2–054** intention is required on a particular element of the actus reus, the prosecution will have to prove that the accused intended to do a particular act, or to bring about a certain result. Sometimes the actus reus consists of surrounding circumstances. You cannot intend a circumstance, and therefore in relation to circumstances we have to say that the defendant *knew* the circumstances existed. Where recklessness is required then the prosecution must prove that the accused consciously took an unjustified risk that he might bring about a particular result, or that he might do a particular act or that certain circumstances existed.

Intention or recklessness were generally the requirements of most common law offences. There are, however, lesser states of mind which may also satisfy the requirement of mens rea. Suppose that the accused has reversed out of his home driveway on to the path and has knocked over a pedestrian who happened to be walking past. If the prosecution can establish that a reasonable person would not have made the same mistake, the defendant can be said to have acted negligently. Of course, this is not truly a state of mind of the defendant. Nevertheless negligence suffices as the mens rea in certain crimes, such as careless driving and manslaughter. Finally, the accused may have made an entirely reasonable mistake so that we can say that he is totally blameless, yet nonetheless he may be convicted of some criminal offences.   We can now examine each of these states of mind in turn.

[267] But see *Dadson* above, para.2–002.
[268] i.e. realised that there might be no justification for hitting X, yet nonetheless hit X with a bar stool.
[269] The accused bears an evidential burden on the issue of justification. See above, paras 1–009—1–011.

A. Intention

2–055 In the majority of crimes it will not be necessary to decide whether or not the defendant intended to do a particular act or to bring about a particular result, since the prosecution will succeed if they can establish intention or recklessness.[270] In such crimes there is no need to draw the line between what constitutes recklessness and what constitutes intention. In the majority of assault offences liability can be founded on either intention or recklessness. In offences under s.18 of the Offences Against the Person Act 1861, however, there is a requirement for the prosecution to establish that the accused intended to do grievous bodily harm or intended to resist arrest; here only intention will suffice. Much of the debate on the meaning of "intention" has centred round the offence of murder.

In *Moloney*,[271] following a fairly drunken family party, M and his stepfather were left alone. M's stepfather challenged him to see who could load a shotgun in the quicker time. M won and his stepfather taunted him for not having the courage to pull the trigger. M pulled the trigger and the blast knocked the victim's head off. M claimed that he had not aimed the gun, but had simply pulled the trigger.[272] The magistrates refused to commit the defendant for trial on a charge of murder; they substituted a charge of manslaughter. Later the charge of murder was reinstated at the Crown Court.[273] The trial judge directed the jury in terms consistent with the earlier decision of the House of Lords in *Hyam v DPP*,[274] but M's subsequent conviction was overturned by the House of Lords. Murder required proof that the accused had intended to kill or had intended to cause grievous bodily harm; nothing short of this would suffice. Foresight of death or grievous bodily harm was not the same as intention, nor was foresight adequate mens rea in itself. This means that in murder we have to isolate intention from recklessness.

Consider, for example, the case of a defendant who insures cargo, which he has fraudulently claimed to be diamonds, against loss while in transit. He has planted a bomb in the cargo which will explode while the aircraft is over the Atlantic thus enabling him to claim the insurance money. All the passengers are killed in the accident, but did he intend to kill them?

2–056 Suppose that the jury conclude that his motive was to gain the insurance money and in order to do that he intended to cause the aircraft to come down in the sea. The likelihood is that people would be killed, but say that he hoped that the plane might be able to land on the sea and that the passengers would escape in life rafts. On these facts would the ordinary man in the street conclude that the bomber intended to kill the passengers? If the bomb had been discovered and rendered safe before it could explode, could you say that the bomber was attempting to kill the passengers? Perhaps the ordinary person would conclude that so inevitable was the death of at least some passengers that he must have intended to kill them. Would the answer be the same if the bomb had been planted not in an aircraft but on a ship where the inevitability of death would not be so great, or if it had been planted in a pub with a short warning to customers? What does the word intention mean to the non-lawyer? Probably that a person intends to kill another when he deliberately sets about to produce that result. The strongest situation is where the accused desires to bring about the prohibited result.

---

[270] Conscious taking of an unjustified risk. See generally A.P. Simester and W. Chan, "Intention Thus Far" [1997] Crim.L.R. 704.
[271] [1985] A.C. 905.
[272] At first he pleaded self-defence but this defence was not pursued. It would have been inconsistent with a defence that the accused had not intended to kill his stepfather.
[273] Lord Hailsham L.C. was highly critical of those responsible for the murder charge. He felt that only the magistrates had shown any common sense.
[274] [1975] A.C. 55.

There will normally be no difficulty where the accused wishes to bring about a certain result but adopts a method which he knows has only a limited chance of success. If, for example, D desires to kill P and to this end tries to shoot him from a distance which he knows will give him little chance of hitting P, if he does hit and kill P there will be no difficulty in holding that D intended to kill P. This form of intention is referred to as *direct intent* in that it is D's *objective, aim* and *purpose* to effect the death of P.

Difficulties begin to arise when the result is not desired for its own sake. In *Steane*,[275] the accused, who had made broadcasts for Germany during the Second World War under threats to the safety of his family, was charged under reg.2A of the Defence (General) Regulations with "doing an act likely to assist the enemy with intent to assist the enemy". Delivering the judgment of the court, Lord Goddard C.J. referred to British prisoners-of-war who had been forced by their brutal Japanese captors to work on the construction of the Burma road and considered what the position would have been had they been charged under the same Regulation. In both cases the men were forced to act against their conscience, and in both cases they knew that what they were doing would assist the enemy even though they had no desire to help that enemy. Lord Goddard concluded that ". . . it would be unnecessary surely . . . to consider any of the niceties of the law relating to duress, because no jury would find that merely by doing this work they were intending to assist the enemy". Allowing Steane's appeal he said that the jury should have been instructed that they could find that Steane lacked the necessary intent if they found that he did what he did in subjection to the power of an enemy.

It is easy to sympathise with Lord Goddard. No one would want to see these soldiers **2–057** charged with, let alone convicted of, any offence. But was he correct? Does a person who acts under duress act unintentionally? The soldiers knew that the building of the railway would assist the enemy, just as Steane knew his broadcasts would help the enemy. They all knew, however, that they would be killed if they refused to carry out their orders. Lord Goddard had confused motive with intention. They had all acted intentionally and the solution should have been found in the defence of duress, not in lack of intention.

The same would be true where A desires to shoot B who is standing behind a plate glass window. A has no desire to damage the window but he knows that is a prerequisite to shooting B. It would be absurd to say that he did not intend to damage the window. This secondary intention is often referred to as *oblique intention*. Similarly C, who wishes to gain his inheritance from his grandfather, decides to poison the old man. He does not desire his grandfather's death, but when he poisons his grandfather's tea he clearly intends his death since this is the only way he can get the inheritance.

It becomes more difficult where the accused intends to bring about consequence A, but realises that in so doing he might well bring about consequence B. He takes the risk and consequence B occurs. Is it possible to say that the accused intended to bring about consequence B? He is reckless as to consequence B and this will often be enough. In some crimes, however, the prosecution will have to prove that the accused intended to bring about consequence B. If we return to our bomb on board the aircraft illustration, we might be tempted to say that the accused did intend to kill the passengers because he foresaw that their deaths were virtually inevitable. Since the death of the passengers and crew is a moral certainty if he is to achieve his primary objective, we can say that this is also an example of an oblique intention. The same, however, could not be said if the bomb was on board an ocean liner or in a pub where a warning had been given. Nor is knowing something is virtually certain to happen the same as intending that it should happen.

---

[275] [1947] K.B. 997.

These problems can arise in any crime in which intention is required on at least one aspect of the actus reus. Most, however, of the cases are concerned with the law of murder. Murder, as we have seen, requires an intention to kill or to cause serious bodily harm. The courts have tried to suggest that the word intention is not a legal word, but a word in everyday use. Lay persons, however, would probably give a rather narrow meaning to the word and this in turn would lead to a rather restricted law of murder.

2–058   In *Moloney*, Lord Bridge said that in the large majority of cases where the prosecution had to establish that the accused intended a certain consequence, it would be sufficient for the trial judge to ask the jury whether they were satisfied that the accused did so intend. In particular, he found it difficult in offences of murder or wounding with intent to conceive of a case in which elaboration or explanation would be required when the offence consisted of a direct attack on the victim with a weapon. This should not be confused with the necessity which frequently arises to explain to the jury that intention is something quite distinct from motive or desire. Lord Bridge said that this could normally be done by reference to the facts of the case or to some homely example:

> "A man who, at London Airport, boards a plane which he knows to be bound for Manchester, clearly intends to travel to Manchester, even though Manchester is the last place he wants to be and his motive for boarding the plane is simply to escape pursuit. The possibility that the plane may have engine trouble and be diverted to Luton does not affect the matter. By boarding the plane the man conclusively demonstrates his intention to go there, because it is a moral certainty that that is where he will arrive."[276]

In other words one can intend certain consequences even though one does not desire them. The golden rule, described by Lord Bridge in *Moloney*, is that in cases of *direct intention* a trial judge ought to "avoid any elaboration or paraphrase of what is meant by intent and leave it to the jury's good sense to decide whether the accused acted with the necessary intent".[277]

However there will be cases, though they should be rare, where a trial judge will be called upon to give further explanation of the meaning of intention by reference to foresight of consequences. Such cases, involving what we previously described as oblique intention, apply where the defendant's ultimate purpose, desire or aim was something other than the prohibited consequence which he has brought about.[278] It must be made clear that murder requires an intention to kill or cause grievous bodily harm; that foresight of death or grievous bodily harm is not the same thing as intention to kill or cause grievous bodily harm. However, the fact that the accused has foreseen a result may be *evidence* that he intended that result, but not according to Lord Bridge unless the probability of the consequence taken to have been foreseen was little short of overwhelming. Thus, in our bomb on the aircraft

---

[276] [1985] A.C. 905 at 926.
[277] [1985] A.C. 905 at 926.
[278] See, G. Williams, "Oblique Intention" (1987) 46 C.L.J. 417 at 421, where he states "Direct intention is where the consequence is what you are aiming at. Oblique intention is something you see clearly, but out of the corner of your eye. The consequence is (figuratively speaking) not in the straight line of your purpose, but a side-effect that you accept as an inevitable or 'certain' accompaniment of your direct intent (desire-intent). There are twin consequences of the act, X and Y; the doer wants X and is prepared to accept its unwanted twin Y. Oblique intention is, in other words, a kind of knowledge or realisation . . . Certainty in human affairs means certainty apart from unforeseen events or remote possibilities. Realisation of practical certainty is something higher in the scale than appreciation of high probability." G. Williams has explained oblique intention as "intention includes not only desire of the consequences (purpose) but also foresight of the certainty of the consequence as a matter of legal definition". See G. Williams, "The New *Mens Rea* for Murder: Leave it Alone" (1989) 105 L.Q.R. 397 at 398.

example, the probability that the passengers will die is so overwhelming, it may be used as evidence that the accused intended to kill the passengers. His Lordship drew attention to a maxim which he said had been of help to judges for more than half a century: "a man is presumed to intend the natural and probable consequences of his acts"[279] In other words if the natural and probable result of chopping a man's head off is that he will die, the perpetrator is presumed to have intended to kill the victim. Such a maxim could still be of use, though Lord Bridge thought that the word "probable" was superfluous, being included in the word "natural". He, therefore, concluded that where a jury need an expanded direction on intention by reference to foresight of consequences they should be asked two questions:

> "First, was death or really serious injury in a murder case (or whatever relevant consequence must be proved to have been intended in any other case) a natural consequence of the defendant's voluntary act? Secondly, did the defendant foresee that consequence as being a natural consequence of his act? The jury should then be told that if they answer yes to both questions it is a proper inference for them to draw that he intended that consequence."[280]

It was not long before one of the supposedly rare cases in which extended guidance would **2–059** be necessary came along in *Hancock and Shankland*.[281] Two miners were charged with the murder of a taxi-driver. It was alleged that they had dropped heavy concrete blocks into the path of an oncoming car from a bridge over the road. The prosecution were, of course, alleging that the defendants had intended at least seriously to injure the occupants of the car. The defendants for their part maintained that they had only intended to prevent the driver from taking his passenger, a strikebreaking miner, to his mine. The defendants were prepared to plead guilty to manslaughter, but this offer was unacceptable to the prosecution. The trial judge rightly held that this was one of those exceptional cases in which it would not be sufficient simply to ask the jury whether they found that the defendants had intended to cause serious bodily injury; it was not a case of direct intention.[282] It is quite likely that the jury would have no difficulty in concluding that the defendants dropped the stones intending to stop the car getting through to the mine. The jury might, without much difficulty, further conclude that H and S foresaw there was a risk of causing serious bodily harm and even that there was a high risk of such harm. But could they find that the defendants intended to cause really serious bodily harm? The judge, therefore, gave them a direction in terms suggested by Lord Bridge in *Moloney* based on natural consequences and the defendants were convicted of murder. Their murder convictions were quashed by the Court of Appeal and this decision was upheld by the House of Lords. So what had gone wrong? Had not the trial judge followed Lord Bridge? Lord Scarman said that Lord Bridge's model direction in *Moloney* was defective in that it referred only to natural consequences and did not advert to the probability of a consequence occurring. A juror might be tempted to think that if a consequence flowed naturally from the act of the accused he would be entitled to infer that the accused intended that consequence. To be fair to Lord Bridge it is clear that he intended

---

[279] One possible interpretation of the controversial decision in *DPP v Smith* [1961] A.C. 290 was that the House of Lords had in that case turned this rebuttable presumption of law into an irrebuttable rule of law. If such was the decision in *Smith*, then it would have been overruled by s.8 of the Criminal Justice Act 1967, see below, para.7–015.
[280] [1985] A.C. 905 at 929.
[281] [1986] 1 All E.R. 641. See generally Lord Goff, "The Mental Element in the Crime of Murder" (1988) 104 L.Q.R. 30; A. Norrie "Oblique Intention and Legal Politics" [1989] Crim.L.R. 793; and N. Lacey "A Clear Concept of Intention: Elusive or Illusory?" (1993) 56 M.L.R. 621.
[282] It was extremely unlikely that the jury would have found that the defendants intended to kill anyone.

the issue of probability to be considered since elsewhere in his speech he had said: "looking on their facts at the decided cases where a crime of specific intention was under consideration . . . they suggest to me that the probability of the consequence taken to have been foreseen must be little short of overwhelming before it will suffice to establish the necessary intent".[283] Elsewhere Lord Bridge had used the phrase "moral certainty" to describe the probability of the event occurring before it would be used as evidence that the accused intended the consequence to occur. His mistake was in thinking that the word "probable" in the phrase "natural and probable consequences" was superfluous, being covered by the word "natural".

Lord Scarman thought that jurors should receive specific guidance on the issue of probability. They should be told that the greater the probability of a consequence occurring, the more likely it is that the consequence was foreseen. That if the consequence was foreseen the greater the probability is that the consequence was intended. Unfortunately even here there is a problem. In *Moloney* Lord Bridge had said that only where the jury conclude that the accused foresaw the probability of the result occurring as little short of overwhelming would they be entitled to infer that the accused intended the result to occur. Elsewhere he said that where the jury conclude that the accused saw the result as a moral certainty they would be entitled to use that as evidence that the accused intended the result to happen. In *Hancock and Shankland* the Court of Appeal spoke of the high likelihood of the consequence occurring. There would seem to be a significant difference between foreseeing a consequence as highly likely and foreseeing it as a moral certainty. It is a pity that Lord Scarman did not resolve the matter.

In *Nedrick*,[284] yet another of those cases which will occur only rarely, Lord Lane C.J. said:

> "Where the charge is murder and in the rare cases where the simple direction is not enough, the jury should be directed that they are not entitled to infer the necessary intention, unless they feel sure that death or serious bodily harm was a virtual certainty (barring some unforeseen intervention) as a result of the defendant's actions and that the defendant appreciated that such was the case."[285]

2–060   This has become the model direction on intention wherever a simple direction is not appropriate.[286] Let us return to the example of the accused who has placed a bomb on board the aircraft. If the jury conclude that he intended to kill all the passengers there is no difficulty. If all they conclude is that the accused saw that there was a chance that passengers would be killed, this in itself will not suffice as an intention to kill, nor should the jury be told that it is evidence from which they can infer an intention to kill. If, however, the jury conclude that the accused foresaw it as virtually certain that the passengers would be killed, this was capable of being evidence from which they would be entitled to infer that he intended to kill.[287]

Despite the fact that the Court of Appeal in *Nedrick* had, in the subsequent eyes of the House of Lords,[288] provided in its model direction excellent guidance for trial judges,

---

[283] [1985] A.C. 905 at 925.
[284] (1986) 83 Cr.App.R. 267; see generally G.R. Sullivan, "Intent, Subjective Recklessness and Culpability" (1992) 12 O.J.L.S. and J. Horder, "Varieties of Intention, Criminal Attempts and Endangerment" (1994) 14 *Legal Studies* 335.
[285] (1986) 83 Cr.App.R. 267 at 271.
[286] See below, para.2–061.
[287] It would appear from the passage quoted that the jury must conclude (a) that it was virtually certain that the passengers would be killed and (b) that the accused foresaw the deaths as virtually certain. Suppose that the aircraft was the very latest model in which the hold had been strengthened to resist explosions; the death of the passengers would not now be a virtual certainty, but the accused might still believe that it was and surely that should suffice to provide evidence of intention.
[288] *Woollin* [1998] 4 All E.R. 103.

evidence that the trial judges were still unsure of themselves was soon provided. In *Walker and Hayles*[289] on a case of attempted murder, where only an intent to kill will suffice as the mens rea,[290] the Court of Appeal held that a direction that the jury were entitled to find that D intended to kill if he knew that it was highly probable that his actions would kill, was acceptable, but not desirable. The court concluded that although this was pitching the requirement lower than a direction in terms of virtual certainty, it did not amount to a misdirection. In *Scalley*[291] the trial judge in a written direction to the jury equated intention to kill or cause grievous bodily harm with foresight that such a result was virtually certain, and this was clearly a misdirection.

In *Woollin*,[292] the House of Lords had occasion to return to the *Nedrick* direction. W had lost his temper and thrown his child, who was aged three months, on to a hard surface and the child died as a result of a fractured skull. The prosecutor had conceded that W had not desired to kill or seriously injure his child; the question, therefore, was whether he had nonetheless intended seriously to injure his son. The trial judge directed the jury in terms of the *Nedrick* direction save that he said that if they were satisfied that the appellant must have realised and appreciated when he threw his son that there was a substantial risk that he would cause serious injury to it, then it would be open to them to find that he intended to cause injury to the child and if they did so find they should convict him of murder. Lord Steyn held that the trial judge had been wrong to depart from the *Nedrick* model direction. By so doing he had blurred the distinction between intention and recklessness and hence between murder and manslaughter. He had increased the scope of the law of murder and this was a material misdirection; the conviction for murder was quashed.

The House of Lords, therefore, gave its general blessing to the *Nedrick* model direction, **2–061** subject to three observations on matters of detail. First, the crux of the direction is the passage quoted above.[293] Lord Steyn thought that the suggestion elsewhere by Lord Lane C.J. that the jury might find it useful to ask themselves "(1) how probable was the consequence which resulted from the defendant's voluntary act? and (2) did he foresee that consequence?" would only detract from the clarity of the direction and could rarely, if ever, be useful.

Secondly, the words "to infer" in the model direction should be replaced for the sake of user friendliness by the words "to find".

Thirdly, Lord Lane C.J. had concluded his judgment in *Nedrick* with the following advice:

> "Where a man realises that it is for all practical purposes inevitable that his actions will result in death or serious harm, the inference may be irresistible that he intended that result, however little he may have desired or wished it to happen. The decision is one for the jury to be reached upon a consideration of all the evidence."[294]

Lord Hope said that whereas the last sentence is clearly correct and a statement the judge should always make to the jury, the remainder of the paragraph formed no part of the model direction.

---

[289] (1990) 99 Cr.App.R. 226.
[290] See below, para.6–008.
[291] [1995] Crim.L.R. 504; see further *Gregory and Mott* [1995] Crim.L.R. 507 as to when a *Nedrick* direction is necessary. In *Woollin* [1998] 4 All E.R. 103 the House of Lords held that a *Nedrick* direction might be appropriate in any case in which the accused might not have desired the result of his act, though the trial judge is the person best placed to decide what direction was required by the circumstances of the case.
[292] [1998] 4 All E.R. 103.
[293] At para.2–059.
[294] (1986) 83 Cr.App.R. 267 at 271.

The case, therefore, appears to be a consolidation of *Nedrick*. It seems that we still have no substantive definition of intention. Once it was decided in *Moloney* that only intention sufficed for murder, trial judges and jurors needed a definition of intention, and this they have not got. From time to time there are statements which appear to come close to a definition of intent. In giving his example of a passenger boarding an aircraft for Manchester, Lord Bridge said that by boarding the plane, the passenger conclusively demonstrates his intention to go to Manchester. There are other statements in the cases which appear to come close to a definition of intention, but at the last minute the courts pull back from such a step and return to the negative point of view that foresight is not the same as intention,[295] *but may be evidence of it,* provided the degree of probability is sufficient. If during a trial the jury were to say to the judge, "we have concluded that the accused did not desire the death of the passengers, but on the other hand he did foresee that their deaths were a virtual certainty. Are we right in thinking that this is an intention to kill? We are still unsure as to what you mean by intention." How should the judge respond? His temptation would be to say that intention was a word in everyday use, but the last thing the House of Lords wants is for the word intent to be given its everyday meaning since this would lead to a very narrow concept of murder. The layman, left to his own devices, would give intention a very narrow purposive definition. The result is that we leave the jury with an almost meaningless direction[296]; we tell them to look for something which even the highest members of the judiciary are not prepared to describe. *Woollin* comes no nearer a direction which can be fully explained to a jury except in so far as Lord Steyn appears to say that a result foreseen as virtually certain is in effect an intended result. Since, however, this statement is in direct opposition to the decision in the case, we should probably conclude that it was a slip of the tongue and not intended to be put to jurors. In the end all the jury can do in the retiring room is to decide whether the accused should be labelled as a murderer or as a person who has committed manslaughter.

That foresight of a virtual certainty does not necessarily equate to intention, but is *evidence* from which intention may be found, was confirmed by the Court of Appeal in *Matthews and Alleyne*.[297] We remain in the curious position where a key criminal law concept lacks a substantive definition.

B. Negligence and Recklessness

2–062   Generally speaking intention is the most culpable of the elements which go to make up the mens rea of a crime. Next in descending order would be recklessness followed by negligence.[298] In the light, however, of complexities which have arisen in relation to recklessness, it will be convenient to deal with negligence first.

---

[295] Unfortunately in *Woollin*, Lord Steyn says: It was not altogether surprising that in *Nedrick* the Court of Appeal had felt compelled to provide a model direction for the assistance of trial judges. The effect was that "a result seen as virtually certain was an intended result". On the face of it this is exactly the mistake the trial judge had made at first instance; the equating of any level of degree of foresight with intention. No doubt Lord Steyn intended to say only that in the vast majority of cases, when a jury found that the accused had foreseen a result as virtually certain, they will conclude he intended that result. It is, however, an unfortunate sentence to find in the middle of what was intended to be a clarification of the whole picture.

[296] Lord Lane C.J. in an extra-judicial pronouncement (HL Paper 78–1, 1989) admitted that *Nedrick* was not as clear as it should have been, but the court had been very concerned not to tread on the toes of the House of Lords. He felt, however, that intention was rightly defined in the Law Commission's Draft Criminal Code.

[297] [2003] EWCA Crim 192; [2003] 2 Cr.App.R. 30.

[298] Negligence is not really a state of mind of the accused, nevertheless it is the required fault element for some crimes and is therefore classified as a form of mens rea.

C. Negligence

In the civil law a classic description of negligence was given by Alderson B. in *Blyth v* **2–063**
Birmingham Waterworks Ltd where he said, "Negligence is the omission to do something
which a reasonable man, guided upon those considerations which ordinarily regulate the
conduct of human affairs, would do, or doing something which a prudent and reasonable
person would not do."[299]

It is, thus, not a defence in a civil action for the defendant to show that he did not foresee
the harm if a reasonable person would have done so; nor even to show that his failure to
foresee was due to physical or mental limitations not shared by the reasonable man.
Nevertheless it seems probable that the defendant's physical and mental defects may be
taken into account in determining whether he is negligent to the extent that they make it
impossible for him to take the necessary precautions. Thus, whereas it would not avail a man
with defective eyesight to attribute a motor accident to his inability to judge distances, if,
however, the same man were to fall over and injure the plaintiff's prize poodle when walking
along the pavement, the appropriate test would be whether, for a man with defective
eyesight, he had taken reasonable care.

In criminal law, negligence is rarely the direct basis of liability, though it may become so
indirectly. It differs from intention and recklessness, in that it is not really a state of mind of
the defendant, and in so far as the criminal law seeks to punish the defendant's culpability it
is questionable whether the criminal law should punish negligent behaviour. At common law
the only example of a crime of negligence is gross negligence manslaughter.[300] The epithet
"gross" indicating that this offence requires a very high degree of negligence; a level
sufficient for civil law negligence will not do.

There are a number of statutory offences in which negligence is the basis of liability.
Perhaps the best known of these is careless driving.[301]

Where the crime is one of negligence, the test to be applied is probably the same as for
negligence in the civil law, though in a criminal case the standard of proof is higher.[302] Thus,
on a charge of careless driving, it is no excuse that the accused is a learner driver on his first
lesson; his driving will be considered to be careless if he fails to measure up to the standard
of the reasonably experienced driver and no allowance is made for the fact that he is a
learner.[303] In *McCrone v Riding*, Lord Hewart C.J. said:

> "That standard is an objective standard, impersonal and universal, fixed in relation to
> the safety of other users of the highway. It is in no way related to the degree of
> proficiency or degree of experience attained by the individual driver."[304]

Although there are few crimes of negligence, liability for negligence might arise indirectly. **2–064**
If a statute expressly provides for a defence of reasonable mistake, it will create in part a
crime of negligence. For example, under s.28 of the Misuse of Drugs Act 1971 it is a defence

---

[299] (1856) 11 Exch. 781 at 784. Since, as we shall see, criminal law recognises degrees of negligence, it is perhaps
better to speak of negligence as falling short of a given standard. It will then be possible to descibe how far short of
the standard the accused has fallen.

[300] See below, para.7–048.

[301] Road Traffic Act 1988 s.3, as amended by the Road Traffic Act 1991 s.2. The offences of causing death by
careless driving, dangerous driving and causing death by dangerous driving in ss.2B, 1 and 2 of the Road Traffic
Act 1988 are also defined in terms of negligence.

[302] The criminal standard of proof is beyond reasonable doubt as opposed to the civil standard of a balance of
probabilities; see above, paras 1–009—1–011.

[303] See, e.g. *McCrone v Riding* [1938] 1 All E.R. 157; (1938) 158 L.T. 253.

[304] [1938] 1 All E.R. 157 at 158.

to a charge of possession of controlled drugs if the accused can prove[305] that he neither believed nor suspected nor had reason to suspect that the substance or product in question was a controlled drug.[306]

Negligence in the form of constructive knowledge[307] has been used as the basis for liability in offences designed to control harassment or stalking.[308] Under s.1(1) of the Protection of Harassment Act 1997 it is provided that it is an offence for a person to pursue a course of conduct which amounts to harassment of another, and which he knows or ought to know amounts to harassment of the other. This offence is a summary only offence. A more serious offence is provided by s.4(1) of the Act whereby it is an offence if the accused's course of conduct causes another to fear, on at least two occasions, that violence will be used against him, if he knows or ought to know that his course of conduct will cause the other so to fear on each of those occasions.[309] The use of constructive knowledge in both provisions can be justified by the difficulties often encountered in proving mens rea against the sort of people who engage in such activities as stalking.[310]

Although it could be argued that holding someone criminally liable for a negligent mistake is objectionable in principle it can be said that in many instances where negligence suffices, it is as mitigation of the harshness of strict liability.[311]

D. Recklessness

2–065   Until 1982 it was generally assumed that the word "recklessness" had the meaning ascribed to it by Byrne J. in *Cunningham*,[312] where he was construing the meaning of "maliciously" in s.23 of the Offences against the Person Act 1861. Malice did not mean that the prosecution must simply prove that the accused had acted wickedly; it indicated that the prosecution must prove either that the accused had intended to administer a noxious substance or that he foresaw that what he was doing would have that effect but had nonetheless gone on to do it. This second state of mind was, he said, recklessness. The 1861 Act does not actually use the term "recklessness" but following *Cunningham* it was gradually accepted that recklessness, as defined in that case, would suffice as a basis of liability where the offence required proof that the accused had acted "maliciously". Later statutes began to use the word "recklessly" in place of "maliciously". For example, in the basic offence of Criminal Damage[313] it is an offence intentionally or recklessly to destroy or damage property belonging to another. After some initial hesitation the Court of Appeal accepted that the word "recklessly" in this new statute should have the subjective meaning ascribed to it in *Cunningham*.[314] However in *Caldwell*[315] the House of Lords held that the word "recklessly"

---

[305] The statute specifically puts the burden of proof on the accused. In *Lambert* [2001] UKHL 37; [2001] 3 W.L.R. 206; [2001] 3 All E.R. 577, the House of Lords took the view that, to ensure compatibility with the presumption of innocence in art.6(2) of the European Convention on Human Rights, a defendant could only be required to raise evidence of, rather than to prove, this issue.

[306] s.28(3)(b)(i); see below, para.3–026.

[307] See below, para.2–073.

[308] See, also *Ireland* [1997] 4 All E.R. 225 and *Burstow* [1997] 4 All E.R. 225, discussed below, at paras 7–065—7–086.

[309] The objective nature of these two provisions is given a subjective aspect in ss.1(2) and 4(2).

[310] See, generally C. Wells, "Stalking: The Criminal Law Response" [1997] Crim.L.R. 463.

[311] For a critique of strict liability and the role of negligence, see below, paras 3–001—3–003.

[312] [1957] 2 Q.B. 396, above, para.2–052.

[313] Criminal Damage Act 1971 s.1(1); See below, para.10–001. Note: it is clear that Parliament had not intended to change the substantive law by the Act. The Act itself was based upon a report by the Law Commission, Offences of Damage to Property, No.29, 1970. Parliament had intended simply to replace the outmoded word "maliciously" with the more modern "recklessly". See also the dissenting judgment in *Caldwell* by Lord Edmund-Davies; [1982] 2 A.C. 341 at 356–362.

[314] See, e.g. *Briggs* [1977] 1 W.L.R. 605; *Parker* [1977] Crim.L.R. 102; and *Stephenson* [1979] Q.B. 695.

[315] [1982] 2 A.C. 341.

had a much wider meaning than that described by Byrne J. in *Cunningham*. While it clearly covered a situation in which the accused had consciously taken an unjustified risk of bringing about the actus reus, it also covered situations in which the accused had done an act without giving any thought to the existence of such a risk. This decision meant that we had two definitions of the word "recklessly". From that time onwards it was necessary to know in which offences the prosecution were required to prove the narrower, subjective state of mind defined in *Cunningham*, and in which offences the wider definition from *Caldwell* was sufficient. Courts began to use the epithets *Caldwell* and *Cunningham* to identify the type of recklessness required.

In this section we shall first consider the two types of recklessness, after which we shall consider the decision of the House of Lords in *R v G*[316] which has, for our purpose, unified the meaning of recklessness along *Cunningham* lines.

(i) Cunningham Recklessness

In *Cunningham*, Byrne J. described recklessness as foreseeing that the particular kind of **2–066** harm might be done, yet going on to take the risk of it. *Cunningham* recklessness thus requires the conscious taking of an unjustified risk. The following will hopefully provide a simple illustration of these requirements. Suppose that D lives opposite a public park. He places a beer can on top of a public toilet in the park which is opposite his bedroom window and, retreating to his bedroom proceeds to fire at the can with an air rifle. One of his shots hits a man who is coming out of the toilets. He is charged with unlawfully and maliciously wounding the man.[317] He has clearly created an obvious risk of injuring people using the toilets, and, further, it is a risk he is not justified in taking. Section 20, however, requires *Cunningham* recklessness and this means that the prosecution must prove that he consciously took the risk of hurting someone.[318] In other words, he must have thought to himself, "There's a chance I might hit someone with a pellet, but that's a risk I am prepared to take; I could not care less."

The risk taken must be one that the defendant is not justified in taking and to this extent *Cunningham* recklessness has an objective element. It is not a question of whether the accused thinks that the risk is one he is justified in taking, but rather whether the risk is one that reasonable people would have taken. A surgeon may operate on a patient in circumstances where he foresees there to be a risk of death. If death does, in fact, result, so long as the risk was one the doctor was justified in taking, we cannot say he has recklessly killed the patient. There is a risk that by driving your car you may kill or seriously injure another, but again this is a risk you are normally justified in taking. Whether or not a risk is one you are justified in taking depends upon the social utility of the act you are performing. There is great social utility in the surgeon taking risks of causing death, even high risks. A heart replacement operation may be the only hope the patient has for a decent lifestyle. On the other hand there can be no justification for putting the public at risk by shooting at an empty beer can placed above the entrance to a public toilet.

These principles were cogently put forward by the Law Commission in their Working Paper on the Mental Element in Crime:

---

[316] [2003] UKHL 50; [2004] 1 A.C. 1034.
[317] Contrary to the Offences Against the Person Act 1861 s.20; see below, para.7–082. See also *Spratt* (1991) 91 Cr.App.R. 362.
[318] We shall see later that the prosecution do not have to prove that he foresaw a wound or the infliction of grievous bodily harm, but merely that he foresaw that his action might cause some harm, albeit slight. Below, paras 7–083—7–084.

"the operation of public transport, for example, is inevitably accompanied by risks of accident beyond the control of the operator, yet it is socially necessary that these risks be taken. Dangerous surgical operations must be carried out in the interests of the life and health of the patient, yet the taking of these risks is socially justifiable."[319]

An allied question is the degree of foresight which must exist in order to constitute recklessness. There is no clear cut answer to this question. An illustration should suffice to demonstrate the likely approach by the court. Suppose, for example, the defendant who is standing on a cliff top at 3am in the middle of winter, throws a rock on to the beach below. He thinks that there is an outside chance of hitting someone on the beach, but that this an extremely remote possibility. Unfortunately P is on the beach and is injured. The likely outcome is that the court would hold that this was not a risk he was justified in taking; it had no social utility whatsoever. In these circumstances foresight of even the remotest possibility of causing harm should be classified as *Cunningham* recklessness. On the other hand a surgeon may conclude that the risk of death is quite high, but in view of the social utility of what he is doing, only if the risk of death is so high that it outweighs the social utility will his action be classified as reckless.

(ii) Caldwell Recklessness

2–067 In *Caldwell*,[320] where, in an act of revenge arising from a quarrel with the owner of a hotel, C had got drunk and set fire to the hotel, the House of Lords was concerned with the interpretation of the Criminal Damage Act 1971. The Act specifically provides that the prosecution must prove that the accused intentionally or recklessly brought about the actus reus of the various offences. In *Caldwell*, Lord Diplock held that the Criminal Damage Act 1971 was a modern statute and should be interpreted accordingly; it was a reforming statute and not one merely designed to incorporate existing legislation. Its predecessor, the Malicious Damage Act 1861 had, like the Offences Against the Person Act, used the word "malicious" to denote the requisite mens rea. The Criminal Damage Act, however, used the word "recklessness" and it was for the courts to interpret the new term.

Lord Diplock did not challenge the correctness of Byrne J.'s interpretation of malicious in the 1861 Act. However, he said that Byrne J. was concerned to define the term "malicious". In doing so he had said that "malicious" indicated that the offence required intention or conscious risk-taking, this latter being a form of recklessness. Lord Diplock said that "recklessness" is a word in everyday use and had a wider meaning than that attributed to it in *Cunningham*. Recklessness was apt to cover not only situations in which the accused consciously took an unjustified risk, but also situations in which the accused had created a risk but had given no thought to it. Lord Diplock concluded:

"In my opinion, a person charged with an offence under s.1(1) of the 1971 (Criminal Damage) Act is 'reckless as to whether or not any property would be destroyed or damaged' if (1) he does an act which in fact creates an obvious risk that property will be destroyed or damaged and (2) when he does the act he either has not given any thought to the possibility of there being any such risk or has recognised that there was some risk involved and has none the less gone on to do it."[321]

---

[319] Law Commission Working Paper No.31, at p.53.
[320] [1982] A.C. 341; see generally G. Syrota, "A Radical Change in the Law of Recklessness" [1982] Crim.L.R. 97; G. Williams, "Divergent Interpretations of Recklessness" (1982) 132 N.L.J. 289; and D.J. Birch, "The Foresight Saga; the Biggest Mistake of All?" [1988] Crim.L.R. 4.
[321] [1982] A.C. 342 at 354.

So a strange situation existed where "recklessness" had two meanings one for criminal damage, and one for other offences. After *Caldwell* trial judges had to make sure they applied the right meaning. Suppose that a defendant was charged with punching P in the face causing him a broken nose and broken glasses. In relation to the offence against the person the judge would have to direct the jury in terms of the restricted *Cunningham* meaning, while in relation to the criminal damage to the glasses the jury would be directed in terms of the wider *Caldwell* meaning. They could be forgiven if they thought the law had taken leave of its senses.

You can see that in *Caldwell,* Lord Diplock refers to an "obvious risk". Clearly, this was **2–068** basically an objective test, but was it totally objective? What if the risk would have been obvious to a reasonable adult, but not to the reasonable teenager, and the defendant was a teenager? What if the defendant had a characteristic which affected their ability to appreciate a risk?

In *Elliott v C (a minor)*[322] a 14-year-old girl had spent the night out of doors. She had entered a shed where she found a bottle of white spirit and some matches. She poured the spirit on to the floor of the shed and set light to it. The shed was destroyed by fire and she was charged with criminal damage. According to her story she thought that it might ignite, but it never occurred to her that it might get out of control and destroy the whole shed. The magistrates took the view that in all the circumstances, including the fact that she had a mental impairment, the risk of the destruction of the shed was not one which was obvious to her and hence she did not fall within the meaning ascribed by Lord Diplock to recklessness. On a case stated following her acquittal, the Divisional Court reluctantly took the view that the risk had only to be obvious to a reasonably prudent person. It did not have to be a risk which would have been obvious to the defendant had she given any thought to it. In *Stephen (Malcolm R)*[323] a further attempt was made to mitigate the harshness of this approach. While accepting that the jury should not be asked to consider whether the risk should have been obvious to the particular defendant, the defence suggested that it would be correct to ask whether the risk would be obvious to a person of the defendant's age with such characteristics of the defendant as affect his ability to appreciate the risk.[324] This time the Court of Appeal held that, however attractive the reasoning was, it did not accord with the clear wording of Lord Diplock's speech in *Caldwell*; the risk had merely to be obvious to a reasonable person. In *Reid*, however, Lord Goff discussed the hypothetical example of a motorist who might have driven dangerously in that his driving had created a serious risk of injury, yet might not be reckless because while he was driving he was affected by illness or shock which impaired his capacity to address his mind to the possibility of the risk.[325] It is hard to reconcile this approach with that adopted in *Elliott v C (a minor)* and *Stephen (Malcolm R)*. If it was not permitted to take account of the child's retarded state in *Elliott v C (a minor)* why should any allowance be made for illness?[326] The test must be the same in all cases. Either it was a simple objective question of whether the risk would have been obvious to a reasonable person, or the question was whether the risk would have been obvious to a reasonable person who shared the characteristics of the accused which might affect the accused's ability to see the risk. The former was supported by *Elliott v C (a minor)*, the latter by Lord Goff's *obiter* remarks. The decision in *Coles*[327] supported the view that the

---

[322] [1983] 2 All E.R. 1005.
[323] [1984] 79 Cr.App.R. 334.
[324] This approach is similar to that accepted in provocation and duress; see below, paras 5–071 and 7–019.
[325] [1992] 3 All E.R. 673 at 687.
[326] Even harder to explain is why, in *Hardie* [1984] 3 All E.R. 848 (discussed below, para.5–038) account was taken of H's consumption of non-dangerous drugs to explain why H did not give any thought to damaging property. See also *Bell* [1984] 3 All E.R. 842.
[327] [1995] 1 Cr.App.R. 157.

test was objective and could not be watered down by concessions to a partially subjective approach.

R v G and the unification of the test for recklessness

2–069   In a previous edition of this book, we pointed out the unpopularity of the decision in *Caldwell*, and we noted the hints in the House of Lords in *Reid*[328] that the opportunity might be taken to review *Caldwell* when next a criminal damage case was before that court.

That opportunity arose in *R v G*.[329] The appellants were aged 11 and 12 at the time of the activities in question. They went camping without their parents' permission, and during the night, they went into the back yard of a shop. There, they found bundles of newspapers which they opened up to read. They then lit some of the newspapers with a lighter and threw some lit newspaper under a large plastic wheelie-bin. They left the yard without extinguishing the fire. The newspapers set fire to the wheelie-bin, from where the fire spread to a second wheelie-bin next to the shop wall. The fire spread up into the roof space of the shop and the roof of the shop and the adjoining buildings caught fire. Approximately £1 million worth of damage was caused. It was accepted that neither of the appellants appreciated that there was any risk of the fire spreading in the way that it did.

The defendants were convicted under s.1 of the Criminal Damage Act 1971, although it is clear from the speech of Lord Bingham in the House of Lords that the trial judge and the jury were not comfortable with the law that they had to apply. The judge had even made a point of letting the appellants know that "nothing unpleasant" would happen to them if the jury convicted, and they duly received only minor penalties.

The defendants appealed unsuccessfully to the Court of Appeal, who certified the following point of law of public importance for the House of Lords:

> "Can a defendant properly be convicted under section 1 of the Criminal Damage Act 1971 on the basis that he was reckless as to whether property was destroyed or damaged when he gave no thought to the risk but, by reason of his age and/or personal characteristics the risk would not have been obvious to him, even if he had thought about it?"

The House of Lords had the opportunity, by virtue of the phrasing of the certified question, to give a relatively narrow answer. It would have been open for them to say that the decision in *Caldwell* stood, but that if a defendant's age or personal characteristics impaired his ability to appreciate risk, then that age or those personal characteristics would be taken into account in applying the *Caldwell* test. Thus, on the question of whether a risk was obvious, a twelve year old defendant would be compared with a reasonable twelve year old.

2–070   However, the House of Lords went further than this, and unanimously overruled *Caldwell*, taking the law back to a position where, for our purposes, there was only one meaning of recklessness, and that was the *Cunningham* meaning. The leading speech was given by Lord Bingham. He identified four reasons behind his decision.[330]

First, he took what might be called a *subjectivist* position, according to which a defendant should be convicted on the basis of the results that *they* intended or *they* foresaw. He suggested that to be convicted of a serious crime, it should be necessary either to intend a prohibited result, or to knowingly disregard an appreciated and unacceptable risk of bringing about that result. The person who did not perceive the risk was less blameworthy. According to Lord Bingham:

[328] [1992] 1 W.L.R. 793.
[329] [2003] UKHL 50; [2004] 1 A.C. 1034.
[330] [2003] UKHL 50; [2004] 1 A.C. 1034 at [31] to [35].

"Such a person may fairly be accused of stupidity or lack of imagination, but neither of those failings should expose him to conviction of serious crime or the risk of punishment."[331]

Secondly, the case demonstrated that the direction given by Lord Diplock in *Caldwell* could lead to obvious unfairness. The law should, wherever possible, reflect general understandings of fairness and the need, according to the law, to convict the boys in *R v G* did not seem to correspond with those general feelings. The problem was not cured by the imposition of a nominal penalty.

Thirdly, the decision in *Caldwell* had been the subject of a barrage of criticism from **2–071** academics, judges and practitioners. Mere disfavour was not a reason to depart from a decision, but the nature of and reasoning behind the criticism, from leading authorities in the field, could not be ignored.

Fourthly, the decision of the majority in *Caldwell* had been a misinterpretation of the term "recklessness" in the Criminal Damage Act. In *Caldwell*, it had been suggested that the 1971 Act redefined the mens rea for criminal damage, such that it no longer corresponded with the *Cunningham* definition. In *R v G*, however, it was held that this was not the case. The work of the Law Commission on which the act was based suggested that the *Cunningham* definition was the proper one. Insofar as the 1971 Act "changed" the mens rea for the offence, it was only by *updating* the archaic term "maliciously" with the more modern "recklessly". As Lord Bingham stated, the mere fact of a misinterpretation was not itself a reason for departing from a previous decision (Lord Steyn also noted that a previous decision of the House of Lords should not be departed from lightly) but the misinterpretation in *Caldwell* was "offensive to principle" and "apt to cause injustice".[332]

Lord Steyn also noted the United Kingdom's international obligations under the Convention on the Rights of the Child, which states, at art.40.1:

"States Parties recognise the right of every child alleged as, accused of, or recognised as having infringed the penal law to be treated in a manner consistent with the promotion of the child's sense of dignity and worth, which reinforces the child's respect for the human rights and fundamental freedoms of others and *which takes into account the child's age* and the desirability of promoting the child's reintegration and the child's assuming a constructive role in society." (Lord Steyn's emphasis.)[333]

He suggested that this meant that it was not acceptable to ignore the special position of children. While the Convention became binding on the United Kingdom after *Caldwell*, it was now a factor which on its own justified a reappraisal of that decision.

So the House of Lords did not restrict themselves to a narrow response to the question **2–072** certified by the Court of Appeal. The decision in *Caldwell* has been consigned to history. And so recklessness now has, in effect, but a single definition, which corresponds, in substance, to that in *Cunningham*.[334] Lord Bingham concluded:

---

[331] [2003] UKHL 50; [2004] 1 A.C. 1034 at [32]. See, also, *Booth* [2006] EWHC 192 (Admin).

[332] [2003] UKHL 50; [2004] 1 A.C. 1034, per Lord Bingham at [35].

[333] [2003] UKHL 50; [2004] 1 A.C. 1034 at [53].

[334] The decision in *R v G* was, of course, a decision on criminal damage. There may be other offences beyond the scope of this book, in which the *Caldwell* definition for recklessness may still be relevant. It must follow from Lord Bingham's approach that if there are any such offences, they must be of a minor nature. They can safely be ignored for our purposes. See, e.g. *Data Protection Registrar v Amnesty International (British Section), The Times,* November 23, 1994, in which the Divisional Court held that in the offence of knowingly or recklessly misusing personal data, the word recklessly had the meaning ascribed by *Caldwell*.

"A person acts recklessly within the meaning of section 1 of the Criminal Damage Act 1971 with respect to:

(i) a circumstance when he is aware of a risk that it exists or will exist;

(ii) a result when he is aware of a risk that it will occur;
and it is, in the circumstances known to him, unreasonable to take the risk."[335]

According to the House of Lords in *R v G*, this is a more principled position than previously. The anomaly and apparent injustice of *Elliott v C (a minor)* has certainly been overcome. Judges no longer have to ponder the question of which definition of recklessness is relevant to a particular case, and, if nothing else, the subject of recklessness should be considerably easier to study than was the case previously.

E. Knowledge

2–073   Where the definition of the crime contains certain surrounding circumstances, the prosecutor may need to prove that the accused:

(a) knew the circumstances existed; or

(b) was wilfully blind as to whether the circumstances existed; or

(c) ought to have known of their existence.[336]

(i) Actual Knowledge

2–074   In relation to circumstances, knowledge is the equivalent of "intention", in that one does not really intend a circumstance.

Many statutes contain the word "knowingly" as part of the definition of the offences. Where this is the case, actual knowledge will normally be required. The main concern will often be the extent to which knowledge will be required. In *Hallam*,[337] where the accused was charged with knowingly possessing explosives, the question for the court was whether the prosecution had to prove merely that the accused knew he was in possession of a substance which in fact was explosives, or whether he must also establish that the defendant knew the substance to be explosives. The court held that knowingly applied not only to possession but also to the nature of the substance.[338] Similarly, in *Westminster City Council v Croyalgrange Ltd*[339] D was charged in that he knowingly used or knowingly caused or permitted the use of premises as a sex establishment without a licence. Robert Goff L.J. remarked:

"Prima facie, as a matter of ordinary construction, when the word knowingly is so introduced in a provision of this kind, it requires knowledge by the accused of each of the facts constituting the actus reus of the offence. On that basis it would follow that, in the present case, a person who is accused of an offence . . . must have knowledge

---

[335] [2003] UKHL 50; [2004] 1 A.C. 1034 at [41].
[336] See, Devlin J. in *Roper v Taylor's Central Garages (Exeter) Ltd* [1951] 2 T.L.R. 284.
[337] [1957] 1 Q.B. 569.
[338] See further below, para.3–009.
[339] [1985] 1 All E.R. 740; [1986] 1 W.L.R. 676; [1986] 2 All E.R. 353 HL.

not only of the fact that the premises in question are being used as a sex establishment but also that they are unlicensed."[340]

The fact that such provisions do not contain the word knowingly should not automatically lead one to suppose that strict liability is being imposed. As a general presumption, the word knowingly only makes explicit that which is normally implied, namely that mens rea is required.[341]

Where the statute requires knowledge of surrounding circumstances, this is sometimes satisfied by proof of wilful blindness. This is a state of mind somewhere between knowledge and recklessness. It describes a situation in which the accused deliberately refrains from asking questions in the belief that if he does not actually know the truth, he cannot be liable. In *Westminster City Council v Croyalgrange*[342] Goff L.J. said:

> "It is well established that, in cases where knowledge is required, knowledge may be proved not only by showing actual knowledge, but also by showing that the defendant in question has deliberately shut his eyes to obvious means of knowledge or deliberately refrained from making enquiries, the results of which he might not care to know."[343]

In many offences the prosecutor will have the option of proving knowledge or a lesser alternative specified in the statutory provision. Examples include "know or suspect" and "know or believe". In these situations "know" is taken to mean actual knowledge; whether or not wilful blindness will suffice depends upon the specified alternative. In handling stolen property, for example, the prosecution must prove that the defendant knew or believed the goods to be stolen. It has been held that "believe" is almost the same as "know" and more difficult to establish than wilful blindness. Wilful blindness will, therefore, not suffice for handling.[344]

(ii) Recklessness as to the Existence of a Circumstance

It is quite common for statutes to require either actual knowledge of or recklessness as to **2–075** the existence of a circumstance. Wilful blindness is a species of recklessness; the accused consciously takes an unjustified risk that certain facts exist.

(iii) Constructive Knowledge

Statutes occasionally require proof that the accused had reason to believe that certain **2–076** surrounding circumstances existed. This is liability for negligence. In wilful blindness the accused deliberately shuts his eyes; in constructive knowledge the accused simply fails to make the enquiries a reasonable person would have made.[345]

3. COINCIDENCE OF ACTUS REUS AND MENS REA

We have seen that each offence is made up of a series of elements. The external elements **2–077** form the actus reus and the internal elements the mens rea. In general, it must be shown that the accused brought about the actus reus with the requisite mens rea. Suppose, for

---

[340] [1985] 1 All E.R. 740 at 743.
[341] See, Devlin J. in *Roper v Taylor's Garage* [1951] 2 T.L.R. 284 at 286.
[342] [1985] 1 All E.R. 740.
[343] [1985] 1 All E.R. 740 at 744.
[344] See, comment by J.C. Smith on *Forsyth* [1997] Crim.L.R. 591.
[345] Examples of such provisions can be seen above, para.2–064 (harassment provisions).

example, D has decided to kill P on Saturday. On Friday while D is cleaning his gun in preparation for Saturday, P enters the room surprising D who accidentally discharges the gun, killing P. D has unlawfully killed P, but he did not do so with the necessary mens rea; the killing was an accidental one. If the accident was brought about by D's gross negligence, D might be liable for gross negligence manslaughter.[346] In result crimes it is not necessary that D had the mens rea at the time the result occurs, so long as D's conduct which brought about the actus reus was accompanied by mens rea. Thus, if D digs a pit and places spikes in the bottom with the intent that P should fall into the pit and be killed, D may well not be thinking about P at the moment when P falls into the pit and dies. Nevertheless D will be liable for the murder of P. He has done everything required of him to bring about the actus reus and he has done this with the necessary mens rea. He will be guilty of attempted murder if P does not fall into the pit[347] and murder when P does so fall. It will make no difference that P does not fall into the pit for several weeks or months; whenever he does D will be guilty of murder.

In *Jakeman*,[348] J had planned to fly from Accra to London via Rome. In Accra she purchased her ticket and checked in two suitcases which contained cannabis. In fact the flight to Rome was cancelled and she travelled to England via Paris where she abandoned the suitcases. Customs officials in Paris, however, sent the suitcases on to London where the cannabis was discovered. She was charged with being knowingly concerned in a fraudulent evasion of any prohibition for the time being in force with respect to the goods,[349] and she pleaded that she had abandoned the plan in Paris. The court held that she was guilty. The full offence is not committed until the aircraft touches down at the London airport. It was not necessary to prove that she had the mens rea at the time the aircraft touched down; what mattered was the state of mind at the time the relevant acts were done. In other words did J have the necessary mens rea at the time she did the acts which would cause the cannabis to be imported into England? If J, in Accra, thought she was doing the last act required of her to bring about the importation of the drugs into Britain, she would be guilty of an attempt at that moment[350] and guilty of the full offence when the aircraft touched down. If, however, J believed that she would be reunited with her bags at some stage and would be again required to check them onwards to London, she would not have had the necessary mens rea. In this case she could probably be held liable by reason of her failure to prevent the bags going onwards from Paris.[351]

At first sight the facts of *Fagan*[352] would seem to be an exception to the general principle that the accused must bring about the actus reus with the necessary mens rea. It will be recalled that in that case F accidentally drove on to a policeman's foot. When asked to move his car he refused to do so immediately. The problem with a charge involving an assault is that the actus reus consists of the application of unlawful violence against the police officer and the mens rea would be that F intentionally or recklessly applied unlawful force to the officer. Now it is clear that unlawful violence was inflicted by F upon the policeman, but at the time when he drove on to the policeman's foot he neither intended to do so nor did he perceive of any risk that he would do so. When he became aware of what he had done and decided to get some fun out of the situation, it could be argued that the act of inflicting violence was already over. The Court of Appeal, however, took a common sense approach in

---

[346] See, below, para.7–048.
[347] See, below, para.6–002.
[348] (1983) 76 Cr.App.R. 223; see also *Latif* [1996] 1 W.L.R. 104, discussed above at para.2–041.
[349] Contrary to the Customs and Excise Management Act 1979 s.170(2).
[350] For attempts, see below, para.6–001.
[351] See, further Professor J.C. Smith [1983] Crim.L.R. 104 at 105.
[352] [1969] 1 Q.B. 439; see above, para.2–027.

holding that an assault was a continuing offence. It lasted from the time he drove onto the policeman's foot until he drove off. If at any time during that period he had the necessary mens rea then the charge was made out.[353]

A more extreme example was provided by *Thabo Meli v R*.[354] The appellants in this case **7-078** had lured the victim to a mountain hut where they attempted to kill him by striking him over the head with a metal bar. Thinking he was dead, they rolled his body over a cliff to simulate accidental death. Evidence showed that the man had been alive when he was pushed over the cliff and that he died later from exposure. The problem here is that at the time the defendants had the intention to kill they did not bring about the actus reus of murder; they had not killed a human being. Furthermore, when they perpetrated the act which led to his death, in other words rolling him over the cliff, they did not intend to kill or seriously injure a human being, because they thought they were merely disposing of a corpse. The Privy Council had no hesitation in finding the defendants guilty of murder. Lord Reid explained:

> "It appears to their Lordships impossible to divide up what was really one series of acts in this way. There is no doubt that the accused set out to do all these acts in order to achieve their plan, and as parts of their plan; and it is much too refined a ground of judgment to say that, because they were under a misapprehension at one stage and thought that their guilty purpose had been achieved before, in fact, it was achieved, therefore they are to escape the penalties of the law."[355]

This is clearly a common sense decision; the public would not readily understand that they had not committed murder. On the facts of this case it would be possible to say that the defendants had formulated a plan to kill the victim and dispose of his body. This was one transaction and everything that was done was done to fulfil the plan. Would the same be true if there had been no preconceived plan? In *Church*,[356] C took a woman in his van to a riverbank for sexual purposes. It appears that C failed to satisfy the woman and she slapped his face. A fight ensued and C said that as a result the woman lay on the floor moaning. When he could not revive her after about half an hour, he panicked and threw what he supposed to be her dead body into the river. Evidence showed that she was still alive when he threw her into the river and that she died as a result of drowning. Despite the absence of a preconceived plan, the Court of Appeal upheld his conviction for manslaughter. Edmund Davies J. held that the law was correctly stated by Professor Glanville Williams when he said "If a killing by the first act would have been manslaughter, a later destruction of the supposed corpse should also be manslaughter."[357] He continued that the jury:

> "[W]ere entitled (if they thought fit) to regard the conduct of the appellant in relation to Mrs Nott as constituting throughout a series of acts which culminated in her death, and that, if that was how they regarded the appellant's behaviour, it mattered not whether he believed her to be alive or dead when he threw her in the river."[358]

---

[353] Following *Miller* [1983] 2 A.C. 161 (discussed above, para.2–027) the court would today probably approach the facts rather differently. It is likely that the accused's action in driving on to the foot gave rise to a duty to get off as soon as possible. He would thus be held liable for failing to act based upon a breach of that duty. See also *Kaitamaki v R.* [1985] A.C. 147 (below para.7–120); *Attorney-General for Northern Ireland v Gallagher* [1963] A.C. 349 (discussed below, para.5–041).

[354] [1954] 1 All E.R. 373.

[355] [1954] 1 All E.R. 373 at 374.

[356] [1966] 1 Q.B. 59; [1965] 2 All E.R. 72.

[357] *Criminal Law*, General Part (2nd) at p.174.

[358] [1996] 1 Q.B. 59 at 76.

The subsequent case of *Le Brun*[359] confirmed that there was no need for an antecedent plan and further that the same principles applied to both murder and manslaughter. Le Brun and his wife were walking home at about 2am when a heated argument developed. L struck his wife on the jaw and rendered her unconscious. It appears that L tried to drag her from the scene, but she fell to the floor and suffered a fractured skull from which she died. The Court of Appeal said that cases such as these can often be approached in two ways; the *transaction* approach and the *causation* approach.

2–079   Under the transaction approach it does not matter that the second act is the sole cause of death. The defendant is guilty of murder or manslaughter if he kills the victim during the course of the transaction. The transaction for these purposes began when he struck her on the jaw and continued so long as he was either trying to move her against her will or to cover up what he had done. So long as he had the necessary mens rea at some time during the period of the transaction he is guilty. Under this approach the transaction would probably have come to an end if, when she slipped out of his grasp, he had been trying to get her to a doctor or into their house if that is where she had wanted to go.

Under the causation approach the first act must have been at least a cause of the victim's death.[360] If this is perpetrated with mens rea, then the only remaining question is whether the second act broke the chain of causation.[361] The question is whether or not the intervening act is foreseeable.[362] It is difficult to see how anything the accused was to do could be regarded as unforeseeable. Suppose, however, that a passing motorist had seen the wife unconscious on the path and had been trying to get her into his car when she slipped and struck her head. Would such an event have been foreseeable?

On the actual facts of *Le Brun* it appears that the sole cause of death was the fracturing of the skull; an act perpetrated without mens rea. Under these circumstances the causation approach would not be applicable since the first blow was not a cause of death. He would, however, be liable under the transaction principle since mens rea accompanied the first part of the transaction and could be linked with the accidental dropping of the wife to produce a conviction for unlawful act manslaughter.[363]

In summary, Lord Lane C.J. concluded:

> "It seems to us that where the unlawful application of force and the eventual act causing death are parts of the same sequence of events, the same transaction, the fact that there is an appreciable interval of time between the two does not serve to exonerate the defendant from liability. That is certainly so when the appellant's subsequent actions which caused death, after the initial unlawful blow, are designed to conceal his commission of the original unlawful assault . . . In short, in circumstances such as the present, . . . the act which causes death and the necessary mental state to constitute manslaughter need not coincide in point of time."[364]

It was clear in *Thabo Meli* and *Le Brun* that the victim had died as a result of the second of two acts. In *Attorney-General's Reference (No.4 of 1980)*[365] the Court of Appeal was faced

---

[359] [1991] 4 All E.R. 673. See generally G.R. Sullivan, "Cause and Contemporaneity of *Actus Reus* and *Mens Rea*" (1993) 52 C.L.J. 487.
[360] There can be more than one cause of death.
[361] As to causation see above paras 2–032—2–050.
[362] For a case based on the causation approach see *S v Masilela* [1968] (2) S.A. 558. D intended to kill P and rendered him unconscious. D, believing P to be dead, set fire to the house and left. P was killed by the fumes from the blaze. Had he not been unconscious he would have been able to escape. Therefore, D's act in knocking P unconscious was a cause of the death and the chain was not broken by D's subsequent actions.
[363] As to unlawful act manslaughter see below, para.7–038.
[364] [1991] 4 All E.R. 673 at 678–679.
[365] [1981] 1 W.L.R. 705.

with a variation on the problem. In this case the defendant was alleged to have slapped his girlfriend on the face. This caused her to fall down the stairs banging her head. He then put a rope around her neck and dragged her back up the stairs, where he placed her in the bath and drained off all her blood. Finally he sawed her up into disposable pieces. It was not clear as to what was the cause of death since very little of her body was found for forensic examination. She might have died from the fall, from strangulation or from having her throat cut. The Court of Appeal held that the jury would have been entitled to return a verdict of manslaughter if they were satisfied that at the time the defendant did any act which might have caused her death he had the necessary mens rea for manslaughter.[366] This seems somewhat generous to the defendant. Assuming that it was all one transaction, it should suffice that he had the necessary mens rea when he committed the first act.

4. TRANSFERRED MALICE

In *Hyam v DPP*,[367] Mrs H was determined to scare off Mrs B, her rival for the affection of **2–080** Mr X. She went round to Mrs B's house, poured petrol through her letter box, stuffed newspapers in and then set light to the petrol. In the ensuing fire, Mrs B escaped but her two young children were suffocated by the fumes. Mrs H was charged with murder. The case is important for what it said about the mens rea of murder.[368] However, it raised another important point. If we accept that the prosecution must prove an intention to cause death or grievous bodily harm, the question can be asked whether the prosecution must prove that the accused intended to kill or seriously injure a particular individual or whether it suffices that the defendant intended to kill another human being. The answer can be traced back to *Latimer*,[369] where L attempted to hit V with his belt. The belt glanced off the intended victim and hit R causing her serious injuries. The jury had found that the injury to R was purely accidental; and that L was not even negligent since it was not a result he could have been expected to have anticipated. Nonetheless the Court for Crown Cases Reserved held that he was properly convicted of unlawfully and maliciously wounding R. Lord Coleridge C.J. stated:[370]

> "We are of opinion that this conviction must be sustained. It is common knowledge that a man who has an unlawful and malicious intent against another, and, in attempting to carry it out, injures a third person, is guilty of what the law deems malice against the person injured, because the defendant is doing an unlawful act, and has that which the judges call general malice, and that is enough."

In *Mitchell*,[371] M had attempted to jump the queue at a post office and had been upbraided by an elderly man, S, whereupon M subsequently pushed S into C, an 89 year old lady. C suffered a broken femur and died following an operation to replace her broken hip. The cause of death was pulmonary embolism caused by the fracture of the femur. M appealed against his conviction for manslaughter, the main point of his argument being that

---

[366] As we shall see later in Ch.7 this would require that in slapping the victim the defendant had intentionally committed an unlawful act which was likely to cause injury, and that when he dragged her up the stairs and cut her throat he was behaving in a grossly negligent manner.
[367] [1975] A.C. 55; see above, para.2–055.
[368] See above, para.2–055. On the issue of the mens rea of murder it is now regarded as defective. Its approach to transferred malice is undoubtedly correct.
[369] (1886) 17 Q.B.D. 359.
[370] (1886) 17 Q.B.D. 359 at 361.
[371] [1983] 2 All E.R. 427.

the person against whom the act was aimed, namely S, was not the person who had died. In rejecting this argument Staughton J. said, "We can see no reason of policy for holding an act calculated to harm A cannot be manslaughter if it in fact kills B. The criminality of the doer of the act is precisely the same whether it is A or B who dies."[372]

A case which, at first, might appear to be against the above authorities is *Pembliton*.[373] P was one of a number of persons engaged in a fight outside a public house. He picked up a stone and threw it at the others. The stone sailed over the heads of the other men and broke a window of the public house. He was charged with unlawfully and maliciously committing damage contrary to s.51 of the Malicious Damage Act 1861. The jury found that he had intended to hit the men with whom he had been fighting and that he did not intend to hit the window which was broken. On those facts the Court for Crown Cases Reserved held that he was not guilty. The case illustrates the limits of the doctrine of transferred malice. In *Hyam*, *Latimer* and *Mitchell*, the accused had intended to injure person A, but had accidentally injured person B. In this situation the malice the defendant bears against A can be transferred to B; he has brought about the actus reus of an offence against the person with the necessary mens rea for that offence. In *Pembliton*, however, on the facts found by the jury, he had brought about the actus reus of an offence against property with the mens rea of an offence against the person, and as such commits neither offence. That does not mean to say that Pembliton is guilty of no offence. Were the facts to arise today, Pembliton could have been charged with attempting to injure the other men[374] or with recklessly causing criminal damage.[375] The trouble in *Pembliton* was that the jury were simply not asked to consider these questions.

A similar rule operates in relation to defences. Suppose that D believing that P is about to shoot him (D), shoots at P but misses P and kills V. If D is charged with murder, had his victim been P he would have been able to say that he believed that he was justified in shooting at P. However, he will be prosecuted for the murder of V, but he can nevertheless raise the defence of justification. In relation to P, D did not intend an unlawful killing; there is thus no mens rea to transfer to the killing of V.

2–081   In the examples we have considered, thus far, the accused might be said to have been at least negligent in relation to the actual victim. In *Hyam* it would be reasonable to assume that there would be others in the house and both *Mitchell* and *Latimer* would have been aware of others present at the time of the alleged offence. Suppose, however, that D shoots at P not knowing that W is standing behind some curtains. If the bullet hits and kills W, D could argue that he could not reasonably have been expected to anticipate someone hiding behind the curtains. Professor Williams has argued[376] that the doctrine of transferred malice should be subject to the limitations that the ultimate victim should be reasonably foreseeable and that there should be no alteration in the mode in which the actus reus is effected. These matters were considered in *Attorney-General's Reference (No.3 of 1994)*.[377] D had stabbed his

---

[372] [1983] 2 All E.R. 427 at 431.
[373] (1874) L.R. 2 C.C.R. 119.
[374] He did an act which was more than merely preparatory to an offence under the Offences Against the Person Act 1861 s.47 (assault occasioning actual bodily harm) and intended to bring about this offence; see below, para.6–002. It has been argued by Professor Ashworth that in most cases involving transferred malice there is the option to convict the defendant of an attempt and this may render the doctrine superfluous; see A.J. Ashworth, "Transferred Malice and Punishment for Unforeseen Consequences" in P. Glazebrook, ed., *Reshaping the Criminal Law* (1978).
[375] Under the Criminal Damage Act 1971 s.1 he has brought about the actus reus of this offence and may have been reckless as to causing that damage within the current definition of that state of mind for criminal damage; see below, para.10–001.
[376] G. Williams, *Criminal Law: The General Part* 2nd edn (1961), paras 44 and 48.
[377] [1996] 2 W.L.R. 412; [1997] 3 All E.R. 936. See generally on the Court of Appeal stage, M. Seneviratne "Pre-Natal Injury and Transferred Malice: The Inverted Other" (1996) 59 M.L.R. 884; J. Beaumont, "The Unborn Child and the Limits of Homicide" (1997) 61 J.C.L. 86.

pregnant girlfriend causing premature birth of her child, which lived for 120 days and then died. D was charged with murder of the child but acquitted on the direction of the judge on the basis that D did not intend to kill or seriously injure a human being.[378] The Court of Appeal ruled that it was possible to use the doctrine of transferred malice to convict D of murder. D's intention to cause the mother serious bodily harm could be transferred to the child once it had been born alive and so long as a causal link between the stabbing and the ultimate death of the child could be established, a conviction for murder could be sustained. The same result would follow if D had intended to injure only the foetus; until birth the foetus was as much a part of the woman as any of her limbs or organs.[379] Lord Taylor C.J. held that Professor Williams' first limitation did not apply to this case since D was aware that his girlfriend was pregnant; thus the ultimate victim was reasonably foreseeable. Nevertheless Lord Taylor C.J. held that it would have made no difference had D been unaware of the pregnancy. Lord Taylor dealt similarly with Professor Williams' second limitation that the doctrine does not apply when the ultimate result is brought about in a manner different from that intended by the defendant. In *Attorney-General's Reference (No.3 of 1994)* the defendant had intended any harm to be caused by a knife wound, whereas the actual cause of death was the result of premature birth. Lord Taylor held that so long as the prosecution could establish a chain of causation between the initial stabbing, to the premature birth and finally to the infant's death, the case was made out.

On appeal to the House of Lords, their Lordships quashed the conviction for murder and substituted one for unlawful act manslaughter.[380] Lord Mustill, whose speech is the leading speech on the issue of murder, concluded that there could be no conviction for murder since this would require an unwarranted extension of the antiquated doctrine of transferred malice. Lord Mustill, however, did accept that the doctrine was well-established in English law and that it was not for the House of Lords to abolish it. It is undoubtedly true that the courts recognise a doctrine of transferred malice in cases such as *Hyam*, *Mitchell* and *Latimer*. The ultimate victim is treated as if he were the intended victim from the start and it is, therefore, possible in these cases to find some compatability between the original intention and the actual result. Lord Mustill continued:

> "There is no such compatibility here. The defendant intended to commit and did commit an immediate crime of violence to the mother. He committed no relevant violence to the foetus, which was not a person, either at the time or in the future, and intended no harm to the foetus or to the human person which it would become. If fictions are useful, and they can be, they are only damaged by straining them beyond their limits. I would not overstrain the idea of transferred malice by trying to make it fit the present case."[381]

There is a clear indication from their Lordships that the doctrine of transferred malice is an anachronistic exception to modern day principles, but that in so far as it is applied to

[378] See below, para.7–004.
[379] [1996] 2 W.L.R. 412: Lord Taylor C.J. was categoric on this point, stating at 422, "In the eyes of the law the foetus is taken to be a part of the mother until it has an existence independent of the mother. Thus an intention to cause serious bodily injury to the foetus is an intention to cause serious bodily injury to a part of the mother just as an intention to injure her arm or her leg would be so viewed. Thus consideration whether a charge of murder can arise where the focus of the defendant's intention is exclusively the foetus falls to be considered under the head of transferred malice, as is the case where the intention is focused exclusively or partially upon the mother herself."
[380] See below, para.7–038.
[381] [1997] 3 All E.R. 936 at 949. Since the House of Lords did not accept the proposition advanced by the Court of Appeal that until birth the foetus was, in effect, the mother (see below, para.7–004), it would have necessitated a double transfer of malice on the facts of the case. First the malice would have to be transferred from the mother to the foetus and then from the foetus to the child as yet unborn.

cases such as *Mitchell* and *Latimer* it is still part of English criminal law. However, it should not be used as the basis for a modern extension of the rule to cover the facts of *Att-Gen's Reference*. It is difficult to see how the doctrine is outdated. Lord Mustill concentrated upon the decisions in *Pembliton* and *Latimer* and said that he found it difficult to construct a modern law of murder on these two cases. But why should we try to found a law of murder on those two cases. Surely the doctrine has worked well in the modern cases of *Hyam* and *Mitchell*. Some years ago drug dealers shot and killed a small boy in Bolton. The killers were trying to shoot the boy's father, but they killed the boy by mistake. The public would be outraged if these killers were not to be found guilty of murder. The killers had the intention to kill a human being and this is what they did. The matter is as simple as that; it only serves to muddy the picture by talking about transferred malice. If D digs a hole and puts spikes in the bottom with the intention that P should fall into it and be killed, when P does eventually fall into the pit and is killed, there is no doubt that D has committed murder. It would make no difference that it is V, a stranger, who falls into the hole and is killed, nor even that V was not alive at the time that D dug the hole.

5. MISTAKE AS A DEFENCE TO CRIME

A. The Basic Problem

2–082   Consider D who mistakenly believes that the dark shape in the bushes is an escaped gorilla and shoots at it. The shape turns out to be P who is killed by D's shot. D may well be charged with murder. The prosecution will have to prove that D intended to kill or seriously injure a human being. If, however, the jury accepts D's version of events, it is clear that D did not intend seriously to injure or to kill a human being. The rule can be stated quite simply; *a mistake will afford a defence if it results in the accused not forming the mens rea required by the offence with which he is charged.* It follows that if the accused makes a mistake as to an issue for which *no mens rea* is required, the mistake will be irrelevant and will afford him no defence. In the famous case of *Prince*[382] the accused was charged with abducting a girl under the age of 16. The Court for Crown Cases Reserved held that the prosecution did not have to prove that he was aware or even ought to have been aware that she was under 16. It was sufficient that he abducted her and that she was in fact under 16. His mistaken belief that she was 19, a belief the court found entirely reasonable, was irrelevant and afforded him no defence since it did not prevent the prosecution from proving all the ingredients of the crime.[383]

The basic point that a mistaken belief will afford a defence if it negatives the required mens rea is further illustrated by those cases in which the accused says that he did not realise a particular act was illegal; this situation is better referred to as ignorance of the law and everyone will know the old maxim that "ignorance of the law is no defence". In *Esop*[384] the accused told the court that buggery between males was not an offence in his country and at the time he committed the act he assumed the same position would apply here. The accused had made a mistake, but the important point is that it was not a mistake which would affect the mens rea required by the offence. Under the law as it then was, on a charge of buggery, the prosecution would have to prove that the accused intended to have sexual intercourse

---

[382] (1875) L.R. 2 C.C.R. 154.
[383] See, also *Hibbert* (1869) L.R. 1 C.C.R. 184. See generally G. Williams, "The Theory of Excuses" [1982] Crim. L.R. 732.
[384] (1836) 7 C&P 456. See also *Lightfoot* (1993) 97 Cr.App.R. 24.

with a male; it was no part of the prosecution's case to prove that the accused knew that buggery was an offence under the laws of this country. His mistaken belief accordingly afforded him no defence.[385] The prosecution must prove that the accused was aware of the facts which made the action criminal, but not that he knew those acts were criminal.[386] The issue has arisen very recently in a controversial context in *Christian v The Queen (The Pitcairn Islands)*,[387] focusing on prosecutions brought against Pitcairn Islands residents for rape and assault against young women on the island. The defendants' contention that they lacked specific awareness of extant offences under English law was disregarded; their conduct, self-evidently, was morally culpable and they appreciated the unlawfulness of their egregious behaviour.[388]

However, it would be wrong to assume that the maxim "ignorance of the law is no defence" is always applicable; the question, as always, is whether the prosecution can establish the necessary mens rea of the offence. The crime of theft requires that the prosecution prove that the accused dishonestly appropriated property belonging to another with the intention of permanently depriving the other of the property. Consider a person from another country who believes that the law which operates in his country, that people of his status may take goods from a supermarket without payment, equally applies here. It would be no defence to a charge of theft that he was unaware that theft was a crime. However, his belief about the applicability of his country's laws would probably mean that he did not act dishonestly. Ignorance of the law in such a situation would negative the mens rea of the offence.

It is easy to overcomplicate the issue of mistake. So, rather than ask *general* questions **2–083** about when the law requires a mistake to be honest, or when a mistake must be honest *and* reasonable, we prefer to ask "*What is the mens rea of the offence under consideration?*" and to work from there. Consider these examples.

Let us start with the crime of murder. The prosecution must prove that the accused intended to kill (or seriously injure) a human being; unless the prosecution can establish this intention it will lose. If the jury accept that the accused honestly believed that he was shooting at a wooden post and not at a human being, the prosecution cannot make out the necessary mens rea. It makes no difference that the jury believe that his mistake is totally unreasonable.[389]

The crime of battery requires that the prosecution prove either that the accused intended to apply unlawful force to the victim or that he consciously took an unjustified risk of so doing.[390] If the jury conclude that it never entered the accused's head that the stone he was throwing at a window might strike an innocent pedestrian, the prosecution have failed to make out the necessary mens rea of battery.

Different considerations apply where the crime requires only proof of negligence. There are not many examples of crimes imposing liability for negligence, but careless driving[391] is

[385] Homosexual acts between consenting males aged 16 or over are no longer offences.
[386] See below, para.7–118.
[387] [2006] UKPC 47.
[388] Note the assertion of Lord Woolf, placing an incumbent responsibility on individuals: "The sheer volume of the law in England, much of which would be inapplicable . . . creates real problems of access even to lawyers unless they are experts in the particular field of law in question. The criminal law can only operate . . . if the *onus is firmly placed on a person*, who is or ought to be on notice that conduct he is intending to embark on may contravene the criminal law, to take the action that is open to him to find out what are the provisions of that law"; [2006] UKPC 47 at [44].
[389] In *Cogan and Leak* (below, para.4–005) the jury were asked whether (a) the accused honestly held a belief and (b) whether his belief was reasonable. The jury concluded his belief was honest but unreasonable, suggesting that jurors are capable of understanding the difference.
[390] *Cunningham* recklessness.
[391] Contrary to the Road Traffic Act 1988 s.3 as substituted by the Road Traffic Act 1991 s.2.

one. Here the prosecution need prove only that the accused's driving fell below the standard of the reasonable motorist. Therefore if D is charged with backing out of his driveway into the path of an oncoming vehicle, it would be no defence to show that he honestly believed the road to be clear. An honestly held belief will not negative an allegation that the accused was driving negligently; only a reasonable mistake will suffice. It follows from this that whenever a court requires that a mistaken belief should be both honestly and reasonably held, the court is in effect imposing liability for negligence on that element of the actus reus. Consider also the crime of rape. The offence is committed where D, who believes the non-consenting victim is actually consenting to penetration, has no reasonable grounds for that belief. Rape is thus a crime of negligence.

Where a court holds that on a given element of the actus reus neither an honest nor a reasonable mistake will afford a defence, the court is indicating that liability on this element of the crime is strict. Thus in *Prince*[392] the accused's reasonable mistake that the girl was over 16 was irrelevant. The prosecution had only to establish that the girl was under 16; mistakes by the accused as to her age were immaterial.

In summary, we can say that when intention or subjective recklessness is required as to an element of the crime, an honest mistake will suffice to negative the mens rea. When the crime requires proof of negligence, a reasonable mistake will be required. Where strict liability exists, mistake is irrelevant. This summary is represented in the following table:

Mens rea of offence in question	Type of mistake which will negative mens rea
Intention	Honest
Recklessness	Honest
Negligence	Honest and reasonable
Strict Liability	None

B. Mistake and Lawfulness

2–084   Under the old (that is prior to the Sexual Offences Act 2003) law on rape, the House of Lords had held, in *DPP v Morgan*,[393] that an honest (albeit unreasonable) belief that the victim was consenting negatived the mens rea for the offence. It is clear from the 2003 Act that such a mistake must now be both honest and reasonable.

Despite dicta in certain cases that the decision in *Morgan* applied only to the crime of rape,[394] it is now clear that it had, and continues to have, wider effect. Until the decision of the House of Lords in *Morgan*, it was generally accepted that an accused who used force in self-defence, or in the defence of another, was entitled to be judged on the facts as he *reasonably* believed them to be. It is conceivable that had the Lords in *Morgan* been asked to consider the line of cases on self-defence and allied defences, they might have held that in defence situations the accused should be judged on facts that he reasonably believed to exist. They were not, however, invited to consider these cases. In *Albert v Lavin*[395] the Divisional

[392] See above, para.2–082.
[393] [1976] A.C. 182.
[394] *Phekoo* [1981] 1 W.L.R. 1117.
[395] [1981] 1 All E.R. 628; affirmed [1981] 3 All E.R. 878.

Court was concerned with the requisite mens rea for a battery arising out of a queue jumping dispute at a bus stop. The accused had used force on another and claimed that, on the facts that he believed to exist, he was justified in using such force. A battery requires proof that the defendant either intended to or recklessly applied unlawful force to another. Defence counsel, basing himself on *Morgan*, argued that he should be judged on the facts he genuinely believed to exist. However, the court held that while lack of consent was part of the core prohibited act of battery,[396] and therefore an honest belief that the person had consented to the touching would be a defence, issues of justification were not part of the core prohibited act[397] and thus a mistaken belief in the existence of circumstances which would justify the use of force had to be based on reasonable grounds. In *Kimber*[398] the accused was charged with indecent assault and he pleaded not guilty on the basis that he believed that the woman was consenting.[399] The Court of Appeal held that the absence of consent was a part of the central prohibited act. The prosecution have to prove that the accused intentionally or recklessly applied non-consensual force. If the jury concluded that the accused genuinely believed that the complainant was consenting, the prosecution could not establish the necessary mens rea.

At this stage the situation was absurd. To establish a battery the prosecution had to prove that the accused had intentionally or recklessly applied unlawful force to another. The word unlawful surely embraces both the lack of consent and the lack of justification. Why is lack of consent any more central to the definition of the offence than the lack of justification? Lawton L.J. in *Kimber* recognised that there was no merit in the distinction taken in *Albert v Lavin*, though his remarks on this issue were obiter since lack of justification was not an issue in *Kimber*.

Finally the matter was resolved by the Court of Appeal in *Gladstone Williams*.[400] W had **2–085** witnessed what he took to be a man, M, beating up a youth. In fact, M was trying to arrest the youth for the mugging of an old lady. M falsely told W that he was a police officer trying to effect an arrest. He was unable to produce his warrant card and so W took it upon himself to protect the youth. In the course of the struggle M received several injuries. W was charged with assault and pleaded that he believed he was behaving properly to protect a youth from a beating. At his trial the recorder told the jury that W would have a defence only if he honestly and reasonably believed that his intervention and action was necessary to save the young man from a beating. On appeal against conviction the Court of Appeal held that the mental element necessary to establish guilt was an intention to apply unlawful force to the victim. Force may be applied lawfully where the victim consents, where the accused is acting in self-defence and where the defendant is using reasonable force either to prevent the commission of a crime or to assist in a lawful arrest.[401] It is for the prosecution to prove that the accused intended to apply the force unlawfully. If the defendant mistakenly believes that the victim is consenting or that it is necessary to defend himself or that a crime is being committed which he intends to prevent, the prosecution have not made out the charge. Lord Lane C.J. then asked whether it made any difference that the mistake the accused had made was one no reasonable person would have made:

---

[396] Just as intercourse with a non-consenting woman is the core prohibited act in rape.
[397] See above, para.2–004, Professor Lanham's definition of crime as being actus reus and mens rea plus the absence of justification.
[398] [1983] 1 W.L.R. 1118.
[399] Indecent assault required proof of a basic battery to which consent may be a defence. For sexual assault see below, para.7–133.
[400] (1984) 78 Cr.App.R. 276.
[401] See, Criminal Law Act 1967 s.3, below, para.5–046.

"The reasonableness or unreasonableness of the defendant's belief is material to the question of whether the belief was held by the defendant at all. If the belief was in fact held, its unreasonableness, so far as guilt or innocence is concerned, is neither here nor there. It is irrelevant. Were it otherwise, the defendant would be convicted because he was negligent in failing to recognise that the victim was not consenting or that a crime was not being committed and so on."[402]

Lord Lane C.J. drew attention to the need to ensure that the jury was aware that the prosecution bore the burden of proving beyond reasonable doubt that the applicaton of force was unlawful. That if the defendant may have been labouring under a mistake as to the facts he must be judged according to his mistaken view of the facts. It was very easy to leave the jury with the impression that it is up to the defendant to prove that he was or thought he was entitled to use force to defend himself or to prevent crime. This is a misunderstanding of the burden of proof and must be guarded against by judges.

This approach has been confirmed by the Privy Council in *Beckford v R*,[403] where in a murder case Lord Griffiths gave approval to a model direction for judges prepared by the Judicial Studies Board. The direction contains the following guidance:

"Whether the plea is self-defence or defence of another, if the defendant may have been labouring under a mistake as to the facts, he must be judged according to his mistaken view of the facts; that is so whether the mistake was, on an objective view, a reasonable mistake or not."[404]

Lord Griffiths remarked that the fears of some, that the abandonment of the objective approach[405] would result in the success of too many spurious self-defence claims, simply had not been realised. It would appear that juries are capable of understanding the difference between an honest mistake and a reasonable mistake.[406]

MENS REA: GENERAL READING

2–086   Birch, D.J., "The Foresight Saga: The Biggest Mistake of All?" [1988] Crim.L.R. 4.

Duff, R.A., *Intention, Agency and Criminal Liability: Philosophy of Action and the Criminal Law* (1990).

Gardner, M.R., "The Mens Rea Enigma: Observations on the Role of Motive in the Criminal Law Past and Present" (1993) Utah L.Rev. 635.

Gardner, S., "Recklessness Refined" (1993) 109 L.Q.R. 21.

Goff, The Rt Hon. Lord, "The Mental Element in the Crime of Murder" (1988) 104 L.Q.R. 30.

Horder, J., "Varieties of Intention, Criminal Attempts and Endangerment" (1994) 14 *Legal Studies* 335.

Kugler, I., "Conditional Oblique Intention" [2004] Crim.L.R. 284.

---

[402] (1984) 78 Cr.App.R. 276 at 281.
[403] [1988] A.C. 130; see generally A. Simester, "Mistakes in Defence" (1992) 12 O.J.L.S. 295.
[404] [1988] A.C. 130 at 145.
[405] i.e. reasonable belief; see also *Dadson* (1850) 175 E.R. 499, above, para.2–002; see also B. Hogan, "The Dadson Principle" [1989] Crim.L.R. 679.
[406] For the effect of mistakes induced by intoxication see, generally, below, paras 5–032—5–033, but especially *O'Grady*, below, para.5–032. For mistake as to the amount of force which is reasonable in the circumstances see below, para.5–052.

Lacey, N., "A Clear Concept of Intention: Ellusions or Illusory" (1993) 56 M.L.R. 621.

Norrie, A., "Oblique Intention and Legal Politics" [1989] Crim.L.R. 793.

Norrie, A., "Between Orthodox Subjectivism and Moral Contextualism" [2006] Crim.L.R. 486.

Parker, J.S., " The Economics of Mens Rea" (1993) 79 Va.L.Rev. 741.

Pedain, A., "Intention and the Terrorist Example" [2003] Crim.L.R. 579.

Robinson P.H. and Grall J.A., "Element Analysis in Defences in Defining Criminal Liability: The Model Penal Code and Beyond" (1983) 35 Stan. L.R. 681.

Simester, A.P.S and Chan, W., "Intention Thus Far" [1997] Crim.L.R. 704.

Sullivan, G., "Intent, Subjective Recklessness and Culpability" (1992) 12 O.J.L.S. 380.

Syrota, G., "A Radical Change in the Law of Recklessness" [1982] Crim.L.R. 97.

Williams, G., "Divergent Interpretation of Recklessness" (1982) 132 N.L.J. 289.

Williams, G., "Oblique Intention" (1987) 46 C.L.J. 417.

Williams, G., "The Mens Rea for Murder: Leave it Alone" (1989) 105 L.Q.R. 397.

Chapter 3

STRICT LIABILITY

In the last chapter we saw that in some situations the courts have imposed what is known as **3–001** strict liability; in other words they have dispensed with the need for mens rea as to at least one aspect of the actus reus. Thus in *Prince*[1] the accused's honest and even reasonable mistake did not provide any defence to the charge of abduction[2] whilst in *Larsonneur*[3] and *Winzar*,[4] involving so-called "status offences", it even appeared that liability was absolute with no defences open to the accused. In this chapter we shall examine in more detail the phenomenon of strict liability, and try to discover whether there is any way of predicting whether a court will find strict liability in a given piece of legislation.

It is an offence under s.5 of the Road Traffic Act 1988 to drive or attempt to drive a motorvehicle on a road or other public place having consumed alcohol to such an extent that the amount of alcohol which has passed into the blood stream at the time a specimen of breath is taken exceeds the prescribed limit, which is at present 35mg of alcohol per 100ml of breath. Most readers will immediately recognise this as the breathalyser legislation under which the motorist who fails a preliminary breath test at the side of the road will be asked to provide a specimen of breath for analysis on an intoximeter. If this analysis proves positive the motorist will be charged with an offence which carries with it the mandatory penalty of disqualification for at least a year. But what mens rea must the prosecution establish in order to gain a conviction? The accused might be pretty sure he is over the prescribed limit; more likely he is aware of the risk but nevertheless drives. Possibly he honestly believes that 10 pints of beer will not take him over the limit—this would be a negligent even if not a grossly negligent belief. In some cases he may honestly and totally reasonably believe that he is not over the limit—for example in the cases where his orange juice has been laced by a "friend". Which of these should the law punish? Probably the man in the street would say that the first three ought to be guilty, but not the man who has had his drink laced. This would be based upon the notion that if you know you have had some alcohol you should know that you may be breaking the law, but the man with the laced drink may be totally unaware of the risk he is taking.

However, the courts have held that even the laced-drink man should be convicted, though he may have a chance of avoiding the disqualification penalty.[5] In other words the courts are

[1] (1875) L.R. 2 C.C.R. 154.
[2] See above, para.2–082.
[3] (1933) 24 Cr.App.R. 74 (above, para.2–014). See generally, D. Lanham, "*Larsonneur* Revisited" [1976] Crim.L.R. 276.
[4] *The Times,* March 28, 1983; see above para.2–014.
[5] See, s.34(1) of the Road Traffic Offenders Act 1988.

saying that not only does the prosecution not have to establish that the accused knew or even should have known that he was over the limit, but also that there is no need to show that he was even aware that he had consumed alcohol. In the language of the previous chapter we have imposed liability for blameless inadvertence.

This raises further questions. Who is responsible for the development of such crimes? How do we know which offences and which elements of those offences will attract strict liability? Is there any defence to such crimes? What justification can there be for such a development?

1. WHO CREATED THIS GENRE OF CRIMES?

3–002   The fact that in almost every case on which strict liability is imposed the offence is created by statute would tend to suggest that it was Parliament who created strict liability, and indeed in many cases the judges have said it was clearly the intention of Parliament to impose strict liability. In some ways this may be true. The courts are expected to give effect to the will of Parliament as expressed in the statutes, but it is extremely unlikely that the drafters of nineteenth-century legislation had any clear cut views that the use of certain words in statutes would lead the courts to impose strict liability. Today parliamentary draftsmen will be, or should be, aware that the use of certain expressions will lead the courts to impose strict liability and so their use can be taken to express Parliament's intention to impose strict liability; if the Law Commission's Criminal Code[6] or something akin to it is passed the legislators will have clear guidance as to how various forms of legislation will be interpreted. In the nineteenth century, however, it would be wrong to suggest that the legislators had any such clear cut ideas. The truth is that it was the nineteenth century judges who began to develop the concept of strict liability, and since that time much has come to depend upon the outlook of the senior criminal judge, the Lord Chief Justice.[7] The haphazard system of the common law has also meant that since courts tend to interpret only that part of the crime which is necessary for the decision in the particular case, completely irrational differences can exist in the elements of the same crime. For instance, in *Hibbert*[8] the court held that the prosecution had to establish that the accused was aware that the girl was in the possession of her parents, while on the same statute in *Prince*,[9] the differently constituted Court for Crown Cases Reserved held that the prosecution did not have to prove that the accused was aware that the girl was under 16. Thus, mens rea was attached to one part of the actus reus, but not to another, and there is no truly logical reason to justify this.

2. HOW CAN CRIMES OF STRICT LIABILITY BE IDENTIFIED?

3–003   With very few exceptions (public nuisance,[10] outraging public decency,[11] criminal libel and parts of contempt of court[12]) crimes of strict liability are statutory offences. It is highly

---

[6] See above, para.2–009.
[7] See, generally, G. Richardson, "Strict Liability for Regulatory Crime: the Empirical Research" [1987] Crim.L.R. 295.
[8] (1869) L.R. 1 C.C.R. 184.
[9] (1875) L.R. 2 C.C.R. 154. Note that s.55 of the Offences Against the Person Act 1861 was replaced by s.20 of the Sexual Offences Act 1956. The s.20 offence has been repealed by the Sexual Offences Act 2003.
[10] *Stephens* (1866) L.R. 1 Q.B. 702; and *Shorrock* [1993] 3 All E.R. 917.
[11] *Gibson* [1990] 2 Q.B. 619.
[12] *Evening Standard Co Ltd* [1954] 1 Q.B. 578.

unlikely that we shall see the creation of any new common law crimes of strict liability. Since, in reality, we can say that strict liability operates only in respect of statutory crimes, the principles of statutory interpretation operate and the courts are supposed to try to discover the intention of Parliament from the wording of the statute. One principle of statutory interpretation is that in statutes creating criminal offences there is a presumption that mens rea will be required even where it is not specifically mentioned. An example of a crime which expressly provides for mens rea is s.1(1) of the Criminal Damage Act 1971, where for the basic offence of criminal damage it is expressly provided that the accused must, without lawful excuse, intentionally or recklessly destroy or damage property belonging to another. On the other hand many offences contain no reference at all to the requirement for mens rea and here the courts should start from the principle that mens rea is required. Thus, common assault under s.39 of the Criminal Justice Act 1988 is punishable with six months' imprisonment and/or a fine not exceeding £5,000. The courts have interpreted this to mean that the prosecution must prove that the accused either intended to cause the victim to apprehend immediate and unlawful violence or that he foresaw that his actions would have this effect.

However this presumption in favour of mens rea is rebuttable and we must now examine the factors which are likely to cause its rebuttal.

A. The Wording of the Act

As with any other statute one of the court's duties is to try to ascertain the intention of **3–004** Parliament, not from any extraneous sources, but from the wording of the Act itself. If the Draft Criminal Code were enacted then the courts would know that certain wording indicated that Parliament intended the crime to be one of strict liability. At present there is no guarantee that any given form of wording will create an offence of strict liability. On the other hand there are one or two discernible patterns. Thus, certain words have received fairly consistent interpretation as requiring or dispensing with the need for mens rea. We will now have a look at some of these "key" words.

"Permitting or allowing"

Where it is an offence to permit or allow another to do a certain act, the prosecution will **3–005** normally be expected to prove that the accused was aware of the circumstances which made the act unlawful or deliberately avoided finding out.[13] Thus, under a statute creating an offence of permitting or allowing another to drive a motorvehicle with defective brakes, the prosecution would have to prove that the accused knew that his vehicle's brakes were defective before he could be said to have permitted or allowed the other to drive it.[14] You must remember, however, that he does not have to know that it is illegal to permit or allow another to drive a vehicle with defective brakes. On the other hand where the statute makes it an offence to *drive* or *use* a vehicle with defective brakes the courts have tended to say that the prosecution need not prove that the driver or user knew that the brakes were defective.[15]

---

[13] But cf. *Gammon (Hong Kong) Ltd v Att-Gen of Hong Kong* [1985] A.C. 1, below, para.3–012.
[14] See, e.g. *James & Son Ltd v Smee* [1955] 1 Q.B. 78. In contrast the offence of "permitting" the use of an uninsured motorvehicle, considered in *DPP v Fisher* [1991] Crim.L.R. 787, was held to be an offence of strict liability. The jurisprudence is not always consistent in this area.
[15] See, e.g. *Green v Burnett* [1955] 1 Q.B. 78; [1954] 3 All E.R. 273.

Cause

3–006 Where statutes create an offence of causing something to happen the courts should, according to the House of Lords in *Alphacell v Woodward*,[16] adopt a common sense approach—if reasonable people would say that the accused has caused something to happen then a conviction is appropriate without the need for mens rea. Thus, in *Wrothwell Ltd v Yorkshire Water Authority*[17] it was held that where the accused had poured a toxic chemical down a drain believing, wrongly, that it would find its way into the main sewer when, in fact, it entered a local stream, it was right to say that he had caused a poisonous matter to enter a stream.

Of course, there are many crimes such as murder which require a prohibited result. What the present line of cases shows is that the express use of the word *cause* in a statute is not likely to lead the court to require mens rea, as exemplified by the House of Lords decision in *Environment Agency v Empress Car Co Ltd*.[18]

Possession

3–007 The word possession has caused many problems for the courts over the years. It is the basis of many offences that the accused be *in possession* of a prohibited substance. Since many of the offences involve the possession of prohibited drugs and since these offences are often interpreted as imposing strict liability, the courts have from time to time attempted to mitigate the severity that would be caused by strict liability by holding that the word "possession" has a mental as well as physical aspect. For example, would we wish to convict an innocent shopper (A) of being in possession of cannabis when the cannabis had been placed in his shopping bag by a drug supplier who believed that he was just about to be arrested? Does the shopper possess the drug? Suppose that just before he left home, and without his knowledge, his wife slipped the keys to the house into his raincoat pocket; is he in possession of these keys while he is walking round the shops? If a pickpocket took the keys out of his pocket, would the pickpocket not have stolen them from him? Yet is he any more in possession of the keys than the cannabis?

In the realms of possession of drugs the House of Lords in *Warner v Metropolitan Police Commissioner*,[19] a case under previous legislation but still applicable to the definition of possession, accepted that A would not be in possession of a drug which had been slipped into his pocket or shopping basket without his knowledge. In these types of case we are saying that the prosecution have failed to establish possession.[20] What then of the situation where the accused knows he is in possession of a substance, but is genuinely unaware of the nature of the substance? Suppose A has been given some tablets and told they are aspirin when they are, in fact, heroin. He is clearly in possession of the tablets and this is as far as the mental element in possession goes. Unless the controlling legislation provides that it is an offence knowingly to possess heroin or unless the statute provides a defence of mistake of fact[21] he is guilty of possessing the prohibited substance. In other words the word "possession" does not involve knowledge of the nature of the thing one possesses.

Does this mean, therefore, that if you know you possess a substance, but you do not know what it is because it is in a locked container, you are in possession of that substance?

---

[16] [1972] A.C. 824; see below, para.3–014.
[17] [1984] Crim.L.R. 43.
[18] [1999] 2 A.C. 22.
[19] [1969] 2 A.C. 256.
[20] By way of contrast consider the scenario where you place an old item of clothing in an attic and, subsequently, have totally forgotten about it. You are still in "possession" of that particular item of clothing.
[21] See, e.g. the Misuse of Drugs Act 1971 s.28, below, para.3–008.

Suppose that you believe that it is some photographic equipment, but in fact it is heroin tablets. Can you be said to be in possession of heroin for purposes of s.5 of the Misuse of Drugs Act 1971?[22] The House of Lords took a more lenient view of such container cases. Their Lordships said that if you were completely mistaken as to the nature but not the quality of the contents, have had no opportunity to examine the contents and do not suspect that there is anything wrong with the contents, then you are not, for the purpose of the type of offences in s.5, in possession of the contents. The reference to a distinction between nature and quality means that if you believed the contents to be photographic equipment and it was heroin, then this would be a mistake as to the nature of the contents. On the other hand if you thought the package contained aspirin and it turned out to be heroin, then this is a mistake as to quality; you thought it was a drug—and it was—you were merely mistaken as to what sort of drug. Although cases such as *Warner* must now be read subject to the provisions of the Misuse of Drugs Act 1971, *Warner* remains as general authority on the meaning of the word "possesses" in situations where the proscribed goods are in a container. Where, however, there is no container, stricter provisions apply. In *Marriott*[23] the accused possessed a penknife to the blade of which adhered 0.03 grains of cannabis. On appeal against conviction the court held that the proper direction to a jury in such a case would be that the accused was guilty of possessing cannabis if he knew that there was a substance on the penknife even if he did not know what that substance was. It was not, however, sufficient to prove that he knew he was in possession of the penknife. A similar approach was adopted in *Searle v Randolph*,[24] a case decided prior to the entry into force of the Misuse of Drugs Act 1971. The defendant was in possession of a number of cigarette ends, one of which was found to contain a foreign substance, some three milligrams of cannabis. It was held that the difference between a cigarette end composed of or filled wholly with tobacco and one filled with a substance including cannabis was the same kind of distinction between an aspirin tablet and a heroin tablet. It was sufficient for the prosecutor to prove that the defendant had possession of the cigarette ends and at least one of them contained a measurable quantity of cannabis; the prosecutor was not required to prove specific knowledge by the defendant that the end contained cannabis.

These cases dealt with the meaning of the word "possess". Section 28 of the Misuse of **3–008** Drugs Act 1971 provides certain defences for those charged with the possession of controlled drugs. For example, s.28(3)(b)(i) provides that the defendant shall be acquitted if he proves that he neither believed nor suspected nor had reason to suspect that the substance or product in question was a controlled drug. In other words, applying the provision to the facts in *Searle v Randolph*, a defendant must be acquitted if the jury or magistrates are satisfied that he believed on reasonable grounds that the cigarette contained only tobacco. The Court of Appeal in *McNamara*[25] appears to have used this provision to find a simpler approach to the container situations which avoids the need to distinguish between differences in kind and quality. The court held that it was for the prosecution to prove that the defendant; (i) had control of the container; (ii) knew that he had control of

---

[22] By s.5(1) it is an offence for an individual to have a controlled drug in his possession. The controlled drugs are specified in the second schedule of the Act and divide into three classes: Class A includes heroin, cocaine and LSD; Class B includes amphetamine and cannabis; Class C includes pemoline and benzphetamine. Unauthorised possession offences are punishable on conviction on indictment with imprisonment for up to seven, five or two years according to whether the drug belongs to Class A, B or C. The supply of such controlled drugs is subject to penalties of life imprisonment, 14 years, or seven years depending on the drug category.
[23] [1971] 1 All E.R. 595.
[24] [1972] Crim.L.R. 779. See also *Champ* [1982] 108 where the appellate court applied a similar rationale, by analogy to "possession" cases, in convicting D of "cultivating" any plant of the genus cannabis.
[25] (1988) 87 Cr.App.R. 246.

the container; and (iii) that the box contained something which was in fact the drug alleged. It was then up to the defendant to bring himself within the provisions of s.28(3)(b)(i) by proving that he neither believed or suspected nor had reason to suspect that the substance or product in question was (any sort of) controlled drug. However, in *Lewis*[26] it was determined that an absent tenant could be convicted of drug possession on their premises, with the only proviso being the existence of a viable opportunity to discover the substances. The decision in *Lewis* serves to highlight that the word "possession" will continue to cause problems.

In the related context of firearm possession the legislation has been purposively interpreted to impose a tight control on the use of highly dangerous weapons. Strict liability has been applied to achieve effective control, and reflect policy concerns over the potentially disastrous consequences of firearm misuse. In *Bradish*,[27] for example, the defendant was found to be in possession of a metal spray aerosol canister marked "Force 10 Super Magnum CS" which contained CS gas. He was charged with possessing a prohibited weapon without the authority of the Secretary of State contrary to s.5(1)(b) of the Firearms Act 1968. The earlier authorities of *Howells*[28] and *Hussain*[29] had clearly established that strict liability applied to s.1(1) of the firearms legislation. This was expanded by the Court of Appeal in *Bradish* to cover the more serious provisions contained within s.5(1).[30] It was not necessary for the prosecution to prove that the defendant had known that it was such a weapon. No similar defence akin to s.28 of the Misuse of Drugs Act 1971 applies to the firearms legislation. Accordingly, it would be no defence for the defendant to prove that he had not known, or could not reasonably have been expected to have known, that an article was a prohibited weapon, even where the weapon was concealed in a container which was not itself a prohibited weapon. A differently constituted appellate court in the later case of *Harrison*[31] has held that strict liability also applies to the offence under s.19 of the Firearms Act 1968, of having a loaded shotgun in a public place. All that need be proved is knowledge of the fact of possession, not of the nature and quality of the thing possessed. The public welfare concerns at issue here were vividly exemplified by Auld J. in *Bradish*:

"To the argument that the innocent possessor or carrier of firearms or prohibited weapons or parts of them is at risk of unfair conviction under these provisions, there has to be balanced the important public policy behind the legislation of protecting the public from the misuse of such dangerous weapons. Just as the Chicago-style gangster might plausibly maintain that he believed his violin case to contain a violin, not a sub-machine gun, so it might be difficult to meet a London lout's assertion that he did not know an unmarked plastic bottle in his possession contained ammonia rather than something to drink."[32]

---

[26] (1988) 87 Cr.App.R. 270; [1988] Crim.L.R. 517.

[27] [1990] 1 Q.B. 981.

[28] [1977] Q.B. 614. It was no defence that D honestly believed that the firearm in his possession was in fact an antique heirloom.

[29] [1981] 1 W.L.R. 416.

[30] Note by s.1(1) it is an offence for a person to have in his possession, or to purchase or acquire, a firearm to which s.1 applies without holding a firearms certificate. By s.5(1) it is an offence to have a "prohibited weapon" without written authority of the Secretary of State, These prohibited weapons are weapons that will not be of general use except by the armed forces. They include self-loading or pump action rifles, smooth-bore guns, smooth-bore revolver guns and rocket launchers.

[31] [1996] Crim.L.R. 200.

[32] [1990] 1 Q.B. 981 at 992.

Knowingly

One would think that the word knowingly could cause few problems and that it would **3–009** indicate an express requirement for mens rea. This is true to the extent that it clearly requires mens rea as to the word or clause it qualifies, but it is not always easy to identify exactly what it does qualify. For example, in *Hallam*[33] the accused was charged with knowingly possessing explosives (gunpowder and gelignite). Does this mean that the accused knows that he is in possession of a substance which is later identified as an explosive even though he thought it was soap powder, or does it mean that he must be both aware that he possesses a substance and that he further knows the substance to be an explosive? In the case cited the court held that the prosecution must prove that the accused knew that the substance was an explosive. Indeed to have held otherwise would have been to render the word "knowingly" superfluous since, as we have seen, the word "possess" is usually held to require at least the knowledge that the accused has something in his possession This was affirmed in *Berry (No.3)*[34] where the Court of Appeal interpreted mens rea, as being a specific ingredient of the offence under s.4 of the Explosive Substances Act 1883. This was particularly important in *Berry (No.3)* because, unlike gunpowder or gelignite, which were self-evidently explosive substances found in *Hallam*, the electronic timer which Berry had manufactured was not so obviously an explosive substance within the statutory definition.[35] It would have been better had Parliament defined the offence as possession of goods knowing them to be explosives. A similar result was reached in *Westminster City Council v Croyalgrange Ltd*[36] where the offence was knowingly to use or knowingly to cause or permit the use of premises as a sex establishment without a licence. The court held that the prosecution must establish that the defendant both knew that the premises were a sex establishment and that they were being so used without a licence.

The word "knowingly" has been used by the courts indirectly to indicate strict liability. In certain offences the word knowingly appears in one section but not in the next, or in some but not all subsections of a given section. Where this happens it is tempting to say that it is a clear indication that Parliament must have intended those sections which do not contain the word "knowingly" to impose strict liability. Thus, in *Neville v Mavroghenis*[37] the accused was the landlord of rented premises and was charged with an offence under s.13(4) of the Housing Act 1961—failure to maintain premises in a proper state of repair. The stipendiary magistrate who tried the case held that since he was unaware of the defects he could not be liable. The prosecutor appealed. The Divisional Court held that s.13(4) could be divided into two limbs. The first limb contained the phrase "knowingly contravenes" and, thus, clearly required that the prosecution prove that he had knowledge of the defects. The second limb was in the form "without reasonable excuse fails to comply with any regulations". The word "knowingly" did not appear, and, thus, it was held to be irrelevant that he was unaware of the defects. The decision in *Cundy v Le Coq*[38] is to the same effect. At issue was an offence under s.13 of the Licensing Act 1872 involving the sale by a landlord to a drunken person. It was determined that the belief of the landlord, albeit reasonably held, in the sobriety of the customer did not save him from conviction. The absence of the word "knowingly" in the

---

[33] [1957] 1 Q.B. 569; see above, para.2–073.
[34] [1995] 1 W.L.R. 7.
[35] By s.4 of the Explosive Substances Act 1883 it is an offence to make or knowingly possess an explosive substance, under such circumstances as to give rise to a reasonable suspicion that the defendant is not making it or does not have it in his possession or under his control for a lawful object. It is subject to a maximum punishment of 14 years' imprisonment.
[36] [1986] 1 W.L.R. 676; [1986] 2 All E.R. 353 HL; see above, para.2–073.
[37] [1984] Crim.L.R. 42.
[38] (1881) 13 Q.B.D. 207.

relevant section of the Act, in contrast to its inclusion in other provisions of the same statute, evinced a legislative desire for the application of a strict approach. It should, however, be noticed that in *Neville v Mavroghenis* that the words "without reasonable excuse" in the second limb did at least provide the accused with a "no negligence" defence which is a decided improvement on strict liability with no such defence.[39]

In *Pharmaceutical Society of Great Britain v Storkwain*[40] the House of Lords followed similar reasoning to hold that a provision of the Medicines Act 1968 which made it an offence to sell certain medicines without the prescription of an appropriate medical practitioner, created an offence of strict liability. The result was that an offence was committed by a pharmacist who had sold medicines on the strength of a forged prescription believing it to be genuine. However, it must be remembered that although the presence of the work "knowingly" in one section and its absence in the next is a pointer in the direction of strict liability it must not be taken to be conclusive. In *Sherras v De Rutzen*[41] the accused was charged with selling alcohol to a police constable on duty. The defence submitted that the constable had removed his duty armband and so it was impossible for the accused to know that he was on duty. Against this it was argued that whereas other surrounding provisions of the statute used the word knowingly,[42] s.16(2) of the Licensing Act 1872 did not. The Divisional Court quashed the conviction largely on the basis that without the requirement of knowledge the accused would be defenceless, since he would be convicted even if he had asked the constable whether he was on duty and the constable had told him falsely that he was not. Wright J. stated:

> "[I]f guilty knowledge is not necessary, no care on the part of the publican could save him from conviction . . . since it would be as easy for the constable to deny that he was on duty when asked, or to produce a forged permission from his superior officer as to remove his armlet before entering the public house."[43]

A similar illustration of this principle is provided by *Lim Chin Aik*.[44] D had been prohibited from entering Singapore, but the prohibition had neither been published nor brought to his attention. His conviction under the Singapore Immigration Ordinance was quashed by the Privy Council. In such a situation it would have been futile to punish Lim Chin Aik; there was nothing he could have done.

Wilfully and Maliciously

3–010 We have already seen that the word "maliciously" generally connotes some degree of subjective awareness as defined in *Cunningham*.[45] This interpretation of the word survives the decision in *Caldwell,* prior to revision in *G,* though it is unlikely that any new statutes will use the word "maliciously".

---

[39] See below, para.3–028.

[40] [1986] 1 W.L.R. 903. See generally, B. S. Jackson, "*Storkwain:* A Case Study in Strict Liability and Self-Regulation" [1991] Crim.L.R. 892.

[41] [1895] 1 Q.B. 918. In a classic statement of general principles Wright J. said (at 921): "There is a presumption that mens rea, an evil intention, or a knowledge of the wrongfulness of the act, is an essential ingredient in every offence; but that presumption is liable to be displaced either by the words of the statute creating the offence or by the subject-matter with which it deals, and both must be considered."

[42] By s.16(1) of the Licensing Act 1872 it was an offence for a licensee "knowingly" to harbour or suffer to remain on his premises any constable on duty.

[43] [1895] 1 Q.B. 918 at 923. Interestingly Day J. asserted that the effect of the deletion of the word "knowingly" from s.16(2) evidenced an intent to shift the burden of proof on the issue upon the accused. However this perspective has not been followed in subsequent authorities.

[44] [1963] A.C. 160; see above, para.2–014.

[45] [1957] 2 Q.B. 396, see above, para.2–066.

"Wilfully", on the other hand, which suggests a full mens rea requirement has been interpreted less consistently by the courts. Thus in *Cotterill v Penn*,[46] D was held unlawfully and wilfully to have killed a house pigeon when he shot a bird honestly thinking that it was a wild pigeon. Clearly the court took the word *"wilfully"* to mean that the prosecution must prove that the accused deliberately shot at the bird in question, but that it did not require the prosecution to prove that the accused knew that the bird was a house pigeon. However, in *Sheppard*[47] the House of Lords held that where an accused was charged with an offence of wilfully neglecting a child in a manner likely to cause him unnecessary suffering or injury to health, contrary to s.1 of the Children and Young Persons Act 1933, the word wilful must be taken to apply both to the prohibited act (i.e. neglect) and to the consequences (i.e. unnecessary suffering). This was not, therefore, an offence of strict liability. Although the word "wilful" was held to apply to both parts of the offence, it was satisfied by what, in effect, amounted to negligence.

It is important to stress that these sort of "key" words are useful guidelines, but it would be wrong to expect complete consistency from the courts.

B. Crimes and *Quasi* Crimes

In *Warner v M.P.C.* the issue of strict liability received attention for the first time from the **3–011** House of Lords in a case relating to possession of drugs. The House of Lords gave its approval to the notion of strict liability. In *Sweet v Parsley*[48] four of the same Law Lords appeared to be suggesting a much stronger adherence to the presumption of mens rea.

The defendant, a subtenant of a farmhouse, had let out several room to tenants, quaintly referred to in the judgment as "beatniks", who shared the use of the kitchen. She herself gave up living there, though she came occasionally to collect letters and rent. Subsequently, quantities of drugs, including cannabis resin, were found in the farmhouse and she was convicted of being concerned in the management of premises used for the purpose of smoking cannabis resin, contrary to s.5(6) of the Dangerous Drugs Act 1965. It was conceded by the prosecution that the defendant, a schoolmistress, had no knowledge whatsoever that cannabis was being smoked on the premises. Nevertheless the Divisional Court held her strictly liable. This produced a public outcry at the time. It caused grave concern, for instance, to landlords of university accommodation! Her appeal to the House of Lords was successful with Lord Reid asserting, "[I]t is firmly established by a host of authorities that mens rea is an essential ingredient of every offence unless some reason can be found for holding that it was not necessary."[49] The *Sweet* case was not, however, in any sense a denial of strict liability. What their Lordships said was that there were two types of criminal offences; the first were those which could truly be said to be criminal such as murder, rape, theft and assault (*mala in se*). These were to be distinguished from those which are not criminal in any real sense, but are acts which in the public interest are prohibited under a penalty. Crimes of this second type have been called regulatory offences, quasi crimes or crimes *mala prohibita*. In other words when Parliament makes regulations to govern the better running of society—such as regulations to ensure that food and drink are sold and served under hygienic conditions or regulations to prevent industry from polluting the environment—then it is common to sanction breaches of such regulations with a penalty,

[46] [1936] 1 K.B. 53.
[47] [1981] A.C. 394.
[48] [1970] A.C. 132.
[49] [1970] A.C. 132 at 149.

though no one really thinks of the offenders as criminals. Strict liability for purely regulatory offences is required in the public interest to protect society as a whole, to promote increased safety and greater vigilance by those carrying out certain activities. In this regard Lord Diplock stated:

> "But where the subject-matter of a statute is the regulation of a particular activity involving potential danger to public health, safety or morals, in which citizens have a choice whether they participate or not, the court may feel driven to infer an intention of Parliament to impose, by penal sanctions, a higher duty of care on those who choose to participate and to place on them an obligation to take whatever measures may be necessary to prevent the prohibited act without regard to those considerations of cost or business practicability which play a part in the determination of what would be required of them in order to fulfil the ordinary common law duty of care."[50]

The significance of the distinction is that in the former category (true crimes) the presumption in favour of mens rea should rarely, if at all, be rebutted, whereas in the second category it is easier to infer that Parliament intended the presumption to be rebutted. Thus, whereas in *Sweet v Parsley* the offence of "being concerned in the management of premises which are used for the purpose of smoking cannabis" was treated as a true crime (*mala in se*) which thus required mens rea, in *Alphacell Ltd v Woodward*,[51] the House of Lords treated the offence of "causing polluted matter to enter a river" as a regulatory offence and dispensed with the requirement for mens rea. The result was that the defendants in *Alphacell*, who had taken great care to ensure that they did not pollute the river, were convicted.

3–012   The principles applicable to the distinction between true crimes (*mala in se*), as opposed to regulatory offences (*mala prohibita*) were considered by the Privy Council in *Gammon (Hong Kong) Ltd v Attorney-General of Hong Kong*,[52] an important decision concerning building regulations in Hong Kong. The charge related to material deviations from approved plans in contravention of the Hong Kong Ordinance; part of a temporary lateral support system had been removed. It was held that it was irrelevant that the defendants did not know that the deviation was material; strict liability applied in order to promulgate social concerns over public safety, to secure greater vigilance and to ensure the exercise of greater control. Lord Scarman found that the law could be summarised as follows:

> "(1) there is a presumption of law that mens rea is required before a person can be held guilty of a criminal offence; (2) the presumption is particularly strong where the offence is 'truly criminal' in character; (3) the presumption applies to statutory offences, and can be displaced only if this is clearly or by necessary implication the effect of the statute; (4) the only situation in which the presumption can be displaced is where the statute is concerned with an issue of social concern; public safety is such an issue; the presumption of mens rea stands unless it can also be shown that the creation of strict liability will be effective to promote the objects of the statute by encouraging greater vigilance to prevent the commission of the prohibited act."[53]

---

[50] [1970] A.C. 132 at 163.
[51] [1972] A.C. 824; see below, para.3–014.
[52] [1985] A.C. 1.
[53] [1985] A.C. 1 at 14.

The final point (4) above that Lord Scarman enunciated is clearly illustrated by the decision in *Brockley*,[54] a case which, incidentally, also highlights the dangers of acting on the basis of unqualified and gratuitous legal advice. The defendant, an undischarged bankrupt, following a discussion with a para-legal solicitor, operated under the belief that he had been automatically discharged under the provisions of the Insolvency Act 1986. However, the Court of Appeal discovered a social concern underlying the provisions of the Company Directors Disqualification Act. The imposition of strict liability would ensure greater vigilance by obliging those adjudged bankrupt to ensure that their bankruptcy was in fact discharged before they engaged in any of the forbidden activities in relation to a company. The defendant was not allowed to escape liability by "burying his head in the sand". Similarly in *Collett*[55] it was held that, for reasons of social concern, it was necessary to impose strict liability where land had been used in breach of enforcement notices, contrary to s.89(5) of the Town and Country Planning Act 1971.

An interesting application of strict liability arose in *Jackson*.[56] D, an active member of the Royal Air Force, had flown a Jaguar aircraft at a height of between 50 and 100 feet, unfortunately thereby colliding with a floodlight tower. The consequential damage, to both aircraft and tower, was of a significant nature. D initially appeared before a General Court-Martial, charged with the offence of unlawful low flying, contrary to s.51 of the Air Force Act 1955, and regulations made pursuant to the Act. The defence was predicated on the argument that as the instrument indicating the height at which he was flying was malfunctioning, this meant that there was a corresponding lack of knowledge or recklessness on his part. It was contended that the judge's ruling was wrong in the context of identification of the offence as imposing strict liability. The appellate court, however, adopting the dichotomy raised in *Gammon*, treated the offence contrary to s.51 of the Air Force Act 1955 as one of *mala prohibita*. Essentially low flying was an activity creating a serious hazard and risk of serious danger to person and property, and one where the strictest possible standards needed to be imposed to ensure the avoidance of such danger occurring. It is difficult to disagree with such a conclusion. In such a scenario the creation of strict liability will be effective to promote the objects of the statute by encouraging greater vigilance to prevent the commission of the prohibited act.

It is, thus, important that we are able to identify these crimes which are classified as "quasi crimes" or "offences of social concern". Clearly no definitive list could be provided, but the following areas should serve to provide some indication, with a particular emphasis on pollution and public welfare.

Sale of Food and Drink

Here there are many complicated regulations, designed to ensure that hygiene prevails and **3–013** also to ensure that customers are not given short measure. This area extends to the rules concerning the licensing of public houses. These crimes are prime examples of "regulatory offences".[57]

Laws Governing the Environment

Like clothing, strict liability has its fashions. At times of economic crisis we see strict liability **3–014** being applied in regulations designed to help the economic situation. In the sixties the concern seemed to be with drugs, while in the seventies pollution of the environment

---

[54] (1994) 99 Cr.App.R. 385.
[55] [1994] Crim.L.R. 607.
[56] [2006] EWCA Crim 2380; [2007] 1 Cr.App.R. 20.
[57] See *Meah v Roberts* [1977] 1 W.L.R. 1187.

became one of the main topics of concern. This concern over pollution has grown during the course of subsequent decades. The argument here seems to be that there is a form of activity which is causing grave public concern and that breaches of the regulations designed to help the community should be subject to sanctions irrespective of whether the transgressor did it innocently or culpably. Such severe action, it is said, will serve to keep people on their toes. The social dangers and harms inherent to these enterprises must be balanced against the need for industrial activities and processes to be carried out for the benefit of all.

3–015   Two competing interests are at stake here. On one side of the coin it is laudable to prevent pollution for the benefit of society as a whole, whilst on the other side it seems harsh and unfair to business enterprises to impose what may be termed, "causal strict liability", i.e. liability imposed on the basis of simple causation. In reality companies may need to balance the dangers of a conviction and fine, no doubt with consequential adverse publicity, as against the practical steps they may take to prevent pollution, potentially at huge detrimental cost. In *Alphacell*, Lord Salmon was not prepared to limit the steps taken to prevent pollution by a requirement of reasonableness and he stated:

> "If this appeal succeeded and it were held to be the law that no conviction could be obtained under the Act of 1951 unless the prosecution could discharge the often impossible onus of proving that the pollution was caused intentionally or negligently, a great deal of pollution would be unpunished and undeterred to the relief of many riparian factory owners not only to take reasonable steps to prevent pollution but to do everything possible to ensure that they do not cause it."[58]

The onus imposed by Lord Salmon on companies to prevent pollution may be unrealistic. Commercial undertakings will need to balance the competing risks. It may appear harsh, but severe penalties can be imposed for strict liability offences despite the fact that they are "quasi-criminal," an issue considered further below.[59]

Drugs

3–016 As previously mentioned, increasing concern over drugs led to strict liability being imposed in the field of possession, etc., of dangerous drugs, but the recognition by the House of Lords that some of these offences fall into the category of true crimes has led to a softer approach being adopted by the courts and by the legislature in the Misuse of Drugs Act 1971, with the defence contained, within s.28. By way of contrast a very hard approach has been applied to the "possession" offences contained within the firearms legislation.[60]

Road Traffic

3–017 Many road traffic offences are created by regulations and provide sanctions for breaches of rules designed to ensure that the vehicles are in a roadworthy condition; it is a good bet that most of these so-called construction and use offences will be interpreted as imposing strict liability.[61] Another group of offences deals with the way in which the vehicles are actually driven on the road. The offences of dangerous and careless driving (ss.2 and 3 of the Road Traffic Act 1988) require proof of at least negligence. Offences of driving under the influence of alcohol, however, attract strict liability.[62]

---

[58] [1972] A.C. 824 at 848.
[59] See below at para.3–020.
[60] See above, para.3–007.
[61] See, generally, Road Traffic Regulation Act 1984.
[62] Road Traffic Act 1988 ss.4 and 5.

Public Safety

An analysis of the consolidated appeals in *Bezzina, Codling and Elvin*[63] reveals how judicial **3–018** construction of a statute, specifically designed to promote public safety, may lead inexorably to the application of strict liability. It also exemplifies the uncertain application of lack of knowledge or control arguments on the part of the defendant, operating causally as a novus actus interveniens, to discharge liability even in relation to strict liability offences. The issue before the Court of Appeal in these three appeals was the proper construction of s.3(1) and s.10(3) of the Dangerous Dogs Act 1991.[64] Did the sections impose strict liability on the owners of dogs of all sorts which were dangerously out of control in public places?[65] Section 3 of the 1991 Act provides:

> "(1) If a dog is dangerously out of control in a public place:
>
> (a) the owner; and
>
> (b) if different, the person for the time being in charge of the dog, is guilty of an offence, or, if the dog while so out of control injures any person an aggravated offence, under this sub-section."

Section 10 provides:

> "(3) For the purposes of this Act a dog shall be regarded as dangerously out of control on any occasion on which there are grounds for reasonable apprehension that it will injure any person, whether or not it actually does so."

On the face of it those sections imposed strict liability on the owners of dogs of all sorts which were dangerously out of control in public places. It was an objective test, applying a standard of reasonable apprehension; which did not relate to the state of mind of the dog owner. The objection taken to that by the defendants was that it involved no element of mens rea on the part of the dog owner as to his state of mind. As they stressed there was a long legal history that criminal offences were rarely of that sort. However, the appellate court, applying the propositions enunciated by Lord Scarman in *Gammon*,[66] held that public safety was the prevalent issue, and in such a scenario the presumption of mens rea can be displaced by strict liability. An objective test applies which does not relate to the state of mind of the dog owner. Ownership of a dog was an activity in which one could choose to participate or not. Hence the inference of parliamentary intention to impose strict liability would be that much stronger. It was akin to quasi-criminal acts not bearing the stigma of criminality.

An interesting hypothetical issue raised by counsel for one of the defendants in the case **3–019** (*Elvin*) was the problem of a third party, of whom the owner knew nothing, releasing a dog which subsequently became dangerously out of control. Unfortunately the Court of Appeal did not consider this matter as the situation did not arise on the particular facts of the case.[67]

---

[63] [1994] 3 All E.R. 964.

[64] The Dangerous Dogs Act 1991 was enacted to deal with what was perceived to be a serious problem of dogs, particularly of an unruly and savage type, attacking particularly children.

[65] In the first case the defendant was exercising his Rottweiler dog when it bit one of a group of teenagers. In the second case the defendant was exercising her dog when it bit another dog owner. In the third case the defendant left two pit bull terriers at large in premises that were inadequately secured so that they escaped and bit a third party.

[66] [1985] A.C. 1, see above, para.3–012.

[67] The issue was hypothetical as in all three cases the owners were in charge of their own dogs.

It raises the interesting conundrum of whether the blamelessly inadvertent dog owner should be convicted of a strict liability offence. Can lack of knowledge or control on the part of the defendant operate causally as a novus actus interveniens or allow an acquittal through involuntariness? The foregoing issues have received extremely limited judicial attention in England. There is, however, Commonwealth authority on the matter. In *Kilbride v Lake*[68] the defendant left his parked car with its current warrant of fitness prominently displayed on the windscreen. Subsequently, when he returned to the car the warrant had inexplicably been removed. A charge was laid under reg.52(i) of the New Zealand Traffic Regulations Act 1956 (SR 1956/217) with operating a motorvehicle (by permitting the car to be on the road) on which there was not displayed a current warrant of fitness. The appeal to the New Zealand Court of Appeal was successful. They held the omission to display the warrant of fitness was not within the defendant's conduct, knowledge or control. Woodhouse J. stated that, "the general purpose (of the regulation) is not likely to be promoted by prosecuting people who cannot reasonably be expected to do more than, in fact, they have done."[69]

The general tenor of the New Zealand Court of Appeal judgment can be applauded. The morally blameless should not be subjected to the stigma of conviction, albeit through pecuniary penalties; strict liability should be curtailed where possible. Impressionistically it seems wrong to punish individuals lacking any opportunity to act to prevent harm, where they have taken all reasonable care. However, we have seen that a robust approach has been applied to the offence of selling alcohol to a police constable on duty in *Sherras v De Rutzen*, and by the Privy Council in *Lim Chin Aik*.[70]

C. Smallness of the Penalty

3–020 Another pointer to the way in which a court will interpret a given offence is the size of the penalty available. As a general rule the larger the penalty the less likely the court is to treat it as a crime involving strict liability. The reasoning behind this is that a heavy maximum penalty is an indication of Parliament's intention that the accused should be shown to be blameworthy. Whereas you can impose fines on blameless individuals, imprisonment should be reserved for those who are at least negligent. In *Gammon (Hong Kong) Ltd v Att-Gen of Hong Kong*, however, Lord Scarman held that where the regulations were concerned with a matter of public safety it was quite proper that severe penalties could be imposed even for strict liability offences. The maximum penalty for breach of the building regulations was a fine of $250,000 and/or imprisonment for three years. He, thus, took the view that strict liability was needed in order to promote greater vigilance among builders, and continued:

> "It must be crucially important that those who participate in or bear responsibility for the carrying out of works in a manner which complies with the requirements of the ordinance should know that severe penalties await them in the event of any contravention or non-compliance with the ordinance by themselves . . ."[71]

It should also be recalled that under the Water Act 1989 a maximum punishment of two years' imprisonment could be imposed. Similar interests of social concern apply to the firearm legislation; in both *Howells* and *Bradish* the potential existed for terms of between

---

[68] [1962] N.Z.L.R. 590. See generally, M. Budd and A. Lynch, "Voluntariness, Causation and Strict Liability" [1978] Crim.L.R. 74.
[69] [1962] N.Z.L.R. 590 at 594.
[70] [1963] A.C. 160, see above, para.2–014.
[71] [1985] A.C. 1, at 17.

three and five years imprisonment for the offences of possessing a firearm without a certificate and of possessing a prohibited weapon.

At the end of the day there is no sure test to discover whether a statute has imposed strict liability. The above principles have been taken from cases. They are not applied consistently, but provide some indication of how the courts will react when confronted with a new criminal offence.

3. MODERN PRINCIPLES FOR STRICT LIABILITY

The debate over the import of strict liability offences was revived by the House of Lords **3–021** decisions in *B (A Minor) v DPP*[72] and *R v K*.[73] Their Lordships in both cases had to consider whether a mistake as to the victim's age afforded a defence in age-based sexual offences or whether the legislation precluded mens rea requirements on specific elements of the offence. The subjectivist principles propounded in these cases remain cogent even though the statutory offences involved have been overtaken by adoption of the Sexual Offences Act 2003.

(i) The Decision in B (A Minor) v DPP

The facts in *B (A Minor)* presented a disturbing picture. B, a 15-year-old boy, repeatedly **3–022** asked a 13-year-old girl to perform oral sex with him, referring colloquially to the act as a "shiner". The girl refused, and B was subsequently charged with inciting a child under the age of 14 to commit an act of gross indecency, contrary to s.1(1) of the Indecency with Children Act 1960 (now replaced by ss.8 and 10 of the Sexual Offences Act 2003).[74] It was accepted that B had honestly believed that the girl was over 14 years, but the justices ruled that his state of mind could not constitute a defence to the charge. As a result, B changed his plea from not guilty to guilty, but subsequently appealed by way of case stated to the Divisional Court. When that appeal was dismissed, B appealed to the House of Lords, and the following point of law of general public importance was involved in the decision, namely, "Is a defendant entitled to be acquitted of the offence of inciting a child aged under 14 to commit an act of gross indecency . . . if he may hold an honest belief that the child in question was aged 14 years or over?" A positive response was elicited from their Lordships.

Lord Nicholls and Lord Steyn, who delivered the leading judgments in *B (A Minor)*, evaluated the general nature of strict liability and distinctions between crimes and "quasi" crimes.[75] Was there a presumption that mens rea was required for the commission of the offence under s.1(1) of the Indecency with Children Act 1960? Was the offence "truly criminal" in character? A distinction had to be made between truly criminal offences (*mala in se*), as opposed to regulatory offences (*mala prohibita*). The more serious the offence the less likely it is that the presumption of mens rea should be rebutted. Lord Nicholls asserted that in view of the presumption of mens rea that applies to truly criminal offences, and age-based sexual offences evidently fit that category, then any necessary implication of Parliament's intention to impose strict liability could only be satisfied by an implication that was "*compellingly clear*". Lord Nicholls set out some illustrations of the sorts of relevant factors in the determination: it might be found in the language used, the nature of the offence; the mischief sought to be prevented and any other circumstances which may assist in determining what intention was properly to be attributed to Parliament.[76]

---

[72] [2000] 1 All E.R. 833.
[73] [2001] 3 All E.R. 897.
[74] See below at paras 7–135—7–136.
[75] [2000] 1 All E.R. 833 at 836–837, 845–847 and 849–854.
[76] [2000] 1 All E.R. 833 at 839.

Thus, in *B (A Minor)* it was determined that where an individual had been charged with the offence of inciting a child under 14 to commit an act of gross indecency contrary to s.1(1) of the 1960 Act, the prosecution was required to prove that the defendant lacked an honest belief that the child was aged 14 years or over. Such a conclusion gave effect to the common law presumption that a statutory offence required a mental element unless Parliament provided to the contrary, either expressly or by necessary implication, i.e. by an implication that was compellingly clear. Moreover, where a mistaken belief would prevent the defendant from having the necessary mental element, that belief did not have to be based on reasonable grounds. As regard s.1(1) of the 1960 Act, Parliament had not expressly negatived the need for a mental element in respect of the age element of the offence. Nor had the presumption been displaced by necessary implication. On the contrary, the application of the presumption was reinforced by the serious nature of the offence and the broad manner in which it was drawn, embracing conduct ranging from predatory approaches by much older paedophiles to consensual sexual experimentation between precocious teenagers of whom the offender might be the younger of the two. In the light of these circumstances the appeal was allowed.

(ii) The Decision in R v K

3–023 The House of Lords in *R v K* considered the applicability of strict liability to the provisions of s.14 of the Sexual Offences Act 1956 (now replaced by s.3 of the Sexual Offences Act 2003.)[77] The defendant, aged 26 at the time of the incident, was charged under s.14 with the indecent assault of a girl aged 16. The complaint made by the schoolgirl was that she was indecently assaulted by K touching her private parts without her consent. K's case was that the girl told him that she was 16 and he had no reason to disbelieve her. She consented to all the sexual activity which occurred between them. The House of Lords, quashing D's conviction, concluded that the language of s.14 did not, as a matter of necessary implication, exclude the presumption of mens rea.

The general issue in *R v K* related to the case of *Prince*,[78] and whether a mistake as to age affords a defence in age-based sexual offences. The specific issue addressed the mens rea requirement of indecent assault. On the former matter direct comparisons were invoked to their Lordships decision a year previous in *B (A Minor)*. The outcome was replicated in *R v K* where Lord Bingham asserted that there was no doubt that indecent assault, with the maximum penalty increased to 10 years' imprisonment, palpably represented a truly "criminal" offence. Thus, following *B (A Minor)*, their Lordships unanimously determined that the prosecution must prove absence of belief of age (16 or over). The belief had to be one that was honestly held, but need not be predicated on reasonable grounds. In reaching that conclusion there was reliance on the established common law assumption that mens rea was an essential ingredient unless Parliament had indicated a contrary intention, either expressly or by necessary implication. Subsequently, in *Deyemi*[79] the Court of Appeal treated this statement as the correct pathway to follow in deciphering whether strict liability (or otherwise) applied to a defendant in possession of an electrical stun-gun, and liability within the confines of firearms legislation.

The impact of the decisions in *B (A Minor)* and *R v K* meant that the case of *Prince*, influential for over a century, has been rendered obsolete. Moreover, the legislative offence has been repealed by the Sexual Offences Act 2003. Additionally, it seems that another side-wind of the decision in *B (A Minor)* is that, not just *Prince*, but also the similarly antediluvian

---

[77] See below at para.7–135.
[78] (1875) L.R. 2 C.C.R. 154; see above, para.2–082.
[79] [2007] EWCA Crim 2060; [2008] Crim.L.R. 327.

case of *Tolson*[80] needs reappraisal. Here the defendant had entered into a second marriage, believing on very reasonable grounds that her first husband had been drowned in a shipwreck more than five years before, and was subsequently charged with bigamy. It was held that she was not guilty of bigamy, but only because her belief was *reasonable*, and hence not negligent. It appears, however, that this must be re-interpreted in light of *B (A Minor)*; an honest belief (albeit mistaken) is now a good defence and the words "and reasonable" must be deleted. This viewpoint accords with Lord Nicholls' summary on the application of mistake as a defence today, put in general terms and not delineated as subject to any specific exceptions:

> "Considered as a matter of principle, the honest belief approach must be preferable. By definition the mental element in a crime is concerned with a subjective state of mind, such as intent or belief. To the extent that an overriding objective limit ('on reasonable grounds') is introduced, the subjective element is displaced."[81]

(iii) Dealing with strict liability: appropriate methodology

If we left discussion at this point a false impression may be created that subjectivism, **3–024** through *B (A Minor)* and *R v K*, has triumphed over strict liability. This is certainly not apposite, and a number of cases have reaffirmed legislative provisions imposing strict liability: in *Barnfather*[82] an offence under s.444(1) of the Education Act 1996 stating, if a child of compulsory school age who is a registered pupil at a school fails to attend at the school his parent is guilty of an offence; in *Muhamad*[83] the defendant contributed to insolvency by gambling carrying two years' imprisonment; and in *Matudi*[84] the offence of importing prohibited animal products contrary to regs 21 and 37 of the Products of Animal Origin (Import and Export) Regulations 1996 (SI 1996/3124).

An examination of the appropriate methodology used in *Barnfather*, *Muhamad* and *Matudi*, identifying strict liability offences in all three cases, is illuminating. It draws together a number of key features highlighted in this chapter and bears reiteration. In determining whether a statute imposes strict liability, attention needs to be paid to two issues. It is necessary to scrutinise the language of the statute; and also to consider the behaviour which the statute seeks to regulate. In shorthand, both the *content* and *context* of the statute are relevant. There is nothing mysterious about these processes; nor are they unique to questions about strict liability. Rather, they refer to general canons of statutory interpretation, in the lexicon of which one might say that both a *literal* and a *purposive* approach need to be adopted. As Lord Nicholls suggested in *B (A Minor)*:

> "The question, therefore, is whether, although not expressly negatived, the need for a mental element is negatived by necessary implication. 'Necessary implication' connotes an implication which is compellingly clear. Such an implication may be found in the language used, the nature of the offence, the mischief sought to be prevented and any other circumstances which may assist in determining what attention is properly to be attributed to Parliament when creating the offence."[85]

---

[80] (1889) 23 Q.B.D. 168.
[81] [2000] 1 All E.R. 833 at 837.
[82] *Barnfather v London Borough of Islington Education Authority, Secretary of State for Education and Skills* [2003] EWHC 418; [2003] 1 W.L.R. 2318; and see B. Fitzpatrick, "Case Comment" (2004) 68 J.C.L. 16.
[83] [2003] EWCA Crim 182.
[84] *Matudi v The Crown* [2003] EWCA Crim 697; and see B. Fitzpatrick, "Case Comment" (2004) 68 J.C.L. 195.
[85] [2000] 2 A.C. 428 at 463H.

It might be instructive, as in *Barnfather* and *Matudi*, to draw attention to the supposed distinction between offences which are "truly criminal" and those which are merely "quasi-crimes", or, to use a relevant vernacular, crimes which are *mala in se* (bad in themselves) and those which are *mala prohibita* (bad only in the sense that they are instances of prohibited behaviour). This distinction is problematic. While there may be a core of criminality that most would agree is "true" crime, as one moves away from the core to the periphery of the criminal law, a search for consensus on that issue would struggle. However, the problems with the true/quasi-crime distinction are perhaps more significant than the mere difficulty one might encounter in "placing" any given offence. The distinction raises the question of the criteria by which one defines "crime", and seems to rest on the notion of moral culpability or turpitude, in the absence of which it is more appropriate to impose strict liability. Clearly, to impose strict liability for the offence of murder would be problematic, because the notion of "murder" is imbued with sufficient moral stigma that the label murderer should be reserved for those who acted with a prescribed mental element. However, does it necessarily follow that the imposition of strict liability carries the implication that the behaviour in question is "not that serious?" As Lord Scarman suggests in *Gammon Ltd v Attorney-General of Hong Kong*,[86] strict liability may be used to address a behaviour which is a matter of social concern (which is itself a difficult proposition given that, on one view, the very essence of the decision to criminalise *any* behaviour is that a social norm is thought to be worth supporting). However, what appears to be meant is that strict liability may be legitimately deployed where some public interest, rather than a particular individual interest, needs protection. Thus, we can observe the use of strict liability to regulate the circulation of currency in times of economic instability,[87] or to regulate potential environmental offenders.[88] A potentially damaging by-product of the true quasi-crime distinction is that the corporate polluter/environmental despoiler might be viewed in some way as not properly criminal, even though they may have caused immense harm, because the offence they committed may have been one of strict liability. This problem is arguably exacerbated by the rhetoric of "regulatory offences" and the practice of their enforcement by the appropriate agencies, such as the Health and Safety Executive or the Environment Agency.[89]

3–025   Lord Scarman suggested in *Gammon* that even if it were acceptable to impose strict liability, it should only be done in circumstances where greater vigilance on the part of potential offenders would be promoted, as in *Harrow London BC v Shah*[90] and sales of national lottery tickets to children under 16. Thus, in *Barnfather* it is more acceptable to impose strict liability if that imposition makes it more likely that potentially recalcitrant parents will think twice before permitting their children to take unauthorised absences from school. Similarly in *Matudi*, on importation of prohibited animal products, Scott Baker LJ's view is that the objects of the legislation will be promoted by the imposition of strict liability. He suggests the kinds of precautions that importers would take in the light of their clear obligations. The suggestion is that the imposition of strict liability would encourage vigilance and dissuade slipshod importers, who might be relatively unconcerned about the contents of their consignments. This contention is perhaps problematic. A rigorously enforced criminal law of negligence could conceivably encourage potential offenders to take all reasonable

[86] [1985] 1 A.C. 1.
[87] See *R v St Margaret's Trust Ltd* [1958] 2 All E.R. 289.
[88] See *Alphacell v Woodward* [1972] A.C. 824; *Environment Agency v Brock Plc* [1998] Env. L.R. 607; *R (on the application of Grundy and Co Excavations Ltd and Sean Parry) v Halton Division Magistrates Court, The Forestry Commission* [2003] EWHC 272.
[89] See, for example, *Davies (David Janway) v Health and Safety Executive* [2002] EWCA Crim 2949.
[90] [1999] 2 Cr.App.Rep. 47; and *Doring* [2002] EWCA Crim 169.

steps to ensure that they were not breaching any prohibition, and indeed this seems to be the position taken in the 2002 Regs. However, the offender who breaches the prohibition in a case of strict liability is not exonerated, even though they may have taken all such (or indeed, greater) steps. It is therefore perhaps difficult to identify the point in taking of precautionary measures beyond those which are reasonable.

It might also be the case that such incentives as are present in instances of strict liability, might in practice operate differentially between individual and corporate potential offenders. While an individual might well respond to the enhanced threat of criminalisation presented by strict liability and adjust their practice accordingly, it is perhaps not especially controversial to suggest that corporate offenders might merely factor in potential liability to their operating costs. In the vernacular, one might as well be hanged for a sheep as a lamb. If, for example, a corporate importer is going to be liable, should it import prohibited goods, even if it has gone to the expense of initiating pre-import checks, then the commercially minded might ask whether it is worth going to that particular expense. Implementation of a possible due-diligence standard is considered further below.

Arguments have been raised that strict liability offences infringe art.6(2) of the ECHR, and the presumption of innocence, as once the prohibited act is proved then D is presumed to be liable. However, in *Barnfather* it is clearly stated that art.6(2) has no role in the evaluation of substantive law, and this is supported by both domestic[91] and European Court of Human Rights authorities.[92] It has recently been confirmed by the House of Lords in the important case of *R v G*.[93] D's conviction for rape of a girl aged 12 under the Sexual Offences Act 2003 s.5 was upheld by their Lordships, although D was 15 at the time of the offence, the complainant had consented to the intercourse and she had told him that she was 15. A majority of the House of Lords also determined that the defendant's rights under art.8 were not violated.[94] The Court of Appeal in *Deyemi*[95] had reached a similar conclusion on the art.6(2) issue. An electrical stun gun had been found on D's possession which was capable of discharging electricity through electrodes, and in it was positioned a lens and a bulb. D's contention that he believed it to be a torch was rejected, and strict liability was applied within the purview of s.5(1) of the Firearms Act 1968. The presumption of innocence declared by art.6(2) did not operate to prevent or restrict strict liability offences; the article was not concerned with the substantive law but with the fairness of the procedure.[96]

4. DEFENCES TO OFFENCES OF STRICT LIABILITY

If we say that the offence is one of strict liability does this mean that the accused can have **3–026** no defence to it? No, for that would be going too far. We have already said that where an offence is held to be one of strict liability, this usually means that the court has dispensed with the need to prove intention, recklessness or negligence as to one element of the actus reus, usually the central element. The practical effect is that on that one element the accused

---

[91] See *Gemmell and Richards* [2002] EWCA Crim 1992; and *Concannon* [2002] Crim.L.R. 213.

[92] See *Z v United Kingdom* (2002) 34 EHRR 3.

[93] [2008] UKHL 37; [2008] Crim.L.R. 818.

[94] Note their Lordships divided 3:2 on this issue. Baroness Hale for the majority emphasised the positive obligation on states to protect young people from the sexual attentions of others and from premature sexual activity: "In view of all the dangers resulting from under-age sexual activity, it cannot be wrong for the law to apply that label [rape] even if it cannot be proved that the child was in fact unwilling"; [2008] UKHL 37 at [55].

[95] [2007] EWCA Crim 2060; [2008] Crim.L.R. 327.

[96] See, generally, V. Tadros and S. Tierney, "The Presumption of Innocence and the Human Rights Act" (2004) 67 M.L.R., 402; and A. Ashworth, "Four Threats to the Presumption of Innocence" (2006) E. & P. 241.

cannot raise the defence of mistake of fact, even if his mistake was reasonable. It possibly also means that the defence of impossibility will not apply to that element; thus where the accused is charged with failing, as the owner of a vehicle, to display the excise licence, it will arguably (although the point has not been judicially determined in England) be of no defence to show that it happened without any default of his own while he was away from the vehicle.[97] However, mistake of fact may well apply to other elements of the actus reus and the remaining general defences such as infancy, duress, necessity and automatism are possible defences to a charge. Let us consider a hypothetical example. The offence of driving over the prescribed alcohol limit requires that the prosecution prove that the accused was driving on a road or other public place.[98] The notion of driving involves a mental element or at least the concept of voluntary conduct. Thus, if the accused were to show that he had received a blow on the head immediately before he started to drive and this had produced a state of automatism, then he would be able to say that he was not "driving" the car.[99] On the other hand a defence that he was unaware that he had consumed any alcohol since a friend had laced his drink would fail; liability on this element is strict and mistake of fact is no defence.[100]

In Australia the courts have made attempts to lessen the rigours of strict liability by allowing the accused to plead by way of defence that he had taken all reasonable care.[101] If we consider the example of a butcher who sells bad meat if such an approach were to be adopted, the prosecution would at first prove that the butcher had sold meat and that this meat had turned out to be bad. If nothing further is said then the butcher will be convicted. However if he can prove, on a balance of probabilities, that he had taken all reasonable precautions to ensure that the meat sold in his shop was sound, then he would be acquitted. Of course, this would be another exception to the rule in *Woolmington's* case which says that it is for the prosecution to prove guilt and not for the accused to prove his innocence. However, if the alternative is strict liability with no such defence, then it is clearly an improvement from the point of view of the butcher. It would be an even greater improvement if the butcher merely had to introduce evidence that he had taken all reasonable care, leaving the prosecution to prove that he had not taken all reasonable care.

The courts in England and Wales have not adopted such a general midway position to offences of strict liability. Occasionally it has been held that a statute, which might have been expected to impose strict liability, did not, in fact, impose strict liability, because there was nothing the accused could have done to protect himself. Thus, in *Sherras v De Rutzen* the court held that a statute making it an offence for a licensee to sell alcohol to a policeman on duty did not impose strict liability since this would have left him defenceless had the constable deliberately lied about being off duty. Similarly in *Lim Chin Aik*,[102] a case where, as previously mentioned, D had been convicted for entering Singapore in breach of a prohibition notice but in circumstances where this prohibition had neither been made known or published to him. The Privy Council took the view that the imposition of strict liability is pointless unless there is something that the accused can do to prevent himself breaching the regulation.

---

[97] See above, para.3–019 for discussion of the New Zealand case of *Kilbride v Lake*; it is argued no liability should attach in such circumstances to the morally blameless.

[98] Contrary to ss.4 and 5 of the Road Traffic Act 1988.

[99] See, e.g. *Watmore v Jenkins* [1962] 2 Q.B. 572; and *Hill v Baxter* [1958] 1 Q.B. 277.

[100] However it might be a reason for not disqualifying.

[101] In *Proudman v Dayman* (1941) 67 C.L.R. 536, at 540 Dixon J. stated: "As a general rule an honest and reasonable belief in a state of facts which, if they existed, would make the defendant's act innocent affords an excuse for doing what would otherwise be an offence."

[102] [1963] A.C. 160; see above, para.2–014.

It is becoming more common today, for statutes which impose strict liability to contain express defences. Thus, a statutory defence might allow the accused to escape conviction if he can prove that the contravention of the regulation was due to the fault of a third party and that he, the accused, took all reasonable precautions against breaking the regulations (see, e.g. the Food and Drugs Act 1955 s.113 as amended by the Food Safety Act 1990 s.21). More generally, statutory defences have taken the form of casting the burden on the accused to prove that he was not negligent; thus we do specifically for some crimes what the Australian approach would suggest we should do for all crimes of strict liability. Examples of statutory provision for a "no-negligence" defence, i.e. a reasonable care standard, include s.24(1) of the Trades Descriptions Act 1968,[103] s.34 of the Weights and Measures Act 1985 and, as we have seen[104] in accordance with s.28 of the Misuse of Drugs Act 1971.

5. WHY DO WE HAVE CRIMES OF STRICT LIABILITY AT ALL?

Clearly from the point of view of the police and the prosecution, strict liability is an **3–027** attractive proposition. It relieves them of the duty of proving mens rea on what is normally the most troublesome aspect of the actus reus. In our hypothetical butcher case, it will rarely trouble the prosecution that they have to prove that the accused intentionally sold a given piece of meat. Proof, however, that he knew or had reason to believe that the meat was bad would be far more difficult to find. Those who support the notion of strict liability would probably argue that to allow the butcher a defence of an honest or even an honest and reasonable mistake would surely undermine the efficacy of the legislation. Regulations relating to food and drink, public hygiene, road safety and pollution are designed for the benefit of the public and strict liability is essential to keep those involved in these areas on their toes by ensuring conviction for any breach, however innocent.[105] It was once said that if a town has built and is maintaining defences against a flood, if X does anything which causes the barrier to fall, it matters not whether he did it innocently or not.[106]

Those who support strict liability would also say that the offences are by and large less serious offences and the penalties imposed are normally very light. In any event where the court is satisfied that the accused took all reasonable care this can be reflected in the sentence—he can be given an absolute discharge. How strong are such arguments? Do we really need crimes of strict liability?

The argument that it might be difficult to prove mens rea on a given element can be taken to extremes. The prosecution often find it extremely difficult to prove the mens rea of a murder charge, but rarely is the argument advanced that, therefore, murder should be a crime of strict liability.

Secondly, it is not very comforting for a butcher, who relies on his reputation, to know **3–028** that the court is sorry for his conviction and has imposed only an absolute discharge. The fact remains that he has been convicted and his conviction will probably be reported in the local press. The reader who may have been a customer of the butcher will not be concerned with the butcher's lack of culpability, merely with the fact that he sold bad meat.

This leaves the argument that strict liability is necessary to keep people on their toes. Such was clearly the major argument used by the Privy Council in the *Gammon* case[107] to support

---

[103] See *Tesco Supermarkets Ltd v Nattrass* [1972] A.C. 153, considered below, para.4–061.
[104] Above, para.3–008.
[105] See, generally, M. Smith and A. Pearson, "The Value of Strict Liability" [1969] Crim.L.R. 5.
[106] *St Margaret's Trust Ltd* [1958] 2 All E.R. 289 at 293 per Donovan J.
[107] [1985] A.C. 1, above, para.3–012.

the imposition of strict liability. This has always appeared to be taking a sledge hammer to crack a nut. Clearly we want to do everything possible to ensure that butchers and those concerned in the sale of food and drink, for example, should take every precaution to ensure that their wares are fit for sale, but does this mean that we need strict liability to achieve it? Obviously the existence of strict liability makes a trader aware that he will need to exercise great care in his trade, but surely so would a defence that allowed him to prove, or raise evidence, that he took all reasonable care. Let us return finally to our neighbourhood butcher. He has sold a piece of meat which an inspector has found to be bad. There are several possibilities as to his mental state in relation to this sale: (i) he may have known that the meat was bad, and yet deliberately sold it; (ii) he may have suspected that the meat was bad, and yet taken the risk in selling it; (iii) he may not have suspected the meat to have been bad, although reasonable steps would have shown this to be the case; (iv) he may not have suspected the meat to be bad and reasonable steps would not have revealed this to him. Clearly we would want to convict those in categories (i) and (ii). In this area we may want to convict in situation (iii) since we would want butchers to take reasonable steps and we would probably not complain if a sloppy butcher was fined. However, what do we achieve by convicting number (iv)? By our very definition we have said that even the taking of reasonable steps would not have revealed to him that his meat was bad. Knowledge that he would be convicted however much care he has taken would keep him on his toes, but so would knowledge that he would be convicted if he could not prove that he had taken all reasonable steps. Common sense would seem to suggest that the line should be drawn between (iii) and (iv) and that nothing is gained from convicting the accused in case (iv).[108]

In conclusion, it is important to address the underlying rationale over the imposition of criminal liability for regulatory matters. The answer lies historically with Dicey and the aversion he instilled into our system for different systems of courts, criminal and civil, to do different types of job. This has created inconsistencies and, arguably, pollution and public health crimes should now be dealt with entirely by administrative bodies who would treat infractions of the laws as violations not crimes. It is instructive to consider the American approach to criticism of strict liability. Many states, following the lead of the Model Penal Code, have reclassified such strict liability regulatory offences as non-criminal "infractions" or "violations" that are punishable only by monetary penalties and that do not, "give rise to any disability or legal disadvantage based on conviction of a criminal offence".[109] Such violations have been applied to traffic and other public health matters. Strict liability for violations is more defensible than strict liability for crimes, and the stigma of criminality is avoided. The time has arrived to consider the range of flexible and appropriate adaptation of civil penalties applicable to particular regulatory concerns. The corollary here is that it seems entirely correct that the negligent corporation who fail to take reasonable steps should be held liable. Punishing the negligent accords with a due diligence (or no negligence) defence to offences of strict liability adopted by the High Court of Australia in *Proudman v Dayman*,[110] and the Supreme Court of Canada in *R v City of Sault Ste Marie*.[111]

---

[108] See, generally, J.C. Smith and B. Hogan, *Criminal Law* (Butterworths, 1996) at 118–119.
[109] See, MPC s.104(5).
[110] (1941) 67 C.L.R. 536.
[111] (1978) 85 D.L.R. (3d) 161. In an important statement by Dickson J., providing the leading judgment of the Supreme Court of Canada, it was asserted (at 181): "The correct approach . . . is to relieve the Crown of the burden of proving mens rea, having regard to . . . the virtual impossibility in most regulatory cases of proving wrongful intention. In a normal case, the accused alone will have knowledge of what he has done to avoid the breach and it is not improper to expect him to come forward with the evidence of due diligence . . . This involves consideration of what a reasonable man would have done in the circumstances. The defence will be available if the accused reasonably believed in a mistaken set of facts which, if true, would render the act or omission innocent, or if he took all reasonable steps to avoid the particular event."

It has the effect of placing the burden of proof on the accused and mitigates the harsh strict liability regime. There are lessons to be learnt here from other jurisdictions.

It may well be, as the Court said in *Sheppard*, that in recent years the climate of judicial opinion has grown less favourable to the recognition of strict liability offences. It remains equally true, however, that this category of offences remains far from being dead and buried.

GENERAL READING

Brett, P., "Strict Responsibility: Possible Solutions" (1974) 37 M.L.R. 417.   **3–029**
Budd, M. and Lynch, A., "Voluntarism, Causation And Strict Liability" [1978] Crim.L.R. 74.
Hogan, B., *Criminal Liability Without Fault* (Leeds University Press, 1967).
Jackson, B.S., "*Storkwain*: A Case Study In Strict Liability and Self-Regulation" [1991] Crim.L.R. 892.
Lanham, D.,"*Larsonneur* Revisited" [1976] Crim.L.R. 276.
Leigh, L.H., *Strict and Vicarious Liability*, (Sweet & Maxwell, 1982).
Richardson, G., "Strict Liability for Regulatory Crime: The Empirical Research [1987] Crim.L.R. 295.
Smith, J.C., "Responsibility in Criminal Law" in Bean and Whynes (eds), *Barbara Wootton, Essays In Her Honour*, (1986) 141.
Smith, M. and Pearson, A., "The Value Of Strict Liability" [1969] Crim.L.R. 5.
Stanton-Ife, J., "Strict Liability: Stigma and Regret" (2007) 27 *Oxford Journal of Legal Studies* 151.

Chapter 4

PARTIES TO CRIMINAL OFFENCES

PRINCIPAL AND SECONDARY OFFENDERS

1. INTRODUCTION

When a criminal offence is committed attention is primarily focused on the perpetrator. In a **4–001** case of murder the police will look for the killer, in a case of burglary the person who entered the building as a trespasser, in a case of criminal damage the person who caused the damage, and so on. However, a moment's reflection tells us that if the criminal law were concerned only with the perpetrator it would be seriously defective. Someone who helps the perpetrator, for example, by providing the gun for a killing, or a key for a burglary, ought also to incur liability for the crime. In some cases the helper may indeed have played a much more significant part than the perpetrator for he may have been the one who conceived and planned the offence.[1]

On the other hand a point is reached at which the assistance given is so remote that it would be unfair or unrealistic to make the helper a party to the crime. In a well-known civil case, *Lloyd v Johnson*,[2] it was held that a laundress could recover from a prostitute the cost of washing expensive dresses and some gentlemen's nightcaps though the laundress knew well that the dresses were used for the purpose of enticing men in public places. In such circumstances the laundress could hardly be regarded as a party to the prostitute's offence of soliciting. Once again the task of the law is to draw the line at the appropriate place.[3]

Our starting point should be s.8 of the Accessories and Abettors Act 1861 (as amended by the Criminal Law Act 1977). This provides: "Whosoever shall aid, abet, counsel or procure the commission of any indictable offence whether the same be an offence of common law or by virtue of any act passed or to be passed, shall be liable to be tried, indicted and punished as a principal offender." There are similar provisions in relation to summary offences.[4] Until 1967 offences were either felonies or misdemeanours and in the case of felonies various

---

[1] For example, consider the major roles played by Marlon Brando and Al Pacino in the *Godfather* trilogy of movies. Note that A is generally used in this chapter to refer to the principal party, whilst B refers to the secondary party.
[2] (1798) 1 Bos. 8 P. 340.
[3] See, generally, K.J.M. Smith, *A Modern Treatise on the Law of Criminal Complicity* (Clarendon, 1991).
[4] Magistrates' Courts Act 1980 s.44.

degrees of participation were identified. The actual perpetrator of the offence was known as the principal in the first degree, anyone who was present at the scene of the crime and gave assistance was known as the principal in the second degree, while anyone who gave assistance before the commission of the crime but who was not present at the scene was designated an accessory before the fact. A person who gave assistance to the felony after the offence was called an accessory after the fact. With the passing of the Criminal Law Act 1967 the distinction between felonies and misdemeanours was abolished and s.8 of the Accessories and Abettors Act became applicable to all indictable offences, with the resulting disappearance of the above classifications. Today it is more normal to refer to the actual perpetrator of the offence as the principal offender and all the others who assisted in the commission of the offence as the secondary parties, or accessories, and these are the terms we shall use in this chapter. Accessories after the fact are not parties to the offence; they are now covered by specific offences.[5]

4–002   From a procedural point of view it is not necessary to distinguish in the indictment between principal and secondary offenders—all can be indicted as having committed the offence—provided that at the trial the prosecution can prove that the offence was in fact committed by someone and that those on trial are either principal or secondary parties.

However, the House of Lords has indicated that it is desirable that in the particulars of the offence given in the indictment the prosecution should indicate whether the accused is charged as a perpetrator or secondary party so that he is better able to meet the evidence to be brought against him.[6] Once convicted all are liable to the same penalty. This was brought home in a dramatic way by the case of *Craig and Bentley*[7] where following a roof top chase Bentley was arrested by police officers following a robbery. He, allegedly, called out to Craig, "Let him have it Chris" and Craig shot and killed a police officer. Both were indicted and convicted of murder. Craig was too young to face the death penalty and he was sentenced to life imprisonment, but Bentley, who was in police custody at the time of the killing, was hanged.

In the case of *Giannetto*[8] the prosecution's case was that the defendant was liable either as a principal offender, or alternatively as a secondary party to the killing of his wife. The Court of Appeal addressed the issue of whether the jury had to be unanimous on the defendant's mode of participation. His wife had been killed by a total of 12 blows to the head which shattered her skull and brain. They had separated prior to her death, and were embroiled in an acrimonious custody dispute. Evidence was presented at trial that D had previously engaged Welch, a tramp, described by the judge as "a rogue and a vagabond"—as executioner, but Welch had reneged on their agreement. In essence, the Crown's case had been that the defendant had either murdered her himself, as a principal offender, or had got someone else to do so, in which case D would be liable as an accessory. Their Lordships,

---

[5] See, below, para.4–047.
[6] See, generally, *Fitzgerald* [1992] Crim.L.R. 66.
[7] *The Times,* December 10–13, 1952. In 1998, 45 years after his hanging in 1953, Derek Bentley received a pardon from the Court of Appeal. In a scathing criticism of the judge, Lord Chief Justice Goddard, who had condemned Bentley to hang, the Court stated that the summing-up had been biased and fatally flawed. Bentley who was 19 at the time but had a mental age of only 11, had an IQ of 66, was tried, convicted and hanged within three months of the bungled robbery: see *The Times,* July 31, 1998.
[8] [1997] 1 Cr.App.R. 1; [1996] Crim.L.R. 722. See also *Taylor* [1998] Crim.L.R. 582; and R. Taylor, "Jury Unanimity in Homicide" [2001] Crim.L.R. 283.

expressly approving the decision of the Supreme Court of Canada in *Thatcher v R*,[9] held that a jury were entitled to convict D if they were all satisfied that if he was not the killer he at least encouraged the killing. Two cardinal principles prevailed. First, that the jury must be agreed upon the basis upon which they find a defendant guilty. Secondly, that the defendant must know what case he has to meet. When the Crown allege that, on the evidence, the defendant must have committed the offence either as principal or as secondary offender, and make it equally clear that they cannot say which, the basis on which the jury must be unanimous (subject to the majority verdict rules) is that the defendant, having the necessary mens rea, by whatever means caused the result which is criminalised by the law. Specification of mode of participation or explicit participatory delineation is not expressly required. Thus, in *Giannetto*, the jury could find D guilty on the basis that he had killed his wife or at least encouraged the actual perpetrator to kill her.[10]

Three important points should be noted before we go any further: (i) a person does not become a secondary party to a crime until that crime is either committed or attempted by the principal. If B supplies A with a gun in order to kill X, B becomes a party to the murder only when A kills X, though he will be a party to an attempt if A attempts to kill X and fails; (ii) both s.8 of the Accessories and Abettors Act 1861 and the Criminal Law Act 1967 were designed to improve criminal procedure and not to affect substantive criminal liability. Thus the old cases are authoritative on the question of who is a participant in a given crime. Today, however, we do not need as a general rule to distinguish between the various types of secondary participation[11]; (iii) with the abolition by the Criminal Law Act 1967 of felonies, the old offence of being an accessory after the fact to a felony automatically lapsed. However section 4 of the Act introduces a new offence of assisting arrestable offenders which has similar features to the old offence.[12]

2. THE PRINCIPAL OR PERPETRATOR

Suppose that A, B and C are charged with the murder of V. The evidence establishes that **4–003** they had agreed to kill V, that all were present at the time of the killing, and that V was killed by a single stab wound. All deny striking the fatal blow and the evidence does not establish which was the perpetrator though it was clearly one of them. It would be the height of absurdity if the law provided in such a case that all three should be acquitted and of course they are not. All three may be convicted of murder and on conviction all three must be sentenced to imprisonment for life.

---

[9] (1987) 39 D.L.R. (4th) 275. T was charged with the murder of his ex-wife. In the alternative it was said by the prosecution that he had had her killed on his behalf. There was evidence of previous attempts to hire an executioner and the trial judge directed the jury that they could find T guilty either on the basis that he had killed his ex-wife himself, or on the basis that he was a party to the offence, having aided and abetted another in the commission of the offence—there being in s.21(1) of the relevant Criminal Code provisions similar to those in s.8 of the Accessories and Abettors Act 1861. On appeal it was argued that the jury should have been directed that they must be unanimous as to the basis upon which they found the accused guilty, but the Supreme Court rejected that argument. It was stated that the Code had been designed to alleviate the necessity for the Crown having to indict D as a principal or secondary offender. The law stipulates that both forms of participation are not only equally culpable, but should be treated as one single mode of incurring criminal liability. Dickson C.J. asserted that: "If there is evidence before a jury that points to an accused either committing a crime personally, or alternatively, aiding and abetting another to commit the offence; provided the jury is satisfied beyond a reasonable doubt that the accused did one or the other, it is "a matter of indifference" which alternative actually occurred . . . s.21 precludes a requirement of jury unanimity as to the particular nature of the accused's participation in the offence. Why should the juror be compelled to make a choice on a subject which is a matter of legal indifference?"
[10] Lack of precision over the indictment in such cases is not incompatible with art.6 of the ECHR vis-à-vis D knowing the case to be presented against him. See *Mercer* [2001] All E.R. (D) 187.
[11] See below, para.4–005.
[12] See below, para.4–047.

In this illustration there is no need to isolate the principal, but sometimes this is necessary because the rules relating to his liability differ from those of secondary parties. One situation in which it is necessary to draw a sharp distinction between the principal offender and secondary party is where the offence is one of strict liability.[13] We have seen that a person may be made liable for certain offences even though he lacks mens rea. But strict liability is imposed *only* on the principal offender and is not imposed on secondary parties. In *Callow v Tillstone*[14] the principal offender was a butcher who was charged with exposing bad meat for sale. He had got a vet to examine a carcass of a heifer which had eaten yew leaves. The vet passed it fit for sale and, relying upon the vet's certificate, the principal offender put it up for sale. The offence was one of strict liability and the principal offender was, therefore, convicted. The justices also convicted the vet as they found that he had been negligent in issuing the certificate. On appeal the vet's conviction was quashed since he did not know nor was he reckless as to the meat being bad. It may strike the reader as a trifle odd that the principal offender was held liable even though he was entirely blameless while the secondary party (the vet) was not liable though he was at fault in the sense that he was negligent. However, the courts have taken the view that strict liability applies only to the principal offender. The reason for all this is that liability for secondary participation arises at common law and criminal liability at common law generally requires mens rea in the form of intention, knowledge or *Cunningham* recklessness. You could argue that this is illogical since if there are good policy reasons for imposing strict liability on the principal there are equally good reasons for imposing it on the secondary offenders—but the law is not always logical.

A similar situation may arise in relation to vicarious liability.[15] Under this doctrine the licensee of a public house who is away from the premises may be held liable for the crimes committed by his employee whom he has left in charge of the pub. However, if the employee is only liable as a secondary party, for example he has aided and abetted customers consuming alcohol after hours, the licensee cannot be vicariously liable.[16] Thus, in this situation, we need to know whether the employee is a principal or secondary party.

4–004   So how is the principal to be marked off from the secondary parties? Normally this presents no problems. A shoots and kills X with a gun provided by B. A is the perpetrator or principal and B is a secondary party to it. C enters a building to steal while D keeps a watch outside; C is the principal offender in the burglary and D is the secondary party. However, it is not always as clear as this. Suppose that E holds Y while F stabs him and Y dies as a result. Is E a principal offender or a secondary party? It is possible to have more than one principal offender. If E had merely decoyed Y to a place where F stabbed him, then E would clearly only be a secondary party. Does he become a principal by holding Y so that Y cannot defend himself against F's murderous attack. This case is clearly right on the borderline. If the crime had been rape and E had held Y down while F engaged in penile penetration, you could hardly say that E was the perpetrator of the rape—you could not really say that E raped Y. On the other hand if E holds Y while F punches him you could say that E and F are co-perpetrators of an assault since for E to hold Y against his will is in itself an assault. But where E holds Y so that F can stab him it may be unrealistic to say that E killed Y: what he had done is to help F kill Y.

The principal offender is, therefore, any person (or persons) who by his own conduct *directly brings about the actus reus of the crime*. This formulation may not, however, suffice for all cases. Suppose that A puts poison in X's medicine knowing that B, a nurse, will

---

[13] See above, para.3–001.
[14] (1900) 64 J.P. 823; 19 Cox C.C. 576.
[15] See below, paras 4–050—4–057.
[16] See, e.g. *Ferguson v Weaving* [1951] 1 K.B. 814; considered below, para.4–056.

innocently administer the poison to X in the course of her duties. Or suppose that C persuades D, a nine year old boy, to steal from Y. Neither B, since she lacks mens rea, nor D, since he is under the age of criminal responsibility[17] can be charged as parties either to the killing of X or the stealing from Y. In both cases it might be said that A and C did not directly bring about the actus reus of the respective crimes. Common sense, however, tells us that A killed X and C stole from Y and the formulation at the beginning of this paragraph should be taken to include such cases. In these cases, B and D are often referred to as innocent agents; thus we say that A killed X through the innocent agency of B. It is probably safer and simpler to ask—can we drop B out of the picture and say A killed X?[18]

3. SECONDARY PARTIES

From the discussion in the preceding section we can say that a secondary party, sometimes **4–005** called an accessory, is, broadly speaking, someone who helps to bring about the crime without being the actual perpetrator.[19] Such a broad definition, though it will probably suffice for most cases, is not sufficiently refined to deal precisely with all the cases that can arise.

It might be thought that the position of a secondary party was exactly the same as that of a principal. After all, s.8 of the Accessories and Abettors Act 1861 provides that he is liable "to be indicted and tried as if he were a principal offender". However this is not really so and the liability of the secondary party turns out to be rather more complex than that of the principal. Suppose that A and B are charged with a crime and it is alleged that A is the perpetrator and that B is the secondary party. Against A it has to be proved that he by his own conduct directly caused the actus reus with the appropriate mens rea. Against B it has to be proved that:

(i) he knew that A would cause the actus reus with the appropriate mens rea; and

(ii) that he helped A to commit that crime knowing that his conduct would be of assistance to A.

You may say that the proposition (ii) includes proposition (i), but this way of setting out the requirements in relation to B serves to emphasise that the mens rea of a secondary party extends not only to knowledge of the principal's mens rea, but also requires a further intention to help the principal; and, in the case of the secondary party, not only has it to be shown that the actus reus of the crime was brought about but also that there was some conduct of the secondary party which helped the commission of that crime.

It follows, therefore, that B cannot be convicted as an accessory to A's crime merely because he knows that A will commit the crime. B may learn that A plans to murder X or burgle Y's premises but this knowledge alone is not enough to make B a party to the killing of X or the burgling of Y's premises. It can make no difference that, on learning of A's

---

[17] See below, para.5–098.

[18] An illustration is provided by *Stringer* (1991) 94 Cr.App.R. 13 where D, duping his fellow employees (accounts staff), facilitated the transfer of bogus invoices to himself through the firm's accounting system, resulting in the debiting of his employer's account. These fellow employees were innocent agents; D had dishonestly appropriated and committed theft; see also *Bourne* (1952) 36 Cr.App.R. 125 and *Cogan and Leak* [1976] Q.B. 217, above at para.2–083.

[19] It is quite common to call the secondary party an accessory and both these terms are used in the book. It is also common practice to refer to this individual as an "aider, abettor, counsellor or a procurer", because these are the activities of an accessory under s.8 of the Accessories and Abettors Act 1861.

intention, B is secretly delighted because he will inherit under X's will or because Y is someone he hates. An even more extreme illustration is provided by the case of *Allan*.[20] Allan was present when some of his friends became involved in a fight. He knew that his friends were committing a crime, but not only did he approve of their conduct, he had secretly resolved to help them should they require his aid. His conviction, however, as a party to the crime committed by his friends was quashed because knowledge of the principal's crime coupled with an intention to aid is not enough unless there is also some conduct of the accessory which helps the principal. Edmund-Davies J. stated:

> "In our judgment, before a jury can properly convict an accused person of being a principal in the second degree to an affray, they must be convinced by the evidence, that, at the very least, he by some means or other encouraged the participants. To hold otherwise would be, in effect . . . to convict a man on his thoughts, unaccompanied by any physical act other than the fact of his mere presence."[21]

So what exactly has to be proved against the accessory to make him a party to the principal's crime? Simply put, it must be shown that with knowledge of the principal's crime the accessory did something to help in its commission with the intention of assisting; though in detail the position may be more complicated.

A. Knowledge of the Type of Crime

4–006   The accessory must have knowledge of the essential matters which constitute the offence; there needs to be some sort of subjective awareness of the elements of the principal crime. This requirement was encapsulated by Lord Goddard C.J. in *Johnson v Youden* who stated:

> "Before a person can be convicted of aiding and abetting the commission of an offence he must at least know the essential matters which constitute that offence. He need not actually know that an offence has been committed, because he may not know that the facts constitute an offence and ignorance of the law is no defence."[22]

What is the nature of this prerequisite? First, the requirement of knowledge of the principal's crime does not require that B should know of every detail of A's planned crime. Take a case where A plans to steal money from a safe at a particular factory and needs cutting equipment for this purpose. He contacts B and purchases this equipment from him making no mention whatever of his plans. B, however, knows that A has a record for burglary, that he has no legitimate business for which such equipment could be required and guesses correctly that it is required to break into a safe on some premises or other. Nevertheless B supplies the equipment. B may be convicted as an accessory to the burglary committed by A though B has no idea when or where the crime is to be committed. The point is that he knows the essentials of the crime. But *Bainbridge*,[23] on which the last illustration is based, shows that it is not enough to make B liable that he knew that A was up to no good—that would be far too vague.

---

[20] [1965] 1 Q.B. 130.
[21] [1965] 1 Q.B. 130 at 138. See also, *S v DPP* [2003] EWHC 2717 (Admin); and *Rose* [2004] EWCA Crim 764 where D2 simply evinced an intent to dissuade D from attacking V.
[22] [1950] 1 K.B. 544 at 546.
[23] [1960] 1 Q.B. 129. B claimed that he thought that the individual on whose behalf he purchased the oxy-acetylene equipment was going to use it for cutting-up stolen property, and had no knowledge that it was going to be used, as indeed it was, to facilitate breaking into the Midland Bank at Stoke Newington.

It was also accepted in that case that B would not be liable if his only suspicion was that A planned to commit some different type of crime, such as receiving stolen metal and that the cutting equipment was to be used to break it up. Bainbridge's counsel contended that since B had no knowledge of the details of the principal crime intended (time, place or date), he did not have the mens rea of an accessory in that crime. This formulation was held by the court to be too constrained. It sufficed that B knew, and not that he merely suspected, that a crime of the *same type* as that actually committed was intended by the principal.

So the accessory will not escape liability by saying that it was a case of no-questions-asked if he, in fact, realised what the principal was up to. Moreover, it is enough that the principal commits one of a range of crimes which was in the contemplation of the accessory. In *DPP for Northern Ireland v Maxwell*,[24] Maxwell's task had been to lead Northern Ireland terrorists to a public house in a village where they left a bomb. He claimed that he could not be convicted as a party to the bombing since he did not know what the terrorists had planned to do. The House of Lords held that from his knowledge of the organisation he knew that the mission would take one of a number of forms and it was sufficient that the actual deed that night fell within the bounds of one of the offences he must have contemplated. In essence, a prescribed "*shopping list*" of offences was in existence; the offence committed being an item on that specific list.

In most cases the test propounded in *Maxwell* will provide a ready answer. However one **4–007** or two questions remain unanswered. For example, if B suspects A is about to commit burglary and the equipment he has supplied (a crowbar) will be used to force open the windows of the premises, will he be liable if A's plan, which he carries out, is to inflict grievous bodily harm on the householder utilising the crowbar. The immediate reaction will be to say that this is an entirely different crime from the one B contemplated. However, where A enters the house as a trespasser with intent to inflict grievous bodily harm on someone inside, this is burglary, contrary to s.9(1)(a) of the Theft Act 1968,[25] and burglary is the very crime B contemplated. Perhaps the courts would take a common sense view in these sorts of cases and hold that B should not be convicted as a party to a particular crime he almost certainly would not have supported. Another problem is that once B has supplied the equipment A can go on using it indefinitely for the type of crime B had in mind. Does B become a party to all the future crimes A commits with the equipment? This may seem rather hard on B but there is nothing technically to stop such liability arising.

We have said so far that the secondary party must know that the principal offender will commit a particular offence or one of a known group of offences. Knowledge here includes wilful blindness and so B would be liable if he guesses that A is about to commit a burglary with the equipment he is supplying and deliberately asks no questions so that he can say that he does not know what A is about.[26] The court appears to have gone even further in *Carter v Richardson*[27] where A was a learner driver under the supervision of B. They were involved in an accident and it was discovered that A was over the prescribed alcohol limit. Here B was held to have knowledge of the crime even though he could not *know* that A was over the prescribed limit; he did, however, know that A might be over the prescribed limit and his subjective *Cunningham* recklessness constitutes sufficient knowledge for this purpose. So far as A in this case was concerned we have already seen that the offence is one of strict liability[28] but, as previously mentioned, mens rea must always be proved in a secondary

---

[24] [1978] 1 W.L.R. 1350; see also *Bryce* [2004] EWCA Crim 1231; [2004] Crim.L.R. 936; considered further below at para.4–013.
[25] See below, para.9–023.
[26] Wilful blindness would seem to lie somewhere between intention and recklessness; see above para.2–073.
[27] [1974] R.T.R. 314.
[28] See above, para.3–001.

party. Presumably what has to be shown against B is that he knew that A had been drinking and deliberately took the risk that A was over the prescribed limit.[29] In *Webster*[30] the defendant was charged with aiding and abetting the offence of causing death by dangerous driving. The Court of Appeal rejected the proposition that a negligence standard of mens rea could suffice for liability for the accessory. The threshold was not set at proving what D, "ought to have foreseen", but rather, "it is the defendant's foresight that the principal was likely to commit the offence which must be proved."[31] It was necessary for the prosecution to establish that D did foresee that the principal offender was likely to drive dangerously, and yet failed to take an opportunity to prevent the occurrence.

B. Aids, Abets, Counsels or Procures

4–008   In addition to providing that the secondary party knew of the crime the principal intended to commit, the prosecution must prove that the secondary party helped the principal with intent to do so. In fact, s.8 uses neither the words "help" nor "assistance" and imposes liability where the accessory, "aids, abets, counsels or procures" the crime. Basically these verbs convey the idea of help or assistance but in the end we have to consider the precise interpretation of the words used in the statute itself. This was the important point made by the Court of Appeal in *Attorney-General's Reference (No.1 of 1975)*[32] when it was said that these words must be given their ordinary meaning. Obviously the words overlap to some extent. If A and B meet X and B encourages A to assault X we may indifferently say that B aids, abets, counsels or procures A to assault X. On the other hand each word may contain nuances of meaning not conveyed by the others; *Attorney-General's Reference (No.1 of 1975)* illustrates the point. B added alcohol to A's drink without A's knowledge and A's subsequent driving of a car resulted in him being prosecuted under the breathalyser provisions. It was held that B had *procured* the commission of the offence by A. The court rejected an argument that secondary participation always requires communication between the accessory and the perpetrator and held that a crime could be procured, that is brought about by endeavour, though there was no communication between the secondary and principal offenders.[33] The court did not attempt an exhaustive definition of the remaining verbs but it would now be unwise to assume that they are synonymous.

The meaning attributable to "counselling" was considered in *Calhaem*.[34] C was charged with counselling Z to kill another, having paid him £5,000 to do so. Z, the principal prosecution witness at C's trial, gave evidence that having been hired by C, he had gone to the victim's house intending to act out a charade so as to keep C happy. When the victim screamed, however, he had gone berserk and killed her. C claimed that she could not be guilty as an accomplice unless there was a substantial causal connection between her acts and the commission of the offence. However, the Court of Appeal held that the ordinary meaning of the word "counsel" did not imply a causal connection; it sufficed that the crime was committed "within the scope of the authority or advice".[35] Similarly it seems that "aid"

---

[29] See, e.g. *Blakely and Sutton v DPP* [1991] R.T.R. 405.
[30] [2006] EWCA Crim 415.
[31] [2006] EWCA Crim 415 at paras [25]–[26].
[32] [1975] 2 All E.R. 684.
[33] No communication or consensus was needed for procuring. However, Lord Widgery stated: "You cannot procure an offence unless there is a *causal link* between what you do and the commission of the offence . . ." (emphasis added): [1975] 2 All E.R. 684 at 687.
[34] [1985] Q.B. 808. See also *Luffmann and Briscoe* [2008] EWCA Crim 1379.
[35] [1985] Q.B. 808 at 813. Their Lordships presented an unusual hypothetical scenario wherein the principal is involved in a football riot during which he assaults and kills V, the very person (although unaware at the time) he has been counselled to kill. The counsellor would clearly not be liable for the killing in such circumstances.

does not require a causal link; in many cases the principal would have gone on to carry out the crime irrespective of any assistance given.

In summary, the words "aiding" and "abetting" are suitable to cover a situation where the principal offender in trying to do the prohibited act, supplies the weapon or proffers encouragement at the time of the crime, and "counselling" suggests that the principal will, after being counselled, attempt to commit the offence. Procuring is the only one of the four words which covers a situation where the principal offender may not have any criminal end in mind. In the Law Commission's Code the terms "procure", "assist" and "encourage" are used in place of aid, abet, counsel or procure.[36]

(i) Conduct Amounting to Aiding, Abetting, Counselling or Procuring

There must be some conduct of the secondary party which can properly be said to amount to **4–009** assistance. *Allan*[37] shows that a secret intention to assist without any assistance in fact is not enough. On the other hand very little assistance may, in fact, be required, and words alone may suffice. It would have been enough had Allan shouted encouragement to the principals or even if he had said "give me a call if you need a hand".

An interesting problem was posed by the speeches of their Lordships in the case of *Gillick v West Norfolk and Wisbech Area Health Authority.*[38] Under the old law, prior to the Sexual Offences Act 2003 and the specific creation of a multiplicity of crimes targeting a wider range of sexual activity with children[39] under 16, an offence existed within s.6 of the Sexual Offences Act 1956 for a man to have intercourse with a girl who is under 16 years of age. It was also clear that it would be an offence for another to aid, abet, counsel or procure that man to have intercourse with the girl. A doctor who prescribes contraceptive pills for a 15-year-old girl knows that he is making it more likely that she will have intercourse. It ought to follow, therefore, that the doctor is a secondary party to that intercourse. Their Lordships recognised this possibility and said that a doctor may, in some circumstances, prescribe contraceptive pills for a 15-year-old girl without attracting secondary party liability. They did not, however, explain how this could be so, although the majority assumed that a doctor in such a scenario lacked the requisite intention. It has been cogently advocated by Professor Smith that the case is better explained as impliedly predicated upon necessity:

> "The answer to this conundrum, it is suggested, is that we have here encountered a concealed defence of necessity. The doctor is acting lawfully if he is doing what he honestly believes to be necessary. All the normal conditions for liability as an aider and abettor may be satisfied; yet the doctor is to be excused. The commission of the offence may be, as Lord Brandon asserts it is, promoted, encouraged or facilitated; but the evil of the encouragement, etc., of the offence is outweighed by the good which flows from the provision of the advice."[40]

---

[36] Clause 27(1) of the Draft Criminal Code provides:
 "A person is guilty of an offence as an accessory if—
 (a) he intentionally procures, assists or encourages the act which constitutes or results in the commission of the offence by the principal; and
 (b) he knows, or (where recklessness suffices in the case of the principal) is reckless with respect to, any circumstances that is an element of the offence; and
 (c) he intends that the principal shall act, or is aware that he is or maybe acting, or that he may act, with the fault [if any] required for the offence."
[37] [1965] 1 Q.B. 130, above, para.4–005.
[38] [1986] A.C. 112.
[39] See below, at paras 7–135—7–136.
[40] J.C. Smith [1986] Crim.L.R. 113 at 117.

4–010 Presence as aiding, etc.   If a shout or two of encouragement is enough to constitute aiding, why should not mere presence suffice? A may be just as much encouraged by the presence of B as by a word of encouragement. Clearly B's accidental presence cannot suffice but the reason for this is that B would then lack any intention to aid. But what if B then stays to watch? When terrorists seized the Iranian Embassy in London, their illegal activities were closely watched for some days by hordes of newsmen and, through the medium of television, by many millions of viewers. In a very real sense the terrorists drew encouragement from this for one of their primary aims was to secure publicity for their cause. Common sense tells us that the newsmen were not accessories to the continued imprisonment of the Embassy staff and the case of *Clarkson*[41] strikingly bears this out. In that case B and C did not become secondary parties to rape merely because, to satisfy their prurient interest, they watched fellow soldiers repeatedly rape a girl in their barracks.

Presence, however, if it is not accidental constitutes some evidence of aiding, etc., though it must be considered along with all the other evidence. Thus presence coupled with evidence of a previous conspiracy between the parties to commit the crime will suffice. Depending on the surrounding circumstances, presence alone may be demonstrative of encouragement. The presence of the accused over a lengthy period while offences are perpetrated can be significant. In *Francom,*[42] for instance, the murder victim was subjected to appalling acts of violence and degradation, involving 48 separate injuries, whilst trapped in a flat over several days by her eventual murderers. According to the evidence before the jury, she was punched, kicked, struck with a snooker cue, had her hair pulled out and burnt, she was struck with an iron, urinated upon, scalded and burnt with cigaretttes. She was also given disinfectant to drink and placed in a kitchen cupboard. Lord Woolf clearly articulated that, having regard to the length of the period which was involved here, even the presence alone of the defendant was capable of demonstrating encouragement.[43] In *Coney,*[44] however, it was held to be a misdirection to direct a jury that non-accidental presence at a fight was conclusive evidence of aiding. No doubt this decision was right, but presence at an illegal activity which requires spectators if it is to prosper at all may more readily give rise to an inference of aiding and abetting than presence at other illegal activities.

In *Wilcox v Jeffrey*[45] B was convicted of aiding and abetting A, the celebrated jazz saxophonist Coleman Hawkins, to play in public contrary to the conditions on which he was allowed to enter England. The Divisional Court thought it right in such a case to invite the jury to infer aiding from B's presence throughout the illegal performance together with the fact that B had met A at the airport and had written an account of the performance in the newspaper for which he worked. Suppose then that in *Allan* the trial judge had directed the jury that Allan's continued presence at the fight could be regarded as evidence of aiding, and that the jury had convicted him. Would the Court of Appeal have quashed his conviction? It is submitted that a defendant ought not to be convicted where the evidence establishes mere presence without any positive act of assistance.

4–011 Aiding, etc., by Omission.   Is B liable for A's crime because he fails to intervene to prevent it or to put a stop to it? The general answer must be "no", because there is no general duty to prevent the commission of a crime by A, but exceptions may apply. In an Australian case, *Russell,*[46] it was held that a father was a secondary party to the homicide of his children

---

[41] [1971] 3 All E.R. 344.
[42] [2001] 1 Cr.App.R. 237; see also, *Miah* [2004] EWCA Crim 63.
[43] [2001] 1 Cr.App.R. 237 at 243.
[44] (1882) 8 Q.B.D. 534.
[45] [1951] 1 All E.R. 464.
[46] [1933] V.L.R. 59.

where he stood by and watched the mother drown them.[47] In this jurisdiction a limited solution to the problem of proving which of two or more defendants attacked a person in the same household has been provided by the Domestic Violence, Crime and Victims Act 2004.[48] By s.5 an offence punishable by a maximum of 14 years imprisonment, has been created to cover causing the death of a child or "vulnerable adult". In effect, the crime is one of negligence as D, if not the direct cause of death, is liable if he *ought to have been aware of the risk*; the risk of which D ought to have been aware is a "significant" one of "serious injury" and the death must have occurred in the circumstances that D ought to have foreseen.

In *Du Cros v Lambourne*[49] it was held that B could be convicted of aiding A to drive dangerously where A was driving B's car with his permission and was, to B's knowledge, driving it dangerously. Similarly in the recent case of *Webster*[50] it was determined that the owner of a motor vehicle could be liable as a secondary party to the offence of causing death by dangerous driving committed by the principal offender. The owner by sitting idly by in the passenger seat and failing to take a legitimate opportunity to intervene may consequently become inculpated. This duty to intervene was replicated in *Forman and Ford*,[51] a case where V was assaulted whilst in police custody in the presence of two officers. This duty to intervene applies to every police constable to prevent the commission of a crime, such as an assault, irrespective of the actual perpetrator. Both officers can be convicted, even where it is unclear which officer struck the blow, provided the jury are sure in respect of each of them that if he himself did not commit the assault he encouraged the other to do so by failing to intervene or to report the offence. Aiding and abetting can, therefore, arise through B's inactivity.

A difficult problem may be experienced where a group of people are sharing a flat and A discovers that B has possession of a controlled drug. Is A expected to leave the flat? If he stays will he be in danger of being held to have given passive encouragement to B? In *Bland*[52] the Court of Appeal held that you could not get evidence of passive assistance merely from the fact that people live together. You would need evidence that A either encouraged B or that A had the right to control B's activities. The nature of the right to control the actions of another was also at issue in *Tuck v Robson*.[53] It was determined therein that a licensee of a public house who stands idly by, and takes no affirmative steps to remove patrons from the premises after closing hours, thereby aids and abets their prohibited drinking.

(ii) The Mental Element in Aiding, etc.

It has been pointed out that a secondary party's mens rea, in a sense, requires two elements: **4–012** (i) knowledge of the principal's mens rea and (ii) an intent to aid the principal in the commission of his crime. The former of these requirements has been examined in some detail above; it is now necessary to say something more about the latter. Clearly B does not become a party to A's crime if, knowing of it, he accidentally helps in its commission as where B, knowing that A intends to steal from C's safe, absent mindedly fails to lock the safe. The words "aids, abets, counsels or procures" suggest purposive conduct on B's part.

It is usually said that the accomplice must be proved to have *intended* to aid, abet, counsel or procure the offence committed by the principal. Is it sufficient that he is reckless as to

---

[47] See, e.g. *Gibson and Gibson* (1984) 80 Cr.App.R. 24.
[48] See below, at para.4–035.
[49] [1907] 1 K.B. 40.
[50] [2006] EWCA Crim 415.
[51] [1988] Crim.L.R. 677.
[52] [1988] Crim.L.R. 41.
[53] [1970] 1 W.L.R. 741.

whether his action will aid, abet, counsel or procure? We saw in *Carter v Richardson*[54] that the driving supervisor was convicted on the basis that he intentionally assisted the learner driver to drive the car being aware that he was likely to be over the prescribed alcohol limit. There is no way that he could actually "know" that the driver was over the limit and it seems subjective *Cunningham* recklessness in relation to a circumstance[55] provides an adequate basis of liability.

In *Blakely and Sutton v DPP*[56] the position was, in effect, reversed. Blakely (B) had been having an affair with a married man, T, who occasionally spent the night with her. On the evening in question B and her friend S were having a drink with T at a pub when he announced that he intended to drive home to spend the night with his wife. B and S added vodka to his drink, planning to tell him he would have to spend the night with B since he was now unfit to drive. Unfortunately the plan back-fired. T went off to the toilet and left to drive home before B and S could tell him what they had done. He was breathalysed and found to be over the limit. There is no question of T's criminal liability for a drink driving offence. He had committed a strict liability offence and his lack of knowledge of the lacing of his drink was no defence, though it might save him from mandatory disqualification. The question for the court was whether B and S were parties to the offence. Whereas in *Carter v Richardson* the accomplice *intended* to aid and abet the learner driver to drive the car, being *reckless* as to whether the level of alcohol in his blood was too high (i.e. reckless as to a circumstance of the offence), Blakeley and Sutton deliberately set about to ensure that T was over the prescribed limit, but the last thing they wanted was for him to drive; they were at most reckless that he might do so (i.e. reckless as to the act of driving). There is, a suggestion in the case that they would have been convicted had it been proved that they were aware that he might drive (i.e. *Cunningham* subjective recklessness). But should *Cunningham* subjective recklessness suffice as the basis for secondary party liability? There is support in the Draft Criminal Code for the proposition that recklessness as to circumstances (as in *Carter v Richardson*) should suffice, but the Code proposes that the prosecution must prove that the accessory intended to "aid, abet, counsel or procure." There are statements in other cases[57] that where at least procure is concerned, the prosecution will need to prove that the accomplice intended to procure the commission of the offence by the principal and it is suggested that this should be the position in relation to the other methods of participation.

4–013   Suppose, however, that A plans to burgle X's house and he asks B to drive him to a specified destination. B does so and A burgles the house. B's liability may be considered on various hypotheses:

(1) B believes that A's enterprise is an innocent one; then B cannot incur criminal liability.

(2) B knows what A plans and is willing to drive him to and from the scene of the crime. B is evidently a party to A's crime.

(3) B is a taxi driver whom A has engaged at the normal commercial rates. B knows that A plans to burgle X's home but considers that this is none of his business. B reasons that if he refuses his service then another taxi driver, who does not have

---

[54] [1974] R.T.R. 314, see, above, para.4–007.
[55] Being over the prescribed limit.
[56] [1991] R.T.R. 405.
[57] See, e.g. *Att-Gen's Reference (No.1 of 1975)* [1975] 2 All E.R. 684; *Reed* [1982] Crim.L.R. 819 and *Millward* [1994] Crim.L.R. 527.

B's knowledge of A's intentions, will readily be found by A. Why, B asks himself, should he lose a fare when the crime will be committed anyway? A problem similar to this arose in *National Coal Board v Gamble*,[58] where the defendants, the National Coal Board, had supplied X with coal. The procedure was that X's drivers filled up their lorries at the Coal Board's depot and then drove the loaded lorries on to a weighbridge. If the weight shown was correct the weighbridge operator issued the driver with a ticket at which time the court held that ownership of the goods passed to X. Under the Motor Vehicle (Construction and Use) Regulations 1955 it was an offence to drive a lorry on a public road when the load exceeds a certain weight. On the occasion in question the weighbridge operator saw that the lorry was overloaded and commented on this fact to the driver. The driver replied that he would take the risk and a ticket was issued. The driver committed the offence immediately he drove on to the road, but the difficult question was whether or not the Coal Board was liable as a secondary party through the action of their employee.[59] It seems clear that the weighbridge operator did not desire to help the driver commit an offence; essentially he could not have cared less whether the driver was picked up for contravening the regulations or not. On the other hand he did know all the facts which constituted the offence and he knew his action in issuing a ticket enabled the driver to commit the offence. The Divisional Court held that this was enough to make the weighbridge operator, and therefore the Board, a secondary party.[60] Thus it is sufficient that B performs an act which he knows will assist A in the commission of a crime.

In a modern context the decision in *J. F. Alford Transport Ltd, Alford and Payne*[61] represents a similar illustration of the principles previously established by *NCB v Gamble*. The three defendants involved in the case were a company, its managing director and its transport manager. Tachograph records of the company were found to have material discrepancies. Nineteen of the company's drivers had pleaded guilty to specimen offences involving the making of false entries on the record sheets contrary to s.99(5) of the Transport Act 1968. The three defendants were charged with having aided and abetted these offences. In his direction to the jury the trial judge stated that passive acquiescence on the defendants' part would suffice for a conviction for aiding and abetting. They were all convicted on that basis and appealed. The Court of Appeal held that passive acquiescence was not sufficient. For a defendant to be convicted it had to be demonstrated that the defendant intended to do acts which he knew to be capable of assisting or encouraging the commission of the crime. Insufficient evidence existed of this knowledge to sustain their convictions, which were quashed. Knowledge of and passive acquiescence in the principal's offence are not, on their own, sufficient to ground liability for aiding and abetting. What has to be proved by the prosecution is that: (1) B had knowledge of the principal offence coupled with (2) B had an ability to control the principal's action and (3) B took a deliberate decision to refrain from exercising that control. If these elements can be proved then B can be convicted of aiding and abetting. They were present in *NCB v Gamble* since B: (i)

---

[58] [1959] 1 Q.B. 11.
[59] On the basis of vicarious liability, see below, para.4–050.
[60] Query whether it would have made any difference had the weighbridge operator been under the belief that he had no power to refuse to issue the ticket.
[61] [1997] Crim.L.R. 745. See also, *Yorkshire Traction Co Ltd v Vehicle Inspectorate, The Times,* March 15, 2001 CA.

did know that the driver's lorry was overloaded and yet the driver still intended to drive on the highway; (ii) B appreciated he had the power and ability not to issue the certificate which empowered the driver to leave with the load; and (iii) B deliberately refrained from exercising that control and issued the requisite certificate. The aiding and abetting charge was logically applied in *NCB v Gamble*, and logically rejected in *J. F. Alford Transport Ltd, Alford and Payne*.

The issues of degree of foresight and specificity of criminal conduct required have arisen more recently in *Reardon*[62] and *Bryce*.[63] In *Reardon*, A shot two men, X and Y, in the bar of a public house and carried them, both dying, into the bar. He returned to the bar, said to Reardon (B) that one of them was still alive and asked B for the loan of his knife. B handed A a knife with a six inch blade which A took into the garden. Medical evidence established that both men would have died from the gunshot wounds but both in fact died from stab wounds inflicted with B's knife. B appealed against his conviction on two counts of murder. In dispute was whether the stabbing of not just one but both victims by A amounted to conduct which B could reasonably, and did foresee, as the type of conduct which A might effect. It was clear that whichever victim A stabbed first, the use of the knife for the purpose of killing the deceased was plainly contemplated. Furthermore, it followed that B would have foreseen at least the strong possibility that if A found the other victim was still breathing and alive, he might use the knife in the same way, and therefore that was an act by A of a type which B had foreseen. The appeal was dismissed: the fact that A used the knife in a foreseen way on two occasions rather than one did not exculpate B.[64] Similarly, liability was established in *Bryce*.[65] The defendant had intentionally transported the killer, D1, to the scene of the crime, but the eventual killing do not occur until 13 hours later. Nonetheless, the Court of Appeal determined that the jury were entitled to infer that the defendant had intentionally assisted, that act was committed knowingly, and with contemplation that D1 would effect the very type of offence actually committed.

(4) B hopes that A will be unable to commit the burglary. Let us say that he hopes that on arrival at X's house they will discover that it is occupied and that A will thereupon call off the enterprise. It seems that this will not save B. In *DPP for Northern Ireland v Lynch*,[66] Lynch drove some terrorists to a place where they shot and killed a man. Lynch said that he was hoping that the crime—or any crime—would not be committed but it was said that this would be no defence. Would it make any difference that B spent the journey to X's house trying to persuade A not to burgle the house? *Fretwell*[67] suggests that it might, for there B was held not guilty of the self-murder by A where he gave A the medication to procure an

[62] [1999] Crim.L.R. 392.

[63] [2004] EWCA Crim 1231; [2004] Crim.L.R. 936.

[64] It is submitted that the principle would appear to apply where the foreseen offence is greater than the offence intentionally encouraged or assisted. B, coming by chance upon his friend A resisting arrest by a constable, trips up another officer coming to the assistance of the first. He intends to assist, and does assist, A to resist lawful arrest. A draws a knife and stabs the constable through the heart. If B knew that A habitually carried a knife and that there was a real risk, a strong possibility, that, in these circumstances, he would use the knife with intent to kill, B would be guilty of murder; see J.C. Smith, Commentary on *Reardon* [1999] Crim.L.R. 392 at 393–394.

[65] [2004] EWCA Crim 1231; [2004] Crim.L.R. 936.

[66] [1975] A.C. 653.

[67] (1862) 28 J.P. 499. Note that prior to amendment by s.1 of the Suicide Act 1961 it was, somewhat bizarrely, an offence to commit suicide.

abortion whilst earnestly entreating her not to use it. This decision is, however, questionable. In *NCB v Gamble*, Devlin J. thought, surely correctly, that if B sold a gun to A knowing that A intended to murder his wife, B would be an accessory to the murder even though his interest was only in the profit he would make on the sale and was utterly indifferent to the fate of A's wife.[68] It is unlikely that Devlin J. would take a different view of B's participation if B sold the gun to A with a plea for matrimonial reconciliation. This brings us full circle to the case we were discussing at the outset of the laundress who washed and returned clothes to a prostitute knowing that she would use them to ply her trade in public. It seems unlikely that we should convict the laundress as a party to the prostitution and, therefore, a line has to be drawn. Of course, in such cases B can always refuse to sell the gun or wash the clothes, but what if A is asking for the return of the gun he lent to B so that he can kill his wife? If B refuses can he be sued for wrongful retention of A's property? It is unlikely that a civil court would uphold such an action and in any case *Garrett v Arthur Churchill (Glass) Ltd*[69] would imply that such a plea would be no defence to B if he returns the gun. How then do we distinguish between the sale of the gun and the washing of the clothes? The only really practical solution is to say that liability in these type of situations will depend upon the severity of the contemplated crime. Thus, if B returns the gun to A knowing that he plans to shoot his wife he will be liable, but not if he knows that A plans a bit of illegal poaching. This seems hardly satisfactory but it is submitted it is the only practicable solution.[70]

4. JOINT ENTERPRISE

A. The Nature of Joint Enterprise

The doctrine of joint enterprise has developed in a haphazard manner and recent case law **4–014** developments have only extended the area of uncertainty. As the Law Commission[71] stressed, the principles have only been subjected to close analysis in comparatively recent times, though its point of origin is to be found in the early case of *Macklin*:

"It is a principle of law that if several persons act together in pursuance of a common intent, every act in furtherance of such intent by each of them is, in law, done by all."[72]

In joint enterprise the allegation is that one defendant participated in the criminal act of another. It renders each of the parties to a joint enterprise criminally liable for the acts done

---

[68] The wider general principle of liability for complicity was stated by Devlin J. in *NCB v Gamble* [1959] 1 Q.B. 11, 20 to the effect that, "a person who supplies the instrument for a crime or anything essential to its commission aids in the commission of it; and if he does so knowingly and with intent to aid, he abets it as well and is therefore guilty of aiding and abetting." Devlin J. also asserted (at 23) that: "An indifference to the result of the crime does not of itself negative abetting. If one man deliberately sells to another a gun to be used for murdering a third, he may be indifferent whether the third man lives or dies and interested only in the cash profit to be made out of the sale, but he can still be an aider and abettor. To hold otherwise would be to negative the rule that mens rea is a matter of intent only and does not depend on desire or motive".
[69] [1970] 1 Q.B. 92.
[70] Under American law the test applied has been to examine the potential seriousness of the contemplated unlawful conduct. This approach may suffer from a lack of certainty but at least it represents a practical solution; see, generally, Perkins and Boyce 3rd edn at p.746.
[71] Law Commission No.131 (1993) *Assisting and Encouraging Crime* at 7 (Consultation Paper).
[72] (1838) 2 Law CC 225, per Alderson B.

in the course of carrying out that joint enterprise. This situation frequently occurs when A and B embark on a planned criminal offence and in the course of that enterprise a "collateral" crime is committed by A; commonly murder during the course of a robbery or burglary.[73] At issue will be whether B can be inculpated in the murder (not simply burglary) committed by A. The same principles apply not simply to the offence of murder but generally to a more serious level of the planned offence. For example, where the concerted plan is to "rough up" V but A actually kills him; or where sexual assault is proposed but rape occurs. Similarly where A rapes V during the course of a planned burglary. Where the criminal liability of any given defendant depends upon the further proof that he had a certain state of mind, that state of mind must be proved against that defendant. Even though several defendants may, as a result of having engaged in a joint enterprise, be each criminally responsible for the criminal act of one of those defendants done in the course of carrying out the joint enterprise, their individual criminal responsibility will, in such a case, depend upon what individual state of mind or intention has been proved against them.[74] The central issue concerns the state of the defendant's mind at the time of his participation in the joint enterprise, but substantial uncertainty still exists over the definition of mens rea required to secure a conviction for the collateral offence.[75]

The key feature of joint enterprise is, thus, that B is inculpated in respect of A's crime even though he does not commit its actus reus. For instance, a planned burglary is thwarted by the householder who is intentionally stabbed to death by A. The question of joint enterprise liability for murder on B's part arises even though he did not have the mens rea of the murder carried out by A. As illustrated below, since these offences often occur during a robbery or burglary enterprise, the wish to implicate every party connected to the killing has appeared at times to outweigh the more stringent demands of legal analysis.

B. Joint Enterprise and Murder

(i) General Principles

4–015 The starting point for consideration of this area is the decision of the Privy Council in *Chan Wing-Siu*,[76] a case where Chan Wing-Siu and two others, armed with knives, had entered the flat of their victim intending to steal from him. The victim refused to surrender any money, upon which the victim was stabbed to death. All three co-defendants were charged with murder and convicted. The nature of secondary liability was addressed, but unfortunately difficulties have ensued from a chance remark made by Sir Robin Cooke who delivered the leading judgment. Having said that, in a murder case, the prosecution must prove that the secondary party had joined the venture foreseeing it as a real possibility, *contemplated by B*, that the principal *might* intentionally kill or cause serious bodily harm, he then added that this could be expressed in terms of authorisation, i.e. the secondary party has authorised the

---

[73] Although many of the cases involve murder arising in the course of burglary, the same principles apply generally where crime X is brought about during the course of committing crime Y.

[74] In *Petters and Parfitt* [1995] Crim.L.R. 501 there was no joint enterprise where A and B came separately to a car park, and one of them had caused V's death through a fatal kick. No communication had occurred between them over common purpose; independent and separate actions do not comprise a joint enterprise and so their manslaughter convictions were quashed.

[75] See, generally, G.R. Sullivan, "Intent, Purpose and Complicity" [1988] Crim.L.R. 641; M. Giles, "Complicity—the Problems of Joint Enterprise" [1990] Crim.L.R. 383; and A Reed, "Joint Participation in Criminal Activity" (1996) 60 J.C.L. 310.

[76] [1985] A.C. 168.

principal to kill or cause serious bodily harm.[77] Now there is potentially a great deal of difference between on the one hand going on a venture foreseeing that the other party might react with violence and on the other authorising the other to use violence; the latter being far more difficult to prove. For example, if the principal believes that the getaway car driver had no knowledge of the gun that he, the principal, is carrying, whereas in fact he is aware and believes that the principal might use it in an emergency to cause death, it is not possible to say the principal is authorised so to act but we say that the secondary party joins the venture foreseeing that it might lead to death or really serious injury.

Following *Chan Wing-Siu* a series of appellate decisions held that the prosecution needed to prove that the secondary party authorised (expressly or tacitly) the use of the violence.[78] Subsequently, in the case of *Hyde*[79] which involved the killing of V through a violent kicking, "like a football", brought about by Hyde and two other main participants, the mens rea for murder by a secondary party was specifically laid out by Lord Lane C.J. He concluded that: "if B realises, without agreeing to such conduct being used, that A may kill or intentionally inflict serious injury, but nevertheless continues to participate with A in this venture, that will amount to a sufficient mental element for B to be guilty of murder if A, with the requisite intent, kills in the course of the venture."[80] In effect, it could be said the secondary party is liable to conviction for murder although he is only reckless, whereas in the case of the perpetrator an intention to kill or cause serious injury must be established; recklessness on the part of the secondary party extending here to the perpetrator's mens rea of murder.[81]

In *Hui Chi-Ming*[82] A's girlfriend claimed that she had been intimidated by a man. A got **4–016** together a group of friends to search for the man responsible; he told them they were going to find someone to hit. Hui Chi-Ming (B), the defendant, was one of the group and was aware that A was carrying a length of metal pipe. Subsequently A hit a man with the pipe and later the man died. A was convicted of manslaughter. Two years later B was put on trial for murder, though it was not alleged that he had himself hit the victim. B refused to plead guilty to manslaughter and stood trial for murder. B was convicted of murder (*Howe* is House of Lords authority for the proposition that the secondary party can be convicted of an offence greater than that of the principal).[83] B appealed against his conviction, inter alia, on the ground that the trial judge had misdirected the jury in telling them that they could convict B of murder if they were satisfied that he thought there was a realistic possibility that A might use the pipe to cause serious injury. The Privy Council held that this was a perfectly acceptable direction; there was no need to look for any authorisation or agreement, express or implied. It was sufficient that the jury were satisfied that the defendant had deliberately lent himself to a venture in which he foresaw that there was a realistic possibility that the principal offender might intentionally cause grievous bodily harm. Additionally, *Hui Chi-Ming* makes it clear that it is not necessary for the prosecution to prove that both parties

[77] Sir Robin Cooke stated: "The case must depend on the wider principle whereby a secondary party is criminally liable for acts by the primary offender of a type which the former foresees but does not necessarily intend. That there is such a principle is not in doubt. It turns on *contemplation* or putting the same idea in other words, *authorisation*, which may be express but is more usually implied. It meets the case of a crime foreseen as a possible incident of the common unlawful enterprise. The criminal culpability lies in participating in the venture with that foresight."

[78] See, e.g. *Slack* [1989] 3 W.L.R. 513 and *Wakely, Symonds and Holly* [1990] Crim.L.R. 119 rejecting the earlier cases of *Barr* (1986) 88 Cr.App.R. 362 and *Smith* [1988] Crim.L.R. 616 which seemed to equate the intent necessary for an accomplice with that needed for a principal.

[79] [1991] 1 Q.B. 134.

[80] [1991] 1 Q.B. 134 at 139.

[81] See, generally J.C. Smith [1991] Crim.L.R. at 133, 134. Note, as discussed below, the secondary party is not merely reckless. He has deliberately given aid to a person he knows could well commit murder.

[82] [1992] 1 A.C. 34.

[83] [1987] A.C. 417, see below, para.4–040.

contemplated the use of violence when they set out on their joint venture, though this will usually be the case. Suppose, for example, A and B set out on a burglary expedition. A is armed with a gun which he intends to use merely to frighten anyone who gets in the way. B, on the other hand, knows that A has a gun and expects that A will use it deliberately to kill or seriously injure such a person. If A later, at the scene of the crime, intentionally kills the night-watchman who intervenes, both will be liable for murder; A because he has intentionally killed the night-watchman and B because he has gone on the venture contemplating that A might do this.

The general principles relating to murder occurring on an unlawful joint enterprise to commit another crime were reaffirmed in *Roberts*,[84] applying principles established in *Hyde* and applied in the Privy Council case of *Hui Chi-Ming*. In *Roberts,* the defendant (B) took part with A in a robbery. Unexpectedly the 69-year-old householder (V) provided resistance and was killed by a blow from A using an implement obtained in V's premises—no weapons were taken as part of the burglarious intrusion. Irrespective of whether the primary unlawful object of the participants is to do some kind of physical injury to the victim or to do some other unlawful act such as burglary and or robbery, as occurred in *Roberts*, the same principles apply. The crucial question for the jury to address on a murder charge is whether the accomplice *contemplated* that the principal *might* kill or intentionally inflict serious bodily injury on the victim and yet continued to participate in the unlawful enterprise. The test of mens rea here is subjective and it is simply what the individual accused in fact contemplated that matters. This approach has been confirmed by the House of Lords in the significant case of *Powell*.[85] As we have said previously it should be remembered that these principles apply whatever the crimes involved, for example, rape during burglary.

(ii) Matters of Proof

4–017   In these cases it is important to keep questions of proof separate from questions of substantive law. In an important sense the Court of Appeal decision in *Roberts* exemplified that there are no restrictions on liability to cases in which some violence was contemplated or weapons taken. Unlike previous case authorities the object of the enterprise was robbery alone, not physical assault, nor were any lethal weapons carried or indeed any weapons whatsoever. That was held to be of no consequence. As Lord Taylor C.J. stated quite categorically:

> "True it will be easier for the Crown to prove that 'B' participated in the venture realising that 'A' might wound with murderous intent if weapons are carried or if the object is to attack the victim or both. But that is purely an evidential difference, not a difference in principle."[86]

Thus, it is a matter of evidence pure and simple as to the defendant's state of mind. Palpably it is far easier for the prosecution to prove against an accomplice that he contemplated extra force and that really serious injury might be inflicted in a situation, such as in *Hui Chi-Ming*, where the object of the expedition is to find someone to hit. It is far more difficult to establish that B contemplated the collateral offence in the case of a new offence, such as murder arising in the course of burglary or robbery. In *Roberts* the

---

[84] (1993) 96 Cr.App.R. 291.
[85] *Powell and another; English* [1997] 4 All E.R. 545; see below, paras 4–019—4–020. In consolidated appeals the House of Lords addressed the issues of requisite mens rea of the secondary party to murder (*Powell*), and also liability for unforeseen consequences arising out of joint criminal enterprises (*English*).
[86] (1993) 96 Cr.App.R. 291 at 297.

defendant admitted that he had contemplated that there might be some violence when they went to the victim's house. He gave inconsistent answers as to the degree of violence he foresaw, but twice said that he foresaw the risk of really serious injury. Without this evidence the prosecution would have been in serious difficulties vis-à-vis a murder charge. In any subsequent case, given similar facts to *Roberts* with no assault planned or weapons carried, if a defendant were to invoke the right to silence, the burden on the prosecution in respect of proof of the defendant's mens rea would appear to be insurmountable. Of course, that situation would not arise in those US states where the felony murder rule is still applicable. All participants are guilty of murder if a death occurs during the commission or attempted commission of any felony.[87] Liability is strict in the sense that no inquiry need be made into the culpability of any of the actors or to the death. This harsh rule has been mitigated by most states, such as Pennsylvania, where felony murder has been retained, by the requirement that the actual felony itself be inherently dangerous, either in general or on the particular facts.

(iii) Remoteness

What level of foresight is required of B regarding the unlawful act to be committed by A? **4–018** The key matter is contemplation on the part of the defendant. The fact that the defendant, as in *Gordon,*[88] merely demonstrates a lack of surprise about the commission of the full substantive by the main perpetrator, does not necessarily equate to the required foresight. The question of remoteness has to be addressed. It was submitted by the defence in *Roberts* that it was wrong or insufficient for the judge to identify the degree of foresight required to be proved against B as foresight that A *might* intentionally kill or inflict really serious injury. It was argued that the trial judge should have emphasised that such an intentional killing or infliction of really serious injury was foreseen as a "real" or a "substantial" or "serious" possibility. Reliance was placed on a passage in the advice of the Privy Council delivered by Sir Robin Cooke in *Chan Wing-Siu*. It was stated, albeit obiter in the case, that where the risk of the principal offender committing a particular act was dismissed by the secondary party as being negligible and too remote to be seriously contemplated the secondary party is not liable for that act of the principal offender. Sir Robin Cooke said:

> "In cases where an issue of remoteness does arise, it is for the jury (or other tribunal of fact) to decide whether the risk *as recognised by the accused* was sufficient to make him a party to the crime committed by the principal. Various formulae have been suggested—including a substantial risk, a real risk, a risk that something might happen . . . What has to be brought home to the jury is that occasionally a risk may have occurred to an accused's mind—fleetingly or even causing him some deliberation—but may genuinely have been dismissed by him as altogether negligible. If they think that there is a reasonable possibility that the case is in that class, taking the risk should not make that accused a party to such a crime of intention as murder or wounding with intent to cause grievous bodily harm."[89]

The court in *Roberts*, relying on the above passage, rejected the defence's proposition that further direction was needed on the issue of the defendant's foresight. It would be extremely rare cases where it was necessary—this was not one of them. A defendant who fleetingly thinks of the risk only to dismiss it from his mind does not have foresight or realisation at

---

[87] See below, para.7–007.
[88] [2004] EWCA Crim 961.
[89] [1985] A.C. 168 at 179.

the time he lends himself to the unlawful criminal enterprise. The risk has gone for all time from his mind. Realisation is a prerequisite for liability in the sense according to Lord Taylor C.J. that, "to realise something may happen is surely to contemplate it as a real not a fanciful proposition".[90] It is unhelpful and unnecessary in most cases to try to distinguish between the fleeting but immediately rejected thought of a risk and the ever-present realisation of risk. The crux of the case anyway was apparently not whether force was contemplated—this was taken for granted given that the defendant knew that the victim was unlikely to yield up his money or goods without resistance—but rather the degree of force to be applied. There had been a clear direction on this point and the jury had held that the defendant realised really serious injury might be used.

In summary, if B has considered the risk of A intentionally causing grievous bodily harm and has dismissed it entirely, he should not be held liable. In reality, however, if he goes on the venture seeing that there is even an outside chance of such an occurrence, it is unlikely that the court will hold that it was a risk he was entitled to take.

(iv) Can Secondary Party Liability Based upon Recklessness be Justified?

4–019 Can it be logically justified that against the principal offender it has to be proved that he intended to kill or cause grievous bodily harm but against the secondary party there is only a need to prove that he contemplated this as a realistic possibility, and not even a probability? It intuitively seems strange that the law appears to allow a substantially reduced blame-worthy mental state for the non-acting party compared with that of the individual who actually commits the actus reus. Arguably the answer is that this approach is perfectly logical. No doubt the underlying premise for the imposition of liability is to implicate all parties in the criminal enterprise. The non-acting co-adventurer is at fault by intentionally lending support to the planned crime and so it can legitimately be asked why he should avoid punishment for any collateral crimes. Protection of society and deterrence theory supports attaching guilt to B in such a scenario. Against the secondary party it has to be proved that he knew that the principal offender might bring about the actus reus of murder with the necessary mens rea and with this knowledge he *intentionally* and deliberately sets out to help the principal offender. If it were to be required that the secondary party foresaw that violence would probably be used, the law would be seriously failing in its duty to protect the public. Consider, for example, a bank robbery in which one of the robbers is, to the knowledge of the others, carrying a gun which in extreme circumstances he will use to kill or seriously injure. It is extremely unlikely that the accomplices could be said to have foreseen death or grievous bodily harm as a probable consequence of the venture since it will only be on rare occasions that someone will intervene to stop them. They do, however, see violence as a possibility and are nonetheless prepared to help. It can be said that they should be guilty if the violence occurs.

The alternative view is that strict legal analysis runs contrary to such an outcome based on the result of collateral crime being committed by the principal party. It arguably seems both harsh and anomalous to punish B in such a manner. It is one thing to think that a person should be guilty of murder if he foresees that A may intentionally kill, but illogical to convict B of murder when he merely foresees that his co-adventurer may intentionally inflict grievous bodily harm. The requisite mens rea of a secondary party on a charge of murder arose before the House of Lords in *Powell*,[91] and very recently in *Rahman* (see below).[92]

---

[90] (1993) 96 Cr.App.R. 291 at 298.
[91] [1997] 4 All E.R. 545; see generally, C.M.V. Clarkson, "Complicity, *Powell* and Manslaughter" [1998] Crim.L.R. 556.
[92] [2008] UKHL 45; [2008] 4 All E.R. 351.

Their Lordships addressed the policy rationale behind secondary party liability. Powell (B) and another (A) were convicted of murder on the basis of joint enterprise. The prosecution case was that they had, with a third man, C, rung the doorbell of the victim, a drugs dealer, and shot him when he answered. The prosecution could not be certain who fired the shot, although they inclined to the view it was A. The trial judge directed the jury that if they found that there was a tacit agreement and parties B and C (the third party) realised, without agreeing to such conduct, that party A (the principal) *may* kill or intentionally inflict serious injury in pursuance of the agreement, but they nevertheless participated, that was a sufficient mental element for B and C to be guilty of murder. This direction was approved by the Court of Appeal who upheld their convictions. The question certified for consideration by the House of Lords was to the following effect: "Is it sufficient to found a conviction for murder for a secondary party to a killing to have realised that the primary party might kill with intent to do so or must the secondary party have held such belief himself?"

The above question, as Lord Hutton identified[93] raised two specific matters. First, the **4–020** issue of whether there was a principle established by the authorities that where there is a joint enterprise to commit a crime, foresight or contemplation by one party to the enterprise (B) that another party to the enterprise (A) may in the course of it commit another crime, is sufficient to impose criminal liability for that crime if committed by A, even if B did not intend that criminal act to be carried out. Second, whether, if there be such an established principle it could stand as good law in the light of previous House of Lords authorities that foresight was not sufficient to constitute the mens rea for murder in the case of the person who actually causes the death and that guilt only arises if that person intends to kill or cause really serious injury. The defendant in *Powell* contended that the constructive form of secondary party liability was inappropriate. It was argued that secondary party liability, predicated simply on foresight and recklessness, stood in contradistinction to principal liability for murder which, following both *Moloney*[94] and *Hancock*,[95] required an intention to kill or to cause grievous bodily harm. However, their Lordships rejected this contention, affirming existing principles on secondary party mens rea established in *Hyde, Hui Chi-Ming* and *Roberts*.[96] It was sufficient to found a conviction for murder for a secondary party to a killing in the course of a joint enterprise to have realised that the principal party *might* kill with intent to do so or with intent to cause grievous bodily harm. Although a lesser mens rea than that required for conviction of the primary party was, therefore, to be proven in the case of the secondary party, that result was required for reasons of public policy which were concerned with the practical need to control crime committed in the course of joint enterprises. These concerns were cogently enunciated by Lord Hutton:

> "A further consideration is that, unlike the principal party who carries out the killing with a deadly weapon, the secondary party will not be placed in the situation in which he suddenly has to decide whether to shoot or stab the third person with intent to kill or cause really serious harm. There is, in my opinion, an argument of considerable force that the secondary party who takes part in a criminal enterprise (for example the robbery of a bank) with foresight that a deadly weapon may be used, should not escape liability for murder because he, unlike the principal party, is not suddenly confronted by the security officer so that he has to decide whether to use the gun or knife or have the enterprise thwarted and face arrest."[97]

[93] [1997] 4 All E.R. 545 at 554.
[94] [1985] A.C. 905; [1985] 1 All E.R. 1025; see above, para.2–058.
[95] [1986] A.C. 455; [1986] 1 All E.R. 641; see above, para.2–059. See now *Woollin* [1998] 4 All E.R. 103.
[96] See above, para.4–017.
[97] [1997] 4 All E.R. 545 at 562.

It is interesting to note that Lord Steyn rejected the notion that the accessory principle *as such* imposes a form of constructive liability. In his view[98] liability is imposed simply because the secondary party is *intentionally* assisting in and encouraging a criminal enterprise which he is aware might result in the commission of a greater offence. Thus, the liability of a secondary party, albeit a lesser form of mens rea than for the principal, requires proof of a subjective state of mind on the part of the participant in the criminal enterprise. This subjective state of mind, foresight that the principal *might* commit a different and more serious offence, can logically form the requisite mens rea for secondary party liability for murder. Lord Steyn adopted Professor Smith's elaboration of relevant principles in his article, "*Criminal Liability of Accessories: Law and Law Reform*":

> "Nevertheless, as critics point out it is enough that the accessory is reckless, whereas, in the case of the principal, intention must be proved. Recklessness whether death be caused is a sufficient mens rea for a principal offender in manslaughter, but not murder. The accessory to murder, however, must be proved to have been reckless, not merely whether death might be caused, but whether murder might be committed; *he must have been aware, not merely that death or grievous bodily harm might be caused, but that it might be caused intentionally, by a person whom he was assisting or encouraging to commit a crime*. Recklessness whether murder be committed is different from, and more serious than, recklessness whether death be caused by an accident (emphasis added)."[99]

(v) Foresight of the principal offender's state of mind and actions

4–021 In the very recent case of *Rahman*[100] the nature of joint enterprise and the mens rea required for accessory liability have been reappraised. Unfortunately earlier clarion calls for greater clarity remain unheeded following the House of Lords judgment. The fatal act transpired in the course of a long-standing dispute between different groups of young men. The defendant (B) and others within their group armed themselves with a variety of weapons including baseball bats, a metal bar and a table leg. The deceased, in the course of this violent attack, sustained three stab wounds, the evidence suggesting that the first two wounds were probably caused by the same knife using similar movements and that it was possible that one knife had been used to inflict all three wounds. B was charged with murder although there was no evidence that he had inflicted the fatal injuries. A conviction followed, upheld by the Court of Appeal, on the premise that B had lent himself to the unlawful criminal enterprise realising that A might kill or cause grievous bodily harm, and that realisation encompassed the use of lethal weapons. The question posited to the House of Lords was as follows:

> "If in the course of a joint enterprise to inflict unlawful violence a principal party kills with an intention to kill which is unknown to and unforeseen by a secondary party is the principal's intention relevant;
>
> > (i) to whether the killing was within the scope of a common purpose to which the secondary party was an accessory?

---

[98] [1997] 4 All E.R. 545 at 551.
[99] (1997) 113 L.Q.R. 453 at 464.
[100] [2008] UKHL 45; [2008] 4 All E.R. 351.

(ii) to whether the principal's act was fundamentally different from the act or acts which the secondary party foresaw as part of the joint enterprise?"[101]

The essential issue between the appellant and the Crown in *Rahman* was the extent to which the proper focus of enquiry was (i) B's foresight of A's *state of mind*; and/or (ii) B's foresight of A's *course of conduct*. B asserted that foresight (or otherwise) as to A's *intention to kill* was a crucial determinant towards culpability. It was argued that if A has inflicted the fatal stab wound with the intention to kill and not merely the intention to inflict serious injury this took A's actions outside the common design and rendered it thus "fundamentally different" (see below), obviating liability for murder. In contradistinction, the Crown argued that A's undisclosed intention was irrelevant, and that B's liability was founded on A's acts.

Their Lordships in *Rahman*, considering the above precedential authorities and historical developments, were unanimous that the appeal should be dismissed. On policy grounds, where a killing was effected by a principal offender with intent to kill, the foresight of the secondary offender that the principal would only effect the intentional causing of serious injury did not automatically invoke the "fundamentally different" rule (see below) to insulate B from liability. The focus of the "fundamentally different" principle was prescribed to the perpetrator's conduct engaging the lethal weapon, not undisclosed intention. Lord Bingham presented two clear reasons for this posited outcome. First, any other perspective would "introduce a new and highly undesirable level of complexity" for jury evaluation.[102] They would be engaged in a mystical speculative engagement as to B's foresight and A's undisclosed intentions or otherwise. Lord Bingham asserted:

> "Given the fluid, fast-moving course of events in incidents such as that which culminated in the killing of the deceased, incidents which are unhappily not rare, it must often be very hard for jurors to make a reliable assessment of what a particular defendant foresaw as likely or possible acts on the part of his associates. It would be even harder, and border on speculation, to judge what a particular defendant foresaw as the intention with which is associates might perform such acts. It is safer to focus on the defendant's foresight of what an associate might do, an issue to which knowledge of the associates possession of an obviously lethal weapon such as a gun or a knife would usually be very relevant."[103]

Secondly, Lord Bingham was concerned not to undermine extant principles on liability for murder; more particularly, the policy concern that the mens rea for murder is predicated upon either an intention to kill or an intention to commit serious injury on the part of the perpetrator: the prosecution does not have to prove a specific basis because if the accused had not embarked on deliberate violence the fatality would not have occurred. Adopting, as Lord Bingham pithily states, "a quality of earthy realism",[104] similar public policy concerns underpin accessorial liability for complicity:

> "To rule that an undisclosed and unforeseen intention to kill on the part of the primary offender may take a killing outside the scope of a common purpose to cause really serious injury, calling for a distinction irrelevant in the case of the primary offender, is in my view to subvert the rationale which underlies our law or murder."[105]

---

[101] See [2008] 4 All E.R. 351 at 354.
[102] [2008] 4 All E.R. 351 at 363.
[103] [2008] 4 All E.R. 351 at 363.
[104] [2008] 4 All E.R. 351 at 363.
[105] [2008] 4 All E.R. 351 at 363.

In their Report *Murder, Manslaughter and Infanticide,*[106] the Law Commission made specific recommendations regarding complicity in homicide, as part of their proposals to fundamentally restructure homicide offences. They proposed that D should be liable in respect of P's offence of first or second degree murder (as appropriate) where:

"(1) D intended to assist or encourage P to commit the relevant offence; or

(2) D was engaged in a joint criminal venture with P, and realised that P, or another party to the joint venture, might commit the relevant offence."[107]

They also recommended that D should be liable for manslaughter where:

"(1) D and P were parties to a joint venture to commit an offence;

(2) P committed the offence of first degree murder or second degree murder in relation to the fulfilment of that venture;

(3) D intended or foresaw that (non-serious) harm or the fear of harm might be caused by a party to the venture; and

(4) a reasonable person in D's position, with D's knowledge of the relevant facts, would have foreseen an obvious risk of death or serious injury being caused by a party to the venture."[108]

The Government has not taken these proposals forward given the other work on participation in crime conducted by the Commission[109] and the position appears to be that a review of complicity in homicide will form part of a general review of the law on complicity.[110]

C. Liability for Unforeseen Consequences

(i) General Principles

4–022 It follows from the foregoing discussion that while B may be liable for such crimes committed by A as were in B's contemplation, he is not liable for crimes committed by A that he does not contemplate at all. It has been highlighted that where B supplies cutting equipment to A knowing of its use in connection with a burglary that B becomes an accessory to the burglary. Suppose then, that as part of the burglary, A attacked X, a night-watchman, and rendered him unconscious. B is not a party to the assault on X which was uncontemplated by him; the fact that B contemplated one crime (burglary) and that during the commission of that crime another (assault) was committed is not enough to make B liable as a party to the further crime. In relation to the assault B is totally lacking in mens rea.

In this example it is assumed that B supplies the equipment some days before the burglary and is not present at its commission. Does it, therefore, make any difference if B

---

[106] Law Com. No. 304, 2006. This followed Law Commission, Consultation Paper No.177 (2005), *A New Homicide Act for England and Wales?*
[107] Law Com. No. 304, 2006 at para.4.4.
[108] Law Com. No. 304, 2006 at para.4.6.
[109] *Participating in Crime* (Law Com. No. 305, 2007).
[110] See Ministry of Justice et al., *Murder, manslaughter and infanticide: proposals for reform of the law* (Consultation Paper CP19/08) (July 2008); and Ministry of Justice et al., *Murder, manslaughter and infanticide: proposals for reform of the law—Summary of responses and Government position* (January 2009).

accompanies A on the burglarious expedition? The answer is that it makes no difference whether B is present or absent from the scene of the crime. B is liable only for such crime or crimes of A that he contemplates A will commit, intending to assist in their commission.[111] Thus, if B had accompanied A but had been totally unaware of the presence of the night-watchman and had never contemplated that force would be used on any person, he could not be a party to A's assault. If, however, it could be proved that B had gone along with A foreseeing that in the unlikely event that someone intervened A would use violence to avoid capture, then B will be an accessory to the use of such violence by A.

In these cases it could be said that what is needed is proof that the secondary party joined in a venture contemplating that, for example, violence was a real possibility. The principles relating to joint ventures or enterprises arise in relation to all types of crime, but the majority of cases reaching the courts tend to centre upon ventures where violence has occurred.

The following examples, largely drawn from decided cases, illustrate how the issue of B's liability for unforeseen consequences has arisen:

1. In a dispute over A's girlfriend both A and B attack V. Unknown to B a knife is carried by A. A stabs V and kills him.[112]

2. A and B are involved in a fist fight with rival gangs on Clapham Common. Unknown to B a "knuckle-duster" is carried by A who punches V killing him.[113]

3. A and B are members of an Irish military organisation. Their concerted plan is to "kneecap" V by firing a bullet into his leg. A departs from this plan by firing a bullet into V's heart killing him immediately.[114]

4. A and B carry out an attack on a police officer with wooden posts. Unknown to B a knife is carried by A who stabs the officer and kills him.[115]

The starting point for their Lordships in *Rahman*[116] was consideration of the earlier decision in *English*,[117] which formed part of a consolidated appeal with *Powell*. The facts therein were as presented in the last scenario above. B was convicted of murder, the trial judge having directed the jury to do so if they found that he had joined in an unlawful attack realising at the time that there was a substantial risk that A might kill the police officer during the attack or at least cause some really serious injury to him. B contended before the House of Lords that where the principal offender kills with a deadly weapon, which the secondary party did not know that he had and, therefore, did not foresee his use of it, the secondary party should not be guilty of murder. He submitted that to be guilty under the principle stated in *Chan Wing-Siu* (see above) the secondary party must foresee an act of the type which the principal party committed, and that in the present case the use of a knife was fundamentally different to the use of a wooden post. The certified question before the House of Lords was to the following effect: "Is it sufficient for murder that the secondary

---

[111] Note that B will be liable for any unforeseen consequence that A is liable for. For example, consider a scenario where A is hired by B to kill V. A shoots to kill V but accidentally misses and kills X. A and B are both liable for the murder of X.

[112] The facts in *Anderson and Morris* [1966] 2 Q.B. 110; considered below, para.4–032.

[113] The facts in *Davies v DPP* [1954] A.C. 378 with the exception that a knife was used not a "knuckle-duster"; considered below, para.4–032.

[114] The facts in *Gamble* [1989] N.I. 268; considered below, para.4–023.

[115] The facts in *English* [1997] 4 All E.R. 545.

[116] [2008] UKHL 45; [2008] 4 All E.R. 351.

[117] [1997] 4 All E.R. 545.

party intends or foresees that the primary party would or may act with intent to cause grievous bodily harm, if the primary act carried out by the primary party is fundamentally different from the acts foreseen or intended by the secondary party?"

4–023   Their Lordships, applying the principles established in *Anderson and Morris*[118] quashed B's conviction for murder; liability still existed for the assault with the wooden posts under the relevant section of the Offences Against the Person Act 1861. B was liable for unusual consequences arising out of the joint enterprise but was not liable for the *unauthorised* acts of A. It was held that the secondary party would not be guilty of murder where he intended or foresaw that the primary party would or might act with intent to cause grievous bodily harm but the lethal act carried out by the primary party was *fundamentally different* from the acts foreseen or intended by the secondary party. However, as Lord Hutton stated,[119] in other cases, if the weapon used by A is simply different to, but as dangerous as, the weapon which B had contemplated he might use, then B should not escape liability for murder because of the difference in the weapon. It should, for example, make no difference if B expected A to kill with a gun and A actually used a knife. Other situations may be more borderline. In *Greatrex and Bates*,[120] for example, a retrial was ordered by the Court of Appeal so that the jury could determine whether hitting someone with a metal bar was a more dangerous act then kicking him with a shod foot. It was arguable that the striking of a heavy blow to the head with the bar was plainly a qualitatively different and more dangerous act than kicking with ordinary shoes. An issue in *Uddin*[121] focused on whether the jury should have addressed the question on dangerousness of the act of using a flick-knife, as opposed to hitting the deceased with clubs or kicking him with shod feet. The central point of whether the use of the weapon to effect the central act is fundamentally different from that envisaged by the secondary party is a question of fact for the jury.[122]

In the case of *Attorney-General's Reference (No.3) of 2004*[123] where P deliberately discharged a firearm at V with intent to kill this was fundamentally different from deliberately discharging a firearm near V with no intent to cause injury. It was only the latter act that D had envisaged, and so, quite correctly, no liability arose for manslaughter on his part.

The outcome in *English* was on one level eminently rational, based simply on the unauthorised activity principles enunciated in *Anderson and Morris*. More surprising is the strong reliance placed by Lord Hutton[124] on the decision of the Irish Crown Court in *Gamble*.[125] The four accused, all members of a terrorist organisation, had a grievance against V. It appears from the facts that a concerted plan arose to cause grievous bodily harm to V by "kneecapping" (firing a bullet into his kneecap). What actually occurred was that V's throat was cut with a knife with great force which rapidly caused his death. In addition he was shot with four bullets into the head, and two of the bullet wounds would have been fatal had his death not been caused by the cutting of his throat. The defendant, a secondary party, had not foreseen killing with a knife or firing bullets into the head, but had contemplated the kneecapping. It was held by Carswell J., supported by Lord Hutton, that as the use of the knife was unauthorised, as in *English*, the defendant was not liable for an act which he did

---

[118] [1966] 2 Q.B. 110, see below, para.4–032
[119] [1997] 4 All E.R. 545 at 566.
[120] [1999] 1 Cr.App.R. 126.
[121] [1999] Q.B. 431; [1998] 2 All E.R. 744; see generally J.C. Smith, "Joint Enterprise and Secondary Liability" (1999) 50 N.I.L.Q. 153.
[122] See *O'Flaherty* [2004] EWCA Crim 526; [2004] Crim.L.R. 751.
[123] [2005] EWCA Crim 1882; [2006] Crim.L.R. 63. See, also *Briggs* [2007] Cr.App.R.(S.) 425.
[124] [1997] 4 All E.R. 545 at 564–565.
[125] [1989] N.I. 268.

not contemplate. Strangely, Lord Hutton also supported the view of the trial judge, on the facts, that where a secondary party foresees the use of a gun to kneecap, and death is then caused by the deliberate firing of the gun into the head or body of the victim, this could also constitute unauthorised activity by the principal exempting the secondary party from murder, but not the relevant offence under the Offences Against the Person Act 1861. Perhaps Lord Hutton was appraised of more facts than appear in the *Gamble* judgment itself. Otherwise the view expressed contradicts acknowledged principles. If B contemplates that A will cause grievous bodily harm by A firing a gun into V's leg, but V fires the gun into V's heart and V subsequently dies, then both parties ought to be guilty of murder. The mens rea for murder is an intention to kill or to cause grievous bodily harm, and B has the requisite foresight. Public policy concerns demand a murder conviction here no less than in the *Powell* type scenario. It is arguable that kneecappings rarely lead to death and, therefore, there is a substantial deviation from the plan. But on our general principles this should make no difference since we do not differentiate between an intention to kill and an intention to cause grievous bodily harm. In *Rahman*,[126] Lords Scott, Neuberger and Brown followed similar type analyses in rejecting the *Gamble* principles.[127] However, Lord Bingham viewed the threat of cutting the victim's throat as "of an entirely different character in an entirely different context."[128]

Interestingly, a reformulated test for the "fundamentally different" qualification was propounded by Lord Brown in *Rahman*, supported by Lord Neuberger and Lord Scott. Lord Brown's template suggested a formula for jury consideration in this opaque arena and both extends and limits the *English* principles:

> "If D realises (without agreeing to such conduct being used) that P may kill or intentionally inflict serious injury, but nevertheless continues to participate with P in the venture, that will amount to a sufficient mental element for D to be guilty of murder if P, with the requisite intent, kills in the course of the venture *unless (i) P suddenly produces and uses a weapon of which D knows nothing and which is more lethal than any weapon which D contemplates that P or any other participant may be carrying and (ii) for that reason P's act is to be regarded as fundamentally different from anything foreseen by D"*[129] (emphasis added).

The majority view in *Rahman* has extended the *English* qualification into novel territory where B foresees that A might kill with intent (not simply cause grievous bodily harm), but nevertheless A's conduct is "unforeseen" in relation to the method of killing. However, the breadth of the *English* test is now restricted to cases where; (a) A "suddenly produces" a weapon; (b) B is "unaware" of the weapon which A uses to kill V; (c) the weapon itself is "more lethal" than any contemplated by B; and (d) because of the change of weapon and its more lethal nature A's acts may be regarded as fundamentally different. Despite numerous statements in *Rahman* that the test as set out has a "plain meaning" it is suggested that it

---

[126] [2008] UKHL 45; 4 All E.R. 351.

[127] [2008] UKHL 45; 4 All E.R. 351: Lord Scott stated at 365, "if parties embark on a punishment exercise that carries with it the foreseeable possibility of death of the victim, the instruments used for that purpose seem to me of much less importance than the purpose itself" Lord Neuberger asserted at 380 that it was, "no different in principle from the reliance on the shooting to the head rather than the knees in the kneecapping case": and Lord Brown said at 374 that *Gamble*, "stretches to breaking point the 'fundamentally different' principle".

[128] [2008] UKHL 45; 4 All E.R. 351 at 364; and see also Lord Rodger's speech (at 368) supporting the view that in *Gamble* there had indeed been a break in causation between the assault on the victim, with the intention of inflicting grievous bodily harm, and his murder by cutting his throat: in effect, it was if two defendants were on the point of kneecapping the victim when two other men suddenly appeared and cut his throat.

[129] [2008] UKHL 45; 4 All E.R. 351 at 375.

raises more questions than answers as to the lethal nature of A's conduct and actions which are unforeseen in the sense of "fundamentally different" such as to insulate B from liability for murder. Even the proposed bright-line test for jury determination set out by Lord Brown seems contradicted by Lord Bingham's assertion, supported by Lord Neuberger on this point, that there can be "no prescriptive formula" for directing juries.[130]

A more logical illustration of unforeseen actions by A absolving B from liability for the greater offence is provided by the case of *Mahmood*.[131] This decision exemplifies the principle that B is not liable for a greater crime committed by A in the course of committing a less serious crime if the act which A did was materially different from any act foreseen or contemplated by B.[132] A and B had participated in an unlawful enterprise where the conduct involved the taking of a car without the consent of the owner. Subsequently, a police chase ensued which is a typical feature attendant to car thefts. In this case A, the driver, abandoned the car whilst still in gear which led to the killing of a bystander, a small baby. This was held by the appellate court to be manslaughter on A's part but not by B who was liable only for the lesser offences under the Theft Act and Road Traffic Act. The Court of Appeal was of the view that B did not contemplate or foresee the greater offence. Thus, B was not responsible for the totally unforeseen consequence. No doubt a different outcome would have transpired if A had killed by means of high speed driving or through failing to adhere to a red light. A's conduct was treated as unauthorised by B, absolving B from liability for manslaughter. The case represents a more logical explanation of unforeseen consequences than the confused reasoning in *English* and *Gamble*.

(ii) Manslaughter and Secondary Party Liability

4–024   Particularly acute problems have recently arisen where A is convicted of murder, but uncertainty prevails over B's liability for manslaughter, where the commission of some form of violence, less than serious injury, forms part of the common design. Can B be convicted of manslaughter where A has gone beyond their common plan to cause V minor injuries, and has in fact caused V serious injury leading to his death? This general issue, B's liability for acts beyond the common design, where A causes serious injury resulting in V's death, arose in *Stewart and Schofield*.[133]

In *Stewart and Schofield,* the co-adventurers took part in the robbery of a shopkeeper. Schofield kept watch outside the shop while Stewart and a co-accused, L, went inside. L was armed with a scaffolding bar and Stewart had a knife. The victim was beaten with the bar and a small amount of cash was stolen. He died some days later in hospital as a result of the injuries he had received. L pleaded guilty to murder and robbery. Schofield and Stewart pleaded guilty to robbery and stood trial on a charge of murder. Their argument at trial was that they were not to be associated with the killing of the victim by L because it went far beyond anything they had contemplated or that they had any reason to contemplate. They averred that L's attack upon the victim was not motivated by the needs of the robbery but by racial hatred and was so excessive that it did not form part of any joint enterprise upon which the three of them were engaged. The jury acquitted them of murder but found them guilty of manslaughter. The defendants appealed and contended that L's acts were unauthorised.

The clearest support for upholding a manslaughter conviction, relied on by the Court of Appeal in *Stewart and Schofield*, derives from the decision in *Reid*.[134] Three men, alleged by

---

[130] [2008] UKHL 45; [2008] 4 All E.R. 351 at 364; and see 381 per Lord Neuberger.
[131] [1994] Crim.L.R. 368.
[132] See, generally, J.C. Smith, "Criminal Liability of Accessories: Law And Law Reform" (1997) 113 L.Q.R. 453 at 455.
[133] [1995] 1 Cr.App.R. 441; see also, *Day* [2001] Crim.L.R. 984.
[134] (1976) 62 Cr.App.R. 109.

the Crown to be supporters of the IRA, went to the house of an army officer at night armed with weapons. When he opened the door one of them shot him. Two were convicted of murder; the third, Reid was acquitted of murder but convicted of manslaughter.[135] His defence had been that he was not part of the joint venture but had gone along with them in order to see whether the other two were really IRA terrorists, which he did not believe they were. The appeal was based on the factual submission that on the evidence it must have been murder or nothing; this was rejected. Lawton L.J., delivering the judgment of the court, said:

> "When two or more men go out together in joint possession of offensive weapons such as revolvers and knives and the circumstances are such as to justify an inference that the very least they intend to do with them is to use them to cause fear in another, there is, in our judgment, always a likelihood that, in the excitement and tensions of the occasion, one of them will use his weapon in some way which will cause death or serious injury. If such injury was not intended by the others, they must be acquitted of murder; but having started out on an enterprise which envisaged some degree of violence, albeit nothing more than causing fright, they will be guilty of manslaughter."[136]

The decision in *Reid* must be taken to be of questionable authority given that the Court of Appeal stated quite clearly that B knew of his co-accused's murderous intent.[137] If this was the case then B ought to have been convicted of murder. However, the breadth of the ratio decidendi is noteworthy; it sufficed for a manslaughter conviction that the secondary party merely contemplated that A would frighten V (a common assault). The decisions of *Smith*[138] and *Betty*[139] are of similar effect to the extent that a manslaughter conviction was substituted against B. Both cases involved death by stabbing arising out of fighting. It was argued in *Betty* that in truth the principal had murdered the victim and this meant that B should not have been convicted of manslaughter as it was outside the scope of the joint criminal enterprise. The argument was rejected by the Court of Appeal who asserted that the point was covered by the earlier decision in *Smith* where the court had correctly approved the following direction:

> "Anybody who is a party to an attack which results in an unlawful killing which results in death is a party to the killing . . . only he who intended that unlawful and grievous bodily harm should be done is guilty of murder. He who intended only that the victim should be unlawfully hit and hurt will be guilty of manslaughter if death results."[140]

The cases of *Reid, Smith* and *Betty* were relied on by the court in *Stewart and Schofield* as **4–025** the foundation for the manslaughter conviction. However, equally persuasive authorities support a directly opposite result. In *Anderson and Morris*,[141] there was an alleged common

---

[135] This conviction was based on unlawful act manslaughter derived from *Church* [1966] 1 Q.B. 59. The unlawful act must be one which, objectively assessed, is dangerous, that is to say, subjects the victim to at least the risk of some harm, albeit not serious harm. The mental element required is no more than an intention to commit the unlawful act; see below, para.7–038.

[136] (1976) 62 Cr.App.R. 109 at 112.

[137] (1976) 62 Cr.App.R. 109 at 113.

[138] [1963] 1 W.L.R. 1200.

[139] (1964) 48 Cr.App.R. 6.

[140] [1963] 1 W.L.R. 1200 at 1206.

[141] [1966] 2 Q.B. 110.

design by A and B to attack V, but in the course of the attack A produced a knife, which unbeknown to B he was carrying, and killed V. The court held that it did not automatically follow that B, who was engaged in the unlawful act, was guilty of manslaughter. It was determined that where two persons embarked on a joint enterprise, each was liable for acts done in pursuance of that joint enterprise including *liability for unusual consequences if they arose from the agreed joint enterprise*, but that, if one of the adventurers went beyond what had been tacitly agreed as part of the common enterprise, his co-adventurer was not liable for the consequence of the *unauthorised act*. It was for the jury in every case to decide whether what was done was part of the joint enterprise or whether it went beyond it and was an act outside the scope of that joint enterprise. Lord Parker C.J. stated:

> "It seems to this court that to say that adventurers are guilty of manslaughter when one of them has departed completely from the concerted action of the common design and has suddenly formed an intent to kill and has used a weapon and acted in a way which no party to that common design could suspect is something which would revolt the conscience of people today . . . considered as a matter of causation there may well be an overwhelming supervening event which is of such a character that it will relegate into history matters which would otherwise be looked upon as causative factors."[142]

In essence, the joint unlawful enterprise is viewed as limited in scope. An act by A causing death wholly outside the contemplation of B, can be viewed according to *Anderson and Morris* as breaking the chain of causation, being the fully voluntary act of another person. Similar analysis underpins the decision in *Lovesey and Peterson*[143] where the ruling was followed and clearly restated. The common design involved the commission of robbery with violence which led to the death of the victim. However, the court refused to substitute a verdict of manslaughter for an unsatisfactory conviction for murder because it considered that the degree of violence used led to the conclusion that if the acts were within the common design it had to be murder and, if they were not, there was no other basis for any finding of guilt:

> "It is clear that a common design to use unlawful violence, short of the infliction of grievous bodily harm, renders all co-adventurers guilty of manslaughter if the victim's death is an unexpected consequence of the carrying out of that design. Where, however, the victim's death is not a product of the common design but is attributable to one of the co-adventurers going beyond the scope of that design, by using violence which is intended to cause grievous bodily harm, the others are not responsible for that unauthorised act."[144]

The decision was also followed in *Dunbar*[145] where the defendant's manslaughter conviction was quashed. The prosecution alleged that she had incited her co-defendants to murder her former lover. The defendant for her part denied inciting murder but said she merely suspected that the co-defendants planned to burgle the victim's flat and that in the course of the burglary some violence, short of the infliction of grievous bodily harm, might be done to her former lover. The extreme violence used meant that the co-defendants must have gone beyond the scope of that design. Of course from the point of view of protecting

---

[142] [1966] 2 Q.B. 110 at 120.
[143] [1970] 1 Q.B. 352.
[144] [1970] 1 Q.B. 352 at 356.
[145] [1988] Crim.L.R. 693.

society such an outcome is unwelcome in that the instigator of violence leading to death can go scot-free. The death would not have taken place if the killers had not been hired. However, a well-founded indictment could charge conspiracy to commit an assault occasioning actual bodily harm or incitement in such a scenario.

The dichotomy between *Smith, Betty* and *Reid* on one side conflicting with *Anderson and Morris, Lovesey and Peterson*, and *Dunbar* on the other seems incapable of resolution by the lower courts.[146] The Court of Appeal in *Stewart and Schofield* have approved the former line of cases allowing a manslaughter conviction to be substituted where B contemplates that carrying out the enterprise may involve V suffering some bodily injury, albeit not a serious injury. The merit of such an approach is that the participant in unlawful criminal activity is inculpated when death occurs. The instigator of violence does not go scot-free as in *Dunbar*. The demerits are that it does not properly accord with legal analysis in that the fully voluntary act of another person ought to break the chain of causation, and the joint enterprise should come to an end at that juncture. There may be a concern among some that parties to the joint enterprise who are not guilty of murder are not guilty of manslaughter either, but it seems right in principle. If B is not responsible for A's unforeseen and fundamentally different act, it makes no difference whether the charge is murder or manslaughter.

The alignment of the defendant's mens rea with specific crime liability occurred in **4–026** *Gilmour*[147] where the Northern Ireland Court of Appeal followed the *Stewart and Schofield* approach. The defendant (B) admitted that he had driven three associates, members of a Protestant terrorist organisation, to a housing estate where a large petrol bomb had been thrown into a house in which six people were in bed asleep. The three adults in the house escaped, not without injury, but three young boys died. The Northern Ireland Court of Appeal, allowing B's appeal against conviction for murder on the premise of *Powell; English*, substituted a conviction for manslaughter. B realised that a petrol bombing was planned but there was insufficient evidence that he knew that anyone would act with intent to kill or cause grievous bodily harm. It was difficult to attribute to B with any degree of certainty an intention that the attack should result in more than a blaze which might do some damage, put the occupants in fear and intimidate them into moving from the house. A conviction for manslaughter was, thus, substituted on the basis that there was no reason "why a person acting as an accessory to a principal who carries out the very deed contemplated by both should not be guilty of the degree of offence appropriate to the intent with which he had acted".[148] Where, therefore, the principals had thrown the petrol bomb intending murder or grievous body harm but the defendant only intended the throwing of the petrol bomb to cause a fire, and the principals were convicted of murder, there was no reason why, according to the Northern Ireland Court of Appeal, the defendant could not be convicted of manslaughter.[149]

The ambit of the judgment in *Stewart and Schofield* is interesting on a number of different levels. The differing case precedents are simply explained away on the basis that a different view was taken on the facts of the cases and whether the act in question was, or was to be treated as being, within or without the scope of the joint enterprise.[150] In essence, the court

---

[146] The issue was not properly addressed by the House of Lords in *Powell; English*.
[147] [2000] 2 Cr.App.R. 407; [2000] Crim.L.R. 763.
[148] [2000] 2 Cr.App.R. 407 at 415 per Carswell L.C.J. See also, *Van Hoogstraaten* (December 2, 2003) CCC.
[149] The court also discussed an example in *Blackstone's Criminal Practice* of the posting by A and B of an incendiary device, A foreseeing that it will cause serious injuries, B that it will cause only superficial injuries. The victim dies. A is guilty of murder and B of manslaughter.
[150] The view to the contrary expressed in Smith and Hogan, *Criminal Law* 6th edn pp.149–150 and 152–153 is expressly rejected by the court.

held that where proof of participation in the joint enterprise during the course of which the relevant act was done was considered to prove 'only the mens rea appropriate to a lesser offence, only the lesser crime would have been proved against that defendant, although the act in question may have involved the commission of a more serious crime by another against whom a specific intent could be proved. Thus, it is submitted that the decision, if subsequently followed, is of wider significance than murder and manslaughter. If B contemplates actual bodily harm but A causes serious injury then B will be liable for the s.47 offence; similarly where B contemplates sexual assault but A rapes the victim then, following *Stewart and Schofield*, the sexual assault charge is applicable to B. The effect is that B is liable for the specific crime that he foresees that A might commit.

D. Is There a Need to Distinguish between Joint Enterprise and Accessoryship Liability?

4–027 The court in *Stewart and Schofield* distinguishes quite clearly between cases of joint enterprise, properly so termed, with cases of counselling or procuring (accessoryship liability). It was determined that different principles apply if the accomplice is physically present (joint enterprise) when the offence was committed, as opposed to merely providing acts of assistance given by B to A prior to the commission of the offence.[151] With respect, such an approach seems incorrect.[152] No mention was made in the decision of the earlier judgments of *Wan and Chan*[153] or *Rook*,[154] considered below. It is disappointing that the latter case, in particular, was not mentioned. Additionally, it is surprising that the proper issue of causation was not addressed by the court. Such an issue is vital to whether the collateral result is within or without the scope of the criminal enterprise.

In *Wan and Chan*[155] the allegation brought against the co-adventurers was that they had arranged for the victim to be beaten up, believing that the victim had previously stolen Chan's watch. They were convicted before the Crown Court of aiding, abetting, counselling or procuring an offence under s.20 of the Offences Against The Person Act 1861 of inflicting grievous bodily harm, but acquitted of the more serious s.18 offence of causing grievous bodily harm with intent to do grievous bodily harm. A matter of fundamental importance was raised on appeal as to whether, where A and B have agreed to assault another, and in the course of the assault one of them causes grievous bodily harm and intends to do so, it is possible for the other to be found guilty of unlawfully inflicting grievous bodily harm even if he was not present and did not himself intend to cause grievous bodily harm or contemplate that it might be used? The question was answered in the negative, and the defendants' convictions were quashed since the court concluded that the jury must have decided that the attackers had gone beyond the scope of what the defendants had asked them to do. It is implicit that the court assumed that the joint enterprise principles, described above, are also directly applicable, by parity of reasoning, to an individual who counselled or procured the commission of an offence but who is absent when that offence is committed, just as they similarly apply to the aider or abettor.[156] Such an approach is undoubtedly correct as it

---

[151] It was determined that the solution in the actual case, substitution of a manslaughter conviction upon B, could only apply in cases where B was actually present.

[152] See, generally, J.C. Smith, "Secondary Participation in Crime—Can We Do Without It"? (1994) 144 N.L.J. 679; and J.C. Smith, "Criminal Liability of Accessories: Law and Law Reform" (1997) 113 L.Q.R. 453.

[153] [1995] Crim.L.R. 296.

[154] [1993] 2 All E.R. 955.

[155] [1995] Crim.L.R. 296. See generally, L. Toczek, "Homicide and Accomplices" (1995) N.L.J. 956.

[156] J.C. Smith [1995] Crim.L.R. 296 at 297.

would be to indulge in invidious semantics to try to distinguish the "participant" actually at the scene of a bank robbery from the party keeping watch outside the bank (aider and abettor) and the accomplice who planned the robbery and disposal of proceeds but who absented himself from the actual participation in the robbery itself (counsellor or procurer). No distinction ought to be made over principles governing accomplice liability where a collateral crime occurs.

The above analysis is in accordance with the important decision in *Rook*.[157] It was established from that case that identical principles apply whether or not the secondary party was present at the scene of the crime or not. The facts bear similarity to a scene from a Hollywood crime movie. It involved a so-called contract killing where three men agreed to kill the wife of a fourth for an agreed sum of £20,000. The four men met the evening before the killing to discuss arrangements and it was decided that on the next day the husband would pick up the three men and drive them to a lake, and that when they were ready he would bring his wife to the lake in his car. *Rook* did not turn up the next day as arranged and the killing was carried out by the others. He contended that he had never intended the woman to be killed, that he hoped to get some money "up front" from the husband and then disappear, and that he had never intended to go through with the killing himself. It was held by the Court of Appeal that the defendant's conviction for murder should be upheld. Lloyd L.J. stated:

> "It is now well established that in a case of joint enterprise, where the parties are both present at the scene of the crime, it is not necessary for the prosecution to show that the secondary party intended the victim to be killed or to suffer serious injury. It is enough that he should have foreseen the event as a real or substantial risk: see *Chan Wing-Siu v R* [1984] 2 All E.R. 877, *R v Hyde* [1990] 3 All E.R. 892 and *Hui Chi-Ming v R* [1991] 3 All E.R. 897. Thus, a secondary party may be liable for the unintended consequences of the principal's acts, provided the principal does not go outside the scope of the joint enterprise. *We see no reason why the same reasoning should not apply in the case of a secondary party who lends assistance or encouragement before the commission of the crime*"[158] (emphasis added).

The principle derived from *Rook* is, thus, that it is totally irrelevant whether or not the **4–028** secondary party lends assistance or encouragement prior to or during commission of the offence. In each scenario the same doctrine applies to govern liability. It should similarly be the case that no distinction applies between each kind of accessoryship liability, i.e. aiding, abetting, counselling or procuring.

Unfortunately a contrary analysis has been applied by the court in *Stewart and Schofield* which drew a distinction between cases of joint enterprise, as described above, and cases of counselling or procuring.[159] Regrettably no mention at all was made therein of the analysis provided in *Rook*; a very strange omission. In *Stewart and Schofield*, Hobhouse L.J. said:

> "The allegation that a defendant took part in the execution of a crime as a joint enterprise is not the same as an allegation that he aided, abetted, counselled or procured the commission of that crime. A person who is a mere aider or abettor, etc., is truly a secondary party to the commission of whatever crime it is that the principal

---

[157] [1993] 2 All E.R. 955; considered further below, para.4–043.
[158] [1993] 2 All E.R. 955 at 960.
[159] [1995] 1 Cr.App.R. 441 at 453.

has committed although he may be charged as a principal. If the principal has committed the crime of murder, the liability of the secondary party can only be a liability for aiding and abetting murder. In contrast, where the allegation is joint enterprise, the allegation is that one defendant participated in the criminal act of another. This is a different principle."[160]

The distinction that Hobhouse L.J. seeks to draw in *Stewart and Schofield* between presence/non-presence on the part of the accomplice seems totally illusory. The prevailing uncertainty over the distinction, if any, between joint enterprise and accessoryship liability merely exemplifies the difficulties attendant to this complex area of the criminal law. It desperately needs further guidance from the House of Lords to resolve underlying conflicts and patent ambiguities.

E. Hypothetical Example

4–029 The complex nature of the ascription of liability in this area can now be illustrated by a hypothetical scenario. Suppose that A, B and C plan to burgle X's house in the night at a time when the occupants are expected to be asleep.[161] They plan to steal certain valuable antiques. A and B are to enter the house and C is to remain outside in his car with the engine running. B knows that A carries a weapon; C does not know this but knows that A has a reputation for violence. A and B enter the house. During the enterprise B commits various acts of vandalism by slashing furniture and furnishings with a razor. As they are about to leave they are surprised by X. A fires at him, misses and the bullet travels through the door killing Y, X's wife, who was standing behind it. If we consider the various crimes in turn:

(i) The Burglary

4–030 This presents no problems. A and B are joint principals and C is an accessory; liability arises as soon as A and B enter the building as trespassers with intent to steal. Though the point is unimportant A and B are also joint principals in theft. Could C say that he was not a party to the theft if some of the articles taken were not antiques? Probably not. He could do so if the compact was for the taking of antiques and nothing else but this is unlikely in the extreme. If C contemplated that other articles would be taken, and he would surely contemplate that A and B would appropriate any money they found lying about the house, he will be a secondary party to the theft of articles other than the antiques.

(ii) Criminal Damage

4–031 B is the principal offender here. Whether C will be held to be an accessory depends upon whether he knows of B's proclivities. It is not at all uncommon for burglars to be given to vandalising the premises they burgle. If C knows that B is given to this activity, he is a party to the criminal damage if he contemplates that B might commit it on this occasion—even if

---

[160] [1995] 1 Cr.App.R. 441 at 447.
[161] There are two categories of burglary in accordance with s.9(1)(a) and s.9(1)(b) of the Theft Act 1968. By s.9(1)(a) it must be shown that a defendant entered a building with the ulterior intent to commit one of the following offences: (a) stealing, (b) inflicting grievous bodily harm, or (c) unlawful damage to the building or anything therein. By s.9(1)(b) it must be shown that the defendant entered a building and committed or attempted to commit one of the following offences: (a) stealing, or (b) inflicting grievous bodily harm.

he hopes that B will not.[162] If C has no such knowledge then he cannot be a party to the criminal damage. A's position as an accessory to criminal damage is essentially the same. It is noteworthy that under s.9(1)(b) it is burglary, having entered premises as a trespasser, to commit criminal damage to the property. Thus the unresolved point discussed at para.4–007. above could arise here. Both A and C contemplate burglary and this has occurred though in a form they did not contemplate.

(iii) Murder and Manslaughter

By virtue of the doctrine of transferred malice A is liable for the death of Y and will be **4–032** liable to be convicted of murder or manslaughter depending upon his mens rea; murder if he intended to kill or cause serious bodily harm, manslaughter if he merely intended to frighten X. As for C, it is clearly not enough to make him liable in respect of Y's death that he knew that A was given to violence. But suppose that C contemplated that the householders might be awakened by the burglary and contemplated that A would use force against anyone who disturbed him. Here the fact that C is unaware of the weapon is crucial. In *Davies v DPP*[163] there was a fight between two rival gangs on Clapham Common. Basically what started as a punch-up ended with a member of one gang, Davies, stabbing to death a member of the rival gang. It was held by the House of Lords that Lawson, another member of Davies' gang, was not an accessory to murder since he did not know that Davies had a knife. It is clear that Lawson was not an accomplice in manslaughter either since it was said that he was not an accomplice "in the use of the knife". If, however, the death had occurred as a result of a blow struck by Davies' fist, then Lawson would have been an accessory to manslaughter. As we have seen in *English* and *Rahman* a secondary party is liable for a consequence unforeseen by him if the crime is one in which the principal is liable for that unforeseen consequence. Manslaughter by an unlawful act is such a crime[164] so that Lawson becomes party to manslaughter if he is a party to the form of violence which causes the death.[165]

It follows in our example that C's ignorance of the gun insulates him from liability for the death of Y. The principles applicable are similar to those in *English* and *Rahman* in that the lethal act carried out by the primary party was fundamentally different from the acts foreseen or intended by the secondary party.

B's position is quite different because he knew that A carried the weapon. The requisite mens rea for a secondary party to be liable for murder has been confirmed by the House of Lords in *Powell and Daniels* and *Rahman*. If B realised that there was a real risk that A, if disturbed, would use the gun to seriously injure or kill another then B would be a party to murder. In this regard it is irrelevant whether B contemplates infliction of serious harm through either shooting or use of the gun in the form of pistol-whipping (a cudgel in effect). The case of *Bamborough*[166] determined that if B knew really serious harm, of whatever type, was going to be inflicted with the gun then he was properly convicted of murder—the legal category was the same. If B realised that there was a real risk that A would use the gun to occasion actual bodily harm and A so used it, then B would be a party to manslaughter, in accordance with *Stewart and Schofield*.[167] In neither case does it make a scrap of difference that Y's death may have been unforeseen.

---

[162] See *C v Hume* [1979] Crim.L.R. 328.

[163] [1954] A.C. 378.

[164] See below, para.7–038.

[165] What if Lawson did not know about the knife but thought that Davies might kill someone with his fists? The point here is that knowledge of the knife relates to the issue of proof of the level of violence Lawson contemplated. If he contemplates that Davies will kill, it can matter little how he does it.

[166] [1996] Crim.L.R. 744.

[167] Assuming that *Stewart and Schofield* is subsequently followed; see above, para.4–024.

Suppose that B thought that A had taken the weapon to give himself "Dutch Courage", and A would not use it, or alternatively he believed that the gun was unloaded, being brought purely to frighten. Strictly speaking B would not be a party to the death of Y, though it has to be said that any jury is likely to give short shrift to such a claim by B when he knew of the loaded gun and knew that they were burgling occupied premises in the night. Does it make a difference that he thought the gun was unloaded? The facts in the case of *Perman*,[168] a killing during the course of a robbery of a newsagent's shop, are identical. B cannot be guilty of murder because he does not share, and indeed is quite unaware of, A's intent to kill. It was held in *Perman* that a joint enterprise to cause fright through threats being made with an unloaded and innocuous gun was *not* sufficient to found a conviction for manslaughter,[169] albeit sufficient to found B's conviction for robbery. Reliance was placed on the important decision in *Anderson and Morris*,[170] considered briefly above,[171] which bears reiterating. B is liable for unusual consequences arising out of the joint enterprise but is not liable for *unauthorised* acts of A. Following an attack by Welch on Anderson's wife, Anderson armed himself with a knife and, accompanied by Morris, went in search of Welch. When Welch was found he was attacked by Anderson who stabbed him to death. The judge instructed the jury that if they were satisfied that Morris took part in the assault they could convict him of manslaughter even if he was unaware that Anderson had a knife. This was clearly wrong and Morris's conviction was quashed, but the Court of Criminal Appeal went on to indicate that even if Morris was aware that Anderson had the knife and that he planned to assault Welch, Morris would incur liability neither for murder nor manslaughter if, unbeknown to Morris, Anderson formed an intention to kill. This may seem a very generous result so far as Morris was concerned; after all if Anderson had used the knife with intent to frighten Welch and had accidentally caused his death, Anderson would have been convicted of manslaughter and Morris would have been an accessory. But the decision can be defended; Morris may have been prepared to help Anderson to assault Welch without being at all prepared to help Anderson to kill him.

F.   Reform

4–033   The above illustrations serve only to exemplify how confused this area has become. If prizes were awarded for the most convoluted and opaque branch of the criminal law then joint enterprise principles would be a strong contender for first place. In 2005 the Law Commission in their Consultation Paper, *A New Homicide Act for England and Wales?*[172] considered whether B should be able, in certain circumstances, to be guilty of "complicity in an unlawful killing" (alternatively manslaughter) instead of first degree murder.[173] Subsequently, additional reform proposals and recommendations in relation to complicity in murder were set out in *Murder, Manslaughter and Infanticide*[174] and *Participating in Crime*.[175] These were consolidated in the Ministry of Justice's 2008 Consultation Paper on *Murder, Manslaughter and Infanticide: Proposals for Reform of the Law*.[176]

---

[168] [1996] 1 Cr.App.R. 24.
[169] See statement by Lord Parker C.J. in *Anderson and Morris* [1966] 2 Q.B. 110; above at para.4–025.
[170] [1966] 2 Q.B. 110.
[171] Above, para.4–025.
[172] Law Com. No.177, November 2005.
[173] Law Com. No.177 at para.5.83.
[174] Law Com. No.304, 2006.
[175] Law Com. No.305, 2007.
[176] See *http://www.justice.gov.uk/docs/murder-manslaughter-infanticide-consultation.pdf*. See above para.4–021.

On the issue of joint enterprise, in terms of the "fundamentally different" rule greater discretion is propounded by addressing the question of whether A's conduct was: "within the scope of the joint criminal venture. This would be the case where the act did not go far beyond that which was planned, agreed to or foreseen by the secondary party."[177] Operation of the qualification would be subject to the stricture that B has not foreseen the death of V as a possibility, and even in circumstances where it is operable it only commutes B's liability to a manslaughter conviction.[178]

A radical overhaul of complicity principles to provide enhanced certainty is urgently needed. Appropriate jury directions still remain opaque as the law continues to develop in an ad hoc fashion. The decisions in *Powell and English* and *Rahman* (complicity for murder) and *Stewart and Schofield* (manslaughter) have failed to satisfactorily provide bright-line guidance. We await with bated breath to see if statutory reform will provide a panacea to current ills.

5. THE NEED FOR AN ACTUS REUS

Thus far an attempt has been made to describe participation in crime and to show why we **4–034** need to distinguish between the principal offender and secondary offenders and how the distinction is to be made. We have also examined joint enterprise principles. This does not exhaust all the problems which arise in connection with participation in crime and some mention must be made of these.

A. The Commission of the Actus Reus

In some cases it is not possible to work out which of several defendants actually brought **4–035** about the actus reus. As previously mentioned,[179] it is possible for the jury in such cases to convict any of the participants against whom it can be proved that he either committed the offence himself or else aided and abetted another to commit the offence (see *Giannetto* and *Forman and Ford*).[180] In *Fitzgerald*[181] it was alleged that the accused had set fire to a motorcycle owned by C. However, at the trial, evidence given by the victim made it unclear as to exactly what had happened. The evidence showed that C had been chased by a car belonging to F in which there was a passenger, H. When C abandoned his scooter on the roadside as he went to seek help from a householder, either F, or, more likely, H, got out of the car and removed the petrol cap from the scooter and then either this same person or the other flicked a match into the tank, thereby setting fire to the scooter. The trial judge left the case to the jury on two factual bases. The first was that it was F who set fire to the scooter by flicking matches out of the car and the second that there was clear evidence of a joint venture. The direction in this case was stricter than in many since the judge directed the jury that they should first consider whether it had been proved that F was the principal. If they could not agree on this they must acquit unless they could all agree that F or H had

[177] See Ministry of Justice et al., *Murder, Manslaughter and Infanticide*, (2008) at para.101.
[178] *ibid.*, cl.4.
[179] See above, para.4–003.
[180] See, generally, G. Williams, "Which of You Did It?" (1989) 52 M.L.R. 179.
[181] [1992] Crim.L.R. 660.

set it on fire as part of a joint venture. In other cases the jury seem to have been told that it is sufficient that they are all sure that one or other basis is made out;[182] i.e. it would be sufficient that six found F to have been the principal and six that he aided and abetted H. For example, in *Smith v Mellors and Soar*,[183] both M and S were spotted by a police officer running from a stationary car, and were found to have consumed alcohol above the prescribed legal limit, a strict liability offence. Both said the other had been driving. It was held that M and S were both liable for conviction if they had the mens rea requirements for an accessory, i.e. the Crown had to show that M and S knew that the other had too much to drink and, thus, was unfit to drive.

In the case of *Strudwick*[184] a three-year-old child suffered fatal injuries whilst in the care of the mother and her co-habitee. Similarly in *Lane and Lane*[185] a 22-month-old child died as a result of a fractured skull in the presence of the mother and stepfather between noon and 8.30 pm. The respective parties involved in these child deaths asserted that there was no case to answer in relation to the charge of manslaughter. This plea was successfully raised before the appellate court in both authorities. The principle was that if two people are jointly indicted for the commission of a crime, and evidence does not point to one rather than the other, and there is no evidence that they were acting in concert (or encouraging) the other, the jury ought to return a verdict of Not Guilty in the case of both because the prosecution have not proved the case.[186] Evidence of encouragement would be harder to demonstrate in "single blow" cases than those where there was a continuing course of conduct. It will be more difficult to establish that the parties acted in concert where there is only one blow rather than an identifiable course of conduct. A limited panacea, however, to difficulties in this arena has been presented by enactment of s.5 of the Domestic Violence, Crime and Victims Act 2004.[187] As previously highlighted, an offence punishable by a maximum of 14 years' imprisonment has been created for causing the death of a child or vulnerable adult within the same household. It is a crime of negligence in that D, if not the direct cause of death, is liable if he *ought to have been aware of the risk.* The identified risk of which D ought to have been cognisant is a "significant" one of serious injury and the death must have occurred in circumstances that D ought to have foreseen. D is liable where they fail to take such steps as could reasonably have been expected to take to protect V from the risk. It remains unclear, however, how a jury will view the criterion of "reasonable steps" for that particular D, where D has also been the subject of abuse in a violent household.

B. No Principal Offender

4–036   It may happen that the police have been unable to catch the principal offender but they have arrested the man they think aided the principal. Is it permissible for them to bring the secondary party to trial in the absence of any principal offender? This raises several related problems which we can now examine.

---

[182] Note: in *Giannetto* it was determined that the jury could find D guilty on the basis that he had killed his wife or at least encouraged the actual perpetrator to kill her; see above, para.4–002.

[183] [1987] R.T.R. 210.

[184] (1994) 99 Cr.App.R. 326.

[185] (1986) 82 Cr.App.R. 5.

[186] See, e.g. *Abbott* (1955) 2 Q.B. 497 at 503 per Lord Goddard.

[187] See above at para.4–011; and see the Law Commission, *Children: Their Non-Accidental Death or Serious Injury (Criminal Trials)* (Law Com. No.282, 2003). See, generally, *Liu and Tan* [2006] EWCA Crim 3321. See also *Khan* [2009] EWCA Crim 2; *Stephens and Mujuru* [2007] EWCA Crim 1249.

Provided that the prosecution is able to prove that the actus reus of the crime in question was caused by someone then the jury are entitled to convict B as a secondary party even though the prosecution have not been able to produce the principal offender.

C. Previous Acquittal of the Principal Offender

If the principal offender has already been tried and acquitted it is still possible for the **4–037** prosecution to bring to trial the secondary offender provided that the evidence against him is not identical to the evidence upon which the previous jury acquitted the principal offender.[188]

D. Joint Trial of Principal and Secondary Parties

It is usual for the principal and secondary parties to the offence to be tried together. So the **4–038** question then arises as to whether the jury could acquit the principal offender and convict the secondary party. This, to an outsider, would look rather odd and indeed there are suggestions that this course is not open. However, such action is probably not as absurd as it may first appear. If the evidence against the parties is the same then it would be improper for the jury to acquit the principal and convict the secondary party. On the other hand, some evidence may only be admissible against the secondary party. For example, the secondary party may have made a voluntary confession to the police which he now denies. This, under the rules of evidence, would be admissible evidence against the secondary party who made it, but not against the others since in relation to them it may be inadmissible hearsay. In these circumstances there would be no illogicality in the jury convicting the secondary party even though they felt that they were not satisfied with the case against the principal offender.

One point needs to be remembered. In any of these cases if the acquittal of the principal is tantamount to a finding that the jury are not satisfied that the actus reus of the crime was committed by anyone, then obviously there can be no secondary party liability. Thus, in *Thornton v Mitchell*[189] the driver of a bus had been trying to reverse his vehicle with the help of signals on the bell from his conductor. On the given signal he reversed the bus and collided with two pedestrians. He was charged with driving without due care and attention and the conductor was charged with aiding and abetting. Now it is quite clear that the responsibility for what happened lay with the conductor, but he could not be charged with careless driving, even through the innocent agency of the driver, since he had not, in fact, been driving the bus. Thus, he was charged as a secondary party to the driver's careless driving. However, the charge against the driver was dismissed, and this could only be on the basis that there was no careless driving, since the offence does not require any subjective mens rea on his part. The finding, therefore, was that no crime of careless driving had been committed. It was consequently impossible to convict the conductor as a secondary party to a non-existent crime. Was there any offence with which the conductor could have been charged? If he had intended or seen as likely the injury to the pedestrians then he could have been prosecuted for some form of assault.[190] Had the pedestrians died he could probably have been prosecuted for manslaughter as the principal offender,[191] but since there

---

[188] See, e.g. *Hughes* (1860) Bell C.C. 242; and *Humphreys and Turner* [1965] 3 All E.R. 689.
[189] [1940] 1 All E.R. 339.
[190] See below, para.7–062.
[191] On the basis that the driver was, in effect, an innocent agent; see above, para.4–002, and below at para.5–098.

is, at present, no offence of negligently causing injury it seems that he committed no offence. If, however, the principal offence has been committed but the principal offender is, for some reason, exempt from prosecution, then it is still possible to prosecute a secondary offender. This was the position in *Austin*[192] where the Court of Appeal held that the effect of a statutory provision was that the perpetrator could not be prosecuted; it did not mean that he had not committed the offence.

In the case of *Bourne*,[193] where a husband forced his wife to have sexual connection with a dog, the wife would be the principal offender in the crime of buggery, but because of the duress factor she was not charged and would have been acquitted had she been charged. There was, however, the actus reus of buggery and it was held that the husband could be charged with and convicted of this offence.

4–039   In *Cogan and Leak*,[194] where the facts were similar to those in *Morgan*,[195] the accused had invited a friend to have intercourse with his wife telling him that his wife was a willing partner. During the intercourse the wife lay passively with her face covered. The jury found that the friend had honestly but unreasonably believed that the woman was consenting and so, following the decision in *Morgan*, his conviction for rape was quashed. At the time of this case a husband could not be indicted as a principal offender in the rape of his own wife and so he had been prosecuted as a secondary offender.[196] The question in *Cogan and Leak* for the Court of Appeal was whether the husband could be convicted as a secondary party to the rape of his wife when the only principal offender had been acquitted on the grounds of lack of mens rea. The Court of Appeal held that he could, but unfortunately based this decision largely upon the doctrine of innocent agency. In other words the court was saying that the husband raped his wife through an innocent agent, namely his friend. This is an unfortunate approach; innocent agency should only be used where the innocent agent is being used as a sort of weapon by the real perpetrator of the crime.[197] Thus A hands B a poisoned apple to give to V. B hands it over to V without any awareness of the poisonous contents and V is killed. In that case it makes complete sense to say that A killed V. It does not make any sense in *Cogan* to say that the husband raped his wife. He did not; his friend raped the wife assisted by the husband. Like the word "drive" in *Thornton v Mitchell* (above) "intercourse" is another word which does not lend itself to the concept of innocent agency. Furthermore the decision is open to the objection that the use of the innocent agent approach would render the husband liable as the principal offender and at that time he could not be indicted as a principal offender in his wife's rape. It would be much more sensible for the court to hold that although the friend had been acquitted of the charge of rape, the wife had nevertheless been raped and the husband had assisted in this offence.

The overall effect of *Bourne* and *Cogan and Leak* would seem to be that if A gets B to commit the actus reus of an offence with the help of A, then A can be convicted as a secondary party to that offence, even though B, the perpetrator, has a defence to the charge.

In *Millward*[198] the driver of a vehicle was acquitted of causing death by reckless driving but his employer was convicted of procuring the commission of the offence. The employee had

---

[192] [1981] 1 All E.R. 374. In this case Austin had assisted a father to snatch his child from his estranged wife. The father was held to have committed the offence under s.56 of the Offences Against The Person Act 1861 of taking away a child by force from the possession of his parent, but was saved from prosecution by the proviso to the section, that no-one who claimed a right to the possession of a child "should be liable to be prosecuted by virtue hereof"; see also conspiracy below, para.6–029.

[193] (1952) 36 Cr.App.R. 125.

[194] [1976] Q.B. 217.

[195] [1975] 1 All E.R. 8, see above, para.2–084.

[196] The marital rape exemption rule for husbands no longer exists. In *R. v R.* the House of Lords declared that it had been based upon a concept of marriage which no longer existed.

[197] For an illustration of innocent agency in relation to burglary see the facts in *Wheelhouse* [1994] Crim.L.R. 756; see generally, *Saunders and Archer* (1573) 2 Plowd. 473.

[198] [1994] Crim.L.R. 527.

been instructed to drive the tractor, which was poorly maintained, with a trailer close behind it when the hitching mechanism was defective. The trailer became detached and collided with an oncoming vehicle, killing a passenger. The case against the driver was confined to the condition of the hitching mechanism, whereas the case against the employer was that he had procured the offence by giving instructions to his employee to drive it. This was a case of procuring, similar to *Cogan and Leak*. The actus reus was the taking of the vehicle in the defective condition on to the road, which was procured by the employer and his requisite mens rea was present in that he caused the employee to drive the vehicle in that condition. By contrast in *Loukes*[199] the relevant offence was that of causing death by dangerous driving. D was charged with being a secondary party to this offence. The Court of Appeal determined that no actus reus had been committed, i.e. an obvious risk to a competent driver that the car was being driven dangerously. With no primary substantive offence D could not be guilty of procuring that offence.[200] In effect, the rationale enunciated in *Thornton v Mitchell* was applied with *Millward* distinguishable.

Thus, it is submitted that provided that the prosecution can satisfy the jury that there was an actus reus of the crime in question, there can be a conviction of the secondary party even though the principal offender: (i) is not known or (ii) is acquitted at the same time or subsequently, provided here that the evidence against the secondary party is not the same as that against the principal. This analysis was applied in the case of *DPP v K and C*.[201] The defendants, two girls aged 14 and 11, had subjected V (aged 14) to threats, false imprisonment and robbery. They ordered V to remove her clothing and have sexual intercourse with a boy who was not apprehended. In a room in a block of flats the boy had sexual intercourse with V without her consent. It was held that the defendants had procured the offence of rape and were in reality secondary parties not principals.[202] It did not matter that the principal was not apprehended or charged. Even if he had been, the magistrate found that the prosecution had failed to negative the presumption of doli incapax[203] in respect of the boy. However, the procurers did not escape conviction when they were found to have the requisite mens rea—the desire that rape should take place and the intention to procure it. Thus, this decision confirms *Millward* and the view that procuring the commission of a mere actus reus is an offence.

Can the secondary party be convicted of an offence greater than that of the principal? **4–040** Suppose that A and B return to A's house one night and discover A's wife in bed with X. Let us suppose that B sees that A is boiling over with rage and so he hands him a poker and urges A to smash in X's skull. If A were to do this, then he would be charged with murder and B would be charged as a secondary party. A, however, is likely to raise, probably successfully, the defence of provocation which will mean that he will be convicted only of manslaughter. B, however, was not provoked and so he cannot rely on such a defence. Can he, therefore, be convicted of murder while A, the principal, is convicted only of manslaughter? Theoretically this would seem quite logical, but until recently it appeared that

---

[199] [1996] Crim.L.R. 341. Loukes was a partner in a firm of haulage contractors. One of the firm's drivers was driving one of their tipper trucks along a motorway when part of the prop shaft broke free, crossed the crash barrier and killed a driver travelling in the opposite direction. The driver was acquitted as the defect in the vehicle was not obvious to him. Loukes, as the driver's employer, was charged with causing death by dangerous driving, contrary to ss.1 and 2A of the Road Traffic Act 1988 (as amended by the Road Traffic Act 1991).

[200] See, e.g. *Roberts and George* [1997] Crim.L.R. 209.

[201] [1997] Crim.L.R. 121.

[202] Note a girl cannot commit rape as a principal but can procure the substantive offence—see below, para.4–041.

[203] By this presumption a boy or girl between 10 and 14 was deemed to be incapable of committing a criminal offence. The onus was on the prosecution to demonstrate that they appreciated their conduct to be seriously wrong—see infancy as a general defence, considered below, para.5–097. The presumption was abolished by s.34 of the Crime and Disorder Act 1998.

the Court of Appeal favoured a general rule that it was not open for a jury to convict the secondary party of an offence greater than that of the principal offender.[204] However, in *Howe*[205] the House of Lords expressed its disapproval of *Richards*. Although the statements concerning *Richards* were obiter dicta, it seems fairly safe to assume that in our example of the adulterous spouse a jury could properly find A not guilty of murder but guilty of manslaughter on the grounds of provocation, while convicting B, who cannot raise the defence of provocation, of murder. In this example both defendants have the same mens rea; the difference lies in a mitigating defence available only to A. However, whilst this still remains an open question, the Court of Appeal in *Marks*,[206] in a converse scenario, recognised that the defence of provocation may be available to an individual who abetted or counselled another to kill, even if inapplicable to the perpetrator who performed the physical act leading to the death of the victim.[207]

The same result should follow in a case where A, the secondary party, has the mens rea of murder, while B, the principal offender, has the mens rea only of manslaughter. For example, A and B were escaping from the scene of the crime in a car driven by B, when a police officer stepped out into the road and signalled to B to stop. Suppose that A had urged B to run over the officer, but B had made an unsuccessful attempt to avoid hitting him and the officer was killed. It may well be, if B's driving were sufficiently bad, that B could be convicted of manslaughter; he cannot be convicted of murder since he lacks the necessary mens rea. A, however, is a party to the actus reus of unlawful homicide[208] and since A possesses the mens rea of murder he should be convicted of that offence.[209] Lord Mackay in *Howe* clearly stated that the accomplice may be convicted of the more serious offence:

> "where a person has been killed and that result is the result intended by another participant, the mere fact that the actual killer may be convicted of the reduced charge of manslaughter for some reason special to himself does not, in my opinion, in any way result in a compulsory reduction for the other participant."[210]

6. VICTIMS AS PARTIES TO AN OFFENCE

4–041   When A is charged with raping B we can say that in a very real sense B is the victim of the crime and no one would suggest that B is a party to the rape. On the other hand, if A is charged with having unlawful sexual intercourse with his 15-year-old girlfriend, B is again the victim, but this time a very willing one and so why should she not be charged as an accessory to A's crime? The reason why B cannot be so charged is the rule in *Tyrell's case*[211] which provides that where a statute is designed to protect a certain class of individual, such an individual cannot be held to be a party to the crime however willing she was for the crime to be committed against her. The scope of the rule is uncertain but it has been applied

---

[204] See *Richards* [1974] Q.B. 776.
[205] [1987] A.C. 417: considered further below, para.5–072.
[206] [1998] Crim.L.R. 676.
[207] This ensures that collinearity exists with the defence of diminished responsibility. An individual charged with murder may be convicted of manslaughter if he successfully raises a defence of diminished responsibility or provocation; see below, para.5–015. By s.2(4) of the Homicide Act 1957 it is provided that the fact that one party to the killing is not guilty of murder on account of his diminished responsibility does not affect the question whether the killing amounted to murder in the case of any other party to it.
[208] The actus reus for murder and manslaughter is the same, see below, para.7–007.
[209] See, e.g. *Hui Chi-Ming* [1992] 1 A.C. 34; above para.4–016.
[210] [1987] A.C. 417 at 445.
[211] [1894] 1 Q.B. 710. In relation to the specific offence see now s.9 of the Sexual Offences Act 2003.

mainly in the sexual area. It only protects the victim of the particular crime. If B, a 15-year-old girl, helps A to have intercourse with C, another 15-year-old girl, then B can be charged as a party to that intercourse, whereas C cannot. In this context it was determined in *Congdon*[212] that a prostitute could not be convicted of aiding, abetting, counselling or procuring a man to live off her immoral earnings, as the offence was specifically brought into force for the protection of prostitutes.

7. REPENTANCE BY A SECONDARY PARTY BEFORE THE CRIME IS COMMITTED

The law has always recognised that a person who has embarked on a criminal enterprise may **4–042** withdraw from it and save himself from a criminal liability in respect of it. This applies, of course, unless he has reached the stage of an inchoate offence such as conspiracy or attempt. The ambits of such a defence are unfortunately extremely unclear, and this provides another illustration of the uncertainty pervading this whole area. The limits of the defence are somewhat controversial. However, as stated by the Law Commission, considerations of social policy support the argument that if an accessory counters his assistance with equally obstructive measures, an acquittal ought to follow given his efforts to right the wrong.[213] Mere repentance subsequent to the commission of the offence is irrelevant, but for centuries the law has to some degree recognised an escape from liability by withdrawal before the crime is committed. Plowden's commentary on *Saunders and Archer* way back in 1576 stated:

> "If I commend one to kill JS and before the fact is done I go to him and tell him that I have repented and expressly charge him not to kill JS and he afterwards kills him, there I shall not be accessory to this murder, because I have countermanded my first command which in all reason shall discharge me . . . but if he had killed JS before the time of my discharge or countermand given, I should have been accessory to the death, notwithstanding my private repentance."[214]

The modern law on withdrawal was addressed in *Becerra and Cooper*.[215] The common design was one of burglary from an elderly householder. While in the house, the tenant of a flat on the first floor surprised them. B, calling "let's go", climbed out of a window and ran away. C, meanwhile, who had been handed a knife by B, stabbed and killed the tenant. They were both charged with murder. B contended by his words and actions he had withdrawn from the joint enterprise before the attack on the tenant and, therefore, was not liable to be convicted of murder. The defence of withdrawal was rejected by the Court of Appeal relying on the earlier authority of *Whitehouse*[216] before the Court of Appeal of British Columbia. Roskill L.J. stated an effective withdrawal must: "serve unequivocal notice on the other party to the common unlawful cause that if he proceeds upon it he does so without the further aid and assistance of those who withdraw."[217] Thus, it is essential that, in order to allow A the opportunity to desist rather than complete the offence, then B must make a timely and unequivocal communication to A of his change of heart and of the fact that, if A continues, he does so on his own account, without the aid and assistance of the person who

---

[212] See (1990) N.L.J. 1221; but offence repealed in Sexual Offences Act 2003.
[213] Law Com. No.131 at 53.
[214] (1576) 2 Plowd. 473 at 476.
[215] (1976) 62 Cr.App.R. 212.
[216] [1941] 1 W.W.R. 112.
[217] (1976) 62 Cr.App.R. 212 at 218.

is purporting to withdraw. The most recent affirmation of this principle occurred in *O'Flaherty*[218] where Mantell L.J. asserted that, "a person who unequivocally withdraws from the joint enterprise before the moment of the actual commission of the crime of murder, should not be liable for that crime." The requirement of unequivocality was held not to be satisfied in *Baker*.[219] In that case, B, a party to a joint unlawful enterprise to kill V, had said, after starting the attack, "I'm not doing it" and then moved a few feet away, whereupon the other parties stabbed V to death. The words uttered were far from serving unequivocal notice that he was dissociating himself from the entire enterprise, and could simply have meant "I will stay but not do anything after having struck my blows". No doubt the lack of timeliness of the countermand was also an implicit factor. In similar vein, the bland statement by the defendant in *Nawaz*,[220] to the effect that he withdrew from the joint enterprise, was also insufficient. To be effective the withdrawal had to be unequivocal, timely, universally notified to other parties, and incorporate an effort to dissuade others from continuing.

4–043   The very question of what actually constituted an effective withdrawal was raised in *Rook*.[221] D contended that his absence on the day of the murder amounted to an effective withdrawal. This was rejected by the court which held that where D had merely changed his mind about participating in the commission of the actual offence, and had failed to communicate his intention to the other persons engaged in the offence, he did not thereby effectively withdraw from the commission of the offence, and was liable as a secondary party. In order to escape liability for the commission of a crime, the secondary party had at least unequivocally to communicate his withdrawal to the other party. His simple absence on the day of the murder did not amount to unequivocal communication of his withdrawal.

The basis and requirements of an effective withdrawal will depend very much on the assistance or encouragement D has given. More is required where D has supplied the very means of the crime as in *Becerra*. It will be easier to withdraw, as in *Grundy*,[222] where the defendant had simply aided the principal through the supply of information concerning a burglary. Here efforts to prevent the principal actually committing the offence were sufficient evidence of a valid withdrawal to have been left to the jury. Verbal communication of withdrawal sufficed without the necessity to warn either the police or the owners of the premises. It may well be that such steps are eminently reasonable to amount to effective withdrawal. Certainly the Law Commission has suggested that in the case of assistance such a defence should only be available if the secondary party takes all reasonable steps to prevent the commission of the crime he has assisted.[223] This mirrors the recommendations made in Australia,[224] although under Canadian law, abandonment, as it is known, is not valid as a defence but simply taken into account as a mitigating factor at the sentencing stage.[225]

In summary, where the accused decides to withdraw long before the commission of the offence, it may suffice that he makes it very clear to the others that any further activity will go ahead without assistance from the accused. Where the offence is about to be committed

[218] [2004] EWCA Crim 526 at [58]; [2004] Crim.L.R. 751.
[219] [1994] Crim.L.R. 444.
[220] Unrep. May 13, 1999.
[221] [1993] 2 All E.R. 955; considered above, para.4–027.
[222] [1977] Crim.L.R. 543.
[223] Law Com. No.131 at 124.
[224] See, Criminal Law Officers' Committee of the Standing Committee of Attorneys General (CLOC). *Model Criminal Code*: Ch.2, General Principles of Criminal Responsibility, at p.86.
[225] See, *Kosh* (1964) 44 Cr. 185 (Sask., CA).

it may well be that the accused must try, by force if necessary, to prevent the commission of the offence. If his assistance has been in the form of supplying a gun for a murder, then the court would certainly require something more than mere communication by the accused to the would-be killer that the accused wants nothing more to do with the offence. In such a case, or where communication with the other parties is impossible, it may be that the only effective action the accused can take to withdraw is to inform the police so that the crime can be stopped. The position is unclear as in *Perman*[226] the Court of Appeal stated, *en passant*, that it was questionable whether once the criminal activity contemplated in a joint enterprise had commenced, it was possible for a party to the joint enterprise to withdraw.[227]

A similar statement, albeit obiter again, was made by the Northern Ireland Court of **4–044** Appeal in *Graham*.[228] The defendant, part of a group of terrorists, had transferred a kidnap victim from a house he had used following an earlier escape, to another house where he realised the terrorists were staying, appreciating the risk that they would kill the terrified hostage. Despite the protestations of Graham, and his refusal to assist the terrorists further, the hostage was subsequently killed. Carswell L.J., who delivered the leading judgment, asserted obiter that in such circumstances even informing the police would most likely fail to constitute an effective withdrawal in the case where terrorist murderers were close to committing the homicide:

> "We consider that at the late stage which the murder plan had reached, and after the appellant had played such a significant part in assisting the killers to accomplish their aim, it could not be a sufficient withdrawal to indicate to them that he no longer supported their enterprise. Something more was required, and the judge was amply justified in holding that what the appellant did was not enough. His pleas were useless and the withholding of co-operation . . . was of minimal effect. We do not find it necessary to attempt to specify what acts would have been required of the appellant in the circumstances. It is sufficient for present purposes for us to say that the steps which he did take cannot be regarded as sufficient for withdrawal."[229]

More recently, the cases suggest that a distinction should be made between pre-planned and spontaneous violence. In *Mitchell*[230] the Court of Appeal determined that communication of withdrawal (the *Whitehouse* direction), while necessary when violence was planned, was not a requirement for withdrawal when the violence was spontaneous. Mitchell (B) and two others (A and C) had been involved in a fight with other customers in an Indian take-away restaurant. The dispute escalated, and the owner of the restaurant and two of his sons became involved. The evidence was to the effect that after leaving V (one of the sons) prostrate on the ground having been the recipient of a concerted attack involving beating with a stick, kicking and stamping on his head, A had returned to effect a further beating to V's head with the stick. The appellate court, however, said that a jury properly directed, could have concluded that B had withdrawn when he stopped fighting, threw down the stick he was carrying and walked away; this desistance may have been sufficient to constitute withdrawal from the joint enterprise leaving A solely responsible for the murder of V. The conviction was, thus, unsafe and a retrial ordered. In a case of spontaneous violence a

---

[226] [1996] 1 Cr.App.R. 24.
[227] [1996] 1 Cr.App.R. 24 at 34 per Roch L.J.
[228] [1996] N.I. 157.
[229] [1996] N.I. 157 at 169.
[230] [1999] Crim.L.R. 496; see, generally, K.J.M. Smith, "Withdrawal in Complicity: A Restatement of Principles" [2001] Crim.L.R. 769.

direction as to the test of communication of withdrawal was not appropriate, since such communication was only a necessary condition for dissociation from pre-planned violence.

Similarly, in *O'Flaherty*,[231] Mantell L.J. followed the *Mitchell* approach, within joint enterprise principles. Hence a jury must be satisfied that the fatal injuries were sustained when the joint enterprise was continuing and "that the defendant was still acting within that joint enterprise". Moreover, Mantell L.J. continued in a case of spontaneous violence such as this where there has been no prior agreement, the jury will usually have to make inferences as to the scope of the joint enterprise from the knowledge and actions of individual participants."[232]

It is submitted that the outcome in *Mitchell* and *O'Flaherty* is overly generous to the defendant. Apart from the unfortunate need to make nebulous distinctions between "spontaneous" and "pre-planned" violence, irrelevant to joint enterprise principles, there is a failure to address concerns over effectiveness and universality of withdrawal. There is also a failure to accord tacit recognition to the element of A's encouragement in the commission of the crime through B's overall involvement which is not directly countermanded:

> "Secondary participation consists in assisting or encouraging the principal offender in the commission of the crime. A party who withdraws from an enterprise, spontaneous or not, usually ceases to assist but he does not necessarily cease to encourage. Suppose that A is encouraged in the fight because he knows that B is there with him. If B decides that he has had enough and quietly slopes off without attracting A's attention, the external element of secondary participation still continues. B's encouragement of A is still operative. Does mere withdrawal then relieve B of responsibility? In principle, it seems that it should not do so. A person who has done an act which makes him potentially liable for a crime cannot relieve himself of responsibility by a mere change of mind. Once the arrow is in the air, it is no use wishing to have never let it go— 'Please God, let it miss!' The archer is guilty of homicide when the arrow gets the victim through the heart. The withdrawer, it is true, does not merely change his mind—he withdraws—but is that relevant if the withdrawal has no more effect on subsequent events than the archer's repentance."[233]

4–045 The impact of the decision in *Mitchell* was limited by a differently constituted Court of Appeal in the subsequent case of *Robinson*.[234] The defendant (B) and a gang of youths followed V taunting him mercilessly. The gang looked to B as their leader and called on him to inflict personal violence on V. B, emboldened by this encouragement, attacked V, whereupon the others actively participated in the assault. B took a back-seat to this further attack, but when concerned that it was going further than he desired, he intervened and the attack ceased. The Court of Appeal reaffirmed the *Whitehouse* direction, as approved in *Becerra*, as determinative in cases where violence was not spontaneous. Thus, withdrawal from pre-planned violence requires, "where practicable and reasonable . . . such communication, verbal or otherwise, that it will serve unequivocal notice upon the other party to the common unlawful cause that if he proceeds upon it he does so without the further aid and assistance of those who withdraw."[235] Otton L.J., who delivered the leading judgment, quite

---

[231] [2004] EWCA Crim 526; [2004] Crim.L.R. 751.
[232] [2004] EWCA Crim 526, at [65].
[233] See J.C. Smith, Commentary on *Mitchell* [1999] Crim.L.R. 496 at 497.
[234] Unrep. February 3, 2000 (Case No.9903443Y3). Note that Otton L.J. delivered the leading judgment in this case as in *Mitchell*.
[235] See *Whitehouse* [1941] 1 W.W.R. 172 (Court of Appeal, British Colombia) per Sloan J.A., approved in *Becerra* (1975) 62 Cr.App.R. 212, and subsequent cases.

clearly stated that there was a clear line of authority that where a party has given encouragement to others to commit an offence it cannot be withdrawn once the offence has commenced. Furthermore, it was articulated that *Mitchell* was an exceptional case: generally communication of withdrawal must be given in order to give the principal offenders the opportunity to desist rather than complete the crime. This is the case even in situations of spontaneous violence unless it is not practicable or reasonable so to communicate as in the exceptional circumstances pertaining in *Mitchell* where the accused threw down his weapon and moved away before the final and fatal blows were inflicted. It seems that if the very attack of personal violence which B has initiated has come to fruition then it is too late for him to effectively withdraw: the exculpatory interlude available for quasi-justificatory extrication from complicity liability has passed.[236] This applied to the defendant in *O'Flaherty*. He was present and, at the very least, providing encouragement or prepared to lend support to the attack.

On occasion our courts have been confused as to the applicability of withdrawal as an issue. In the recent case of *Rafferty*,[237] B and other co-adventurers, carried out an attack on V at a beach. B elbowed V in the back and stole his debit card. Before decamping from the scene for over forty minutes to find a cash dispenser he called out "come on boys, leave it." In his absence the violence escalated, V was stripped down then drowned. The trial judge left for jury consideration whether B had withdrawn from the unlawful joint enterprise. In reality this was a non-issue. The appellate court, quite legitimately, concluded that B was not a principal offender as he was not a substantial cause of V's death. The application of *Rahman* and *Powell* meant that B could also not be categorised as a secondary party—the fatal act of drowning effected by the principals was of a fundamentally different nature from the unlawful robbery enterprise contemplated by B and within which he was engaged. As such consideration of withdrawal principles were rendered otiose.

A final point to note is that the mere fact that the police have already arrested the secondary party does not mean that he can no longer give assistance to the principal.[238]

8. REFORMING THE LAW ON COMPLICITY AND JOINT ENTERPRISE

As part of a broader review of the law of assisting and encouraging crime, the Law   **4–046** Commission recommended at one point that the framework of liability for complicity, in which it was necessary that a principal offence be committed, be fundamentally reappraised, such that liability for "accomplice-type behaviour" would no longer depend on the commission of a principal offence.[239] That radical proposal is no longer on the table but the issue of complicity remains a key issue for the Commission, and has been given further impetus recently by the various pieces of work on the law of homicide with which it has been involved.

The most recent general offering from the Commission proposes, inter alia, two forms of offence.[240] First, for basic complicity/accessoryship situations—that is to say, those where there is assistance or encouragement but no element of joint enterprise—D must intend P to commit the conduct element of the principal offence and must believe that P would be

---

[236] See K.J.M. Smith, [2001] Crim.L.R. 769 at 772–774.
[237] [2007] EWCA Crim 1846; [2008] Crim.L.R. 218.
[238] See, *Craig and Bentley, The Times,* July 31, 1998, above para.4–002.
[239] Law Com. No.131 (1993) *Assisting and Encouraging Crime.*
[240] *Participating in Crime* (2007) Law Com. No.305. See especially Pt 3.

acting with a fault element required for the offence.[241] The second form is relevant to joint enterprise situations. For such a situation to arise, D must agree with P to commit an offence or share a common intention with P to commit an offence. In relation to the further offence committed by P, for D to be liable in respect of that offence, D must intend that P or another party to the joint enterprise should commit the conduct element of the offence; or must believe that P or another party would or might commit the conduct element. D must also believe that P might be acting with the fault required for the offence.

9. ASSISTANCE GIVEN AFTER THE COMMISSION OF THE CRIME

4–047 In this chapter we have been concerned with the situation in which someone has given help to the principal offender which has aided him in the commission of the offence. The giving of such assistance may, as we have seen, render the giver liable to be dealt with as if he were a principal offender. In other words, he may become a party to the actual crime. Help given after the offence has been committed will not normally render a person a party to the offence, but may nevertheless merit punishment in so far as it hinders the apprehension of criminals by the police. There are, therefore offences, to cover just this problem.

By s.4 of the Criminal Law Act 1967 it is provided that:

> "Where a person has committed a relevant offence, any other person who, knowing or believing him to be guilty of the offence or of some other relevant offence, does without lawful authority or reasonable excuse any act with intent to impede his apprehension or prosecution shall be guilty of an offence."

In order to gain a conviction under this section the prosecution must prove first that an relevant offence[242] has been committed. It is not necessary that someone has been convicted of the offence and it would presumably be no defence that the principal offender was, for some reason, exempt from prosecution. Secondly, the prosecution must prove that the accused knew or believed that the principal offender had committed this or some other relevant offence. This does not mean that the accused must know that what A has done amounts to an relevant offence, but it suffices that he knows of the facts which, in law, constitute an relevant offence. Thus it would suffice that the accused knew that the principal offender had forced a girl to have intercourse with him by threatening her with a knife. Thirdly, the prosecutor must establish that the accused has done any act with the intention of impeding the arrest or prosecution of the principal offender. It is clear that nothing short of intention suffices here. It is not sufficient that the accused realises that what he is doing will have the effect of impeding the arrest of the principal offender. Finally the prosecution must show that there was no lawful authority or reasonable excuse for the accused's action.

Under s.5 of the Criminal Law Act it is an offence to conceal information which may be of material assistance in securing the prosecution or conviction of a person who has committed a relevant offence where this has been done for any consideration (reward) other than the making good of the loss caused by the offence, or the making of reasonable compensation for that loss or injury.

We should conclude by saying that there are several other offences which might be used by the police against those who have, in some way, given aid to those who have committed

---

[241] Or D's state of mind must be such that if he were actually performing the conduct constituting the principal offence he would have the fault required for that offence.
[242] "Relevant offence" is defined in s.4(1A) of the Act.

criminal offences. Among these offences are: attempting to pervert the course of justice, obstructing the police in the execution of their duty, causing wasteful employment to the police, and contempt of court.[243]

GENERAL READING

Alldridge, P., "The Doctrine Of Innocent Agency" (1990) 2 *Criminal Law Forum* 45.   **4–048**

Clarkson, C.M.V., "Complicity, *Powell* and Manslaughter" [1998] Crim.L.R. 556.

Dressler, J.,"Reassessing The Theoretical Underpinnings Of Accomplice Liability: New Solutions To An Old Problem" (1985) 37 Hastings L.J. 91.

Giles, M., "Complicity—The Problems Of Joint Enterprise" [1990] Crim.L.R. 383.

Herring, J., "Familial Homicide, Failure to Protect and Domestic Violence: Who's the Victim?" [2007] Crim.L.R. 923.

Kadish, S., "Complicity, Cause And Blame: A Study In The Interpretation Of Doctrine" (1985) 73 Calif.L.Rev. 323.

Lanham, D., "Primary and Derivative Criminal Liability: An Australian Perspective" [2000] Crim.L.R. 707.

Simester, A., "The Mental Element in Complicity" (2006) 122 L.Q.R. 578.

Smith, J.C., "Criminal Liability Of Accessories: Law And Law Reform" (1997) 113 L.Q.R. 453.

Smith, J.C., "Secondary Participation In Crime—Can We Do Without It?" (1994) 144 N.L.J. 679.

Smith, J.C., "Joint Enterprise and Secondary Liability" (1999) 50 N.I.L.Q. 153.

Smith, K.J.M., "Withdrawal In Complicity: A Restatement of Principles" [2001] Crim.L.R. 769.

Smith, K.J.M., *A Modern Treatise On The Law of Criminal Complicity* (Clarendon, 1991)

Smith, K.J.M., "The Law Commission Consultation Paper On Complicity: (1) A Blueprint For Rationalism" [1994] Crim.L.R. 239.

Spencer, J., "Trying To Help Another Person To Commit A Crime", in *Criminal Law Essays* (Smith ed., 1987) p. 148.

Sullivan, G.R., "Intent, Purpose And Complicity" [1988] Crim.L.R. 641.

Sullivan, G.R., "The Law Commission Consultation Paper On Complicity: (2) Fault Elements And Joint Enterprise [1994] Crim.L.R. 252.

Sullivan, G.R., "Participating in Crime" [2008] Crim.L.R. 19.

Taylor, R., "Jury Unanimity In Homicide" [2001] Crim.L.R. 283.

Taylor, R., "Procuring, Causation, Innocent Agency and the Law Commission" [2008] Crim.L.R. 32.

Williams, G., "Complicity, Purpose And The Draft Code" [1990] Crim.L.R. 4 and 98.

Williams, G., "Which Of You Did It?" (1989) 52 M.L.R. 179.

Wilson, W., "A Rational Scheme of Liability for Participation in Crime" [2008] Crim.L.R. 3.

VICARIOUS AND CORPORATE LIABILITY

We shall conclude this chapter with a look at the way in which an employer can be **4–049** prosecuted for the crimes of his employees and a limited company can be prosecuted as if it were a human defendant.

---

[243] See, generally, Ormerod, *op. cit.* Ch.9.

1. VICARIOUS LIABILITY

4–050 In civil actions a master, usually covered today by the word "employer", is liable for the wrongs of his servants (employees) which were committed by the servants during the course of their employment. This usually enables the victim of the torts to sue the tortfeasor's employer who is more likely to be able to pay should liability be proved. But is such a concept really needed in the criminal law? After all, in criminal law, we are trying to attach liability to the person who is responsible for the commission of the offence. We are not normally concerned with trying to compensate the victim. Thus, if X drives a lorry belonging to his boss and the lorry has defective brakes, X is the wrongdoer and should be punished accordingly, but, surely, so should the boss. In general, the rule that liability is personal not vicarious is a long-established principle of the common law. This is exemplified by the old case of *Huggins*[244] where H, the warden of Fleet prison, was acquitted of murder where the prisoner's death had been caused by the gaoler's neglect, and incarceration in an unhealthy cell. H, who had no knowledge of these facts, was not vicariously liable.[245] Two exceptions to this principle are the common law offences of public nuisance[246] and criminal libel.[247] The third important exception, that relating to statutory offences, is examined below.

The rationale for vicarious liability being imposed is based upon social welfare. By enabling the court to punish the employer it is thought that the law will keep him on his toes and ensure, for example, that he carries out regular safety checks on his fleet of lorries. This is an argument very similar to the one put forward in Ch.3 for the justification of strict liability, and again much the same sort of effect could be achieved by carefully worded legislation based on liability for negligence. However, there is another reason for one form of vicarious liability, namely that under the Licensing Acts many offences can be committed only by the holder of the licence. Thus, for example, it is an offence for a licensee to sell alcohol to a person under the age of 18. If there was no concept of vicarious liability it would mean that in order to obtain a conviction the prosecution would have to prove that the licensee personally sold the drink. The relevant principles governing this area were enunciated by Lord Evershed in *Vane v Yiannopoullos*:

> "Where the scope and purpose of the relevant Act is the maintenance of proper and accepted standards of public order in licensed premises or other comparable establishments, there arises under the legislation what Channell J. in *Emary v Nolloth* [1903] 2 K.B. 264, called a 'quasi-criminal offence' which renders the licensee or proprietor criminally liable for the acts of his servants, though there may be no mens rea on his part. On the other hand, where the relevant legislation imports the word 'knowingly' . . . the result will be different . . . In the absence of proof of actual knowledge, nevertheless, the licensee or proprietor may be held liable if he is shown . . . effectively to have '*delegated*' his proprietary or managerial functions."[248]

It is possible that had the courts not adopted a form of vicarious liability to cover these cases it would have forced Parliament to enact more sensibly worded legislation, but this is

---

[244] (1730) 2 *Strange* 883; and see *Nottingham City Council v Wolverhampton and Dudley Breweries* [2004] 2 W.L.R. 820.

[245] Raymond C.J. stated at 885: "It is a point not to be disputed but that in criminal cases the principal is not answerable for the act of his deputy, as he is in civil cases; they must each answer for their own acts, and stand or fall by their own behaviour."

[246] See, e.g. *Stephens* (1886) L.R. 1 Q.B. 702.

[247] Note: this was modified by the Libel Act 1843 s.7 which introduced a defence that publication was made without the defendant's authority, knowledge or consent and (in effect) without negligence on her part. See, e.g. *Holbrook* (1878) 4 Q.B.D. 42.

[248] [1965] A.C. 486 at 504.

one area in which the courts have come to the aid of the legislature. We can now look in more detail at the forms of vicarious liability which have emerged.

A. Express Statutory Vicarious Liability

Occasionally, Parliament provides expressly for the imposition of vicarious liability. For example, s.163(1) of the Licensing Act 1964 provides: "A person shall not, in pursuance of a sale by him of intoxicating liquor, deliver that liquor, either himself or by his servant or agent, from any van, barrow, basket or other vehicle or receptacle unless . . ." It is clear from the emphasis of the statute that express statutory vicarious liability is to be applied.   **4–051**

B. Implied Vicarious Liability

The courts have sometimes held that although a statute has not expressly provided for vicarious liability, the wording is such as to indicate that this must have been Parliament's intention. This they will do when the word used in the statute is one which, without too much of a strain on its meaning, can be interpreted to cover persons other than the actual perpetrator. Such words as "sell", "supply" and "use"[249] have frequently received this extended meaning. Thus, when a lorry driver takes a lorry out for his employer, it is not unreasonable to say that both the driver and the employer "use" the lorry. So both could be said to have used a lorry with defective brakes. It is necessary to examine the ambit of the duty, explicit words used, and expectations of the Act, as stated by Atkin J. in *Mousell Bros v LNWR*:   **4–052**

> "While prima facie a principal is not to be made criminally responsible for the acts of his servants, yet the legislature may prohibit an act or enforce a duty in such words as to make the prohibition or the duty absolute; in which case the principal is in fact liable if the act is in fact done by his servants. To ascertain whether a particular Act of Parliament has that effect or not, regard must be had to the words used, the nature of the duty laid down, the person upon whom it is imposed, the person by whom it would in ordinary circumstances be performed and the person upon whom the penalty is imposed."[250]

This form of vicarious liability is found only in cases where the statute imposes *strict liability*. It cannot be used in offences requiring mens rea to transfer the mens rea of the actual perpetrator to his employer. Two cases will serve to show how this principle works.

In *Coppen v Moore (No.2)*[251] the accused owned six shops which sold food supplies. In these shops he sold American ham, but he told all his managers that they were to call them "breakfast hams". Unfortunately a shop assistant in one of the shops, without the knowledge of the shop manager or the accused owner, sold some of this ham as "Scotch ham". Now clearly she committed the offence, but the Divisional Court held that the accused was also liable since he could in reality be said to be the seller of the wrongly described ham, even if he was not the actual salesman.[252]

---

[249] See, e.g. *Green v Burnett* [1955] 1 Q.B. 78; and *Hallett Silberman Ltd v Cheshire CC* [1993] R.T.R. 32.
[250] [1917] 2 K.B. 836 at 845.
[251] [1898] 2 Q.B. 306.
[252] Note that D continues to be liable even in the scenario where he has forbidden the employee to commit the prohibited activity. See, e.g. *Director General of Fair Trading v Pioneer Concrete (UK) Ltd* [1995] 1 A.C. 456.

In *James & Sons Ltd v Smee*[253] the offence in question was using, or causing or permitting to be used a vehicle in contravention of the Motor Vehicle (Construction and Use) Regulations 1951. The Divisional Court held that there were in effect three different crimes of which "permitting to be used" clearly required mens rea and "using" clearly did not. Thus if A, an employee, sets out in one of his employer's lorries which has defective tyres, the employer, B, can only be convicted of permitting the use of the vehicle if he knows that the tyres are defective, whereas A can be charged with using the vehicle even if he is unaware of the defect. Furthermore, if the police rely on the "using" offence they can hold B vicariously liable—they can, in effect, say that B was using the lorry. They may charge both A and B in which case they will be co-principals. If, however, the regulation had provided that it was an offence to drive a vehicle with defective tyres, then the police could charge only A as a principal offender. B could not be held vicariously liable[254] since the word "drive" is not capable of an extended meaning—you could not really say that B had driven the lorry.[255]

C. The Licensee Cases

4-053 Most people are aware that before a public house can sell alcohol to the public there will have to be a licence obtained from the local magistrates permitting such a sale. This licence has to be issued to a person and not to a company so it will be issued either to the tenant of the public house or, in most cases today, to the manager who draws his salary from one of the breweries. The sale of alcohol is governed in the main by the Licensing Act 1964 under which there are many offences which can only be committed by the holder of the justices licence. This means that if he cannot be named as the principal offender there is no chance of charging the actual perpetrator, e.g. a barman, as a secondary party.[256] There are not many pubs or establishments operating under these licenses where the licensee is the sole person working. Most places employ staff and so there is a good chance that it will be these staff who perpetrate the acts which, if done by the licensee, would be an offence. If the courts had not come to the aid of Parliament with a form of vicarious liability much of the legislation would by now have been rewritten in a more sensible way to cover offences committed by employees.

Some of the offences under the Licensing Act are offences of *strict liability* and where this is the case it may be possible to hold the licensee vicariously liable under the principles discussed in the above sections. For example, it is an offence to sell drinks to a person under the age of 18 or to sell alcohol to a person who is already drunk. Both of these offences are offences of strict liability, and we have already seen the word "sell" is capable of an extended meaning. Thus, if a barman sold a drink to a 17-year-old, it would be possible to say that it was really a sale by the licensee through the agency of the barman.[257]

On the other hand some of the offences are offences requiring mens rea. We saw in Ch.3[258] that the offence of selling alcohol to a policeman on duty requires that the offender knows that the policeman is, in fact, on duty. The offences of permitting drunkenness and permitting prostitutes to congregate also require mens rea. The courts have not allowed the type of vicarious liability we saw in the previous section to be used where the offence requires mens rea. To remedy this lacuna the courts have developed a second type of

---

[253] [1955] 1 Q.B. 78.
[254] See, e.g. *Thornton v Mitchell* [1940] 1 All E.R. 339.
[255] [1940 1 All E.R. 339.
[256] See above, para.4–003.
[257] This form of vicarious liability does not appear to have been used in licensee cases.
[258] See above, para.3–001.

vicarious liability which is now used almost entirely to impute the guilty mind of the licensee's employees to the licensee himself. This operates only when the licensee has delegated general responsibility to his staff for at least part of the pub and is himself not present in that part when the offence is committed. The principle is not restricted to the Licensing Act but this is where it has been largely developed.

The Delegation Principle

To reiterate, the nature of this principle is that the mens rea of employee B is imputed to **4–054** employer A where there has been a delegation of duties. Effectively, as Lord Coleridge C.J. affirmed in the old case of *Somerset v Hart*,[259] it is permissible that a man may put another in his position so as to represent him for the purpose of knowledge. The matter of delegation by a licensee is well illustrated by the decision in *Allen v Whitehead*.[260] The owner and licensee of a refreshment house, while receiving the profits of the business, did not himself manage the refreshment house, but employed a manager for that purpose. A number of women, known to the manager to be prostitutes, resorted to the refreshment house on a number of consecutive days and stayed there for several hours during the night time between the hours of 8pm and 4am. The owner had expressly instructed his manager that no prostitutes were to be allowed to congregate on the premises, but he only visited the premises once or twice a week and had no personal knowledge of what had taken place. It was held that the licensee (owner) was liable to be convicted under s.44 of the Metropolitan Police Act 1839, of knowingly suffering prostitutes to meet together in his refreshment house and remain therein, in as much as having delegated his duty, so far as the conduct of the house was concerned, to his manager, the knowledge of the manager must be imputed to the employer. Similarly, in *Linnett v Metropolitan Police Commissioner*[261] where the offence involved was knowingly permitting disorderly conduct contrary to s.44 of the Metropolitan Police Act 1839. The licensee of the premises had absented himself from the premises and left the control to another man (a co-licensee in fact). It was held that although L, the licensee, had no knowledge, the man he had appointed manager or controller did have knowledge and on the principle of delegation L was liable. Lord Goddard C.J. said:

> "The principle underlying these decisions does not depend upon the legal relationship existing between master and servant or between principal and agent; it depends on the fact that the person who is responsible in law, as for example, a licensee under the Licensing Acts, has chosen to delegate his duties, powers and authority to another."[262]

It is possible to see how the distinction between vicarious liability arising impliedly from statute, as opposed to via delegation, operates in practice by considering two hypothetical examples. Suppose A is the landlord of the Fox and Hounds, a public house with both a bar room and a lounge. He employs B and C to look after the lounge and he is normally in charge of the bar room with the help of D. If, on one occasion, E, who is 17-years-old, asks for a drink, it does not matter who serves him, in which bar, or whether A is present or not. This is an offence of strict liability and the sale by any of the staff could, under the principle discussed in section (B) above, be regarded as the sale of the licensee. Since, however, the principal offender can only be a licence holder, if the sale was made by one of his

---

[259] (1884) 12 Q.B.D. 360 at 362 per Lord Coleridge C.J.
[260] [1930] 1 K.B. 211. See, generally, P.J. Pace, "Delegation—A Doctrine in Search of a Definition" [1982] Crim. L.R. 627.
[261] [1946] K.B. 290.
[262] [1946] K.B. 290 at 294.

employees, for example B, then B could only be liable as a secondary party, and then only if he knew E was under 18.

Now let us consider an offence requiring mens rea. Let us suppose that members of the local rugby club are in the lounge celebrating a victory that day. They are now all well and truly drunk. It is an offence for the licensee to permit drunkenness on the licensed premises (Licensing Act 1964 s.172(1)). B, who is the senior barman on duty in the lounge, has been instructed by A that under no circumstances must he permit such behaviour. B, however, knows most of the players and consequently does nothing. Has an offence been committed? This will depend upon whether we can impute B's knowledge to A under the delegation principle. This raises two questions. Has A delegated authority for the general running of the lounge to B and is A absent? Of course, if he has gone out for the night he will have delegated authority to someone and he will not be present. But is it enough that he is simply in another room? Most of the cases on this topic suggest that it is sufficient that the licensee is not in the room in question at the time the offence is committed, and that in his absence another is in charge. However, in *Vane v Yiannopoullos*[263] the House of Lords held that there had not been delegation when the licensee of a restaurant was not in the room in question, but had gone up on to another floor. Since there was no delegation the House of Lords did not give a final ruling on the delegation principle, but their comments suggested that they were not altogether happy about the idea of imputing mens rea to a licensee in this way. As Lord Donovan said, "If a decision that 'knowingly' means that 'knowingly' will make the provision difficult to enforce, the remedy lies with the legislature."[264] It seemed their Lordships were looking for strict requirements involving a total transfer of responsibility and authority, allied with total non-presence of the licensee in any part of the public house.

4–055   The lower courts have, however, continued to apply the delegation principle without the strictures set out above. In *Howker v Robinson*[265] a barman in the lounge bar of licensed premises sold beer to a boy who was not quite 15 years old. The licensee was present in another bar on the premises at the time of the sale but was not present in the lounge bar and had no knowledge of what had taken place. Nonetheless his conviction for "knowingly" selling intoxicating liquor to a person under the age of 18, contrary to s.169(1) of the Licensing Act 1964 was upheld by the Divisional Court. It was possible for a licensee effectively to delegate his managerial functions and responsibilities in respect of *part* of the premises to his employee even though he himself remained on *another part* of the premises. The outcome therein is surprising given that the licensee was still actively involved in managing the business. Any delegation, if it occurred, could only be partial delegation, applying a wide reading to that concept. A certain degree of ambiguity now prevails as the court stated that it was a question of fact in every case for magistrates or the jury as to whether delegation had occurred, irrespective of the presence on the premises of the licensee. Delegation as a factual matter was clearer in *Winson*[266] where the licensee visited the premises rarely and had specifically forwarded control to a manager. Lord Parker clearly stated that the delegation principle becomes operative where the offence requires mens rea, where the statute uses words which import knowledge or intent.[267] Provided that a direct line of causation can be established between the licensee and the sub-delegate, for example a barmaid, then the delegation principle may be operative, and liability for mens rea offences imposed on the licensee. It suffices that a chain of delegation can be established (see *Sopp v Long*).[268]

[263] [1965] A.C. 486.
[264] [1965] A.C. 486 at 512.
[265] [1972] 2 All E.R. 786.
[266] [1969] 1 Q.B. 371.
[267] [1969] 1 Q.B. 371 at 382.
[268] [1970] 1 Q.B. 518.

To return to our hypothetical example, if the drunken men were in the room where A, the licensee, was clearly in charge then the delegation principle does not operate. If only B, the barman, was aware of their drunken state, his knowledge cannot be imputed to A. In such a case the prosecution will have to prove that it was A who personally permitted the drunken men to remain and that he knew that they were drunk.

D. Inapplicability of Vicarious Liability

Vicarious liability will not apply in the following three situations: **4–056**

1. A licensee will not be liable where an unauthorised individual behind his back does something which contravenes the terms of the license. In *Adams v Camfoni*[269] a licensee was charged under s.4 of the Licensing Act 1921 of selling alcohol during prohibited hours. An employee, an errand boy, had sold in the licensed premises two bottles of whisky to a customer outside permitted hours. He had no authority to do so, was not employed in that capacity, nor did the licensee have knowledge. The licensee was not liable to be convicted under the section; he was not an insurer that no unauthorised person on the premises will do the acts prohibited by the statute.

2. When various customers continue to drink after closing time with the knowledge of the bar staff, the point to remember is that the offence is drinking after hours and not permitting customers to drink after hours. Thus, it is the customer who is the principal offender. Any of the staff who knowingly permit this to continue will be liable as secondary parties, but if A is absent the knowledge of his staff cannot be imputed to him under the delegation principle; you cannot be vicariously liable as a secondary party without knowing the essential facts that constitute the offence (see *Ferguson v Weaving*).[270]

3. Vicarious liability does not apply to attempts to commit a substantive offence (see *Gardner v Akeroyd*).[271]

E. Summary

The doctrine of vicarious liability means the imposition on the defendant of criminal liability **4–057** in relation to physical acts committed by another individual. It relates to offences created by statute and is imposed for social welfare concerns. These objectives are achieved through two mechanisms:

(1) Legislation attaching strict liability for certain activities interpreted in the sense that the employer is imputed to "sell", "supply" and "use" even where all physical manifestations involved in those processes are performed by the employee. In effect, principal liability is ascribed to the employer for the acts of another. No mens rea is needed, so lack of knowledge is no defence for these strict liability offences, with the conviction predicated on attribution of the physical actus reus to the employer; and

[269] [1929] 1 K.B. 95.
[270] [1951] 1 K.B. 814.
[271] [1952] 2 Q.B. 743.

(2) Liability may be imposed where the employer (licensee) has *delegated* to another individual the performance of certain duties imposed upon him by statute; for example the duty imposed in *Allen v Whitehead* that cafe proprietors do not knowingly permit prostitutes to congregate on their premises, or the duty imposed in *Winson* not to sell alcohol to unauthorised persons. Here mens rea may be imputed.

F. Conclusion

4–058 It is to be hoped that under any future code of criminal liability the need for a concept of vicarious liability can be avoided. As we said earlier, a properly drafted statute could impose liability for negligence on employers where this is thought necessary. Thus, in the case where an employer is held vicariously liable for the use by an employee of a vehicle with defective brakes, the same result could be achieved by liability for failing to provide a proper system of vehicle maintenance.

2. CORPORATE LIABILITY

A. General Principles

4–059 Limited companies possess what is known as legal personality. This means that the company can hold property as if it were an ordinary human being and that it can sue and be sued in the civil courts in its own name. The question for us to consider now is whether the company can be a party to criminal proceedings. Of course, when a criminal offence is committed, the actual act must have been perpetrated by an ordinary human being and he will be liable as an individual for the criminal act, but the courts have held that in certain circumstances the limited company can also be held liable in the criminal law for the acts of one of the member individuals.[272] Supporters of corporate liability argue that there is a need for it to affect: curtailment of careless company procedures; improvement in company regulation and safety procedures; deterrence of future egregious conduct through the stigma attached to adverse publicity and fines; deprivation of unjust enrichment; and the promulgation of greater control by shareholders who ultimately bear the financial penalties imposed. It has been suggested that as many large corporations have complex structures which make it difficult for outsiders to determine who is responsible for a particular decision, the effective punishment of a company can trigger the most appropriate institutional response since the company is in the best position to identify and discipline its recalcitrant employees.[273] Other leading academic criminal law commentators remain unconvinced of the need for this form of liability, asserting that "the necessity for corporate criminal liability awaits demonstration."[274] The need for reform and proposals advocated are examined further below.

For most purposes, there are two ways in which a limited company can be held liable for a criminal act—through vicarious liability or the doctrine of identification.

---

[272] Of course no difficulties apply over the imposition of liability for strict offences, for example, those of public nuisance and criminal libel.

[273] C.M.V. Clarkson, "Kicking Corporate Bodies and Damning Their Souls" (1996) 59 M.L.R. 557 at 563.

[274] J.C. Smith and B. Hogan, *Criminal Law* (Butterworths, 1996), p.190. Essentially, the argument is that punishment of a company via the imposition of a fine simply constitutes punishment of innocent shareholders, creditors and employees who might be made redundant, or the public who will ultimately be faced with the burden of the fine through higher prices.

(i) Vicarious Liability

The company can be held to be vicariously liable for the crimes of its employees in just the **4–060** same way that a human employer can be held responsible for the crimes of his employee.[275] Thus, as we saw earlier,[276] this will only apply in statutory crimes of strict liability where the court has been able to give an extended meaning to words such as "sell", "supply" or "use".[277] For example, in *Tesco Stores Ltd v Brent London Borough Council*[278] the defendant company was charged with "supplying" a video with an "18" classification certificate to a youth of 14 in violation of the Video Recordings Act 1984 s.11(1). The statute provided a defence within s.11(1)(b) to a defendant who neither knew nor had reasonable grounds to believe that the purchaser had not attained the designated age. Tesco argued that none of the directing mind of the company under the *Nattrass* test[279] had the requisite knowledge, even though the cashier who sold the video may have been aware of the boy's age. The Divisional Court dismissed Tesco's appeal holding that it was unrealistic to expect those in control of a large company to have knowledge or information about the age of every video purchaser. The knowledge of the employee could properly be attributed to the company as a contrary conclusion meant that the efficacy of the statute would be destroyed.[280] In essence, this interpretation meant that the offence was one of vicarious liability. In a similar vein are the decisions in *R v British Steel Plc*[281] and *National Rivers Authority v Alfred McAlpine Homes East*.[282] The former case involved construction by the Court of Appeal of s.3(1) of the Health and Safety at Work Act 1974. The charge related to an accident at a British Steel plant where sub-contractors had cut away the platform supports without securing them to a crane or temporary supports. It collapsed killing two men. An identified British Steel employee was responsible for the supervision. The Court of Appeal upheld the conviction of the company determining that, subject to the words "so far as is reasonably practicable", s.3(1) created an absolute prohibition, with consequential imposition of vicarious liability.[283] Similarly, the Divisional Court in *National Rivers Authority v Alfred McAlpine Homes East* applied vicarious liability to a regulatory offence concerning pollution contained within s.85(1) of the Water Resources Act 1991. In this case two employees of the company, the site manager and the site agent, admitted responsibility for "causing" wet cement to enter controlled waters. In such circumstances it is necessary to resort to statutory construction on the applicability of vicarious liability to companies.[284] Clarkson has cogently stated:

---

[275] See, e.g. *Mousell Bros. Ltd v London and North-Western Railway Co* [1917] 2 K.B. 836; *Chuter v Freeth & Pocock Ltd.* [1911] 2 K.B. 832; and *Griffiths v Studebakers Ltd* [1924] 1 K.B. 102.

[276] See above, para.4–052.

[277] This general principle received approval from the House of Lords in *Director General of Fair Trading v Pioneer Concrete (UK) Ltd* [1995] 1 A.C. 456.

[278] [1993] 2 All E.R. 718. See generally, J. Gobert, "Corporate Criminality: Four Models of Fault" (1994) 14 *Legal Studies* 393 at 407.

[279] See below, para.4–061.

[280] See *Coppen v Moore (No.2)* [1898] 2 Q.B. 306; see above, para.4–052.

[281] [1995] I.C.R. 586; [1995] Crim.L.R. 654.

[282] [1994] 4 All E.R. 286.

[283] The Court of Appeal concluded that: "If . . . (an offence was one of) absolute criminal liability, it would drive a juggernaut through the legislative scheme if corporate employers could avoid criminal liability where the potentially harmful event is committed by someone who is not the directing mind of the company" [1995] I.C.R. 586 at 593.

[284] It is not the position that vicarious liability be applied as a matter of course to strict liability offences. By way of contrast to *British Steel* and *National Rivers Authority* consider *Seaboard Offshore Ltd v Secretary of State for Transport* [1994] 2 All E.R. 99, where the company was prosecuted under s.31 of the Merchant Shipping Act 1988. The House of Lords held that as a matter of interpretation of the statute and its policy implications the company could not be vicariously liable for a breach of duty under s.31 for the acts of its servants or agents, i.e. it was viewed as incongruous for company liability to be based on activities of lowly employees such as the failure of a bosun to close the portholes.

"whether the doctrine of vicarious liability applies or not is a matter of statutory interpretation, taking into account the language, content and policy of the law, and whether vicarious liability will assist enforcement".[285]

It has been criticised as a doctrine on the grounds that it is too wide, in attributing wrongdoing of all and any employees to the company, and too narrow, in leaving no opportunity to explore company policies.[286]

In summary, a corporate entity may be vicariously liable in the same manner as a natural person. It will be liable for strict liability offences to the same degree as a natural person where vicarious liability is applicable, when liability applies for the actions of all employees, even minor employees in the corporate structure. It is not limited to those who actually control the company.

(ii) Identification

4–061 The company can be held liable by what is known as the doctrine of identification, also known as the *alter ego* doctrine.[287] What this means is that in each company the court recognises certain senior individuals as being the company itself and the acts of these individuals when acting in the company's business are treated as the acts of the company. The identification doctrine was fully received into our law in a trio of cases in 1944 dealing with various forms of deception perpetrated at senior management levels in the respective corporations.[288] It has been said that certain members of the company can be regarded as its "brain" and the others as merely its "hands". This tells us that we are looking for people who have the power to control the company's actions. Thus, in most companies, we can say that the managing director and the other directors will be regarded as being in a position of control and this might even extend to the company secretary and non-director managers if they have sufficient executive power; these will be the brains of the company. The anthropomorphic delineation between "brains" and "hands" was provided by Lord Denning in one of his typically vivid metaphors in the civil case of *H.L. Bolton (Engineering) Co Ltd v T.J. Graham & Sons Ltd*:

"A company may in many ways be likened to a human body. It has a brain and a nerve centre which control what it does. It also has hands which hold the tools and act in

[285] C.M.V. Clarkson, (1996) 59 M.L.R. 557 at 565.
[286] C. Wells, "The Corporate Manslaughter Proposals: Pragmatism, Paradox and Peninsularity" [1996] Crim.L.R. 545, 547. Colvin has stated that: "It is under inclusive because it is activated only through the criminal liability of some individual. Where offences require some form of fault, that fault must be present at the individual level. If it is not present at that level, there is no corporate liability regardless of the measure of corporate fault. Yet vicarious liability is also over inclusive because, if there is individual liability, corporate liability follows even in the absence of corporate fault. The general objection to vicarious liability in criminal law—that it divorces the determination of liability from an inquiry into culpability—applies to corporations as it does to other defendants. The special characteristics of corporations do not insulate them from the stigmatising and penal consequences of a criminal conviction"; E. Colvin, "Corporate Personality and Criminal Liability" (1995) 6 Criminal Law Forum 1 at 8.
[287] See generally, C. Wells, "Corporations: Culture, Risk and Criminal Liability" [1993] Crim.L.R. 551 at 559. This new form of liability, distinct from vicarious liability, was based on the idea of the company itself being *identified* with the acts of senior officers, rather than being accountable for the transgressions of its employees.
[288] *DPP v Kent and Sussex Contractors Ltd* [1944] 1 K.B. 146; *ICR Haulage Ltd* [1944] K.B. 551; and *Moore v Bresler* [1944] 2 All E.R. 515. See, generally, G.R. Sullivan, "Expressing Corporate Guilt" (1995) 15 O.J.L.S. 281. Sullivan asserts (pp.282–283) that given the factual circumstances involved in the three cases in 1944 the *alter ego* doctrine was perfectly well-adapted to secure convictions against the companies but is singularly ill-adapted to generate convictions against companies for manslaughter by gross negligence. Save in the smallest of companies, senior corporate officials are unlikely to be involved in those "sharp-end" incidents which give rise to death or injury, thereby largely precluding the finding of any corporate culpability arising from the specifics of any particular incident. Considerable difficulties prevail in inculpating companies of any organisational size and complexity.

accordance with directions from the centre. Some of the people in the company are mere servants and agents who are nothing more than hands to do the work and cannot be said to represent the mind or will. Others are directors and managers who represent the directing mind and will of the company, and control what it does. The state of mind of these managers is the state of mind of the company and is treated by the law as such."[289]

But the line between "brains" and "hands" is not easy to draw with any degree of certainty and this was illustrated by the decision in *Tesco Supermarkets Ltd v Nattrass*.[290] In that case an old age pensioner was trying to buy a packet of soap powder at the reduced price being offered by one of Tesco's shops. He could not find any packets priced at the lower price and the shop refused to sell him a packet at anything other than the full price. He complained to the inspector of weights and measures who brought a prosecution against Tesco Supermarkets Ltd. under the Trade Descriptions Act 1968 s.11(2). A statutory defence was provided by s.24 of the Act which provided that no liability applied if a person charged under the Act could show that the commission of the offence was due to the act or default of another person and that the defendant himself, i.e. in this case, Tesco Ltd, took all reasonable precautions to prevent the commission of such an offence by itself or any person under its control.[291] Tesco sought to put the blame on the branch manager who had failed to ensure that packets at the reduced price were on display, despite the control exercised by the firm and its detailed instructions to managers as to how to deal with such matters. One of the issues confronting the House of Lords was whether or not the store manager could be identified as the company. If this was the case then Tesco would be liable for the offence. Lord Reid described the identification principle of liability in the following terms:

"A living person has a mind which can have knowledge or intention or be negligent and he has hands to carry out his instructions. A corporation has none of these: it must act through living persons, though not always one or the same person. Then the person who acts is not speaking or acting for the company. He is speaking as the company and his mind which directs his acts is the mind of the company. There is no question of the company being vicariously liable. He is not acting as a servant, representative, agent or delegate. He is an embodiment of the company, one could say, he hears and speaks through the persona of the company, within his appropriate sphere, and his mind is the mind of the company. If it is a guilty mind then that guilt is the guilt of the company."[292]

In *Tesco*, the House of Lords held that because of the strict controls exercised by the company over its branch managers they were left with so little power that they could not be regarded as part of the "brains" of the company, not a directing mind and will.[293] This meant that Tesco Ltd was able to show that the offence was, in fact, committed by a third party—namely their manager—and, thus, it could rely on the defence provided by s.24 of the Act.

[289] [1957] 1 Q.B. 159 at 172.
[290] [1972] A.C. 153.
[291] See defences to strict liability, above, para.3–026.
[292] [1972] A.C. 153 at 170.
[293] The directing mind and will test derives from *Lennard's Carrying Co Ltd v Asiatic Petroleum Co Ltd* [1915] A.C. 705 and the oft-cited passage of Viscount Haldane L.C. (at 713): "A corporation is an abstraction. It has no mind of its own any more than it has a body; its active and directing will must consequently be sought in the person of somebody who for some purposes may be called an agent, but who is really the directing mind and will of the corporation; the very ego and centre of the personality of the corporation."

This is not a true example of the third party defence since there is no need for the third party to be joined in the proceedings. It is sufficient that the defendant can give sufficient information to the prosecution to enable the true culprit to be prosecuted.

4–062   Later cases have shown pervading difficulties in applying the identification test down the chain of corporate command. A controlling officer is not simply one who engages in brain work rather than manual duties.[294] In this regard companies have escaped liability for activities carried out by weighbridge operators,[295] depot engineers,[296] transport managers[297] and more recently in *Redfern*[298] the Court of Appeal held that the European sales manager of Dunlop (Aviation) Ltd was insufficiently senior to be identified with the company. It has been judicially suggested that the doctrine be restricted for limited companies to those individuals identified by the memorandum and articles of association as entrusted with the exercise of the powers of the company.[299]

The contextual ambit of the *alter ego* doctrine needs to be evaluated in the light of the important Privy Council decision in *Meridian Global Funds Management Asia Ltd v Securities Commission*.[300] In this case, two senior management managers (K and N), employed by Meridian, improperly used their authority to invest in a New Zealand company. As a consequence Meridian were in breach of s.20(3) of the Securities Amendment Act 1988, a New Zealand statute, necessitating notice of substantial investments to be given both to the company and the stock exchange. The breach of the securities legislation depended upon whether the company had knowledge of the activities of its investment managers. The Privy Council rejected the application of vicarious liability in this scenario, but held that an individual had to be found within the company whose acts and knowledge could be *attributed* to the company. Moreover, Lord Hoffmann suggested that the "directing mind and will" test was not always appropriate, and attribution of knowledge was not constrained by anthropomorphisms, namely brains and hands of a company.[301] They were a generalisation that only applied in certain cases.[302] In this situation the knowledge of the senior investment managers was to be attributed to the company. The policy of the statute was to compel disclosure of a substantial security holder, and thus the relevant knowledge was possessed by the individual who acquired the relevant interest. Attribution will be determined by examining the language of the particular statute, its content and policy. Lord Hoffmann stated:

> "their Lordships would wish to guard themselves against being understood to mean that whenever a servant of a company has authority to do an act on its behalf, knowledge of that act will for all purposes be attributed to the company. It is a question of construction in each case as to whether the particular rule requires that that knowledge that an act has been done, or the state of mind with which it was done, should be attributed to the company."[303]

---

[294] *Tesco Supermarkets Ltd v Nattrass* [1972] A.C. 153 at 171 per Lord Reid.
[295] *John Henshall (Quarries) Ltd v Harvey* [1965] 2 Q.B. 233.
[296] *Magna Plant Ltd v Mitchell* [1966] Crim.L.R. 394.
[297] *Readhead Freight Ltd v Shulman* [1988] Crim.L.R. 696.
[298] [1993] Crim.L.R. 43.
[299] *Tesco Supermarkets Ltd v Nattrass* [1972] A.C. 153 at 200 per Lord Diplock, and also followed in *Seaboard Offshore Ltd v Secretary of State* [1994] 2 All E.R. 99 at 104.
[300] [1995] 2 A.C. 500.
[301] [1995] 2 A.C. 500 at 507. Lord Hoffmann said: "the court must fashion a special rule of attribution for the particular substantive rule. This is always a matter of interpretation: given that it was intended to apply to a company, how was it intended to apply? Whose act (or knowledge or state of mind) was *for this purpose* intended to count as the act etc. of the company?"
[302] C.M.V. Clarkson, (1996) 59 M.L.R. 557 at 565.
[303] [1995] 2 A.C. 505 at 511.

Lord Hoffmann then proceeded to give as an illustration of the relevant construction, that a company would not be guilty of manslaughter because its employee, authorised to drive a lorry, killed someone by reckless driving.[304] However, difficulties still pertain to the attribution test adopted in *Meridian*. The case clearly stretches the ambit of the identification model beyond the anthropomorphic directing mind and will of a company, but it is unclear how the test will be determined or deployed.[305] We are thrown back to construe inferences from legislative intent, and to construe language, content and policy of relevant statutes. Wells has asserted that the decision in *Meridian* is "a step of uncertain dimensions (and much depends on the unpredictable judicial divining rod for legislative intent) taking us closer to a new model of corporate liability".[306] We await the clarification that a series of appellate decisions will hopefully provide on the contextual ambit of the identification model. At this juncture, the doctrinal perspective adopted in *Meridian* has yet to be applied by an English court in a reported case concerning a corporation's criminal liability. In any event, it was determined in *Attorney-General's Reference (No.2 of 1999)*[307] that it was inapplicable to common law offences, such as manslaughter, because it is constrained to the interpretation of statutory offences. Thus, the identification doctrine remains the rule of attribution for this common law offence, and others such as conspiracy to defraud.

B. Liability of Individual

If the firm is held to be liable because of the acts of one of its members, can the member be **4–063** joined as a party to the proceedings? The answer to this, with a notable exception,[308] is clearly yes. In both types of corporate liability the member may be joined as a co-principal. Additionally, company officers may be made directly liable through statutory provisions; this is illustrated by statutes such as s.20 of the Trades Descriptions Act 1968 and s.53 of the Betting, Gaming and Lotteries Act 1963 which contain the following terms:

> "Where an offence under this Act which has been committed by a body corporate is proved to have been committed with the consent or connivance of, or to be attributable to any neglect on the part of, any director, manager, secretary and other similar officer of the body corporate or any person who was purporting to act in any such capacity, he as well as the body corporate shall be guilty of that offence."

C. Are There any Crimes a Company Cannot Commit?

A company can be convicted of any offence provided that the sentence can be in the nature **4–064** of a fine. You clearly cannot send a company to jail, let alone hang it. Thus, the penalty must take the form of a fine and/or a compensation order which will fall upon the shareholders.

---

[304] [1995] 2 A.C. 505 at 512.
[305] C.M.V. Clarkson, (1996) 59 M.L.R. 557 at 566. Clarkson identifies two particular problems with this approach: "First, it is unclear when the acts of a person not representing the directing mind and will of the company are to be attributed to the company. How does one tailor this new attribution rule to fit the 'terms and policies' of the substantive rule? How, for instance, is this to be done for a common law offence such as manslaughter? Or is the subtext here that this can only be done for white-collar offences such as those in the *Meridian* case? Secondly, it must be stressed that this is still a rule of attribution. Someone (a human being) must be found within the corporate structure who did the criminal act before liability can be attributed to the company. In other words, in complex organisations such as P and O where no such person can be identified, there will still be no criminal liability."
[306] C. Wells, "The Corporate Manslaughter Proposals: Pragmatism, Paradox and Peninsularity" [1996] Crim.L.R. 545 at 548.
[307] [2000] 3 All E.R. 182; [2000] 1 Cr.App.R. 207.
[308] See Corporate Manslaughter, below at para.4–066.

The only crimes where this will not be possible are treason, murder and some forms of piracy where imprisonment is mandatory.

Theoretically this means that a company can be convicted of all offences against the person except for murder. However, early English case law took the view that a corporation could not be guilty of manslaughter, because homicide required the killing to be done by a human being. This was the underlying reasoning of a decision in 1927, *Cory Bros Ltd*,[309] in which Finlay J. quashed an indictment against a company for manslaughter, considering himself bound by authorities which demonstrated that an indictment would not lie against a corporation for a felony involving personal violence.[310] Of course, the case of *Cory Bros Ltd* was decided prior to the development of the identification doctrine in the trio of 1944 cases. The issue of corporate liability for manslaughter was raised in public consciousness through a series of widely publicised disasters during the course of the 1980s. In 1987 there was the Zeebrugge tragedy in which the ferry, *Herald of Free Enterprise*, capsized killing 192 people. Also in 1987 there was the King's Cross fire in which 31 people died, the cause being the inability of various groups of people within the overall organisational corporate network to identify and implement their areas of responsibility; and in 1988 the Piper Alpha oil rig explosion led to the death of 167 people.[311] At this time the decision of a coroner, who had determined that a corporation could not be indicted for manslaughter, was challenged in an application for judicial review.[312] Although not fully argued, Bingham L.J. was tentatively of the opinion that an indictment would lie.[313] The issue was subsequently argued in depth in *P and O European Ferries (Dover) Ltd*[314] involving the successor company of the firm which owned the *Herald of Free Enterprise*.

The prosecution of P & O and seven employees for manslaughter followed the Zeebrugge disaster. The Herald of Free Enterprise had capsized just outside Zeebrugge harbour in March 1987 after leaving port with its bow doors open. It was found that the assistant bosun, whose job was to ensure that the doors were shut, was asleep in his cabin, and there were no means by which the captain could confirm from the bridge whether or not the doors were shut.[315] Ultimately the prosecution against P & O European Ferries (Dover) Ltd was terminated when Turner J. directed the jury that, as a matter of law, there was no evidence upon which they could properly convict six of the eight defendants, including the company, of manslaughter.[316] There was no case to answer to that charge. In essence, this was based, vis-à-vis the company, on the ground that in order to convict it of manslaughter, one of the individual defendants who could be identified with the company would have to be guilty of manslaughter. Because there was inadequate evidence to convict any individual defendant, this meant the case against the company had to fail.[317] However, in the reported portion of the trial, Turner J. comprehensively reviewed existing authorities and came to the conclusion that an indictment for manslaughter could lie against a corporation. It was held by Turner J. that:

> "[T]here is nothing essentially incongruous in the notion that a corporation should be guilty of the offence of unlawful killing . . . [W]here a corporation, through the

[309] [1927] 1 K.B. 810.
[310] [1927] 1 K.B. 810 at 817–818.
[311] C.M.V. Clarkson, (1996) 59 M.L.R. 557 at 557.
[312] *H.M. Coroner for East Kent, Ex. p. Spooner* (1989) 88 Cr.App.R. 10.
[313] (1989) 88 Cr.App.R. 10 at 16. See, e.g. Legislating the Criminal Code: Involuntary Manslaughter, Law Com. No.237 (hereafter Law Com. No.237) at 80.
[314] (1991) 93 Cr.App.R. 72.
[315] See generally, C. Wells, "Corporations: Culture, Risk and Criminal Liability" [1993] Crim.L.R. 551.
[316] *Stanley and Others,* Unrep. October 19, 1990 (C.C.C. No.900160). See Law Com. No.237 at p.83.
[317] Unreported, October 19, 1990 (C.C.C. No.900160).

controlling mind of one of its agents, does an act which fulfils the prerequisites of the crime of manslaughter, it is properly indictable for the crime of manslaughter."[318]

The decision in *P & O*, despite the termination of the prosecution on the factual basis **4–065** therein, signalled the liability of companies for offences against the person. This was crystallised by the first conviction of a company of manslaughter under English law in 1994, in *Kite and OLL Ltd*,[319] following the death of four teenagers during a canoeing trip in Lyme Bay. Both the company, OLL Ltd, which organised the canoeing trip and its managing director, Kite, were convicted of manslaughter. The perceived risks involved were obvious and serious, and the company had received a number of written warnings from former instructors that fatalities could result unless safety was improved at the centre; these warnings had not been heeded. In effect, as the company was a one-man concern whose directing mind was plainly its managing director, the company's liability was established automatically by his conviction. It will be more problematic to secure a corporate conviction for manslaughter where a complex operational structure prevails, as in *P & O*, with attendant difficulties in identifying the controlling individuals.

It is a truism that the establishment of relevant principles to sustain a conviction of a corporation for manslaughter have proved enduringly controversial in recent years. The matter has arisen in several high-profile disasters, especially involving alleged breaches of safety by railway management, which have engendered pulic outcry and strong demands for appropriate remedial action. There was, for instance, a media outcry after the CPS confirmed that it would not bring any manslaughter charges after the Ladbroke Grove crash.[320] The most recent case to evaluate the guiding rationale is that of *Attorney-General's Reference (No.2 of 1999)*[321] which derived from the Southall rail disaster.[322] On September 19, 1997 a high speed train from Swansea crashed into a freight train at Southall. Seven people were killed and many others injured. The operator responsible for the high speed train was indicted in seven counts with manslaughter. The trial judge ruled that it was a condition precedent to a conviction for manslaughter by gross negligence for a guilty mind to be proved, and that where a non-human defendant was prosecuted it could only be convicted via the guilt of a human being with whom it could be identified. No trial took place; the defendant was sentenced only for an offence under s.3(1) of the Health and Safety at Work etc. Act 1974,[323] to which it pleaded guilty, and was fined £1.5m for what the judge described as a "serious fault of senior management". No employee of the defendant, apart

---

[318] (1991) 93 Cr.App.R. 72, 83–84.

[319] Unreported Winchester Crown Court, December 8, 1994. Subsequent convictions have followed in at least two other cases involving small corporations; see *Jackson Transport (Ossett) Ltd* (1996) (November) Health and Safety at Work 4; and *Roy Bowles Ltd, The Times,* December 11, 1999.

[320] See, generally, Walker, H., "Criminalising companies—will corporate killing make a difference?" (2001) 151 N.L.J. 1404.

[321] [2000] 3 All E.R. 182; [2000] 1 Cr.App.R. 207.

[322] See Trotter, S., "Corporate Manslaughter" (2000) 150 N.L.J. 454.

[323] Penalties under the Health and Safety at Work, etc., Act 1974 include unlimited fines and/or up to two years imprisonment for certain offences. Professor Sullivan has argued that the import of this Act needs fresh consideration: "Liability under the 1974 Act is not triggered by causing death, thus avoiding all the elements of chance and luck entailed. In terms of the application of consistent standards of safety, the forensic issue arising under the Act is commendably straightforward—was it reasonably practicable for the company to provide a safe system of work? Case law and regulations made under the 1974 Act make this virtually a strict standard; effectively the defendant company has to demonstrate that, all things considered, it was not possible to attain a higher standard of safety . . . Large fines are now imposed under the Health and Safety Act 1974"; see G.R. Sullivan, "Corporate Killing—Some Government Proposals" [2001] Crim.L.R. 31. The 1974 Act has been recently amended by the Health and Safety (Offences) Act 2008. The Act has extended the range of health and safety offences in respect which a £20,000 maximum fine is available in magistrates' courts, and has made custody available in respect of more offences.

from the driver, was prosecuted. The Attorney-General, on a reference under s.36 of the Criminal Justice Act 1972, sought the opinion of the court, inter alia, on the following question:

> "Can a non-human defendant be convicted of the crime of manslaughter by gross negligence in the absence of evidence establishing the guilt of an identified human individual for the same crime?"

It was determined that a non-human defendant, such as a corporation, could not be convicted in the absence of evidence establishing the guilt of an identified human individual for the same crime. It seemed to their Lordships that there was no sound basis for suggesting that, by their recent decisions, the courts had started a process of moving from identification to personal liability as a basis for corporate liability for manslaughter. Indeed, Lord Hoffmann's speech in *Meridian Global Funds Management Asia Ltd v Securities Commission*,[324] in fashioning an additional special rule of attribution geared to the purpose of the statute, proceeded on the basis that the primary "directing mind and will" rule still applied, although it was not determinative in all cases. In other words, he was not departing from the identification theory, but reaffirming its existence. With respect, the result is an uncertain and convoluted approach to corporate liabilty for manslaughter. It is submitted that the appellate court's conclusion is incorrect in assuming that there can be no corporate liability in the absence of an identifiable human offender; compare the earlier authorities of *Birmingham and Gloucester Railway*[325]; *Great North of England Railway Co,*[326] and *Tyler and the International Commercial Co.*[327] No such general principle exists at common law. Certainly other jurisdictions, particularly a number of US states, have had no difficulty imposing criminal liability on corporations although no specific person is identifiable as the culprit. La Fave and Scott, leading American commentators, assert in this regard:

> "[O]ften no one other than the corporation could be convicted, either because the offence is an omission of a duty imposed only on the corporation, or because [citing Glanville Williams, The Criminal Law, The General Part, 2nd edn (1961) s.283] the division of responsibility is so great that it is difficult to fix on an individual."

D.   A New Offence: the Corporate Manslaughter and Corporate Homicide Act 2007

4–066   The identification doctrine was proving, in most situations, an insuperable obstacle to securing convictions for corporate manslaughter. While it was possible for smaller organisations to be caught by virtue of the relative ease of identifying a relevant "directing mind and will" in respect of the corporate failure leading to death, there was a real danger of a two-tier criminal law emerging, in which larger organisations, by virtue of their structure, were effectively insulated from the offence. This could have thrown the very credibility of the law into question. It is not surprising therefore that there has been pressure for a change to the law for some time.

---

[324] [1995] 2 A.C. 500; [1995] 3 W.L.R. 413 PC. The aggregation principle has also been rejected in Scotland; see *Transco v HM Advocate* [2004] S.L.T. 41.
[325] (1840) 3 Q.B. 223.
[326] (1846) 9 Q.B. 315.
[327] [1891] 2 Q.B. 588.

The Law Commission in 1996 proposed the introduction of a new offence of "corporate killing."[328] The Government in 2000, with certain variations, published a Consultation Paper on Involuntary Manslaughter which endorsed the proposal for a new offence.[329] Previous editions of this textbook have commented on these initiatives. In 2005 when the Government published a new version coupled with a draft Bill[330] which proposed the abolition of the common law offence of manslaughter by gross negligence as it applied to companies, to be replaced by a statutory offence of "corporate manslaughter". The Select Committee on Home Affairs and Work and Pensions produced a Report[331] on the Bill in that year, and the Government responded in March 2006.[332] In due course the Corporate Manslaughter and Corporate Homicide Act 2007 received Royal Assent in July 2007, and most of the provisions of the Act came into force in April 2008.

The Act abolishes the common law liability of corporations for manslaughter.[333] The new offence of corporate manslaughter is set out in s.1 of the Act. Prosecutions require the consent of the Director of Public Prosecutions, although the reason for this is not clear.[334] An organisation to which the Act applies commits the offence if "the way in which its activities are managed or organised" causes death and constitututes a "gross breach" of a "relevant duty of care". The "way in which its activities are managed or organised by its senior management"[335] must make a substantial contribution to the breach. The breach is "gross" if the conduct in question "falls far below what can reasonably be expected of the organisation in the circumstances".[336] The application of the Act is not limited to corporations. It also applies to police forces, government departments and other Crown bodies, to partnerships, trade unions and employers' associations which are employers.

Section 18 provides that individuals within the organisation cannot be liable as secondary **4–067** parties to the corporate manslaughter offence. Their conduct may of course attract individual liability for other offences. These include gross negligence manslaughter, subject to the requisite degree of fault and the proof of a causal link with the death. Individuals may also be liable for health and safety offences. Section 19 of the CMCHA 2007 makes it possible for an organisation to be convicted of corporate manslaughter and a health and safety offence on the same facts, "if the interests of justice so require". In respect of individual liability, this brings into play s.37 of the Health and Safety at Work, etc., Act 1974, which creates individual liability in respect of the health and safety offence committed by the organisation if it is committed with "the consent or connivance of", or is "attributable to any neglect on the part of", "any director, manager, secretary or other similar officer".[337]

The offence turns significantly on the existence of a "relevant duty of care", a notion derived from the law of negligence. In broad terms, the organisation owes such a duty as an

---

[328] Law Com. No.237 (1996), *Legislating the Criminal Code: Involuntary Manslaughter*.

[329] Home Office, *Reforming the Law on Involuntary Manslaughter: the Government's Proposals* (2000).

[330] Home Office, *Corporate Manslaughter: the Government's Draft Bill for Reform*, Cm.6497 (2005). See, generally, C.M.V. Clarkson, "Corporate Manslaughter: Yet More Government Proposals" [2005] Crim.L.R. 677.

[331] Select Committee on Home Affairs and Work and Pensions First Report: Draft Corporate Manslaughter Bill (2005–06) HC 540–II. Professors Chris Clarkson and Celia Wells were appointed as Specialist Advisers to the Committee.

[332] The Government Reply to the First Joint Report from the Home Affairs and Work and Pensions Committees, Session 2005–06 HC 540: Draft Corporate Manslaughter Bill (Cm 6755).

[333] Corporate Manslaughter and Corporate Homicide Act 2007 s.20.

[334] CMCHA 2007 s.17. The *Explanatory Notes* to the Act give no guidance as to why consent is required. There was no such requirement in the old common law.

[335] CMCHA 2007 s.1(3).

[336] CMCHA 2007 s.1(4)(b).

[337] See F.B. Wright, "Criminal liability of directors and senior managers for deaths at work" [2007] Crim.L.R. 949–968.

employer or contractor, as an occupier, as a commercial operator, or as a custody operator.[338] Whether a duty of care exists is a question of law, to be decided by the judge.[339]

The Act countenances a variety of contexts in which a relevant duty of care will not exist. These include the making of public policy decisions and the conduct of certain public functions,[340] the conduct of various military[341] and law enforcement activities,[342] the response to emergencies of the emergency services,[343] and the exercise of certain child-protection or probation functions.[344]

The most innovative structural feature of the new offence is its move away from the individualism of the identification doctrine. Whereas formerly it was necessary to fix liability on a corporation by way of an identified guilty individual, now the focus is on management and its failings. This seems to capture more effectively the "corporateness" of corporate manslaughter and is embodied most vividly in s.8 of the Act, which sets out a variety of factors which a jury must and may consider when determining whether a breach of duty was gross. The jury must consider whether there has been a breach of health and safety legislation, and if so, how serious the breach was and how great was the risk of death caused by the breach. Most strikingly, the Act opens up and makes relevant the workings of the organisation in a way which the old law never could, by permitting the jury to consider "the extent to which the evidence shows that there were attitudes, policies, systems or accepted practices within the organisation that were likely to have encouraged" the relevant failure or "to have produced tolerance of it".[345]

4–068   The penalty for corporate manslaughter is an unlimited fine. There are additional options open to a court on conviction. A "remedial order" may be imposed under s.9 of the Act. Such an order can only be made following an application by the prosecution and can require the organisation to remedy the breach or associated deficiencies within a specified time. Failure to comply with a remedial order is an indictable offence, punishable by a fine.

The most interesting penalty set out in the Act is not available yet, as s.10 has not been brought into force. If it is implemented, the provision will allow a court to impose a "publicity order" on conviction, which can require the organisation to publicise its conviction, the particulars of the offence, the fine imposed and the terms of any remedial order. Failure to comply will be an indictable offence, punishable by a fine.

There is much to commend in the new offence. The focus is turned away from individual misconduct and towards the organisation as a collective actor (albeit with a focus on senior management activity), and its aggregated organisational failings. Organisations should not be able to avoid liability simply through the adoption of diffuse management structures and it ought to be easier than was previously the case to secure convictions against larger organisations who were effectively beyond the reach of the old law by virtue of their size.

---

[338] The provision imposing a duty on custody operators (who may be public (e.g. the police or Prison Service) or private providers) is not yet in force. Indeed, arguments about this provision almost derailed the entire Bill. A compromise was reached whereby the government, who had originally opposed such a duty, committed to the implementation of the duty at a point where custody providers had had the opportunity to prepare themselves for the new legal regime, and where necessary, to raise their standards. The projected timescale for implementation was three years from commencement of the Act. That the standards were not already adequate to countenance the implementation of the new regime is a damning admission. See *Hansard*, HL Debates, (July 23, 2007) for the reaching of the compromise.

[339] CMCHA s.2(5).

[340] CMCHA 2007 s.3. Such decisions might relate, for example, to the allocation of public resources. They are, in orthodox terms, not justiciable in the law of negligence either.

[341] CMCHA s.4.

[342] CMCHA s.5.

[343] CMCHA s.6.

[344] CMCHA s.7.

[345] CMCHA s.8.

Some will find the exclusion of individual liability for secondary participation in the offence an unsatisfactory omission, although there are other avenues available for the criminalisation of individuals. Causes for concern remain. The drive to bring custody operators within the offence must retain focus.[346] It is important that vigilance is exercised to ensure that providers' commitments to upskill, and government commitments to implementation are honoured in due course. That the publicity order is not yet available is disappointing as the threat of reputational damage to companies is potentially of significant deterrent effect. A remaining doctrinal matter is of course that the new offence only applies to fatalities. Thus, corporate liability for other offences continues to be pursued by way of the identification doctrine. So, if, for example, a workplace incident results in both death and serious injury, it is possible that two doctrinal schemes will be brought into play simultaneously: the management failure approach in relation to corporate manslaughter, and identification in respect of other offences.

E. Summary

It may be said that although a company is a separate legal person, nevertheless it has no **4–069** physical existence; and consequently can act only through individuals who are its employees or agents. Initially it was conceived under our law that for matters of procedure a corporation was not indictable.[347] However, these procedural reasons have evaporated over time, and now as a matter of substantive law, three doctrinal approaches have been developed for attribution of corporate liability for conduct and mental states of employees: (i) vicarious liability—in accordance with this doctrine a company is vicariously liable for the acts of any employee wherever an individual employer would be so liable; (ii) identification—this originated in a trio of cases in 1944 and the model has been developed in later cases; and (iii) in cases of corporate manlaughter, liability based on management failings. The management failure approach applies only to manslaughter and so the significance of identification remains. Essentially, under this theory those who *control* the corporation are identified, vis-à-vis criminal liability, as the embodiment of the company. Broadly speaking the acts and states of mind of individuals who control a company are fictionally treated in law as those of the company itself.

GENERAL READING

Bergman, D., *Deaths At Work: Accidents Or Corporate Crime* (London, WEA, 1991).   **4–070**

Clarkson, C.M.V., "Kicking Corporate Bodies And Damning Their Souls" (1996) 59 M.L.R. 557.

Clarkson, C.M.V., "Corporate Manslaughter: Yet More Government Proposals" [2005] Crim.L.R. 677.

Colvin, E., "Corporate Personality and Criminal Responsibility" (1995) 6 *Criminal Law Forum* 1.

Fisse, B. and Braithwaite, J., *Corporations and Accountability*, (Cambridge University Press, 1994).

Fisse, B. and Braithwaite, J., "The Allocation Of Responsibility For Corporate Crime: Individualism, Collectivism and Accountability" (1988) 11 Sydney L.Rev. 468.

---

[346] See Ministry of Justice, *Corporate Manslaughter and Corporate Homicide Act 2007: Progress towards implementation of custody provisions* (2008).
[347] Law Com. No.237 at 67.

Gobert, J., "Corporate Criminality, Four Models Of Fault" (1994) 14 *Legal Studies* 393.

Hainsworth, A., "The Case For Establishing Independent Schemes Of Corporate and Individual Fault In Criminal Law" (2001) 65 J.C.L. 420.

Jefferson, M., "Corporate Criminal Liability: The Problem of Sanctions" (2001) 65 J.C.L. 235.

Jefferson, M., "Corporate Criminal Liability in the 1990s" (2000) 64 J.C.L. 106.

Mujih, E., "Sentencing for Health and Safety Offences: Is the Court of Appeal Going Soft?" (2008) 72 J.C.L. 370.

Ormerod, D., and Taylor, R., "The Corporate Manslaughter and Corporate Homicide Act 2007" [2008] Crim.L.R. 589.

Pace, P.J., "Delegation—A Doctrine In Search Of A Definition" [1982] Crim.L.R. 627.

Simester, A.P. and Sullivan, G.R., *Criminal Law Theory and Doctrine* (Hart Publishing, 2000) at 235–255.

Sullivan, G.R., "Corporate Killing—Some Government Proposals" [2001] Crim.L.R. 31.

Sullivan, G.R., "Expressing Corporate Guilt" (1995) 15 O.J.L.S. 281.

Wells, C., "Corporations: Culture, Risk And Criminal Liability" [1993] Crim.L.R. 551.

Wells, C., *Corporations and Criminal Responsibility* 2nd edn (Oxford: Oxford University Press, 2001).

Wells, C., "The Corporate Manslaughter Proposals: Pragmatism, Paradox and Peninsularity" [1996] Crim.L.R. 545.

Wright, F.B., "Criminal Liability of Directors and Senior Managers for Deaths at Work" [2007] Crim.L.R. 949.

Chapter 5

GENERAL DEFENCES

THE MENTALLY ABNORMAL OFFENDER: INSANITY AND UNFITNESS TO PLEAD

The defence of insanity is raised by a defendant who is claiming that at the time he was **5–001** alleged to have committed the offence he was suffering from a mental condition which would excuse him from criminal responsibility. Where a court reaches such a conclusion it returns a verdict of not guilty by reason of insanity. If it is obvious that the defendant is totally unfit to stand trial, there are powers to commit him directly to a mental hospital (ss.47 and 48 of the Mental Health Act 1983).[1] Where it is less obvious and he is sent for trial, the court may determine that he is unfit to plead.[2] A person is unfit to plead when he is unable to recognise the charges that have been brought against him, to challenge jurors, to instruct counsel, and is unable to appreciate the difference between pleas of guilty and not guilty.[3] If he is able to understand these issues he is fit to stand trial even if he is unable to recall any of the events to which the charges relate; this was claimed in the case of *Podola*[4] where D sought to rely on hysterical amnesia preventing him from remembering events material to the commission of the crime which involved the murder of a police officer. This emphasises that it is the state of the person's mind *at the time of the trial* that is in issue. By the time of the trial Podola was clearly able to understand the charges that had been brought against him and knew the difference between pleading "guilty" or "not guilty". In his case, if his claims as to hysterical amnesia were true, his difficulty lay in knowing whether to plead "guilty" or "not guilty" since he could not recall what had happened. Where the issue is raised by the defendant he has the burden of proving on a balance of probabilities that he is

[1] The Home Secretary is empowered to order that D be detained in a hospital in the public interest if he is of the view, following reports from at least two medical practitioners, that D is suffering from mental illness or severe mental impairment.

[2] This will be on arraignment under ss.4 and 4A of the Criminal Procedure (Insanity) Act 1964, as substituted by s.2 of the Criminal Procedure (Insanity and Unfitness to Plead) Act 1991, and as amended by s.22 of the Domestic Violence Crime and Victims Act 2004. See generally, R.D. Mackay. "The Trial of Facts and Unfitness to Plead" [1997] Crim.L.R. 644.

[3] For an interesting historical perspective on unfitness to plead see D. Grubin, "What Constitutes Fitness To Plead" [1993] Crim.L.R. 748.

[4] [1960] 1 Q.B. 325.

unfit to plead[5]; where it is raised by the judge[6] or prosecution, the prosecution bears the burden of proving beyond reasonable doubt that the accused is unfit.[7]

The issue of unfitness to plead may be raised by either party or by the judge prior to trial. The issue, at that stage, was until recently one for jury evaluation.[8] However, revision occurred in s.22 of the Domestic Violence, Crime and Victims Act 2004, by which the matter is one for the court without a jury. The proceedings are viewed as providing effective dual protection for both the public and the particular defendant. In general, the question of a defendant's fitness for trial ought to be considered as expeditiously as possible, with attendant medical evidence. Where the judge finds D fit to stand trial then the case will be tried by a jury in accordance with normal practice. In exceptional circumstances, where the issue arises for determination later in the procedure, then it is to be determined by the same jury by which the defendant is being tried.[9]

In s.4A of the Criminal Procedure (Insanity) Act 1964 (introduced by the 1991 Act, and amended by the 2004 Act), are the relevant governing principles which apply where it is determined by a jury that the defendant is unfit to be tried (a finding of disability). It is stated in s.4A(2) that the trial must not proceed or further proceed but it must be determined by a jury whether they are satisfied, as respects the counts or each of the counts against the accused, "that he did the act or made the omission charged". In the House of Lords case of *Antoine*[10] the issue arose whether this terminology meant that the jury need *only* be satisfied that the accused committed the actus reus of the offence, and need not address whether he did so with the mens rea for it? The suggestion from the earlier authority of *Egan*[11] was that both elements were necessary. This was rejected by their Lordships in *Antoine*. The victim was brutally murdered by the defendant and another, apparently as a sacrifice to the devil. Antoine was charged with murder. After hearing psychiatric evidence, the jury found the appellant unfit to plead by reason of mental disability. A different jury later proceeded to determine under s.4(A)(2) of the Criminal Procedure (Insanity) Act 1964 whether Antoine did the act charged against him as murder, and so found. On the appeal to the House of Lords the defendant invited their Lordships to consider the question whether the jury had to be satisfied as to mens rea, in the sense of establishment·that the defendant had done the act with the requisite state of mind for criminal liability.

---

[5] This raises an important question of principle, considered further below, para.5–023 and at para.5–024, as to whether there is a conflict between the fundamental human right of the presumption of innocence and the requirement that the accused prove that he or she is not guilty on the basis of insanity at the time of bringing about the actus reus of the offence; this is the burden of proof at the trial of the case. See generally, T.H. Jones, "Insanity, Automatism, And The Burden Of Proof On The Accused" (1995) 111 L.Q.R. 475.

[6] *MacCarthy* [1967] 1 Q.B. 68.

[7] *Robertson* [1968] 1 W.L.R. 1767, and see *M* [2003] EWCA Crim 3452.

[8] See Criminal Procedure (Insanity) Act 1964 s.4(5).

[9] See s.22 of the Domestic Violence, Crime and Victims Act 2004, amending the Criminal Procedure (Insanity) Act 1964 s.4, as substituted by the Criminal Procedure (Insanity and Unfitness to Plead) Act 1991 s.2.

[10] [2001] 1 A.C. 340; [2000] 2 All E.R. 208 HL.

[11] [1998] 1 Cr.App.R. 121; [1997] Crim.L.R. 225. In this case a man snatched a handbag from a woman while she was travelling on a train. The defendant was arrested but denied the offence. He was found by a jury to be unfit to plead. There was then a trial of the issue of fact. Nobody was formally appointed by the judge to put the case for the defence on the issue of fact, although the defendant was nonetheless represented by counsel. The jury found that the defendant had done the act charged against him as theft and an admission order to hospital, not accompanied by a restriction order, was made pursuant to s.5 of the Criminal Procedure (Insanity) Act 1964. He appealed against the finding of fact. It was determined by the appellate court, dismissing the appeal, that the prosecution had to prove all the ingredients of what would otherwise be an offence. Ognall J. stated (at 124–125): "although the words "the act' are used in the relevant legislation, the phrase means neither more nor less than proof of all the necessary ingredients of what otherwise would be an offence."

Their Lordships determined in *Antoine* that by using the word "act" and not the word **5–002** "offence" in s.4A(2) of the 1964 Act, Parliament had made it clear that the jury was not to consider the mental ingredients of the offence.[12] A measure of protection was given by a person suffering from mental disability at the time of his trial by s.4 of the 1964 Act. If the defence considered that facts relied on by the prosecution did not give rise to the prima facie inference that the defendant had had the requisite mens rea for the offence charged, it could request the court under s.4(2) to permit the trial to proceed and at the conclusion of the prosecution case make a submission of no case to answer. The purpose of s.4A was to strike a fair balance between the need to protect a defendant who had in fact done nothing wrong and was unfit to plead at the trial, and the need to protect the public from a defendant who had committed an injurious act that would have constituted a crime if done with the requisite mens rea. That was particularly important where the act had caused death or physical injury and there was a risk that the defendant might carry out a similar act in the future. If there was "objective" evidence that raised the issues of mistake, accident, self-defence or involuntariness, the jury should not find that the defendant had done the "act" unless it was satisfied that the prosecution had negatived the defence. This addendum was, with respect, particularly surprising:

> "it is difficult to see how admissible objective evidence of mistake or accident, in particular, could come before the jury when the determination of whether the accused did the act or made the omission charged is made at the start of the trial".[13]

More generally, their Lordships reserved their opinion on the question whether, on a determination under s.4A(2), it would be open to the defence to call witnesses to raise the issue of provocation.[14] In *Grant (Heather)*,[15] however, it was stated that a defendant cannot invoke the defence of provocation. The familiar burden of proof applies in that the onus is on the prosecution to establish beyond a reasonable doubt that the defendant did the act or made the omission charged.[16]

Until very recently, once a trial court held that the defendant was insane or unfit to plead, it had no discretion but to make an order admitting him to a mental institution coupled with a restriction direction forbidding his release without the Home Secretary's approval. As a result very few defendants were inclined to use these pleas.[17] For this reason the Criminal Procedure (Insanity and Unfitness to Plead) Act 1991[18] made important changes by way of amendment to the Criminal Procedure (Insanity) Act 1964, and further reforms have recently taken place under s.24 of the Domestic Violence, Crime and Victims Act 2004. An interesting study on unfitness to plead has revealed that since the coming into force of the 1991 Act the number of successful pleas have doubled.[19] In a period covered by the study the

---

[12] For comment suggesting that s.4A of the Criminal Procedure (Insanity) Act 1964 falls foul of art.6 of the European Convention of Human Rights and Fundamental Freedom guaranteeing the right to a fair trial see Johnson P., "Unfit To Stand Trial" (2000) 150 N.L.J. 930.

[13] See R. Card, *Criminal Law* 15th edn (Butterworths, 2001) at p.591.

[14] Note in *Antoine* their Lordships also determined that the appellate court had been correct to hold that the provisions of s.2 of the Homicide Act 1957 (diminished responsibility) could not apply to the hearing under s.4A(2) of the 1964 Act and that at that hearing the defendant could not raise the defence of diminished responsibility.

[15] [2002] Q.B. 1030.

[16] [2000] 2 All E.R. 208 at 211 per Lord Hutton. Note in *M* [2003] 2 Cr.App.R. 21 it was cogently asserted that a basic actus reus division from mens rea was not feasible given the diverse nature of respective offences.

[17] An evaluation of this area by R.D. Mackay, "Fact And Fiction About the Insanity Defence" [1990] Crim.L.R. 247, cogently affirms this point in that between 1975–88 there were only 49 verdicts of not guilty by reason of insanity; only 14 of these 49 pertained to verdicts in murder trials.

[18] See, generally, R.D. Mackay and G. Kearns, "The Continued Underuse of Unfitness To Plead And The Insanity Defence" [1994] Crim.L.R. 576.

[19] R.D. Mackay and G. Kearns, "An Upturn in Unfitness to Plead? Disability in Relation to the Trial Under the 1991 Act" [2000] Crim.L.R. 532.

number of findings of unfitness to be tried has averaged 24 per year.[20] Of these the largest proportion who were successful were schizophrenics; those featured among the diagnostic groups included sufferers from dementia, psychosis, brain damage and depressive states. A startling finding was that some 90 per cent of those found unfit to plead were male defendants.

5–003   The 1991 Act provides that no jury may make a finding that the accused is insane or unfit to plead unless they have received evidence from at least two qualified medical practitioners, at least one of whom must be approved by the Home Secretary as having special experience in the diagnosis or treatment of mental disorder. In the case of unfitness to plead, where the issue arises exceptionally at a later time, it is to be determined by the exact same jury by which the accused is being tried in accordance with s.22 of the 2004 Act. However, the trial judge may delay consideration of the issue of unfitness to plead right up until the start of the defence case.[21] If before the defence opens, the jury have already acquitted the defendant on a submission of no case to answer, the issue of unfitness to plead may not be tried. Once a jury have returned a finding that the defendant is under a disability and hence unfit to plead, the jury will then determine, on the evidence already received or now adduced, whether they are satisfied that the defendant did in fact do the act or make the omission charged against him.[22] The jury will either make such a finding or return an acquittal.[23] In the event that all relevant evidence presented at trial points to D being insane, but the jury convicts, this conviction will be overturned on appeal on the premise that no reasonable jury could have reached such a conclusion.[24] It is insufficient in this regard that only the medical evidence supports the defence if other evidence is presented at trial to the contrary.[25]

Where the court reach a verdict of not guilty by reason of insanity or unfitness to plead coupled with a finding that he did the act or made the omission with which he was charged, they are no longer restricted to making an order confining the defendant indefinitely to a mental hospital. The court may, in accordance with s.5 of the Criminal Procedure (Insanity) Act 1964 (as substituted by the Criminal Procedure (Insanity and Unfitness to Plead) Act 1991), and amended by s.24 of the Domestic Violence, Crime and Victims Act 2004 make (i) an order admitting him to a hospital (with or without a restriction order); (ii) a supervision and treatment order under sch.2 to the Criminal Procedure (Insanity and Unfitness to Plead) Act 1991—this is similar to a psychiatric probation order whereby the supervisee is to be under the supervision of a social worker or probation officer for a period specified, but which is not longer than two years, during which the "supervisee" "shall submit" to treatment by or under the direction of a registered medical practitioner, usually a consultant psychiatrist, with a view to the improvement of his medical condition[26]; or (iii) an absolute discharge. In murder, prior to the 2004 Act, a court had to make an admission order coupled with an indefinite restriction direction. This indefinite restriction was recognised as possibly falling foul of art.5(1) of the ECHR. Consequently it has been abrogated by s.24 of the 2004 Act in cases where the sentence for the crime to which the finding relates is fixed by law which, in essence, means murder.

---

[20] R.D. Mackay and G. Kearns, [2000] Crim.L.R. 532 at 534.

[21] This is to check the strength of the prosecution evidence; if it is weak it would be unfair to deprive D of a trial he might win. This is particularly cogent where the prosecution is making a submission of unfitness to plead.

[22] See, e.g. *O'Donnell* [1996] 1 Cr.App.R. 286.

[23] Empirical research conducted by R.D. Mackay, "The Decline of Disability In Relation to Trial" [1991] Crim. L.R. 87, revealed that between 1979–89 there were 229 findings of unfitness to plead, the preponderance of defendants being male, within the 20–39 age range, with 81% possessing a psychiatric history and 71% previous criminal records. Trials for unfitness to plead declined by half during the 1980s.

[24] *Matheson* (1958) 42 Cr.App.R. 145.

[25] *Latham* [1963] Crim.L.R. 434.

[26] R.D. Mackay and G. Kearns, [2000] Crim.L.R. 532 at 576–577.

Where under its powers under ss.6 and 14 of the Criminal Appeal Act 1968 the Court of Appeal, on an appeal against conviction or acquittal on the grounds of insanity, substitutes a verdict of not guilty by reason of insanity or unfitness to plead together with a finding that the accused did the act, it may make any of the orders available to the court of trial.

It is hoped that these new provisions will make the defence of insanity more acceptable to **5–004** defendants who could benefit from the wide treatment which is now available. It is notable, however, that an order under s.5 can only be made if it is proven that the accused committed the act alleged and so they are punitive in nature. In no sense can they be considered protective, as was the case under the pre-1991 procedure. If an obviously dangerous person is found not to have committed the act (acquitted) the court has no power to order him to be admitted to a hospital. If, however, an individual is found to have committed the act, but poses little risk to the public, an order under s.5 may be imposed. As a consequence it remains an open question whether this procedure is in breach of art.6 of the ECHR. The relevant parts read as follows:

> "(1) in the determination of his civil rights and obligations or of any criminal charge against him, everyone is entitled to a fair and public hearing within a reasonable time by an independent and impartial tribunal established by law . . .
>
> (3) Everyone charged with a criminal offence has the following minimum rights:
>
> > (a) to be informed promptly, in a language which he understands and in detail, of the nature and cause of the accusation against him;
> >
> > (b) to have adequate time and facilities for the preparation of his defence;
> >
> > (a) to defend himself in person or through legal assistance of his own choosing or, if he has insufficient means to pay for legal assistance, to be given it free when the interests of justice so require;
> >
> > (c) to examine or have examined witnesses against him and to obtain the attendance and examination of witnesses on his behalf under the same conditions as witnesses against him;
> >
> > (d) to have the free assistance of an interpreter if he cannot understand or speak the language used in court."

The European Court of Human Rights has asserted that art.6 implies a right for an accused to effectively participate in his trial.[27] Later jurisprudence has gone further in making it explicit that if a defendant is unable to participate *effectively* in the criminal proceeding against him, he is denied a fair trial, and hence art.6 is breached.[28] Furthermore, it seems to be self-evident that an individual who is unfit to plead is unlikely to understand the charges he faces, which is potentially a further breach of art.6(3)(a). There may also be an argument that such proceedings would breach art.6(3)(c)—by compelling the accused to have a court appointed lawyer and not a lawyer of his choosing. In summary, a defendant found unfit to plead or stand trial is by that very finding unable to participate effectively in any proceedings. In order to square the circle the logical corollary of this may be that proceedings for determining whether the accused did "the act or omission alleged" under s.4A may be in breach of art.6. If this is the case then it has been cogently asserted that the violation could only be remedied by new domestic legislation.[29] A cathartic panacea may be

---

[27] *Ekbatini v Sweden* (1988) 13 E.H.R.R. 504 ECtHR.
[28] See *V and T v UK* (1999) 30 E.H.R.R. 121 ECtHR.
[29] See Johnson, P. "Unfit to Stand Trial?" (2000) 150 N.L.J. 930.

to return to a slightly amended pre-1991 procedure—if someone is found to be unfit to plead the judge could either pass a hospital order, a guardianship order or no order—essentially a protective rather than a punitive measure. The proposal adduced is that this response would be compatible with the Convention, provided that there is a periodic review of the patient's condition and the right to challenge the continuation of any order.[30] If the tribunal, as a consequence of the review procedure, conclude that the patient is fit to plead, then a fresh appraisal could be taken of whether or not commencing a new prosecution is in the public interest.

1. THE DEFENCES OF INSANITY AND DIMINISHED RESPONSIBILITY

5–005   Now we can look at the scope of the defence of insanity, under which the accused claims that because of his mental state *at the time he allegedly committed the offence*, he was not truly responsible for his actions. The defence of insanity is of common law origin and its requirements are to be found in the answers by the judges to a series of questions posed by the House of Lords. A man by the name of M'Naghten had tried to kill Sir Robert Peel but had killed his secretary by mistake. His acquittal on the ground of insanity provoked an outcry and the questions by the House of Lords to the judges were an attempt to clarify the position in relation to the defence of insanity.[31] The questions and answers form what are known as the M'Naghten Rules. Although they are not technically binding as a source of law, they have been treated as authoritative since 1843, and are the basis for the defence of insanity today. We shall see that insanity is a relatively narrow defence and does not provide for many mentally abnormal offenders. This led Parliament in s.2 of the Homicide Act 1957 to provide a special defence, applicable only to murder, known as diminished responsibility which, when successfully pleaded, means that the accused will be convicted not of murder, but of manslaughter.

A. Insanity

5–006   The word "insanity" is not a medically recognised term which describes a particular mental state; it is a legal term for a legally defined state of mind which will lead in any criminal offence to a verdict of not guilty by reason of insanity.

   The starting point is the presumption that the accused is presumed sane until the contrary is proved. The burden of proving insanity lies on whoever wishes such a finding to be made by the jury. Thus if the accused raises the defence he must prove, applying the civil law standard of a balance of probabilities, that it is more likely than not that he is insane.[32] If the accused pleads diminished responsibility the prosecution will be entitled to argue that the accused was insane. If the jury decide that the accused was insane they will return a verdict of not guilty by reason of insanity. Since this is technically an acquittal it is provided by s.12 of the Criminal Appeal Act 1968 that the accused may appeal against the verdict.

---

[30] *ibid.*

[31] A similar outcry occurred in the USA following the jury's acquittal of John Hinckley, who had attempted to assassinate President Reagan, on the grounds of insanity. Many US states responded by abolishing or restricting the use of the insanity defence. See generally, R.G. Frey, "The Guilty But Mentally Ill Verdict And Due Process" (1982) 92 Yale L.J. 475; and R.D. Mackay. "Post-Hinckley Insanity In The USA" [1988] Crim.L.R. 88.

[32] The same position may apply if the judge determines that D is raising the defence of insanity. When it is raised by the prosecution then the onus is on them.

More recently, the Court of Appeal in *Attorney-General's Reference (No.3 of 1998)*[33] have concluded that where the issue of insanity is raised during a trial, the prosecution are relieved of the duty of proving mens rea. In accordance with the provisions of s.2(1) of the Trial of Lunatics Act 1883 it is only required to be proved that the accused "did the act or made the omission charged".[34] In this context there is equiparity with unfitness to plead as in *Antoine* the House of Lords subsequently determined that in construing s.4A of the Criminal Procedure (Insanity) Act 1964 (finding of disability) the jury need only be satisfied that the accused committed the actus reus of the offence, and need not address whether he did so with the mens rea for it.[35] The earlier approach effected in *Egan*[36] has been resiled from in the clearest possible terms in relation to both insanity and unfitness to plead. In *Attorney-General's Reference (No.3 of 1998)*, however, there was no evaluation of the problem of the burden of proof on the accused and compatibility with the European Convention on Human Rights.[37]

The fact that before the Criminal Procedure (Insanity and Unfitness to Plead) Act 1991 a **5–007** verdict of not guilty by reason of insanity meant hospitalisation, very few defendants chose to raise it directly, except as a defence to very serious charges. In murder cases it was virtually superseded by the defence of diminished responsibility. However, it may arise indirectly. First, as we have already seen, it may be raised by the prosecution in answer to the defendant's plea of diminished responsibility, as Lord Denning said in *Bratty v Att-Gen for Northern Ireland*:

> "I think that Devlin J. was right in *Kemp's* case in putting the question of insanity to the jury, even though it had not been raised by the defence. When it is asserted that the accused did an involuntary act in a state of automatism, the defence necessarily puts in issue the state of mind of the accused man: and thereupon it is open to the prosecution to show what his true state of mind was. The old notion that only the defence can raise a defence of insanity is now gone. The prosecution are entitled to raise it and it is their duty to do so rather than allow a dangerous person to be at large."[38]

Secondly the accused, in seeking to raise some other defence such as non-insane automatism[39] or even lack of mens rea, may provide an explanation for his conduct which may be seen by the trial judge as evidence of insanity. In such a case the trial judge will be bound to leave the defence of insanity to the jury. Where the defendant realises that this will

---

[33] [1999] 3 All E.R. 40.

[34] Trial of Lunatics Act 1883 s.2, as amended by s.1 of the Criminal Procedure (Insanity) Act 1964, provides that where at the trial of a person for an offence: "it is given in evidence . . . that he was insane so as not to be responsible, according to law, for his actions at the time when the act was done or omission made, then, if it appears to the jury . . . that he did the act or made the omission charged, but was insane as aforesaid when he did or made the same, the jury shall return a special verdict that the accused is not guilty by reason of insanity."

[35] See above at p.172. Note, however, contrary to the situation under s.4A of the Criminal Procedure (Insanity) Act 1964, which also refers to the jury being satisfied that the accused, "did the act or omission charged", the prosecution vis-à-vis insanity does not have to disprove evidence that an accused might have been acting under a mistake, by accident, or involuntarily.

[36] [1998] 1 Cr.App.R. 121, see above, at para.5–001.

[37] See below, para.5–023.

[38] [1963] A.C. 386 at 411.

[39] Lord Denning defined automatism [1963] A.C. 386 (at 409) as being: "an act which is done by the muscles without any control of the mind, such as a spasm, a reflex action or a convulsion; or an act done by a person who is not conscious of what he is doing, such as an act done whilst suffering from concussion or whilst sleep-walking". It will be recalled that automation involves allegations of involuntary conduct by D and lack of conscious willed movements—see above, para.2–007.

happen, he may change his plea to guilty to avoid any possibility of a verdict of not guilty by reason of insanity and the risk of incarceration in a psychiatric hospital.

The side bearing the burden of proof must prove, in accordance with the M'Naghten Rules, that the accused was, at the time he committed the act, *"labouring under such a defect of reason, from disease of the mind, as not to know the nature and quality of the act he was doing, or if he did know it, that he did not know he was doing what was wrong."* It is necessary that the following elements of the defence be established.

(i) Defect of Reason

5–008 The defendant (or prosecutor if it is the prosecutor who is seeking to establish the defendant is insane) must show that the defendant was suffering from such a defect of reason that he did not know the nature and quality of the act he had committed, or, if he did know, that he did not know that what he was doing was wrong. This has been confirmed by the Court of Appeal in *Johnson*.[40] There is no specific defence to the effect that the accused was simply operating under irresistible impulses.[41]

Clearly anyone who is acting in a state of automatism will not know the nature and quality of his act. More generally, the reference to nature and quality of the act is another way of saying that the accused lacked the necessary mens rea for the crime. Traditional examples given include the man who cut a woman's throat thinking it was a loaf of bread, and the nurse who put the baby on the fire thinking it was a log of wood.

If the accused is relying on the second limb—that he did not know he was doing what was wrong—then he must prove that he did not know that it was legally wrong. Thus, even though the accused believed that what he was doing was morally abhorrent and that people in general would not approve, he is entitled to a verdict of not guilty by reason of insanity if he can show that he thought that it was legally permissible. This principle, which is subject to criticism,[42] was held to be correct in the case of *Windle*.[43] D, the subject of a very unhappy marriage, killed his certifiably insane wife by the administration of 100 aspirin tablets. Subsequently he gave himself up to the police, saying to them when arrested: "I suppose they will hang me for this?" Medical evidence was given at Windle's trial to the effect that he was suffering from a communicated form of insanity known as *folie-à-deux*, but medical experts on both sides were in agreement that he knew that he was doing an act that was legally wrong. His conviction was consequently upheld by the Court of Criminal Appeal, with Lord Goddard C.J. asserting:

> "Courts of law can only distinguish between that which is in accordance with the law and that which is contrary to law . . . The law cannot embark on the question, and it would be an unfortunate thing if it were left to juries to consider whether some particular act was morally right or wrong. The test must be whether it is contrary to law . . . In the opinion of the court there is no doubt that in the M'Naghten Rules 'wrong' means contrary to law and not 'wrong' according to the opinion of one man or a number of people on the question whether a particular act might or might not be justified."[44]

---

[40] [2007] EWCA Crim 1978.
[41] See, e.g. *Kopsch* (1925) 19 Cr.App.R. 50; and *Sodeman v R.* [1936] 2 All E.R. 1138.
[42] Note that it was rejected by the High Court of Australia in *Stapleton v R.* (1952) 86 C.L.R. 358 which held that where the defendant believed his act to be right *according to the ordinary standards of reasonable men* he was entitled to be acquitted even if he knew it to be legally wrong.
[43] [1952] 2 Q.B. 826.
[44] [1952] 2 Q.B. 826 at 833–34.

Thus, if X's disease of the mind caused him to think that three of his friends, A, B and C were members of an assassination squad who had to be killed before they could kill him, then he would succeed on a defence of insanity, because his delusion caused him to think that he was legally entitled to kill A, B and C. If, on the other hand, his disease of the mind caused him to think that he was Jack the Ripper and so led him to go round killing prostitutes, he would not succeed with a plea of insanity because, as Jack the Ripper, he would know that he was not entitled to kill prostitutes. He might now, however, be able to plead diminished responsibility.

(ii) Disease of the Mind

Not every defect of reason will lead to a defence of insanity. The defect of reason must have **5–009** been caused by a disease of the mind. Where, for example, the defect of reason has been brought about by the defendant consuming 15 pints of beer, he may be able to plead intoxication but the defence of insanity will not be available. Where, therefore, the accused has relied on a blackout at the time of the alleged crime, the court will want information as to the cause of the blackout. If this explanation reveals that the cause was a disease of the mind, then the defendant will be taken to have raised the defence of insanity. What, therefore, constitutes a disease of the mind?

The starting point for consideration of this issue is the case of *Bratty v Att-Gen for Northern Ireland*.[45] Bratty was charged with murdering a girl by strangulation. He claimed to have been unconscious of what he was doing at the time he strangled the girl and he sought to run as alternative defences non-insane automatism and insanity. The only evidential foundation that he laid for either of these pleas was medical evidence that he might have been suffering from psychomotor epilepsy which, if he were, would account for his having been unconscious of what he was doing. No other pathological explanation of his actions having been carried out in a state of automatism were supported by evidence. The trial judge first put the defence of insanity to the jury. The jury rejected it and declined to bring in the special verdict. Thereupon, the judge refused to put to the jury the alternative defence of automatism. His refusal was upheld by the Court of Criminal Appeal of Northern Ireland and subsequently by the House of Lords. Their Lordships drew a fundamental distinction between two types of automatism, namely non-insane and insane automatism. The former allows an outright acquittal but the latter meant incarceration in a mental hospital.[46] Lord Denning elaborated upon the nature of disease of the mind, as being, "any mental disorder which has manifested itself in violence and is prone to recur is a disease of the mind. At any rate it is the sort of disease for which a person should be detained in hospital rather than be given an unqualified acquittal."[47] Later cases have tended to treat the propensity of violence to recur as merely one of a number of indicators of a disease of the mind. Self-evidently this is an appropriate response given that diseases of the mind may become apparent in ways other than through "violence" per se, for example, through arson, criminal damage or repeated theft.

The leading decision on what constitutes a disease of the mind is *Sullivan*[48] which again involved drawing a distinction between insane and non-insane automatism. D had kicked a man violently on the head and body while suffering a seizure due to psychomotor epilepsy. At his trial he pleaded not guilty to causing grievous bodily harm with intent and inflicting grievous bodily harm. Medical evidence was presented to the effect that it was in the post-

[45] [1963] A.C. 386; see above, para.2–007.
[46] Note that a judge has wider powers today; see above, para.5–005.
[47] [1963] A.C. 386 at 412.
[48] [1984] A.C. 156.

octal stage of a seizure of psychomotor epilepsy when D would make automatic movements of which he was not conscious. The trial judge, at the close of the evidence, ruled this amounted to a defence of insanity, at which point Sullivan changed his plea to guilty of assault occasioning actual bodily harm and was convicted accordingly. It was held by the House of Lords that the trial judge had been correct in equating the defence to insanity. Lord Diplock provided the following definition of disease of the mind:

> "'mind' in the M'Naghten Rules is used in the ordinary sense of the mental faculties of reason, memory and understanding. If the effect of a disease is to impair these faculties so severely as to have either of the consequences referred to in the latter part of the rules, it matters not whether the aetiology of the impairment is organic, as in epilepsy, or functional, or whether the impairment itself is permanent or is transient and intermittent, provided that it subsisted at the time of the commission of the act."[49]

(iii) Insane and Non-insane Automatism: A Division Between Internal and External Factors

5–010 Any condition which produces the effects on the mind outlined in *Sullivan* can and will be classified as a disease of the mind. It should be remembered that it is a disease of the mind and not a disease of the brain which is required. This point was enunciated by Devlin J. in *Kemp*,[50] a case where D, suffering from arteriosclerosis (a condition which affects blood flow to brain), carried out motiveless bodily injuries to his wife by attacking her with a hammer. This, according to Devlin J., was a prima facie illustration of the raising of the defence of insanity, not non-insane automatism, and he asserted:

> "The law is not concerned with the brain but with the mind, in the sense that 'mind' is ordinarily used, the mental faculties of reason, memory and understanding. If one read for 'disease of the mind' 'disease of the brain', it would follow that in many cases pleas of insanity would not be established because it could not be proved that the brain had been affected in any way, either by degeneration of the cells or in any other way. In my judgment the condition of the brain is irrelevant and so is the question whether the condition of the mind is curable or incurable, transitory or permanent."[51]

Thus, disease of the mind incorporates epilepsy, arteriosclerosis, a tumour on the brain, senility, organic psychosis (for example, caused by syphilis), schizophrenia, and even diabetes is within the definition where they all operate as catalysts to the malfunctioning of the mind. In their decisions in *Quick*[52] and *Hennessy*[53] the Court of Appeal made it clear that the basic question for the courts is whether the condition was caused by *external factors* (non-insane automatism) or *internal factors* (insane automatism); a potentially crucial distinction for an accused between outright acquittal or incarceration in a mental institution.[54] It is clear that where the condition is caused by illness such as epilepsy or diabetes it will be classified as a disease of the mind. In this regard the case of *Charlson*,[55] in which a state of automatism

---

[49] [1984] A.C. 156 at 172.
[50] [1957] 1 Q.B. 399.
[51] [1957] 1 Q.B. 399 at 407.
[52] [1973] Q.B. 910.
[53] [1989] 2 All E.R. 9.
[54] The dichotomy between internal and external factors was impliedly approved of by Lord Diplock in *Sullivan* [1984] A.C. 156 at 172–173 who referred to non-insane automatism applying, "in cases where temporary impairment (not being self-induced by consuming drink or drugs) results from some external factor such as a blow on the head causing concussion or the administration of an anaesthetic for therapeutic purposes".
[55] [1955] 1 All E.R. 859; also considered above, para.2–007.

produced by a brain tumour was held to be non-insane automatism, must now be considered to be wrong. The distinction between internal and external factors is not, however, entirely straightforward. This is illustrated, in particular, by the way the courts have treated diabetes, engaging in an exercise of semantic line-drawing of the worst possible kind. Defendants may be placed in different legal categories in spite of the fact that they acted in a similarly involuntary manner, and a diabetic may perform the actus reus of an offence and yet be unaware of his actions either because of hyperglycaemia (high blood sugar level) or hypoglycaemia (low blood sugar level). Diabetes itself is clearly an internal factor. Hyperglycaemia is usually caused by failure to take insulin; in its absence the disease causes the blood sugar level to rise. It is, therefore, held that the blackout is caused by a disease of the mind. If D acts as an automaton as a result of a hyperglycaemic attack then he is insane within the meaning of the M'Naghten Rules. Hypoglycaemia on the other hand is not the result of the initial disease of diabetes but is caused either by treatment in the form of too much insulin, or by insufficient food to counter-balance the insulin. The administration of insulin is an external factor. Thus where involuntariness is the result of hypoglycaemia the defence of non-insane automatism is available; it is simply the equivalent of automatism being caused by a blow on the head.[56]

This distinction between internal and external factors vis-à-vis diabetes is well illustrated by comparing the decisions in *Quick* and *Hennessy*. In *Quick*, D, a male nurse who had inflicted actual bodily harm on a paraplegic spastic patient in his care, sought to rely on medical evidence to establish that he was a diabetic and that he was suffering from hypoglycaemia and was unaware of what he was doing. The trial judge ruled that he had raised a defence of insanity, whereupon the defendant pleaded guilty. On appeal it was established that the alleged mental condition was brought about not by Quick's diabetes but rather his use of insulin prescribed by the doctor. As such this was an external factor and so the defence of non-insane automatism, not insanity, ought to have been left to the jury. Lawton L.J. defined "disease of the mind" in the following manner:

"[T]he fundamental concept is a malfunctioning of the mind caused by disease. A malfunctioning of the mind of transitory effect caused by the application to the body of some external factor such as violence, drugs including anaesthetics, alcohol and hypnotic influences cannot fairly be said to be due to disease."[57]

The decision in *Quick* was followed in *Bingham*[58] where the defendant committed theft during the course of a hypoglycaemic attack.

By way of contrast, in *Hennessy*, D, a diabetic was charged with taking a car and driving **5–011** while disqualified. At his trial he pleaded not guilty, his defence being that at the relevant time he had failed to take his proper dose of insulin because of stress, anxiety and depression, and was as a result suffering from hyperglycaemia and in a state of non-insane automatism. The trial judge rejected the defence of non-insane automatism on the ground that if it existed D's mental condition was caused by disease, namely diabetes, and therefore fell within the legal definition of insanity under the M'Naghten Rules. Following the judge's ruling Hennessy changed his plea to guilty and was convicted. The judge's ruling on insanity was upheld by the Court of Appeal. The hyperglycaemia was brought about not by any external factor, but by the illness (diabetes) itself. It was therefore a disease of the mind.

---

[56] See, generally, T.H. Jones, "Insanity, Automatism And The Burden Of Proof On The Accused" (1995) 111 L.Q.R. 475.
[57] [1973] Q.B. 910 at 922–23.
[58] [1991] Crim.L.R. 433.

In cases where the condition has been triggered by external factors such as alcohol, medicinal drugs, failure to eat properly or administration of too much insulin, the jury should consider whether this is the first time it has happened. If it has happened in the past, the accused might be said to have been reckless in his behaviour. Overall it has been suggested that an egregious position has been reached by our courts in treatment of diabetes as a defence:

"If the jury has a reasonable doubt external factor (hypoglycaemia), he or she will be acquitted. But if the reasonable doubt is as to an internal factor (hyperglycaemia), the accused should be convicted. This is because, if the automatism is the result of an internal factor, it will be incumbent on the accused to prove this on the balance of probabilities. Quite apart from the absurdity of labelling a diabetic as insane, both accused may have acted in precisely the same way and with precisely the same state of mind (though with differing aetiologies). Sane and insane automatism are thus, in Hall Williams's singular phrase, 'ranged on opposite sides of an evidential chasm'. It is, as Smith and Hogan have pointed out, "difficult to see why a man whose alleged disability arises from a disease of the mind should be convicted whereas one whose alleged disability arises from some other cause, would, in exactly the same circumstances, be acquitted."[59]

Until recently sleepwalking (somnambulism) had been cited as an example of non-insane automatism, indeed, one of the clearest according to Lord Denning in *Bratty v Att-Gen for Northern Ireland*.[60] However, unless it stems from external factors it will be treated as arising from internal causes and hence insane automatism. If the defendant has killed or injured another while sleepwalking the public clearly need protection. Hence the matter was reappraised by the Court of Criminal Appeal in *Burgess*.[61] D fell in love with the victim, who lived in a flat directly above his own. One night, after watching a violent video together, they both fell asleep. The victim awoke to find that Burgess had broken a bottle over her head. He then hit her with the video recorder and finally grasped her round the throat. She stopped all this only by having the presence of mind to shout out that she loved him. D was tried on a count of wounding with intent to do grievous bodily harm, contrary to s.18 of the Offences Against the Person Act 1861. His defence was that he lacked the necessary intent, in that, during undisputed violence to the victim, he was sleepwalking and suffering from non-insane automatism. However, it was held by the Court of Appeal that a defence of somnambulism constituted insane automatism. It was a disease of the mind because it arose from an internal cause. In this regard it was irrelevant that it was only temporary and that there was no recorded case of recurrence with serious violence, in contrast to the earlier dictum of Lord Denning in *Bratty* imposing such a requirement. Their Lordships determined that the mandatory hospital order was justified because sleepwalking was a mental disorder which had manifested itself in violence and suitable medical treatment was available.

5–012 It is suggested that the approach adopted by the court in *Burgess* is consistent with general developments in the law of insanity.[62] For example, in *Sullivan* (see above), the House of Lords had decided that it was irrelevant whether the disease of the mind was organic or

---

[59] T.H. Jones, (1995) 111 L.Q.R. 475 at 499.
[60] [1963] A.C. 386 at 409 where Lord Denning quoted with approval the dictum of Stephen J. in *Tolson* (1889) 23 Q.B.D. 168, 187 that: "Can anyone doubt that a man who, though he might be perfectly sane, committed what would otherwise be a crime in a state of somnambulism, would be entitled to be acquitted? And why is this? Simply because he would not know what he was doing."
[61] [1991] 2 Q.B. 92. See generally, G. Virgo, "Sanitising Insanity—Sleepwalking And Statutory Reform" (1991) 50 C.L.J. 386, 387–388.
[62] (1991) 50 C.L.J. 386 at 388.

functional,[63] permanent or transient, or intermittent. Consistent it may be but that does not prevent the stigma of insanity from being somewhat incongruously attached to sleepwalkers. That does not end the dilemma, since whilst sleepwalking is generally regarded as coming from within, "some anecdotal evidence suggests that one possible cause of sleepwalking may be eating cheese before sleep. If this could be proven, it would mean that the defence would become one of non-insane automatism, by virtue of an external cause."[64] It serves to exemplify difficulties pervading this area of law.

Insanity is a legal and not a medical term. Its use in many of these cases is highly offensive. Clearly the courts need to have the power to protect the public from possible danger, but is it essential to label as insane a diabetic whose illness has caused him to take goods from a shop while in a state of automatism?

As a final point in this particular section it should be noted that the question of whether a given condition amounts to a disease of the mind is a question of law for the judge.[65]

(iv) Insanity as a Defence Today

We said at the beginning that insanity was a defence to criminal charges in general. So, in **5–013** theory, it could be raised as a defence to even the most trivial assault. However, the result of a successful defence of insanity may be committal to a mental institution for an indeterminate length of time. In effect, therefore, insanity will rarely be raised by the accused on anything but a charge of murder and even there a plea of diminished responsibility would normally be preferred which could lead to a determinate prison sentence.[66]

Although insanity is rarely raised expressly as a defence today, it may arise indirectly. This could occur because the accused has attempted to plead that he did not possess the necessary mens rea for the offence only to find that the judge has ruled that as a matter of law the reason he is advancing amounts to a disease of the mind. In *Clarke*,[67] the accused was charged with stealing from a shop. She pleaded that she had taken the items from the shelf absent-mindedly as a result of the depression that she was suffering. If Mrs Clarke had simply rested her case on absent-mindedness, all would probably have been well. Unfortunately, medical evidence was called to support her statements and it was the effect of this evidence which led the trial judge to decide she was raising the defence of insanity. Mrs Clarke changed her plea to one of "guilty". The Court of Appeal were not disposed to decide whether or not the trial judge was entitled to hold that the evidence pointed to a disease of the mind. The M'Naghten Rules required that the disease of the mind had led to a defect of reason which meant that she was unable to appreciate the nature and quality of her acts. Ackner J. said that the M'Naghten Rules were designed to cover persons who have lost the power of reasoning, not persons who retain the power of reasoning but in moments of stress fail to use these powers to the full. Since the trial judge's ruling had caused Mrs Clarke to change her plea to one of guilty, the Court of Appeal felt bound to quash the conviction.

In *Dickie*[68] the Court of Appeal said that courts should bear in mind the fact that insanity was a defence and as such should in most cases be raised specifically by the accused. However, there might be occasions on which it would be permissible for a judge to raise the

[63] Meaning nervous as opposed to physical or organic.
[64] *ibid*. If medical evidence of this could be produced then the defence would be one of non-insane automatism and the burden of proving that D was not an automaton would be on the Crown.
[65] See, e.g. *Kemp* [1957] 1 Q.B. 399.
[66] See above, para.5–005.
[67] [1972] 1 All E.R. 219.
[68] [1984] 3 All E.R. 173.

issue on his own volition. This should only occur where there was relevant evidence which goes to all elements of the M'Naghten test. It was inappropriate and an unnecessary complication for the jury in *Thomas*[69] where the trial judge, contrary to the wishes of the defendant, ruled that the question of insanity should be left to the jury. The defendant had been indicted for burglary and adduced medical evidence to the effect that she had a mental condition, hypomania, aggravated by drink and drugs, rendering her so confused as to be incapable of forming the specific intent required for the offence of burglary. Essentially this was a simple defence that she was incapable of forming the requisite mens rea of the offence, insanity was inapposite and irrelevant.

5–014   It would seem that a trial judge ought only unilaterally to raise insanity where clear evidence of the defence has been produced in the court, but the accused has sought to avoid the consequences of such a plea by not classifying the evidence as insanity. This was apparent in *Sullivan* where the defendant sought to avoid a charge of inflicting grievous bodily harm by adducing evidence that the attack had happened while he was in the last stages of a minor epileptic seizure; the trial judge was clearly right, on the evidence before him, to rule that the defence amounted to one of insanity rather than automatism. If the judge has doubts in his mind on the evidence before him, he should seek clarification from the witnesses to enable him to reach his conclusion. He should not, however, embark on a fishing expedition for further evidence. In *Dickie*, the Court of Appeal thought that the prosecutor should not raise the issue of insanity, but it must be the position that had the judge in *Sullivan* not raised the matter, the prosecutor would have been entitled to ask for a ruling. The court was clearly anxious that, as far as possible, insanity should be seen as a defence to be raised by the accused, and that we should not have the spectacle of the prosecution trying to get an acquittal on the grounds of insanity so that the accused will be put away for an indeterminate period. A special provision contained within s.12 of the Criminal Appeal Act 1968 allows the accused to appeal against such an acquittal.[70]

The nature of the insanity defence arose in *DPP v H*[71] where the Divisional Court addressed its applicability to a crime of strict liability, where mens rea was not an issue. The defendant was charged with driving with an excess of alcohol in his blood. Evidence was presented that he suffered from manic depressive psychosis, with symptoms of distorted judgment and impaired sense of time and of morals. The accused had been behaving particularly irrationally on the day that the "offence" had occurred. Although the magistrates acquitted him on the grounds of insanity the prosecution appealed by way of case stated to the Divisional Court. It was determined, very surprisingly, that the defence of insanity was available only where mens rea was required as part of the offence. As the offence of driving with an excess of alcohol is a strict liability offence requiring no proof of mens rea hence insanity was no defence to the charge.[72] In the light of this finding the case was remitted to the magistrates with a direction to convict. It is submitted, however, that the decision in *DPP v H* was incorrect, and it is to be hoped that it will not be followed by higher courts as this would lead to a further unacceptable anomaly between insanity and non-insane automatism. As we have already seen an automatism defence effectively denies the commission of the actus reus of an offence[73]; it encompasses a wider defence that D's

---

[69] [1995] Crim.L.R. 314.
[70] Note that the right of appeal is subject to the same prerequisites as generally apply to criminal appeals from the Crown Court.
[71] *The Times*, May 2, 1997. See, generally, T. Ward, "Magistrates, Insanity And The Common Law" [1997] Crim. L.R. 796.
[72] It is noteworthy that in *R v Horseferry Road Magistrates Ex. p. K* [1996] 3 W.L.R. 68; [1996] 3 All E.R. 719, it was acknowledged by the court that insanity could be a defence to a summary offence.
[73] The meaning of voluntary conduct is considered above within the actus reus section, above, paras 2–004—2–012. It does not matter whether automatism relates to actus reus or mens rea—the requirement of voluntary conduct is a sine qua non of all crimes and applies in crimes where mens rea is not required.

actions were not truly voluntary. If it comprises an involuntary action then presumptively it is not D's own commission, and thus no actus reus is effected. The rationale is that a non-insane automatism defence, predicated on involuntary conduct, will apply to *all* crimes not simply those requiring proof of mens rea. However, the defences of insanity and automatism are closely related concepts, either can be based on automatic conduct, with the judicial distinction the derivation of the cause as external or internal (see above). Consider the examples Dobson provides concerning drivers who have passed a red traffic light (a strict liability offence).[74] In each case the driver has suffered a complete lack of self-control. In the first situation the driver's lack of self-control has occurred because a piece of masonry has fallen from a building and knocked the driver unconscious; an external cause constituting non-insane automatism.[75] The second driver has lost self-control because, for the first time in his life and without any prior warning, he has suffered an epileptic fit; an internal cause constituting insane "automatism".[76] The application of *DPP v H*, if followed, would allow a defence in the former scenario, but not the latter, as insanity was denied therein as a defence to strict liability offences. Such a division is logically uncompelling.[77] Insanity and automatism defences ought to apply to *all* offences, including crimes of strict liability.[78]

B. Diminished Responsibility

Such was the narrowness of the legal test for insanity that Parliament introduced a special **5–015** defence which would apply to charges of murder only. This was known as diminished responsibility and a successful plea leads to the accused being convicted of manslaughter rather than murder. As stated by their Lordships in *Antoine,*[79] diminished responsibility applies only where the accused would otherwise be guilty of murder because the actus reus and mens rea of that offence have been proved or admitted. More specifically, it was determined by the House of Lords in *Antoine* that the defence of diminished responsibility could not be inter-linked with that of unfitness to plead; we are left with the scylla of unfitness to plead as one option and with the charybdis of diminished responsibility as another. The rationale for this clear dichotomy is dependent on the terminology in s.4A of the Criminal Procedure (Insanity) Act 1964 which procedure governs unfitness to stand trial. It will be recalled that s.4A of the 1964 Act states that, if a defendant is found unfit to plead, the trial cannot proceed, and hence an individual accused of murder who is found unfit to plead is no longer susceptible to a murder conviction, irrespective of the jury determination that he did the act charged within the procedure laid down by s.4A.[80] Diminished responsibility is a defence which only applies to murder charges. Thus, the concomitant of this is that the defendant cannot raise the defence of diminished responsibility in an effort to avoid the mandatory hospital admission order with the direction restricting discharge which necessarily follows a finding that the defendant is unfit to be tried on a charge of murder.[81] This constitutes a finding of disability and precludes diminished responsibility.

[74] P. Dobson, "Criminal Law" (1997) Student L.R. 26.
[75] See above, para.5–010.
[76] *Ibid.*
[77] Note that in *Antoine* [2001] 1 A.C. 340 Lord Hutton, delivering the sole speech, asserted that when insanity is successfully pleaded, D does not have the mens rea of the offence charged.
[78] The statement in *Hill v Baxter* [1958] 2 W.L.R. 67 at 80 per Goddard L.C.J. is contradictory to the outcome in *DPP v H*: "I agree that there may be cases where the circumstances are such that the accused could not really be said to be driving at all. Suppose he had a stroke or an epileptic fit, both instances of what may properly be called acts of God; he might well be in the driver's seat even with his hands on the wheel, but in such a state of unconsciousness that he could not be said to be driving."
[79] [2001] 1 A.C. 340; [2000] 2 All E.R. 208 HL.
[80] See above, para.5–001.
[81] See R. Card, *op. cit.,* at p.607.

There is no statutory requirement for medical evidence of diminished responsibility, unlike for the insanity defence in murder, but it was clearly stated in *Dix*[82] that this evidence is a practical necessity if the defence is to begin to run at all. As with insanity, the burden of proof lies on the accused to prove that it was more likely than not that he was suffering from diminished responsibility at the time he committed the offence. The imposition of this burden of proof on a defendant was determined in *Lambert, Ali and Jordan*[83] not to contravene art.6(2) of the ECHR.[84] The Human Rights Act 1998 and the European Convention have to be construed by a "broad purposive approach" in the light of what was required by justice and the public interest. On this basis, the appellant could not require the prosecution to prove that he was *not* suffering from diminished responsibility, as that would lead to injustice and would conflict with the public interest.[85] Thus, if justice to both sides (and not merely to the defendant) were considered, there was no conflict between the Homicide Act 1957 and the Convention.

In *Campbell*[86] the Court of Appeal held that a trial judge who thought that the evidence raised the issue of diminished responsibility should inform the counsel for the defence of his opinion in the absence of the jury. In effect, it is rather like provocation[87] in that it enables the jury to return a verdict of guilty of manslaughter but not a complete acquittal. A number of cases, for example that of *Cox*,[88] have shown that the defences of provocation and diminished responsibility may often arise on the same facts. Indeed, the defences of diminished responsibility and provocation are not mutually exclusive, as was confirmed by their Lordships in *Morgan Smith*,[89] but recent cases such as *Holley, Mohammed (Faqir)* and *James and Karimi* have highlighted the division between the defences. They may clearly overlap, although a marked difference is that provocation may be more beneficial to the accused in that, unlike for diminished responsibility, the burden of proof rests firmly on the prosecution.[90] Once the jury has returned a verdict of guilty of manslaughter, the judge then has a wide discretion over what should happen to the accused. He can commit him to prison for up to life, he can have him detained in a mental institution, he can put him on probation

---

[82] (1981) 74 Cr.App.R. 306.

[83] [2001] 1 All E.R. 1014; [2001] 2 W.L.R. 211 CA.

[84] [2001] 1 All E.R. 1014; [2001] 2 W.L.R. 211 CA.

[85] art.6(2) of the ECHR states: "Everyone charged with a criminal offence shall be presumed innocent until proved guilty according to law". Note that the House of Lords have subsequently considered in *Lambert* [2001] 3 W.L.R. 206 the compatibility of s.28(2) and (3) of the Misuse of Drugs Act 1971 (D required to establish defence on balance of probabilities, see above, p.119 cf. *McNamara* (1988) 87 Cr.App.R. 246) with ECHR. Their Lordships determined (Lord Slynn dissenting) that the relevant provisions of the Human Rights Act 1998 were not intended to apply to things happening before the date when they came into force and decisions of courts or tribunals before that date were not to be impugned under s.6 on the ground that the Court or tribunal had acted in a way incompatible with Convention rights. A dichotomy, however, existed in that the 1998 Act was retrospective in respect of proceedings brought by or at the instigation of a public authority, but not in respect of appeals in those proceedings. In any event no incompatibility existed with the provisions of the Misuse of Drugs Act 1971. On retrospectivity and the ECHR in general see also the conflicting House of Lords decisions in *R v DPP Ex p. Kebilene* [2000] 2 A.C. 326 and *Kansal (No.2), The Times,* December 4, 2001.

[86] (1987) 84 Cr.App.R. 225.

[87] In cases where provocation applies D is provoked into losing self-control and kills V. Provocation effects a change in the offence, reducing it from murder for which the penalty is imprisonment for life, to manslaughter for which the penalty is at the discretion of the judge; considered below, para.7–019.

[88] [1995] 2 Cr.App.R. 513. See generally, R.D. Mackay, "Pleading Provocation And Diminished Responsibility Together" [1988] Crim.L.R. 411; See also *Ahluwahlia* and *Thornton (No.2),* discussed below, para.7–021.

[89] [2001] 1 A.C. 146; [2000] 4 All E.R. 289 HL; see below, para.7–029.

[90] On the overlap between defences of diminished responsibility/provocation see R. Mackay and B. Mitchell, "Provoking Diminished Responsibility: Two Pleas Merging Into One" [2003] Crim.L.R. 745; J. Chalmers, "Merging Provocation and Diminished Responsibility: Some Reasons for Scepticism" [2004] Crim.L.R. 198; J. Gardner and T. Macklem, "No Provocation Without Responsibility: A Reply to Mackay and Mitchell" [2004] Crim.L.R. 213; and R. Mackay and B. Mitchell, "Replacing Provocation: More on a Combined Plea" [2004] Crim. L.R. 219.

or even give him an absolute discharge. In truth, where an accused on a murder charge was suffering from a mental incapacity then the practicalities are that diminished responsibility is an easier defence to establish than insanity.

What, then, must the accused prove in order to establish the defence? Section 2(1) of the Homicide Act 1957 provides:

"Where a person kills or is a party to the killing of another, he shall not be convicted of murder if he was suffering from such abnormality of mind (whether arising from a condition of arrested or retarded development of mind or any inherent causes or induced by disease or injury) as substantially impaired his mental responsibility for his acts and omission in doing or being a party to the killing."

This all looks very technical. What is the judge supposed to do? Is he to try to define the terms of the section for the jury? In *Byrne*[91] the Court of Criminal Appeal eventually resolved that it was wrong for a trial judge simply to read the section to the jury and leave them to make what they could of it. He should give them whatever guidance they require to understand it. Basically, three factors have to be established:

(i) The Accused must have been Suffering from an Abnormality of Mind

In many cases it will be sufficient for the judge to ask the jury whether the accused's mind **5–016** seems normal—would they say that he appeared to them to be normal. If he appears "mad" or "insane" as a layman would use these words, then he can be said to be suffering from an abnormality of mind. Thus, it was apt to cover the accused in *Byrne* who had strangled a young girl and had then horribly mutilated her body. His defence was that from early years he had suffered from overwhelming perverted desires which he found very difficult, if not impossible, to resist. He submitted that he had killed the girl under the influence of such an urge. Lord Parker C.J. provided the following definition of abnormality of mind, embracing Byrne, who was self-evidently a sexual psychopath:

" 'Abnormality of mind', which has to be contrasted with the time-honoured expression in the M'Naghten Rules 'defect of reason', means a state of mind so different from that of ordinary human beings that the reasonable man would term it abnormal. It appears to us to be wide enough to cover the mind's activities in all its aspects, not only the perception of physical acts and matters, and the ability to form a rational judgment as to whether an act is right or wrong, but also the ability to exercise will power to control physical acts in accordance with that rational judgment . . . [T]he aetiology of the abnormality of mind (namely, whether it arose from a condition of arrested or retarded development of mind or any inherent causes, or was induced by disease or injury) does, however, seem to be a matter to be determined on expert evidence."[92]

It is interesting to pause here for a moment. Could Byrne have successfully pleaded insanity? The answer is that he could not. Whether or not he could have established that he was suffering from a disease of the mind, the evidence suggested that not only did he appreciate what he was doing, but that he also realised that it was wrong. His trouble was that he found it very difficult to stop himself.

[91] [1960] 2 Q.B. 396.
[92] [1960] 2 Q.B. 396 at 403.

In *Seers*[93] where the defendant had pleaded diminished responsibility on the basis of reactive depression the Court of Appeal said that *Byrne* should not be taken as laying down an immutable rule that juries should, in every case where diminished responsibility is raised, be asked whether or not the defendant could be described in popular language as partially insane or on the borderline of insanity. Even if "insane" were given a broad meaning, it was inappropriate to describe every condition which might properly be described as an "abnormality of mind". The trial judge should always relate his direction to the jury to the particular evidence in the case, otherwise there were dangers that a jury might take a mistaken view of the criteria by which they were to judge abnormality of mind. This principle was clearly stated in *Brown*[94] where "mind" was taken to include perception, understanding, judgment and will. This has meant that diminished responsibility has been benevolently applied to prevent murder convictions despite a paucity of medical evidence; cases encompass mercy killings, for example, where D killed his severely handicapped son,[95] killing where D suffered from PMT,[96] and even fits of jealousy.[97]

(ii) Cause of the Abnormality of Mind

5–017   The abnormality of mind must have arisen from a condition of arrested or retarded development of mind or any inherent causes or must have been induced by disease or injury. This is clearly a very wide provision. Is it wide enough to cover an abnormality of mind caused by excessive drink (alcohol dependency syndrome) or drugs?

The recent appellate decision in *Wood*[98] presented a complex analysis of the inter-relationship between alcohol dependency syndrome and diminished responsibility as a partial defence. The conclusions reached have produced a test for the jury which is delineated more by mud than by crystal. On behalf of the appellant it was contended that he suffered from alcohol dependency syndrome, and had a strong craving for alcohol throughout his working life and if alcohol was available he would drink it until it was finished. Although the medical experts called at trial were in unanimity vis-à-vis the existence of the syndrome there was dispute as to whether there had been consequential damage to his brain. He had been drinking for an extensive period over at least 36 hours prior to the fatal act, and consumed vast quantities of alcohol. D asserted that, after falling asleep on the sofa at the victim's flat, he had been awoken by the deceased making unwelcome homosexual advances to him, thereupon he had lost his self-control and hit the victim repeatedly with a meat cleaver. On appeal against D's conviction for murder it was contended that the trial judge had misdirected the jury on the issue of "involuntariness" of D's consumption of alcohol. Prior to *Wood* the intimations from case precedents suggested that D would have to argue that the alcohol had injured his mind: possibly, therefore, a condition such as alcoholism caused by long-term drinking might be covered, but not an accused who was simply drunk at the time he committed the offence.

In *Gittens,*[99] where D was tried for the murder of his wife and rape and murder of his stepdaughter, the court was faced with a situation in which the abnormality of mind had been caused in part by inherent causes (depressive illness) and in part by drink and drugs. Subsequently, in *Dietschmann*[100] the House of Lords has established the correct analysis to

[93] (1984) 79 Cr.App.R. 261.
[94] [1993] Crim.L.R. 961.
[95] *Price, The Times*, December 22, 1971.
[96] *Smith* [1982] Crim.L.R. 531.
[97] *Miller, The Times*, May 16, 1972. Note in the notorious case of Peter Sutcliffe, also known as the Yorkshire Ripper, who killed 13 victims, the trial judge categorically refused to accept a plea of s.2 diminished responsibility.
[98] [2008] EWCA Crim 1305; [2008] 3 All E.R. 899.
[99] [1984] 1 Q.B. 698.
[100] [2003] 1 A.C. 1209; [2003] Crim.L.R. 550.

apply in cases like *Gittens*, involving evidence of both mental disorder and intoxication. The essence of their decision involves a primordial focus on the underlying mental abnormality which is distilled from the intoxication. The issue is not whether the defendant would have carried out the killing in the absence of intoxication, but whether, if he did kill, he killed under diminished responsibility. As Lord Hutton adumbrated in *Dietschmann*, even if the jury believes that the drinking had a role in the killing and that D might not have killed if he had not been intoxicated, nonetheless they must still be presented with this question: "has the defendant satisfied you that, despite the drink, his mental abnormality substantially impaired his mental responsibility for his fatal acts?" In referring to substantial impairment of mental responsibility the subsection did not require the abnormality of mind to be the sole cause of a D's act in doing the killing. This represented a crystallisation of extant law since the enactment of the partial defence.[101] The primary focus herein on the mental disorder rather than the intoxication is in keeping with the concessionary nature of the partial defence. How do such principles operate, as in *Wood*, where the "mental disorder" itself involves intoxication, or rather alcohol dependency syndrome (chronic alcoholism)? Moreover, how does *Dietschmann*, and the clear principles therein, stand against the apparently contradictory authority in *Tandy*?

In *Tandy*[102] the appellate court had to consider the case of an alcoholic defendant who **5–018** strangled her 11-year-old daughter having drunk almost a whole bottle of vodka, and who at her trial set up the defence of diminished responsibility.[103] It was held that for a craving for drink in itself to produce an abnormality of mind induced by the disease of alcoholism, within s.2(1) of the 1957 Act, the alcoholism had to have reached such a level that the brain was damaged so that there was gross impairment of her judgment and emotional responses, or the craving had to be such as to render the accused's use of drink involuntary because she was no longer able to resist the impulse to drink. In essence, this formed the basis of the contradicted trial judge direction in *Wood*. Watkins L.J. in *Tandy* stated:

> "So in this case it was for the appellant to show: (1) that she was suffering from an abnormality of mind at the time of the act of strangulation; (2) that the abnormality of mind was induced by disease, namely the disease of alcoholism, and; (3) that the abnormality of mind induced by the disease of alcoholism was such as substantially impaired her mental responsibility for her act of strangling her daughter."[104]

In effect, the appellate court in *Tandy* said that the issue for the jury was whether her abnormality of mind was induced by disease, namely the disease of alcoholism.[105] She would have to prove that the drink taken on the day in question had been taken involuntarily as a result of her condition. If the jury found that she took the first drink of the day voluntarily, they should conclude that the defence of diminished responsibility was not open to her. The strictures of such a high threshold test in *Tandy* for the legitimisation of "chronic" alcoholism (alcohol dependency syndrome) as a relevant mental disorder has been the subject of hostile and intemperate academic criticism prior to *Dietschmann*, and subsequent re-evaluation in *Wood*. Goodliffe stated that:

> "[T]he decision . . . illustrates the inability of most lawyers and judges to understand the concept of alcoholism as a disease . . . the Court of Appeal . . . were able to accept

---

[101] See *Hendy* [2006] EWCA Crim 1305; [2008] 3 All E.R. 899.
[102] (1988) 87 Cr.App.R. 45.
[103] See, generally, J. Goodliffe, "*R v Tandy* And The Concept Of Alcoholism As A Disease" (1990) 53 M.L.R. 809.
[104] (1988) 87 Cr.App.R. 45 at 51.
[105] In *Inseal* [1993] Crim.L.R. 35 the existence of alcohol dependence syndrome was implicitly accepted by the court.

the doctrine of diminished responsibility as it applies to alcoholism only in terms of black and white rather than shades of grey: either the defendant was wholly incapable of resisting the impulse to drink or she was responsible for her actions and should be convicted of murder."[106]

In light of this criticism, and following the House of Lords concessionary bifurcation of "mental disorder" and intoxication in *Dietschmann*, the appellate court in *Wood* re-assessed the earlier decision in *Tandy*. The effect is to impose a two-tier system in terms of the threshold test for alcohol dependency syndrome within section 2 of the Homicide Act 1957. The first tier focuses on the applicability of chronic alcoholism as an "abnormality of mind". The contextual perspective addressed in *Wood*, the leading judgment provided by Sir Igor Judge P., is to widen the boundaries of jury evaluation of alcohol dependency syndrome beyond the delimiting strictures in *Tandy*, and away from any requirement for identifiable brain damage or involuntariness:

> "In our judgment *R. v Dietschmann* requires a re-assessment of the way in which *R. v Tandy* is applied in the context of alcohol dependency syndrome where observable brain damage has not occurred. The sharp effect of the distinction drawn in *Tandy* between cases where brain damage has occurred as a result of alcohol dependency syndrome and those where it is not, is no longer appropriate. Naturally, where brain damage has occurred the jury may be more likely to conclude that the defendant suffers from an abnormality of mind induced by disease or illness, but whether it has occurred or not, logically consistent with *R. v Dietschmann*, the same question (i.e. whether it has been established that the defendant's syndrome is of such an extent and nature that it constitutes an abnormality of mind induced by disease or illness) arises for decision. This is for the jury."[107]

5–019 The second tier question for the jury arises in the event that they conclude that the syndrome does constitute an abnormality of mind. If so, the question as to whether the defendant's mental responsibility for his actions at the time of the killing was "substantially impaired" as a result of the alcohol dependency syndrome (see effects below). The trial judge's directions in *Wood* had implied that unless every drink consumed by D on the fatal day was involuntary, his syndrome was to be disregarded. This was incorrect in light of the concessionary liberalisation affirmed in *Dietschmann*. The primordial focus should be on the effect of alcohol consumed by D as a *direct result* of his illness or disease and ignore the effect of any alcohol consumed voluntarily. Sir Igor Judge P. concluded as follows:

> "Assuming that the jury has decided that syndrome constitutes an abnormality of mind induced by disease or illness, its possible impact and significance in the individual case must be addressed. The resolution of this issue embraces questions such as whether the defendant's craving for alcohol was or was not irresistible, and whether his consumption of alcohol in the period leading up to the killing was voluntary (and if so, to what

---

[106] See, generally, J. Goodliffe, "*R. v Tandy and the Concept of Alcoholism as a Disease*" (1990) M.L.R. 809 at 809–810. Note in similar vituperative language Tolmie criticises the lack of understanding shown in *Tandy* to the inherent nature of the disease: "to have required that the defendant, to benefit from the defence, conform to a model of alcoholism that even the most hardened alcoholic would find it difficult to meet . . . even if the alcoholic in question does not have choice about whether or not they will drink they will often have an apparent choice about when and where they commence drinking. Furthermore the court focused on only one aspect of the model—the loss of control over drinking—without placing that phenomenon in the context of the other symptoms and mental processes described by the disease model"; see J. Tolmie, "Alcoholism and Criminal Liability" (2001) M.L.R. 688.
[107] [2008] 3 All E.R. 899 at 909.

extent) or was not voluntary, and leads to the ultimate decision, which is whether the defendant's mental responsibility for his actions when killing the deceased was substantially impaired as a result of the alcohol consumed under the baneful influence of the syndrome."[108]

Undoubtedly, the decision in *Wood*, re-interpreting earlier precedential authorities in *Tandy* and *Dietschmann*, was a difficult one for the appellate court in a complex substantive area. Unfortunately the perplexed jury has been left with an uncertain and convoluted dual test. In terms of reform the government proposals for reform contained in *Murder, Manslaughter and Infanticide: Proposals for Reform of the Law*[109] leave the influence of alcohol dependency syndrome unclear. The jury is charged to consider two issues. First, whether the "recognised mental condition" (not abnormality of mind) substantially impairs D's ability to (a) understand the nature of D's conduct; or (b) to form a rational judgment; or (c) to exercise self-control. Secondly, the jury would have to assess whether the mental impairment provides an explanation for the killing. Moreover, it is asserted in cl.1(1B) that an explanation will be provided if, "it causes, or is a significant contributory factor in causing the person to carry out that conduct." Thus, in real terms the dual two-tier test from *Wood* seems unaltered. In practical terms it will relate to which of two or more medical experts are convincing before the jury. Our juries are left with an unenviable task and a duty replicated for gross negligence manslaughter[110] and dishonesty in theft,[111] whereby the governing template is lacking in certainty, arguably fails retrospectivity challenges and urgently requires further clarification.

The nature of "inherent causes" within the statutory test was addressed in *Sanderson*.[112] The accused, who had a stormy relationship with his girlfriend, killed her following a violent argument by hitting her 100 times with a cricket bat and hockey stick. On appeal, at issue was whether paranoid psychosis, a condition causing incorrect and abnormal beliefs about people, which D contended he was suffering from at the relevant time, was an inherent cause under s.2(1) of the 1957 Act? It was held by the Court of Appeal that paranoid psychosis did fit within inherent causes; the latter covered functional mental illness as well as organic or physical injury or disease of the body, including the brain. Sanderson's conviction of murder was quashed and a verdict of manslaughter by reason of diminished responsibility was substituted.

(iii) Effect of the Abnormality of Mind

The accused must prove that the abnormality of mind substantially impaired his mental **5–020** responsibility for his acts and omissions in doing or being a party to the killing. In *Byrne*, the accused had relied on perverted sexual urges which he alleged caused him to kill the girl. Clearly, if the evidence had shown that he found these urges to be irresistible, the defence would have been established. But this would amount to a total impairment of his responsibility and the Act says that he need only prove a substantial impairment. What, therefore, does the Act mean by "substantial"? In *Egan*[113] the Court of Appeal approved directions given in *Lloyd*[114] to the effect that (i) the jury should approach the word in a broad, commonsense way or (ii) the word meant "more than some trivial degree of

---

[108] [2008] 3 All E.R. 899 at 910.
[109] See Consultation Paper CP18/08, 2008.
[110] See below at para.7–048.
[111] See below at para.8–039.
[112] (1994) 98 Cr.App.R. 525.
[113] [1993] Crim.L.R. 131.
[114] [1966] 2 W.L.R. 13.

impairment which does not make an appreciable difference to a person's ability to control himself, but it means less than total impairment". In essence, it is a matter for the jury deploying their common sense, rather than a matter for psychiatrists. The defence was rejected in *Tulloch*.[115] The defendant, as part of a joint criminal enterprise,[116] had planned the killing of the victim, then returned home for a hammer and used it brutally to effect the killing. He subsequently provided a totally fabricated alibi to the police. Even though the accused had a manifest personality disorder caused by physical and sexual abuse by his stepfather, it was apparent in this case of pre-planned violence that there was no substantial impairment of his mental responsibility.

Procedural Note

5–021 Under s.6 of the Criminal Procedure (Insanity) Act 1964, it is clearly provided that if the accused raises the defence of insanity or diminished responsibility the prosecution shall be entitled to prove the alternative defence. But here the standard of proof required of the prosecution is the criminal standard—proof beyond reasonable doubt.[117]

C. Hospital Orders

5–022 After a successful plea of diminished responsibility has resulted in a manslaughter conviction, the court, as one of the sentencing options, may make a hospital order under the Mental Health Act 1983. Where the court, in such a case, feels that the accused is particularly dangerous, it can make a restriction order which has the effect of necessitating the consent of the Home Secretary before he can be moved or released.

D. Conclusions

5–023 It is interesting to note that one of the reasons for the introduction of the defence of diminished responsibility was the notion that the defence of insanity was not wide enough to cover all those mentally abnormal persons who were charged with criminal offences. It should be remembered that insanity is unlikely to be pleaded outside murder cases and diminished responsibility can be pleaded only in murder cases. However, it was to be expected that following the 1957 Act the numbers of accused pleading some form of mental disorder as a defence would increase. In fact, the number has remained almost the same as before 1957. The major change is that those who before 1957 pleaded insanity, now plead diminished responsibility, which tends to suggest that the courts before 1957 managed to subsume under insanity all those who are now found to be suffering from diminished responsibility.

This whole area now seems ready for some far-ranging reform. It has been criticised on a number of grounds. To stigmatise those suffering from epilepsy, diabetes, hyperglycaemia and somnambulism as insane seems intuitively to be incongruous. It is the result of the way in which the courts have developed the concept of a "disease of mind" by reference to internal and external factors which has been so fundamental to the development of the insanity defence during the last 25 years. One should recall that where a defendant seeks to excuse conduct on the basis of mental incapacity arising from an internal factor, the appropriate defence is insanity, but in contrast pleading incapacity due to an external factor

---

[115] Unrep. February 25, 2000 CA; see also *Weekes* [1999] Crim.L.R. 907.
[116] See above, para.4–014.
[117] See, e.g. *Bastian* [1958] 1 W.L.R. 413.

opens the door to other defences. This vice-like dichotomy is at the root of the current incompatibility between the legal and medical definitions of disorder.[118] It has also been suggested that our law may be in breach of art.5 of the European Convention on Human Rights in two respects. First in placing the burden of proof on the accused (contrary to other general defences). Secondly, and more specifically, in the absence of explicit guidance as to when hospital orders should be imposed. These two principles operate extremely harshly against D.[119] It is, however, beneficial that the revision in s.24 of the Domestic Violence, Crime and Victims Act 2004, has removed the mandatory admission order with an indefinite restriction direction. Nonetheless, the imposition of hospital orders in general has been subject to heightened scrutiny. It is argued that the public interest does not require protection from an individual whose temporary "insanity" at the time of the commission of the offence is unlikely to be reactivated. In this context art.5 of the ECHR provides as follows:

> "1. Everyone has the right to liberty and security of person. No one shall be deprived of his liberty save in the following cases and in accordance with a procedure prescribed by law; . . .
>
> (a) the lawful detention . . . of persons of unsound mind . . ."

The European Court of Human Rights, in the seminal case of *Winterwerp v The Netherlands* asserted that interpreting this provision requires consideration of balanced criteria:

> "In the Court's opinion, except in emergency cases, the individual concerned should not be deprived of his liberty unless he has been reliably shown to be of "unsound mind". The very nature of what has to be established before the competent national authority—that is, a true mental disorder—calls for objective medical expertise. Further, the mental disorder must be of a kind or degree warranting compulsory confinement. What is more, the validity of the continued confinement depends upon the persistence of such a disorder."[120]

The requirements set out by the court in *Winterwerp v The Netherlands* seem to clash with **5–024** current domestic perspectives on insanity. First, consider the requirement for "objective medical expertise". The Criminal Procedure (Insanity and Unfitness to Plead) Act 1991 provides that no jury may make a finding that the accused is insane or unfit to plead unless they have received evidence from at least two qualified medical practitioners, at least one of whom must be approved by the Home Secretary as having special experience in the diagnosis or treatment of mental disorder. This evidence, however, only has to be considered by the jury, but it does *not* have binding effect. Furthermore, the court in *Winterwerp* also highlighted the need for a strong correlation between the legal and medical criteria used to assess the issue of "unsound mind". This, as discussed, is inapt from a domestic perspective in relation to treatment of somnabulism, epilepsy, and hyperglycaemia. Additionally, the European Court has consistently determined that both the initial deprivation of a psychiatric patient's liberty and the continued detention of a patient can only be lawful under art.5 of the Convention if it can "reliably be shown" that he or she suffers from a mental disorder

[118] See, e.g. E. Baker, "Human Rights, M'Naghten And The 1991 Act [1994] Crim.L.R. 84 at 89–90.
[119] See, e.g. P.J. Sutherland and C.A. Gearty, "Insanity And The European Court Of Human Rights [1992] Crim. L.R. 418.
[120] (1979) 2 E.H.R.R. 387 at para.39.

sufficiently serious to warrant detention.[121] In *R (H) v N & E London Mental Health Tribunal*[122] the applicant (H) had been convicted of manslaughter in 1988, diagnosed as suffering from schizophrenia, and admitted to Broadmoor Hospital. Over a decade later he has successfully obtained a declaration before the Court of Appeal that s.72 of the Mental Health Act 1983 was incompatible with art.5(1)(4) of the ECHR in so far as it imposed the burden of proof on the patient to establish the criteria for his discharge. Interesting times lie ahead for the insanity defence under the auspices of the ECHR, and reforms are needed to bridge the chasm identified by MacKay and Kearns between legal and psychiatric definitions:

> "[T]he overwhelming impression is that the question the majority of psychiatrists are addressing is: if the delusion that the defendant was experiencing at the time of the offence was in fact reality, then would the defendant's actions be morally justified— rather than the narrow cognitive test of legal wrongness required by the M'Naghten Rules . . . In so doing, it may be argued that psychiatrists in many respects are adopting a common sense or folk psychology approach and that the courts by accepting this interpretation are, in reality, expanding the scope of the M'Naghten Rules."[123]

A committee under the Chairmanship of Lord Butler made major proposals for reform which have been broadly incorporated into the Draft Code.[124] If implemented the provisions would ameliorate criticism that current law is out of step with modern medicine in concentrating purely on defects of reason to the detriment of emotional or volitional factors. The proposed reforms would replace insanity by new terms of "severe mental illness" and "severe mental handicap" derived from the Mental Health Acts, and would insert terminology actually used in practice by psychiatrists. Clause 35 of the Code provides:

> "(1) A mental disorder verdict shall be returned if the defendant is proved to have committed an offence but it is proved on the balance of probabilities (whether by the prosecution or by the defendant) that he was at the time suffering from severe mental illness or severe mental handicap."

The term "severe mental illness" is defined by cl.36, which states:

> "A mental disorder verdict shall be returned if—(a) the defendant is acquitted of an offence only because, by reason of evidence of mental disorder or a combination of mental disorder and intoxication, it is found that he acted or may have acted in a state of automatism, or without the fault required for the offence, or believing that an exempting circumstance existed; and (b) it is proved on a balance of probabilities (whether by the prosecution or by the defendant) that he was suffering from mental disorder at the time of the act."

5–025   However, given the delay over implementing these proposals, which continue to gather dust on library shelves, this seems yet another area in which governments are unwilling to find parliamentary time for legislative reform. Any change in our law on insanity seems as

---

[121] See *Winterwerp v The Netherlands* (1979) 2 E.H.R.R. 387 at 402–403, paras 39–40; and *Johnson v United Kingdom* (1997) 27 E..H.R.R. 296 at 322, para.60.
[122] [2001] 3 W.L.R. 512.
[123] See R.D. MacKay and G. Kearns, "More Fact(s) about the Insanity Defence" [1999] Crim.L.R. 714 at 723.
[124] Report of the Committee on Mentally Abnormal Offenders, Cmnd. 6244 (1975).

far away today as ever. In relation to diminished responsibility the Law Commission in their Report on *Partial Defences to Murder*[125] asserted that:

> "there was overwhelming support from those consultees who addressed the issue for the retention of a partial defence of diminished responsibility for as long as there is the mandatory life sentence for murder."

The Commission broadly kept to the proposals in the 2004 Report when they published their further Report, *Murder, Manslaughter and Infanticide.*[126] They recommended that the defence be "modernised, so that it is both clearer and better able to accommodate developments in expert diagnostic practice"[127] and reformed as follows:

(a) a person who would otherwise be guilty of first degree murder is guilty of second degree murder if, at the time he or she played his or her part in the killing, his or her capacity to:

    (i) understand the nature of his or her conduct; or

    (ii) form a rational judgement; or

    (iii) control him or herself, was substantially impaired by an abnormality of mental functioning arising from a recognised medical condition, developmental immaturity in a defendant under the age of eighteen, or a combination of both; and

(b) the abnormality, the developmental immaturity, or the combination of both provides an explanation for the defendant's conduct in carrying out or taking part in the killing.

At the time of writing, the Government has taken the view that dealing with the defences takes priority over the Commission's more fundamental proposals for restructuring homicide offences, and so the role for diminished responsibility which is countenanced in the Coroners and Justice Bill currently before Parliament is as a defence which will, as is the case at present, reduce murder to manslaughter.[128] The Bill proposes the substitution of the current s.2 of the Homicide Act 1957 with the new proposals based broadly on the Law Commission's proposals, with the exception that the Government declined to take forward the "developmental immaturity" element of the proposed defence.

---

[125] See Law Com. Consultation Paper No.173 (2004) *Partial Defences to Murder,* at para.12.74.
[126] Law Com. No.304 (2006).
[127] Law Com. No.304 (2006) at para.5.107.
[128] Cls 42–43. For policy discussion leading to the Bill, see Ministry of Justice et al., *Murder, manslaughter and infanticide: proposals for reform of the law* (Consultation Paper CP19/08) (July 2008); and Ministry of Justice et al., *Murder, manslaughter and infanticide: proposals for reform of the law—Summary of responses and Government position* (January 2009).

THE MENTALLY ABNORMAL OFFENDER: GENERAL READING

5–026   Baker, E., "Human Rights, M'Naghten And The 1991 Act" [1994] Crim.L.R. 84.

Boland, F., "Intoxication And Criminal Liability" (1996) 60 J.C.L. 100.

Boland, F., *Anglo-American Insanity Defence Reform* (Ashgate, 1999).

Dell, S., "Diminished Responsibility Reconsidered" [1982] Crim.L.R. 809.

Frey, R.G., "The Guilty But Mentally Ill Verdict And Due Process" (1982) 92 Yale L.J. 475.

Goodliffe, J., "*R. v Tandy* And The Concept of Alcoholism As A Disease" (1990) 53 M.L.R. 809.

Grubin, D., "What Constitutes Fitness To Plead" [1993] Crim.L.R. 748.

Jones, T.H., "Insanity, Automatism And The Burden Of Proof On the Accused (1995) 111 L.Q.R. 475.

Loughnan, A., "Manifest Madness: Towards a New Understanding of the Insanity Defence" (2007) 70 M.L.R. 379.

Mackay, R.D., Mitchell, B., and Howe, L., "Yet More Facts About the Insanity Defence" [2006] Crim.L.R. 399.

Mackay, R.D., Mitchell, B., and Howe, L., "A Continued Upturn in Unfitness to Plead— More Disability in Relation to the Trial under the 1991 Act" [2007] Crim.L.R. 530.

Mackay, R.D., and Reuber, M., "Epilepsy and the Defence of Insanity—Time for a Change" [2007] Crim.L.R. 782.

Mackay, R.D., *Mental Condition Defences In The Criminal Law* (Clarendon, 1995).

Mackay, R.D., "Pleading Provocation and Diminished Responsibility Together" [1988] Crim.L.R. 411.

Mackay. R.D., "Post-Hinckley Insanity in the USA" [1988] Crim.L.R. 88.

Mackay, R.D., "The Trial of Facts and Unfitness to Plead" [1997] Crim.L.R. 644.

Mackay, R.D. and Kearns, G., "More Fact(s) About the Insanity Defence" [1999] Crim.L.R. 714.

Mackay, R.D. and Kearns, G., "An Upturn in Unfitness to Plead? Disability In Relation To The Trial Under the 1991 Act" [2000] Crim.L.R. 532.

Sutherland, P.J. and Gearty, C.A., "Insanity And The European Court Of Human Rights" [1992] Crim.L.R. 418.

Virgo, G., "Sanitising Insanity—Sleep-Walking And Statutory Reform" (1991) 50 C.L.J. 386.

Ward, T., "Magistrates, Insanity And The Common Law" [1997] Crim.L.R. 796.

2. INTOXICATION

5–027   We saw in Chapter 2[129] how a mistake might result in the prosecution being unable to prove that the accused brought about the actus reus with the necessary mens rea. A factor which is likely to make it more probable that the defendant was labouring under a mistaken belief is the presence in the accused of a large quantity of alcohol or drugs. In the majority of occasions where the accused is intoxicated, the effect of the intoxication will be to remove his inhibitions. He will do something he would not have done had he been sober, but he will nonetheless possess the necessary mens rea.[130] On other occasions he will be so drunk that

---

[129] See above, paras 2–082—2–085.

[130] In *Bowden* [1993] Crim.L.R. 380 it was held that provided D forms the necessary mens rea it will not be of any relevance that he did an act he would not have performed had he been sober; see also *Kingston* [1994] 3 All E.R. 353; see below, para.5–035.

he does not form the necessary mens rea. We need to ask whether either of these states of mind will afford the accused a defence to a criminal charge. The general rule can be stated that intoxication[131] will provide a defence only when it negatives the required mens rea, and even here the defence is severely restricted. We can say that where the effect of intoxication is simply to remove the inhibitions, it will be no defence; an intoxicated or drugged intent is still an intent.[132] The defendant will have a defence in these circumstances only if he can bring himself within a defence such as diminished responsibility.[133]

Section 8 of the Criminal Justice Act 1967 provides that where the definition of the offence requires proof that the defendant intended or foresaw a result of his actions, the jury are entitled to take account of all the evidence drawing such inferences from the evidence as appear proper in the circumstances. Thus, in the crime of battery, the prosecution must prove that the defendant intended to apply unlawful force or foresaw that this would be the result of his conduct. Under s.20 of the Offences Against the Person Act 1861,[134] the prosecution must prove that the accused intended or foresaw some harm to another. If the jury are entitled to reach this conclusion by reference to all the relevant evidence, then it would seem that evidence of intoxication might be very relevant. A defendant who was very drunk might well stagger into an elderly person knocking that person over. He has clearly applied unlawful force to the victim, but the prosecution would have a hard time proving that the defendant either intended to touch the victim or even that he consciously took the risk of so doing.

Can the jury take note of the accused's intoxication and draw from it the inference that he lacked the necessary mens rea? If the contact had been brought about by a perfectly sober person tripping over the edge of a carpet and hurtling headlong into the victim, the jury would undoubtedly be entitled to take account of all the evidence. Why should it make any difference that the accused is intoxicated? The reason is not hard to find. The courts have adopted the view that the public at large would find it intolerable that a person who brought about the actus reus of a crime should have a complete defence on the basis of a condition for which he himself was entirely to blame. They have, therefore, placed severe restrictions on the use of voluntary intoxication as a defence to most criminal charges. Where, however, the accused was not responsible for his intoxicated or drugged state, the courts have been able to take a more sympathetic approach. We shall, therefore, have a look first at those cases in which the defendant has been responsible for his intoxicated state. Thereafter we shall look at the defendant who was intoxicated at the time of committing the offence, but who cannot be blamed for that intoxicated state.

A. Voluntary Intoxication

Voluntary intoxication can at best afford a defence only if it negatives the mens rea required **5–028** of the offence; it can be no defence if it causes the accused to form the necessary mens rea, nor if it simply removes his inhibitions.[135] It therefore follows that there are certain situations in which it is totally irrelevant. In *Prince*[136] the Court for Crown Cases Reserved held that the accused's honest and reasonable belief that the girl he abducted was 19 years of

---

[131] Intoxication here relates to conditions brought about by the consumption of either alcohol or drugs.
[132] See, *Bowden* [1993] Crim.L.R. 380.
[133] See above, paras 5–015—5–020. This defence may be open to a drug addict or alcoholic, but not to someone who is simply drunk.
[134] Unlawful wounding or infliction of grievous bodily harm.
[135] See, generally P. Robinson "Causing the Conditions of One's Own Defences" (1985) 73 Virginia L.R. 1.
[136] (1875) L.R. 2 C.C.R. 154; above, para.2–082.

age was no defence; liability on that aspect of the actus reus was strict. There being no mens rea to negate, intoxication is totally irrelevant. It would have made no difference that Prince made his mistake because he had been drunk. Where liability is based upon negligence, as in the offence of careless driving,[137] it would be of little avail for the accused to plead that had he been sober he would not have made the mistake. The proof that the accused had been under the influence of drugs or alcohol would be all the evidence of negligence that the court would require.[138]

So we can make the point that unless the evidence of intoxication is capable of negativing the requisite mens rea, it is of no relevance. In the above situations no special rules relating to intoxication are necessary. Where, however, the crime requires proof of intention or subjective recklessness,[139] evidence of intoxication could clearly negative the necessary mens rea. If D is charged with the murder of P, the fact that he had consumed large quantities of alcohol could explain why he thought P was a waxwork model, and thus prevent the prosecution from proving he intended to kill a human being. The question, therefore, is whether the courts are prepared to allow D to introduce his intoxicated state as a means of negativing the necessary mens rea. As we said above, s.8 of the Criminal Justice Act 1967 would appear to permit the jury to consider any evidence which would help them decide whether the accused intended or foresaw a result, and logic would suggest that a similar rule should operate in relation to knowledge or foresight of circumstances. Against this, however, is the issue of public policy which would condemn any approach purporting to allow a drunken defendant to escape liability on the grounds of his own self-induced intoxication.

The general position can be stated thus. Where the prosecution has to establish intention or subjective recklessness, the relevance of intoxication depends upon whether the crime in question is classified as one of *basic* or *specific* intent. In *DPP v Majewski*,[140] following an incident in a public house, the defendant was convicted of three offences of assault occasioning actual bodily harm and three offences of assaulting a police constable in the execution of his duty. He had previously to the alleged assaults consumed large quantities of drugs and alcohol as a result of which he said that he had been totally unaware of what he was doing. Nevertheless, the trial judge directed the jury to ignore the subject of drink or drugs as being in any way a defence to the assaults. The House of Lords held that the authority which had been relied upon for the last half century was the speech of Lord Birkenhead in *DPP v Beard*,[141] where he said that the cases:

> "establish that where a specific intent is an essential element in the offence, evidence of a state of drunkenness rendering the accused incapable of forming such an intent should be taken into consideration in order to determine whether he had in fact formed the intent necessary to constitute the particular crime. If he was so drunk that he was incapable of forming the intent required he could not be convicted of a crime which was committed only if the intent was proved."[142]

5–029   Lord Birkenhead took murder as an example. If the accused did not form the intention to kill or cause grievous bodily harm because he was intoxicated, he could not be convicted of murder, but no such intent was required in manslaughter and he would thus be convicted of

---

[137] Road Traffic Act 1988 s.3.
[138] The same would be true of gross negligence manslaughter.
[139] *Cunningham* [1957] 2 Q.B. 396.
[140] [1977] A.C. 443. See generally S. Gardner, "The Importance of *Majewski*" (1984) 4 O.J.L.S. 279.
[141] [1920] A.C. 479. Beard had suffocated a girl during the course of raping her. He was charged with murder on the basis of the felony murder rule which meant that the only mens rea required was that of rape. As to felony murder rule, see below, para.7–015.
[142] [1920] A.C. 479 at 499.

that offence. The position would appear to be that voluntary intoxication is a defence only to crimes requiring a specific intent; voluntary intoxication is irrelevant to crimes, such as assault, which require only what is described as a basic intent. In *Majewski*, Lord Elwyn-Jones defended the position in relation to basic intent crimes:

"His (the defendant's) course of conduct in reducing himself by drugs and drink to that condition in my view supplies the evidence of mens rea, of guilty mind certainly sufficient for crimes of basic intent. It is a reckless course of conduct and recklessness is enough to constitute the necessary mens rea in the assault cases: see *Venna*.[143] The drunkenness itself is an integral part of the crime, the other part being the evidence of the unlawful use of force against the victim. Together they add up to criminal recklessness."[144]

Where the defendant wishes to claim that voluntary intoxication deprived him of the mens rea, it will be necessary to decide whether the crime is one of basic or specific intent.[145] What, therefore, is a crime of specific intent? Generally speaking they are crimes where, on at least one element of the actus reus, the prosecution will succeed only if it can establish intention. Following *Moloney*[146] murder requires proof of an intention to kill or cause grievous bodily harm; recklessness will not suffice. Murder is, therefore, a crime of specific intent.[147] A crime with an ulterior intent will also be a crime of specific intent for these purposes; e.g. wounding with intent to do grievous bodily harm contrary to s.18 of the Offences Against the Person Act 1861. A crime of basic intent is one in which on all elements of the actus reus liability will be satisfied by proof of recklessness.[148] Crimes of specific intent include murder, offences under s.18 of the Offences Against the Person Act 1861, theft, obtaining property by deception, robbery, burglary with intent, and criminal attempts.[149] The following have been held to be crimes of basic intent; manslaughter; rape; offences under s.20 of the Offences Against the Person Act 1861, assault occasioning actual bodily harm; common assault; criminal damage[150]; kidnapping and false imprisonment.[151] The effect of these rules is that where the defendant is charged with a crime of basic intent, the court will not allow him to assert that he lacked the mens rea required of the offence when the reason alleged is self-induced intoxication. This is a rule of substantive law which, in effect, holds that in crimes of basic intent once it is established that the accused was intoxicated, the prosecution no longer need to prove recklessness; this is supplied by his conduct in getting drunk. Section 8 of the Criminal Justice Act 1967 is, therefore, irrelevant.

Despite the outrage these rules perpetrate upon the general principles of mens rea, it is possible to see some sort of logic, at least in relation to offences against the person. Where

---

[143] [1976] Q.B. 421, per James L.J. at 429.

[144] [1977] A.C. 443 at 474–475.

[145] Technically speaking the division into crimes of basic or specific intent is needed only in crimes requiring subjective recklessness or intention. In other crimes evidence of intoxication would not affect the mens rea; this is seen most clearly in crimes of strict liability where there is no mens rea requirement. However, it will be convenient to use the term basic intent to cover all crimes in which there is no specific intent.

[146] [1985] A.C. 905; see above, para.2–055.

[147] Murder has always been perceived as a crime requiring a specific intent, even though during the period between *Hyam v DPP* and *Moloney*, it seems recklessness as to death or grievous bodily harm sufficed. It does, however, serve to show that the courts have not been consistent in the definition of specific intent.

[148] A more watertight definition would be to say that crimes of specific intent are those in which the defence of voluntary intoxication has been allowed and crimes of basic intention are those where it has not.

[149] But see *Khan* [1990] 2 All E.R. 783; below, para.6–010.

[150] Except where the charge is aggravated criminal damage contrary to s.1(2)(b) of the Criminal Damage Act 1971 and the prosecution is relying solely upon intention, see below, para.10–001.

[151] These last two were added to the list by the case of *Hutchins* [1988] Crim.L.R. 379.

the accused is charged with murder, a crime of specific intent, he will be able to plead that he did not form the necessary intent due to intoxication. This may result in his acquittal for murder, but the jury will be able to convict him of the alternative offence of manslaughter[152] which is a basic intent crime. Similarly a person charged with wounding with intent could plead intoxication; the jury would nevertheless be able to convict him of the basic intent offence of unlawful wounding to which intoxication is irrelevant. In this way the law has mitigated against the draconian rule that intoxication may never be raised as a defence, while keeping an eye on the public outrage that would follow were such defendants to be totally exonerated on the basis of a lack of mens rea caused solely by a self-induced state.

5–030   So far we have said that voluntary intoxication is a defence to crimes of specific intent, but is irrelevant in crimes of basic intent. We need to examine this in rather more detail. In the first place, what is meant by intoxication? Many people have reached a level of intoxication which would be regarded by others as drunkenness, but they nevertheless are still fully aware of what they are doing; the alcohol has simply made them more aggressive or less inhibited. A person charged with murder in a drunken brawl would have no defence if he admitted intentionally causing grievous bodily harm, but claimed that seven pints of beer had deprived him of self-restraint. A drunken intent is still an intent. Intoxication will *only* be a defence if it means that the accused did not form the intent to kill or cause grievous bodily harm. Some of the authorities would appear to say[153] that intoxication must have deprived the accused of the ability to form the necessary mens rea. This is going too far. It is sufficient that the accused did not form the mens rea,[154] though of course evidence that he was incapable of forming the mens rea would be good proof that he did not.

There are suggestions in *Majewski*[155] that the prosecution may be entitled to lead evidence of drunkenness in basic intent crimes in substitution for proving the required mens rea. If the accused is indeed so drunk that he does not form the mens rea of a basic intent crime, the prosecution will be unable to establish mens rea. In such circumstances the prosecution should be entitled to prove that the accused did not form the mens rea for the offence, but that had he not been drunk he would have done so. This would achieve the same result as the US Model Penal Code, which provides "When recklessness establishes an element of the offence, if the actor, due to self-induced intoxication, is unaware of a risk of which he would have been aware had he been sober, such unawareness is immaterial."[156] Any suggestion, however, that the prosecutor can avoid the need to prove mens rea by simply adducing some evidence that the accused had been drinking would clearly be unacceptable. However, it can be said that where a defendant is charged with a crime of basic intent, little will be gained by the defendant introducing evidence of the consumption of alcohol. It will be no defence to the charge and most judges would see it as an aggravating rather than a mitigating factor in terms of sentence.

An unorthodox perspective, contrary to acknowledged principles on the divide between specific and basic intent crimes for intoxication purposes, has recently been applied by the Court of Appeal in *Heard*.[157] This case addressed the significance of intoxication as a defence to sexual assault within s.3 of the Sexual Offences Act.[158] In terms of voluntary intoxication a constrained ambit has been determined, identifying the extant offence as a

---

[152] Manslaughter is always an alternative verdict on a murder indictment.
[153] See, above for example, Lord Birkenhead in *Beard* [1920] A.C. 479 at 499.
[154] *Cole* [1993] Crim.L.R. 300; see generally J. Horder, "Pleading Involuntary Lack of Capacity" (1993) 52 C.L.J. 298.
[155] [1977] A.C. 443, above, para.5–028.
[156] M.P.C. s.208(2).
[157] [2007] EWCA Crim 125; [2007] 3 All E.R. 306.
[158] See below at para.7–133 for discussion of this offence.

basic intent crime, and for public policy concerns denying the reach of the defence. The facts demonstrate the appropriate balancing act applicable in this substantive area. Whilst drunk, the defendant rubbed his genitals against the complainant police officer's leg. In interview, he said that he could not remember whether he did what had been attributed to him due to his drunkenness. D appealed against conviction on the basis that the offence under s.3 of the Sexual Offences Act 2003 was of specific intent, as it required intentional touching, and the issue of D's intoxication should have been left to the jury as negating his mens rea of an intention to touch.

Their Lordships in *Heard* determined that self-induced intoxication per se could not   **5–031** remove the element of intention in a charge of sexually assaulting another person. In the leading judgment, provided by Hughes L.J., it was asserted that the defendant could not contend that his voluntary intoxication prevented him from intending to touch in the sense of willed muscular movement. The trial judge's direction that the touching must be deliberate was correct, and to touch another person accidentally is outwith this offence.[159] This may occur through an accidental fall as in *Brady*[160] where D fell from the balcony in a night-club injuring a dancer below, or through stumbling inadvertently into someone in an intoxicated state. As such, the defence can raise evidence that the act, as opposed to relevant consequences, transpired in an accidental manner. This point was adduced in *Heard* by Hughes L.J.:

> "To flail about, stumble or barge around in an uncoordinated manner which results in an unintended touching, objectively sexual, is not this offence. If to do so when sober is not this offence, then nor is it this offence to do so when intoxicated. It is also possible that such an action would not be judged by the jury to be objectively sexual, on the basis that it was, clearly accidental, but whether this is so or not, we are satisfied that in such a case this offence is not committed. The intoxication, in such a situation, has not impacted on intention. Intention is simply not in question. What is in question is impairment of control of the limbs . . . [T]he judge might well find it useful to add to the previously mentioned direction that "a drunken intent is still an intent", the corollary that "a drunken accident is still an accident."[161]

More opaquely, Hughes L.J. in *Heard*, albeit obiter, sought to create a workable modern delineation between crimes of specific intent and those of basic intent.[162] Apparently, specific intent crimes require an intention as applied to acts considered in relation to their purposes, in the sense of "the offence requires proof of a state of mind, addressing something beyond the prohibited act itself, namely its consequences". Hughes L.J. placed in this category the offence of aggravated criminal damage,[163] albeit that the mens rea of the crime may involve ulterior recklessness. The construction of the offence is predicated upon proof that the defendant intentionally or recklessly damaged property, being reckless as to whether life was endangered thereby. In contradistinction, basic intent crimes require intention (or recklessness) as applied to acts apart from the purposes. The "intentional touching" element of the offences prescribed by s.3 of the Sexual Offences Act 2003

---

[159] [2007] EWCA Crim 125; [2007] 3 All E.R. 306 at [23].
[160] [2006] EWCA Crim 2413; [2007] Crim.L.R. 564. The offence herein related to the basic intent offence within OAPA 1861 s.20 of inflicting grievous bodily harm. As presented, before the appellate court the issue focused on the fall (accidental) rather than D climbing and perching on the balcony ledge (non-accidental). The perching on the ledge seems self-evidently to constitute reckless action.
[161] [2007] 3 All E.R. 306 at [23].
[162] [2007] 3 All E.R. 306 at [30].
[163] See below at para.10–008 for discussion of this offence.

correspondingly fell into the category of basic intent; the mens rea of the crime does not go beyond the actus reus of the offence and no requirement exists to "bolt-on" a further fault element.

Confusion now reigns supreme, but it is important to remember that the statements in *Heard* are simply obiter dictum at this juncture. The bifurcation between specific intent (intention) and basic intent (recklessness) predicated from *Majewski* on policy grounds has operated in a pragmatic and successful fashion, with legitimate alternative indictments. The Sexual Offences Act 2003 has not altered the law so as to make voluntary intoxication available as a defence to an allegation of intentional touching (a basic intent crime). The convoluted reasoning adduced in *Heard*, however, simply muddied the waters. In reality the law in this arena has been mandated by public policy reasons, and this provides a better rationale for the outcome; Hughes L.J. admitted as much when he stated: "[T]here is a great deal of policy in the decision whether voluntary intoxication can or cannot be relied upon."[164]

The position has been further obscured by the decisions of the Court of Appeal in *O'Grady*[165] and *O'Connor*.[166] We saw earlier[167] that the actus reus of most crimes comprises various elements and that normally mens rea is required as to each part of the actus reus. In murder, for example, the prosecution must prove that at the time the accused killed another human being he intended either to kill or cause grievous bodily harm: the specific intent. However, the accused may raise the issue of self-defence as justification for the killing. Where this happens the prosecution must prove that there was no justification and that the killing was unlawful. In relation to this element the prosecution must prove that the accused either knew that there was no justification or that he consciously took an unjustified risk that the killing might not be justified. A sober defendant is to be judged on the issue of justification on the facts he honestly believed to exist, however unreasonable his belief. Since murder is a crime of specific intent, may a drunken defendant plead that because he was drunk he mistakenly believed there was a need to defend himself? This was basically the position in *O'Grady*. G and a friend had been drinking heavily and later fought each other. G said that he could remember being attacked by his friend and that he had taken what steps he had considered necessary to save his own life. When he awoke in the morning he found his friend to be dead. He was convicted of manslaughter and appealed to the Court of Appeal. Lord Lane C.J. concluded that:

> "[w]here the jury are satisfied that the defendant was mistaken in his belief that any force or the force which he in fact used was necessary to defend himself and are further satisfied that the mistake was caused by voluntarily induced intoxication, the defence must fail. We do not consider that any distinction should be drawn on this aspect of the matter between offences involving what is called specific intent, such as murder, and offences of so-called basic intent, such as manslaughter."[168]

5–032   As far as manslaughter is concerned the decision is in line with the general principle that intoxication is irrelevant in a basic intent crime. Just as it would not avail an alleged rapist to say that because of drink he had mistakenly believed that the woman was consenting, so it will not avail someone charged with manslaughter to say that drink caused them to believe

---

[164] [2007] 3 All E.R. 306 at [32].
[165] [1987] Q.B. 995; [1987] 3 All E.R. 420.
[166] [1991] Crim.L.R. 135.
[167] Above, paras 2–004—2–006.
[168] [1987] Q.B. 995 at 999.

that force was necessary, or that the amount of force that was used was reasonable. However, Lord Lane C.J. goes on, obiter, to say that the position is exactly the same in murder, and this is startling. Surely murder is a crime of specific intent to which intoxication is an available defence? Lord Lane C.J. draws a distinction, "the question of mistake can and ought to be considered separately from the question of intent."[169]

With the greatest of respect to Lord Lane, such a statement is highly misleading. Mistake is nothing more than a denial of mens rea; the two cannot be separated. What the Court of Appeal appears to be saying is that voluntary intoxication is a defence only if it means that the accused did not form the specific intent of the crime in question and this is certainly in line with the way in which the rules were formulated in *DPP v Beard* and *Majewski*.[170] If this interpretation is correct it means that not only do we have to identify crimes of specific intent, but we have to be able to isolate the specific intent element in that crime since the defence of intoxication is relevant only to that element. Consider, for example, the crime of wounding with intent to resist arrest under s.18 of the Offences Against the Person Act 1861. This is a crime of specific intent and the prosecution must prove that the accused foresaw, at least, that he would cause some harm and that he had the intent to resist arrest.[171] On our interpretation of *O'Grady*, an accused charged under s.18 would be able to rely upon intoxication to show he did not intend to resist arrest since this is the specific intent element of the crime, but not to show that he did not foresee any harm since this is a basic intent element which is satisfied by recklessness. In murder the specific intent is the intent to kill or cause grievous bodily harm and so the accused would be able to raise intoxication to show that he did not intend to kill or seriously injure a human being, but not to show that he believed he was acting in self-defence or that he believed the victim not to be within the Queen's Peace.

Is there any other explanation of the decision in *O'Grady*? It cannot be that the court is saying that a mistaken belief induced by intoxication is irrelevant; if O'Grady killed his friend because in his intoxicated state he mistook him for a gorilla he would have a defence because he did not form the specific intent to kill a human being. The only other possibility is that drunken mistakes relating to issues of justification are for some reason irrelevant even in specific intent crimes. The only explanation for this would be that justification is not a part of the core element of the crime, but there appears little logical justification for such a view.[172] It is suggested that the position is that intoxication is relevant only if it relates to that element of the offence which makes that offence a crime of specific intent. This makes the defence an extremely narrow defence, but that is in keeping with the public policy approach adopted by the courts.

Despite vigorous attacks on the decision in *O'Grady*,[173] the Court of Appeal seemed to **5–033** hold themselves bound by it in *O'Connor*,[174] though again the statements appear to be obiter since the decision in the case was that the trial judge had misdirected the jury by telling them that intoxication was a defence only if it deprived the accused of the ability to form the specific intent. The issue for the jury is not whether the accused could form the specific intent, but rather whether he did. Most recently, in *Hatton*[175] the Court of Appeal specifically relied upon the statements of Lord Lane in *O'Grady*. In *O'Grady* the defendant

[169] [1987] Q.B. 995 at 999.
[170] *Beard* [1920] A.C. 479; *Majewski* [1977] A.C. 443, above, para.5–038.
[171] See, below para.7–090 for a discussion of this offence.
[172] It would also appear to be inconsistent with the approach to justification taken in *Gladstone Williams* and *Beckford*, below para.5–046.
[173] See, for example J.C. Smith's commentary in [1987] Crim.L.R. 706 at 707.
[174] [1991] Crim.L.R. 135.
[175] [2005] EWCA Crim 2951.

had been convicted only of manslaughter, but nonetheless the guiding principles were transposed in *Hatton* to a case of murder. The court felt obliged to follow *O'Grady* and to reject the defendant's contention that the judge should have directed the jury to consider whether the defendant's drunkenness might have led him to make a mistake as to the severity of any attack to which he might have been subjected to by the victim. The effect is that it is not open to a defendant seeking to establish self-defence for murder to rely on a mistake induced by voluntary self-induced intoxication. Nevertheless until the Court of Appeal decides otherwise we might now say that the rule is that voluntary intoxication is relevant in crimes of specific intent, but only in so far as it relates to the requirement of intention, rather than to the belief in circumstances of justification.

A further muddying of the waters has occurred through the decision of the Court of Appeal in *Richardson and Irwin*.[176] The defendants and the eventual victim, their friend, were all university students. After consuming four or five pints each at the student union bar they went to a flat belonging to one of the defendants. There was some horseplay and the defendants lifted their friend over the edge of the balcony and dropped him. He fell about 10 or 12 ft and suffered injuries. The defendants were convicted of inflicting grievous bodily harm contrary to s.20 of the Offences Against the Person Act 1861 (a basic intent offence). They appealed against conviction on the grounds that the judge wrongly directed the jury that the intention of each defendant should be on the basis of a reasonable, (i.e. not under the influence of drink) man and not (as they were) under the influence of drink. They also contended that they believed that their stricken friend had consented to all aspects of the horseplay. One might have logically anticipated that s.20, being a basic intent offence, the appellate court would have determined that intoxication was not relevant to such a charge. Not so, was the staggering response of the Court of Appeal. The defendants' appeals against conviction were allowed on the premise that the trial judge had failed to tell the jury that they had to be sure that the defendants foresaw that their friend might slip or be dropped and suffer some bodily harm, or would have foreseen this particular risk if sober and had not consumed four to five pints. A jury is, thus, tasked to engage in a question involving mental gyrations on foreseeability of a sober (but in reality drunk) defendant.

Moreover, the court in *Richardson and Irwin* held that the trial judge, on the issue of the defendants' belief in their friends consent, should have directed the jury to take account of evidence that the defendants' minds were affected by alcohol. No consideration was given to the earlier authorities of *O'Grady* and *O'Connor*, nor was there any attention paid to the decisions of *Woods*[177] and *Fotheringham*,[178] in the context of rape, which asserted that for a basic intent crime (rape) that intoxicated beliefs over victim's consent could not be relied upon. The outcome in *Richardson and Irwin* must, thus, be highly questionable. The general proposition is that self-induced intoxication by drink or drugs is no defence, except to offences requiring a specific intent. If the decision in *Richardson and Irwin* proves to be apposite this requires severe modification. The position would be that intoxication is a defence if it causes the defendant, as in circumstances therein, to believe that the victim is consenting, although, if he had been sober, he would have known that this is not so. The alternative is to treat *Richardson and Irwin*, together with *Aitken*,[179] and *R v A*,[180] as *sui generis* and delimited by specific circumstances relating to rough horseplay and excess of alcohol on the part of defendant(s) and "willing" complainant.

---

[176] [1999] 1 Cr.App.R. 392 CA.
[177] (1982) 74 Cr.App.R. 312.
[178] (1988) 88 Cr.App.R. 206.
[179] See below, para.7–112 for discussion of *Aitken* in the context of consent and rough horseplay; see also *Jones* (1986) 83 Cr.App.R. 375.
[180] See below at para.7–112.

As far as basic intent crimes are concerned intoxication is totally irrelevant. Rape, for **5–034** example, is a crime of basic intent even though the prosecution must prove that the defendant intended to engage in penile penetration. Intoxication is, therefore, irrelevant whether the defence is that he thought the victim was consenting or, as in one case, he thought that he was having intercourse with his wife, when in fact it was a young babysitter.[181] Irrelevant, that is, unless the wording of a particular statutory defence to a basic intent crime leads the court to believe that Parliament must have intended otherwise. In *Jaggard v Dickinson*[182] the defendant had damaged property belonging to another because in her drunken state she thought that she was entering the property of X who had told her to treat the house as her own, whereas in fact she was damaging the property of Y. She was charged under s.1(1) of the Criminal Damage Act 1971[183] which makes it an offence intentionally or recklessly to damage another's property without lawful excuse. Whether you regard this as an offence of basic intent or simply as an offence requiring only recklessness, it is clear that it would have been of no avail for her to plead that in her drunken state she had not realised that she was damaging property belonging to another. However, under s.5(2)[184] of the Act it is provided that the defendant would have a lawful excuse if:

> "at the time of the act or acts alleged to constitute the offence he believed that the person or persons whom he believed to be entitled to consent to the destruction or damage to the property in question had so consented, or would have so consented to it if he or they had known of the destruction or damage and its circumstances."

She thought that the person entitled to consent to the damage would have done so had he known the circumstances. The Divisional Court held that the provision was so worded that it provided her with a defence even though her mistaken belief was due to intoxication. With respect to the court this does create very anomalous results and it is very hard to follow the actual statutory interpretation adopted by the court. It means that the person who, because he is drunk, does not intend to damage property or believes that it is his own will be found guilty; but a person who, because he is drunk, mistakenly believes that the owner would have consented will not. Such a distinction has little merit to commend it.

B. Involuntary Intoxication

As we have seen the law takes a very unsympathetic view of the defendant who has **5–035** voluntarily become intoxicated. What is the position where the defendant is not responsible for his intoxicated state? A person may become involuntarily intoxicated in a variety of ways; his drinks may have been laced or he may have been tricked into taking drugs without his knowledge. He may have been prescribed medicine by a doctor who has failed to warn him of the side-effects, especially the effect of consuming any alcohol in conjunction with the drugs.[185] Another possibility is that the drugs may have been forcibly administered.[186] On the other hand a person who has been voluntarily consuming alcohol cannot claim that his drunkenness was involuntary simply because he underestimated the strength of the drink.[187]

---

[181] *Fotheringham* (1988) 88 Cr.App.R. 206.
[182] [1981] Q.B. 527; [1980] 3 All E.R. 716.
[183] See below, para.10–001.
[184] See below, para.10–015.
[185] See, e.g. *Bailey* [1983] 1 W.L.R. 760.
[186] See generally, J. Horder, "Pleading Involuntary Lack of Capacity" (1993) 52 C.L.J. 298; and W. Wilson "Involuntary Intoxication: Excusing the Inexcusable" (1995) 1 *Res Publica* 25.
[187] *Allen, The Times*, June 10, 1988.

The main feature that such situations have in common is that the defendant is not to blame for his condition. Is it, therefore, right that the rules relating to voluntary intoxication laid down in *Majewski* should apply to such defendants?

The House of Lords had the opportunity to review the position in *Kingston*.[188] P had lured a 15-year-old boy to his flat and had rendered him unconscious by means of a drugged drink. He then invited K to indulge in sexual abuse of the unconscious boy. While K was so engaged P took photographs and made an audio-recording. Both P and K were charged with indecent assault.[189] K pleaded that he had been drugged by P, otherwise he would never have acted in the way that he did. The trial judge directed the jury, correctly it is submitted in the light of what little authority existed at that time, that if they found that because of intoxication P had not formed the necessary mens rea, he should be acquitted. If, on the other hand, they found that he had formed the intent indecently to assault the boy, they should convict him whether or not they thought he was acting under the influence of a drug; because a drugged intent is still an intent. His appeal to the Court of Appeal was allowed on the basis that if a defendant forms an intention after being involuntarily intoxicated, where such intention would not have been formed had he been sober, then he ought to be acquitted. The prosecutor appealed to the House of Lords where their Lordships restored K's conviction.[190]

Lord Mustill examined the various ways in which the Court of Appeal had reached its decision. He said that it seems fairly clear that they had relied upon a supposed principle that "an accused person may be entitled to be acquitted if there is a possibility that, although his act was intentional, the intent itself arose out of circumstances for which he bears no blame".[191] Lord Mustill said that however attractive such a principle might be, it did not represent the law. In the majority of criminal offences, proof of the necessary mens rea will also establish the necessary culpability of the accused. Nevertheless, once the prosecution have established that the accused brought about the actus reus of the crime with the required mens rea, they are entitled to a conviction even if there was no moral blame attaching to the defendant and society would not censure him for what he had done.[192]

5–036   The second line of reasoning applied by the Court of Appeal appeared to be that there was a defence of involuntary intoxication which would provide a defence where the defendant has the necessary mens rea for the offence, but would not have committed the deed but for involuntary intoxication. Lord Mustill concluded that there was no such authority, but that it was necessary to see involuntary intoxication in the light of intoxication as a whole. Voluntary intoxication is controlled by *Majewski*[193] where, as we have seen, it was held that voluntary intoxication is no defence to a crime of basic intent such as indecent assault. Such a rule could be justified on one of two grounds. The first is that in a crime of basic intent the absence of the necessary intent is cured by treating the intentional taking of drink without regards to its possible effects as a substitute for the mental element ordinarily required by the offence. The second ground is that a defendant cannot rely upon the absence of the mens rea when it is absent because of his own voluntary acts; a sort of

---

[188] [1994] 3 All E.R. 353; see generally G.R. Sullivan, "Involuntary Intoxication and Beyond." [1994] Crim.L.R. 272; S. Gardner, "Criminal Defences by Judicial Discretion" (1995) 111 L.Q.R. 177; and J.R. Spencer, "Involuntary Intoxication as a Defence" (1995) 54 C.L.J. 12.

[189] The offence would now be "sexual assault", under s.3 of the Sexual Offences Act 2003.

[190] The point was affirmed, following *Sheehan* [1975] 1 W.L.R. 739, that a drunken intent is still an intent. See also *Pordage* [1975] Crim.L.R. 575.

[191] [1994] 3 All E.R. 353 at 359.

[192] A good illustration is provided by *Buckoke v Greater London Council* [1971] 2 All E.R. 254. The fire-engine driver committed an offence by deliberately driving through a red traffic light even though society would congratulate him for saving a life. See below, para.5–064, fn.299. See also *Yip Chiu-cheung* [1994] 2 All E.R. 924.

[193] [1977] A.C. 443, see above, para.5–028.

estoppel. Where, however, the intoxication is involuntary, the first rationalisation disappears because there is no intentional drinking to substitute for the necessary mens rea. As far as the second is concerned, there is no good reason why a person should not rely on a mental condition which he had not himself brought about. Lord Mustill concluded:

> "Thus once the involuntary nature of the intoxication is added the two theories of *Majewski* fall way, and the position reverts to what it would have been if *Majewski* had not been decided, namely that the offence is not made out if the defendant is so intoxicated that he could not form an intent.[194] Thus, where the intoxication is involuntary *Majewski* does not *subtract* the defence of absence of intent; but there is nothing in *Majewski* to suggest that where intent is proved involuntary intoxication adds a further defence."[195]

This returns us to the position prior to the decision of the Court of Appeal in *Kingston*. While it may be grudgingly admitted that there are reasons of public policy for severely restricting the defence of voluntary intoxication, the reasons do not apply to involuntary intoxication. It follows that the defendant should be able to rely on involuntary intoxication as evidence that he did not form the necessary mens rea of any crime of which he stands accused, whether it be a crime of basic or specific intent. But that is as far as it goes; it does not provide a new defence for the person who possesses the necessary mens rea even if this was entirely due to an involuntary consumption of alcohol or drugs. As we have said before; a drugged intent is still an intent.

Finally, the House examined the question of whether it should create a new defence to cover a situation such as that in *Kingston*. Since there was no suggestion that the drug had caused him to form the mens rea, but that the drug had removed his inhibitions which would normally have prevented him from giving way to his paedophilic urges, this would be a defence of disinhibition. It would protect a defendant whose restraint against committing the offence was removed by involuntary intoxication. Their Lordships, while appearing ready to create new defences where needed,[196] concluded that such a step should only be taken in straightforward situations. The issue in *Kingston* did not admit of a simple solution; the issues both medical and legal were complex. Lord Mustill said that it would be far more appropriate for the Law Commission to expand their work on intoxication to take such issues on board.

C. Self-induced Automatism and Non-harmful Drugs

The general principles developed largely in cases of alcoholic intoxication apply also to **5–037** intoxication brought about by the consumption of drugs. In relation to drugs, however, the courts have drawn a distinction between intoxication caused by the taking of dangerous drugs and intoxication caused by taking non-harmful drugs used for medicinal purposes. The case of *Lipman*[197] provides a good illustration of intoxication caused by the taking of a dangerous drug. L killed his girlfriend while on an hallucinatory trip brought about by his consumption of L.S.D. He imagined that he was travelling to the centre of the Earth and

---

[194] It is suggested that Lord Mustill should, consistently with the position in relation to voluntary intoxication, have said that the defendant was so intoxicated that he did not form an intent and not that he could not form an intent. Above para.5–028; and see also *Cole* [1993] Crim.L.R. 300.

[195] [1994] 3 All E.R. 353 at 364–365.

[196] See below para.5–093.

[197] [1970] 1 Q.B. 152.

was fending off dangerous serpents. When he awoke he discovered that he had shoved several inches of bedding sheet down his girlfriend's throat and she had suffocated. The Court of Appeal upheld his conviction for manslaughter on the basis that the *Majewski* rules applied even where the voluntary intoxication had brought about a state of automatism. Manslaughter was a crime of basic intent and evidence of voluntary intoxication was irrelevant.

In *Bailey*,[198] however, B was a diabetic who claimed that he had assaulted the victim during a period of unconsciousness caused by hypoglycaemia because of his failure to eat sufficient food following his last dose of insulin. He was convicted of wounding with intent[199] and appealed to the Court of Appeal. The Crown argued that the approach in *Lipman* should be adopted for all cases of self-induced automatism; in other words his failure to eat sufficient food should be treated in the same way as voluntary intoxication under the *Majewski* rules. Even if such an approach were to be adopted, it would not apply to an offence of wounding with intent since this was an offence of specific intent and evidence of his self-induced automatism would be admissible to show that he had not formed the specific intent of that offence. This should have been left to the jury. The question for the Court of Appeal was whether such a defence was also available to the lesser offence of unlawful wounding under s.20 of the Act, which is an offence of basic intent.

The Court of Appeal held that there was a difference between the failure to eat sufficient food following an injection of insulin and the consumption of drugs or alcohol. It is common knowledge that those who take alcohol to excess, or certain sorts of drugs, may become aggressive or do dangerous or unpredictable things. Yet with this knowledge they still persist in their conduct. But the same cannot be said, in general, of the person who fails to eat sufficient food after an insulin injection. The jury should have been instructed to look for recklessness. If Bailey was aware that the failure to take in sufficient food might lead to him becoming aggressive or dangerous and yet he still persisted in his conduct then this would be evidence of recklessness required by the offence of unlawful wounding. However, most people would not expect that the failure to eat sufficient food would lead to aggression and there was no evidence that Bailey was so aware. Most would probably assume that such conduct would probably lead to unconsciousness, but nothing more.

5–038   Griffiths L.J. concluded that self-induced automatism, other than that brought about by the voluntary consumption or drugs or alcohol, should be a defence even to a crime of basic intent:

> "The question in each case will be whether the prosecution have proved the necessary element of recklessness. In cases of assault, if the accused knows that his actions or inaction are likely to make him aggressive, unpredictable or uncontrolled with the result that he may cause some injury to others and he persists in the action or takes no remedial action when he knows it is required, it will be open to the jury to find that he is reckless."[200]

This approach was taken further in the case of *Hardie*[201] where H had been given some old Valium tablets by the woman with whom he was living. She had told him that they were totally harmless. Later, having consumed some of the tablets, he set fire to a bedroom while the woman and her child were in the sitting-room. He was charged with causing damage to

[198] [1983] 2 All E.R. 503; (1983) 77 Cr.App.R. 76.
[199] Offences Against the Person Act 1861 s.18.
[200] (1983) 77 Cr.App.R. 76 at 81.
[201] [1984] 3 All E.R. 848.

property being reckless as to whether life would thereby be endangered; a basic intent crime.[202] The Court of Appeal held that the *Majewski* rules only applied to alcohol and dangerous drugs. Where the drug was non-dangerous in the sense that it was not likely to cause unpredictability or aggression,[203] the defendant should be entitled to rely upon it, even in a crime of basic intent, to explain the absence of recklessness; in this case *Caldwell* recklessness. It is quite extraordinary that in determining whether or not the accused gave no thought to a serious and obvious risk, the jury may take account of the consumption of non-dangerous drugs by the defendant, but not that the defendant would have been unable to give any thought to such a risk because she suffered from a mental impairment, at least prior to revision in *R v G*.[204]

The Court of Appeal is, in effect, treating the consumption of non-dangerous drugs in the same way as involuntary intoxication. If, however, the defendant is aware that the consumption of such a drug in his case will lead to aggression or unpredictable behaviour, yet nevertheless persists in taking the drug, this will satisfy the requirement of recklessness in the Offences Against the Person Act 1861.

Summary

It would appear that the following principles can be obtained from the cases.   **5–039**

(1) Involuntary intoxication, the consumption of non-dangerous drugs and self-induced automatism not arising through voluntary intoxication may be used as evidence to show that the accused did not form the mens rea of any offence of which he is charged. There is no distinction here between basic and specific intent offences.

(2) Voluntary intoxication due to alcohol or dangerous drugs is a defence only in so far as it negatives the specific intent in crimes of specific intent. It has no relevance to other mens rea requirements in specific intent crimes and no relevance at all in crimes of basic intent.[205]

(3) Intoxication, voluntary or involuntary, is only relevant in so far as it negatives the required mens rea. It, therefore, has no relevance where liability is strict nor where liability is based upon negligence. Evidence that the intoxication caused the accused to form the mens rea or removed his inhibitions is irrelevant; a drugged intent is still an intent.

D. Insanity and Diminished Responsibility Produced by Intoxication[206]

Where the defendant's drinking brings him within the terms of the M'Naghten Rules[207] he **5–040** will be acquitted on the grounds of insanity.[208] This will mean, of course, that the court will have to be satisfied that the drinking amounted to a disease of the mind and not an external cause. If the court rules that the defence is one of insanity as opposed to intoxication it will apply to any charge, whether the offence is one of basic or specific intent. Where the

---

[202] Criminal Damage Act 1971 s.1(2)(b). Only where the prosecution relies on intention is aggravated criminal damage a specific intent crime.

[203] e.g. sedative or soporific drugs.

[204] See, above at para.2–069.

[205] Unless there is a specific statutory exception; *Jaggard v Dickinson* [1981] Q.B. 527, discussed below, para.10–016.

[206] See, e.g. G.R. Sullivan, "Intoxicants and Diminished Responsibility" [1994] Crim.L.R. 156.

[207] See above, para.5–005.

[208] *Davis* (1881) 14 Cox C.C. 563.

defendant has pleaded that he was unaware that what he had done was legally wrong, it will be a defence only if he falls within the M'Naghten Rules, otherwise such a plea is irrelevant.

The courts will be reluctant to find that excessive drinking has caused diminished responsibility.[209] However, it is possible that he could prove that he was suffering from an abnormality of mind on the basis that the effects of alcohol have injured his mind.[210] This does not totally exclude the possibility, as stated by the High Court of Justiciary in Scotland in *Finnegan v Heywood*,[211] that sleepwalking may on rare occasions be attributable to an external factor, as in the case of excessive consumption of alcohol over the course of an evening. If so regarded it would fall into the category of non-insane automatism.

E. Drinking with Intent

5–041 If the defendant formed an intention to kill his wife and then drank heavily to give himself the courage to do the deed, he would undoubtedly be guilty of murder if, when he shot his wife, he intended to kill her; the fact that the alcohol had removed his fear of doing the deed would be totally irrelevant. If, however, the alcohol did remove his mens rea, yet he still managed to kill his wife, the position might be different. Now we would have a situation where the mens rea had ceased to exist before the accused perpetrated the actus reus. However unlikely this hypothetical example is, we should be able to state how the courts would react. A similar situation would occur if the accused, having formed an intent to kill his wife, drinks a large amount of alcohol which induces a latent disease of the mind so that he is unable to appreciate the nature and quality of his acts and in this state kills his wife.

Both situations were addressed by Lord Denning in *Att-Gen for Northern Ireland v Gallagher*[212] where he said:

> "If a man, whilst sane and sober, forms an intention to kill and makes preparation for it knowing that it is a wrong thing to do, and then gets himself drunk so as to give himself Dutch courage to do the killing, and whilst drunk carries out his intention, he cannot rely on his self-induced drunkenness as a defence to a charge of murder, nor even as reducing it to manslaughter. He cannot say that he got himself into such a stupid state that he was incapable of an intent to kill. So also, when he is a psychopath, he cannot by drinking rely on his self-induced defect of reason as a defence of insanity. The wickedness of his mind before he got drunk is enough to condemn him, coupled with the act which he intended to do and did do."

In both situations envisaged by Lord Denning, there is a problem in that at the time the defendant perpetrated the actus reus he did not possess the necessary mens rea and at the time he had the mens rea, he did not bring about the actus reus. On the other hand it seems entirely reasonable to say that if a man plans to kill his wife, drinks to such an extent that he loses his ability to appreciate what he is doing and then while in this state for which he is responsible, kills his wife, he should be convicted of murder. It is almost as if he is using himself as an innocent agent.[213] A fortiori this should be the case if the defendant is aware that excessive drinking triggers in him a dangerous and aggressive pattern of behaviour.

---

[209] See above, para.5–017.
[210] *Tandy* (1989) 87 Cr.App.R. 45; see above, para.5–017 and also the decision in *Wood*.
[211] 2000 S.C. 444.
[212] [1963] A.C. 349 at 382.
[213] See, Smith and Hogan at p.236. There are also similarities to the approach taken by the majority in *Ryan*; see above, para.2–007.

The main point to remember is that if, at the time of the killing, the accused intended to kill his wife, it is irrelevant that the alcohol on its own or coupled with a latent mental condition has made it difficult for the accused to desist from his plan.

F. Proposals for Reform

Various bodies have made suggestions for reform of the law relating to intoxication and criminal liability,[214] including, on more than one occasion, the Law Commission.[215] The Commission's latest report on the subject was published in January 2009,[216] and its approach, like the 1995 Report is in favour of codification of the law "with clarification and modifications"[217] but with less complexity than the earlier Report. The Report recommends, codification which broadly reflects the different approaches currently taken by the law to offences of so-called "specific" and "basic" intent, but which makes clearer the basis for that distinction. Thus, it is proposed that certain fault elements will always need to be proved, even if the defendant is voluntarily intoxicated, but that actual subjective recklessness will not need to be proved if the relevant lack of awareness or foresight arises because of voluntary intoxication.

5–042

INTOXICATION: GENERAL READING

Gardner, S., "Criminal Defence By Judicial Discretion" (1995) 111 L.Q.R. 177.

5–043

Gardner, S., "The Importance of *Majewski*" (1984) 4 O.J.L.S. 279.

Gough, S., "Intoxication And Criminal Liability: The Law Commission's Proposed Reforms", (1996) 112 L.Q.R. 335.

Gough, S., "Surviving Without *Majewski*" [2000] Crim.L.R. 719 (see also [2001] Crim.L.R. 258 for Reply letter).

Horder, J., "Pleading Involuntary Lack of Capacity" (1993) 52 C.L.J. 298.

Orchard, G., "Surviving Without *Majewski*—A View From Down Under", [1993] Crim.L.R. 426.

Paton, E., "Reformulating The Intoxication Rules: The Law Commission Report" [1995] Crim.L.R. 382.

Robinson, P., "Causing The Conditions Of One's Own Defence" (1985) 73 Virginia L.R. 1.

Simester, A.P., "Intoxication is Never a Defence" [2009] Crim.L.R. 3.

Spencer, J.R., "Involuntary Intoxication as a Defence" (1995) 54 C.L.J. 12.

Sullivan, G.R., "Intoxicants and Diminished Responsibility" [1994] Crim.L.R. 156.

Sullivan, G.R., "Involuntary Intoxication and Beyond" [1994] Crim.L.R. 272.

Virgo, G, "The Law Commission On Intoxication And Criminal Liability" [1993] Crim.L.R. 415.

Wilson, W., "Involuntary Intoxication: Excusing the Inexcusable" (1995) 1 Res Publica 25.

3. SELF-DEFENCE, NECESSITY AND DURESS

These defences all have a common feature; they are all based on the concept of necessity. In other words the defendant is alleged to have committed a criminal offence but he pleads that he was forced to commit the offence. The three defences reflect the different ways in

5–044

---

[214] These include the Committee on Mentally Abnormal Offenders, the "Butler Committee", which reported in 1975 (Cm. 6244), the Criminal Law Revision Committee (see its Fourteenth Report, *Offences Against the Person*, (1980) Cm. 7844).

[215] See *Legislating the Criminal Code: Intoxication and Criminal Liability* (1995), Law Com. No.229.

[216] *Intoxication and Criminal Liability* (2009) Law Com. No.314.

[217] *Intoxication and Criminal Liability* (2009) Law Com. No.314 at para.1.67.

which this "force" arises. For example, suppose that D (the defendant) is a member of a mountain climbing team. As they ascend the mountain they are roped together. Ahead of D are A, B and C and behind D is E. D is alleged to have cut the rope between himself and E, sending E hurtling down the mountainside and seriously injuring him. D has been charged with causing grievous bodily harm with intent contrary to s.18 of the Offences Against The Person Act 1861.[218] If his defence was self-defence, D might, for example, plead that E had a gun and was about to shoot D, and so D cut the rope to protect himself. If the defence was duress, D might plead that both he and his family had been threatened with violence if he did not seriously injure E. If the defence was necessity, he might plead that E had slipped and was gradually pulling the others with him and so D cut the rope to protect the others. We shall see that although the concept of necessity is the basis of the well recognised defences of self-defence and duress, until recently the courts have been reluctant to admit the existence of a general defence of necessity per se.

A. Self-Defence: The Use of Force in Public and Private Defence

5–045 The following material in this section on the operation of the common law defence of self-defence has been supplemented, but we suggest, not substantively altered by s.76 of the Criminal Justice and Immigration Act 2008.[219] Section 76 merely reflects the status quo approach taken earlier by our courts. As such, it is difficult to countenance why this legislative response was needed or helpful, but it has been adumbrated that it is:

> "aimed at ensuring that those who seek to protect themselves, their loved ones and their homes, as well as other citizens, have confidence that the law is on their side."[220]

This defence operates, if raised successfully, as a *justification* for the defendant's behaviour thereby rendering it *lawful*. We have seen that a common element in offences against the person is a requirement that the use of force was unlawful. The law recognises that the use of force is sometimes justified and when this occurs, the act will not be unlawful. The best known justification for the use of force is the common law defence of self-defence. Allied to this is the defence of property, also a creation of the common law. Under s.3 of the Criminal Law Act 1967 there is a provision for the use of force in the prevention of crime and in the effecting of lawful arrests. Today it is common to refer to the common law defences as private defence and the defences under s.3 as public defence. Thus we talk of the use of force in public and private defence. It will be a defence to any crime of which the use of force is an element, or alternatively to offences alleged to have been committed by the use of force.[221] Let us suppose that X has been charged with unlawfully and maliciously inflicting grievous bodily harm on Y; he may plead one of the following factual situations by way of justification:

---

[218] See below, para.7–090.

[219] The provisions came into force on July 14, 2008. As stated, they relate to the private common law defence, but the public law defence in s.3 of the Criminal Justice Act 1967 remains unaffected.

[220] Jack Straw, Minister for Justice, 2006/2007, October 1, 2007. Note revisions were introduced at Report Stage.

[221] See, e.g. *Renouf* [1986] 2 All E.R. 449 involving reckless driving (now dangerous driving). D, peacefully working at home on the forecourt of his garage was disturbed when occupants of a Volvo motorcar threw objects at him and damaged his car windscreen. He chased after them, drew alongside the Volvo, forced it off the carriageway on to the grass verge and rammed it when it was stationary. He was charged with reckless driving. Could D rely on s.3 of the Criminal Law Act 1967 in that he was assisting in the lawful arrest of offenders, using reasonable force in the circumstances? It was held this section was capable of constituting a valid defence, D's actions, i.e. acts alleged to amount to reckless driving, formed the very constituents of the use of force under s.3. It ought to have been left to the jury to determine whether it was reasonable. No defence would be applicable where the reckless acts were antecedent to the use of force. [1986] 2 All E.R. 449 at 524 per Lawton L.J.

(i) X may say that he was trying to prevent Y from committing a crime which may or may not have involved X;

(ii) he may claim that Y was about to attack him and that he had to injure Y in order to protect himself;

(iii) he may claim that Y was about to attack a member of his family (or anyone else) and that X simply did all that was necessary to protect the would be victim;

(iv) he may claim that Y was in the process of burgling his house and that he simply used sufficient force to restrain him until the police arrived.

These factual situations cover defence of self, others, property and prevention of crime. Each is subject to the same requirement in that the force used in defence must be *reasonable* in the prevailing circumstances. It is for the prosecution to prove that there was no justification[222]; the defendant bears an evidential burden to introduce evidence of justification.

B. Prevention of Crime

This was originally covered by common law rules, but is now covered by s.3 of the Criminal Law Act 1967 which provides: **5–046**

"(1) A person may use such force as is reasonable in the circumstances in the prevention of crime, or in effecting or assisting in the lawful arrest of offenders or suspected offenders or of persons unlawfully at large."

The question of fact for the jury is to determine what force was reasonable in the circumstances of the particular case being tried. Thus, for instance, where the accused is charged with assaulting another and seeks to rely on s.3, the question for the jury is:

". . . Are we satisfied that no reasonable man (a) with knowledge of such facts as were known to the accused or [honestly] believed by him to exist (b) in the circumstances and time available to him for reflection (c) could be of the opinion that the prevention of the risk of harm to which others might be exposed if the suspect were allowed to escape, justified exposing the suspect to the risk of harm to him that might result from the kind of force that the accused contemplated using."[223]

In the above question, in para.(a) the word [honestly] has been substituted for the word "reasonably" which appeared in the original quotation. This, it is suggested, is necessary in the light of the decisions of the Court of Appeal in *Gladstone Williams*,[224] and Privy Council in *Beckford v R*,[225] on mistaken belief. The principle is illustrated by the decision of the

---

[222] See, e.g. *Chan Kau v R* [1955] A.C. 206; and *Khan* [1995] Crim.L.R. 78.

[223] *Reference under s.48A of the Criminal Appeal (Northern Ireland) Act 1968 (No.1 of 1975)* [1976] 2 All E.R. 937 at 947 per Lord Diplock. In this case D was a soldier who had shot dead a member of the public, falsely believing him to be an active member of the IRA. At issue for the jury was whether D's conduct was "reasonable in the circumstances" for the aim of crime prevention. The ambit of s.3 was considered by the House of Lords in *Jones* [2006] UKHL 16. It was held that "crime" referred to a crime as recognised by domestic law. Thus, D could not rely on s.3 as a defence to a charge of conspiracy to commit criminal damage at a military airbase, where D claimed she was seeking to prevent the *international* crime of aggression. See below, para.5–095; para.10–017.

[224] (1984) 74 Cr.App.R. 276; see above, para.2–085.

[225] [1988] A.C. 130; see above para.2–085. See generally, W. Wilson, "The Structure of Defences" [2005] Crim.L.R. 108.

Court of Appeal in *Cousins*[226] which held, that, in appropriate circumstances, it could be reasonable to threaten to kill another when, for example, it is believed that this would forestall a planned attack on oneself. Whether or not such a threat is reasonable is always a question of fact for the jury. Clearly a threat to kill may be reasonable in circumstances where the implementation of such a threat would not be.

What then, if the accused was mistaken in thinking that the man he assaulted was about to commit a crime? Suppose that X was drinking in a bar when he saw Y pick up a broken glass and wave it menacingly in front of Z. It would not be unreasonable for X to suppose that Y meant to harm Z and for him to take action to prevent such injury to Z. However, it turns out that Y was just telling Z of an incident which had happened in the bar on the previous evening. Lord Diplock's statement would indicate that the jury must consider the facts as they were known to X or as he honestly believed them to be. Thus, in our example, if the jury considers that X honestly thought that Y was about to attack Z, they should proceed to consider whether on the facts X believed to exist it was reasonable for him to have acted in the way he did.[227]

C. Self-defence and Defence of Others

5–047 In many cases where the accused pleads self-defence the situation could be covered by s.3 in that if the accused's story is correct he is merely trying to prevent the other man from committing a crime, namely attacking the accused. This is, however, not necessarily so. If D is attacked by a child he knows to be below the age of criminal responsibility then he cannot say that the force he used on the child to stop the attack was force used in the prevention of crime. He would, however, be able to rely on the common law defence of self-defence. It is clear that the common law defence of self-defence survives s.3, but since the area of overlap is, to all intents and purposes, total, it would be absurd if the common law defence were to be governed by principles different from those controlling s.3. It is, therefore, submitted that where the accused, who is charged with an offence against the person, relies on the common law defence of self-defence, the court will approach the question in the same way as a defence raised under s.3. In this regard, if the mistake in either public or private defence is caused by intoxication, then D will have no defence.[228] Self-defence will, however, be available to render conduct lawful where D mistakenly applies force to a police officer or court official which would otherwise be reasonable if that person were not an officer.[229]

Self-defence is perhaps rather a narrow term to describe the defence since it applies to force used to protect members of the accused's family, his friends or even a total stranger he sees being unlawfully attacked.[230] This point is illustrated by the case of *Duffy*[231] wherein it was determined that a woman could justifiably use reasonable force to prevent her sister being attacked. This force was necessary in the prevailing circumstances, it was no less necessary just because it was a family member under attack since, "there is a general liberty as between strangers to prevent a felony."[232] In each case, the question should be the same, "did he use such force as he believed to be reasonable in the circumstances as he knew them to be or honestly believed them to be?"

---

[226] [1982] Q.B. 526. Note that D may not have used the force personally. For example, see *Pollard v Chief Constable of West Yorkshire* [1999] P.I.Q.R. 219 (use of highly trained police alsatian dog to effect an arrest).
[227] See below, paras 5–052—5–055, for problems relating to the case of excessive force.
[228] See, e.g. *O'Grady* [1987] Q.B. 995; [1987] 3 All E.R. 420; above, para.5–033.
[229] See, e.g. *Blackburn v Bowering* [1984] 3 All E.R. 380.
[230] *Rose* (1884) 15 Cox C.C. 540.
[231] [1967] 1 Q.B. 63.
[232] Ormerod, op. cit., at p.367.

(i) Duty to Retreat?

The old cases on self-defence established that the accused who sought to rely on self-defence **5–048** had to show that he retreated as far as was safely possible before using serious force. In *Bird*,[233] however, Lord Lane C.J. made it perfectly clear that it was not an essential part of the defence that the accused had demonstrated by her actions that she did not want to fight. The law, he said, had been correctly stated by Smith and Hogan to the effect that:

> "A demonstration by D at the time that he did not want to fight is, no doubt, the best evidence that he was acting reasonably and in good faith in self-defence, but it is no more than that. A person may, in some circumstances so act without temporising, disengaging or withdrawing; and he should have a good defence."[234]

In essence, the duty to retreat is not a prerequisite for the application of the defence but will be a factor in the jury equation as to whether D's use of force was necessary and reasonable. Suppose that the accused is standing at a bar when the man next to him suggests that if he does not want a beer glass rammed in his face he should go and drink elsewhere. If the accused were seriously to injure the man who made the threats, then it would be open for the jury to take the view that this was unreasonable in the circumstances since he could simply have walked away, however undignified that course of action may have seemed. The possibility of retreat should be treated in the same way as the proportionality rule in provocation.[235] The issue of proportionality was central in the recent case of *Rashford*.[236] D had instigated a dispute with P who responded with violence, and acting in self defence D killed P. The appellate court concluded that a defence was still operative, even against a provoked attack created by D's own blameworthy conduct, but only if the escalated violence in P's response was disproportionate to D's initial actions.

(ii) Restriction to Imminent Violence

It is sometimes said that the defence is available only against imminent violence, which **5–049** implies that it cannot be used against violence which will occur sometime in the future. Again this should be regarded as a question affecting the reasonableness of the accused's action. Clearly, if A has been kidnapped by B and he knows B will kill him if a ransom is not paid in so many hours, it should be permissible for A to use force against B to prevent the future killing. On the other hand if the facts were different and A has the opportunity of putting the matter in the hands of the police before B carries out his threats, then the use of violence by A against B may be seen as unreasonable and this in turn may be evidence that A did not in fact believe his actions to be reasonable.

Normally self-defence describes a situation in which X has been attacked by Y and takes action to defend itself. There may, however, be situations in which it will be justified to take pre-emptive action. In *Finch and Jardine*[237] two police officers approached a car in which they believed was an armed man who was extremely dangerous. It was held that in such situations it may be unreasonable for the police officers to wait for the suspect to shoot first.

It is not a requirement that the act of self-defence need be spontaneous; preparatory activities to justifiable acts of self-defence may be permissible in some circumstances. For

---

[233] [1985] 2 All E.R. 513.
[234] [1985] 2 All E.R. 513 at 516. See J.C. Smith and B. Hogan *Criminal Law* 5th edn (1983) at p.327. Note civil damages may now be recoverable against D where he acts negligently in public or private defence, but these may be reduced by V's contributory negligence; see *Revill v Newbery* [1996] 2 W.L.R. 239.
[235] See below, para.7–020.
[236] [2005] EWCA Crim 3377; [2006] Crim.L.R. 547.
[237] Unreported, 1983.

example, in *Attorney-General's Reference (No.2 of 1983)*[238] the Court of Appeal held that it might be justifiable for a man to make and possess a petrol bomb, an act which would normally be an offence, where this was done to protect his family or property by way of self-defence against an imminent and apprehended attack. If, however, he continued to possess the bomb after the threat had passed, his possession would no longer be justified. A correlation exists here with the defence of duress of circumstances, restricted to where D's will is overborne by threats of death or serious injury, and where a corresponding duty to desist operates once the threat is no longer operative.[239]

5–050   Self-defence will be inapplicable where D has personally created the situation of danger. This is illustrated by *Malnik v DPP*,[240] where D and three others set out to pay a visit to J., who they believed had stolen cars belonging to a friend. J was known to have a tendency to violent and irresponsible behaviour. D armed himself with a rice flail for the purpose of self-defence, a weapon used in connection with martial arts; it was tucked into the waistband of his trousers. He was arrested before he reached J's house. D contended that he was justified in carrying the weapon since he was fearful of being attacked. This was rejected by the Court of Appeal who concluded that the risk of violence could have been avoided, and thus the need to carry weapons, by inviting the appropriate agency to repossess the cars by the usual means. In effect, as it was D who had created the situational source of danger, the defence was negated. The principle that an individual cannot be driven off the streets and compelled not to go to a place where he might lawfully be because of the danger of confrontation by people intending to attack him, established by a serious of case precedents,[241] is consequentially more circumscribed. If it is not safe to go to that place except by possessing an offensive weapon it seems D must not take this hazardous step.[242]

It is unclear to what extent self-defence (and also public defence) applies to offences other than those involving the use of force. Although the justifications are generally raised in relation to charges of offences against the person, they are not restricted to such offences, as illustrated by *Renouf*,[243] a case of reckless driving, where on the facts of that case the circumstances encompassing the offence involved the use of force.[244] It has been suggested that the defence ought to be widened beyond the use of force criterion:

"... [A]cts immediately preparatory to public or private defence are better regarded as justified or excused by those defences ... The fears of the courts regarding a general defence of necessity probably militate against a recognition that public and private defence may constitute a defence to crime generally; but, where contravention of *any* law is (i) necessary to enable the right of public or private defence to be exercised, and (ii) reasonable in the circumstances, it ought to be excused. It is open to the courts to move in this direction."[245]

D. Defence of Property

5–051   Again this is probably covered sufficiently by s.3 of the Criminal Law Act 1967 and, thus, the same principles should apply; was the force used by D to protect his property reasonable in the circumstances? Can it ever be reasonable to kill in order to defend your property? The

---

[238] [1984] Q.B. 456.
[239] See below, at para.5–093.
[240] [1989] Crim.L.R. 451.
[241] See, e.g. *Beatty v Gillbanks* (1882) 9 Q.B.D. 308; *R v Fegan* [1972] N.I. 80; and *Evans v Hughes* [1972] 1 W.L.R. 1452.
[242] J.C. Smith, "Case Comment" [1989] Crim.L.R. 451, 452.
[243] [1986] 2 All E.R. 449.
[244] Above, para.5–045, fn.221.
[245] J.C. Smith and B. Hogan, *Criminal Law,* 8th edn (London: Butterworths, 1996) at p.268.

old case of *Hussey*[246] said that this was permissible, but with modern means of legal redress for the dispossessed householder it is inconceivable that this applies today. Where D is charged with perpetrating criminal damage, not an offence against the person, in protection of his property then the issue is regulated by the statutory provisions contained in the Criminal Damage Act 1971.[247] The protection of property issue arose in *Faraj*[248] before the Court of Appeal. D had threatened and detained an entrant into his property with a knife, believing that the individual was a burglar. It transpired that V was a gas repair man. Their Lordships held where D acted out of a genuinely held belief in an honest fashion,[249] and the detention was conducted reasonably, then the defence was operative.

E. Excessive Force

Now that we have looked at the various forms of public and private defence, we can turn to **5–052** a problem that has been hinted at in the preceding sections. We have seen that if the accused mistakenly believes that there is a need for force, he will be able to rely on the defence provided that he used only so much force as was reasonable in the circumstances he believed to exist. Thus, if the accused rightly believes X is about to attack him, but wrongly, though honestly, believes that X plans to use a knife, the amount of force which would be reasonable will be assessed on the facts the accused believed to exist. But the more difficult problem is the one in which the amount of force used was unreasonable even in the circumstances he believed to exist.

Two types of problem may arise here. First, X believes that he is about to be attacked by Y and reasonably decides to shoot Y in the leg as he approaches. Unfortunately, his aim is bad and Y is killed. If X is charged with murder, the first thing to remember is that the prosecution must prove that X had the necessary mens rea. That aside, the jury should be asked to consider the reasonableness of what the accused contemplated doing. In our case, they should ask whether it was reasonable for X to try to shoot Y in the legs to prevent the attack.

Secondly, X believes that poachers are taking trout from his lake during the night. He, therefore, lies in wait with a 12-bore shotgun and when he sees Y taking trout from the lake he shoots at him and kills him. In other words, we have a situation in which the jury would probably have sanctioned the use of some force, but not the killing of Y. Where does X stand now? Does this finding mean that he has no defence at all? The problem is only likely to be acute in the cases where the charge is murder, since in all other cases, if it is held that excessive use of force means that the defence fails, the judge can take the facts into account when passing sentence. However, where the accused is charged with murder, if the defence fails the accused will be convicted of murder, if the prosecution establishes the necessary mens rea, in which case D receives life imprisonment.

The two points raised above have been the subject of recent significant case law developments considered below.

(i) Mistake of Fact and the Objective Approach to Excessive Force

The private and public defences are predicated on establishing that the force used is such as **5–053** is necessary and reasonable in the circumstances. These criteria, adopting proportionality, derive from the Report of the Royal Commission appointed to consider the law relating to indictable offences:

---

[246] (1924) 18 Cr.App.R. 160.
[247] Note that s.5 of the Criminal Damage Act 1971 allows property to be destroyed or damaged in the defence of other property; see below, para.10–015.
[248] [2007] EWCA Crim 1033.
[249] See *Gladstone Williams* (1984) 78 Cr.App.R. 276; discussed below at para.5–053 and above at para.2–085.

"We take one great principle of the common law to be, that although it sanctions the defence of a man's person, liberty and property against illegal violence, and permits the use of force to prevent crimes, to preserve the public peace, and to bring offenders to justice, yet all this is subject to the restriction that the force used is necessary; that is, that the mischief sought to be prevented could not be prevented by less violent means; and that the mischief done by, or which might reasonably be anticipated from the force used is not disproportionate to the injury or mischief which it is intended to prevent."[250]

Who decides this proportionality test (accused, judge or jury) where D, operating under a mistaken belief as to the prevailing circumstances, uses excessive force in private or public defence? Do we apply subjective or objective principles to this dilemma?[251] The matter has been the subject of an important decision by the Court of Appeal in *Owino,*[252] rejecting the earlier approach of Beldam L.J. in *Scarlett.*[253] In *Owino*, D was convicted on two counts of assaulting his wife occasioning her actual bodily harm under s.47 of the Offences Against the Person Act 1861 (injuries to her thumb and her head). D contended that any injuries his wife had sustained through his actions were caused by reasonable force used to restrain her and to stop her from assaulting him. No direction was given to the jury on self-defence until, about an hour-and-a-half after retiring, they sent a note that, in practical terms, asked for such a direction. The judge then directed them on the issue to the effect that the prosecution must prove that the defendant did not believe that *he* was using unreasonable force, a test derived from *Scarlett*. On appeal, it was argued that the judge inadequately directed the jury on self-defence, by reason of (a) his failure to state that the test of what force was reasonable was subjective, and (b) the delay of an hour-and-a-half before the direction was given.

Essentially, the case involved consideration of the issue central to any successful self-defence plea, focusing on the reasonableness of the force used by the accused. It was held by the Court of Appeal in *Gladstone Williams*, and by the Board of the Privy Council in *Beckford* that, at common law, an individual does not commit an offence by using force which is reasonable in the circumstances as he, reasonably or unreasonably, believes them to be, in defence of himself or any other person.[254] The accused was entitled to be acquitted if he mistakenly believed that he was justified in using force. Even if the jury came to the conclusion that the mistake was an unreasonable one, if the defendant may honestly have been labouring under it, he was entitled to rely upon it. Of course, the more unreasonable the mistake then the more unlikely it is that the jury will believe him. Clearly a subjective test is applied as to whether D believes he is under attack given the prevailing circumstances.

5–054   However, it was established prior to the decision in *Scarlett* that an objective test was applied to D's reaction to the threat, requiring the force used to be necessary and proportionate to prevent the harm which D believed was threatened. Whether the force used was reasonable in the circumstances, which D believed to exist, was a matter for the determination of the jury, an objective standard being applied, so that acts beyond the necessity of the occasion imposed liability. The objective standard of reasonableness would be relaxed to reflect the anxiety of the situation in which the defendant acted. As Lord Morris stated in *Palmer v R*:

---

[250] (1879) 36 HL Papers 157 at 167, para.11.
[251] See, generally, A. Reed, "Self-Defence—Applying The Objective Approach To Reasonable Force" (1996) 60 J.C.L. 94; and S. Parish, "Self-Defence: The Wrong Direction?" [1997] Crim.L.R. 201.
[252] [1995] Crim.L.R. 743; and see also *DPP v Armstrong-Braun* (1998) 163 J.P. 271.
[253] [1993] 4 All E.R. 629.
[254] See above, para.2–085. A series of cases has followed this approach. See, e.g. *Jackson* [1985] R.T.R. 257; *Asbury* [1986] Crim.L.R. 258; and *Fisher* [1987] Crim.L.R. 334.

"If there has been attack so that defence is reasonably necessary it will be recognised that a person defending himself cannot weigh to a nicety the exact measure of his necessary defensive action. If a jury thought that in a moment of unexpected anguish a person attacked had only done what he honestly and instinctively thought was necessary that would be most potent evidence that only reasonable defensive action had been taken."[255]

Thus, *Palmer* holds that the fact that D believed himself to be acting reasonably constitutes "most potent evidence" that he was doing so, albeit that the jury objectively determines whether the force used was both necessary and proportionate to prevent the harm. A directly contrary approach seemed to be adopted in *Scarlett*, supporting the subjectivist position on criminal liability. In *Scarlett*, D, the landlord of a public house, was convicted of unlawful act manslaughter following his use of force to eject the victim who had entered the public house after closing time, and the worse for drink. In directing the jury the trial judge stated that if *the jury* concluded that D had used more force than was necessary in the circumstances in the bar, and if *they* were satisfied that had caused the deceased to fall and strike his head, D was guilty of manslaughter. That was held by the Court of Appeal to be a misdirection. The court ordained that not only is D to be judged on facts as he believed them to be but that even if the jury concludes that the force was excessive on those facts, D is entitled to an acquittal if he honestly believed that the circumstances called for the degree of force he used even if his belief was unreasonable. Beldam L.J. concluded by asserting that:

"Further [the jury] should be directed that the accused is not to be found guilty merely because he intentionally or recklessly used force which they consider to have been excessive. They ought not to convict him unless they are satisfied that the degree of force used was plainly more than was called for by the circumstances as he believed them to be *and, provided he believed the circumstances called for the degree of force used, he is not to be convicted even if his belief was unreasonable* (emphasis added)."[256]

It seemed, according to *Scarlett*, that D could justify the most extravagant actions provided he subjectively believed the circumstances warranted it. The decision seems to elevate D's belief as to the circumstances giving rise to the need for self-defence from "potent evidence" to an overreaching new substantive defence.[257] However, it is now evident from *Owino*, as subsequently followed in *DPP v Armstrong-Braun*,[258] that this totally subjective approach is unsound, and the prevailing orthodox principles established in *Palmer v R* and *Gladstone Williams* are to be followed.

The defendant's appeal was rejected in *Owino*. Their Lordships asserted that when read in **5–055** context and properly understood, Beldam L.J. in *Scarlett* was not saying that a person was entitled to use any degree of force he believed to be reasonable, however ill-founded the belief. Possibly a kind way of inviting courts quietly to forget it. The law was as set out by Lord Lane L.J. in *Gladstone Williams* which was referred to in *Scarlett*: *a person may use such force as is (objectively) reasonable, determinable by a jury, in the circumstances as he*

---

[255] [1971] A.C. 814 at 832. There is no imposed requirement demanding exact proportionality. See, e.g. *Rivolta* [1994] Crim.L.R. 694; and *Oatridge* (1991) 94 Cr.App.R. 367—look to whether D's actions were commensurate with the degree of danger created by the attack.
[256] [1993] 4 All E.R. 629 at 636.
[257] See, generally, B. Hogan, "Defence of Property" [1991] N.L.J. 466.
[258] (1998) 163 J.P. 271; and see further recent confirmation in *Drane* [2009] Crim.L.R. 202.

(subjectively) believes them to be. It followed that the trial judge's direction actually went further in the defence's favour than the law required. Hence, it seems that we must now take it that *Scarlett* added nothing to the law as stated in *Gladstone Williams* vis-à-vis jury determination of necessary and reasonable force in the circumstances. This is reaffirmed by the later decision in *Hughes*,[259] provided by the very same Beldam L.J., to the effect that a defendant cannot simply rely on his estimation of reasonable force. This is eminently logical; it is fallacious to allow D the most extravagant claims provided he believes the circumstances warranted it.

In relation to mistaken belief the principle established in *Dadson*[260] is applicable. In a scenario where D does not himself believe that he is acting reasonably in self-defence or prevention of crime, but circumstances exist which, if he knew of them, would justify his use of force, D cannot take advantage of the unknown circumstances as a justification. Consider, for example, a situation where D, wishing to kill V, arranges to meet him at the top of a multi-storey building. D plans to push V off the top of the building, then claim that he acted in self-defence. However, unknown to D, a similar evil motive is possessed by V who plans to murder D by shooting him dead with a handgun concealed in his coat pocket. Suppose that before V has an opportunity to press the trigger D pushes him to his death off the top of the building. In such a hypothetical situation D cannot rely on the unknown circumstances as a justification. He did not act in self-defence for the purpose of resisting an unlawful attack upon himself, he was in fact entirely ignorant of such an attack.[261] D will be liable for the murder of V.

(ii) Murder and the Use of Excessive Force in Self-defence and Prevention of Crime

5–056   The hypothetical scenario presented above, para.5–052, in relation to the trout lake, addresses the inter-relationship between murder and the use of excessive force in self-defence/prevention of crime. The issue arose before the House of Lords in *Clegg*.[262] The case of Pte Lee Clegg, who was sentenced to life imprisonment for the murder of Karen Reilly, has attracted much media attention because it involved the killing by a member of the security forces in Northern Ireland of an unarmed civilian in circumstances which led many to believe that murder was an inappropriate label for the killing. In brief, the facts were that Clegg had been on patrol with some 14 other soldiers and a police officer. The purpose of the mission was to look for joy riders, although it would appear that this was not explained to Clegg. A car approached the checkpoint and ignored a request to stop. It sped towards Clegg and another soldier, Pte Aindow, with its headlights full on. Clegg fired three shots through the windscreen as the car approached, but a fourth bullet was allegedly fired by Clegg when the car had travelled some 50 feet past Clegg. The bullet ended up in the back of a rear seat passenger, Karen Reilly, and was a substantial cause of her death.

At his trial before a judge sitting without a jury, the court accepted that Clegg fired the first three shots to protect either himself or his colleagues from injury. This could not be the explanation of the firing of the fourth shot. He admitted that he had no reason to think that the car was full of terrorists on their way to carry out terrorist offences and that he had no

---

[259] [1995] Crim.L.R. 957. Note that references to *R. v Clegg* in this section all relate to this judgment; but subsequently there was a retrial, after the Court of Appeal in Northern Ireland held that new evidence suggesting that Clegg may not have fired when the car had passed the patrol after all was "capable of belief": *Guardian*, February 28, 1998. Clegg, in March 1999, was cleared of murder.

[260] [1850] 175 E.R. 499; [1850] 14 J.P. 754; considered above, para.2–002. See, generally, B. Hogan, "The *Dadson* Principle" [1989] Crim.L.R. 679.

[261] See, generally, W. Wilson, *Criminal Law* (Longman, 1998) at p.67.

[262] [1995] 1 A.C. 482; [1995] 1 All E.R. 334. See generally, P. Seago, "Criminal Law" [1995] All E.R. Annual Review 149 at 156.

reason to fire once the car had passed himself and Aindow. It was, at best, a case of an escaping criminal and the use of an automatic weapon aimed to kill or cause serious bodily harm was grossly disproportionate to the danger. The trial judge had no option but to convict Clegg of murder and this conviction was upheld by the Court of Appeal. The Court of Appeal, however, held that since there was some evidence that Clegg might have fired the fourth shot to stop the car after it had injured Aindow, the trial judge should have considered whether he was acting in public defence. The following important question was certified for the House of Lords:

> "Where a soldier or police officer in the course of his duty kills a person by firing a shot with the intention of killing or seriously wounding that person and the firing is in self-defence or in defence of another person, or in the prevention of crime, or in effecting or assisting in the lawful arrest of offenders or suspected offenders or of persons unlawfully at large, but constitutes force which is excessive and unreasonable in the circumstances, is he guilty of manslaughter and not murder?"

On the facts of *Clegg* no question of excessive force used in self-defence or defence of another arose, since Clegg admitted that once the car had gone past there was no longer any danger to himself or to Pte Aindow. Nevertheless, the House felt that it should examine the law in relation to self-defence since it formed the background to the other issues. The unanimous judgment, that of Lord Lloyd, was a reaffirmation of the generally accepted approach of the English courts. Despite the development of a half-way house approach in the Australian case of *Howe*,[263] in which a killing would be reduced from murder to manslaughter when a plea of self-defence was rejected because the accused had used excessive force, the Privy Council in *Palmer v R*,[264] and the Court of Appeal in *McInnes*[265] held that either a plea of self-defence succeeded or it failed; there was no half-way position.[266] This approach has been strengthened by the fact that the Australian courts have now turned their backs on *Howe* because jurors were finding its application too complex. In *Zekevic v DPP (Victoria)*[267] the High Court decided to revert to the law as stated in *Palmer v R*. The effect of the decisions, in *Palmer v R* and *McInnes*, which now receive the approval of the House of Lords, is that where the defendant relies upon the use of force in self-defence, that force must be reasonable and whether it is or not is a question to be determined by the tribunal of fact. If it can be proved that he intended to defend himself by killing or seriously injuring the assailant and this is considered by the tribunal of fact to be excessive, he must be convicted of murder. If the force is not considered excessive he will be acquitted completely. Of course, as Lord Lloyd pointed out, the verdict may be reduced from murder to manslaughter on other grounds. This would be the case, for example, if the prosecution were to fail to negative provocation, where it arose, or were to fail to prove the requisite intent for murder. But so far as self-defence is concerned, it is all or nothing. The defence either succeeds or it fails.

Lord Lloyd went on to confirm that since there was such a large overlap between the use **5–057** of force in self-defence and the use of force to prevent crime or arrest offenders, the degree of permissible force should be the same under the common law and s.3. Any alteration in

[263] (1958) 100 C.L.R. 448.
[264] [1971] 1 All E.R. 1077.
[265] [1971] 3 All E.R. 295.
[266] A form of half-way house will be created if the relevant provisions of the Coroners and Justice Bill, currently before Parliament, come into force. The Bill proposes a defence of "loss of control" which is principally designed as a reform to the defence of provocation. See para.7–035 below. However, one of the "qualifying triggers" for the offence is "D's fear of serious violence from V against D or another identified person" (cl.45(3)), which will reduce murder to manslaughter in what would now be viewed as excessive force in self-defence and hence murder.
[267] [1987] 162 C.L.R. 645.

the law relating to excessive force was a matter for Parliament not judicial legislation.[268] Lord Lloyd's reference, *en passant*, to parliamentary intervention over this issue simply mirrors the previous approach by Viscount Dilhorne, who asserted in *Attorney-General for Northern Ireland's Reference (No.1 of 1975)* that:

> "If a plea of self-defence is put forward in answer to a charge of murder and fails because excessive force was used though some force was justifiable, as the law now stands the accused cannot be convicted of manslaughter. It may be that a strong case can be made for an alteration of the law to enable a verdict of manslaughter to be returned where the use of some force was justifiable but that is a matter for legislation and not for judicial decision."[269]

Lord Lloyd concluded that on the law as it stood the trial judge regrettably had no option but to convict Clegg of murder. The only question remaining was whether the House of Lords should alter the law so as to permit a conviction for manslaughter in these circumstances. It has often been said that the issue of the use of excessive force is bound up with the existence of the mandatory life sentence for murder. It is, however, a separate question. As with killings under provocation, the first question is whether such killings should be classified or stigmatised as murder or something else. Even if the trial judge had flexibility in his sentencing powers for murder, we still need to ask whether a killing perpetrated under provocation or involving the use of excessive force in self-defence should result in a conviction for murder or whether it should be something less. In the second place, it is not entirely clear that a half-way house would be generally welcomed. At present, where a person uses force to defend himself from attack, there is every chance that a jury[270] will be very sympathetic towards the defendant and that he will be completely acquitted. The existence of compromise in the form of a possible conviction for manslaughter might well stand in the way of a complete acquittal.

In this context it is suggested that the outcome in the *Martin*[271] case was atypical, and was peculiar to the facts therein. The original murder verdict against Tony Martin was seized on by politicians and commentators alike as the case became a *cause célèbre* for those who believed that the law had been tilted too far in favour of the criminal. Martin was convicted of murdering a 16 year-old engaged on a burglarious intrusion into his ramshackle and deserted farmhouse in Norfolk, and of wounding another burglar with an illegally held pump-action shotgun.[272] On appeal, the appellate court have determined that extant principles on "reasonable force" and "excessive force" remain unaltered, and no explicit set of guidelines on any "reasonable force" criteria should be promulgated by trial judges to juries.[273] However, Martin's appeal against the original murder conviction was accepted on the ground of diminished responsibility. Lord Woolf said he was satisfied that fresh evidence presented during the appeal showing that Martin had a paranoid personality disorder would have led to the original trial jury finding him guilty of manslaughter by reason of diminished responsibility. Lord Woolf asserted:

> "Mr Martin was entitled to use reasonable force to protect himself and his home, but the jury were surely correct in coming to their judgment that Mr Martin was not acting

---

[268] See below, para.5–060, for consideration of developments in this area.
[269] [1977] A.C. 105 at 148.
[270] *Clegg* was tried by judge alone.
[271] [2002] Crim.L.R. 136. Martin was originally convicted in April 2000.
[272] He was sentenced to life for murder and ten years in prison for wounding with intent.
[273] See [2002] Crim.L.R. 136.

reasonably in shooting one of the intruders dead and seriously injuring the other. We must make it clear that an extremely dangerous weapon cannot be used in the manner in which it was used by Mr Martin that night."

In other situations the use of deadly force, lacking the apparently premeditated elements of the *Martin* case, may still lead to an outright acquittal of a defendant. It remains for the jury (often householders themselves), as representatives of the public, to decide the amount of force which is reasonable or unreasonable to use in the circumstances in which they found the defendant believed himself to be in.

In deciding whether a defendant had used reasonable force in self-defence it is not **5–058** appropriate, as stated by the Court of Appeal in *Martin*, to take into account the fact that he was suffering from some psychiatric condition (such as paranoid personality disorder), except in exceptional circumstances which would make such evidence especially probative. This mirrors novel recent developments with the defence of provocation in *Holley, Mohammed (Faqir)* and *James and Karimi*,[274] where it has been determined that the jury are not entitled to take into account some characteristics (such as clinical depression), whether temporary or permanent, which affect the degree of control which society could reasonably expect of a defendant. It, however, contradicts the position in relation to duress which applies to virtually all crimes except murder and is a complete defence. In *Martin (David Paul)*,[275] for example, psychiatric evidence was admitted that D was suffering from a schizoid affective disorder which made him more likely than a normal person to regard things said as threatening and to believe that threats would be carried out. It is difficult to see why the same perspective should not similarly apply to private defence. Overall there is a palpable need to clarify the legitimate ambit of our laws on duress, provocation and private defence, which all raise issues on the importance of the defendant's personal characteristics but lack consistency of treatment.

In general, the vagueness of the "reasonable force" test has adventitious benefits. The inherent flexibility allows for appropriate responses to deal with novel situations that would be precluded by a more rigid template. Indeed, the avenue presented by the defence of private defence may have been further widened by the recent decision of a strong Board of the Privy Council in *Shaw (Norman) v R*.[276] It was held that the jury must have regard not only to the circumstances as D believed them to be but also to the consequent *danger* as he believed it to be. If subsequently followed it appears to open up consideration of medical evidence relating to D's personal characteristics pertaining to his judgment as to the degree of danger involved.

(iii) Onus on the Judge

It should be reiterated that where the defendant pleads the justification of private or public **5–059** defence then the onus is on the prosecution to disprove it beyond reasonable doubt. If the Crown fails to do so it will be because the defendant's use of force is *lawful*. These principles were asserted by Lord Griffiths in *Beckford v R*:

"It is because it is an essential element of all crimes of violence that the violence or the threat of violence should be unlawful that self-defence, if raised as an issue in a criminal trial, must be disproved by the prosecution. If the prosecution fail to do so the accused is entitled to be acquitted because the prosecution will have failed to prove an

---

[274] See below at para.7–033 for full discussion.
[275] [2000] 2 Cr.App.R. 42; and see below, para.5–087.
[276] [2002] Crim.L.R. 140.

essential element of the crime namely that the violence used by the accused was unlawful."[277]

What is the position where self-defence is not raised by the defence but prima facie arises on the facts? In such a case is an onus imposed on the judge to give an appropriate jury direction on the defence? This very issue arose for determination in *DPP (Jamaica) v Bailey*[278] before the Board of the Privy Council. D, a special constable in Jamaica, had an altercation with V, his brother, and other young men in the street. The following day D met the deceased and his brother, and shot the deceased dead. He was charged with murder. It was the defence case that there had been a struggle in which the brothers had tried to take D's gun away from him and that D had fired a shot accidentally. The alternative defence was provocation. The issue of self-defence was not raised by the defence. In his summing-up the judge specifically withdrew the issue of self-defence from the jury. D was acquitted of murder but convicted of manslaughter. The appeal was based on the ground that the jury ought to have been directed on self-defence.

Their Lordships held that if the shooting was deliberate then it was necessary to consider whether the shot had been fired by way of self-defence. It followed that self-defence arose on the facts even though it had not been raised by the defence and accordingly the jury should have been directed to consider the issue. Since the judge had not given such a direction the conviction for manslaughter could not stand. The guiding principles, relied on in *Bailey*, were contained in *Bonnick* where the Court of Appeal said:

> "When is evidence sufficient to raise an issue, for example, self-defence, fit to be left to a jury? The question is one for the trial judge to answer by applying common sense to the evidence in the particular case. We do not think it right to go further in this case than to state our view that self-defence should be left to the jury when there is evidence sufficiently strong to raise a prima facie case of self-defence if it is accepted. To invite the jury to consider self-defence upon evidence which does not reach this standard would be to invite speculation. It is plain that there may be evidence of self-defence even though a defendant asserts that he was not present, and in so far as the judge told the jury the contrary, he was in error . . ."[279]

It is clear that perfectly hopeless defences which have no factual basis of support do not have to be left to the jury. But is it no less clear, in their Lordships' view, that if the accused's account of what happened includes matters which, if accepted, could raise a prima facie case of self-defence this should be left to the jury, even if the accused has not formally relied upon self-defence.[280]

F. Summary

5–060   The same principles underpin defence of self, others, property or prevention of crime. They share the same requirement that force used is such as is *reasonable* in the circumstances. It has now been established following *Owino,* which clarifies *Scarlett,* that while the defendant

---

[277] [1988] A.C. 130 at 144.
[278] [1995] 1 Cr.App.R. 257.
[279] (1978) 66 Cr.App.R. 266 at 269 per Stephenson L.J.
[280] Even where D specifically requests the judge not to mention self-defence, as it may conflict with the main defence contention, it is incumbent upon the judge to leave the matter to the jury. A corollary exists here with the provocation defence, considered below, para.7–019, in that D may not wish to harm his assertion that he acted in self-defence by putting forward evidence of provocation. Nonetheless where evidence exists that D may have been provoked to lose his self-control then the judge *must* give the jury a direction on provocation; see, e.g. *Newell* (1980) 71 Cr.App.R. 331 and *Dhillon* [1997] Crim.L.R. 295.

is judged according to what he believed the circumstances to be, he will only be able to claim the benefit of this defence if he has acted (objectively) reasonably in the light of those circumstances. It is not for the defendant himself to determine unilaterally the reasonableness of the actions that he takes to prevent crime, because that would unfairly and incorrectly exculpate defendants who had an irresponsible or illogical notion of the extent to which it is legitimate to use force to prevent crime.

In *Clegg*, the very issue which the House of Lords considered was whether current law allows a verdict of manslaughter instead of murder where the force used in self-defence is excessive. Their Lordships, applying *Palmer v R* and *McInnes,* viewed the matter as settled and were not prepared to change the law, regarding it as a matter purely for Parliament. A specially appointed Interdepartmental Steering Group established by the Home Secretary to review this area, against a background of media publicity attached to the *Clegg* decision, has not come down strongly in favour of the need for parliamentary reform.[281] In light of the furore surrounding the *Martin* case a number of proposals were laid before Parliament for reform. They have all come to nothing and our basic law remains unaltered. However, in 2005 a Joint Public Statement was issued from the Crown Prosecution Service and the Association of Chief Police Officers on *Guidance published on the use of force by householders against intruders.*[282] The guiding proposition is:

> "So long as you only do what you *honestly and instinctively* believe is necessary in the heat of the moment, that would be the strongest evidence of you (a householder) acting lawfully in self-defence. As a general rule, the more extreme the circumstances and fear felt, the more force you can lawfully use in self-defence."[283]

The Joint Statement is reflective of current thinking that no reform of self-defence is needed, and the "reasonable force" criterion remains unaltered.[284]

As a final point it ought to be repeated that in the light of *Bailey* a presumptive duty appears to exist on a judge to give an appropriate jury direction on self-defence. This occurs if the accused's account of what happened includes matters which, if accepted, could raise a prima facie case of self-defence, even if the accused has not formally relied upon self-defence.

GENERAL READING

Clarkson, C.M.V., "Necessary Action: A New Defence" [2004] Crim.L.R. 81.   **5–061**
Elliott, D.W., "Necessity, Duress And Self-Defence" [1989] Crim.L.R. 611.
Hogan, B., "Defence Of Property" (1994) N.L.J. 466.
Jefferson, M., "Householders And The Use of Force Against Intruders" (2005) 69 J.C.L. 405.
Lanham, D., "Offensive Weapons and Self-Defence" [2005] Crim.L.R. 85.
Leverick, F., "Defending Self-Defence" (2007) 27 *Oxford Journal of Legal Studies* 563.
Parish, S., "Self-Defence: The Wrong Direction?" [1997] Crim.L.R. 201.
Pichhadze, A., "Proposals for Reforming the Law of Self-Defence" (2008) 72 J.C.L. 409.
Quick, O., and Wells, C., "Getting Tough with Defences" [2006] Crim.L.R. 511.

---

[281] See, e.g. *The Report of the Inter-Departmental Review of the Law on the Use of Lethal Force in Self-Defence or the Prevention of Crime* (Home Office, 1996).
[282] Accessible at *http://www.cps.gov.uk/publications/prosecution/householders.html.*
[283] See, generally, M. Jefferson, "Householders and the Use of Force against Intruders" (2005) 69 J.C.L. 405.
[284] (2005) 69 J.C.L. 405 at 406.

Reed, A., "Self-Defence—Applying The Objective Approach To Reasonable Force" (1996) 60 J.C.L. 94.

Rogers, J., "Justifying The Use of Firearms By Policemen And Soldiers: A Response To The Home Office's Review Of The Law On The Use Of Lethal Force" (1998) 18 *Legal Studies* 486.

Seago, P., "Criminal Law" [1995] All E.R. Annual Review 149.

Waddington, P.A.J., "Overkill Or Minimum Force?" [1990] Crim.L.R. 695.

Wilson, W., "The Structure of Criminal Defences" [2005] Crim.L.R. 108.

4. NECESSITY

5–062 Let us start discussion of the concept of necessity as a defence to a criminal prosecution by considering a hypothetical example. You are driving home one night when you see in the distance a child in difficulties in a river which runs alongside the road. Unfortunately, before you can reach the child you have to pass through some traffic lights which have just turned to red. You drive through the lights to rescue the child only to find that you were being followed by a police car and that despite your heroic rescue you are to be prosecuted for driving through a red light. Have you any defences? Do you consider that you ought to have a defence? You clearly cannot plead that you did not intend to disobey the traffic signal, and in any case it is an offence of strict liability. You cannot plead that it was an involuntary action. Your only hope would be that the law provides that in such circumstances you have a lawful excuse and in our example this would have to be based on a concept of necessity. Of course, as we shall soon seen there are dangers in such a general defence, so possibly some might argue that it would be better to leave it up to the common sense of individual Crown prosecutors not to prosecute. But discretion is rarely a satisfactory means of solving legal problems. Either the law should recognise such a defence or it should not. The question, therefore, is should we have such a general defence and do we, in fact, have such a defence? There would be very few who would be unwilling to see a defence of necessity applied to an example such as the one given above. Once, however, the crime becomes more serious, the problem with such a defence becomes more apparent.

A. Necessity and the Killing of Another

5–063 In the famous case of *Dudley and Stephens*[285] three men and a cabin boy were forced to take to a lifeboat following a storm at sea. There was very little food in the lifeboat and the four grew very weak. After 20 days, the last eight of which were without any food, D and S killed the cabin boy with a knife and for the next four days the three men lived off his flesh and blood. On that fourth day they were picked up in a very low state of health by a passing ship. They were put on trial for murder but the jury refused to convict them. Instead, they returned a statement of the facts they found to be proved. They found that there was no food left and there was little chance of survival for much longer. The cabin boy was in the worst state and was likely to have died first. D and S killed the cabin boy who did not consent to being killed, but had they not lived off his flesh they would probably all have died before they were picked up. There was no greater reason for killing the cabin boy other than the fact that he was the weakest. This statement of facts was referred to the Queen's Bench Division, who convicted D and S of murder. Their death sentences were commuted to six months' imprisonment without hard labour.

[285] (1884) 14 Q.B.D. 273.

Clearly this case raises the defence of necessity in its most extreme form—can such extreme circumstances ever justify the killing of a human being? The answer of the court in *Dudley and Stephens* is that necessity cannot possibly justify such an act—and circumstances are unlikely to get more compelling than in that case. If we imagine for one moment that the court had acquitted D and S on the ground that necessity justified their action, what sort of precedent would it have set? At what stage could people in the future resort to such acts. Are there any rules for choosing the victim? Would the cabin boy have the right to kill either D or S in self-defence? Would we test D and S's act on subjective or objective grounds?

Why did the judges reject the defence of necessity in *Dudley and Stephens*? Unfortunately, the answer to this question is not clear. It is possible to read into the case the view that no real necessity existed in that case at all (Coleridge C.J.) and it was, therefore, unnecessary to rule on the defence of necessity in English law. Alternatively, it might have been based on the view that there was no reason as to why the cabin boy should have been selected as the victim—thus implying that had there been a democratic choice of victim the court might have taken a different view. Or possibly, as the majority of writers would seem to believe, the court was in fact saying that there was no defence of necessity to a charge of murder, or possibly to any charge.

If the court was saying that no real necessity existed in that case, then when would such a **5–064** necessity exist? It is hard to imagine a more extreme case than *Dudley and Stephens*. Of course, they may have been picked up within the hour, but this hardly seems relevant. On the facts known to them there was no real hope of being picked up, coupled with the very real knowledge that if no action were taken it would soon be too late to act at all. It, thus, seems unrealistic to hold that *Dudley and Stephens* was based on a finding that no necessity existed in that case.

Would, then, the court have taken a different view had a more democratic method been used to select the food? Clearly, the reason for the selection of the cabin boy was that he was the least likely to resist and the most likely to die first, but there is no reason to suppose that he would not have recovered given nourishment. Should they have drawn lots? This was the suggestion made in the American case, *US v Holmes*.[286] There, the Supreme Court held that the crew ought to have left the overcrowded life-boat first, leaving just enough crew to look after the passengers. If more needed to be thrown overboard, then these should have been passengers chosen by lot.

It seems fairly clear that this view would not have appealed to the judges in *Dudley and Stephens*, though they might have taken a different view had all four consented to the drawing of lots, for then the killing would have been by consent. Normally consent is no defence to a murder charge, but it might have just been accepted in these circumstances.[287] The court obviously expected the four to lie back and gracefully accept the inevitable.

If we take the third possible view, that English criminal law knows no defence of necessity, how far was the court influenced by the fact that the crime in question was murder? Can it be regarded as a holding that necessity cannot excuse murder, but might excuse less serious crimes? We shall shortly be looking at the defence of duress which closely resembles the defence of necessity, but which the courts have been prepared to allow as a general defence to practically all crimes. It seems rather illogical to recognise the defence of duress but not that of necessity.[288] If a doctor who was not on night duty, and who had consumed a large quantity of alcohol, drove his car to the scene of a road accident to help the victim, should

---

[286] (1842) 26 Fed. Cas. 360.
[287] See below, para.7–098.
[288] In this regard see Report of the Law Commission on Defences of General Application: No.83 (1977) which recommended that necessity should not be a defence.

he not have a defence of necessity to a charge of being over the prescribed limit?[289] If a diabetic, desperate for insulin, breaks into a chemist because he can find no one to help, should he not be able to plead necessity? In the modern world, post September 11, 2001, would it be lawful through necessity to shoot down a hijacked plane destined for Canary Wharf? Could the loss of life aboard the plane be juxtaposed against the thousands of lives saved through the extreme action taken?[290] Is the safer answer to say that we can leave it to the police and Crown Prosecution Service to exercise their discretion sensibly or to the trial judge to show clemency following a conviction? It may be easier to do that, but it is hardly a satisfactory answer.

B. Necessity and Medical Treatment

5–065   It needs to be reiterated that in cases of necessity the defendant does not rely on any allegation that the circumstances placed an irresistible pressure on him, but rather claims that his conduct, although falling within the definition of an offence, was not unlawful because it was, in the circumstances, justified.[291] Beyond the very extreme circumstances in *Dudley and Stephens*, has "necessity" been recognised as providing a defence? The answer here is that whilst it has not been expressly acknowledged, a series of decisions have implicitly affirmed the existence of the doctrine in prevailing circumstances, albeit very strictly confined in ambit. Three medical cases provide examples of its operation in connection with the very difficult decisions that have to be taken in relation to medical treatment. The effect has been to characterise the individual actor's conduct as "lawful", legitimate responses to dilemmatic situations, and thus not criminal. For example, in *Bourne*[292] a charge was brought against a surgeon of unlawfully using an instrument with intent to procure a miscarriage, contrary to s.58 of the Offences Against The Person Act 1861. D had performed an abortion on a 14-year-old girl who was the victim of a gruesome rape. D was acquitted after a direction from the judge that, "the unborn child in the womb must not be destroyed unless the destruction of that child is for the purpose of preserving the yet more precious life of the mother".[293] Effectively the surgeon's actions were justified and hence within the umbrella of lawful activity. Similarly in *Gillick v West Norfolk and Wisbech AHA*[294] it was held that in certain circumstances it was lawful, and justified, for a doctor to provide contraceptive advice or treatment to a girl under the age of 16 without her parents' consent. Provided the doctor acted bona fide in what he clinically judged to be in the best interests of the girl then no offence within s.6 of the Sexual Offences Act 1956 would be committed, i.e. the doctor aiding, abetting, counselling or procuring the offence of unlawful sexual intercourse.

[289] See, e.g. *Buckoke v GLC* [1971] Ch. 655, 668 where Lord Denning stated: "A driver of a fire engine with ladders approaches the traffic lights. He sees 200 yards down the road a blazing house with a man at an upstairs window in extreme peril. The road is clear in all directions. At that moment the lights turn red. Is the driver to wait for 60 seconds, or more, for the lights to turn to green? If the driver waits for that time, the man's life will be lost. I suggested to both counsel that the driver might be excused in crossing the lights to save the man. He might have the defence of necessity. Both counsel denied it. They would not allow him any defence in law. The circumstances went to mitigation, they said, and did not take away his guilt. If counsel are correct—and I accept that they are—nevertheless such a man should not be prosecuted. He should be congratulated." In relation to necessity and road traffic offences see also *Johnson v Phillips* [1976] 1 W.L.R. 65 and *Wood v Richards* [1977] R.T.R. 201.
[290] See M. Bohlander, "Of Shipwrecked Sailors, Unborn Children, Conjoined Twins and Hijacked Airplanes—Taking Human Life and the Defence of Necessity" (2006) 70 J.C.L. 147.
[291] Law Com. No.122 at 61.
[292] [1938] 3 All E.R. 615.
[293] [1938] 3 All E.R. 615 at 620 per MacNaghten J.
[294] [1986] A.C. 112; considered above, para.4–009.

The final case in the trilogy concentrating on medical "necessity" is that of *Re F (Mental Patient: Sterilisation)*.[295] The House of Lords, in the leading judgment of Lord Goff, invoked recourse to necessity to allow sterilisation for persons unable because of mental handicap (and similarly unconsciousness) to give informed consent. The conclusion in that case was that, in all the circumstances, the operation was justified; otherwise the well established general rule is that the performance of a medical operation upon a person without his or her consent is unlawful, as constituting both the crime of battery and the tort of trespass to the person. Lord Goff enunciated three categories of circumstances where "necessity" has been acknowledged under the common law[296]:

1. Public necessity: this applies where an individual interferes with another man's property in the public interest—for example, the destruction of another man's house to prevent the spread of a catastrophic fire, as occurred in the Great Fire of London in 1666.

2. Private necessity: this occurs when an individual interferes with another's property to save his own person or property from imminent danger—for example, when he enters upon his neighbour's land without his consent, in order to prevent the spread of fire on to his own land.

3. General cases of necessity: for example, where an individual seizes another and forcibly drags him from the path of an oncoming vehicle, thereby saving him from injury or even death, he commits no wrong. Lord Goff clearly embraced medical treatment, including sterilisation, within this latter category.

The debate over the ambit of the necessity defence has been enervated in recent times by the controversial issues that arose in the tragic case of *Re A (Children) (Conjoined Twins: Medical Treatment) (No.1)*.[297] In a judgment running to 163 pages their Lordships were severely troubled by the legal, moral and ethical considerations upon which they were asked to decide; they had to rule on whether surgical separation of conjoined twins that would lead to death of the non-viable twin was lawful. The dilemma presented is, no doubt, familiar to most students. Jodie and Mary were conjoined twins. Separation of the twins would lead to the death of Mary because her lungs and heart were too deficient to oxygenate and pump blood through her body. Had she been a singleton she would have died shortly after birth. She remained alive because a common artery enabled Jodie, who was stronger, to circulate the blood for both of them. Separation would involve the severing of the common artery. The parents of the twins were devout Roman Catholics who refused to consent to the operation because they believed it was God's will that the children were born conjoined and that they should be left in God's hands. The parents were also concerned that if Jodie survived she might have a serious disability, and as they lived in a remote area with limited medical facilities they were worried that they would find it very difficult to cope. The doctors were convinced that if they separated the twins they could save Jodie. Without the operation it was thought that Jodie would die within three to six months. The hospital therefore sought

[295] [1990] 2 A.C. 1.
[296] [1990] 2 A.C. 1 at 74.
[297] [2000] 4 All E.R. 961; see J. Rogers, "Necessity, private defence and the killing of Mary" [2001] Crim.L.R. 515; and C. Elliott, "Murder and Necessity following the Siamese Twins litigation" (2001) 65 J.C.L. 66.

a declaration that the operation might be lawfully carried out.[298] The judge granted that declaration and the parents appealed against that order.

5–066   The Court of Appeal had initially to determine whether, in its inherent jurisdiction over the welfare of minors, it was in the interests of *both* of the children that it should consent to the treatment. This being answered in the affirmative, then secondly whether the operation could in fact *lawfully* be performed as it could be viewed as constituting the murder of Mary.[299] In this context the Court of Appeal overruled Johnson J. in the High Court by asserting that the "invasive treatment" propounded could not be classified as an omission akin to *Bland*,[300] and stated that Mary was not, in any event, being kept alive by medical treatment which was capable of being withdrawn.[301] The killing of Mary, a human being, could not be legitimised under the *Bland* principles on omission identifying, the "best interests of the patient" to withdraw treatment. The definitional elements for murder were satisfied here, but nonetheless the killing could be categorised as "lawful" under the utilitarian concept of necessity. Like Phoenix from the flames this defence arose again and was seized upon by their Lordships—the doctrine presupposes that an individual may effect a prima facie criminal act in order to bring about a greater good, i.e. the future prospects of life fulfilment for Jodie contrasting with Mary's certain death regardless of invasive treatment.

It is significant that their Lordship's judgments differed in the degree they embraced the utilitarian concept of necessity. Brooke L.J. was quite explicit in this regard and went much further than the other two, although they both did not demur on its applicability.[302] Brooke L.J. set out the parameters of the defence by invoking the three prerequisites set out by Stephen in his *Digest of the Criminal Law*[303]:

"(i) the act must be needed to avoid inevitable and irreparable evil, and

 (ii) it should be no more than is reasonably necessary for the purpose to be achieved, and

 (iii) the evil inflicted must not be disproportionate to the evil avoided."

One may safely argue that the above test is apposite for future cases involving necessity. In the exceptional facts before their Lordships they were in broad consensus that this formulaic test was satisfied. How then was it possible to square the circle over the hurdle presented by *Dudley and Stephens* in that necessity was no defence to murder? Were the cases distinguishable? A positive response was elicited. Unlike *Dudley and Stephens* there was no

---

[298] Note that in *Secretary of State for the Home Department v Robb* [1995] 1 All E.R. 677, Thorpe L.J. effectively overruled *Leigh v Gladstone* [1909] 26 T.L.R. 139 by holding that the prison authorities have no liberty to forcibly feed a starving prisoner, and in *St George's Healthcare NHS Trust v S* [1998] 3 All E.R. 673, the Court of Appeal overruled *Re S* [1992] 3 W.L.R. 806 by holding that a woman has an absolute right to refuse a Caesarian section, even when this refusal will result in the death of her foetus; and see, also, *R v Bournewood Community and Mental Health NHS Trust Ex. p. L* [1998] 3 All E.R. 289; and *Re Y (Mental Patient: Bone Marrow Donation)* [1997] Fam. 110.

[299] Mary died a few minutes after the aorta was severed, towards the end of complex surgery which lasted for more than 15 hours: see *The Daily Telegraph,* November 7, 2000. Jodie went on to develop at a rate that was ahead of many babies of her age: see *The Daily Telegraph,* December 16, 2000.

[300] *Airedale NHS Trust v Bland* [1993] A.C. 789; [1993] 1 All E.R. 821; see above, para.2–029 (held that the artificial feeding of a person in a persistent vegetative state may be lawfully discontinued, as it is characterised as an omission to struggle rather than a positive act which causes death, provided that to do so is in the best interests of the patient).

[301] [2000] 4 All E.R. 961 at 1003.

[302] [2000] 4 All E.R. 961 at 1052.

[303] Note that Stephen said that the "extent of this principle is unascertained in his *Digest of the Criminal Law* 4th edn (1987). For a helpful discussion of Stephen's viewpoint see, G. Williams "Necessity" [1978] Crim.L.R. 128.

dilemmatic problem in selecting one person to die in *Re A*—nature had made that choice. No dispute existed over steps needed to be taken to save Jodie, and more fundamentally no margin of choice existed that it would have to be Mary and not any other person whose life needed to be sacrificed. It is submitted that, "the absolute prohibition of murder does not apply if the victim is already designated by fate or by the circumstances, and is not chosen as an alternative to anyone else".[304] This fine but crucial demarcation has been cited by Sir John Smith as a way of explaining why, during the attempted climb to safety by passengers from the sinking Zeebrugge ferry, it might have been lawful to push the man who had remained immobile from the top of a ladder into the freezing water.[305] The breadth of this distinction should be limited to murder cases only where the impacted concerns invoke sanctity of life principles. Moreover, the outcome in *Re A* did not "mark an absolute divorce of the law from morality"; in truth, there was no overriding consensus as to the "morally correct" path to follow.[306]

Although Ward L.J. accepted that the defence of necessity was applicable his judgment highlights the belief that more empathitically valid is *private defence against an innocent person*.[307] This represents a novel departure; Mary was not an "unjust aggressor" against Jodie but nonetheless amounted to a bodily invasion killing her. Private defence, unlike duress and necessity, has long been recognised as a defence to all crimes including murder. Ward L.J. drew an interesting comparison between Jodie's situation and a hypothetical postulation of a six year old boy, below the age of criminal responsibility, shooting indiscriminately in the playground with a firearm[308]:

> "What I am however competent to say is that, in law, killing the six-year-old boy in self-defence [sic] of others would be fully justified and the killing would not be unlawful. I can see no difference in essence between the resort to legitimate self-defence and the doctor's coming to Jodie's defence and removing the threat of fatal harm to her presented by Mary's draining her life blood. The availability of such a plea of *quasi self-defence*, modified to meet the quite exceptional circumstances nature has inflicted on the twins, makes intervention by the doctors unlawful" (cf. *Malcherek* [1981] 2 All E.R. 422 [authors' emphasis in italics].

Walker L.J., rejected the private defence argument, but accepted a limited form of the **5–067** necessity defence. His judgment is confusing in that, by focusing explicitly on the purpose (intention) for surgery, he inadvertently condones what, in effect, is unlawful euthanasia: "Mary's death would be foreseen as an inevitable consequence of an operation which is intended and is necessary, to save Jodie's life. But Mary's death would not be the purpose or intention of the surgery, and she would die because tragically her body, on its own, is not and never has been viable."[309]

---

[304] J. Rogers, *loc. cit.*, at p.521.
[305] Professor Sir J.C. Smith, *Justification and Excuse In the Criminal Law* (Hamlyn, 1989) at 77–78 and J. Rogers, *loc. cit.*
[306] [2000] 4 All E.R. 961 at 1051 per Brooke L.J.
[307] [2000] 4 All E.R. 961 at 1016–1017. Ward L.J. asserted: "Mary is killing Jodie. That is the effect of the incontrovertible medical evidence . . . Mary uses Jodie's heart and lungs to receive and use Jodie's oxygenated blood. This will cause Jodie's heart to fail and cause Jodie's death as surely as a slow drip of poison. How can it be just that Jodie should be required to tolerate that state of affairs?"; and, see, also S. Uniacke, *Permissible Killing: The Self-Defence Justification of Homicide* (Cambridge University Press, 1994) at pp.157–166.
[308] [2000] 4 All E.R. 961.
[309] [2000] 4 All E.R. 961 at 1057.

Their Lordships agreed in *Re A* that the defence of necessity was uniquely available to provide justification for what would otherwise be an offence of murder.[310] The relevant definitional elements of the defence, and balancing of harms test, were cogently enunciated by Brooke L.J. It is suggested that the ratio decidendi of the case may be articulated in the following terms:

"Where A is, as the defendant knows, doomed to die in the near future but even the short continuation of his life will inevitably kill B as well, it is lawful to kill A, however free of fault he may be".[311]

It will be fascinating to observe whether the revived defence of necessity is extended beyond the tragic and unique facts in *Re A*, beyond the medical arena per se, and into other avenues of substantive criminal law. If so the vital question posed by Lord MacKay in *Howe*,[312]—whether the law should recognise in any individual in any circumstances, however extreme, the right to choose that one innocent person should be killed rather than another—will be nearer to a definitive answer over a widened playing field.

C. Necessity and Statutory Legislation

5–068 Statute may impose an absolute prohibition on the existence of necessity or on rare occasions, specifically allow the defence. The former principle is highlighted by the decision in *Cichon v DPP*.[313] D was convicted of allowing a pit bull terrier to be in a public place without being muzzled, contrary to s.1(2)(d) of the Dangerous Dogs Act 1991. He appealed against sentence to the Crown Court arguing that he had removed the muzzle because the dog had kennel cough, which made it cruel to keep it muzzled whilst it was coughing. This amounted to the common law defence of necessity. It was held, dismissing the appeal, that the aim of the 1991 Act was the security of the public; neither the Act nor the common law allowed a person in control of a dog to make a value judgment as between what was good for the dog and what was good for the public. The prohibition imposed by s.1(2)(d) of the Dangerous Dogs Act 1991 was, in this respect, absolute and Parliament evidently did not intend that a defence of necessity was applicable.

Another illustration of statutory denial is evidenced by *DPP v Harris*.[314] D, a detective constable, driving an unmarked police car, was covertly following a vehicle carrying persons believed to be planning an armed robbery. In order to keep up with the suspects D crossed a road junction against a red traffic light and collided with another vehicle. He was charged with driving without due care and attention contrary to s.2 of the Road Traffic Act 1991 and reg.34 of the Traffic Signs Regulations and General Directions 1981. This regulation provides that the general prohibition against crossing a red light does not apply when a vehicle is being used for police purposes, but that the vehicle shall not proceed beyond the stop line in such circumstances that it is likely to cause danger to the driver of any other vehicle. The justices accepted his defence that his actions arose out of necessity and acquitted him; the DPP appealed by way of case stated to the Divisional Court. The court, applying criteria of reasonableness and proportionality, refused to allow necessity as a

[310] [2000] 4 All E.R. 961, see J. Rogers, *loc. cit.*
[311] See J.C. Smith, "Commentary on *Re A (Children) (Conjoined Twins: Medical Treatment) (No.1)* [2001] Crim. L.R. 400 at 405.
[312] [1987] 1 A.C. 417 (duress by threats; no defence to charge of murder); see below, para.5–072.
[313] [1994] Crim.L.R. 918.
[314] [1995] 1 Cr.App.R. 170.

defence to driving without due care and attention. D, in carrying on across the junction, posed the risk of a dangerous collision with serious resulting injuries, and possibly even death. Additionally, the court referred, *en passant*, to the absolute prohibition imposed by the statutory regulations, acting to prevent the necessity defence to a charge of driving without due care and attention.[315]

It has been determined in *Quayle*[316] and *Altham*[317] that a defence of necessity is not available to a defendant charged with possession of cannabis contrary to the Misuse of Drugs Act 1971. Even where D is in possession of the drug for the purpose of alleviating pain, of either another or himself, the defence is excluded as otherwise individuals could undertake unlawful activities without medical intervention or prescription.

A number of statutory exceptions apply to the principle that generally necessity is no defence. A lawful excuse is provided by s.5 of the Criminal Damage Act 1971 where property is destroyed or damaged in order to protect property; for instance where a building is demolished in order to create a firebreak. Similarly, driving a vehicle elsewhere than on the roads can be excused under s.34 of the Road Traffic Act 1988 if the driver was doing so in order to save life, extinguishing fire or meeting any other emergency.[318]

D. Necessity as a General Defence

The traditional position under English law has been to take a very restricted view of the defence of necessity. From the legal writings of Hale onwards the defence has been circumscribed, and no defence to the theft of food or clothes: "if a person being under necessity for want of victuals or clothes, shall upon that account . . . steal another man's goods . . . it is a felony, and a crime by the laws of England punishable by death".[319] More recently, this rule has been supported by Lord Denning on the basis that, "if hunger were once allowed to be an excuse for stealing it would open a door through which all kinds of lawlessness and disorder would pass."[320] Gearty has also supported such a rationale: **5–069**

> "In science, necessity is the mother of invention. In law, it fathers confusion and fosters subversion. Should the homeless be allowed to squat? Are the hungry to be permitted to steal? Does the poor student who nicks a little of the College silver to pay next year's new tax on his existence deserve a full acquittal? Well-meaning people who think the world is fair believe a defence of necessity would make it fairer still. The judges, who know better, realise that it would parade for public view the inequalities and iniquities inherent in our affluence, without ever threatening to remove them—the Crown Court is hardly the place, after all, to abolish the law of property. So the courts prefer fairness within the system to revolution through it. And, within this constraint they have achieved a large measure of success."[321]

---

[315] For a contrary recent decision where necessity, in a situation in which D acted through duress of circumstances, was available to a charge of careless driving see *Backshall* [1999] Crim.L.R. 662; see below, para.5–093.

[316] [2005] 1 W.L.R. 3642.

[317] [2005] EWCA Crim 1415. The appellate court ruled that no breach occurred of either art.3 or art.8 of ECHR in denying the defence.

[318] G. Slapper, "Public Policy under Duress" (1995) N.L.J. 1063.

[319] Matthew Hale in P.R. Glazebrook (ed.), *The History of the Pleas of the Crown* (1971).

[320] *Southwark London Borough v Williams* [1971] 2 All E.R. 175, 179. At issue in this civil action was homelessness and entry into unoccupied houses in local authority ownership. In similar vein Lord Denning stated: "If homelessness were once admitted as a defence to trespass, no one's house could be safe. Necessity would open a door which no man could shut."

[321] C. Gearty, "Necessity: A Necessary Defence in Criminal Law?" (1989) 48 C.L.J. 356.

However, on occasions, closing the door to necessity has led to wholly perverse results, defendants convicted where they acted appropriately, legitimately and rationally. A prime example of this perversity is represented by the case of *Kitson*.[322] D was a passenger in a car who, having been drinking, had fallen asleep in the vehicle. He awoke to find no driver in the vehicle and the car coasting rapidly downhill. In these circumstances, he acted expeditiously, grabbing hold of the steering-wheel and in so doing averting a crash. Unfortunately he was subsequently prosecuted and convicted of driving while under the influence of drink. Ludicrously the verdict of the court would seem to suggest he ought instead to have endangered the lives of himself and many others. It seems unrealistic to place reliance on the discretion of prosecuting authorities not to bring prosecutions where common sense demands. The case stands as one of the most ridiculous in the criminal law arena.

Thus, at present, we must conclude that English law does not generally recognise a defence of necessity in its straightforward form. However, as we shall see in the next section, recently the courts have been prepared to allow a limited version of the defence of necessity in what is called duress of circumstances—the factual scenario in *Kitson* may now fit within this umbrella. In classifying this as a variant of duress the court have been able to allow what, in reality, is a defence of necessity, but a defence subject to all the stringent requirements of the defence of duress.

GENERAL READING

5–070　Bolander, M., "Of Shipwrecked Sailors, Unborn Children, Conjoined Twins, and Hijacked Airplanes—Taking Human Life and the Defence of Necessity" (2006) 70 J.C.L. 147.

Brudner, A., "A Theory Of Necessity" (1987) 7 O.J.L.S. 339.

Elliott, "Murder and Necessity Following The Siamese Twins Litigation" (2001) 65 J.C.L. 66.

Elliott, D.W., "Necessity, Duress And Self-defence" [1989] Crim.L.R. 611.

Gardner, S., "Necessity's Newest Inventions" (1991) 11 O.J.L.S. 125.

Gardner, S., "Direct Action and the Defence of Necessity" [2005] Crim.L.R. 371.

Gearty, C., "Necessity: A Necessary Defence In Criminal Law?" (1989) 48 C.L.J. 356.

Glazebrook, P., "The Necessity Plea In English Criminal Law" (1972) 31 C.L.J. 87.

Ost, S., "Euthanasia and the Defence of Necessity: Advocating a More Appropriate Legal Response" [2005] Crim.L.R. 355.

Rogers, J., "Necessity, Private Defence And The Killing Of Mary" [2001] Crim.L.R. 515.

Slapper, G., "Public Policy Under Duress" (1995) N.L.J. 1063.

Smith, J.C., *Justification And Excuse In The Criminal Law* (1989).

5. DURESS

A. General Background

5–071　The defence of duress *per minas* (by threats) can be analogised as operating as a concession to human frailty. It is predicated upon "confession and avoidance". The defendant actually admits the completion of the actus reus with attendant mens rea (confession) but seeks to excuse his conduct to deny criminal liability (avoidance).[323] As a general matter when an

---

[322] (1955) 39 Cr.App.R. 66.

[323] J. Horder, "Autonomy, Provocation and Duress" [1992] Crim.L.R. 707. The onus of disproving duress is on the Crown: see *Gill* [1963] 2 All E.R. 688; *Giaquento* [2001] EWCA Crim 2696, and *Bianco* [2002] 1 *Archbold News* 2.

individual pleads duress he is claiming that, although committing the actus reus of an offence with the requisite mens rea nonetheless such conduct ought to be excused.[324] In *Abdul-Hussain and Others*[325] the appellate court rephrased this choice of evils rationale by asserting that the alleged crime must be "a reasonable and proportionate response" to the threat. The accused claims that his will has been overborne by the wrongful threats imposed by another to inflict harm on himself or his family. An analysis of the correct operation of the duress defence was provided by Lord Wilberforce in *DPP for Northern Ireland v Lynch*[326] where he asserted:

> "At the present time, whatever the ultimate analysis in jurisprudence might be, the best opinion . . . seems to be that duress . . . is something which is superimposed on the other ingredients which by themselves would make up an offence, i.e. on the act and intention. *Coactus volui* sums up the combination: the victim completes the act and knows that he is doing so; but the addition of the element of duress prevents the law from treating what he has done as a crime."[327]

The problem here is rather similar to that in the previous section on necessity. Again extraneous factors lead the accused intentionally to perform an act which is contrary to the criminal law. The difference here is that the extraneous facts are deliberately produced by a third party with a view to persuading the victim to break the criminal law. Let us start by posing a hypothetical situation which is, unfortunately, all too familiar today. X is visited by members of a terrorist organisation. They have discovered that X is to drive a well-known politician on his forthcoming visit to the country. They tell X that unless he stops the car at a given point on the route they will kill his wife and children (or himself). They further tell X that they intend to kill the politician. X does what he is ordered to do and the politician is killed. X is then charged as a secondary party to the killing. The question raised by this problem is whether X will be able to plead that he acted under duress and that it would not, therefore, be possible to say that his action was truly voluntary? In other words, does English law recognise duress as a general defence, and if such a defence is recognised, what are its essential ingredients?

A summary of the key elements of the defence of duress has been provided by Lord Bingham in *Hasan*[328]: (a) duress does not afford a defence to charges of murder, attempted murder and, perhaps, some forms of treason; (b) to found a plea of duress the threat relied upon must be to cause death or serious injury; (c) the threat must be directed against D or his immediate family or someone close to him or, someone for whom D would reasonably regard himself as responsible; (d) the relevant tests pertaining to duress have been largely stated objectively, with reference to the reasonableness of the defendant's perceptions and conduct and not, as is usual in many other areas of the criminal law, with primary reference to his subjective perceptions[329]; (e) the criminal conduct which the defence is sought to

---

[324] See, generally, J. Dressler, "Exegis of the Law of Duress: Justifying the Excuse and Searching for its Proper Limits" (1989) 62 Southern California L.R. 1331; E. Colvin, "Exculpatory Defences in Criminal Law" (1990) 10 O.J.L.S. 381; and K.J.M. Smith and W. Wilson, "Impaired Voluntariness and Criminal Responsibility: Reworking Hart's Theory of Excuses—The English Judicial Response" (1993) 13 O.J.L.S. 69.

[325] [1999] Crim.L.R. 570; see below, para.5–094.

[326] [1975] A.C. 653.

[327] [1975] A.C. 653 at 680; see also, *Fisher* [2004] EWCA Crim 1190.

[328] [2005] 4 All E.R. 685 at 694–695, [21].

[329] Baroness Hale in *Hasan* [2005] 4 All E.R. 685, contrary to Lord Bingham, favours a more subjective perspective: "I accept that even the person with a knife at her back has a choice whether or not to do as the knifeman says. The question is whether she should have resisted the threat. But perhaps because I am a reasonable but comparatively weak and fearful grandmother, I do not understand why the defendant's beliefs and personal characteristics are not morally relevant to whether she could reasonably have been expected to resist"; see p.714, [73].

excuse must be directly caused by the threats which are relied upon; (f) D may excuse his criminal conduct on grounds of duress only if, placed as he was, there was no evasive action he could reasonably have expected to take, and (g) D may not rely on duress to which he has voluntarily laid himself open. These ingredients and principles are explored more fully in the following sections: the overriding thread is that our courts, where possible, have constrained the nature and ambit of the defence.[330] This was explicitly stated by the House of Lords in *Hasan*.[331]

B. The Ambit of the Duress Defence

(i) Duress and Murder

5–072   The denial of duress as an excuse to murder reflects an unbroken tradition of legal writing dating back to Hale's *The History of the Pleas of the Crown*[332] and repeated by Blackstone's *Commentaries on the Laws of England*.[333] Hale stated that as a matter of principle:

> "[I]f a man be desperately assaulted, and in peril of death, and cannot otherwise escape, unless to satisfy his assailant's fury he will kill an innocent person then present, the fear and actual force will not acquit him of the crime and punishment of murder, if he commit the fact; for he ought rather to die himself, than kill an innocent . . ."[334]

Despite the clear statement in legal writings denying duress as a defence to murder, no clear judicial authority was operative on this issue until relatively recently. A series of cases have appraised this matter over the course of the last 20 years. In *DPP for Northern Ireland v Lynch*,[335] a police officer had been fatally wounded in Northern Ireland by the IRA. The appellant, Lynch, had not taken part in the actual shooting but he had driven the terrorists to and from the garage where the murder took place. His participation in the murder was therefore, as a secondary party. He claimed that he had participated under duress. By a bare majority the House of Lords held that he could rely on the defence. However, in *Abbott v The Queen*[336] the decision in *Lynch* was distinguished by the Privy Council, and the Judicial Committee held that the defence was not available to the principal in the first degree, the actual killer. Thus, a man charged with murder could plead duress, but the jury would be instructed that if they found him to be a principal offender in the crime they must ignore the plea. The reasoning behind this distinction between the principal and secondary offender to murder was that the law could excuse a person who had a "subsidiary" role in the killing of another human being, but that it could not excuse the actual killer. In other words no threat could be serious enough to cause you to take another person's life. The dividing line between a principal and a secondary offender may be exceedingly hard to draw, but on it could rest the difference between a conviction for murder, or a complete acquittal. This was clearly an unsatisfactory state of affairs and the House of Lords took the opportunity to

---

[330] See, generally, W. Wilson "The Structure of Criminal Defences" [2005] Crim.L.R. 108.
[331] Lord Bingham stated: "I must acknowledge that the features of duress to which I have referred above, incline me, where policy choices are to be made, towards tightening rather than relaxing the conditions to be met before duress may be successfully relied upon."; see [2005] 4 All E.R. 685 at 695, [22].
[332] Matthew Hale *The History of the Pleas of the Crown* in P.R. Glazebrook (ed.) (1971) (1736), p.51.
[333] William Blackstone, *Commentaries on the Laws of England* (1809), p.30.
[334] *The History of the Pleas of the Crown, op. cit.* at 51.
[335] [1975] A.C. 653. Note in the notorious case of *Kray* [1970] 1 Q.B. 125, it had been asserted, albeit obiter, by Widgery L.J. that duress could be available as a defence even to an individual charged with being an accessory to murder.
[336] [1977] A.C. 755.

review the position in *Howe*.[337] In effect, the House saw the decision lying between an extension of the defence to all murders or a complete withdrawal of the defence in murder cases. While prepared to consider making the defence available to one who has played a minor role in a murder, the House could not see any practical and reliable way of isolating such defendants. The previous attempt to do so by reference to principal and secondary offenders did not necessarily identify the importance of the various roles; a secondary party may well have played the major role. In the result the House, overruling its own decision in *Lynch*, decided that it should not be available to anyone charged with murder whether as principal or secondary offender. The decision clearly simplifies the law, but has some unfortunate deleterious consequences, and creates anomalies. An analysis of the five main arguments advanced by their Lordships in *Howe* illuminates these difficulties.[338]

(i) Heroism and Sanctity of Human Life. This argument can be expressed quite simply. 5–073 The prima facie reason involved the special sanctity that the law attaches to human life and which denies to a man the right to take an innocent life even at the price of his own or another's life.[339] Lord Hailsham's analysis was quite unrestrained on this issue. According to his view, the law is neither:

> "just [n]or humane which withdraws the protection of the criminal law from the innocent victim and casts the cloak of its protection upon the coward and the poltroon in the name of a concession to human frailty".[340]

Therefore, the ordinary man, rather than kill another, might be expected to sacrifice his own life.[341] It is suggested that such a view imposes a fundamentally false standard on criminal conduct. There is palpably no duty of heroism in the criminal law; the standard is that of the reasonable man, not the reasonable hero.[342] To suggest otherwise is absurd and this requirement makes obligatory a form of self-sacrifice which should be regarded as supererogatory: i.e. as being above and beyond the call of duty.[343]

---

[337] [1987] A.C. 417. See generally, H.P. Milgate, "Duress and the Criminal Law: Another About Turn by the House of Lords" (1988) 47 C.L.J. 61; and I.H. Dennis, "Developments in Duress" (1987) 51 J.C.L. 463.

[338] See, Law Commission Consultation Paper No.122, *Legislating the Criminal Code: Offences Against the Person and General Principles* (1992), p.56 [hereinafter Consultation Paper No.122].

[339] [1987] A.C. 417, per Lord Griffiths at 439.

[340] [1987] A.C. 417 at 432.

[341] [1987] A.C. 417.

[342] As Joshua Dressler has stated:
"[S]ince duress is an excuse rather than a justification, the real issue (it bears repeating with some additional emphasis) is whether a coerced person who unjustifiably violates the moral principle *necessarily, unalterably and unfailingly* deserves to be punished as a murderer, as the common law insists. If a murderer were insane, involuntarily intoxicated, or especially young, society would not necessarily, unalterably and unfailingly demand punishment.
. . .
. . . I am afraid that such a rule, like Lord Hailsham's opinion, has the imprint of self-righteousness, which the law should avoid. The rule asks us to be virtuous; more accurately; it *demands* our virtual saintliness, which the law has no right to require. It is precisely in the case of kill-or-be-killed threats that the criminal law ought to be prepared in some cases to assuage the guilt feelings of the homicidal wrongdoer by excusing him—by reminding him that he acted no less valiantly than any person of reasonable moral strength would have done."
Joshua Dressler, "Exegis of the Law of Duress: Justifying the Excuse and Searching for its Proper Limits" (1989) 62 Southern California L.R. 1331, 1372–1379.

[343] R. Mullender, "Murder, Attempted Murder and the Defence of Duress: Some Objections to the Present State of the Law" (1993) 25 Bracton L.J. 15. He vividly asserts (at 18) that: "Examination of this issue, bearing as it does, on the relationship between law and morality, involves making a hazardous journey, to use Jhering's striking image, around the Cape Horn of jurisprudence".

5–074   **(ii) Terrorism.**   The second argument in *Howe* focused on the dangers of terrorism and the importance of the law standing firm against an increase in violence and terrorist threat.[344] Their Lordships were particularly concerned that terrorists, via human tools, could kill many innocent victims if duress were embraced as a viable defence to murder. Lord Lane in the Court of Appeal, supported by Lords Bridge and Griffiths in the House of Lords, viewed duress as a:

> "highly dangerous relaxation in the law allowing a person who has deliberately killed, may be a number of innocent people, to escape conviction and punishment altogether because of a fear that his own life or those of his family might be in danger if he did not."[345]

This danger, according to Lord Lane, was exacerbated because "the defence of duress was so easy to raise and may be so difficult for the prosecution to disprove beyond a reasonable doubt".[346] However, as Lord Hailsham admits in *Howe*, juries have been commendably robust in rejecting duress where appropriate, as the verdicts in the trials of Howe, Bannister and Burke clearly demonstrate.[347] Additionally, the charter for terrorism argument has lost much of its force as a result of more recent Court of Appeal decisions, discussed below, which establish that where a defendant voluntarily joins a terrorist group or criminal gang, and is forced by pressure of violence to commit an offence for that group or gang, he cannot raise the defence of duress if, when he joined the gang, he knew that it took part in violent crime or that violence might be used against him to take part in the gang's activities.[348]

5–075   **(iii) Executive Discretion.**   Thirdly, their Lordships recognised the extreme rigour of the complete denial of the defence but argued that this could simply be ameliorated by the exercise of executive discretion.[349] Flexibility could prevail by executive discretion not to prosecute or, alternatively, by the expeditious release by licence of an individual serving a life sentence for murder.[350] Such an argument is not convincing. Axiomatically, as Lord Wilberforce stated in *Lynch*, "if the defence is excluded in law, much of the evidence which would prove the duress would be inadmissible at the trial, not brought out in court, and not tested by cross-examination".[351] The discretion not to prosecute does not, in any event, ensure that the law is saved from irrationality. For example, the accused was prosecuted in *Anderton v Ryan*[352] on the basis of a factual scenario in which the Law Commission had predicted no prosecution would take place. There would be nothing to stop such a result occurring in duress.

5–076   **(iv) The Comparison with Necessity.**   Fourthly, their Lordships noted that apart from the majority decision in the *Lynch* case, duress, dating back to Hale and Blackstone, had uniformly not been a defence to murder.[353] In *Dudley and Stephens*[354] in 1884 the House of

---

[344] [1987] A.C. 417 at 443–444 per Lord Griffiths (Lord Bridge concurring at 438). Griffiths L.J. states: "we face a rising tide of violence and terrorism against which the law must stand firm recognising that its highest duty is to protect the freedom and lives of those that live under it."
[345] [1986] Q.B. 626 at 641.
[346] [1986] Q.B. 626.
[347] [1987] A.C. 417 at 434.
[348] H.P. Milgate, "Duress and the Criminal Law: Another About Turn by the House of Lords" (1988) 47 C.L.J. 61 at 73.
[349] [1987] A.C. 417 at 433 per Lord Hailsham. See generally, A. Reed, "Duress and Provocation as Excuses to Murder: Salutary Lessons from Recent Anglo-American Jurisprudence" (1996) 6 Florida State University, Journal of Transnational Law and Policy 51.
[350] [1987] A.C. 417 at 433 (per Lord Hailsham); see also 454 (Lord Griffiths concurring).
[351] [1975] A.C. 675 at 685.
[352] [1985] A.C. 560; for discussion see below, para.6–016.
[353] [1987] A.C. 417 at 423.
[354] (1884) 14 Q.B.D. 273.

Lords had decided that necessity could not be a defence to murder, whatever the degree of participation. According to the argument propounded by Lords Hailsham and Mackay in *Howe*, necessity and duress are analogous, and duress cannot be available on a murder charge whilst *Dudley and Stephens* remained part of the common law.[355] Whilst this is the strongest argument advanced in *Howe* it is not without weaknesses. The two defences of necessity and duress, although conceptually linked, are not identical. For example, whereas duress can be raised as a defence to theft, the thief cannot successfully rely on necessity.[356] Moreover, the parallels drawn here are arguably no stronger than those between duress and provocation; provocation is a defence to murder but duress is not! Indeed it can be argued that the individual who kills under duress, a morally involuntary actor, is *less* blameworthy than the provoked killer.

(v) The Legislative Argument. The Law Commission Report No.83, *Defences of General* 5–077 *Application*, had recommended 10 years previously that duress should be available in *all* cases of murder. Since Parliament had taken no action in the light of this report it was propounded by Lords Bridge and Griffiths that neither the legislative will nor public pressure existed to extend the defence to the actual killer.[357] Of course, it is self-evident that such an analysis cuts both ways. Parliamentary inactivity was also illustrative of a wish not to abrogate the *Lynch* decision, which only 12 years previously extended duress as a defence to secondary participation even for murder. This argument raises the important issue of the proper role of "judicial legislation" in the criminal area, and the balance between legislative and case precedent reforms.

Conclusions. The duress defence to murder requires the law to consider the type of 5–078 conduct legitimately expected of our fellow citizens who are threatened by dire consequences and coerced into completely atypical behaviour that is morally repugnant to them and their previous code of conduct. Lord Hailsham demands heroism and rejects the "coward" in such a scenario. However, the criminal law does not require or demand heroism but imposes the reasonable man standard. It is suggested that to demand more and attach liability when such a demand is not met is unsupportable. This rule, which an individual is likely to be unaware of or unable to comply with, does not effectively protect human life.[358]

Consider the following hypothetical scenario, presented by Professor Smith, which represents an odious dilemmatic choice.[359] A female army officer is driving her two young children to school when gunmen hijack the car and tell her that both children will be shot unless she drives the car back to the army barracks where they intend to shoot a guard. The woman, constrained by the threat to her children and the imminent peril of their deaths, acts as an accomplice by driving the vehicle; the gunmen accomplish the plan and kill the guard. Since duress is inapplicable to murder under prevailing doctrine, the woman would be guilty of murder.[360]

The logical corollary, however, must be that no criminal liability should be attached when individuals cannot reasonably be expected to behave other than the way they did. In such a scenario, no *real* choice exists because the actions involve moral involuntariness. Lord Morris in *Lynch* arguably provides the correct analysis:

---

[355] See above, para.5–063.
[356] See above, para.5–069.
[357] [1987] A.C. 417, 437 (Lord Bridge) and 443 (Lord Griffiths).
[358] Consultation Paper No.122, above, fn.337, at 57. A. Reed, *loc. cit.*, at p.62.
[359] J.C. Smith, "Case Comment, *R v Gotts*" [1992] Crim.L.R. 724 at 726.
[360] Of course, it may be possible through prosecutorial discretion for the individual not to be prosecuted; nevertheless, by strict analysis, liability is incurred for murder.

"[I]t is proper that any rational system of law should take fully into account the standards of honest and reasonable men. By those standards it is fair that actions and reactions may be tested. If then someone is really threatened with death or serious injury unless he does what he is told to do is the law to pay no heed to the miserable, agonising plight of such a person? For the law to understand not only how the timid but also the stalwart may in a moment of crisis behave is not to make the law weak but to make it just. In the calm of the courtroom measures of fortitude or of heroic behaviour are surely not to be demanded when they could not in moments for decision reasonably have been expected even of the resolute and the well disposed."[361]

5–079   In essence, the criminal law demands that a person who killed another under duress, whatever the circumstances, has to comply with a higher standard than that demanded of the average person.[362] Such an exception to the general rule in criminal law is not justified. Nor is it sufficient to rely simply on executive discretion not to prosecute or on quick release on licence as a mitigating device. As the Law Commission stresses most cogently, such a rationale is improper both in principle and in practice.[363] Clearly, even when a prosecutor is aware of the duress plea, he may believe it incorrect to rule on its merits. Additionally, those with the duty to rule on a prisoner's release would have to do so without recourse to a proper trial on the defendant's claim of duress.[364] The strictures of the defence, and harsh operation to young offenders, were clearly illustrated in the recent case of *Wilson*.[365] D, aged thirteen at the time of the fatal act, had assisted his father in a brutal attack on his mother. V died from a stab wound to her lung, but she had also been attacked by an axe, a sock filled with pebbles, and a metal bar. D had been present at the scene and fetched the axe on his father's behalf. D contended that his whole course of conduct was motivated by fear and terror, and did not represent the exercise of his own independent free will. The Court of Appeal, however, determined that the inapplicability of duress as a defence to murder reigned supreme despite the susceptibilities and maturity levels of a child defendant. Despite obvious misgivings they were left with no alternative other than to apply extant law.[366]

It is eminently logical that current law does not make duress available to members of criminal or terrorist gangs. However, it is illogical to deny it to innocent tools of such groups, as in the earlier postulation. It is suggested that, as for gross negligence manslaughter,[367] these matters ought to be left for jury determination, and there is no doubt that juries are commendably robust in rejecting the defence where appropriate.[368] When the offence is more heinous and a greater number are killed, juries are best placed to determine the desert of punishment. The jurors are peculiarly well situated to determine society's legitimate expectations of moral courage, so they should be charged with applying duress to murder. A jury applying Lord Hailsham's demand of heroism would leave the current law unaltered; however, a less rigorous test, applying the reasonable man standard would be more humane and compassionate. Thus, the jury ought to be charged with making such determinations.[369]

---

[361] [1975] A.C. 653 at 670.
[362] See, *State v Goliath* (1972) S.A.L.R. 1, 25 (S.A.) (per Rumpff J.).
[363] See, Consultation Paper No.122, above, n.26 at 57.
[364] Consultation Paper No.122.
[365] [2007] EWCA Crim 1251.
[366] The court stressed that there might be grounds for criticising the principle that a child remained liable despite parental duress, but nonetheless were bound by the House of Lords decision in *Howe*.
[367] See below, para.7–048.
[368] Even Lord Hailsham was prepared to accept that juries are commendably robust!.
[369] A. Reed, "Duress and Provocation as Excuses to Murder: Salutary Lessons from Recent Anglo-American Jurisprudence" (1996) 6 Florida State University, Journal of Transnational Law and Policy 51, 60–63.

In this regard, the renewed onus on jury determination would replicate the excusing decision imposed on juries under the Model Penal Code in the United States.[370]

(ii) Duress and Attempted Murder

The defence is inapplicable to murder, but does it extend to attempted murder? This issue **5–080** was addressed in *Gotts*,[371] a few years after the decision of the House in *Howe*. D, aged 16, was threatened by his father that he would be shot unless D killed his mother. The mother had fled the marital home to a woman's refuge in order to escape from domestic violence. D stabbed, but did not kill his mother—although but for prompt medical attention she may have died. The accused was charged with attempted murder and with wounding with intent to do grievous bodily harm contrary to s.18 of the Offences Against the Person Act 1861. The jury convicted D of attempted murder and on appeal the House of Lords, by a bare majority, held that duress was no defence to attempted murder. There was no evidence that the common law had drawn a line under murder and treason as the only offences to which duress could not be raised as a defence; there was no reason to distinguish attempted murder, in which the defendant must be proved to have had the intention to kill, from murder. The Court of Appeal, however, thought that different reasoning might be applied to incitement or conspiracy to murder since they were a stage further away from the completed killing than attempted murder.[372]

The major problem, it is suggested, is whether duress should be allowed on a charge under s.18 where the prosecution is alleging that the accused intended to cause grievous bodily harm. This problem did not face the court in *Gotts* since the jury convicted the defendant of attempted murder and thereby must have found that he had an intention to kill. However, a flagrant anomaly clearly applies under current English law. Duress may be pleaded on a charge under s.18 of the Offences Against the Person Act. The mens rea of murder embraces this latter constructive liability, i.e. an intention to cause grievous bodily harm suffices. Accordingly, a defendant may be acquitted of wounding with intent to cause grievous bodily harm based on the defence of duress, and yet on the very day after his acquittal the victim could die rendering D liable to a murder charge to which duress would be no defence! In each scenario the culpability of the coerced criminal action is identical but liability is imposed depending purely on the victim's survival.[373]

---

[370] The most significant difference between English law and the Model Penal Code is that the Code allows duress as a defence, even for murder [s.2.09(1)]. Additionally, the Model Penal Code vastly enhances the jury's role in the determination of the excuse. Under the M.P.C; the jury must consider "whether the hypothetical person of reasonable firmness would have resisted the threat". Within that choice is, in essence, a moral judgment regarding the ambit of fortitude of individuals constrained by prevailing circumstances. Thus, a fundamental dichotomy exists between the M.P.C. and the jury's limited role at English common law.

The material part of the M.P.C., unfortunately adopted by only a minority of states [see for example Alaska Stat. S. 11.81.440 (1995); Haw. Rev. Stat. S. 702–231 (1995); N.J. Rev. Stat. S. 2C: 2–9 (1995); and Utah Code Ann. S. 76–2–302 (1995)], defines duress as follows:

"(1) It is an affirmative defence that the actor engaged in the conduct charged to constitute an offence because he was coerced to do so by the use of, or threat to use, unlawful force against his person or the person of another, that a person of reasonable firmness in his situation would have been unable to resist.

(2) The defence . . . is unavailable if the actor recklessly placed himself in a situation in which it was probable that he would be subjected to duress. The defence is also unavailable if he was negligent in placing himself in such a situation, whenever negligence suffices to establish culpability for the offence charged."

[371] [1992] 2 A.C. 412. See generally, S. Gardner, "Duress in Attempted Murder" (1991) 107 L.Q.R. 389; and S. Gardner, "Duress in the House of Lords" (1992) 108 L.Q.R. 349.

[372] The Law Commission has recommended that duress should be a defence to its proposed offences of first degree and second degree murder, and to attempted murder. See *Murder, Manslaughter and Infanticide* (2006) Law Com. No.304, Pt 6.

[373] A. Reed, *loc. cit.*, at p.63.

(iii) Duress and Other Criminal Offences

5–081 Duress is not a defence to murder either as principal or secondary party, attempted murder nor to some forms of treason.[374] In a sense we need to draw a line in the sand. Above the line are those offences outlined above, but below this line will be grouped together *all* other criminal law offences. The effect of a successful plea is that the accused escapes conviction. Duress has been relied upon to excuse manslaughter,[375] non-fatal offences within the Offences Against the Person Act, incitement and conspiracy to murder, theft,[376] criminal damage,[377] perjury,[378] contempt of court,[379] possessing ammunition[380] and handling.[381] In this regard the burden of proof lays firmly upon the Crown to disprove duress. However, if no facts supporting the defence of duress appear in the presentation of the prosecution's case, or might reasonably be inferred, then it falls to the defendant, who bears simply an evidential burden, to lay a foundation that duress was operative upon his mind.[382]

C. The Constituents of Duress

(i) Nature of the Threat

5–082 In order for a defendant to be able to rely upon duress as a defence the nature of the operative threat suborning his will must be of a particular nature. It seems from case precedents that this threat must be of death or serious personal injury, as stated by Lord Widgery C.J. in *Hudson and Taylor*,[383] and is so stated in the draft criminal code. In both *Conway*[384] and *Martin*,[385] cases on the analogous defence of duress of circumstances, considered below, the courts imposed this requirement of death or serious injury. In *Baker and Wilkins*[386] the Court of Appeal determined that a threat of serious psychological damage, not bodily physical injury, would not be regarded as serious injury for the purposes of the duress defence. The threat of injury merely to property has historically been deemed insufficient. For example, in *McGrowther*[387] the defendant was guilty of treason when compelled to join the rebellion through friends of Bonnie Prince Charlie under a threat to burn his house and drive off his cattle.[388] A line is drawn here between threats to the person

[374] *Steane* [1947] K.B. 997.
[375] *Evans and Gardiner* [1976] V.R. 517 and *Evans and Gardiner (No.2)* [1976] V.R. 523.
[376] *Gill* [1963] 2 All E.R. 688.
[377] *Crutchley* (1831) 5 C. & P. 123.
[378] *K* (1983) 78 Cr.App.R. 82.
[379] *Lewis* (1992) 96 Cr.App.R. 412.
[380] *Subramaniam* [1956] 1 W.L.R. 965.
[381] *Att-Gen v Whelan* [1934] I.R. 518.
[382] As to burden of proof see above, para.1–010.
[383] [1971] 2 Q.B. 202. Note in *Sephakela v R* [1954] Crim.L.R. 723 the Privy Council asserted that duress was constrained to either the threat to kill or to cause serious bodily injury. More recently in *Quayle* [2005] EWCA Crim 1415, it was asserted that a threat of death or serious injury was required.
[384] [1989] Q.B. 290. See also, *Aikens* [2003] EWCA Crim 1573; and *Radford* [2004] EWCA Crim 2878.
[385] [1989] 1 All E.R. 652.
[386] [1997] Crim.L.R. 497. A direct corollary exists here with the determination in *Chan-Fook* [1994] 2 All E.R. 552 that psychiatric injury can constitute "actual bodily harm" for the purposes of s.47 of the Offences Against The Person Act 1861 (see below, para.7–076), and similarly in *Burstow* [1997] 1 Cr.App.R. 144 the House of Lords have recently determined that serious psychiatric injury can constitute "grievous bodily harm" under s.20 of the 1861 statute (see below, para.7–082). It is submitted that in the light of these developments it is incongrous that a threat of serious psychological injury should remain inapt for the duress defence; see generally, J.C. Smith [1998] Crim.L.R. 498.
[387] (1746) 18 State Tr. 391.
[388] See, also *DPP v Milcoy* [1993] *Crown Office Digest* 200. Threats to expose sexual immorality or dire financial straits are similarly insufficient in nature, cf. *Valderrama-Vega* [1985] Crim.L.R. 220.

as opposed merely to property. In many respects the law here is not logically consistent since a threat to cause the defendant economic harm, to damage his reputation or to harm his property, might constitute overwhelming pressure in some circumstances. Lord Simon stressed this point in *DPP for Northern Ireland v Lynch* in his dissenting judgment:

> "But a threat to property may, in certain circumstances be as potent in overbearing the actor's wish not to perform the prohibited act as a threat of physical harm. For example, the threat may be to burn down his house unless the householder merely keeps watch against interruption while a crime is committed. Or a fugitive from justice may say, I have it in my power to make your son bankrupt. You can avoid that merely by driving me to the airport. Would not many ordinary people yield to such threats, and act contrary to their wish not to perform an action prohibited by law?"[389]

The Law Commission, whilst acknowledging that a sliding scale of threats depending on the offence with which the defendant was charged might be fairer, have stated it would inevitably introduce an air of uncertainty. It is for this reason that the Law Commission has recommended that the defence of duress should, generally, be limited to threats to cause death or serious injury.[390] However, in more recent Law Commission proposals, insofar as whether duress should apply to murder or attempted murder, the provisional proposal is that for the plea to be successful D must have been threatened with death or life-threatening harm.[391] But what about the scenario where mixed motives may apply to overbear the mind of the defendant? This issue was considered in *Valderrama-Vega*.[392] The accused had been charged with being knowingly concerned in the fraudulent evasion of the prohibition on the importation of a controlled drug; it appeared that his will may have been overcome by a combination of factors including (1) threats of death or serious injury against him and his family, (2) threats to expose his homosexual tendencies and (3) fear of financial ruin. It was held that the defence of duress was available so long as it was reasonably possible to say that the threat of death or serious bodily injury was a sine qua non of his decision to offend, although it need not have been the only factor. However, in *Ortiz*[393] the court thought it inadvisable to use the word "solely" in relation to relevant threats. In essence, the threat need not be the sole cause of the defendant's acting as he did. The defence will apply if the defendant would not have committed the offence *but for* the threat.

Threat Against Whom?   It is generally accepted that the threats do not have to be against **5–083** the safety of the defendant himself. Threats to kill or seriously injure the defendant's family, and possibly anyone with whom he has a special relationship will suffice. In *Hurley and Murray*[394] the Supreme Court of Victoria held that threats to kill or seriously injure the accused's common law wife could amount to duress; in *K*[395] the threat involved the defendant's mother. The court in *Ortiz*[396] assumed that a threat to a wife and child was sufficient. In the analogous doctrine of duress of circumstances, threats to a passenger in D's car,[397] and D's wife's threat to commit suicide if he did not drive while disqualified[398] had

---

[389] [1975] A.C. 653 at 686.
[390] See, generally, N.M. Padfield, "Duress, Necessity and the Law Commission" [1992] Crim.L.R. 778.
[391] See generally, Law Com. No.304, *Murder, Manslaughter & Infanticide* (2006) at paras 6.73 et seq.
[392] [1985] Crim.L.R. 220.
[393] (1986) 83 Cr.App.R. 173.
[394] [1967] V.R. 526.
[395] (1984) 78 Cr.App.R. 82.
[396] (1986) 83 Cr.App.R. 173.
[397] *Conway* [1989] Q.B. 290; see below, para.5–093.
[398] *Martin* [1989] 1 All E.R. 652; see below, para.5–093.

sufficient causative nexus. More recently, in *Baker and Ward*[399] the Court of Appeal stated, obiter, that the pressure on the accused must be one which took the form of violence or the threat of violence either to the accused or to a member of his immediate family; in *Abdul-Hussain and Others,*[400] Rose L.J. spoke of "imminent peril of death or serious injury to the defendant or those to whom he has responsibility". The concept of "responsibility" was followed in *Shayler,* and supported by Lord Bingham in *Hasan.*[401] Logically the defendant ought to be able to rely on a threat against a third party, with no special relationship, provided the ordinary reasonable person would similarly have acceded to the threat. It is provided by the Draft Criminal Code cl.42(3)(a)(i) that the defence be allowed where the threat is made to the life or safety of D "or another", thus embracing complete strangers.

5–084 Specificity of the Threat. How specific must the relationship be between the threats made to D and the offence(s) committed in relation to those threats? What nexus must exist over threat and criminal conduct? That particular issue was addressed by the appellate court in *Cole.*[402] D's defence to robbing two building societies was his inability to repay money lenders, who had threatened him, hit him with a baseball bat, and threatened his girlfriend and child. It was held that duress was only available where the threats were directed to the commission of the particular offence charged. Here the threat related to the debt, and it was not contended that he was threatened with the unpleasant consequences if he did not commit the robbery. The money lenders had not stipulated that he commit robbery to meet their demands. Additionally, the imminent peril, which was a necessary pre-condition to the defence properly arising, was lacking. D had said that he had no choice, and had to have the money by a particular time, but that fell short of the degree of directness and immediacy required of the link between the suggested peril and the offence charged; a defence of duress of circumstances was, thus, also inapplicable (see below).

The decision in *Cole* stands for the proposition that duress *per minas* (by threats) is only available where the duressor has actually *nominated* the specific crime(s) to be committed. Nomination as a concept may be difficult to apply. At one end of the spectrum a threat to "Get the money from the Nationwide Building Society or else" is self-evidently specific enough. But, what about, "Go and rob a bank or a building society" and, at the other end of the spectrum, "Get it any way you want, but I must have it tomorrow or else."[403] This latter demand would arguably fail the specificity test, with no nominated offence. It illustrates the difficulties and uncertainty over an applicable nexus test. For example, will a duressor's nominated offence of "steal X" also embrace criminal conduct covering robbery, blackmail or fraud?[404] The question does not admit of any obvious reply.

It is clear, however, that no requirement exists for there to be a threat in fact: the defence is still apposite where D believes that there is a threat of the relevant gravity. In *Safi and Others,*[405] for example, a group of Afghan hijackers landed at Stansted airport asserting a defence of duress deriving from their fear of persecution at the hands of the Taliban. The

---

[399] [1999] 2 Cr.App.R. 335.
[400] [1999] Crim.L.R. 570. See, also, *Wright* [2000] Crim.L.R. 510 where the accused alleged that a threat had been made to kill her boyfriend. The appellate court determined that a threat need not be made to harm the accused himself or herself. The court specifically referred to the Judicial Studies Board's specimen direction which indicated that the threat could relate to a "person for whom [the accused] would reasonably regard himself as responsible". Note in *Rogers* [1999] 9 *Archbold News* 1, it was assumed that a threat against the accused's "close friend" could be sufficient.
[401] [2005] 4 All E.R. 685 at 694, [21]; and see *Shayler* [2001] 1 W.L.R. 2206, para.49.
[402] [1994] Crim.L.R. 582.
[403] J.C. Smith, "Case Comment, *R v Cole*" [1994] Crim.L.R. 582 at 583.
[404] See below, para.9–003.
[405] [2003] EWCA Crim 1809.

Court of Appeal determined that it is not necessary to establish that there actually was a threat, it sufficed that D believed there was a threat. This belief must be reasonable as well as genuine.[406]

Immediacy of the Threat. In order to rely upon duress as a defence D must have **5–085** committed the offence whilst under the threat of "immediate" or "imminent" harm. Illustrative of this proposition is the decision in *Gill*[407] where the court considered that D would not have this defence if the threat was not to be carried out immediately because he could have sought police protection. However, in *Hurley and Murray*[408] it was determined that the defence of duress could be relied upon by D, even though he had ample opportunity to place himself under the protection of the police and was out of the range of the duressors, since his common law wife was being held hostage, and thus the threats were presently operative on the mind of D.

A rather benevolent application of this rule was seen in the case of *Hudson and Taylor*[409] where two girls were charged with committing perjury. They claimed that they had been threatened with injury if they made certain statements at the trial in question, and that during the course of the trial they had seen one of the men who made the threats in the public gallery. Of course, they would have been able to have asked, then and there, for police help, but the Court of Appeal held that the defence of duress should have been left to the jury. The decision seems to have been based upon the notion that police protection could not guarantee to be effective and that the threats were no less immediate because they could not be carried out until the girls had left the courtroom, if they could be carried out in the streets of Salford the same night. However, police protection will rarely, if ever, be able to guarantee permanent protection, and the outcome in *Hudson and Taylor* seems to be understandable. Lord Widgery C.J. made the following cogent points on the matter of police protection:

> "The argument does not distinguish cases in which the police would be able to provide effective protection, from those when they would not, and it would, in effect, restrict the defence of duress to cases where the person threatened had been kept in custody by the maker of the threats, or where the time interval between the making of the threats and the commission of the offence had made recourse to the police impossible. We recognise the need to keep the defence of duress within reasonable bounds but cannot accept so severe a restriction on it."[410]

In *Abdul-Hussain and Others*[411] the Court of Appeal confirmed the decision in *Hudson and Taylor* and decided that the threat must be "imminent", but need not be immediate. The case involved a group of Shiite Muslims who were fugitives from the Saddam Hussein regime living in Sudan. They were overstayers in Sudan, and so in fear of being arrested and returned to Iraq where they expected to be tortured and executed, they boarded a plane bound for Jordan and hijacked it. They forced the pilot to fly to London where they sought political asylum. They were arrested at Stansted Airport and charged with hi-jacking contrary to s.1(1) of the Aviation Security Act 1982. They sought to rely on the defence of

---

[406] See below at para.5–087.
[407] [1963] 1 W.L.R. 841.
[408] [1967] V.R. 526.
[409] [1971] 2 Q.B. 202.
[410] [1971] 2 Q.B. 202 at 207. See, also, *Aldridge* [2006] EWCA Crim 1970 where D participated in a robbery subsequent to a terrifying threat that his children would be beheaded by a samurai sword.
[411] [1999] Crim.L.R. 570.

duress of circumstances[412]—the charge of hi-jacking was admitted but they contended that they had done so as a last resort to escape death, either of themselves or of their families, at the hands of the Iraqi authorities. The trial judge, however, ruled that the defence of duress of circumstances should not be left to the jury because the threat was insufficiently close and immediate to give rise to a virtually spontaneous reaction to the physical risk arising. The appeal of the accused to the Court of Appeal proved successful.[413] Their Lordships determined that, as in *Hudson and Taylor, imminent* peril of death or serious injury to the defendant or his dependants had to operate on the mind of the defendant at the time he committed the act so as to overbear his will, but the execution of the threat *need not be immediately* in prospect.[414] The trial judge had incorrectly limited the availability of the defence by requiring a virtually spontaneous reaction. Rose L.J. gave a vivid and persuasive illustration to support this rationale:

> "If Anne Frank had stolen a car to escape from Amsterdam and been charged with theft, the tenets of English law would not, in our judgment, have denied her a defence of duress of circumstances, on the ground that she should have waited for the Gestapo's knock on the door."

5–086 In *Hasan*,[415] Lord Bingham has carefully reasserted the significance of the imminent and immediacy requirements. The decision in *Hudson and Taylor* was viewed as "indulgent". According to Lord Bingham the defence would be inapposite where a delay of a day existed between D being threatened with being shot and his commission of the offence. His Lordship stated that execution of a threat must be reasonably believed to be imminent and immediate if it is to support a plea of duress.[416]

The defence is inapplicable to the timorous defendant if an avenue of escape is available which the ordinary reasonable person would have taken. In this regard the Law Commission in their Report, No.218 of 1993[417] rejected their earlier opinion in Consultation Paper No.122 over the irrelevance of the criterion of "effective" official protection. It is now their view that the question whether D "knows or believes" that the police would be able to provide effective protection is relevant to the duress equation.[418] Clause 25(2)(b) of their Draft Bill provides:

> "A person does an act under duress by threats if he does it because he *knows or believes* . . . that the act will be carried out immediately if he does not do the act or, if not immediately, before he or that other can obtain *effective* official protection."

---

[412] See below for discussion of this defence; a similar rationale also applies to duress by threats.

[413] Note that this outcome does not provide a blank cheque to hijacking activities under some form of duress. The decision only determines that the defence of duress was wrongly withheld from the jury on this occasion. If the defence had been properly left to the jury, they would have had to consider whether the hijacking was a reasonable and proportionate response to the threat (an objective question). Of course, the onus would have been on the prosecution to establish this not to be the case, but in light of the terrifying dangers attached to such conduct the prosecution might well have been successful.

[414] The court, obiter, resiled from the decision in *DPP v Rogers* [1998] Crim.L.R. 202; see below, para.5–086. It is submitted that it is still the law that D cannot rely on an unreasonable belief of fact in order to found a defence of duress by threats or duress of circumstances.

[415] [2005] 4 All E.R. 685.

[416] [2005] 4 All E.R. 685 at 697–698 [27–28]. See, also, *N* [2007] EWCA Crim 3479.

[417] See, Law Commission No.218, *Legislating the Criminal Code: Offences Against the Person and General Principles* 49–50 (1993).

[418] This reiterates the statement made by Lord Griffiths in *Howe* [1987] A.C. 417 at 443 that: "if duress is introduced as a merciful concession to human frailty it seems hard to deny it to a man who knows full well that any official protection he may seek will not be effective to save him from the threat under which he has acted."

In both *Baker and Ward*[419] and *Heath,*[420] the Court of Appeal have affirmed that the defence is not available to a defendant who unreasonably failed to take advantage of an opportunity to escape from the duress. In *Baker and Ward,* where the accused had an opportunity to put himself under the protection of the police but did not because he believed the police could not have afforded effective protection, the conviction was quashed because it was not left to the jury to decide whether any reasonable person would have done so. It may well have been the case that police protection may not have stopped the duressors to whom the duressees owed money for cannabis. A different perspective applied in *Heath* where the accused alleged that he had been pressured into transporting drugs. The court held that more than one avenue of escape was open to him (going to the police, which he was reluctant to do because he was a drug addict and scared, or returning to the safety of his parents' home in Scotland, which he did not wish to do because he did not want them to know about the position he was in). Certainly, Lord Bingham in *Hasan*[421] regarded it as a fundamental principle that it should be made clear to juries that unless D reasonably expects the threat of retribution to be carried out "immediately or almost immediately" on his failure to comply with the threat, there may be little if any room for doubt that he could have taken evasive action. This action involves going to the police, or in some other way to avoid committing the crime with which he is charged. Yet again, his Lordship was concerned to constrain the nature of the defence.

(ii) The Apposite Test for Duress

Subjective and Objective Elements.   Duress operates as a concession to human weakness.   **5–087**
The defendant elects one evil, the apparent breaking of the law, when faced with a choice of two evils, the other dilemmatic choice being to suffer serious injury or death. The question is what test ought to be applied against which the conduct of the defendant can be assessed. Judicial opinions have culminated in the development of a two-prong test with subjective and objective elements determining when duress may be used as a defence. Lord Lane C.J. clearly enunciated this test in *Graham,*[422] and the House of Lords has since affirmed it in *Howe.* The defence is available only if, from an objective standpoint, the accused can be said to have acted reasonably and proportionately to avoid a threat of death or serious injury. Assuming the defence is available to the accused based on the facts, the defence should be a question for the jury, with instructions to determine two questions:

> "(1) Was the defendant, or may he have been, impelled to act as he did because, as a result of what he reasonably believed [the person issuing the threat] had said or done, he had good cause to fear that if he did not so act [that person] would kill him . . . or cause him serious personal injury?
>
> (2) If so, have the prosecution made the jury sure that a sober person of reasonable firmness, sharing the characteristics of the defendant, would not have responded to whatever he reasonably believed [the person making the threat] said or did by taking part in the killing? The fact that a defendant's will to resist has been eroded by the voluntary consumption of drink or drugs or both is not relevant to this test."[423]

The objective test involves the standard of the reasonable man. Three objective elements are contained within the overall direction, i.e. D must have *reasonably* believed that he was

---

[419] [1999] 2 Cr.App.R. 335.
[420] [2000] Crim.L.R. 109.
[421] [2005] 4 All E.R. 685 at 698, [28].
[422] [1982] 1 All E.R. 801 at 806.
[423] [1982] 1 All E.R. 801.

impelled to act as he did because of the threat; the belief needs to constitute a *good cause* for his fear, and most importantly the response needs to be one which might have been expected of a *sober person of reasonable firmness*.[424] It is noteworthy that the requirement imposed by Lord Lane C.J., that a mistaken belief as to the relevant act of the duressor must be "reasonable" so that D had "good cause" to fear the supposedly threatened harm, is out of line with other defences. In most defences today a mistaken belief may be a defence even if it is *unreasonably* held. For example, in both *Gladstone Williams*[425] and *Beckford*[426] the courts recognised, vis-à-vis private defence and prevention of crime, a defendant ought to be judged on the facts as he believed them to be, whether the belief was reasonably held or not. No logical basis exists to exclude this rationale to duress.[427] The Law Commission have until recently consistently advocated the abolition of this anomaly in relation to mistaken belief and duress.[428] However, the existing position is that when a defendant pleads duress a factual belief will not be of relevance unless it is based on reasonable grounds. This principle, which was imported into the law of duress by the Court of Appeal in *Graham*, and confirmed by the House of Lords in *Howe*,[429] was surprisingly recently overlooked by the Divisional Court in *DPP v Rogers*,[430] and by the Court of Appeal in *Martin (David Paul)*.[431] The statement therein that the mistaken belief does not have to be a reasonable one is flatly contradictory to both *Graham* and *Howe*, the two leading cases which form the basis of our law.[432] Whatever the merits of this position it is firmly entrenched by case law authorities and remains the law until remedied by either the House of Lords or Parliament. In *Hasan*[433] it was implicitly accepted by Lord Bingham stating that there was no warrant for relaxing the requirement that the belief must be reasonable as well as genuine.

Prior to the decision in *Graham* the Law Commission had asserted that, "threats directed against a weak, immature or disabled person may well be more compelling than the same threats directed against a normal healthy person".[434] This was accepted in part only by Lord Lane in *Graham* when stating that the resistance to be expected was that of one "sharing the characteristics of the accused". This was suitably qualified by the addition of the requirement that the resistance should match that of a "sober person of reasonable firmness", seeking in this way to "limit the defence . . . by means of an objective criterion formulated in terms of reasonableness".[435] Thus, the test is that if an ordinary person sharing the characteristics of the accused would have resisted the threats, D will be convicted. The characteristics of D which are to be attributed to the ordinary person are, by analogy with provocation, presumably age, sex and other non-transitory mental or physical attributes which would affect the gravity of the threat to him.[436] Difficulties associated with identifying relevant characteristics in the defence of provocation are well known. The next section focuses on similar problems pertinent to duress.[437]

---

[424] J.C. Smith and B. Hogan, *Criminal Law* (Butterworths, 1996) at p.245.
[425] [1987] 3 All E.R. 411; (1994) 78 Cr.App.R. 276; see above, para.2–085.
[426] [1988] A.C. 130; see above, para.2–085.
[427] N.M. Padfield, *loc. cit.*, at p.782.
[428] See, Consultation Paper No.122, and Law Commission No.218, but now Law Com. No.304, *Murder, Manslaughter and Infanticide* (2006).
[429] [1987] A.C. 417 at 459.
[430] [1998] Crim.L.R. 202.
[431] [2000] 2 Cr.App.R. 42; see, also, *Cairns* [1999] 2 Cr.App.R. 137 (duress of circumstances).
[432] Note that the view of the Divisional Court in *DPP v Rogers* that the defendant's mistake need not be a reasonable one was based on a false assumption that the present law on duress is accurately defined by a proposed codification of the law set out in cl.26(2) of the draft Criminal Law Bill annexed to the 1993 L.C. *Report on Offences Against The Person*, No.218.
[433] [2005] 4 All E.R. 685 at 696, [23].
[434] Law Com. No.83, para.2.28.
[435] [1982] 1 All E.R. 801 at 806.
[436] N.M. Padfield, *loc. cit.*, at p.783.
[437] See, generally, K.J.M. Smith, "Must Heroes Behave Heroically?" [1989] Crim.L.R. 622.

Relevant Objective Criteria.   The ambit of relevant characteristics of D, attributable to the   **5–088** "ordinary person" were considered by the Court of Appeal in *Bowen*,[438] their Lordships reviewing extant principles from previous case law.[439] D was convicted of five counts of obtaining services by deception for which he was sentenced to 18 months' imprisonment concurrently on each count. These charges related to the purchase of electrical goods on credit. In giving evidence D accepted that he had received the goods on credit, and had made few payments, but asserted that throughout the period he had acted under duress. It was suggested that he had been accosted by two men in a public house who had threatened him that he and his family would be petrol-bombed if he did not obtain goods for them. He was also told that if he went to the police his family would be attacked.

On appeal, it was submitted on behalf of D that the judge misdirected the jury in relation to the defence of duress. The claim was that the judge should have included in his direction on duress that the sober person of reasonable firmness was someone who shared D's characteristics, incorporating a low IQ of only 68. What were the relevant characteristics of the accused to which the jury should have regard in considering the objective test? It seemed clear to the Court of Appeal in *Bowen* that age and sex were, and physical health or disability might be, relevant characteristics, but beyond that the court considered that it was not altogether easy to determine from the authorities what others might be relevant. In the leading judgment, that of Stuart-Smith L.J., it was stated that the following guiding principles could be extricated from the leading authorities in the area.[440]

(a) The mere fact that the accused was more pliable, vulnerable, timid or susceptible to threats than a normal person did not make it legitimate to invest the reasonable/ordinary person with such characteristics for the purpose of considering the objective test. In *Horne*[441] D had conspired with others to make fraudulent claims for Income Support. During his trial he had applied for leave to call a psychiatrist whose evidence was designed to show that D was a man unusually pliant and vulnerable to pressure. The Court of Appeal held such evidence was rightly excluded. If the standard for comparison was a person of reasonable firmness it must be irrelevant for the jury to consider any characteristics of D which showed that he was not such a person, but was "pliant" or "vulnerable to pressure". Similarly in *Hegarty*[442] medical reports suggesting that D was "emotionally unstable" and "in a grossly elevated medical state" were excluded. This trilogy of cases is completed by the decision in *Hurst*[443] where D was charged with being knowingly concerned in the fraudulent evasion of the prohibition on the importation of cocaine, a class A controlled drug. She raised the defence of duress and sought to call evidence from a psychiatrist, not of any psychiatric disorder, but of the possible effects of sexual abuse as a child. This expert evidence, viewed as mere speculative opinion, was excluded.[444] The only exception here will be where an expert testifies to a relevant issue which is outside the knowledge and experience of a judge and jury, affirming principles enunciated in *Turner*.[445] Medical

---

[438] [1996] 2 Cr.App.R. 157.

[439] See, generally, A. Reed, "The Irrelevance of a Low Intelligence Quotient to a Claim of Duress "(1997) 67 *The Criminal Lawyer* 1.

[440] [1996] 2 Cr.App.R. 157 at 166–167.

[441] [1994] Crim.L.R. 584.

[442] [1994] Crim.L.R. 353.

[443] [1995] 1 Cr.App.R. 82.

[444] [1995] 1 Cr.App.R. 82: Beldam L.J. stated (at 90) that: "we find it hard to see how the person of reasonable firmness can be invested with the characteristics of a personality which lacks reasonable firmness . . ."

[445] The well-known dictum of Lawton L.J. in *Turner* (1975) 60 Cr.App.R. 80 at 83 is that: "An expert's opinion is admissible to furnish the court with scientific information which is likely to be outside the experience and knowledge of a judge or jury. If on the proven facts a judge or jury can form their own conclusions without help, then the opinion of an expert is unnecessary. In such a case, if it is given dressed up in scientific jargon, it may make judgment more difficult."

evidence which goes only to show that D's mental state was such that he was exceptionally "vulnerable" to threats is irrelevant.

(b) The defendant might be in a category of persons whom the jury might think less able to resist pressure than people not within that category. Obvious examples were age, where a young person might not be as robust as a mature one; possibly sex, although many women would doubtless consider that they had as much moral courage to resist pressure as men; pregnancy where there was an added fear for the unborn child; serious physical disability, which might inhibit self-protection; and recognised mental illness of psychiatric condition, such as post-traumatic stress disorder leading to learnt helplessness. The last category pertains to the decision in the important case of *Emery*.[446] The female D was convicted of cruelty to a child who died at the age of 11 months. Both mother and father blamed each other for the severe physical abuse. The appellate court held that evidence that D was subject to a condition in which she was unable to resist or stand up to the father as a result of his treatment of her, a condition of learnt helplessness, was relevant in mitigation. In essence, the history of violence committed by the child's father, causative of D's condition, was part of the duress. It was stated, albeit obiter, by Lord Taylor C.J. that it was relevant to allow evidence, "to give an expert account of the causes of the condition of dependent helplessness, the circumstances in which it might arise and what level of abuse would be required to produce it."[447]

An interesting case in this area is that of *Rogers*[448] where the accused was found to be suffering from Asperger's syndrome, a developmental disorder of autistic personality which apparently renders sufferers from the syndrome vulnerable, more susceptible to threats, and easier to exploit than non-sufferers. In this context the appellate court quashed the accused's conviction and ordered a retrial when evidence of D's mental condition, unavailable at trial, came to light when the case was adjourned for reports prior to sentencing. The fact that D suffered from Asperger's syndrome may well have altered the jury's view on his plea of duress if it had been allowed into evidence.

(c) Characteristics which might be relevant in considering provocation, because they related to the nature of the provocation itself would not necessarily be relevant in cases of duress. Thus homosexuality might be relevant to provocation if the provocative words or conduct were related to that characteristic. However, it could not be relevant in duress, since there was no reason to think that homosexual people were less robust in resisting threats of the kind that were relevant in duress cases.

(d) Characteristics due to self-imposed abuse such as alcohol, drugs or glue-sniffing could not be relevant to duress.

In *Flatt*,[449] it was determined that drug addiction was a self-induced condition, not a characteristic, and was not a relevant characteristic because it did not affect an individual's ability to resist threats. A dichotomy prevails here with the House of Lords decision in *Morhall* relating to provocation directed specifically at the "characteristic" of drug addiction.[450] Substance abuse may be a relevant characteristic in provocation where the taunt is

---

[446] (1993) 14 Cr.App.R. (S) 394. This category of mental illness was added here for the first time.
[447] (1993) 14 Cr.App.R.(S.) 394 at 398.
[448] Unrep., June, 15, 1999 (Case No: 99/2314/W4); see, generally, A. Buchanan and G. Virgo, "Duress and Mental Abnormality" [1999] Crim.L.R. 517; and K.J.M. Smith, "Duress and Steadfastness: In Pursuit of the Unintelligible" [1999] Crim.L.R. 363. In *Moseley* [1999] 7 *Archbold News* 2 CA it was determined that "learned helplessness", not resulting from post-traumatic stress disorder or any other mental disorder, but where it arose from D's previous relationships with violent men, including the duressor, was not a relevant characteristic; see also, *Walker* [2003] EWCA Crim 1837; and *Antar* [2004] EWCA Crim 2708.
[449] [1996] Crim.L.R. 576.
[450] See below, para.7–028.

targeted at this very abuse since it may be relevant to the response of the defendant in losing self-control.

The Court of Appeal in *Bowen*, adopting the above guidelines, held that a low intelligence quotient, short of mental impairment or mental defectiveness, was not a relevant characteristic since it did not make those who had it less courageous or less able to withstand threats and pressure than an ordinary person. A low IQ of 68 was treated as irrelevant to the defence of duress.[451]

Proposals for Reform.   The objective test involves the standard of the reasonable man, the **5–089** standard of "a sober person of reasonable firmness". Under current law, as applied in *Bowen*, the defence is denied to those of low intelligence, the subjectively weak or timorous accused who fails to meet the reasonable person standard. A welcome development, from a subjectivist perspective, would be to apply a test of simply whether in all the circumstances the individual in question could reasonably be expected to resist the threat.

Impressionistically, the incumbent characteristics of low intelligence or timidity in an individual, a consequence of which makes him more willing to accede to the particular threat and undertake criminal activity, ought to be circumstances that are evaluated when pressure through duress is considered. On that view, a welcome reform of the law would be to adopt the earlier proposals of the Law Commission back in 1993, whereby "the threat is one which in all the circumstances, including any of his personal characteristics that affect its gravity, he cannot reasonably be expected to resist".[452] It must be remembered that duress operates as a concession to human frailty, and included within that group are undoubtedly those of low intelligence, the timid and the weak. By adopting a subjectivist approach, focusing on the peculiarities of the individual, it might be argued that more logical and humane principles can be adopted.

Most importantly, in cl.25 of their draft Criminal Law Bill, the Law Commissioners in 1993 set out significant proposals to deal with duress by threats. They suggested that a legal burden of proof be placed on *defendant*s to establish their pleas of duress on a balance of probabilities, and also to show, where relevant, that they did not knowingly and without reasonable excuse expose themselves to the risk of the threat being made:

"25—(1) No act of a person constitutes an offence if the act is done under duress by threats.

(2) A person does not act under duress by threats if he does it because he knows or believes:

(a) that a threat has been made to cause death or serious injury to himself or another if the act is not done, and

(b) that the act will be carried out immediately if he does not do the act or, if not immediately, before he or that other can obtain effective official protection, and

(c) that there is no other way of preventing the threat being carried out.

and the threat is one which in all the circumstances (including any of his personal characteristics that affect its gravity) he cannot reasonably be expected to resist."

---

[451] It is submitted that this principle may operate harshly against D in that it is arguable that a low IQ inhibits D's ability to seek the protection of the police. D would not think it necessary to seek help.
[452] Law Com. No.218, cl.25.

5–090   It could be suggested that similar subjectivist alterations ought to be adopted in the United States where the common law, in contrast to jurisdictions applying the Model Penal Code, has demonstrated anomalies, vacillations and inconsistencies over adopting an applicable test for duress. For example, in *United States v Jennell*[453] the Ninth Circuit Court of Appeal set out three essential requirements of duress:

> "(1) an immediate threat of death or serious bodily injury; (2) a well-grounded fear that the threat will be carried out; and (3) no reasonable opportunity to escape threatened harm."

Such a test has pervading difficulties in that it palpably fails to expound whether the test for a "well-grounded" fear is an objective or subjective one, nor is any specification made as to which individual the threat has to be made against.

Most recently, in 2006, the Law Commission published its significant report suggesting a restructuring of the homicide offences and of a number of defences. The Commission proposes a three-tiered approach to homicide, with offences of first degree murder; second degree murder; and manslaughter.[454] Departing from the position it took in *A New Homicide Act for England and Wales?*[455] the Commission now proposes[456]:

- that duress should be a full defence to its proposed offences of first and second degree murder, and attempted murder;

- that for the defences to be available to these offences, the threat in question should be one of death or life-threatening harm;

- that the defendant's belief in the existence of the threat and as to it being implemented must be both honestly and reasonably held;

- that for the purpose of comparing the actions of D with those of a notional person of reasonable firmness, all the circumstances of D are relevant, including age, but not any other characteristics affecting his ability to resist duress;

- that the defendant should bear the burden of proving the defence on the balance of probabilities.

D. Duress and the Voluntary Joining of Criminal Associations

5–091 An individual who voluntarily joins a criminal gang knowing of its nature and knowing that it might bring pressure on him to commit an offence, will be unable to rely on duress if he did commit an offence in response to such pressure.[457] This principle was established by the

---

[453] 749 F 2d. 1302 (9th Cir., 1985).
[454] *Manslaughter and Infanticide* (2006) Law Com. No.304. See below, para.7–017.
[455] Law Com. No.177 (2005). In the earlier report the Commission suggested that duress should be a partial defence to first degree murder.
[456] See generally *Manslaughter and Infanticide* (2006) Law Com. No.304, Pt 6.
[457] See, generally, I.H. Dennis, "Developments in Duress" (1987) 51 J.C.L. 463, 478–479.

Court of Appeal in *Sharp*.[458] The appellate court upheld a trial judge who had refused to leave to the jury a defence of duress put forward by one of three armed robbers.[459] D asserted that he had participated only because the leader of the gang threatened to kill him if he did not. Evidence, however, existed that he had voluntarily joined the gang which had then committed an earlier robbery in which shots had been fired. It was held that the defendant's extreme culpability in knowingly exposing himself to the risk of duress destroyed any claim of duress as an excuse.[460] These principles were extended in *Ali*[461] where a heroin dealer and addict, in debt to the duressor, was threatened with death unless he participated in a conspiracy directed at robbing a bank or building society. It was determined that duress was inapplicable as a defence where D voluntarily joined himself to a violent individual. Application of the rule extended to where D realised he would become part of a crime and need not know precisely which violent offence he would be ordered to carry out where a range of violent offences were in contemplation at the outset.

In *Sharp,* the issue did not arise whether duress was available as a defence where a defendant was unexpectedly faced with the prospect of committing a wholly different type of offence outside the scope of the initial gang enterprise. Nor did it arise whether the defence was available where unexpected pressure was applied to coerce D into an offence within the enterprise. These matters arose directly in the subsequent case of *Shepherd*,[462] wherein the Court of Appeal determined that a distinction prevailed between joining on the one hand a gang promulgating violence as a political end or one tacitly prepared to resort to violence for other criminal means, and joining on the other hand a gang where D's absence of knowledge of a propensity to violence on the part of one gang member would not lead him, "to suspect that a decision to think better of the whole affair might lead him into serious trouble". In the first scenario the voluntary act of joining the gang prevented D, from relying upon duress as he freely undertook the risk of duress. By way of contrast in the second type of case the question ought to be left to the jury whether, via gang participation, D had knowingly taken the risk of violence against himself. In the event that duress materialised unexpectedly, then the jury could find that the risk of it had not been freely undertaken. For example, D, who participates in a small money transfer bank fraud may legitimately claim no contemplation of threats of death or serious injury being imposed upon him as catalysts to the facilitation of violent offence(s).[463] It may credibly be asserted that coercion to commit such offence(s) was unexpected, although such a defence will rarely succeed in practice.

In essence, if D is aware of or ought to be aware of the risk of compulsion by threats of death or grievous bodily harm at the time he voluntarily associates with the ultimate duressor(s) then the defence may not be available although he may not have foreseen the particular type of crime the duressor(s) would require him to commit. In recent times the relevant principles have been developed in relation to drug-dealing, where the accused in debt to violent drug-dealers has engaged in the transportation or supply of dangerous drugs on their behalf. In *Heath*,[464] the accused, indebted to drug dealers, was charged with possessing a Class B drug with intent to supply, an offence committed under serious threats

---

[458] [1987] 1 Q.B. 853.

[459] Reliance was placed upon codes in other common law jurisdictions and the decision of the Northern Ireland Court of Appeal in *Fitzpatrick* [1977] N.I. 20.

[460] [1977] N.I. 20 Lord Lane C.J. asserted (at 861) that: "where a person has voluntarily, and with knowledge of its nature, joined a criminal organisation or gang which he knew might bring pressure on him to commit an offence and was an active member when he was put under such pressure, he cannot avail himself of the defence of duress."

[461] [1995] Crim.L.R. 303.

[462] (1988) 86 Cr.App.R. 47.

[463] I.H. Dennis, *loc. cit.*, at p.479.

[464] [2000] Crim.L.R. 109.

from his erstwhile "creditor". The court held that the defendant could not rely on duress as a defence because although he was not a member of any criminal organisation or gang, by becoming indebted to a drug dealer he had voluntarily exposed himself to unlawful violence. There was credible evidence that the defendant appreciated that he had put himself in what he described as a "bad position" and exposure to the risk of violence. He said, "[i]t's the drugs world. It can be heavy. People collect their debts in one way". The defence is, thus, excluded where the risk of duress is freely undertaken and voluntary association has occurred which does not necessarily have to incorporate joining their gang or association.

5–092   Prior to the recent House of Lords decision in *Hasan*,[465] however, confusion existed because a differently constituted appellate court in *Baker and Ward*[466] adopted a flatly contradictory view to *Heath*. In *Baker and Ward* it was asserted that, what D has to be aware of is the risk that the group might try to coerce him into committing criminal offences of the *type* for which he is being tried by the use of violence or threats of violence. On this perspective the vice of voluntary association is that it renders D liable to pressure to commit a crime of the relevant degree of seriousness. Thus, there had to be an anticipation on the part of D of pressure to commit a crime of the type charged before the defence was unavailable. *Heath* illustrated the more general proposition that it is the awareness of risk of compulsion that matters:

> "[A]n awareness of what criminal activity those exercising compulsion might offer as a possible alternative to violence is irrelevant."[467]

The decision of their Lordships in *Hasan* is significant in constraining further the ambit of the duress defence. In the context of a defendant voluntarily joining a criminal association it is no defence that "he" did not foresee exposure to the risk of the application of duress if it "ought" to have been foreseen.[468] This is reflective of an external standard of liability equated to the amorphous test of the reasonable person. The defendant was an individual who had voluntarily surrendered his will to the domination of another. In holding that there had to be foresight of coercion to commit crimes of the kind with which he was charged, the appellate court in *Baker and Ward* had, apparently, misstated the law. The defence is precluded where the risk to which D exposes himself is pressure compelling him to commit *any type of crime*. Lord Bingham asserted:

> "The defendant is, *ex hypothesi*, a person who has voluntarily surrendered his will to the domination of another. Nothing should turn on foresight of the manner in which, in the event, the dominant party chooses to exploit the defendant's subservience. There need not be foresight of coercion to commit crimes, although it is not easy to envisage circumstances in which a party might be coerced to act lawfully."[469]

---

[465] [2005] 4 All E.R. 685.

[466] [1999] 2 Cr.App.R. 335.

[467] [2000] Crim.L.R. 109, quoted in *Hasan* per Lord Bingham. Note that *Heath* was followed in *Harmer* [2001] EWCA Crim 2930.

[468] Note that Baroness Hale in *Hasan* reveals an inclination towards a more subjective approach, see 714 at [73].

[469] [2005] 4 All E.R. 685 at 702, [37]. An objective test is propounded by Lord Bingham at 703, [38] on policy grounds: "The policy of the law must be to discourage association with known criminals, and it should be slow to excuse the criminal conduct of those who do so. If a person voluntarily becomes or remains associated with others engaged in criminal activity in a situation where he knows or ought reasonably to know that he may be the subject of compulsion by them or their associates, he cannot rely on the defence to excuse any act which he is thereafter compelled to do by them".

E. Duress of Circumstances

In *Jones*[470] the court was not prepared to allow a defence of duress in a situation where D **5–093** claimed to have driven dangerously because he thought that he was being chased by men who wanted to attack him; his pursuers were, in fact, police officers. The court ruled that the defence was only open to someone who had been ordered to commit a crime, and no one had ordered Jones to drive dangerously. However, more recent decisions have facilitated the possibility of a defence of "duress" in similar dilemmatic factual circumstances. In this regard English courts have never expressly recognised a general defence of necessity, where an individual commits an offence to avoid the greater evil to himself or another that would occur from the dangerous circumstances in which he or the other person is placed. The gap has been remedied by several recent appellate decisions allowing a form of necessity as an excuse, albeit within the duress terminology, and, therefore, through the backdoor by judicial sleight of hand.

The limited defence of duress of circumstances, i.e. necessity, has developed in English law in relation to road traffic cases involving reckless driving and driving while dis-qualified.[471] For example, in *Willer* the defendant, in order to escape from a gang of youths who threatened to kill both him and his car passenger, had driven along a pavement and into a shopping precinct in order to escape from them. The defence of duress was available to a charge of reckless driving where D had been compelled to drive in such a manner by force of circumstance.[472] In *Conway*[473] D was charged with and convicted of reckless driving.[474] He claimed that he honestly believed that the two-plain clothes police officers who approached his car planned to kill his passenger, T. T had been involved in a shooting incident several weeks earlier and D believed that T had been the real target for the attack at that time. After a high speed chase through a built up area D was eventually forced to stop. On his appeal against conviction D argued that the jury should have been directed on the defence of necessity. The Court of Appeal was of the opinion that it was not entirely clear whether or not there was a general defence of necessity and if so when it was available. The court held that it was only available in cases of reckless driving where it amounted to duress of circumstances. What this means is that the court is saying that it would accept a defence of duress, provided that all the requirements of that defence were satisfied, but that this defence was unlike the ordinary defence of duress *per minas* (by threats) where D is told to do something "or else". In duress of circumstances the duress is applied by the surrounding circumstances. Woolf L.J. agreed with the comment of Lord Hailsham in *Howe* where he remarked that it could make no difference whether the accused does something because he is told to "or else" or whether he does it because he perceives that in view of the circumstances he has no choice. The court treated the defence of duress of circumstances (necessity) as a logical corollary of duress *per minas* (by threats) because the duress defence was similarly limited by the fact that the harm sought to be avoided must be death or serious

---

[470] *The Times,* December 18, 1963.

[471] See, e.g. *Willer* (1986) 83 Cr.App.R. 225; *Conway* [1989] Q.B. 290 and *Martin (Colin)* [1989] 1 All E.R. 652.

[472] It was stated by Watkins L.J. that: "[T]he assistant recorder upon those facts should have directed that he would leave to the jury the question as to whether or not . . . the appellant was wholly driven by force of circumstances into doing what he did and did not drive the car otherwise than under that form of compulsion, i.e., under duress"; (1986) 83 Cr.App.R. 225 at 227.

[473] [1989] Q.B. 290.

[474] Note that reckless driving has been replaced by the offence of dangerous driving.

injury.[475] Subsequently, in *Backshall*,[476] the court determined that duress of circumstances was also available as a defence to driving without due care and attention.

The elements of duress of circumstances were further considered in *Martin (Colin)*,[477] a case where D was charged with driving while disqualified. The trial judge refused to allow the defence of necessity and so D pleaded guilty and introduced, by way of mitigation, the facts he would have used to support his defence of necessity. He said that on the morning in question his wife asked him to drive her son (his stepson) to work as he was late and in danger of being fired. His wife had previously tried to commit suicide and she now threatened to do so again if he refused. He, thus, felt obliged to drive, although he had been disqualified. Allowing his appeal against conviction the Court of Appeal said that D had discharged his evidential burden in relation to the defence of duress of circumstances and the trial judge should therefore, have left it to the jury. Simon Brown J. affirmed the existence of such a defence:

> "[F]irst, English law does, in extreme circumstances, recognise a defence of necessity. Most commonly this defence arises as duress, that is pressure upon the accused's will from the wrongful threats of violence of another. Equally, however, it can arise from other objective dangers threatening the accused or others. Arising thus it is conveniently called 'duress of circumstances'."[478]

5–094   The jury should have been asked two questions: (1) Was the accused, or may he have been, impelled to act as he did, because as a result of what he reasonably believed to be the situation he had good cause to fear that otherwise death or serious bodily injury would result. (2) If so, would a sober person of reasonable firmness, sharing the characteristics of the accused, have responded to that situation by acting as the accused did? The defence is only available if, from an objective standpoint, the accused can be said to be acting reasonably and proportionately in order to avoid a threat of death or serious injury.[479] Derived from the subjective and objective principles established by *Graham*, the test for necessity is essentially identical to that for duress by threats, with the exception of the situational source from which the threat emanates. In this regard, it is only through these recent significant developments that English law has caught up with a limited number of US jurisdictions that have adopted the Model Penal Code provisions requiring a balancing of competing evils:

> "Conduct that the actor believes to be necessary to avoid a harm or evil to himself or to another is justifiable, provided that: (a) the harm or evil sought to be avoided by such conduct is greater than that sought to be prevented by the law defining the offence charged."[480]

---

[475] Woolf L.J. stated that: "We conclude that necessity can only be a defence to a charge of reckless driving where the facts establish 'duress of circumstances' . . . i.e. where the defendant was constrained by circumstances to drive as he did to avoid death or serious bodily harm to himself or some other person. [T]o admit a defence of 'duress of circumstances' is a logical consequence of the existence of the defence of duress as that term is ordinarily understood, i.e. 'do this or else'." [1989] Q.B. 290 at 297.

[476] [1998] 1 W.L.R. 1506; *The Times*, April 10, 1998.

[477] [1989] 1 All E.R. 652.

[478] [1989] 1 All E.R. 652 at 653.

[479] A. Reed, "The Need for a New Anglo-American Approach to Duress" (1997) 61 J.C.L. 209 at 222.

Note on the factual scenario in *Martin (Colin)* the case should more properly be viewed as involving duress *per minas* (threats) not circumstances.

[480] Model Penal Code s.3.02(1)(a) (1985). This test arguably allows flexibility and compassion for the coerced actor.

The guiding principles have been affirmed by the Court of Appeal in *Abdul-Hussain and Others*.[481] In that case the Iraqi hijackers apprehended at Stansted Airport asserted that their desperate operation sprung from their perceived fear of being arrested and returned to Iraq where they expected to be tortured and executed.[482] There is a distinction here with duress by threats where the offence committed is in response to the specified threats of the duressor; in duress of circumstances the offence springs from the perceived threat in the prevailing circumstances. This demands the jury to address the question whether the proportionality criterion is satisfied. The jury will have to evaluate whether the commission of the offence was a reasonable and proportionate response that was consonant with the perceived threat in the prevailing circumstances. This constitutes objective consideration of whether the amorphous reasonable person would have so acted. Hence, in *Rodger and Rose*[483] the appellate court determined that the appellants' own suicidal tendencies, in effect the threats made to themselves personally of suicide, could not constitute a defence to the offence of prison breaking. The use of a purely subjective element therein was precluded by the objective requirement.[484] Moreover, the defence of duress of circumstances will be inapplicable when the defendant had an alternative course of action available that does not involve breaking the law.[485]

The ambit of duress of circumstances, closely related to duress by threats, was previously determined by the Court of Appeal in *Pommell*.[486] Therein, police officers had entered D's house to execute a search warrant, and they found him lying in bed with a loaded gun in his right hand. He was convicted under the Firearms Act 1968 of possessing a prohibited weapon and ammunition without a firearms certificate.[487] D contended that during the night, someone carrying a gun had come to see him with the intention of shooting some people because they had killed his friend. D said that he had persuaded the man to give him the gun, which he took upstairs; he took the bullets out, then put them back, having decided to wait until morning to give the gun to his brother to hand to the police. The trial judge held that necessity could not be an issue because, even assuming that D was originally driven by necessity to take possession of the gun, his failure to go immediately to the police robbed him of the defence. The Court of Appeal stressed that no grounds existed for limiting the necessity defence to road traffic offences.[488] On the contrary, since the necessity defence was

---

[481] [1999] Crim.L.R. 570. Note it should be recalled that in *DPP v Rogers* [1998] Crim.L.R. 202, see above, para.5–087, it was asserted that the defendant's belief need not be reasonable. This conflicts with all other cases dealing with the issue in respect of duress of circumstances. In respect of duress by threats it is contradictory with the House of Lords decision in *Howe* [1987] A.C. 417 and, of course *Graham*. There is support for such a view in *Martin (David Paul)* [2000] 2 Cr.App.R. 42, criticised above at para.5–087, but as it contradicts *Howe* it must be incorrect until altered by the House of Lords or Parliament.

[482] See above, para.5–085.

[483] [1998] 1 Cr.App.R. 143. There must be an extraneous source: D cannot rely on the defence where cannabis is independently cultivated to alleviate pain from MS; see *Brown* [2003] EWCA Crim 2637.

[484] In *Rodger and Rose* earlier jurisprudence on the applicability of the defence of duress of circumstance was reviewed by Sir Patrick Russell who asserted: "All these authorities had one feature in common which is not present in the instant appeals. The feature which was causative of the defendants committing the offence was in all the authorities extraneous to the offender himself. In contrast, in these appeals it was solely the suicidal tendencies, the thought processes and the emotions of the offenders themselves which operated as duress. That factor introduced an entirely subjective element not present in the authorities ... We do not think that such a development of the law would be justified, nor do we think that such an extension would be in the public interest. If allowed it could amount to a licence to commit crime dependent on the personal characteristics and vulnerability of the offender. As a matter of policy that is undesirable and in our view it is not the law and should not be the law".

[485] In this regard an interesting illustration is provided by the Scottish decision in *Moss v Howdle* 1997 S.L.T. 782 wherein D, in response to cries of pain from a passenger, broke the speed limit in racing to the nearest available service station to engage medical attention. Duress of circumstances as a defence was denied; alternatives to breaching the law were reasonable courses of action such as stopping on the hard shoulder.

[486] (1995) 2 Cr.App.R. 607.

[487] Firearms Act 1968, (c.27) (Eng.).

[488] See, generally, G. Slapper, "Public Policy under Duress" (1995) N.L.J. 1063.

closely related to the defence of duress by threats and appeared to be general in nature, the court held that it applied to all crimes except murder, attempted murder, and some forms of treason.[489] The same line in the sand is drawn as for duress by threats.

5–095   A related matter that arose in *Pommell* is that of a duty to desist. In their Lordships' judgment, a person who had taken possession of a gun, in circumstances where he has the defence of duress of circumstances, must desist from committing the crime as soon as he reasonably can. It is a factual question on the evidence for determination by the jury. Clearly D must desist from the unlawful conduct as soon as he is aware that the threat is no longer operative. In *DPP v Jones*,[490] D may have had a defence of duress when he began to drive with an excess of alcohol, seeking to avoid a confrontation in a public house car park, but it was held that there was no necessity for him to drive the entire two miles to his home.[491] Similar principles have been applied in cases involving driving with excess alcohol where the factual circumstances have involved unwelcome homosexual advances or threats made by a violent partner.[492] In essence, the position is that on the possibility of duress becoming operative, the burden is imposed on the prosecution to demonstrate that it had ceased to be operative at the time of the criminal activity and that D failed the duty to desist.[493] This applied in *Arnaot*[494] where the defendant had driven away at high speed subsequent to a road traffic fracas, but it was questioned whether a genuine fear was prevalent which prompted her dangerous driving.

The ambit of duress as a defence arose in the high profile case of *Jones*.[495] The defendants committed various acts of criminal damage at RAF Fulford. Their contention, inter alia, was that duress of circumstances was apposite. The war on Iraq was submitted to be illegal in international law and by necessity their actions were necessary to prevent crimes being committed on civilians in Iraq. In essence, they asserted that they were preventing acts of aggression by Allied forces. The Court of Appeal, on an interlocutory appeal, determined that duress of circumstances did not apply as no "offence of aggression" was operative in our national law, even if it were an offence in international law. In the sense that the court limited the defence to situations where a defendant is presented with a crime in national law, and responds accordingly, this is unduly restrictive and contrary to earlier precedents.[496]

In conclusion, we can say that the defence of duress of circumstances is a limited form of a defence of necessity. Limited in that by classifying it as duress it means that it is not available on a charge of murder or attempted murder, and the requirements of the defence are the partially objective requirements of the defence of duress.[497] It seems fairly clear that the fear of death or serious bodily injury does not have to be for oneself,[498] and it is suggested that it could cover a situation in which there is no relationship between D and the person for whose safety he fears (for example, the motorist who goes through a red light to save a child from a drowning). Later cases may need to explore the relationship between this

---

[489] In this regard the Court of Appeal approved Professor Smith's commentary on *DPP v Bell*; see J.C. Smith, "Case Comment, *DPP v Bell*" [1992] Crim.L.R. 176, 177; see *Pommell* (1995) 2 Cr.App.R. 607 at 615.
[490] [1990] R.T.R. 34.
[491] See, e.g. *DPP v Bell* [1992] Crim.L.R. 176.
[492] *DPP v Davis; DPP v Pittaway* [1994] Crim.L.R. 600. See, generally, *Brown v CPS* [2007] EWHC 3274 (Admin).
[493] J.C. Smith, "Case Comment, *DPP v Bell*" [1992] Crim.L.R. 176 at 177.
[494] [2008] EWCA Crim 121.
[495] [2004] EWCA Crim 1981; [2005] Crim.L.R. 122. The case has since been heard, with the principal focus on issues other than duress, by the House of Lords. See [2006] UKHL 16. The House of Lords agreed that there was no offence of aggression in domestic law. See above, para.5–046; below, para.10–017.
[496] See, e.g. *Martin* [1989] 1 All E.R. 652—no "crime" of suicide.
[497] Note that in Law Com. No.218, draft bill, cl.26 similar proposals for reform of duress of circumstances have been made as for duress *per minas*.
[498] See *Conway*, above, para.5–093.

new defence and existing defences such as self-defence and prevention of crime.[499] The relationship between the alternative defences of self-defence and duress of circumstances arose in *Symonds*.[500] The defendant was charged with inflicting grievous bodily harm and dangerous driving in that he had driven away from a drunken pedestrian, C, whilst C's hand was trapped in his car, and consequently C was dragged for a distance and suffered injury. Symonds' defence was that C forced him to stop by staggering into the road. C had tried to pull him from the car and so, very frightened, he had driven off to escape. The Court of Appeal, in an obiter statement, enunciated that the same factual situation may be sufficient to support defences of self-defence and also duress of circumstances.[501] Their Lordships believed any problems caused by leaving a jury with these alternative defences would be more theoretical than substantial. However, with respect, this fails to recognise that under current law when self-defence is adduced D ought to be judged on the facts he honestly even if unreasonably believes[502]; in contradistinction for duress by threats or circumstances a factual belief will not be of relevance unless it is predicated on reasonable grounds. This distinction will, of course, be abrogated if *Martin (David Paul)*[503] on duress by threats and lack of requirement for reasonable grounds for mistaken belief was subsequently followed, but in *Hasan* it was implicitly rejected by Lord Bingham.[504] At present, substantial difficulties do still apply in directing a jury on these alternative defences. It has been submitted that a panacea to these difficulties may be for the trial judge simply to leave the defence of self-defence for consideration by the jury; it is more favourable to the accused in relation to mistaken factual beliefs and applies to all crimes.[505] This, indeed, was the perspective adopted by the Court of Appeal in *Burley*[506] It will be interesting to observe how these practical difficulties are ameliorated in the future.

GENERAL READING

Buchanan, A. and Virgo, G., "Duress And Mental Abnormality" [1999] Crim.L.R. 517.   **5–096**

Colvin, E., "Exculpatory Defences In Criminal Law" (1990) 10 O.J.L.S. 381.

Dennis, I.H., "Developments In Duress" (1987) 51 J.C.L. 463.

Dressler, J., "Exegis Of The Law Of Duress: Justifying The Excuse And Searching For Its Proper Limits" (1989) 62 Southern California L.R. 1331.

Elliott, D.W., "Necessity, Duress And Self-Defence" [1989] Crim.L.R. 611.

Gardner, S., "Duress In Attempted Murder" (1991) 107 L.Q.R. 389; and "Duress In The House Of Lords" (1992) 108 L.Q.R. 349.

Horder, J., "Autonomy, Provocation And Duress" [1992] Crim.L.R. 707.

Horder, J., "Occupying The Moral High Ground? The Law Commission On Duress" [1994] Crim.L.R. 334.

Milgate, H.P., "Duress And The Criminal Law: Another About Turn By The House Of Lords" (1988) 47 C.L.J. 61.

Padfield, N.M., "Duress, Necessity And The Law Commission" [1992] Crim.L.R. 778.

Reed, A., "The Need For A New Anglo-American Approach To Duress" (1997) 61 J.C.L. 209.

---

[499] Query in this regard whether self-defence was available in *Willer*? Did Willer use *force* to protect himself or prevent crime?
[500] [1998] Crim.L.R. 280.
[501] See, e.g. the facts in *Willer*, above.
[502] See *Gladstone Williams*, above, para.2–085.
[503] [2000] 2 Cr.App.R. 42; see above, at para.5–087.
[504] See above at para.5–087.
[505] J.C. Smith [1998] Crim.L.R. 281.
[506] [2000] Crim.L.R. 843.

Smith, K.J.M., "Must Heroes Behave Heroically?" [1989] Crim.L.R. 622.

Smith, K.J.M., and Wilson, W., "Impaired Voluntariness And Criminal Responsibility: Reinventing Hart's Theory Of Excuses—The English Judicial Response" (1993) 13 O.J.L.S. 69.

Smith, K.J.M., "Duress And Steadfastness: In Pursuit Of The Unintelligible" [1999] Crim.L.R. 363.

6. INFANCY

A. Children Under 10 Years of Age

5–097   The criminal law provides that children who are under the age of 10 when they commit the act which, had they been adults, would have been a criminal offence, are irrebutably to be presumed incapable of committing the crime.[507] In other words it is a total answer to a criminal charge that the accused was under the age of 10 at the time the act was perpetrated. Since the child is completely absolved from criminal liability it means that if X persuades a child to enter a house and to steal property from within, X will be guilty of burglary as a principal offender acting through the innocent agency of the child.[508]

B. Children 10 Years Old and Above

(i) Doli Incapax and the Age of Criminal Responsibility

5–098   Children who are 10 years old and above may be the subject of criminal proceedings though until they reach their eighteenth birthday they are likely to be tried in Youth Court of the magistrate's court. It should be noted that the appropriate court is determined by the age on the date of trial, whereas the question of liability is determined by the age at the time of the act was allegedly committed.

Prior to its abolition by s.34 of the Crime and Disorder Act 1998, the position at common law was that a child 10 years or over and under the age of 14 at the time of the alleged offence was presumed not to have reached the age of discretion and to be doli incapax; but this evidence may have been rebutted by the prosecution presenting strong and clear evidence of a mischievous discretion. Between 10 and 14 years a child was presumed not to know the difference between right and wrong, and therefore to be incapable of committing a crime because of lack of mens rea. In this regard "wrong" meant gravely wrong, *seriously wrong,* evil or morally wrong.[509] The continued vitality of such a presumption, set against a changed social, educational, moral, and political, background, was the very issue before the House of Lords in *C (A Minor) v DPP*, three years before the abrogation of the doctrine by Parliamentary legislation,[510] and the case raised the important issue of the proper role for

---

[507] See, s.50 of the Children and Young Persons Act 1933, as amended. The doctrine is summarised in Archbold, *Criminal Pleading Evidence and Practice*, Vol.1, p.52, para.1–96. It should be noted that no such presumption operates in Scotland where normal criminal responsibility attaches to a child over eight years of age.

[508] It may be that the non-commission of any criminal offence serves to negate the criminal liability of other parties. See, e.g. *Walters v Lunt* [1951] 2 All E.R. 645 where a child, aged seven, took another child's tricycle in factual circumstances which would have constituted the act of theft but for the child's age. No offence being committed the child's parents had to be acquitted of the offence of what is now handling. Of course, if the parents instigated the taking they would be liable for stealing it via the innocent agency of the child.

[509] See, e.g. *R v Gorrie* (1918) 83 J.P. 136; *B v R* (1958) 44 Cr.App.R. 1; and *R v Smith (Sidney)* (1845) 1 Cox C.C. 260.

[510] [1995] 2 W.L.R. 383. See generally, T. Crofts, "Rebutting the Presumption of *Doli Incapax*" (1998) 62 J.C.L. 185.

judicial law-making. The common law doctrine itself dated back to the legal writings of Hale[511] and Blackstone,[512] the latter stating:

> "But by the law, as it now stands, and has stood at least ever since the time of Edward the Third, the capacity of doing ill, or contracting guilt, is not so much measured by years and days, as by the strength of the delinquent's understanding and judgment. For one lad of eleven years old may have as much cunning as another of fourteen; and in these cases our maxim is, that 'malitia supplet aetatem' . . . under fourteen, though an infant shall be prima facie adjudged to be doli incapax, yet if it appears to the court and the jury, that he was doli capax, and could discern between good and evil, he may be convicted and suffer death. But, in all such cases, the evidence of that malice, which is to supply age, ought to be strong and clear beyond all doubt or contradiction."[513]

In *C (A Minor) v DPP*, D aged 12, and another boy were seen by police officers using a crowbar to tamper with a motorcycle in a private driveway. As the police approached the boys ran off but D was arrested. The motorcycle was found to be damaged and D was charged with interfering with a motorvehicle with intention to commit theft, contrary to s.9(1) of the Criminal Attempts Act 1981.[514] From these facts the justices inferred that D knew that he was in serious trouble and that what he had done was seriously wrong. Accordingly, although D was under 14, the presumption of doli incapax was rebutted, and D was convicted and fined. On appeal by way of case stated, the Divisional Court dismissed the appeal holding the presumption that a child between the age of 10 and 14 was doli incapax was outdated and no longer to be regarded as part of the law of England.[515] D appealed to the House of Lords, contending that the Divisional Court in holding that the presumption was no longer part of the law of England had engaged in unjustified judicial law-making and was bound by authority to recognise and apply the presumption.

The central issue for determination by the House of Lords in *C (A Minor) v DPP* was **5–099** thus, whether there continued to be a presumption that a child between the ages of 10 and 14 is doli incapax and, if so, whether that presumption could only be rebutted by clear positive evidence that he knew that his act was seriously wrong, such evidence not consisting merely in the evidence of the acts amounting to the offence itself. Certainly, Laws J. in the Divisional Court had regarded the presumption as insupportable, seeing it as a serious disservice to our law.[516] It meant that a child over 10 who committed an act of obvious dishonesty, or even of grave violence, was to be acquitted unless the prosecution proved by discrete evidence that he understood the obliquity of what he was doing. This was viewed by the Divisional Court as incongruous, unreal and contrary to common sense,[517] referring to modern judges—Forbes J. in *JBH and JH (Minors) v O'Connell*[518] and Bingham L.J. in *A v*

---

[511] (1788) 6th edn, Leach.

[512] (1769) Book IV, 1st edn.

[513] (1769) Book IV, 1st edn, at 23–24.

[514] s.9(1) of the Criminal Attempts Act 1981 provides: "(1) A person is guilty of the offence of vehicle interference if he interferes with a motorvehicle or trailer or with anything carried in or on a motorvehicle or trailer with the intention that any offence specified in subs. (2) below shall be committed by himself or some other person. (2) The offences mentioned in subs. (1) above are—(a) theft of the motorvehicle or trailer or part of it, (b) theft of anything carried in or on the motorvehicle or trailer; and (c) an offence under s.12(1) of the Theft Act 1968 (taking and driving away without consent); and, if it is shown that a person accused of an offence under this section intended that one of those offences should be committed, it is immaterial that it cannot be shown which it was. (3) A person guilty of an offence under this section shall be liable on summary conviction to imprisonment for a term not exceeding three months or to a fine not exceeding £500 or to both."

[515] [1994] 3 W.L.R. 888.

[516] [1994] 3 W.L.R. 888 at 894.

[517] [1994] 3 W.L.R. 888.

[518] [1981] Crim.L.R. 632. The Ds, two boys aged 13 and 11, broke into a school and caused £3,000 worth of damage.

DPP[519]—looking upon the rule with increasing unease. It was seen as out of step with the modern world since children now grow up more quickly through compulsory education. The rule was also viewed by the Divisional Court as divisive, as it bears harshly on perhaps isolated acts of wrongdoing done by children from "good homes", and also perverse because it absolves children from "bad homes" who are most likely to commit "criminal acts".[520]

The House of Lords refused to countenance the abolition of the presumption through the exercise of judicial law-making. In the leading speech of Lord Lowry, the objections of the Divisional Court, outlined above, although pertinent, were held to be no basis for judicial legislation but rather a classic case for parliamentary investigation, deliberation and initiative.[521] It was obvious, with support dating back to Hale and Blackstone, that the presumption was still universally recognised as an effective doctrine which the previous Conservative government had reaffirmed to be part of the criminal law. It was stated in *Crime, Justice and Protecting the Public* that:

> "between the ages of 10 and 13 a child may only be convicted of a criminal offence if the prosecution can show that he knew that what he did was *seriously wrong*. The Government does not intend to change these arrangements which make proper allowance for the fact that children's understanding, knowledge and ability to reason are still developing."[522]

The imperfections attributable to the doctrine could not, according to Lord Lowry, provide a justification for saying that the presumption was no longer part of our law. To sweep it away under the doubtful auspices of judicial legislation was viewed as quite impracticable.[523]

Whilst the House of Lords in *C (A Minor)* were wary of abolishing the doli incapax presumption, no such reluctance was demonstrated by the new Labour Government. By s.34 of the Crime and Disorder Act 1998 the doli incapax presumption was abolished. The Government believed that in presuming that children aged over 10 but under 14 generally did not know the difference between naughtiness and serious wrongdoing, the notion of doli incapax was contrary to common sense. Further it was submitted that practical difficulties which the presumption presented for the prosecution could stop some children who have been prosecuted and punished for their offences from being convicted or even coming to court. A child aged 10 and above is now treated the same way as an adult for the purposes of criminal liability; no preferential assumptions apply in their favour.[524]

7. ENTRAPMENT

5–100   Suppose that X approaches Y and says that he has heard that Y is an expert forger. Y denies that he possesses these skills, but X persists and says that he needs a fake passport and that he is willing to pay a high price for one. Y begins to show signs of being interested and so X tells him that it is a matter of life and death and says that he will pay £5,000 at

---

[519] [1992] Crim.L.R. 34.
[520] [1995] 2 W.L.R. 383 at 399.
[521] [1995] 2 W.L.R. 383 at 403.
[522] Cm. 965 at para.8.4. See generally, C. Ball, "Youth Justice: Half A Century of Response to Youth Offending" [2004] Crim.L.R. 167.
[523] [1995] 2 W.L.R. 383 at 401.
[524] See further *CPS v P* [2007] EWHC 946 (Admin); and *I* [2008] EWCA Crim 815. Most recently, see the decision of the House of Lords in *R v JTB* [2009] UKHL 20, confirming the abolition of doli by s.34 of the 1998 Act.

which point Y does forge such a passport. It is quite clear that Y is guilty of forgery and also that X is a party to that forgery. Under normal circumstances X will also be guilty of encouraging Y to commit forgery,[525] and conspiring with Y to commit forgery.[526] But suppose that X is an undercover police agent who was merely trying to get evidence of forgery against Y. Does this make any difference to Y's liability?[527]

A. Y's Liability

Let us suppose that Y has now been charged with forgery, can he raise, by way of defence, **5–101** that X lured him into the crime and that without X's incitement no crime would have been committed? In some countries, notably the United States, this would constitute the defence of entrapment. In such countries it is normal to draw a line between a police officer who merely joins in an existing venture and one who positively promotes a crime which would otherwise not have been committed; only in the latter case would the accused have the defence of entrapment. However, in this country the courts have positively rejected any defence of entrapment and furthermore the evidence received as a result of such police activity will be admissible evidence against the accused.[528] This does not mean to say that the courts approve of such conduct, and they may reflect their disapproval by giving the accused a light sentence.

B. X's Liability

Suppose X, the police officer, is also prosecuted. He could be charged with encouraging or **5–102** assisting Y to forge, conspiring with Y to forge and as a party to Y's forgery. Is it any defence for him to say that he was merely trying to collect evidence against Y, a suspected forger?

As regards complicity in the commission of the offence, it would seem that the courts distinguish between participation by law entrapment officers in those crimes which are already planned and situations in which the law enforcement officer positively encourages and brings about the commission of a crime which otherwise would not have occurred. For example, it would appear quite in order for plain clothes officers to put themselves in a position where they can be solicited by prostitutes, but it would be improper for an officer to try to make the running.[529] The House of Lords in *Sang*[530] suggests that officers who by their

---

[525] See, the encouragement offences under the Serious Crime Act 2007, para.6–021 below.
[526] See, below, para.6–029.
[527] There are also issues beyond the scope of this book to do with the admissibility of evidence obtained by such means. See *Looseley; Attorney-General's Reference (No.3 of 2000)* [2001] 4 All E.R. 897.
[528] See, e.g. *Sang* [1979] 2 All E.R. 1222. Note also *McCann* (1971) 56 Cr.App.R. 359 and *McEvilly and Lee* (1973) 60 Cr.App.R. 150.
[529] See generally, *Mullins* (1843) 3 Cox C.C. 526; and *Birtles* (1969) 53 Cr.App.R. 469, 473 where Lord Parker C.J. stated: "[I]t is vitally important to ensure so far as possible that the informer does not create an offence, that is to say, incite others to commit an offence which those others would not otherwise have committed. It is one thing for the police to make use of information concerning an offence that is already laid on . . . But it is quite another thing, and something of which this court thoroughly disapproves, to use an informer to encourage another to commit an offence, or indeed an offence of a more serious character, which he would not otherwise commit, still more to do so if the police themselves take part in carrying it out."
[530] [1979] 2 All E.R. 1222 at 1236 per Lord Salmon who asserted: "I would now refer to what is, I believe, and hope, the unusual case in which a dishonest policeman, anxious to improve his detection record, tries very hard with the help of an *agent provocateur* to induce a young man with no criminal tendencies to commit a crime and ultimately the young man succumbs to the inducement . . . The policeman and the informer who acted together in inciting him to commit the crime . . . should both be prosecuted and suitably punished."

encouragement bring about the commission of an offence where otherwise one would not have occurred should be prosecuted as parties to the offence.

The same answer would probably be reached in relation to any charge of conspiracy[531] Where the officer has persuaded another to commit a crime he would not otherwise have committed, the officer should be liable to be convicted of an encouragement offence.

GENERAL READING

5–103   Allen, M., "Entrapment: Time For Reconsideration" (1984) 13 Anglo-Am.L.R. 57.

Ashworth, A., "Testing Fidelity To Legal Values: Official Involvement In Criminal Justice" (2000) 63 M.L.R. 633.

Ashworth, A., "Re-drawing The Boundaries of Entrapment" [2002] Crim.L.R. 161.

Ormerod, D. and Roberts, A., "The Trouble with *Teixera*: Developing a Principled Approach to Entrapment" [2002] Int. Jnl. E & P. 38.

8. SUPERIOR ORDERS

5–104   If X is charged with a criminal offence can he plead by way of defence that he was simply following the orders of somebody in authority over him? Until recently there were few judicial statements on this matter, but the House of Lords[532] and the Privy Council[533] have now held, albeit obiter, that there is no defence of superior orders in English law. A question that arose in *Clegg*[534] was whether it made any difference that Pte Clegg was a member of the armed forces acting in the course of his duty. It is clear that where force is used by a civilian or an ordinary police officer, there is a choice of the degree of force used, albeit a choice which may have to be exercised on the spur of the moment. In the case of an armed soldier in Northern Ireland, there was no such scope for graduated force. Either he does nothing or he uses his high-velocity rifle which will almost certainly result in death. Nevertheless, the House concluded that from the legal point of view there were no special rules for members of the armed forces.

We are envisaging here a situation in which X has the requisite mens rea for the offence, but simply says that he thought he was obliged to follow his orders. It may well be that the effect of an order by a superior is to deprive the accused of the requisite mens rea. Thus, if X's employer tells him to go and take some wood from Y's yard, X may well believe that the employer has the right to the wood in which case X would not be acting dishonestly (a necessary requirement for theft). Even if X knew that his employer was not entitled to the wood, his belief that he had to do what he was told might lead a jury to find that he was not acting dishonestly. Where the prosecution have to prove that the accused acted negligently, the fact that he was following orders might be evidence that he did act negligently. Beyond these types of example, however, it is submitted that there is no general defence of acting under superior orders (whether military or civilian). The court may, however, take such a factor into account when passing sentence.

---

[531] See below, para.6–029.
[532] *Clegg* [1995] 1 A.C. 482; see above, para.5–056.
[533] *Yip Chiu-Cheung* [1994] 3 W.L.R. 514; [1994] 2 All E.R. 924; see below, para.6–049.
[534] See above, para.5–056.

GENERAL READING

Brownlee, I.D., "Superior Orders—Time For A New Realism" [1989] Crim.L.R. 396.   **5–105**
Eden, P., "Criminal Liability And The Defence Of Superior Orders" (1991) 108 South African L.J. 640.

Chapter 6

THE INCHOATE OFFENCES

In Chapter 4 we saw that a secondary party to a criminal offence could be held liable for acts **6–001** of assistance he had performed sometime before the commission of the offence; but his liability does not arise until the offence is actually committed or attempted. The law would be seriously deficient if liability only arose when the offence was actually committed. It would mean that if the police were aware that X intended to assault Y they would have to choose between preventing the offence and prosecuting X. Obviously we would not wish to prosecute a man simply for dreaming up criminal plans in his head, but as soon as he begins to commit overt acts which evidence his intention to put the plan into operation it is arguable that the law should be able to intervene. This, basically, is the role of the inchoate[1] offences of encouragement or assistance; conspiracy; and attempt. Consider, for a moment, the following set of events; (i) X conceives in his mind a plan to burgle Barclays Bank; (ii) he approaches Y and tells him of his plans; (iii) he encourages Y to help him and to find a getaway driver; (iv) Y agrees to help and they formulate a plan in collaboration with Z who will be the getaway driver; (v) on the night in question they render the alarm on the outside of the bank inoperative and start to force open a door; and (vi) they enter the bank.

Clearly at stage (vi) they commit the completed offence of burglary the moment they enter the bank with intent to steal from it.[2] No offence is committed at stage (i) for our law has never punished a man for his thoughts; nor at (ii) in disclosing his thoughts to Y does X commit a crime because this is still too remote from the commission of the contemplated crime. But at stage (iii) X oversteps the mark; in seeking to persuade Y to join him he commits the crime of encouragement. At stage (iv) the agreement reached by X, Y and Z is a crime; they have conspired to commit burglary. At stage (v) they are guilty of attempting to burgle the bank. When the prosecution gain a conviction of encouragement, conspiracy or attempting to commit a criminal offence the convicted person is, generally speaking, liable to receive the same penalty he would have incurred had he been convicted of the completed offence. On completion of the full substantive offence then X, Y and Z will all be parties to the offence.

It is important to remember that these offences do not exist in the abstract; the indictment must always contain reference to the completed offence. Thus, it would be wrong to say in the indictment "X is charged with conspiracy"; it should be "X" is charged with conspiracy to murder, steal, etc."

---

[1] Inchoate derives from Latin, meaning "just begun" or "undeveloped".
[2] See, Theft Act s.9(1)(a) and s.9(1)(b), below, para.9–023.

The law relating to each of the inchoate offences has been subject to legislative reform, with new offences of encouragement and assistance being created in Pt 2 of the Serious Crime Act 2007.

ATTEMPTS

1. GENERAL PRINCIPLES

6–002 Liability for attempted crimes is generally covered by s.1(1) of the Criminal Attempts Act 1981, which provides:

> "If, with intent to commit an offence to which this section applies, a person does an act which is more than merely preparatory to the commission of the offence, he is guilty of attempting to commit the offence."

Under this provision a person can be convicted of attempting to commit any offence which is either indictable or triable either way (see s.1(4)).[3] Thus, whenever Parliament creates an offence which is triable on indictment, attempted liability for the offence is automatically created at the same time without any specific words in the statute creating the offence.[4] It is not, however, possible, under this Act, to be convicted of attempting to commit an offence which is purely summary. For example, under the Criminal Justice Act 1988, common assault (s.39) was made an offence that is triable only summarily, and thus ceased to be an offence in respect of which there could be liability for an attempt. In this situation Parliament may decide that this gap must be filled by a specific statutory attempt. The offence of driving over the prescribed limit (i.e. the breathalyser offence) is a purely summary offence, but under s.5 of the Road Traffic Act 1988, it is specifically made an offence "to drive or attempt to drive having consumed . . .".

There are further restrictions on the scope of attempted liability. These can be summarised as follows:

1. it is possible to attempt to incite another to commit a substantive crime, but it is not possible to attempt to conspire, (s.1(4)(a) of the Criminal Attempts Act 1981)[5];

2. it is possible to be convicted as an accomplice to an attempted offence, but it is not possible to attempt to aid, abet, counsel, procure or suborn the commission of an offence (see s.1(4)(b) of the Criminal Attempts Act 1981). These points were reiterated by the appellate court in *Dunnington*[6] which upheld the defendant's

---

[3] Note in *Velasquez* [1996] 1 Cr.App.R. 155 it was determined that an individual convicted on indictment of attempt may not subsequently be charged with the full substantive offence.

[4] It is provided by s.1(4) that:
"This section applies to any offence which, if it were completed, would be triable in England and Wales as an indictable offence, other than—
    (a) conspiracy (at common law or under s.1 of the Criminal Law Act 1977 or any other enactment);
    (b) aiding, abetting, counselling, procuring or suborning the commission of an offence;
    (c) offences under s.4(1) (assisting offenders) or 5(1) accepting or agreeing to accept consideration for not disclosing information about an arrestable offence) of the Criminal Law Act 1967."

[5] See, e.g. *Rowley* [1991] 1 W.L.R. 1020 involving the offence of attempting to incite a child under the age of 14 to commit gross indecency.

[6] [1984] Q.B. 472. In substance the purpose of s.1(4)(b) was to make it apparent that it is not an offence to attempt to aid, abet, counsel or procure whilst leaving unaltered the established principle that aiding, abetting, counselling or procuring an attempt is an offence.

conviction for attempted robbery. He had acted in the role of getaway driver. The general rule of common law is that it is an offence to aid, abet, counsel or procure a crime, and, of course, an attempt is a crime. In contrast, aiding, abetting, counselling and procuring are not, in themselves, criminal offences. There are, however, certain offences where the perpetrator is someone who aids and abets; for example, aiding and abetting suicide contrary to the Suicide Act 1961. Where this is the case it is possible to attempt to aid and abet under s.1(1) of the Criminal Attempts Act 1981 (see *Attorney-General v Able*).[7] This principle is also exemplified by the decision in *McShane*.[8] The defendant was an avaricious daughter who persuaded her own mother, residing in a convalescent home, to take nembutal tablets to hasten her death so that the defendant would inherit under a trust fund. The mother survived and McShane was convicted of attempting to counsel or procure suicide contrary to s.2(1) of the Suicide Act 1961.[9] By this provision the substantive (principal) offence is defined in the nature of an attempt so no problem existed in upholding McShane's conviction. Her bizarre contention that her mother fantasised about committing suicide, and that pinning nembutal tablets to her clothing was merely an exercise in "play-acting", was not surprisingly rejected by the jury;

3. it is not possible to attempt the commission of offences under ss.4(1) and 5(1) of the Criminal Law Act 1967[10];

4. there are certain offences which, by their very nature, it is impossible to attempt. For example, it is generally accepted that it is not possible to attempt to commit involuntary manslaughter.[11] This is because in a prosecution for an attempted offence the prosecution must prove that the defendant intended to bring about the offence. Since any intentional killing in the absence of mitigating factors, such as provocation or diminished responsibility, will be murder there is, thus, no scope for attempted involuntary manslaughter, where the constituent of the crime is that the killing is unintentional. It would also seem impossible to attempt to commit any offence which is defined as an omission and where the actus reus does not include any consequences of the omission.

By and large the mode of trial and possible sentence for a person charged with an attempt is that of the completed offence. Indeed a verdict of not guilty of the substantive offence, but guilty of the attempted offence, is always an alternative verdict for the jury provided, of course, that the prosecution have established the ingredients of the attempt. There is no need specifically to charge the accused with the attempted offence. Thus, where the accused is charged with rape, the statement of the offence in the indictment will read "rape, contrary to s.1 of the Sexual Offences Act 2003" and on such indictment the jury may return a verdict

---

[7] [1984] Q.B. 795. The supply of a booklet entitled, "a guide to self-deliverance", informing individuals of the most effective and painless method to end their life, could amount to an offence under s.2(1) of the Suicide Act 1961. It had to be proved: (1) that the supplier intended the booklet to be used by, and to assist or otherwise encourage, a person actually contemplating suicide; and (2) that while so intending he supplied the booklet to such a person; and (3) that that person then read it and was assisted or encouraged by reading it to commit suicide or to attempt to do so.

[8] (1977) 66 Cr.App.R. 97; and see also, *S* [2005] All E.R. (D) 339.

[9] By s.2(1) of the Suicide Act 1961 it is provided that, "a person who aids, abets, counsels or procures the suicide of another, or an attempt by another to commit suicide shall be liable on conviction or indictment to imprisonment for a term not exceeding 14 years."

[10] See above, para.6–002, fn.4 and s.1(4)(1) of the Criminal Attempts Act 1981.

[11] See, e.g. *Bruzas* [1972] Crim.L.R. 367; for involuntary manslaughter see below, paras 7–038—7–048.

of guilty of attempted rape. Where, from the outset, the prosecution intends to prosecute the accused for attempted rape the indictment will read "attempted rape, contrary to s.1(1) of the Criminal Attempts Act 1981." As we mentioned earlier, certain statutory offences expressly prohibit attempted conduct (see, e.g. s.5 of the Road Traffic Act 1988), but this is by virtue of the particular statute and not under the provisions of the Criminal Attempts Act. Section 3 of the Criminal Attempts Act 1981, however, provides that the principles governing these specific statutory attempts shall be those of the 1981 Act in so far as there is no express inconsistency between the statutes.

We must now look at the various ingredients of attempted offences. In simple language we are looking at situations in which the defendant has tried to do an act, which if completed would constitute a criminal offence, but has failed. In looking at the actus reus we must ask, how close must the defendant have got to completing the full offence before he can be convicted of an attempt? Is the mens rea of the attempted offence the same as that for the completed offence? In murder we can convict a defendant who merely intended to cause the victim serious bodily harm, but if the victim had not died would it make sense to charge the defendant with attempting to murder the victim? Finally we must consider cases where the defendant was trying to do something he could not possibly achieve, such as stealing from an empty pocket. Can he be convicted of attempted theft since he could never have committed the completed offence?

2. ACTUS REUS

6–003   Suppose that X wishes to kill Y. He buys a gun, loads it, goes to Y's house, rings the doorbell, points the gun at Y and pulls the trigger. If the bullet strikes and kills Y, X will be convicted of murder. Suppose, however, either that Y does not die from the wounds, or that X is stopped before he can pull the trigger. At what stage can we say that he has attempted to kill Y?[12] The 1981 Act says that he must do an act which is more than merely preparatory to the commission of the offence, and s.4(3) of the Act says that when there is evidence sufficient in law to support a finding that he did an act falling within s.1(1), it is a question of fact whether or not his act came within that subsection.[13] This may seem unduly vague and not particularly helpful, but the view is held that it is for the jury and not for the judge to decide whether the accused can be said to have attempted to kill. It would be wrong for a judge to say to the jury, "if you find the following acts proved, then you will find that the acts of the accused go beyond mere acts of preparation." This would be usurping the jury's function.[14] On the other hand the judge may tell the jury that certain acts are mere acts of preparation and not sufficiently proximate to the completed offence to constitute an offence. Thus, in *O'Brien v Anderton*, Kerr L.J. said:

> "The words 'more than merely preparatory' have replaced the various ways of seeking to define the concept of an attempt which one finds in many earlier authorities. In my view, whether an act is more than merely preparatory to the commission of an offence must be a question of degree in the nature of a jury question. Obviously, acts which are merely preparatory, such as a reconnaissance of the scene of the intended crime,

---

[12] See, generally, G. Williams, "Wrong Turnings On The Law Of Attempt" [1991] Crim.L.R. 416; and K.J.M. Smith, "Proximity In Attempt: Lord Lane's Midway Course" [1991] Crim.L.R. 576.
[13] The terms of s.4(3) provide: "Where, in proceedings against a person for an offence under s.1 above, there is evidence sufficient in law to support a finding that he did an act falling within subs.(1) of that section, the question whether or not his act fell within that subsection is a question of fact."
[14] See *DPP v Stonehouse* [1978] A.C. 55.

cannot amount to attempts. They must be more than merely preparatory. If they go close to the actual commission of the offence, they may still form part of the acts necessary to carry out the complete offence, and may, in that sense, still be preparatory. But if they are properly to be regarded as more than merely preparatory, then they constitute an attempt."[15]

In other words the jury should ask themselves "is he getting ready to commit an offence or is he in the process of attempting to commit it?" The Court of Appeal may intervene if it considers that the trial judge was wrong in law in directing a jury that the defendant's act might be regarded as more than merely preparatory. There will be many cases in which a jury, properly directed, could reasonably convict or acquit. In these situations the appellate court will not interfere. Essentially the judge's task is to decide whether there is evidence upon which a jury could reasonably come to the conclusion that the defendant had gone beyond the realm of mere preparation and had embarked upon the actual commission of the offence. If he considers that the relevant circumstances could not amount to an attempt, he should withdraw the matter from the jury. If he concludes that, although the matter is not as conclusive as that, it nevertheless would be unsafe to leave the evidence to the jury, he should direct a verdict of not guilty. Only where the judge is satisfied that there is evidence upon which a jury can properly and safely consider whether there has been an attempt should he allow the case to continue.[16] The position may helpfully be summarised by means of the following diagram:

No evidence of Acts which are more than merely preparatory.	Evidence on which the jury might find acts that are more than merely preparatory.	Conclusive evidence of acts which are more than merely preparatory.
Judge withdraws issue from jury.	Issue left to jury.	Issue left to jury but with strong hint from judge.

Before the passing of the Criminal Attempts Act the courts had evolved several tests designed to help a jury to decide whether the stage of a criminal attempt had been reached. One of those tests was the so-called "last act" test derived from *Eagleton*,[17] i.e. has the defendant with the intent to commit the full offence, done the last act in his power towards committing that offence, or, as Lord Diplock put it in *DPP v Stonehouse*,[18] has he "crossed the Rubicon and burnt his boats". The other test derived from *Stephen's Digest of the Criminal Law*[19] was, did the act done with intent to commit the full offence form part of a series of acts which would constitute its actual commission if not interrupted. However, Lord Lane clearly stated in *Gullefer*,[20] in a passage relied on by the appellate court in *Jones*,[21] that

---

[15] [1984] Crim.L.R. 483. Note that it seems incumbent upon a trial judge, in making a determination of whether an act was capable of being "more than merely preparatory" to bear in mind the quintessential nature of the offence attempted. The trial judge ought to examine the essential act or transaction on which it is predicated and any consequence needed to effect it; see *Nash* [1999] Crim.L.R. 308.

[16] See *Wang* [2005] UKHL 9.

[17] (1855) 6 Cox C.C. 559.

[18] [1978] A.C. 55 at 68. Lord Diplock's test is not necessarily the last act test but is in similar vein. It concentrates on examining whether D has gone too far to pull back when caught.

[19] 1894, 5th edn, art.50.

[20] [1990] 1 W.L.R. 1063 at 1066.

[21] See below, para.6–004.

one must now look first at the natural meaning of the statutory words contained within the Criminal Attempts Act 1981:

> "It seems to us that the words of the Act of 1981 seek to steer a midway course. They do not provide, as they might have done, that the *Eagleton* test is to be followed, or that, as Lord Diplock suggested, the defendant must have reached a point from which it was impossible for him to retreat before the actus reus of an attempt is proved. On the other hand the words give perhaps as clear a guidance as is possible in the circumstances on the point of time at which Stephen's 'series of acts' begins. *It begins when the merely preparatory acts come to an end and the defendant embarks upon the crime proper.* When this is will depend of course upon the facts in any particular case" (emphasis added).[22]

6–004 The issue now is simply whether or not the defendant has embarked upon the commission of the offence itself.[23] In most cases if the judge were simply to ask the jury whether they thought that the defendant was merely getting himself ready to commit the crime or whether he was attempting to commit the crime, they would be able to reach a sensible conclusion. Where, however, the trial judge feels that there is no evidence upon which a jury could find that the defendant had got beyond acts of preparation he can direct the jury to find that the prosecution had failed to make out an attempt.

It is a matter of fact and degree whether a defendant has actually embarked upon the crime or merely engaged in preparatory activities. A series of post-Act appellate decisions have exemplified the difficulties in establishing where the dividing line comes between acts of preparation and attempts. They serve to illustrate that the cases in this area are hard to reconcile, with contradictory outcomes. In *Gullefer*[24] the accused had placed money on a dog race. When he realised that his dog would not win, he ran on to the race track in order to distract the dogs. His intention was to cause the race stewards to declare the race null and void and so entitle those who had bet on the race to claim back their stakes. He was as unsuccessful in distracting the dogs as he had been in picking the winner. In fact the stewards did not declare the race void, but instead Gullefer was charged with and convicted of attempted theft. The Court of Appeal held that there was no evidence on which a jury could find that he was attempting to steal; there was much more he needed to do. He was simply making preparations. It is interesting to consider the position if a no race had been declared in *Gullefer*. Would the defendant have taken a more than merely preparatory step when he set off for the bookmaker's stall, or when he joined the queue of punters waiting for refunds, or would he embark on the crime proper only when he presented his betting paper to the bookmaker? The request for repayment of his £18 stake would clearly have been his "last act". It seems that Gullefer's actual conduct in trying to stop the race was similar in many respects to the pre-Act cases of *Robinson*[25] and *Comer v Bloomfield*.[26] In each of these authorities there had been a fabrication of events by the defendant in order to set the scene for a fraudulent insurance claim at a future point. In neither case was it

---

[22] [1990] 1 W.L.R. 1057 at 1061 per Taylor L.J.
[23] The Law Com. No.102 at para.245 had stated that there was "no magic formula" which could be produced to define precisely what constituted an attempt, and that there was always some degree of uncertainty in answering that question.
[24] [1990] 1 W.L.R. 1063.
[25] [1915] 2 K.B. 342. D, a jeweller, staged a fake robbery from his premises, but still had to make a claim from the insurers.
[26] (1970) 55 Cr.App.R. 305. D crashed his own van then pretended it had been stolen. Preliminary inquiries only were made to the insurance company about a future claim.

considered that the attempted offence had been committed where the relevant claim form had yet to be completed or forwarded to the insurance company.[27] Similar principles underpinned the decision in *Bowles and Bowles*[28] where the defendant's had denuded an old lady into preparing a testamentary disposition with them as beneficiaries. However, it had yet to be executed and gathered dust in a bedside drawer. The appellate court determined that their conduct was "merely preparatory" towards making a false instrument.

In *Jones*[29] the defendant's mistress had left him in favour of another man, F. Jones purchased several guns and shortened the barrel of one. He went to where he knew he would find F and got into F's car with him. He then pulled out the gun with the sawn-off barrel and pointed it at F at close range. F managed to get the gun away from Jones and threw it out of the car. On a charge of attempted murder Jones argued that the stage of attempt had not been reached; he had still to remove the safety catch, put his finger on the trigger and pull it. The trial judge rejected his submission and the Court of Appeal agreed that there was sufficient evidence on which a jury could find that Jones was attempting to kill. Expressly adopting Lord Lane's "midway course" in *Gullefer* and looking at the plain natural meaning of the statutory words, the court concluded that:

> "Clearly [the appellant's] actions in obtaining the gun, in shortening it, in loading it, in putting on his disguise, and in [lying in wait] could only be regarded as preparatory acts. But, in our judgment, once he had got into the car, taken out the loaded gun and pointed it at the victim with the intention of killing him, there was sufficient evidence for consideration of the jury on a charge of attempted murder. It was a matter for them to decide whether they were sure those acts were more than merely preparatory. In our judgment, therefore, the judge was right to allow the case to go the jury."[30]

A more difficult decision to comprehend is that in *Campbell*[31] where the police had **6–005** received a tip-off that a post office was to be robbed. They kept the post office under surveillance and saw C behaving suspiciously. He eventually walked towards the entrance and put his hand in his pocket where the police thought he had a heavy object. They arrested him one yard outside the post office and he was charged with attempted robbery. When he was searched he was found to be carrying an imitation pistol, sunglasses and a threatening note. The Court of Appeal held that he was still in the act of preparing to commit the crime of robbery; he was not, as yet, on the job[32] since he had not even entered the building.[33] It was viewed as significant that the defendant had not entered the post office premises in which he intended to commit the offence. Thus one yard either side of the post office entrance door was viewed as of importance. However logical this decision might be it will be worrying for the police and those like the counter assistants in the post office who are at risk of being the victims of armed robbery. By acting too early the police had lost the chance to gain a conviction for attempted robbery. This presumably means that the suspect must be allowed to proceed further before he is apprehended with all the risks to the safety

[27] See, e.g. *Widdowson* (1985) 82 Cr.App.R. 314.

[28] [2004] EWCA Crim 1608.

[29] [1990] 1 W.L.R. 1057. See also *Litholetors* [2002] EWCA Crim 1154. D poured petrol on V's door but had yet to set it alight—held that the offence of attempted arson was established.

[30] [1990] 1 W.L.R. 1057 at 1062 per Taylor L.J.

[31] (1990) 93 Cr.App.R. 350.

[32] A phrase used by Rowlatt J. in *Osborne* (1919) 84 J.P. 63.

[33] Watkins L.J. stated: "if a person in circumstances such as this has not even gained the place where he could be in a position to carry out the offence, it is extremely unlikely that it could ever be said that he had performed an act which could properly said to be an attempt; (1919) 84 J.P. 63 at 352.

of the assistants that this will entail. Fortunately, in this case, the court was able to convict him of unlawfully possessing an imitation firearm.[34]

There is also a problem over the jury's determination of more than merely preparatory acts. Once the trial judge rules that there is evidence that the accused has gone beyond mere acts of preparation, it is for the jury to decide whether he had attempted to commit the offence. Here it is possible for two juries on the same facts to reach entirely opposite conclusions and there is little the trial judge can do to help them. In *Jones*, for instance, it was open to the jury to take the view that since the defendant had not released the safety catch they did not regard his acts as more than merely preparatory. So it is possible that, on the facts of *Jones*, while the jury at Leicester Crown Court convicted the defendant, a jury at Newcastle Crown Court may have acquitted him. This seems, however, to be an inevitable and unfortunate consequence of the Criminal Attempts Act. Moreover, it would be a safe bet that any jury if left by the court to consider the facts in *Campbell* would return a verdict of attempted robbery. The decision, as previously mentioned, is a worrying one for police officers who have to consider the safety of those such as post office workers. It could be cogently argued that a law of attempt which requires the police to wait until the armed robber is in the shop is seriously defective.[35] If D can be proved to have in his possession a hammer with which to commit criminal damage he is guilty of an offence under s.3 of the Criminal Damage Act 1971 long before he reaches the stage of attempted criminal damage.[36] If, however, he has the hammer to cause grievous bodily harm to another we have to wait until he goes beyond acts of preparation before he commits an offence. Perhaps the time is right to consider either the modification of the law of attempt so that the attempted offence is committed at an earlier stage, or the creation of a more general preparatory offence along the lines of s.3 of the Criminal Damage Act 1971.[37]

An interesting case to contrast with *Campbell* is *Griffin*,[38] where a significantly more generous approach in favour of the prosecution was propounded by the appellate court. The defendant, who was the mother of two children who were in care, was convicted of attempting to abduct her own children and take them out of the United Kingdom. She had bought single ferry tickets to the Republic of Ireland for herself and the two children and made preparations for travel, and falsely told the children's teacher that she was taking them to the dentist. However, at no point had she taken possession or control over the children nor had she embarked on the journey to the port. Nonetheless it was determined that the judge had ruled correctly that a jury could conclude that Griffin had started to commit the offence when she asked the teacher for the children. This seems a surprising conclusion in that her acts were much less proximate in time, place and the number of acts to be performed for commission of the full substantive offence than in *Campbell*. As stated at the outset, the views of differently constituted appellate courts are not easy to reconcile in this area. A leading commentator has helpfully suggested the following examples where activities are more remote and which appear likely to be regarded as "merely preparatory"[39]:

---

[34] Could Campbell have been convicted of attempted burglary. Was he attempting to enter under s.9(1)(a) of the Theft Act 1968? See *Tosti and White* [1997] Crim.L.R. 746, considered below, para.6–007.

[35] See, e.g. P. Seago, "Criminal Law" [1992] All E.R. *Annual Review* 136.

[36] By s.3 of the Criminal Damage Act 1971 it is an offence, subject to a maximum of 10 years' imprisonment, for an individual who has anything in their custody or under their control, intending without lawful excuse to use it or cause or permit another to use it—(a) to destroy or damage any property belonging to some other person; or (b) to destroy or damage his own or the user's property in a way which he knows is likely to endanger the life of some other person. Thus an intention suffices for the offence where D merely intends to use the thing to cause damage should it prove necessary. For further consideration see below, para.10–014.

[37] See below, para.6–007 for potential reform of attempt.

[38] [1993] Crim.L.R. 515.

[39] K.J.M. Smith, *loc. cit.,* at p.580.

(i) a gunman, or person with a remotely detonatable bomb, lying in wait for his victim to appear;

(ii) the prospective burglar positioning his ladder prior to entering a building; and

(iii) the would-be insurance fraudster who, having faked the insurance event, writes to his insurers indicating an intention to submit a claim in the near future.

The question for the Court of Appeal in *Attorney-General's Reference (No.1 of 1992)*[40] was **6–006** at what point could a jury find that a defendant had attempted to rape the woman complainant? The facts alleged by the prosecution were that the complainant and the defendant were walking home late at night and that both had been drinking. The defendant had dragged her off the path and behind a hedge where he forced her to the ground and lay on top of her, threatening to kill her if she did not stop screaming. A nearby householder raised the alarm when he saw a man dragging a woman away from the road. When the police arrived, the complainant was on her back, her skirt pulled up and her breasts exposed. Her knickers were found nearby. The accused was kneeling on the ground a little way off. When he stood up it was seen his trousers were round his ankles, but his penis was not erect. Medical examination revealed that the complainant had bruising around her private parts and the defendant had corresponding bruising to his penis, though this had not necessarily been caused by the accused trying to penetrate the complainant. He said that he accepted that the complainant had been in no fit state to consent and that he had not asked her. He had been unable, due to drink, to have intercourse. On these facts the trial judge ruled initially that there was evidence which could be left to a jury to decide whether he had in fact gone beyond acts which were merely preparatory to the commission of rape. Later, however, he changed his mind and told the jury that for attempted rape there had to be some evidence of an attempt by the accused to insert his penis into the complainant's vagina. On this basis he directed the jury to acquit. The Court of Appeal was asked "whether on a charge of attempted rape, it is incumbent upon the prosecution, as a matter of law, to prove that the defendant physically attempted to penetrate the woman's vagina with his penis." At this time, prior to changes effected by the Sexual Offences Act 2003,[41] the actus reus of the full substantive offence of rape included unlawful sexual intercourse, which by s.7(2) of the Sexual Offences (Amendment) Act 1976 was deemed to be complete upon proof of penetration only. Sexual intercourse was proved if the jury were satisfied that any degree of actual penetration took place irrespective of whether the man ejaculated or not.

However, the Court of Appeal held in *Attorney-General's Reference (No.1 of 1992)* that for attempted rape it was not necessary for the prosecution to prove that the defendant, with the requisite intent, had necessarily gone as far as to attempt physical penetration of the vagina—contrary to the judgment at first instance. It was sufficient that there was evidence that the defendant had the necessary intent and that the prosecution had established facts from which a jury could conclude that the accused had gone beyond mere acts of preparation; the evidence in this case satisfied those requirements. In his commentary on this case in the *Criminal Law Review*, Professor Smith asks whether, since rape is the physical penetration of the woman's vagina by the man's penis, it is not a contradiction in terms to say he did not attempt to penetrate her, but he did attempt to rape her?[42] The

---

[40] [1993] 2 All E.R. 190; see, generally, A. Reed, "Attempted Rape" (1993) 57 J.C.L. 364. See also *Patnaik* Unreported, November 5, 2000, CA, where D had verbally threatened V and straddled her, but had not removed any of his own clothing and had not striven to touch V intimately. However, the appellate court determined that there was sufficient evidence of an attempted rape for jury consideration; see also *MH* [2004] WL 137.

[41] See below at para.7–119.

[42] [1993] Crim.L.R. 274 at 275.

answer he suggests is that in the law of attempt we must give the word "attempt" a wider meaning than we have so far allowed. For example, "if D is pulling his gun from his holster with intent to kill P when he is arrested we do not need the Criminal Attempts Act to tell us that D is attempting to kill P, although D still has to aim the gun and pull the trigger. It is the same if D takes out his penis with intent to insert it into P. He is attempting to penetrate her even though he may still have more than one physical movement to make before he does so."[43]

Of course, this represents another illustration of an authority hard to fit with *Campbell*. It is illogical that in Campbell's situation, where all he needed to do was to take one more step into the premises for the full offence to be committed, he should be acquitted, as he had not entered the requisite criminal arena, whereas a defendant who had not even begun to put his penis in close proximity to the woman's vagina should be convicted. As a matter of public policy, it is entirely laudable to prevent would-be rapists at as early a stage as possible on the criminal enterprise, but would-be robbers should similarly be prevented.[44]

6–007   The actus reus of attempt also arose in *Geddes*[45] and *Tosti and White*[46] which have both exemplified that the matter is a question of fact and degree. There are problems of demarcation over how proximate the defendant's completed acts need be to the commission of the full substantive offence. In *Geddes* the defendant appealed against his conviction for attempted false imprisonment, in that he attempted unlawfully and injuriously to imprison a person unknown, for which he had been sentenced to four years' imprisonment. The defendant had entered school grounds and was found in the boys' toilet by a member of staff. He ran away and a rucksack discarded by him was found to contain lengths of string, sealing tape, a knife and other items. The Court of Appeal stressed that there was no rule of thumb test to distinguish merely preparatory acts and acts which amount to an attempt. It involves an exercise of judgment based on the particular facts of the case. Had Geddes moved from the role of intention, preparation and planning into the area of execution or implementation? Their Lordships answered this question in the negative. He had entered the school but never had any communication or contact with any pupil. In essence, the court concluded that the evidence was not sufficient in law to support a finding that the defendant did an act which was more than merely preparatory to imprisoning a person wrongfully. It seems that "lying in wait", with intent to commit an offence if and when the victim comes along, does not constitute a 'more than merely preparatory act".[47] This represents the antithesis of efficient law enforcement as it seems incumbent upon the police to wait as late as possible in the criminal transaction before effecting an arrest.

More satisfactory on policy grounds is the decision in *Tosti and White*, albeit contradictory in outcome to *Campbell*. The defendants were convicted of attempted burglary. They had been seen by the owners of a farm, just before midnight, walking to the door of a barn and examining the padlock. When they realised that they were being watched they took fright and ran off. Some oxyacetylene equipment for breaking into premises was subsequently found near the barn. It has long been established that once a more than merely preparatory

---

[43] [1993] Crim.L.R. 274.

[44] A. Reed, *loc. cit.,* at p.365.

[45] [1996] Crim.L.R. 894. Note the relevant offence herein is now contained in s.63 of the Sexual Offences Act 2003—trespass with intent to commit a sexual offence.

[46] [1997] Crim.L.R. 746. See also *Quadir and Khan* Unreported, July 24, 1997, Case No.9602311. Unhelpfully, Potter L.J. sought to distinguish between different offences by focusing upon the nature of the crime attempted delineating between offences where the epicentre is upon an act and those where it is upon a transaction. In truth, it is a factual question on a case by case basis.

[47] See, e.g. J.C. Smith [1996] Crim.L.R. 895.

act has been performed then no defence of withdrawal will be available.[48] Were the defendant's acts sufficiently proximate to constitute attempted burglary? Their Lordships on this occasion answered in the affirmative. The facts proved in evidence were sufficient for the judge to leave to the jury. The decision stands in tandem with *Griffin* on the basis that a more generous interpretation in favour of the Crown was applied. However, it represents yet another example of the difficult factual choice for our courts over attempt; it remains a question of degree whether the defendant has embarked on the criminal enterprise.

As previously mentioned, one of the old tests, which was used to determine whether the stage of an attempt had been reached, was known as the "last act" test. Under this the question for the jury was whether the accused had done the last act required of him to bring about the crime; if so he was guilty of an attempt to commit that crime. This test has been rightly criticised as being too restrictive since there will be occasions where the defendant is guilty of an attempt before he does the last act. For example, a poisoner who is slowing administering arsenic to his wife will be guilty of attempted murder when he administers the first of many doses. The decision in *Jones* is another example of a case in which an attempt was correctly found even though the accused had several more acts to do. However, in the case of the principal offender, it is probably safe to say that where the accused has, in fact, done the last act required of him, there will be evidence upon which a jury can find he has gone beyond mere acts of preparation. This will not necessarily be true of secondary parties. Consider, for instance, a wife who has hired a killer to murder her husband. She has done the last act required of her, but she cannot be liable for attempted murder until the principal offender attempts to kill her husband.

In conclusion, it is interesting to consider how the actus reus of attempt may be reformed. The English case authorities are difficult to reconcile and problems exist over what acts will be, "more than merely preparatory". Some commentators have propounded the need for express new legislation adopting a "substantial step" definition of an attempt. This approach has been embodied in the Model Penal Code of the American Law Institute, which has been widely accepted in legislation in the United States. By s.5.01 of the Code it is stated that, "conduct shall not be held to constitute a substantial step . . . unless it is strongly corroborative of the actor's criminal purpose". The Code then helpfully provides in paragraph (2) a crystallised set of examples of what amounts to a substantial step:

> "(2) The following, if strongly corroborative of the actor's criminal purpose, shall not be held insufficient as a matter of law:
>
> > (a) lying in wait, searching for or following the contemplated victim of the crime[49];
> >
> > (b) enticing or seeking to entice the contemplated victim of the crime to go to the place contemplated for its commission;
> >
> > (c) reconnoitring the place contemplated for the commission of the crime;
> >
> > (d) unlawful entry of a structure, vehicle or enclosure in which it is contemplated that the crime will be committed;
> >
> > (e) possession of materials to be employed in the commission of the crime, which are specially designed for such unlawful use or which can serve no lawful purpose of the actor under the circumstances;

---

[48] For example, consider the nineteenth-century authority of *Taylor* (1859) 1 F. & F. 511. D abandoned his plan to set fire to some property when he realised he was being observed. He had approached the property with a lighted match, and thus had completed an attempt. No defence of withdrawal was applicable at a subsequent stage.

[49] This is clearly in conflict with the decision of our Court of Appeal in *Geddes.*

> (f) possession, collection or fabrication of materials to be employed in the commission of the offence, at or near the place contemplated for its commission, where such possession, collection or fabrication serves no lawful purpose in the circumstances; and
>
> (g) soliciting an innocent agent to engage in conduct constituting an element of the crime."[50]

The advantage of the series of examples provided by the Model Penal Code is that it provides a concrete list of conduct which qualifies for the inchoate offence. It has the merit of certainty and can be expeditiously applied in practice. The Law Commision's Working Party published a paper advocating the adoption of the substantial step test,[51] but this was rejected in the ultimate Law Commission Report No.102, 1980, which formed the general basis for the Criminal Attempts Act 1981. The "more than merely preparatory test" was preferred, but as we have seen it has led to problems of demarcation between preparatory acts and attempt. As part of a broader review of liability for inchoate offences, the Commission has more recently proposed the creation of two offences dealing with preparatory conduct.[52] First, an offence of "attempt" is proposed, which would be limited to situations in which D was engaged in the last acts required to commit an offence. More novel is the second proposal, which is for an offence of "criminal preparation", which would cover "acts of preparation which are properly to be regarded as part of the execution of the plan to commit the intended offence."[53]

3. MENS REA

6–008 In many respects it might be thought desirable in the interests of simplicity to require that the mens rea for the attempted offence should be the same as that for the completed offence. On the other hand that might lead to odd results. If a terrorist who is torturing a prisoner shoots him in the kneecaps, he clearly intends to cause him serious bodily harm and if the victim dies there is nothing wrong in holding that the terrorist should be guilty of murder. However, if the victim does not die, it might sound odd to hold the terrorist liable for attempting to murder him because this would imply that the terrorist was trying to kill the victim, which he was not. In other words if you say that someone is attempting to bring about a result you are saying that he intends to achieve that result.

Section 1(1) of the Criminal Attempts Act 1981 says that the prosecution must prove that the accused did the act with the *intention* to commit an offence to which the section applies. This will clearly be interpreted to mean that, for example, in the crime of attempted murder, the prosecution must prove that the accused intended to kill the victim; proof that he intended to cause the victim serious bodily harm will not suffice. This principle was enunciated at common law by the appellate court in *Whybrow*,[54] a case where the defendant had wired up the bath in an attempt to electrocute his wife. When the charge is one of attempt, "the intent becomes the principal ingredient of the crime".[55] Hence the prosecution had to establish in *Whybrow* that the defendant had the intention to kill his wife; it was not

---

[50] See, e.g. A. Ashworth (1988) 19 Rutgers L.J. 725 at 752; and G. Williams, *loc. cit.* at pp.420–421.
[51] See L.C. Working Paper No.50.
[52] Law Commission Consultation Paper No.183, *Conspiracy and Attempts* (2007).
[53] Law Commission Consultation Paper No.183, *Conspiracy and Attempts* (2007) proposals 15, paras 16.1 et seq.
[54] (1951) 35 Cr.App.R. 141.
[55] (1951) 35 Cr.App.R. 141, per Lord Goddard C.J.

enough merely to show that he intended to cause her grievous bodily harm. It is also clear that in the basic offence of criminal damage, contrary to s.1(1) of the Criminal Damage Act 1971, which provides that it is an offence intentionally or recklessly to damage property belonging to another, the attempted offence will require proof that the defendant intended to damage property belonging to another. There is no room for reckless damage to property when the offence itself is an attempt because the attempt must have the necessary intent (see *Millard and Vernon*,[56] considered below).

The crime of attempted offences, thus, inevitably confronts the trial judge with the meaning of intention. In straightforward cases it will probably be simplest to ask the jury if the prosecution has satisfied them that the accused was trying to bring about the prohibited result. This was expressed at common law by the Court of Appeal in *Mohan* in the following terms, "a decision to bring about, in so far as it lies within the accused's power, the commission of the offence which it is alleged the accused attempted to commit, no matter whether the accused desired that consequence of his act or not".[57] However, problems have been encountered over the adoption of suitable directions that trial judges ought to make for attempted murder. It will be recalled from the discussion of mens rea in Chapter 2 that intention for murder itself may be either *direct intention* or *oblique intention*. Direct intention applies where it is the defendant's objective, aim or purpose to bring about the death of V. The "golden rule" in such cases, asserted by Lord Bridge in *Moloney*,[58] is to "avoid any elaboration or paraphrase of what is meant by intent, and leave it to the jury's good sense to decide whether the accused acted with the necessary intent". Only in exceptional cases, involving *oblique intention*, where the defendant's ultimate purpose, desire or aim was something other than the prohibited consequence which he had brought about, should further explanation or elaboration be presented to the jury, relating to foresight of consequences as inferential evidence of intention.[59] However, both the trial judge and the appellate court were confused by this distinction in *Walker and Hayles*,[60] in relation to attempted murder. The defendants were involved in a dispute with V over his affair with Walker's sister. During a fight they banged V's head against a wall and threatened to kill him, finally dropping him from a third-floor balcony to the ground below. V survived and the defendants were charged with his attempted murder. The jury were directed that they were entitled to draw the inference that the defendants intended to kill the victim, if they were sure the perpetrators knew that there was a "very high degree of probability" that he would be killed.

On appeal, it was argued that the judge had misdirected the jury on the mental element **6–009** necessary to sustain a charge of attempted murder, in that (1) he led them to equate probability of death and foresight of death with an intention to kill, and (2) he should have used the words "virtual certainty", derived from *Nedrick*,[61] instead of "high degree of probability". Their Lordships, however, dismissed the appeal and held that the trial judge had properly directed the jury that foresight was something from which they could infer

---

[56] [1987] Crim.L.R. 397; and see also *O'Toole* [1987] Crim.L.R. 759. On a charge of attempting to commit the basic criminal damage offence under s.1(1) of the Criminal Damage Act 1971 it must be established that D *intended to destroy or damage property belonging to another*, recklessness will not suffice, although recklessness will suffice for the full substantive offence, see below, para.10–002.

[57] [1976] Q.B. 1 at 11; see, e.g. *Pearman* (1984) 80 Cr.App.R. 259 for application of this direction to an attempt to cause grievous bodily harm with intent.

[58] [1985] 1 A.C. 905 at 926.

[59] See above, paras 2–055—2–061.

[60] (1990) 90 Cr.App.R. 226; see above, para.2–060.

[61] [1986] 83 Cr.App.R. 267; above, para.2–060; see also *Woollin* [1999] 1 A.C. 82; [1999] 1 Cr.App.R. 8, discussed above, at para.2–060. Note implicit within an indictment for attempted murder is also an attempt to cause grievous bodily harm with intent; see *Morrison* [2003] All E.R. (D) 281.

intent. It was determined that whilst it was better to use the term "virtual certainty" the court did not regard the difference of degree, if indeed there was one, between a very high degree of probability on the one hand and virtual certainty on the other, as being sufficient to render the verdict unsafe. Provided it was made clear that it was a question for the jury to infer from the degree of probability in the particular case whether the defendants intended to kill, the use of the words "very high degree of probability" was not a misdirection.

With respect, it is submitted that their Lordships were confused in *Walker and Hayles*, which was, it seems a clear case involving *direct intention*, i.e. the defendants' objective was to cause V's death. For attempted murder an intention to kill must be shown, and an intention to cause grievous bodily harm, although a sufficient mens rea for the full offence of murder, is not enough on the attempt charge. Thus, in cases of direct intention where the defendants are *trying to kill* it is superfluous to require death as a virtual certainty, high possibility or even possibility—evidentially it only bears upon the question of whether D was actually trying to kill.

The judge should follow Lord Bridge's advice and avoid any elaboration or paraphrase of what is meant by intent, and leave it to the jury's good sense to decide whether the accused acted with the necessary intent. It is only in more complex cases where the attempted crime is merely the means of achieving some ulterior purpose (oblique intention) that a trial judge should give the jury the type of direction outlined in *Nedrick*, with foresight of death as being "virtually certain" being inferential evidence on the intention of the defendant.[62] For example, if the defendant is charged with attempted murder for trying to blow up a passenger airliner in mid-flight in order to recover insurance money on the cargo, the judge should tell them that if they find that the defendant saw it as virtually certain all the passengers on the aircraft would be killed, they were entitled to draw the conclusion that he intended to kill them.

6–010   Unfortunately this is not the end of the matter. The analysis, thus far, has concentrated on the mens rea of attempt in relation to a consequence or result. It will, however, be recalled that we said that the actus reus of most crimes comprises several elements (conduct, results and circumstances) and that mens rea might be required on each of the elements. Additionally, the degree of culpability required might vary from element to element. Take, for example, the crime of rape. The actus reus consists of penile penetration of the vagina, anus or mouth of the victim who is not consenting.[63] As far as the mens rea for the completed offence is concerned, the prosecution must prove that the accused intended to penetrate, and the absence of a reasonable belief in the consent of the victim. The victim's consent is a circumstance of the actus reus of rape.[64] Suppose, however, that a defendant is charged with attempted rape. It is clear that the prosecution must prove he intended penile penetration of the victim but will recklessness or negligence as to her lack of consent suffice? Section 1(1) of the Criminal Attempts Act requires that the accused intends to commit the offence and in the context of rape that would seem to mean he intended penile penetration of a non-consenting victim. In *Khan*,[65] prior to the Sexual Offences Act 2003 revisions, the Court of Appeal held that in the crime of attempted rape the prosecution had to prove that the accused intentionally had intercourse with a woman, but that as far as her lack of consent was concerned it was sufficient to prove that he was reckless. Russell L.J. stated:

[62] See, e.g. *Fallon* [1994] Crim.L.R. 519 where the trial judge confused the jury by giving three directions on the intent necessary for the offence of attempted murder. D had shot a police officer who was in the process of searching him. It ought to have been a clear case for the application of the "golden rule". At issue was D's *direct intention*, i.e. whether he intended to kill.

[63] s.1 of the Sexual Offences Act 2003, see below at para.7–119.

[64] See, generally, G. Williams, "The Problem Of Reckless Attempts" [1983] Crim.L.R. 365; and R. Buxton, "Circumstances, Consequences and Attempted Rape" [1984] Crim.L.R. 25.

[65] [1990] 2 All E.R. 783.

"The only 'intent', giving that word its natural and ordinary meaning, of the rapist is to have sexual intercourse. He commits the offence because of the circumstances in which he manifests that intent, i.e. when the woman is not consenting and he either knows it or could not care less about the absence of consent."[66]

What the Court of Appeal in *Khan* appears to be saying is that in every crime there is *a central prohibited act* and where the charge is attempting to commit a particular crime, the prosecution must prove that the defendant intended to bring about that prohibited act. Thus, according to *Millard and Vernon*, in criminal damage the defendant must intend to damage or destroy property belonging to another; it would not be sufficient that he was reckless as to the ownership of the property. In rape the prohibited act is the penile penetration; lack of consent is *outside the core element* of the offence which constitutes the prohibited act. *As far as the elements outside the prohibited act are concerned it would appear that whatever mens rea suffices for the completed offence will suffice for the attempted offence.*[67]

With the greatest respect to the Court of Appeal this decision is likely to cause great confusion. Is the decision to be confined to the crime of attempted rape? That seems unlikely. How, then, are we to decide exactly what constitutes the prohibited act—the core of the crime? Did not the House of Lords in *Morgan*[68] say that the prohibited act in rape was having intercourse with a non-consenting woman. Suppose that I find a book and I do not know whether it belongs to me or to you. I decide that I am going to burn it irrespective of the ownership. If I am stopped just as I am about to throw it on the fire, am I guilty of attempting to destroy your book? It would appear not since in *Millard and Vernon* (above) it was clearly held that the prosecution must prove that I intended to destroy property belonging to another, which means that they must establish that I knew the book was yours. It seems absurd that I can be convicted of attempted rape if the prosecution can establish that I could not care less whether the woman was consenting, but not of criminal damage if the prosecution can prove I could not care less whether the book belonged to you or to me.

The Court of Appeal had another chance to review this area of law in *Attorney-General's Reference (No.3 of 1992)*[69] and appeared to find yet another way to identify the mens rea in attempted crime. This case takes us back to criminal damage; this time to aggravated criminal damage under s.1(2) and (3) of the Criminal Damage Act 1971.[70] The decision pre-dates the abrogation of *Caldwell* recklessness in *R v G* but principles remain relevant.[71] The owners of a factory, which had been the subject of attacks, had arranged for a night-time watch to be kept from a patrol car. The defendants arrived upon the scene in a van containing petrol bombs, matches, a petrol can and some rags. The defendants threw a petrol bomb towards the night patrol car, its four occupants and two people talking to them on the pavement. Fortunately the bomb missed the car and hit a garden wall behind. No one was injured. The defendants were charged, inter alia, with the offence of attempted aggravated arson contrary to s.1, subss.(2) and (3) of the Criminal Damage Act 1971. To gain a conviction for the completed offence the prosecution has to prove that the defendant intentionally or recklessly damaged or destroyed property (this property may belong either

---

[66] [1990] 2 All E.R. 783 at 788.
[67] Note that the Draft Code cl.49(2) provides as follows: "For the purposes of subs.(1) [attempt to commit an offence], an intention to commit an offence is an intention with respect to all the elements of the offence other than fault elements, except that recklessness with respect to circumstances suffices where it suffices for the offence itself."
[68] [1976] A.C. 182; considered above, para.2–084.
[69] [1994] 2 All E.R. 121; see, generally, P. Seago, "Criminal Law" [1994] All E.R. *Annual Review* 130.
[70] See below, para.10–008.
[71] See above at para.2–069.

to another or to the defendant) with intent to endanger life or being reckless as to whether life was thereby endangered. Subsection (3) provides that if the damage is caused by fire, the charge is arson. The trial judge had directed the jury that for the prosecution to succeed on the attempted offence they must prove not only that the defendant *intended* to damage or destroy property,[72] but also that the defendant *intended to endanger life*. In other words, recklessness was insufficient on any limb of the attempted offence. Following the acquittal of the defendants on this charge, the Attorney-General sought the opinion of the Court of Appeal as to whether the trial judge's direction had been correct, and whether she had been right to say that this case was distinguishable from *Khan*. The court held that there was no reason to distinguish *Khan*. The mens rea of an attempt was an intention to bring about that which was missing from the completed offence. In attempted rape it is the penile penetration which is missing; the prosecution, therefore, have to prove an intention to have penile penetration. In attempted aggravated damage (or arson) it is the damage or destruction which is missing; it has, therefore, to be proved that the defendant intended to damage or destroy property. As far as the mens rea of the other elements of the actus reus was concerned or any ulterior intent, it sufficed that the prosecution could establish the mens rea required of the completed offence. Thus, in relation to the absence of consent in attempted rape it sufficed than that the prosecution could prove the accused knew or was *Cunningham* reckless as to the lack of consent. In aggravated damage, beyond the need to prove an intention to damage property, it was sufficient that the prosecution could prove that the defendants *intended or were reckless as to endangering life*. It would seem to be the position, therefore, that if D does an act intending to endanger life, but not intending in the process to damage property, he cannot be convicted of attempted aggravated damage endangering life, but that if he intends to damage property he can be convicted even though he was unaware that anyone was inside the property he was trying to damage as long as a reasonable person would have realised that what he was doing created an obvious and serious risk of endangering life.

6–011 It would be tempting to leave the discussion here in the hope that on the surface there is some glimmer of understanding. However, we ought to dig just a little deeper. If we go back to *Khan*, it will be recalled that the court held that in attempted rape the prosecution must prove the accused intended the central or core element of the offence, but that on other aspects a lesser state of mind would suffice. Thus, in rape, the accused must intend to have penile penetration, but he can be negligent—because negligence suffices for the completed offence—as to the lack of consent. How are we supposed to determine this central element in any given offence? Why, in attempted basic criminal damage, do we need to prove that the accused intended to damage property *belonging to another*, but in rape we do not have to prove that the accused intended to have penile penetration *with a non-consenting victim*? After all, as previously mentioned, in *DPP v Morgan* the House of Lords held that the prohibited act in rape was not intercourse, but intercourse with a non-consenting woman. What makes "belonging to another" more central to the crime than the lack of consent in rape? Perhaps Schiemann J., who delivered the leading judgment in *Attorney-General's Reference (No.3 of 1992)*, had in mind the distinction between conduct and result on the one hand and surrounding circumstances on the other and that in attempted crimes intention must be proved as to the former, but something less will suffice for the latter. If so, why did he not say so? But even this will not do, since the fact that property belongs to another is a surrounding circumstance in criminal damage just as the lack of consent is in rape.

In *Attorney-General's Reference (No.3 of 1992)*, however, Schiemann J. advances an alternative way of expressing what Russell L.J. had said in *Khan*. He said:

---

[72] See *Millard and Vernon* [1987] Crim.L.R. 397, discussed above, para.6–008, fn.56.

"One way of analysing the situation is to say that a defendant, in order to be guilty of an attempt, must be in one of the states of mind required for the commission of the full offence, and did his best, as far as he could, to supply what was missing from the completion of the offence."[73]

Thus, in *Khan*, what was missing from the full offence was the act of intercourse, (penile penetration in terms of the Sexual Offences Act 2003) and it is this that the defendant must intend to accomplish. Similarly, in the crime of attempted aggravated damage, it is the physical damage that is missing and which the defendant must be proved to have set out to achieve. This works well on the facts of *Khan* and *Attorney-General's Reference (No.3 of 1992)*. Suppose, however, D intends to have intercourse with C. He believes that she is not consenting, whereas, in fact, she is. If he has intercourse in these circumstances, he cannot be guilty of rape since there is no actual lack of consent. However, according to *Shivpuri*[74] he would commit attempted rape. What is missing is not a physical act of intercourse, but the state of mind of the victim. Does this mean that the accused must intend that the woman is not consenting? Would recklessness as to her lack of consent now be insufficient? Suppose that Prince believed that Annie was 15 whereas she was in fact 17. Can he be charged with attempted abduction? The missing element is the girl's age. Does the prosecution for attempted abduction have to prove in these circumstances that he intended or knew she was 16? These questions do not admit to obvious solutions.

It would be possible to support a law of attempts in which intention was required on every aspect of the actus reus and in an ulterior intent over and above the actus reus as in aggravated criminal damage. It would be equally supportable to require, despite the problems for attempted murder outlined at the beginning of this section, that in a prosecution for attempt the prosecutor must establish the same mens rea as is required by the completed offence. What we have in England at present is a sort of half-way house in which no one is sure of where to draw the line. It is suggested that the preferred solution should be to require the same mens rea for the attempt and the completed offence.[75] It would make it far easier for trial judges in their directions to juries and it can surely not be thought to operate unfairly against the accused.

4. ARE ALL ATTEMPTED OFFENCES CRIMES OF SPECIFIC INTENT?

It will be recalled that earlier we said that attempted offences were crimes of specific intent **6–012** and that, therefore, the defence of intoxication was a relevant defence if it negatived the specific intent.[76] This was true even where the completed offence was a crime of basic intent since in the attempted offence the prosecution has to prove that the accused intended to bring about the completed offence. Thus, in the offence of battery, the prosecution must prove that the accused either intentionally or recklessly applied unlawful force, but in the attempted offence only an intention to apply unlawful force will suffice. The picture is no longer so clear. The statement would still seem to be true in relation to criminal damage since the completed offence can be committed either intentionally or recklessly, but the attempted offence is satisfied only by an intention to damage or destroy property. The same

---

[73] [1994] 2 All E.R. 121 at 126.
[74] [1987] A.C. 1; see below, para.6–016.
[75] P. Seago, *loc. cit.,* at p.134.
[76] See above, para.5–028.

cannot, however, be said in relation to attempted rape. The completed offence requires intentional penile penetration of the vagina, anus or mouth of the victim who is not consenting; and a lack of a reasonable belief in consent. By analogy with *Khan* (above) this is also the mens rea for the attempted offence. Since the completed offence is a crime of basic intent, it is hard to see how the attempted offence could be said to be different. It, therefore, seems that the crime of attempted rape is an offence of basic intent. It is no longer the case that all attempted crimes are crimes of specific intent.

5. ATTEMPTING THE IMPOSSIBLE

6–013 Sometimes an accused fails to commit the full offence because he is either stopped before he can do so or because his plan goes astray. These are examples of straightforward criminal attempts and will depend upon whether he has gone beyond acts of mere preparation. On the other hand he may fail to commit an offence because what he is trying to do is impossible. In this section we shall look at four different situations in which the accused may be said to have tried to do something which is impossible. In each case the question to be asked is whether the Criminal Attempts Act 1981 renders his activity criminal.[77]

Example 1

6–014 A is caught trying to open the night safe at a bank with a can opener. It is quite clear that the bank's money is safe from him. On the other hand, if he were to succeed he would commit the offence of theft. This is not so much a case of attempting the impossible, as incompetently attempting the possible. Provided that the jury think that he is beyond merely preparing to commit the offence, he can be convicted.[78]

Example 2

6–015 B is a pickpocket. He sneaks up behind V and inserts his hand into V's pocket, but it is empty. Once again, if B were to achieve his purpose he would commit the offence of theft, but since there is nothing in the pocket this is impossible. This type of case is sometimes referred to as attempting the factually impossible. It is fairly certain that the general public would view this conduct as attempted theft and would be highly surprised if the law provided otherwise.[79] In *Anderton v Ryan*[80] the House of Lords held, obiter, that such conduct amounted to attempted theft. Had the accused been able to achieve his purpose he would have committed theft, he only fails because there is nothing in the pocket.[81] The effect of s.1(2) and (3) of the Criminal Attempts Act 1981 on impossibility is to focus on the intention of the defendant; he will be liable provided he intended to commit the offence and, on the facts he believed to exist, his actions could bring about the offence. It is not a

---

[77] See, generally, B. Hogan, "The Criminal Attempts Act And Attempting The Impossible" [1984] Crim.L.R. 584; G. Williams, "Attempting The Impossible—The Last Round"? (1985) N.L.J. 337; G. Williams, "The Lords Achieve The Logically Impossible" (1985) N.L.J. 502; and G. Williams, "The Lords And Impossible Attempts or *Quis Custodiet Ipsos Custodes*" (1986) 45 C.L.J. 33.

[78] See, e.g. *Haughton v Smith* [1975] A.C. 476. Under the common law the "inadequate means" scenario was not viewed as a matter of impossibility. D could have brought about the offence by using adequate means.

[79] However, prior to the Criminal Attempts Act 1981, it was determined by the House of Lords in *Haughton v Smith* that no attempt occurred in such a situation. The defendant had taken possession of a consignment of baked beans under the impression that they were stolen when in reality they were not. It was determined that he could not be guilty of attempting to handle stolen goods with Lord Reid asserting, "The crime is impossible in the circumstances so no acts could be proximate to it."

[80] [1985] A.C. 560.

[81] See, e.g. *Partington v Williams* (1975) 62 Cr.App.R. 225. A defendant will be guilty where he tries to take money from V's wallet, but the wallet, as a matter of fact, is empty.

bar to conviction that D's acts were factually incapable of effecting the commission of the substantive offence.

Section 1(2) and (3) of the Criminal Attempts Act provide as follows:

"(2) A person may be guilty of attempting to commit an offence to which this section applies even though the facts are such that the commission of the offence is impossible.

(3) In any case where—

(a) apart from this subsection a person's intention would not be regarded as an intent to commit an offence but

(b) if the facts of the case had been as he believed them to be, his intention would be so regarded, then, for the purposes of subs.(1) above, he shall be regarded as having had an intent to commit that offence."[82]

The above s.1(2) was clearly intended to cover such cases as trying to steal from empty pockets and it is suggested that it is quite adequate to do so. The pickpocket has clearly got beyond the stage of preparation and it makes perfect sense to say that he is attempting to steal from the pocket. A similar illustration is provided by the would-be assassin who fires at a bed with intent to kill V, but in fact the bed is empty. It is perfectly logical to convict the defendant of attempted murder in such a scenario.

Example 3

D has intercourse with his girlfriend. Although she is, in fact, 16 she has always told him she **6–016** is 12 in order to dampen his approaches. On the evening in question, however, he has broken down her resistance and they have had intercourse, but she has not informed him that she is 16 and that he will not be committing any offence. Now if the girl had been 12 he would have committed the offence of rape of a child under 13 contrary to s.5 of the Sexual Offences Act 2003. Unlike the situation in *Example 2*, D has done everything he set out to do; it is unlikely that he will feel disappointed when he realises that she is 16. This type of case is sometimes said to be attempting the legally impossible and occurs most frequently where the accused receives non-stolen goods in the belief that they are stolen.[83] Again it is clear that the drafters of the Act thought that such conduct should constitute a criminal attempt and that the Act, as drafted, would criminalise such conduct. However, in *Anderton v Ryan*,[84] the House of Lords reached a contrary conclusion. In that case Mrs Ryan had received a video-cassette recorder believing it to be stolen property, whereas it was not, in fact, stolen. She could not be charged with the offence of handling stolen property contrary to s.22 of the Theft Act 1968 (see below) since that requires proof that she handled property which was, in fact, *stolen*, knowing or believing it to be stolen. She was therefore, charged with attempted handling. She was convicted, but when her appeal reached the House of Lords her conviction was quashed. Their Lordships held that handling non-stolen property was no offence and that a belief that the property was stolen could not render the person liable for attempted handling unless such liability was created by the Criminal Attempts Act. They could find nothing in the Act which was sufficiently clear to do this.

---

[82] The s.1(3) provision is, in essence, of a superfluous nature, in that it adds nothing of substance to s.1(2). However, its import is to counteract any possibility of D raising a fallacious argument derived from *Haughton v Smith*, i.e. I intended to handle stolen baked beans—the baked beans I handled were not stolen—hence in relation to those *specific* baked beans I intended to handle "non-stolen" goods. The effect of s.1(3) means that D will be deemed to handle stolen goods *on the facts which he believed to exist*.

[83] See, e.g. *Walker* [1984] Crim.L.R. 112.

[84] [1985] A.C. 560.

In *Shivpuri*[85] the House of Lords had another chance to examine this area of law. Here the accused was convicted of an attempt to be knowingly concerned in dealing with and harbouring a prohibited drug.[86] Shivpuri admitted that he thought that the substance in his possession was such a drug, but on investigation it turned out to be a harmless substance rather like snuff. The House of Lords said that they considered that they had reached the wrong conclusion in *Anderton v Ryan*, and although Lord Hailsham said that he could distinguish the two cases on the facts, their Lordships preferred to invoke their power to overrule previous decisions of the House of Lords. Lord Bridge said that the correct way to approach such problems was first of all to ask whether the defendant intended to commit the offence which he was alleged to have attempted; in *Shivpuri* he clearly intended to be knowingly concerned in dealing with and harbouring prohibited drugs with intent to evade the prohibition on their importation. The second question is whether he, in relation to these offences, did an act which was more than merely preparatory to the commission of the offences? Lord Bridge held that the acts relied on were more than merely preparatory to the commission of the *intended* offence and this was sufficient. Where the facts were such that the commission of the offence was impossible, it would never be possible to prove that the accused had done an act which was more than merely preparatory to the commission of the actual offence and this would render s.1(2) otiose. Lord Bridge thought that he and other members of the House in *Anderton v Ryan* had gone astray in describing Mrs Ryan's conduct in purchasing a non-stolen video recorder as "objectively innocent". The mistake was to categorise the purchase of a non-stolen article as "innocent" without regard to Mrs Ryan's belief that it was stolen. Lord Bridge asserted:

> "[T]he concept of 'objective innocence' is incapable of sensible application in relation to the law of criminal attempts. The reason for this is that any attempt to commit an offence which involves an act which is more than merely preparatory to the commission of the offence but which for any reason fails, so that in the event no offence is committed, must *ex hypothesi*, from the point of view of the criminal law, be 'objectively innocent'. What turns what would otherwise, from the point of view of the criminal law, be an innocent act into a crime is the intent of the actor to commit an offence . . . A puts his hand into B's pocket. Whether or not there is anything in the pocket capable of being stolen, if A intends to steal his act is a criminal attempt; if he does not so intend his act is innocent . . . These considerations lead me to the conclusion that the distinction sought to be drawn in *Anderton v Ryan* between innocent and guilty acts considered 'objectively' and independently of the state of mind of the actor cannot be sensibly maintained."[87]

There has been much heated debate over this matter; suffice it to say that *Shivpuri* seems to have settled this issue for the moment in favour of the prosecution. However, in *Galvin*[88] the Court of Appeal quashed the defendant's conviction for unlawfully receiving a document contrary to s.2(2) of the Official Secrets Act 1911 because there was evidence that the Government's own wide distribution of the document may have impliedly authorised anyone who came into possession of it to use the document as he saw fit. Thus, to put it simply, Galvin believed he was receiving the document unlawfully, when, in fact, he was not. It is strange that with *Shivpuri* still ringing in their ears, it did not occur to the Court of Appeal that this was a case of attempting to receive the document unlawfully.

---

[85] [1987] A.C. 1.
[86] Contrary to the Customs and Excise Management Act 1979 s.170.
[87] [1987] A.C. 1 at 21–22.
[88] [1987] Q.B. 862.

A similar situation arose in *DPP v Huskinson*.[89] In this case the defendant was charged **6–017** with theft of £279 from the Housing Services Department. He had applied for housing benefit and had been sent a cheque for £479. Although he was already £800 in arrears with his rent, he gave only £200 to his landlord and spent the remainder on himself even though he believed that he was under a legal obligation to use all the money for rental purposes. The problem for the court in this case was that theft is the dishonest appropriation of property belonging to another with the intent permanently to deprive the other of the property. It was clear that, in law, the money became his on receipt and, thus, he had, on the face of it, appropriated his own money. Under s.5(3) of the Theft Act 1968 he can be treated as having appropriated property belonging to another if the prosecution could prove that he was under a legal obligation to use that property in a specific way.[90] The court held that the defendant was not on the facts of this case under an obligation to use the £479 in a specific way, even though he thought he was under such an obligation. He could not, therefore, be convicted of theft. The court did not consider whether he should have been convicted of attempted theft; but was he guilty of attempted theft? Is not this case just like *Shivpuri*? Arguably there is a significant difference. In both *Shivpuri* and *Anderton v Ryan* it is arguable that the defendants made a mistake of fact; one believed the substance was a controlled drug, the other that a video recorder was stolen property. Huskinson's mistake, however, was one of law. He was fully aware of the facts, namely that he had been given a sum of money by the Housing Services Department; he was mistaken as to the legal effect of this transaction. The court might say that s.1(2) of the Criminal Attempts Act 1981 is not appropriate to cover this type of situation—it only relates to mistakes of fact. However, the position is not entirely straightforward. It is very tempting to suggest that the answer the court would give would depend upon whether they wish to impose a penalty for the conduct. What is clear, however, is that the court should have at least adverted to the issue; it would appear that just as with *Galvin* the court simply did not think that this looked like a criminal attempt.

The problems engendered in this area may be illustrated by means of a hypothetical illustration. Suppose Parliament, as part of the smoking ban in public places, makes it an indictable criminal offence to smoke in public restaurants. The statute is to come into effect on April 1. D, intending to break the law in protest on behalf of the smoking lobby, (a) smokes on March 1 in a public restaurant believing March 1 to be the date on which the Act comes into effect. He can clearly commit no indictable offence in such a scenario. Has he committed an attempt? It is submitted that, as in *DPP v Huskinson*, the defendant has made a *mistake of law* and this might be a reason for distinguishing *Shivpuri*. Alternatively, suppose (b) that D smokes in a public restaurant on March 31 believing it to be April 1; his watch has gone wrong and it is only March 31. He has, similar to *Shivpuri*, made a *mistake of fact* and s.1(2) of the Criminal Attempts Act would suggest he is guilty of an attempt. Had the facts been as he believed them to be he would be guilty of an offence. However, the difficulty remains that the offence is alleged to be committed on March 31 and on this day there is no substantive indictable offence he could be guilty of committing; there is as yet no offence in the statute books of smoking in a public restaurant. It seems that great care must be demonstrated by prosecution authorities in bringing indictments where D has attempted the impossible.

Since nearly all the examples of this type of attempting the legally impossible occur in the area of handling of drugs, it would be more satisfactory to amend the substantive offences so

---

[89] [1988] Crim.L.R. 620.
[90] See below, para.8–033.

that the accused commits a full offence. Thus, if handling were amended so that it was an offence to receive property knowing or believing it to be stolen, Mrs Ryan would have committed the offence of handling—there would have been no need to rely on attempts at all.

Example 4

6–018 E has intercourse with his 17-year-old girlfriend believing it to be an offence to have sexual intercourse with a girl under the age of 18. Although this may be morally indistinguishable from *Example 3* it is suggested that the answer is clear. There is no crime known to English law with which he could be charged. The indictment (the formal document containing the charges at the trial) must accuse the defendant of attempting to commit an offence which is triable on indictment. In *Example 3* the indictment would refer to the offence of rape of a child under 13 which is an offence under s.5 of the Sexual Offences Act 2003. In this example, there is no offence which is triable in this country on indictment. This becomes even more obvious if the defendant, believing it to be an offence to wear a red bow tie on Thursdays, deliberately sets out to break the law. Can it be seriously imagined that he has attempted to commit an offence which is indictable in English law? The question demands a negative reply in the same manner, that no offence is committed where D commits adultery, personally believing that this constitutes a criminal offence. It seems, as Professor Glanville Williams suggested,[91] that the only form of "impossibility defence" that can now be rationally regarded as surviving the Criminal Attempts Act 1981 is what may be called abstract legal impossibility—the "imaginary crime" rule. In this regard abstract legal impossibility will transpire where the crime attempted, meaning the very crime that the defendant thought he was attempting, does not exist as a crime in the books. The proposition is illustrated by *Taaffe*[92] where the defendant believed that he was importing foreign currency into England contrary to express prohibitions. In reality no such crime existed on the books, and so no liability could exist for attempting the commission of a totally imaginary crime.

6. ACTS OF PREPARATION

6–019 Section 6 of the Criminal Attempts Act 1981 makes it clear that the offence of attempt at common law and any offence at common law of procuring materials for crime are abolished (see *Gurmit Singh*).[93] However, Parliament has specifically provided that certain acts which would be described as acts of preparation to commit offences shall, in themselves, amount to crimes. Examples of such provisions are going equipped for stealing contrary to s.25 of the Theft Act 1968[94] and possessing anything with intent to use it to damage or destroy property contrary to s.3 of the Criminal Damage Act 1971.[95]

---

[91] G. Williams, "Attempting the Impossible—The Last Round?" (1985) N.L.J. 337 at 346.
[92] [1983] 2 All E.R. 625.
[93] [1966] 2 Q.B. 53.
[94] Below, para.9–057.
[95] Below, para.10–014.

GENERAL READING

Ashworth, A., "Criminal Attempts And The Role Of Resulting Harm Under The Code, **6–020** And In The Common Law" (1988) 19 *Rutgers Law Journal* 725.

Buxton, R., "Circumstances, Consequences And Attempted Rape" [1984] Crim.L.R. 25.

Dressler, J., "Reassessing The Theoretical Underpinnings Of Accomplice Liability: New Solutions To An Old Problem" (1985) 37 Hastings L.J. 91.

Hogan, B., "The Criminal Attempts Act And Attempting The Impossible" [1984] Crim.L.R. 584.

Palmer, P., "Attempt By Act or Omission: Causation And The Problem Of The Hypothetical Nurse" (1999) 63 J.C.L. 158.

Rogers, J., "The Codification Of Attempts And The Case For Preparation" [2008] Crim.L.R. 937.

Smith, K.J.M., "Proximity In Attempt: Lord Lane's Midway Course" [1991] Crim.L.R. 576.

Williams, G., "Attempting The Impossible—The Last Round" (1985) N.L.J. 337; and Williams, G., "The Lords Achieve The Logically Impossible" (1985) N.L.J. 502.

Williams, G., "The Lords And Impossible Attempts, Or *Quis Custodiet Ipsos Custodes*" (1986) 45 C.L.J. 33.

Williams, G., "The Problem of Reckless Attempts" [1983] Crim.L.R. 365.

Williams, G., "Wrong Turnings On The Law Of Attempt" [1991] Crim.L.R. 416.

ENCOURAGEMENT OR ASSISTANCE

The law has recently undergone significant change, through the enactment of Pt 2 of the **6–021** Serious Crime Act 2007, in relation to the provision by a defendant of encouragement or assistance to another to commit an offence. Where D encourages or assists the commission of an offence by another, and that other goes on to commit an offence, the criminal law rules regarding complicity are triggered, and the question will be whether D becomes a party to that offence.[96] Liability for participation in the crime of another is rather different from what is being considered in this chapter—albeit that liability for the offences we are about to discuss and liability for participation in the crime of another can both arise on the same facts. We are concerned here with inchoate offences, the commission of which do not depend on whether the person, in this case assisted or encouraged, goes on to commit an offence at all.

We saw at the beginning of this chapter that if X were to conceive in his mind a plan to burgle Barclays Bank and even if he were to outline his plan to Y he would commit no offence. However if the prosecution can prove that he tried to persuade Y to join him in the venture this would amount to the offence of encouraging Y to commit, in this case, burglary. In the old case of *Higgins* Lord Kenyon stated, "it is argued that a mere intent to commit evil is not indictable, without an act done; but is there not an act done, when it is charged that the defendant solicited another to commit a felony?"[97] Prior to the 2007 Act, liability for encouraging or assisting the commission of offences was addressed by the common law offence of incitement. In essence, incitement meant encouragement[98] and D would commit

---

[96] See Ch.4.

[97] (1801) 2 *East* 5 at 170.

[98] The oft-quoted definition provided by Lord Denning M.R. in *Race Relations Board v Applin* is that, "to incite means to urge or spur on by advice, encouragement and persuasion" [1973] Q.B. 815 at 825. Although the actual case itself focused on the statutory offence of incitement to racial hatred under s.12 of the Race Relations Act, Lord Denning's definition was generally accepted as applicable to the inchoate common law offence.

it if he encouraged another to commit an offence, whether or not that offence was committed.

An inciter was an individual who reached and sought to influence the mind of another to the commission of a crime, by means of persuasion or pressure.[99] The nature of incitement arose in *Marlow*.[100] The defendant was the author of a book on the cultivation and production of cannabis. Some 500 copies were sold and several customers followed the methodology advocated in the book. He was convicted, inter alia, of incitement to commit an offence, contrary to s.19 of the Misuse of Drugs Act 1971, which charge was based on his admitted authorship and publication of the book. The appeal against conviction was predicated on the grounds that there was no evidence that he had incited anyone to commit an offence. However this was rejected by the Court of Appeal which determined that Marlow had incited the offence by means of encouragement. He had, in effect, emboldened others to engage in criminal activity. It seems that if the book was capable of encouraging or persuading, and was published with that particular purpose in mind, then it constituted incitement.

6–022   The decision in *Marlow* illustrates the point that incitement could be directed to a particular person or to people in general. It could be to the world at large. For example, a general article in a newspaper would qualify as incitement if put in sufficiently clear terms. In *Most*[101] an article was published by the defendant in a London newspaper which solicited the reader audience to copy the lead of those engaged in the uprisings in Russia and murder their Heads of State. This was determined to be a case of the statutory offence of incitement to murder under s.4 of the Offences against the Person Act 1861.

Another illustration of the principle that incitement could be directed at people in general is provided by *Invicta Plastics v Clare*,[102] which also makes clear that incitement could be *implied*, not simply of an express nature. At issue was the defendant's advertisement in a motoring magazine of its manufactured device called "Radatec", which emitted a high-pitched whine when within some half-mile range of radio transmissions on a band of frequencies allocated to a number of services including amateurs, airports and police radar traps for speeding vehicles. In effect, the only sensible use of the device was for the detection of police radar traps, and it was held that this constituted an offence under s.1(1) of the Wireless Telegraphy Act 1949. Indeed the advertisement itself depicted a picture of a road through a car windscreen to which the device was attached and a speed restriction sign immediately ahead. The company was convicted of inciting readers of a magazine to commit the offence of using unlicensed apparatus for wireless telegraphy. Invicta Plastics had impliedly encouraged or persuaded the world at large (readers of the magazine) to engage in criminal activity.[103] Similarly in *James and Ashford*[104] the appellate court held that the supply to householders of "black boxes" whose design purpose was to allow electricity meters to under-record and consequentially facilitate the dishonest abstraction of electricity

---

[99] *Nkosiyana* 1966 (4) S.A. 655 at 658 per Holmes J.A. It was further stated that, "[T]he machinations of criminal ingenuity being legion, the approach to the other's mind may take various forms such as suggestion, proposal, request, exhortation, gesture, argument, persuasion, inducement, goading, or the arousal of cupidity." See, generally, J.C. Smith and B. Hogan, *Criminal Law* (Butterworths, 1996) at p.273.
[100] [1997] Crim.L.R. 897.
[101] (1881) 7 Q.B.D. 244. The offence of incitement becomes complete on communication reaching the incitee; see, generally, *Krause* (1902) 66 J.P. 121 and *Ransford* (1874) 13 Cox C.C. 9.
[102] [1976] Crim.L.R. 131.
[103] See, generally, *CBS Songs v Amstrad* [1988] A.C. 1013, where the defendants' manufacture for sale of hi-fi systems with facilities for, inter alia, recording at high speed from pre-recorded cassettes on to blank tapes did not constitute copyright infringement or the incitement thereof under the Copyright Act 1956. This was because of the unfortunate wording of this much-criticised statute.
[104] (1985) 82 Cr.App.R. 232.

contrary to s.13 of the Theft Act 1968, could constitute incitement to commit that offence. In a modern context, it was determined in *O'Shea*[105] that a defendant subscribing to a website containing indecent images of children thereby "incites" the business supplier of the egregious site. The subscription facilitates the continuation of supply and is tantamount to encouragement.

These cases also demonstrate the flexibility of the notion of incitement as some of them arguably involved behaviour which was better characterised as assistance than encouragement.

The basic position on the mens rea of incitement was that the prosecution had to show **6–023** that the accused intended that as a result of his persuasion another person would commit an act which would be a criminal offence, though, of course, there was no need to prove that the accused knew that the act in question was a crime. In essence, the inciter must know all the circumstances of the act incited that would make it criminal, including the necessary mental element of the principal offender. However, the Court of Appeal managed to confuse itself on more than one occasion on this issue.

In *Curr*[106] the defendant was engaged in the egregious practice of trafficking in family allowance vouchers by purchasing them at a substantial undervalue from their holders, as security against loans he had given them, and then sending different women agents to cash them on his behalf. Curr was charged with soliciting the commission of an offence under s.9(b) of the Family Allowance Act 1945. The feature of this offence was that it prohibited an individual from receiving money in payment of an allowance which that individual knew was not properly payable. This meant that the women agents, who collected the payments, would only be guilty if knowledge on their part was ascertainable. Hence Curr's conviction was quashed since it was not proved that the woman agents knew that they were not allowed to receive the moneys, as the definition of the offence required. This meant that Curr could not be shown to have known the circumstances of the offence, and consequentially the appellate court determined that he did not fulfil the necessary requirements for inciting it. With respect, the Court of Appeal added here an unnecessary ingredient to the mens rea for incitement. We have seen that the offence of incitement was completed irrespective of whether or not the incitee carried out the incited offence or intends to commit it. Thus the actual state of mind of the incitee was not of consequence. The relevant question ought to have been simply whether Curr believed, if the offence were to be carried out, that the incitees would have the requisite mens rea for the substantive offence. It is submitted that belief on the inciter's part that the incitee had the mens rea of the principal crime should have been sufficient. The incitee's actual mens rea should have been of no consequence to the inciter's liability for incitement.

In *Shaw* the defendant incited a fellow employee (K) to obtain property by deception from their common employer, a car leasing company. Shaw contended that he had emboldened K to accept bogus invoices simply to demonstrate the inadequacies of the company's invoice system. He hoped by perpetrating the scheme to gain esteem and perhaps promotion in the company. He did not tell K what his purpose was behind the scheme but affirmed that he would eventually have done so. His conviction was quashed by the Court of Appeal, apparently on the basis that an inciter needs to have the mens rea of the full principal offence, and the jury ought to have been allowed to consider whether Shaw intended to deprive the owners of their property permanently (a requirement for the full offence) and make a profit of his own. Again it seems that the Court of Appeal analysis, like

---

[105] [2004] Crim.L.R. 948.
[106] [1968] 2 Q.B. 944.

that in *Curr*, was misconceived. As Professor Smith commented, the court confused the mens rea of incitement with the mens rea required for the full offence itself.[107] In essence, Shaw was not charged with obtaining property by deception (full offence) but with inciting K to obtain property by deception (an inchoate offence). This meant that, "it was necessary to show that he intended K to act dishonestly and with intention permanently to deprive but quite unnecessary to show that Shaw had any such dishonest intention."[108]

6–024   More recently, the Divisional Court in *DPP v Armstrong*[109] rejected the requirement for parity of mens rea between the parties, and diverged from the conceptual analysis provided in *Curr* and *Shaw*. The defendant was convicted of inciting a person to distribute indecent photographs of children.[110] The incitee was an undercover police officer ("John") with whom the defendant had been put in touch by a police informer. The defendant had requested from "John" pornography involving girls no younger than 12 years. At the trial "John" testified that he had no intention of supplying the material but that he did have access to it from police stores. The deputy stipendiary magistrate acquitted the defendant on the basis, following *Curr* and *Shaw*, that the incitee should have parity of mens rea with Armstrong. Since the material would not have been supplied, the full offence could not have been committed. The Divisional Court, however, held that the mens rea of the inciter is only a *belief* or *intention* that the incitee will have the necessary fault. There was no requirement that the incitee should act at all, let alone that he should act with the necessary mens rea. The court distinguished *Shaw* and *Curr*, denying that they laid down any general rule that the law required parity of mens rea.[111] In principle, the necessary mens rea for incitement was an intention that if the person did what was asked he would commit an offence.[112]

As part of a broader review of the law of assisting and encouraging crime, the Law Commission recommended at one point that the framework of liability for complicity, in which it was necessary that a principal offence be committed, be fundamentally reappraised, such that liability for "accomplice-type behaviour" would no longer depend on the commission of a principal offence. The inchoate offences of encouragement and assistance emerged from that body of work, and although the general framework of liability for accomplices remains "derivative"—that is to say, it depends on the commission of a principal offence—the new inchoate offences remained on the agenda and came into being in some rather technical provisions in the Serious Crime Act 2007. The common law offence of incitement has been abolished.[113]

Part 2 of the 2007 Act sets out three offences of encouragement and assistance. The first of these is contained in s.44. D commits this offence if "he does an act capable of

---

[107] J.C. Smith [1994] Crim.L.R. 366.

[108] J.C. Smith [1994] Crim.L.R. 366.

[109] [2000] Crim.L.R. 379; see also *Goldman* [2001] Crim.L.R. 894; see, generally, J. Holroyd, "Incitement—A Tale of Three Agents" (2001) 65 J.C.L. 515. See also, *El Faisal* [2004] EWCA Crim 343, where D incited all believers to kill Americans.

[110] Contrary to the Protection of Children Act 1978 s.1(1).

[111] It was held that *Shaw* could be explained on its facts and was not general authority for the proposition that there must be parity of mens rea, while in *Curr* the defendant was not guilty of soliciting a woman to collect some family allowance from a post office, which was not properly receivable by her, because the offence required knowledge by the woman, which she did not have, that collecting the money was an offence. The court in that case made no general pronouncement about whether incitement required that the person incited, as well as the inciter, had the full mens rea for the offence.

[112] Tuckey L.J. asserted that if the law were otherwise, all the cases regarding an *agent provocateur* would have been wrongly decided, as in each case a defendant could argue that the person incited never intended to commit the offence and that no offence of incitement had been committed.

[113] Serious Crime Act 2007 s.59. Specific statutory forms of incitement remain including incitement to murder contrary to s.4 of the Offences Against The Person Act 1861 or the Incitement to Mutiny Act 1797 or the Incitement to Disaffection Act 1934. See *Abu Hamza* [2006] EWCA Crim 2918.

encouraging or assisting the commission of an offence" and "he intends to encourage or assist its commission". Section 44(2) states that intention to encourage or assist cannot be inferred merely from the foreseeability of D's actions giving encouragement or assistance.

The second offence is contained in s.45. It is committed by D who "does an act capable of **6–025** encouraging or assisting the commission of an offence" and who believes "that the offence will be committed" and "that his act will encourage or assist its commission".

The third offence is set out in s.46 and addresses the question of the degree of specificity which must accompany encouragement or assistance. It is committed by D who "does an act capable of encouraging or assisting the commission of one or more of a number of offences" and who believes "that one or more of those offences will be committed (but has no belief as to which)" and "that his act will encourage or assist the commission of one or more of them". In respect of the final requirement, it does not matter whether D "has any belief as to which offence will be encouraged or assisted".

Section 47 sets out in further detail what must be proved to establish the commission of offences under ss.44–46. So, to establish that a person intended to encourage or assist the commission of an offence,[114] "it is sufficient to prove that he intended to encourage or assist the doing of an act which would amount to the commission of that offence". Therefore, it is not necessary to show that D knew that what he or she intended to assist or encourage was actually an offence—as usual, ignorance of the law is no defence. Likewise, where D believed that an offence would be committed and that his act would encourage or assist its commission[115] it is not necessary to prove that D believed that what would occur and what he believed he was assisting was an offence, merely that in fact what was encouraged etc. would amount to an offence. Similarly, where D believes that one or more offences would be committed and that his act would assist or encourage one or more of them,[116] it is enough to prove that he believed "that one or more of a number of acts would be done which would amount to the commission of one or more of those offences" and that his act would encourage or assist the doing of one or more of those acts. It is not necessary to prove that D had any belief in the criminality of anything he was encouraging or assisting.

Section 47(5) addresses the issue of D's mental element in respect of the mental element **6–026** required for the offence being encouraged or assisted. If the offence in question requires proof of fault, it must be proved that D believed that if the act were done, it would be done with that fault; that D was reckless as to whether it would be done with that fault; or that D's state of mind was such that if he did that act constituting the offence himself, it would be done with the fault required for the offence. Section 47(5) also demands that if the offence encouraged or assisted requires proof of particular circumstances or consequences, it must be proved either that D believed that if the act were done, it would be done in the required circumstances or with the required consequences; or that D was reckless as to whether to would be done in the required circumstances or with the required consequences.

So, where D is alleged to have encouraged or assisted an offence of strict liability, the offence of encouragement or assistance still has a distinct mens rea requirement of its own, namely belief in or recklessness as to the prohibited circumstances or consequences attending the offence encouraged or assisted. The Explanatory Notes provide a helpful example of D who asks P to drive him home as D has been drinking. Unknown to D and P, P has just been disqualified from driving. P commits the strict liability offence of driving while disqualified, but D is not liable for encouragement of that offence because of a lack of belief in or recklessness as to the circumstances in question—namely that P was disqualified.[117] The need to prove belief in or recklessness as to consequences is also illustrated

---

[114] For the purposes of s.44.
[115] For the purposes of s.45.
[116] For the purposes of s.46.
[117] Explanatory Notes at para.156.

by an example in the Explanatory Notes in which D gives P a weapon and intends that P use it to inflict minor harm on the victim. In the event, P intentionally kills the victim with the weapon. D would not be liable for encouraging or assisting murder unless he believed that or was reckless as to whether the victim would be killed.[118]

Section 47(6) states that where s.47(5)(a)(iii) is being relied on—in which liability for encouragement or assistance is provided for in the situation where the person encouraging or assisting has the mens rea necessary for the offence being encouraged or assisted—the person encouraging or assisting "is to be assumed to be able to do the act in question". It is suggested in the Explanatory Notes that this caters for the situation in which D (a woman) encourages P (a man) to penetrate V with his penis, and believes that were that to occur, V would not be consenting. The example in the Explanatory Notes posits a situation in which P has a reasonable belief in consent and therefore avoids liability. The Notes continue:

> "[t]herefore, D's fault is determined under s.47(5)(a)(iii) in that if she were to commit the act, she would do it with the fault required. However, it is not possible for a woman to commit the act of penetration with a penis so were it not for this subsection, D would escape liability".[119]

6–027   The aim is laudable here but there seems to be an error. It does not follow that just because P lacks mens rea for the offence we have to fall back on s.47(5)(a)(iii) to determine the liability of the 'encourager'. The encourager must believe that the act (of P) will be dome with the fault required for the offence (in this example, of rape) or be reckless as to whether it is done with that fault. It matters not that P's act is not *actually* done with that fault. The Explanatory Notes appear to be making the same kind of mistake which the Court of Appeal made with the old law on incitement. The reference point is not the mens rea which the person encouraged (P) actually has. Rather, it is the mens rea which *D believes etc. that P will have*. If D believes that P will act with the fault required for the offence or is reckless as to whether P will so act, that suffices for the offence of encouragement or assistance.

Section 48 sets out in further detail still what must be proved to establish the commission of offences under s.46. It is enough for the purposes of s.46 that the matters referred to in s.47(5) (belief in or recklessness as to fault, circumstances and consequences etc.) be proved in relation to one offence.

There are two defences set out in the Act itself to a charge of encouraging or assisting. Section 50 sets out a defence of acting reasonably. The s.50 defence is available to D who proves that he knows that certain circumstances exist, and that it was reasonable for him to act as he did under those circumstances; or to D who proves that he has a reasonable belief in the existence of certain circumstances, and that it was reasonable to act as he did under the circumstances as he believed them to be. Section 50(3) refers to a (seemingly non-exhaustive) list of factors which affect whether it is reasonable for D to act as he did: "the seriousness of the anticipated offence"; "any purpose for which he claims to have been acting"; and "any authority by which he claims to have been acting". This limited purpose-based defence to encouragement might conceivably be used as a result of law enforcement operations in which an undercover agent or informer is deployed whose actions (perhaps in facilitating the commission of an offence) might otherwise amount to offences under the 2007 Act.

---

[118] And indeed unless he believed or was reckless as to whether D would act with the mens rea for murder. Query whether under the circumstances in the example from the Explanatory Notes (see para.157) D might be liable for encouraging or assisting manslaughter, by analogy with *Stewart and Schofield* (1995) 1 Cr.App.Rep. 441.
[119] At para.159.

Section 51 restates the so-called *"Tyrrell"* principle—under which exemption from liability **6–028** for an offence is provided for classes of persons whom that offence was designed to protect.[120] So, if D, aged 12, encourages P to have sexual intercourse with her, D cannot be liable for encouraging rape of a child under 13[121] because that offence is designed to protect her. In the example given in the Explanatory Notes, P is a 40-year-old man, but it is submitted that the result would be the same if P were 14, or even 10-years-old.

Part 2 of the 2007 Act also contains some fairly complicated provisions on territorial application and jurisdiction, which are, in their detail, beyond the scope of this book.[122] Suffice to say that these will come into play in a variety of situations. These situations are, in broad terms:

- when an act capable of amounting to encouragement or assistance is done outside England and Wales in respect of an offence which is to take place within England and Wales;

- when an act capable of amounting to encouragement or assistance is done within or outside England and Wales in respect of conduct to be undertaken outside England and Wales but in respect of which the perpetrator of that conduct could be tried in England and Wales even though it did not take place within England and Wales[123];

- where an act capable of amounting to encouragement or assistance is done in England and Wales in respect of actions to be committed in another country which would constitute an offence in that country.

Where these issues of territoriality and jurisdiction arise, prosecution in England and Wales requires the consent of the Attorney-General.[124]

The maximum penalty available for encouragement or assistance is the same as that available for the offence encouraged or assisted.[125]

CONSPIRACY

1. GENERAL OVERVIEW

The inchoate offence of conspiracy represents one of the most complex and confusing areas **6–029** of our criminal law. In this respect it may be helpful to outline a general overview of the topic before considering specific issues in more detail. While a decision by one person to commit a crime, even if there is clear evidence of his intention, is not an offence, it has long been the law that an *agreement* by two or more to commit a crime is an offence. Perhaps the reason is that where two or more persons have agreed on a course of action it is more likely that the planned course of action will be carried out. Certainly courts have taken the view that confederacies are especially dangerous. So dangerous, in fact, that criminal conspiracies

---

[120] *Tyrrell* [1894] 1 Q.B. 710. See para.4–041.
[121] Rape of a child under 13 is an offence under s.5 of the Sexual Offences Act 2003. See para.7–135.
[122] See Schedule 4.
[123] The most obvious application here is to the offence of murder, where there is extra-territorial jurisdiction at common law in relation to defendants who are "subjects of her Majesty".
[124] s.53.
[125] s.58.

were not restricted to agreements to commit crimes. In *Kamara v DPP*,[126] for example, it was held by the House of Lords that an agreement to commit the tort of trespass to land, if accompanied by an intention to inflict more than merely nominal damage, was indictable as a criminal conspiracy.

That it should be a crime in certain circumstances even to agree to commit a civil wrong was thought by many to be objectionable. The Law Commission[127] considered the matter and at first the Commission essentially expressed the idea that only agreements to commit crimes should be indictable as conspiracies. This proposal was in turn criticised as being too narrow. In particular, it would have restricted the operation of conspiracy to defraud because, on the common law view of this crime, there could be a conspiracy to defraud even though there was no conspiracy to commit a crime. Consider, for example, the case of *Scott v Metropolitan Police Commissioner*.[128] A, B and others made copies of films without the consent of the copyright holders with a view to making a profit for themselves by showing the films without paying the copyright holders. In such a case as this it may have been difficult to prove that A and B had committed some crime under the Theft Acts. They did not steal anything from the copyright holders nor was there any deception of the holders. But it was held that their conduct fell within the wide net of the common law offence of conspiracy to defraud in that they had prejudiced the economic interests of another.

The Law Commission, therefore, proposed that criminal conspiracy should extend to: (i) agreements to commit crime, and (ii) that the common law conspiracy to defraud should be retained, at least for the time being. Had this proposal been accepted all common law conspiracies other than conspiracy to defraud would have ceased to be criminal. But the government of the day thought it best to postpone a final decision on conspiracies to corrupt public morals and conspiracies to outrage public decency pending the outcome of another review. The result, not altogether a happy one, is embodied in the Criminal Law Act 1977 (see below). The Law Commission's proposals have been implemented to create statutory offences of conspiracy but the common law conspiracy to defraud was retained and agreements to corrupt public morals and outrage public decency were excepted from the statutory scheme as well. We thus have statutory conspiracies and common law conspiracies.

6–030   One problem that has troubled the courts since the introduction of statutory conspiracies in 1977 is the question of overlap between statutory and common law conspiracies. Suppose that X, Y and Z agree to a plan under which they will obtain possession of a rental television set from a local company by giving false names and addresses and that once in possession of the set they will sell it and keep the money. If the plan is put into operation they will clearly commit the offence of fraud by false representation contrary to s.2 of the Fraud Act 2006. At present, however, they have only agreed to do this. Should the prosecutor therefore charge them with conspiracy to commit fraud by false representation, a statutory conspiracy under s.1 of the Criminal Law Act 1977, or should he charge them with conspiracy to defraud (a common law conspiracy not abolished by the statute of 1977), or does he have a choice? It seems fairly clear that the drafters of the Act intended that in such a case the accused should be charged with the statutory conspiracy. Conspiracy to defraud was meant to be retained as a long stop for those cases where the commission of the agreed plan by one person would not necessarily amount to a substantive criminal law offence. The real solution envisaged was that these loopholes would eventually be filled by substantive criminal offences and the need for conspiracy to defraud would then disappear. An example of the closing of this type of loophole can be seen in s.3 of the Theft Act 1978. Before that Act if X simply left a hotel

---

[126] [1974] A.C. 104.
[127] *Conspiracy and Criminal Law Reform* (1976) Law Com. No.76, H.C. 176.
[128] [1975] A.C. 819.

at the end of his holiday without paying he might possibly have committed no criminal offence. If, however, he agreed with Y that they should leave without paying, this would amount to conspiracy to defraud the hotel. Under s.3 of the Theft Act 1978 a new criminal offence of making off without payment was created so that if X dishonestly leaves the hotel without paying he will commit a substantive criminal offence.[129]

It is one thing for legislators to have a certain objective in mind. It does not necessarily follow that the legislation they pass will achieve that objective. The Criminal Law Act 1977 could not be described as the clearest of statutes. Since the Act was passed there have been conflicting decisions of the Court of Appeal as to whether the prosecution can still charge an accused with conspiracy to defraud when the agreement is to commit a substantive criminal law offence. After two attempts by the House of Lords to resolve the matter in *Ayres*[130] and *Cooke*[131] the position was still far from clear. Happily the matter has now been resolved by statute. Section 12 of the Criminal Justice Act 1987 provides that it is perfectly permissible to charge the defendant with conspiracy to defraud even though the facts reveal a statutory conspiracy. Although this was not the intention of the drafters of the original statute it does seem the simplest solution to a potentially complex issue. The other common law conspiracies, those of outraging public decency and corrupting public morals, may not be charged when the facts reveal a statutory conspiracy. These offences, however, make only rare appearances before the courts and are not, therefore, likely to cause serious difficulties.

2. THE ACTUS REUS IN CONSPIRACY

A. Rationale and the Requirement of an Agreement

The rationale behind imposition of liability for criminal conspiracy has never been clearly **6–031** articulated by our courts. It has, however, been cogently suggested that it derives from the culpable nature of the plot which is the focus of the criminal partnership.[132] This accords with the approach adopted by the US Supreme Court in *Pinkerton v United States* where factors were enunciated justifying the punishment of these partnerships in crime:

> "A conspiracy is a partnership in crime. *US v Socony Vacuum Oil Co.*, 310 US 150, 253. It has ingredients, as well as implications, distinct from the completion of the unlawful project. As stated in *U.S. v Rabinowich*, 238 US 78: 'For two or more to confederate and combine together to commit or cause to be committed a breach of the criminal laws, is an offence of the gravest character, sometimes quite outweighing, in injury to the public, the mere commission of the contemplated crime. It involves deliberate plotting to subvert the laws, educating and preparing the conspirators for further and habitual criminal practices. And it is characterised by secrecy, rendering it difficult of detection, requiring more time for its discovery and adding to the importance of punishing it when discovered."[133]

An alternative rationale, upon which the Law Commission implicitly relied, is to view conspiracy as akin to attempt in that it is based upon an act of preparation auxiliary to the substantive offence. In effect, the offence of conspiracy is viewed as a stage-back derivation

---

[129] See below, para.9–015.
[130] [1984] A.C. 447.
[131] [1986] A.C. 909. See also *Att-Gen Ex p. Rockall* [1999] 4 All E.R. 312 DC.
[132] I. Dennis, "The Rationale of Conspiracy" (1977) 93 L.Q.R. 39 at 51.
[133] (1945) 328 U.S. 640 at 644.

from the full crime contemplated.[134] However, whatever the basis for criminal conspiracy what is clear is that the very essence of the offence is the *agreement* between the parties on a course of conduct. What is required is a compact which may be manifested by writing, words or deeds. Negotiations, however far advanced, will not suffice without a compact to effect a criminal purpose. For instance, in *Walker*[135] the defendant had discussed with others a proposal to carry out a robbery, but his conviction of conspiracy to rob was quashed as it was not demonstrated that the parties had gone beyond the stage of discussing the possibility of committing the ulterior offence and had come to a definite decision to do so. Nor is it enough that A simply gives help to B knowing of his criminal purpose. In *Bainbridge*,[136] B in knowingly supplying oxygen cutting equipment to A became a secondary party to the burglary committed by A, but, on those facts alone, it could hardly be said that B had agreed with A to commit burglary. However, the crime of conspiracy is complete as soon as agreement is reached and it is irrelevant that, after the agreement, one or all of the parties decides to abandon it.[137]

This point has recently been affirmed by Lord Hope in *Saik*[138] who stated:

> "A conspiracy is complete when the agreement to enter it is formed, even if nothing is done to implement it. Implementation gives effect to the conspiracy, but it does not alter its essential elements. The statutory language adopts this approach. It assumes that implementation of the agreement lies in the future. The question whether its requirements are fulfilled is directed to the stage when the agreement is formed, not to the stage when it is implemented."[139]

The statutory conspiracy offence is defined by s.1(1) of the Criminal Law Act 1977, as amended by s.5 of the Criminal Attempts Act 1981:

> "[I]f a person agrees with any other person or persons that a course of conduct shall be pursued which, if the agreement is carried out in accordance with their intentions, either—
>
> (a) will necessarily amount to or involve the commission of any offence or offences by one or more parties to the agreement, or
>
> (b) would do so but for the existence of facts which render the commission of the offence or any of the offences impossible,[140]
>
> he is guilty of conspiracy to commit the offence or offences in question."

6–032   In relation to statutory conspiracy, s.1(1) above requires that A and B should have agreed on a course of conduct which if it is carried out as planned will necessarily amount to a crime. In this regard conspiracy is a continuing offence with no actual requirement that the conspiracy be effected.[141] Suppose, for example, that A and B agree to go on a shoplifting

---

[134] I. Dennis, (1977) 93 L.Q.R. 39 at 63.
[135] [1962] Crim.L.R. 458.
[136] [1960] 1 Q.B. 129; above, para.4–006.
[137] See *El Ghazal* [1986] Crim.L.R. 52.
[138] [2006] UKHL 18; [2007] 1 A.C. 18.
[139] [2006] UKHL 18; [2007] 1 A.C. 18, at [75].
[140] Note here that statutory conspiracy has been put on the same footing over impossibility as attempt; see also Criminal Attempts Act 1981 ss.1(2) and (3) discussed above, paras 6–013—6–018.
[141] See, e.g. *Barnard* (1980) 70 Cr.App.R. 28. Note that because s.1 of the 1977 Act stipulates that a conspiracy may involve the commission of a substantive offence by one or more, but not all, of the conspirators, D can be convicted of conspiracy where he is the intended "object" of the substantive offence, e.g. D agrees with others for the supply to himself of a controlled drug; see *Jackson, The Times,* May 13, 1999 CA, and *Drew* (2000) 1 Cr.App.R. 91.

expedition tomorrow. Between now and tomorrow many things may go wrong and thwart the plan. They may fall ill, or the shops may be closed by a strike or by a power failure. Have they, then, agreed on a course of conduct which if carried out in accordance with that intention will *necessarily* result in the commission of a crime? Of course they have and the fact that their intentions are thwarted for some reason cannot affect the matter. Nor are they any the less guilty of conspiracy to steal because they have not decided upon the particular shop or shops from which they will steal, nor because they have not yet specified the goods they will steal. Similarly, they remain liable for conspiracy to steal if between their compact and commission of the ulterior offence they abandon the plan because of a shared massive win on the National Lottery. Within a single common plan may be embraced a number of distinct crimes, such as conspiracy to rob, burgle or steal. As determined in *Hussain*[142] it is permissible, and not bad for duplicity, for charges to be laid for conspiracy to commit theft, burglary or robbery within the common agreement.

When A and B are the only parties to the alleged conspiracy it is necessary to show a meeting of their minds. But if there are three or more parties it is unnecessary to show that each conspirator was in contact with every other conspirator. For instance, suppose that A agreed with B to rob X leaving it to B to get someone to provide transport, and B engaged C in the enterprise. A and C have now conspired to rob X though neither may have met or even known of the other's identity, provided C knew he was joining such an enterprise and that there were other members of the gang even if he did not know their names. On the other hand, there must be a *nexus* between A and C in relation to the conspiracy charged. If A and B plan to kill X as well as rob him but only the intention to rob X is disclosed to C, A has conspired with C to rob X but there is no agreement between them to murder X.

It should be noted that as a practical matter under a Practice Direction,[143] if full substantive offence counts and a related inchoate conspiracy offence count are joined in the indictment, the prosecution must elect to proceed *either* on the substantive counts or on the conspiracy count (unless, in the interests of justice, the judge directs otherwise). So where a conspiracy count adds nothing to the full substantive offence, it has no place in the indictment, and will be unduly prejudicial to the accused.[144]

B. The Object of the Agreement

Criminal conspiracies are now confined to agreements: (i) to commit a criminal offence[145] **6–033** (ii) to defraud; (iii) to corrupt public morals; and (iv) to outrage public decency. For the sake of completeness it should be added that an agreement (v) to commit murder abroad is indictable here as are some agreements to commit other crimes abroad.[146] Thus it is important to consider in some detail the ambit of the extant conspiracy offences that remain governed by the common law, and which have survived the enactment of the Criminal Law Act 1977.

(i) Conspiracy to Corrupt Public Morals and Outrage Public Decency

The nature of these offences can be illustrated by the House of Lords decisions in *Shaw v* **6–034** *DPP*[147] and *Knuller v DPP*[148] In *Shaw v DPP* the defendant published a booklet, the *Ladies Directory*, of some 28 pages, most of which were taken up with the names and addresses of

---

[142] [2002] Crim.L.R. 407.
[143] *Practice Direction (Crime: Conspiracy)* [1977] 1 W.L.R. 537.
[144] See, e.g. *Jones* (1974) 59 Cr.App.R. 120.
[145] See s.1(1)(a) above. Note in the recent case of *Kenning* [2009] Crim.L.R. 37 it was determined that no offence existed of conspiracy to aid and abet.
[146] See below, para.6–051, on territorial jurisdiction. See also s.5 of the Criminal Justice (Terrorism and Conspiracy) Act 1998.
[147] [1962] A.C. 220.
[148] [1973] A.C. 435.

prostitutes; the matter published left no doubt that the advertisers could be got in touch with at the telephone numbers given and were offering their services for sexual intercourse and, in some cases, for other sexual practices. It was determined by their Lordships, Lord Reid dissenting, that there was an offence at common law of conspiracy to corrupt public morals. In essence, the offence will be committed if the jury, upon whom the onus rests to determine on the facts that the crime has been established, believe that the conduct is outrageously indecent because it would "disgust and annoy them", and similarly ordinary citizens whom they embody.[149] Lord Simon in *Knuller* asserted that, "the words 'corrupt public morals' suggest conduct which a jury might find to be destructive of the very fabric of society."

In *Knuller v DPP*[150] the defendants were directors of a company which published a fortnightly magazine. On an inside page under a column headed "Males", advertisements were inserted inviting readers to meet the advertisers for the purpose of homosexual practices. They were convicted on counts of conspiracy to corrupt public morals and conspiracy to outrage public decency. Their convictions were affirmed by the House of Lords on the first premise, but whilst the conviction of conspiracy to outrage public decency was quashed on the grounds of an inadequate direction by the trial judge, nevertheless a majority of their Lordships affirmed the existence of the common law offence, Lords Reid and Diplock dissenting on this point. Here again it is a matter for jury consideration in the light of Lord Simon's statement in *Knuller*:

> "It should be emphasised that 'outrage' . . . is a very strong word. 'Outraging public decency' goes considerably beyond offending the susceptibilities of, or even shocking, reasonable people. Moreover the offence is, in my view, concerned with recognised minimum standards of decency, which are likely to vary from time to time. Finally, notwithstanding that 'public' in the offence is used in a locative sense, public decency must be viewed as a whole; and I think the jury should be invited, where appropriate, to remember that they live in a plural society, with a tradition of toleration towards minorities, and that this atmosphere of toleration is itself part of public decency."[151]

These offences have been preserved at common law by the terms of s.5 of the Criminal Law Act 1977, which provides:

> "(1) Subject to the following provisions of this section, the offence of conspiracy at common law is hereby abolished . . . (3) Subs.(1) above shall not affect the offence of conspiracy at common law if and in so far as it may be committed by entering into an agreement to engage in conduct which—
>
> (a) tends to corrupt public morals or outrages public decency; but
>
> (b) would not amount to or involve the commission of an offence if carried out by a single person otherwise than in pursuance of an agreement."

A peculiar difficulty with the definition of these extant offences, provided by s.5 above, is that it is difficult, if not impossible, to see what conduct amounts to a conspiracy to outrage public decency if a compact exists between two people, but will not involve the full substantive offence of outraging public decency when done by one individual. Of course where the conduct, if committed by one individual, constitutes a criminal offence then this

---

[149] J.C. Smith [1991] Crim.L.R. 785.
[150] [1973] A.C. 435.
[151] [1973] A.C. 435 at 495.

means it ought to be charged as a statutory conspiracy. Whatever the problems attendant to this anomaly, a series of appellate decisions have affirmed the continued existence of the full substantive offence of outraging public decency. This is exemplified by the cases of *Gibson*,[152] where the defendant exhibited in an art gallery an item known as "Human Earrings" consisting of two frozen foetuses made into earrings which were attached to a model's head, and *Lunderbech*[153] in which the defendant, in view of two small children, covered his lap with a cloth and his actions indicated that he was masturbating. Both defendants' convictions for outraging public decency were upheld with the acts calculated to disgust and annoy, as interpreted by the respective juries.[154]

(ii) Conspiracy to Defraud

The meaning of defraud. The Law Commission in their 1976 Report on conspiracy **6–035** recommended that, in general, conspiracy should be limited to agreements to commit a substantive offence. This was implemented by the Criminal Law Act 1977 which, as we have seen, embodied the general principle that conspiracy was to be an offence only if the object of the conspiracy would necessarily amount to the commission of a crime. An exception was created for conspiracy to defraud on the basis that to abolish the offence without any statutory replacement would have left an unacceptable lacuna in the law. Hence conspiracy to defraud was specifically excluded by s.5(2) of the 1977 Act, which provides:

> "subs.(1) above [abolishing the offence of conspiracy of common law] shall not affect the offence of conspiracy at common law so far as relates to conspiracy to defraud, and s.1 above shall not apply in any case where the agreement in question amounts to a conspiracy to defraud at common law."

As previously mentioned, confusion prevailed over whether a conspiracy to defraud which would involve the commission of a substantive criminal offence could be charged as common law conspiracy, with *Ayres*[155] authority for their mutual exclusiveness. This uncertainty was ended by s.12 of the Criminal Justice Act 1987 whose effect was to recognise that each form is not mutually exclusive.[156] Prosecutors have a discretion how to charge a particular form of conspiracy, and as to the circumstances in which it is appropriate to change conspiracy to defraud, but this discretion needs to be exercised in accordance with the guidance issued by the Director of Public Prosecutions under s.10 of the Prosecution of Offences Act 1985.

The continued existence of the offence of conspiracy to defraud, which involves a compact to commit a fraud, is of significance in filling loopholes left by existing theft and fraud offences. Whilst the boundaries of the offence are uncertain, involving the causing of financial and economic prejudice to another, it does fulfil an important function.[157] The Law

---

[152] [1991] 1 All E.R. 439.
[153] [1991] Crim.L.R. 784.
[154] See also *Hamilton* [2007] EWCA Crim 2062. This case raised the question of whether the act in question actually needed to be seen. The answer was no, but it had to have been capable of being seen by two or more persons who were actually present.
[155] [1984] A.C. 447; see above, para.6–030.
[156] By s.12 of the Criminal Justice Act 1987 it is provided that:
   "(1) If—
      (a) a person agrees with any other person or persons that a course of conduct shall be pursued; and
      (b) that course of conduct will necessarily amount to or involve the commission of any offence or offences by one or more of the parties to the agreement if the agreement is carried out in accordance with their intentions, the fact that it will do so shall not preclude a charge of conspiracy to defraud being brought against any of them in respect of the agreement."
Note that the maximum punishment for conspiracy to defraud is a sentence of 10 years' imprisonment.
[157] See the case of *R v K* [2004] EWCA Crim 2685; [2005] Crim.L.R. 298, where it was asserted that the alleged agreement itself should be set out with specificity in the indictment.

Commission in their report on conspiracy to defraud, Law Com. No.228, (1994),[158] present an interesting hypothetical example, involving a gambling swindle, of conduct which falls outside the law of theft and deception, but for which a suitable panacea exists through conspiracy to defraud:

> "If A lays a bet with B that C's horse will win a race and, later, to make this more likely, A drugs the other horses in the race, with the result that C's horse does win and B pays A a sum of money, there is neither an appropriation nor an operative deception. It is, however, arguable that A's behaviour is dishonest and deserving of criminal sanction and that if A acted following an agreement with another the conduct would be within the scope of conspiracy to defraud."[159]

The leading authority on the meaning of "defraud" is that of *Scott v Metropolitan Police Commissioner*[160] which, it will be recalled, involved the unauthorised copying of films for distribution. Deception was not an essential prerequisite for the offence. Viscount Dilhorne provided the following synopsis of conspiracy to defraud:

> "[A]n agreement by two or more by dishonesty to deprive a person of something which is his or to which he is or would or might be entitled and an agreement by two or more by dishonesty to injure some proprietary right [of the victim's]."[161]

In essence, a victim will be taken to be defrauded where they have been induced to take an economic risk that otherwise would not have been taken. This proposition was endorsed by the appellate court in *Allsop*.[162] In this case the appellant, a sub-broker for a hire-purchase company, acting in tandem with others, entered false particulars on application forms in order to induce the company to accept applications that it might otherwise have rejected. Allsop's conviction of conspiracy to defraud the company was upheld by the Court of Appeal. Although the position was that if the debtors met their obligations under the agreements, the hire-purchase company would make a profit, this fact did not negative defrauding, since the debtors constituted a higher risk than the company would normally accept. The company, as the victim of the fraud, had been induced to take an *economic risk* that otherwise would not have been taken since, "interests which are imperilled are less valuable in terms of money than those same interests when they are secure and protected."[163]

6–036   The decision in *Allsop* was affirmed by the Privy Council in *Wai Yu-Tsang v R.*[164] Indeed the meaning attributable to defrauding was expanded in this later case as it sufficed for the offence that the company, which was the victim of the fraud, had been put at risk that it would be induced to take an economic risk that it would not otherwise have taken. The defendant, who was the chief accountant of a bank in Hong Kong, colluded with others dishonestly to conceal in the accounts of the bank the dishonouring of cheques the banks had purchased to the sum of US $124m. The defendant's purpose was to stop a run on the

---

[158] *Conspiracy to Defraud* (1994) Law Com. No.228. See also *Legislating the Criminal Code: Fraud and Deception* (1999) Law Com. Consultation Paper No.155.
[159] ibid. at 48 (para.4.53); see also Working Paper No.104, para.4.30.
[160] [1975] A.C. 819; see above, para.6–029.
[161] [1975] A.C. 819 at 840 per Viscount Dilhorne (with whom the other law lords agreed).
[162] (1977) 64 Cr.App.R. 29; see, generally, Law Com. No.228 at 11–16.
[163] (1977) 64 Cr.App.R. 29 at 32. In relation to conspiracy to defraud and allegations of price-fixing by cartels see *Norris v USA* [2008] UKHL 16.
[164] [1992] 1 A.C. 269.

bank assets; his motive was meritorious and he certainly did not desire to cause the company any loss, indeed quite the reverse. Nonetheless his conviction of conspiracy to defraud was upheld by the Privy Council. It was of no consequence that the conspirators did not wish to harm the company. They had intentionally prejudiced or risked prejudicing the victim's interests. Lord Goff, who delivered the leading judgment, stated that it sufficed that:

"the conspirators have dishonestly agreed to bring about a state of affairs which they realise will *or may* deceive the victim into so acting, or failing to act, that he will suffer economic loss or his economic interests will be put at risk".[165]

This was followed in *Adams v R.*[166] where company directors abused their positions to make secret profits at the company's expense. Clearly the victim's assets were actually imperilled in the case, but the court stressed that prospective loss is all that is required. The prerequisite here is that there must exist some right or interest in the victim which is capable of being prejudiced whether by actual loss or by being put at risk.

It will also be fraud, as the House of Lords established in *Welham*,[167] to deceive a public official into doing something that he would not have done but for the deceit. This is exemplified by *Moses*[168] which provides an illustration of the use of conspiracy to defraud to deal with an agreement to deceive a public official into acting contrary to his public duty. The appellants colluded together to facilitate applications for work permits by immigrants who were barred by a passport stamp from obtaining such permits. The central feature of the deception comprised the withholding from departmental supervisors of information about the applications, which consequentially increased the likelihood of a national insurance number being issued to them.

The mens rea of conspiracy to defraud. It is necessary to show that the defendant *intended* **6–037** *to defraud* and that he acted dishonestly.[169] It ought to suffice that the defendant intended to cause economic loss or risk prejudicing the economic assets of the victim. Motive, purpose or object of the defendant's actions are not relevant, as was held by the Privy Council in *Wai Yu-tsang v R.*, where the fact that D was operating from a good motive, not a base cause, was of no relevance. A difficult authority to reconcile with this principle is the case of *Attorney-General's Reference (No.1 of 1982)*.[170] The defendants colluded in England to affix labels of a company to bottles of whisky that did not contain whisky produced by the company. The whisky was to be sold abroad in the Lebanon. It was determined by the Court of Appeal that the defendants had not conspired to defraud the company since this was not their purpose, but had conspired simply to obtain money by deception from the ultimate whisky purchasers. Thus, it seemed implicit that where the victim only suffered damage as a "side effect or incidental consequence" of the fraudulent plan then conspiracy to defraud a company was not sustainable. What seemed necessary was that the infliction of such damage had to be the "true object" or "very purpose" of the fraudulent scam. This authority, although cited in argument in *Wai Yu-tsang*, was not referred to by Lord Goff. It must be viewed now as extremely questionable in the light of Lord Goff's statement that:

---

[165] [1992] 1 A.C. 269 at 280.
[166] [1995] 1 W.L.R. 52.
[167] [1961] A.C. 103.
[168] [1991] Crim.L.R. 617.
[169] See, generally, A.T.H. Smith, "Conspiracy To Defraud: The Law Commission's Working Paper No.104" [1988] Crim.L.R. 508; J.C. Smith, "Conspiracy to Defraud: Some Comments On The Law Commission's Report" [1995] Crim.L.R. 209; and J.C. Smith, "More On Proving Conspiracy" [1997] Crim.L.R. 333.
[170] [1983] Q.B. 751; see, generally, Law Com. No.228, para.2–9.

"It is however important . . . to distinguish a conspirator's intention (or immediate purpose) . . . from his motive (or underlying purpose). The latter may be benign in that he does not wish the victim or potential victim to suffer harm; but the mere fact that it is benign will not of itself prevent the agreement from constituting a conspiracy to defraud."[171]

The meaning of dishonesty in this context has also proved troublesome, at least prior to *Ghosh*.[172] It was unclear whether a different test applied to conspiracy to defraud as opposed to theft, with *McIvor*[173] authority for a different approach, in tandem with *Landy*[174] propounding a purely subjective analysis from the defendant's viewpoint above. The position has been clarified by *Ghosh* in that the same test now applies as for theft. A person is dishonest when: (a) his conduct would be regarded as dishonest by ordinary decent people and (b) he is aware that it would be so regarded. If the defendant is dishonest in that sense, it is irrelevant that he did not himself regard the conduct as dishonest.

6–038 Reform of conspiracy to defraud.   The Law Commission in an interim Report on this area, No.228, 1994, pending a full review of dishonesty in general,[175] considered whether conspiracy to defraud ought to be abolished. It had been subjected to criticism on the basis that it criminalises an agreement which if carried out would not necessarily amount to a crime if committed by one person.[176] In general terms the Law Commission had stressed, as we have seen, that the object of a conspiracy should be limited to the commission of a substantive offence. Opposition had also focused on the width and uncertainty in ambit of the constituents of "defrauding". However, the Commission initially concluded that conspiracy to defraud ought to continue, at least until their more general review of dishonesty offences was completed. It fulfils an important function in buttressing undesirable gaps that would otherwise exist in the criminal law. Practical benefits also apply in that a charge of conspiracy to defraud may more realistically embody the "overall criminality" of the defendant's conduct, rather than a substantive offence or a statutory conspiracy. Conspiracy to defraud may paint a better picture of the overall fraud.[177] Conspiracy to defraud has been retained, ever since the coming into force of the Fraud Act 2006.[178]

C. Parties to the Agreement

6–039 It is common ground to both statutory and common law conspiracy that there must be an agreement by two or more persons. It is a truism to say that a man cannot conspire with himself. It was accordingly held in *McDonnell*[179] that A, the managing and sole director of A Ltd., could not be convicted of conspiring with A Ltd even though A Ltd could have been convicted of the substantive crime committed by A.[180] On the other hand it is perfectly

---

[171] [1992] 1 A.C. 269 at 280. It has been commented that: "A requirement of purpose to defraud is unnecessarily limiting and was rightly rejected by the Privy Council in *Wai Yu-tsang*. Intention to do the acts that will defraud, with proof of dishonesty, should suffice to demonstrate culpability, without an additional requirement of foresight of a risk of loss; see G. Virgo, "Conspiracy To Defraud—Intent And Prejudice" (1992) 52 C.L.J. 208 at 210.
[172] [1982] Q.B. 1053; considered below, para.8–043; see, e.g. *Withers* [1975] A.C. 842.
[173] [1982] Crim.L.R. 312.
[174] [1981] 1 All E.R. 1172.
[175] On the development of the law of fraud, see Ch.9 below.
[176] Law Com. No.228 at 21–28.
[177] Law Com. No.228 at 58–62.
[178] See below at para.9–001.
[179] [1966] 1 Q.B. 233.
[180] See above, para.4–059.

possible to convict A, A Ltd and B on a charge of conspiracy; or to convict A Ltd of conspiring with B Ltd.

(i) Husband and Wife

For reasons of policy one spouse cannot be convicted of conspiring with the other spouse if **6-040** these are the *only* parties to the agreement. So husband and wife do not commit a crime in agreeing to murder X, but if their son, A, becomes a party to the agreement then all three are guilty of conspiracy. This was the rule for common law conspiracies applied in *Mawji v R.*,[181] and by s.2(2)(a) of the Criminal Law Act 1977 the same rule is applied to statutory conspiracies. However, a wife will be guilty of conspiracy where she enters into a compact with her husband, knowing that her husband is also conspiring with other parties. In *Chrastny (No.1)*,[182] it was held that it was sufficient that the wife was aware that others were conspiring with her husband and that she had also conspired with her husband. It is not necessary to prove that she entered into an agreement with a person other than her husband. However, where the parties marry at a point after the agreement has been concluded then they remain liable. This exemption is predicated on policy grounds and it will be interesting to observe whether, like the abolition of the marital rape exemption, it will be abrogated through a changed perception of the marital union. It seems incongruous today that marriage should provide a shield for criminal behaviour.[183]

(ii) Where One of the Parties is Exempt

It is also provided in s.2(2) of the Criminal Law Act 1977 that a person cannot be convicted **6-041** of conspiracy if the *only* other party is (b) a person under the age of criminal responsibility; or (c) an intended victim of the offence.[184] A child under the age of 10 will, as a matter of law, be conclusively presumed to be incapable of forming the necessary intention of a criminal offence. Between the ages of 10–14 a child has historically been liable under the *doli incapax* presumption only where the prosecution could establish a mischievous discretion. This presumption was abolished by the Crime and Disorder Act 1998; an individual between the age of 10–14 is now treated no differently in the criminal law.[185] There is no direct common law authority on agreements falling within (b) or (c). The Law Commission was of the view that at common law a conviction for conspiracy was at least theoretically possible in both cases. They further proposed that a person should not be liable for conspiracy if the only other person was himself or herself exempt from liability for conspiracy to commit the offence in question. If this proposal had been implemented it would have reversed the decision in *Duguid*[186] where it was held that A could be convicted of conspiracy with B to abduct a child from his guardian even though B, as the mother of the child, was exempt from liability. Another illustration is the offence under the Offences against the Person Act 1861 s.58 whereby a woman who is not pregnant is not liable to conviction for attempting to procure her miscarriage, although any other person who

---

[181] [1957] A.C. 126. Note in *Midland Bank Trust Co v Green (No.3)* [1979] 2 All E.R. 193 at issue in this civil authority was a claim by a son that he had been defrauded over an agreed land purchase option. It was held that the assumed common law rule that H and W, where they were the only alleged conspirators, could not be indicted for the crime of conspiracy because of the fiction of unity of H and W, did not apply to the civil liability of a H and W for the tort of conspiracy, because the essence of the tort was the damage which flowed from the overt act, whereas the essence of the crime was the conspiratorial agreement.

[182] [1992] 1 All E.R. 189.

[183] The Law Commission have proposed the abolition of spousal immunity. See Law Commission Consultation Paper No.183, *Conspiracy and Attempts* (2007).

[184] See, e.g. *Tyrrell* [1894] 1 Q.B. 710, discussed at para.4–041.

[185] See above, para.5–097.

[186] (1906) 70 J.P. 294.

attempted to do so believing the woman to be pregnant would be guilty of the offence. However, in *Whitchurch*[187] the Court for Crown Cases Reserved held that the woman can be convicted of conspiracy with the non-exempt party to procure her abortion. Since the Law Commission proposal was not implemented in the Criminal Law Act 1977 it continues to be the law that a non-exempt party can conspire with an exempt party even though the exempt party cannot be convicted of the full substantive offence.

It may well be the case that whilst the exempt party cannot be convicted of the full offence, nonetheless a conspiracy charge may lie against them. This will depend on a purposive interpretation of the statute by the court to determine whether the breadth of the exemption from the principal offence extends to cover the conspiracy to commit that offence. This evaluation was applied in *Burns*[188] by the Court of Appeal where the defendant, the child's father, broke into his former wife's home in collusion with a posse of men to snatch back his own child. It was held that despite his exemption from prosecution for the full substantive offence, in accordance with s.56 of the Offences Against the Person Act 1861 (now repealed by the Child Abduction Act 1984) he was justifiably convicted of conspiracy.

D. Acquittal of a Co-conspirator

6–042 In a scenario where two parties, A and B, comprised the criminal conspiracy, and where they were tried separately, there was no difficulty as was held by the House of Lords in *DPP v Shannon*,[189] that A be acquitted and B convicted or vice versa. Of course the evidence could be much stronger against one of the parties rather than the other, for example a highly probative confession by only one of the parties. What was unclear prior to the passing of the Criminal Law Act 1977 was whether it was possible to convict A but acquit B when they were tried together. The doubts over this matter have been removed by s.5(8) and (9) of the Act which govern both common law as well as statutory conspiracies:

> "(8) The fact that the person or persons who, so far as appears from the indictment on which any person has been convicted of conspiracy, were the only other parties to the agreement on which his conviction was based have been acquitted of conspiracy by reference to that agreement (whether after being tried with the person convicted or separately) shall not be a ground for quashing his conviction unless after all the circumstances of the case his conviction is inconsistent with the acquittal of the other person or persons in question.
>
> (9) Any rule of law or practice inconsistent with the provisions of subs.(8) above is hereby abolished."

The impact of these provisions, as subsequently considered in *Merrick*[190] and *Roberts*,[191] is that a trial judge where the evidence against A and B is of roughly equivalent proportion should direct a jury that they should either convict or acquit both. The conviction of A but acquittal of B in such a scenario would be inconsistent. Where the weight of the evidence differs between A and B then a trial judge ought to direct the jury to consider each party separately.

---

[187] (1896) 24 Q.B.D. 420.
[188] (1984) 79 Cr.App.R. 173.
[189] [1975] A.C. 717.
[190] (1980) 71 Cr.App.R. 130.
[191] (1984) 78 Cr.App.R. 41.

3. THE MENTAL ELEMENT IN CONSPIRACY

A. Recklessness as to Circumstances Will Not Do

It was established by the House of Lords in *Churchill v Walton*[192] that conspiracy at common **6–043** law involves mens rea in the full sense of intention—strict liability, recklessness or negligence does not apply. Section 1(2) of the Criminal Law Act 1977 was intended to embody the identical principle for statutory conspiracies and provides:

> "(2) Where liability for any offence may be incurred without knowledge on the part of the person committing it of any particular fact or circumstance necessary for the commission of the offence, a person shall nevertheless not be guilty of conspiracy to commit that offence by virtue of subs.(1) above unless he and at least one other party to the agreement intend or know that that fact or circumstance shall or will exist at the time when the conduct constituting the offence is to take place."

The effect of the above provision is that arguably it is an insufficient mens rea for a conspiracy offence that the defendant is merely reckless as to circumstances which form part of the elements for the full offence. This proposition can be exemplified by two examples. First, let us consider the facts in *Prince*, involving the offence of abduction of a minor (a strict liability crime) but where D legitimately believed the girl to be over 16. Although the offence is now repealed the underlying principle has enjoyed longevity.[193] Suppose that Prince and another agreed to take the girl out of the possession of her parents, both believing she was over 16. Neither Prince nor his friend would be guilty of a statutory conspiracy to abduct the girl. Section 1(2) makes it clear that even if the completed offence can be committed without knowledge of a "particular fact or circumstance" (in this case that the girl is under 16) there can be no conviction for conspiracy unless that fact or circumstance is known to those charged with conspiracy.

In statutory conspiracy intention as to circumstances is required, not merely recklessness. On this matter consider the offence of rape prior to revision in the Sexual Offences Act 2003. It has been illustrated[194] that for attempted rape recklessness as to the circumstance of the victim's consent would suffice as the mens rea for attempt, where it was adequate for the full offence of rape itself (see *Khan*[195]). This is not the position for statutory conspiracies where intention is required. Suppose, for instance, that A and B plot to have intercourse with C's wife (V). Although C has initiated this planned intercourse, both A and B are uncertain whether V is truly consenting or has been coerced by C. If intercourse occurs, and V does not consent, then A and B have committed the full offence of rape. However, there would have been no conspiracy to rape, as was discussed in *Mir*,[196] since applying s.1(2) generally it was determined by the court that liability for conspiracy only transpires where the accused knows, intends or believes that a circumstance exists. In this context mere recklessness is insufficient. Similarly for basic criminal damage within s.1(1) of the Criminal Damage Act 1971. The full substantive offence encompasses definitional elements of destroying or damaging property belonging to another with the requisite mens rea of either intention or recklessness.[197] The requirement that property belongs to another can be

---

[192] [1967] 2 A.C. 236.
[193] (1875) L.R. 2 C.C.R. 154; above, para.2–082.
[194] See above, para.6–010.
[195] [1990] 2 All E.R. 783.
[196] *The Independent*, May 23, 1994.
[197] See below at para.10–002.

delineated as a circumstance of the offence[198]; although recklessness suffices for the full crime it is not sufficient for a conspiracy to commit the offence as it is incumbent upon the prosecution to demonstrate that the accused knows, intends or believes that a circumstance exists. It is inapt for the conspiracy offence that a defendant merely suspected (recklessness) that the property belonged to another.[199] Consider, by way of example, a situation where D1 (a tenant) has installed kitchen units in a rented property. At the end of the tenancy D1 and D2 agree to remove the fixed items with knowledge that consequential damage will be effected. They are uncertain whether the fixed items belong to D1 or the property owner—in that sense they are "reckless" as to a circumstance of the offence (property belonging to another). However, they do not possess the required mens rea to be inculpated for a conspiracy offence given a lack of requisite mens rea of intention or knowledge as to prescribed circumstances.

6–044   Confusion has reigned supreme in recent times over conspiracies involving money laundering and wrongful retention of the proceeds of crime, at least in regards to the statutory regime that existed prior to the amendments made by the Proceeds of Crime Act 2002 revisionary legislation.[200] In *Sakavickas*[201] the D's were convicted of a statutory conspiracy to assist another to retain the benefit of criminal conduct. The conspiracy alleged was an agreement to commit the offence contrary to s.93A of the Criminal Justice Act 1988, which prohibited a person from entering into or being otherwise concerned in an arrangement whereby the retention or control of another person's criminal proceeds were facilitated, when he knew or suspected that the other person had been engaged in or had benefited from criminal conduct. The appeal centred upon whether mere suspicion of the nefarious activities of other "conspirators" sufficed, or whether more direct knowledge had to be identified. The D's thus, contended that the alleged offender and at least one other party to the conspiracy had to know (the direct provenance) or intend to know that the money to be laundered was or was to be the proceeds of another person's crime when the conduct constituting the offence contrary to s.93A of the 1988 Act was to take place. Their Lordships in *Sakavickas*, contrary to the above analysis and appropriate identification of the insufficiency of recklessness as to circumstance, dismissed the appeals. Apparently, it was the mere suspicion, as opposed to the knowledge of the fact that an individual was engaged in nefarious behaviour which crystallised liability. This meant that for the purposes of s.1(2) of the 1977 Act the mere suspicion equated to a "fact or circumstance necessary for the commission of the offence". In essence, although it was a pre-requisite for the offence that an alleged conspirator had to have knowledge of that suspicion, nonetheless *such "knowledge" could be transplanted from his own state of mind*. To require proof of D's knowledge or awareness of his own state of mind as part of the conspiracy offence seems incongruous. As Ormerod has cogently stated, no one in a murder trial would suggest that D has to intend to kill or commit grievous bodily harm *and be aware that he has a state of mind of intention*![202]

---

[198] See below at para.10–002.

[199] Note the principles vis-à-vis conspiracy to commit aggravated criminal damage within s.1(2) of the Criminal Damage Act 1971 are particularly complex. The actus reus involves destroying or damaging any property, whether belonging to the defendant or another. D must intend or be reckless by that destruction or damage to endanger the life of another. See below at para.10–008. However in *Parker* [1993] Crim.L.R. 856 it was held that life endangerment was not a "circumstance" forming part of the actus reus of the crime. See below at para.10–010. As such the principle from *Mir* that "intention" was needed on this element for the conspiracy offence is no longer apposite. Lord Nicholls in *Saik* [2007] 1 A.C. 18 at [4] stated obiter. "Conspiracy to commit this offence requires proof of an intention to damage property, and to do so recklessly indifferent as to whether this would endanger life". In essence, life endangerment is not a circumstance of the full offence—intention or knowledge is thus, not a pre-requisite for the conspiracy offence— recklessness will suffice.

[200] See, generally, D. Ormerod (2006) C.L.P. 185.

[201] [2004] EWCA Crim 2686; [2005] Crim.L.R. 293.

[202] See D.C Ormerod, *Smith and Hogan, Criminal Law* 11th edn (Oxford: Oxford University Press, 2005) at p.380.

Post-*Sakavickas* a trio of cases have restored the orthodox position in strictly construing the words of s.1(2) of the Criminal Law Act 1977 to require "intention" or "knowledge"; recklessness as to circumstances is inapposite.[203] In *Ali*[204] the appellate court determined that, subject to the other ingredients being satisfied, a defendant would only be guilty of a conspiracy under the relevant money laundering offences where he *knew* (or intended) that the property concerned was criminal property; suspicion (objective or subjective) was insufficient. The House of Lords in *Saik*[205] were not prepared to dilute the clear mens rea requirement laid down in the legislation despite the attractions of inculpating defendants for conspiracy to launder the proceeds of crime based upon their "suspicions" around the provenance of received monies. Neither belief nor suspicion would be equiparated with the requirement of knowledge[206]; Lord Nicholls clearly asserted that, "it is not for the courts to extend the net of conspiracy beyond the reach set by Parliament."[207] Subsequently in *Suchedina*,[208] applying *Saik*, it has been further clarified that, even if the full substantive offence has a necessary fact or circumstance required for commission of the actus reus element, which can be satisfied by either recklessness (see, for example, property belonging to another in criminal damage) or negligence (see for example, consent in rape), this is inadequate to satisfy the mens rea for conspiracy to effect that offence. The requirement of intention or knowledge presented in s.1(2) of the Criminal Law Act 1977 was designed to, "eliminate the risk that someone could be guilty of conspiracy just because he was reckless as to the existence or otherwise of the circumstances that would make the conduct criminal."[209]

It is reflective of the essence of inchoate offences centred around a strong focus on the requirement of full mens rea as the crucial determinant of D's liability, given the absence of the direct harm which would flow from effecting the actus reus (conduct) of the full substantive offence.[210]

Following the decision in *Saik*, the Government asked the Law Commission to review the offence of statutory conspiracy. The Commission published a lengthy consultation paper[211] setting out a variety of proposals, the most significant for present purposes being to broaden the mental element for conspiracy to include recklessness as to the circumstance elements of the offence conspired to.[212]

B. Course of Conduct

The central feature of a conspiracy is that the parties agree on a course of conduct that will **6–045** necessarily amount to or involve the commission of an offence by one or more of the conspirators. We look here at the *intended consequences* of the planned course of conduct

---

[203] See, also, *M* [2004] UKHL 50; *Harmer* [2005] EWCA Crim 1; [2005] Crim.L.R. 482; and *Rizzvi* [2003] EWCA Crim 3575. See relevant offences in Drug Trafficking Act 1994, Criminal Justice Act 1998 and Proceeds of Crime Act 2002.

[204] [2005] EWCA Crim 87; [2005] Crim.L.R. 864. See, generally, D. Corker, "Conspiracy to Launder: Revisited" (2005) 155 N.L.J. 1070; J. Barnard, "A Stupid Agreement" [2005] 2 *Archbold News* 5. And S. Shaw Q.C. and D. Ormerod [2005] 7 *Archbold News* 7.

[205] [2006] UKHL 18; [2007] 1 A.C. 18.

[206] [2006] UKHL 18; [2007] 1 A.C. 18 at [26] and [30] per Lord Nicholls, at [78] per Lord Hope, and at [119] per Lord Brown.

[207] [2006] UKHL 18; [2007] 1 A.C. 18 at [33].

[208] [2006] EWCA Crim 2543; [2007] Crim.L.R. 301.

[209] *Saik* [2006] UKHL 18; [2007] 1 A.C. 18 at [58].

[210] A point expertly made by Professor Ormerod; see D Ormerod, *Smith and Hogan: Criminal Law*, 12th edn (Oxford University Press, 2008) at p.416.

[211] Law Commission Consultation Paper No.183, *Conspiracy and Attempts* (2007).

[212] Law Commission Consultation Paper No.183, *Conspiracy and Attempts* (2007) at paras 4.42 et seq. Where a substantive offence has a more culpable fault element than recklessness on a circumstance element, the Commission proposes that conspirators should also have that fault element. at paras 4.133 et seq.

that forms their compact. It is essential to review the actions they intend to carry out, but additionally the consequences of their actions. Section 1(1) is intended to make it clear that on a charge of statutory conspiracy, for example to murder or to cause criminal damage, it must be shown that the alleged conspirators had agreed on a course of conduct which will necessarily result in murder or criminal damage if the agreement is carried out in accordance with their intentions. There is no difficulty whatever if A and B agree to kill X by poisoning or to break Y's windows. But suppose that A and B agreed to "knee-cap" X. A and B would here be guilty of a conspiracy to cause grievous bodily harm and if X dies they would be guilty of murder since an intention to cause grievous bodily harm forms part of the mens rea of murder. Are A and B, therefore, guilty of conspiracy to murder? They are not. The course of conduct they have agreed on will not necessarily result in death; indeed it is rare for death to occur as a result of "knee-capping". Another example could be where, in a street fight, A and B agree to attack X and Y by throwing stones at them, both realising that they might miss X and Y and break windows in the street. A and B are guilty of a conspiracy to assault X and Y but they are not guilty of a conspiracy to commit criminal damage. In other words conspiracy is an intentional crime in the same general sense as attempt. The conspirators' liability will be limited to the intended consequences of their actions. This point was reinforced in *Siracusa* by O'Connor L.J. who stated:

> "The mens rea sufficient to support the commission of a substantive offence will not necessarily be sufficient to support a charge of conspiracy to commit that offence. An intent to cause grievous bodily harm is sufficient to support the charge of murder, but is not sufficient to support a charge of conspiracy to murder or of attempt to murder."[213]

In *Siracusa* the defendant was charged with conspiracy to import heroin from Thailand contrary to s.170(2)(b) of the Customs and Excise Management Act 1979. The Court of Appeal concluded that the onus was on the prosecution to establish that the agreed course of conduct was the importation of heroin. Whilst a defendant could be convicted of the full substantive offence under the 1979 Act merely by the establishment of the belief that he was importing another substance, such as cannabis, this was insufficient for conspiracy where intention is required as to consequences.

C. Intention on the Part of Each Conspirator

6–046   The position at common law, following *Thomson*,[214] was that it was incumbent upon the prosecution to demonstrate not only a compact to effect an unlawful purpose, but also *an intention on the part of each conspirator to bring about the unlawful purpose*. The Law Commission Report No.76, which preceded the Criminal Law Act 1977, thought that this was what the law ought to be. The law should require full intention and knowledge before a conspiracy can be established:

> "A person should be guilty of conspiracy if he agrees with another person that an offence shall be committed. *Both must intend that any consequence specified in the*

---

[213] (1990) 90 Cr.App.R. 340 at 350. Note also the decision of the Court of Appeal in *Broad* [1997] Crim.L.R. 666. See also *El-Kurd* [2001] Crim.L.R. 234; and *Taylor* [2002] Crim.L.R. 205 (one does not prove an agreement to import Class A drugs by proving an agreement to import Class B drugs).
[214] (1965) 50 Cr.App.R. 1.

definition of the offence will result and both must know of the existence of any state of affairs which it is necessary for them to know in order to be aware that the course of conduct agreed upon will amount to the offence." (Emphasis added).[215]

However, in the leading case after the 1977 Act, that of *Anderson*,[216] Lord Bridge asserted that it sufficed for a conspiracy conviction that the defendant had simply entered a compact with another that a course of conduct be followed. It was deemed to be unnecessary to prove the conspirator actually intended that the course of conduct be fully carried out. No doubt Lord Bridge was influenced by the desire to assist prosecutors in this area by reducing the mens rea prerequisites, but his result corrupts the statutory intent for conspiracy. In *Anderson* the defendant was an individual on remand in custody. He was charged with conspiracy to effect a prisoner's release in that he agreed for an initial fee of £2,000 to supply diamond wire to cut through prison bars to enable another prisoner to escape. Anderson contended that he had never intended that the escape plan should be carried out nor believed that it could succeed; accordingly, he had lacked the mental element necessary for the conviction. Although their Lordships could have upheld his conviction on the ground that he had aided and abetted the conspiracy as other conspirators in the plot did have intent that the full offence be carried out, they refused to do so. Instead Anderson's conviction was affirmed on the basis of conspiracy to effect the escape of a prisoner. Lord Bridge, whose judgment was agreed upon by all other members of the House, stated:

"I am clearly driven by consideration of the diversity of roles which parties may agree to play in criminal conspiracies to reject any construction of the statutory language which would require the prosecution to prove an intention on the part of each conspirator that the criminal offence or offences which will necessarily be committed by one or more of the conspirators if the agreed course of conduct is fully carried out should in fact be committed."[217]

The bizarre effect of Lord Bridge's statement above is to remove the requirement that *any* **6–047** of the conspirators intended the full substantive offence to be carried out. If we remove the requirement, as Lord Bridge would, that it is necessary to prove an intention on the part of one of the parties to an agreement that the course of conduct be followed, then the logical corollary is that none of them need have this intent. The outcome is that no compact exists to commit any substantive offence at all! Perhaps unsurprisingly *Anderson* was resiled from in this respect both by the Court of Appeal in *Edwards*,[218] and also by the Privy Council in *Yip Chiu-Cheung v R.*[219] For example, in *Edwards* the conspirator had agreed to supply amphetamine but there was uncertainty whether any intention existed to supply ephedrine instead. It was determined that the trial judge had correctly directed the jury that they could convict only if they were sure that Edwards intended to supply amphetamine. A mere agreement to supply amphetamine was not sufficient for a conspiracy conviction, unlike *Anderson*, unless Edwards *intended to carry it out*. This requirement reflects the implicit meaning behind the statutory words contained within s.1(1)(a) of the Criminal Law Act 1977. In *Saik* it received the support of the House of Lords. It was asserted by Lord Nicholls,

---

[215] See para.7.2.
[216] [1985] 2 All E.R. 961. The decision, however, was overlooked in *Ashton* [1992] Crim.L.R. 667; and *Harvey* [1999] Crim.L.R. 70 CA.
[217] [1985] 2 All E.R. 961 at 38.
[218] [1991] Crim.L.R. 45.
[219] [1994] 3 W.L.R. 514; see below, para.6–048.

with the express agreement of Lord Steyn, that "conspirators must intend to do the act prohibited by the substantive offence."[220]

D. Active Participation in the Course of Conduct

6–048 Further problems have been engendered over the mens rea of conspiracy by Lord Bridge's concern in *Anderson* to exempt from liability general law-abiding citizens, such as law enforcement officers, who "participate" in criminal conspiracies to frustrate crime. Because Lord Bridge considered it unnecessary for a conspiracy conviction that D actually intended the commission of the substantive offence, he believed it necessary to expand on the mens rea of conspiracy to exempt "respectable citizens". To achieve that he added a further mens rea criterion, derived neither from common law nor statutory authority, to exculpate them from liability. This new ingredient was dependent upon active or passive roles in the conspiracy:

> "[T]he necessary mens rea of the crime is, in my opinion, established if, and only if, it is shown that the accused when he entered into the agreement, *intended to play some part in the agreed course of conduct in furtherance of the criminal purpose* which the agreed course of conduct was intended to achieve. Nothing less will suffice; nothing more is required."[221]

Lord Bridge seemed to be adding a requirement that D intended to play some form of active role in the planned course of conduct; presumptively if this was lacking then a conspiracy charge would fail.[222] Of course, no difficulty existed in *Anderson* itself in satisfying this criterion as D intended to actively supply the cutting wire. More problematic is that this apparent test would seem to exclude the "brains" or "leader" of a conspiratorial plot. Consider, for instance, the part of I.R.A. gang leaders. Suppose that A simply plots with B and requests that B carries out the murder of C, A expressing that he intends to play no active role in bringing about the agreed killing.[223] There is no conspiracy in accordance with a strict interpretation of Lord Bridge's dictum in *Anderson*. This, of course, is the exact opposite of what Lord Bridge was hoping to achieve in making a conspiracy charge easier for prosecutorial authorities, but excluding "respectable citizens" engaged in law enforcement. Subsequent cases have re-evaluated the mens rea of conspiracy. In *Siracusa* (see above) the Court of Appeal determined that Lord Bridge should not be taken as saying that the organiser of a crime who recruited others to carry it out would not himself be guilty of conspiracy unless it could be proved that he intended to play some active part himself thereafter. By judicial sorcery O'Connor L.J. in *Siracusa* reappraised the meaning of "play some part in" to mean merely to continue to concur in the activity of another or others, or the failure to stop this unlawful conduct:

> "Participation in a conspiracy is infinitely variable: it can be active or passive. If the majority shareholder and director of a company consents to the company being used for drug smuggling carried out in the company's name by a fellow director and minority shareholder, he is guilty of conspiracy. Consent, that is the agreement or

---

[220] [2006] UKHL 18; [2007] 1 A.C. 18 at [4].
[221] [1985] 2 All E.R. 961 at 965.
[222] This raises the question of whether the accused must intend to further the criminal purpose. Undercover police officers normally intend to frustrate it.
[223] See, e.g. J.C. Smith [1989] Crim.L.R. 713.

adherence to the agreement, can be inferred if it is proved that he knew what was going on and the intention to participate in the furtherance of the criminal purpose is also established by his failure to stop the unlawful activity. Lord Bridge's dictum does not require anything more."[224]

The mens rea of a co-conspirator who was in fact an undercover agent arose in *Yip Chiu-Cheung v R.*,[225] before the Privy Council, and here again a directly contradictory approach to *Anderson* was applied. The undercover agent was a US drugs enforcement officer who agreed to act as a courier of heroin on behalf of the accused. The heroin was to be carried from Hong Kong to Australia, but Yip Chiu-Cheung was arrested at the airport in Hong Kong. He contended that since the law enforcement officer lacked sufficient mens rea to be a co-conspirator, thus, no conspiracy was in being; conspiracy, of course, requires at least two participants. On the facts it was held that the agent did intend to commit the substantive offence of trafficking in drugs, albeit that he would be exculpated through prosecutorial discretion. As the officer *intended to commit the crime* the actus reus and mens rea of conspiracy were both present in the compact that the parties entered. It is submitted that, contrary to *Anderson*, the implicit assumption upon which the outcome in *Yip Chiu-Cheung v R.* was predicated is that there is a conspiracy between A and B only if both A and B *intend that the agreement they have made will be carried into effect*. Lord Griffiths asserted that, "the crime of conspiracy requires an agreement between two or more persons to commit an unlawful act with the intention of carrying it out. It is the intention to carry out the crime that constitutes the necessary mens rea for the offence."[226] The decision in *Anderson* has been distinguished to such an extent that its impact has been severely diluted.[227]

As a final point it is interesting to consider the decision in *Hollinshead*.[228] In this case the defendants had agreed to make and sell devices which were known as "black boxes", whose only function was to affect the proper functioning of electricity meters and consequentially conceal the amount of electricity actually used. It was determined by the Court of Appeal that the compact was neither a conspiracy to defraud nor a statutory conspiracy, on the basis that the contemplated fraud was to be committed by third party individuals who were strangers to the actual agreement. However, the House of Lords held that as the sole purpose of the defendants was dishonest thus a conspiracy to defraud was made out; they did not resile from the Court of Appeal's view that a conspiracy to aid and abet an offence is inapt as it is not an offence known to the law.

E. Conditional Intention

The parties may make a conditional form of compact between themselves. For example, they **6–049** may agree to commit a robbery on V provided he is alone and the street is deserted in the early evening. Where alternative courses of action are proposed, dependent on future ascertainable fact(s), can it be said that A and B have agreed on a course of conduct that will

---

[224] (1990) 90 Cr.App.R. 340 at 349.
[225] [1994] 3 W.L.R. 514.
[226] [1994] 3 W.L.R. 514 at 518.
[227] By cl.52 of the Draft Criminal Code Bill a person would be guilty of conspiracy to commit an offence or offences if: "(1) (a) he agrees with any other person or persons that an act or acts shall be done which, if done, will involve the commission of the offence or offences by one or more of the parties to the agreement; and (b) he and at least one other party to the agreement intend that the offence or offences shall be committed. (2) For the purposes of subs.(1), an intention that an offence shall be committed is an intention in respect of all the elements of the offence."
[228] [1985] 1 All E.R. 850.

necessarily result in the commission of an offence? Three appellate cases have addressed this issue.

In *Jackson*,[229] A and B agreed with C that he would be shot in the leg if he was convicted of the burglary offence for which he was being tried. This extreme action was to provide mitigation over sentencing so that he would receive leniency. Their convictions of conspiring to pervert the course of justice were upheld by the Court of Appeal. In effect, if the conspiracy was carried out in accordance with their plan, then there must be the commission of the offence referred to in the conspiracy court. Planning was taking place for a contingency, and if that contingency transpired then the conspiracy would necessarily involve the commission of an offence. Similarly in *Reed*[230] where the convictions of A and B of conspiring to aid and abet suicide were upheld. The conspirators planned to visit individuals considering the taking of their own life and A would either help or dissuade them depending on what he considered the appropriate approach. General principles in this arena were referred to, *en passant*, by Lord Nicholls in the House of Lords decision in *Saik*[231]:

> "An intention to do a prohibited act is within the scope of s.1(1) even if the intention is expressed to be conditional on the happening, or non-happening, of some particular event. The question always is whether the agreed course of action, if carried out in accordance with the parties' intentions, would necessarily amount to or involve an offence. A conspiracy to rob a bank tomorrow if the coast is clear when the conspirators reach the bank is not, by reason of this disqualification, any less a conspiracy to rob."[232]

In *O'Hadhmaill*,[233] the appellant was a lecturer in sociology at the University of Central Lancashire in Preston. It was the prosecution's case that he was to have played a controlling role in a planned I.R.A. bombing campaign to have taken place in the early part of 1994. The items found in his possession suggested that up to 17 semtex-based explosive devices, including two under-car booby traps, were to be planted. O'Hadhmaill contended that a settled agreement and intention to carry out a bombing campaign had not been proved; it was advanced that such a campaign was extremely unlikely when the whole peace process was under discussion. However, his conviction of conspiracy to cause an explosion with other I.R.A. co-conspirators was upheld. As with the outcome in *Jackson* if the planned conspiracy was effected in accordance with the agreement it necessarily involved the commission of a substantive offence. By way of contrast it is instructive to consider the hypothetical example presented in both *Reed* and *Jackson*. This example is intrinsically different to the case authorities previously considered in that the commission of any driving offence is wholly incidental and extraneous to the primary object of the agreed course of conduct between the parties:

> "A and B agree to drive from London to Edinburgh in a time which can be achieved without exceeding the speed limits, but only if the traffic which they encounter is exceptionally light. Their agreement will not necessarily involve the commission of any offence, even if it is carried out in accordance with their intentions, and they do drive from London to Edinburgh within the agreed time. Accordingly the agreement does not constitute the offence of statutory conspiracy or indeed of any offence."

---

229 [1985] Crim.L.R. 442.
230 [1982] Crim.L.R. 819.
231 [2006] UKHL 18; [2007] 1 A.C. 18.
232 [2006] UKHL 18; [2007] 1 A.C. 18 at [5].
233 [1996] Crim.L.R. 509.

It has been submitted by Professor Smith that it seems unlikely that an indictment for conspiracy to murder would succeed where A and B set out to commit a burglary, having agreed that B will shoot to kill if, but only if, it is necessary to enable them to carry out the plan or to escape.[234] The intention is circumscribed by a condition precedent which may be inadequate to constitute a defined agreement on a planned course of action. If this is the case then it is wholly unfortunate that a charge of conspiracy to murder will not lie. By analogy to the law on joint participation in crime which, as we have seen, turns on the *contemplation* of the respective parties[235] a contemplated condition precedent should be sufficient to ground liability. The public policy arguments for liability where parties engage in joint unlawful activity[236] are no less prevalent for conspiracy.

4. IMPOSSIBILITY

As with attempts, so with conspiracy, issues of impossibility may arise; it is possible for **6–050** persons to agree to steal from a safe which turns out to be empty, or to receive goods which are no longer stolen. By s.1(1)(b) of the Criminal Law Act 1977 (inserted by s.5 of the Criminal Attempts Act 1981) statutory, though not common law, conspiracies are brought into line with the law on attempts; there can be a conviction for conspiracy in both of these cases. The position at common law remains governed by the authorities of *Haughton v Smith*[237] and *DPP v Nock*[238] in that legal and factual impossibility may be a defence, with the proviso that it would be no defence where it is based on inadequacy of the means employed.

5. TERRITORIAL JURISDICTION

A conspiracy to defraud in England and Wales is triable here, wherever the conspiracy is **6–051** formed.[239] In accordance with s.5 of the Criminal Justice (Terrorism and Conspiracy) Act 1998, which came into force on September 4, 1998, the English courts may now have jurisdiction to try a conspiracy to commit offences outside the United Kingdom.[240] Where a British citizen agrees with another to effect a murder abroad that is indictable here subject to the exception provided by s.1(4) of the Criminal Law Act 1977.[241] An agreement abroad to carry out an offence in England will be indictable provided an overt act can be established, it is unnecessary that the prosecution prove this overt act was actually done in England (see *Liangsiriprasert v Government of the USA*).[242]

---

[234] [1996] Crim.L.R. 511.
[235] See above, paras 4–015—4–017.
[236] See above, para.4–019—4–021.
[237] [1975] A.C. 476.
[238] [1978] A.C. 979.
[239] *Sansom* [1991] 2 Q.B. 130; see, generally, Law Com. No.228 at p.19. For an excellent discussion of this general area see M. Hirst, *Jurisdiction and the Ambit of the Criminal Law* (Oxford University Press, 2003) at pp.142–148.
[240] The Act inserts a new section into s.1 of the Criminal Law Act 1977. The new provisions are not retrospective; see also *Board of Trade v Owen* [1957] A.C. 602; and *Att-Gen's Reference (No.1 of 1982)* [1983] Q.B. 751 in relation to conspiracy to defraud.
[241] By s.1(4) of the Criminal Law Act 1977 it is provided: "(4) In this Part of this Act 'offence' means an offence triable in England and Wales, except that it includes murder notwithstanding that the murder in question would not be so triable if committed in accordance with the intentions of the parties to the agreement."
[242] [1991] A.C. 225. Lord Griffiths stated: "Why should an overt act be necessary to found jurisdiction? In the case of conspiracy in England the crime is complete once the agreement is made and no further overt act need be proved as an ingredient of the crime. The only purpose of looking for an overt act in England in the case of a conspiracy entered into abroad can be to establish the link between the conspiracy and England or possibly to show the conspiracy is continuing. But, if this can be established by other evidence, for example the taping of conversations between the conspirators showing a firm agreement to commit the crime at some future date, it defeats the preventative purpose of the crime of conspiracy to have to wait until some overt act is performed in pursuance of the conspiracy."

A significant development on territorial jurisdiction has been legislation to specifically deal with child prostitution and "sexual tourism". The Sexual Offences (Conspiracy and Incitement) Act 1996 extended liability for conspiracy to commit, or inciting the commission of, sexual offences against children to the case where the act conspired or incited is to be performed outside the jurisdiction. As Alldridge has stated, there is now increased consciousness that huge numbers of children in relatively poor nations are being exploited by tourists from rich ones.[243] The legislation was specifically designed to curtail paedophile activities, and to promulgate convictions of such culprits in this jurisdiction. It is laid down that the agreement or incitement to commit a designated sexual offence against a person under the age of 16 became punishable in England and Wales provided that conduct also amounted to a crime in the country where it was to be committed. The specific provisions relating to conspiracy were repealed by the Criminal Justice (Terrorism and Conspiracy) Act 1998, but those relating to incitement remain operative.[244]

In order to allow for territorial jurisdiction of English courts over transnational offences constituting fraud or deception, planned here but effected abroad, there was passed specific legislation in Pt I of the Criminal Justice Act 1993. This Act was designed to counteract growing concerns over international crimes involving elements of dishonesty. A conspiracy to commit a "group A" offence in England or abroad is triable in England whether the accused became a party to the conspiracy in England or abroad.[245] The group A offences include, inter alia, theft, various offences involving obtaining by deception, blackmail, handling stolen goods and a range of offences under the Forgery and Counterfeiting Act 1981.[246] Jurisdiction is arrogated where any "relevant event" occurs in England. A relevant event is defined as "any act or omission or other event (including any result of one or more acts or omissions), proof of which is required for conviction of the offence".[247] Consider, by way of illustration, a scenario where A in England conspires with B in France to steal a Van Gogh painting from the Louvre in Paris. A and B may both now be tried in England, pursuant to the jurisdictional provisions of the 1993 Act. The jurisdictional net has been tightened in recent times by specific legislation to deal with inchoate offences which have an international flavour.

GENERAL READING

6–052   Campbell, C., "Two Steps Backwards: The Criminal Justice (Terrorism and Conspiracy) Act 1998" [1999] Crim.L.R. 941.

Cohen, M., "Inciting The Impossible" [1979] Crim.L.R. 239.

Dennis, I., "The Rationale Of Conspiracy" (1977) 93 L.Q.R. 39.

Holroyd, J., "Incitement—A Tale Of Three Agents" (2001) 65 J.C.L. 515.

Ickler, N.L., "Conspiracy To Violate RICO: Expanding Traditional Conspiracy Law" (1982) 58 Notre Dame L. Rev. 587.

Johnson, R., "The Unnecessary Crime Of Conspiracy" (1973) Cal.L.Rev. 1137.

Jones, A., *Conspiracy, Attempt and Incitement* (Sweet and Maxwell, 1997).

---

[243] P. Alldridge, "The Sexual Offences (Conspiracy and Incitement) Act 1996" [1997] Crim.L.R. 30.
[244] Note by the Sex Offenders Act 1997, Pt. II, Parliament extended jurisdiction to cover substantive sexual offences where they were committed against children under 16 outside the jurisdiction by a British citizen or person resident in the UK.
[245] This provision, in effect, confirms the earlier decisions in *Sansom* and *Liangsiriprasert*.
[246] The jurisdictional provisions also apply to Group B offences which are listed in s.1. Group B offences are incitement, conspiracy or attempt to commit a Group A offence or conspiracy to defraud.
[247] s.2(1).

Ormerod, D. and Fortson, R., "Serious Crime Act 2007: the Part 2 Offences" [2009] Crim.L.R. 389.

Smith, A.T.H., "Conspiracy To Defraud: The Law Commission's Working Paper No.104" [1988] Crim.L.R. 508.

Smith, J.C., "Conspiracy To Defraud: Some Comments On The Law Commission's Report" [1995] Crim.L.R. 209.

Smith, J.C., "More On Proving Conspiracy" [1997] Crim.L.R. 333.

Virgo, G., "Conspiracy To Defraud—Intent And Prejudice" (1992) 52 C.L.J. 208.

Chapter 7

OFFENCES AGAINST THE PERSON

GENERAL INTRODUCTION

In this section the composition of offences against the person will be examined. These can **7–001** be divided into (a) fatal and (b) non-fatal offences. All offences will require proof of some conduct by the defendant, though as we have seen liability for most can be based on a failure to act when there exists a duty to act. In the majority, but not all, the prosecution will have to establish that the accused's unlawful conduct brought about a prohibited result. Murder, for example, requires proof that the accused caused death and the offence under s.47 of the Offences Against the Person Act 1861 requires proof that the accused caused actual bodily harm. On the other hand the crime of battery (generally prosecuted under the name of assault) requires simply that the accused applied unlawful force to the victim; it does not require proof of any harm.[1]

It will be immediately apparent that there will be an enormous variation in the heinousness of conduct which can attract criminal liability, from the intentional causing of death to the accidental causing of a slight degree of harm, and in an ideal system one would expect to find a graded system of offences to tackle the various possibilities. Unfortunately this is not presently the case in England and Wales. The main statute governing these offences, the Offences Against the Person Act 1861, was simply a consolidating Act, thrown together without any attempt at a rational scheme. The result is that the courts have had to make repeated efforts to achieve some semblance of a scheme of offences.

It will be useful at the outset to have an overall picture of crimes dealing with offences against the person. A given set of facts may give rise to liability for a number of offences. Crimes which come under the heading of offences against the person seek to impose criminal liability for the infliction of violence by one person on another. Where X causes serious injury to Y, X may be prosecuted for the offence of unlawfully and maliciously inflicting grievous bodily harm on Y.[2] If the incident, however took place in the bar of a pub, it may have the effect of terrorising the other customers and there are a series of offences known as Public Order Offences[3] whose object is to impose criminal liability for the effect such activity has upon public order. So Y may be prosecuted for an affray,[4] and there the court will be concerned not directly with the injuries X has inflicted upon Y, but with the effect this activity has had upon ordinary law-abiding citizens.

---

[1] See below, para.7–062.
[2] Contrary to s.20 of the Offences Against the Person Act 1861.
[3] Public Order Act 1986.
[4] Public Order Act 1986 s.3.

Offences against the person are normally divided into those involving death and non-fatal offences. Those involving death are generally categorised as unlawful homicides and include murder and manslaughter. There are a whole range of offences to deal with non-fatal offences but the ones most frequently encountered are common assault,[5] assault occasioning actual bodily harm,[6] unlawfully and maliciously wounding or inflicting grievous bodily harm[7] and unlawfully and maliciously wounding or causing grievous bodily harm with intent to do grievous bodily harm or with intent to resist arrest.[8] Where X forces a woman or a man to have sexual intercourse, X could be charged with one of the non-fatal offences just outlined, but there is a special category of non-fatal offences to deal with conduct where the main behaviour is sexual. Such offences include rape and sexual assault.[9] One major difference between the sexual offences and the general non-fatal offences is that whereas the non-fatal offences are generally concerned with proving that the accused's unlawful conduct has produced a prohibited result, the sexual offences are generally concerned with proving unlawful conduct. In other words the sexual offences are not result crimes and issues of causation are not normally involved.

Before proceeding to look at the particular offences in turn, it will be useful to consider two questions which are applicable to all the offences, namely who can commit such offences, and who can be the victim of such offences? Although these two issues appear to have been discussed almost exclusively in the context of murder they are of general application. Coke C.J., attempting to define murder, said:

> "Murder is when a man of sound memory, and of the age of discretion, unlawfully killeth within any county of the realm any reasonable creature in *rerum natura* under the King's peace, with malice aforethought, . . ."[10]

1. WHO CAN COMMIT AN OFFENCE AGAINST THE PERSON?

7–002   Coke's reference to "a man of sound memory, and of the age of discretion" is taken to mean a human being who has reached his tenth birthday and who is not suffering from insanity or diminished responsibility.[11] It was the position that where the person had not attained his fourteenth birthday the prosecution had, in addition to proving the actus reus and mens rea required to establish the offence, prove a mischievous discretion.[12] Under the presumption of *doli incapax* children in this age group could be convicted only if the prosecutor could prove that the child knew that what he was doing was not simply naughty, but that it was seriously wrong. The presumption of *doli incapax* has now been abolished by s.34 of the Crime and Disorder Act 1998.

2. WHO CAN BE THE VICTIM OF AN OFFENCE AGAINST THE PERSON?

7–003   All offences against the person require a victim and this will generally present no problems. Again Coke's reference to any reasonable creature *in rerum natura* can be taken to mean a human being. However, does the term human being cover an unborn child which is

---

[5] Criminal Justice Act 1988 s.39; see below, para.7–062.
[6] Offences Against the Person Act 1861 s.47; see below, para.7–076.
[7] Offences Against the Person Act 1861 s.20; see below, para.7–082.
[8] Offences Against the Person Act 1861 s.18; see below, para.7–090.
[9] See below, paras 7–119—7–134.
[10] 3 Inst. 47.
[11] s.2 of the Homicide Act 1957. See above, paras 5–005—5–020 for consideration of the defences of insanity and diminished responsibility.
[12] See above, paras 5–097—5–099.

developing in its mother's womb or a person whose bodily functions are being maintained by a respirator? Or, to put it another way, are such entities protected by the law relating to offences against the person?

A. The Unborn Child

The general rule is that a child becomes a human being only when it achieves an existence **7–004** independent of its mother.[13] It seems safe to say that this involves the whole body of the child being expelled from its mother and its being alive.[14] It has been argued that the child should have established a circulation independent of its mother and that it should have begun to breathe independently. The independent circulation requirement is now recognised to be irrelevant since the infant has established a circulation independent of it mother before being born alive. Independent breathing is more problematical. It is not uncommon for a child to be born alive yet not breathe independently for several minutes.[15] It is clear that the cord and afterbirth need not be expelled from the mother nor severed from the child.[16] In the significant case of *Re A (Conjoined Twins: Surgical Separation)*[17] the conjoined twins, each with a brain and nearly complete bodies, were treated by the appellate court, and rightly so, as separate individuals from a legal perspective.

It follows that the intentional destruction of the foetus before it has achieved an existence independent of its mother cannot amount to murder or manslaughter nor can the intentional or reckless injuring of a foetus within the womb amount to an offence against the person. It may constitute the specific statutory offences of unlawful abortion or child destruction.[18]

Problems may arise where the foetus is born alive but dies due to injuries inflicted while in the womb. Lord Mustill in *Attorney-General's Reference (No.3 of 1994)*[19] remarked that there were so many possible factual situations it would take a lengthy book to provide answers to them all.[20] However, we can try to identify the more likely scenarios. Caution should be observed in relying upon earlier precedents. The reasoning behind some of the earlier convictions was based upon the existence of the felony murder rule[21] and this was abolished by s.1 of the Homicide Act 1957.

1. We can say with confidence that where the foetus does not achieve an existence independent of its mother, there can be no charge of unlawful homicide. The prosecution will be restricted to offences such as unlawful abortion[22] and child destruction.[23] This will be the answer whether the attack was aimed at the mother

---

[13] *Enoch* (1833) 5 C. & P. 539.

[14] *Poulton* (1832) 5 C. & P. 329.

[15] *Brain* (1834) 6 C. & P. 349.

[16] In *Rance v Mid Downs Health Authority* [1991] 1 Q.B. 587, a civil case, Brooke J. thought that the meaning of the phrase "independent existence" was that a baby will be born alive if: "after birth, it exists as a live child, that is to say breathing and living by reason of its breathing through its own lungs alone, without deriving any of its living or power of living by or through any connection with its mother".

[17] [2000] 4 All E.R. 961, see above, para.5–065.

[18] Basically unlawful abortion contrary to s.58 of the Offences Against the Person Act 1861 can be committed at any time after conception. Child destruction contrary to s.1 of the Infant Life (Preservation) Act 1929 is the destruction of a foetus which is capable of being born alive.

[19] [1996] 2 W.L.R. 412; [1997] 3 All E.R. 936 HL, see above, para.2–081.

[20] He said that the purpose of the Att-Gen's Reference procedure was to provide answers to issues which had arisen at the trial; it was not intended as a vehicle to discuss hypothetical problems.

[21] See below, para.7–015.

[22] See Offences Against the Person Act 1861 s.58.

[23] See Infant Life (Preservation) Act 1929 s.1.

or the foetus or both. The prosecution cannot establish the actus reus of unlawful homicide.

2. Perhaps the most likely scenario is that the accused's attack was directed at a pregnant woman, and this has caused a premature birth in which the child is born alive but dies later as a result of being born too early. We have seen that even if the accused intended seriously to injure the mother or even if he intended to kill her, he cannot be guilty of murder[24] but he can be convicted of unlawful act manslaughter.[25] It would appear to make no difference whether or not the accused knew that the woman was pregnant.[26]

3. An intent to destroy the foetus in the womb which results in a live birth followed by death as a result of the antenatal injuries cannot constitute murder; there is no intention to kill or seriously injure a human being. If the intent is to injure the foetus in the womb in a way which would result in a live birth but death shortly thereafter, there would seem to be no reason why this should not be murder. This would appear to be like a man who digs a pit for his enemy to fall into and be killed, but where several months later a mother with her one-month-old baby falls in and both are killed. D has unlawfully killed the mother and baby and he dug the pit with intent to kill a human being.[27]

4. If, as a result of grossly negligent driving D runs down P, who is pregnant, and she later gives birth to a child who is very premature and who dies as a result, there would appear to be no reason why D should not be convicted of involuntary manslaughter.[28] Would the courts be willing to follow this line of reasoning and hold liable for manslaughter a mother who grossly neglected herself while pregnant and who thereby caused the premature birth and subsequent death of the child she was carrying? It is suggested that for reasons of personal autonomy the principle ought not to be extended as far as that. Matters of causation will also make it difficult to sustain such a conviction.

B. When do you Cease to be a Human Being?

7–005 If D shoots at what he imagines is a human being, but it turns out to be a corpse, he cannot be prosecuted for murder or manslaughter.[29] The body is no longer subject to the protection of these offences. But at exactly what moment does this change from a living human being to a corpse take place? Is it when breathing stops or when the heart ceases to beat? What would be the position if D shot at P at a time when P's heart had ceased to beat but the surgeons expected that they would be able to re-start it? Breathing and heartbeats can be maintained artificially by means of a respirator; is it murder for a doctor or anyone else to switch off the respirator?

There is no legally recognised definition of the time of death for the purposes of unlawful homicide. The courts are rarely faced with criminal cases in which the timing of death is

[24] See above, para.2–081.
[25] See below, para.7–038. Why did the House of Lords consider it was unlawful act manslaughter? Would not gross negligence have been simpler for a jury? See below, para.7–048.
[26] See, generally J. Beaumont, "The Unborn Child and the Limits of Homicide" (1997) 61 J.C.L. 86.
[27] See, generally M. Seneviratne, "Pre Natal Injury and Transferred Malice: The Invented Other" (1996) 59 M.L.R. 884.
[28] See *Senior* (1832) 1 Mood C.C. 346.
[29] It may be attempted murder; see above, para.6–002.

important and so they are reluctant to say more than is necessary for the decision on the particular facts. However, the medical community does support the concept of "brain stem death". This test is reached when recognisable tests show that none of the centres of the brain stem is functioning.[30] Although the matter has not been directly at issue in any case, there is clear indication from the House of Lords in *Airedale NHS Trust v Bland* that this would be the test the courts would adopt.[31] It is suggested that once this stage is reached the person is no longer a human being and, therefore, no longer capable of being the victim of any future unlawful homicide. The doctors may keep the body ventilated beyond this stage in order to preserve the condition of organs which will be removed for transplants, but this does not alter the fact that the person has been pronounced dead. If P has been brought in to hospital having been shot by D, a decision by the doctors to turn off the life support machines on the basis that P is brain stem dead will not affect D's responsibility for P's death.[32]

The problem of the legal definition of death does not seem, in practice, to have greatly troubled the courts. The leading authority on this point is *Malcherek and Steel*.[33] In that case the defendant, following a quarrel, stabbed his wife nine times with a kitchen knife, causing a deep wound in the abdomen. After surgery she seemed to be making an uneventful recovery, and was confidently expected to survive, but collapsed a few days later. The diagnosis was a massive pulmonary embolism. During surgery a large clot of blood, 12 inches long, was removed from the pulmonary artery and her heart started again. Her heart had not been beating for a period of 30 minutes and anoxic damage to the brain was feared. The life of the victim was sustained by means of a life support machine. Subsequently, when the doctors treating her concluded, after extensive tests, that she was "brain dead", they switched off the machine. The Court of Appeal upheld the conviction for murder. Lord Lane stated:

> "There is no evidence in the present cases here that at the time of conventional death, after the life support machine was disconnected, the original wound or injury was other than a continuing, operating and indeed substantial cause of the death of the victim."[34]

In essence, their Lordships determined that a body of opinion existed in the medical profession that there is only one true test of death, and that is the irreversible death of the brain stem, which controls the basic functions of the body such as breathing.

You will recall in *Airedale NHS Trust v Bland*[35] that B was in what was described as a persistent vegetative state (PVS) following the Hillsborough Stadium disaster. Although he was comatose and it was concluded he would never recover, he was not brain stem dead. People in the persistent vegetative state can still breathe on their own and can react to light and noise, though they will have to be fed by a nasal drip since they cannot swallow. If any person, whether it be the doctor, relatives of the patient or simply a homicidal interloper, deliberately accelerates the appearance of the remaining features of full brain stem death he or she will be guilty of murder. A court, at this stage, may be prepared to say that the continuation of treatment is no longer in the patient's interest, but even then the patient must be allowed to die; he cannot be killed.[36]

---

[30] See [1976] 2 *British Medical Journal* 1187. Royal College of Physicians' Working Group "Criteria for the Diagnosis of Brain Stem Death" (1995) *Journal of the Royal College of Physicians* 381–1.

[31] [1993] A.C. 789.

[32] *Malcherek & Steel* [1981] 1 W.L.R. 690; (1981) 73 Cr.App.R. 173.

[33] [1981] 1 W.L.R. 690; (1981) 73 Cr.App.R. 173. This was the combined hearing of two appeals.

[34] [1981] 1 W.L.R. 690; (1981) 73 Cr.App.R. 173 at 696.

[35] See above, para.2–029.

[36] See above, para.2–030.

UNLAWFUL HOMICIDE

7–006 The word homicide means simply the killing of a human being by another human being and in itself is not a criminal offence. Unlawful homicide is a killing which is contrary to the law. In countries which use the death penalty, the killing by the executioner of the condemned person in the prescribed manner is clearly authorised by law and not, therefore, a criminal offence. A killing in self-defence may be held to be justified[37] and such a killing will not therefore be unlawful, though it might require a trial to reach this conclusion. An accidental killing may on the other hand be described as unlawful in the sense that there is no justification for it, though the perpetrator may escape criminal liability on the basis that he lacked the necessary mens rea.

A criminal code could simply provide one offence of unlawful homicide to cover all unlawful killings, in which a person convicted of an offence would be sentenced by the judge according to the judge's perception of the culpability of the killing. However, it is more normal to sub-divide unlawful homicides into more specific offences according to our perception of their gravity. In this country we have attempted to identify those killings which we regard as the most serious and to these we have attached the name "murder". Those we regard as less serious we classify as manslaughter, infanticide and causing death by dangerous driving. There are other offences akin to unlawful homicide such as abortion and child destruction. Once it has been decided that unlawful homicides must be sub-divided, it is necessary to specify the criteria upon which a given killing will be assigned to one category or to another, and this will form the basis of this section of the chapter.

Before we look at the way in which we assign unlawful homicides to one category or another it may be useful to have a look at the criminal statistics in order to get some idea of the size of the problem. For the moment, if we use the term "homicide" to cover murder, manslaughter and infanticide, we can say that in 2004–05, 839 deaths were initially recorded as homicides.[38] This represents a decrease of two per cent on 2003–04. By November 28, 2005, 820 were still listed as homicides (19 deaths initially listed as homicides were no longer so regarded). In general terms, it is not wise to rely exclusively on the figures for a single year to get a picture of the extent of homicide. Because it remains a relatively rare occurrence, the figures are susceptible to distortion. Thus, in 2002–03, the figures were greatly affected by the recording of the deaths of 172 victims of Dr Harold Shipman. Accordingly, it is preferable to consider trends over a number of years. Returning to the data for 2004–05, over 70 per cent of homicide victims were male. The most common method of causing death was with a sharp instrument. This accounted for 29 per cent of all killings. For male victims, the next most common method involved hitting or kicking. This accounted for 19 per cent of killings of male victims. For female victims, the next most common method was strangulation or asphyxiation. This accounted for 19 per cent of killings of female victims. Nine per cent of homicides were brought about by shooting. For nearly half of male victims, the principal suspect was a stranger. For nearly half of female victims, the principal suspect was a partner or ex-partner. Nearly two-fifths of homicides arose out of quarrels, acts of revenge or loss of temper, a proportion rising to over half when the victim and suspect were known to each other. The homicide figures need to be seen in the context of approximately 1,118,000 violent crimes in total recorded by police in 2004–05.[39]

---

[37] See, for example *Beckford v R.* [1988] A.C. 130; see above, para.2–085.
[38] This use of the term "homicide" corresponds with relevant official publications.
[39] It should be noted that the criteria employed by police for recording crimes have changed recently which makes the analysis of long term trends more complicated.

In excess of 4 million property crimes were recorded in the same period. Of these, for example, over 320,000 were domestic burglaries; nearly 740,000 were thefts of and from vehicles; over 275,000 fraud and forgery and around 1,185,000 criminal damage. Obviously murder attracts more media coverage than any other crime because of its extremely serious and potentially sensational nature. On the other hand, it makes fewer courtroom appearances than media coverage might tend to lead one to expect.[40]

MURDER AND MANSLAUGHTER

In England and Wales, as in most common law jurisdictions, the law categorises most **7–007** unlawful killings as either murder or manslaughter. However, once the view is taken that there is a need to categorise unlawful homicides, it is then necessary to decide upon the criteria to be used. We have traditionally taken the view that the most heinous killings should be labelled as murder and that the less serious killings be called manslaughter (or possibly infanticide or causing death by dangerous driving). It would, of course, be quite feasible for Parliament to provide that in future there should be only one category known as unlawful homicide and that the sentence should vary according to the severity of the offence. This would have the effect of rendering the law a great deal more simple, though it would be open to the criticism that it would leave too much discretion in the hands of the sentencer. In any case, there is no serious possibility that Parliament would ever be attracted to such a drastic change which would remove from our law the opportunity to stigmatise the worst killers as murderers. How, therefore, do we decide which killings merit the label "murder"? In England and Wales we have normally, though not invariably, distinguished murder from manslaughter by reference to the state of the accused's mind at the time of the killing. Thus we have held it to be murder where the accused has intentionally brought about the death of the victim. This however, is not the only workable method for classifying killings. It would be possible to hold that murder—the most serious of the homicide offences—should include all killings committed in the furtherance of thefts, terrorism and rapes or any killings where the victim was a police officer or killings which involved the use of guns or explosives. This type of approach has been discarded on the basis that we find it to be unacceptable that a chance killing can be held to be murder simply because it happened during the commission of another offence or because the victim happened to be a police officer.[41] Other jurisdictions have taken the view that to treat as murder any killing which results from the furtherance of, for example, robbery, serves as a deterrent to would-be robbers; they will be convicted of murder if any death results from the robbery, even if the victim is shot by a policeman who is chasing the robbers.[42]

Whatever criteria are selected to distinguish murder from manslaughter the problem remains the same; you must identify factually those killings which you consider to be the most heinous and then find a form of statutory provision which will cover those and no

[40] This data is taken from sources available via the website of the Home Office: *http://www.homeoffice.gov.uk*. See particularly Nicholas, S., Povey, D., Walker, A. and Kershaw, C., *Crime in England and Wales 2004/2005* (2005); Coleman, K., Hird, C., and Povey, D., *Violent Crime Overview, Homicide and Gun Crime 2004/2005* 2nd edn (2006).
[41] The felony murder rule under which killings caused by the defendant while committing a felony would be classified as murder; the mens rea for murder here being the mens rea of the crime being committed; see, for example, *DPP v Beard* [1920] A.C. 479 where B suffocated a girl during the course of rape. He was convicted of murder upon the basis of an intention to rape. See further below, para.7–015. This category of murder was abolished by s.1 of the Homicide Act 1957. It, or modified versions of it, is still the basis for murder in several states of the USA; see, for example, Pennsylvania and Indiana.
[42] But see below, para.7–015.

others.[43] The complexity of the problem can be seen by a consideration of two types of killing. If we assume for the moment that only a killing in which the accused has deliberately taken the life of his victim shall be murder, then in the absence of any mercy killing defence, a father who deliberately kills his child, who is terminally and painfully ill, will be a murderer. The bank robber, however who sprays bullets round the bank will not necessarily be covered because he may not intend to kill anyone.[44]

1. THE PENALTY FOR MURDER AND MANSLAUGHTER

7–008   The development of the law of murder and manslaughter has been profoundly affected, some would say hindered, by the issue of sentencing those who commit these offences. As you may know, those who are found guilty of murder receive a mandatory sentence of life imprisonment. Politically, this is proving to be non-negotiable: no government is likely to suggest altering this position for fear of appearing "soft" on murderers, this despite the fact that "life imprisonment" rarely means life in prison.

The sentencing of those who commit murder has recently been the site of a fascinating turf war between the government and the judiciary. Historically, when an offender was convicted of murder, they would be required to serve a minimum term of imprisonment—known as a "tariff"—which was fixed by the Home Secretary, after which they became eligible for release on licence. This position was constitutionally untenable as it involved a member of government carrying out a sentencing exercise which was properly a judicial function. Politicians might be influenced by the perceived need to appear tough on murderers, and it was only a matter of time before the Home Secretary was ousted from the tariff-setting role.[45] The role was then fulfilled by the Lord Chief Justice, in accordance with a judicial Practice Direction. However, the Criminal Justice Act 2003 places the sentencing regime for murder on a statutory footing. To some extent it represents the retrenchment of government power, acting through Parliament, in an attempt to limit the role of judges in sentencing in murder cases.

According to s.269 and Sch.21 to the 2003 Act, the trial judge must now set the minimum term of imprisonment in open court. In doing so, the trial judge must take into account the appropriate "starting point" for fixing the minimum term—the Act identifies the characteristics of murders of different levels of seriousness, and designates the appropriate term for such a murder in the absence of any specific aggravating or mitigating factors. Examples of such factors are also set out in the legislation and, if they are present, the judge departs from the "starting point" in an appropriate fashion. Detailed consideration of the sentencing regime for murder is beyond the scope of this book, but you may be interested to know that, insofar as there is a "normal" murder, free of aggravating or mitigating factors, the minimum term of imprisonment set by the Act is 15 years.

The purposes of the minimum term are punishment and deterrence. Upon completion of the minimum term, the convicted murderer remains in prison until the Parole Board deems him or her suitable for release on licence. The criterion governing such release is the

---

[43] See, generally, B. Mitchell, "Distinguishing Between Murder and Manslaughter" (1991) N.L.J. 935.
[44] For further discussion and proposals for future reform see: 14th Report of the Criminal Law Revision Committee; Offences Against the Person; Law Commission No.177—A Criminal Code for England and Wales; Clause 54 and commentary thereon; The Report of the Select Committee of the House of Lords on Murder and Life Imprisonment; HL Paper 78–1, 1989; Law Commission, Consultation Paper No.177, *A New Homicide Act England and Wales?* (2005); Law Commission, *Murder, Manslaughter and Infanticide* (Law Com. No.304, 2006).
[45] See *V and T v UK* (2000) 30 E.H.R.R. 121; *R v Home Secretary, ex p. Anderson* [2002] UKHL 46; [2003] 1 A.C. 837.

prospect of public safety. Release on licence means that the offender can be recalled to prison if he or she does not comply with the conditions of their licence.

While murder, for principally political reasons, has its own specific sentencing regime, manslaughter does not. The offence of manslaughter, as we will see, covers a whole range of killings, from those which may approximate to murder, to those which may almost appear to be accidental. The trial judge sentencing for manslaughter may accordingly impose any sentence, from life imprisonment to an absolute discharge.

2. THE ACTUS REUS OF MURDER AND MANSLAUGHTER

The actus reus for murder and manslaughter[46] is the same; the unlawful killing of a **7–009** reasonable creature (human being) within the Queen's Peace.[47] Until fairly recently there was a further requirement: the death must have occurred within a year and a day of the last act of the accused which caused the victim's death.[48] This may appear a rather odd requirement but it was, in effect, an early rough and ready test of causation. If the victim lived longer than a year and a day after, for example, the last dose of poison administered by the accused, there was an irrebuttable presumption that the death was not caused by the acts of the accused.[49] Such a rule was clearly out of place in a time when it is possible to injure a victim in such a way that it will take him longer than a year and a day to die. Further, modern medical techniques will, in many cases, be able to establish a causal link between the act of the accused and the death of the victim even though these are more than a year and a day apart. Where the accused was saved from a murder or manslaughter conviction by this rule, it would often be possible to convict him of an alternative offence. A person charged with murder would almost certainly have also committed the offence or wounding or causing grievous bodily harm with intent to do grievous bodily harm contrary to s.18 of the Offences Against the Person Act 1861. Thus if D deliberately inflicted P with the AIDS virus intending to cause death, he would instantly be guilty of attempted murder and an offence under s.18 and would remain so even after a year and a day had elapsed.[50] However, a person charged with gross negligence manslaughter[51] is probably guilty of no other offence against the person since such offences require at least *Cunningham* recklessness.[52] In such a case if a patient who had received grossly negligent treatment at the hands of a surgeon died within the year and a day period, the doctor would commit manslaughter, but if the death occurred after the period had expired the doctor would walk free. This year and a day requirement for all homicide and suicide offences was abolished by the Law Reform (Year and a Day Rule) Act 1996.[53] The Act provides that in any proceedings against a person for a fatal offence (murder, manslaughter, infanticide, or any other offences of which one of the elements is causing a person's death, or the offence of aiding, abetting, counselling or procuring a person's suicide) the proceedings must be instituted by or with the consent of

---

[46] And infanticide, see below, para.7–058. Note *Coutts* [2006] 1 W.L.R. 2154 on manslaughter as an alternative count on the event that the jury fail to agree on a murder conviction.

[47] Coke. 3 Inst 47. The Queen's Peace element means, in essence, that the killing of an enemy alien in time of war will not be a criminal homicide; in conditions other than the exercise of war then presumptively it will be unlawful. It still remains the case though that it will be murder where the defendant kills a prisoner of war.

[48] See, generally D. Yale, "A Year and a Day in Homicide" (1989) 48 C.L.J. 202.

[49] See, e.g. *Dyson* [1908] 2 K.B. 454.

[50] See, generally S. Bronitt, "Spreading Disease and the Criminal Law" [1994] Crim.L.R. 24.

[51] For example, a surgeon who has killed a patient by treating him in a highly negligent manner.

[52] See above, para.2–066.

[53] See, Law Commission Consultation Paper No.136, "The Year and a Day Rule in Homicide". The Act applies where the act or omission causing death occurred after June 17, 1996.

the Attorney-General where one of two situations is present. The first is where the injury alleged to have caused the death was inflicted more than three years before the death occurred. The second is where the person to be charged has previously been convicted of an offence committed in circumstances alleged to be connected with the death. If, for example, D shoots P and seriously injures him, D may be convicted of wounding with intent to do grievous bodily harm. If the victim subsequently dies, D may now be prosecuted for murder, but only with the consent of the Attorney-General.

7–010 Jurisdiction. The jurisdiction in most criminal cases is limited to offences committed in England and Wales. However, murder and manslaughter are exceptions to this general rule. Where murder or manslaughter is committed by a British subject anywhere in the world, the offence is triable here.[54] Also, where murder or manslaughter is committed on a British ship or aircraft, the offence is triable in this country irrespective of whether or not the defendant is a British Citizen.

7–011 Unlawful killing. The prosecution must prove that the defendant has killed the victim and that the killing was unlawful. As we have already seen[55] the prosecution must establish a causal link between the unlawful conduct of the defendant and the death of the victim. In most cases this will cause no problems, but occasionally the court will have to determine whether the conduct of the defendant is in law capable of amounting to a legal cause of the victim's death. The prosecution will also have to establish that the killing was unlawful. In the majority of cases this will cause no problems, however, where the defendant has introduced evidence that the killing was justified (e.g. self-defence, defence of property or prevention of crime[56]) the prosecution will have to prove, beyond reasonable doubt, that the killing was unlawful.

7–012 A reasonable creature in rerum natura. The prosecution must prove that the defendant unlawfully killed a reasonable creature *in rerum natura* which, as we have seen,[57] is normally translated to mean "human being".

7–013 The mens rea of Murder and Manslaughter. The actus reus of murder and manslaughter is the same. The distinction between the two offences arises in two ways. In some cases the prosecution is able to prove that the defendant unlawfully killed the victim with the mens rea required for murder, but there exists a partial defence (provocation, diminished responsibility or suicide pact) which reduces the crime to manslaughter. This type of manslaughter is known as voluntary manslaughter. In other cases the prosecution establishes that the defendant unlawfully killed the victim, but is able to establish only the mens rea of manslaughter; this type of manslaughter is known as involuntary manslaughter. In this section we shall examine first the mens rea of murder and then of the various types of manslaughter.

3. THE MENS REA OF MURDER

7–014 The prosecution in order to establish a charge of murder must prove that the defendant possessed the necessary mens rea on each element of the actus reus.[58]

---

[54] See, s.9 of the Offences Against the Person Act 1861 and s.3 of the British Nationality Act 1948.
[55] See above, para.2–032.
[56] See above, paras 5–044—5–059.
[57] Above, para.7–004.
[58] See, generally G. Williams, "*Mens rea* for Murder: Leave it Alone" (1989) 105 L.Q.R. 387; and W. Wilson, "A Plea for Rationality in the Law of Murder" (1990) 10 *Legal Studies* 307.

A. The Killing of a Human Being

We have already seen that on this central element of the actus reus nothing short of **7–015** intention suffices and that murder is, therefore, a crime of specific intent.[59] However, since the passing of s.1 of the Homicide Act 1957, it has been generally accepted that the mens rea is not restricted to an intention to kill; an intention to cause grievous bodily harm will also suffice.[60] Thus if D is torturing V to obtain information, he may well intend to cause V grievous bodily harm, but equally he may have every intention that V should remain alive. If, in these circumstances, V dies as a result of the torture, D will be guilty of murder; it would not avail him that the jury were satisfied that it never even occurred to D that there was a risk of death. Why, it should be asked, when intention alone suffices, should a prosecution for murder succeed when the defendant's intention is not to cause death? The explanation is mainly historical and not altogether clear. Until the passing of the Homicide Act 1957 it was generally accepted that malice aforethought could take one of three forms. Express malice meant an intention to kill and implied malice meant an intention to cause grievous bodily harm. The third was known as constructive malice and covered killings committed in the course of a felony (or possibly only a violent felony) or killings perpetrated in an attempt to resist lawful arrest or to escape from lawful arrest or custody. Where the prosecution relied on constructive malice the mens rea for murder was satisfied either by an intention to commit the felony or the intention to prevent arrest or escape from arrest or custody. Thus in *DPP v Beard*[61] the accused suffocated the girl he was raping and the killing amounted to murder, the mens rea being the intention to rape. Both types of constructive malice were abolished by s.1 of the Homicide Act 1957. Deaths brought about while the accused was intentionally committing a felony would no longer be murder simply on the basis that the defendant intended to commit the felony. Today in *Beard* the Crown would have to prove that the accused had express malice (an intention to kill) or possibly implied malice (an intention to cause grievous bodily harm). Section 1 of the Homicide Act 1957 provides:

"(1) Where a person kills another in the course or furtherance of some other offence, the killing shall not amount to murder unless done with the same malice aforethought (express or implied) as is required for a killing to amount to murder when not done in the course or furtherance of another offence.

(2) For the purpose of the foregoing subsection, a killing done in the course or for the purpose of resisting an officer of justice, or of resisting or avoiding or preventing a lawful arrest, or of effecting or assisting an escape or rescue from legal custody, shall be treated as a killing in the course of furtherance of an offence."

What, therefore, of implied malice? An intention to cause grievous bodily harm was the mens rea of the offence created by Lord Ellenborough's Act of 1803, namely the felony of causing grievous bodily harm with intent to do so. If the defendant is alleged to have committed murder on the basis of an intention to cause grievous bodily harm, is this not an illustration of the felony murder rule? This problem was posed for the court in *Vickers*[62] where the Court of Criminal Appeal held that an intention to cause grievous bodily harm was not an example of constructive malice and, therefore, did not fall within s.1 of the 1957

[59] Above, paras 2–055—2–057.
[60] See, for example *Vickers* [1957] 2 Q.B. 664.
[61] [1920] A.C. 479.
[62] [1957] 2 Q.B. 664.

Act.[63] It is clear that the courts acted upon this decision for many years after the decision in *Vickers*. However, in *Hyam v DPP*[64] Lords Diplock and Kilbrandon challenged the correctness of the decision in *Vickers* and held that an intention to cause grievous bodily harm was, after all, an example of constructive malice and, therefore, abolished in 1957; malice aforethought required either an intention to kill or an intention to do grievous bodily harm which the defendant knew was likely to kill. This was a rather alarming proposition since presumably several convictions and possibly even executions for murder were based upon implied malice. The position in *Hyam* was obscured because Viscount Dilhorne and Lord Hailsham supported the correctness of the decision in *Vickers* and the fifth judge, Lord Cross, felt unable to express any opinion on the matter since it had not been fully argued before the House. The matter was resolved by the House of Lords in *Cunningham*[65] where the House held that implied malice had been a recognisable head of malice aforethought before Lord Ellenborough's Act and hence was not a form of constructive malice. *Vickers* had, therefore, been correctly decided.[66] The decision in *Cunningham* has subsequently been approved by the House of Lords in *Moloney*[67] where it was said that the restricted definition of malice aforethought supported by Lords Diplock and Kilbrandon could only be achieved by legislation. In *Attorney-General's Reference (No.3 of 1994)* Lord Mustill, despite his dislike of the rule that murder can be committed by someone who intends only to inflict grievous bodily harm, accepted that it would now be unthinkable for the House of Lords to abolish the rule.[68]

B. Mens Rea on the Other External Elements of Murder

7–016   It is clear that the specific intent element of murder is the intention to kill or cause really serious bodily harm.[69] The mens rea required to establish the remaining elements is less clear, but it is probably safe to say that intention or recklessness will suffice. Once the accused has introduced some evidence that the killing was lawful, it is for the prosecution to prove that there was no justification for the killing. It is clear from cases such as *Gladstone Williams*[70] and *Beckford*[71] that the prosecution will succeed if it can prove that the defendant either knew that there were no circumstances of justification or consciously took an unjustified risk that there was no justification.[72]

It would also appear that where D, due to voluntary intoxication, mistakenly believes he is justified in attacking a victim, he may not rely upon his mistaken belief. The defence of

---

[63] Since s.1 of the Homicide Act 1957 preserved both express and implied malice, a decision that an intention to cause grievous bodily harm was not the mens rea of murder would leave open the question of what, therefore, constituted implied malice.

[64] [1975] A.C. 55.

[65] [1982] A.C. 566.

[66] It is noteworthy that the American Model Penal Code equates an intention to cause grievous bodily harm as the malice for murder only where a defendant demonstrates the extreme degree of recklessness required for what they call "depraved heart" malice; in this regard see M.P.C. s.210.2(1)(b).

[67] [1985] A.C. 905 at 925 per Lord Bridge. See generally Lord Goff, "The Mental Element in Murder" (1988) 104 L.Q.R. 40.

[68] [1997] 3 All E.R. 936 at 945. However, he added "but when asked to strike out into new territory it is, I think, right to recognise that the grievous harm rule is an outcropping of old law from which the surrounding strata of rationalisations have weathered away. It survives but exemplifies no principle which can be applied to a new situation."

[69] In *Janjua and Chaudhury* (1999) 1 Cr.App.R. 91 the Court of Appeal inclined to the view that "really" serious bodily harm in this context means "very".

[70] (1984) 78 Cr.App.R. 276, above, para.2–085.

[71] [1988] A.C. 130, above, para.2–085.

[72] In cases such as *Dadson* (1850) 175 E.R. 499 (above para.2–002) where there are, unknown to the defendant, circumstances of justification, the prosecution will have to prove that D was unaware of the existence of justification.

intoxication would seem to apply only to the specific intent element of murder, namely the intention to kill or cause grievous bodily harm.[73]

It is suggested that the mens rea required in relation to the victim being within the Queen's Peace is intention or *Cunningham* recklessness. It is to be remembered, however, that whereas the prosecution in any murder case will have to introduce and lead evidence that the accused intended to kill or cause grievous bodily harm, only if there is evidence that the killing was lawful or that the victim was not within the Queen's Peace will the prosecution need to address these issues.[74]

4. REFORMING THE LAW OF MURDER

The law of murder has long been a matter of controversy. For some it is too wide—the rule **7–017** in *Vickers* and *Cunningham* means that a defendant can be convicted of murder if he or she intends grievous bodily harm—even if he or she does not even contemplate the possibility of the victim's death. For others, the definition is too narrow—the requirement that the prosecution prove *intention* to kill or to do grievous bodily harm means that those who exhibit a flagrant disregard for human life short of such an intention do not fall within the ambit of the offence.

In 2006, following a consultation exercise, the Law Commission published the Report *Murder, Manslaughter and Infanticide,*[75] which made a number of recommendations regarding the structure of the law of homicide and the operation of a variety of defences to charges of homicide. At the time of writing, the Government has taken the view that dealing with the defences is a priority and so the radical restructuring of the homicide offences which is proposed by the Commission is not an immediate-term prospect.[76] The proposals, which involve a three-tier approach to homicide offences, are worthy of note nonetheless[77]:

- first degree murder, which would carry a mandatory life sentence, would be constituted by intentional killings and killings where there was both an intention to do serious injury and an awareness of a serious risk of causing death;

- second degree murder, which would carry a discretionary life maximum sentence, would be committed where D killed intending to do serious injury; where D killed intending to cause some injury or a fear or risk of injury and was aware of a serious risk of causing death; and where D had a partial defence to what would otherwise be first degree murder;[78]

- manslaughter, which would also carry a discretionary life maximum sentence, would be committed, inter alia, where D kills through gross negligence as to a risk of causing death; or where D kills through a criminal act intended to cause injury or where D was aware of a serious risk of causing injury by the act.

---

[73] See *O'Grady* and *O'Connor*, above, para.5–031.

[74] On these issues the defendant is said to have an evidential burden. If there is no evidence that the defendant acted in self-defence or that the victim was not within the Queen's Peace, the trial judge will not put the issues before the jury. See above, para.1–009.

[75] Law Com. No.304. This followed Law Commission, Consultation Paper No.177 (2005), *A New Homicide Act for England and Wales?*

[76] See Ministry of Justice, *Murder, manslaughter and infanticide: proposals for reform of the law* (Consultation Paper CP19/08) (July 2008); and Ministry of Justice, *Murder, manslaughter and infanticide: proposals for reform of the law—Summary of responses and Government position* (January 2009).

[77] See Law Com. No.304, paras 9.5—9.9.

[78] These defences would be provocation; diminished responsibility (the scope of which defences is also considered in the proposals) and suicide pact. It is also proposed that duress be a complete defence to first and second degree murder.

Under the Law Commission's proposed scheme, other specific homicide offences would remain, such as infanticide and assisted suicide and the offences involving causing death by driving.

Given that the clear message from government, and indeed from Parliament, is that the mandatory life sentence is here to stay, it is imperative that it attaches only to those unlawful killings which properly merit it. It may just be that the Law Commission's approach provides a sensible way of identifying such killings.

VOLUNTARY AND INVOLUNTARY MANSLAUGHTER

7–018   Manslaughter is the name given to a sort of rag bag of unlawful homicides which for one reason or another do not constitute murder. On the one hand there are those killings where the prosecution are able to prove the necessary actus reus and mens rea for murder, but where there is a mitigating factor such as provocation,[79] diminished responsibility, or the existence of a suicide pact which reduces the offence to manslaughter. This category is usually known as voluntary manslaughter.[80] On the other hand there are unlawful killings where the prosecution is unable to prove the necessary mens rea for murder, but can establish a lesser mens rea which the courts have found sufficient to warrant a conviction for manslaughter. This second category is known as involuntary manslaughter. There is, however, only one offence of manslaughter and the statement of offence in the indictment will simply allege manslaughter,[81] but the prosecution will have to establish that the killing comes within one of the two categories.

In this chapter we shall examine first of all the cases in which the offence is reduced from murder to manslaughter on the basis of provocation and then we shall examine the scope of involuntary manslaughter. As we will see, provocation has been the subject of significant recent development.[82]

VOLUNTARY MANSLAUGHTER

1. THE NATURE OF PROVOCATION

7–019   The defence of provocation in crimes of homicide has always represented an anomaly in English law. Usually, the fact that a defendant has been provoked into committing a crime will only be relevant at the sentencing stage. In homicide, however, provocation effects a change in the offence, reducing it from murder for which the penalty is life imprisonment, to manslaughter for which the penalty is at the discretion of the judge.[83] Historically, the

---

[79] Provocation is the only mitigating factor at common law. The other two are creatures of statute, namely diminished responsibility in accordance with the Homicide Act 1957 s.2 (see above, para.5–015); and killings committed in furtherance of a suicide pact under the Homicide Act 1957 s.4 (see below, para.7–057).

[80] In some jurisdictions this has been known as mitigated murder.

[81] See, for example Archbold ss.19–123.

[82] For consideration of the other mitigating factors relevant to voluntary manslaughter, i.e. diminished responsibility see above, para.5–015; for suicide pacts, see below, para.7–057.

[83] DPP v Camplin [1978] A.C. 705 at 713 per Lord Diplock; see generally, T. Macklem, "Provocation and the Ordinary Person" (1987) 11 Dalhousie L.J. 126; and A. Reed, "Duress and Provocation as Excuses to Murder: Salutary Lessons from Recent Anglo-American Jurisprudence" (1996) 6 Florida State University, Journal of Transnational Law and Policy 51.

defence developed in the common law at a time when the carrying of weapons was routine, and when, as a consequence, the potential for fatalities to arise from angry altercations was high. Provocation allowed the strictness of the murder laws—in particular, the mandatory death penalty—to be avoided. By the early 20th century, a two-stage approach had begun to develop, whereby it was asked, first, whether a defendant had been provoked, and, second, whether a reasonable person would have acted in the same way as the defendant.[84] The decision in *Lesbini* established a dual test applied, engrafting subjective and objective elements. The conduct of the deceased towards the defendant had to be evaluated in light of this two-prong approach. This objective criterion, the "reasonable person" test, evolved for policy considerations, designed to set a standard of self-control which must be complied with before the defendant is able to rely on the defence of provocation.

The first question to ask is what is meant by provocation; or what it means for a defendant to be provoked. This is sometimes referred to as the "subjective" question in provovation, because it asks about the state of mind of the defendant *himself or herself*. The classic definition is usually taken to be that of Devlin J. in *Duffy* where he said: "Provocation is some act, or series of acts, done by the dead man to the accused, which would cause in any reasonable person, and actually causes in the accused, *a sudden and temporary loss of self-control*, rendering the accused subject to passion as to make him or her for the moment not master of his mind."[85] We shall see later that this definition has been somewhat modified by subsequent legislation and cases, but it nevertheless provides us with a useful starting point. We are concerned here with, for example, a situation in which A insults B about B's deformed nose, a characteristic about which B has very strong feelings. B loses his self-control and smashes A over the head with a beer glass he happens to be holding, thereby killing A. It is worth making the point at this stage that only if B is charged with murder will the defence of provocation be of any relevance; the prosecution must prove the necessary mens rea of murder. The defence only becomes necessary if the jury are prepared in the first place to return a verdict of murder.

The defence of provocation is now partially covered by s.3 of the Homicide Act 1957, which modifies common law rules. The section provides:

> "Where on a charge of murder there is evidence on which the jury can find that the person charged was provoked (whether by things done or by things said or by both together) to lose his self-control, the question whether the provocation was enough to make a reasonable man do as he did shall be left to be determined by the jury; and in determining that question the jury shall take into account everything both done and said according to the effect which, in their opinion, it would have on a reasonable man."

Before the 1957 Act the judge was entitled to withdraw the issue of provocation from the **7–020** jury on the ground that even if the accused had himself been provoked no reasonable man would have reacted in the way he did to the provocation. It is quite clear that s.3 has removed that power. The judge must leave the issue to the jury if there is evidence that the accused was provoked to lose his self-control, however unreasonable his actions might appear to the judge.[86] Thus in *Doughty*[87] the Court of Appeal held that there was evidence

---

[84] *Lesbini* [1914] 3 K.B. 1116.
[85] [1949] 1 All E.R. 932 (emphasis added).
[86] This embraces acts directed against third parties provided they would have provoked the reasonable man. For example, in *Pearson* [1992] Crim.L.R. 193, two brothers (M and W) had suffered abuse over a number of years from their violent father, and they killed him. It was held that the ill-treatment of M over a period of eight years when W, the older brother, was away from the home was relevant to W's defence of provocation, i.e. the acts and conduct of the father directed against M.
[87] (1986) 83 Cr.App.R. 319.

that the accused had been provoked by the crying of his 17-day-old child; the trial judge was, therefore, under an obligation to leave the defence of provocation to the jury. The case seems to illustrate that the phrase in s.3, "whether by things done or by things said or by both together" is wide enough to cover a baby crying. It is probably not wide enough to cover a pure "act of God", such as damage caused by lightning, which causes the accused to lose his self-control.

In summary, the changes effected by s.3, as interpreted by the courts, are of fundamental importance because this section: (1) establishes that *words alone* may be sufficient provocation if the jury decides that they would have provoked a reasonable man[88]; (2) treats the "proportionality" of a defendant's response to provocation as only one factor in judging whether a reasonable man would have acted as the actor did[89]; (3) takes away the power of the judge to withdraw the defence from the jury on the grounds that there was no evidence on which the jury could find that a reasonable man would have been provoked to do as the defendant had done[90]; (4) authorises the defence to be used if a third person, not the victim, is the provoker.[91] The section makes it clear that a dual test applies. The provocation must not only have caused the accused to lose his self-control but must also be such as might cause a reasonable man to react to it as the accused did.[92]

On the issue of provocation the defendant bears an evidential burden. This means that it is up to the defendant to make sure that by the time the judge sums up to the jury, there is some evidence that he was provoked. It does not mean that he must specifically raise the defence as part of his case; evidence of provocation may emerge from the prosecution evidence.[93] Why might an accused not specifically raise and develop a defence? The reason is usually a matter of strategy; evidence necessary to substantiate provocation may contradict the evidence relied upon to support self-defence. Furthermore, a successful plea of self-defence will lead to an acquittal, whereas a plea of provocation will only reduce the conviction from murder to manslaughter. The defence will wish to concentrate their efforts on self-defence and will not wish to send conflicting messages to the jury.[94] On the other hand, if the judge is seen to raise the possibility of another defence, this may not harm the defence's case. In *Wellington*,[95] for example, the accused pleaded that he had knifed the victim in self-defence and that he had not used more force than was reasonably necessary. He appealed against his conviction for murder on the ground that the trial judge should have left the issue of provocation to the jury, even though he had not raised it specifically. He argued that there was evidence that he had been provoked to lose his self-control. The Court of Appeal, however, held that there was no such evidence. His plea of self-defence had been made on the basis of a reasoned use of force and the forensic evidence revealed only one wound inflicted without much force. The evidence pointed against a frenzied attack by someone who had lost control.

---

[88] *Phillips v R.* [1969] 2 A.C. 130, 137 (P.C. 1968) (appeal taken from Sup. Ct Judicature of Jam.).

[89] Contrast the old case of *Mancini v DPP* [1942] A.C. 1; see also *Brown* [1972] 2 Q.B. 229.

[90] *DPP v Camplin* [1978] A.C. 705.

[91] J. Dressler, "Rethinking Heat of Passion: A Defence in Search of a Rationale" (1982) 73 J.Crim.L. & Criminology 429; see also *Davies* [1975] Q.B. 691, 701.

[92] The doctrine of transferred malice applies, i.e. D aims a blow at V, the provoker, but by accident kills B, an innocent bystander, then D may be guilty of manslaughter only. See, e.g. *Gross* (1913) 23 Cox C.C. 455.

[93] The burden of proof remains upon the prosecution. That is to say, if provocation is a live issue, the prosecution must *disprove* it. See, e.g. *Lee Chun Chuen v R.* [1963] A.C. 220; *Rolle v R.* [1965] 1 W.L.R. 1341; and *Cascoe* [1970] 2 All E.R. 833. Note there is a duty on the trial judge to leave the defence of provocation to the jury even when it conflicts with the defence actually raised by the accused.

[94] Although it is permissible for a defendant to run defences of provocation and self-defence together if they wish: see *Kromer* [2002] EWCA Crim 1278.

[95] [1993] Crim.L.R. 616.

A. Cooling-off period: A Gender Issue?

The essence of the provocation defence is that the defendant suffers "a sudden and **7–021** temporary loss of self-control".[96] The longer the period between the provoking behaviour and response the weaker the cogency of the defence. For example, in *Ibrams and Gregory*[97] the defendants had been terrorised by V over a lengthy period up to October 7. They concocted a plan to kill him on October 10 and carried out this killing on October 14. The cooling-off period, conscious formulation of a plan, desire for revenge and self-control of the defendants, precluded the application of the provocation defence. The appellate court expressly approved the dictum of Devlin J. in *Duffy* that:

> ". . . circumstances which induce a desire for revenge are inconsistent with provocation, since the conscious formulation of a desire for revenge means that a person has had time to think, to reflect, and that would negative a sudden temporary loss of self-control which is of the essence of provocation."[98]

That the killing should have been carried out during a sudden and temporary loss of self-control may be seen as making the defence more suitable for male rather than for female defendants. This may be because, in general, males are physically stronger, and may react instantaneously to provocation, whereas females tend to demonstrate "slow-burn" responses. Female responses to taunts, although no less apparent, tend to be slower to ignite than male reactions. It has been submitted that their anger simmers more or less constantly and then is unleashed in a sudden eruption, typically when the danger has subsided and the neutralising effect of fear has passed.[99] Where there is evidence that the person provoked took steps to arm themselves before killing the person who was provoking them, it may well point to a premeditated rather than provoked killing. A series of high-profile cases in relation to "battered women" have addressed this issue. In *Thornton*[100] a husband had subjected his wife to a very long period of brutal treatment. On the night of the killing, Sara Thornton found her husband asleep on the sofa. When she asked him to come to bed, he said he would kill her if she had been with another man. She fetched a knife from the kitchen for her own protection and sharpened it. Her husband told her he would kill her while she was asleep, at which point she stabbed him once in the stomach, which resulted in his death. At her trial she pleaded diminished responsibility, but the trial judge left the issue of provocation to the jury, though in a way which suggested that he did not see much in the defence. The defence tried unsuccessfully to argue that the trial judge had been wrong to direct the jury that, for the defence to succeed, the provocative words or conduct had to have caused in the defendant "a sudden and temporary loss of self-control". *Ahluwalia*[101] also involved a long period of mistreatment by the husband of the defendant wife; after the last provocative act she filled a bin full of petrol and threw it into the bedroom where her husband was and then threw in a match. The husband was killed. In both *Thornton* and

---

[96] Inability of D to restrain himself suffices; it is not necessary to show that he did not know what he was doing. See, e.g. *Richens* [1993] Crim.L.R. 384: judge's direction which implied that for provocation the defendant must have involved "complete loss of self-control to the extent that you do not know what you are doing" was a misdirection. In any event if an accused "did not know what he was doing" then he could not be convicted of murder.

[97] (1981) 74 Cr.App.R. 154.

[98] [1949] 1 All E.R. 932 at 932.

[99] W. Wilson, *Criminal Law* (Longman, 1998) at p.382.

[100] [1992] 1 All E.R. 306.

[101] [1992] 4 All E.R. 889.

Ahluwalia there was evidence of premeditation; both defendants left the scene to fetch a weapon. Both defendants argued that it was inappropriate today to require a sudden and temporary loss of self-control, particularly in cases where the defendant had suffered a long course of provocative conduct. The Court of Appeal in *Ahluwalia*, however, was of the opinion that the requirement had so long been a part of the defence, that only Parliament could now alter it. Nonetheless, the Court suggested that a "cooling time" between provocation and killing, a slow-burn reaction, did not constitute an absolute bar to the application of the defence:

> "We accept that the subjective element in the defence of provocation would not as a matter of law be negatived simply because of the delayed reaction in such cases, provided that there was at the time of the killing a 'sudden and temporary loss of self-control' caused by the alleged provocation. However, the longer the delay and the stronger the evidence of deliberation on the part of the defendant, the more likely it will be that the prosecution will negative provocation."[102]

7–022   The principles in *Ahluwalia* were affirmed in *Humphreys*,[103] where the appellate court considered the matter of "cumulative provocation" over a period of time. Emma Humphreys had left home at the age of 16, became a prostitute and moved in with V. V, who was jealous and possessive and had previous convictions for violence, began seriously to assault her, and to mentally and sexually abuse her. On the evening in question Emma met V, his son, and two friends in a pub, where he said that they would be "all right for a gang bang tonight". Emma and V then returned to the latter's house. Here she took two knives and cut both her wrists; Emma had a history of cutting her wrists to gain attention. V undressed to his shirt, causing her to fear rape. V then taunted her that she had not made a very good job of wrist-slashing, whereupon she lost self-control and stabbed him. She was tried and convicted of murder, notwithstanding evidence of abuse by the deceased and a psychiatrist's report that she was of "abnormal mentality with immature, explosive and attention-seeking traits". Her appeal succeeded, inter alia, on the basis that the judge misdirected the jury to consider *only* the deceased's taunts about her wrist-slashing in deciding whether she had been provoked and whether her reaction was reasonable. The Court of Appeal held that a history of violence (cumulative provocation) suffered by the killer at the hands of the victim may be extremely relevant evidence that the accused did in fact lose her self-control at the time of the killing.

There is no reason why the provocation should not be cumulative. It is the *loss of self-control* which must be sudden not the provocation. For example, if D has been bullied over a period of time by V, it is quite possible that one final incident, not obviously the sort of incident which would be likely to cause someone to lose their self-control, may nonetheless cause D to lose her self-control. A history of violence may explain why the defendant lost her self-control in the face of what was not, objectively, particularly strong provocation. Indeed, in Sara Thornton's second appeal to the Court of Appeal, *Thornton (No.2)*,[104] it was held that cumulative provocation was relevant. Battered woman syndrome, the effect of a husband's abuse over a period of time on a woman's mental state, was a relevant

---

[102] [1992] 4 All E.R. 889 at 896 per Lord Taylor C.J. The Court of Appeal allowed her appeal on the diminished responsibility ground, achieving a "desirable" and "sympathetic" result. This decision was followed two months later by that of *Gardner* (1992) 14 Cr.App.R.(S) 364, where the five-year sentence of D for the provoked manslaughter of her partner was reduced to probation on the grounds of fresh evidence of diminished responsibility.

[103] [1995] 4 All E.R. 1010.

[104] [1995] 4 All E.R. 1008.

characteristic which could be considered in a murder trial, although a defendant could still not succeed in relying on provocation unless the jury considered she had suffered or might have suffered a sudden and temporary loss of self-control at the time of the killing.

The requirement of a sudden and temporary loss of self-control has drawn a hostile response from academic commentators on both sides of the Atlantic in operating capriciously against women with slow-burn reactions to provocation.[105] A requirement that defendants must suddenly lose their self-control will continue to pose difficulties for battered women who tend to kill with an outwardly calm demeanour. Battered woman syndrome has been criticised as politically objectionable in stereotyping women as passive, helpless and prone to physical and mental illness.[106] A number of commentators have suggested that the situation may be ameliorated for battered defendants through the panacea of developing the existing law on self-defence, allowing an outright acquittal.[107] Wells, for example, has propounded that:

> "[O]ne form of departure would be to recognise that domestic violence does not merely invade a person's physical integrity, it is an instrument of psychological and emotional control. This might be better addressed by a defence of psychological self-defence."[108]

The issue of battered woman syndrome is considered further when we examine the so-called "objective question" in provocation.

B. The Role of Judge and Jury

Since the passing of the 1957 Act, the role of the jury has been integral to determining the **7–023** availability of the provocation defence. This policy has been reinforced specifically by the cases (above) validating the relevance of "cumulative provocation",[109] and generally by a judicial recognition of the primacy of the the jury in this context. In *Rossiter,* Russell L.J. said of s.3:

> "The emphasis in that section is very much on the function of the jury as opposed to the judge. We take the law to be that wherever there is material which is capable of amounting to provocation, however tenuous it may be, the jury must be given the privilege of ruling on it."[110]

---

[105] See, generally, M. Wasik, "Cumulative Provocation and Domestic Killing" [1982] Crim.L.R. 29; J.R. Castel, "Discerning Justice for Battered Women Who Kill" (1990) 48 *University of Toronto Faculty of Law Review* 229; A. McColgan, "In Defence of Battered Women Who Kill" (1993) 13 O.J.L.S. 508; D. Nicholson and R. Sanghvi, "Battered Women and Provocation: The Implications of *R. v Ahluwalia*" [1993] Crim.L.R. 728. For an interesting review of the US position see A.M. Coughlin, "Excusing Conduct" (1994) 82 California L.R. 1.

[106] D. Nicholson and R. Sanghvi, "More Justice for Battered Women" (1995) N.L.J. 1124 at 1125.

[107] See, e.g. Edwards, S.S.M., "Abolishing provocation and reframing self defence: the Law Commission's options for reform" [2004] Crim.L.R. 181.

[108] C. Wells, "Battered Women Syndrome and Defences to Homicide: Where Now?" (1994) 14 *Legal Studies* 266, 273; see also Talbot, "Is Psychological Self-Defence a Solution to the Problem of Defending Battered Women Who Kill"? (1988) 45 Washington and Lee L.R. 1527.

[109] See also *Baillie* [1995] 2 Cr.App.R. 31 in which the Court of Appeal stated that provocation should have been left to the jury even though, as the trial judge had pointed out there was time for reflection and time for cooling-off given that D, although angry, had gone to the attic, collected a gun, brought it down and placed it in the car, driven from his house a distance of some miles via a petrol filling station to the street where the victim resided, and then walked, albeit a short distance, from the car to the house.

[110] (1992) 95 Cr.App.R. 326 at 333. This applies even though neither counsel for D nor for the Crown are of the view that it was necessary to leave the issue of provocation to the jury: see, e.g. *Dhillon* [1997] 2 Cr.App.R. 104.

Similarly, in *Stewart,* Stuart-Smith L.J. said:

> "In our judgment, where the judge must, as a matter of law, leave the issue of provocation to the jury, he should indicate to them, unless it is obvious, what evidence might support the conclusion that the appellant lost his self-control. This is particularly important where counsel has not raised the issue at all. In many cases it may be obvious, for example if there has been a fight and a defence of self-defence is rejected by the jury, or if there is evidence of a row or violence and the defence is nevertheless one of accident, however improbable that may be."[111]

Nonetheless, in cases where no evidence emerges, from whatever source, which suggests the reasonable possibility that the defendant might have lost his self-control due to words or deeds of another, or a combination of the two, the question of provocation does not arise and should not be put to the jury. This was affirmed by the House of Lords in *Acott*,[112] a case where a 48-year-old defendant, financially dependent upon his mother and treated like a child, was charged with her murder, but claimed the injuries were sustained as a result of a fall and his unskilled efforts to resuscitate her. A loss of self-control caused by fear, panic, sheer bad temper or circumstances (for example, a slow down of traffic due to snow) would not be enough. There must be some evidence, albeit slight, tending to show that the killing might have been an uncontrolled reaction to provoking conduct rather than an act of revenge. A frenzied attack is more likely to point to a sudden and temporary loss of self-control, than is evidence of a solitary wound. Lord Steyn concluded in *Acott* that what was required was a *specific provoking event*; it was insufficient that the issue of loss of self-control may simply have been raised by the prosecution in cross-examination of the defendant.[113]

2. SELF-INDUCED PROVOCATION

7–024 A question which has given arguably unnecessary trouble to the courts for several years is that of self-induced provocation. The situation envisaged is where the accused, by his acts, causes the victim to act in a provocative way towards the accused who thereupon loses his self-control and kills the victim. It had been felt by some that it would be wrong to allow the accused to rely on the provocation when he had caused it. However, such a position would be clearly against the wording of the Act which simply says that once there is evidence that the accused has been provoked to lose his self-control the issue of provocation must be left to the jury. The Act does not say that this is restricted to provocation for which the accused was not responsible.

A rule which would *sometimes* have accepted the validity of self-induced provocation was suggested in *Edwards v R.*:

> "On principle it seems reasonable to say that: (1) a blackmailer cannot rely on the predictable results of his own blackmailing conduct as constituting provocation

---

[111] [1995] 4 All E.R. 999 at 1007. D was charged with murder and raised a defence of accident, which he said had occurred when he threw his wife on to the bed in an attempt to restrain her from leaving the house because he believed she was going to commit suicide. He admitted that he had been "fed up" with his wife's illness, but denied losing his self-control or being provoked by anything his wife said to him during their struggle.

[112] [1997] 1 All E.R. 706; [1997] 2 Cr.App.R. 104; and see also *Van Dongen* [2005] EWCA Crim 1728; [2005] 2 Cr.App.R. 38.

[113] [1997] 1 All E.R. 706 at 712. See generally, P. Seago and A. Reed, "Criminal Law" [1997] All E.R. Annual Review 117 at 124.

sufficient to reduce his killing of the victim from murder to manslaughter, and the predictable results may include a considerable degree of hostile reaction by the person sought to be blackmailed, for instance vituperative words and even some hostile action such as blows with a fist; (2) but, if the hostile reaction by the person sought to be blackmailed goes to *extreme lengths*, it might constitute sufficient provocation even for the blackmailer; (3) there would in many cases be a question of degree to be decided by the jury."[114]

However, the Court of Appeal, in the later case of *Johnson*,[115] expressly disapproved the restrictive approach in *Edwards*. The *Edwards* "extreme lengths" justification of self-induced provocation was held to be inconsistent with the words of s.3 of the Homicide Act, which requires that when there is any evidence that the accused was provoked, the issue must be left to the jury. In *Johnson* both the defendant and the victim had been drinking at a nightclub. The defendant made threats of violence to the victim's female friend and to the victim himself. A fight developed, and the defendant, who was carrying a flick knife, stabbed the victim and killed him. On his appeal against a conviction for murder, the defendant asserted that the judge should have instructed the jury on the issue of provocation, albeit self-induced. The Court of Appeal quashed the murder conviction, substituting one of manslaughter. Watkins L.J. stated the guiding principles on self-induced provocation:

"In view of the express wording of section 3, as interpreted in *DPP v Camplin*, which was decided after *Edwards v R* we find it impossible to accept that the mere fact that a defendant caused a reaction in others, which in turn led him to lose his self-control, should result in the issue of provocation being kept outside a jury's consideration. Section 3 clearly provides that the question is whether things done or said or both provoked the defendant to lose his self-control. If there is any evidence that it may have done, the issue must be left to the jury."[116]

Thus in *Johnson*, the Court of Appeal accepted that the accused was not debarred from relying on the defence of provocation even though he had caused the victim to act in a provocative manner. It would, however, be a factor that the jury would take into consideration in deciding whether the provocation was such as to make a reasonable man act in the way that the accused had acted. It would also be taken into account by the trial judge in determining sentence.

3. THE DUAL TEST FOR PROVOCATION

Thus far, we have been considering the issue of what, in effect, counts as provocation. This has **7–025** principally involved looking at the subjective question—trying, as it were, to look through the eyes of the defendant himself or herself—of what it means to be provoked. However, there is a second limb in the test for provocation, the so-called objective question—would a reasonable person have done as the defendant did under the circumstances?

A. The Objective Question

Whenever an objective test is used in criminal law, what is being suggested is that there is a **7–026** benchmark of acceptable behaviour against which the defendant's behaviour can be measured. Thus, in the context of provocation, it is not enough for the defendant, however

---

[114] (1972) 57 Cr.App.R. 157 at 168 per Lord Pearson.
[115] (1989) Cr.App.R. 148.
[116] (1989) Cr.App.R. 148 at 152.

convincingly, to claim that he or she lost self-control. If that were the only part of the test, then defendants with short tempers would be able to benefit from the defence without any reference to the question of whether they *should* have controlled themselves. By requiring the jury to consider whether a reasonable person would have acted as the defendant did, the law sets a level of self-control which *all* are supposed to exercise, however difficult they may find it.

There has been considerable recent development in this aspect of the law on provocation. However, the question which has underpinned this development throughout is superficially quite straightforward. Who is the reasonable person against whom we are measuring the conduct of the defendant?

The story of the modern law can legitimately be begun in different places, but we will begin our consideration with the decision of the House of Lords in *DPP v Camplin*.[117] In that case, the defendant was 15 years old. He killed a man who had both buggered him and then laughed about it. The accused ran the defence of provocation. The major issue was whether the defendant's age was relevant to the objective question—that is to say, should the jury have been required to consider the effect of the provocation on a reasonable person of 15 years? The judge directed the jury to consider the effect of the provocation on a reasonable adult—suggesting that the defendant's age was not relevant to the objective question. The defendant was convicted. He won his appeal, and the Court of Appeal certified a point of law of general public importance, namely "whether on the prosecution for murder of a boy of 15, where the issue of provocation arises, the jury should be directed to consider the question, under s.3 of the Homicide Act 1957, whether the provocation was enough to make a reasonable man do as he did by reference to a "reasonable adult" or by reference to a "reasonable boy". The House of Lords confirmed the decision of the Court of Appeal and the most significant speech was delivered by Lord Diplock, who suggested that a jury should be directed in the following terms:

> "The judge should state what the question is, using the very terms of the section. He should then explain to them that the reasonable man referred to in the question is a person having the power of self-control to be expected of the person of the sex and age of the accused, but in other respects sharing such of the accused's characteristics as they think would affect the gravity of the provocation to him, and that the question is not merely whether such a person in like circumstances would be provoked to lose his self-control, but also would react to the provocation as the accused did."[118]

You can see that Lord Diplock suggests that the reasonable person, against whom we measure the conduct of the defendant, has two relevant dimensions.

Power of self-control

7–027 The first of these dimensions is the power of self-control to be expected of a person of the sex and age of the accused. Thus, in *Camplin* itself, the age of the defendant was relevant because he was particularly young and would thus have found it particularly hard to control himself. Age is, of course, only an issue insofar as it is relevant to the ability of a defendant to exercise self-control. Thus, a defendant of 35 will gain nothing by raising the issue of their age, as by that age, it is appropriate that their conduct be measured against the reasonable adult of no particular age.[119]

---

[117] [1978] A.C. 705.
[118] [1978] A.C. 705, at 718.
[119] See, e.g. *Ali* [1989] Crim.L.R. 736, in which it was stated that a 20-year-old defendant was to be measured against the standard of a reasonable adult.

Such characteristics, which affect the ability of a defendant to exercise self-control, have been referred to as *control characteristics*.[120] We will return to them below.

Sharing such of the accused's characteristics as they think would affect the gravity of the provocation to him

The second dimension of the reasonable person to which Lord Diplock draws attention **7–028** requires the jury to consider whether there is something about the defendant which makes a particular form of provocation especially grave to him or her. Thus, a person who wears glasses may feel particularly aggrieved at being called "four-eyes"; a person with a prosthetic leg may feel particularly resentful at being referred to as "hopalong"; a person with a mental impairment may take great exception to being addressed as a "nutter". What these rather flippant examples seek to illustrate is that the jury are being asked to consider provocation which is, so to speak, *directed at* a particular trait of the defendant, or, to put it another way, to consider a situation in which the trait of the defendant is the *subject-matter* of the provocation. These traits, affecting the gravity of the provocation, and hence, the defendant's response, have been referred to as *response characteristics*.[121]

A useful illustration is *Morhall*.[122] The defendant was addicted to glue-sniffing, and had killed the victim who had taunted him about his inability to kick the habit. Thus, the provocation was directed at a particular trait of the defendant. The question was whether an addiction to glue-sniffing was to be taken into account in addressing the issue of how a reasonable person would have responded to the provocation. Was the addiction a relevant "characteristic [which the jury thought] would affect the gravity of the provocation"? In effect, should the jury be required to ask how a reasonable person addicted to glue-sniffing would have responded to a taunt about being addicted to glue-sniffing?

Not surprisingly, the Court of Appeal struggled with the very idea of a reasonable person addicted to glue-sniffing. Lord Taylor C.J. stated that the addiction could not be relevant because it was a characteristic repugnant to the concept of a reasonable person. He suggested:

> "It is to be noted, and we emphasize, that s.3 refers to 'a reasonable man', not just to a person with the self-control of a reasonable man. Whilst *DPP v Camplin* decided that the 'reasonable man' should be invested with the defendant's characteristics, they surely cannot include characteristics repugnant to the concept of a reasonable man. Quite apart from the incongruity of regarding glue, or drug addiction, or paedophilia, as characteristic of a reasonable man, the problem of getting a jury to understand how possession of any of those characteristics, and being bated [*sic*] about it, would affect the self-control of a reasonable man who *ex hypothesi* would not have such a characteristic, seems to us insuperable."[123]

However, the House of Lords reversed the decision of the Court of Appeal, suggesting that the "reasonable person", in this context, was merely a yardstick against which to measure the conduct of the defendant, taking into account all the relevant circumstances. That is to say, the reasonable person was not necessarily reasonable in the sense that they were absolutely morally upstanding. Lord Goff stated:

[120] See Seago, P., "Criminal Law" [1995] All E.R. Annual Review 149, at p.152.
[121] Seago [1995] All E.R. Annual Review 149.
[122] [1996] 1 A.C. 90.
[123] [1993] 4 All E.R. 888 at 893.

"At all events in the present case, when the judge turned to the second and objective inquiry, he was entitled to direct the jury that they must take into account the entire factual situation (and in particular the fact that the provocation was directed at a habitual glue sniffer taunted with his habit) when considering the question whether the provocation was enough to cause a man possessed of an ordinary man's power of self-control to act as the defendant did."[124]

Thus, it is possible, in the context of this dimension of the reasonable man, to take into account traits which might be morally neutral (consider the defendant with acne taunted about their condition) but also those which might be more morally problematic (see *Morhall* itself).

B.   Control Characteristics: Recent Developments

7–029   We stated earlier that we would return to the issue of control characteristics. It is in this area that the law on provocation has been subject to significant recent change. We have seen, based on Lord Diplock's description of the reasonable person in *Camplin*, that there are two ways in which the characteristics of the defendant may be relevant to the question of how a reasonable person might react to provocation. First, insofar as they may affect his or her self-control, Lord Diplock only mentioned age and sex. Secondly, insofar as they affect the gravity of the provocation (in effect, insofar as they are the subject-matter of the provocation), Lord Diplock did not mention any specific characteristics and, it follows from *Morhall*, that almost any characteristic may be relevant in this context.

The key issue in the recent development of the law on provocation has concerned defendants with mental conditions which impair their self-control. Clearly, where a defendant is taunted *about* a mental condition, the condition may be relevant insofar as it affects the gravity of the provocation (consider the defendant with a mental impairment who is called a "nutter"). However, where the subject-matter of the provocation is entirely unconnected with the defendant's mental condition, can that mental condition be relevant to the issue of the defendant's (reduced) ability to exercise self-control?

The issue came before the House of Lords in the highly significant case of *Smith (Morgan)*.[125] In that case the defendant was charged with the murder of a friend whom he suspected of stealing some of his garden tools. He pleaded "not guilty" on the ground that he was suffering, at the time of the killing, with clinical depression, which had lessened his ability to control himself in the face of provocation. The trial judge instructed the jury that a depressive state was a characteristic to be taken into account when considering the gravity of the provocation, but no account was to be taken of the fact that the depressive illness might have reduced S's powers of self-control. S was convicted but his appeal was allowed by the Court of Appeal, which in turn certified the following point of law of general public importance:

"Are characteristics other than age and sex, attributable to a reasonable man for the purpose of s.3 of the Homicide Act 1957, relevant not only to the gravity of the provocation to him but also to the standard of self-control to be expected."

By a majority of three to two, the House of Lords supported the Court of Appeal. Thus, the jury could take into account, in addition to age and sex, other characteristics of the

---

[124] [1996] 1 A.C. 90 at 98.
[125] [2001] 1 A.C. 146.

defendant which affect powers of self-control, whether or not they are also relevant to the gravity of the provocation. In *Smith,* the distinction between acts which increase the gravity of the provocation and acts which explain the defendant's loss of self-control was rejected as being far too complex for the jury to understand. Lord Hoffmann, suggested that it would be to trespass on the jury's role to tell them to ignore any factor or characteristic as it is the right of the jury to act upon its own opinion of whether the objective element of provocation has been satisfied.

The majority stressed in *Smith* that the issues in s.3 of the Homicide Act 1957 were **7–030** principally for the jury and the trial judge had overstepped the mark in telling them they were not entitled to take account of the defendant's depression in deciding why he lost his self-control. The trial judge can always provide guidance, just so long as the role of the jury is not usurped. The trial judge must not instruct the jury that they cannot use this or that characteristic. Lord Steyn asserted that the vital question for the jury is whether the defendant had exercised the degree of self-control to be expected of someone in his situation.

Their Lordships were of the view that the jury might not necessarily find that directions in terms of the reasonable man were always helpful, nor is it necessary to use the exact wording of the statute. Lord Hoffmann said that it was not the principle in the second part of the test which has become unworkable, but a particular way of explaining it. He continued:

> "In my opinion, therefore judges should not be required to describe the objective element in the provocation defence by reference to a reasonable man, with or without attribution of personal characteristics. They may instead find it more helpful to explain in simple language the principles of the doctrine of provocation. First it requires that the accused should have killed while he had lost self-control and that something should have caused him to lose self-control. Secondly, the fact that something caused him to lose self-control is not enough. The law expects people to exercise control over their tantrums. A tendency to violent rages or childish tantrums is a defect in character rather than an excuse. The jury must think the circumstances were such as to make the loss of self-control sufficiently excusable to reduce the gravity of the defence from murder to manslaughter. This is entirely a matter for the jury. In deciding what should count as a sufficient excuse they have to apply what should count as a sufficient excuse they have to apply what they consider to be appropriate standards of behaviour, on the one hand making allowance for human nature and the power of the emotions but, on the other hand, not allowing someone to rely on his own violent disposition."[126]

Smith was received with scepticism in a previous edition of this book. We were not convinced that it would add clarity to the law. The decision has also been the subject of widespread academic criticism. However, it was followed by the Court of Appeal in *Rowland*,[127] where the defendant's mental impairment was relevant to the question of the degree of self-control which would be exercised by the reasonable person in the defendant's position. More controversially, in *Weller*[128] it was accepted by the Court of Appeal that a consequence of *Smith* was that a defendant's jealousy and possessiveness could be relevant.

Although the decision in *Smith* was the subject of considerable hostility, on one view it **7–031** was quite in keeping with the trajectory of the developing law in the 1990s. You will recall from our earlier discussion of the need for a sudden and temporary loss of self-control (part

---

[126] [2000] 4 All E.R. 289 at 312.
[127] [2003] EWCA Crim 3636.
[128] [2003] EWCA Crim 815; [2004] 1 Cr.App.R. 1.

of the subjective question) that the law had proved problematic for battered women who wished to frame their experiences in terms of the defence of provocation. We noted how the "slow burn" reaction, more typical of a female than a male response to provocation, did not rule out the possibility of the defence as a matter of law, but might make it harder to establish. The objective question in provocation has also been a site for debate as to how battered women ought to be treated by the law.

In *Thornton (No.2)*[129] the Court of Appeal had suggested that on the objective question, the fact that a defendant suffered from the clinically diagnosable condition "battered woman's syndrome" could be relevant on the issue of the level of self-control. Thus, applying Lord Diplock's requirements from *Camplin*, a defendant with battered woman's syndrome who was provoked as a result of abuse during a relationship would have their conduct measured against the reasonable (1) woman (2) who suffered from battered women's syndrome. A similar result was reached in *Humphreys*[130] where the defendant's attention-seeking and immaturity were held to be relevant; and in *Dryden*,[131] where the defendant's obsessional relationship with his property was held to be relevant. Viewed in this light, not only was *Smith* the logical application of principles developed by the Court of Appeal, but had it been decided the other way, with the effect that mental characteristics impairing self-control were not relevant, the liberalisation of the law in favour of battered women would have been undone.

Nonetheless, the line of authority in the Court of Appeal had not stood unchallenged. In *Luc Thiet Thuan*,[132] a majority of the Privy Council, sitting as a five-judge court, held that mental characteristics might be relevant on the issue of the gravity of the provocation, but not on the issue of self-control. In that case, the defendant introduced evidence of organic brain damage, which, it was claimed, made it difficult for him to resist impulses. For the majority, Lord Goff drew on the work of Professor Ashworth, who had observed:

> "The proper distinction . . . is that individual peculiarities which bear on the gravity of the provocation should be taken into account, whereas individual peculiarities bearing on the accused's level of self-control should not."[133]

This was neatly expressed by Professor Smith in his commentary to *Morhall*: "It is suggested that increased provocativeness is relevant, increased provocability is not."[134]

7–032   Lord Steyn dissented in *Luc Thiet Thuan*. In his view the logic of the majority led to a conclusion that in addressing the first and subjective question, the jury should be directed to look at the evidence of mental infirmity. However, they must be told to disregard it when they come to the second and objective question. This they will find puzzling. Youthfulness is relevant because of the lesser degree of self-control associated with it. Why should there not, therefore, be a different standard for the immature 21-year-old, or indeed a mentally impaired 21-year-old? There is nothing in the speeches in *Camplin* to suggest that relevant control characteristics are limited to age and sex[135]; if they were the House could have said so. Nor was Lord Steyn impressed with the argument that allowing the jury to take into account the mental infirmity of the defendant in answering the objective question would lead

---

[129] [1996] 2 Cr.App.R. 108.
[130] [1995] 4 All E.R. 1008.
[131] [1995] 4 All E.R. 987.
[132] [1996] 2 All E.R. 1033.
[133] A. Ashworth, "The Doctrine of Provocation" (1976) 35 C.L.J. 292 at 299.
[134] J.C. Smith, "Case Comment" [1995] Crim.L.R. 892.
[135] But see the actual wording of the relevant passage in *Camplin* [1978] A.C. 705, above, para.7–026 with authors' emphasis added.

to too great an overlap between provocation and diminished responsibility. Diminished responsibility is limited to an abnormality of mind which substantially impairs the defendant's mental responsibility for his acts. It does not cover the whole field of significant mental attributes which might be relevant to provocation.

If the contribution of the Privy Council to the law on provocation pre-*Smith* was interesting, its contribution post-*Smith* has been extraordinary. In *Attorney-General for Jersey v Holley*[136] the Privy Council was called on to interpret a Jersey statute which was identical in substance to s.3 of the Homicide Act 1957. The defendant in that case had killed his girlfriend after an argument. There was evidence that he had a number of personality traits: he suffered from depression; from strong feelings of worthlessness; he had an avoidant personality; he suffered from anxiety, and from alcoholism. At trial, the judge pointed out these characteristics, and went on to note that the fact that a person was drunk at the time of a killing, and hence more susceptible to provocation than he would be when sober, was not relevant. The Court of Appeal of Jersey held that a distinction should have been drawn between being drunk, which was not relevant to the question of provocation, and suffering from alcoholism, which was to be taken into account. That is to say, the characteristic of alcoholism was, in the view of the Court of Appeal of Jersey, a relevant characteristic on the issue of the level of self-control which could be reasonably expected of the defendant.

The Privy Council accepted that the approach of the Court of Appeal of Jersey was an entirely proper application of the decision of the House of Lords in *Smith*. However, by a majority of six to three, they held that the decision itself in *Smith* was wrong. Lord Nicholls, for the majority, suggested:

> "[H]owever much the contrary is asserted, the majority view [in *Smith*] does represent a departure from the law as declared in section 3 of the Homicide Act 1957. It involves a significant relaxation of the *uniform, objective standard adopted by Parliament* [emphasis added]. Under the statute the sufficiency of the provocation ('whether the provocation was enough to make a reasonable man do as [the defendant] did') is to be judged by one standard, not a standard which varies from defendant to defendant. Whether the provocative act or words and the defendant's response met the 'ordinary person' standard prescribed by the statute is the question the jury must consider, not the altogether looser question of whether, having regard to all the circumstances, the jury consider the loss of self-control was sufficiently excusable. The statute does not leave each jury free to set whatever standard they consider appropriate in the circumstances by which to judge whether the defendant's conduct is 'excusable'".[137]

Thus, for the Privy Council, while the defendant's alcoholism may have been relevant had the provocation been directed at it—in the manner of *Morhall*—it was not to be taken into account as a control characteristic. The Privy Council endorsed their own earlier decision in *Luc* and disavowed the decision in *Smith*.

What then of the basic position that a decision of the Privy Council is persuasive, and that **7–033** a decision of the House of Lords must take precedence? *Holley* in fact represents a consciously taken judicial decision to subvert the authority of *Smith*. While *Luc* was always likely to lose out, so to speak, when being considered in comparison with the line of Court of Appeal decisions including *Thornton (No.2)* and *Humphreys*, which allowed for the taking into account, on the issue of self-control, of characteristics other than the age and sex of the

[136] [2005] UKPC 23; [2005] 2 A.C. 580.
[137] [2005] UKPC 23 at [22].

defendant, it needs to be recalled that it was a decision of a slender majority, in which the two senior judges, Lord Goff and Lord Steyn, found themselves on opposing sides. *Holley* on the other hand involved a court of nine judges—all of them from the House of Lords—convened for the express purpose of clarifying the law.

The status of *Holley* is a matter of some controversy. It might be taken to pose something of a quandary for the Court of Appeal hearing a "control characteristic" case. Does the Court of Appeal follow *Holley*, or does it follow *Smith*; the assumption being that if the latter course were taken, leave to appeal would be granted and the House of Lords would subsequently be highly likely to depart from the decision in *Smith*? The Court of Appeal has in fact short-circuited the doctrine of precedent by already following the decision in *Holley*. In *Mohammed (Faqir)*[138] and *James and Karimi*[139] the Court of Appeal expressly preferred the approach in *Holley*. The constitutional propriety of this approach must be doubted, however laudable the result. For the Privy Council to be taken to have overruled a decision of the House of Lords—even where the Privy Council is of a particularly powerful and persuasive composition—is a notion which has ramifications way beyond the law on provocation. It is likely that this issue will be live for some time to come.

There are two principal arguments surrounding the correctness or otherwise of the decisions in *Smith* and *Holley*. One is to do with the extent to which, by allowing the characteristics of the defendant to be relevant to the objective question in provocation, one actually ceases any longer to have a truly objective test. The more characteristics are allowed, the more like a replica of the defendant the reasonable person appears. The implication of *Holley* is that the relevance of the defendant's characteristics other than age or sex to the question of how the reasonable person would respond to provocation constitutes an unwarranted dilution of the objective standard which the law should be setting.

7–034   The second argument concerns the relationship between the defences of provocation and diminished responsibility (see para.5–015 above). A criticism levelled at the majority position in *Smith* was that it blurred the distinction between the two defences. The essence of the criticism was that defendants with mental impairments should seek to avail themselves of the defence of diminished responsibility. However, there are two notable reasons why provocation might appear more attractive as a defence. The first is practical. Section 2 of the Homicide Act requires a defendant to prove diminished responsibility on the balance of probabilities; while provocation must be disproved by the prosecution if it is a live issue. The second reason is to do with labelling. By running a defence of diminished responsibility, the defendant invites the court to apply an essentially psychiatric label to them and their behaviour—they did it because they were mad. Defendants may be uncomfortable with the stigma associated with such a label. This is an issue which is, once again, significant to the context of battered women. In *Ahluwalia*,[140] the appeal succeeded on the grounds of diminished responsibility. It should of course be noted that defendants running provocation in similar situations risked being required to accept some level of psychiatric labelling. If the defendant wanted to have the objective question tailored to their situation, then it had to be on the basis that they were labouring under a "syndrome" which affected their mental make-up. It has been suggested that defendants who have suffered long-term abuse and consequently kill their abuser are in fact responding to their predicament in a rational manner with a view to defending themselves. As a consequence, some commentators take

---

[138] [2005] EWCA Crim 1880.
[139] [2006] EWCA Crim 14; [2006] 1 All E.R. 759.
[140] [1992] 4 All E.R. 889.

the view that the most appropriate defence for battered women who kill is neither diminished responsibility nor provocation, but a form of self-defence.[141]

The position taken in *Holley* attempts to draw a line between provocation and diminished responsibility, although it should be noted that not everybody views an overlap between the defences as problematic.[142] It also leaves open a situation where a defendant is not *sufficiently* mentally impaired to benefit from the defence of diminished responsibility, but can also not make use of provocation because, on the issue of self-control, no characteristics other than age or sex are relevant.

A final note of caution on *Holley* might be sounded. The case seeks to draw a clear distinction between characteristics of the defendant which are relevant to the degree of self-control exercised by the reasonable person (age and sex only are relevant); and characteristics which affect the gravity of the provocation to the defendant (any characteristics might be relevant). It may be difficult for a jury to understand the difference: in a case where a drunken defendant was taunted about his alcoholism, the jury would be instructed to ignore his intoxicated state. However, they would be expected to take into account his alcoholism insofar as it affected the gravity of the provocation to him but not insofar as it might have affected his ability to control himself. The yardstick against which the jury would be expected to measure the conduct of the defendant would be the "reasonable (sober, non-alcoholic) person being taunted about their alcoholism"! Also, there may be situations where it is not clear whether a particular characteristic is being invoked on the self-control issue or on the issue of the gravity of the provocation. Consider a defendant with a pathological sensitivity to noise, who is provoked by the sound of loud shouting. Is such a defendant saying "My self-control is lowered by my sensitivity to noise" (in which case a court would be required to ignore it) or "Noise affects me in an especially grave manner because of my sensitivity" (in which case it could be taken into account)?

4. REFORM

Clearly, the law of provocation is a matter of considerable controversy, and it should come **7–035** as no surprise that it has been the subject of proposals for reform in recent years. In 2004, the Law Commission published their Report, *Partial Defences to Murder*.[143] This sought to reappraise the defences of provocation and diminished responsibility (and also the application to murder of the general defence of self-defence). In respect of provocation, the Law Commission broadly kept to the proposals in the 2004 Report when they published their further Report, *Murder, Manslaughter and Infanticide*.[144] They recommended that provocation be reformed as follows:

> "(1) Unlawful homicide that would otherwise be first degree murder should instead be second degree murder if:
>
> > (a) the defendant acted in response to:
> >
> > > (i)   gross provocation (meaning words or conduct or a combination of words and conduct) which caused the defendant to have a justifiable sense of being seriously wronged; or

---

[141] See, e.g. Edwards, S.S.M., "Abolishing provocation and reframing self defence—the Law Commission's options for reform" [2004] Crim.L.R. 181–197.

[142] Mackay, R.D. and Mitchell, B.J., "Provoking diminished responsibility: two pleas merging into one?" [2003] Crim.L.R. 745–759.

[143] *Partial Defences to Murder: Final Report* (Law Commission Report No.290, 2004).

[144] Law Com. No.304 (2006).

       (ii)   fear of serious violence towards the defendant or another; or

       (iii)   a combination of both (i) and (ii); and

   (b) a person of the defendant's age and of ordinary temperament, i.e., ordinary tolerance and self-restraint, in the circumstances of the defendant might have reacted in the same or in a similar way.

(2) In deciding whether a person of the defendant's age and of ordinary temperament, i.e. ordinary tolerance and self-restraint, in the circumstances of the defendant, might have reacted in the same or in a similar way, the court should take into account the defendant's age and all the circumstances of the defendant other than matters whose only relevance to the defendant's conduct is that they bear simply on his or her general capacity for self-control.

(3) The partial defence should not apply where:

   (a) the provocation was incited by the defendant for the purpose of providing an excuse to use violence; or

   (b) the defendant acted in considered desire for revenge.

(4) A person should not be treated as having acted in considered desire for revenge if he or she acted in fear of serious violence, merely because he or she was also angry towards the deceased for the conduct which engendered that fear.

(5) A judge should not be required to leave the defence to the jury unless there is evidence on which a reasonable jury, properly directed, could conclude that it might apply."

It can be seen from the second principle suggested by the Law Commission that it prefers the approach in *Holley* to that in *Smith*. At the time of writing, the Government has taken the view that dealing with the defences takes priority over the Commission's more fundamental proposals for restructuring homicide offences, and so the role for provocation which is countenanced in the Coroners and Justice Bill currently before Parliament is as a defence which will, as is the case at present, reduce murder to manslaughter.[145] The Bill proposes the abolition of the common law defence of provocation and its replacement with a statutory partial defence to murder of "loss of control". In the definition of the defence, the Bill broadly uses the scheme set out in the Commission's work, with the additional point that sexual infidelity cannot be a so-called "qualifying trigger" for the defence of loss of control.

It should be noted that if the Commission's full homicide proposals become law, a "provocation" defence[146] will no longer be available to a person who kills, having intended to cause serious bodily harm, because such a killing will itself be second degree murder to which the "provocation" defence would not be available.

---

[145] Cls 44—46. For policy discussion leading to the Bill, see Ministry of Justice, *Murder, manslaughter and infanticide: proposals for reform of the law* (Consultation Paper CP19/08) (July 2008); and Ministry of Justice, *Murder, manslaughter and infanticide: proposals for reform of the law—Summary of responses and Government position* (January 2009).
[146] The Coroners and Justice Bill labels the defence "loss of control".

PROVOCATION: GENERAL READING

Allen, M., "Provocation's Reasonable Man: A Plea For Self-Control" (2000) 64 J.C.L. 216. **7–036**

Chalmers, J., "Merging Provocation Dimished Responsibility: Some Reason for Scepticism" [2004] Crim.L.R. 198.

Dressler, J., "Rethinking Heat Of Passion: A Defence In Search Of A Rationale" (1982) 73 J. Crim. L. & Criminology 421.

Edwards, S., "Descent Into Murder: Provocation's Stricture—The Prognosis For Women Who Kill Men Who Abuse Them" (2007) 71 J.C.L. 342.

Elliott, C., "What Future for Voluntary Manslaughter" (2004) 68 J.C.L. 253.

Gardner, J. and Macklem, T., "Compassion Without Respect? Nine Fallacies In *R v Smith*" [2001] Crim.L.R. 623.

Herring, J., "Provocation And Ethnicity" [1996] Crim.L.R. 490.

Holton, R. and Shute, S., "Self-Control in the Modern Provocation Defence" (2007) 27 Oxford Journal of Legal Studies 49.

Horder, J., *Provocation And Responsibility* (Clarendon, 1991).

McColgan, A., "In Defence Of Battered Women Who Kill" (1993) 13 O.J.L.S. 508.

Mackay, R.D., and Mitchell, B.J., "Replacing Provocation: More on a Combined Plea" [2004] Crim.L.R. 219.

Mackay, R.D., and Mitchell, B.J., "But is this Provocation? Some Thoughts on the Law Commission's Report on Partial Defences to Murder" [2005] Crim.L.R. 85.

Macklem, T., "Provocation And The Ordinary Person" (1987) 11 Dalhousie L.J. 126.

Mitchell, B.J., Mackay, R.D. and Brookbanks, W.J., "Pleading for Provoked Killers: In Defence of *Morgan Smith*" (2008) 124 L.Q.R. 675.

Nicholson, D. and Sanghvi, R., "Battered Women And Provocation: The Implications Of *R v Ahluwalia*" [1993] Crim.L.R. 728.

Oliver, S., "Provocation—Pushing The Reasonable Man Too Far?" (2000) 64 J.C.L. 409.

Simone, C.J., "Killer(er) Man Was A Battered Wife": The Application Of Battered Women Syndrome To Homosexual Defendants (1997) 19 Sydney L.R. 230.

Wasik, M., "Cumulative Provocation And Domestic Killing" [1982] Crim.L.R. 29.

Wells, C., "Battered Woman Syndrome And Defences To Homicide: Where Now?" (1994) 14 Legal Studies 266.

Yeo, S., "Sex, Ethnicity, Power Of Self-Control And Provocation Revisited" (1996) 18 Sydney L.R. 304.

Involuntary Manslaughter

Involuntary manslaughter is the name given to those unlawful homicides where the **7–037** defendant brings about the actus reus of murder but without the necessary mens rea. Thus, a defendant who consciously undertook an unjustified risk of killing another would fall outside the definition of murder.[147] It is clear, however, that such a killing should amount at least to manslaughter, but the problem for the courts has been to formulate the requirements for involuntary manslaughter. Traditionally, involuntary manslaughter has tended to fall into two categories. The first can be described as constructive or unlawful act manslaughter. This

---

[147] See above, para.7–007.

category is based upon the defendant deliberately committing an unlawful and dangerous act; dangerous in the sense that it is likely to cause some injury to another person. Although its present formulation has many shortcomings and opponents,[148] in that it is akin to the much disliked felony murder rule, it is firmly established as a category of involuntary manslaughter and could only be removed by legislation.[149] The second category is much harder to pin down. It covers unlawful homicides which result from activities which are prima facie legal but which are done with such a degree of negligence that the court holds that the defendant should receive punishment for his behaviour. To take a simple example, the running of a fun-fair is not, in itself, a criminal activity. If, however, the owners of the fair fail to maintain the equipment to an appropriate standard they could be sued for negligence in tort for any resulting injuries suffered, including death.[150] In criminal law, however, there are no offences covering the negligent infliction of harm; offences against the person generally require intention or recklessness.[151] However, it has been generally accepted that if the negligent conduct results in death and a jury finds that the negligence is of a very high degree such as to merit punishment, they can return a verdict of manslaughter. This is illogical; whether the result is very serious bodily injury or death may be totally fortuitous. If the victim suffers serious injuries as a result of the fun-fair owner's negligence, there may well be no criminal offence. If, however, the victim dies the owners may be jailed for manslaughter. However illogical it may be, the fact of death is seen as highly important by the average person in the street[152] and hence this residual category of involuntary manslaughter to deal with such deaths.

In the remaining part of this section we shall look at these two categories of involuntary manslaughter and ask whether there are any further categories.

1. UNLAWFUL ACT MANSLAUGHTER

7–038   Until 1957,[153] the felony murder rule provided that any killing caused by the defendant in the commission by him of a violent felony was automatically murder. The mens rea required was the mens rea of the felony he was committing. Thus, in *DPP v Beard*,[154] B suffocated a girl during the course of raping her. Under the rule B was guilty of murder so long as the prosecution could prove that he had the necessary mens rea for rape and that the death occurred during the course of the rape.[155] Alongside this rule there existed a similar one for killings brought about by the commission of lesser offences. This rule is variously known as constructive manslaughter, unlawful act manslaughter or, in some of the jurisdictions where the distinction between felonies and misdemeanours still exists, misdemeanour manslaughter.

During the last century a defendant could be convicted of unlawful act manslaughter if he was proved to have caused the death of another while engaged upon any wrongdoing, and this included wrongdoings that were merely tortious and not criminal.[156] However, this rule

---

[148] See, for example Law Com. Report No.177 and Law Com. Report No.237.
[149] This form of manslaughter is clearly acknowledged by the House of Lords in *Att-Gen's Reference (No.3 of 1994)* [1996] 2 W.L.R. 412; [1997] 3 All E.R. 936; considered above, para.2–081, and below, para.7–047.
[150] See, for example, the statements in *Behrens v Bertram Mills Circus Ltd* [1957] 2 Q.B. 1 on civil liability.
[151] See above, para.2–065.
[152] See the findings of the North Report on road traffic offences; Department of Transport, Home Office, Road Traffic Law Review Report, (HMSO, 1988).
[153] Homicide Act 1957 s.1.
[154] [1920] A.C. 479, see above, para.5–028.
[155] The felony murder rule is still operational in some states in the USA; see, for example, Pennsylvania and Indiana.
[156] See, for example, *Fenton* (1830) 1 Lew C.C. 179.

has been severely restricted in subsequent decisions. It is now clear beyond any argument that the unlawful act must at least constitute a crime.[157] In *Larkin*[158] the Court of Criminal Appeal held that the unlawful act must also be a dangerous act.[159] Thus the prosecution must prove that the death was brought about by the performance by the accused of an unlawful and dangerous act and that he intended to commit the unlawful act. Most recently in *Kennedy (No.2)*[160] it was asserted by Lord Bingham, delivering a unanimous judgment on the part of the House of Lords, that the offence of unlawful act manslaughter invoked the following elements: (a) that the defendant committed an unlawful act; (b) that such unlawful act was a crime; and (c) that the defendant's unlawful act was a significant cause of the death of the deceased.[161]

A. The Act must be Unlawful in Itself

It is important to distinguish between an act which is unlawful in itself and an act which is **7–039** prima facie lawful, but may become unlawful because of the negligent way it is performed. Only an act which is unlawful in itself may form the basis for unlawful act manslaughter.

An assault is an example of an act which is unlawful in itself so long as the prosecution can establish that there was no justification for the application of force.[162] On the other hand, driving a car or the performance of medical surgery are prima facie lawful acts which, if performed with a sufficiently high degree of negligence, may become unlawful.[163] Thus consider, for example, the case of D who is driving at 10mph in excess of the speed limit for that stretch of road when he knocks down and kills a child. It might be tempting to say that he knew that he was exceeding the speed limit and that is an unlawful act which has caused the child's death. It might be that he could be charged with the criminal offence of careless driving[164] which requires proof of a low level of negligence, equivalent to negligence in civil law. It is quite clear that this is an unlawful piece of driving. Nonetheless according to Lord Atkin in *Andrews v DPP*[165] it is not to be treated as an unlawful act for the purposes of unlawful act manslaughter:

> "There is an obvious difference in the law of manslaughter between doing an unlawful act and doing a lawful act with a degree of carelessness which the legislature makes criminal. If it were otherwise a man who killed another while driving without due care and attention would *ex necessitate* commit manslaughter."

This passage is poorly drafted; it is clear that an act done with a degree of carelessness the law makes criminal is an unlawful act. However, it is submitted that the distinction Lord Atkin was seeking to make and the reason for the distinction is clear enough. Where it is sought to base manslaughter upon negligence, then the appropriate charge is one of gross

---

[157] *Franklin* (1883) 15 Cox C.C. 163.
[158] [1943] K.B. 174.
[159] "Where the act which a person is engaged in performing is unlawful, then if at the same time it is a dangerous act, that is, an act which is likely to injure another person, and quite inadvertently the doer of the act causes the death of that other person by that act, then he is guilty of manslaughter." Per Humphreys J. (1943) 29 Cr.App.R. 18 at 23.
[160] See below, para.7–047.
[161] [2007] UKHL 38; [2007] 4 All E.R. 1083.
[162] [2007] UKHL 38; [2007] 4 All E.R. 1083 at 1087.
[163] See, *Andrews v DPP* [1937] A.C. 576 HL.
[164] Contrary to the Road Traffic Act 1988 s.3 (as amended by Road Traffic Act 1991 s.2).
[165] [1937] A.C. 576 at 585.

negligence manslaughter which, of course, requires a very high degree of negligence. Take, for example, Lord Atkin's example of a death caused by careless driving. Driving is a lawful activity but if performed with a degree of negligence required for the tort of negligence, the driver commits the offence of careless driving. If because of his careless driving the defendant kills a pedestrian it might be tempting to say that he has committed unlawful act manslaughter. However, despite the unlawful act, what you are really faced with is an allegation of killing by negligence and the House of Lords holds that killing by negligence is only manslaughter if the level of negligence is very high or gross. The prosecution should, therefore, prove gross negligence or fail. This is made even clearer if you consider the case of a surgeon who has killed a patient through negligence. At the point at which he kills the patient through negligence sufficient to found a civil action for damages, there is no criminal charge which could be brought; there is no criminal offence of negligently causing death unless the negligence is gross. His act is, therefore, not criminal unless the negligence is gross.

7–040   It is suggested that the same is true even if the motorist intentionally commits a moving traffic offence such as speeding, or driving with defective brakes or steering. This is yet another way of alleging that the lawful activity of driving a car has become negligent and it is submitted that the death of a pedestrian caused by a speeding motorist should only be treated as manslaughter if the prosecution can establish gross negligence. On the other hand if the motorist deliberately drives his car at a pedestrian to give the pedestrian a scare and accidentally hits the pedestrian causing his death, he has committed an unlawful act, namely an assault, and this is properly charged as unlawful act manslaughter.

In practice the majority of prosecutions for unlawful act manslaughter are based upon some form of assault. Thus, in *Lamb*,[166] two young boys were playing about with a revolver. Lamb knew that there were two bullets in the chambers, but he believed that the chambers revolved after the shot had been fired and since neither bullet was opposite the firing pin, he believed it would be safe to pull the trigger since the gun would not fire. For a joke he aimed the gun at his friend, who also saw the whole thing as a joke, and pulled the trigger. This brought one of the bullets to a position opposite the firing pin and the bullet was fired killing his friend. He was convicted of manslaughter.[167] In so far as the charge was based upon an unlawful act, it was clear to the Court of Appeal that the only possible unlawful act was an assault.[168] However, the Court of Appeal held that there was no evidence of an assault of any kind. Lamb did not intend to put his friend in fear of any immediate application of unlawful force, nor was he reckless in this regard. Furthermore his friend did not in fact anticipate any threat since he thought the whole thing was a joke. There being no assault, nor any other possible unlawful act, the prosecution could not establish unlawful act manslaughter.[169]

It is generally said that the prosecution must prove that the accused intended to do the unlawful act, but the meaning of this requirement is not altogether clear. Certain passages in *DPP v Newbury*[170] and *Attorney-General's Reference (No.3 of 1994)*[171] suggest that the prosecution simply have to prove that the accused deliberately did the act which constituted the unlawful act and that it is not necessary to prove that he did the act with the mens rea necessary to constitute the criminal offence. In other words, it is enough to prove that the

---

[166] [1967] 2 Q.B. 981.
[167] See below, para.7–048 for a discussion of gross negligence manslaughter.
[168] For assaults see below, paras 7–062—7–068.
[169] Could he be convicted of gross negligence manslaughter? See below, para.7–048.
[170] [1977] A.C. 500 at 509.
[171] [1997] 3 All E.R. 936 at 944–946.

accused voluntarily did the act which in law constitutes an unlawful act. It is suggested that this cannot be right. The defendant in *Lamb* clearly intended to point the gun at the defendant and to pull the trigger; this was a voluntary act on his part. It could not, however, constitute an unlawful act unless he intended to cause his friend to apprehend the immediate application of unlawful violence.[172] Perhaps the answer is that the accused must be proved to have deliberately thrown a punch and that he has the necessary mens rea for battery, namely an intent to apply unlawful force or consciously take an unjustified risk of applying unlawful force.[173]

It is not always easy to identify the unlawful act upon which the court has based its finding **7–041** of unlawful act manslaughter. In *DPP v Newbury*[174] the defendant was charged with manslaughter on the basis that he had killed a guard on a railway train by dropping paving slabs from a bridge across a railway on to a passing train. It has been generally assumed that the unlawful act was criminal damage to property, but the matter is not discussed by the Law Lords who were mainly concerned with another issue.[175] It is simply assumed that there was an unlawful act.[176]

This assumption also applied in *Andrews*[177] in the context of a strict liability offence, not requiring mens rea proper. D gave V, with her full consent, an injection of insulin in order to give her a "rush" or "pick me up". V had drunk large quantities of cider prior to the insulin injection, and continued drinking post the injection. She died as a result of the injection of insulin. D appealed against conviction on the premise that the trial judge was wrong to rule that he would direct the jury that V's consent to the injection did not render D's act lawful. There was a further argument, not raised in the case, that no "base" unlawful act requiring mens rea was effected to trigger the involuntary manslaughter offence.[178] D's conviction was upheld as the injection of insulin, albeit consensual, was an unlawful act contrary to ss.58(2)(b) and 67 of the Medicines Act 1968. The fact that the "unlawful" act was one of strict liability was not reviewed or challenged by the court. The ambit of the Medicines Act 1968, and the variety of strict liability offences contained therein, was to constrain the distribution and use of prescription only medicines in question.

In the recent case of *Carey*[179] the Court of Appeal determined that affray, a public order offence,[180] could form the unlawful act for the charge of manslaughter. An affray requires a

---

[172] See also *Scarlett* [1993] 4 All E.R. 629; [1994] 98 Cr.App.R. 290. In *Att-Gen's Reference (No.3 of 1994)* where Lord Hope suggests that all that is required is an intention to do the act, he says that the act acquires its unlawful nature by the fact of the accused foreseeing that it will cause harm. Since, however, he also states, at p.957, that foresight by the accused of harm is not an essential part of the offence, this would appear to be somewhat inconsistent.

[173] A further possibility would be that the prosecution must prove that the accused intended to do the prohibited act; thus in *Lamb*, where the basis of the unlawful act would have been a technical assault, the prosecution would have to prove that the accused intended to make his friend apprehend the immediate application of unlawful violence; recklessness which generally suffices for an assault would not be sufficient as the basis for unlawful act manslaughter. It is suggested, however, that this is equally wrong and that on the facts of *Lamb*, the prosecutor would have to prove that Lamb deliberately pulled the trigger, which he did, and that at the time he either intended to cause his friend to apprehend the immediate application of unlawful violence or consciously took an unjustified risk of so doing, which he did not.

[174] [1977] A.C. 500.

[175] Whether it had to be proved that the defendant had foreseen the possibility of causing injury to another; see below, para.7–046.

[176] It is possible that the unlawful act was an assault or the offence of "endangering the safety of any person conveyed upon a railway" contrary to the Offences Against the Person Act 1861 s.34. The prosecution should today specify the unlawful act; see *Jennings* [1990] Crim.L.R. 588.

[177] [2002] EWCA Crim 3021.

[178] If similar facts reoccur then in light of recent developments a charge under s.23 of the Offences Against the Person Act 1861 seems logical; see discussion below of the unlawful act in drug administration.

[179] [2006] EWCA Crim 17; [2006] Crim.L.R. 842.

[180] See Public Order Act 1986 s.3(1).

person to use or threaten another in such a way as to cause a person of reasonable firmness present at the scene to fear for his personal safety.

The Unlawful Act In Drug Administration

7–042   In *Cato*,[181] the accused injected the victim with heroin at the victim's request and the victim died. Cato was charged with unlawfully and maliciously administering a noxious substance contrary to s.23 of the Offences Against the Person Act 1861 and with manslaughter. There is no problem with a conviction for unlawful act manslaughter based upon s.23. However, the court added that had it not been possible to rely upon s.23, the manslaughter charge could still have been upheld on the basis of another unlawful act. Lord Widgery C.J. said:

> "we think that the unlawful act would be described as injecting the deceased Farmer with a mixture of heroin and water which at the time of the injection and for the purposes of the injection the accused had unlawfully taken into his possession."[182]

This is not without difficulties. There is no offence under the Misuse of Drugs Act 1971 of administering a controlled drug. The Court of Appeal appears to be relying on the offence of possessing a controlled substance but since, as we shall see below,[183] the unlawful act must be such as would be likely to cause some harm to another, it is hard to see how merely possessing the drug could have such an effect. The victim, after all, did not die through Cato's possession of the drug. To the extent that the case suggests that conduct not actually forming the actus reus of any offence can constitute the unlawful act it is irreconcilable with existing authorities and should not be followed. It was explicitly rejected by the House of Lords in *Kennedy (No.2)*.[184] Prior to this reaffirmation of orthodox principles our courts in this arena seemed more concerned with the moral fault attached to drug administration than with strict legal principles. Another illustration of problematic reasoning being applied is the case of *Kennedy (No.1)*.[185] D prepared for V a syringe containing heroin and water. V knew the contents and injected herself—in this respect there was a material difference from the factual scenario in *Cato*. The outcome of the injection was identical in that V died. The Court of Appeal, upholding D's conviction for manslaughter did so on the basis either that D was guilty of the s.23 offence or that the self-injection of heroin by V was unlawful and D had assisted and wilfully encouraged this conduct. This seems bizarre in as much as the appellate court should have asserted that the voluntary act of V was a novus actus interveniens, breaking the chain of causation, as she was fully aware of what she was injecting into herself.[186] Thus, D did not cause V's death.

Problems in this area were subsequently highlighted in *Dias*[187] where, on similar facts to *Kennedy (No.1)*, it was asserted no offence exists of self-injection. Thus, V is not a principal to self-manslaughter and D does not become liable as a secondary party through assistance and encouragement.[188] When the Criminal Cases Review Commission referred the case of

---

[181] [1976] 1 All E.R. 260.
[182] [1976] 1 All E.R. 260 at 267.
[183] See also Smith and Hogan, *loc. cit.*, at p.342.
[184] [2007] UKHL 38; [2007] 4 All E.R. 1083.
[185] [1999] Crim.L.R. 65.
[186] See above, paras 2–043—2–045 on causation.
[187] [2001] EWCA Crim 2986; (2001) 165 JP 1010; see above at para.2–044.
[188] See, also, *Rogers* [2003] 2 Cr.App.R. 10; [2003] EWCA Crim 945; see above at para.2–044. D in that case applied a tourniquet to V's arm—V then injected himself. It was held that D had actively participated in the injection process. It was viewed that he had caused in part an injection which in turn led to death.

Kennedy (No.1) back to the Court of Appeal it was accepted that an error had occurred in predicating liability of a drug supplier on accessory principles.[189] However, the conviction was upheld through adoption of a novel doctrine on participatory engagement. In preparing a syringe of heroin and handing it to V for injection the parties ought to be viewed as engaged in the one activity of administering the heroin. They are "acting together in concert" to effect the unlawful act contrary to s.23 of the Offences Against the Person Act 1861. There is a "joint engagement" in the administration of the substance.

Subsequently, of course, the House of Lords in *Kennedy (No.2)*[190] has recently declared **7–043** that the Court of Appeal had fallen into error imposing liability for unlawful act manslaughter in such a scenario. D commits an unlawful act in supplying the heroin, but this in itself is not "harmful" to V unless administration transpires. It is the administration which "causes" death. The "free and voluntary" self-administration by V, an act to which freedom of choice applies, insulates D from liability for unlawful act manslaughter. It is insufficient for liability that D "facilitated or contributed" to the administration. In a sense D here merely provided the "backdrop" for V's own act. It is only where D has "administered" the drug that the s.23 unlawful act is activated. It is not enough to impose liability that D assists V, as in *Rogers*,[191] by holding the tourniquet around V's arm. The supply of a controlled drug, per se, is not dangerous, but the danger element is attached to the administration.

It is generally accepted that the unlawful act must be one of commission; unlawful act manslaughter cannot be based upon an omission.[192] In *Khan and Khan*[193] P went to get heroin from the flat belonging to the Ks. After snorting what may have been her first dose of heroin, she went into a coma and was left by the Ks in their flat. When they returned the next day she was dead and they dumped her on some waste ground. The trial judge withdrew the charge of murder from the jury on the ground that there was no evidence of mens rea. However, he told the jury that they could convict of manslaughter. The Court of Appeal allowed their appeal against conviction. Manslaughter by omission was a type of manslaughter arising from a breach of duty coupled with gross negligence.[194] It required proof of a relationship between the accused and the victim which created a duty to act. In this case the prosecution were arguing that a duty to summon assistance arose out of the incident at the flat. The Court of Appeal held that the trial judge had failed to direct the jury as to whether the facts were capable of giving rise to such a duty and in any event it would also have the effect of adding to the categories of person to whom such a duty was owed.[195]

B. The Act Must Not Only be Unlawful; It Must Also be Dangerous

This requirement received its clearest enunciation in *Church*[196] where the accused was **7–044** alleged to have caused the death of a woman by throwing her into a river. He had taken her down to the river in his van for the purposes of sexual intercourse. When she jeered at him for failing to satisfy her he struck her and, thinking he had killed her, he threw her "body" into the river, where she drowned. In so far as the manslaughter charged was based upon an unlawful and dangerous act, Edmund Davies L.J. held:

[189] See *Kennedy (No.2)* [2005] EWCA Crim 685; see above at para.2–044.
[190] [2007] UKHL 38; [2007] 4 All E.R. 1083.
[191] [2003] 2 Cr.App.R. 10; [2003] EWCA 945; [2003] Crim.L.R. 555.
[192] *Lowe* [1973] Q.B. 702.
[193] *The Times,* April 7, 1998; [1998] Crim.L.R. 830.
[194] In other words the Court of Appeal is saying that manslaughter based upon a failure to act must be prosecuted as gross negligence manslaughter, the requirements of which are set out below; see para.7–048.
[195] As to omissions, generally, see above, paras 2–015—2–027. Would not the facts of *Khan and Khan* fall within the established principles of *Miller,* see above, para.2–027.
[196] [1966] 1 Q.B. 59.

"[T]he conclusion of this court is that an unlawful act causing the death of another cannot, simply because it is an unlawful act, render a manslaughter verdict inevitable. For such a verdict inexorably to follow, the unlawful act must be such as all sober and reasonable people would inevitably recognise must subject the other person to, at least, the risk of some harm resulting therefrom, albeit not serious harm . . ."[197]

Thus if P punches D in the face the act is both unlawful and also dangerous in the way described by Edmund Davies L.J. above; all sober and reasonable persons would inevitably see that such a blow could cause some physical harm. At one stage there was support for the view that the prosecution must prove that P himself foresaw that his act would lead to some harm.[198] However, the issue was put beyond doubt by the House of Lords in *DPP v Newbury*[199] where their Lordships held that there was no need to prove that the accused foresaw any harm; the test was a purely objective one of whether a reasonable person would have recognised that the unlawful act must inevitably expose the other to the risk of at least some harm. We said earlier that the accused must have deliberately done the act which constitutes the unlawful act with the necessary mens rea of that act. Should the mens rea of that offence require that the accused foresaw harm as a result of the act, then this would have to be established otherwise the act would not be unlawful. However, since most cases of constructive manslaughter are based upon an assault or battery which require no proof that the accused foresaw harm, the statement in *DPP v Newbury* is generally true. In any event it is highly unlikely that a prosecutor would choose to base constructive manslaughter upon an unlawful wounding allegation which requires foresight of harm, when he could equally rely upon assault occasioning actual bodily harm which requires no foresight of harm.

Harm in this context means actual bodily harm;[200] emotional disturbance is not enough. In *Dawson*[201] three men held up a petrol station and the station attendant died from a heart attack shortly afterwards. The Court of Appeal held that it was not sufficient that the reasonable person would foresee that the victim would suffer emotional distress; he must foresee actual harm. It would, however, suffice, if the reasonable person foresaw that the emotional distress was so severe it might cause a heart attack.[202] In *Dhaliwal*[203] the appellate court reaffirmed that the infliction of mere psychological harm was an insufficient predicate for a manslaughter conviction.[204]

7–045   A further point was raised in *Dawson*. The petrol station attendant suffered from a heart complaint which made it more likely that emotional distress would lead to a heart attack. Should the reasonable person be taken to be aware of any special facts which might make it more likely that the victim will suffer actual physical harm? The Court of Appeal held that since the accused had no reason to know that the victim had a heart complaint, that factor should not be taken into account by the jury in deciding whether the attack was likely to cause physical harm. In *Watson*,[205] however, the Court of Appeal held that since by the end

---

[197] [1966] 1 Q.B. 59 at p.70.
[198] *Gray v Barr* [1971] 2 Q.B. 554.
[199] [1977] A.C. 500; see above, para.7–041.
[200] For discussion of actual bodily harm see below, paras 7–078—7–079.
[201] (1985) 81 Cr.App.R. 150.
[202] See, further M. Stallworthy, "Can Death by Shock be Manslaughter?" (1986) 135 N.L.J. 51.
[203] [2006] 2 Cr.App.R. 24.
[204] Note, however, the appellate court in an obiter dictum left open the possibility of a manslaughter conviction where V takes their own life subsequent to a final act of violence by D: "where a decision to commit suicide has been triggered by a physical assault which represents the culmination of a course of abusive conduct, it would be possible . . . to argue that the final assault played a significant part in causing the victim's death" [2006] 2 Cr.App.R. 24.
[205] [1989] 2 All E.R. 865. See generally A. Busutill and A. McCall Smith, "Fright, Stress and Homicide" (1990) 54 J.C.L. 257.

of the burglary the defendant had realised that the victim who was in the house was a frail and elderly man, the jury should ask themselves whether the burglary and subsequent visit of the police was likely to cause some harm to such a frail person. In *Carey*[206] the defendant's conviction for manslaughter was quashed as the threshold level of shock for liability could not have been foreseen by a reasonable bystander from the relevant acts and threats imposed. A confrontation had occurred between two groups of young girls. As part of this meleé V had been punched in the face. She ran away over a distance of 109 metres. Tragically V, who had a weak heart, suffered a ventricular fibrillation and died. It was determined that the trial judge had rightly declined to leave the charge to the jury on the basis that the affray had caused V to suffer from shock leading to her heart attack. Even had the affray caused V to suffer shock as opposed to emotional upset the parameters required for the concept of dangerousness were lacking. As Dyson L.J. stated, "it would not be recognised by a sober and reasonable bystander that an apparently healthy 15-year-old was at risk of suffering shock as a result of this affray."[207]

In *Ball*,[208] after an altercation between B and the victim, B shot and killed her as she was climbing over a wall into his garden accompanied by two young men. B claimed that he was frightened by them and that on the fateful occasion he had grabbed a handful of cartridges from the pocket of his overall. He knew that the pocket contained both live rounds and blanks, but he said he thought he had put blanks into the shotgun and had only meant to frighten her off. He was acquitted of murder but convicted of manslaughter. On appeal, he argued that where the accused was labouring under a mistaken belief, then the sober and reasonable person must also share that belief. Stuart-Smith L.J., however, disagreed:

> "Once these matters are established, namely that the act was both unlawful and that he intended to commit the assault, the question whether the act is a dangerous one is to be judged not by the appellant's appreciation but by that of the sober and reasonable man, and it is impossible to impute into his appreciation the mistaken belief of the appellant that what he was doing was not dangerous because he thought he had a blank cartridge in the chamber. At that stage the appellant's intention, foresight or knowledge is irrelevant."

C. Must the Unlawful Act be "Aimed at" the Particular Victim?[209]

In *Dalby*,[210] D was lawfully in possession of a controlled drug (Diconal) which he unlawfully **7–046** supplied to his friend, O. O later injected himself with the drug and died as a result. The situation is similar to that discussed in *Cato*[211]; the unlawful act is the supply of a controlled drug contrary to s.4(1) of the Misuse of Drugs Act 1971. The problem is that, in itself,

---

[206] [2006] EWCA Crim 17; [2006] Crim.L.R. 842; and see, generally, L. Cherkassky, "Kennedy and Unlawful Act Manslaughter: An Unorthodox Application of the Doctrine of Causation" (2008) 72 J.C.L. 387.

[207] An interesting point in this regard is presented by Professor Ormerod in favour of aggregation of D's conduct to constitute dangerousness: "If D1 and D2 use violence against V, their acts can surely be aggregated in assessing the dangerousness posed. This aggregation will be most important in case of physical harm through shock. Thus, where D1 and D2 threaten violence against V who is obviously frail, and he dies from the shock, their conduct can be *aggregated* when evaluating the dangerousness"; see D. Ormerod, "Case Comment on *R v Carey*" [2006] Crim.L.R. 842 at 847.

[208] [1989] Crim.L.R. 730.

[209] The House of Lords in *Moloney* [1985] A.C. 905 (above, para.2–055) held that there was no such requirement in the offence of murder.

[210] (1982) 74 Cr.App.R. 348.

[211] See above, para.7–042.

supplying drugs to another is not dangerous in the sense that reasonable people would not recognise it as an act which would inevitably subject the other person to the risk of some harm from the act itself. For harm to occur, it was necessary for the deceased to administer the drug to himself in a form and quantity which was dangerous. Waller L.J. thought it was not in any way similar to the normal run of unlawful act manslaughter cases where, for example, the victim is struck a blow which causes him to fall and strike his head against a wall causing death, or where slabs are dropped from a railway bridge causing death to the guard. He concluded ". . . where the charge of manslaughter is based upon an unlawful and dangerous act, it must be directed at the victim and likely to cause immediate injury, however slight."[212]

The requirement that the act be directed at the victim[213] raises certain problems. It is difficult to reconcile with the approach taken in *DPP v Newbury*;[214] indeed it is very hard to see that the act in *Newbury*, of dropping the paving stones, was directed at anyone. On the other hand Smith and Hogan argue[215] that the approach is to be welcomed on the ground that it introduces a subjective test into the law of manslaughter; an act cannot be directed at someone unless the defendant so intends it to be directed. Against this approach are the cases of *Mitchell*,[216] and *Goodfellow*.[217] In *Goodfellow* the defendant wanted to move from his council house to another. He felt he had little chance of being allowed to do so, and therefore deliberately set out to make the council believe that his house had been burned down by a petrol bomb. Unfortunately his plan went badly wrong and two members of his family together with his girlfriend were killed. Goodfellow tried to argue that unlawful act manslaughter required that the unlawful act be directed against the victim and that his plan had in no way been directed at the victims, but the Court of Appeal held that there was no such requirement. Lord Lane C.J., commenting upon the earlier passage of Waller L.J. in *Dalby*,[218] said:

> "However, we do not think that he was suggesting there must be an intention on the part of the defendant to harm or frighten or a realisation that his acts were likely to harm or frighten. Indeed it would have been contrary to the dicta of Lord Salmon in *DPP v Newbury* if he was. What he was, we believe, intending to say was *that there must be no fresh intervening cause between the act and the death*."[219]

The Court of Appeal, thus, interprets the problem as one of causation; in *Dalby*[220] the act of the victim injecting himself with the drugs provided by the defendant was a novus actus interveniens. This would be a neat solution, but it is suggested that the matter is not quite so straightforward. In the first place it contradicts the clear words used in *Dalby* to indicate the requirement that the act of the defendant should be aimed at the victim; it is clear that the

---

[212] (1982) 74 Cr.App.R. 348 at 352.
[213] (1982) 74 Ar.App.R. 348.
[214] Above, para.7–044.
[215] Smith and Hogan, *loc. cit.*, at p.384.
[216] [1983] Q.B. 741; see above, para.2–080.
[217] (1986) 83 Cr.App.R. 23. See also *Watson* [1989] 2 All E.R. 865 where, as we have seen, the Court of Appeal held that the defendant who had disturbed an obviously frail old man during a burglary could be liable for unlawful act manslaughter when the old man later died, so long as it could be proved that the burglary caused his death. The act of burglary was not directed at the old man, but this did not prevent a conviction.
[218] (1982) 74 Cr.App.R. 348 see below, fn.218.
[219] (1982) 74 Cr.App.R. 348 at p.27. (authors' italics). See also *Att-Gen's Reference (No.3 of 1994)* [1997] 3 All E.R. 936 at 957 *per* Lord Hope; and *Kennedy (No.1)* [1999] Crim.L.R. 65 where D was guilty of manslaughter of V to whom he had supplied a controlled drug.
[220] Below, para.7–046.

court in *Dalby* did not see the issue as one of causation. The certified question in *Dalby* assumes that the act of the defendant caused the death of the victim and that the only issue was whether the act of the accused must be aimed at the victim. Further, the later decision of the Court of Appeal in *Ball*[221] appears, in certain obiter dicta, to reaffirm the aimed at test. In *Ball* it was clear that the act of the accused, the firing of the shotgun, was aimed at the victim and, therefore, the Court of Appeal was able to avoid answering certain hypothetical situations proposed by defence counsel in which the act of the accused was not so directed. Counsel, for example, posed the question of whether a defendant, who was knowingly storing stolen goods, but which, unbeknown to him, contained explosives, and which exploded killing another, should be liable for the ensuing death. Stuart-Smith L.J. declined to suggest any answer to this example because it did not contain issues raised in *Ball* where the accused had deliberately shot at the victim.

It is suggested that for the moment courts should follow the approach of the Court of Appeal in *Goodfellow* and wait to see whether the Court of Appeal has an opportunity to raise this issue before the House of Lords. The aimed at test was rejected by the House of Lords in murder as being unnecessarily complex and it is suggested that the same should be true for manslaughter. As suggested by Clarkson and Keating:

> "assuming that the unlawful act is dangerous in itself and likely to cause some injury, there is no particular reason to require it to be directed at the victim."[222]

Applying this to the explosives example the case would turn upon whether sober and reasonable people would have known of the danger. If they would as reasonable people know of the danger, the defendant would be liable for a death resulting from the explosion even though in no way could you say that the unlawful act (handling stolen property) was aimed at another. Only if you could show a break in the chain of causation, for example a stranger tossing a lighted match into the store, would the defendant escape liability.

D. The Unlawful and Dangerous Act must be the Cause of Death

This would appear to be self-evident, but there must be no intervening cause which breaks **7–047** the chain of causation between the unlawful act of the accused and the death. In most cases this will be straightforward. Occasionally the matter may be more complex. In *Williams,*[223] a hitch-hiker leapt to his death from a car in which he had accepted a lift. The prosecution alleged that he had done so because of an unlawful threat to rob the hitch-hiker made by the other occupants of the car.[224] The Court of Appeal said that in such a case the jury would first have to decide whether the victim's reaction was foreseeable in the light of what was being done to him or whether it was a daft thing to do. In reaching this conclusion the jury should bear in mind any relevant characteristic of the victim and the fact that in the agony of the moment he may do the wrong thing. In other words the court is saying that the jury should first decide the issue of causation and then move on to the law relating to manslaughter. With all due respect, this seems rather cumbersome. A direction based on *Church* would cover all the issues that need to be raised.

It would appear from the decision in *Attorney-General's Reference (No.3 of 1994)*[225] where a defendant perpetrates an unlawful act against a pregnant woman, the act may also be

---

[221] Above, para.7–045.
[222] Clarkson and Keating, *Criminal Law: Text and Materials* 4th edn (1998), at p.668.
[223] [1992] 2 All E.R. 183; [1992] 1 W.L.R. 380; see above, para.2–038.
[224] For fright and flight cases generally, see above, paras 2–037—2–038.
[225] See above, para.2–081.

sufficiently wide to cover the child when it is born alive so as to render the defendant liable for manslaughter if the child subsequently dies as a result of that injury.[226] In recent times discussion has also focused on drug administration, with D preparing a syringe for self-injection by V.[227] In the Court of Appeal, liability was based on a revolutionary perspective of joint engagement in the administration process, with an unlawful act committed by D under s.23 of the Offences Against the Person Act 1861. However, this was rejected by the House of Lords in *Kennedy (No.2)*.[228] It is not the supply of a drug which causes death but the act of administration. D will not be liable for unlawful act manslaughter through assisting or contributing to V's self-injection. The fully informed and autonomous act of a responsible adult operates as a *novus actus interveniens*. Is this also apposite to a scenario where V, after suffering psychological trauma in an abusive marriage, took her own life after a final episode of violence by D? In *Dhaliwal*,[229] albeit in an obiter dictum, the Court of Appeal determined that unlawful violence on an individual with a fragile and vulnerable personality which was proved to be a material cause of death (even if the result of suicide) would at least arguably be capable of amounting to manslaughter. The case needs to be treated with great caution as no analysis occurred of causation principles. A suggestion, however, is that as with our discussion of fright and flight cases on causation we apply the test of reasonable foresight.[230] The question would be whether suicide was within the foreseeable range of responses which might be expected from a person in this situation.

2. GROSS NEGLIGENCE MANSLAUGHTER

7–048 Traditionally in this category of involuntary manslaughter the mens rea was considered to be that of gross negligence, indicating a requirement of a very high degree of negligence. Lord Hewart C.J. in *Bateman* observed:

> "In explaining to juries the test which they should apply to determine whether the negligence, in the particular case, amounted or did not amount to a crime, judges have used many epithets, such as 'culpable', 'gross', 'wicked', 'clear', 'complete'. But whatever epithet be used and whether an epithet be used or not, in order to establish criminal liability the facts must be such that, in the opinion of the jury, the negligence of the accused went beyond a mere matter of compensation between subjects and showed such disregard for the life and safety of others, as to amount to a crime against the State and conduct deserving punishment."[231]

Despite certain reservations about Lord Hewart's test, it was accepted as a workable direction for juries by Lord Atkin in *Andrews v DPP* where he said:

> "Simple lack of care such as will constitute civil liability is not enough. For the purpose of the criminal law there are degrees of negligence, and a very high degree of

---

[226] It is difficult to see why this does not involve transferred malice whereas a charge of murder on these facts does; see above, para.2–081. The speech of Lord Hope on the issue of unlawful act manslaughter is far from being readily understandable. As Professor Smith says in his commentary [1997] Crim.L.R. 829 at 831 it is as well that these cases make only rare appearances. See also P. Seago and A. Reed, "Criminal Law" [1997] All E.R. Annual Review 117 at 127.

[227] See above at para.7–042.

[228] [2007] UKHL 38; [2007] 4 All E.R. 1083.

[229] [2006] 2 Cr.App.R. 24; and see, generally, J. Horder and L. McGowan, "Manslaughter by Causing Another's Suicide" [2006] Crim.L.R. 1035.

[230] See above at paras 2–037—2–038.

[231] (1925) 19 Cr.App.R. 8 at 11.

negligence is required to be proved before the felony is established. Probably of all the epithets that can be applied 'reckless' most nearly covers the case."[232]

Even recklessness was not a complete definition since Lord Atkin noted that recklessness generally connotes indifference to a risk, "whereas the accused may have appreciated the risk, and intended to avoid it, and yet shown in the means adopted to avoid the risk such a degree of negligence as would justify a conviction".

An illustration should indicate the nature of the offence. Suppose that there is a very sharp bend in the road and a sign indicates that the maximum speed at which this bend should be negotiated is 20mph. It would be possible to say that a motorist who drives round the bend at 30mph is to a certain extent negligent. As his speed increases so too does the level of negligence and also the risk of death or grievous bodily harm to another road user coming in the opposite direction. At some point it could be said that the negligence is so bad that there is a serious risk of causing death or grievous bodily harm and that if someone is killed as a result of this driving the defendant would deserve to be punished for his driving. When this point is reached the jury should convict the motorist of manslaughter. This reasoning is, however, circuitous. In murder and unlawful act manslaughter the trial judge will direct the jury that if certain elements are proved they will convict the defendant. In gross negligence manslaughter the judge must tell the jury that the offence is made out if they consider that the defendant's conduct deserves to be treated as criminal.

The key case is now *Adomako*.[233] The appellant had been acting as an anaesthetist during **7–049** an eye operation and had failed to notice that the supply of oxygen had become disconnected. As a result the patient died. It was conceded at his trial that he had been negligent but the issue was whether or not his conduct was criminal?[234]

In the House of Lords, Lord Mackay signalled clearly the approach which was needed in these cases:

> "The task of trial judges in setting out for the jury the issues of fact and the relevant law in cases of this class is a difficult and demanding one. I believe that the supreme test that should be satisfied in such directions is that they are comprehensible to an ordinary member of the public who is called to sit on a jury and who has no particular prior acquaintance with the law. To make it obligatory of trial judges to give directions in law which are so elaborate that the ordinary member of the jury will have great difficulty in following them, and even greater difficulty in retaining them in his memory for the purpose of application in the jury room, is no service to the cause of justice."[235]

Lord Mackay held that in future judges should direct juries in accordance with the following principles. First, the general principles of negligence apply to determine whether or not the defendant was in breach of a duty of care owed to the victim who had died. If such a breach of duty is established, the second question is whether that breach of duty caused the death of the victim. If so, should that breach of duty be categorised as gross negligence and therefore as a crime? This will depend upon the seriousness of the breach committed by the defendant in all the circumstances in which the defendant was placed

---

[232] [1937] A.C. 576 at 585.
[233] [1995] A.C. 171. See generally S. Gardner, "Manslaughter by Gross Negligence" (1995) 111 L.Q.R. 22; G. Virgo, "Reconstructing Manslaughter on Defective Foundations" (1995) 54 C.L.J. 14.
[234] There was no suggestion that he had been performing an act which itself was unlawful; thus this was not a case of unlawful act or constructive manslaughter. In any event, the facts of *Adomako* pointed to a failure to act and, according to *Lowe* [1973] 1 All E.R. 805, constructive manslaughter cannot be based upon a failure to act.
[235] [1995] A.C. 171 at 189.

when the breach occurred.[236] In essence, it is permissible for gross negligence manslaughter to be established without the necessity to inquire into the defendant's state of mind, and this was so held in *Attorney-General's Reference (No.2 of 1999)*.[237] Inevitably this overall approach involves an element of circularity. However, this has always been the case in gross negligence manslaughter[238] and will continue to be so even under the Law Commission's proposals.[239]

Lord Mackay concluded[240]:

> "The essence of the matter, which is supremely a jury question, is whether, having regard to *the risk of death involved*, the conduct of the defendant was so bad in all the circumstances as to amount in their judgment to a criminal act or omission."

7–050   Consider, for example, the conduct of *Lamb*[241] in the context of gross negligence manslaughter. Was the defendant's conduct in firing the revolver, albeit as a practical joke, behaviour that was so bad that a jury would stigmatise it as criminal?

The passage of Lord Mackay reveals a further requirement. The jury must be satisfied that the conduct of the defendant created a risk of death.[242] Since virtually any conduct carries some slight risk of death, it would be sensible to require that the defendant's conduct must carry a serious or significant risk of death and it is suggested that this is what Lord Mackay intended. The jury will need to be careful in reaching this decision. The very fact that death occurred may well lead the jury to conclude that there must, therefore, have been *a* risk of death. It must be made clear to them that their task is to determine whether the defendant's conduct caused a serious risk of death. It is also important to keep separate the seriousness of the risk from the culpability of the defendant for that risk. The Law Commission cites an illustration of this from the case of *Prentice*.[243] It was accepted that the mistaken injection of vincristine into the patient's spine created a very serious risk of death, as witnessed by Dr Prentice's reaction when he realised what had happened. Nevertheless he should only be convicted of manslaughter if his conduct in allowing this to happen was grossly negligent.

The Duty of Care Requirement and Ex Turpi Causa

7–051   As previously stated, Lord Mackay in *Adomako*[244] asserted that "ordinary principles of negligence" apply to determine whether or not D has been in breach of a duty of care to V. Later cases have demonstrated that all the technicalities of the tort of negligence are inapplicable in establishing the criminal law offence. Civil and criminal law functions are different.

Human tragedy occurs in a variety of different guises. Rarely is it as starkly presented as the events that occurred in *Wacker*.[245] D, a Dutch national, drove a lorry from Rotterdam on which 60 Chinese illegal immigrants had been hidden in a refrigerated container behind a

---

[236] In a case such as the present where the death occurred as a result of the defendant exercising his professional skills, the jury should assess his culpability, not by comparing him with more skilled doctors but by the standard of a reasonably competent doctor. This amounts to an affirmation of the *Bateman* test (see above, para.7–048); the level of negligence remains a matter for determination by the jury.

[237] [2000] 3 All E.R. 182, see above, para.4–062.

[238] See above, para.7–048.

[239] See below, para.7–055.

[240] [2000] 3 All E.R. 182 at 338; authors' italics.

[241] See above, para.7–040. Lamb shot his friend while they were "messing about" with a revolver.

[242] This criterion was endorsed by the appellate court in *Singh* [1999] Crim.L.R. 582 in approving the trial judge's direction that the mere risk of injury, even serious injury, was not adequate. Moreover, the Court of Appeal held that whether D owed a duty of care was a question of law for the judge to determine.

[243] [1993] 4 All E.R. 935.

[244] See above, para.7–049.

[245] [2003] Q.B. 1203; [2002] EWCA Crim 1944; [2003] Crim.L.R. 108.

load of tomatoes. Their journey was organised by others, whose involvement was manifestly to make a profit out of the desire of people in China to leave that country and settle elsewhere. The container was sealed apart from a small air vent which was closed prior to the ferry crossing Dover to preserve secrecy. On disembarkation custom officers examined the container and found the bodies of 58 of the immigrants, who had suffocated. It was contended that no duty of care could be said to be owed by the defendant to the victims because they shared the same joint illegal purpose which (a) displaced the duty of care; (b) made it impossible for the court to define the content of the relevant duty of care; and (c) made it inappropriate for the court to define the content of a relevant duty of care. In essence, D submitted that one of the general principles of the tort of negligence, known by the Latin maxim of *ex turpi causa non oritur actio*, was that the law did not recognise the relationship between those involved in a criminal enterprise as giving rise to a duty of care.

In *Wacker* the Court of Appeal adopted a more constrained definition of gross negligence manslaughter. Kay L.J., who delivered the leading judgment, asserted that when Lord Mackay in *Adomako* referred to all general principles of negligence being applicable he, apparently, did not mean to embrace all tortious elements per se.[246] *Wacker's* conviction for manslaughter was upheld. The criminal law would not decline to hold a person as criminally responsible for the death of another simply because the two were engaged in some joint unlawful activity at the time or because there might have been an element of acceptance of a degree of risk by the victim in order to further the joint unlawful enterprise. As Kay L.J. stressed, the criminal law should not be disapplied just because the civil law is inoperable. It has its own public policy aim which may require a different approach. There is a functional need to protect individuals even where the civil law is disapplied. The criminal law will not hesitate to act to prevent serious injury or death even where the persons subjected to such injury or death may have consented to or willingly accepted the risk of actual injury or death. For example, the criminal law makes assisting another to commit suicide a criminal offence and denies a defence of consent where significant injury is deliberately caused to another in a sexual context: see *Brown*.[247] The state in such circumstances is viewed as having an overriding duty to act to prevent such consequences.[248] The fact that keeping the vent shut increased the chances of the victims entering the United Kingdom without detection was not a factor to be taken into account in deciding whether D had acted reasonably or not.

On a practical level the outcome in *Wacker* is eminently logical. The difficulty, however, is **7-052** that the Court of Appeal has driven a coach and horses through the clear statement of Lord Mackay in *Adomako* that all general principles of the law of negligence apply to determine whether or not D was in breach of a duty of care. A demarcation has been made between different kinds of actions. Basic negligence principles on duty of care will apply, for example, to cases of medical malpractice, but not, following *Wacker*, to illegal activities where all parties are engaged. In the latter scenario it is public policy concerns which will now mandate the establishment of a duty of care irrespective of the consensual accedance of the participants. This chasm was highlighted in *Willoughby*,[249] where a further issue also arose as to whether it was for the trial judge to determine the duty question as a pure question of

---

[246] Kay L.J. stated that when Lord Mackay in *Adomako* made reference to "ordinary" principles of negligence he was, "not intended to decide that the rules relating to ex turpi causa were part of those ordinary principles, he was doing no more than holding that in an "ordinary" case of negligence the question whether there was a duty of care was to be governed by whether there was a duty of care in the law of negligence."

[247] [1994] 1 A.C. 212; see discussion below at para.7–102.

[248] Note in Law Commission Report No.237, *Involuntary Manslaughter*, it is asserted that precepts of tort law are best avoided altogether.

[249] [2004] EWCA Crim 3365.

law,[250] or whether it was a matter for jury determination. D and V had engaged in illegal activity involving the spreading of petrol around D's property with an express intent to burn it down and claim on the insurance. The petrol, when ignited, caused an explosion killing V and injuring D. The Court of Appeal concluded that no duty arose simply from D's ownership of the property, but despite the illegal nature of the participatory conduct of both parties, nonetheless a duty existed through the engagement in setting fire to the premises for D's benefit.

Their Lordships in *Willoughby* stated that, in general, it is for the jury to decide whether a duty of care exists once the trial judge has decided that there is evidence capable of establishing a duty. However, there will be "exceptional cases" where a judge can properly direct a jury that a duty of care existed. Two examples are provided in *Willoughby* where judge intervention would be logical: (1) where a duty of care obviously exists such as that arising between doctor and patient[251]; and (2) where Parliament had imposed a statutory duty. Other categories are open for future development on an incremental basis, as with public policy exceptions where consent exculpates a willing participant.[252]

Compability with ECHR, article 7 and Circularity of the Test

7–053 The difficulty with the conclusions in *Willoughby* is that they fit uneasily with the outcome in *Misra*.[253] In the latter case, addressing medical malfeasance in the context of post-operative care, the Court of Appeal determined that the ingredients of the offence of manslaughter through gross negligence were sufficiently clearly defined[254] and did not offend against the retrospectivity provisions of ECHR. This is difficult to countenance following *Willoughby* whereby public policy considerations can trump negligence principles on establishment of a duty of care irrespective of the status of participants, where the trial judge can instruct the jury to "find" a duty of care in unspecified "exceptional" cases and where Lord Mackay's determination of guiding principles in *Adomako* is supplanted at will by legal legerdemain.

A particular problem for the court in *Misra* involved the circularity of the test for gross negligence manslaughter laid down in *Adomako*.[255] The issue of circularity has generally been taken to mean that the jury is involved not merely in deciding whether a defendant has committed certain acts which fall within a given definition of an offence, but that the jury is required to ask whether the defendant's conduct is such as to merit the label of criminality through the gross quality of the defendant's negligence—effectively the jury is required not merely to make a decision of fact on the evidence, but also to evaluate the definition of the crime itself. If the question is "What degree of negligence is sufficiently gross as to attract the attention of the criminal law?", the answer is "Negligence of a sufficiently gross degree

---

[250] See *Singh* [1999] Crim.L.R. 582.

[251] On doctor/patient duty see *Adomako* and also *Misra* [2004] EWCA Crim 2375; consider also other categories such as captain of ship to sailors cf. *Litchfield* [1998] Crim.L.R. 507; employer/employee cf. *Clothier* [2004] EWCA Crim 2629 and *Dean* [2002] EWCA Crim 2410; engagement in hazardous activities such as drug-taking, on which, see the recent decision in *Evans* [2009] EWCA Crim 650, cf. *Ruffell* [2003] Cr.App.R.(S.) 330 (taking of heroin) and illegal smuggling of immigrants cf. *Wacker* [2002] EWCA Crim 1944; and also spousal relationships cf. *Hood* [2004] 2 Cr.App.R.(S.) 73 (failure to summon medical assistance).

[252] See *Brown* [1994] 1 A.C. 212, discussed below at para.7–102, and cases on consent.

[253] [2004] EWCA Crim 2375; [2005] Crim.L.R. 234.

[254] A test that the court applies in addressing the issue of certainty is the test of notional legal advice—could the defendant find out, using a lawyer if needs be, whether his or her conduct would render him or her liable? As was stated in the European Court of Human Rights, in the context of a statutory provision, in *Kokkinakis v Greece* (1993) 17 E.H.R.R. 397 at [52], the criminal law must not be construed excessively to the disadvantage of an accused, but the requirement of certainty is met "where the individual can know from the wording of the relevant provision and, if need be, with the assistance of the courts' interpretation of it, what acts and omissions will make him liable."

[255] See above at para.7–049.

to attract the attention of the criminal law". The jury is thus required to take a view on the degree of negligence which would render the conduct of the defendant criminal. The suggestion is thus that a question of law—or at least a question of mixed fact and law—is left to the jury.

The answer given to the circularity problem by the court in *Misra* is that the jury are not required to decide that the conduct was criminal *in addition* to its being grossly negligent, but that the gross negligence of the conduct was *what made it criminal*.[256] The court treats this as a question of fact rather than law. However, the problem of circularity is not a problem of "criminality" being a separate element in the definition of the offence of gross negligence manslaughter—rather, it is a problem of there being no external criteria by which to measure the notion of "gross"-ness. The members of the jury are left to define this for themselves and thus not merely to determine whether the offence has been committed, but also *to determine the definition of the offence*. The court in *Misra* dismisses the appellants' arguments on certainty by suggesting that there is adequate certainty in Lord Mackay's definition of the offence in *Adomako* (what one might call legal certainty) and that any uncertainty that did exist would be in relation to the conclusion that a tribunal would reach in determining whether a given behaviour met that definition (what one might call factual or evidential uncertainty).[257] However, that fails to engage with the dual function—of finding facts and defining the offence—of the jury in a gross negligence manslaughter case. It is not merely a question of a defendant convicted of manslaughter not knowing what specifically about his conduct was viewed as grossly negligent by the jury, but also of that same defendant not knowing what standard of "gross"-ness was being applied by the jury in reaching that decision. It is submitted that the relatively short shrift given to the certainty argument in *Misra* makes it likely that the issue will be revisited in due course.

3. FURTHER CATEGORIES OF INVOLUNTARY MANSLAUGHTER?

We can safely assert that there are at least two categories of involuntary manslaughter; **7–054** unlawful act and gross negligence. It is conceivable that there are others. Until the decision of the House of Lords in *Moloney*[258] the mens rea of murder included foresight of death and foresight of grievous bodily harm. The House of Lords made it clear that these states of mind were not sufficient to constitute murder. It is clear, however, that if D kills P having consciously taken the risk that he would kill or seriously injure P, this must constitute manslaughter. It is likely that such activity would fall within the category of unlawful act manslaughter and possibly gross negligence manslaughter. However, it would be simpler to regard these states of mind as a category of manslaughter on their own.

The continued existence of manslaughter predicated upon D's subjective recklessness as to death or serious bodily harm was questioned by two post-*Adomako* cases.[259] The appellate

---

[256] At [62] The Court of Appeal in *Misra* asserts: "The decision whether the conduct was criminal is described [in *Adomako*] not as 'the' test, but as 'a' test as to how far the conduct in question must depart from accepted standards to be 'characterized as criminal'. On proper analysis, therefore, the jury is not deciding whether the particular defendant ought to be convicted on some unprincipled basis. The question for the jury is not whether the defendant's negligence was gross, and whether, additionally, it was a crime, but whether his behaviour was grossly negligent and consequently criminal. This is not a question of law, but one of fact, for decision in the individual case."

[257] Judge L.J. suggests in the context of the question of certainty and decisions made by juries (at [63]): "If he made enquiries in advance, at most an individual would be told the principle of law which the jury would be directed to apply: he could not be advised what a jury would think of the individual case, and how it would be decided. That involves an element of uncertainty about the decision-making process, but not unacceptable uncertainty about the offence itself".

[258] See above, para.2–055.

[259] *Khan and Khan* [1998] Crim.L.R. 830; and *Inner South London Coroner Ex. p. Douglas-Williams* [1999] 1 All E.R. 344.

court in the decisions, albeit obiter, intimated that only two kinds of involuntary manslaughter existed: constructive manslaughter and gross negligence manslaughter. More recently, however, in *Lidar*[260] the Court of Appeal have explicitly asserted that a separate category exists of involuntary manslaughter based upon subjective recklessness.

Lidar involved a dispute between two groups of young men in a public house, which continued in the car park after they had been thrown out of the premises. D got into the driving seat of his Land Rover with his brother in the front passenger seat. The victim then went over to the front passenger window, which was open, and leaned in so that half of his body was in the car. A fight ensued between the victim, D, and a rear passenger. D drove off with the victim still half in the window. The car reached over 30mph when the victim's feet caught the rear wheel and he fell to the ground, suffering severe crush injuries to his chest, from which he died. The Court of Appeal, upholding D's conviction, held that the trial judge had been correct to treat this case as one of reckless manslaughter and that the judge had not been required to give the jury a direction on gross negligence manslaughter which would have been "superfluous and unnecessary". The key issue was whether D, the driver of the motor vehicle, was aware of the necessary degree of risk of serious injury to the victim and nevertheless chose to disregard it.

At one time it would appear that the law recognised a category of manslaughter where the accused had consciously taken a risk of causing actual bodily harm.[261] In *Pike*[262] the accused had discovered that if he could get his girlfriends to sniff a common household cleanser before sexual intercourse their sexual performance was improved. He had, however, observed that this occasionally caused unconsciousness. On one occasion the girl died and he was convicted of manslaughter. It is generally accepted that this was on the basis that D had done an act foreseeing that it might cause the victim actual bodily harm. It is not clear whether this category survives *Adomako* though Lord Mackay did give approval to *Stone and Dobinson* in that case.[263] In *Lidar,* however, the Court of Appeal affirmed that D must have been subjectively reckless as to the risk of serious injury.[264] D must foresee the risk of serious injury as highly probable and take the unjustified risk of it. The trial judge should have specified that there had to be a high probability of serious physical injury, and not just of some "injury to health" and "some physical harm, however slight".

4. THE FUTURE OF INVOLUNTARY MANSLAUGHTER

7–055   It is easy to point out the perceived faults of the present offences of gross negligence manslaughter and unlawful act manslaughter. We saw that if D causes serious bodily harm to P by gross negligence, he is probably not guilty of any offences against the person since these require subjective recklessness. Yet if the victim dies, D will be liable for gross negligence manslaughter which carries life imprisonment.[265] Equally if D assaults P by punching him in the face, should the victim die as a result of this minor offence, D will be

---

[260] [2000] 4 *Archbold News* 3, CA.
[261] In *Stone and Dobinson* [1977] Q.B. 354 the Court of Appeal held as sufficient mens rea for manslaughter that the accused had consciously taken the risk of causing injury to health and welfare; see also above, para.2–026.
[262] [1961] Crim.L.R. 547.
[263] [1961] Crim.L.R. 547 at 187.
[264] [2000] 4 *Archbold News* 3, CA. The corollary is that if D foresees the risk of death as highly probable and unjustifiably takes that risk he is criminally liable for the offence of involuntary manslaughter based upon a test of subjective recklessness.
[265] See above, para.7–048.

liable for unlawful act manslaughter. Death is obviously a serious factor, but the average lay person finds it hard to accept that the occurrence of death does not necessarily make the defendant's conduct more culpable. As previously highlighted, a recent Report from the Law Commission, *Murder, Manslaughter and Infanticide*[266] has proposed significant wide-ranging reforms. The paper is substantial, running to 336 pages. The Commission proposes to retain murder and manslaughter, but to establish a new hierarchical structure of offences with murder divided into two degrees and to narrow the scope of manslaughter. In accordance with the Commission's scheme manslaughter would be committed only where a person caused death by gross negligence as to the risk of death, or by a criminal act, intending to cause injury, or being aware of a serious risk of causing injury. The penalty for second degree murder and manslaughter would be discretionary up to life imprisonment.

OTHER UNLAWFUL HOMICIDES

In this section we provide a brief outline of other offences involving death.   **7–056**

1. SUICIDE

It is no longer an offence for a person to kill himself or to attempt to kill himself. However, **7–057** the abolition of the crime of suicide was thought to leave an unacceptable gap in the law, namely that if a person who killed or attempted to kill himself did not commit a crime, then someone who helped him to do this could not be a party to the death and there might be good reasons for wanting to bring such a helper within the scope of the criminal law. Thus s.2 of the Suicide Act 1961 provides that:

> "A person who aids, abets, counsels or procures the suicide of another or an attempt by another to commit suicide, shall be liable on conviction on indictment to imprisonment for a term not exceeding fourteen years."

The words "aids, abets, counsels or procures" are the words which are used to describe liability generally for secondary parties to crimes.[267] They cover a wide variety of situations from the man who urges another to kill himself for some ulterior motive to the fond relative who obtains for his dying wife some poison so that she can put herself out of pain. The section must be interpreted to mean that no liability arises until the suicide is committed or at least attempted. However, one who unsuccessfully urges another to commit suicide will be guilty of an attempt.[268]

Where the accused has killed or been a party to the killing of another, it will be manslaughter and not murder if he can establish that the killing was part of a suicide pact in which he also, at the time of the killing, intended to die.[269]

---

[266] Law Com. No.304 (2006).
[267] See above, para.4–008; see *Att-Gen v Able* [1984] Q.B. 795. On assisted suicide of an incurably ill spouse see *Pretty v UK* [2002] 35 E.H.R.R. 1—the protection of art.2 is a right to life and not to death. See also, *Re Z* [2004] EWHC 2817 (Fam). See also *R. (Purdy) v DPP* [2009] EWCA Civ 92 for a recent attempt to secure clarification of the position of "assisters" with regard to the threat of prosecution. The case has gone to the House of Lords.
[268] See above, para.6–002; see also *McShane* (1977) 66 Cr.App.R. 97; and see also *S* [2005] All E.R. (D) 339 (Mar).
[269] Homicide Act 1957 s.4. It has been held that a defendant must establish the existence of a suicide pact on the balance of probabilities: *Att-Gen's Reference (No.1 of 2004)* [2004] EWCA Crim 1025.

2. INFANTICIDE

7–058   Under the provisions of the Infanticide Act 1938, where a woman has caused the death of her child which was under the age of 12 months in circumstances which would amount to murder but for the fact that at the time of her act or omission the balance of her mind was disturbed by reason of not having recovered from the effect of giving birth to the child or by reason of the effect of lactation consequent upon the birth of the child, she may be either:

(i) prosecuted for murder at which trial she may raise the defence of infanticide; or

(ii) she may be tried directly for infanticide.

In either case a conviction for infanticide shall be treated as a conviction for manslaughter and, thus, the maximum sentence will be life imprisonment, though, of course, the judge will be able to take account of the mitigating factors. Unlike the defences of insanity or diminished responsibility, the defence of infanticide does not place the burden of proof on the accused woman. She must introduce evidence of the defence, but it is for the prosecution to show that the defence has not been made out.[270]

3. CAUSING DEATH BY DANGEROUS DRIVING[271]

7–059   Until 1956, where a motorist killed another by bad driving, the only charge that could be brought was that of manslaughter, or, in extreme cases, murder. Jurors were very reluctant to convict motorists of a crime such as manslaughter which carried with it a possible sentence of life imprisonment together with the stigma that attaches to a serious criminal offence. In 1956 Parliament introduced the offence of causing death by dangerous driving and this is now covered by s.1 of the Road Traffic Act 1988 (as amended).[272] The prosecutor must first prove that the defendant was guilty of the basic offence of dangerous driving contrary to s.2 of the 1988 Act. Secondly he must prove that the dangerous driving caused death. It is not sufficient to prove that the defendant was driving dangerously at the time he killed the victim; it must be established that the death was caused by the dangerous nature of the driving.[273] There is no requirement for the prosecution to prove mens rea in respect of the death; it suffices that the dangerous driving caused the death.[274] The result is that there is no difference in the law of culpability between dangerous driving and causing death by dangerous driving; the difference between the two offences lies simply in the fortuitous occurrence of death. As with manslaughter, there is no offence of causing serious bodily harm by dangerous driving; both these offences recognise the fact that the general public view the causing of death as highly significant.[275] The offence of dangerous driving carries a maximum penalty of two years' imprisonment. The penalty for causing death by dangerous driving is a maximum of 10 years' imprisonment.[276] Thus if two drivers (A and B) were to

---

[270] See *Gore* [2007] EWCA Crim 2789.
[271] See, generally S. Cooper, *Blackstone's Guide to the Road Traffic Act 1991*; also Elliott and Street, *Road Accidents* (Penguin 1968).
[272] In the years since 1956 the offence has been variously known as dangerous and/or reckless driving. In the period up to the 1991 Act when the Road Traffic Act of 1988 was amended, the offence had been causing death by reckless driving, the term reckless being defined in terms of *Caldwell* objective recklessness.
[273] See, the discussion of *Dalloway*, above, para.2–033.
[274] In this respect the offence resembles assault occasioning actual bodily harm; see below, para.7–076.
[275] See, the North Committee's Road Traffic Law Review (HMSO, 1988); see *Spencer* [1988] Crim.L.R. 707.
[276] Previously the maximum for causing death by reckless driving was five years.

drive round a hairpin bend at an excessively high speed and on the wrong side of the road and if A runs over a pedestrian thereby killing him, both are equally culpable but A can be sentenced far more heavily.

We said that the first step is for the prosecution to prove that the defendant is guilty of dangerous driving. This is defined in ss.2 and 2A of the 1988 Act. Section 2 makes it an offence for a person to drive a mechanically propelled vehicle dangerously on a road or other public place. Section 2A(1) describes "dangerously" to mean that (a) "the way that he drives is far below what would be expected of a competent and careful driver, and (b) it would be obvious to a competent and careful driver that driving in that way would be dangerous". There is a similar provision in subs.(2) to cover the person whose driving is dangerous because of the dangerous state of his car. Subsection 3 provides that:

> "dangerous refers to danger either of injury to any person or of serious damage to property; and in determining . . . what would be expected of, or obvious to, a competent and careful driver in a particular case, regard shall be had not only to the circumstances of which he could be expected to be aware but also to any circumstances shown to have been within the knowledge of the accused."

It will still be possible for a motorist to be charged with manslaughter or, if the Law Commission proposals are enacted, one of the new homicide offences.[277] However, now that causing death by dangerous driving carries 10 years, it is going to be only in an exceptional case that a prosecutor would consider it worthwhile to charge a defendant with manslaughter.

It is worth noting that there are a similar pair of offences contained in ss.3 and 3A of the Act. Section 3 provides for the offence of careless and inconsiderate driving, an offence which requires proof of negligence which would satisfy the civil law level of negligence. Section 2B creates a new offence of causing death by careless driving. Again there is no equivalent for causing serious injuries by driving in this state.

HOMICIDE: GENERAL READING

Ashworth, A., "Reforming the Law of Murder" [1990] Crim.L.R. 75.   **7–060**

Ashworth, A., "Principles, Pragmatism and the Law Commission's Recommendations on Homicide Law Reform" [2007] Crim.L.R. 333.

Beaumont, J., "The Unborn Child And The Limits Of Homicide" (1997) 61 J.C.L. 86.

Bronitt, S., "Spreading Disease And the Criminal Law" [1994] Crim.L.R. 24.

Busutill, A., and McCall Smith, A. "Fright, Stress And Homicide" (1990) 54 J.C.L. 257.

Childs, M., "Medical Manslaughter And Corporate Liability" (1999) 19 *Legal Studies* 316.

Gardner, S., "Manslaughter By Gross Negligence" (1995) 111 L.Q.R. 22.

Goff, The Rt Hon Lord, "The Mental Element In Murder" (1988) 104 L.Q.R. 40.

Herring, J. and Palser, E., "A Duty of Care in Gross Negligence Manslaughter" [2007] Crim.L.R. 24.

Horder, J. and McGowan, L., "Manslaughter by Causing Another's Suicide" [2006] Crim.L.R. 1035.

Keating, H., "The Law Commission Report on Involuntary Manslaughter: (1) The Restoration Of A Serious Crime" [1996] Crim.L.R. 535.

Mitchell, B., "Distinguishing Between Murder and Manslaughter in Practice" (2007) 71 J.C.L. 318.

---

[277] See above, para.7–055.

Mitchell, B., "Minding the Gap In Unlawful and Dangerous Act Manslaughter: A Moral Defence of One-Punch Killers" (2008) 72 J.C.L. 537.

Padfield, N., "Manslaughter: The Dilemma Facing the Law Reformer" (1995) 59 J.C.L. 291.

Seneviratne, M., "Pre-Natal Injury and Transferred Malice: The Invented Other" (1996) 59 M.L.R. 884.

Tadros, V., "The Homicide Ladder" (2006) 69 M.L.R. 601.

Virgo, G., "Reconstructing Manslaughter on Defective Foundations" (1995) 54 C.L.J. 14.

Wells, C., "The Law Commission Report on Involuntary Manslaughter: (2) The Corporate Manslaughter Proposals: Pragmatism, Paradox and Peninsularity" [1996] Crim.L.R. 545.

Williams, G., "Mens Rea For Murder: Leave It Alone" (1989) 105 L.Q.R. 387.

Wilson, W., "A Plea For Rationality In The Law Of Homicide" (1990) 10 *Legal Studies* 307.

Yale, D., "A Year and a Day in Homicide" (1989) 48 C.L.J. 202.

NON-FATAL OFFENCES AGAINST THE PERSON

1. THE GENERAL FRAMEWORK

7–061   There are many offences whose function is to deal with unlawful harm being inflicted upon another individual. In the first part of this section we shall be concerned mainly with the four offences most commonly seen in our courts. These are, in order of increasing gravity, common assault,[278] assault occasioning actual bodily harm,[279] unlawful wounding and the unlawful infliction of grievous bodily harm,[280] unlawful wounding and unlawful causing of grievous bodily harm with intent to do grievous bodily harm or with intent to resist lawful arrest, etc.[281] We shall also need to consider the general question of the effect of consent by the victim to any activity which would constitute one of these offences. In the second section we shall look at the offences such as rape and sexual assault which seek to control certain sexual activity. Here we shall need to look at both heterosexual and homosexual activity and we shall see that the issue of consent is particularly important in this area.

It is important to appreciate from the outset that although we spoke of an ascending hierarchy of offences in the previous paragraph, there is, in reality, no such neatly ordered set of offences. The Offences Against the Person Act 1861, which contains most of the current existing offences against the person, is now 148 years old. Even when it was drafted, it was merely a consolidating statute of existing offences; it was not an attempt to reform or codify the law. The result is the existence of certain anomalies such as the fact that whereas unlawful wounding under s.20 is clearly to be seen as more serious than an assault occasioning actual bodily harm, they both carry a maximum penalty of five years' imprisonment. The Law Commission and the Government have both put forward draft

---

[278] Criminal Justice Act 1988 s.39. This is a summary only offence with a maximum sentence of six months' imprisonment and/or a fine at level 5 (currently £5,000). See, e.g. *DPP v Little* [1992] 1 All E.R. 299 (asserting that this was a statutory offence); but by way of contrast, see *Haystead v Chief Constable of Derbyshire* [2000] 3 All E.R. 890 where Laws L.J. stated that common assault by beating remains a common law offence. The authorities are in conflict and need to be reconciled.

[279] Offences Against the Person Act 1861 s.47. An either way offence punishable on indictment with a maximum of five years' imprisonment and/or an unlimited fine.

[280] Offences Against the Person Act 1861 s.20. An either way offence, punishable on indictment with a maximum of five years' imprisonment and/or an unlimited fine.

[281] Offences Against the Person Act 1861 s.18. Triable only on indictment and punishable with a maximum of life imprisonment and/or an unlimited fine.

proposals which would create a rational hierarchy of offences against the person.[282] In the combined appeals of *Savage and Parmenter*,[283] the House of Lords had an opportunity to effect some interim rationalisation of these offences; unfortunately, as will become clear in the following sections, it was not taken.

2. COMMON ASSAULT

At common law the phrase common assault covered two separate offences; assault and **7–062** battery. In *Collins v Wilcock*, Robert Goff L.J. describing the difference said:

> "The law draws a distinction, in terms more easily understood by philologists than by ordinary citizens, between an assault and a battery. An assault is an act which causes another person to apprehend the infliction of immediate unlawful force on his person; a battery is the actual infliction of unlawful force upon another person."[284]

Thus if D puts up his fists to strike P in the face and P fears that D is about to punch him on the nose, this is an assault and when D actually strikes P on the nose, that is a battery.[285] In criminal law, lawyers have come to use the expression "assault" to cover both assault and battery. It is important to remember that they are separate offences and any charge which accused the defendant of assault and/or battery would be bad for duplicity.[286]

A. Assault

(i) The Actus Reus

In the previously cited passage, Goff L.J. said that an assault was an act which causes **7–063** another to apprehend the application of immediate force. Thus as we said above, if D raises his fist to strike P, P is assaulted when he apprehends that he is about to be struck. It is sometimes said that an assault is an attempted battery, and although this may often be the case, it is not necessarily true.[287] An attempted battery requires that the defendant intended to apply unlawful force to the victim, whereas a person who is guilty of a technical assault may have no such intention. For example, if D points an imitation revolver at P intending P to think he was about to be shot, this would be an assault, but not an attempted battery. Equally if D threw a rock at P who is sleeping, and if the rock were narrowly to miss P, this

---

[282] *Legislating the Criminal Code: Offences Against the Person and General Principles* (Law Com. No.218). Home Office; *Violence: Reforming the Offences Against the Person Act 1861, Draft Offences Against the Person Bill 1998.* See below, para.7–114 for a note on reform of these offences.

[283] [1992] 1 A.C. 699.

[284] [1984] 3 All E.R. 374 at 377.

[285] In *Faulkner v Talbot* [1981] 3 All E.R. 468 at 471 Lord Lane J.J. said a battery is "any intentional touching of another person without the consent of that person and without lawful excuse. It need not necessarily be hostile, rude or aggressive . . ." Note s.79 of the Sexual Offences Act 2003 defines touching as including with any part of the body, with anything else or through anything cf. *H* [2005] EWCA Crim 732, where touching clothes of another constituted a touching for the purposes of the Act.

[286] Where D is indicted in the Crown Court, the indictment is, in effect, the charge sheet which is read out to the court. Each charge is put into a separate count (paragraph) of the indictment and any count which reveals more than one offence is bad for duplicity. A similar rule applies to informations before the magistrates' court. Common assault and battery are offences which, in general, are triable only summarily; they may occasionally be tried in the Crown Court when linked with either way offences; ss.40 and 41 of the Criminal Justice Act 1988.

[287] In the USA it is common for the criminal codes to identify two types of assault; the one being an attempt to commit a battery and the other is placing another in reasonable apprehension of a battery. In some states the definition of assault is limited to one or the other, but in more states both versions are found. See LaFave and Scott, *Criminal Law* 2nd edn (1986), at p.691.

would be an attempted battery, but not an assault since P does not apprehend the infliction of immediate violence.

It must be remembered that all an assault requires is that the victim should apprehend the application of immediate force. Force, as we shall see in the section on battery, requires only non-consensual contact; a tap on the shoulder will suffice.

It does not matter that D was incapable of carrying out the threat; the essential question is the view formed of D's conduct by P. Thus if D points an imitation gun at P and says he is about to shoot him, if P anticipates the immediate infliction upon himself of unlawful violence, the actus reus of assault has been brought about. On the other hand in *Lamb*,[288] where L had pointed a gun at his friend and pulled the trigger believing that there was no bullet opposite the firing pin, there was no assault since the friend did not believe that the gun would fire.[289]

7–064   Does the word "act" in Goff L.J.'s definition of assault mean that an assault in the technical sense could not be brought about by an omission? By analogy with *Fagan v Metropolitan Police Commissioner*[290] there seems no reason in principle why an assault should not be based upon a failure to act. For example, if D inadvertently causes P to think that D is about to hit him, a deliberate failure by D to correct the impression should constitute an assault.

In *DPP v Santana-Bermudez*[291] a female police officer, stopping a suspect who she believed had committed drug offences, enquired whether they possessed any needles. The suspect replied that he was not carrying any "sharps" but on effecting the search the officer stabbed her finger on a hypodermic needle. The court, upholding D's conviction for an assault occasioning actual bodily harm, applied principles established earlier in *Fagan* and *Miller*.[292] Where a defendant, by act or word or a combination of the two, creates a danger and thereby exposes another to a reasonably foreseeable risk of injury which materialises, there is an evidential basis for the actus reus of an assault. The offence may be committed in circumstances of omission.

It is sometimes said that an assault cannot be committed by words alone. This view would appear to be based upon a dictum from the old case of *Meade and Belt*[293] and has very few supporters today.[294] In many situations where the assault might seem to consist of words alone, there may well be some action on the part of D which constitutes an act which is coupled with the words. However if, to take a rather fanciful example, D telephones P and tells P that D has placed an explosive device in the base of the telephone which will explode within seconds, this is a situation in which D, by words alone, has caused P to fear the immediate application of unlawful force and it would seem absurd if this were not to constitute an assault. Similarly if at night D hid in the shadows and whispered to P as she walked past, that he was the son of Jack the Ripper, this would be more terrifying than many forms of assault where there is an act involved.

7–065   The issue has now been resolved by the decision of the House of Lords in *Ireland*.[295] In this case the accused had terrorised three women by telephoning them, normally at night, and when they answered the phone he remained silent or occasionally he resorted to heavy

---

[288] [1967] 2 Q.B. 981, above, para.7–040.
[289] Nor did Lamb intend to cause, or consciously take an unjustifed risk of causing, his friend to apprehend harm.
[290] Above, para.2–027 where the defendant accidentally parked on a policeman's foot and then refused to drive off; this constituted a battery. Following *Miller* [1983] 2 A.C. 161 (above para.2–027) this would almost certainly be treated as a failure to discharge a duty which had been created by the defendant's inadvertent conduct.
[291] [2004] Crim.L.R. 471; [2003] EWHC 2908 (Admin).
[292] See above at para.2–027.
[293] (1823) 1 Lew C.C. 184.
[294] See, e.g. Glanville Williams, *op. cit.*
[295] [1997] 4 All E.R. 225. See generally J. Herring, "The Criminalisation of Harassment" (1998) 57 C.L.J. 10; and S. Gardner "Stalking" (1998) 114 L.Q.R. 33.

breathing. As a result the women suffered psychiatric illness.[296] Counsel for Ireland argued that the making of silent telephone calls could not, under any circumstances, constitute an assault, just as words alone could not constitute an assault. He argued that the Court of Appeal had fallen into error by assuming that it was sufficient that when the women lifted the telephone they were immediately afraid and that this fear resulted in psychiatric injury. The Court had, according to D's submission, overlooked the essential requirement of a psychic assault that the victim's fear should be that he or she is at risk of the immediate application of unlawful force.

Lord Steyn reflected upon the scarcity of authority on the issue of whether words alone could constitute an assault.[297] He concluded:

> "The proposition that a gesture may amount to an assault, but that words can never suffice, is unrealistic and indefensible. A thing said is also a thing done. There is no reason why something said should be incapable of causing an apprehension of immediate personal violence, e.g. a man accosting a woman in a dark alley saying 'come with me or I will stab you'. I would, therefore, reject the proposition that an assault can never be committed by words."[298]

Lord Steyn said that it was necessary to consider the words or gestures in their context. If the person making the telephone call said that he would be on the victim's doorstep within a minute, this could clearly cause the victim to fear the immediate application of unlawful force. A similar message could just as easily be conveyed to the victim by the caller remaining silent. Lord Hope said:

> "He was using his silence as a means of conveying a message to his victims. This was that he knew who and where they were, and that his purpose in making contact with them was as malicious as it was deliberate. In my opinion silent telephone calls are just as capable as words or gestures, said or made in the presence of the victim, of causing an apprehension of immediate and unlawful violence."[299]

Their Lordships were concerned that the law was not capable, as it stood, of protecting **7–066** victims of this sort of attack. Under the Telecommunications Act 1984 it was an offence persistently to make use of a public telecommunications system for the purpose of causing annoyance, inconvenience or needless anxiety to another. Unfortunately the maximum penalty for this offence is six months' imprisonment and that may be well short of what is needed to deal with persons who make obscene telephone calls. Equally the provisions of the Protection from Harassment Act 1997 may fall well short of what is required. The offence under ss.1 and 2 of the Act of pursuing a course of conduct which amounts to harassment of another and which the defendant knows or ought to know amounts to harassment of another carries a penalty of only six months' imprisonment. The more serious offence under s.4, which carries a maximum of five years' imprisonment, requires that the victim fears on at least two occasions that violence will be used against her; it may well be difficult to prove any more than that the victim feared that violence might (not will) be used

---

[296] As to whether psychiatric illness can constitute bodily harm, see below, paras 7–078—7–079.
[297] Note in *Gelder, The Times,* May 24, 1994 a bank clerk, who subjected a woman customer to a series of obscene telephone calls thereby causing the victim to suffer sickness and diarrhoea, was convicted at Chester Crown Court of causing grievous bodily harm.
[298] [1997] 4 All E.R. 225 at 236.
[299] [1997] 4 All E.R. 225 at 240–241.

against her. The decision in *Ireland* at least permits a charge to be brought under s.47 of the Offences Against the Person Act 1861 (assault occasioning actual bodily harm) so long as there is a fear of immediate unlawful violence, though Lord Steyn conceded that this requirement was a considerable complicating factor in bringing such a charge. Enactment of cl.4 of the Law Commission's Draft Criminal Code[300] which provides that, "A person is guilty of an offence if he intentionally or recklessly causes injury to another" would greatly simplify matters.

It now seems clear that the view that assaults cannot be by word alone is no longer tenable.[301] It is equally clear that words can negative an assault. In *Tuberville v Savage*[302] the defendant took hold of his sword saying, "If it were not assize time, I would not take such language from you." The grabbing of the sword could clearly have constituted an assault, but the words indicated that the defendant had no intention of using his sword. The victim had no reason to apprehend the infliction of immediate and unlawful force. It is, however, important to see that there is an important distinction between the words uttered in *Tuberville v Savage* and those of a highwayman who demands, "Your money or your life." In one sense the victim knows that there will be no assault so long as he hands over his money, but to deny criminal liability in such a situation would be preposterous. In *Tuberville v Savage* the victim knew that there would be no application of force, but in the case of the highwayman the victim does apprehend the application of unlawful force; it will follow quickly unless he takes steps to appease the robber. In these cases the courts will hold that there has been an assault. Thus in *Read v Coker*[303] the defendant and his servants advanced on P, rolling up their sleeves, tucking in their aprons and threatening to break P's neck if he did not leave the premises. The court had no doubt that this was an assault.[304]

(ii) The Apprehension Must be of the Application of Immediate Force

7–067   It is said that the victim must apprehend that unlawful force is to be applied immediately to the victim. A threat to apply force sometime in the future is not an assault.[305] For this reason courts have been prepared to give a fairly wide meaning to the word "immediate".[306] Thus in *Smith v Chief Superintendent, Woking Police Station*[307] the Divisional Court held that magistrates were entitled to find that a woman who saw the defendant looking through the window of her bed-sitting room late at night apprehended immediate violence. Similarly in *Lewis*,[308] where the husband was threatening violence to his wife who was on the other side of a locked door, the court held that the woman, who suffered grievous bodily harm when she leapt from the window of her flat, had apprehended the application of immediate

---

[300] *Legislating the Criminal Code: Offences Against the Person and General Principles* (Law Com. Consultation Paper No.218, 1993).

[301] See, also *Wilson* [1955] 1 All E.R. 744, Lord Goddard C.J. said obiter of the accused "He called out 'Get out the knives,' which itself would be an assault, in addition to kicking the gamekeeper", at 745.

[302] (1669) 1 Mod. Rep. 3; 86 All E.R. 684; and see, generally, J. Horder, "Reconsidering Psychic Assault" [1998] Crim.L.R. 392.

[303] (1853) 13 C.B. 850; see also *Blake v Barnard* (1840) 9 C. & P. 626.

[304] If, as was the case, P was a trespasser, why would the threat amount to an assault? See below, para.7–069.

[305] There is an offence of threatening to kill under Offences Against the Person Act 1861 s.16, as amended by the Criminal Law Act 1977 s.12, but this does not extend to threats to cause lesser injuries in the future. The Law Commission has recommended that it should be extended to cover threats of serious injury (Law Commission; Consultation Paper No.122 *Legislating the Criminal Code: Offences Against the Person and General Principles*).

[306] Until the decision of the House of Lords in *Wilson* [1984] A.C. 242, it was assumed that use of the word "inflict" in the offence under s.20 of the Offences Against the Person Act 1861 meant that the offence of inflicting grievous bodily harm necessarily involved an assault. This also led the courts to find an assault in situations where there was no apprehension of immediate force. See below, para.7–085.

[307] (1983) 76 Cr.App.R. 234.

[308] [1970] Crim.L.R. 647.

force[309] As we have seen in *Ireland*,[310] an assault can be committed by a caller on a telephone so long as the call conveys the fear of the infliction of immediate and unlawful violence to the victim, and this is a question of fact for the jury to determine by reference to all the surrounding circumstances. In *Constanza*,[311] where the defendant had bombarded the victim with unsolicited letters and telephone calls, and had followed her about for two whole years, the Court of Appeal appears to say that there may be an assault where the apprehension of violence extends over a longer period, provided that it includes violence in the immediate future.

(iii) The Force Apprehended Must be Unlawful

If P was attacking D, a threat by D to take his knife to P if P did not desist might not **7–068** amount to an assault. It would all depend upon whether the violence threatened was excessive in the circumstances. Persons may use such force as is reasonable in the circumstances to prevent crime, to defend themselves or another or to defend their property.[312] Thus D would have every right to use reasonable force to eject a trespasser from his property. A threat, however, to use a knife on him to get him to go might be a threat of an unreasonable degree of violence and hence an assault.[313]

B. The Actus Reus of Battery

We saw earlier[314] that Lord Goff said that a battery "is the actual infliction of unlawful force **7–069** upon another person". Various points need to be appreciated from the outset, otherwise the offence is likely to be misconstrued. In the first place the word "force"[315] does not necessarily require that the victim suffers any harm or injury; the slightest touching of another constitutes force.[316] Secondly, in complete contrast to a psychic or technical assault, the victim of a battery does not have to see the force coming. It is just as much a battery if the defendant creeps up behind the complainant and applies force from behind. In fact, a battery does not even require that the complainant was aware of the force at the time it was applied. For example, in *Kingston*,[317] the House of Lords held that the defendant's sexual abuse of an unconscious youth constituted an assault.[318] The courts have also held that it is just as much a battery to apply force to the clothes the complainant is wearing, as to apply force to the actual person of the complainant.[319]

In the most common sort of case, the defendant will apply force directly to the victim, for example by striking him with a fist or weapon. In *Savage*,[320] Glidewell L.J. held that the defendant committed an intentional battery by drenching the complainant with beer. The impact of the beer on the complainant constituted the application of force; it was irrelevant that the complainant suffered no bodily harm. It would also constitute a battery to set a dog to attack the complainant.

---

[309] The decision in *Lewis* was almost certainly influenced by the need to find an assault to substantiate a charge under the Offences Against the Person Act 1861, s.20. See below, para.7–084.

[310] Above, para.7–065.

[311] [1997] Crim.L.R. 576.

[312] See above, paras 5–047—5–059.

[313] *Read v Coker* (1853) 13 C.B. 850; see above, fn.303.

[314] Above, para.7–063.

[315] Others use the word "violence" in place of force, but that is even more likely to mislead.

[316] But see below, para.7–070 and the quote from Lord Goff. See also, s.79 of the Sexual Offences Act 2003.

[317] [1994] 3 All E.R. 353; see above, para.5–035.

[318] In fact the charge was of an indecent assault, but this required proof of a basic assault; See below, para.7–134 for a discussion of the offence of sexual assault.

[319] *Thomas* (1985) 81 Cr.App.R. 331.

[320] (1990) 91 Cr.App.R. 317; [1991] 2 All E.R. 220 (CA).

There is some authority to support the view that battery requires the direct application of force to another, either by means of the defendant's fists or by a weapon in the control of the defendant. According to these authorities the indirect application of force could not constitute a battery. Other authorities, however, have held less direct applications of force to constitute a battery. In *Clarence,*[321] Stephen and Wills JJ. thought it would constitute an assault to dig a hole for another to fall into. In *Martin,*[322] M blocked the exit door to a theatre with an iron bar. He then turned the lights out and yelled "fire". He was convicted of inflicting grievous bodily harm contrary to s.20 of the Offences Against the Person Act 1861[323] in relation to several persons who were crushed against the doors in the ensuing panic.[324]

An affirmation was provided by the Divisional Court in *Haystead v Chief Constable of Derbyshire*[325] that there can be a battery by the indirect application of force. The facts were straightforward and not in dispute. D had struck the victim twice in the face while she was, to his knowledge, holding her three-month-old child. The blows caused V to drop the child and it was injured when it struck the floor. D was charged with common assault by beating. No challenge was made to the meaning of battery given in *Archbold's Criminal Pleading, Evidence and Practice*, "an act by which a person intentionally or recklessly applies unlawful force to the complainant".[326] D sought to persuade the court that the phrase "application of force" required the prosecution to prove that the defendant had had direct physical contact with the complainant either through his body, e.g. a punch, or through a medium controlled by his actions, e.g. a weapon. The Divisional Court, upholding D's conviction, asserted that a causal link could be established between D's act and the consequence that unlawful force had been applied to the baby when it struck the floor.[327] Laws L.J. concluded:

> "In a case such as the present, it seems to me plain that it is right that the offence of assault by beating should be available for criminal condemnation of the defendant's conduct."[328]

(i) Can Liability for a Battery be Founded Upon an Omission?

7–070 It is generally accepted that a battery may be committed where D digs a hole for P to fall into. Even though this could be phrased in terms of an omission,[329] the subsequent injury of P is brought about by a positive act on the part of D and not simply by his failure to act. Suppose, however, that D's gardener has dug a large hole and has told D about it when he leaves. D knows that P will be visiting him later and deliberately fails to warn him of the hole hoping that he will fall into it. Is D guilty of a battery when P falls into the hole? In *Fagan v Metropolitan Police Commissioner*[330] James J. said, "To constitute this offence,[331]

---

[321] (1888) 22 Q.B.D. 23, discussed below, para.7–084.

[322] (1881) 8 Q.B.D. 54, discussed below, para.7–084.

[323] An offence which, at that time, was considered to include a common assault as an essential element.

[324] Until *Wilson* [1984] A.C. 242 it was assumed because s.20 required proof that the accused had "inflicted" grievous bodily harm, whereas s.18 required that the accused had caused grievous bodily harm, the word "inflict" meant that the harm had to be produced in a violent rather than surreptitious manner and therefore *ex necessitate* involved a common assault. One reading of *Martin*, therefore, is that it is authority for his conduct constituting an assault. See further below, paras 7–083—7–085 and discussion of the offence under s.20.

[325] [2000] 3 All E.R. 890.

[326] 2000 edn at para.19–166a.

[327] It was accepted that D foresaw injury to both the mother and the child and so there was no issue relating to mens rea. Note also the dropping of the child by the mother was involuntary and not a novus actus interveniens.

[328] [2000] 3 All E.R. 890 at 896.

[329] Namely D has omitted to tell P of the hole.

[330] [1969] 1 Q.B. 439, above, para.2–027.

[331] James J. uses the word assault, but in the context of *Fagan* he was concerned with a battery.

some intentional act must have been performed; a mere omission to act cannot amount to an assault." In *Fagan* D had accidentally parked his car on the foot of a police constable. When asked to drive forward to release the foot he refused to do so. The Divisional Court held that a battery was a continuing offence and, therefore, the requirements of the offence were met so long as the defendant formed the mens rea to apply unlawful force during the time the car was on the constable's foot. The case was not treated as one of omission. However, following the decision of the House of Lords in *Miller*,[332] it is suggested that the position is less clear cut. In *Miller* the House of Lords held a tramp liable for damage to property he had caused by dropping a lighted cigarette. His liability was based upon his duty to act which arose out of the danger which he was aware he had created. Thus if D applies unlawful force to P, and if when he becomes aware of what he has done he deliberately or recklessly takes no action to remove the unlawful force, his omission will render him liable for a battery. Support for this view can be found in *DPP v K*[333] where K, a schoolboy, in order to avoid detection for removing sulphuric acid from the classroom to the toilet, poured it into a hot air dryer. He had intended to remove it as soon as possible. However, before he was able to get back to remove the acid, another pupil used the dryer and was permanently scarred by the acid which was blown into his face. Parker L.J. bases K's liability for assault on the fact that K knew full well that he had created a dangerous situation. It is suggested that were the facts of *Fagan* to come before the courts today, it would be dealt with along the same lines. Once he realised he had driven on to the constable's foot a duty to drive off would arise. Thus, in this type of situation, it would seem that a battery can be based upon an omission. This was recently confirmed in *DPP v Santana-Bermudez*,[334] asserting that the offence may be effected in circumstances of omission, failure therein to warn the lady police officer about the presence of the hypodermic needle.

The same type of approach might be taken to a hypothetical situation discussed by Ormerod.[335] Having stated that it is generally accepted that it would not be a battery for D merely to stand his ground in the street so that P has to come into contact with D in order to get past, they suggest that it might be different if D is sitting around the corner of a corridor with his legs outstretched when he hears P approaching. It would undoubtedly be a battery if D stuck out his legs in order to trip up P, so why should it not be a battery if D deliberately leaves his legs sticking out when he knows that P is likely to fall over them when he rounds the corner? It would seem plausible to argue that once D realises that he has created a dangerous situation by sitting with his legs outstretched he is under a duty to remove the danger. Would not the position be the same if D stands on the pavement in such a way as to force P to choose between coming into contact with D or stepping on to a very busy road? The answer must surely be "yes".

(ii) Consent and Allied Issues[336]

Since a battery does not require proof that the victim has suffered any harm, only that the **7–071** defendant has touched (applied force to) the victim, the law recognises that the complainant may consent to the touching. Where the person to whom the force was applied consents, there is no battery. It would make more sense to treat the absence of consent as an element of the offence rather than as a defence, but the House of Lords in *Brown*[337] seem to regard it

---

[332] [1983] A.C. 161; discussed above, para.2–027.
[333] [1990] 1 All E.R. 331.
[334] See above at para.2–027.
[335] Ormerod, *op. cit.*, p.586.
[336] The issue of consent generally in the area of offences against the person is considered below, paras 7–098—7–116.
[337] [1994] 1 A.C. 212.

as a defence. There is little practical difference, save that by treating it as a defence the defendant who wishes to rely upon consent will have to discharge an evidential burden.[338] Thus each of us expressly consents to being touched by others possibly several times a day. Consent is given, for example, to the hairdresser and to the shop assistant who is taking body measurements.

Modern life, however, means that we come into contact with possibly scores of people each day. For example, anyone living in London and travelling to work each day by the underground will need to make physical contact with others merely to get into the train. It is clearly not expected that we should give express consent in such situations. Such contacts were generally said to be based upon implied consent. However, "it is more common nowadays to treat them as falling within a general exception embracing all physical contact which is generally acceptable in the ordinary conduct of daily life."[339]

We generally accept that people will touch us in order to attract our attention, some more forcibly than others. Some will initiate a handshake and others will find the need to touch you as they speak. Unless we make it clear that such contact is unwanted, we will be taken to have accepted it as part of everyday life. A police officer may have the power to detain a member of the public using his lawful powers of arrest, but unless he is exercising such powers he is subject to the same restraints as ordinary citizens. He may well be able to touch the suspect to indicate that he wishes to speak to him, and this may include touching him a second time. However, in *Kenlin v Gardiner*[340] it was held that where a constable grabbed hold of two schoolboys he was doing so not to arrest them, but simply to detain them for questioning and this was unlawful.[341]

(iii) The Force Applied Must be Unlawful

7–072 As in most offences against the person the presence of the word "unlawful" indicates the existence of certain defences. In the context of battery we have already seen that the application of force must be without consent. It would also be a defence that the force used was reasonable in the circumstances in the exercise of self-defence, defence of property or to prevent the commission of a criminal offence.[342]

Where P is brought unconscious into a hospital emergency room, the doctor who operates to save P's life will not be guilty of a battery. This may be on the basis of a general defence of necessity[343] or on the basis that the patient would have consented had he been conscious.[344] Lord Brandon sets out the position in *F v West Berkshire Health Authority*:

> ". . . a doctor can lawfully operate on, or give other treatment to, adult patients who are incapable, for one reason or another, of consenting to his doing so, provided that the operation or other treatment concerned is in the best interests of such patients. The operation or other treatment will be in their best interests if, but only if, it is carried out in order either to save their lives or to ensure improvement or prevent deterioration in their physical or mental health."[345]

---

[338] See above, para.1–009.

[339] per Robert Goff L.J. in *Collins v Wilcock* [1984] 3 All E.R. 374 at p.378. See generally, R. Leng, "Consent and Offences Against the Person" [1994] Crim.L.R. 480.

[340] [1967] 2 Q.B. 510.

[341] In *Donnelly v Jackman* [1970] 1 All E.R. 987 it was held lawful for a police officer to continue tapping the suspect on the shoulder in order to attract his attention, even though the suspect had made it clear he did not want to be touched; possibly an over-generous decision. In *Collins v Wilcock*, [1984] 3 All E.R. 374, the officer who had detained a prostitute in order to caution her was held to be acting illegally. There was no power to detain for cautioning.

[342] See above, para.5–044.

[343] See above, para.5–062.

[344] *F. v West Berkshire Health Authority* [1989] 2 All E.R. 545.

[345] [1989] 2 All E.R. 545 at 551.

This principle is not limited to medical cases. Lord Goff suggests the same principle would apply where D pulls P clear of an oncoming vehicle. It would appear, however, that if D knows that P does not want to be pulled clear, it would be a battery for D to apply any force to P to save his life. The suicide patient who arrives unconscious at a hospital provides a potential problem for the medical staff, particularly if he has pinned a message to himself which says that under no circumstances are the hospital staff to try to save him.[346]

The application of force would not be unlawful where it is administered as reasonable and **7–073** moderate chastisement of a child. At common law parents have had the right to chastise their children so long as the degree of force is not excessive and that it is inflicted for the right motive. In *A v United Kingdom*[347] a stepfather was acquitted by a jury of assault occasioning actual bodily harm. The jury obviously accepted that the stepfather's use of a garden cane constituted reasonable chastisement. The European Court of Human Rights held that the conduct had breached art.3 of the Convention which provides, "No one shall be subjected to torture or to inhuman or degrading treatment or punishment." The case does not say that the use of force in reasonable chastisement is in itself wrong; each case turns upon its own facts. However, the punishment here did offend the Convention and English Law had provided no protection. Subsequently in *H*,[348] the Court of Appeal, purporting to follow the doctrine established in *A v United Kingdom*, laid down a list of nebulous factors for the jury to consider on the issue of "reasonableness": the duration of the behaviour; the child's age and personal characteristics; the nature and context of D's behaviour; the physical and mental consequences for the child; and D's reasons for administering the punishment. Moreover, the Department of Health issued a consultation document, *Protecting Children, Supporting Parents: A Consultation Document on the Physical Punishment of Children (2000)*, and a degree of clarification of this area has occurred through legislation. In accordance with s.58 of the Children Act 2004, the defence of lawful chastisement is still operable provided the punishment amounts only to the level of an assault or battery that does not involve cruelty. The punishment must be reasonable and proportionate and touching of a child constituting actual bodily harm or cruelty is excluded. Uncertainty still pervades, of course, regarding the division between assault and actual bodily harm. The further difficulty, is delineating what constitutes excessive force, identified as inhuman or degrading treatment or punishment, for the purposes of art.3. When, if ever, does a smack on the bottom, hand or leg meet this threshold, and in what circumstances? How significant is "good motive"? No certain response can be elicited to this controversial question of legitimate/illegitimate force.

Teachers in state schools are no longer authorised to administer corporal punishment, whereas teachers in private schools which receive no state funding or support may do so.[349] Where teachers may inflict corporal punishment their position, like parents, is controlled by the common law subject to the qualification that no corporal punishment may be inflicted which is inhuman or degrading.[350] A parent may authorise a teacher to inflict corporal

---

[346] In practice the staff would ignore the message; the risk of legal action or prosecution is probably remote. However, in the civil case of *St George's Healthcare National Health Service Trust v S, The Times*, May 8, 1998 it was held that even when her own life depended upon receiving medical treatment, an adult of sound mind was entitled to refuse it. That right of a pregnant woman was not diminished merely because her decision to exercise it would result in the death of an unborn child.

[347] [1998] 27 E.H.R.R. 611.

[348] [2001] EWCA Crim 1024, *The Times*, April 25, 2001 CA.

[349] See Education Act 1996 s.548, as substituted by the School Standards and Framework Act 1998.

[350] See, the Education Act 1993 s.293 which, in effect, incorporates art.3 of the European Convention on Human Rights; and see further Education Act 1996 by which teachers remain empowered to use reasonable force to restrain a pupil from causing or continuing to cause injury to a person or damage to property, or behaving or continuing to behave in a way prejudicial to good order and discipline at the school or among its pupils.

punishment on his or her child in which case the teacher would act with the common law authority of a parent and not by virtue of his position as teacher.

C. Mens Rea of Assault and Battery

7–074 It was generally assumed after *Venna*[351] that the offences of assault and battery required intention or at least *Cunningham* recklessness. In other words, for an assault the prosecution would have to prove that the defendant intended to cause another to apprehend the immediate infliction of unlawful force or consciously took an unjustified risk that his conduct would cause this to happen. For a battery the prosecution would have to prove that the accused either intended to inflict unlawful force on another person or at least consciously took an unjustified risk that his conduct would have this effect. Following *Caldwell*,[352] uncertainty prevailed as to the mens rea for the range of non-fatal offences in general. However, Lord Diplock had recognised that for many of the offences covered by the 1861 Act the relevant mens rea was defined by the word "maliciously" and that was accepted as requiring either intention or the conscious taking of an unjustified risk. Common assault and battery, however, were not defined in the Act and it was generally thought that these required proof of intention or recklessness, though at least since *Venna* recklessness was taken to mean a conscious risk taking. In *DPP v K*,[353] Parker L.J. in the Divisional Court held that recklessness sufficed for battery and that recklessness should be defined to mean that the defendant gave no thought to the serious and obvious risk he had created. This was subsequently overruled by the Court of Appeal in *Spratt*,[354] which in turn was supported by the Court of Appeal in *Parmenter*.[355] In the subsequent appeal by *Parmenter* to the House of Lords, their Lordships were not faced with an issue involving common assault, but it is very clear that the House supported the position taken in *Venna*, that recklessness in these two offences required proof that the defendant had consciously taken an unjustified risk of either inflicting unlawful force or of causing the victim to fear the immediate application of unlawful force. We can confidently treat *DPP v K* as overruled on the issue of mens rea, reinforced by the recent House of Lords decision in *R v G*.[356]

7–075 **An Element of Hostility?**   In the civil case of *Wilson v Pringle*[357] the Court of Appeal held that the prosecution must, in order to establish a battery, prove that the touching was "hostile". Although this was approved in *Brown*[358], the only real explanation of what this means was that if the touching was unlawful it was hostile. In *Brown*, however, the House of Lords had held that consensual infliction of harm in the course of sado-masochistic activities was unlawful. The touching was, therefore, hostile even though there was consent. What possible meaning does this leave for the word "hostile". It is perhaps safe to say that even if there ever was a requirement for an element of hostility, this is no longer the case.

3. ASSAULT OCCASIONING ACTUAL BODILY HARM

7–076 It is an offence punishable with up to five years' imprisonment and/or an unlimited fine to assault another thereby causing actual bodily harm. This offence requires first that the prosecutor establish a common assault. In other words he must prove the actus reus and

[351] [1976] Q.B. 421.
[352] See above, para.2–067.
[353] (1990) 91 Cr.App.R. 23; above, para.7–070.
[354] [1991] 2 All E.R. 210.
[355] [1991] 2 All E.R. 225.
[356] See above at para.2–069.
[357] [1986] 2 All E.R. 440.
[358] [1994] 1 A.C. 212; see below, para.7–102.

mens rea of a technical assault or battery as we have just described in the preceding section.[359] In the majority of cases the prosecution will rely on establishing a battery, but as we have seen in the case of *Ireland*[360] this offence may also be based upon a technical assault. In that case the accused had caused bodily harm by a series of silent telephone calls. If D waves a knife in P's face and P falls and injures himself in the process of escaping what he believes will be the immediate infliction of violence, D will have committed the offence under s.47.

A. Occasioning Actual Bodily Harm

The feature which distinguishes this offence from that of common assault and battery is the **7–077** requirement that the prosecution prove that by the assault the defendant occasioned (caused) actual bodily harm. You will recall that we stressed in dealing with the offence of battery that there was no requirement of harm or injury. Unfortunately, in describing battery as the unlawful application of force or violence, it is sometimes forgotten that any non-consensual and unjustified touching of another is a battery. The offence of assault occasioning actual bodily harm, however, has as its essential ingredient the causing of some bodily injury.

Two issues must be discussed. The first is the meaning of the phrase "actual bodily harm" and the second is whether there is any requirement for mens rea over and above that required for common assault.

B. Actual Bodily Harm

In *DPP v Smith*[361] Viscount Kilmuir L.C. said, of the phrase "grievous bodily harm", that the **7–078** words "bodily harm" needed no explanation and that grievous meant "really serious". It was, thus, taken to follow that "actual bodily harm" means something less than "really serious harm". In *Chan-Fook*[362] Hobhouse L.J. said that the word "harm" was a synonym for "injury" and that "actual" indicated that, although there was no requirement that the injury should be permanent, it should not be so trivial as to be wholly insignificant. The question of whether an injury is serious enough to be described as "actual" is a question of fact and degree for a jury. This is somewhat vague. A judge will be able to give some guidance, but he must be careful not to usurp the jury's function to decide what is an issue of fact.

A bruise, a graze and a cut would all be capable of being described as actual bodily harm, but drenching someone with beer, while it would be the application of force and, therefore, sufficient for a battery, would not constitute harm.[363] More recently, the courts have been occupied with the question of whether the word "bodily" restricts this offence to the causing of physical as opposed to psychological or psychiatric injuries. In *Miller*,[364] where a husband forced his wife to have sexual intercourse, it was held that actual bodily harm was not limited to skin, flesh or bones, but included any hurt or injury calculated to interfere with the health or comfort of the victim. Subsequently, in *Chan-Fook*,[365] the defendant (C-F) had suspected

---

[359] See above, para.7–074.
[360] See above, para.7–065.
[361] [1961] A.C. 290.
[362] [1994] 2 All E.R. 552.
[363] See, *Savage* [1991] 2 All E.R. 220, CA. The trial judge could, of course, rule that drenching with beer was not capable of constituting actual bodily harm. However, once he rules something is capable of being actual bodily harm, whether it is actual bodily harm is a jury issue.
[364] [1954] 2 Q.B. 282.
[365] [1994] 2 All E.R. 552.

that the complainant had stolen a ring belonging to C-F's fiancée. He questioned the complainant aggressively and then locked him in an upper room. The complainant, fearful that C-F might return, effected an escape through the window and sustained injuries when he fell. The prosecution's case was that even if the complainant had suffered no physical injuries as a result of C-F's conduct, he had nonetheless been reduced to a mental state which, in itself, constituted bodily harm.

Hobhouse L.J. commented that the word "bodily" does not restrict harm to injuries to the flesh, skin and bones. "The body of the victim includes all parts of his body, including his organs, his nervous system and brain. Bodily injury therefore may include injury to any of those parts of his body responsible for his mental and other faculties."[366] Hobhouse L.J. concluded that that the phrase "actual bodily harm" is capable of including recognisable psychiatric injury, but it does not include mere emotions such as fear, distress or panic, nor does it include, as such, states of mind that are not themselves evidence of some identifiable clinical condition. The phrase "interference with the health or comfort of the victim" which has regularly been used in directions to juries, should not be used as it is likely to lead jurors into thinking that this is sufficient whether or not any injury has occurred. No psychiatric evidence was produced in *Chan-Fook* and Hobhouse L.J. said that, in the absence of psychiatric evidence, a question of whether or not an assault occasioned psychiatric injury should not be left to the jury.[367] The decision of the Court of Appeal was endorsed by the House of Lords in the combined appeals of *Ireland* and *Burstow*.[368] It was argued that a Victorian statute passed nearly 140 years ago could not be taken to cover recognisable psychiatric injuries. Lord Steyn, however, said that such statutes are meant to last for a long time and therefore statutes needed to be interpreted "in the light of the best current scientific appreciation of the link between bodily and psychiatric injury."[369] In *Dhaliwal*[370] the appellate court were not prepared to extend the definition of bodily harm to include emotional distress, psychological trauma or indeed any condition less than a "recognisable psychiatric injury". There was a concern expressed that the present clear line should not be blurred, nor that any degree of elasticity should be introduced to it.

7–079   It can safely be said, therefore, that the phrase "bodily harm" in ss.18, 20 and 47 of the Offences Against the Person Act 1861 is capable of including recognisable psychiatric illness. In *R (On the application of T) v DPP*,[371] the Administrative Court determined that momentary loss of consciousness fell within the compass of the word "harm" as it embraced, "an injurious impairment to [the victim's] sensory functions", and thus it followed that the bodily harm was "actual." Harm would, however, not be within the definition where it was so trivial as to be wholly insignificant. This template applied in *DPP v Smith (Michael)*[372] where D malevolently cut off his former girlfriend's ponytail without consent. The Divisional Court held that "actual bodily harm" applied in a similar sense to *Chan-Fook* as an individual's hair was part of the whole body; harm encompasses hurt or damage provided it is not so trifling as to be insubstantial. Even if, medically and scientifically speaking, the hair above the surface of the scalp was no more than dead tissue, it remained part of the body and was attached to it. Moreover, it was intrinsic to each individual and to the identity of each individual. Hence, it fell within the meaning of "bodily" in the phrase "actual bodily harm" as it was concerned with the body of the individual victim. Sir Igor Judge P. in rather colourful language, asserted:

---

[366] [1994] 2 All E.R. 552 at 558–559.
[367] [1994] 2 All E.R. 552 at 559.
[368] [1997] 4 All E.R. 225.
[369] [1997] 4 All E.R. 225 at 233.
[370] [2006] 2 Cr.App.R. 24.
[371] [2003] EWHC 226 (Admin).
[372] [2006] EWHC 94 (Admin.); [2006] 2 All E.R. 16 DC.

"An individual's hair is relevant to his or her autonomy. Some regard it as their crowning glory. Admirers may so regard it in the object of their affections . . . In my judgment, the respondent's actions in cutting off a substantial part of the victim's hair in the course of an assault on her—like putting paint on it or some unpleasant substance which marked or damaged it without causing injury elsewhere—is capable of amounting to an assault which occasions actual bodily harm."[373]

The lessons from *DPP v Smith (Michael)* are, thus, self-evident. Protection is given to an individual's "crowning glory", and an unrequited lover who effects revenge on a former paramour by non-consensual hair cutting thereby commits "actual bodily harm". Individual autonomy and integrity is consequently protected, and rightly so. Cresswell J. provided an important summary of the matter:

"The body, for the purposes of the word 'bodily' in s.47 of the Offences Against the Person Act 1861, includes all parts of the body, including the hairs upon the scalp. On the evidence called by the prosecution, there was a case to answer of actual bodily harm. As the President has said, to a woman her hair is a vitally important part of her body. Where a significant portion of a woman's hair is cut off without her consent, this is a serious matter amounting to actual (not trivial or insignificant) bodily harm."[374]

Finally it has to be proved that the actual bodily harm was occasioned (caused) by the assault or battery. In *Savage*[375] the defendant deliberately threw a glass of beer over the complainant. At the same time the glass left the defendant's hand, broke on the bar-room table and a fragment of it cut the complainant's wrist. Both the Court of Appeal and House of Lords held that the drenching with the beer constituted a deliberate battery (application of unlawful force) and that the act which constituted the battery also caused the glass to shatter and cut the complainant. The battery had, therefore, occasioned actual bodily harm. Equally in the fright and flight cases,[376] where in a reasonable response to a battery or psychic assault the complainant is injured in escaping, the defendant will be held by his assault to have occasioned actual bodily harm. Where, however, the response to the battery or to threat of immediate violence is totally unreasonable, the assault will not be held to be the cause of the subsequent bodily injuries.

C. Mens Rea

The prosecution must first prove the mens rea necessary to establish an assault or battery. Is **7–080** it also required that the prosecution should prove that the defendant intended to cause or consciously took an unjustified risk of causing actual bodily harm? This would be the logical expectation; the mens rea should accompany each element of the actus reus. In *Roberts*,[377] R had given a lift to a female hitchhiker and had then suggested that she might like to go on the back seat with him and made a grab at her coat. The complainant was terrified and jumped from the moving car, thereby injuring herself. Roberts was charged with assaulting the complainant thereby occasioning actual bodily harm. He claimed that he had not

---

[373] [2006] EWHC 94 (Admin); [2006] 2 All E.R. 16 DC at [18]–[19].
[374] [2006] EWHC 94 (Admin); [2006] 2 All E.R. 16 DC at [21].
[375] See [1991] 2 All E.R. 220; [1992] 1 A.C. 699. See generally, A. Ashworth and K. Campbell, "Non-Fatal Offences: Mend and Make Do?" (1992) 108 L.Q.R. 187.
[376] See above, para.2–037.
[377] (1972) 56 Cr.App.R. 95; see above, para.2–037.

intended to cause any harm, nor had he foreseen that harm would result. Nevertheless his conviction was upheld on the basis that the section required only that actual bodily harm had, in fact, been caused by the assault; there was no requirement of mens rea on this aspect of the actus reus.[378] The only issue in relation to "occasioning actual bodily harm" is whether the harm was caused by the assault. In *Roberts*, the victim's attempts to get away from the clutches of D would not break the chain of causation unless the response could have been described as daft in the circumstances.[379]

Confusion was caused in 1991 by two contemporaneous decisions of the Court of Appeal. In *Savage*[380] Glidewell L.J. held that all that was required under s.47 was the mens rea of the assault or battery. Once this had been established it remained only to show a causal connection between the assault or battery and the actual bodily harm. In *Spratt*,[381] however, the Court of Appeal appeared to say that the prosecution must establish that the accused had foreseen that his conduct gave rise to the risk of causing harm. Later in *Parmenter*[382] the Court of Appeal said that there was a clear conflict between *Savage* and *Spratt* on this point and *Spratt* was to be preferred. In the combined appeals of *Savage and Parmenter*, the House of Lords upholding Glidewell L.J. in *Savage*, said[383] that none of the courts had referred to *Roberts* which had stated the law correctly; the only mens rea required for the offence of assault occasioning actual bodily harm, was the mens rea required to establish the assault or battery.

While it is suggested that the decision of the House of Lords does indeed return us to the position as it was before *Spratt* and *Parmenter*, the question remains as to which approach is the more logical. We said at the outset of our consideration of non-fatal offences against the person that there needs to be a ladder of non-fatal offences which is linked to the gravity of the offence. A defendant who commits an intentional battery but who causes no harm is liable to a maximum sentence of six months' imprisonment. A person who with the same mens rea causes slight, but unforeseen, injury by his intentional battery is guilty of an offence with a maximum sentence of five years. In *Savage* the defendant deliberately threw beer over a woman and in doing so let go of the glass. Bodily injury (the cut on the wrist) flowed directly from the intentional battery. It was, however, unclear from the trial court whether Savage had foreseen the risk of causing bodily injury. On this basis Savage would under *Parmenter* be liable only for battery and a maximum sentence of six months. Under *Roberts* and *Savage* she commits the offence of assault occasioning actual bodily harm, an offence carrying five years' imprisonment. Arguably, *Parmenter* is more logical. If Savage did not foresee the risk of bodily injury she should only be liable for a battery. If she foresaw harm, then she is clearly more culpable and should be exposed to a greater sentence.

Parmenter, it is suggested, would have produced a more logical ladder of offences. Assault and battery would have remained minor offences in which no harm is anticipated. Assault occasioning actual bodily harm would have been the next offence up the ladder where the courts have a dramatically increased power of sentence, but only for persons who have foreseen that they might cause harm. However, we shall see that this would have caused problems in relation to s.20 of the Act.[384]

---

[378] s.23 of the Offences Against the Person Act 1861 has a similar provision, the words "so as thereby to endanger the life of such person" being interpreted to require proof only of factual causation.
[379] See, further on the fright and flight cases, above para.2–037.
[380] [1991] 2 All E.R. 220.
[381] [1991] 2 All E.R. 210.
[382] [1991] 2 All E.R. 225 at 232.
[383] [1991] 4 All E.R. 698 at 713.
[384] See below, para.7–082.

4. THE OFFENCES UNDER SECTIONS 20 AND 18 OF THE OFFENCES AGAINST THE PERSON ACT 1861

Section 20 provides: **7–081**

> "Whosoever shall unlawfully and maliciously wound or inflict any grievous bodily harm upon another person, either with or without any weapon or instrument, shall be guilty of an offence triable either way and being convicted thereof shall be liable to imprisonment for five years."

Section 18 provides:

> "Whosoever shall unlawfully and maliciously by any means whatsoever wound or cause grievous bodily harm to any person *with intent to do some grievous bodily harm to some person, or with intent to resist or prevent the lawful apprehension or detaining of any person*, shall be guilty of an offence, and being convicted thereof shall be liable to imprisonment for life."[385]

By way of introduction to these offences we can say that today, for all intents and purposes, the actus reus of the two offences is the same. The main distinction lies in the ulterior intent within s.18 (italicised). It should also be noted that s.18 carries a possible life sentence while s.20 has a maximum sentence of five years, the same as that provided for the offence of assault occasioning actual bodily harm (s.47). This may seem odd since s.20 is clearly regarded by all as a far more serious offence than the s.47 offence. The reason is simply that the 1861 Act was a consolidating statute, into which a whole host of existing offences were placed without any rationalisation.

A. Section 20

There are two separate offences within this section—(1) unlawful and malicious wounding **7–082** and (2) unlawful and malicious infliction of grievous bodily harm.

(i) Actus Reus

The prosecution must prove that the defendant wounded or inflicted grievous bodily harm. **7–083** A wound requires that the continuity of the skin must be broken.[386] The whole skin must be severed, not just the mere cuticle or upper skin.[387] It is not sufficient that internal bleeding is caused, though this may amount to grievous or actual bodily harm.[388] On the other hand, a cut on the inside of the mouth has been held to constitute a wound.[389] The difference is that the inside skin of the lips and cheek is readily accessible from the outside; you can trace the continuity of the skin with your finger. Although most wounding will be caused by sharp instruments, the actual implement is of no concern; it is the rupturing of the skin that is important and not the means by which it was achieved. Nor does it matter how big the cut is; a pin prick will suffice if it penetrates the whole skin.

---

[385] Authors' italics.
[386] *Wood* (1830) 1 Mood. 278.
[387] *M'Loughlin* (1838) 8 C. & P. 635.
[388] See *C (A Minor) v Eisenhower* [1984] Q.B. 331. Note also that a mere bruising of the skin cannot be classified as a wound.
[389] *Shadbolt* (1835) 5 C. & P. 504. See also *Waltham* (1849) 3 Cox 442; a rupture of the lining of the urethra was classified as a wound.

It has been asserted,[390] "the wound must be given by the act of the defendant; for if in self-defence the prosecutor forces a part of his body against an instrument in the defendant's hands, and so cuts or wounds himself, it is not within the statute: *Beckett.*"[391] It is suggested, however, that Ormerod is correct when he says that this was a decision under a statute of 1837 which did not contain the words "by any means whatsoever" and that today the prosecutor would be held to have been wounded by the defendant.[392]

The second offence within s.20 requires proof that the defendant inflicted grievous bodily harm. We have already seen that bodily harm is a synonym for bodily injury and that it can include recognisable psychiatric injuries or illnesses.[393] The word grievous means nothing more than serious and it is a question for the jury as to whether the injury is grievous.

7–084   More problematical is the word "inflict" and the fact that in s.18 the word used in this context is "cause". Is there any difference between inflicting grievous bodily harm and causing grievous bodily harm? Is one expression wider than the other? The answer must be that cause is a wider concept merely requiring proof of a causal link between the defendant's unlawful conduct and the prohibited result. If one were faced today by a statute in which different words were used, and if the statute had been drawn up as a coherent whole with the clear legislative intention that its provisions should be consistent, then it would be entirely appropriate to conclude that Parliament had intended the two words to receive different meanings. However the Act of 1861 is not such an Act. It was merely a consolidating Act which gathered together a whole host of unrelated provisions from existing statutes. No attempt was made to rationalise the provisions and this is why ss.47 and 20 carry the same maximum penalty even though s.20 is clearly seen as the more heinous offence. Under these circumstances, the House of Lords in *Ireland and Burstow*[394] accepted as correct a passage from Greaves, the draftsman, where he said:

"... any argument as to a difference in the intention of the legislature, which may be drawn from a difference in the terms of one clause from those in another, will be entitled to no weight in the construction of such clauses; for that argument can only apply with force where an Act is framed from beginning to end with one and the same view, and with the intention of making it thoroughly consistent throughout."[395]

Nevertheless the courts have endeavoured to find a difference in scope between the two words. The word "inflict" was considered to indicate the need to prove that the grievous bodily harm had been brought about in a violent manner and this led the courts to decide that the grievous bodily harm must be brought about by an assault or battery.[396] Thus in the leading case of *Clarence*,[397] C, knowing he was suffering from a venereal disease, had intercourse with his wife who was totally ignorant of his condition. There is no doubt that the condition was capable of constituting grievous bodily harm and there would be no problem in proving that he had "caused her grievous bodily harm". However, he was charged under s.20 with inflicting grievous bodily harm and this could not be established

---

[390] Archbold *Criminal Pleading, Evidence and Practice* 1996 edn para.19–217. The passage does not appear in the 1998 edition.
[391] (1836) 1 M. & Rob. 526.
[392] Smith and Hogan, *Criminal Law* 8th edn, p.609.
[393] See above, paras 7–078—7–079. On unconsciousness as grievous bodily harm see *Hicks* [2007] EWCA Crim 1500; and injection of a needle as a s.47 offence see *Gower* [2007] EWCA Crim 1655.
[394] [1997] 4 All E.R. 225 at 234.
[395] The Criminal Law Consolidation and Amendment Acts 2nd edn (1862), at pp.3–4.
[396] It was held that a wound must be the result of a battery. But now see below, para.7–085.
[397] (1888) 22 Q.B.D. 23.

since his wife consented to having sexual intercourse, albeit under a mistake, and this meant that he had not assaulted her. His conviction was, therefore, quashed.

This narrow interpretation of the word "inflict" led to a line of cases in which the courts either strained the meaning of the word assault or ignored the need to find an assault. Thus in *Lewis*,[398] L shouted threats at his wife through a locked door. She heard the sound of breaking glass and attempted to escape through a window, thereby suffering serious injuries. His conviction for inflicting grievous bodily harm was upheld. If the court was relying on a technical assault, then it would have to find that the complainant was in fear of the immediate application of violence and this is stretching the concept of immediacy a long way. In *Martin*[399] M, shortly before the end of a theatre performance, placed an iron bar across one of the exit doors, turned out the lights and yelled "fire". In the ensuing panic, several persons were seriously injured by being crushed against the doors which were barred. Martin's conviction for inflicting grievous bodily harm was upheld. Earlier decisions on battery had indicated it required a direct application of force by D on the complainant. The case of *Martin* can, therefore, be seen either as saying that an indirect application of force will suffice for a battery or that the word "inflicting" in s.20 does not require proof of an assault or battery.

The position was far from satisfactory. However the case of *Clarence Wilson*[400] gave the **7–085** House of Lords a chance to review the situation. The matter arose on an issue of procedure concerning alternative verdicts. The question was whether a jury trying a defendant upon a charge of inflicting grievous bodily harm could acquit him of that charge and convict of assault occasioning actual bodily harm. In general a jury may do that if the allegations in the indictment amount to or include (whether expressly or by implication) an allegation of another offence falling within the jurisdiction of the court.[401] It had generally been assumed that the s.20 charge of inflicting grievous bodily harm necessarily involved proof of an assault occasioning actual bodily harm and, thus, the alternative verdict was permissible. However, in *Wilson* the House of Lords, following *Salisbury*,[402] a decision of the Supreme Court of Victoria, held that while the word "inflict" did not have such a wide meaning as "cause", neither was its meaning so limited that it always required proof of an assault. A defendant could inflict grievous bodily harm on someone without necessarily assaulting them. The Supreme Court of Victoria had concluded:

> ". . . grievous bodily harm may be inflicted . . . either where the accused has directly and violently 'inflicted' it by assaulting the victim,[403] or where the accused has 'inflicted' it by doing something intentionally, which though is not itself a direct application of force to the body of the victim, does directly result in force being violently applied to the body of the victim, so that he suffers grievous bodily harm."[404]

We can now say that *Martin* and *Lewis* can both be regarded as cases where there was no assault in the strict sense, but nonetheless we can say that the accused have inflicted grievous bodily harm in an indirect way. The House of Lords held that although this would now mean an assault or battery was no longer a requirement under s.20, in the vast majority of cases there would be an assault and, therefore, it would be possible to say that the allegations

[398] [1970] Crim.L.R. 647.
[399] (1881) 8 Q.B.D. 54; above, p.370.
[400] [1984] A.C. 242.
[401] See further the Criminal Law Act 1967 s.6.
[402] [1976] V.R. 452.
[403] An assault.
[404] Not an assault.

impliedly include an assault; s.47, therefore, remains an alternative verdict.[405] But what is the position in one of these rare cases in which there is no assault or battery? Would today a jury hearing charges of inflicting grievous bodily harm against *Martin* or *Lewis* have open to them the alternative verdict of assault occasioning actual bodily harm? Would a jury be able to convict Martin or Lewis if they were prosecuted on an indictment which charged them with assault occasioning actual bodily harm? If the answer is "no" in *Martin*, because there is no battery and "no" in *Lewis*, because of the absence of immediacy, why should they be able to return an alternative verdict of assault occasioning actual bodily harm on an indictment which charges only a s.20 offence and does not even mention s.47?[406]

It would seem that following *Wilson* the position is that there is less difference in the meaning of the words "cause" and "inflict" though it is still recognised that cause may be slightly wider.[407]

7–086   This was not to be the end of the story. In *Burstow*,[408] B, who had had a relationship with the victim, refused to accept it was over. Following his release from prison for harassing her, he continued to pester her by a variety of conduct which included stalking her, turning up at her place of work, making silent and abusive phone calls to her, scattering condoms in her garden and stealing her clothes and sending her a note which he meant to be menacing and which was taken to be menacing by her. As a result of all this conduct over a five-month period, she suffered a serious psychiatric illness. He was convicted of inflicting grievous bodily harm and his appeal eventually reached the House of Lords where his counsel argued that, despite decisions such as *Clarence Wilson*, a Victorian statute dealing with grievous bodily harm was inappropriate to cover the infliction of psychiatric illness. There was universal agreement that there would be no difficulty had Burstow been charged with "causing" grievous bodily harm. The endorsement, however, given in *Wilson* to the statement from *Salisbury*[409] would seem to suggest that "inflict" required at least an indirect application of violence to the body. However, Lord Steyn, in *Burstow*, said that the issue is one of construction:

> "The question is whether as a matter of current usage the contextual interpretation of 'inflict' can embrace the idea of one person inflicting psychiatric injury on another. One can without straining the language in any way answer that question in the affirmative. I am not saying that the words cause and inflict are exactly synonymous. They are not. What I am saying is that in the context of the 1861 Act one can now quite naturally speak of inflicting psychiatric injury."[410]

The overall result is that there is possibly little or no difference between the meanings of the two words, and this was an essential conclusion to avoid absurd distinctions being drawn between ss.18 and 20. Lord Hope said that there was possibly one difference; the word "inflict" implies that the consequence of the act is something that the victim is likely to find unpleasant or harmful, but the word "cause" may, however, embrace some result which is

---

[405] This was supported in *Savage and Parmenter*.

[406] See, Clarkson and Keating, *op. cit.* p.596.

[407] See, e.g. Lord Mackay L.C. in *Mandair* [1995] 1 A.C. 208 at 215 where he said with the agreement of the majority of the House "In my opinion . . . the word 'cause' is wider or at least not narrower than the word 'inflict'". See generally J. Gardner, "Rationality and the Rule of Law in Offences Against the Person" (1994) 53 C.L.J. 502; A. Reed, "Offences Against the Person: The Need for Reform" (1995) 59 J.C.L. 187.

[408] [1997] 4 All E.R. 225; [1997] 1 Cr.App.R. 144; see generally C. Wells, "Stalking: The Criminal Law Response" [1997] Crim.L.R. 463; P. Seago and A. Reed [1997] All E.R. Annual Review 117. Burstow was again sentenced to custody on January 4, 1999 for similar offences against the same victim.

[409] Above, para.7–085.

[410] [1997] 4 All E.R. 225 at 235.

pleasant and enjoyable. It would, however, be unwise to say that "inflict" involves the absence of pleasure. In *Brown*[411] the House of Lords ruled that the deliberate infliction of injury was an offence, irrespective of the consent or pleasure of the victim unless the act was covered by a recognised exception such as medical or sporting activities. It would be nonsensical if consent could be no defence to a charge of assault occasioning actual bodily harm, yet it could be a defence to inflicting grievous bodily harm.

The case of *Clarence*[412] remains problematical. On what basis could it be said that *Clarence* did not inflict grievous bodily harm on his wife. It will no longer be an answer that he did not commit an assault. Clarence's wife, unlike the complainants in *Ireland* and *Burstow*, did consent to the conduct of the accused, but is this a relevant distinction? The decision in *Clarence* is no longer authoritative and today the defendant could be charged with inflicting grievous bodily harm. This result was recently posited by the Court of Appeal in the significant case of *Dica*.[413] Their Lordships determined that grievous bodily harm *can* be inflicted through consensual sexual intercourse. Liability will be incurred in the context of a defendant, knowing that he himself was HIV infected, recklessly transmitting that disease to a person who did not know of, and did not consent to, the risk of infection. In effect, *Burstow* established that even when no physical violence has been applied, directly or indirectly to the victim's body, an offence under s.20 may be committed. This according to Judge L.J. who delivered the leading judgment in *Dica*, meant that *Clarence* was finally overruled. He stated:

> "Whether the consequences suffered by the victim are physical injuries or psychiatric injuries, or a combination of the two, the ingredients of the offence prescribed by s.20 are identical. If psychiatric injury can be inflicted without direct or indirect violence, or an assault, for the purposes of s.20 physical injury may be similarly inflicted. It is no longer possible to discern the critical difference identified by the majority in *R v Clarence*, and encapsulated by Stephen J. in his judgment, between an 'immediate and necessary connection' between the relevant blow and the consequent injury, and the 'uncertain and delayed' effect of the act which led to the eventual development of infection. The erosion process is now complete."[414]

Unlawful

As we have said before the word "unlawful" is an element of offences against the person **7–087** in general. It indicates the availability of defences of justification such as self-defence, defence of property and prevention of crime.[415] In offences of common assault and battery the word "unlawful" also indicates the availability of consent as a defence. Where, however, bodily injury is intended or caused, and this will be the case in nearly all offences apart from common assault and battery, consent will be a defence only if the case comes within an exception to the general rule.[416]

(ii) *Mens Rea*

The mens rea of most of the offences in the Offences Against the Person Act is provided by **7–088** the word "maliciously". We saw in *Cunningham*[417] that this means the prosecution must prove that the accused intended to bring about the prohibited result or was reckless as to so

---

[411] [1994] 1 A.C. 212; see below, para.7–102.
[412] Above, para.7–084.
[413] [2004] 3 All E.R. 593; [2004] EWCA Crim 1103.
[414] [2004] 3 All E.R. 593; [2004] EWCA Crim 1103 at [30].
[415] See above, para.5–044.
[416] For discussion of consent as a defence to offences against the person see below, para.7–098.
[417] Above, para.2–065.

doing. The word reckless was accepted by Byrne J. as meaning that the defendant had foreseen that the particular type of harm might be done, and yet had gone on to take the risk of it. It might have been thought that, on a s.20 charge, the prosecution would therefore have to prove either that the accused intended to wound or inflict grievous bodily harm, or that he consciously took an unjustified risk of so doing. In *Mowatt*,[418] however, Diplock L.J. said this was to misunderstand what Byrne J. had meant when he had used the phrase "particular kind of harm". He had simply meant that the accused must see that what he was doing would lead to personal injury as opposed to, for example, damage to property. He continued:

> "It is quite unnecessary that the accused should have foreseen that his unlawful act might cause physical harm of the gravity described in the section, i.e. wound or serious physical injury. It is enough that he should have foreseen that some physical harm to some person, albeit of a minor character, might result."[419]

This extract from Lord Diplock's judgment raises two important issues. First, in purporting to follow Byrne J. in *Cunningham*, Lord Diplock had used the phrase "*should have foreseen*" which would suggest an objective test was being applied and, secondly, by saying that the prosecution need prove only that the accused should have foreseen some harm, albeit slight, he would appear to be stating mens rea more appropriate to the charge of assault occasioning actual bodily harm rather than to that of s.20. A chance for the House of Lords to review the position occurred in the combined appeals of *Savage* and *Parmenter*.[420] In both *Savage* and *Parmenter* the trial judge had directed the jury that it was enough that the accused *should have foreseen* that what he was doing would result in harm to some other person. In doing so the trial judges would simply appear to have been following the words of Lord Diplock in *Mowatt* which laid down an objective approach to the question. However, Lord Ackner said that when Lord Diplock's speech was read as a whole it was clear that he meant the courts to take a subjective approach. It was not enough that the accused should have foreseen some harm to another (an objective approach); the prosecution must prove that he actually did foresee some harm to another (a subjective approach). This is yet another example of the dangers of relying upon the words of a judge as if they were a statutory provision. In the passage quoted above Lord Diplock was purporting to deal with the issue of exactly what the accused must foresee and in doing so he lost sight of the fact that he had already spent considerable time in ruling that the word "maliciously" meant that the accused must actually foresee some harm. It is clear that where courts are interpreting the word "maliciously" in the Offences Against the Person Act 1861 they should be guided by the definition given in *Cunningham*; it must be proved that the accused actually foresaw the requisite degree of harm.[421]

7–089 In dealing with the second issue of exactly what degree of harm the accused must foresee to be guilty of a s.20 offence, the House also confirmed that there was no need to prove that the accused had foreseen a wound or the infliction of grievous bodily harm. It was sufficient

[418] [1968] 1 Q.B. 421.
[419] [1968] 1 Q.B. 421 at 426.
[420] [1991] 4 All E.R. 698.
[421] Unfortunately Lord Ackner, in summing up, concluded, "It is enough that he *should have foreseen* that some physical harm to some person, albeit of a minor character, might result." Again all that can be said is that in the context of his speech as a whole this has to be seen as a slip of the tongue, and another reminder that it is dangerous to treat extracts from judgments as if they were the carefully thought out provisions of a statute. Just as with Lord Diplock in *Mowatt*, Lord Ackner in *Savage* and *Parmenter* clearly intended to rule that the accused must actually see the requisite degree of harm.

that he foresaw some harm albeit of a minor character. This is, in effect, constructive liability; the accused is convicted on the basis of mens rea which is more appropriate for the offence under s.47 of assault occasioning actual bodily harm and this is objectionable in principle.[422] It would appear, therefore, that the House of Lords shares Lord Diplock's view that when Byrne J. referred to *"the particular type of harm"* in *Cunningham*, he meant that the accused must foresee physical injury as opposed to property damage. There does, however, seem to be very little to support such a view. It is far more likely that in relation to s.23[423] Byrne J. had meant that the accused must foresee that what he was doing would cause a noxious substance to be administered to another, and that if he had been invited to express a view about s.20 he would have said that the accused must foresee a wound or the infliction of grievous bodily harm.

Had the House rejected *Mowatt* in favour of a requirement that the accused be proved to have foreseen that a wound or the infliction of grievous bodily harm might occur, the way would have been clear to hold that for s.47 the accused must foresee that his actions might occasion actual bodily harm. In this way a more coherent ladder of offences would have been created. Unfortunately the opportunity was missed.

One final point should be mentioned. The prosecution need prove only that the accused foresaw that some harm "might" result. It is not necessary to prove that he foresaw that it "would" result; this would be too heavy a burden on the Crown and far too generous to the accused. It is perhaps preferable to phrase recklessness in terms of risk taking; the prosecution must prove that the accused took an unjustified risk of causing some harm.[424]

B. Section 18

(i) Actus Reus

We have already referred to the use of the word "cause" in s.18 in contrast to "inflict" in s.20 and this may mean that the actus reus of s.18 may be wider than that of s.20.[425] That apart we can safely say that there are no other significant differences.   **7–090**

(ii) Mens Rea

The prosecution must prove firstly that the accused maliciously wounded or caused grievous bodily harm and secondly that he possessed an ulterior intent.   **7–091**

(a) Maliciously Wounded or Caused Grievous Bodily Harm: (The Basic Intent)

In *Mowatt*[426] Diplock L.J., said, obiter, that the word "malicious" was superfluous in s.18. This is only partially true. Presumably Diplock L.J. was thinking of the usual type of s.18 case where the accused is indicted for maliciously causing grievous bodily harm with intent   **7–092**

---

[422] Lord Ackner argued that there were several examples where the requisite mens rea did not accord with the *actus reus*. Murder was one example; the accused could be convicted on the basis of an intention to cause grievous bodily harm. In assault occasioning actual bodily harm, the prosecution did not have to prove that the accused intended or foresaw any harm. This, however, can be defended upon the wording of s.47; it can be argued that the word "occasioning" merely requires proof of causation. It is likely also that in s.23 of the 1861 Act (see above, para.7–042), the prosecution need only prove mens rea on the administration of a noxious thing; the wording "so as thereby to endanger the life of such person" suggests only the need to prove a causal link. Lord Ackner's argument that a requirement that the accused be proved to have intended or foreseen a wound or the infliction of grievous bodily harm would make the offence too difficult to prove is equally unconvincing.

[423] s.23 of the Offences Against the Person Act 1861 provides; "Whosoever shall unlawfully and maliciously administer or cause to be administered to or taken by any other person any poison or other destructive or noxious thing, so as thereby to endanger the life of such person, or so as thereby to inflict on such person any grievous bodily harm, shall be guilty of an offence . . ."

[424] See above, para.2–065.

[425] See above, para.7–083. Secretive poisoning might amount to the causing of grievous bodily harm but not the infliction of it.

[426] Above, para.7–084.

to do grievous bodily harm. In this case the word is redundant since the prosecution will have to prove the ulterior intent—with intent to do grievous bodily harm—recklessness will not suffice here. Equally where the accused is charged with wounding with intent to do grievous bodily harm, the word "malicious" is probably redundant.

Where, however, the accused is charged with wounding or causing grievous bodily harm with intent to resist arrest the word "maliciously" has a full role to play. Consider a situation in which it is alleged that the defendant in trying to escape lawful arrest pushes the police officer who is seriously injured in a fall.[427] If the word malicious is given no role to play, it would mean that the only mens rea required of the defendant would be his intent to resist arrest and this would be satisfied even if he had used only the slightest force to break away from the officer. This would surely be wrong. The word maliciously should mean that the prosecutor, in addition to proving the intent to resist arrest, should also have to prove that the accused also foresaw that what he was doing might result in some physical injury, albeit slight. This would give maliciously the same meaning as in s.20 under the *Mowatt* gloss. Some have argued that in s.18, an offence carrying life imprisonment, the prosecution should have to prove that the accused intended or foresaw a wound or the causing of grievous bodily harm. This, however, would mean that the word maliciously would have different meanings in ss.20 and 18 and is unlikely to find support in the courts; especially since the word has been the subject of recent scrutiny by the House of Lords in *Savage* and *Parmenter*.

(b) With Intent to . . . (the Ulterior Intent)

7–093   In addition to the basic intent the prosecution must prove that the defendant either intended to do some grievous bodily harm to any person or that he intended to resist or prevent the lawful apprehension or detainer of any person.

The word intend in this section should be given the same meaning as intends to kill bears in the law of murder.[428] In other words it is not enough that the accused foresaw that what he was doing was virtually certain to cause grievous bodily harm; such a state of mind is, however, evidence from which a jury may infer that the accused intended to cause grievous bodily harm.

If the prosecution rely on proving that the defendant intended to prevent the lawful arrest of himself or another, they must prove that the defendant was aware of the facts that made the arrest lawful. If, on the facts the defendant believed to exist, the arrest would have been unlawful, the intent is not made out. On the other hand, if on the circumstances known by D to exist the arrest is lawful, though for some reason D believes it to be unlawful, the prosecution will have made out the allegation.[429]

Like s.20, s.18 provides for two separate offences; wounding and causing grievous bodily harm. It would be duplicitous to include both allegations against a defendant in the same count of the indictment, even in the alternative. However, the two versions of the ulterior intent are seen not as separate offences, but different ways of wounding or causing grievous bodily harm.Thus it is permissible to allege in one count that the defendant unlawfully and maliciously wounded the victim with the intent to do some grievous bodily harm or with the intent to resist arrest.

---

[427] See, e.g. *Morrison* (1989) Cr.App.R. 17.
[428] *Bryson* [1985] Crim.L.R. 669; see also *Belfon* [1976] 3 All E.R. 46. Only in exceptional cases will a direction on oblique intent be appropriate; see, e.g. *Phillips* [2004] EWCA Crim 112.
[429] See, e.g. *Blackburn v Bowering* [1995] Crim.L.R. 38.

5. MISCELLANEOUS NOTES ON OFFENCES AGAINST THE PERSON

A. Alternative Verdicts

In some situations it is possible for the trial judge to tell the jury that they would be entitled **7–094**
to find the defendant not guilty of the offence charged, but guilty of another offence which is
not specifically included in the indictment.[430] Thus where the defendant is charged with an
offence under s.18 of the Offences Against the Person Act 1861, the jury may acquit him of
that charge and convict him of an offence under s.20 or s.47. Similarly, a person charged
with an offence under s.20 may be convicted instead of an assault occasioning actual bodily
harm under s.47. Although the words "greater" and "lesser" offences do not occur in the
statutory provisions, the alternative offence will almost always be a lesser offence than the
offence charged.

It is not, however, open for a jury to acquit a defendant charged with assault occasioning
actual bodily harm and convict him of common assault or battery. This is because common
assault is outside the jurisdiction of the Crown Court, being a summary only offence.[431]

B. Laser Pointers

It is worth noting the relatively recent arrival on the scene of a new weapon, the laser **7–095**
pointer. This device, which was originally intended for use by lecturers, can, if pointed into
another's eyes, cause temporary blindness and possibly even permanent serious damage.
What charges may be brought against such a defendant? It would seem that depending upon
the extent of the injuries it would be possible to say that the defendant had "caused"
grievous bodily harm (s.18). Following *Ireland* and *Burstow*[432] a charge of inflicting grievous
bodily harm would also be tenable. Could it, however, constitute a battery? Does it
constitute the application of unlawful force to the body of the victim? It is suggested that
there is no reason to distinguish it from applying force by means of a bullet, or a splashing
with sulphuric acid.[433] Another possible offence would be possession of an offensive
weapon.[434]

C. A Hierarchy of Offences[435]

Although to a certain extent the offences we have examined provide the courts with a ladder **7–096**
of offences, there are, as we have seen, anomalies which arise out of the ragbag nature of
the statute. A further example is worth mentioning. If D sticks a pin into P's hand drawing
blood, D may be convicted of common assault, assault occasioning actual bodily harm,
malicious wounding and, if he has stuck the pin in intending to resist lawful arrest by P, of
wounding with intent which carries life imprisonment.

D. Racially or Religiously Aggravated Assaults

A significant increase during the 1990s of crimes involving incidents of racial violence and **7–097**
harassment prompted the Government to take action. New remedial legislation was
introduced in the Crime and Disorder Act 1998 to counteract this unfortunate trend. This

---

[430] See, generally, the Criminal Law Act 1967 s.6(3).
[431] It may, however, be possible to specify the common assault in the indictment under the provisions of ss.40 and
41 of the Criminal Justice Act 1988.
[432] [1997] 4 All E.R. 225 above, para.7–086.
[433] *DPP v K* (1990) 91 Cr.App.R. 23, above, para.7–070.
[434] Prevention of Crime Act 1953 s.1.
[435] See below, para.7–114 for note on reform.

has been twinned together with specific legislation to deal with religiously aggravated offences. This was promulgated by the events in America in 2001 prompting the Anti-Terrorism Crime and Security Act 2001.[436] A new s.28(1) of the Crime and Disorder Act established two offences to deal with the prevalent issues. It is a crime where at the time of committing the offence or immediately before or after doing so, D demonstrates towards the victim of the offence racial or religious hostility based on the victim's membership of a racial or religious group.[437] Liability also applies where the offence is motivated wholly or partly by hostility towards members of a racial or religious group based on their membership of that group. The Crime and Disorder Act 1998 created new offences of racially aggravated assaults—all of them are based on pre-existing offences but carry a higher maximum punishment.[438] Section 29(1) of the Act provides that:

> "A person is guilty of an offence under this section if he commits—
>
> (a) an offence under s.20 of the Offences Against the Person Act 1861 (malicious wounding or grievous bodily harm);
>
> (b) an offence under s.47 of that Act (actual bodily harm); or
>
> (c) common assault,
>
> which is racially aggravated for the purposes of this section."

It is significant that s.29(1) does not create one offence which can be committed in various ways but a number of separate ones. In relation to maxima punishment available for these offences then in the case of assaults based on s.20 or s.47 the maximum penalty of five years is increased to seven years and for common assault the maximum penalty is increased from six months to two years. Interpretative difficulties attach to the issue of whether a crime is or is not racially aggravated. This problem was illuminated in sharp focus in *DPP v Pal*.[439] The victim, a man in his 60s of Asian appearance, was a caretaker at a community centre. He sought to eject D, an Asian youth from the centre, whereupon D assaulted him and called him a "white man's arse licker" and a "brown Englishman". D was subsequently charged with an offence of racially aggravated common assault contrary to s.29(1)(c) and (3) of the Crime and Disorder Act 1998. However, the justices acquitted, determining that D used the words because he was aggrieved at being asked to leave and thus he was not demonstrating racial hostility. The appeal by the prosecution was dismissed by the Divisional Court who held that D was not demonstrating hostility towards Asians in general, but hostility towards V's conduct that night in seeking to remove him from the premises. The words used certainly displayed hostility to brown people who associate too closely with white, but did not display hostility towards V's membership of the Asian racial group (the defendant's own group). Although the words used had a race element attached to them they did not fall within the confines of the statutory definition of racial aggravation. Moreover, the assault may have been motivated solely by D's resentment of V's conduct—it may be that he would have attacked V whatever his race. More recently, however, in *Rogers*[440] the House of Lords

---

[436] See M. Idriss, "Religion and the Anti-Terrorism Crime and Security Act 2001" [2002] Crim.L.R. 890.

[437] See, e.g. *Parry v DPP* [2004] EWHC 3112 (Admin).

[438] See Malik, M., "'Racist Crime': Racially Aggravated Offences in the Crime and Disorder Act 1998, Part II" (1999) 62 M.L.R. 409.

[439] [2000] Crim.L.R. 756. see also, *DPP v M* [2004] EWHC 1453; and *Att.-Gen.'s Reference (No.4 of 2004)* [2005] EWCA Crim 889 and *Rogers* [2007] UKHL 8. See, also, *Howard v DPP* [2008] EWHC 608 (Admin); and *Johnson v DPP* [2008] EWHC 509 (Admin).

[440] [2007] UKHL 8; [2007] 2 A.C. 62 HL.

have adopted a broad purposive interpretation to the statutory provisions. The requirements of s.28(1)(a) are satisfied where D refers to P as a "bloody foreigner", and where P is of Spanish descent. The words in the section are consequently transmogrified to embrace those of non-British origin, and they are capable of forming a defined "racial group".

6. CONSENT AS A DEFENCE TO OFFENCES AGAINST THE PERSON[441]

The question we need to answer in this section is how far the presence of consent on the **7–098** part of the victim of an alleged offence against the person may prevent the prosecution establishing the offence. This involves two distinct questions; to what offences is consent relevant,[442] and what do we mean by consent?[443]

A. To Which Crimes is Consent a Defence?

It has to be said at the outset that the law in this area is not altogether free from confusion. **7–099** This stems from the need to balance the freedom of the individual to chose what he wants to do with his body against the right of the state to protect the individual from harming himself and thereby harming society in general. At one extreme there is the view, based on personal autonomy, that our bodies are our own and we should be entitled to do as we please with them. At the other extreme is the view that the state should be able to interfere to prevent an individual doing anything which might be thought to be harmful to him or her self. A paternalistic approach could be defended upon the basis either that society simply has the right to lay down certain limits to behaviour or that self-inflicted injuries use up valuable medical resources which could be used on more deserving cases. A cogent illustration of this balancing equation occurred in the recent high profile cases of *Dica*[444] and *Konzani*[445] involving transmission of sexual disease. Their Lordships, on policy grounds, considered comparable issues of protection and autonomy.

The law as to the limits of consent represents an attempt to strike a balance between individual freedom and the interests of the state.

It is probably safe to say that the law does not permit citizens to consent to being killed. Even here, however, certain qualifications need to be made. While it is clear that euthanasia is not permitted in this country, there is nothing to stop an individual refusing to accept medical treatment. But as we have seen,[446] the law draws a sharp line between omission and commission. We are entitled to consent to being allowed to die peacefully without further treatment, but we may not consent to being killed.[447]

Consent may also be relevant in determining a secondary party's liability for murder. In the South African case of *S v Robinson*[448] the defendants agreed to kill the victim with his

---

[441] See generally *Consent in the Criminal Law*, Law Commission Consultation Paper, No.139 (1995).

[442] Consent may be relevant as a defence or lack of consent by the victim might be an essential ingredient of the definition of an offence. If it is classified as a defence then the accused would bear an evidential burden on the issue. In *Brown* ([1994] 1 A.C. 212; see below, para.7–102, the House of Lords appears to support the view that in the non-sexual offences against the person such as common assault, consent is a matter of defence.

[443] See, generally R. Leng, "Consent and Offences Against the Person" [1994] Crim.L.R. 480.

[444] [2004] 3 All E.R. 593; [2004] EWCA Crim 1103.

[445] [2005] EWCA Crim 706.

[446] See, section on omissions, above paras 2–015—2–031.

[447] See also *Bodkin Adams* [1957] Crim.L.R. 365. Painkilling drugs often accelerate death and here the law may have a fine distinction to draw. So long as the doctor's purpose is the relief of suffering, it will not constitute an unlawful killing if the drugs incidentally accelerate death. Where, however, acceleration of death is the prime motive, the doctor will be guilty of murder.

[448] 1968 (1) S.A. 666, Supreme Court of South Africa, Appellate Division.

consent. When at the last minute the victim withdrew his consent, the principal offender nevertheless carried out the killing. It was held that the accessories were not liable for murder since the defendant had exceeded the agreed plan to kill the victim with his consent. Thus while the principal offender was guilty of murder since, even had consent not been withdrawn, it would not protect the actual killer, the accessories were, in effect, protected by the deceased's consent.[449]

7–100   In *Dudley and Stephens,*[450] the defendants were convicted of the murder of a cabin boy whose body they had fed upon to save themselves from starvation after having been adrift in a lifeboat without food for eight days and water for six days. It is clear that the cabin boy did not assent to being killed, but were the same facts to recur today, it is possible that the court would take a different approach if it were established that the victim had consented to be killed to save the others.

In boxing the contestants clearly consent to the risk of serious bodily injury being inflicted upon themselves. Outside of the ring if A were to render B unconscious by a blow on the head, a jury would be entitled to find that A had caused B grievous bodily harm. Today, however, the contestants know that such a blow might cause death and they must be taken to have consented to the, albeit highly unlikely, risk of death.[451]

It is also fairly safe to say that consent is a defence to common assault. In practice this will be relevant only to the crime of battery, which as we have seen[452] requires proof that the defendant has applied unlawful force to the victim. Battery does not require the infliction of harm; any non-consensual touching can amount to a battery, however slight. Earlier cases tended to treat absence of consent as an element of the offence of battery[453] in the same way that absence of consent is part of the crime of rape. In *Brown*[454] the majority of the House of Lords thought that consent was more properly referred to as a defence. The practical effect of this decision is that as a defence it places an evidential burden[455] on the accused to produce evidence of consent before the judge is obliged to put it before the jury.

As we have already seen,[456] the law assumes consent in the contact between persons in everyday life. Whether this is based on implied consent or a sort of doctrine of necessity is not very important. It would be absurd to expect express consent to the bodily contact experienced in busy streets, shops and public transport. Apart from such instances of necessary social contact, it is clear that we can consent to being touched; for example we may give consent to the hairdresser cutting our hair. Equally we can consent to sexual contact, though this generally limited to those over the age of 16.[457] We can, thus, say that consent is generally a defence to battery where no injury is involved.

7–101   The major problem for the courts is whether consent will be available as a defence where bodily harm has been caused. A minute's thought will show that the law does allow persons to consent to the infliction of bodily injury or at least to the risk of it; the most obvious example is in violent sports such as boxing and rugby football. There must also be some way in which a surgeon who opens up a patient on the operating table with a very sharp knife is protected against a charge of unlawful wounding.

---

[449] They were, however, guilty as accessories to attempted murder since this stage had been reached before the victim withdrew consent.

[450] (1884) 14 Q.B.D. 273, above, para.5–063.

[451] See, Law Commission No.134. The Law Commission noted that between 1945 and 1992, 361 deaths had been brought about worldwide as a result of boxing bouts conducted in accordance with the Marquess of Queensbury's Rules.

[452] Above, para.7–069.

[453] See, e.g. *Kimber* [1983] 1 W.L.R. 1118.

[454] [1994] 1 A.C. 212; [1993] 2 W.L.R. 556; 2 All E.R. 75.

[455] See above, para.1–009.

[456] Above, para.7–062.

[457] See below, paras 7–122—7–128 for a discussion of consent in sexual cases.

Until 1993 the position was covered by the case of *Attorney-General's Reference (No.6 of 1980)*.[458] In that case two youths had resolved to settle a dispute by a fight, during the course of which the defendant caused the other to suffer a bleeding nose and a bruised face. It would appear that the defendant was charged with a common assault.[459] The Court of Appeal held that while consent would normally be a defence to common assault, there might be cases where the public interest demanded otherwise:

". . . it is not in the public interest that people should try to cause or should cause each other actual bodily harm for no good reason. Minor struggles are another matter. So, in our judgment, it is immaterial whether the act occurs in public or private; it is an assault if actual bodily harm is intended and/or caused. This means that most fights will be unlawful regardless of consent."[460]

The phrase "for no good reason" is a reference to the exceptions to the general rule where there is deemed to be a public interest in allowing activities where harm is caused or intended. Boxing matches would be a prime example of such an exception.[461] Lord Lane C.J. commented:

"Nothing which we have said is intended to cast doubt upon the accepted legality of properly conducted games and sports, lawful chastisement or correction, reasonable surgical interference, dangerous exhibitions, etc. These apparent exceptions can be justified as involving the exercise of a legal right, in the case of chastisement or correction, or as needed in the public interest, in other cases."[462]

The position could be summarised as laying down a general rule that consent was irrelevant wherever bodily injury was intended and/or caused, unless the case fell within one of the well-known exceptions.

The whole issue of consent was brought dramatically before the House of Lords in **7–102** *Brown*.[463] In that case a group of homosexual males had been discovered participating in sado-masochistic practices. These practices usually involved the recipient of the activity being manacled so as to be powerless while another member of the group carried out such activities as the nailing of the recipient's scrotum to a board or the burning of his penis with a candle. It is clear that all the recipients gave their full consent to what was done. The group had a series of code words which could be used by the recipient to stop the procedures at any stage. It also appeared that younger persons had been introduced to these practices and that video recordings were made, not for sale, but for viewing by members who had missed that evening's events. The defendants were charged with a variety of offences, but the House of Lords was concerned primarily with the charges of assault occasioning actual bodily harm and unlawful wounding brought under the Offences Against the Person

---

[458] [1981] 2 All E.R. 1057. Previously in *Donovan* [1934] 2 K.B. 498 D had given a 17-year-old girl a caning in his garage for purposes of sexual gratification; the girl had consented. Swift L.J. stated that in general but with some exceptions "It is an unlawful act to beat another person with such a degree of force that the infliction of bodily harm is a probable consequence and when such an act is proved, consent is immaterial."

[459] This is not entirely clear from the report and also the speeches in *Brown* [1994] 1 A.C. 212 at 507. In *Brown*, Lords Jauncey and Lowry said that the charge was assault occasioning actual bodily harm, while Lord Mustill was of the opinion that it was common assault.

[460] [1981] 2 All E.R. 1057 at 1059, per Lord Lane C.J.

[461] [1981] 2 All E.R. 1057. For further treatment of the exceptions, see below, paras 7–107—7–112.

[462] [1981] 2 All E.R. 1057.

[463] [1994] 1 A.C. 212. See generally M.J. Allen, "Consent and Assault" (1994) 58 J.C.L. 183; H. Power, "Consensual Sex, Disease and the Criminal Law" (1996) 60 J.C.L. 412.

Act 1861.[464] The Court of Appeal, in dismissing their appeals against conviction, had certified the following question:

"Where A wounds or assaults B occasioning him actual bodily harm in the course of a sado-masochistic encounter, does the prosecution have to prove lack of consent on the part of B before they can establish A's guilt under s.20 or s.47 of the Offences Against the Person Act 1861?"[465]

It was argued for the defendants that since the injuries fell short of being serious, the prosecution could only succeed if it could establish a lack of consent on the part of the victims. In other words the law should respect the privacy of people's homes. By a majority of three to two the House held that consent was irrelevant. The majority took the view that the conduct was presumptively unlawful in that it involved violence, cruelty and abnormal and perverted homosexual activity. For example, Lord Templeman commented:

"In my opinion sado-masochism is not only concerned with sex. Sado-masochism is also concerned with violence. The evidence discloses that the practices of the appellants were unpredictably dangerous and degrading to body and mind and were developed with increasing barbarity and taught to persons whose consents were dubious or worthless . . ."[466]

The majority concluded that on the face of it the activities fell within the definition of the offences and that since injury was both intended and caused, consent was irrelevant unless the court could find that there was a good reason to allow the activity. In other words the majority considered that consent was not an integral part of the definition of these offences, but was a defence to charges where injury was either intended or caused only if the facts fell within one of the well known exceptions such as sporting activity or medical treatment. The Lordships were, therefore, being invited to create a new exception to cover the intentional infliction of bodily harm in the course of sado-masochistic practices. The majority held that there were several good reasons why the defence should not be extended to cover these activities. In the first place it was simply good luck that these men had not suffered any really serious infections or injuries. Secondly there was a risk of spreading such diseases as AIDS. Thirdly there was the danger that young persons might be drawn into these unnatural practices. There was therefore no public interest in permitting such practices.[467]

7–103   The defence argued that the law should draw a line between grievous bodily injuries and actual bodily injuries, allowing consent as a defence to the latter. This would, however, cause a problem in relation to s.20 of the Offences Against the Person Act 1861. Wounding in s.20 may not necessarily constitute grievous bodily harm.[468] It would, therefore, result in a line being drawn with s.47 and those woundings which fell within s.20 but did not amount to grievous bodily harm on the one side, and grievous bodily harm and those woundings which also amounted to grievous bodily harm on the other. The majority were not prepared to lend their support to such a suggestion. It was far easier to draw a line between assaults involving no injury and assaults occasioning actual bodily harm.

[464] It is worth noting that four of the men had pleaded guilty to keeping a disorderly house and had received a custodial sentence. One was also sentenced for publishing an obscene article (the video recording).
[465] The House of Lords stated that the men had indulged in even more revolting sexual practices, but that no charges had been brought in respect of these activities since the activities would constitute only common assaults (battery) and, as no harm was caused, consent would have been a complete defence.
[466] [1994] 1 A.C. 212 at 235.
[467] Would the answer have differed had the defendants been a group of heterosexual men and women?
[468] A pin prick would constitute a wound.

The result would seem to be that consent is a defence only to common assault (and battery), and then only if there is no injury caused and/ or intended.[469] Where harm is intended and/or caused consent will be no defence unless there is some good reason to justify it in the public interest.

The minority, led by Lord Mustill, approached the matter from an entirely different angle. Lord Mustill remarked, "This is a case about the criminal law of violence. In my opinion it should be about the criminal law of private sexual relations, if about anything at all."[470] He was clearly influenced by the fact that the prosecution had trawled the statute books in order to find some offences with which to charge the defendants. The offences under the Offences Against the Person Act 1861 were daily visitors to the courts, but the subject-matter of the charges was usually far removed from the activities in this case. Charges under ss.47 and 20 normally involved violence inflicted on unwilling victims. Here the activities were carried out on persons who had given their assent to what was done. Obviously, if the wording of the sections or previous decisions of the courts clearly indicated that this sort of activity was covered by the Act, then Lord Mustill would not be prepared to decriminalise it. However, after a full review of the previous decisions he came to the conclusion that there was nothing which would prevent the House of Lords from looking again at whether public interests required that s.47 be interpreted so as to include the conduct of these men. Neither he nor Lord Slynn thought that there was any clear public interest argument which would necessitate the extension of liability under the act to cover these activities, though both stressed that they were not to be taken as condoning the defendants' conduct.

The defendants sought to persuade the European Court of Human Rights that their prosecutions and convictions were a contravention of art.8 of the European Convention on Human Rights, which covers the right to respect for private life. The Court, however, held that although their private life had been interfered with, this was in pursuance of a legitimate aim, namely the protection of the health and morals of the community.[471]

In 1997, seven men from Bolton (known as the Bolton 7) were prosecuted for buggery **7–104** within the group. Here the prosecution were able to rely upon sexual offence legislation. One of the group was 17½ at the time of the activity and so six months below the age at which he could, as the law then stood, consent to buggery; any activity with this youth would, therefore, constitute a criminal offence. The case had come to the attention of the police because of the discovery of a video recording of their activity and this led the police to infer that since a third person must have been present to work the camera, the men contravened the law that buggery between consenting males was, at the time, legitimate only where it was done in private; the presence of the cameraman made the activity illegal. All the activity was consensual and there was no suggestion of sado-masochistic practices. On the other hand, the prosecution had no need to dredge the statute books to find appropriate offences. This case, however, raises very clearly the issue of whether the law should interfere in such a manner when the activity was clearly not aggressive or harmful. As far as the youth was concerned he was only just short of the then age of homosexual consent. Moreover, the European Court might have viewed the distinction between the then age of homosexual (18) and heterosexual (16) consent to be a breach of human rights.

---

[469] A court hearing a charge of common assault where consent is raised must consider whether injury was caused or intended. If this were not the case then an odd result would follow. Suppose that the accused who has caused some harm is charged under s.47. Consent would be irrelevant and an unlawful assault would be made out. However if, as is possible, for the same activity he is charged with common assault and the defence of consent is permitted, the activity would not constitute an assault. How can the same activity be an assault or not depending upon the section under which he is charged? It follows that a line has to be drawn through the common assault offence; where injury is intended and/or caused, consent is irrelevant.

[470] [1994] 1 A.C. 212 at 256.

[471] *Laskey, Jaggard and Brown v United Kingdom* [1997] 24 E.C.H.R.R. 39.

In *Wilson*,[472] W was asked by his wife to tattoo his initials on her breasts. He refused, but she persuaded him to burn his initials with a hot knife on her buttocks. It is clear that the wife was not only a willing partner, she was the instigator of the activity. The matter was reported to the police by her doctor who had discovered it during a routine examination. W was charged with an assault occasioning actual bodily harm.

Russell L.J. drew an analogy with tattooing. That is a perfectly lawful activity so long as it is carried out with the consent of an adult, even though actual bodily harm is deliberately inflicted. On this basis the case can be squared with *Brown*. Branding, like tattooing, can be classified as one of the recognised exceptions to the rule that consent is no defence where injury is deliberately inflicted. However, Russell L.J. appeared to go further. He said:

> "[W]e are firmly of the opinion that it is not in the public interest that activities such as the appellant's in this appeal should amount to criminal behaviour. Consensual activity between husband and wife, in the privacy of the matrimonial home, is not, in our judgment, a proper matter for criminal investigation, let alone criminal prosecution."[473]

This is more akin to the reasoning of the minority in *Brown*; can *Brown* be distinguished on the basis that the certified question in *Brown* was set firmly in the context of sado-masochism? There is little else that can distinguish the two cases. Russell L.J. said that not only did Mrs Wilson consent to the activity, she instigated it. In *Brown* also the victim in each activity instigated the activity and fully consented to it. Indeed the injury to Mrs Wilson was perhaps as serious as any suffered in *Brown*. In the end one is forced to speculate whether the true distinction was the fact that in *Wilson* the activity was that of a married heterosexual couple in the privacy of their bedroom. Would the result have been different had the participants been a lesbian or homosexual couple? Would it have made a difference had the motive been not to adorn the wife, but sexual gratification?

7–105   The preference of our courts has been to develop this area solipsistically, on a case-by-case analysis, rather than through rigid bright-line rules on consent to criminal/non-criminal activity. This incremental perspective was highlighted again by the Court of Appeal decision in *Emmett*[474] involving sado-masochistic acts between unmarried parties at the time of the conduct; they were, however, married by the time of the trial. D was convicted of two counts of assault occasioning actual bodily harm arising from consensual sexual activity with his fiancée. The sexual activity was of an unusual and atypical nature. On the first occasion D had tied a plastic bag over the woman's head during sexual activity; on the second, D had poured lighter fluid on his fiancée's breasts and set light to it. The injuries were reported not by the woman but by her doctor. Through these peculiar activities she suffered "subconjunctival haemorrhages in both eyes and some petechial bruising around her neck" and "a burn, measuring some 6cm × 4cm" on her breast. No treatment was needed in relation to the former injuries, and for the latter, contrary to earlier expectations, no skin graft was required. D contended that consent negated liability.

The Court of Appeal in *Emmett*, adopting the perspective of the majority in *Brown*, determined that the trial judge was correct in asserting that consent was no defence to this harm. In principle, their Lordships asserted that there was no rationale, "to draw any distinction between sado-masochistic activity on a heterosexual basis and that which is

---

[472] [1996] 2 Cr.App.R. 241.
[473] [1996] 2 Cr.App.R. 241 at p.244; see generally P. Roberts "Consent to Injury: How Far Can You Go?" (1997) 113 L.Q.R. 27.
[474] *The Times*, October 15, 1999, CA.

conducted in a homosexual context". Furthermore, the appellate court drew a distinction with the branding that occurred in *Wilson*, and held that the, "actual or potential damage to which the appellant's partner was exposed in this case, plainly went far beyond that which was established by the evidence in *Wilson*". It will be a line-drawing exercise in each case as to whether valid consent can be given by an individual and its effect on personal autonomy over their own bodies.

The position would, however, appear to be that consent is no defence to those offences where there is a requirement of proof of any harm, albeit slight. It can be a defence to common assault or indecent assault provided that harm is not caused and/or intended. This raises another question. If the prosecution in seeking to prove an assault, argue that consent is irrelevant because the conduct of the accused actually caused injury, should the prosecution be required to prove that the defendant at least foresaw that his conduct might cause injury? Statements in *Attorney-General's Reference (No.6 of 1980)*[475] to the effect that consent is not relevant where injury is intended and or caused, which were approved by the majority in *Brown*, and the case of *Boyea*,[476] suggest that there is no such requirement. In *Boyea* the defendant inserted his hand into the complainant's vagina and twisted it thereby causing her injury. His conviction for indecent assault[477] was confirmed on the basis that the conduct was likely to cause injury. The Court reasoned by analogy with *Savage and Parmenter*[478] that since on a charge of assault occasioning actual bodily harm no mens rea was required as to the occasioning of actual bodily harm, there was no need in the present case to prove that the defendant foresaw that his conduct was likely to cause harm. This reasoning is at least questionable. In *Savage and Parmenter* there was a clear intentional battery.[479] In *Boyea* the issue was whether there was a battery at all and a battery is the intentional or reckless infliction of non-consensual force. It would, of course, be no defence for the defendant to say that he did not know that the law did not permit the defence of consent when injury was caused, but surely he must at least be aware of the facts which made consent irrelevant. In other words, unless he consciously took the risk of harming the girl, he foresaw only a consented to, non-injurious application of force, and that is not a battery.

On the other hand in *Slingsby*,[480] S, during the course of vigorous consensual sexual **7–106** activity, inserted his hand into V's vagina and rectum. Unfortunately the signet ring he was wearing caused several cuts. Only later did V realise that the injuries were serious and although she was admitted to hospital, she died from septicaemia. S was charged with unlawful act manslaughter. The prosecution needed to establish an unlawful act and this would have to be a battery on the facts of this case. The question for the court was whether the consensual sexual activity became a battery because injury resulted accidentally through S's wearing of a signet ring? Judge J. held that it did not since, "It would . . . be contrary to principle to treat as criminal, activity which would not otherwise amount to assault merely because in the course of the activity an injury occurred."[481] *Slingsby* differs from *Donovan* and *Brown* in that, in those two cases, the defendant had intended to inflict injuries, whereas in *Slingsby* no injury was intended or even foreseen. It is suggested that *Boyea* and the dicta from *Attorney-General's Reference* are wrong in principle, despite the approval of the House

---

[475] See below, para.7–110.
[476] [1992] Crim.L.R. 574.
[477] An indecent assault required proof of an assault or battery. See below, at para.7–133 for discussion of sexual assaults.
[478] Above, para.7–092.
[479] e.g. the deliberate drenching of the complainant with beer in *Savage*.
[480] [1995] Crim.L.R. 570.
[481] [1995] Crim.L.R. 570.

of Lords, and that the prosecution should have to prove that the accused was at least aware of the circumstances that made consent irrelevant. In other words, on facts such as those in *Slingsby*, only if the prosecution could establish that S intended to cause injury to V or at least foresaw that he might, should consent be irrelevant. It should not suffice that injury was, in fact, caused.

The interaction between consent and transmission of sexual disease arose in the important recent case of *Dica*.[482] D was charged with unlawfully and maliciously inflicting grievous bodily harm contrary to s.20 of the Offences Against the Person Act 1861. D knowing he was HIV positive, had unprotected sexual intercourse with two long-term sexual partners, infecting each of them with the disease. The trial judge determined, inter alia, that whether or not the victims knew of D's condition, their consent, if any, was irrelevant.[483] This, it was propounded, was the effect of the House of Lords decision in *Brown* whereby a "victim" cannot consent to the infliction of a s.20 level harm upon themselves for public policy reasons. However, the Court of Appeal, ordering a retrial, asserted that the primary issue for the jury was one of *informed consent*. The deliberate and intentional infliction of bodily harm is unlawful irrespective of consent, but an individual with informed consent may lawfully engage in an activity which merely carried the risk of injury or harm. The Court of Appeal in *Dica* have, thus, drawn a distinction between, on the one hand, violent sexual conduct (see *Brown*, *Boyea* and *Emmett*) embodied as per se unlawful irrespective of consent, and on the other hand, informed sexual autonomy where consent remains of crucial significance in relation to the taking of known risks and lawfulness of the conduct. Judge L.J., on this premise, held that the *Brown* principle was not determinative:

> "In our judgment the impact of the authorities dealing with sexual gratification can too readily be misunderstood. It does not follow from them, and they do not suggest, that consensual acts of sexual intercourse are unlawful merely because there may be a known risk to the health of one or other participant. These participants are not intent on spreading or becoming infected with disease through sexual activity. They are not indulging in serious violence for the purpose of sexual gratification. They are simply prepared, knowingly, to run the risk—not the certainty—of infection, as well as all the other risks inherent in and possible consequences of sexual intercourse, such as, and despite the most careful precautions, an unintended pregnancy."[484]

Their Lordships in *Dica* provided two interesting examples of the class of exceptions, both involving known risks attendant to sexual intercourse, outwith the *Brown* general principles. First, one partner suffers from HIV and the other partner is aware of this state of affairs. However, they are both devout Roman Catholics and are conscientiously unable to use artificial contraception. Both are aware that each time they have sexual intercourse there is a risk that the healthy partner may become infected with HIV. Secondly, a young couple are desperate to have a baby. Medical advice is to the effect that if the wife were to become pregnant and give birth her life would be at risk. They decide to take a chance, but sadly the wife is injured, perhaps fatally, in child birth. In each illustration, according to Judge L.J., the "victim's" consent would validate the activity, and interference with personal autonomy would be inappropriate

The Court of Appeal in *Dica* used informed consent as the pivotal issue in deciding when there will be liability for reckless transmission of HIV. The exact method of acquisition of

---

[482] [2004] 3 All E.R. 593; [2004] EWCA Crim 1103.
[483] Note the trial judge also determined that *Clarence* was no longer authoritative in light of *Ireland, Burstow*. This was confirmed by the appellate court in *Dica*; see above at para.7–086.
[484] [2004] 3 All E.R. 593 at [46].

the necessary knowledge to found informed consent was left equivocal. It was conceded, obiter, that there may be situations where D had concealed his condition, but V was nonetheless able to give informed consent. This loophole was subsequently revealed in *Konzani*[485] with situations envisaged as raising this issue including where V may have learnt of D's HIV status from a mutual friend or by virtue of having been hospitalised with him. Despite D's concealment of the condition no liability is attached to infliction of a sexual disease. This, with respect, seems unduly lenient to D and raises the spectre of unknown justification as a defence, precluded since *Dadson*.[486] For the future the decision in *Dica* is significant in establishing that reckless infliction of grievous bodily harm through sexual intercourse imposes liability for the s.20 offence, but consistent principles still need incremental development.

B. The Exceptions to the General Rule

In *Attorney-General's Reference (No.6 of 1980)* it was said that it was not in the public **7–107** interest that people should try to cause or should cause each other actual bodily harm for no good reason.[487] The phrase "for no good reason" is a reference to the acceptance by the courts that the interests of the public require that individuals be allowed to consent to the infliction of bodily injury. The two major situations where this is so are rough sports and medical treatment.[488]

(i) Sporting Activities

Without some relaxation of the general rule, most contact sports would be illegal. It is in the **7–108** public interest that people engage in sporting activity both as a means of gaining exercise and also in the cause of providing entertainment for the public at large. The law has to strike a balance between acceptable and unacceptable risks. Brutality cannot be licensed under the name of sport. In many sports there is an acknowledgment that the participants may sustain injuries, though the expectation is that this will be rare. This is true for such sports as athletics and tennis. At the other end of the spectrum, however, is boxing in which each opponent is aware that the other intends to cause him serious bodily injury.[489] In the middle lie contact sports such as rugby and soccer in which players are aware that deliberate contact in the form of tackles may have unintended effects, conceivably of sufficient severity to amount to serious bodily harm.

(a) Boxing

It is tempting to say that in sport the participants consent to injuries received within the **7–109** rules of the game, but this would be going too far. If the sports governing body was to introduce a new rule which the courts felt likely to lead to numerous serious injuries, it would be open to them to say that the participants had not consented to those injuries.

---

[485] [2005] EWCA Crim 706.

[486] See above at para.2–002.

[487] Above, para.7–101.

[488] "Surgery involves intentional violence resulting in actual or sometimes serious bodily harm, but surgery is a lawful activity. Other activities carried on with consent by or on behalf of the injured person have been accepted as lawful notwithstanding that they involve actual bodily harm or may cause serious bodily harm. Ritual circumcision, tattooing, ear-piercing, and violent sports including boxing are lawful activities", per Lord Templeman at 231. See also *Re A (Conjoined Twins: Surgical Separation)* [2000] 4 All E.R. 961 on balancing of evils, consent, and least detrimental choice; above para.5–066.

[489] An intention to render another unconscious outside the ring would surely be seen as an intention to cause serious bodily harm.

Boxing, however, shows us that the legislature and the courts are unwilling lightly to invoke their powers.[490] In *Brown*,[491] Lord Mustill said of boxing:

> "For money, not recreation or personal improvement, each boxer tries to injure the opponent more than he is hurt himself, and aims to end the contest prematurely by inflicting a brain injury serious enough to make the opponent unconscious, or temporarily impairing his central nervous system through a blow to the midriff, or cutting his skin to a degree which would ordinarily be well within the scope of s.20. The boxers display skill, strength and courage, but nobody pretends that they do good to themselves or others. The onlookers derive entertainment, but none of the physical and moral benefits which have been seen as the fruits of engagement in manly sports."[492]

If as a result of a knockout blow the recipient dies, the winner would be able to rely on the consent of his opponent to the infliction of grievous bodily harm. Hence consent in these circumstances would be a defence to a charge of murder.

Boxing's predecessor, prize-fighting, which involved fighting with bare fists, was made unlawful in the last century. It was felt to be no longer in the interests of the public to tolerate it. In *Attorney-General's Reference (No.6 of 1980)*[493] where two boys had fought to resolve a dispute the courts refused to allow the defence of consent. Had they taken the trouble to go to a gymnasium, put on boxing gloves and entered a boxing ring, they could have knocked hell out of each other with impunity in the name of sport.[494]

(b) Soccer and Rugby

7–110 Sports such as soccer and rugby often involve quite violent bodily contact. Obviously those who take part in such sports consent to fair tackles even though these may sometimes lead to quite serious but unintentional injuries. Do they consent to injuries received from tackles which constitute fouls under the rules of the sport? Today it is generally accepted that tackles from behind in soccer are dangerous and often lead to serious injuries. For this reason they not only constitute a foul, but will normally result in the player being booked or even sent off the pitch. It is suggested that players do not consent to the deliberate infliction upon themselves of any degree of bodily harm and that courts would be unwilling to allow consent as a defence. However, it is much more likely that the injury will be a result of recklessness. Experienced players will know that virtually any tackle can lead to injury and to this extent any player making a tackle consciously takes a risk of so doing. Players are well aware that tackles from behind a player who is moving at speed could well cause a broken leg, similarly a player who jumps for a ball in the penalty area with his elbows raised will be aware that this could cause serious facial injuries. It is suggested that players do not consent to such reckless injuries and that the perpetrators should be criminally liable for having consciously taken an unjustified risk of causing actual or grievous bodily harm.

In the case of other tackles which are not seen as dangerous, it is still possible that injuries may be caused. However, in the vast majority of tackles so long as the allegation is that the accused was reckless, the risk would be considered to have been one he was justified in taking.

---

[490] For an excellent account of the lawfulness of boxing, see D.C. Ormerod and M.J. Gunn, "The Legality of Boxing" (1995) 15 *Legal Studies* 181.

[491] Above, para.7–101.

[492] [1994] 1 A.C. 212 at 265.

[493] Above, para.7–101.

[494] Or would evil motive have nullified consent?

A degree of guidance has been provided in *Barnes*.[495] D was charged with unlawfully and maliciously inflicting grievous bodily harm contrary to s.20 of the Offences Against the Person Act 1861 after seriously injuring the right ankle and calf bone of an opposing player during an amateur football match. The Court of Appeal, accepting that there had been a misdirection, stressed that the jury needed to consider whether the conduct had been so obviously late and/or violent that it was not to be regarded as an instinctive reaction, error or misjudgement in the heat of the game.[496] Their Lordships set out unequivocally that, given most organised sports have their own standards of conduct and their own disciplinary proceedings for enforcing the rules of the game, allied to availability of civil redress, criminal prosecution should be limited to situations where the conduct is "sufficiently grave to be properly categorised as criminal".[497] In determining whether reckless infliction of injury should properly be labelled as criminal, consideration should be given to whether the injury occurred during play, in the heat of the moment when play has ceased or "off the ball"; an injury occurring during play can still be criminal if it results from unreasonable risk-taking. Hence the more the act that causes injury is spatially or temporally remote from play, the more likely it is that the act will attract criminal liability.[498]

Whether D's conduct is within the defence of consent is a matter for arbiters of fact, magistrates or the jury. Following *Barnes* there are myriad factors to evaluate: the type of sport; the level at which it was played; the nature of the act; the degree of force used; the extent of the risk of injury; and the state of mind of the defendant. In a sense it mirrors the 'so bad' justification for the imposition of criminal liability for manslaughter based on gross negligence that was established in *Adomako*,[499] and similarly in the context of contact sports it is fundamentally a jury question. The approach, of course, is inherently uncertain and further guidance is required. *Barnes* illustrates, however, that a significant level of dissonance from accepted rules of play is required before implied consent to injury is abrogated, and before criminal law becomes operational superceding proceedings of the sport's disciplinary body or civil redress.

(ii) Medical Treatment

With the express or implied consent of the patient a surgeon may do things to the patient **7-111** which, if performed by a lay person, would constitute very serious bodily harm. We allow such activity to be performed by the surgeon because of the therapeutic value to the patient. While we do not permit euthanasia, we do permit patients to consent to treatment where there is a risk of death or serious injury. For example, a patient may consent to a heart transplant operation even though this might not be successful. The risk of death is considered one that is worth taking in that the treatment is the only way in which the patient can be given the chance of leading a normal life. Where there is no perceived public benefit from the operation, a doctor is in the same position as any other member of the public. A doctor who, for instance, at the request of the patient removed the patient's leg so that the patient could take part in the disabled person's Olympic Games, would be guilty of causing grievous bodily harm with intent to do so.

Until relatively recently the courts were unwilling to include cosmetic surgery within this exception, on the basis that only therapeutic surgery would be permitted. However, it is now

---

[495] [2004] EWCA Crim 3246; [2005] 1 W.L.R. 910.
[496] The trial judge directed the jury in terms of whether D's conduct fell within "legitimate sport".
[497] [2005] 1 W.L.R. 910, at [5].
[498] See, generally, S. Fafinski, "Consent and the Rules of the Game: the Interplay of Civil and Criminal Liability for Sporting Injuries" (2005) 69 J.C.L. 414.
[499] [1995] 1 A.C. 171; see above at para.7-049.

recognised that providing the patient with a more attractive nose has clear therapeutic value. The same is true of sterilisation and sex change surgery; these were once seen as being against the public interest, but are now fully accepted as proper medical treatment.

(iii) Rough Horseplay

7–112   The courts apparently believe that young people have a need for the sort of rough horseplay that occurs in school playgrounds and in military barracks, usually among males. In *Jones*[500] two young boys were thrown into the air by two other youths in a school playground and were seriously injured when they hit the ground. It was held to be a defence that the defendant believed, however unreasonably, that the victims were consenting. In *Aitken*[501] the defendants, who were RAF officers, set fire to the clothing of another officer at a mess party. Two other men had been previously set alight but had suffered no injuries. The third officer suffered severe burns. It was held on appeal that it would be a defence if the defendants had believed that the victim had consented to the activity. Commenting on these amazing cases Clarkson and Keating say:

> "This seems to be a bully's charter. It is extremely far-fetched to suggest that boys being held by several others *to prevent them running away* are genuinely consenting to being thrown in the air. To say that boys in such a situation can consent to *grievous bodily harm*, but that sado-masochists, who are genuinely consenting, cannot consent to *actual bodily harm* provides an interesting insight into the way some of our judiciary view the world. Violence in the playground or barrack room is what is expected and normal in the male world; it is a 'manly diversion'. Two men wishing to express their sexuality together and in private are not doing the sort of thing 'real men' do. It is an 'evil thing' and 'uncivilised' and cannot be the subject of valid consent."[502]

These cases must, it seems, be viewed as an area in which the courts feel that the public interest demands a relaxation of the normal principles enunciated in the *Attorney-General's Reference case.*[503] Most recently, in *R v A*[504] the Court of Appeal upheld the notion of the availability of consent as a defence in horseplay, even in a case resulting in death.[505]

C. What is Consent?

7–113   Most of the contentious issues concerning what constitutes a valid consent arise in the area of sexual offences and are better dealt with in that context. However, the principles are the same for both sexual and non-sexual offences and a brief outline will be given here.

In some situations the law holds that a consent which has been given is not valid. This might be because the victim who has purported to give the consent is too young to appreciate what he is consenting to; in sexual offences there are offences which specify the age at which a valid consent might be given.[506] In the non-sexual field, age limits are rarely specified,[507] but the court will decide whether the person could be expected to understand

---

[500] (1986) 83 Cr.App.R. 375.
[501] [1992] 1 W.L.R. 1006. See also *Richardson and Irwin* [1999] Q.B. 444; [1998] 2 Cr.App.R. 200; and see above, para.5–033.
[502] Clarkson and Keating, at p.299.
[503] Above, para.7–109.
[504] [2005] All E.R. (D) 38.
[505] Note that D's asserted belief in consent was not believed in the light of other witness statements.
[506] See below, paras 7–133—7–134.
[507] One example is provided by tattooing. It seems clear that a person who is under the age of 18 cannot consent to being tattooed except for bona fide medical purposes; Tattooing of Minors Act 1969.

the consent he or she was giving. Consent may also be invalid because the person is mentally incapable of making a sound decision. Parents and guardians may give consent on behalf of their children, for example, in relation to surgical operations.

Where the consent is obtained by force or threats of force it will be invalid. The law draws a line between real consent and mere submission.

Where the victim has given consent due to a mistake as to the nature and quality of the act or the identity of the person with whom it is to be performed the consent will be ineffective. This will normally occur due to fraud by the accused, but not necessarily so; the nature of fraud vitiating consent is strictly construed. If a patient, for instance, gave her consent to an operation on the basis that there would be no medical students present, if when the patient was unconscious the doctor admitted medical students, the consent would be valid. She has consented to a particular operation being carried out by a competent surgeon and that is what has happened; no mistake has occurred as to the nature of the act, i.e. the operation itself. If however, the doctor performed an entirely different operation her consent would be invalid.[508] In *Richardson*[509] a dentist who had been suspended from dental practice by the General Dental Council was convicted of assault occasioning actual bodily harm for treatment given to patients whilst disqualified. The Court of Appeal accepted the defendant's argument that the patients had consented to receiving proper dental treatment and that is what they received. It was immaterial that the patients would not have consented to treatment had they realised the dentist had been struck off the Register. Would, however, the answer have been the same had the person performing the treatment no qualifications whatsoever. Would she have received proper dental treatment or would this now be a mistake as to the nature of the act and identity of the person? Would it make any difference whether or not the treatment given was the correct treatment albeit at the hands of a complete amateur? It is suggested that a different outcome would follow; the act consented to was construed to be proper dental treatment by a dental practitioner. There must be a fundamental deception of the very attributes of the criminal act before it will vitiate consent. In *Tabassum*,[510] for instance, the denuded women victims consented to the defendant touching their breasts because they believed that he was engaged in a breast cancer survey. The Court of Appeal determined that whilst the victims had consented to the *nature* of the act, which constituted the touching of the breasts, they had not consented to the *quality* of the act since they falsely believed that he was medically qualified and they were being touched for sound medical reasons. In truth, the women would not have submitted to the defendant's acts if they had not believed that he had medical qualifications; and that he knew that this was so. The victim's mistake as to the *quality* of the act was fundamental rather than the fact that the mistake derived from any misrepresentation by the defendant that was material. If followed subsequently this represents a novel distinction between lack of consent as to either nature or quality of the act vitiating consent. In *Dica* it was determined that whilst the victims had been fraudulently deceived as to the risk of infection (*quality*), they had not been defrauded as to the act of sexual intercourse itself (*nature*).[511] Fraud applied to the infection in contradistinction to the intercourse.[512]

---

[508] See *Bolduc and Bird* below, para.7–116. If a patient consents to an injection of a flu vaccine and the doctor injects poison, there will be no consent. If, however, he injects the flu vaccine with a blunt needle, she would be deemed to have consented, even if she would not have allowed him to give the injection had she known the state of the syringe.

[509] [1999] Crim.L.R. 62.

[510] [2000] Crim.L.R. 686.

[511] It is noteworthy that under s.76 of the Sexual Offences Act 2003 a fraud as to the "nature or purpose" of the act (not quality) is conclusively presumed to vitiate consent. See below at para.7–127.

[512] The logically corollary is that V does not commit rape; the "act" of penetration is consensual.

7. FUTURE REFORMS OF THE OFFENCES AGAINST THE PERSON AND CONSENT[513]

A. Reform of Non-fatal Offences Against the Person

7–114 Following extensive work in the area of non-fatal offences, the Government published a draft Offences Against the Person Bill,[514] and this indicated that at long last codification of the criminal law might get under way. This seems, however, to be as far away as ever. If enacted the offences in the Bill will replace the basic offences of common assault and ss.47, 20 and 18 of the Offences Against the Person Act 1861, imposing a new hierarchical structure. In outline the four new offences are as follows:

Under cl.1(1), a person is guilty of an offence if he intentionally[515] causes serious injury to another. This is to be the most serious of the non-fatal offences against the person and will replace s.18 of the 1861 Act. The offence is triable only on indictment and carries life imprisonment. Clause 1(2) specifically provides that this offence can be brought about by omission.

Under cl.2(1), a person is guilty of an offence if he recklessly causes serious injury to another. This offence will replace s.20 of the 1861 Act. It is an either way offence which will carry a maximum sentence of seven years' imprisonment on conviction on indictment and, on summary conviction, a maximum term of six months' imprisonment and/or a fine not exceeding the maximum at level five.

Under cl.3(1), a person is guilty of an offence if he intentionally or recklessly causes injury to another. This will replace s.47 of the 1861 Act. It is an either way offence which carries a maximum of five years' imprisonment on conviction on indictment and a maximum of six months' imprisonment and/or a fine at the maximum of level five on summary conviction.

7–115 Injury is defined in s.15 to cover both physical and mental injury. Physical injury does not include anything caused by disease but (subject to that) it includes pain, unconsciousness and any other impairment of a person's physical condition. Mental illness does not cover anything caused by disease but (subject to that) it includes any impairment of a person's mental health. The exceptions relating to disease do not apply to charges brought under cl.1.

Under cl.4(1), a person is guilty of an offence if:

(a) he intentionally or recklessly applies force to or causes an impact on the body of another, or

(b) he intentionally or recklessly causes the other to believe that any such force or impact is imminent.

Under cl.4(2), no such offence is committed if the force or impact, not being intended or likely to cause injury, is in circumstances such as are generally acceptable in the ordinary conduct of ordinary life and the defendant does not know or believe that it is in fact unacceptable to the other person.

This clause replaces common assault and battery. It is triable only summarily and the maximum sentence is six months' imprisonment and/or a fine not exceeding £5,000. There is

[513] See generally Law Com. No 177, *Criminal Law; A Criminal Code for England and Wales* (1989); Law Com. No. 218: *Legislating the Criminal Code; Offences Against the Person and General Defences* (1993).
[514] Home Office (1998), *Violence: Reforming the Offences Against the Person Act 1861.* See generally J.C. Smith, "Offences Against the Person: The Home Office Consultation Paper" [1998] Crim.L.R. 317.
[515] For the definition of fault terms see cl.14.

no reference to consent in this draft. The issue has been left to await the recommendations of the Law Commission.[516]

The Draft Bill also includes clauses dealing with fault terms,[517] the retention of general defences as well as supervening and transferred fault. It also includes a variety of other non-fatal offences including offences against those who are effecting lawful arrests, dangerous substances, threats to kill, torture, and administering substances capable of causing injury.

The enactment of even this limited amount of the Law Commission's Draft Code would be a welcome change. It would provide prosecutors with a clear hierarchy of basic non-fatal offences against the person.

B. Reform of Consent

As mentioned above, the Government chose not to include any provisions relating to **7–116** consent in their draft Offences Against the Person Bill. The Law Commission has produced two consultation papers. The first[518] consultation paper turned out to be too limited in scope and in 1995 the Law Commission produced a far more wide-ranging exploration of the subject.[519] On the subject of the offences to which consent should be a defence it proposes that consent should be no defence to the intentional or reckless causing of a serious disabling injury. A serious disabling injury is defined[520] as one which causes serious distress and involves the loss of a bodily member or organ or permanent bodily injury, or permanent functional impairment, or serious or permanent disfigurement, or severe and prolonged pain, or serious impairment of mental health, or prolonged unconsciousness; and, in determining whether an effect is permanent, no account should be taken of the fact that it may be remediable by surgery. Consent, however, should be a defence to injuries not amounting to serious disabling injuries. The paper proposes that consent may be given to any level of injury if it occurs during proper medical treatment or proper medical research. The paper continues to see the need to allow persons to consent to injury in the course of rough horseplay, but otherwise the intentional or reckless causing of injuries during undisciplined fighting should continue to constitute a criminal offence, even if the victim consents. Boxing, however, and other recognised sports continue to be protected.

On the issue of what constitutes consent, the Law Commission has resiled from its former proposal to reverse the decision in cases such as *Bolduc* and *Bird*.[521] You will recall that the position is that consent procured by fraud was still a valid consent unless it produced a mistake as to the nature of the act or as to the identity of the other party. The later Report proposes that position should be largely retained; the mere fact that a person had consented to intercourse because of a promise of payment and would not otherwise have consented, should not alter the fact she had consented to intercourse. The Commission, however, seeks views as to whether a false statement that the person is not infected with the AIDS virus should nullify consent. The Court of Appeal in *Richardson*[522] adopted the Law Commission proposal that consent procured by fraud was nevertheless a valid consent where it did not

---

[516] See discussion below, para.7–119.

[517] See above, para.7–114.

[518] *Consent and Offences Against the Person* (Law Com. 134, 1994).

[519] *Consent in the Criminal Law: A Consultation Paper*, Law Com. No.139 (1995). See generally S. Shute, "The Second Law Commission Consultation Paper on Consent: Something Old, Something New, Something Borrowed: Three Aspects of the Project" [1996] Crim.L.R. 684; and D.C. Ormerod and M.J. Gunn, "The Second Law Commission Consultation Paper—A Second Bash" [1996] Crim.L.R. 694.

[520] See, para.4.51.

[521] See below, para.7–127.

[522] See above, para.7–113.

produce a mistake as to the nature of the act or identity of the person; consent to proper dental treatment was not vitiated by the practitioner's disqualification. In *Tabassum*, however, the defendant at no point had any medical qualification whatsoever.

GENERAL READING

7–117   Allen, M., "Consent and Assasult" (1994) 58 J.C.L. 183.

Anderson, J., "No Licence For Thuggery: Violence, Sport and the Criminal Law" [2008] Crim.L.R. 751.

Ashworth, A., and Campbell, K., "Non-Fatal Offences: Mend and Make Do?" (1992) 108 L.Q.R. 187.

Cooper, S. and Reed, A., "Informed Consent and the Transmission of Sexual Disease: *Dadson* Revivified" (2007) 71 J.C.L. 461.

Davies, M., "Lawmakers, Law Lords and Legal Fault: Two Tales from the (Thames) River Bank: Sexual Offences Act; R v G and Another (2004) 68 J.C.L. 130.

Davies, M., "R v Dica: Lessons in Practising Unsafe Sex" (2004) 68 J.C.L. 498.

Elliott, C. and De Than, C., "The Case for a Rational Reconstruction of Consent in Criminal Law" (2007) 70 M.L.R. 225.

Gardner, J., "Rationality and the Rule of Law in Offences Against the Person" (1994) 53 C.L.J. 502.

Gardner, S., "Stalking" (1998) 114 L.Q.R. 33.

Genders, E., "Reform Of The Offences Against The Person Act: Lessons From The Law In Action" [1999] Crim.L.R. 689.

Giles, M. "R v Brown: Consensual Harm and the Public Interest" (1994) 57 M.L.R. 101.

Gunn, M. and Ormerod, D., "The Legality Of Boxing" (1995) 15 *Legal Studies* 181.

Herring, J., "The Criminalisation Of Harassment" (1998) 57 C.L.J. 10.

Hirst, M., "Assault, Battery And Indirect Violence" [1999] Crim.L.R. 557.

Leng, R., "Consent And Offences Against The Person" [1994] Crim.L.R. 480.

Livings, B., "A Different Ball-Game" (2007) 71 J.C.L. 534.

Mullender, R., "Sado-Masochism, Criminal Law and Adjudicative Method: *R v Brown* in The House of Lords" (1993) 44 N.I.L.Q. 380.

Power, H., "Consensual Sex, Disease And The Criminal Law" (1996) 60 J.C.L. 412.

Reed, A., "Offences Against the Person: The Need for Reform" (1995) 59 J.C.L. 187.

Roberts, P., "Consent To Injury: How Far Can You Go?" (1997) 113 L.Q.R. 27.

Ryan, S., "Reckless Transmission of HIV: Knowledge and Culpability" [2006] Crim.L.R. 981.

Smith, J.C., "Offences Against the Person: The Home Office Consultation Paper" [1998] Crim.L.R. 317.

Weait, M., "Knowledge, Autonomy and Consent" [2005] Crim.L.R. 763.

Wells, C., "Stalking: The Criminal Law Response" [1997] Crim.L.R. 463.

Sexual Offences

1.   GENERAL

7–118   While sexual offences can, technically, be subsumed under a broader heading of non-fatal offences against the person, it is generally considered appropriate to give them separate treatment in criminal law texts. There are various reasons for this: not only are sexual offences governed by a distinct body of law, but it is also generally accepted that the consequences of being a victim of a sexual offence are different from those that follow being the victim of a non-sexual assault.

Until 2003, the principal statute governing sexual offences was the Sexual Offences Act 1956. In January 1999, the then Home Secretary, Jack Straw, announced a review of sexual offences, with the following terms of reference:

"To . . . make recommendations that [would]:

- provide coherent and clear sex offences which protect individuals, especially children and the more vulnerable, from abuse and exploitation;
- enable abusers to be appropriately punished; and
- be fair and non-discriminatory in accordance with the ECHR and Human Rights Act."

Following an extensive consultation process, the Review, entitled *Setting the Boundaries: Reforming the law on sex offences,*[523] was published in July 2000. In November 2002, the Government published the paper *Protecting the Public: Strengthening protection against sex offenders and reforming the law on sexual offences,*[524] which flagged up, in broad terms, the contents of the subsequent Sexual Offences Act 2003.

The ambit of the Sexual Offences Act 2003 is extremely broad. In this part of the book, we will limit ourselves to consideration of the principal offences which may be of relevance on a criminal law course. We will spend the majority of this part of the book considering the offence of rape, but we will also consider the following offences:

- Core offences:

    (a) Assault by penetration.
    (b) Sexual assault.
    (c) Causing sexual activity without consent.

- Rape and other offences against children under 13.
- "Child sex offences" committed by those 18 years old or over, against victims under 16.

2. RAPE

Section 1 of the Act states: **7–119**

"*1 Rape*

(1) A person (A) commits an offence if—

    (a) he intentionally penetrates the vagina, anus or mouth of another person (B) with his penis,

    (b) B does not consent to the penetration, and

    (c) A does not reasonably believe that B consents.

[523] Home Office, 2000.
[524] TSO, 2002, Cm 5668.

(2) Whether a belief is reasonable is to be determined having regard to all the circumstances, including any steps A has taken to ascertain whether B consents.

(3) Sections 75 and 76 apply to an offence under this section.

(4) A person guilty of an offence under this section is liable, on conviction on indictment, to imprisonment for life."

It can thus be seen that the elements of the offence of rape are as follows:

Actus reus

- Penile penetration of the vagina, anus or mouth of the victim.
- The victim's lack of consent.

Mens rea

- Intentional penetration.
- The absence of a reasonable belief in the consent of the victim.

A.   ACTUS REUS:

(i) penetration

7–120 The actus reus of rape has been substantially developed in recent years. Until the Criminal Justice and Public Order Act 1994, rape could only be committed by penile penetration of the vagina. The 1994 Act made anal penetration a possible element of rape, and thus allowed men to be victims of rape. The 2003 Act developed the definition still further by bringing within it penile penetration of the mouth. (It is worthy of note that penile-oral penetration is an element in the definition of rape in some other jurisdictions.) It will be noted that although there may be various ways of committing rape, they all involve penile penetration. It follows that rape can only be committed, as a principal offender, by a man (although a woman can commit rape as a secondary party).[525]

According to s.79(2) of the Act, penetration is a continuing act from entry to withdrawal. Thus, even if there is consent at the moment of entry, if, for example, a woman ceases to consent during an act of sexual intercourse, penetration becomes non-consensual. This, in essence, gives statutory effect to the earlier decisions in *Kaitamaki v R*[526] and *Cooper and Schaub*.[527] Of course, whether the man is guilty of rape will depend on his state of mind at the relevant time.

---

[525] This was also the position prior to the 2003 Act. See *DPP v K and C* [1997] 1 Cr.App.R. 36.
[526] [1985] A.C. 147.
[527] [1994] Crim.L.R. 531.

(ii) lack of consent

At the outset, it is worthy of note that consent is relevant to the offence of rape in two ways: **7–121**

- lack of consent is part of the actus reus of rape;
- the defendant's lack of a reasonable belief in consent is part of the mens rea.

Consent is at the heart of the offence of rape, and the issue of whether there was consent, or whether a defendant believed there was consent, forms the key area of dispute in a significant proportion of rape cases.[528]

Section 74 of the 2003 Act provides a non-exhaustive definition of consent:

". . . a person consents if he agrees by choice, and has the freedom and capacity to make that choice."

A person might lack the capacity to make the relevant choice by virtue, for example, of their age or because of a mental disorder.[529]

Consent is principally a question of fact; it is either given or it is not, although proving whether it is or is not given may be tremendously difficult. Historically, there was some dispute over what kind of behaviour would be sufficient to negative the victim's consent. The position taken by the common law was that a victim's consent would only be negatived by "force, fear or fraud". This was an unsatisfactory position for victims, who risked being treated as if they had consented unless they demonstrated some active resistance to their attacker. In *Olugboja*,[530] the Court of Appeal made clear that there was no need for the use of force to be proved before consent could be treated as being negatived.

In that case J, who had already been raped by O's friend L, was told by O that he was **7–122** going to have sexual intercourse with her and that she should take her trousers off. She did so as she said she was frightened. She put up no resistance until some time after penetration when she thought he was going to ejaculate within her. He withdrew and she got dressed. On a charge of rape, O was convicted and appealed on the basis that rape required that the prosecutor should prove that the girl's submission should have been obtained by force or fear of force. Rejecting this argument Dunn L.J. said:

"Accordingly in so far as the *actus reus* is concerned, the question now is simply: at the time of the sexual intercourse did the woman consent to it? It is not necessary for the

---

[528] It is hard to comprehend that, until 1991, a husband who knowingly had non-consensual sexual intercourse with his wife did not commit rape, on the basis of an anachronistic presumption that the wife gave ongoing consent to sexual intercourse through marriage. This affront to women was removed by the House of Lords in *R* [1992] 1 A.C. 599. A legitimate argument remained as to whether it was the proper constitutional function of the House of Lords to develop the law in this way. However, the decision was endorsed by the European Court of Human Rights in *SW and CR v UK* (1996) 21 E.H.R.R. 363 as being compatible with art.7 of the European Convention on Human Rights, which proscribes retrospective lawmaking. Moreover, the decision in *R* was effectively ratified by Parliament in s.142 of the Criminal Justice and Public Order Act 1994 which explicitly removed the so-called "marital immunity" from the offence of rape. In s.1 of the Sexual Offences (Amendment) Act 1976, the offence of rape was only committed where the sexual intercourse was "unlawful". The word "unlawful" was interpreted to denote sexual intercourse which took place outside marriage. The 1994 Act removed the word "unlawful" from the definition.
[529] It seems that a lack of knowledge, of itself, will not vitiate consent for the purposes of s.74. Thus, in *EB* [2006] EWCA Crim 2945, where D knowingly concealed his HIV positive status from V, the concealment did not vitiate the consent to sexual intercourse given by V. Contrast the lack of relevance of concealment of HIV status to s.74 with the possible liability of D for infliction of grievous bodily harm in respect of the transmission of HIV (see *Dica* [2004] EWCA Crim 1103; and *Konzani* [2005] EWCA Crim 706). See the discussion of consent and fraud below para.7–128.
[530] [1982] Q.B. 320.

prosecution to prove that what might otherwise appear to have been consent was in reality merely submission induced by force fear or fraud, although one or more of these factors will no doubt be present in the majority of cases of rape."[531]

The courts have drawn a line between consent and submission, but "the dividing line between real consent on the one hand and mere submission on the other may not be easy to draw. Where it is to be drawn in a given case is for the jury to decide, applying their combined good sense, experience and knowledge of human nature and modern behaviour to all the relevant facts of the case."[532]

Jheeta[533] involved an appellant and complainant who were very good friends who had entered into a consensual sexual relationship. The complainant started to receive threatening text messages and telephone calls. The appellant assured the complainant that she would be protected by him and his friends. When the complainant decided to inform the police, the appellant purported to do this on her behalf. The complainant subsequently received text messages from a series of sources representing themselves as police officers who were working on her case.

The complainant attempted to break off her relationship with the appellant, but whenever she tried, she received messages from the police officers, claiming that the appellant had tried to commit suicide, and stating that she should stay with him. Messages advised her to have sexual intercourse with the appellant, and that she would be liable to a fine if she did not do so. When she received these messages, she complied with the advice, and had intercourse with the appellant.

7–123   The appellant had in fact been responsible for the entire scheme, and had generated the text messages himself. He was convicted of rape and his appeal was unsuccessful. The complainant did not consent to the acts of intercourse for the purposes of s.74 of the 2003 Act.

While cases of this nature might be reasonably rare, where they do arise, a significant amount of probative work must be done by the rather loose definition of consent in s.74. It is not clear what type of pressures, and of what magnitude, must be exerted on a complainant before their freedom to choose is compromised to the extent that consent is vitiated, but in *Jheeta* the court had no difficulty in bringing the appellant's conduct within the required parameters. This is understandable on the facts; the appellant had, through his deceptive behaviour, effectively locked the complainant into a cycle of dependency. That the complainant might have felt little option other than to accede to the advice that she have intercourse with the appellant is entirely plausible.

Section 1 of the Act states that ss.75 and 76 of the Act apply to the offence of rape. This is a significant issue in the definition of consent, not only for the purposes of the offence of rape, but also for a number of other offences under the 2003 Act. Sections 75 and 76 state, respectively, that there are a number of so-called "evidential presumptions" and "conclusive presumptions" which apply to the issue of consent. The relevance of the presumptions depends on the circumstances under which intentional penetration takes place.

Under s.75, the complainant (this is a term often used in discussions about sexual offences to refer to the alleged victim) is presumed not to have consented to the penetration (referred to in the section as "the relevant act") where any of the following circumstances, listed in s.75(2), are proved to exist:

---

[531] [1982] Q.B. 320 at 331.
[532] [1982] Q.B. 320 at 332, per Dunn L.J.
[533] [2007] EWCA Crim 1699.

(a) any person was, at the time of the relevant act or immediately before it began, using violence against the complainant or causing the complainant to fear that immediate violence would be used against him;

(b) any person was, at the time of the relevant act or immediately before it began, causing the complainant to fear that violence was being used, or that immediate violence would be used, against another person;

(c) the complainant was, and the defendant was not, unlawfully detained at the time of the relevant act;

(d) the complainant was asleep or otherwise unconscious at the time of the relevant act;

(e) because of the complainant's physical disability, the complainant would not have been able at the time of the relevant act to communicate to the defendant whether the complainant consented;

(f) any person had administered to or caused to be taken by the complainant, without the complainant's consent, a substance which, having regard to when it was administered or taken, was capable of causing or enabling the complainant to be stupefied or overpowered at the time of the relevant act.

Paragraphs (a) and (b) refer to the actual or threatened use of violence against the victim or against a third party. Paragraph (c) refers to the situation where the victim is falsely imprisoned. Paragraphs (d), (e) and (f) refer to situations in which circumstances which ought to be obvious to the defendant hinder the ability of the victim to communicate his or her lack of consent. **7–124**

Just because one of the listed circumstances exists, the defendant can rebut the presumption that the complainant has not consented by adducing sufficient evidence to raise an issue as to whether there was consent. That is to say, the defendant need not *prove* that there was consent, but must at least present a realistic argument to the court that there was consent, at which stage the prosecution must prove that there was no consent. If, in a situation listed in s.75(2), the defendant does not present such an argument, then the complainant is taken not to have consented.

In the important recent decision in *Bree*[534] the Court of Appeal had the opportunity to consider the relevance of the complainant's intoxication to the issue of consent in rape. D, aged 25, was convicted of rape before Bournemouth Crown Court. It was not in issue that, after a very heavy evening drinking together, he had sexual intercourse with the complainant, a woman aged 19 years. The prosecution had alleged at the commencement of the trial that D had raped the complainant when her level of intoxication was so great that she was effectively unconscious. In essence, it was argued that she lacked the capacity to consent, and therefore did not consent. The case, however, by the end of the evidence had shifted to the effect that the jury were no longer invited to conclude that the complainant had been unable to consent to sexual intercourse because she was unconscious,[535] rather that she did not in fact consent to sexual intercourse. On the part of the appellant it had been contended that, outwith the alcohol consumption on the part of the complainant, and even perhaps

[534] [2007] EWCA Crim 804; [2007] 2 All E.R. 676. See, generally, E. Finch and V. Munro, "Breaking Boundaries; Sexual Consent in the Jury Room" (2006) 26 *Legal Studies* 303; and P. Rumney and R. Fenton. "Intoxicated Consent in Rape: *Bree* and Juror Decision-Making" (2008) 71 M.L.R. 279.
[535] See s.75(2)(d) of the Sexual Offences Act 2003.

because of this drinking, she was consenting and was conscious throughout; and that he had reasonably believed that she was consenting. The appeal focused upon a misdirection by the trial judge in addressing the effect of voluntary heavy alcohol consumption as it applies to rape. The trial judge, in summing up, had directed the jury in terms simply of the specificity of the complainant's alcohol consumption, but only in the context of possible relevance to her reliability as a witness. The appeal, more directly, required consideration and elaboration of the import of s.74 of the Sexual Offences Act 2003.

7–125   Their Lordships in *Bree* determined that a misdirection had occurred and that the appeal be allowed. Sir Igor Judge P., who delivered the leading judgment, viewed it as unrealistic to endeavour to create some kind of grid system which would enable the answer to questions about consent to be related to some prescribed level of alcohol consumption.[536] It was viewed, surprisingly, that the clear definition in s.74 sufficiently addressed the issue of consent in the context of voluntary consumption of alcohol by the complainant. The central tenet of the decision, as articulated by Sir Igor Judge P.,[537] is that s.74 of the Sexual Offences Act 2003 without further elaboration does provide a workable definition of consent. It defines it with reference to "capacity to make that choice"; and this remains the template in the context of voluntary consumption of alcohol by the complainant. Difficulties are viewed, not as pertaining to the definitive test, but through the private consensual nature (or otherwise) of sexual intercourse, and irreducible problems of evidence pertaining to the activity. On this fundamental matter of capacity or otherwise, Sir Igor Judge P. stated:

> "In our judgment, the proper construction of s.74 of the 2003 Act, as applied to the problem now under discussion, leads to clear conclusions. If through drink (or for any other reason) the complainant has temporarily lost her capacity to choose whether to have intercourse on the relevant occasion, she is not consenting, and subject to questions about the defendant's state of mind, if intercourse takes place, this would be rape. However, where the complainant has voluntarily consumed even substantial quantities of alcohol, but nevertheless remains capable of choosing whether or not to have intercourse, and in drink agrees to do so, this would not be rape. We should perhaps underline that, as a matter of practical reality, capacity to consent may evaporate well before a complainant becomes unconscious. Whether this is so or not, however, is fact specific, or more accurately, depends on the actual state of mind of the individuals involved on that particular occasion."[538]

As the focus of *Bree* involved the capacity, or otherwise, of the complainant to make an informed consensual decision, the jury required assistance on this point. Direction was required on the meaning of "capacity" in the context where the complainant had been affected by her own voluntarily induced intoxication, and on whether, and to what extent, they could take that into account in deciding whether she consented. Moreover, as Sir Igor Judge P. asserted:

> "[T]he questions whether she might have behaved differently drunk than she would have done sober, and whether, although and perhaps because drunk, she might have

---

[536] [2007] 2 All E.R. 676 at [35].
[537] [2007] 2 All E.R. 676 at [36], See, also, *Wright* [2007] All E.R. (D) 267.
[538] [2007] 2 All E.R. 676 at [34]. See, also, *Hysa* [2007] EWCA Crim 2056 where the Court of Appeal, relying on the pre-Act case of *Malone* [1998] 2 Cr.App.R. 447, asserted: "there is no requirement that the absence of consent has to be demonstrated or that it has to be communicated to the defendant for the actus reus of rape to exist . . . It is not the law that the prosecution in order to obtain a conviction for rape have to show that the complainant was either incapable of saying no or putting up some physical resistance, or did say no or put up some physical resistance."

behaved as the appellant contended, and the way in which the jury should consider these important issues were not mentioned at all."[539]

It was a misdirection to focus upon the complainant's alcohol consumption as relevant only to her reliability as a witness.

It seems, however, that the true meaning behind s.74 of the Sexual Offences Act 2003 **7–126** remains as opaque as ever following the decision in *Bree*. Arguably, necessarily so given the fact specific, and evidential difficulties presented by private behaviour. We are left with incremental case-by-case ad-hocery and the search continues for an appropriate definitional test for consent to be left for jury deliberation. The extant position has been expertly summarised by Professors Temkin and Ashworth:

> "it might be thought that 'freedom' and 'choice' are ideas which raise philosophical issues of such complexity as to be ill-suited to the needs of criminal justice—clearly these words do not refer to total freedom or choice, so all the questions about how much liberty of action satisfies the 'definition' remains at large."[540]

While s.75 deals with "evidential presumptions", which can be rebutted by the defendant, s.76 contains "conclusive presumptions". If the defendant is proved to have intentionally penetrated the victim, and particular circumstances are proved to exist, the victim is presumed not to have consented, and the defendant cannot rebut the presumption. The circumstances are set out in s.76(2):

(a) the defendant intentionally deceived the complainant as to the nature or purpose of the relevant act;

(b) the defendant intentionally induced the complainant to consent to the relevant act by impersonating a person known personally to the complainant.

Section 76 was discussed in *Jheeta*,[541] where it was held that the defendant's impersonation (by message) of a police officer did not bring s.76 into play. There was no deception as to the "nature or purpose" of the relevant act—sexual intercourse—and so the issue of consent fell to be resolved under s.74.

In *Devonald*,[542] a case brought under s.4 of the 2003 Act,[543] D posed as a 20-year-old woman, "Cassie", and corresponded with V online. V masturbated on a webcam at D's behest, thinking he was doing so for the gratification of "Cassie". However, D's aim was in fact to humiliate V, who had broken up with D's daughter. Although V had not been deceived as to the nature of the act (masturbation), the jury could have properly concluded that there had been a deception as to the *purpose* of the act. That is, V thought it was for Cassie's pleasure, whereas it was in fact to serve D's goal of humiliation.

Under the law prior to the 2003 Act consent was negatived only if the victim was mistaken **7–127** about the *nature* of the act to which she was consenting or as to the *identity* of the person with whom she was consenting to have intercourse. In *Williams*[544] W, a choirmaster, had

---

[539] [2007] 2 All E.R. 676 at [42].
[540] J. Temkin and A. Ashworth, "The Sexual Offences Act 2003: (1) Rape, Sexual Assault and the Problem of Consent" [2004] Crim.L.R. 328 at 336.
[541] [2007] EWCA Crim 1699. See para.7–127.
[542] [2008] EWCA Crim 527.
[543] Causing sexual activity without consent. Sections 75 and 76 apply to this offence.
[544] [1920] 1 K.B. 340; see also *Flattery* (1877) 2 Q.B. 410.

intercourse with a 16-year-old chorister on the pretext that it was a medical operation to create an air passage to improve her voice projection. The girl, who trusted W, was completely ignorant of sexual matters and so her consent to what occurred was ineffective; she had been raped. Had she been aware that what was happening was sexual intercourse, but wrongly believed that sexual intercourse had voice improving side effects, she would have given a valid consent to intercourse and, therefore, would not have been raped.[545] The latter scenario would be covered by s.76(2)(a) of the Act if there had been deception as to the *purpose* for which sexual intercourse was to take place.

It was long accepted that if a woman consented to intercourse with a man she wrongly believed to be her husband, there was no valid consent. It was not clear to what other relationships this rule extended. In *Elbekkay*[546] the complainant had lived with her boyfriend for about 18 months. On the night in question E was staying as a guest and all three had had too much to drink. During the course of the night the complainant became aware of someone touching her and felt herself being entered by a penis. For about 20 seconds she assumed it was her boyfriend, but then realised it was E. V thereupon punched E and cut him with a knife. At E's trial for rape the complainant alleged that she had consented only so long as she thought it was her boyfriend. The Court of Appeal held that the rule was not restricted to the impersonation of husbands. Sexual intercourse is a highly personal act and it cannot be said that a woman who consents to intercourse with A has consented to intercourse with B. The amendments to s.1 of the Sexual Offences Act 1956, which were effected by s.142 of the Criminal Justice and Public Order Act 1994, post-dated *Elbekkay* and there was no change to s.1(3) which provides that a man commits rape if he induced a married woman to have sexual intercourse with him by impersonating her husband. Section 76(2)(b) of the Act is a noticeable improvement on what went before, providing for a conclusive presumption of a lack of consent where D impersonates "a person known personally" to the complainant. It is not absolutely clear who counts as "a person known personally to the complainant" for the purposes of s.76(2)(b). While the section is designed to deal with the defendant who impersonates a partner or spouse, the section probably does not cover the defendant who seeks to pass himself off as a famous person for the purposes of persuading the complainant to have sexual intercourse with him. Although the complainant may know who the famous person is, their knowledge of the famous person is not of a personal nature. However, what of *Jheeta*?[547] The defendant's impersonation of the (non-existent) police officers was clearly designed to facilitate instances of sexual intercourse with the complainant. Why was the complainant willing to follow the advice of the "police officers" to have sexual intercourse with the defendant? Was it purely because of their apparent status as police officers? If so, it might be unlikely that s.76(2)(b) would apply as the question of being "known personally" would not arise. However, if, through her interactions with the "police officers" some kind of substantive relationship of trust had developed (and we know from the facts that the complainant did correspond with the officers, albeit principally for formal purposes), whereby she would be more likely to follow

---

[545] *Williams* can be contrasted with *Bolduc and Bird*, a decision of the Supreme Court of Canada, where B1, a doctor, persuaded V, a woman patient, to allow B2 to watch B1 perform a vaginal examination on V. B2 was, in fact, a jazz musician who simply wanted to see such an examination, but B1 introduced him to V as a medical student and on that basis V gave her consent. When V discovered the truth she reported the incident and both defendants were charged with indecent assault. It was held, however, that she had consented to a proper medical examination by B1 and that is what happened. Her consent was real; it was irrelevant that she would not have consented had not B1 lied about B2. There was no mistake as to the nature of the act that was actually perpetrated, that is to say the medical examination itself.

[546] [1995] Crim.L.R. 163.

[547] See above para.7–125.

their advice than that of an unknown officer, could it be said that her actions were affected by the extent to which the officers were "known personally" to her? Perhaps unlikely, and the argument was not actually run in that case. However, the situation in *Jheeta* might appear on one level to be different from the impersonation of a famous person, because of the possible use of the impersonation to facilitate personal trust. The underlying question of statutory interpretation is whether somebody who does not exist can be known personally to one.[548]

At common law, fraud which did not induce a mistake about the nature of the act or of the identity of the man was irrelevant. Thus in *Linekar*,[549] L persuaded a prostitute to have intercourse with him on the basis that she would receive a sum of money. After the intercourse he walked off without paying and she claimed that she had been raped. The Court of Appeal held that the issue was not that of fraud, but of whether the woman had consented to sexual intercourse with L. This she clearly had done; the fact that she would not have had intercourse but for the promise of money was irrelevant. There was no fraud relating to the nature of the act or to the identity of the person. It is clear that many people allow another to have intercourse with them because of some promise that has been made. This might be that the victim is offered money, status or marriage in return for sexual intercourse. However, on one view, the position may now be different under s.76(2)(a) of the 2003 Act. The deception as to payment may be viewed as altering the nature *or purpose* of the act in question, consequently it could be argued that D should be classified as a rapist under the new provisions.[550]

In *Tabassum*,[551] the parameters of consent obtained by fraud in the context of sexual **7–128** activity were re-evaluated by the Court of Appeal. It was the prosecution case that D had asked several women to take part in a breast cancer survey he was carrying out in order to prepare a database software package to sell to the doctors. The three complainants consented to D showing them how to carry out a breast self-examination, which involved taking off their bras and allowing D to feel their breasts. D had no medical qualifications or training and each of the victims said that they had only consented because they thought he was so qualified. There was no evidence of a sexual motive. On behalf of Tabassum it was contended that the case should be discontinued on the premise that the complainants had undoubtedly consented, and such consent was not negatived by deception, except where identity was in issue and the nature and quality of the act done was different from that for which consent was given. Furthermore, it was submitted that lack of medical qualifications on the part of D did not change the nature and quality of the act, which equiparated to what had been consented to by the women.

The Court of Appeal, in upholding D's conviction, on three counts of indecent assault, determined that the women were consenting to touching for medical purposes and not indecent behaviour. Hence, there was consent to the *nature* of the act but not its *quality*. In the absence of a sexual motive, *Tabassum* would not be covered by s.76(2)(a) of the 2003 Act, as there was no deception as to either the nature or the purpose of the relevant act. Moreover, it was fundamental that an intimate examination for the purpose of creating a

---

[548] See also *Devonald* [2008] EWCA Crim 527, a case under s.4 of the 2003 Act (causing sexual activity without consent) where V was induced into sexual activity through impersonation. The case was turned on the different issue of D's deception as to the nature and purpose of the activity. See below, para.7–134.

[549] [1995] Q.B. 250; [1995] Crim.L.R. 320. See generally A. Reed, "An Analysis of Fraud Vitiating Consent in Rape Cases." (1995) 59 J.C.L. 310.

[550] Note under the old law the conduct of D in *Linekar* may have amounted to the offence of procuring a woman by false pretences to have intercourse contrary to s.3 of the Sexual Offences Act 1956. The 2003 Act contains no similar provision.

[551] [2000] Crim L.R. 686.

database by a medically qualified person is an act of a different *quality* from the same act done for the same purpose by a person not medically qualified. A by-product of the decision is that the outcome in *Clarence*[552] is thrown into even graver doubt. The wife may have consented to sexual intercourse which was the nature of the act, but following *Tabassum* it may be that she did not consent to the risk of contracting venereal disease which is embodied by the quality of the act.[553] Similar analysis applied in *Dica* to the risk of HIV infection.[554]

Confusion now reigns as to which types of fraud vitiate consent in the context of sexual activity. The decision in *Dica*,[555] following *Tabassum*, in allowing qualitative mistakes to negate consent is palpably inconsistent with a long line of authority dating back to *Clarence*. If qualitative errors destroy consent then the logical corollary may be that the victim has endured either a rape or an assault.[556] If a qualitative error as to D's state of health destroys consent then, by parity of reasoning, other mistakes as to 'quality' also destroy consent. Embraced herein will be collateral matters such as suppression of the truth as to D's lack of intention to pay for sexual services, D's wealth, or even a promise of marriage. The difficulty, of course, is that the core transaction itself has been the subject of consent.

A similar rationale to that in *Dica*, qualitative mistakes vitiating consent, was adopted in *Cort*.[557] At issue was the offence of kidnapping. D made false allegations to individuals waiting at bus stops that the bus had broken down and offered to give women on their own a lift. Invariably the offer was rejected, but on one occasion he took a woman to her destination. He contended that, given the consensual nature of the journey, no offence of kidnapping could be made out. This was rejected by the Court of Appeal, and Buxton LJ asserted that kidnapping may be established by carrying away by fraud:

> ". . . it is difficult to see how one could ever consent to that once fraud was indeed established. The nature of the act here is therefore taking the complainant away by fraud. The complainant did not consent to that even. All that she consented to is a ride in the car, which in itself is irrelevant to the offence and a different thing from that with which Mr Cort is charged."[558]

The decisions in *Tabassum*, *Dica* and *Cort*, operating in tandem, represent an important change in judicial mindset on consent. The consistent line of authority dating back to *Clarence* has been resiled from in an explicit manner. We await with interest developments in this area, and look forward to clarification from the House of Lords as to the relationship between fraud and consent beyond the provisions of s.76 of the 2003 Act.

---

[552] (1888) 22 Q.B.D. 23; see above, para.7–084. It will be recalled that D had intercourse with his wife, knowing that he had venereal disease, and thereby infected her. It was determined that no assault occurred, even though D's conduct did amount to a fraud it did not vitiate the wife's consent because she understood the nature of the act and her ignorance of D's disease was not sufficient for criminal liability.

[553] In *Tabassum* the Court of Appeal, obiter, sought to distinguish *Clarence* on spurious lines. It was asserted that the wife in *Clarence* did consent to sexual intercourse knowing both the nature and quality of D's act despite the "additional unexpected consequences of infection". Additionally, the appellate court, obiter, stated that in *Linekar* a prostitute who consented to intercourse with a man who had deceived her into believing that she would be paid for her services did not make a mistake as to the quality of the act in question.

[554] See above at paras 7–107—7–109.

[555] [2004] 3 All E.R. 593; [2004] EWCA Crim 1103.

[556] It is noteworthy, of course, that in accordance with s.76 of the Sexual Offences Act 2003 a fraud as to the "nature or purpose" (no reference to quality) of the act is conclusively presumed to vitiate consent.

[557] [2003] EWCA Crim 2139; [2004] 4 All E.R. 137.

[558] [2003] EWCA Crim 2139 at [20].

B. MENS REA:

(i) Intentional penetration

For the offence of rape to be committed, the penetration must be intentional. It is difficult **7–129** to imagine that this will create a serious argument in many cases. However, there may be a question of intention in circumstances where the defendant is intoxicated to the extent that he does not appreciate the nature of what he is doing, or when he is having a hallucinatory episode.

(ii) No reasonable belief that the victim is consenting

It is in this regard that the mens rea of rape has been significantly changed by the 2003 Act. **7–130** Prior to the Act, the decisions in *DPP v Morgan*[559] and *Satnam and Kewal*[560] had created a situation where the mens rea for rape on the issue of the victim's lack of consent was, in effect, a modified form of subjective recklessness. A defendant would be guilty of rape if he intended that there be no consent; or if he knew that there was a risk that the complainant was not consenting; or if he "could not care less" whether the complainant was consenting. A defendant would avoid conviction through an honest belief in the existence of consent.

   This was a matter of considerable controversy. The decision of the House of Lords in *DPP v Morgan* meant that even if a defendant's honest belief in consent was not based on reasonable grounds, the offence would not be committed. The Heilbron Committee was convened to consider the law of rape in the aftermath of *Morgan,* and the Sexual Offences (Amendment) Act 1976 was the ultimate result of its deliberations. The committee endorsed the position in *Morgan,* but the 1976 Act made specific reference, in s.1(2), to the question of the reasonable grounds for a defendant's belief in consent. The jury was instructed by that provision to use the reasonableness or otherwise of a defendant's claimed belief in the existence of consent as evidence on the issue of whether the belief was in fact genuine. The facts of *Morgan* itself are instructive:

   D had invited several friends back to his house after an evening's drinking. He had informed them that they could have intercourse with his wife who would consent. He provided them with condoms and told them that they should not be put off by any apparent signs of resistance since these were just her way of increasing her sexual enjoyment. The facts revealed that the wife put up tremendous resistance but was eventually overcome by the men who then had intercourse with her. The men were charged with rape, but pleaded that they genuinely thought that she was consenting.[561] The trial judge directed the jury that the men would have a defence if they believed on reasonable grounds that the woman was consenting to intercourse. Not surprisingly the men were convicted and appealed.[562] The House of Lords held that the trial judge should have directed the jury that if the men honestly, albeit unreasonably, believed that the woman was consenting to intercourse, they were not guilty of rape.

---

[559] [1976] A.C. 182.

[560] (1983) 78 Cr.App.R. 149.

[561] At that time the husband could not be convicted as the principal offender in the rape of his wife; Morgan was therefore indicted as a secondary party. See further, above, para.4–005.

[562] At the time *Morgan* was bound for the House of Lords, a trial judge was confronted with almost identical facts in *Cogan and Leak* [1976] Q.B. 217; a husband invited a friend to have intercourse with his wife who, he said, had consented. Although the trial judge directed the jury that only a reasonable belief in consent would afford a defence, he realised that if the House of Lords were to allow the appeal in *Morgan,* the friend might, if convicted, appeal; the husband clearly knew that the wife was not consenting. He, therefore, asked the jury to indicate whether they thought that the friend honestly believed that the woman was consenting and, if so, whether the belief was a reasonable one. The jury replied that they thought the friend had genuinely believed the woman was consenting, but that he had no reasonable grounds for so believing.

7–131   The 2003 Act has now consigned the *Morgan* test to history. The defendant's belief in consent must now be reasonable. The mens rea for rape on the issue of consent has thus moved from being a modified form of subjective recklessness to being negligence. It is argued that this provides better protection for victims and less opportunity for defendants to escape liability by running questionable arguments about their belief in consent. Nonetheless, the change effected by the 2003 Act is controversial, as it can be argued that one ought not to be convicted of a serious crime such as rape on the basis of anything less than a subjective form of mens rea. It is interesting to note that around the time that Parliament was moving away from the subjective test in rape, the House of Lords were moving towards a subjective test in criminal damage, in *R v G*.[563]

It should be noted that there is no duty on a defendant to actively seek an expression of consent from the complainant, but s.1(2) of the 2003 Act makes clear that whether steps have been taken by the defendant to establish the existence of consent is relevant, along with all the other circumstances, to the question of whether there was a reasonable belief in consent.

The evidential and conclusive presumptions about consent, in ss.75 and 76, are also relevant to the question of the defendant's reasonable belief in consent.[564] If one of the circumstances in s.75 is proved to exist, then not only is the complainant presumed not to have consented, but also the defendant is presumed not to have had a reasonable belief in consent, unless he can rebut that presumption with evidence. Similarly, where the defendant practises a deception or impersonation of the type referred to in s.76, not only is the complainant presumed not to have consented, but the defendant is presumed not to have had a reasonable belief in consent. Where it is proved that the defendant intentionally penetrated the complainant and the circumstances in s.76 are proved, it follows that the offence of rape is inevitably committed.

3.   ASSAULT BY PENETRATION

7–132 Section 2 of the Act states:

"(1) A person (A) commits an offence if—

(a) he intentionally penetrates the vagina or anus of another person (B) with a part of his body or anything else,

(b) the penetration is sexual,

(c) B does not consent to the penetration, and

(d) A does not reasonably believe that B consents.

(2) Whether a belief is reasonable is to be determined having regard to all the circumstances, including any steps A has taken to ascertain whether B consents.

(3) Sections 75 and 76 apply to an offence under this section.

(4) A person guilty of an offence under this section is liable, on conviction on indictment, to imprisonment for life."

---

[563] [2003] UKHL 50; [2004] 1 A.C. 1034. See above, para.2–069.
[564] See above, para.7–130.

Thus, the elements of this offence are:

Actus reus

- Sexual penetration of the vagina or anus of the victim.
- The victim's lack of consent.

Whether penetration is "sexual" is determined by reference to s.78 of the Act. According to that provision, an activity is "sexual" if a reasonable person would consider that:

(a) whatever its circumstances or any person's purpose in relation to it, it is because of its nature sexual, or

(b) because of its nature it may be sexual and because of its circumstances or the purpose of any person in relation to it (or both) it is sexual.

Mens rea

- Intentional penetration.
- No reasonable belief that the victim is consenting.

Although the offence of rape can only be committed by penile penetration, s.2 of the Act recognises the distinctively harmful quality of penetrative assaults, however they are perpetrated. The offence is, in effect, a mirror of the offence of rape without the specific requirement that penetration be penile. It may also be a useful offence for prosecutors who are able to prove that penetration took place, but who are not able categorically to prove that penetration was penile.

It is worthy of note that there are other offences in the Act—some beyond the scope of this book—which involve the defendant "touching" the victim. Touching, according to s.79(8) of the 2003 Act, includes penetration. It should also be noted that some offences under the Act carry an enhanced penalty where the behaviour in question is proved to be penetrative.

4. SEXUAL ASSAULT

Section 3 of the 2003 Act states:

7–133

"(1) A person (A) commits an offence if—

    (a) he intentionally touches another person (B),

    (b) the touching is sexual,

    (c) B does not consent to the touching, and

    (d) A does not reasonably believe that B consents.

(2) Whether a belief is reasonable is to be determined having regard to all the circumstances, including any steps A has taken to ascertain whether B consents.

(3) Sections 75 and 76 apply to an offence under this section.

(4) A person guilty of an offence under this section is liable—

    (a) on summary conviction, to imprisonment for a term not exceeding 6 months or a fine not exceeding the statutory maximum or both;

(b) on conviction on indictment, to imprisonment for a term not exceeding 10 years."

The elements of this offence are:

Actus reus

- Sexual touching.
- The victim's lack of consent.

Mens rea

- Intentional touching.
- No reasonable belief that the victim is consenting.

Prior to the 2003 Act, the principal sexual offences other than rape were the offences of indecent assault, under the Sexual Offences Act 1956. Those offences, like the new offence, covered a wide range of behaviours of different levels of seriousness. The wide ambit of the new offence is denoted by its triable either way status.

This is one of the offences in the 2003 Act where the Court of Appeal has already been involved. In *R v H (Karl Anthony)*,[565] the defendant grabbed the victim's tracksuit bottoms. His submission that the mere touching of clothing did not amount to "touching" for the purposes of the 2003 Act was rejected. To touch the clothes worn by a person is to touch that person for those purposes.

The court also considered the meaning of "sexual" in s.78 of the Act (see discussion of s.2 above).[566] Unambiguously sexual touching would be covered by s.78(a), other, possibly sexual touching by s.78(b). Where touching was not unambiguously sexual, the jury ought to be asked to undertake a two stage inquiry. First, they should consider whether they, as twelve reasonable people, considered that the nature of the touching meant that it might be sexual; and second, whether, in light of the circumstances and/or the purpose of any person in relation to it, the touching was in fact sexual. Section 78(b) leaves the possibility for a wide range of behaviours to be deemed "sexual" by factfinders.

In *Heard*,[567] D, while drunk, rubbed his exposed genitals against the leg of a police officer. He lost his appeal against conviction for sexual assault. In the context of deciding that the defence of voluntary intoxication was not available to a defendant charged under s.3,[568] the court took the view that an intentional touching was one that was done deliberately rather than accidentally.

5. CAUSING A PERSON TO ENGAGE IN SEXUAL ACTIVITY WITHOUT CONSENT

7–134   Section 4 of the Act states:

"(1) A person (A) commits an offence if—

(a) he intentionally causes another person (B) to engage in an activity,

(b) the activity is sexual,

---

[565] [2005] EWCA Crim 732; [2005] 2 Cr.App.R. 9; [2005] Crim.L.R. 734–737.
[566] See above, para.7–132.
[567] [2007] EWCA Crim 125.
[568] The decision is problematic on this point. See above, para.5–031.

   (c) B does not consent to engaging in the activity, and

   (d) A does not reasonably believe that B consents.

(2) Whether a belief is reasonable is to be determined having regard to all the circumstances, including any steps A has taken to ascertain whether B consents.

(3) Sections 75 and 76 apply to an offence under this section.

(4) A person guilty of an offence under this section, if the activity caused involved—

   (a) penetration of B's anus or vagina,

   (b) penetration of B's mouth with a person's penis,

   (c) penetration of a person's anus or vagina with a part of B's body or by B with anything else, or

   (d) penetration of a person's mouth with B's penis,

is liable, on conviction on indictment, to imprisonment for life.

(5) Unless subsection (4) applies, a person guilty of an offence under this section is liable—

   (a) on summary conviction, to imprisonment for a term not exceeding 6 months or to a fine not exceeding the statutory maximum or both;

   (b) on conviction on indictment, to imprisonment for a term not exceeding 10 years."

The elements of this offence are:

Actus reus

- Causing another person to engage in sexual activity.
- The victim's lack of consent.

Mens rea

- Intentionally causing another person to engage in sexual activity.
- No reasonable belief that the victim is consenting.

One function of this offence is to fill in the gaps left by the definition of assault. This offence covers behaviours which might not constitute an assault (i.e. in most cases, the non-consensual touching (i) *of the victim* (ii) *by the defendant*) but which do result in non-consensual sexual activity. Thus it covers the coerced performance of sexual acts by the victim on the defendant, or by the victim on himself or herself, and coerced sexual activity with third parties. Prosecutions have recently been brought in respect of unlawful text messaging where the content of the message is indecent, and where the words utilised by the defendant incite another to engage in sexual activity.[569] The ubiquity of communications technologies make it likely that this will be a recurrent issue.

---

[569] See, generally, *Hinton-Smith* [2005] EWCA Crim 2575; and *A* [2006] EWCA Crim 2103.

In *Devonald*,[570] D sought to humiliate V, who had broken up with D's daughter. Through correspondence online, D posed as a 20-year old woman, "Cassie", and encouraged V to masturbate on a webcam for "Cassie's" pleasure. V did so. D's conviction under s.4 was upheld: there had been a proper basis for deciding that V had not consented to the activity—he thought he was engaging in the activity for Cassie's gratification when this was not in fact the case.[571]

The offence is triable either way, although the distinctive nature of penetrative activity is recognised by making an offence involving such activity triable on indictment, and punishable by life imprisonment.

6.   SECTIONS 5 TO 8: OFFENCES AGAINST CHILDREN UNDER 13

7–135   Sections 5 to 8 create a set of offences which, in broad terms, mirror ss.1 to 4 respectively, but which apply when the victim of the offence is under 13 years old. There are two key points to note about the offences in ss.5 to 8. First, they make no mention of the consent of the victim; the prosecution need not prove that the victim did not consent. The issue of consent does not feature in the elements of the offences. Second, the offences are designed with the intention that the prosecution need not prove that the defendant knew that the victim was under 13 years old.

Under the law prior to the 2003 Act, the offences of indecent assault against a victim under the age of sixteen,[572] and the offence of inciting a child under the age of fourteen to commit an act of gross indecency[573] were deemed by the House of Lords to require proof that the defendant did not honestly believe that the victim was of age. This position was reached despite the acknowledgement, in *K*, that the intention of Parliament (that the belief of the defendant that the victim was of age was immaterial) was being subverted.[574]

Sections 5 to 8 suggest an attempt by Parliament to create offences in respect of which liability on the issue of the age of the victim is strict. The evidence for this is that whereas the later sections in the Act which deal with victims under the age of sixteen, provide that the defendant can escape liability of he or she reasonably believes that the victim is sixteen, there is no corresponding provision in ss.5 to 8.

The upshot of this is, for instance, that a defendant who has sexual intercourse with a girl of twelve, believing, on good grounds, that she is sixteen, will be liable for the offence of rape of a child under thirteen. It is controversial that such a serious offence can be committed without the need for the prosecution to prove any mens rea on the part of the defendant. It will be interesting to see whether the courts are minded to conduct the same sort of interpretive exercises as in *B* and *K* and to try to "read in" a requirement to prove some kind of mens rea on the issue of the age of the victim. The decision of the House of Lords in *G*[575] suggests that, in the immediate term, they may not be so minded. In *G*, D, who was 15-years-old, pleaded guilty to an offence under s.5 in respect of a 12-year-old complainant. The basis of the plea was that V consented and that D thought that V was 15-years-old. D claimed that his right under art.6(2) of the European Convention on Human Rights (presumption of innocence) was violated by the fact that the offence was one of strict

---

[570] [2008] EWCA Crim 527.
[571] See also the discussion of fraud and consent at para.7–127—7–128 above.
[572] *R v K* [2001] UKHL 41; [2002] 1 A.C. 462.
[573] *B v DPP* [2000] 2 W.L.R. 452.
[574] Lord Millett suggested in *R v K*, at [41], "I have little doubt that we shall be failing to give effect to the intention of Parliament and will reduce s.14 of the Sexual Offences Act 1956 [indecent assault on a woman] to incoherence."
[575] [2008] UKHL 37.

liability. This ground of appeal was unanimously rejected by the House of Lords. Article 6(2) is concerned with the processes by which allegations of criminal conduct are proved, not with the substantive definitions of offences themselves. He also claimed a violation of art.8 (privacy) on the basis that he should not have been prosecuted under s.5 when the behaviour could more properly have been dealt with under the less serious s.13.[576] The House of Lords rejected that ground of appeal by 3 to 2, the majority holding either that art.8 was not engaged or that if it was engaged the prosecution under s.5 was not disproportionate.

7. CHILD SEX OFFENCES

For the purposes of this book, we will note the existence of some of these offences, although **7–136** we will not consider them in much detail. The offences labelled as "Child sex offences" in the 2003 Act are committed only by those aged eighteen or over.

Sections 9 and 10 of the Act cover "Sexual activity with a child" and "causing a child to engage in sexual activity". The former is, broadly speaking, a sexual touching offence along the lines of ss.3 and 7, and the latter mirrors ss.4 and 8. The offences are committed irrespective of the existence of the victim's consent. If the victim is under thirteen, then the belief of the defendant that he or she is older is immaterial. If the victim is 13 to 15 years' old, the prosecution must prove that the defendant did not reasonably believe that he or she was 16 or over. The offences are, in their basic form, triable either way. However, if the behaviour alleged involves penetration, then they are triable on indictment and carry a maximum penalty of fourteen years.

Sections 11 and 12 cover, respectively, engaging in sexual activity in the presence of a child, and causing a child to watch a sexual act.[577] The position regarding the victim's age is as in ss.9 and 10.

There are many other offences in the 2003 Act, covering issues such as grooming, abuse of trust, sexual relationships within families, and sexual relations with persons whose competence to enter into such relations may be compromised by mental impairment. Specific offences of voyeurism and sexual interference with a corpse are also created. To cover much more of the Act in any detail would not be feasible in a book of this length. However, we would like to conclude this section by reference to s.13 of the Act, which reads as follows:

"(1) A person under 18 commits an offence if he does anything which would be an offence under any of sections 9 to 12 if he were aged 18.

(2) A person guilty of an offence under this section is liable—

    (a) on summary conviction, to imprisonment for a term not exceeding 6 months or a fine not exceeding the statutory maximum or both;

    (b) on conviction on indictment, to imprisonment for a term not exceeding 5 years."

This is a controversial provision because it potentially criminalises low level consensual sexual activity between young people of similar ages. It is, of course, a sad reality that young people are capable of acting abusively towards one another. However, this offence is so broad that it would cover the fifteen year old boy who kisses his girlfriend of the same age.

---

[576] See below para.7–136.
[577] On s.12, see *Abdullahi* [2006] EWCA Crim 2060.

Although the Government has attempted to make clear in the policy documents leading to the passing of the 2003 Act that prosecutorial discretion would be exercised sensibly in such cases, it does not seem satisfactory that such behaviour is even capable of being criminal.

GENERAL READING

7–137   Bohlander, M., "Mistaken Consent to Sex, Political Correctness and Correct Policy" (2008) 72 J.C.L. 412.

Brooks, R., "Marital Consent In Rape". [1989] Crim.L.R. 877.

Elvin, J., "The Concept of Consent Under the Sexual Offences Act 2003" (2008) 72 J.C.L. 519.

Finch. E., and Munro, V.E., "The Sexual Offences Act 2003: Intoxicated Consent and Drug Assisted Rape Revisited" [2004] Crim.L.R. 789.

Gardner, S. "Appreciating *Olugboja*". (1996) 16 *Legal Studies* 275.

Giles, M., "Judicial Law-Making In The Criminal Courts: The Case of Marital Rape" [1992] Crim.L.R. 407.

Gross, H., "Rape, Moralism and Human Rights" [2007] Crim.L.R. 220.

Hall, J., "Can Children Consent to Indecent Assault?" [1996] Crim.L.R. 184.

Herring, J., Human Rights and Rape: A Reply to Hyman Gross" [2007] Crim.L.R. 228.

Hicks, M. and Branston, G., "Transsexual Rape—A Loophole Closed?" [1997] Crim.L.R. 565.

Horder, J., "Rethinking Non-Fatal Offences Against the Person" (1994) 14 O.J.L.S. 335.

Lacey, N., "Beset By Boundaries: The Home Office Review Of Sex Offences" [2001] Crim.L.R. 3.

Rumney, P. and Fenton, R., "Intoxicated Consent in Rape: *Bree* and Juror Decision-Making" (2008) 71 M.L.R. 279.

Tadros, V., "Rape Without Consent" (2006) 26 O.J.L.S. 515.

Temkin, J., and Ashworth, A., "Rape, Sexual Assaults and the Problems of Consent" [2004] Crim.L.R. 328.

Temkin, J., *Rape and the Legal Process*, 2nd ed, (Oxford University Press, 2002).

Williams, G., "The Meaning of Indecency" (1992) 12 *Legal Studies* 20.

Williams, G., "Rape Is Rape" (1992) N.L.J. 11.

Williams, R., "Deception, Mistake and the Vitiation of the Victim's Consent" (2008) 124 L.Q.R. 132.

Chapter 8

OFFENCES AGAINST PROPERTY I

STEALING UNDER THE THEFT ACT 1968

The Theft Acts of 1968 and 1978 provide us with a fairly comprehensive list of offences **8–001** which, broadly speaking, involve the dishonest dealing with other people's property. They do not, however, provide a complete code on what might be termed as property offences. Forgery, for example, is covered by the Forgery and Counterfeiting Act 1981, and offences involving damage or destruction of property are contained in the Criminal Damage Act 1971 which will be examined in Chapter 10. Included in the Theft Acts are such offences as theft, burglary, robbery, blackmail and handling.[1]

The Theft Act 1968 represents an overhaul of the existing assortment of offences which had become rather complex and unwieldy. The 1978 Act created three new offences to replace a subsection of the 1968 Act which had been found to be unworkable. Between them the Acts have produced a simplification of the law in this area, though not as much as first expected, and we can say from the outset that the great majority of cases brought under them present very few difficult legal problems. They may present difficult problems of proof for the court of trial—but this is a totally different issue. For example, many cases involving thefts from supermarkets may hinge upon the ability of the prosecution to prove that the defendant deliberately tried to avoid paying for a given item and that it was not simply a case of absentmindedness. We all know how easy it is to arrive at the other side of the checkout counter without having paid for an item, because, for instance, it has become hidden in another item. Hence the difficulty in individual cases of proving that the defendant was dishonest. But to repeat what was said earlier, this is not a difficulty arising from the interpretation of the Act itself; it is one of proving that the essential elements of the offence exist. That is not to say that the Theft Acts have got rid of all the legal difficulties; this is probably an impossible task given the complex nature of the rights the law is seeking to protect. Take theft itself, for example; this consists in the interference with the property rights of another. These property rights are controlled at the outset by the civil law, and so in theft cases it is sometimes necessary to take account of difficult civil law rules before criminal liability can be sorted out. Occasionally judges have said that complex rules relating to property rights have no place in the criminal law, but it would be impossible to divorce the law of theft from the property rights it is seeking to protect.

[1] See, generally, A.T.H. Smith, *Property Offences* (Sweet and Maxwell, 1994); E. Griew, *The Theft Act* (Sweet and Maxwell, 1995); A. Arlidge and J. Parry, *Arlidge & Parry on Fraud* 2nd edn (1996); and J.C. Smith, *The Law of Theft* (Butterworths, 1997).

One of the major problems in this area has been the failure of prosecutors to make full use of the wide range of offences created by these Acts. In many cases which have led to questionable appellate decisions, the problem would not have arisen had the prosecutor selected a more appropriate offence.[2] The judiciary, for their part, should avoid strained interpretations of the law in their attempts to uphold convictions where the prosecutor has selected the wrong offence. As it is there is a grave danger that the Theft Acts will become as complex as the law they were designed to replace. The golden rule in every case is that the prosecutor must be able to establish each of the required elements of the actus reus andmens rea. In nearly every case where the court has got itself into difficulty there was a more appropriate charge which could have been successfully brought against the defendant. Nowhere is this more true than in the approach of the courts, particularly the House of Lords, to theft itself, where muddled thinking has resulted in a definition of theft which virtually renders redundant the offence of obtaining property by deception (now fraud).

8–002   Since we shall occasionally have to get involved in some of these property rights it will be useful at the outset to mention certain concepts which will be in use throughout the chapter. Let us stay with the crime of stealing. When we say X has taken Y's book what do we mean by Y's book? Normally we would mean that Y is the owner of the book. It is common for judges to say that the property or title in the book is in Y. This is another way of say that Y owns the book. If Y now sells the book we can say that the property or title in the book passes to whoever buys it. Ownership is the ultimate right over property; it usually means that Y will have the right to determine what happens to the book. It does not, however, mean that Y has possession of the book or even that he has the right to possess it. He may have lent the book to Z. Under normal circumstances Y would be able to demand the return of the book, but this is not always so. Consider a common everyday situation. Y has rented a car from B company. He is paying £100 a week for the loan of the car. Y is therefore in possession, but B company is still the owner of the car. Although B company is still the owner of the car, it will not be in possession of it and nor will it have the right to immediate possession unless Y defaults on his payments or breaks some other clause in the rental agreement.

It will also be useful to say a few words about money as a form of property. If Y lends B his book, the ownership remains with Y; B merely gets possession. B cannot make X the owner of the book by purporting to sell it to him because B has no "property" in the book to pass on to X, this is still with Y. On the other hand if Y lends B a twenty pound note, B's only obligation is to restore an equivalent amount of money. If B passes on the twenty pounds to X, X receives ownership of the money. This goes even further. If B steals the note from Y, ownership in the twenty pounds remains with Y, but if B passes on the note to X for valuable consideration and X is acting in good faith X will receive a good title to the money which he can pass on to others. What is the difference between the book and the twenty pound note? The answer is that money is negotiable whereas a book and most other forms of property are not. If B had stolen Y's book he could not pass on a good title to the book to X even if X was acting in good faith and paid a fair price. The need for such a rule in relation to money is obvious; it will usually be very hard to identify your particular pound coin or note and one could only imagine the havoc that could be caused if one's right to spend money could be made dependent upon showing that you received it from someone who was in a position to pass ownership in it to you.

The word "possession" can also be hard to pin down. Normally it means control over property. Thus in the example of the rental car we can clearly say that Y is in possession.

---

[2] The difficulties caused over interpretation of the 1968 Theft Act were highlighted by the Court of Appeal in *Hallam* [1995] Crim.L.R. 323, calling for urgent reform, and asserting that much time was wasted on "hours of semantic argument divorced from the real merits of the case".

When, however, an employee is cleaning his employer's silverware it would be odd to say that he was in possession of the silverware. It is probably more accurate to say that he is in control of it as long as he is engaged on its cleaning.

In this chapter we shall concentrate upon the offence of theft. Fraud and related offences will be considered in the next chapter.

2. THEFT

The offence is defined by s.1 of the Theft Act 1968 as follows: 8–003

> "(1) A person is guilty of theft if he dishonestly appropriates property belonging to another with the intention of permanently depriving the other of it; and 'thief' and 'steal' shall be construed accordingly."

Sections 1 to 6 of the Act amplify the meaning of words and phrases used in this definition and s.7 provides that the offence of theft shall be punishable with a maximum of seven years' imprisonment. Originally, theft carried ten years' imprisonment, but this was reduced to seven years by s.26 of the Criminal Justice Act 1991, which substituted a new s.7 to the Theft Act. It should be borne in mind that the offence of theft covers all cases of stealing whether it be of a great or a small sum; we have no division into petty theft and grand theft; though theft is an offence which is triable either way.[3] There is no separate offence of shoplifting; this is a colloquialism used to describe a particular form of theft, which has the unfortunate tendency of suggesting that there is a separate, less serious offence.

From the definition in s.1 we can see that the actus reus comprises (a) an appropriation (b) of property (c) which property belongs to another. The mens rea requires (a) dishonesty and (b) an intention permanently to deprive the other of the property.[4]

1. THE ACTUS REUS OF THEFT

A. Appropriates

Attempts to define the word "appropriates" have probably caused more problems for the   8–004
courts than the rest of the Act put together. It is clear from the Eighth Report of the Criminal Law Revision Committee, *Theft and Related Offences*, upon which the 1968 Theft Act was based, that the phrase "dishonestly appropriates" was chosen as a direct modern equivalent of the phrase "fraudulently converts to his own use or benefit, or for the use or benefit of any other person". In so doing the Committee clearly envisaged that it conveyed the notion of unauthorised dealing with another's property, and hence they saw no need to incorporate the words "without the consent of the owner" which appeared in the old Larceny Act, because an unauthorised dealing clearly would be without the consent or authority of the owner. The courts, nevertheless, appear in this instance to have ignored the Committee's report. This is somewhat strange in view of the House of Lords' new-found willingness, revealed in *Pepper v Hart*,[5] to consider parliamentary debates as an aid to

---

[3] See above, para.1–006.
[4] The mens rea also presumably requires an intention to appropriate.
[5] [1993] A.C. 593.

discovering the intention of the legislature. The result has been, as we shall see, a very wide interpretation of the notion of "appropriation".

The word "appropriates" is partially defined by s.3(1) of the Act which provides:

"Any assumption by a person of the rights of an owner amounts to an appropriation, and this includes, where he has come by the property (innocently or not) without stealing it, any later assumption of a right to it by keeping or dealing with it as owner."

Clearly, the owner of property has a variety of rights in relation to that property, including in most cases the right to destroy it. It was held by the House of Lords in *Morris*,[6] and not challenged by the House of Lords in *Gomez*,[7] that the assumption of any of these rights amounts to an appropriation within the meaning of the Act. It is not essential that the defendant has assumed all of the owner's rights.

To illustrate the meaning of appropriation we can consider the most commonly occurring form of appropriation, the case of appropriation by taking. A enters B's bookshop and takes a book belonging to B; C enters D's room and takes D's watch; E puts his hand in F's pocket and removes F's wallet. In these cases it is as clear as can be that A has appropriated the book, C the watch and E the wallet. A, C and E are treating themselves as owners of property which belongs to B, D and F.

8–005   But two things need to be noticed. The first is that although taking is so far the most common mode of appropriation that laymen still think of theft as a taking, it is not the only mode of appropriation. The definition says that "any" assumption of the rights of an owner amounts to an appropriation.[8] Strictly, therefore, it amounts to an appropriation to destroy another's property. Thus if A pushes B's car over a cliff and thereby destroys it, it can properly be said that he has appropriated the car. Most laymen would not recognise this as a case of theft, and no doubt A would be charged under the Criminal Damage Act 1971,[9] but a charge of theft could be supported on such facts.[10] This is clearly an appropriation—what could be a clearer assumption of B's rights than destroying his car—and s.1(1) makes it clear that the prosecution does not have to establish, on a charge of theft, that A intended to make any gain from his action. A similar illustration would be if D, a mischievous Sunderland football supporter, were to throw V's prized Newcastle United season ticket down a disused mine shaft at Seaham Colliery. The wide meaning given to "appropriates" is probably at odds with many people's instinctive, though erroneous, feeling that theft involves some form of unauthorised taking. This may have led the Court of Appeal into error in *Gallasso*[11] (see below) and *Briggs*[12] (see below).

The second point to note is that while the layman might think that, in the examples first given, A, C and E appropriate the property when they take it away, i.e. when they remove the goods from the control of B, D and F into their own control, in law the appropriation has occurred at an earlier stage. When, for example, E put his hand on the wallet inside F's pocket, and before he removes it, he may be said to have appropriated it because, at that

---

[6] [1984] A.C. 320.
[7] [1993] A.C. 442; [1993] 1 All E.R. 1.
[8] The owner has a number of rights and the following have been treated as an appropriation: *Pitham and Hehl* (1976) 65 Cr.App.R. 45 (D offering to sell P's furniture in P's absence, right to sell a right of ownership); *Pilgram v Rice-Smith* [1977] 2 All E.R. 658 (D, a supermarket assistant in cahoots with a customer, acting to understate price of goods on wrapper so goods sold for less than true price); and *Rogers v Arnott* [1960] 2 Q.B. 244 (bailee offering to sell tape recorder); see further *Tomsett* [1985] Crim.L.R. 369.
[9] See below, para.10–001.
[10] But, of course, the prosecution would also have to establish that it was dishonest.
[11] (1992) 98 Cr.App.R. 284.
[12] [2004] EWCA Crim 3662; [2004] Crim.L.R. 455.

instance, he is assuming the rights of the owner, F. One of F's rights is to enjoy the undisturbed possession of his wallet; in asserting a right to possess it himself, E is assuming F's right. This point may be further illustrated by reference to *Corcoran v Anderton*.[13] A and B attacked a woman intending to take her bag. A got his hands on the bag and there was a struggle for its possession during which the bag fell to the ground. A and B then ran off emptyhanded. This to the layman might look like a case of attempted robbery because the youths failed to get what they were after but they were convicted of the full offence. Robbery is theft accomplished with force[14] and the theft was complete when the handbag was appropriated, i.e. when A grabbed it and tried to take it from her—that conduct was an assumption by A of the owner's rights.

Before examining the important House of Lords judgment in *Gomez* on the meaning of appropriation, it is instructive to examine earlier case precedents which exemplify the confused doctrinal approaches. A useful starting point is the decision in *Skipp*.[15] The defendant, who had passed himself off as a genuine haulage contractor, was instructed to pick up three loads of oranges from different places in London and to deliver them to Leicester. It was his intention all along to abscond with the fruit and in pursuance of this plan he collected the oranges from the three pick-up points but then did not take them to Leicester. The question for the court was whether he stole the oranges at the time he loaded them on to his lorry with a dishonest intention or only when he deviated from the route to Leicester. It may legitimately be questioned why the court should be at all bothered with this type of point so long as he could be said to have stolen them at some time. In fact it stemmed from a procedural issue. The defendant had been charged on an indictment alleging only one count of theft. If a count is found to contain more than one offence it is said to be bad for duplicity and any conviction based upon it will almost certainly be quashed. It is quite clear that he obtained each load of oranges by deception and this was an offence under s.15 of the Theft Act 1968. The court held, however, that so long as he was doing what he was *authorised* to do by the owner of the oranges he could not be said to have appropriated them, even though the owner would not have let him touch the oranges had he known what was in his mind. Only when he failed to take the load to Leicester can he be said to have exceeded his authority. Hence, although there were clearly three offences of obtaining property by deception, there was only one theft and the indictment was sound. Similarly in *Fritschy*[16] the defendant was authorised to collect krugerrands in England and to take them to Switzerland which he did. The prosecution alleged he had collected the coins with the dishonest intention of keeping them. Nevertheless the reasoning in *Skipp* led to the conclusion that no *unauthorised* act had occurred in this country. Theft, if it had been committed at all, had been committed in Switzerland. It may be considered that this type of situation will be rare and only arose in *Skipp* and *Fritschy* because of procedural points. However, exactly the same problem arises in everyday events. Consider, for example, the case of *Eddy v Niman*[17] in which the defendant and a friend had spent some time drinking before they entered a large self-service store. There they formed the intention to steal some goods. They took items from the shelves and placed them in a trolley and wire basket. At this point the defendant said he had changed his mind and that the plan was stupid. He abandoned the trolley and wire basket and left the shop without taking anything. Had he committed any offence? He had certainly not tried to take goods past the checkout. In

---

[13] (1980) 71 Cr.App.R. 104; see below, para.9–021.
[14] See below, para.9–020.
[15] [1975] Crim.L.R. 114.
[16] [1985] Crim.L.R. 745.
[17] (1981) 73 Cr.App.R. 237.

putting the goods into the trolley and basket he was assuming some of the owner's rights—the right to touch and move his property. On the other hand he was simply doing that which the shop owner authorised him to do, namely to select produce from the shelves and to place it in a trolley. Of course, the defendant would never have been allowed to touch the property had the owner realised what he was up to. It was held that he could not be convicted of theft because there was nothing that could be described as an appropriation; in doing what he was authorised to do, albeit with a dishonest intention, he had not yet assumed the rights of the owner.

8–006   A case that was hard to reconcile with *Skipp* and *Eddy v Niman*, but would now be seen as correct in its result, was *Monoghan*.[18] There a checkout cashier was seen to place money given to her by a customer for the purchase of goods in the till but without ringing up the purchase. When questioned she admitted that she was acting dishonestly and that it was her intention to take from the till an equivalent sum of money at a later stage. It was held that she had appropriated the money when she failed to ring it up[19] and she was convicted of theft. It seems that there was an appropriation at the time she took delivery of the cash.

Unfortunately two conflicting approaches had developed on the meaning of appropriation, both of which could claim House of Lords authority in support.[20] These approaches were helpfully summarised by Lord Lane C.J. in the Court of Appeal in *Morris, Anderton v Burnside*[21]:

> "As to the meaning of the word '*appropriation*' there are two schools of thought. The first contends that the word '*appropriate*' has built into it a connotation that it is some action inconsistent with the owner's rights, something hostile to the interests of the owner or contrary to his wishes or intention or without his authority. The second school of thought contends that the word in this context means no more than to take possession of an article and that there is no requirement that the trading or appropriation should be in any way antagonistic to the rights of the owner. Support can be found for each of those two points of view both in the authorities and also amongst the textbook writers."

The second school of thought owes its authority to the decision of the House of Lords in *Lawrence v Commissioner of Police for the Metropolis*.[22] The accused, a taxi driver, picked up an Italian student, Occhi, who had just arrived at Victoria station and whose grasp of English was very poor. Occhi showed Lawrence a piece of paper with an address in Ladbroke Grove written on it. Once inside the taxi Occhi took out his wallet and produced a £1 note. Lawrence said it was much more expensive and took out a further £6 from the wallet which Occhi was still holding open. The correct fare would have been about 50p. Had he been charged with obtaining the excess fare by deception he would have had little answer to the charge. However, he was charged with theft, and that, of course, is the charge the prosecution had to substantiate.

Lawrence was convicted of theft and his appeal against conviction was dismissed by both the Court of Appeal and House of Lords. Much of the argument in both courts centred round the question of whether the words "without the consent of the owner", which had

---

[18] [1979] Crim.L.R. 673.
[19] The authorised act was putting money in the till together with ringing it up.
[20] See for example, M. Giles and S. Uglow, "Appropriation and Manifest Criminality in Theft" (1992) 56 J.C.L. 179.
[21] [1983] 2 All E.R. 448 at 451.
[22] [1972] A.C. 626.

been part of the definition of larceny (the predecessor of theft), should be implied into s.1(1) of the 1968 Theft Act. Quite understandably both courts took the view that Parliament must have intended to omit the words and there was, therefore, no reason to imply them into the new legislation. Lawrence had appropriated property which, at the time he took it from the wallet, belonged to Occhi; he was clearly dishonest and intended permanently to deprive Occhi of the money. The charge of theft was, therefore, made out.

On the issue of consent, the House held that the facts of the case fell far short of **8–007** establishing that Occhi consented, but in any event even had Occhi consented, Lawrence's conduct would still have amounted to appropriation. Viscount Dilhorne added that an appropriation may occur even though the owner has permitted or consented to the property being taken.

It was argued that consent was relevant for another reason. If Occhi had consented to Lawrence having the notes, then ownership in the £6 would have passed to Lawrence who would, therefore, have been appropriating his own property. This difficulty was avoided on the actual facts of *Lawrence* by holding that the appropriation occurred when Lawrence took the notes out of the wallet and until he took the notes they belonged to Occhi and therefore, it was possible to say that he had appropriated property belonging to Occhi. In other words, the transfer of ownership and appropriation were simultaneous and effected by the same act.

In *Morris*[23] the court was faced with the question of label switching in a supermarket. The defendant had removed the price from a joint of meat and had replaced it with a label showing a lesser price which he had removed from another joint. He was detected at the checkout before he had paid for the piece of meat. Clearly once he had paid for the joint he would have committed the offence of obtaining property by deception, but the question for the court was whether on the facts before it he had stolen the meat, and if so, when? The view of the Court of Appeal was that the mere removal of an item from the shelf with an intention to steal the item amounted to theft. This view, which admittedly has the merit of simplicity and is clearly consistent with the views expressed in *Lawrence*, would clearly be hard to reconcile with the decision in *Skipp* (above).

In the House of Lords, Lord Roskill held that the view expressed in the Court of Appeal, **8–008** that the mere removal of the meat from the shelf amounted to theft, was clearly wrong. The customer, said Lord Roskill, is merely doing what he is invited to do by the owner of the meat. Lord Roskill concluded that while it was not necessary for the prosecution to prove that the defendant had assumed all of the rights of the owner, appropriation "involves not an act expressly or impliedly authorised by the owner but an act by way of adverse interference with or usurpation of those rights". Thus an "appropriation" is viewed in a pejorative and unilateral sense as hostile to the owner's interest; this was the authority for the alternative school of thought.

In other words Lord Roskill is saying that so long as the customer is acting with the authority bestowed upon him by the shop, he cannot be said to have assumed any of the owner's rights. Clearly picking up an item in a supermarket is something which the owner has the right to do; but it is also something which he expressly allows his customers to do. This view is clearly in line with decisions such as *Skipp* and *Eddy v Niman*.

Try as courts in subsequent cases did to reconcile these two House of Lords decisions, the plain fact of the matter was that they were irreconcilable. The courts were forced to choose between them. In *Dobson v General Accident Fire and Life Assurance Corporation*,[24] a civil case in which it was relevant to determine whether conduct amounted to theft since the

---

[23] [1984] A.C. 320.
[24] [1990] 1 Q.B. 274; [1989] 3 All E.R. 927; see below, para.8–012.

policy protected the insured against theft but not deception, the Court of Appeal thought that *Lawrence* should be treated as correct, whereas in *Shuck*[25] the Court of Appeal said that *Morris* was to be preferred. It was left to the House of Lords in *Gomez* to sort out the mess.

8–009   Few decisions can have had such a polarising effect as the decision of the House of Lords in *Gomez*[26] on the meaning of the word "appropriates" in s.1(1) of the Theft Act 1968. Crown prosecutors have hailed it as achieving a great simplification of the law while others, particularly academics, have deplored the cavalier manner in which their Lordships have ignored what was seen as the clear intention of Parliament to implement the Eighth Report of the Criminal Law Revision Committee, *Theft and Related Offences*.[27] The respondent (G) was the assistant manager of an electrical retailers. He was approached by and asked to supply B with some goods on the strength of two stolen building society cheques. G asked the manager if he could complete the transaction and the manager asked him to find out from the bank whether they would accept the cheques. G later pretended he had contacted the bank and told his manager that the cheques were as good as cash, whereupon the manager authorised the supply of goods. B was supplied with goods to the value of over £16,000 and the cheques were dishonoured on presentation. An obvious case of obtaining property by deception (under the old law) if ever there was one, but G and B were charged with theft. G's appeal against his conviction for theft was allowed by the Court of Appeal, relying on the approach taken in the House of Lords in *Morris*. The House of Lords reviewed both its earlier decisions and came to the view, despite a vigorous dissent by Lord Lowry, that *Lawrence* was correctly decided and that the contradictory statements in *Morris* were obiter dicta and incorrect. Lord Roskill had been wrong in *Morris* to indicate that an act expressly or impliedly authorised by the owner could never amount to an appropriation and in any case this part of his speech was obiter dicta, since the act of label switching was clearly unauthorised. It is surprising that Lord Keith takes Lord Roskill to task for going beyond what was necessary to dispose of the appeal in *Morris*, since this is precisely what the majority do in *Gomez*. The certified question merely asked for clarification of the situation where the owner is tricked by a false representation into handing over his property; there was no need to consider, for example, the case of shoplifters who simply take the goods from the shelves. Lord Keith said that it served little purpose to seek at the present time to construe the provisions of the Theft Act by reference to the Report which preceded it. *Lawrence* was a clear decision of the House of Lords on the meaning of the word "appropriates" which had stood for 12 years before it was challenged by the obiter dicta in *Morris*.

The effect of *Gomez* is that the concept of appropriation means any "dealing" with the property of another. It is entirely neutral, being an "objective description of the act done irrespective of the mental state of either the owner or the accused".[28] By way of contrast, Lord Lowry in his dissenting judgment enunciated the word in a pejorative sense, hostile to owner interests, not neutral but a unilateral act performed by the defendant. The outcome of such a broad definition to the term, applied by the majority, has been the corresponding

---

[25] [1992] Crim.L.R. 209.

[26] [1993] A.C. 442.

[27] See generally, P. Seago, "Criminal Law" [1993] All E.R. Annual Review 146; S. Shute and J. Horder, "Thieving and Deceiving: What is the Difference?" (1993) 56 M.L.R. 548; C.M.V. Clarkson, "Theft and Fair Labelling", (1993) 56 M.L.R. 554; and S. Cooper and M.J. Allen, "Appropriation After *Gomez*" (1993) 57 J.C.L. 186. For an academic opinion in support of the decision see P.R. Glazebrook "Revising The Theft Acts" (1993) 52 C.L.J. 191, who states: "Holding swindlers to be thieves does no injustice, will save much inconvenience in cases where it transpires only late in the day that a crook has resorted to deception, and avoids the extreme absurdity of denying the name of thief to those who misappropriate property received as a result of a mistake that they have induced while according it to those who had done nothing to bring about the mistaken transfer."

[28] [1993] A.C. 442 at 495 per Lord Browne-Wilkinson.

diminution in importance to the actus reus requirement, such that, "appropriation has become almost meaningless with the entire emphasis being shifted to whether the defendant was dishonest or not".[29] When taken in conjunction with the House's approval of the statement in *Morris* that it is not necessary to prove that the defendant has assumed all the rights of the owner, it is sufficient that he assumed just one of the owner's rights, it becomes clear that "appropriates" has a very wide meaning. Let us take the case of the person who switches labels on goods in a supermarket. It would appear that he is now guilty of theft when he first gets hold of the item whose label he intends to remove. This is so even though he is merely doing what all shoppers are authorised to do. It is also difficult to argue that by picking up the item he intends by that act permanently to deprive the owner of property, since it is his plan to present the item at the counter. However, the courts will now presumably hold that by picking up the goods with a dishonest intent he has appropriated the property of the store owner and it is sufficient that it is his ultimate aim to deprive the owner permanently of the property. Of course, there may be problems of proof at this stage, and the prosecutor would be wise to look for some more substantial evidence of dishonesty, such as label switching, but there seems to be little doubt that the theft occurs at the time he dishonestly takes the goods from the shelf. This means that the ordinary shopper appropriates property belonging to another every time he handles items in the supermarket, though he will not be guilty of theft because he will not have a dishonest intent.

The significance of the outcome in *Gomez* needs to be considered, as further interpreted in the light of recent developments. The following points are important to address:

(i) Gomez *and Previous Case Precedents*

The case of *Skipp* (above) was expressly considered by the House of *Gomez* and held to be **8–010** wrong. *Skipp* appropriated the oranges when he loaded them on to his lorry, despite the fact that he was authorised to do this. There were, therefore, three separate thefts and presumably no further theft occurred when he departed from the authorised route to Leicester since he had already stolen the property. He had assumed a right of the owner in taking delivery; the fact that the act was to outward appearances, only what he was authorised to do is irrelevant. Coupled with the required mental element it was theft. Similarly, in *Fritschy* where the House of Lords, in overruling this case, made clear in *Gomez* that there was a theft of the gold in England. Authorisation or consent is irrelevant to whether or not there has been an appropriation. It follows that the case of *Eddy v Niman* (above) must also be wrong. The youths would have appropriated the whiskey when they removed it from the shelves and since, at this time, they had the intention to leave the shop without paying for it, theft would have occurred at this moment. A fortiori label switching will constitute appropriation. In this regard an interesting case to consider is *Dip Kaur v Chief Constable for Hampshire*.[30] The defendant was looking at a display of shoes in a department store. She noticed that one pair of shoes had been incorrectly labelled. On one heel was a price label for £6.99 while on the other heel was a price label for £4.99. She realised that the higher price was correct. She took the shoes and placed them on the counter with the cheaper label uppermost and she was sold the shoes for £4.99. She was obviously behaving strangely since a store detective stopped her after she had gone through the checkouts; he thought she had been switching labels. She told him that she had been dishonest and she was ultimately prosecuted for theft. The Divisional Court held that the mistake on the part of the cashier rendered the contract voidable, and so Kaur became

---

[29] C.M.V. Clarkson (1993) 56 M.L.R. 554 at 557.
[30] [1981] 2 All E.R. 430.

owner of the goods before she did any act which could amount to an appropriation. Suffice it to say that before *Gomez* the facts had been the subject of discussion by all levels of courts with as many different conclusions. Following *Gomez* it would seem that the view of Lord Lane C.J., in the Court of Appeal in *Morris* is correct; namely that she committed theft when, having formed the dishonest intent, she took the shoes to the cashier. Lord Lane added that perhaps the real answer to the case lies in a closer examination of whether the defendant's conduct was dishonest. Nevertheless, it seems that the appropriation on these facts now clearly precedes any point at which ownership of the goods might have passed.

(ii) Theft, Attempted Theft and Deception

8–011 The result of following *Lawrence,* coupled with the very wide definition given to what may constitute an appropriation, means, in effect, that virtually all cases of obtaining property by deception (s.15 of the Theft Act 1968—see below), can be charged as theft. The only exceptions are those instances where s.4 excludes certain property from the scope of theft[31]; it will still be necessary to rely on s.15 for items such as land, wild flowers and animals. In all other cases it will not be necessary for the prosecution to worry whether they are dealing with a case of theft or one of deception; s.1 will cover them all. It should be noted that by s.26 of the Criminal Justice Act 1991 the maximum penalty for theft is reduced from 10 to seven years; obtaining property by deception continues to be subject to a maximum penalty of 10 years.

A corollary of the decision in *Gomez* is that acts that previously would have formed the actus reus of attempted theft, being merely preparatory to the commission of the offence, will now constitute the actus reus of the full substantive offence. The hotel clerk who puts a customer's suitcase under the desk ready to take it away feloniously at a later date; the British rail porter who puts a suitcase in a rack to purloin when opportunity presents itself; and even the shopper who places the baked beans tin in his shopping basket with intent to place in his coat pocket when the store detectives back is turned, will in each scenario have "appropriated" property. The theft conviction will consequentially depend on establishing the mens rea ingredients, namely dishonesty and an intention permanently to deprive.

(iii) Appropriation and the Civil Law

8–012 It was noted at the beginning of this chapter that some of the intricacies of the Theft Act stem from the involvement of civil law concepts concerning right of ownership over property. On most occasions fraud renders a contract voidable, but nevertheless property will pass and, therefore, the fraudulent buyer who obtains a voidable title to goods may obtain ownership of the goods.[32] Generally speaking one cannot steal one's own property[33] so the precise point when an appropriation occurs might before *Gomez* have been crucial. In other words if the appropriation took place after the contract of sale it was hard to see how one could be appropriating anybody else's property and therefore be guilty of theft (see *Dip Kaur* above).

It is now clearly established that an accused will appropriate property even where the owner transfers ownership to him under the terms of a contract negotiated between them. In *Dobson v General Accident Fire and Life Assurance Corporation*[34] the complainant was insured by the defendant company against loss of property by theft. He advertised items for

---

[31] See below, paras 8–020—8–027. See generally, R. Heaton, "Deceiving Without Thieving" [2001] Crim.L.R. 712; and *Clarke v CPS* [2007] EWHC 2228 (Admin).
[32] Note in relation to when property passes under the civil law see ss.17–18 of the Sale of Goods Act 1979.
[33] Although see below, para.8–029.
[34] [1990] 1 Q.B. 274.

sale and a rogue telephoned expressing an interest. They provisionally agreed that the complainant would sell them to the rogue in return for a building society cheque. The next day the complainant handed the items over in return for the cheque. The cheque turned out to be worthless and the complainant claimed on his insurance policy. The defendant firm refused payment on the basis that the items had not been stolen but obtained by deception and he was not covered for deception. The Court of Appeal held that the items had been stolen and the complainant was, therefore, covered against his loss. This expressly raises the problem of the time at which the items become the rogue's under the voidable contract of sale? The prosecution must prove that the rogue appropriated property belonging to another and, therefore, the act of appropriation must occur before the property in the goods has passed to the rogue. In a case such as *Dobson*, property would pass when the parties agreed it would pass or, at the latest, upon delivery by the complainant to the rogue. It would seem, therefore, that the appropriation and passing of property would occur at the same instant and this according to Viscount Dilhorne in *Lawrence* is sufficient since the rogue can be said to be appropriating property which until that instant belonged to another. In any event, Parker L.J., in *Dobson*, said that if it were to be held that property passed on contract, then the result would merely be that the making of the contract constituted the appropriation. The decision in *Dobson* was expressly approved in *Gomez*, but its wisdom is not so certain. The insurance company had clearly offered to protect the complainant against having his property taken by another without his consent; they had not agreed to cover him against the voluntary handing over of his property by him to a confidence trickster. These are seen as two distinct crimes and many might take the view that they do not wish the added insurance expense of being covered against their own gullibility.

(iv) Gomez and the Court of Appeal Decision in Gallasso

The argument was heard by the Court of Appeal in *Gallasso*[35] on the very same day that **8–013** judgment was delivered in *Gomez*. Unfortunately the decision is inconsistent with the House of Lords authority. Gallasso, a state-enrolled nurse, was the house leader of a residential home for mentally handicapped adults. The issue, inter alia, related to the opening of a new bank account and payment therein of a cheque belonging to a patient who could not look after himself. The prosecution's case was that *Gallasso* had done this to facilitate later unauthorised withdrawals. The Court of Appeal held that this was not an appropriation. According to Lloyd L.J. by paying in the cheque the appellant was not assuming the rights of an owner, but rather "affirming those rights, by placing the cheque in trust accounts of which he was the named beneficiary". It seems that the Court of Appeal thought that Gallasso's activities seemed more like an act of preparation which had not yet reached the stage of an attempt. But payment in of the cheque was the exercise of a *right* of the owner. It may have been an act authorised by the patient but authorisation is, according to *Gomez*, irrelevant for the purposes of appropriation. The Court of Appeal was clearly wrong to hold that a taking was required; the defendant in the light of *Gomez* had indeed appropriated the cheque. Lloyd L.J. enunciated a series of examples of situations which, in his opinion, did not constitute "appropriation"; self-evidently he was concerned about stopping the camera too soon in the full picture of theft. These examples included the shopper carelessly knocking an article off the shelf then bending down and replacing it on the shelf, a lady dropping her purse in the street being picked up and returned to her by a passer by, and the hall porter keeping a customer's suitcase under his desk instead of locking it up in the cloakroom (see (ii) above).[36] In all three situations he believed that "appropriation" had yet to occur.

[35] (1992) 98 Cr.App.R. 284.
[36] (1992) 98 Cr.App.R. 284 at 288.

Following *Gomez*, as we have seen, any "dealing" with property belonging to another constitutes appropriation; it is simply an objective description of the act done. There will, contrary to Lloyd L.J.'s view, be an appropriation in all three cases; whether theft has transpired depends on dishonest intention. To the extent that *Gallasso* contradicts the House of Lords judgment in *Gomez* it should be disregarded.

(v) The Company as a Victim of Theft

8–014   It was established in *Bonner*[37] that one partner can appropriate partnership property belonging to others within the enterprise. However, prior to *Gomez*, the situation was unclear where those in de facto control of a company, sole directors and shareholders, have been charged with theft from it. A dichotomy existed pre-*Gomez* between case authorities denying and allowing individual liability. The former line of authorities, exemplified by *Roffel*,[38] and *McHugh and Tringham*,[39] concentrated on consent to wrongdoing by the governing mind and will of the company, thereby rendering nugatory any "appropriation" of the company's property. This approach applies a *Morris* rationale in that no appropriation can occur where the "victim" (the company) consents to the taking of the property. In this sense the consent of the governing company officers precludes theft. In contradistinction it was held in *Attorney-General's Reference (No.2 of 1982)*,[40] and *Philippou*,[41] adopting a *Lawrence* type approach, that the consent or authorisation of governing officers was irrelevant to the charge of theft. The consent of such dishonest directors to illegal activities was not to be attributed to the corporate entity. An illustration of the denial of liability is provided by the decision of the Supreme Court of Victoria in *Roffel*.

In *Roffel* the facts involved a husband and wife partnership who were engaged in a small clothing manufacturing business. Subsequently, they formed a limited company of which they became the sole directors and shareholders, and sold the business to the company, although the price remained unpaid. Sadly, the company's premises were destroyed by fire and the insurance proceeds were paid into the company's bank account. However, the company's debts exceeded the proceeds of the insurance. The husband drew cheques on the company's account and was prosecuted and convicted of theft from the company. On appeal a majority of the Supreme Court of Victoria quashed the conviction. It was stated that appropriation, a vital element for theft, necessitated proof of adverse interference with or usurpation of some right or rights of the owner. In essence, the company was a separate legal entity, and consequentially (through its directing mind and will) had consented to the husband's drawing of the cheques, it could not be said that he had appropriated the company's property.

The principles applied in *Roffel*, and similarly in *McHugh and Tringham*, were categorically rejected by their Lordships in *Gomez*, the leading judgment on this issue that of Lord Browne-Wilkinson. It is now incorrect to assert that no theft can occur under s.1 of the Theft Act 1968 if the owner (company) consents to what is done. An appropriation will be established and the issue will relate to other necessary elements upon which a theft offence is predicated, namely was such appropriation dishonest and whether it was committed with the intention of permanently depriving the company of such property. A policy issue is at stake here to safeguard company assets from pillaging directors. The fundamental delineation was made by Lord Browne-Wilkinson when he asserted:

---

[37] [1970] 2 All E.R. 97.
[38] [1985] V.R. 511.
[39] (1988) 88 Cr.App.R. 385.
[40] [1984] Q.B. 624.
[41] (1989) 89 Cr.App.R. 290.

"Where a company is accused of a crime the acts and intentions of those who are the directing minds and will of the company are to be attributed to the company. That is not the law where the charge is that those who are the directing minds and will have themselves committed a crime against the company: see *Attorney-General's Reference (No.2 of 1982)* [1984] Q.B. 624 applying *Belmont Finance Corp Ltd v Williams Furniture Ltd* [1979] 1 All E.R. 118 . . . In any event, your Lordships' decision in this case, re-establishing as it does the decision in *Lawrence*, renders the whole question of consent by the company irrelevant. Whether or not those controlling the company consented or purported to consent to the abstraction of the company's property by the accused, he will have appropriated the property of the company."[42]

(vi) Appropriation and Jurisdictional Matters

The decision in *Atakpu*[43] illustrates one possibly unforeseen consequence of the *Gomez* **8–015** approach. In this case the defendants were involved in a conspiracy to obtain hire cars in mainland Europe (Germany and Belgium), which would then be brought to this country to be sold. They were charged with conspiracy to steal and in order to establish jurisdiction the prosecution had to prove that the conspiracy would result in theft of the cars in this country. Not so, argued the defendants. We obtained them by deception on the continent and so they were stolen abroad. This being the case they cannot be stolen again in this country. The Court of Appeal, despite referring to the defendants as "a pair of thoroughly dishonest rascals" and "utterly devoid of merit", nonetheless held that where a person comes by property by stealing it then his later dealing with it is, by implication, not included among the assumptions of the right of an owner which amount to an appropriation within the meaning of s.3(1). Since, on the authority of *Gomez*, the property had been stolen abroad it could not be stolen again in this country and so the conspiracy charged failed. Under the *Morris* approach, the cars would not have been stolen when they were driven away from the owners, since the owners expressly authorised those hiring cars to do just that. Whether they would have been stolen before they reached this country would depend upon the terms of the rental agreement. If the contract provided that the car should not be taken out of the country then the rogues would have appropriated them when they drove them into another country. The Court of Appeal commented that, had *Morris* been the correct authority, the appropriation would have occurred when the cars were first used after the expiry of the hire agreement and that would have been in England. The theft would, therefore, have occurred in England (see *Fritschy* above). The outcome reached in *Atakpu* has been criticised by Sullivan and Warbrick who argue that the case could and should have been decided differently.[44] In their view the so-called theft abroad would not be theft under extant English criminal law. They argue that if the defendant had done in England what they did in Belgium or Germany, the cars would clearly have been stolen here. However, because the Theft Act does not reach conduct in Belgium or Germany, the cars were not in this sense, "stolen" there; in effect, theft abroad does not constitute theft for the purposes of English law. Hence they could be "stolen" when they were kept and dealt with by the defendants within the English jurisdiction; theft occurred when the defendant first assumed the rights of ownership in England.[45] In any event the problem raised by *Atakpu* has ameliorated by s.5 of the Criminal Justice (Terrorism and Conspiracy) Act 1998, which inserts a new s.1 into the

[42] [1993] A.C. 442 at 496.
[43] [1994] Q.B. 69.
[44] G.R. Sullivan and C. Warbrick, "Territoriality, Theft and *Atakpu*" [1994] Crim.L.R. 650.
[45] [1994] Q.B. 659 at 659–660.

Criminal Law Act 1977, by which it would be possible to charge an agreement made in England to steal abroad as an indictable conspiracy.[46]

A jurisdictional issue was also involved in the important case of *Sui Soi Ngan*[47] which addressed the question of when the theft of a credit balance occurred, with appropriation by means of a cheque payment. The defendant appreciated that money had been paid into her bank account in error.[48] However, she did not notify the bank authorities of this error, but rather decided to write three blank cheques on that account and sent them to her sister in Scotland, the sister knowing that the defendant's account had been credited with the extra money. Subsequently, two of these cheques were presented for payment in Scotland, and one of them was presented in England. The defendant was convicted of stealing money mistakenly credited to her own bank account. The court held that the drawing and signing of the cheque amounted to merely preparatory acts; no right was assumed to the part of the defendant's credit balance which was not hers, until a cheque was presented for payment. The court, expressly approving the decision in *R. v Governor of Pentonville Prison Ex. p. Osman*,[49] held that the theft was committed on the presentation of the cheque. This meant that on the two occasions when the cheque was presented in Scotland, no offence was committed within English jurisdiction and the convictions on those two counts were quashed.[50] However, an offence was committed within the jurisdiction when the cheque was presented in England and the conviction on that count was, therefore, upheld. It is submitted that a defendant will logically assume the rights of an owner when he presents the cheque since by that act he intends to deprive the owner of all his rights in that portion of the bank balance with which he deals.[51]

(vii) Appropriation and Gifts

8–016   It is important to state again that it would be wrong to assume that *Gomez* has ended all difficulties in relation to s.3(1). The House of Lords decision in *Hinks*,[52] interpreting earlier appellate cases of *Mazo*[53] and *Hopkins and Kendrick*,[54] demonstrates that pervading problems still apply to the concept of appropriation, when applied to gifts of property, and this confusion is exacerbated by the intricacies of the inter-relationship of civil and criminal law. An individual who receives a gift from a donor whose mental capacity is impaired, but not to the extent of rendering the donor mentally incapable of making a valid gift, acquires an indefeasible right to the property. Can it, thus, be capable of being "stolen"? A positive response to this dilemma was elicited from their Lordships in *Hinks*. If the prosecution can establish the relevant the mens rea ingredients (dishonesty and intention permanently to deprive) at the time of the acquisition, then the donee will be guilty of theft, despite the fact that an indefeasible right to receive the property applies under civil law, and as a consequence that the donee can retain it or even legitimately recover it if divested from

---

[46] See generally, Hirst, M., *Jurisdiction and the Ambit of the Criminal Law* (Oxford University Press, 2003), pp.24–26. See also, *Ashcroft* [2003] EWCA Crim 2365.

[47] *The Times*, July 24, 1997.

[48] See s.5(4) of the Theft Act, considered below.

[49] (1990) 90 Cr.App.R. 281. For appropriation by computer means see also *R. v Governor at Brixton Prison Ex. p. Levin* [1996] 4 All E.R. 350.

[50] Note that if s.2(1) of the Criminal Justice Act 1993 had been in force at the time of D's conduct then the English courts would have had jurisdiction over all 3 counts. By the terms of s.2(1) it will be sufficient for the effect, i.e. here the debiting of the bank account of the Scottish appropriation, had occurred in England.

[51] See below, para.9–001, for consideration of *Preddy* and obtaining of money transfers by deception.

[52] [2000] 4 All E.R. 833; [2000] 3 W.L.R. 1590 HL.

[53] [1996] Crim.L.R. 435.

[54] [1997] 2 Cr.App.R. 524; [1997] Crim.L.R. 359. See generally, S. Gardner, "Property and Theft" [1998] Crim.L.R. 35.

them. Such an outcome is counter-intuitive, and the position we have reached is eminently regrettable.

In *Mazo,* the defendant, a maid to Lady S, was charged with theft in connection with cheques totalling £37,000. The Crown asserted that she took dishonest advantage of S's mental incapacity and that the transfers were not valid gifts. It was contended by the defendant that the donee of property could not be convicted of stealing that very property where the donor intended and carried out the intention to make a gift and had the mental capacity to do so. In *Hopkins and Kendrick* the two defendants ran a residential home, one of whose residents was a frail 99-year-old lady. She was virtually blind and was incapable of managing her affairs. The defendants were charged with theft of the assets of the old lady totalling £127,500. They sold her stock at a disadvantageous time, refused to allow other friends to see her and effected a will which the old lady signed making them the principal beneficiaries. Money from the sale of her stock was paid into an account in the name of one of the defendants. Their defence was that they were at all times acting with the resident's authorisation and in her best interests. The judge directed the jury that they could be dishonest notwithstanding the resident's consent if she was not able to give unconfused and proper consent. The defendants were convicted and appealed on the basis that the judge should have directed that the issue of consent was relevant not just to dishonesty but also to appropriation.

On one level the cases of *Mazo* and *Hopkins and Kendrick* were distinguishable. There was ample evidence in the latter case relating to the old lady's incapacity which did not exist in the former case. The appeal was allowed in *Mazo* but not in *Hopkins and Kendrick*.[55] However, in the course of their judgment in *Mazo* the Court of Appeal stated that: "it is common ground that the receiver of a valid gift *inter vivos* could not be the subject of a conviction for theft." How then can this statement be reconciled with *Gomez,* where, as we have seen, appropriation is a neutral concept, and an individual can be guilty of theft notwithstanding that he obtained the property in question with the consent of the owner. Does the acquisition of an indefeasible title in the property in question through, for example, a fully valid gift, negate the possibility of a conviction for theft?[56] The problem has been cogently identified by Professor Smith who stresses that the implication is that *Gomez* must be subject to rights arising under civil law:

> "The answer seems to be that, however all-embracing *Gomez* may seem, a line must be drawn where a conviction of theft would cause a conflict with the civil law—in this case, the law of gift. If the effect of the transaction is that D gets an absolute, indefeasible right to the property in question, it would be unacceptable for a criminal court to hold that the transaction amounted to a theft of the property by him. If D has a right to retain the property, or even to recover it from the alleged victim, it can hardly be held to be theft for him to take and keep it. Otherwise the civil law would be assisting D to recover or to retain the fruits of his crime."[57]

---

[55] The appeal in *Mazo's* case was allowed on the basis that the jury had been inadequately directed by reference simply to reduced mental state of the donor. The jury ought to have been directed on the issue of whether the donor's mental deterioration was so extensive as to vitiate her gifts to the donee. In contrast the Court of Appeal is far more damning of the defendant's conduct in *Hopkins and Kendrick*. It did not matter that the trial judge failed to provide any jury direction on the issue whether the defendants had acquired an indefeasible title to the property in question.

[56] See S. Gardner, "Property and Theft" [1998] Crim.L.R. 35 at 35–37.

[57] J.C. Smith [1996] Crim.L.R. 437. Professor Smith stated following *Mazo* and *Hopkins* that, "it is submitted that the Act must be subject to a narrower qualification: an act by which D acquires from V an indefeasible title to V's entire proprietary interest is not an 'appropriation' of that interest. Only thus can the conflict with civil law be avoided"; see further J.C. Smith [1997] Crim.L.R. 361.

8–017   In *Hinks*,[58] the appellant, aged 38 and the mother of a young son, had befriended John Dolphin, aged 53, who was of limited intelligence. Dr Fuller, a consultant psychiatrist, assessed Mr Dolphin's IQ as in the range between 70 and 80 and described him as naïve and trusting and having no idea of the value of his assets or the ability to calculate their value. Dr Fuller said he thought Mr Dolphin was capable of making the decision to divest himself of money, but that it was unlikely that he could make the decision alone. The appellant described herself as Mr Dolphin's main carer. Between April and November 1996 Mr Dolphin withdrew sums totalling around £60,000 from his building society account, which was most of his savings, and the money was deposited into Hinks' account. She was charged with theft of these sums of money and of a television. It was the prosecution case that the appellant had dishonestly influenced and coerced Mr Dolphin into giving her the property. The defence submitted that, in reality, the property had been a gift from Mr Dolphin, voluntarily given, thus transferring proprietary interests, and consequently no "appropriation" within s.3 of the Theft Act had transpired. The jury, however, unanimously found Hinks guilty of theft and her appeal was rejected by the Court of Appeal. A further appeal was allowed to the House of Lords where the certified question at issue was:

> "Whether the acquisition of an indefeasible title to property is capable of amounting to an appropriation of property belonging to another for the purposes of s.1(1) of the Theft Act 1968".

In effect, their Lordships had to determine whether an individual could appropriate property belonging to another where the other person has made an indefeasible gift of property. In addressing this dilemmatic issue, their Lordships had to reconcile extant principles on the meaning of "appropriation", and its symbiotic relationship with gifts by transfer.

The House of Lords, by a majority of three to two, dismissed Hinks' appeal. The three Law Lords in the majority plus Lord Hutton[59] answered the certified question in the affirmative. Lord Steyn, who delivered the leading majority judgment (concurred by Lord Slynn and Lord Jauncey), asserted that appropriation was a neutral word comprising any assumption by a person of the rights of an owner. This followed from his approval of a dictum of Lord Browne-Wilkinson in *Gomez* that the word "appropriation" is an objective description of the act done irrespective of the mental state of either the owner or the accused. This meant that it did embrace, as in the case at hand, the acceptance of indefeasible gifts of property. He rejected a narrower definition of appropriation as he was concerned about policy implications, "placing beyond the reach of the criminal law dishonest persons who should be found guilty of theft".[60] Lord Steyn opined that the law as settled in *Gomez* and *Lawrence* could be applied by judges and juries in a way which, in the absence of human error, did not result in injustice.[61] In practice, the mental requirements of theft (dishonesty and intention to permanently deprive) were, in the eyes of the majority, an adequate protection against injustice. Furthermore, Lord Steyn refused to restrict the decision in *Gomez* by interpolating "unlawfully" before "appropriates" or by acceding to the

---

[58] [2000] 4 All E.R. 833; [2000] 3 W.L.R. 1590 HL.
[59] Note that Lord Hutton dissented on the gound that the trial judge had misdirected the jury on dishonesty. Although Lord Hutton answered the certified question in the affirmative, he went on to hold that whilst the acquisition of an indefeasible title may amount to an appropriation, it will not amount to the actus reus of theft unless it is also a dishonest appropriation. Lord Hutton asserted: "A direction based only on *Ghosh* is inadequate because it fails to make clear to the jury that if there was a valid gift there cannot be dishonesty"; see below, para.8–043.
[60] [2000] 4 All E.R. 833 at 843.
[61] [2000] 4 All E.R. 833.

proposition that an individual does not appropriate property unless the owner retains, beyond the instant of the alleged appropriation, some proprietary interest or the right to resume or recover some proprietary interest.[62]

A serious aspect of the decision in *Hinks* is the conflict that it effects between the civil and the criminal law. It seems the apotheosis of absurdity that the performance of a perfectly valid contract should be a crime.[63] This real conflict is accepted by Lord Steyn with unswerving unconcern. He asserts, "In any event, it would be wrong to assume on *a priori* grounds that the criminal law rather than the civil law is defective". The outcome, as Lord Hobhouse intimates in his powerful and logical dissenting judgment, is totally bizarre. It is illogical that an individual should be guilty of stealing property which is his and in which no one else has any legal interest whatever. In essence, there is theft, but there are no stolen goods because the donor, *ex hypothesi*, never had any right to restitution.[64] As Professor Smith asserted:

"If the property were seized from [D] by the police, D, not the donor or anyone else would be entitled to recover it. [D] would have an action in conversion against the police—or the donor, if the police returned the property to [the donor]".[65]

Certainly, Lord Hobhouse considered that it was still necessary for a court to take into account whether a gift was invalid due to the incapacity of the donee or the use of undue influence or coercion to obtain the gift. Lord Hobhouse pointed out that if a valid gift occurs, then "appropriation" is absent; in such a scenario a donee is not "assuming the rights of an owner" (a prerequisite for liability) but she already has those rights.[66]

Lord Hobhouse clearly articulated that the word appropriation must be read in its context. He was conscious of the danger of construing each word or phrase in s.1(1) of the Theft Act in isolation from its context.[67] It is submitted that this approach is preferable to that of the majority view in *Hinks* which fails to accord due significance to the civil law underpinnings of proprietary interests. Their Lordships have laboured mightily in *Gomez* and *Hinks* but have sadly given birth to an mouse! It now suffices for an appropriation that we have *any* dealing or exercise in the property of another. The essence of the theft charge becomes a question of establishing dishonesty (see s.2(1) below). This view means that the receiver of a valid gift inter vivos can thereby be guilty of theft, and whether or not he is guilty will depend upon whether, on the particular facts of the case, it can be established that the donee was dishonest. In most situations no problem accrues where a valid gift is made to the donee. However, on rare occasions, it will be necessary to consider the receiver's mens rea relating to circumstances attached to the gift, and the donee's appreciation of the validity of the authorisation given by the donor in the light of the known circumstances.

Section 3(1): Keeping or Dealing as Owner. Thus far it has been suggested that an **8–018** appropriation requires some *conduct* on the accused's part. Certainly it is difficult to see how a pure omission could amount to an assumption of the user's rights. If, for example, A has

---

[62] See Card, *op. cit.*, at p.297 where this point is cogently articulated.
[63] See J.C. Smith, "Case Commentary on *Hinks*" [2001] Crim.L.R. 162 at 165.
[64] [2001] Crim.L.R. 162 at 164; see Theft Act 1968 s.24(3).
[65] J.C. Smith, *The Law Of Theft* 8th edn para.2–22.
[66] [2000] 4 All E.R. 833 at 865.
[67] Lord Hobhouse affirmed that once the item had been given there was no property belonging to another in the context of s.5; moreover even if the acceptance of the gift constitutes an appropriation (which he denied) D is not dishonest through the effect of s.2(1)(a). Additionally, D does not intend to act regardless of the donor's rights within the context of s.6(1) because he has relinquished those rights. On this perspective the donor has already surrendered his rights.

mislaid his umbrella, B could hardly be said to have appropriated it because he knows where it is and fails to tell A—even if B hopes that A will fail to find it so that he, B, can make off with it later on. On the other hand s.3 goes on to say that there is an appropriation where a person has come by the property (innocently or not) but without stealing it and has assumed a right to it " . . . by keeping it or dealing with it as owner". This is meant to deal with the sort of case where A "comes by" B's property and decides to keep it. A may have borrowed it, or found it or had it delivered to him by mistake, etc. A's mental resolution to keep it is probably not enough; the section says that A must keep it "as owner". Suppose then that A borrows B's lawnmower or bicycle or book for a week. At the end of the week A fails to return the goods and his intention is never to do so. Probably this will not make A a thief; but A will become a thief if, with the necessary intent, he removes the lawnmower to his new premises, or he continues to drive the bicycle, or he writes his name in the book. On the other hand, the fact that the draftsman specifies that there may be an appropriation in these circumstances when A has come by the property without stealing it rather implies that there is no fresh appropriation when a person has already stolen the property and subsequently deals with it. This was the approach taken by the Court of Appeal in *Atakpu* (see above).

The issue of appropriation and remoteness arose in *Briggs*[68] where, similar to *Gallasso*, a more constrained definition of appropriation was propounded. D, by deception, had induced her elderly relatives to transfer a credit balance, amounting to the sum of £49,950, representing the proceeds of their house sale. The appellate court, however, quashed D's conviction for theft of the credit balance. Their Lordships concluded that appropriation is a word which connotes a "physical act" which must not be a remote action triggering the payment which gives rise to the charge. In order for the offence of theft to be committed then D must be viewed as having committed an identifiable act of appropriation.[69] It is difficult, however, to countenance why no appropriation occurred in *Briggs*. In light of *Gomez* and *Hinks* the authority and consent of the denuded victim in transferring the property is now irrelevant. The defendant, by initiating the whole transaction, can be viewed as effecting the continuing act of appropriation. Appropriation embraces not simply possession of physical goods such as electrical items in *Gomez*, or receipt of money as in *Hinks*, but also intangibles which are property for the purposes of theft.[70]

8–019   **Section 3(2): The Bona Fide Purchaser Protected from Liability.** Where, however, A receives the property in good faith from B for consideration, if it later turns out that B had no right to sell the property, no assumption of the rights of an owner by A over that property can amount to an appropriation for the purpose of a charge of theft against him (see s.3(2)).[71] Thus if A buys a car from B in circumstances where A believes that B is the lawful owner of the car, then if he is later told that C is the rightful owner of the car and that B had stolen it, A's refusal to restore the car to C would not amount to theft. However, if A later sells the car to D, he may be guilty of fraud contrary to s.2 of the Fraud Act 2006[72] since he will have impliedly represented that he had title to sell, when he clearly did not. The

---

[68] [2004] EWCA Crim 3662; [2004] Crim.L.R. 455.

[69] See Sir John Smith's commentary in *Caresena* [1996] Crim.L.R. 667: "It is true that D procures the whole course of events resulting in V's account being debited; but the telegraphic transfer is initiated by V and his voluntary intervening act break the chain of causation. It is the same as if V is induced by deception to take money out of his safe to pay D. D does not at that moment 'appropriate' if—V is not acting as his agent. D commits theft only if and when the money is put into his hands."

[70] See below at para.8–022. See, also, *Gresham* [2003] EWCA Crim 2070.

[71] s.3(2) of the Theft Act 1968 provides as follows: "where property or a right or interest in property is or purports to be transferred for value to a person acting in good faith, no later assumption by him of rights which he believed himself to be acquiring shall, by reason of any defect in the transferor's title, amount to theft of the property."

[72] See below, para.9–005.

effect of s.3(2) is clearly illustrated by the case of *Adams*.[73] The defendant had a special interest in motorcycles and bought for the sum of £350 certain parts for his bike, these parts having in fact been stolen. D had been falsely told that the parts came from a motorcycle previously written off in a crash. He had no suspicions on their true origin until 2–3 days after their initial acquisition by him. It was held that there was no actus reus of theft at the precise moment D acquired the parts.

B. Property

(i) The General Position

The definition of what can amount to property for the purposes of being stolen is to be **8–020** found in s.4. The general position is covered by s.4(1) which provides that "property" includes money and all other property, real or personal, including things in action and other intangible property. The reference to real property means that land is included in the definition of property, but subs.(2) specifically provides that with one or two exceptions land cannot be stolen.[74] Before we look at the special problem with land we ought to mention one or two points in relation to the general definition. The effect of subs.(1) is that virtually all tangible property with the exception of land is capable of being stolen. One or two difficulties may, however, arise:

Gas, Water and Electricity.   Gas and water are clearly within the definition of property in **8–021** s.4(1) and are thus capable of being stolen, as was held in *Low v Blease*.[75] Electricity, on the other hand, does not constitute property and cannot, therefore, be stolen. There is a separate offence to deal with the unlawful abstraction of electricity.[76]

Intangible Property.   Section 4(1) makes it clear that choses in action and other intangible **8–022** property are capable of being stolen. Choses in action are rights which can only be enforced by taking legal action. Thus if X owes Y £50, X can sue Y for the £50 and this right to sue is known as a chose in action. Other examples of choses in action are copyrights and trade marks; patents are not choses in action but they are clearly a form of intangible property. In *Attorney-General for Hong Kong v Nai Keung*[77] the Privy Council held that export quotas fell within the meaning of other intangible property. They are transferable for value and can be bought and sold. Since the defendant had sold export quotas belonging to another at a gross undervalue he was rightly convicted of stealing them.

   The correct delineation of credit balances and theft of cheques as "property" present special difficulties in this area.[78] In *Kohn*,[79] for instance, the defendant accountant drew cheques on his employer's bank account which he knew to be in credit. It was held that by paying the company cheque into his own bank account he was appropriating a thing in action, specifically the debt which the bank owed the company. There was an obligation imposed upon the bank to meet the drawing, and the debt itself can be regarded as property.

---

[73] [1993] Crim.L.R. 72.
[74] It can, however, be obtained by fraud; see para.9–001.
[75] [1975] Crim.L.R. 513.
[76] See below, para.9–054.
[77] [1987] 1 W.L.R. 1139.
[78] A bank account creates a debt between the bank and the customer. The bank does not keep an identifiable sum of money for each customer, but each customer has the right to sue the bank for the sum represented by their credit balance.
[79] (1979) 69 Cr.App.R. 395.

Similarly, in *Chan Man Sin v Attorney-General of Hong Kong*[80] where the appellant, while employed as an accountant for two Hong Kong companies, forged 10 cheques to withdraw some $HK 4.8M from the companies' bank accounts, which he then deposited in his personal account or to the account of a business which he owned. His defalcations were discovered and he was charged with theft of choses in action, namely debts owed by the companies' bank to the companies. The Privy Council determined that by drawing, presenting and negotiating forged cheques on the companies' accounts at their bank the appellant was assuming the companies' rights as owners of the credit in the account. It would also have been theft if the companies were in overdraft but had an agreed credit facility, the sums withdrawn by the appellant up to the level of that facility.[81]

Furthermore, it has been held in *Williams (Roy)*[82] that the presentation of a cheque by or on behalf of the defendant, causing a diminution of the victim's credit balance or his bank account, amounts to an appropriation of the victim's property. The defendant was a builder, who was alleged to have defrauded many elderly householders over a five year period. He would initially charge a modest price for carrying out work, to gain the trust of a customer, but as work continued the price would rise, to the point at which it far exceeded what might properly have been charged. It was alleged inter alia, that the defendant stole a chose in action by cashing the householder's cheque. The Court of Appeal upheld D's conviction. Where D presents the cheque and it is honoured D steals a chose in action, namely V's credit balance or right to overdraw his account. In presenting the cheque D had destroyed V's property, and the exercise of the power to destroy is the clearest possible assumption of the rights of an owner with intent permanently to deprive, because it extinguishes all of V's rights.[83]

8–023 Intellectual Property. In *Oxford v Moss*[84] a student borrowed an examination paper and photographed the questions. He could not be charged with stealing the question paper since he intended to return it and the court held that he could not be charged with theft of the confidential information since this did not amount to property under s.4(1). It would seem to follow that trade secrets are not property which is capable of being stolen.

8–024 Human Remains and Property of the Deceased. Under the previous legislation it appears to have been accepted that it was not possible to steal a corpse since corpses are incapable of being the subject of ownership by anyone. There seems no logical reason why a corpse should not be capable of being stolen. Where a person has expended time or money in preserving a corpse or parts of a corpse (such as kidneys for use in transplants) it would seem sensible to hold that these should be capable of being stolen. Presumably where a corpse has been cremated and the ashes retained by a relative, the ashes should be capable of being stolen. While it is quite reasonable to hold that a living body cannot be stolen, there seems no logic in the rule that the position continues after death. It has been established that a blood sample[85] and urine specimen[86] are capable of being stolen; similar principles will apply to sperm from a sperm bank. In *Kelly*,[87] a human skeleton was deemed to be

---

[80] [1988] 1 All E.R. 1.
[81] An interesting decision to contrast here is *Navvabi* [1986] 3 All E.R. 102. It was held therein that no theft occurs, because no specific debt (property) accrues, where D knowing he has no credit or overdraft facility writes a cheque backed by a banker's card in favour of V; but see the offence of fraud (below, para.9–006).
[82] [2001] 1 Cr.App.R. 362; [2001] Crim.L.R. 253.
[83] See also *Hilton* [1997] 2 Cr.App.R. 445; [1997] Crim.L.R. 761.
[84] (1978) 68 Cr.App.R. 183.
[85] *Rothery* [1976] R.T.R. 550.
[86] *Welsh* [1974] R.T.R. 478.
[87] [1998] 3 All E.R. 741. It was determined that parts of corpses were capable of being property within the meaning of s.4 of the 1968 Act if they had acquired different attributes by virtue of the application of skill, such as dissection and preservation techniques, for exhibition and teaching purposes.

capable of being stolen from the Royal College of Surgeons. The Human Tissue Act 2004, a specific legislative response to the outcry propagated by the notorious events at Bristol Royal Infirmary and Alder Hey hospital in Liverpool, deals with restrictions on improper retention of tissue and organs without legitimate consent.[88]

The issue of "property" of the deceased arose in *Sullivan and Ballion*.[89] The case for the prosecution was that the Ds, acting in concert, had together stolen £50,000. Apparently, V, a notorious drug dealer, had arrived in Kent with the money, the provenance of which was proceeds of drug dealing on behalf of a group of local drug dealers known as "The Firm". Unfortunately for V he had no opportunity to "enjoy" the fruits of his apparently ill-gotten gains. He went to the home of the Ds, and there died. Most likely from the effect of a drug overdose. It was alleged by the prosecution that the Ds, recovering well from their grief, took the money. The trial judge dismissed the charge of theft of the money ruling that the property did not belong to another when it was taken. Theft, however, may be committed against anyone who has a proprietary interest of any kind, legal or equitable in the property.[90] Moreover, at the time of the alleged theft, the money could no longer belong to V because he was dead. Clearly the two defendants did not own the money which they took. So who did? The property was not *res nullius*, the property of no one, and it is submitted that the logical outcome is that it belonged to the Crown as *bona vacantia*, in the event that no one was entitled as V's principal or under V's will or intestacy.

(ii) Land

Although land is contained in the definition of property in subs.(1), subs.(2) provides that **8–025** "A person cannot steal land, or things forming part of land and severed from it by him or by his directions" except in certain cases. Before we look at the exceptions we should note that in law, land includes not only the earth, but also things attached to it so as to become part of the land. Whether or not something is sufficiently attached to the land so as to be counted as part of the land depends upon the degree of annexation and the degree of permanency. Clearly trees and other growing things can be treated for this purpose as land; equally houses which are not only well and truly fixed to the soil but are usually designed with a degree of permanency in mind. On the other hand a workman's portakabin which is just erected on the land while the workmen are there would not be regarded as part of the land; it can, therefore, be stolen as ordinary property. In between the distinction sometimes becomes rather blurred. It should, however, be noted that land for the purposes of the s.4(2) definition does not embrace incorporeal hereditaments, and thus rents, easements and profits are all capable of being stolen by any individual.

When can land be stolen? There are three exceptions to the general rule that land cannot be stolen, these are:

(a) Section 4(2)(a). A person who falls into a certain category of individual, for example, a trustee or personal representative who deals with the property in breach of the confidence reposed in him can steal land or things forming part of it.

(b) Section 4(2)(b). A person who is not in possession of the land and appropriates anything forming part of the land by severing it or causing it to be severed, or after it has been severed. Thus this section does not apply to an owner who is living on the land or someone living on the land by virtue of a tenancy.

---

[88] See also, Department of Health Guidelines: *The Removal, Retention and Use of Human Organs and Tissue from Post-Mortem Examination* (2001).
[89] [2002] Crim.L.R. 758.
[90] See below at para.8–029.

(c) Section 4(2)(c). A person in possession of the land under a tenancy who appropriates the whole or any part of a fixture or structure let to be used with the land. In this regard a tenant who takes a fixture, for example a fitted kitchen or Adams fireplace, will commit theft.

We can see how these provisions work in practice by considering the following situations:

(a) X has moved a boundary fence so that two acres of Y's land now appear to belong to X. Since this involves the land itself and no act of severance is involved, only if X falls within s.4(2)(a) can this amount to theft. In fact persons falling within s.4(2)(a) would be guilty of theft in all the following situations and so no further mention will be made of them.

(b) X removes a layer of turf from Y's land which he then sells. If X is not in possession of the land he will be guilty of theft by virtue of s.4(2)(b). If he is in possession of the land by virtue of a tenancy he will not be guilty of theft since turf cannot be regarded as a fixture or structure under s.4(2)(c).

(c) X cuts down a tree on land belonging to Y and removes it for firewood. Again, unless he is in possession as a tenant, he will be guilty by virtue of s.4(2)(b)—he has severed the tree and removed it from Y's land. A tenant in possession would not be guilty of theft since this is presumably not what is meant by a fixture or structure let for use by the tenant.[91]

(d) X dismantles Y's brick garage and gives it to Z. X will be guilty by virtue of s.4(2)(b) if he is not in possession of the land and s.4(2)(c) if he is a tenant in possession of the land. It is noteworthy that a person in possession of the land under a tenancy will be guilty of theft if he merely sells it to Z with a promise to dismantle it later; s.4(2)(c) does not require severance.

(e) X dismantles Y's greenhouse and gives it to Z. The answer is the same as in (d) except that if the greenhouse is of a temporary nature and not fixed to the land it may be regarded as an ordinary item of property and stealable by virtue of s.4(1).

(iii) Wild Plants, etc.

8–026 If the section stopped at subs.(2) then a trespasser who picked wild flowers would be guilty of stealing them. Section 4(3) therefore provides:

"A person who picks mushrooms growing wild on any land, or who picks flowers, fruit or foliage from a plant growing wild on any land does not (although not in possession of the land) steal what he picks, unless he does it for reward or for sale or for other commercial purpose."[92]

A few illustrations will show how this section works.

(a) X goes on to Y's land and picks some mushrooms and some strawberries. If these are wild and if X intends them for his own domestic use he commits no offence. If, however, they are cultivated or he intends to sell them he commits an offence. It is

---

[91] See s.4(3) below for further rules relating to wild trees and plants. In the case of *Chelsea Yacht and Boat Club Ltd v Pope* [2001] 2 All E.R. 409 it was determined that a houseboat attached to the river bed, a pontoon and the river wall by mooring lines did not form part of the land.
[92] Mushrooms includes any fungus, and plant includes any shrub or tree.

suggested that a purposive approach needs to be applied to this section. The altruistic individual who picks the mushrooms or strawberries to sell on behalf of a "Children in Need" appeal, in contrast to the street trader selling for personal gain, will be viewed sympathetically by the courts. The former may not even be viewed as "commercial" and is unlikely to be held to be dishonest (see s.2 below).

(b) X goes on to Y's land and digs up a holly tree and saws the top off a fir tree. He has committed theft in both instances since the exemption in the subsection refers only to picking from plants, and neither digging up the whole tree nor sawing a portion off a tree can be regarded as picking.

(iv) Wild Creatures

These are covered by s.4(4) which provides: **8–027**

> "Wild creatures, tamed or untamed, shall be regarded as property; but a person cannot steal a wild creature not tame nor ordinarily kept in captivity, or the carcass of any such creature, unless either it has been reduced into possession by or on behalf of another person and possession of it has not since been lost or abandoned, or another person is in the course of reducing it into possession."

There are Roman Law origins to this section, with treatment of wild animals a part of *Justinian's Digest*.

Thus it is theft to steal a wild animal which has been tamed or which is in captivity. Therefore if X takes a rattlesnake from London Zoo he is guilty of theft.

Where the creature has not been tamed or placed in captivity it is not capable of being stolen unless it has been reduced into possession or it is in the process of being reduced into possession. Thus if X shoots rabbits on Y's land he will not be guilty of theft. If, however, Y has already shot and stored the rabbits or if they are in traps set by Y or even another trespasser and X takes them he will be guilty of theft (poaching is covered by other legislation).[93]

C. Belonging to Another

(i) Introduction

The prosecution must establish that at the time of the appropriation the property belonged   **8–028** to another. This seems an obvious requirement as theft is generally understood to be the taking of someone else's property. What then do we mean by the phrase "belonging to another"? Clearly it must include the case where the property is owned by the victim at the time when the accused takes it. But that alone would be too restricting. Suppose that X dishonestly appropriates a television set which A rents from B. Does X steal the set from A or from B? If we said that belonging to another meant only "owned by another" then the indictment would have to charge X with stealing the television from B. This might present few problems in our illustration, but there will be cases where the true owner would be hard to identify. In any case a law of theft which in our example would allow X to defeat a charge

---

[93] See *Cresswell v DPP* [2006] EWHC 3379 (Admin) addressing the similarly worded term in the Criminal Damage Act 1971 s.10(1)(a). Keane L.J. stated that where a trap has been established a wild animal will *not* be "in the course of reducing into possession" until the point at which the animal enters the trap; it is at this juncture that the nexus becomes operative; see below at para.10–005.

of stealing from A on the ground that A was not the real owner would be open to ridicule. Suppose that it was B, the owner of the television set, who secretly took it back from A, intending both to resell the set and claim the cost of a new set from A. Should we not in such a case be able to charge B with stealing the set from A? It is for reasons such as these that the phrase "belonging to another" receives a much wider definition in s.5 of the Act.

(ii) Section 5(1) of the 1968 Act

8–029 Section 5(1) provides as follows:

> "(1) Property shall be regarded as belonging to any person having possession or control of it, or having in it any proprietary right or interest (not being an equitable interest arising only from an agreement to transfer or grant an interest)."

Thus property can be stolen from a person who owns, possesses or has control over it. In the example of the television set it can, therefore, be stolen from either A, who has possession of it under a rental agreement, or from B who owns it. If A takes the set to C for repairs it could also be stolen from C while it was in his premises awaiting repairs. But then the question arises, can one of the persons with a recognised interest in the property steal it from one of the others? If A, the person renting the set, sold it and told B that it had been stolen, could A be charged with stealing it from B? If B, the owner, took it from A and claimed that A had lost it and was, therefore, under a contractual obligation to pay for it, could B be charged with stealing it from A even though B is the owner? An affirmative answer can be given to both of these questions. In *Turner (No.2)* [94] the accused had left his car for repair with a garage. Later he returned after it had been repaired and took it from outside the garage intending not to pay the bill. Despite the fact that the car belonged to Turner it was held that the garage had sufficient control of it to come within the phrase "belonging to another," and so Turner's conviction for theft was upheld. [95] A wide perspective needs to be applied to the words "possession or control". In a similar vein the owner may be convicted of theft where he removes his own shoes from the cobblers' shop without paying for the repairs carried out, and also where a defendant removes his own goods from a pawnbroker's shop without redeeming them. However, in *Meredith* [96] it was held not to be theft where an owner of a motorvehicle recovered it from a police compound; in the factual circumstances of the case the police had no right to retain it as against the owner. The entitlement of the police to remove a vehicle blocking a highway did not extend to keeping the vehicle from the owner. Another example of "possession or control" is provided by *Philippou*. [97] In that case the sole directors and shareholders of a company were convicted of theft from that company. Although the case was once thought to present difficulties on the issue of appropriation, its correctness was confirmed by *Gomez* and it illustrates the principle that a limited company is a separate "person" from whom property can be stolen even by those who control it.

Subject to situations like those in *Turner* (above) and those which are covered by s.5(3) and (4) [98] it will not be possible to convict of theft someone who has appropriated property which at the time of the appropriation belonged to himself. In some situations it will,

---

[94] [1971] 2 All E.R. 441.
[95] The outcome has been subject to criticism. The trial judge directed the jury to ignore the matter of liens. As a consequence the car repairer was merely a bailee at will, and it has long been the case that bailment may be ended whenever the bailee so desires. Turner on that rationale could have removed the car at any point in time.
[96] [1973] Crim.L.R. 253.
[97] (1989) 89 Cr.App.R. 290; see above, para.8–014.
[98] See below, paras 8–033—8–036.

therefore, be necessary to examine rules of civil law in order to determine to whom the property belonged at the moment of appropriation. Consider the following situation. D has just filled up his car at P's self-service garage when he discovers that he has left his wallet at home. He decides to drive off without paying. On the face of it this looks like theft of the petrol by D. However, the civil law provides that property (i.e. ownership) in the petrol passes to the motorist when it enters the petrol tank. This merely reflects common sense, since once it is mixed with other petrol in the tank, how could it be argued that the garage still owned the petrol? He commits the offence of making off without payment[99] but he has not stolen the petrol. He can be said to have appropriated the petrol when he poured it into his tank, but at this time he is not dishonest and so theft is not committed. By the time he forms his dishonest intent he is owner of the petrol and so any appropriation at the time would be appropriation of property belonging to himself and, again, not theft; he is merely a civil law debtor. Had he intended all along not to pay, then he could be convicted of theft. Here the act of dishonest appropriation is the pouring of the petrol into the tank. The fact that the garage has authorised him to put petrol in his car does not prevent his act from amounting to an appropriation of the petrol,[100] and as in *Lawrence*,[101] where the act of appropriation and the transfer of ownership are simultaneous, the courts will hold that D has appropriated property belonging to another. He would also be guilty of making off without payment and probably fraud.[102]

Where D uses fraud to obtain property from another, whether he obtains ownership, **8–030** possession or control of the property by that fraud, it was the intention of the drafters of the Act that he should be prosecuted for fraud. However, prosecutors seem to prefer to charge theft wherever possible and unfortunately the appellate courts have been prepared to go to extreme lengths to save theft convictions where the more appropriate charge would have been deception. *Lawrence* is a classic example of a situation where a deception charge should have been laid and not theft and it is the approach of the House of Lords in that case that has led to so much confusion and unnecessary litigation ever since. Suppose that D goes to an electrical store and on the basis of a dud cheque induces the store to part with a television set which he intends to sell. If the transaction between D and the store was a rental agreement then D would not obtain ownership of the television, and when he leaves the shop with the set he has dishonestly appropriated property belonging to another and is, thus, guilty of theft. If, however, the transaction is one of sale of the television then D would become owner of the set under a voidable contract. The problem for the court is to determine whether D dishonestly appropriated the television before he became owner of the set. From time to time the appellate courts have said that these intricacies of civil law have no part to play in the criminal law. With respect, however, consideration of the rules of civil law is unavoidable.[103] The Theft Act says that the accused must be proved to have appropriated property belonging to another and whether or not property belongs to a given individual can only be determined by reference to civil law. So when does ownership in the television pass to D? As a general rule property passes under a contract when the parties to the contract intend it to pass. In the absence of a contrary intention it is likely that the courts will hold that the ownership passes with delivery of the goods to the customer whose act of accepting the goods will constitute the appropriation.[104] The House of Lords held in

---

[99] See below, para.9–015.
[100] See *Gomez* [1993] A.C. 442, above, para.8–009.
[101] [1972] A.C. 626, see above, para.8–007.
[102] See *Coady* [1996] Crim.L.R. 518; below, para.9–006, fn.23 for further discussion.
[103] See above, para.8–012.
[104] Following *Gomez* [1993] A.C. 442, above, para.8–009, an authorised act may constitute an appropriation.

Lawrence and *Gomez* that so long as the goods belonged to another right up to the moment of appropriation that was sufficient. In *Dobson v General Accident Fire and Life Assurance Co*, Parker L.J. held, as we have seen, that if it were concluded that property passed with the concluding of the contract and before delivery, he could hold that in making the contract the defendant was assuming the rights of the owner and hence had appropriated goods belonging to another.

The result of this would seem to be that many cases of fraud can be prosecuted as theft. There are some situations, however, where a charge of theft is not appropriate. For example, land cannot be stolen, but it may be obtained by fraud.

Does the victim need to be aware of the property? It is obvious that most people have property in their homes that they have long forgotten that they possess. In *Woodman*[105] the X company was running down one of its factories and sold off a quantity of scrap metal to Y company. This gave Y company the right to enter the factory and remove the metal. Y company did, in fact, remove most of the scrap metal but left some there as not being worth the cost of salvaging it. X company remained owners of the site and put up a barbed wire fence and notices to discourage trespassers. It became clear that X company was not aware that any metal remained at the site. Some two years after X company's business had ceased at the factory, Woodman entered the site and took some of the scrap metal. He was charged with stealing the metal from X company. The trial judge took the view that there was no case to go to the jury on the basis that X company owned or possessed the property, but that there was a case of theft which could be left to the jury on the basis that X company controlled the property. The accused was convicted and appealed on the basis that X company could not be said to control the scrap metal since they were under the impression that it had all been removed by Y company. The Court of Appeal held that in the ordinary case if "it is once established that a particular person is in control of a site such as this, then prima facie he is in control of items on the site even though they were unaware of the existence of specific items." It might be that, if the scrap metal had been placed there by a third party after the barbed wire had been erected, a different result would follow, but that was not the case here. In one sense the property was abandoned, but at least in relation to Woodman, X company could be said to be in control of it.

8–031   Similarly where householders throw rubbish into a dustbin for collection by the corporation, they have in a sense abandoned the property; but not for the purposes of theft. This does not give the public the right to rummage through the bin to see if there is anything worth taking. Thus even in a situation where the householder is expected to place his dustbin in the street outside his house for collection, if X, a passerby, or even the dustman, takes anything from the bin there is a prima facie case of theft from the householder.[106] For those students who are keen golfers an interesting case in this regard is that of *Hibbert v McKiernan*.[107] The defendant, a trespasser on the private links of a golf club, who *animo furandi* had taken eight golf balls, was held to be rightly convicted of larceny under the old Act. The larceny related to the golf balls which were determined as being the property of the secretary and members of the golf club. They had possession and control to exclude trespassers. In the bizarre case of *Rostron*[108] the defendant, at dead of night and in sub-aqua gear, retrieved golf balls from golf course lakes. This profitable entrepreneurship produced

---

[105] [1974] Q.B. 754.
[106] See, e.g. *Williams v Phillips* (1957) 41 Cr.App.R. 5. In relation to proprietary interests generally see *Hancock* (1990) Cr.App.R. 422 (treasure trove) and *Waverley Borough Council v Fletcher* [1996] Q.B. 334 (use of metal detector on council land).
[107] [1948] 2 K.B. 142.
[108] [2003] All E.R. (D) 269; [2003] EWCA Crim 2206.

turnover of £15,000–£30,000 per annum. The appellate court reiterated that it was fundamental from an evidentiary perspective to establish that these lake balls were property belonging to another meaning the club owning the course. Problems are also engendered over establishment of the dishonesty requirement and claim of legal right.[109] It is possible that under civil law a lawful playing visitor to the course, or an individual exercising a public right of way over the course, would have a better right to the golf balls than the club.[110]

Equitable interests in property are also protected. If T is the trustee of property under a trust and B is the beneficiary, the property can be stolen from either T who has the legal interest or from B who has the equitable or beneficial interest. However, it does not cover a person who has an equitable interest which arises solely from an agreement to transfer property (see also s.5(2)).[111] The section covers "proprietary rights or interest". In *Shadrokh-Cigari*,[112] the Court of Appeal, expressly relying upon the civil case of *Chase Manhattan Bank N.A. v Israel British Bank (London) Ltd*,[113] held that where an individual receives money from V under a mistake of fact, there still remains on behalf of V an equitable proprietary interest in the property that has been transferred. The defendant was guardian to his nephew, whose father in Iran arranged for money to be paid to the child's bank account from the United States. Through an error by the US Bank $286,000 was credited to the account instead of $286. The uncle, acting as if the bank account represented an unexpected lottery windfall, drew on it to such an extent that by the time of his arrest some three weeks later only £21,000 remained. It was determined that the appellant was under an obligation to make restoration of the sums withdrawn on the basis that the English bank retained an equitable proprietary interest in the drafts under s.5(1).[114] The effect of *Shadrokh-Cigari* is that an equitable interest arising under, what must have constituted a constructive trust, was considered to be a proprietary interest for the purposes of s.5(1).[115] Equitable interests within s.5(1) were also considered by the appellate court in *Clowes (No.2)*,[116] wherein the defendant had mixed investors' money with those of his own. A trust was thereby created with investors having first charge on this fund; subsequent withdrawals by the defendant were appropriations against which investors had an equitable interest.

(iii) Section 5(3) and (4)

Subsections (3) and (4) of s.5 provide for two situations in which the phrase "belonging to **8–032** another" is given an extended meaning in order to widen the scope of the offence in s.1. It should be remembered that in both cases the provisions of s.5 enable the accused to be prosecuted for the offence of theft under s.1; they do not create separate offences of theft, the tendency to speak of charging the accused under s.5(4) is therefore inaccurate. It is arguable that in the factual situations covered by s.5(3) and (4), the victim retains an equitable interest in the property, which means the property belongs to him under s.5(1). If this is the case s.5(3) and (4) are superfluous.[117] However even if this is correct the provisions are useful in that they describe two situations in which an equitable interest remains vested in the victim.

[109] See below at para.8–040.
[110] See generally, J.C. Smith, *The Law of Theft* (Butterworths, 1997) at pp.42–44.
[111] s.5(2) provides:
   "Where property is subject to a trust, the persons to whom it belongs shall be regarded as including any person having a right to enforce the trust, and an intention to defeat the trust shall be regarded accordingly as an intention to deprive of the property any person having that right."
[112] [1988] Crim.L.R. 465.
[113] [1979] 3 All E.R. 1025.
[114] The same result could be achieved under s.5(4); see below, para.8–035.
[115] For a contrasting decision see *Att.-Gen's Reference (No.1 of 1985)* [1986] Q.B. 491, below, para.8–037.
[116] [1994] 2 All E.R. 316.
[117] See, e.g. *Chase Manhattan Bank N.A. v Israel-British Bank (London)* [1979] 3 All E.R. 1025.

8-033 Section 5(3).   It is provided by s.5(3) that:

> "Where a person receives property from or on account of another, and is under an obligation to the other to retain and deal with that property or its proceeds in a particular way, the property or proceeds shall be regarded (as against him) as belonging to the other."[118]

This is intended to cover the situation in which the accused has been given property, money or otherwise, and is supposed to act in a particular way with that property and where he has acted against his instructions. Why is this a problem? Let us assume a case in which X's fellow employees have given him twenty pounds to go and buy some fish and chips for lunch. Clearly they are not making a present of the twenty pounds to X, but, under the civil law, ownership in the twenty pounds passes to X upon delivery of the money to him. He is under an obligation either to buy the fish and chips or to restore the money, but in the latter case any twenty pound note will do. The same is true when you deposit money in a bank; the bank's only obligation is to restore an equivalent amount. The ownership in the money you leave with the bank passes to the bank. If then X, on the way to buy the fish and chips, suddenly decides to put it all on a horse at the local betting shop, he is using money of which he is now the owner and he will pass a good title in the twenty pounds to the bookmaker. He is, therefore, appropriating money which belongs to himself—the fellow employees have neither ownership nor possession nor control of the money. Thus under the definition of belonging to another in s.5(1) he cannot steal the money. However, under s.5(3) the money will be, for the purposes of theft, regarded as belonging to the employees if X was under an obligation to use that particular twenty pounds in a particular way. This means that the property, though it may be owned only by D, must be, as it were, earmarked in D's pocket for certain specific purposes of V. Does this mean, *ex hypothesi*, that D can be convicted of theft? The position is not quite so simple as it appears. Was he expected to use that particular money, or any money so long as he came back with the chips and change? The subsection and the problem it is supposed to solve are probably best explained by looking at the facts of one of the leading cases, that of *Hall*.[119] The accused had set up as a travel agent and had taken various sums of money from customers for the purpose of booking them on flights to America. He paid all the monies into the general trading account. Later he was forced to tell these customers that his business was in trouble, that he had not booked the flights and that there was no money with which he could refund their deposits. He was charged under s.1 with theft, the prosecution relying on s.5(3) to prove that the money belonged to the customers. On the face of it this looks like a classic example of s.5(3), but a moment's reflection will show that it is not quite so simple. Was Hall supposed to use the actual monies paid in, or was his sole duty to use the firm's money to make the bookings? Clearly in the world of business it would be unreasonable for him to put each sum of money into an envelope and book each customer's flight with their own particular money. Nor would you expect the travel agent to put the money in a specific fund for that particular flight. His sole duty is to make sure the booking is made and if this is impossible to return an equivalent amount of money to the customer. But s.5(3) says the property or its proceeds; does this not cover *Hall*? This must be answered in the negative since this is intended to cover a situation in which the rogue has converted the original property into something equally identifiable. For example, if a shopkeeper gives his assistant a £20 note to "pop next

---

[118] For an application of s.5(3) in relation to bills of exchange see *Arnold* [1997] Crim.L.R. 833.
[119] [1973] Q.B. 126; see also *Klineberg* (1999) 1 Cr.App.R. 427.

door to the bank and get it changed" the change he receives from the bank will be the proceeds of the £20 note and if he absconds at this stage he will be caught by s.5(3). Thus Hall's conviction was quashed. Our example of the twenty pounds for the fish and chips is probably nearer the line and it could be argued that it might be possible for a jury to find that he was expected to use *that* twenty pounds. Where, for any reason, the ownership is not transferred to the accused, s.5(3) is not needed, for instance, in the case of a loan of a book between two friends at university.

More recently, a different outcome to *Hall* arose in *Re Kumar*[120] in a scenario where the defendant was also a travel agent, but on this occasion was obligated to a trust that he would, after deducting commission, transfer money from the agency's account to another body. It was determined by the Divisional Court that he was under an obligation to retain and deal with the money in a particular way.

An application of the same principle applied in *Hall* is found in *DPP v Huskinson*.[121] There a tenant spent his housing benefit on himself rather than in payment of rent. He was acquitted of theft because the relevant legislation imposed no legal duty to use the money only for payment of rent and s.5(3) was, therefore, again of no assistance to the prosecution.[122] By way of contrast, in *McHugh*,[123] where a financial consultant mixed client money into the general trading account of his business, it was determined that both McHugh and the client had clearly understood that the client's investment was to be kept separate from the appellant's own money and that of his business. Therefore the Court of Appeal held that s.5(3) was applicable to their legal arrangement.

In *Klineberg and Marsden*[124] it was determined that there was an obligation imposing specific constituents when purchasers of timeshares paid money into a trust which was charged with the duty of safeguarding income received. Where individuals were induced to contract or did contract, by virtue of implied terms or otherwise, on the basis that their money would be safeguarded by trusteeship, there was clearly a legal obligation within the meaning of s.5(3). Similarly a legal obligation arose in *Floyd v DPP*[125] in a scenario where D collected money in weekly premiums from dyspeptic colleagues at work who had ordered goods from a food hamper company, then dissipated received income on herself. A legal obligation was held by the Divisional Court to exist between D and the food hamper company.[126]

So what sort of situation will generally be covered by s.5(3)? It applies only where **8–034** ownership in the property has been transferred to the accused and where he must use that very property in a particular way. The property will nearly always be money, so we are looking for a situation in which the accused was expected to use *that* money for a particular purpose. Thus if the accused is painting A's house and asks A for £20 to buy more paint, it is likely that the court will hold that he was expected to use that £20 note to buy the paint. Similarly the treasurer of a social club might be held to receive money which he is to put in a special fund for the club's purposes only. If this is the case, any appropriation of that money will be theft.

It is sufficient that an individual is obliged to keep in existence a fund equivalent to that which he has received. Thus in *Davidge v Bunnett*[127] the Divisional Court held that it was

[120] [2000] Crim.L.R. 504 DC.
[121] [1988] Crim.L.R. 620; similarly in *Cullen* (1974), unreported, where an "obligation" was held to arise where V gave D his mistress certain money to buy food but it was dissipated on D herself.
[122] See above, para.6–017, for consideration of *DPP v Huskinson* in the context of attempting the impossible.
[123] (1993) 97 Cr.App.R. 335; see, for example, *Brewster* (1979) 69 Cr.App.R. 375, *Wakeman v Farrar* [1974] Crim.L.R. 136, and *Hallam* [1995] Crim.L.R. 323.
[124] [1999] 1 Cr.App.R. 427.
[125] [2000] Crim.L.R. 411.
[126] In relation to civil law and contractual rights of third parties see the Contract (Rights of Third Parties) Act 1999.
[127] [1984] Crim.L.R. 297.

sufficient the defendant was under an obligation to keep a fund of money which would cover the gas bill. However, a differently constituted Divisional Court in *Lewis v Lethbridge*[128] determined that where the defendant had collected money on behalf of the London Marathon Charity, he merely owed a debt to the charity. He could not become a thief merely by not paying the debt. This decision was overruled in the case of *Wain*.[129] The appellant had taken part in raising money for a "Telethon" held for charity by Yorkshire Television ("The Telethon Trust"). He organised a number of events, including two discotheques, but then dissipated proceeds amounting to nearly £3,000. The appellant was under an obligation to retain at least the proceeds of the actual notes and coins collected. When he took money credited to a separate account into which he had paid those receipts, and moved it to his own personal bank account, he had appropriated what was still the proceeds of the money collected, and accordingly s.5(3) applies. McCowan L.J. stated:

> "[I]t seems to us that by virtue of s.5(3), the appellant was plainly under an obligation to retain, if not the actual notes and coins, at least their proceeds, that is to say the money credited in the bank account which he opened for the trust with the actual property. When he took the money credited to that account and moved it over to his own bank account, it was still the proceeds of the notes and coins donated which he continued to use for his own purposes, thereby appropriating them."[130]

Whether or not an obligation arises is a matter of law for the judge since the obligation referred to is a legal obligation.[131] The nature of street collections on behalf of particular charities arose in *Dyke and Munro*.[132] Their Lordships confirmed that property in the money passed from the donor member of the public to the charity when the money was put in the collecting tin. It was then stolen by whoever acted in a way inconsistent with the charity's ownership of that money. However, it was not stolen from the donor public, it was the charity's as soon as it was placed in the collecting tin. While it is for the jury to find the facts, it is for the judge to rule on which facts give rise to a legal obligation. In *Mainwaring* the court said:

> "Whether or not an obligation arises is a matter of law, because an obligation must be a legal obligation. But a legal obligation arises only in certain circumstances, and in many cases the circumstances cannot be known until the facts are established. It is for the jury, not the judge to establish the facts.
>
> What, in our judgment, a judge ought to do is this: if the facts relied upon by the prosecution are in dispute he should direct the jury to make their findings on the facts and then say to them: 'If you find the facts to be such-and-such, then I direct you as a matter of law that a legal obligation arose to which s.5(3) applies'."[133]

8–035   Section 5(4).   This is possibly one of the most complex provisions of the entire Act yet, like s.5(3), probably superfluous. It covers the situation in which, due to a mistake by the victim, ownership in the property passes to the rogue before any act of appropriation, so that when the appropriation occurs he is appropriating his own property. The section provides:

---

[128] [1987] Crim.L.R. 59.
[129] [1995] 2 Cr.App.R. 660.
[130] [1995] 2 Cr.App.R. 660 at 666.
[131] See, for example, *DPP v Huskinson* [1988] Crim.L.R. 620, discussed above, para.6–017.
[132] [2002] Crim.L.R. 153 CA.
[133] (1981) 74 Cr.App.R. 99 at 107 per Lawton L.J. Obligation here is considered to be in the sense of a legally enforceable obligation; see *Meech* [1974] Q.B. 549.

"Where a person gets property by another's mistake, and is under an obligation to make restoration (in whole or in part) of the property or its proceeds or of the value thereof, then to the extent of that obligation the property or proceeds shall be regarded (as against him) as belonging to the person entitled to restoration, and an intention not to make restoration shall be regarded accordingly as an intention to deprive that person of the property or proceeds."

It might be easiest to understand the workings of the section if we first consider the case of *Moynes v Coopper*[134] which it was designed to overrule. In that case the accused was given an advance on his wages during the course of the week. At the end of the week the wages clerk paid him a full salary, totally unaware that he ought to have made a deduction for the amount already advanced. When Moynes later discovered the error he decided to keep all the money.

At this point is is necessary to consider the civil law. No one can doubt but that Moynes was acting in a thoroughly dishonest way but, as we have just seen, dishonesty is not enough. So far as the civil law is concerned the fact that the person delivering property makes a mistake does not necessarily prevent ownership from passing and, of course, if ownership passes the recipient cannot steal the property because it is his own property.[135] Generally, a mistake will prevent ownership from passing only where the deliverer is mistaken as to the identity of the recipient or the identity of the property. The clerk in *Moynes v Coopper* was mistaken in neither of these senses; he intended to pay to *Moynes* the exact amount he in fact paid.

Prima facie, therefore, Moynes was merely a dishonest debtor—he owed his employers **8–036** the seven pounds approximately which had been overpaid—but the law stops short of making thieves out of dishonest debtors. Moynes, however, was not quite like other dishonest debtors. He did not merely owe seven pounds to his employers; he was under a quasi-contractual obligation to restore either the actual seven pounds or its proceeds or its value. Section 5(4) is there to deal with this sort of case. It is not there to deal with the case where A is under an obligation to pay money to B, because that would make thieves of all dishonest debtors, but only where A is under an obligation to restore to B the very property which he received from B or the proceeds or value of that property.[136] Whether A is under such an obligation can be a very complicated question but the complications arise in the civil law not the criminal law. For our purposes it is enough to note that s.5(4) comes into play only in an unusual sort of case because:

(1) If the ownership does not pass to the accused but remains with the person handing over the property, then the property still belongs to another without the need for s.5(4). Thus if X asks Y if he can give him a 10-pence piece in exchange for pennies and Y mistakenly hands over a 50-pence piece it is arguable that Y retains ownership in the 50-pence and, thus, it is property belonging to Y.[137] It is

---

[134] [1956] 1 Q.B. 439.

[135] The same sort of point arose in *Mazo* and *Hopkins and Kendrick*, considered above at para.8–016.

[136] An example is provided by *Att-Gen's Reference (No.1 of 1983)* [1985] 1 Q.B. 182. D a woman police officer, was mistakenly overpaid by the sum of £74. On realising that an error had occurred she decided to keep the extra payment for herself. It was held by the appellate court that from the moment when D became aware that the mistake had been made and her account credited she became subject to an obligation to restore; s.5(4) was applicable.

[137] An interesting case in this context is *Gilks* (1972) 56 Cr.App.R. 734 which affirms that a legal obligation to restore is a pre-requisite for the application of s.5(4). D, a betting enthusiast, received payment from a bookmaker predicated on the belief his horse had won the race. This was not the case. As wagering transactions themselves were void no legal obligation to repay consequentially arose.

conceivable also that the effect of the decision in *Chase Manhattan Bank N.A. v Israel-British Bank (London)*,[138] a civil law case, is that whenever money is paid under a mistake, the payer retains an equitable proprietary interest in the property which would satisfy s.5(1), thus rendering reliance on s.5(4) unnecessary.[139]

(2) In many cases where ownership in the property does pass despite the mistake, it has been caused to pass by fraud on the part of the recipient. In cases where this has happened the effect of *Gomez* is likely to mean that the court will hold that the property still belonged to the victim at the time when the defendant did an act which could be said to be a dishonest appropriation. In other words the ownership will pass when the victim delivers the goods to the defendant and the defendant's acceptance will constitute the appropriation. At the moment of appropriation the property still belongs to the victim and satisfies s.5(1). If in any doubt the prosecution can avoid these problems simply by charging the rogue with fraud.[140]

The application of s.5(4) is illustrated by *Davis*.[141] The defendant was in receipt of housing benefit from his local authority. Through a computer error he had received two weekly housing benefit cheques, over a period of time during which his entitlement to benefit ceased to exist. The charge related to theft of the money received when he cashed the cheques received by mistake, i.e. proceeds of the error. It was held by the Court of Appeal that Davis was under an obligation to restore the proceeds of all cheques cashed during the period after his benefit entitlement had ceased. This meant that the theft conviction was upheld. A similar case is *Gresham*.[142] Pension payments were made into an account of D's mother for more than 10 years after her death. D failed to inform her employer, the Department of Education, or the bank holding his mother's credit account. A theft conviction was upheld on the premise that these payments had been made by mistake and consequently s.5(4) was applicable.

8–037 **Bribes, Secret Profits and Constructive Trusts.**   A bribe is a gift accepted by a fiduciary as an inducement to him to betray his trust. A secret benefit, which may or may not constitute a bribe, is a benefit which the fiduciary derives from trust property or obtains from knowledge which he acquires in the course of acting as a fiduciary. Constructive trusts are imposed under the principles of equity where a profit is made egregiously by an individual in a fiduciary position. The inter-relationship of these principles has caused difficulties in establishing whether such constructive trusts form the constituents of property belonging to another within s.5. The leading civil law case, that of *Lister & Co v Stubbs*,[143] determined that where an employee abused his position and received bribes from another company, the relationship created was that of debtor and creditor; it was not that of trustee and *cestui que trust*. This was followed in the criminal law case of *Attorney-General's Reference (No.1 of 1985)*[144] where the Court of Appeal asserted that even if an employee did hold a secret profit on constructive trust for his employer (which was rejected in any event), the employer's proprietary interest under that trust was not a proprietary interest for the purposes of s.5(1). The defendant was a salaried manager of a tied public house, who by his

---

[138] See above, para.8–031.
[139] See discussion below, para.8–037.
[140] See below, para.9–001.
[141] [1988] Crim.L.R. 762.
[142] [2003] EWCA Crim 2070.
[143] (1890) 45 Ch.D. 1.
[144] [1986] Q.B. 591; see also *Powell v MacRae* [1977] Crim.L.R. 571.

contractual terms was required to sell only the stock provided by his employers and to pay takings into the latter's account. In contravention of this he brought his own beer into the public house for sale. It was held that D was not a trustee for the secret profit produced by the sales. This conclusion was contradicted in the later case of *Shadrokh-Cigari* where, as we have seen, it was determined that D's receiving of money from V under a mistake of fact, created a constructive trust of the proceeds; an equitable property interest iniured for the benefit of V against D under s.5(1). This outcome has been followed in the Privy Council decision of *Attorney-General for Hong Kong v Reid*.[145] Therein, the defendant, a Crown servant in Hong Kong, was convicted of accepting bribes as an inducement to him to exploit his official position by obstructing the prosecution of certain criminals.[146] Their Lordships in a civil suit for recovery of assets purchased with the bribe proceeds, held that equity considers as done that which ought to have been done. As soon as the bribe was received, whether in cash or in kind, the false fiduciary held the bribe on a constructive trust for the person injured.[147] V had an equitable proprietary interest as against D.

In summary, the Privy Council decision in *Attorney-General for Hong Kong v Reid* is contradictory to the long established civil law case of *Lister & Co v Stubbs*, and also the Court of Appeal decision in *Attorney-General's Reference (No.1 of 1985)*. If followed subsequently by our courts it would represent the extension of the criminal law by a civil court; an extension which Parliament has thus far declined to make. The dichotomy between the Privy Council on the one hand, and our appellate courts on the other, over the issue of constructive trusts, mirrors the confusion between these courts over attribution of relevant characteristics to the objective test for the provocation defence.[148] The initial approach by the appellate courts in relation to provocation was to follow their own precedent to the detriment of Privy Council authority, as confirmed subsequently by the House of Lords, but latterly the Privy Council has held sway.[149]

2. THE MENS REA OF THEFT

The Act provides that the prosecution must prove that the appropriation of property **8–038** belonging to another was dishonest and that at the time of the appropriation the accused had the intention of permanently depriving the other of the property. The effect of the dishonesty requirement is, in part, that the prosecution must be able to establish intention or subjective recklessness in relation to each element of the actus reus. There is no requirement that the accused did it for personal gain; it would equally be theft if the defendant takes property belonging to another or simply throws it on the fire.[150]

A. Dishonesty

Dishonesty is peculiarly difficult to define. Dishonest conduct is conduct which is regarded **8–039** by people generally as dishonest. In most cases, of course, there is general agreement as to what is viewed as honest or dishonest. No one doubts but that it is dishonest to take goods

---

[145] [1994] 1 A.C. 324. See generally, J.C. Smith, "*Lister v Stubbs* And The Criminal Law" (1994) 110 L.Q.R. 180.
[146] The value of D's assets derived from bribes was no small amount, but equated to the grand sum of HK$12.4M!
[147] [1994] 1 A.C. 324 at 333 per Lord Templeman.
[148] See above, para.7–026.
[149] See, e.g. *Campbell (No.2)* [1997] 1 Cr.App.R. 199; and *Parker* [1997] Crim.L.R. 760 and *Smith* [2000] 1 A.C. 146; [2000] 4 All E.R. 289; and see above at para.7–029.
[150] See s.1(2). It is provided by s.1(2) that: "It is immaterial whether the appropriation is made with a view to gain, or is made for the thief's own benefit."

from a store without paying for them, or surreptitiously to remove books from a library, or to get goods from a machine by using a washer instead of coinage, and so on. But cases can arise, and arise not infrequently, where views may differ as to whether particular conduct is dishonest.

The Theft Act does not attempt a comprehensive definition of dishonesty. Section 2 provides only a partial definition and details three cases where a person's conduct is not to be regarded as dishonest. Before these are examined, it will be noted that, in addition, it is provided by s.2(2) that a person's appropriation of property may be dishonest notwithstanding an intention to pay for it, and by s.1(2) that it is immaterial that the appropriation is not made with a view to gain. Suppose A wants to purchase a painting from B which B refuses to sell; A may be convicted of theft if he takes the picture though he leaves in its place money which more than represents its value. Alternatively A may wish merely to deprive B of the painting without intending to enjoy it himself or to see it for his own profit; A may be convicted of theft because he intends the painting to be lost to B though he has no view to gain for himself.

Section 2(1) states that an appropriation is not be regarded as dishonest in three cases: (i) where be believes that he has in law the right to deprive the other of it on behalf of himself or another; (ii) where he appropriates the property in the belief that he would have the owner's consent; and (iii) where he appropriates the property in the belief that the owner cannot be traced by taking reasonable steps.

(i) Belief in Legal Right

8–040 The only belief that is relevant here is a belief in a legal right. That A feels that he has a moral claim to the property, or that he is in some vague way justified in taking it, is not relevant under this head though it may be otherwise relevant to the issue of dishonesty. If A believes he has a legal right, his conduct cannot be accounted dishonest though his claim is entirely unreasonable or even though the claim is one which the law does not recognise. An honest belief in legal right, however arrived at, is inconsistent with dishonesty.[151] It is evident from *Wootton*[152] that the trial judge is well advised to direct the jury specifically in terms of s.2(1) when there is any evidence that those terms might be satisfied. The defendant in *Rostron*, a bizarre case involving retrieval of golf balls from lakes at dead of night through use of sub-aqua equipment, asserted that he had a legal right to collect these "lost" balls. The jury should have been specifically directed under the terms of the section.[153]

(ii) Belief in Consent

8–041 If A honestly believes that B, the owner, would have consented to his appropriation, his conduct cannot be regarded as dishonest. That A's belief is unreasonably arrived at is irrelevant except to the extent that it may cast doubt on the genuineness of his belief, as was determined in *Holden*.[154] Consider, for example, the facts in *Flynn*.[155] D had been employed for over 18 years as manager of a cinema. He had cashed a cheque which had not been met and was ordered to repay the money without delay. He took about £6 belonging to the cinema in order to do so. In giving evidence he asserted that he took it as a loan in the form of an advance on his salary for the following week, something he frequently did in favour of

---

[151] See, e.g. *Robinson* [1977] Crim.L.R. 173; considered below, para.9–020. It is apparent from *Kell* [1985] Crim.L.R. 239 that a full direction is needed from the trial judge to the jury using the words of s.2(1)(a).
[152] [1990] Crim.L.R. 201.
[153] Note in *Rostron* [2003] All E.R. (D); [2003] EWCA Crim 2206 the appellate court approved a general *Ghosh* type direction—surely inapposite in that reference to s.2 alone was required.
[154] [1991] Crim.L.R. 478.
[155] [1970] Crim.L.R. 118.

junior employees, and he believed that his employers would have consented to the taking of the money if they had known about it. The judge failed to direct the jury that under s.2(1)(b), a person's appropriation of property belonging to another was not to be regarded as dishonest if he appropriated the property in the belief that he would have the other's consent if the other knew of the appropriation and the circumstances of it.[156] Flynn's appeal against conviction was allowed.

It is useful to remember here that the law also requires that the accused must intend permanently to deprive the owner of the property so that unlawful borrowing of another's property, even where you know the other would most certainly have refused to lend the property, does not amount to theft. Unlawful borrowing may be a social nuisance but it has long been held that this is not an appropriate subject for criminal sanctions.[157] It should also be remembered that where the property "borrowed" is consumable such as money or cups of sugar, the borrower will intend permanently to deprive the other of that money or sugar, he will have an intention merely to replace an equivalent amount.

Suppose that X enters a shop intending to purchase a bottle of milk. He finds that there is no one serving in the shop and so he simply takes the bottle of milk and leaves. His criminal liability will depend upon the circumstances. For example:

(i) if he honestly believed that the shopkeeper would not object to his taking the milk and paying up later then he will have a defence under s.2(1)(b);

(ii) if, however, he does not know the shopkeeper and has no reason to believe that the shopkeeper would consent to his simply taking the milk, he might suppose that it would be all right if he either left a note of his name and address and a message that he would call in to pay later, or more likely that the owner would not object if he left the money on the counter. The only difficulty here is that s.2(2) says that the appropriation may be dishonest notwithstanding that he is willing to pay for the property. Thus if A owns a valuable Ming vase which B has always wanted, if B were to go to A's house and take the vase, leaving a cheque for the market value of the vase, a jury would be entitled to find that B dishonestly appropriated A's vase despite his willingness to pay. But in the example of the bottle of milk, a jury would be equally entitled to find that the leaving of the money or IOU was evidence that X honestly believed that the owner would have consented or simply that X was not dishonest.[158]

(iii) Belief That the Owner Cannot be Traced

This provision essentially deals with property which is found by A; he is not to be treated as **8–042** a thief if he appropriates that property in the belief that the owner cannot be traced by taking reasonable steps. If, for example, A finds a £5 note in the street it could only be exceptionally that he would believe that the owner can be traced so that in appropriating it he would not be guilty of theft. If, however, A finds in the same street Goya's portrait of the Duke of Wellington, he is unlikely to believe that the owner cannot be traced by taking reasonable steps. Nevertheless, if A is a philistine who regards the painting as worthless so that it does not occur to him to take steps to trace the owner, he cannot be convicted of theft. If it does occur to A that the owner might be traced, he may be convicted of theft if he

---

[156] Where D provides evidence, as in *Flynn*, to the effect that he possesses a s.2(1)(b) belief, then the onus will be on the prosecution to prove beyond reasonable doubt that he did not so believe.
[157] But see s.6 below, para.8–046; unlawful borrowing of a motor vehicle may amount to a separate offence under s.12 (see below, para.9–053).
[158] See below, para.8–044.

fails to take reasonable steps. He is not required to take every conceivable step; no doubt the most usual reasonable step would be to hand the property to the police on the assumption that the owner, if he cares about his loss, will have reported it to them.

(iv) Dishonesty in Other Cases

8–043   The partial definition does not of course provide for all cases and the question arises as to how dishonesty is to be defined in circumstances not falling within the partial definition. The courts have considered the matter in a number of cases; and in *Ghosh*[159] the Court of Appeal, recognising that the law was in a complicated state, attempted a restatement.

The defendant in *Ghosh* was a surgeon acting as a *locum tenens* in a hospital. He claimed fees were due for certain operations that had never been performed. The Court of Appeal adopted a compromise test of dishonesty. They followed the objective standard of dishonesty found in *Feely*, predicated upon the standards of ordinary decent people, but qualified it by the subjective requirement of *Boggeln* that D must have been aware that his behaviour would be regarded as dishonest according to the objective criterion. Whether conduct is to be regarded as dishonest is a matter for the jury to determine. The judge should, however, direct the jury that A acts dishonestly if (a) his conduct would be regarded as dishonest by the ordinary standards of reasonable people; and (b) A realises that his conduct is so regarded. If (a) and (b) are satisfied then (c) A's conduct is dishonest however he might regard his conduct; A cannot set up a personal standard which he knows to be at variance with the general standard.

The test set out in *Ghosh* provides two avenues for the defendant to establish that he was not dishonest. These possibilities may helpfully be set out in diagrammatic form[160]:

The dual test for dishonesty

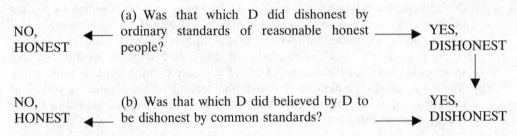

The dual test was necessary, according to Lord Lane, to avoid two extremes. At one end of the spectrum, a purely objective test would ensnare the inadvertent foreigner who came from a country where public transport was free and who did not pay the requisite fare in this country. The objective standards approach would, it was considered, avoid liability being attached to, "conduct to which no moral obloquy could possibly attach".[161] At the other end of the scale it was deemed inapposite to apply a purely subjective test allowing, for example, the ardent anti-vivisectionist to impose his own standards. It was believed this was prevented

---

[159] [1982] 2 All E.R. 689; see also *Feely* [1973] Q.B. 530; *Boggeln v Williams* [1978] 2 All E.R. 1061; *Landy* [1981] 1 All E.R. 1172; and *McIvor* [1982] 1 All E.R. 491.
[160] See K. Campbell, "The Test of Dishonesty in *R. v Ghosh*" (1984) 43 C.L.J. 349 at 351; and A. Halpin, "The Test for Dishonesty" [1996] Crim.L.R. 283 at 287.
[161] [1982] 2 All E.R. 689 at 696. The difficulty, of course, is that it is opaque whether the *Ghosh* perspective contravenes art.5 of the ECHR (right to liberty or security) or art.7 (no punishment without law). There is infringement where D is unable to foresee to a reasonable degree whether or not their conduct is criminal. Does *Ghosh* provide sufficient certainty on dishonesty to avoid contravention? Clarification is needed on this unresolved issue.

by adopting the objective common standards approach. The weight of these arguments is considered subsequently.

As to (a) the issue is one for the jury who have only their own knowledge and experience **8–044** to guide them. No doubt on any given set of facts most juries would reach the same decision, but on certain facts juries may reach different conclusions. Take cases, where A, C and D "borrow" money from B without permission. A may take £5 from the till of his employer B to pay a taxi driver because he has no small change. C may take £10 from B's till to lay a wager on a horse (*Feely);* D may take £200 from B's safe to pay a deposit on his holiday (*McIvor*). All intend to make up the till money at a later stage, but, of course, the money which they take is not "borrowed" but is taken permanently, since B is deprived permanently of the notes and coins taken.[162] The circumstances of the appropriation may be crucial. For example, bank employees are expressly told that in no situation may they borrow money from the till. In *Gohill v DPP*[163] the defendant, a tool hire shop manager, had allowed customers to use store items for a period without payment, and had received individuals' tips thereby. D had falsified store records to cover these transactions. It was presumptively determined that D's conduct was dishonest by ordinary standards of reasonable honest people.

Would any or all of these takings be regarded as dishonest by the generality of reasonable people? No doubt the jury would wish to consider such factors as whether B had expressly forbidden "borrowing", as in the case of bank officials above, the extent to which A, C and D had an ability to repay, whether the borrowing was done openly or secretly and so on. It seems difficult to lay down a general principle for such cases so it may be that different juries would reach different conclusions. A jury in Newcastle may adopt a differing approach on dishonesty than, say, juries in London, Nottingham or Leeds. Thus, Professor Elliott has propounded that the best solution may be the abrogation of "dishonesty" altogether, with the replacement by a new subs.(3) to s.2:

> "No appropriation of property belonging to another which is not detrimental to the interests of the other in a significant practical way shall amount to theft of the property."[164]

As to (b) it is not simply a question of whether the defendant regards his conduct as dishonest according to his own standards. It is a question of whether he knew that ordinary people would regard his conduct as dishonest. It is generally regarded as dishonest to travel on buses with intent to avoid paying the fare but, as suggested above, the court pointed out in *Ghosh* that a person who came from a country where public transport was free, would not act dishonestly if he boarded a bus believing that public transport here was similarly free; he would not be aware that ordinary people in this country would regard the conduct as dishonest.

If, then, a modern Robin Hood thought it was right for him to rob the rich in order to **8–045** feed the poor, he would be acting dishonestly if he realised, as is the fact, that people generally regard such a taking as dishonest.[165] But if he is out of touch with community

---

[162] In *Velumyl* [1989] Crim.L.R. 299 D had taken the sum of £1,050 out of the safe where he was employed in order to lend the amount to a friend. He anticipated that the money would be returned to the safe after the weekend. The court determined that as D clearly would not return the *very same* bank notes he had an intention permanently to deprive contrary to s.6 (see below, para.8–046). An intention to return the sum taken related to dishonesty not to the s.6 criterion.

[163] [2007] EWHC 23 (Admin).

[164] D.W. Elliott, "Dishonesty in Theft: A Dispensable Concept" [1982] Crim.L.R. 395 at 410.

[165] An example is provided by the "professional" thief who stole personal belongings and other items of value from Prince Charles' private apartment. D stated that he intended to sell such items to feed the homeless in London.

standards and genuinely thinks that people generally do not regard such conduct as dishonest, then his conduct cannot, it seems, be accounted dishonest. Cases where the defendant is mistaken about the prevailing standards of dishonesty will be exceptional, but they may occasionally happen.

In *Roberts*[166] the Court of Appeal held that it would not, in every case, be necessary for the trial judge to give a full *Ghosh* direction. If the defendant did not raise an issue with regard to the second part of the test, the judge need not leave it to the jury.[167] A *Ghosh* direction is only applicable where the defendant might have believed that what he was alleged to have done was in accordance with the ordinary person's idea of honesty. Thus there is a burden on the defendant to introduce evidence that he did not think that ordinary people would regard his conduct as dishonest. Once the defendant says that this is what he did and that he does not consider that he has acted dishonestly, the *Ghosh* direction should be given. Furthermore, it should, following *Green*[168] and the decision in *Hyam*,[169] be given in the right order, namely the objective part first, followed by the subjective part. A trial judge would be well advised to stick to the exact words used by Lord Lane C.J. in *Ghosh*. It was a misdirection in *Green* for the trial judge to use a witness, apparently shocked by what she felt was G's dishonesty, as a yardstick for measuring the objective standard of honesty.

B. With Intention Permanently to Deprive

8–046   During the period of debate before the Theft Act 1968 was enacted, it was suggested that the prosecution should no longer have to prove the accused intended permanently to deprive the other of his property. This would have had the effect of making dishonest borrowing theft. It was finally decided that the requirement should be retained and that cases of unlawful borrowing were better dealt with by the civil law.[170]

Thus the prosecution must prove that at the time of the appropriation the accused intended permanently to deprive the owner of the property. This ordinarily presents no problems because when A takes money from B's pocket or when C takes a book from D's shop the prosecution is usually not hard pressed to prove that A and C intended permanently to deprive. Equally, where the accused believed that the property had been abandoned, he cannot be said to have intended permanently to deprive another of it. For example, in *Small*[171] the defendant gave evidence that he had seen the dilapidated motorcar (subject of the theft indictment) every day for two weeks. It had the keys in the ignition; it had a flat tyre, the petrol tank was empty, the wipers did not work. He gave evidence that at the time of taking the motorcar, he thought that it had been abandoned by its true owner. It is submitted that if a defendant believes that the property has been abandoned this belief is incompatible with the intent, which the Act requires, of permanently depriving another of property to that other. But evidential difficulties can occur in other cases. Where C takes the book from the university library, his claim that he intended to return the book at the end of term may be plausible and the prosecution may in such a case have difficulty in proving the

---

[166] (1987) 84 Cr.App.R. 117.
[167] See e.g. *Squire* [1990] Crim.L.R. 341 (D involved in VAT evasion over a gold smuggling exercise); and *Price* [1990] Crim.L.R. 200 (D falsely told his bank that he was a beneficiary under a trust fund—a modern day Billy Bunter who persuaded others to lend him money on the strength of a postal order which was always going to arrive and never did!)
[168] [1992] Crim.L.R. 292.
[169] [1997] Crim.L.R. 439.
[170] But see below, para.9–053 for special provisions for some instances of unlawful borrowing, especially of motorvehicles.
[171] [1987] Crim.L.R. 777.

intent. It has been known even for law students to take books from the law library without signing for them and then to leave them at the end of term outside the library door. This is a deplorable practice but it is not theft for it is obvious that the miscreant does not intend the university to lose the books permanently. What, then, if the miscreant left the books in the students' union or on the London underground? Given that the books were stamped as the property of the university of X, the probability is that they would be returned to the university in the first case, though this is much less likely in the second. But in either case the test of C's liability is the same: did he intend permanently to deprive the university of its books? If C believes that by leaving the books where he does they will be returned to the university he cannot be said to intend permanent deprivation even if he leaves them in a place which makes it highly unlikely that they will ever be returned.

In the normal run of case, then, the intent permanently to deprive raises only evidential problems. But in exceptional cases it can raise legal problems. Such cases tend to be those where A takes the property of B which, in a sense, he returns to B but only after A has treated himself as owner of that property. It is for these exceptional cases that s.6 is there to provide (this is broken down below into two limbs for ease of exposition):

> "A person appropriating property belonging to another without meaning the other permanently to lose the thing itself is nevertheless to be regarded as having the intention of permanently depriving the other of it (i) if his intention is to treat the thing as his own to dispose of regardless of the other's rights; and (ii) a borrowing or lending of it may amount to so treating it if, but only if, the borrowing or lending is for a period and in circumstances making it equivalent to an outright taking or disposal."

Consider the following examples:

(1) A is a shopkeeper who stores empty beer bottles, on which he has paid the refund, in **8–047** his yard. B enters the yards, takes some bottles and then enters A's shop where he gets a refund on the bottles. Such a case as this is perhaps best treated as obtaining by deception, but B may alternatively be convicted of stealing the bottles. In a sense he intends that A should get his bottles back but only after A has paid for them, B is clearly treating the bottles as his own to dispose of regardless of A's rights. A can get his own bottles back only by paying for them. This is just the situation the first part of s.6(1) was designed to cover, according to Lord Lane C.J. in *Lloyd* (see below), and it illustrates the fact that the crucial words in s.6(1) are "to dispose of"—without these words the remainder of the subsection adds nothing to the definition of "appropriates" (see *Cahill*[172]). It applies to a taking and resale or attempted resale to the owner of his own property. For instance, in *Hall*,[173] where the defendant took fat from a candle maker and then offered it for sale to the owner. His conviction for larceny was affirmed. In a more modern context it applied to the appellant in *Scott*[174] who appropriated without paying for a set of curtains from a department store, but then returned them the very next day demanding a full refund.

(2) D, a first-year medical student, takes a copy of *Gray's Anatomy* from the library intending to return it on completion of his course in five years' time. Five years is a long time, so can it be said that D's "borrowing . . . was for a period and in circumstances which

---

[172] [1993] Crim.L.R. 142. The appellate court expressly approved the following statement of Professor Smith: "It is submitted, however, that an intention to use the thing as one's own is not enough and that 'dispose of' is not used in the sense in which a general might 'dispose of' his forces but rather in the meaning given by the *Shorter Oxford Dictionary*: "To deal with definitely: to get rid of, to get done with, finish. To make over by way of sale or bargain, sell."

[173] (1848) 1 Den. 381.

[174] [1987] Crim.L.R. 235.

made it equivalent to an outright taking or disposal", within the second limb of the statutory provision? The difficulty with this view is that it could leave the courts with an impossible task in determining what period of borrowing would be so equivalent. The section says it must be equivalent to an outright taking. Borrowing for a fixed term falls short of being so equivalent and the courts have held it to be a misdirection for a judge to direct a jury that X may be convicted of stealing Y's goods where X intends to keep those goods indefinitely (see *Warner*[175]). A taking or borrowing is equivalent to an outright taking probably only where all the value of the property is consumed. So if X takes Y's season ticket to a football ground, intending to use it for all the games for which it is valued and then return the ticket to Y, X has stolen the ticket, for the borrowing is now equivalent to an outright taking.

For example, in *Coffey*[176] the prosecution alleged that the defendant had obtained a machine from the victim by deception (a worthless cheque). Although this was a charge under the old law, of obtaining property by deception, it also required that the prosecution prove that the defendant intended permanently to deprive the other of the machine. It appeared that the defendant was in dispute with the owner of the machine and had obtained the machine so as to give himself a bargaining counter in the negotiations. It was not altogether clear what would have happened to the machine if the negotiations were not settled to the defendant's satisfaction. It was held that this was a situation in which the trial judge should give the jury a full direction on s.6(1). The prosecution would have to satisfy the jury that the defendant intended not to return the machine until he got what he wanted, or, at least, that he intended to keep it so long as to be regarded as an outright taking of it, in other words, till all the virtue had gone out of the thing.

8–048   The leading authority, upon which the principle enunciated above is based, is that of *Lloyd*.[177] There the defendant, a cinema projectionist, clandestinely removed feature films due to be shown in the cinema. He lent them to a group of accomplices who made master videotape copies of the films. The films were returned before their absence from the cinema was noticed. Many pirated videotape versions of the films were made and sold, and the continued success of their scheme depended on their ability to return the films as rapidly as possible. The matter that arose, inter alia, for determination by the Court of Appeal was whether they possessed an intention to permanently deprive under s.6(1) of the Theft Act, in that the borrowing of the tapes focused on their return to the owner as expeditiously as possible. Their Lordships, the leading judgment that of Lord Lane C.J., clearly affirmed that a mere borrowing was insufficient to constitute the necessary guilty mind under s.6(1) unless the intention was to return the thing in such a changed state that it had *lost all its goodness or virtue*. The feature films did not fall into that category, since they had not diminished in value as they could still be projected to paying audiences, so that their value to their owners had not been lost. The borrowing was not for such a period or in such circumstances as made it equivalent to an outright taking or disposal. Lord Lane stated that this provision:

"is intended to make clear that a mere borrowing is never enough to constitute the necessary guilty mind unless the intention is to return the thing in such a changed state that it can truly be said that all its goodness or virtue has gone".[178]

---

[175] (1970) 55 Cr.App.R. 93; see further *Mulligan* [1990] S.T.C. 200 and *Downes* (1983) 77 Cr.App.R. 260 (sale of Inland Revenue vouchers or certificates by D forms the constituents of s.6 irrespective of the fact that the vouchers or certificates eventually return to the Inland Revenue—their essential characters were destroyed thus depriving the owners of the substance of their property).
[176] [1987] Crim.L.R. 498.
[177] [1985] Q.B. 829.
[178] [1985] Q.B. 829 at 836. Nor did the defendant treat the films as his own to dispose of regardless of the other's rights. See also *Clinton (Chief Inspector of RUC) v Cahill* [1998] N.I. 200, NICA.

He gave as examples the use and return of a railway ticket or a torch battery.

However, the Court of Appeal court in the decision of *Fernandes*[179] has now rejected the proposition that s.6(1) is limited in its application to the illustrations in *Lloyd*, but is expressed in general terms. The defendant was a disreputable solicitor who had transferred money from his clients' account to his bookkeeper, R, for investment in a firm of back-street moneylenders of which R was a partner. Fernandes knew the investment was unsafe and as a consequence the money had disappeared. It was determined that the second limb of s.6(1) could apply to a person in possession or control of another's property who, dishonestly and for his own purpose, dealt with that property in such a manner that he knew that he was *risking its loss*. Someone who deals with property knowing that he is doing so in a way which risks its loss may be intending to "treat the thing as his own to dispose of regardless of the other's rights" and may, thus, be regarded as having an intention of permanently depriving the other of it. This may, if followed, represent an important extension of the ambit of the section. Hypothetically an individual who takes, for instance, a photocopying card from A, unaware as to the remaining units on the card, and then returns it to A after use, uncaring as to the existence of the units left, would presumptively be outside the *Lloyd* limitations, but within *Fernandes*, risking loss. On a wide reading it would even cover the individual who contrary to my wishes throws my prized Crown Derby ornament for me to catch; subject, of course, to the proviso that D appreciates that his planned course of conduct puts the thing or its virtue completely at risk of a total loss.

The nature of s.6(1) was considered in the consolidated appeals of *Marshall, Coombes and Erren*.[180] The defendants were convicted of theft at Southwark Crown Court after being caught on closed circuit television at Victoria station reselling to members of the public unexpired London underground tickets and travel cards, which they had obtained from passengers leaving stations. They appealed against conviction, arguing that the Theft Act 1968 s.6(1) did not apply as they had no intention of permanently depriving London underground of the tickets. They contended that the issuing of a ticket was analogous to the drawing of a cheque in that it created a chose in action belonging first to the passenger and second to the payee. Hence it was argued that the property belonged to the passenger and not to London underground, so that there could be no intention of permanently depriving London underground of the ticket, which would eventually be returned to its possession.[181] However, the Court of Appeal dismissed their appeals. It was determined that on the issuing of a ticket, a contract was formed between the underground and the buyer, carrying rights and obligations. The buyer had an enforceable right to travel on the underground and the latter had an entitlement to demand that no one other than the actual buyer use the ticket. According to the Court of Appeal that last right was disregarded when the defendants obtained the tickets but then sold them on. In essence, the defendants by obtaining and reselling the tickets had the necessary intention to treat the tickets as their own to dispose of regardless of London underground's rights. The decision may have important implications for all ticket touts and even for the ordinary motorist who passes on the benefit of an unexpired parking ticket.[182] Would an altruistic motorist who passes on his unexpired parking ticket now be convicted of theft? Is such a motorist acting dishonestly? It presents an interesting question upon which different juries in varying parts of the country may come to inconsistent conclusions.[183]

---

[179] [1996] 1 Cr.App.R. 175.
[180] [1998] 2 Cr.App.R. 282; (1998) J.P. 488; see generally, J.C. Smith, "Stealing Tickets" [1998] Crim.L.R. 723.
[181] An argument derived from *Preddy* [1996] A.C. 815; considered below, para.9–001. See also *Clark* [2002] 1 Cr.App.R. 14 (no intention on the part of D permanently to deprive the drawer of the cheque form, which would on presentation of the cheque for payment be returned to the drawer via his bank).
[182] See generally, G. Slapper, "Stealing Time is now a Crime", *The Times*, May 26, 1998.
[183] No question of dishonesty arose in *Marshall, Coombes and Erren* as the defendants had admitted acting dishonestly by pleading guilty before Southwark Crown Court.

8–049   It seems obvious that s.6 still has attendant difficulties for courts. Unfortunately, it is impossible to disagree with Professor Spencer when he refers to the section as one which "sprouts obscurities at every phrase".[184] The best approach, referred to *en passant* by the court in *Lloyd*, is to refer to s.6 only in exceptional cases when directing a jury. In the vast majority of cases involving theft, no necessity exists to refer to or consider it.

(3) E, knowing that F is out of town for the day and is in no position to interfere, takes G to F's home. There, representing himself as the owner of the house and contents, he sells F's furniture to G. E is obviously guilty of theft if he anticipates that G will remove the furniture, but what if E knows that F will return in time to prevent removal? The simple answer would be to charge E with fraud but it is arguable that he would still be guilty of stealing. E may not "mean" F to lose the thing (the furniture) itself but by purporting to sell it to G he has treated the furniture as his own to dispose of (see *Pitham v Hehl.*) This conclusion is supported by the decision of the Privy Council in *Chan Man-sin v Attorney-General for Hong Kong.*[185] In that case the defendant had, by means of forged cheques, caused money to be transferred from M and H's accounts with S.C. Bank into his own personal account with O.T. Bank. The defence argued that once it was discovered that the cheques were forgeries, M and H would be able to insist on having the transactions reversed, and would, thus, lose nothing. Since the defendant, who was an accountant, would know this to be the position, it could not be said that he intended permanently to deprive them of their property.[186] The Privy Council held that this was covered by a provision in the Hong Kong statute which was identical to s.6 of our Theft Act 1968. The defendant's intention was to treat the thing as his own to dispose of regardless of the rights of M and H.

(4) H hires a car from J for a week. K takes the car, uses it for a week and then returns it to J. No doubt K would be charged under s.12,[187] but he may also be guilty of theft. He has not stolen the car from J but so far as H is concerned he has deprived H of the whole of his interest.

(5) A takes B's silver goblets and pawns them. He keeps the money he receives from the pawnshop intending to redeem it later. This is covered by s.6(2) which gives a further extended meaning to the phrase "with the intention permanently to deprive":

> "If any person in possession of another's property (whether lawfully, or not) parts with that property under a condition he may not be able to perform he may be regarded as treating the property to dispose of regardless of the other's rights."

A case which might be thought of as rather over extending the meaning of "dispose of" in s.6 is *DPP v Lavender.*[188] The defendant took two doors from a council property undergoing repair and used them to replace two damaged doors in another council property. He was convicted of theft on the basis of disposing of the doors regardless of the owner's right not to have them removed. But is this really a "disposal" of the property in the natural sense of the word? If I swap the door on my office for the door on another office of the same company's building, which could be regarded as essentially the same as this case, I may have rearranged the property but it seems somewhat harsh to say that I have stolen it.

---

[184] J.R. Spencer, "The Metamorphosis of Section 6 of the Theft Act" [1977] Crim.L.R. 653; for an article propounding the abolition of an intention permanently to deprive see G. Williams, "Temporary Appropriation Should be Theft" [1981] Crim.L.R. 129.

[185] [1988] 1 All E.R. 1; see also *Re Osman* [1989] 3 All E.R. 701.

[186] The property in this case was the debts owed by the bank to M and H, i.e. choses in action; see above, para.8–022.

[187] Taking a conveyance, see para.9–053.

[188] [1994] Crim.L.R. 297.

3. CONDITIONAL INTENTION

A problem which has caused much controversy in recent years has been that of so-called **8–050** conditional intent. In a sense all intention may be said to be conditional. A may set out with the firm intention of stealing B's painting but his intention will be subject to certain conditions such as that he will be able to effect an entry to the place where the painting is kept or that B will not be guarding the painting. But it would be quite unrealistic to say that if A leaves empty handed because he cannot effect an entry or because B was on guard that he therefore did not intend to steal the painting.

But what if the painting is not in the building at all because B has moved it to another place? Until recently this sort of case caused a problem because of the House of Lords ruling in *Haughton v Smith*[189] that a person could not be convicted of an attempt to commit a crime which was a physical impossibility. This position has been reversed by the Criminal Attempts Act 1981[190] and now a person may be convicted of an attempt even though, in the circumstances, he could not have effected the complete crime. So if A is found in the room where the painting used to hang he may be convicted of attempting to steal it; moreover, in entering the building with intent to steal it he commits the crime of burglary.[191]

A somewhat similar problem arises where A has not yet made up his mind whether and what to steal.[192] Take the case of the rogue, A, whose practice it is to search other people's cars to see whether there is anything that takes his fancy. In B's car he finds nothing at all; in C's car he notices that there is a copy of the Bible but he is not interested in that; in D's car he finds a handbag but having ascertained that the contents (lipstick, handkerchief, nail file) are of no value to him he returns the handbag to its place. In none of these cases can A be convicted of theft since he has stolen nothing. Now that the rule in *Haughton v Smith* has been changed by statute, A may be convicted even though it was impossible for him to commit the completed crime (theft) owing to the fact that there was nothing he was remotely interested in stealing. But there is another matter to consider. A cannot be charged with stealing nothing, nor with attempting to steal nothing. He must be charged with attempting to steal some property belonging to another. Nor can he be properly charged with attempting to steal property which he just does not intend to steal. A cannot be charged with attempting to steal C's Bible or the lipstick from D's handbag because his conduct proves that he had no intent to steal these.

But when A saw the handbag in D's car he no doubt hoped that it would contain money **8–051** and, had it done so, it is certain that he would have taken it. If so, A can be charged with and convicted of attempting to steal money from D. In the other two cases it may be that A had no expectation of finding money, nor did he find anything else that took his fancy. But if A had found something that had taken his fancy he would certainly have taken it, and in such a case it is proper to charge him, as occurred in *Bayley v Easterbrook*,[193] with attempting to steal "property belonging to" B or C without specifying any particular property.

It really boils down to this—if, in the indictment, you charge A with stealing or attempting to steal a specific item of property, you must prove that he actually intended to steal that item. In a case where you are alleging that A has committed the completed offence of theft, you will obviously need to specify the property, alleged to have been stolen, in the indictment. In cases of attempted theft, however, where you are faced with the sort of

[189] [1975] A.C. 476; see above, para.6–015, fn.82 in relation to attempting the impossible.
[190] Above, para.6–013.
[191] See below, para.9–023.
[192] See, e.g. *Easom* [1971] 2 Q.B. 315.
[193] [1980] Crim.L.R. 503.

problem illustrated above in which A has been looking through the boots of cars, the court will allow an indictment which simply alleges that A has attempted to steal property from B. A similar problem occurs in burglary where the accused is charged under s.9(1)(a) of the Theft Act 1968.[194] In this type of burglary the prosecution may have to prove that at the time the accused entered the building he intended to steal property from within. Again it has been held that there is no need to specify particular items of property in the building, nor would it be fatal to the prosecution that the building turned out to be empty.[195]

GENERAL READING

8–052   Arlidge, A. and Parry, J., *Arlidge & Parry on Fraud* 2nd edn, (1996).
Campbell, K., "The Test of Dishonesty In *R v Ghosh*" (1984) 43 C.L.J. 349.
Christie, A.L., "Should the Law of Theft Extend to Information?" (2005) 69 J.C.L. 361.
Clarkson, C.M.V., "Theft And Fair Labelling" (1993) 56 M.L.R. 554.
Cooper, S. and Allen, M.J., "Appropriation After *Gomez*" (1993) 57 J.C.L. 186.
Elliott, D.W., "Dishonesty In Theft: A Dispensable Concept" [1982] Crim.L.R. 395.
Gardner, S, "Property And Theft" [1998] Crim.L.R. 35.
Giles, M. and Uglow, S., "Appropriation And Manifest Criminality In Theft" (1992) 56 J.C.L. 179.
Griew, E., "Dishonesty: Objections To *Feely* And *Ghosh*" [1985] Crim.L.R. 341.
Griew, E., *The Theft Act* (Sweet and Maxwell, 1995).
Halpin, A., "The Test For Dishonesty" [1996] Crim.L.R. 283.
Heaton, R., "Deceiving Without Thieving" [2001] Crim.L.R. 712.
Heaton, R., "Cheques and Balances" [2005] Crim.L.R. 747.
Hickey, R., "Stealing Abandoned Goods: Possessory Title in Proceedings for Theft" (2006) 26 *Legal Studies* 584.
Horder, J., "Thieving And Deceiving: What Is The Difference?" (1993) 56 M.L.R. 548.
Parsons, S., "Dishonest Appropriation after *Gomez* and *Hinks*" (2004) 68 J.C.L. 533.
Smith, A.T.H., *Property Offences* (Sweet and Maxwell, 1994).
Smith, J.C., "*Lister v Stubbs* And The Criminal Law." (1994) 110 L.Q.R. 180.
Smith, J.C., *The Law Of Theft*, (Butterworths, 1997).
Smith, J.C., "Stealing Tickets" [1998] Crim.L.R. 723.
Spencer, J.R., "The Metamorphosis Of Section 6 of The Theft Act" [1977] Crim.L.R. 653.
Sullivan, G.R. and Warbrick, C., "Territoriality, Theft And *Atakpu*" [1994] Crim.L.R. 650.
Williams, G., "Temporary Appropriation Should Be Theft" [1981] Crim.L.R. 129.

[194] See below, para.9–023.
[195] *See Att-Gen's Reference (Nos 1 and 2 of 1979)* [1980] Q.B. 180.

Chapter 9

OFFENCES AGAINST PROPERTY II

FRAUD UNDER THE FRAUD ACT 2006 AND OTHER OFFENCES UNDER THE THEFT ACTS

1. INTRODUCTION

The offence of theft under s.1 of the Theft Act 1968 was originally conceived as applying to **9–001** dishonest non-consensual interference with another's property. The ambit of a counterpart to such an offence would be dishonest interference with another's property which may have had the consent of the other, but where the consent was brought about by some form of false representation or deception. From the coming into force of the 1968 Act, a scheme of offences existed which reflected that structure—theft for non-consensual interference; and a range of so-called "deception offences" for consensual interference. Deficiencies in the 1968 Act led to the enactment of a second Theft Act in 1978, and a menu of deception offences was on offer until relatively recently. As we also know, over the years, the offence of theft colonised behaviours significantly beyond the borders of "non-consensual interference".[1]

The range of deception offences was broad. There were offences of:

- obtaining property by deception (TA 1968 s.15)

- obtaining a pecuniary advantage by deception (TA 1968 s.16)

- procuring the execution of a valuable security by deception (TA 1968 s.20(2))

- obtaining services by deception (TA 1978 s.1)

- evasion of liability by deception (TA 1978 s.2)

A further offence of obtaining a money transfer by deception was created by the Theft (Amendment) Act 1996, and inserted into the 1968 Act as s.15A. This was enacted following the decision of the House of Lords in *Preddy*[2] to the effect that s.15 (obtaining property by deception) could not apply to a situation where D made false representations as to his creditworthiness in order to persuade a mortgage company to lend, because the credit made to D's account on the act of lending was a different "piece" of property from the debit

---

[1] See especially *Gomez* and *Hinks*, above at paras 8–009 and 8–017.
[2] [1996] A.C. 815; [1996] Crim.L.R. 726.

incurred by the mortgage lender, and hence D had not obtained property "belonging to another", as required by s.15.[3]

The proliferation of offences was problematic. Prosecutors had to grapple with the technicalities of the law and could be tripped up if they opted for the wrong charge. There is, of course nothing intrinsically wrong with requiring prosecutors to grapple with law, but what was interesting about the deception offences was that their technical nature, and the overlaps and distinctions between them were not connected to the essential nature of the wrongful conduct which they were regulating. The offences were "over-particularised",[4] even in the face of a strong link between them. What characterised all the offences was the need for a dishonest deception.[5] What differentiated them was the result which was actually *caused* by the deception. But these differences were technical rather than morally significant. What "mattered" about the deception offences was the dishonest interference with another's economic interests.

9–002 This analysis suggests that a general offence of deception might have done the job just as well. But that would still have left problems. It was accepted (not for the first time, and not without reluctance) relatively recently that a deception at law required a human mind to be deceived.[6] This position was more readily suited to a pre-information technology age,[7] but as the prevalence of automated and electronic business grew, and as human minds became progressively less involved on the supply side of individual transactions in contexts such as internet shopping and banking, it became clear that "deception" was no longer a suitable doctrinal focus for understanding and legislating against fraudulent behaviour.

The possibility of change had been a discussion point for many years and did not merely accompany the rise of the information society.[8] The over particularisation problem and the vulnerability of the law to so-called "technical assaults"[9] by unmeritorious defendants diminished the attraction of a list of offences which were unnecessarily adrift from the real essence of the wrong they were designed to deal with. The tide began to turn in favour of a general offence of fraud.[10]

The utility of a general offence to prosecutors was obvious. No longer would they have to worry about getting caught up in and caught out by the web of deception offences. Moreover, the shift of focus away from the technical means by which a fraud was perpetrated or the technical outcome which was sought (which the old law impelled), and onto the fact that it was fraudulent was arguably better in terms of fair labelling. Nonetheless, it would be wrong to uncritically accept the merits of a general fraud offence, and the counter arguments were strong. Most notable is the concern that generality in criminal law leads to over-criminalisation. A general offence might unjustifiably widen the net of the criminal law to cover behaviours which we might find dubious in some respects, but which might not necessarily truly merit a criminal sanction. Generality also militates

---

[3] The 1996 Act also created a new offence of dishonestly retaining a wrongful credit (inserting a new s.24A into the Theft Act 1968), which is still in force.

[4] Law Commission, *Fraud*, (Law Com. No.276, 2002), at paras 3.11 et seq.

[5] This is not a tautology. The notion of an honest deception might apply to a situation where D claims a right to property held by V, and makes a deceptive statement to V in order to persuade V to relinquish it.

[6] See *Re Holmes* [2004] EWCA Crim 2020.

[7] Although there remained practical and philosophical arguments about whether a machine could be deceived.

[8] The Law Commission consulted on conspiracy to defraud as long ago as 1974 (Law Commission Consultation Paper No.56). For discussion of conspiracy to defraud, see para.6–035 above.

[9] Law Commission, *Fraud*, (Law Com. No.276, 2002), at para.3.19.

[10] See Law Commission Consultation Paper No.155, *Legislating the Criminal Code: Fraud and Deception* (1999). This did not advocate a general fraud offence. For discussion, see Ormerod, D., "A Bit of a Con? The Law Commission's Consultation Paper on Fraud" [1999] Crim.L.R. 789–804. The template for the general offence appeared in Law Commission, *Fraud* (Law Com. No.276, 2002), and was taken forward in the Home Office paper *Fraud Law Reform: Consultation on proposals for legislation* (2004).

against fair labelling, by bringing disparate behaviours which may be significantly morally different from one another under the same label (the question of course would be as to what it is that makes behaviours significantly morally different from each other). There was also a constitutional concern, arising from the perceived heavy dependence of a general fraud offence on the concept of dishonesty. (If the offence was general, and not defined according to the technical means of perpetration or the technical outcome brought about then it would have to turn largely on the state of mind of the defendant.) Because dishonesty is a vague term in law, and because factfinders have a key role to play in defining it in any given case[11] the question arises as to whether an offence so reliant on dishonesty will violate art.7 of the European Convention on Human Rights, which requires an appropriate level of certainty in law and prohibits retrospective law-making.

Despite these concerns, the idea of a general fraud offence generated significant traction, and the Fraud Act 2006 received the Royal Assent on November 8, 2006, coming into force on January 15, 2007.

2. THE FRAUD ACT 2006

Whatever the legal and other merits or demerits of the new fraud offence, it is likely that **9–003** this and future generations of law students will be glad that the old offences have, for most purposes, gone. Piecemeal and at its margins approaching impenetrable, the old regime of offences abolished by the 2006 Act will now only need to be used in cases of historic frauds alleged to have been committed prior to the coming into force of the Act are prosecuted.

All the offences referred to in the previous section have been abolished. In their places now stand the general offence of fraud, an offence of obtaining services dishonestly, and a variety of ancillary offences.[12]

A. Fraud

There is a single offence of fraud,[13] which can be committed in three different ways. These **9–004** ways of committing fraud are set out in the subsequent sections:

- fraud by false representation[14];
- fraud by failing to disclose information[15];
- fraud by abuse of position.[16]

Fraud is triable either way, attracting a possible sentence on indictment of ten years' imprisonment (and/or a fine).[17]

Fraud by false representation

This is the form of the offence which probably corresponds most closely (at least in its **9–005** name) to what the public understand by the term "fraud". The offence requires that the defendant makes a false representation, dishonestly and with the intention by making the

---

[11] See *Ghosh* [1982] Q.B. 1053, above at para.8–043
[12] It is worth noting that the offence under s.3 of the Theft Act 1978—making off without payment—has survived the cull. We consider this offence below, at para.9–015.
[13] Fraud Act 2006 s.1.
[14] FA 2006 s.2.
[15] FA 2006 s.3.
[16] FA 2006 s.4.
[17] FA 2006 s.1(3).

representation to make a gain for himself or another or to cause loss to another or to expose another to a risk of loss.

According to s.2(2), a representation is false if it is "untrue or misleading" and "the person making it knows that it is, or might be, untrue or misleading". A representation can be as to fact or law, and as to the state of mind of either the maker or another person,[18] and can be express or implied.[19]

Thus the definition of falsity incorporates a supplementary element of mens rea—knowledge that the representation is or might be untrue or misleading.[20] Neither "untrue" or "misleading" are defined in the Act. The former is, for this purpose (although doubtless not for many philosophical purposes) relatively unproblematic, while the latter may leave some scope for interpretation.

9–006   A representation which is express may be made orally or in writing and through any medium. It makes sense (and indeed, mirrors the old law) that a representation can be implied by conduct. Thus, for example, the decision in *DPP v Ray*,[21] where D ate a meal in a restaurant and left without paying, remains useful, and dining in a restaurant will be taken to be an implied representation of an intention to pay at the appropriate point. Similarly, the presenter of a payment card represents that he or she has the authority to use the card,[22] and activating a self-service pump at a petrol station forecourt should be capable of amounting to a representation that payment will be made for the petrol in due course.[23]

A key departure from the old law on deception is that the representation need not actually "work". It suffices that there is an *intention* to make gain or cause loss through the representation. Under the old law, the deception had to produce a result. Indeed, in *Laverty*[24] it was held that it was crucial for the prosecution to identify the specific representation which it alleged caused the obtaining. D had sold V a stolen car on which he had changed the number plates. The prosecution alleged that V was induced to buy the car because of D's representation by his conduct that this was the original car with those number plates. However, the Court of Appeal held that V bought the car because he thought that the accused was authorised to sell it and that there was no evidence to prove that V would have been in any way influenced by the knowledge of the change of number plates. The deception had to be operative—it had to contribute to the decision-making of the person deceived. Thus, if A and B went to a buffet car on a train, where a bystander suggested that the attendant was selling his own sandwiches and keeping the money, A might take the view that he would only buy an official railway company sandwich whereas B might be ambivalent as to the provenance of the sandwich. If the attendant dishonestly told A and B that the sandwiches were official railway company products when they were in fact his own, and A and B subsequently bought sandwiches, then we might properly say that both had been deceived. However, only in respect of A would the deception be operative, because B would

---

[18] FA 2006 s.2(3).

[19] FA 2006 s.2(4).

[20] It has been suggested that this is potentially confusing for jurors, who may conflate a knowingly false representation with a dishonestly false representation. See Withey, C, "The Fraud Act 2006—Some Early Observations and Comparisons with the Former Law" (2007) 71 J.C.L. 220–237.

[21] [1974] A.C. 370.

[22] See *MPC v Charles* [1977] A.C. 177, discussed in more detail below at para.9–006. In *Gilmartin* [1983] Q.B. 953 the Court of Appeal held that where the accused had written a post-dated cheque he was making a representation that he had no reason to believe that the cheque would not be honoured when presented.

[23] See the discussion in *Coady* [1996] Crim.L.R. 518. Under the old law, problems could arise if the petrol at a self-service station was obtained prior to a deception operating on the mind of the petrol station employee—because then the petrol would not have been obtained by deception. In *Coady*, D put petrol in his car, and then instructed the petrol station worker to charge the petrol to an account which D was in fact no longer authorised to use. Property in the petrol had already been transferred to D by the time the deception took place.

[24] [1970] 3 All E.R. 432.

have bought the sandwich regardless of the deception.[25] The need under the old law to establish a causal link between the deception and the relevant obtaining led the courts on some occasions to strain to find it. Thus, in *MPC v Charles*,[26] the House of Lords suggested that a casino manager's acceptance of cheques guaranteed by a card from a customer who had in fact exceeded the authorisations given by his bank was induced by the customer's implied representation that he had the authority to use the card. There may well have been such a representation, but it is a stretch to claim that that was what induced the acceptance of the cheque. The manager surely accepted the cheque because it was guaranteed by the card and because he knew that as a consequence of the guarantee he would be paid by the bank regardless of the actual state of the customer's relationship with his bank, in respect of which he may quite understandably have been utterly indifferent. The point of guarantee cards was after all to facilitate transactions without the need for sellers and suppliers to inquire specifically into the creditworthiness of purchasers.

Causation and "operativeness" are no longer concerns. Under the 2006 Act the "gain" or "loss" referred to in the fraud offence does not in fact need to occur at all. Subject to mens rea, the offence is complete at the moment the representation is made. "Gain" and "loss" are defined in s.5. Only money or other property (including real or personal property, including things in action and other intangible property) can be gained or lost for these purposes, but gain or loss can be either temporary or permanent. Under s.5(3), gain includes keeping what one has as well as getting what one does not, while loss includes not getting what one might get as well as parting with what one has.

The offence is pertinent to an almost limitless variety of scenarios. The more obvious of **9–007** these include statements made in mortgage or benefit applications, in company prospectuses, and in curricula vitae. Ormerod has suggested that the offence might stray improperly from the obviously fraudulent into what is "merely" the standard (sharp?) practice of salespersonship and trade "patter". He asks whether the normal puffing up of products by sellers risks falling foul of the offence and he questions the role of the doctrine of *caveat emptor*. He notes that certain stereotyped trades including car dealing and estate agency may be particularly at risk.[27] (At the time of writing, banking appears to be a strong candidate for joining that list.) On the issue of excessively sharp business practice, the old law recognised that, at least under certain circumstances, an excessively high quotation for work could amount to a deception, and presumably the same position pertains with the new offence and the requirement of a false representation—the falsity of the representation being constituted through the implication that the quotation is a fair price, when in fact it is not. In *Silverman*,[28] D gave an excessively high quotation for work to be done on property owned by two elderly sisters. It was significant to the finding that this could amount to a deception that

---

[25] A sandwich venture of this nature was the subject of *Rashid* [1977] 2 All E.R. 237. The charge in that case was under s.25 of the Theft Act 1968, i.e. going equipped for stealing etc. It provides: "(a) A person shall be guilty of an offence if, when not at his place of abode, he has with him any article for use in the course of or in connection with any burglary, theft or cheat". (See above at para.9–057.) D was not guilty of the offence because the purchasers were not concerned about the provenance of the sandwiches. Compare *Doukas* [1978] 1 All E.R. 1061, another case under s.25 of the 1968 Act, where a waiter in a hotel sold his own wine instead of the house wine. The Court of Appeal approached the matter by looking at the effect of the deception on the hypothetical ordinary person who is honest and intelligent. They considered whether this hypothetical reasonable person would have bought the wine if he had known the truth; clearly not, thought the court.

[26] [1977] A.C. 177. See also *Lambie* [1981] 1 All E.R. 332.

[27] On one view he is unduly sympathetic to practitioners whose behaviour imperils the economic interests of others in transactions where there is already an asymmetry of knowledge. If there is a problem with certain trades becoming 'suspect communities' then the better target for criticism might be the policing and law enforcement function rather than the substantive law. See Ormerod, D, "The Fraud Act 2006—Criminalising Lying?" [2007] Crim.L.R. 193–219 for a searching critique of the Act.

[28] (1988) 86 Cr.App.R. 213; see also *Jeff and Bassett* (1966) 51 Cr.App.R. 28.

D had worked for the family in the past, and that it was clear that the negotiations had taken place in an atmosphere of trust, of which D had taken advantage.

The Explanatory Notes make clear that "phishing" is a target for the new offence.[29] Phishing is the practice of sending of multiple (often automated) email messages requesting (fraudulently) that the recipients of the messages transfer money to a supposedly worthy beneficiary, or seeking sensitive data from the recipients of the messages (for example, bank account details) to enable the "phishers" to obtain access and remove money from their bank accounts.

The offence is expressly brought into the technological age by s.2(5), which states:

> "(5) For the purposes of this section a representation may be regarded as made if it (or anything implying it) is submitted in any form to any system or device designed to receive, convey or respond to communications (with or without human intervention)."

This, coupled with the completion of the offence at the point of the making of the statement, disposes of the difficulties caused by the requirement under the old law that a human mind by deceived, which created especial difficulties when the deception was practised in the context of a mechanical or automated process (whether that be using a foreign coin in a vending machine, or transferring funds without authorisation via an electronic banking interface).[30] Ormerod suggests that it also has the effect of broadening the offence in the context of electronic communication, because whereas in the context of oral communication the representation does need to actually emanate from the defendant into the world outside his control, in the electronic context it appears to be made at the point at which it is "submitted . . . to any system [etc.] . . . designed to receive, convey or respond to communications". Thus, the fraudster who drafts a phishing email commits the offence while drafting.[31]

The representation must be made dishonestly. There is no equivalent in the 2006 Act of s.2 of the Theft Act 1968 (setting out a partial definition of dishonesty) and so the entire content of dishonesty for the purposes of fraud is determined by the decision in *Ghosh*.[32] Under the *Ghosh* test, which is discussed extensively above in the context of theft, a defendant will be dishonest if (a) his conduct would be regarded as dishonest by ordinary decent people and (b) he is aware that it would be so regarded.

Fraud by failing to disclose information

9–008   The absolute extent to which silence can constitute a representation for the purposes of s.2 is not clear. Many instances of "silence" will in fact amount to representations which can be implied from conduct, but there may conceivably be situations where a defendant makes a representation which is true at the time it is made, but which subsequently becomes false. Does any failure to correct the now false representation itself constitute a representation for the purposes of s.2? The answer is not clear.

However, s.3 of the 2006 Act provides for the possibility of "fraud by silence" in a limited range of situations (and it might be thought that the express (limited) provision in s.3 makes it inappropriate to develop a further (broader) route via s.2). The s.3 offence is committed by a defendant who "dishonestly"[33] fails to disclose to another person information which he

---

[29] At para.16.
[30] See, e.g. *Re Holmes*, above at para.9–002, fn.6.
[31] See Ormerod, D, "The Fraud Act 2006—Criminalising Lying?" [2007] Crim.L.R. 193 at 200.
[32] [1982] Q.B. 1053. See above at para.8–043.
[33] See *Ghosh* [1982] Q.B. 1053, discussed above.

is under a legal duty to disclose" and who intends by that failure to intend to make a gain or cause a loss.[34]

The notion of a legal duty is not defined in the Act, and the Explanatory Notes direct us back to the Law Commission Report, in which it is suggested:

". . . [s]uch a duty may derive from statute (such as the provisions governing company prospectuses), . . . from the fact that the transaction in question is one of the utmost good faith (such as a contract of insurance), from the express or implied terms of a contract, from the custom of a particular trade or market, or from the existence of a fiduciary relationship between the parties (such as that of agent and principal). . . . [T]here is a legal duty to disclose information not only if the defendant's failure to disclose it gives the victim a cause of action for damages, but also if the law gives the victim a right to set aside any change in his or her legal position to which he or she may consent as a result of the non-disclosure. For example, a person in a fiduciary position has a duty to disclose material information when entering into a contract with his or her beneficiary, in the sense that a failure to make such disclosure will entitle the beneficiary to rescind the contract and to reclaim any property transferred under it.[35]

There is a degree of overlap between ss.3 and 2. For example, is a failure to disclose as **9–009** requested on an application form one's adverse disciplinary record in a previous job a failure to disclose under s.3 or is the putting together of the form without this information a false representation under s.2? The answer is probably both.

This is also an area in which judges in criminal cases will need to be sufficiently conversant with issues of private law (property and contract) in order to be able to determine whether the case before them is one where a duty to disclose actually exists.

Fraud by abuse of position

A potentially very broad version of fraud is created by s.4. It applies to a person who **9–010** "occupies a position in which he is expected to safeguard, or not to act against, the financial interests of another person". The defendant who occupies such a position commits the offence if he "dishonestly[36] abuses that position" and intends by so doing, to make a gain or cause a loss.[37]

The offence can be committed by omission as well as by a positive act, and would appear to be capable of being invoked in a very broad range of relationships.[38] The Explanatory Notes refer to the defendant who "has been put in a privileged position" and who must therefore safeguard, etc. the other's financial interests.[39] It most obviously has the potential to apply in professional-client relationships, but the type of relationship countenanced by the offence will also arise, for example, between director and company, and between employee and employer. The Law Commission also suggested that it would be possible for the type of relationship to arise "within a family, or in the context of voluntary work, or in any context where the parties are not at arm's length".[40]

---

[34] As with s.2, read with s.5.
[35] Law Commission, *Fraud* (Law Com. No.276, 2002).
[36] See *Ghosh* [1982] Q.B. 1053, discussed above.
[37] As with s.2, read with s.5.
[38] "Position" is not defined in the statute, and is only elaborated upon within s.4 itself.
[39] At para.20.
[40] Law Commission, *Fraud*, (Law Com. No.276, 2002), at para.7.38. A situation such as that in *Silverman* (1988) 86 Cr.App.R. 213 (see above at para.9–007), where a business-consumer transaction takes place against the background of an ongoing relationship of trust developed over a history of such transactions, might be such a context.

The examples cited in the Explanatory Notes include the employee of a software company who clones software products and sells them on privately; and the employed carer who abuses their access to their client's bank account. The offence has an almost boundless sphere of potential application—whether the behaviour of an employee who "fails to take up the chance of a crucial contract in order that an associate or rival company can take it up instead at the expense of the employer"[41] is properly the object of the criminal law at all is questionable—even though the employee-employer relationship clearly has fiduciary qualities. The boundaries of the offence will ultimately be determined by judicial interpretation in those relationships where it is not absolutely clear whether the defendant occupies a relevant position.

B. Obtaining services dishonestly

9–011   The offence in s.11 of the Fraud Act 2006 of obtaining services dishonestly replaces the offence under s.1 of the Theft Act 1978 of obtaining services by deception.

The offence is committed by the defendant who by a dishonest[42] act[43] obtains services which "are made available on the basis that payment has been, is being or will be made for or in respect of them", "without any payment having been made for or in respect of them or without payment having been made in full". It is necessary to prove that when the defendant obtains the services, he knows that the services are or might be being made available for payment and that he "intends that payment will not be made, or will not be made in full".

The offence is triable either way and the maximum punishment on indictment is five years' imprisonment and/or a fine.

The offence, like fraud, does not require the deception of a human mind and so can be committed through interaction with an automated process. However, it does require that a service actually be obtained (unlike fraud, where the "gain" or "loss" need not actually occur).

9–012   The Explanatory Notes resurrect the rather hoary example of climbing over a wall to watch a football match for which other spectators have paid an entrance fee.[44] Hoary it may be, but it does clearly illustrate the utility of the new offence. Under the old law it would not be possible to charge obtaining services by deception, because there is no deception. The offence under s.11 focuses on the dishonest acquisition of the services, which may or may not be brought about by deception. A further example given is of the defendant who attaches a decoder to their television to access subscription services such as satellite channels.[45]

Another contemporary example referred to in the Explanatory Notes is of the person dishonestly using false credit card details to access some form of service over the internet (the "humanless" transaction driving so much of the reform in this area). However, as Ormerod suggests, the drafting of s.11 may have gone awry here.[46] The difficulty is that the offence requires that the services be obtained "without any payment having been made for or in respect of them or without payment having been made in full".[47] However the service

---

[41] Explanatory Notes, at para.21.
[42] See *Ghosh* [1982] Q.B. 1053, discussed above.
[43] FA 2006 s.11(1)(a). The use of the word "act" would suggest that the offence cannot be committed by omission, and this is the position countenanced by the Explanatory Notes (at para.34).
[44] At para.35.
[45] Explanatory Notes, at para.36.
[46] Ormerod, D., "Letter to the Editor" [2007] Crim.L.R. 662–664.
[47] FA 2006 s.11(2)(b).

is obtained precisely because payment *is* made—by the card issuer. Ormerod suggests that such behaviour would nonetheless be caught by s.2 (fraud by false representation) on the basis that the defendant intends to expose the card issuer to a risk of loss of a nature which would be covered by s.5 (a loss of property—in this case money).[48] Notice that the service itself is not "property" for the purpose of s.5 and hence could not be the proper basis of a fraud charge.[49]

C. Ancillary offences under the Act

Section 6 creates an offence of possession, etc., of articles for use in frauds. It is intended to **9–013** be modelled on the offence of "going equipped" under s.25 of the Theft Act 1968.[50] No mens rea is actually stated for the offence but the Explanatory Notes suggest that the way forward is by analogy with the decision in *Ellames*[51] in the context of going equipped, which, if transposed to the s.6 offence would require that the articles be possessed with a *general* intention to commit fraud; it would not need to be proved that a specific fraud was countenanced.[52] This is supported by the reference to "any fraud" in s.6(1). Ormerod wonders why mens rea could not have been written explicitly into the provision and notes that if construed very literally anybody knowingly in possession[53] of a pen or paper falls within its ambit.[54]

The s.6 offence is triable either way and the maximum sentence on indictment is five years' imprisonment and/or a fine.

Section 7 creates an offence of making or supplying articles for use in frauds. It is committed by a defendant who "makes, adapts, supplies or offers to supply any article", "knowing that it is designed or adapted for use in the course of or in connection with fraud", or "intending it to be used to commit, or assist in the commission of, fraud".

Again, this is potentially a very broad offence and it should be noted that there are two **9–014** forms of mens rea: knowledge and intention. Each of those forms of mens rea attaches to slightly different object. Thus, "knowledge" must be as to the design or adaptation of the article for use in the course of or in connection with fraud, whereas intention is as to the article's use to commit or assist in fraud. Ormerod captures one implication of the distinction by noting that:

> "articles used only preparatory to the commission of the fraud or after the commission of the fraud may be articles connected with fraud, but are not articles used to commit the offence or assist in its commission".[55]

The s.7 offence is triable either way and the maximum sentence on indictment is ten years' imprisonment and/or a fine.

Both ss.6 and 7 are supported by s.8 which states that "article" includes any program or data held in electronic form.

---

[48] Ormerod, D., "Letter to the Editor" [2007] Crim.L.R. 662–664.
[49] Ormerod, D., "Letter to the Editor" [2007] Crim.L.R. 662–664.
[50] See below, para.9–057.
[51] [1974] 3 All E.R. 130; [1974] 1 W.L.R. 1391; 60 Cr.App.R. 7.
[52] See Explanatory Notes, at para.25.
[53] Possession requires that the defendant knows that he is in possession of an item. Difficulties have arisen elsewhere in the law where there has been a question as to whether the defendant knew specifically what he was in possession of: see, e.g. *Warner v Metropolitan Police Commissioner* [1969] 2 A.C. 256. See above, at para.3–007.
[54] See Ormerod, D., "The Fraud Act 2006—Criminalising Lying?" [2007] Crim.L.R. 193 at 211.
[55] See Ormerod, D., "The Fraud Act 2006—Criminalising Lying?" [2007] Crim.L.R. 193 at 213.

Section 9 creates on offence of knowing participation in fraudulent business where the business is not carried out by a company (an offence already exists to cover the situation where the business is carried out by a company[56]). The business must be carried on "with intent to defraud creditors of any person or for any other fraudulent purpose" and the maximum sentence on indictment is ten years' imprisonment and/or a fine.

MAKING OFF WITHOUT PAYMENT

9–015   Before the Theft Act 1978 came into effect there was a common, and quickly growing, fraud for which the 1968 Act made inadequate provision. The fraud was simplicity itself and consisted merely in making off without paying for goods or services provided. Typical examples are provided by the motorist who, having filled up his tank with petrol, drives away without paying;[57] or by the customer who, having consumed a meal in a restaurant, runs off without settling his bill; conduct referred to as "bilking". If the goods or services are obtained by deception there will usually be an offence under s.15 of the 1968 Act or under s.1 of the 1978 Act (formerly there may have been an offence under s.16(2)(a) of the 1968 Act), but if no deception is made before the goods are obtained or the service provided then these provisions are inapplicable.

On the other hand the law does not in general make it an offence for a debtor dishonestly to resolve not to pay his debts. It is not an offence dishonestly to resolve not to pay the quarterly gas or electricity bill. But since the gas and electricity board know with whom they are dealing, they can be left to pursue their civil remedies and there is no need to make a crime of such conduct. Moreover, if such conduct was made criminal there is a real danger that people who cannot pay, as opposed to those who will not pay, would find themselves in the criminal courts.

Section 3 is accordingly not aimed at dishonest debtors in general but at the kind of debtor who, if he cannot be brought to book on the spot, may never be traced and made to pay. Hence the offence of making off is made an arrestable one because without a power of arrest it would, as a practical matter, be impossible to give effect to the section. However, unlike the power of arrest conferred in the case of arrestable offences, s.3(4) does not permit the arrest of a person who has already completed the offence under s.3.[58]

Section 3 provides:

"(1) Subject to subsection (3) below, a person who, knowing that payment on the spot for any goods supplied or service done is required or expected from him, dishonestly makes off without having paid as required or expected and with intent to avoid payment of the amount due shall be guilty of an offence.

(2) For purposes of this section 'payment on the spot' includes payment of the time of collecting the goods on which work has been done or in respect of which service has been provided.

(3) Subsection (1) above shall not apply where the supply of the goods or the doing of the service is contrary to law, or where the service done is such that payment is not legally enforceable."

---

[56] See Companies Act 1985 s.458.
[57] See *Coady*, above, para.9–006, fn.23.
[58] See *Drameh* [1983] Crim.L.R. 322.

It is noteworthy that s.3(1) does not impose a requirement of a deception in the **9–016** constituents of the offence; it suffices that D dishonestly makes off without payment. The offence is subject to a maximum punishment of up to two years on indictment, and on summary conviction up to a six months' imprisonment and/or a fine not exceeding £5,000.[59]

The issue under review in the recent case of *Vincent*[60] was whether an agreement that payment would be made later defeated the expectation that payment would be made "on the spot". The defendant stayed at two hotels in Windsor, and left without paying the hotels' bills, save that he made a part-payment to one hotel. He was charged with making off without payment, contrary to s.3(1) of the Theft Act 1978. His contention was that, in both cases, he had discussed with the hotel proprietor as to when payment would be made and had claimed to be waiting for money due to him. Thus, he had made an arrangement with the hotel proprietor that he would pay when he could, and he was not asked to pay on leaving the hotel. The trial judge, however, directed the jury that a genuine agreement in good faith on both sides to postpone payment would mean that payment on the spot was not required or expected, but that was not the case if the agreement to postpone payment was a result of the defendant's dishonesty. The defendant was convicted and appealed.

The Court of Appeal in *Vincent* determined that the appeal should be allowed. It was held that an agreement made before the time when payment would normally be expected was capable of defeating the expectation of an "on the spot" payment. In such circumstances it was irrelevant that the agreement was dishonestly obtained by the defendant's deception. The section did not permit or require an analysis of whether the agreement actually made was obtained by deception; it did not contemplate what could be a complex investigation of alleged fraud underlying the agreement. The outcome is consequently an affirmation of Parliament's stated intention that making off without payment be a relatively straightforward offence. There were at the time a multiplicity of other theft offences, assuming the defendant's dishonesty, which might cogently have been brought by the prosecution. D, by continuing to stay at the hotel, once he had formed a dishonest intention of not paying the full bill, would appear to have been guilty of obtaining services by deception, contrary to s.1 of the Theft Act 1978 (see *DPP v Ray*[61] involving a continuing representation by conduct of an initial statement of an intention to pay). Additionally, if Vincent intended to make a payment default in payment, then he could have been guilty of evasion of liability, contrary to s.2(1)(b) of the Theft Act 1968, in that he dishonestly by deception induced the hotel proprietor to wait for payment. If the services that Vincent obtained were to include the serving to him of food or drink, then he would presumptively also have been guilty of obtaining property by deception, contrary to s.15 of the Theft Act 1968. This plethora of other offence possibilities reveal the importance of s.3 of the Theft Act remaining applicable only in straightforward cases as was intended by the import of the legislation.

Again we can examine the working of the offence by reference to some hypothetical **9–017** examples:

(i) A eats a meal in a restaurant fully intending to pay. At the end of the meal he discovers that he has come out without any means of paying and so he simply runs out intending to avoid payment. Before the Theft Act 1978 the prosecution would have had to discover some deception on A's part which enabled him to make his escape.[62] Under s.3 no such mental gymnastics are required. The prosecution must prove that the accused knew that payment on the spot was required. It is clear that people eating in a restaurant will

---

[59] See s.4(3).
[60] [2001] Crim.L.R. 488.
[61] [1974] A.C. 370; see above, at para.9–006.
[62] As in *DPP v Ray*, above, para.9–006.

expect to pay before they leave. Even if they expect to arrange for credit or to use a credit card, this will clearly be covered by the section as long as the customer knows that he must make some deal with the restaurant owner before he leaves. Secondly, the prosecutor must prove that the accused made off from that spot. The nature of where payment is expected or required has been considered in a trio of cases where individuals decamped, or tried to do so, from restaurants and subsequent to a taxi journey. In *McDavitt*[63] the court held that the "spot" was constituted by the restaurant itself; although the exact location will depend upon the circumstances of each case. In moving towards the door intending to decamp without paying, D had taken more than merely preparatory steps towards the commission of the full substantive offence. In another restaurant case, that of *Brooks and Brooks*,[64] the appellate court implicitly treated the "spot" as being embodied by the actual cash point rather than the restaurant itself. In vivid language the court referred to making off from that spot as an exercise which may be "accompanied by the sound of trumpets or a silent stealing away after the folding of tents".[65] In *Aziz*,[66] a dispute arose at the conclusion of a lengthy taxi journey. The passenger had reached his agreed destination, contrary to *Troughton*,[67] but refused to pay. The aggrieved taxi driver headed back towards the police station, but D alighted from the vehicle and tried to decamp. It was held that it was for the jury to say on the evidence whether the offence was made out; expectation of payment of the fare was a continuing one throughout the agreed journey, and thus it seems that the concept of "spot" was a vacillating one. What will constitute making off will depend upon the facts of the individual case; but there will be no difficulty in holding that a person who runs out of a restaurant without paying has "made off". Thirdly, the prosecutor must establish that the accused was dishonest, and fourthly that in making off he did so *with intent to avoid payment*. This last phrase is somewhat ambiguous. It could be interpreted to mean that it was sufficient that the accused intended not to pay when expected or it could mean that the prosecutor must establish that the accused intended never to pay. In *Allen*[68] the House of Lords held that this ambiguity should be resolved in favour of the defendant; no offence shall be committed unless the prosecutor proves that the accused intended never to pay.

From a practical point of view it may be easier to use this offence even where you suspect that the accused intended to avoid payment even before he ate the meal. Technically, he should be charged with fraud which carries a much higher penalty. On the other hand where it is obvious that no use will be made of this greater sentencing power, it may well prove attractive to the prosecution to avoid the need to prove that there was a fraudulent intention from the outset. Similarly where the accused drives off from a petrol station without having paid, he may well have committed offences of theft, fraud and making off, but the prosecution may well settle for the making off charge.

(ii) G pays for a repair to his car with a cheque which he knows will be dishonoured when presented. The garage owner, however, is quite happy and hands G the keys to the car and G leaves intending never to pay. The issue raised by this example is whether the concept of "making off" is satisfied when the accused leaves with the consent of a person who has been tricked into thinking that he has been paid or does "making off" cover only those cases where the accused leaves without the consent of the victim. This point has not yet been settled by the courts. It is submitted that the offence ought to be committed even when the

[63] [1981] Crim.L.R. 843.
[64] [1982] 76 Cr.App.R. 66.
[65] [1982] 76 Cr.App.R. 66 at 69 per Kilner Brown J.
[66] [1993] Crim.L.R. 708.
[67] [1987] Crim.L.R. 138; see below, para.9–018.
[68] [1985] A.C. 1029.

defendant leaves with the victim's acquiescence, but the analysis in *Vincent* runs contrary to this proposition.

(iii) X travels each evening between Leeds and Menston on a local pay train (on such **9–018** trains the guard issues tickets in the same way that tickets are issued on buses, there being no station staff to collect such tickets at local stops such as Menston). One evening the train is particularly full and the guard has not reached X by the time the train reaches Menston. X gets out of the train and walks off without paying.

This may seen an obvious example of an offence under s.3, but is it? He clearly makes off without paying (would hiding in the toilet constitute a making off?); a service has been provided for him and payment on the spot was expected. However, the section requires that the accused should have acted dishonestly and with intent to avoid payment. You will recall that the word "dishonestly" is a question of fact for the jury[69]; they will have to consider whether people in general would regard such conduct as dishonest and, if so, whether the defendant knew that this conduct would be so regarded by people in general. It is therefore quite on the cards that a jury would not find the accused to have acted dishonestly. Further it is rather hard to say that he made off with the intention of avoiding payment. Experience may have taught him that it is not advisable to stay on the train to look for the guard since the train will probably move on as soon as other passengers have dismounted. Clearly if he gets off at an earlier station because he sees that the guard will reach him before the train gets to Menston then it will be possible to say that he has dishonestly made off with intent to avoid payment. This may also be the position if, when he alights from the train at Menston, he sees the guard standing on the platform ready to receive fares from those who have not yet paid and then deliberately avoids taking the opportunity to pay. This problem clearly raises issues as to the duties owed by persons travelling on buses or such pay trains; is there a duty to seek out the fare-collector? Considerations such as these will affect how the jury tackles the requirements of dishonesty.

(iv) X has just had intercourse with a prostitute who now requires payment. X simply walks off saying, "Take me to court and try to get your money." There is no difference in principle between this example and that in number (i). However, s.3(3) provides that if the supply of goods or the doing of the service is contrary to law, or if the service done is such that payment is not legally enforceable, then the offence is not committed. Here the prostitute would not be able to sue X to recover damages for breach of contract and so X commits no offence when he walks off. Thus, in *Troughton*,[70] where the defendant had allegedly made off without paying a taxi fare, it was fatal to the prosecutor's case that the taxi driver had broken his contract by not taking the accused to the desired destination.[71] In those circumstances he was in no position to demand payment on the spot. However, if from the outset X and Troughton intended not to pay, they would probably commit the offence of fraud.

GENERAL READING

Elliott, D.W., "Director's Thefts And Dishonesty" [1991] Crim.L.R. 732.   **9–019**
Griew, E., "Theft And Obtaining By Deception" [1979] Crim.L.R. 292.
Holroyd, J., "Reform of Fraud Law Comes Closer: Fraud Bill 2005" (2005) 69 J.C.L. 507.
Kirk, D., "Fraud Trials: A Brave New World" (2005) 69 J.C.L. 513.

[69] See above, para.8–043.
[70] [1987] Crim.L.R. 138.
[71] Contrast *Aziz* [1993] Crim.L.R. 708, above, para.9–017.

Ormerod, D., "A Bit Of A Con? The Law Commission's Consultation Paper On Fraud" [1999] Crim.L.R. 789.

Ormerod, D., "The Fraud Act 2006—Criminalising Lying?" [2007] Crim.L.R. 193.

Palfrey, T., "Is Fraud Dishonest? Parallel Proceedings And The Role of Dishonesty" (2000) 64 J.C.L. 518.

Parsons, S., "Mortgage Fraud And The Law Of Theft" (1999) 63 J.C.L. 474.

Smith, A.T.H., "The Idea Of Criminal Deception" [1982] Crim.L.R. 721.

Smith, J.C., "Obtaining Cheques By Deception Or Theft" [1997] Crim.L.R. 396.

Sullivan, G.R., "Fraud—The Latest Law Commission Proposals" (2003) 67 J.C.L. 139.

Thompson, M.P., "Is Mortgage Fraud A Crime?" [1996] 60 Conv. 441.

White, S., "Continuing Representations In The Criminal Law" (1986) 37 N.I.L.Q. 255.

Wilson, S., "Collaring the Crime and the Criminal?: 'Jury Psychology' and Some Criminological Perspectives on Fraud and the Criminal Law" (2006) 70 J.C.L. 75.

Withey, C., "The Fraud Act 2006—Some Early Observations and Comparisons with the Former Law" (2007) 71 J.C.L. 220.

ROBBERY

9–020   Section 8 of the Theft Act 1968 provides:

"(1) A person is guilty of robbery if he steals, and immediately before or at the time of doing so, and in order to do so, he uses force on any person or puts or seeks to put any person in fear of being then and there subjected to force.

(2) A person guilty of robbery, or of an assault with intent to rob, shall on conviction on indictment be liable to imprisonment for life."

In order to succeed on a charge of robbery the prosecution must establish (a) that the property was stolen; and (b) that the stealing of it was accomplished by force. The Court of Appeal in *Forrester*[72] surprisingly remarked that it was an open question whether in referring to "steal" in s.8 the drafters had meant to incorporate the definition of theft (ss.1–6) into the crime of robbery. It is suggested that there is no doubt that steal in s.8 should be interpreted in accordance with ss.1–6 of the Act. Thus, all the defences open to one charged with theft are open on a charge of robbery. If the jury believe that the accused honestly thought that he had the right to take the property they must acquit him of theft, and therefore of robbery. In *Robinson*[73] the accused was owed £7 by I's wife. The prosecution alleged that R and two others approached I in the street and that R was brandishing a knife. In the course of a fight which followed, I dropped a £5 note. R picked it up and asked for the remaining £2 he was owed. The judge directed the jury that for a defence under s.2(1) of the Theft Act the accused should honestly believe he had the right to take the money in the way he did. His appeal against conviction for robbery was allowed by the Court of Appeal. The prosecution had to establish the basic offence of theft and it would be a defence to that charge that the accused honestly believed he had a right in law to deprive I of the money, even if he knew he was not entitled to use a knife to get it. If the prosecution failed to prove theft, then an indictment for robbery must also fail, because robbery is an aggravated form of theft.

---

[72] [1992] Crim.L.R. 792.
[73] [1977] Crim.L.R. 173.

What then turns an act of theft into one of robbery? In the first place the prosecution must prove that in order to steal the accused used force on any person or sought to put any person in fear of such force being then and there used on him. As stated by the Divisional Court in *R v DPP*[74] it is not incumbent upon the prosecution to demonstrate that V was put in fear through D's actions, but it is necessary to show that there was an apprehension on the part of V that force would be used.

It is important to note that the section does not say that the force or threat has to be used **9–021** on the person from whom the property is stolen. It can be used on any person provided that it is used "in order to steal". Thus if the accused sees Mr and Mrs A walking along the street, it would be robbery if he knocked Mr A unconscious and snatched Mrs A's handbag. It is not sufficient that the defendant has simply taken advantage of a victim by stealing, when the victim has been rendered powerless by others without any complicity on the part of the defendant.[75] The prosecution must, however, establish that the force was used against a person, and not just against the property, though very slight force will suffice. It is enough to constitute robbery that there is a struggle for possession of the goods and that A pulls them from B's hands. It will be recalled, for example, that in *Corcoran v Anderton*[76] it was held that a robbery had occurred where the defendant's conduct involved tugging a handbag from the victim's grasp, although he then dropped it and decamped. An appropriation had transpired through the defendant taking hold of the handbag. In *Clouden*[77] the defendant followed a woman and then, coming up behind her, grabbed the shopping bag which she was carrying in her left hand. He wrenched it from her grasp. Before the Theft Act 1968 the prosecution would have had to prove not merely that the force was used to gain possession of the goods, but that it was used to overpower the victim and prevent resistance. It is clear that the drafters of the Act intended to preserve this distinction. However, the Court of Appeal said that the trial judge should not concern himself with these distinctions of the old law, but should direct the jury's attention to the wording of s.8. Whether or not the defendant used force on any person in order to steal was an issue for the jury. This approach had been adopted in *Dawson* where the judge had left it to the jury to decide whether jostling to an extent which caused a person to have difficulty in keeping his balance amounted to the use of force. The defendant had nudged V and whilst he was thus unbalanced another stole his wallet. It is possible, on facts such as those in *Clouden*, where the defendant had grabbed a bag which was strapped around V's shoulder, to say that the force needed to break the strap will also constitute force applied to V's body, but it is surely more akin to pickpocketing than robbery. It can be effectively dealt with by the offence of theft, not robbery, with theft itself subject to a maximum punishment of seven years' imprisonment.

The Act, says that the force or threat of force must be used immediately before or at the time of stealing, and this raises difficult problems of fact and degree.[78] What does the Act mean by immediately before? If a gang intend to break into a factory and one of the gang knocks out the nightwatchman before the main part of the gang break in to steal, this would be robbery. If, on the other hand, they were to threaten the nightwatchman with a beating up if he did not draw them a plan of the factory so that they could steal from it a week later,

---

[74] [2007] EWHC 739 (Admin).
[75] See, e.g. *Harris* (1987) 84 Cr.App.R. 75.
[76] (1980) 71 Cr.App.R. 104; see above, para.8–005.
[77] [1987] Crim.L.R. 56; confirming *Dawson* [1976] Crim.L.R. 692.
[78] An illustration of this dilemma is provided by *Donaghy* [1981] Crim.L.R. 644. D demanded that V, a taxidriver, take him from Newmarket to London. Threats were made against V's life, and once the London destination was reached D stole £22 from V. It was determined, rather surprisingly, that since the threats had not been made *in order* to steal the money this meant that the offence of robbery had not been made out.

this would not be robbery since force or threat of force was not used immediately before the stealing. An interesting case in this regard is the pre-Act decision of *Smith v Desmond*.[79] D attacked a nightwatchman and maintenance engineer in a bakery and then stole from the cash office some distance from the bakery. It was held by the House of Lords that the offence of robbery had been committed. Force had been used on individuals who had property stolen from their immediate care and protection.

At the other end of the time-span, the Act says that the force must be used (immediately before or) at the time of the stealing. Here it is important to remember the other qualification that the force or threat must be used in order to steal. A strict interpretation would mean that once the theft is complete, in the sense that the accused could be charged with the substantive offence of theft, the use of force will not turn the crime into an offence of robbery. For example, if X is a pickpocket and has got his hands round Y's wallet and is in the process of removing it from Y, we have said that since he has now assumed rights of an owner over (i.e. appropriated) the wallet, the offence of theft is complete even though he has not yet removed it totally from Y. If Y now realises what is being done, resists and is hit in the stomach by X, does this mean that it is not robbery because the force is used after X has stolen the wallet? Could one argue that since the theft was complete the force was not used "in order to steal?" Clearly, the words must be given a wider meaning than "up to the time when there is a completed act of appropriation". Similar problems arise in handling[80] where the phrase "otherwise than in the course of stealing" appears and presumably a uniform answer should be given. It must be robbery when the accused uses force on the victim to enable him to get the wallet out of his control, or to get the goods off the premises in a bank raid (see *Hale* below). Even though there is already a completed act of theft when the accused appropriated the property, it would probably still be robbery if X hit Y to stop him immediately recovering the wallet, and the House of Lords decision in *Gomez* on appropriation does not affect the principle that appropriation is a continuing act.[81] On the other hand, if X has got hold of Y's wallet and is running down the street when he is stopped by police officer Z, force now used on police officer Z would be after the commission of the theft and would not turn the offence into robbery. "At the time of" committing the theft must be viewed in a commonsense way; the test is whether X can sensibly be said to be stealing the goods when the force is used on Y.

The above proposition is illustrated by the case of *Hale*[82] on the continuing nature of appropriation. The defendants had entered V's house wearing stocking masks. One of them put his hand over V's mouth to stop her screaming whilst the other went upstairs, returned carrying a jewellery box, and tied V up before leaving. Appropriation was determined to be a continuing act. The jury were entitled to find D guilty of robbery relying on the force used by him when he put his hand over V's mouth to restrain her from calling for help. Eveleigh L.J. stated:

> "It is conduct which usurps the rights of an owner. To say that that conduct is over and done with as soon as he lays hands upon the property, or when he first manifests an intention to deal with it as his, is contrary to common-sense and to the natural

---

[79] [1965] A.C. 960. Note this widened the existing common law position in that previously the theft had to be from the person or in the presence of the victim. By s.8 of the Theft Act it is clear that force may be used against *any* person.

[80] See below, para.9–037.

[81] Above, para.8–009; see, e.g. *Lockley* [1995] 2 Cr.App.R. 554.

[82] (1978) 68 Cr.App.R. 415.

meaning of words. A thief who steals a motor car first opens the door. Is it to be said that the act of starting up the motor is no more a part of the theft? In the present case there can be little doubt that if the appellant had been interrupted after the seizure of the jewellery box the jury would have been entitled to find that the appellant and his accomplice were assuming the rights of an owner at the time when the jewellery box was seized. However, the act of appropriation does not suddenly cease. It is a continuous act and it is a matter for the jury to decide whether or not the appropriation has finished."[83]

SUMMARY

1. The word "force" was preferred in the Theft Act 1968 to "violence" (applied in **9–022** the 1916 Larceny Act). Force signifies any exercise of physical strength and has a wide interpretation.

2. By s.8 of the Theft Act 1968 it is necessary that force or the threat of force be used *in order to* steal.

3. It is not robbery where D has a claim of right to the property which he takes by force even if he appreciates that he has no right to use force (see *Robinson*, 1977).

4. It is a matter for the jury to determine whether the act of appropriation has finished (see *Hale*, 1978).

5. It is a question of fact for the jury as to what amounts to force (see *Dawson*, 1976).

6. To use force when theft has been, but is no longer being, committed, for example, in order to escape, does not constitute robbery.

BURGLARY

Burglary is traditionally thought of as breaking and entering a dwelling house in the night **9–023** with intent to steal. It was once so defined and separate provision was made for less serious entries where the building was entered by day or where buildings other than dwelling houses were entered. All these distinctions have been swept away by s.9 of the Theft Act 1968.

Burglary can now be committed in buildings generally, and nothing turns upon whether the entry, for there is no longer any requirement for a breaking, was during the day or night except that the more alarm the burglars cause the heavier the eventual sentence they may receive. However, the maximum sentence that is available will depend on the type of building that the defendant enters. By s.26 of the Criminal Justice Act 1991 new subss.(3) and (4) were added to s.9 of the Theft Act 1968. By these amendments a two division system was created. Higher penalties apply if the building burgled is a "dwelling"[84] which is subject to a maximum penalty of fourteen years imprisonment, whereas for any other building it is limited to ten years imprisonment. The relevant substantive provisions provide as follows:

---

[83] (1978) 68 Cr.App.R. 415 at 418.
[84] This is on the basis of the greater level of personal victimisation that can be experienced by victims of this type of burglary. See *Lees* [2007] EWCA Crim 1640 on new properties and the meaning of a dwelling.

"(1) A person is guilty of burglary if —

    (a) he enters a building or part of a building as a trespasser and with intent to commit any such offence as is mentioned in subsection (2) below.

    (b) having entered any building or part of a building as a trespasser he steals or attempts to steal anything in the building or that part of it or inflicts or attempts to inflict on any person therein any grievous bodily harm.

(2) The offences referred to in subsection (1)(a) above are offences of stealing anything in the building or part of a building in question, of inflicting on any person therein any grievous bodily harm, and of doing unlawful damage to the building or anything therein.

(3) References in subsections (1) and (2) above to a building shall apply also to an inhabited vehicle or vessel and shall apply to any such vehicle or vessel at the times when a person having a habitation in it is not there as well as at times when he is.

(4) A person guilty of burglary shall on conviction on indictment be liable to imprisonment for a term not exceeding fourteen years."

Burglary is, in effect, a form of aggravated trespass. There are two different types of burglary under s.9(1)(a) and s.9(1)(b).[85] They share a common feature that the prosecution have to prove that the accused has entered a building (or part of the building) either knowing, or being reckless as to the fact that, he is a trespasser. If the charge is brought under s.9(1)(a) the prosecution must, in addition, prove that at the time he entered the building the accused intended (and here recklessness will not suffice) to commit one of the offences specified in s.9(2) which are listed above. There must be an ulterior intent to commit one of the three specified offences. It is noteworthy that the offence of entering a building with intent to commit rape was repealed by the Sexual Offences Act 2003 Sch.7 para.1. It has been replaced by new legislation contained within s.63 of that Act introducing a much wider offence of trespass with intent to commit a sexual offence.[86] If the charge is brought under s.9(1)(b) of the Theft Act 1968 the accused must be shown to have actually committed one of the offences specified in para.(b) and at the time of committing the offence he either knew that he entered as a trespasser or was reckless as to that fact.

In summary, it must be shown that D, either:

    (1) entered as a trespasser with the ulterior intent to commit one of the following offences:

        (a) stealing;

        (b) inflicting grievous bodily harm;

        (c) unlawful damage to the building or anything therein.

    [This constitutes the s.9(1)(a) form of burglary.]

---

[85] Note that in *Hollis* [1971] Crim.L.R 525 it was considered that on an indictment for one category of burglary there could not be a conviction for the other. However the s.9(1)(b) variety incorporates the s.9(1)(a) variety where D is charged with entering with intent to steal or to inflict grievous bodily harm. Hence it is possible for a person charged under s.9(1)(b) to be convicted under the former section; see, e.g. *Taylor* [1979] Crim.L.R. 649 and *Whiting* (1987) 85 Cr.App.R. 78.

[86] See above at para.7–119.

(2) entered as a trespasser and actually committed or attempted to commit one of the following:

    (a) stealing;

    (b) inflicting grievous bodily harm.

[This constitutes the s.9(1)(b) form of burglary.][87]

We shall now consider the elements which are common to both forms of burglary, namely entry; trespassing; a building; and part of a building.

1. ENTRY

In both forms of burglary the prosecution must prove that the accused entered the building **9–024** as a trespasser. Under s.9(1)(b) the prosecution must prove that at the time of committing the specified offence he knew that he had entered as a trespasser or was at least reckless as to that fact.

The prosecution must prove that the accused actually entered the building in question. As with many elements of criminal offences this will pose no great problems in the general run of cases since the accused will be apprehended in the building or some days later when he has actually removed property from the building. However, on occasion, it may be difficult to say whether or not there has actually been an entry into the building within the meaning of s.9.

There are various possible views as to what constitutes an entry. One view is that entry requires that the accused, A, should be entirely within the building. On this view, if he still had so much as a foot on the window ledge outside the building he would not be guilty of the complete offence though he would be guilty of an attempt. Another view is that A has entered if any part of his body is within the building; on this view A would be guilty should his hand, or even his fingertips, penetrate beyond the door or window. The old common law approach was simplicity itself. The insertion of any part of the defendant's body, however small, sufficed to constitute an entry. For example, in *Bailey*[88] the introduction of a hand between shutter and window to undo the window latch was determined to be an entry. Similarly in *Davis*,[89] where the defendant, a young boy, pushed his finger against a glass pane in the corner of a window of a dwelling house. This pressure caused the glass to fall inside the property. An entry had transpired for the purposes of burglary. After the enactment of the Theft Act 1968 the question arose as to whether the old common law rules were still determinative, in a scenario where the Act itself was silent as to the definitional meaning of entry. The first case to address the point was that of *Collins*,[90] a salacious authority that has passed into folklore as far as law students are concerned, and which was primarily concerned with the notion of trespassing for the purposes of the burglary offence.[91] It held that there must be "an effective and substantial" entry which seems to suggest a halfway house between the two views, set out above. As a practical test it seems to be less satisfactory than either of the two first suggested tests because it is not clear cut. Whether A's body is entirely

---

[87] J.C. Smith, *The Law of Theft* (Butterworths, 1997), p.201.
[88] (1818) Russ & Ry 341. See *Horncastle* [2006] EWCA Crim 1736 in a modern context involving D utilising a cane through V's letterbox to trap V's keys perched on a shelf.
[89] (1823) Russ & Ry 499.
[90] [1973] Q.B. 100 CA.
[91] See below, para.9–026.

within the building or whether any part of his body has penetrated the building, admit of definite answers; but whether enough of his body is within the building so as to constitute an effective and substantial entry must be something on which views may differ. The subsequent decision of the Court of Appeal in *Brown*,[92] in which it was said that "substantial" did not materially assist in the matter, but that a jury should be directed that in order to convict they must be satisfied that the entry was "effective", would appear to add little in the way of clarification to the matter. In *Brown* a witness, having heard the sound of breaking glass, saw the defendant partially inside a shopfront display. The top half of the defendant's body was inside the shop window as though he were rummaging inside it. It was assumed by the witness that the defendant's feet were touching the ground outside the shop, although his direct view of this was obscured. The Court of Appeal rejected the contention that the whole of the defendant's body had to be within a building, and refuted the dictum of Edmund Davies L.J. in *Collins* that an entry has to be both effective and substantial:

> "In our judgment the word 'substantial' does not materially assist in arriving at a conclusion as to whether or not there has been an entry. It is otherwise, however, with the word 'effective' and we see much force in the proposition that a jury should be directed that there should be an effective entry before a conviction can be made under this subsection."[93]

9–025   The issue arose again before the Court of Appeal in *Ryan*[94] but unfortunately the picture still remains unclarified. In the early hours of the morning an elderly householder found the defendant stuck in the downstairs window of his house. The defendant had his head and right arm inside the window and was trapped by the window itself, which rested on his neck. The rest of his body remained outside the window. In explaining his presence there the defendant, quite unbelievably, told the householder that he was trying to get his baseball bat, which his friend had put through the window! The police and the fire brigade were called and he was eventually extricated from his parlous situation. The defendant found himself charged with burglary and was in due course convicted. He contended that, as a matter of law, his action was not capable of constituting an entry within the meaning of s.9(1)(a) of the Theft Act 1968 since he could not have stolen anything from within the building because he was stuck firmly by his neck in the window. However, the Court of Appeal, following *Brown*, held that a person could enter a building even if only part of his body was actually within the premises. Further, it was totally irrelevant whether he was or was not capable of stealing anything because he was trapped halfway through the window. Consequently the law is now left in an extremely uncertain state. It seems impossible to state following this decision that the entry need be either "substantial" or "effective". If the question of whether an entry was effective or not relates to whether D is enabled to commit the ulterior offence, it would be difficult to say that the defendant in *Ryan* made such an entry. Moreover, by leaving the matter for jury determination it raises the potential for similar cases to be decided differently by differently constituted juries. There is much merit in adopting the old and simple common law rule to remedy these uncertainties, whereby the insertion of any part of the body, however small, is sufficient to constitute an entry.[95]

Further complications are introduced where A employs an innocent agent, or where A gains entry by means of an instrument. This occurred in 1979 when transvestites who hooked

[92] [1985] Crim.L.R. 212.
[93] [1985] Crim.L.R. 212.
[94] [1996] Crim.L.R. 320; see, generally, J. Beaumont, "Getting 'Stuck' Into Burglary: The *Ryan* Case" (1996) 67 *The Criminal Lawyer* 4.
[95] J. Beaumont, "Getting 'Stuck' Into Burglary: The Ryan Case" (1996) 67 *The Criminal Lawyer* 4 at 5.

dresses worth £600 through letter boxes of shops pleaded guilty to burglary in a Magistrates' Court.[96] In the innocent agent scenario A might, for example, employ a boy below the age of criminal responsibility to enter the building and bring out property to him. In such a case it must be tempting to use the innocent agency principle[97] and conclude that this is to be treated as an entry by A himself. Suppose, then, that A, while remaining outside the building, uses some instrument to withdraw property from the building. Is it to be said that, by parity of reasoning, the implement is to be regarded like the boy so that its insertion into the building is to be regarded as an entry by A himself? Since burglary may now be committed when there is an entry with intent to do serious bodily harm, is A guilty of burglary when the bullet from his gun, fired from the highway, enters the victim's house?[98]

If regard is paid to the wording of s.9, it would appear that these last two illustrations cannot constitute burglary. A person is guilty of burglary if "he enters" with certain intents, or "having entered . . . he" commits certain offences. To hold that "he" enters or has entered when an instrument is inserted by him would seem to be at odds with what the section expressly requires.

It is further suggested that the natural meaning of the words employed in the section require a complete entry by A. "Enters" or "having entered" means just that; it can hardly be supposed to mean "being in the process of entering" or "having half-entered." If A is in the process of entering he may always be convicted of an attempt. Where an innocent agent (the boy under the age of criminal responsibility) is employed the same argument should hold good. The "he" referred to in s.9 is the person who is charged with burglary and "he" has not entered the building. However, the old common law rules were to the effect that if an instrument was inserted into the building with intent to commit the ulterior offence, there was in law an entry even though no part of the defendant's body was introduced into the building. These rules went on to state that if the instrument was inserted for the purpose of gaining entry and not in order to commit the ulterior offence, then this was not in law an entry if no part of the body entered.[99] None of these results in relation to innocent agents, instruments or firing of a gun seem satisfactory. It has been submitted that once the device is seen as an extension to the defendant it becomes very difficult to defend the distinction under consideration. These situations should be treated as an entry for the purpose of burglary with the substantive provisions of s.9 of the Theft Act 1968 amended accordingly.[100] We await clarification on these matters by the courts.

2. AS A TRESPASSER

The word trespass is largely a civil law concept. It basically means entry on to property which **9–026** is in the possession of another without the consent of that other. At civil law it would not be a defence to show that you had entered by mistake. So does this mean that for purposes of burglary the prosecution need show only that the accused was, by civil law definition, a trespasser? Fortunately the Theft Act seems to be one area in which the courts have adopted a subjective approach and in prosecutions under s.9 the prosecution will have to prove that the accused was at least subjectively reckless as to the fact of being a trespasser; in other words he was aware of facts which might mean he was trespassing. Recklessness is,

---

[96] See, *Daily Telegraph*, March 4, 1979.
[97] See above, para.5–098.
[98] East provides this example of a muzzle of a gun being introduced into a building with a view to shooting someone inside; see 2 East P.C. 492.
[99] See, e.g. *Hughes* (1785) 1 *Leach* 406, and *O'Brien* (1856) 4 Cox C.C. 398.
[100] J. Beaumont, "Getting 'Stuck' Into Burglary: The Ryan Case" (1996) 67 *The Criminal Lawyer* 4 at 6.

thus, applied in the *Cunningham* sense, as considered by the House of Lords in *R v G*.[101] If the prosecution is brought under s.9(1)(a) of the Theft Act the prosecution must prove that he was reckless as to being a trespasser at the time he entered the building. In the case of a prosecution under s.9(1)(b) the prosecution would have to prove that at the time he committed the offence inside the building he was reckless as to his entry being as a trespasser. If the accused mistakenly thinks that he has the consent of the owner to entering, even if his mistake is unreasonable, he should not be convicted; equally if he believes that he is entering his own house, since then he would not even consider the issue of consent. More problematical is the situation where the accused is invited into the house by a person who has no right to give that consent. Again the answer should be that if the accused honestly believes that he has entered with consent he should not be convicted. In *Jones and Smith*[102] the accused and an accomplice were charged with and convicted of burglary, the offence consisting of stealing TV sets from the house of Smith's father. At the trial it was accepted that Smith's father had given his son a sort of blanket permission to enter his house. So how could you say he entered as a trespasser? James L.J. said that the jury were entitled to hold that the son and his friend were trespassing if they found they had entered the premises of another knowing that they were entering in excess of the permission that had been given to them, or being reckless whether they were so entering. Here it is clear that his father's permission to enter did not extend to entry for the purpose of stealing and the son and friend knew this full well.[103] The jury were entitled to conclude that in entering his father's house with intent to steal the defendant had knowingly exceeded the permission given to him. His conviction for burglary was consequently affirmed.

Where X is charged under s.9(1)(b) it would seem that mens rea to entry as a trespasser is not needed until the moment the crime is committed. So that if X enters a building thinking he has the consent to enter it would suffice that he realised that he did not have consent by the time he committed the theft inside. Usually a trespasser enters by stealth but it is by no means unknown for a person to gain entry by tricking the owner into giving his assent to entry. X may, for example, gain entry to Y's house by pretending to be the gas meter reader. In a way he enters not by stealth but with the consent of the owner, but on the other hand he is fully aware that the owner would not have let him in had he known the truth. It is suggested that there should be no difficulty in saying that X entered knowing that he was a trespasser. Does this mean that if X enters a supermarket intending to steal from within, he commits burglary as he enters? X knows that if the shopkeeper knew of his intentions he would not allow him into the shop and his case is thus not really different from the example of the gas meter reader. The major difficulty here is that the jury will have to be sure that he had that intention when he entered the store, and once the rogue has actually hidden a bottle of Scotch in his coat, the offence of theft is usually sufficient to deal with him. Additionally, the requisite intention will be difficult to prove unless X is specially equipped for stealing, as where, as once happened, an enterprising rogue inserted false arms in the sleeves of his overcoat so that store detectives would not notice what his real arms were doing.

Now that we have considered some of the rules surrounding the offence of burglary it might be helpful to examine a decision in which many of the above points arose in a somewhat bizarre factual setting. In *Collins*,[104] the defendant was a young man who had

---

[101] See above at para.2–069.
[102] [1976] 3 All E.R. 54.
[103] Scrutton L.J. cogently made the same point in the civil law case of *The Carlgarth* [1927] P. 93 at 110: "When you invite a person into your house to use the staircase you do not invite him to slide down the banisters."
[104] [1973] Q.B. 100.

been out drinking heavily into the early hours of the morning. On his way home he passed the house where he knew lived a woman he rather fancied. He found a ladder in the garden of the house and placed it against a window he thought might be the girl's bedroom. He climbed the ladder and seeing her lying naked on the bed he climbed down again, removed all his clothes, except for his socks, and climbed back up.[105] The girl awoke to see the frame of a naked man with an erect penis silhouetted against the window. She took it to be her boyfriend who was in the habit of paying her ardent nocturnal visits. She therefore bade him enter. He climbed into the room and had intercourse with the girl. It was only after the act of intercourse that the girl realised that it was not her boyfriend. Collins was charged with burglary. It seems that there was evidence upon which the jury were entitled to find that he intended to have intercourse with her whether or not she consented, but the Court of Appeal held that the jury had not been properly directed on the question of entry as a trespasser. It was clear that Collins was kneeling on the window sill when the invitation was made, but it was not clear whether at that moment he was on the part of the sill which was inside the bedroom. To a layman this is just the sort of distinction which causes the law to seem absurd. However, the fact remains that if he had crossed the centre line of the sill before the invitation was made, he had entered the building as a trespasser and then the jury would have had to consider whether or not he did intend to have sexual intercourse with the girl whether or not she consented. The Court of Appeal ruled that since the jury had not been asked to consider the question of whether he entered as a trespasser, the conviction had to be quashed. Clearly, the girl made the invitation under a mistake and possibly Collins should have realised this, but so long as he honestly believed he had consent to enter before he made "an effective and substantial entry" he did not commit the offence of burglary.

Edmund-Davies L.J. stated:

> "In the judgment of this court, there cannot be a conviction for entering premises 'as a trespasser' within the meaning of s.9 of the Theft Act 1968 unless the person entering does so knowing that he is a trespasser and nevertheless deliberately enters, or, at the very least, is reckless whether or not he is entering the premises of another without the other party's consent."[106]

This decision can be contrasted with *Jones and Smith*; in that case they knew that they had no permission to enter and to steal; here, Collins must have assumed that any girl who would invite a naked male with an erect penis into her bedroom was giving consent to his entry for the purpose of intercourse. It was up to the prosecution to prove that he did enter before he was invited. As one commentator put it, this case lends a new meaning to the old maxim that the law varies with the length of the Chancellor's foot.[107]

3. A BUILDING

Under the law before 1968 burglary could only be committed from a dwelling-house. The **9–027** new Act is not so restricted, and burglary can be committed in a building or part of a building. However, as previously explained, different maximum punishments have pertained

[105] Edmund-Davies L.J. displayed a lightness of touch in his judgment. In relation to the bizarre factual scenario he stated: "Were they put in a novel or portrayed on the stage, they would be regarded as being so improbable as to be unworthy of serious consideration and as verging at times on farce"; [1973] Q.B. 100 at 101. He also provided an interesting (!) explanation for the presence on D of only the socks, "because apparently he took the view that if the girl's mother entered the bedroom, it would be easier to effect a rapid escape if he had his socks on than if he was in his bare feet"; [1973] Q.B. 100 at 102–103.

[106] [1973] Q.B. 100 at 105.

[107] See, generally, F.J. Odgers, "On Rape Intent" (1972) C.L.J. 194 at 196 who pithily commented: "*Collins* type burglary may well become such a roguish thing that it will vary with the length of a part much more private than the prisoner's foot!"

since the 1991 Criminal Justice Act to dwelling house burglary in contrast to burglary from other types of buildings.

Little would be gained here in trying to give an exhaustive definition of what constitutes a building. It is a word generally used to convey some idea of permanence, and probably there is a requirement of a roof, but beyond this no firm guidelines can be given. Clearly burglary can now be committed from such places as offices, barns and garages. A tent, on the other hand, although it may constitute a dwelling is probably not sufficiently permanent to be regarded as a building. An interesting case in this regard is that of *B and S v Leathley*.[108] The defendants were convicted of burglary. The goods had been stolen from a freezer container in a farmyard. The only question for the court was whether such a container was a building within s.9 of the Theft Act 1968. It was argued by the defendants that it was a piece of industrial plant, which had been delivered by a crane and could be so removed if the farmer sold his farm. Further, it was contended that it was not a building since it merely rested on railway sleepers and was without permanent or purpose-built foundation. However, the court rejected their arguments. The particular points of fact relied on to designate the freezer container as a building were: (1) the container was about 25 feet long with 7 feet square cross-section, weighed about three tons and had been in position for two or three years. The owner intended to leave it there for the foreseeable future. It was, therefore, "a structure of considerable size and intended to be permanent or at least to endure for a considerable time"[109]; (2) its doors were equipped with locks to keep trespassers out; and (3) it was connected to an outside source of electricity.

The Act by s.9(3) specifically extends the definition of buildings to cover inhabited vessels or vehicles, including the times when the person who inhabits them is not there. The word "inhabited" does, however, seem to require that the vehicle at the time of the entry is used as a dwelling, and it would not, therefore, cover an ordinary car or a dormobile which is being used as a form of transport at the time. But if a family use their dormobile as an ordinary form of transport for 50 weeks in the year, but as a holiday home for the other two, it would be an inhabited vehicle for those two weeks. However, the section will not cover a mobile library or mobile shop which are not in use as a dwelling. In *Norfolk Constabulary v Seeking and Gould*[110] the definition of "building" did not extend to two articulated lorry trailers which for a year were used by a supermarket as temporary storerooms. Although they remained static, with steps attached and with an electricity supply, the court held they were still vehicles and as such they only constituted "buildings" if they were inhabited. This case can be contrasted with *B and S v Leathley* where the freezer container, which was identified as being a "building", was self-evidently not a vehicle in any real sense, being totally immobile and without any wheels.

4. PART OF A BUILDING

9–028 The Act provides that the accused must have entered a building or part of a building as a trespasser. This second part is designed to cover situations where the accused is lawfully entitled to be in one part of the building but not in another. For example, if X is a student in a hall of residence he will be entitled to enter his own room and those parts of the hall designed for common use and connecting corridors, but he will not be entitled to enter a fellow student's room without permission. Thus if he goes into student Y's room to steal

---

[108] [1979] Crim.L.R. 314.
[109] *Stevens v Gourley* (1859) 7 C.B.N.S. 99 at 112 per Byles J.
[110] [1986] Crim.L.R. 167.

money from his desk, he would enter Y's room as a trespasser. He has, therefore, entered a part of the building as a trespasser and, thus, he would commit burglary as well as theft. One problem arising out of the use of the concept of parts of a building is that where the prosecution are alleging that the accused has entered part of a building as a trespasser with intent to steal contrary to s.9(1)(a), they must prove that he intended to steal from that part.[111] Suppose that X enters a department store intending only to purchase some gardening equipment. While in the store, where he is legally entitled to be, he conceives a plan to steal money from the manager's office. To reach this office he must first pass through the staff common room which like the manager's office is out of bounds. If X is apprehended in the staff room and confesses that he was on his way to the manager's office can we say that he has entered a part of the building intending to steal in that part, or is the manager's office another part? Possibly the most sensible answer in cases such as these is to treat the building as having two parts—one part where customers are entitled to be, and the other part which is for staff only. If this interpretation is adopted, then as soon as X enters the staff room he has entered a part of the building he is not entitled to enter, and this part includes the manager's office. In *Walkington*[112] the accused was charged with burglary from a till in a department store. The till was standing on a three-sided counter and the questions for the jury were (1) did the management regard the floor area within the three sides of the counter as being restricted to staff; (2) if the answer to (1) was yes, then did the accused realise that this area was so restricted; and (3) if he did, did he enter it with intent to steal from it? It was determined that there was ample evidence on which the jury could come to the conclusion that there was a prohibited area and the defendant knew of it. He was intending to steal the cash contents of the till and the fact that the till happened to be empty did not destroy his intention. The case demonstrates that there is a sufficient "part of a building" where a defined area exists which the defendant appreciates that he may not enter. Permanent division of the building into separate parts is not a prerequisite but a temporary manifestation of division will suffice.

5. MENS REA

Apart from a trespassory entry, which has already been considered, the offence of burglary **9–029** requires, under s.9(1)(a), an ulterior intention to commit one of the three specified offences (stealing, inflicting grievous bodily harm, or criminal damage) and under s.9(1)(b), both the actus reus and mens rea of one of the two specified ulterior offences (stealing and inflicting grievous bodily harm).[113] Burglary is no longer confined to cases where the intention is to commit theft and it will be noted that this range of specified offences is wider under s.9(1)(a) than under s.9(1)(b). As determined in *Attorney-General's References (Nos 1 and 2 of 1979)*[114] a conditional intent will suffice in relation to the s.9(1)(a) offence. Thus, where D

---

[111] An unresolved dilemma in this respect is the extent to be given to a "building". For example, a block of flats may contain 100 individual flats. Does D commit burglary where he enters Flat 1 with intent to steal in Flat 100? Similarly a row of terraced houses in a road may have common rafters. D may enter No.1 but crawl along the rafters to No.7. It is suggested that by applying a purposive approach, looking at the natural and ordinary meaning of "building", there are strong policy grounds to treat "building" as the whole terrace or block of flats. See generally, J.C. Smith, *The Law Of Theft* (Butterworths, 1997) pp.199–200.

[112] [1979] 2 All E.R. 716.

[113] Note that in *Jenkins* [1983] 1 All E.R. 993 the Court of Appeal held that reference in s.9(1)(b) to grievous bodily harm did not necessarily mean the offence to be found in s.20 of the Offences Against the Person Act 1861. On this point the decision seems incorrect as Parliament clearly intended s.20 to be incorporated. Note also that the greater ought to include the lesser here so when D kills V, where murder can also be raised, this palpably covers "inflicting" grievous bodily harm.

[114] [1979] 2 All E.R. 716; see above, para.8–051. Intention at the point of entry to commit the ulterior offence must be proved cf. *A v DPP* [2003] All E.R. (D) 393.

enters a building as a trespasser intending to steal if he finds any item of value, but finds nothing, or intends to inflict grievous bodily harm upon a person who turns out to be absent, then a sufficient intent for burglary has been made out.

AGGRAVATED BURGLARY

9–030 Section 10 of the Theft Act provides for the offence of aggravated burglary which carries a possible maximum sentence of life imprisonment. A person is guilty of aggravated burglary if he commits any burglary and at the time has with him any firearm, any weapon of offence, or any explosive.[115] The section provisions are as follows:

"(1) A person is guilty of aggravated burglary if he commits any burglary and at the time has with him any firearm or imitation firearm, any weapon of offence, or any explosive; and for this purpose—

(a) 'firearm' includes an airgun or air pistol, and 'imitation firearm' means anything which has the appearance of being a firearm, whether capable of being discharged or not[116]; and

(b) 'weapon of offence' means any article made or adapted for use for causing injury to or incapacitating a person, or intended by the person having it with him for such use[117]; and

(c) 'explosive' means any article manufactured for the purpose of producing a practical effect by explosion, or intended by the person having it with him for that purpose.[118]

(2) A person guilty of aggravated burglary shall on conviction or indictment be liable to imprisonment for life."

Whereas burglary under s.9 is, in some senses, a form of aggravated trespass, s.10 is designed both to deter would-be burglars from taking offensive weapons with them when they burgle a house and to enable the court to reflect in the sentence the fact that burglary where offensive weapons are carried is a far more serious offence than when they are not.

A distinction applies to the moment when the defendant must have the article of aggravation (firearm, weapon of offence or explosive) at the "time of committing the burglary" in accordance with s.10 provisions. It depends on whether the actual burglary is of the s.9(1)(a) type or the s.9(1)(b) category. When it is the former then the crucial time to

---

[115] The defendant must actually know that he has the weapon, for example, a flick knife with him at the relevant time; see, e.g. *Cugullere* (1961) 45 Cr.App.R. 108. It does not constitute "knowingly" where D has forgotten the existence of the weapon, for example, a cosh; see, e.g. *Russell* [1985] Crim.L.R. 231.
[116] Guidance on the meaning of firearm may be gleaned from the definition in the Firearms Act 1968 s.57(1). Whether an item constitutes an imitation firearm will be a matter for the jury: see, e.g. *Morris and King* (1984) 79 Cr.App.R. 104; and see also *Bentham* [2005] UKHL 18.
[117] The meaning here is wider than the term in s.1(4) of the Prevention of Crime Act 1953 since it includes items made or adapted for use for incapacitating a person or intended for such use. Hence it would seem to include items such as a broken bottle, hammer, rope, cloth soaked in chloroform, handcuffs, razor blades, a sandbag and a bicycle chain. Generally, it is a jury question whether the particular article has been made or adapted for use for causing injury: see, e.g. *Williamson*(1977) 67 Cr.App.R. 35. However, in *Simpson* [1984] Crim.L.R. 39 it was held that a flick knife came into the category of a weapon that was offensive per se.
[118] Guidance on the meaning of explosive can be gleaned from the definition provided in s.3(1) of the Explosives Act 1875.

evaluate whether an article of aggravation is carried by the defendant is the time of his *entry* into the building as a trespasser with the requisite ulterior intent. It is essential to consider this point in time. This was determined by the Court of Appeal in *Francis*.[119] The defendants, armed with sticks, demanded entry to a dwelling-house by banging and kicking the door. It was unclear whether these sticks were discarded before entering the house or soon after they had entered. Once inside they stole items from the house and committed other offences against the occupant. They were charged with aggravated burglary under s.10. Their Lordships clearly stated that if at the time of entry Francis had with him a weapon of offence he was guilty of aggravated burglary.[120]

In contradistinction, where the s.9(1)(b) variety of burglary is committed, by which a **9–031** defendant enters as a trespasser then commits the ulterior offence of stealing or grievous bodily harm upon V, the relevant time to evaluate whether an article of aggravation is carried will be the very time he *actually commits the ulterior offence*. This was laid down by the court in *O'Leary*.[121] The defendant entered unarmed as a trespasser into a dwelling-house. Subsequently he picked up a knife from the kitchen and proceeded upstairs where he was confronted by the occupants, a husband and wife. He inflicted injuries on the occupants and also stole cash and a bracelet. The Court of Appeal held that the time at which a defendant must be proved to have with him a weapon of offence to make him guilty of aggravated burglary was *the time at which he actually stole*; i.e. in the instant case when he confronted the householders and demanded their cash and jewellery, which was the theft, when he still had the kitchen knife in his hand. Similar principles were applied in *Kelly*[122] where a screwdriver was used as a weapon of offence inside a dwelling-house.

It is not a prerequisite for the offence of aggravated burglary that the prosecution need demonstrate that the article of aggravation was intended to be actually used by the defendant during the burglary. The focus of the statutory provision is directed simply at the presence of the weapon rather than use. This point was made apparent by the court in *Stones*,[123] although it has been subjected to criticism. The defendant was arrested when running away from a house that he had burgled. A search revealed that he was carrying a household knife which he claimed was "for self-defence because some lads from Blyth are after me". His conviction for aggravated burglary was upheld. In his leading judgment Glidewell L.J. held that the mischief at which the section was aimed was that if a burglar had a weapon of offence with him which he intended to use to injure some person unconnected with the premises burgled, he might be "tempted to use it if challenged during the course of the burglary".[124] Consequently, the prosecution had to prove that the defendant at the time of the burglary knowingly had with him the knife and that he had the intention of using it to cause injury or incapacitate some person. It was not necessary for the prosecution to prove that the defendant, if necessary, intended to use the knife during the course of the burglary.[125]

---

[119] [1982] Crim.L.R. 363.
[120] Note that it seems apparent that where D enters with a weapon of offence but lacking an intent to steal, discards the weapon of offence inside the building, then decides to steal, liability will exist for burglary but *not* aggravated burglary.
[121] (1986) 82 Cr.App.R. 341.
[122] (1992) 97 Cr.App.R. 245.
[123] [1989] 1 W.L.R. 156; see, generally, N.J. Reville, "The Mischief Of Aggravated Burglary" (1989) N.L.J. 835.
[124] [1989] 1 W.L.R. 156 at 160.
[125] This is criticised by Reville, "The Mischief of Aggravated Burglary" (1989) N.L.J. 835 at 836 as being contrary to the view adopted by the Criminal Law Revision Committee in its *Eighth Report*, which saw robbery and aggravated burglary as comparable. However, it seems for the s.10 offence that no need exists for the weapon to be used or threatened to be used in the course of the burglary.

In *Klass*[126] the Court of Appeal applied a purposive interpretation to s.10 of the Theft Act 1968. The defendant and two other men, one of whom had a piece of pole in his hand, wrenched open the door of a caravan and demanded money from the occupant who told them he did not have any. The man with the pole then hit the occupant of the caravan over the head and pursued him as he ran away, hitting him repeatedly. When the defendant was subsequently arrested he admitted being outside the caravan (building) but denied entering it. On the appeal, the question of law raised was whether the offence of aggravated burglary could be committed if the weapon was not being carried by the burglar or one of the burglars who entered the building. The Court of Appeal determined that the gravamen of the offence was entry into a building with a weapon. The purpose of s.10 was to deter people from taking weapons into buildings and other people's houses while committing burglary. For example, the fact that a getaway driver had a weapon with him in the car would not, in their Lordships' judgment, be sufficient to turn an offence of burglary into one of aggravated burglary. Although there were certain academic attractions in the strict interpretation, the purposive approach was to be preferred. In the circumstances, the conviction of aggravated burglary had to be quashed. To commit an offence of aggravated burglary contrary to s.10 of the Theft Act 1968, a person must have with him a weapon of offence at the time of entry (for s.9(1)(a) type of burglary). *The offence could not be committed if the weapon was not being carried by one of the people effecting entry to the building.*

MAKING UNWARRANTED DEMANDS WITH MENACES: BLACKMAIL

9–032   Section 21 of the Theft Act 1968 provides:

> "(1) A person is guilty of blackmail if, with a view to gain for himself or another or with intent to cause loss to another, he makes any unwarranted demand with menaces; and for this purpose a demand with menaces is unwarranted unless the person making it does so in the belief:
>
> (a) that he has reasonable grounds for making the demand; and
>
> (b) that the use of the menaces is a proper means of reinforcing the demand."

The word "blackmail"[127] is a word commonly used in everyday language to describe a situation in which X is threatening Y with unpleasant consequences unless Y does what X wants. This is, in fact, the gist of blackmail under s.21, but as we shall see the scope of the offence is somewhat more restricted than the everyday use of the term.

Suppose that one evening as he was driving home X is involved in an accident with Y. X demands that Y admit liability for the accident but Y refuses, whereupon X says he will call the police. Y asks him not to do this as he has been drinking that evening and he cannot risk a breath test since he is a driving instructor. X repeats his demand that unless Y signs a written statement admitting liability, X will now certainly call the police. Y agrees. Has X committed an offence under the section? We can examine each element that the prosecution must prove in turn:

---

[126] *The Times,* December 17, 1997.
[127] The term blackmail started life in Elizabethan times to refer to money paid under an English/Scottish borders protection racket; see, generally, P. Alldridge, "Attempted Murder Of The Soul: Blackmail; Piracy And Secrets" (1993) 13 O.J.L.S. 368.

1. THERE MUST BE A DEMAND

This will generally present no problems and the word will be given its ordinary meaning. The **9–033** nature of the act or omission demanded is not of relevance. By s.21(2) it is provided that:

> "The nature of the act or omission demanded is immaterial, and it is also immaterial whether the menaces relate to action taken or to be taken by the person making the demand."

However, this criterion is subject to the requirement that the demand has to be made with a view to gain or intent to cause loss. For example, in *Collister and Warhurst*[128] two police officers (A and B) made intimations to V that he would be prosecuted for an offence, but suggested to V that this report would only be filed if he failed to keep an appointment with them for the next day. At this subsequent meeting A and B demanded the sum of £5 with the connotation being this was payment to suppress the report. They were convicted of demanding money with menaces. It was not necessary to show that a demand had been made directly and expressly to V:

> "[T]he demeanour of the accused and the circumstances of the case were such that an ordinary reasonable man would understand that a demand for money was being made upon him and that demand was accompanied by menaces so that his ordinary balance of mind was upset."[129]

What is required is that the accused acts in such a way as to demonstrate that he wants the victim to do something. A demand implicitly occurred in the recent case of *Miah*[130] where D, after sending videos of child pornography to Vs asserting that their fingerprints were present on the tapes, then invited them to call a specific telephone number for instructions. It does not matter whether the request is made in the form of an order or a humble plea. The offence is demanding with menaces and so it does not matter whether the request is complied with or even that it was heard, provided that it was made. It is immaterial whether it was made orally or in writing. Where it is made in writing and sent through the post the demand is made as soon as the letter is posted and it continues to be made until it is received. Thus if A posts, in England, a demand to B in America, the demand is made and, therefore, the offence is committed in England; if the facts are reversed the offence is committed in England at the latest when the letter reaches England. In *Treacy v DPP*,[131] for instance, a letter was posted by the defendant in England containing a demand to V in Germany. It was determined by the House of Lords that the demand was made when the letter was posted, which allocated jurisdiction to the English courts. It is clear in our hypothetical example that X has made a demand to Y.

2. THE DEMAND MUST BE ACCOMPANIED BY MENACES

This does not mean that there must be a threat of violence; it is sufficient that something **9–034** detrimental or unpleasant is threatened. This was enunciated in *Thorne v Motor Traders Association*[132] by Lord Wright:

---

[128] (1955) 39 Cr.App.R. 100.
[129] (1955) 39 Cr.App.R. 100.
[130] [2003] 1 Cr.App.R.(S.) 379.
[131] [1971] A.C. 537.
[132] [1937] A.C. 797 at 817.

"I think the word 'menace' is to be liberally construed and not as limited to threats of violence but as including threats of any action detrimental to or unpleasant to the person addressed. It may also include a warning that in certain events such action is intended."

The use of the word "menaces" however rather than "threats" suggests that there might be certain threats which would be too trivial to be classed as menaces. The point that trivial threats do not constitute menaces was exemplified by the case of *Harry*.[133] The over zealous student who sent letters to 115 local shopkeepers containing posters to the effect that, "These premises are immune from all rag '73 activities whatever they may be", with immunity proffered in return for charitable donations, was held not to have used "menaces". A distinction applies between trivial and non-trivial threats which Sellers L.J. stated in *Clear*[134]:

"Words or conduct which would not intimidate or influence anyone to respond to the demand would not be menaces and might negative any intent to steal, but threats and conduct of such a nature and extent that the mind of an ordinary person of normal stability and courage might be influenced or made apprehensive so as to accede unwillingly to the demand would be sufficient for a jury's consideration."

A further twist to the above statement was added in *Garwood*[135] where the Court of Appeal considered threats made by the defendant to a youth the jury considered to be unduly timid. The defendant who believed that V may have burgled his house had aggressively demanded £10 in order to "make it quits". The court held that in the majority of cases the judge would not need to spend time in defining "menaces". However, there were two cases where guidance would be needed. The first was where the threats, although likely to affect the mind of a normal person, did not affect the defendant's; this would clearly amount to "menaces". The second is where the threats are unlikely to have affected the mind of a person of normal stability, but have affected the particular victim because he was unduly susceptible. In this type of case it all depends upon the knowledge of the defendant. If he knows the likely effect of his actions on the victim, then what he has done constitutes menaces. Thus a threat to expose A's sexual perversions would probably influence most stable citizens, but a threat to poison A's pet budgie may be an example of a threat which would only be a menace if the accused knew that A, an old lady, was very timid and devoted to the budgie. Where a false allegation of homosexuality is made by D against V to extort money this clearly constitutes a demand accompanied by menaces for the purposes of s.21 of the Theft Act 1968. This occurred in *Christie*[136] where the defendant saw the photograph of a man who was a stranger to him in a local paper. The defendant wrote to the man, demanding £5,000 under the threat to expose him as homosexual, which he was not. V reported the matter to the police, and D was arrested. It was held that the threat to make a false allegation constituted blackmail for which a sentence of two years was appropriate.

In our hypothetical example X had clearly reinforced the demands with menaces which he knows will influence Y to comply with the demands.

---

[133] [1974] Crim.L.R. 32.
[134] [1968] 1 All E.R. 74 at 80.
[135] [1987] 1 All E.R. 1032. Note that following *Lawrence and Pomroy* (1971) 55 Cr.App.R. 64 at 72 it is not generally incumbent on a trial judge to spell out the meaning of the word "menaces" for the jury since it is an ordinary English word that a jury can be expected to understand.
[136] (1990) 12 Cr.App.R.(S.) 540.

3. THE DEMAND MUST BE MADE WITH A VIEW TO GAIN FOR THE MAKER OR ANOTHER, OR WITH INTENT TO CAUSE LOSS TO ANOTHER

The words gain and loss are defined by s.34(2) of the Act as being restricted to gains and **9–035** losses in money or other property; the gain or loss may be temporary or permanent. Gain includes a gain by keeping what one has, as well as a gain by getting what one has not; and loss includes a loss by not getting what one might get as well as a loss by parting with what one has. Thus if A threatens to expose B's cheating in an examination if she does not have sexual intercourse with him, this will not be a gain under s.21, but if his demand is for the £50 which she owes him then it may be an offence under s.21 even though the money is legally owed to him. It was established by *Parkes*[137] that "gain" includes the obtaining of hard cash as opposed to the mere right of action in respect of the debt owed by V to D. It would appear that so long as the defendant is demanding money or other property, his ulterior motive will be irrelevant. Thus, in *Bevans*,[138] B, who was crippled with osteo-arthritis, went to a doctor's surgery and, at gun point, demanded to be injected with a painkilling drug. The Court of Appeal upheld the trial judge's direction to the jury that "with a view to gain" related to money or other property and that the drug could clearly constitute property. It was irrelevant that his ulterior motive had been the relief of pain and not economic gain. He had clearly made his demand with a view to gain and he certainly intended to cause the doctor loss.

Difficulties may arise when the thing demanded is not money or other property. Here it may be necessary to examine the defendant's motives. For example, if he is demanding that the woman marry him, his demand could properly be said to be made with a view to gain if she was an heiress and the demand was made with a view to getting his hands on her money. However it may be that the monetary gain can become too remote, as where A threatens Professor B that he will expose him as homosexual if he does not give him a place as a student in the university law school. Presumably A will be hoping to earn good money with the law degree he will obtain in a few years' time—but it is likely that the court would hold that this monetary gain is too remote. This contrasts with the simple demand for hard cash, £5,000 in the case of *Christie*, where no issue of remoteness arose.

Thus again in our original example it would appear that the demand is made by X with a view to monetary gain.

4. THE DEMAND MUST BE UNWARRANTED

If the accused raises the issue that the demand was not unwarranted then the prosecution **9–036** must prove either that the accused did not believe that he had reasonable grounds for making the claim or, if he did, that he did not believe that it was proper to use menaces as a means of reinforcing the demand.[139] In the majority of cases it is likely that the accused will believe that he had reasonable grounds for making the claim. Even a prostitute or bookmaker, who knows that the courts would not enforce the demand, may genuinely believe that they have the right to demand payment for a "debt of honour". However, it is

---

[137] [1973] Crim.L.R. 358.
[138] (1987) 87 Cr.App.R. 64.
[139] An interesting case in this regard is that of *Lambert* [1972] Crim.L.R. 422 where D threatened V that he would expose the affair between V and D's wife to V's employers unless he was paid the sum of £250 representing his interests as a husband. The jury, no doubt blinded by V's disreputable conduct, acquitted D.

far more likely that the accused will know that he should not have used menaces as a means of reinforcing the demand. In *Harvey and Others*[140] the defendants paid over £20,000 to V for what they believed to be a consignment of cannabis, but which in reality proved to be a worthless substance. Retribution was swiftly enacted as they kidnapped V's wife and child and threatened V that they would rape, maim and kill them unless their money was returned. They were convicted, inter alia, of blackmail and appealed on the basis that the judge had misdirected the jury that their threats could never be a proper means of reinforcing the demand. However, the Court of Appeal held that no act which the accused believed to be a crime could be considered by him to be a proper means of enforcing the demand.

Bingham J. asserted:

> "Proper . . . is, however, plainly a word of wide meaning, certainly wider than (for example) 'lawful'. But the greater includes the less and no act which was not believed to be lawful could be believed to be proper within the meaning of the subsection. Thus no assistance is given to any defendant, even a fanatic or a deranged idealist, who knows or suspects that his threat, or the act threatened, is criminal, but believes it to be justified by his end or his peculiar circumstance."[141]

It is submitted, however, even here, and despite the restriction in *Harvey* regarding criminal activities never constituting proper means, that it is for the jury to decide what the accused actually believed. Thus, in practice, the more serious the threat, the less likely the jury are to believe that the accused considered his conduct to be "proper". The standard against which the appropriateness of the menaces applied by the accused will be measured is his understanding of what is morally and socially acceptable in accordance with our society norms. Certainly the Criminal Law Revision Committee, Eighth Report, *Theft and Related Offences*, would have allowed a defence only when the defendant's act was "morally and socially acceptable". A corollary prevails here with the English society norm test adopted by the Court of Appeal in *Ghosh* for dishonesty.[142]

In our example X probably believes he has the right to demand a statement admitting liability—if he believes that Y was the cause of the accident. More likely the crucial question will be whether he honestly believed that the use of menaces was a proper means of backing up the demand. In our illustration it is quite possible that X believed his threats were proper. The test is for the jury to ask themselves did the accused actually believe that he was acting in a socially acceptable way. Thus the lower the accused's standards, the less likely he is to be convicted. If X had said he would have Y beaten up if he did not sign a statement, it is less likely that the jury would believe that he honestly thought this was a proper way of reinforcing his demands.

HANDLING

9–037   When thieves have got away with their stolen property, the next step is to dispose of it. Clearly, if the stolen property is money there will be no difficulty, but where the property is readily identifiable there is every danger that the thief will get caught trying to sell it or use

---

[140] (1981) 72 Cr.App.R. 139. See also, *St. Q* [2002] 1 Cr.App.R.(S.) 440, where D's improper threat was to disseminate videos of consensual sexual intercourse with his wife to "encourage" a divorce settlement.
[141] (1981) 72 Cr.App.R. 139 at 142.
[142] See above, para.8–043.

it. It is for this reason that specialist criminals exist whose function is to dispose of the goods for the original thieves. These are the persons regularly known as "fences". In some respects these people are a greater social menace than the original thieves since without them the thieves would have to dispose of the stolen property personally and might find the whole enterprise less attractive and rewarding. This point was enunciated by the Criminal Law Revision Committee's *Eighth Report* which stated that an offence of handling was necessary, "to combat theft by making it more difficult and less profitable to dispose of stolen property".[143] As the court in *Shelton*[144] made clear, the offence of handling is more serious than that of theft. Most fences probably commit theft in relation to the property they deal with, but this is not always the case and this fact, coupled with the generally accepted need to be able to punish big time fences more severely than the thieves for whom they act, has led to the creation of a separate offence. Until 1968 this was known as "receiving" but under the Theft Act 1968 its scope has been increased and it is now termed handling. The basic offence is defined by s.22 of the Act which provides:

"(1) A person handles stolen goods if (otherwise than in the course of the stealing) knowing or believing them to be stolen goods he dishonestly receives the goods, or dishonestly undertakes or assists in their retention, removal, disposal or realisation by or for the benefit of another person, or if he arranges to do so."

A person who is convicted under this section is liable to up to 14 years' imprisonment, which contrasts with the maximum punishment of only seven years for theft. It should be noted that while there are about 18 methods of handling stolen goods outlined in this section, there is only one offence of handling.[145]

1. THE ACTUS REUS OF HANDLING

A. Stolen Goods

"Goods" for the purpose of s.22 are defined to include "money and every other description **9–038** of property except land, and includes things severed from the land by stealing".[146] Subject to minor exceptions goods which may be handled extends to the same property that may be the subject of theft.

Such goods must be "stolen" and for this purpose goods are not only stolen when obtained in circumstances amounting to theft but also when they are obtained by blackmail or by fraud (within the meaning of the Fraud Act 2006).[147] Provision is also made for goods stolen abroad which are brought to this country. However, it must be proved by the prosecution that the behaviour complained of actually amounted to an offence (stealing, blackmail or fraud) under the relevant foreign jurisdiction. The prosecution failed to establish this in *Ofori and Tackie (No.2)*[148] where it was simply alleged that the defendants

---

[143] See, para.127.
[144] (1986) 83 Cr.App.R. 379.
[145] Handling itself is a generic term which embraces the various methods in which the offence may be committed; see, e.g. *Nicklin* [1977] 2 All E.R. 444. However, a properly drawn indictment should specifically itemise the form of handling involved, see, e.g. *Griffiths v Foreman* [1970] 1 All E.R. 1117; *Alt* (1972) 56 Cr.App.R. 457; and *Sloggett* [1972] 1 Q.B. 430.
[146] See, s.34(2)(b).
[147] See, s.24(4).
[148] (1994) 99 Cr.App.R. 223; see also, *Iqbal v DPP* [2004] All E.R. (D) 314; and *Defazio v DPP* [2007] EWHC (Admin)—prosecution failed to establish that credit card retained by D had been stolen in fact when it came into possession.

had handled stolen cars in Germany and Belgium, with the plan to return them to England, but for eventual exportation to West Africa for sale. It was impermissible for the prosecution to rely on a supposedly irrebuttable presumption that foreign law was the same as English law in any relevant respect.

Not only must the prosecution establish that the goods were at some time "stolen" as defined in s.24, they must prove that they were "stolen" at the time of the handling. Problems can arise when the act which is alleged to constitute the handling occurs either before the goods have been stolen or at a time when the law deems that the property has ceased to have the characteristics of stolen property. Thus in *Park*[149] the defendant, a solicitor, was charged with handling certain property in that he had arranged to deal with the property in a way prohibited under s.22. His conviction was quashed because at the time he made the arrangement the money could not yet be described as stolen property. The defendant must know or believe the goods to be stolen goods and it is not sufficient for the full substantive offence, although as determined in *Shivpuri*[150] and *Haughton v Smith*[151] it is for the attempt, that he believes that they have been stolen when they have not. There is a requirement here that the elements of the offence need to be contemporaneous.[152] For example, in *Brook*[153] the defendant was found in possession of a carrier bag containing stolen cheque books and cards inside his briefcase in his car. His weak explanation was that one evening during a car journey his wife had found a bag in a public lavatory and told him what was in it, and had put it in the back of the car while deciding what to do with it the next day. He was charged with dishonest handling and the issue was whether he believed the goods to be stolen. In quashing his conviction the Court of Appeal held that a defendant was guilty of handling only if he believed goods to be stolen at the time he received them (the point of handling); supervening belief/dishonesty after receipt was not enough. The time Brook came into possession, i.e. control of the goods, was the crucial time as this was the time at which the actus reus of receiving was committed, and thus also it was the time at which mens rea had to be proved. In the event that the contemporaneity required for handling itself cannot be shown then a suitably drafted indictment may allege conspiracy to handle. This was the charge in *Slater and Suddens*,[154] where the defendants were engaged in a car-ringing network involving numerous vehicles.

9–039 In relation to handling property after it has ceased to be stolen, s.24(3) provides that goods which may have been "stolen" within the meaning of s.24 (by stealing, fraud or blackmail), may cease to be stolen in one of three ways, namely where:

(i) they have been restored to the person from whom they were stolen; or

(ii) they have been restored to other lawful possession or custody; or

(iii) the person from whom they were stolen (or anyone claiming through him) ceases to have any right to restitution of the goods.

Other lawful possession or custody in (ii) covers the situation in which the police recover the stolen property. Here and in (i) the major difficulty is to decide when the property has actually been restored either to its owner or to other lawful possession. It will be important

---

[149] (1987) 87 Cr.App.R. 164.
[150] [1987] A.C. 1; see above, para.6–016.
[151] [1975] A.C. 476; para.6–014, fn.79.
[152] See, generally, M. Jefferson, *Criminal Law* (Pitman, 1997) at p.435.
[153] [1993] Crim.L.R. 455.
[154] [1996] Crim.L.R. 494.

to determine whether the police are purporting to assume either possession or control over the goods. This was not the case in *Greater London Metropolitan Police Commissioner v Streeter*[155] where stolen cigarette cartons were initialled and marked in order to ease future identification. The simple marking of the goods to identify them when they were subsequently transferred from thief to handler was insufficient exercise of control over them to restore the cigarettes to lawful possession. The problem was considered in *Attorney-General's Reference (No.1 of 1974)*.[156] A police officer suspecting, correctly as it turned out, that the goods in the back of a car were stolen, immobilised the car and kept watch for the driver. When the driver arrived the officer questioned him and, because the driver's replies were unsatisfactory, he arrested him. It was held that in such a case the jury should be invited to consider whether the officer had taken custody of the goods before the driver returned or whether he had postponed the decision to take custody until he had the chance of confirming or disaffirming his suspicions by questioning the suspect. Merely to prevent the suspect from having access to the goods until questions are asked is not necessarily to take possession of the goods. In essence, whether a police officer has taken possession will depend primarily on the intentions of the police officer. This point was made by Lord Widgery C.J.:

> "If the police officer seeing these goods in the back of the car had made up his mind that he would take them into custody, that he would reduce them into his possession or control, take charge of them so that they could not be removed and so that he would have the disposal of them, then it would be a perfectly proper conclusion to say that he had taken possession of the goods. On the other hand, if the truth of the matter is that he was of an entirely open mind at that stage as to whether the goods were to be seized or not and was of an entirely open mind as to whether he should take possession of them or not, but merely stood by so that when the driver of the car appeared he could ask certain questions of that driver as to the nature of the goods and why they were there, then there is no reason whatever to suggest that he had taken the goods into his possession or control."[157]

Sometimes the owner, or the police, become aware that A has stolen the goods but, with a view to catching the handler as well, follow the goods to their destination. Such conduct by the owner or police does not constitute a resumption of possession and the receiver may be convicted of handling.

An illustration of property ceasing to be stolen under (iii) would be where X has obtained **9–040** property from Y under a contract which is voidable because of X's fraud. If, when he realises what has happened, Y ratified the contract, he would cease to have any rights in the property and at that stage the property would cease to be stolen.

Section 24(2) contains some rather complex rules concerning the proceeds of stolen goods.[158] It provides as follows:

---

[155] (1980) 71 Cr.App.R. 113.

[156] [1974] Q.B. 744. Another interesting case on this issue is *King* [1938] 2 All E.R. 662. A police officer was in the process of examining the contents of a parcel, which contained a stolen fur coat, when his search was interrupted by a telephone call from the proposed handler to the thief. As planned the receiver took possession of the coat. His conviction for handling was confirmed. The fur coat, on the facts, had not been restored to lawful custody or possession.

[157] [1974] Q.B. 744 at 753.

[158] Note also at this point the effect s.3(2), previously considered above, para.8–019, which protects the bona fide purchaser; see, e.g. *Wheeler* (1990) 92 Cr.App.R. 279.

"(2) For purposes of those provisions references to stolen goods shall include, in addition to the goods originally stolen and parts of them (whether in their original state or not),—

(a) any other goods which directly or indirectly represent or have at any time represented the stolen goods in the hands of the thief as being the proceeds of any disposal or realisation of the whole or part of the goods stolen or of goods so representing the stolen goods; and

(b) any other goods which directly or indirectly represent or have at any time represented the stolen goods in the hands of a handler of the stolen goods or any part of them as being the proceeds of any disposal or realisation of the whole or part of the stolen goods handled by him or of goods so representing them."

An example will serve to illustrate the general idea of the section. If X steals a car and then sells that car, the money he receives in exchange will be stolen goods and so will the car. Equally, if the handler of stolen property exchanges it for other property, the newly acquired property will be classified as stolen goods. Where, however, stolen property comes into the hands of someone who is not a thief or handler (for example because he is totally unaware that the property is stolen) then although the property is still stolen property, anything he acquires in exchange for it does not become stolen property.

B. Handling

9–041   The prosecution must prove that the accused handled the stolen property. While goods may be handled in a wide variety of ways, these ways fall into two groups:

(i) Received or Arranged to Receive

9–042   This is the clearest example of handling. If the prosecution allege that the accused received the goods they will have to show that he took them into his possession whether personally or by his agents. It is a question of fact and degree for the jury to decide whether the alleged receiver had possession or control of the goods. If the accused has not actually received the goods and has not yet done enough to be charged with an attempt he may nevertheless have arranged to receive. Thus a typical case of arranging to receive would be where the thief has got in touch with a fence and has arranged to deliver the property to the fence who will then dispose of it. But you should remember that the goods must be stolen at the time of the arrangement, as *Park* determined that arranging to receive goods before they have been stolen does not constitute handling. Additionally, it was held in *Haider*[159] that where a defendant simply finds stolen goods and takes possession of them this does not amount to receiving.

(ii) Undertakes or Assists in Their Retention, Removal, Disposal or Realisation by or for the Benefit of Another Person, or Arranges to Do So

9–043   This form of handling casts the net very wide. Assist would seem to suggest a situation in which the accused joins forces with the thief or other handlers and works with them; undertakes on the other hand would seem more suitable to cover the situation where the accused has acted on his own. A few illustrations will serve to show how this part of the section works:

[159] March 22, 1985 (Unreported).

(i) X negotiates with Y that Y will buy stolen property from the thief Z. X has undertaken the disposal of stolen goods for the benefit of Z;

(ii) X helps Y, the thief, store stolen property in a barn where it will stay until the police search dies down. X will have assisted Y in the retention of the stolen goods; and

(iii) X lends Y, the thief, a van to take the stolen goods abroad. X has assisted Y in the removal of the stolen goods.

The section, however, goes further; if X arranges to do any of the above acts he will also be guilty of handling. Thus, in the first example, if X agreed with Z that he would try to find him a buyer, X has arranged to undertake the disposal of the goods for Z.

The word "retention" in the section denotes a positive act carried out by the defendant to assist the thief. It will cover the deliberate telling of lies to the police or actual concealment of the stolen goods. There is a requirement for a purposive intent whereby a defendant acts, "intentionally and dishonestly for the purpose of enabling the goods to be retained".[160] In this regard the cases of *Kanwar* and *Brown* may be distinguished. In *Kanwar*[161] a deliberate deception was practised by the defendant. Her husband had, to her knowledge, bought some stolen furnishings into the house. Aware of the provenance of these goods she deliberately told lies to the police to persuade them that they were lawfully hers. The Court of Appeal determined that there was no reason why assistance should be restricted to physical acts, nor need it be successful in its object. The defendant lied to protect her husband, but nonetheless she was dishonestly assisting in the retention of the stolen property. A refusal to answer questions might also, in fact, have assisted the husband to retain possession but it would not have amounted to an offence. This point was made in *Brown*[162] where the defendant, when questioned at his flat by the police in relation to some stolen cigarettes, told them to "get lost" and he refused to answer any further police questions. His omission to act did not constitute an offence unless the criminal law recognised a duty to act; and it does not recognise any general duty to answer questions put by the police or anyone else.[163] However, the defendant was convicted on the alternative basis that he had provided "accommodation" for the stolen goods knowing or believing that they were stolen. A duty to act was implied in *Pitchley*[164] where the defendant, the father of the thief, paid money stolen by the son into a bank account. At a subsequent date he became aware of the provenance of the money. By omitting to withdraw this money and return it to the owner it was held that he had assisted in the retention of stolen money for the benefit of his son, the thief.

The positive act of deception in *Kanwar* was entirely different from the omission in **9–044** *Brown*. Moreover, it has been acknowledged that merely to use stolen goods does not in itself constitute an offence for the obvious reason that it does not necessarily amount to assistance in the retention of the goods. For example, in *Sanders*[165] it was held that the defendant did not assist the retention of stolen goods, a heater and battery charger, by using them in his father's garage. Similarly in *Coleman*[166] it was asserted that the defendant did not assist in the disposition of stolen property merely by accepting the beneficial consequences of his wife's dispositions. The meaning ascribed to "assisting" required an act of

[160] *Kanwar* [1982] 2 All E.R. 528 at 529, per Cantley J.
[161] [1982] 2 All E.R. 528.
[162] [1970] Q.B. 105.
[163] See, e.g. *Rice v Connolly* [1966] 2 Q.B. 414.
[164] (1972) 57 Cr.App.R. 30.
[165] (1982) 75 Cr.App.R. 84.
[166] [1986] Crim.L.R. 56.

encouraging or helping. His wife had used stolen money to pay for solicitor's fees in relation to the purchase of a flat in their joint names, and also had bought certain household items. There had to be either affirmative or circumstantial evidence that the husband had helped or encouraged the wife. It was possible that, on a proper direction, the jury would have inferred help or encouragement by the husband on the facts of the case.

Where the prosecution is relying on forms of handling other than receiving or arranging to receive, it must prove that the acts were done by or for *the benefit of another person*. If these words were not present it would mean that thieves who tried to dispose of their goods would automatically become handlers. Thus, if X had stolen a painting and he approached Y to see if Y would buy the painting, he would have undertaken the disposal of the painting. However, the addition of the words by or for the benefit of another mean that X is not a handler since he has only undertaken the disposal of the painting for his own benefit. In each of the hypothetical examples discussed above the acts were done by or for the benefit of another. It will not be for the "benefit of another person" in a scenario where the seller of goods, which he suspects to be stolen, sells to a bona fide purchaser. This transpired in *Bloxham*[167] where the defendant, extremely suspicious about the provenance of his motorvehicle, sold it to a purchaser for the sum of £200. It was held that a purchaser, as such, of stolen goods could not be "another person" within s.22(1) since his act of purchase could not sensibly be described as a disposal or realisation by him of the stolen goods.[168]

(iii) Otherwise Than in the Course of the Stealing

9–045 All forms of handling are subject to the requirement that the act which constitutes the handling must not be in the course of the stealing. If these words were not present, it would mean that if X and Y were to burgle Barclays Bank and X handed Y the money from the safe, Y would be guilty of handling. It is necessary here to delineate between the thief, still engaged in a conduct which constitutes stealing, from the actual handler. This phrase is similar to that used in the definition of robbery and it is suggested that it should be given the same interpretation.[169] Thus, in our example of X and Y burgling Barclays Bank, the stealing would presumably be deemed to continue until at least they have left the premises and possibly whilst they are making their getaway. In essence, it is a factual question when the course of stealing has come to an end. It will be recalled that problems have already been encountered as to whether "appropriation" constitutes an instantaneous course of conduct, as in *Pitham and Hehl*,[170] or a continuing one as in *Hale*[171] for robbery.[172]

It is noteworthy that in *Cash*[173] the Court of Appeal held that the prosecution do not always have to prove this element in every case. Only where the jury have to decide whether the accused is a thief or a handler is it likely to be relevant. This has been followed by the Privy Council in *Attorney-General for Hong Kong v Yip Kai-Foon*.[174] This case also considered how a jury ought to be directed where alternative counts of theft and handling are brought

---

[167] [1983] 1 A.C. 109. Note that where the indictment charges "by or for the benefit of another" this excludes the particular person accused of handling or someone who is a co-accused on the same charge of handling; see *Tokeley-Parry* [1999] Crim.L.R. 578 and *Gingell* (2000) 1 Cr.App.R. 88.

[168] See, generally, J.R. Spencer, "The Mishandling of Handling" [1981] Crim.L.R. 682.

[169] See above, para.9–020.

[170] (1976) 65 Cr.App.R. 45. See, e.g. *Gregory* (1982) 77 Cr.App.R. 41.

[171] (1978) 68 Cr.App.R. 415.

[172] See above, para.9–020.

[173] [1985] Q.B. 801. Note in *Cash* stolen goods were found in D's possession nine days after the actual burglary whilst in *Greaves, The Times,* July 11, 1987 this time period was 17 days but it was still permissible to leave it for jury consideration whether D was a burglar. See, generally, J.C. Smith, *op. cit.* at 29. See also, *Wells* [2004] EWCA Crim 79, affirming the *Cash* principle.

[174] [1988] A.C. 642.

by the prosecutor. The matter should be approached by the jury in two stages. First, they should consider whether they were satisfied beyond reasonable doubt that the defendant was guilty of the first offence (theft); if they were not they should then proceed to consider whether the defendant was guilty of the alternative offence (handling). A jury should not be directed, as occurs in some jurisdictions,[175] to convict of the offence which it seems more probable to them that the defendant committed. The Privy Council dual approach in *Yip Kai-Foon* has been adopted by the Divisional Court in *Ryan v DPP*[176] and by the Court of Appeal in *Foreman*.[177]

2. THE MENS REA OF HANDLING

A person is guilty of handling if he dishonestly receives, etc. the stolen goods knowing or **9–046** believing them to be stolen. Notice that the goods must be proved to be stolen goods at the time of the handling. A person may believe goods to be stolen even where they are not; such a person cannot be convicted of the completed offence of handling, but may be convicted of attempted handling.

A. Knowing or Believing That the Goods Were Stolen

The expression "knowing or believing" that the goods are stolen has caused many problems **9–047** for the courts and the Court of Appeal has shown a great reluctance to give clear guidance to trial judges in the correct way to direct juries on this issue.[178]

Particular difficulties have focused on the meaning attributed to "believing". The Criminal Law Revision Committee in their Eighth Report, *Theft and Related Offences*, clearly intended that wilful blindness on the part of the defendant would suffice:

> "In many cases indeed guilty knowledge does not exist, although the circumstances of the transaction are such that the receiver ought to be guilty of an offence. The man who buys goods at a ridiculously low price from an unknown seller whom he meets in a public house may not *know* that the goods were stolen, and he may take the precaution of asking no questions. Yet it may be clear on the evidence that be *believes* that the goods were stolen. In such cases the prosecution may fail (rightly as the law now stands) for want of proof of guilty knowledge. We consider that a person who handles stolen goods ought to be guilty if he believes them to be stolen."[179]

However, in a series of cases, our courts have stated that it was a misdirection to tell a jury to convict a defendant who suspected that the goods were stolen,[180] that he was suspicious and deliberately closed his eyes,[181] or even that he thought the goods were more probably stolen than not.[182] The issue arose in *Hall*,[183] involving a disreputable rogue antique dealer.

[175] See, *Langmead* (1864) Le. & Ca. 427.
[176] [1994] Crim.L.R. 457.
[177] [1991] Crim.L.R. 702.
[178] See, generally, J.R. Spencer, "Handling, Theft And The Mala Fide Purchaser" [1985] Crim.L.R. 92 and 440; and G. Williams, "Handling, Theft And The Purchaser Who Takes A Chance" [1985] Crim.L.R. 432.
[179] See, para.134.
[180] *Grainge* [1974] 1 W.L.R. 619.
[181] *Griffiths* (1974) 60 Cr.App.R. 14; and *Ismail* [1977] Crim.L.R. 557.
[182] *Reader* (1977) 66 Cr.App.R. 33; see J.R. Spencer, "Handling, Theft And The Mala Fide Purchaser" [1985] Crim.L.R. 92 at 93.
[183] (1985) 81 Cr.App.R. 260.

He was found by police in his mother's flat in London with two other men and some articles worth about £26,000 which had been stolen the previous night from a mansion in Gloucestershire. His appeal against conviction was unsuccessful before the Court of Appeal. The court referred to "belief" in the following terms:

> "A man may be said to know that goods are stolen when he is told by someone with first-hand knowledge (someone such as the thief or the burglar) that such is the case. Belief, of course, is something short of knowledge. It may be said to be the state of mind of a person who says to himself: 'I cannot say I know for certain that these goods are stolen but there can be no other reasonable conclusion in the light of all the circumstances, in the light of all that I have heard and seen."[184]

9–048   It would seem, following *Hall*, that it would even be enough that the defendant had said to himself, "despite all that I have seen and heard, I refuse to believe what my brain tells me is obvious". What will certainly not suffice is a finding that the accused suspected that the goods were stolen. It is suggested that the trial judge will not go far wrong if he follows the statement of Professor Glanville Williams:

> "The preferable view is that [the section] extends the notion of knowledge to the case where the defendant, while lacking explicit information, is virtually certain in his own kind that the fact exists"[185]

In *Toor*[186] the Court of Appeal said that it will often be unnecessary for the trial judge to give a full direction along the lines of *Hall*. However, where in the trial much reference has been made to "suspicion" the trial judge should ensure that the jury fully appreciate the meaning of the word "believing".

The approach in *Hall* was criticised in *Forsyth,*[187] where the Court of Appeal struggled to reconcile the requisite mens rea requirement. The matter arose out of the Polly Peck allegations against Asil Nadir who had created a Cayman Island settlement for himself and his family's interests. After the collapse of Polly Peck, investigations revealed complex transactions involving alleged movements of money through a complex group of companies in Switzerland, and other European countries, Turkey and Northern Cyprus. Specimen theft charges were brought against Mr Nadir, who left the country. The defendant was the director of the company which looked after Mr Nadir's and his family interests in the United Kingdom. She was charged, inter alia, with handling in relation to transfer instructions made over a £400,000 payment from London to Switzerland.[188] It was alleged that, knowing or "believing" it had been stolen from Polly Peck by Mr Nadir, she had disposed of or assisted in its disposal by arranging for it to be sent to Switzerland. The trial judge had directed the jury applying the test enunciated in *Hall* above. This was held to be potentially confusing for juries and the test was criticised. It seems that in practical terms a judge should now simply leave it to jury determination without any further enunciation of what is meant by "believing". In reality juries may then treat "wilful blindness" as a sufficient mens rea for the handling offence, where they deem it appropriate. Professor Smith has made the following cogent explanation of the effect of the Court of Appeal decision in *Forsyth*:

---

[184] (1985) 81 Cr.App.R. 260 at 264.
[185] G. Williams, *Textbook of Criminal Law* 2nd edn (1983), p.875.
[186] (1986) 85 Cr.App.R. 116.
[187] [1997] Crim.L.R. 581 and 589.
[188] Another issue in the case related to whether Mr Nadir ought to have been allowed to give evidence from Northern Cyprus, via a video link, on behalf of the defendant.

"What the judge may do is to tell the jury that turning a blind eye to the obvious inference that the goods were stolen is *evidence* that he believed they were stolen; but then he would be advised to stress that they must be sure that he really did believe that. If the jury ask him what is this state of mind of which they must be sure, probably all he can properly do is tell them that 'believing' is an ordinary word of the English language and that, provided they remember it is not suspicion, however great, its meaning is a matter for them not him."[189]

It is clear that, following *Stagg*,[190] a subjective test applies to whether a defendant "knows or believes" that the goods are stolen goods. It is insufficient that he ought to have known that they were stolen or that the reasonable man would have realised their provenance. This was established in *Atwal v Massey*.[191] Admissions made by a defendant as to the circumstances in which the goods were acquired may provide the basis for a jury inference that they were in fact stolen. For example, in *Barnes*[192] the defendant knew that her cohabitee, who had given her sums of cash, had a propensity for stealing large sums of money. Inferences may also be drawn as to the provenance of goods where a defendant sells them at a fraction of their true market value. In *Korniak*,[193] for instance, D sold jewellery in a public house for the sum of £100 when the real value of the jewellery was over £2,000. Similarly in *McDonald*[194] where D sold a television set for less than a third of the market value. Finally, it is noteworthy that it is not necessary for a defendant to know of the exact nature of the stolen goods. If he takes possession of a brown parcel which he realises contains stolen goods, it will be irrelevant that he is mistaken as to the nature of the goods. This proposition is illustrated by the case of *McCullum*.[195] The defendant knew that the contents of a suitcase had been stolen by her husband, but when the case was opened by police officers was surprised to learn that the items were in fact stolen guns and ammunition. It was determined that usually an individual charged with handling knew the nature of the goods, but such knowledge was not necessarily essential.

B. Dishonesty

This is a question of fact for the jury though it will normally add nothing to the requirement **9–049** that the prosecution must prove that the accused knew or believed that the goods were stolen. However, if X received goods knowing that they were stolen, but intending to return them to their true owner, the jury would no doubt find that X was not dishonest. The test for dishonesty applied in *Ghosh* has already been considered.[196] However, in *Roberts*[197] it was determined that for the handling offence the second part of the *Ghosh* test was not a prerequisite in the situation where no evidence existed that D believed he was not dishonest by the standards of ordinary decent people.[198] It was assumed in *Roberts* that selling back two stolen pictures to the original owner for a proposed "commission" was presumptively dishonest.

[189] [1997] Crim.L.R. 589 at 591.
[190] [1978] Crim.L.R. 227.
[191] (1971) 56 Cr.App.R. 6.
[192] [1991] Crim.L.R. 132.
[193] (1983) 76 Cr.App.R. 145.
[194] (1980) 70 Cr.App.R. 288.
[195] [1973] Crim.L.R. 582.
[196] See above, para.8–043.
[197] (1987) 84 Cr.App.R. 117.
[198] See, generally, M. Jefferson, *Criminal Law* (Pitman, 1997), p.441.

C. Proof of Mens Rea

9–050   Assistance may be given to the prosecution in proving the commission of a handling offence by either the common law doctrine of "recent possession" or by s.27(3) of the Theft Act 1968. The former doctrine was explained in the following terms by McCullough J. in *Ball*:

> "Stolen goods pass frequently quickly from hand to hand. Many of those who deal in them knowing or believing them to be stolen tell lies when they are asked to explain how the goods came into their possession. Others prefer to give no explanation. This has been the experience of the courts for generations. So when a defendant is found to have been in possession of goods recently stolen and either gives no explanation of how he came to acquire them innocently or gives an explanation which is patently untrue, it is the practice of judges to tell juries that they may, if they think it right, infer that he acquired them knowing or believing that they were stolen".[199]

This so-called doctrine of recent possession is really misnamed since it has nothing to do with goods recently possessed, but with goods recently stolen. It is not even a doctrine, but simply an application of general principles relating to circumstantial evidence. In other words it is an invitation to the jury to draw certain commonsense conclusions if they see fit to do so. The principles derive from *Abramovitch*,[200] and apply where a defendant has been found in possession of goods which have been recently stolen and, though he has an opportunity to do so, he offers no explanation, or no explanation which could reasonably be true, of how he came to be in possession. It will then be open to a jury to infer either that he was the thief, or that he was a receiver, depending upon the prevailing circumstances. However, it should be noted that a jury are not obliged to draw such an inference and it is still essential for them only to convict a defendant where they are satisfied beyond reasonable doubt that he had such knowledge or belief. The following illustration is presented by Professor Smith:

> "If the lead is stolen off the church roof at midnight and D is found dragging it across a field at 1 a.m. this is very cogent evidence that he stole the lead. If it is found in his backyard next day and he offers no explanation as to how he came by it, this is slightly less cogent but still very persuasive that he either stole it or received it, knowing it to be stolen."[201]

In addition to this common law doctrine of recent possession, s.27(3) of the Theft Act 1968 provides for the reception of evidence, which would otherwise be inadmissible, to assist the jury in their search for the mens rea of handling. This section provides:

> "Where a person is being proceeded against for handling stolen goods (but not for any offence other than handling stolen goods), then at any stage of the proceedings, if evidence has been given of his having or arranging to have in his possession the goods the subject of the charge, or of his undertaking in assisting in, or arranging to undertake or assist in, their retention, removal, disposal or realisation, the following evidence shall be admissible for the purpose of proving that he knew or believed the goods to be stolen goods:

---

[199] [1983] 1 W.L.R. 801 at 805.
[200] (1914) 11 Cr.App.R. 45.
[201] [1985] Crim.L.R. 313.

(a) evidence that he has had in his possession, or has undertaken or assisted in the retention, removal, disposal or realisation of, stolen goods from any theft taking place not earlier than twelve months before the offence charged; and

(b) (provided that seven days' notice in writing has been given to him of the intention to prove the conviction) evidence that he has within the five years preceding the date of the offence charged been convicted of theft or of handling stolen goods."

It has been determined that because of the potential for this subsection to operate in an unduly prejudicial manner against a defendant it needs to be strictly circumscribed. For example, in *Bradley*[202] the Court of Appeal interpreted s.27(3)(a) in such a manner that it was only permissible for the prosecution to tender evidence of actual handling, i.e. evidence that the defendant was in possession of stolen goods on some other occasion. It did not allow evidence to be adduced that he knew or believed these goods to be stolen. In essence, the only evidence to be admitted is the *bare fact of possession,* not extremely relevant inferential evidence relating to knowledge or belief of the defendant that the *present goods* (subject of the charge) were stolen *because* he was knowingly in possession of stolen goods on a previous occasion. The circumstances surrounding the previous possession may not be adduced in the light of the decision in *Bradley.* Additionally, under s.27(3)(b) it is only permissible, in accordance with *Fowler,*[203] for the prosecution to prove the fact that the defendant has been previously convicted. This is subject to the prosecution giving seven days' notice in writing of intention to tender any previous conviction(s).

3. SUMMARY ON HANDLING

The following general points can be made on the offence of handling: **9–051**

1. Handling is subject to a maximum punishment of 14 years' imprisonment. It is viewed as a more serious offence than theft, which is subject to a maximum of seven years' imprisonment.

2. For the offence of handling the prosecution must establish that the goods were "stolen goods" as defined in s.24, and they must prove that they were "stolen" at the time of the handling. The defendant must know or believe the goods to be stolen goods and it is not sufficient for the full substantive offence (although it may be for attempted handling) that he believes that they have been stolen when they have not (see *Park*).

3. Goods cease to be stolen goods in accordance with the provisions of s.24(3). Consider here the case of *Attorney-General's Reference (No.1 of 1974)* which determined that whether a police officer has taken control or possession of the goods will depend primarily upon the intentions of the police officer.

4. There are a number of different forms of handling. The cases of *Kanwar* and *Brown* are useful for the purposes of comparison. It is noteworthy that in *Kanwar* the conviction was upheld on the grounds that: (a) assistance did not have to take

---

[202] (1979) 70 Cr.App.R. 200. See, also, *Adenusi* [2006] EWCA Crim 1059.
[203] (1988) 86 Cr.App.R. 219.

the form of physical assistance and merely verbal assistance would suffice; and (b) telling lies to the police (even though the police were not deceived by them) amounted to such assistance when made for the purpose of protecting the defendant. However, in *Brown* the simple refusal to answer police questions did not make the defendant a handler. This was a simple omission where no duty of care existed. The defendant was convicted on the alternative basis that he had provided accommodation for the stolen goods knowing or believing that they were stolen goods.

5. *Mens rea.* It must be shown that the defendant acted: (a) dishonestly; and (b) knew or believed that the goods were stolen. Particular difficulties have focused on the meaning to be attributed to "believing" with inconsistent appellate decisions on this issue. In *Forsyth* (1997) the Court of Appeal held that "believing" was an ordinary English word that should be left to the jury to determine without any further direction.

6. In relation to proof of mens rea for the handling charge remember the so-called doctrine of "recent possession" and the presumptions created by s.27(3).

MISCELLANEOUS PROVISIONS

9–052   In this chapter on the offences under the Theft Acts we have concentrated on the basic offences. It is important to remember that there are other offences under the Theft Act 1968 which have not been covered in detail. In outline these offences are as follows:

1. OFFENCES OF TEMPORARY DEPRIVATION

9–053   It will be recalled that a charge of theft requires that the prosecution prove that the accused intended permanently to deprive the other of the property. There were those who argued that this element should be dropped from the definition of theft in the 1968 Act, but it was finally decided that it should form part of the new definition of theft. However it was decided that specific offences should be provided for two examples of temporary deprivation. Under s.11 it is an offence to remove articles from places open to the public. This is clearly designed to cover such cases as where a rogue removes a famous painting from an art gallery and offers to return it only upon payment of a ransom.[204] Under s.12 it is an offence to take a motorvehicle or other conveyance without the consent of the owner. Before this provision there was very little the police could do about the rogue who "borrowed" another's car for a joyride and then left it where it was eventually found and returned to the owner. With a car it was very difficult to show that such a rogue intended permanently to deprive the other of the car. Of course it was possible to charge him with stealing the amount of petrol used, but this was hardly satisfactory. Under s.12 he now commits a substantive offence.[205] It is also an offence for a person who knows that a motorvehicle has been taken without the owner's consent, to drive it or to allow himself to be driven in it.

---

[204] See, e.g. *Durkin* [1973] Q.B. 786.
[205] See, e.g. *Stokes* [1982] Crim.L.R. 695; and *Spriggs* [1993] Crim.L.R. 622.

Section 12 offences were originally either way offences carrying a maximum of three years imprisonment, but were reclassified as summary only offences in 1988, thereby reducing the maximum sentence to six months. Unfortunately a dramatic increase in what today is commonly referred to as "joy riding" forced the Government to introduce the Aggravated Vehicle Taking Act 1992 which inserted a new s.12A into the Theft Act 1968. The purpose of this provision is to create an aggravated version of s.12 thereby enabling the courts to pass heavier sentences where, following the commission of the basic s.12 offence, (i) the defendant drove the vehicle dangerously, or (ii) the driving of the vehicle led to an accident which caused injury to another or damage to property other than the vehicle or (iii) damage was caused to the vehicle which was taken. It should be noted that in (ii) and (iii) it is not a requirement that the defendant was at fault in causing the accident or damage. Where the aggravated form of vehicle taking is made out the defendant is liable to imprisonment for up to two years, or up to 14 if death was caused by the accident.[206]

The clear policy behind s.12A is to impose heavier sanctions on those who take vehicles unlawfully and then cause an accident, irrespective of whether or not the accident involves any fault in the driving of the defendant. This strict approach was vividly illustrated by the case of *Marsh*.[207] The defendant was charged with aggravated vehicle taking contrary to s.12A, the aggravating circumstance being, "that owing to the driving of the vehicle, an accident occurred by which injury was caused to any person". While the defendant had been "joy-riding" a woman ran across the road and he knocked her down. She was not seriously injured, and there was no evidence of fault in the manner in which D had driven the car. D submitted that he could not be liable unless it were proved that the accident in question had been caused by culpable driving on his part. This was rejected by the Court of Appeal which determined that on a proper construction of the subsection the question was simply whether the driving of the vehicle was a *cause* of the accident. A very strict liability test is applied, dependant simply on causation, with no requirement whatsoever of fault in the actual driving of the vehicle.

2. ABSTRACTING ELECTRICITY

Under s.13 it is an offence dishonestly to use electricity without authority, or dishonestly to cause the electricity to be diverted or wasted. It is subject to a maximum punishment of five years' imprisonment. Such a section was needed because electricity is not property within the definition of property under s.4 of the Act; it cannot therefore be stolen. Gas and water, on the other hand, are items of property within s.4 and are capable of being stolen. Thus, provided dishonesty is established, it would be an offence under this section for a tramp who has broken into premises for a night's shelter to turn on the electric fire (if it was a gas fire he could be charged with stealing the gas) or for students involved in a sit-in to operate without authority any electrical equipment. **9–054**

3. BUSINESS FRAUDS

Sections 17 to 19 provides for a number of offences relating to commercial fraud such as false accounting (s.17) and to the liability of company officers (ss.18 and 19). **9–055**

---

[206] As inserted by Criminal Justice Act 2003 s.285(1).
[207] [1997] Crim.L.R. 205.

4. ADVERTISING REWARDS

9–056 Under s.23 of the Act it is an offence to advertise publicly a reward for the return of stolen property or lost property, where the words used have the effect of promising immunity from apprehension or inquiry, or that any money paid for the purchase of the goods or advanced by way of loan on the goods will be repaid. The offence is committed by anyone who advertises the reward and anyone who publishes or prints it. This offence is a summary only offence with a limited fine the maximum punishment.

5. GOING EQUIPPED FOR STEALING

9–057 Under s.25 of the Act it is an offence for a person not at his place of abode to have with him any article for use in the course of or in connection with any burglary, theft or cheating. This offence clearly allows the police to stop a suspected burglar well before he has begun to force open the window of a dwelling-house, though the maximum sentence of three years is far less than that available if they apprehend him having entered a building as a trespasser. The width of the offence is illustrated by the conduct of the disreputable hotel waiter in *Doukas*[208] who passed off his own wine as that of house wine. By substituting his own wine, which he had brought on to the premises for that very purpose, he committed the s.25 offence of going equipped for stealing. The offence was also committed in *Minor v DPP*[209] where the defendant was apprehended by police officers in possession of petrol cans and a siphoning tube, having forced off the petrol caps of two cars, but was disturbed before he could actually siphon off any petrol. For the s.25 offence it was immaterial whether or not the actual theft was achieved. A broad definition needs to be applied to the offence. In *Goodwin*[210] the defendant was convicted of going equipped for theft when he used Kenyan 5 shilling coins, identical in size, shape and weight to a 50-pence piece but about half the value, to play gaming machines in an amusement arcade. The case gives new meaning to the expression "coining it in"!

6. RESTITUTION AND COMPENSATION

9–058 Section 28 of the Theft Act 1968 allowed a court to make an order that the stolen property should be returned to its rightful owner or if that were not possible that the victim should be compensated by money from the convicted offender. Further, also that when the court ordered that restitution be made, the convicted person should compensate the person who gave good value for the goods which were being taken from him to be returned to the rightful owner. In effect, a restitution order may be made in favour of any individual with a pre-existing claim of entitlement to recover the stolen goods.

GENERAL READING

9–059 Alldridge, P., "Attempted Murder Of The Soul: Blackmail, Piracy And Secrets" (1993) 13 O.J.L.S. 368.

Beaumont, J., "Getting Stuck Into Burglary: The *Ryan* Case" (1996) 67 *The Criminal Lawyer* 4.

---

[208] [1978] 1 W.L.R. 372; see above, para.9–006, fn.25; and *Rashid* [1977] 1 W.L.R. 298; see above, para.9–006, fn.25.
[209] (1988) 86 Cr.App.R. 378.
[210] [1996] Crim.L.R. 262; see also *M* [2005] Crim.L.R. 479.

Odgers, F.J., "On Rape Intent" (1972) 31 C.L.J. 194.

Reville, N.R., "The Mischief Of Aggravated Burglary" (1989) N.L.J. 835.

Spencer, J.R., "Handling, Theft And The Mala Fide Purchaser" [1985] Crim.L.R. 92 and 440.

Spencer, J.R., "The Mishandling of Handling" [1981] Crim.L.R. 682.

Williams, G., "Handling, Theft And The Purchaser Who Takes A Chance" [1985] Crim.L.R. 432.

Chapter 10

OFFENCES AGAINST PROPERTY III

CRIMINAL DAMAGE

In the two preceding chapters we have examined the offences which deal with the dishonest **10–001** dealing with property. In this chapter we shall look briefly at some of the provisions of the Criminal Damage Act 1971 which cover, amongst other matters, the damaging or destroying of property. As we have already seen[1] it is possible to steal property belonging to another by destroying it so that he is permanently deprived of the property. However, where the property is not destroyed, theft would not be committed and in any case it is asking too much of the law of theft to cover all instances of vandalism and damage to property. Until 1971 offences of damage to property were known as offences of malicious damage; these were to a large extent repealed by the Criminal Law Act 1971 and the offence is now called criminal damage.[2] We shall now look at the basic offences and defences in this Act.[3]

1. THE BASIC OFFENCE

Section 1(1) provides that "A person who without lawful excuse destroys or damages any **10–002** property belonging to another intending to destroy or damage any such property or being reckless as to whether any such property would be destroyed or damaged shall be guilty of an offence."[4]

---

[1] See above, para.8–033.
[2] The 1971 Act is based on the earlier report and proposals of the Law Commission: see Law Com. No.29 *Criminal Law Report on Offences of Damage to Property* (1970).
[3] For an excellent survey of these offences see D.W. Elliott, "Criminal Damage" [1988] Crim.L.R. 404 and "Endangering Life by Destroying or Damaging Property" [1997] Crim.L.R. 382.
[4] See above, para.1–005 for consideration of the trial venue of criminal damage offences. The basic offence under s.1(1) is triable either way if the value of the damage or destruction exceeds £5,000, otherwise it is triable only summarily. If tried on indictment the maximum penalty is 10 years' imprisonment in accordance with s.4(2) of the 1971 Act. If tried summarily because the value of the damage is not more than £5,000 it carries a maximum of 3 months' imprisonment and or a fine not exceeding £2,500. If tried summarily in a case where the value of the damage is greater than £5,000 (either way offence), then the maximum punishment is the magisterial norm, six months' imprisonment and or a fine not exceeding £5,000. *Bristol Magistrates' Court Ex p. E* [1998] 3 All E.R. 798; *Fennell* [2000] Crim.L.R. 677; and *R (on the application of Abbott) v Colchester Magistrates' Court* [2001] Crim.L.R. 564.

A. Actus Reus

10–003 The prosecution must establish (i) damage or destruction of (ii) property belonging to another and (iii) absence of lawful excuse.[5]

(i) Damage or Destruction

10–004 The word destroy would tend to suggest some irreparable damage which renders the property in question useless. Thus if D sets fire to P's car so that it is completely burned out, it can properly be said that D has destroyed the car, even though there may still be a metal shell. Damage, on the other hand, suggests any physical harm which produces impairment of the property's use or value. If D scratched his name on P's car, this can clearly be described as damaging the car in that its value has been clearly reduced. On the other hand the Divisional Court in *Morphitis v Salmon*[6] held that the scratching of a scaffolding bar did not constitute criminal damage, but was merely an incidental effect of the common use of scaffolding components. Difficulties may arise when the harm inflicted is trivial and may, for example, be easily rectified. Several cases concerning graffiti have appeared before the courts and the results are not easy to reconcile.[7] In *Roe v Kingerlee*[8] the court held that, "What constitutes criminal damage is a matter of fact and degree, and it is for the justices, applying their common sense to decide whether what has happened was damage or not." It is not necessarily fatal to the prosecution's case that the harm is rectifiable. However, where the harm can be easily remedied, as in *A. (Juvenile) v The Queen*[9] where the defendant spat on a policeman's raincoat, it might be a reason for holding that there has been no damage. The case might have been different if the coat had required dry cleaning to restore it to its former state.[10]

In *Cox v Riley*[11] it was held to be damage to erase the memory from a plastic circuit card which controlled a computerised saw; although the information stored was intangible property the court took the view that the card itself had been damaged. Similarly, impairment of use was treated as damage in *Whiteley*.[12] W, a computer hacker, gained unauthorised access to a computer network and altered data contained in disks in the system. Relying on s.10, which defines property as "property of a tangible nature" W argued his activities affected only the intangible information contained on the disk. Lord Lane C.J. disagreed:

> "It seems to us that that contention contains a basic fallacy. What the act requires to be proved is that tangible property has been damaged, not necessarily that the damage itself should be tangible."

---

[5] If the offence (either basic criminal damage or aggravated criminal damage) is committed by fire, then the offence is charged as arson which carries life imprisonment, Criminal Damage Act s.1(3).

[6] [1990] Crim.L.R. 48.

[7] Note in *Hardman v Chief Constable of Avon and Somerset Constabulary* [1986] Crim.L.R. 330 it was held that drawing on a public pavement using water soluble chalk or paints did constitute damage; the local authority was put to expense cleaning the substance from the pavement. Motive did not exculpate the defendant; he was a C.N.D. activist who daubed human silhouettes on the pavement to commemorate the Hiroshima anniversary.

[8] [1986] Crim.L.R. 735. The court held that mud graffiti which had been daubed on the walls of a prison cell were capable of constituting damage, despite the fact that they could be easily washed off. The court held that it was not relevant that inexpensive remedial action could be taken to wash the wall; cf. *Hardman*, [1986] Crim.L.R. 735.

[9] [1978] Crim.L.R. 689.

[10] Does it constitute criminal damage for D without P's permission to fill with his own rubbish a skip hired by P?

[11] (1986) 83 Cr.App.R. 54.

[12] (1991) 93 Cr.App.R. 25; see also *Tracey* (1821) 168 E.R. 893 and *Fisher* (1865) L.R. 1 C.C.R. 7.

The particles Whiteley altered were undoubtedly part of the disk and the disk was rendered less valuable to its owner as a result. It was clear, therefore, that he had damaged the disks. Following the implementation of the Computer Misuse Act 1990 in so far as these cases deal with computer disks they would no longer constitute criminal damage for the purpose of s.1(1) of the Criminal Damage Act 1971.[13] They are, however, still authoritative in relation to such items as audio and video tapes on which information is magnetically stored. Erasure of material from such tapes would still constitute criminal damage.

Property can undoubtedly be damaged by the removal of part of it, even though the removal does not physically damage either the part removed or the part left[14]; it would, for example, amount to criminal damage to remove a door from someone's house or to render a car immobile by the removal of its battery. It has been argued that it would equally constitute damage to render a car inoperable by the addition of a wheel clamp, but it seems that the courts would be unlikely to accept this argument.[15]

(ii) Property Belonging to Another

Section 10 says that property of a tangible nature, whether real or personal, and including **10–005** money, may be the subject of a charge of criminal damage. Wild animals, which are covered by s.4(4) of the Theft Act 1968, are covered but not wild flowers as under s.4(3) of the Theft Act.[16] An interesting recent case regarding possession of wild animals is *Cresswell v DPP*.[17] The defendants, acting in protest against badger traps set by DEFRA officials on farmland, had entered the property and destroyed the traps in order to safeguard "wild" badgers. In defence they contended that the badgers were no longer wild but formed "property" within s.10 and as such they were acting to safeguard the property (badgers reduced into possession). This argument was rejected by the Divisional Court.[18] Keane L.J. asserted that where a trap has been established a wild animal will *not* be "in the course of being reduced into possession" until the point at which the animal enters the trap; at this juncture the nexus within the statutory provision becomes operative.[19] It was noted earlier that there is no clear answer to the question of whether or not a corpse is capable of being stolen.[20] If, as was suggested above, there is no good reason why a corpse should not be capable of being stolen, then it should be equally capable of being damaged or destroyed.[21]

In general terms you cannot be guilty of destroying your own property under this provision. Thus if you own a valuable building you may knock it down to build a car park without committing an offence under this provision.[22] (You may, however, have committed an offence against other regulations designed to preserve particular buildings or property.)

---

[13] Section 3(6) of the 1990 Act reverses the effects of these two decisions as far as computer disks are concerned. The accused would now be guilty of a specific computer offence under s.3. Section 3(6) provides: "For the purposes of the Criminal Damage Act 1971 a modification of the contents of a computer shall not be regarded as damaging any computer or any computer storage medium unless its effect on that computer or computer storage medium impairs its physical condition." A new s.3 has since been substituted by the Police and Justice Act 2006.

[14] See, *Morphitis v Salmon* [1990] Crim.L.R. 48, discussed above.

[15] See, *Lloyd v DPP* [1992] 1 All E.R. 982; [1992] All E.R. Annual Review at 105–106.

[16] See above, paras 8–026—8–027.

[17] [2006] EWHC 3379 (Admin).

[18] No individual had any proprietary right or interest in the badgers, or had possession or control of them.

[19] Walker J. in the Divisional Court was more reticent in crystallising the nature of property.

[20] See above, para.8–024. Body parts used as anatomical specimens for exhibition purposes, and for teaching intending doctors, have been deemed capable of being stolen; see *Kelly* [1998] 3 All E.R. 741: considered above, para.8–024.

[21] In *The Times* December 27, 1984, it was reported that a Welsh presbyterian Minister had been charged, inter alia, with criminally damaging a corpse. See also *Kelly* [1998] 3 All E.R. 741.

[22] The section clearly requires that the basic offence can be committed only in relation to another's property. It makes no difference that D has burned his own house down in order to make a fraudulent insurance claim; see *Denton* [1982] 1 All E.R. 65.

However s.10(2) goes on to provide that in certain cases you may be guilty of an offence of damaging your own property if the property is in the custody or control of another or if another has a proprietary right or interest in it or if another has a charge over it. Thus a landlord who has leased his house to Y may be guilty of criminal damage to that property if he deliberately damages it.

(iii) Without Lawful Excuse

10–006 It is part of the prosecution's case that they prove that the accused had no lawful excuse either by virtue of common law or under s.5 of the Criminal Damage Act 1971. This will be discussed after we have considered the other offences.[23]

B. Mens Rea

10–007 You may recall from the earlier chapter on mens rea that the offences of criminal damage were the site of argument about the proper meaning of recklessness; and that for some time, on account of the decision of the House of Lords in *Caldwell*,[24] the meaning of recklessness in criminal damage was different from its meaning in the context of other offences. That is no longer the case since *R v G*,[25] in which the House of Lords effectively unified the meaning of recklessness across the criminal law, along the lines of the decision in *Cunningham*.[26] Lord Bingham concluded his speech in *G* by stating:

> "A person acts recklessly within the meaning of section 1 of the Criminal Damage Act 1971 with respect to—
>
> (i) a circumstance when he is aware of a risk that it exists or will exist;
>
> (ii) a result when he is aware of a risk that it will occur;
>
> and it is, in the circumstances known to him, unreasonable to take the risk."[27]

2. AGGRAVATED DAMAGE

10–008 Section 1(2) provides that:

> "A person, who without lawful excuse destroys or damages any property, whether belonging to himself or another—
>
> (a) intending to destroy or damage any property or being reckless as to whether any property would be destroyed or damaged; and
>
> (b) intending by the destruction or damage to endanger the life of another or being reckless as to whether the life of another would thereby be endangered; shall be guilty of an offence."

Under s.4 this offence is punishable with life imprisonment.

---

[23] Below, para.10–015.
[24] [1982] A.C. 341.
[25] [2003] UKHL 50; [2004] 1 A.C. 1034.
[26] [1957] 2 QB 396.
[27] [2003] UKHL 50 at [41].

The actus reus of this offence is basically the same as that for the offence under s.1(1) with the exception that under this section the offence can be committed in respect of one's own property. Thus if X knows that Y is asleep inside X's house but nonetheless sets fire to it in an attempt to swindle the insurance company, if he is reckless as to Y's life being endangered he is guilty of an offence under s.1(2).

It is essential that the precise wording of the subsection is appreciated. Although we are concerned with life endangerment this is not, in essence, an offence against the person; it is an offence against property. This was made clear by the House of Lords' discussion of the facts in *Steer*,[28] where S had fired a rifle at the bedroom window and door of the bungalow belonging to his former business partner who was in the bedroom at the time. It is clear that the defendant committed the basic criminal damage offence under s.1(1) of the Act. He was charged, however, with being reckless as to whether the life of another was endangered contrary to s.1(2). The House of Lords held that the danger to life has to stem from the damage caused by the accused's conduct and not from the conduct itself. In this case the threat to the victim's life arose from the bullets fired by the defendant and not from the damage he had caused to the property. It may have been different had he been firing into a room full of explosives or if the prosecution had been alleging that the danger to the victim's life stemmed from the flying glass. Lord Bridge remarked:

". . . on the true construction of s.1(2)(b) of the Criminal Damage Act 1971 the prosecution are required to prove that the danger to life resulted from the destruction of or damage to property; it is not sufficient for the prosecution to prove that it resulted from the act of the defendant which caused the destruction or damage."[29]

Similarly, in an arson case, it is not the match or inflammable material which causes the **10–009** danger to life; it is the ensuing conflagration which occurs as the property which has been set on fire is damaged or destroyed. In *Steer* the prosecution should have charged the defendant with an offence against the person arising from the use of the gun.

This distinction was well illustrated by the combined appeals in *Webster and Warwick*.[30] In *Webster* the accused had dropped a heavy paving slab on to a train. The stone only partially penetrated the carriage, but the passengers were showered with debris from the roof. It was not sufficient for the prosecution to prove that W intended to endanger the lives of the passengers by means of being hit by the stone, or that he was reckless as to such endangerment. On the other hand, if the prosecution could prove that W intended the passengers' lives to be endangered by being struck by the roof which W's act had caused to collapse or that W was reckless that lives would be so endangered, there would be a case to answer. Lord Taylor C.J. commented:

"The effect of the statute may be thought to be strange. If the defendant's intention is that the stone itself should crash through the roof of a train or motorvehicle and thereby directly injure a passenger or if he was reckless only as to that outcome, the section would not bite . . . If, however, the defendant intended or was reckless that the stone would smash the roof of the train or vehicle so that metal or wood struts from the roof would or obviously might descend upon a passenger, endangering life, he would surely be guilty. This may seem to many a dismal distinction."[31]

[28] [1987] 2 All E.R. 833.
[29] [1987] 2 All E.R. 833 at 837.
[30] [1995] 2 All E.R. 168; see also Seago, P., "Criminal Law" [1995] All E.R. Annual Review, at p.164; and D.W. Elliott "Endangering Life by Destroying or Damaging Property" [1997] Crim.L.R. 382, esp. 389ff.
[31] [1995] 2 All E.R. 168 at 173.

The Court of Appeal held that since the jury had found that W had intended the stone itself to endanger life by descending into the carriage, he must at least have been reckless that the stone might endanger life by bringing down parts of the roof on passengers thereby endangering life. In *Warwick*, W was charged with aggravated criminal damage by throwing bricks at police cars and also by ramming police cars. The Court of Appeal held that life endangerment could be caused by the damage W had perpetrated on the police cars. A police officer showered with glass or rammed by another car might well lose control of that car due to the damage. Again if the only allegation is that the officer was injured by being hit by the brick, the proper charge would be one under the Offences Against the Person Act 1861.

10–010   The Court of Appeal in *Parker*[32] confirmed what seems clear from the wording of the Act, namely that s.1(2) does not require that the prosecution prove as part of the actus reus that any life was, in fact, endangered. It suffices that the defendant intended by his destruction of or damage to property to endanger life or that he was reckless as to such life endangerment.

As far as the mens rea of this offence goes, the prosecution must prove that the defendant (1) intentionally or recklessly damaged or destroyed property and that (2) he intended by the destruction or damage to endanger the life of another or that he was reckless as to whether the life of another would be endangered by that damage.[33] Recklessness is as defined in *R v G*.[34]

Until the decision of the House of Lords in *Caldwell* aggravated criminal damage under s.1(2) was regarded as a crime of specific intent to which the defence of voluntary intoxication could apply. This was certainly in keeping with an observable pattern, namely that in many cases voluntary intoxication would provide a defence to a very serious charge, but still leave the accused liable to conviction for a lesser charge. However, the decision in *Caldwell* meant that voluntary intoxication would only be a defence where the accused was charged with intentionally seeking to endanger life. This must still be the case after *R v G*, and commonsense would suggest that it will be only in the rarest of cases that the prosecution would so restrict the charge. It is much more likely that the defendant will be charged with either *recklessly* endangering life, or with *intentionally or recklessly* endangering life, in which case the intoxication will be relevant only so far as the allegation of *intentionally* endangering life. *Cunningham*[35] would today be charged with an offence under s.1(2) of the Criminal Damage Act 1971. It is fairly clear that he intentionally damaged the gas meter and that this created a serious and obvious risk that life would be thereby endangered. It is unlikely that he could have any defence to an allegation that he gave no thought to such a risk.[36]

10–011   Whether or not the defendant intended to endanger life or was reckless in this respect must be determined at the time he does the act which causes the damage to or destruction of the property, and not by reference back from the damage or destruction actually caused.

[32] [1993] Crim.L.R. 856.
[33] See, *Merrick* [1996] 1 Cr.App.R. 130; [1995] Crim.L.R. 802. The Court of Appeal held that if M wishes to allege that the taking of precautions meant that he was not reckless, then those precautions must be directed towards preventing the risk occuring at all, rather than remedying it once it has arisen. M had left a live electric wire exposed for six minutes.
[34] See above, para.2–069.
[35] Above, para.2–066 damage of gas meter causing noxious fumes to escape.
[36] From a procedural point of view it is likely that where the prosecution is relying on "intention or recklessness as to endangerment of life" the indictment will contain two counts, one containing a charge that the accused intended to endanger life and the alternative count that he was reckless as to endangering life. In this way the jury will be forced to indicate which of the two states of mind they found to be proved since this will be of relevance in the sentencing; see *Hoof* (1980) 72 Cr.App.R. 126, a decision on arson under s.1(3) which seems equally applicable to s.1(2).

Thus in *Dudley*[37] the accused threw a fire bomb at the complainant's house. This clearly created the risk of serious damage to the property likely to endanger life. However, the complainants managed to extinguish the fire before it had caused more than trivial damage to the house. The defendant argued that there was no evidence that the damage which was actually caused was either intended to or likely to endanger life.

The Court of Appeal held that the words "destruction or damage" in s.1(2)(b) referred back to the damage or destruction intended or as to which there was recklessness, in s.1(2)(a). In this case it was clear that the defendant's conduct created a serious and obvious risk that the property would be damaged in a way likely to endanger life and he, therefore, committed the aggravated offence under s.1(2) even though the actual damage caused was not likely to have this effect. The reverse is equally true. If D is reckless as to causing damage which is not at all likely to endanger life, the fact that a chance happening causes a serious life endangering destruction of the property will not render him liable to the more serious charge.

It must, however, be remembered that the offence under s.1(2) requires some actual damage to the property. If the complainants in *Dudley* had managed to extinguish the bomb before any damage had been caused to their property, the offence under s.1(2) would not have been committed even though his conduct was likely to endanger life.

3. ARSON

Arson was a common law offence of damaging property by fire. It is abolished by the **10–012** Criminal Damage Act 1971 but the term arson is retained to describe the situation where offences under s.1 are committed by means of fire. Where the damage has been perpetrated by fire the offence shall be charged as arson and whether the conduct contravenes s.1(1) or s.1(2) the penalty available is life imprisonment. This reflects the law's great disapproval of the use of fire which of course is a completely uncontrollable means of destroying property.[38]

4. THREATENING TO DESTROY OR DAMAGE PROPERTY (SECTION 2)

If a person threatens without lawful excuse to commit an offence under s.1 intending that **10–013** the other shall fear that the threat will be carried out, he commits a separate offence of threatening damage which is punishable by 10 years' imprisonment. You should note that he must intend that the other should be put in fear that he will carry out the threat; recklessness that the other will be put in fear is not enough.

5. POSSESSION OF ANYTHING WITH INTENT TO DAMAGE OR DESTROY PROPERTY (SECTION 3)

It is an offence for a person to have anything in his custody or under his control intending **10–014** without lawful excuse to use it or to cause or permit another to use it to commit an offence under s.1 of the Act. This offence is punishable by 10 years' imprisonment. Thus if X buys matches from a shop intending to burn down the local public house, he has already

---

[37] [1989] Crim.L.R. 57.
[38] See, *Hoof* (1980) 72 Cr.App.R. 126, above, para.10–011, fn.36; and *Booth* [1999] Crim.L.R. 144.

committed an offence contrary to s.3 of this Act, though there may be difficulty in proving that he had the requisite intent.

6. THE DEFENCE OF LAWFUL EXCUSE

10–015 Section 5 of the Criminal Damage Act 1971 states:

> "5.—(1) This section applies to any offence under s.1(1) above and any offence under s.2 or 3 above other than one involving a threat by the person charged to destroy or damage property in a way which he knows is likely to endanger the life of another or involving an intent by the person charged to use or cause or permit the use of something in his custody or under his control so to destroy or damage property.
>
> (2) A person charged with an offence to which this section applies shall, whether or not he would be treated for the purposes of this Act as having a lawful excuse apart from this subsection, be treated for those purposes as having a lawful excuse—
>
> (a) if at any time of the act or acts alleged to constitute the offence he believed that the person or persons whom he believed to be entitled to consent to the destruction of or damage to the property in question had so consented, or would have so consented to it if he or they had known of the destruction or damage and its circumstances; or
>
> (b) if he destroyed or damaged or threatened to destroy or damage the property in question or, in the case of a charge of an offence under s.3 above, intended to use or cause or permit the use of something to destroy or damage it, in order to protect property belonging to himself or another or a right or an interest in property which was or which he believed to be vested in himself or another, and at the time of the act or acts alleged to constitute the offence he believed—
>
> (i) that the property, right or interest was in immediate need of protection; and
>
> (ii) that the means of protection adopted or proposed to be adopted were or would be reasonable having regard to all the circumstances.
>
> (3) For the purposes of this section it is immaterial whether belief is justified or not if it is honestly held.
>
> (4) . . .
>
> (5) This section shall not be construed as casting doubt on any defence recognised by law as a defence to criminal charges."

In all the offences we have considered the prosecution have to establish that the accused acted without lawful excuse. For all offences except those under s.1(2) and s.1(3) and those under s.2 where the threat was to cause destruction or damage in a way likely to endanger life and s.3 where the possession was with intent to destroy or damage in a way likely to endanger life, the defence receives a partial definition under s.5 of the Act. In addition to the defence under s.5 the phrase lawful excuse in the definition of the offences means that the general common law defences are available to offences under the Act.[39]

---

[39] This is expressly provided for in s.5(5). See also *Merrick,* para.10–010, fn.33 above and the comment by J.C. Smith [1995] Crim.L.R. at 804.

A. Lawful Excuse Under Section 5

Under s.5(2)(a) the accused shall be treated as having a lawful excuse if at the time of the **10–016** acts alleged to constitute the offence he honestly (s.5(3) makes it clear it need not be a reasonably held belief) believed that the person whom he believed to be entitled to give consent to the destruction of the property had or would have given consent. Thus if, following a storm, X sees that his neighbour's garage is in a dangerous condition and likely to fall causing injury to passers-by, if X pulls down the garage to prevent such possible injuries in the belief that Y would have consented, he will have a lawful excuse. In *Denton*[40] it was held that where any employee damaged property belonging to his employer at the request of his employer who wished to make a fraudulent claim in relation to the property, the employee was entitled to rely on his honest belief that the person entitled to give consent to the damage to the property had, in fact, done so.

In *Blake v DPP*[41] a vicar was prosecuted for writing a biblical quotation on a concrete pillar at the perimeter of the Houses of Parliament. He had been one of a group of protesters against the use of force by the allies in the Gulf War. Part of his defence was that he was carrying out the instructions of God, and that he believed God to be the person entitled to give permission to damage the property. The Divisional Court held that however powerful and genuine his belief that God was the person entitled to give permission, this did not amount to a lawful excuse under the domestic law of England.

In *Jaggard v Dickinson*[42] the accused had gained entry to what she thought was a friend's house by breaking a window and damaging a net curtain. Later it transpired that the house belonged to someone else altogether. She had her friend's permission to treat his house as her own and her mistake as to which house it was clearly stemmed from intoxication. She was charged under s.1(1) of the Act and the justices held that she was not entitled to rely on s.5(2), since the belief relied on was induced by intoxication. The Divisional Court held that the conviction should be quashed. Section 5(3) directed the court to focus on the existence of the belief and not its intellectual soundness. A belief could be just as much honestly held if it was induced by intoxication as if it stemmed from stupidity, forgetfulness or inattention. This case highlights the absurdity of the rules relating to intoxication. If this woman had stumbled against the window in a blind intoxicated stupor she would have had no defence, but since her defence was based on a more specific claim of right which is interpreted as requiring no more than an honestly held belief, she is acquitted despite the fact that she is charged with a crime of basic intent. However, it is suggested that until it is expressly held to be wrong, it should be regarded as representing the present law.

Section 5(2) confers a defence upon a defendant who is charged with an offence under **10–017** ss.1, 2 or 3 of the Act and who acted in order to protect property belonging either to himself or to another which he believed to be in immediate[43] need of protection and that he believed the means adopted were reasonable having regard to all the circumstances. The defence will be inoperative, as in *Cresswell v DPP*[44] (the badger case), where D seeks to protect property which belongs neither to another nor himself, or where no vested interest

---

[40] [1982] 1 All E.R. 65.
[41] [1993] Crim.L.R. 587.
[42] [1981] Q.B. 527; [1980] 3 All E.R. 716; see above, para.5–034.
[43] In *Mitchell* [2003] EWCA Crim 2188; [2004] R.T.R. 14, D accepted that his damaging a wheel clamp which had been attached to his car did not fall within s.5(2), because of the lack of immediacy.
[44] [2006] EWHC 3379 (Admin): see above at para.8–027, fn.93.

prevails. Again the provision would seem very clearly to indicate a subjective test, but the courts have found such an approach to be unduly favourable to the defendant and have therefore found ways of introducing an objective element. They have done this by holding that the phrase "in order to protect property" required the court to ask whether the acts done did, in fact, protect property or were capable of so doing. In *Jones and others*,[45] D was charged with conspiracy to commit criminal damage at a military airbase. She claimed that she was acting in order to protect property in Iraq against unlawful aggression. The availability of the defence under s.5(2)(b) did not depend on whether the war on Iraq was lawful. However, its lawfulness might impact on the jury's assessment of D's belief that her actions were reasonable in the circumstances. To what extent would a court find credible a suggestion that D's actions would protect property in Iraq, and consequently that D did believe in the reasonableness of her actions?

In *Blake v DPP*,[46] where B claimed that he had damaged the property in the belief that it would protect property in the Gulf, but the Divisional Court held that even if he did believe that he had a lawful excuse under s.5(2)(b), the court must objectively assess whether, on the facts believed by the defendant, the action taken by him was capable of protecting the property or had, in fact, protected the property. It is easy to understand why, in the context of *Blake,* the court wished to impose an objective test, but it is extremely difficult to find such a test in the wording of the statute. At best it could be said that an objective assessment of the facts might assist the court in determining what belief the defendant did, in fact, hold.[47]

In both s.5(2)(a) and 5(2)(b) it would appear that the accused must raise the issue, but the prosecution must prove beyond reasonable doubt that the accused was acting without lawful excuse.

B. Lawful Excuse Outside Section 5

10–018   As we said earlier, s.5(5) makes it quite clear that the partial definition of lawful excuse provided by s.5(2) must not be taken as casting doubt on any defence recognised as a general defence to criminal charges. Where the offence is one involving intention or recklessness as to endangering life the accused must rely on the general defences since s.5(2) does not apply. Thus the defences of self-defence, defence of property, prevention of crime, duress, etc., all apply to offences under the Act. If X were being pursued by Y and he picked up Z's garden gnome and flung it at Y, he would be able to plead self-defence. It would seem in keeping with the Act and the way it has been interpreted that if, in such a case, X were mistaken about Y's intentions, it should suffice that he honestly believed he was about to be attacked.

---

[45] [2004] EWCA Crim 1981; [2005] Q.B. 259. The court did not consider it necessary to rule on the lawfulness of the Iraq war. The case has since been heard by the House of Lords: [2006] UKHL 16. Section 5 of the Criminal Damage Act 1971 is a marginal issue before that court. The discussion in the House of Lords focuses on the availability or otherwise of the defence of prevention of crime, under s.3 of the Criminal Law Act 1967. D's appeal was dismissed. See above, para.10–016.

[46] [1993] Crim.L.R. 587; see above, para.5–095. See also *Hill and Hall* [1989] Crim.L.R. 136.

[47] See, also *Johnson v DPP* [1994] Crim.L.R. 673. In *Chamberlain v Lindon* [1998] 2 All E.R. 538 D had demolished a wall built on V's land as D honestly believed such action was necessary to protect his right of vehicular access across V's land and that delay would prejudice his rights. The Divisional Court held that D had a lawful excuse; objectively determined, he was protecting his right of way.

GENERAL READING

Birch, D.J., "The Foresight Saga: The Biggest Mistake of All?" [1988] Crim.L.R. 4. **10–019**

Davies, F.G., "The Extension of the *Caldwell* Principle" (1990) 54 J.C.L. 374.

Elliott, D.W., "Criminal Damage" [1988] Crim.L.R. 403.

Elliott, D.W., "Endangering Life by Destroying or Damaging Property" [1997] Crim.L.R. 382.

Jefferson, M., "Recklessness: The Objectivity Of The Caldwell Test" (1999) 63 J.C.L. 57.

Gardner, S., "Reckless Refined" (1993) 109 L.Q.R. 21.

Leigh, L.H, "Recklessness After Reid" (1983) 56 M.L.R. 208.

Williams, G., "Two Nocturnal Blunders" (1990) 140 N.L.J. 1564.

INDEX

(all references are to paragraph number)

This index has been prepared using Sweet & Maxwell's Legal Taxonomy. Main index entries conform to keywords provided by the Legal Taxonomy except where references to specific documents or non-standard terms (denoted by quotation marks) have been included. These keywords provide a means of identifying similar concepts in other Sweet & Maxwell publications and online services to which keywords from the Legal Taxonomy have been applied. Readers may find some minor differences between terms used in the text and those which appear in the index. Suggestions to *sweetandmaxwell.taxonomy@thomson.com*

Abandonment
theft, 8–031
Abstraction of electricity
generally, 9–054
Abetting
See **Aiding and abetting**
Abnormality of mind
See **Diminished responsibility**
Accessories
And see **Secondary parties**
actus reus, 4–005
aiding and abetting, 4–008—4–013
assistance after commission of crime, 4–047
background, 4–001
counselling and procuring, 4–008—4–013
introduction, 4–005
knowledge of type of crime, 4–006—4–007
mens rea, 4–005
reform proposals, 4–046
repentance before commission of crime, 4–042—4–045
Accomplices
attempts, 6–002
Acquittals
co-conspirators, 6–042
"Active participation"
conspiracy, 6–047—6–048
Actual bodily harm
actus reus, 7–076
bodily harm, 7–078—7–079
introduction, 7–076
mens rea, 7–080
occasioning actual bodily harm, 7–077
racially aggravated offences, 7–097
religiously aggravated offences, 7–097

Actual knowledge
mens rea, 2–074
Actus reus
assault
generally, 7–063—7–066
omission to act, 2–020
assault by penetration, 7–132
attempts
generally, 6–003—6–007
'last act' test, 6–007
preparatory acts, 6–005
reform proposals, 6–007
automatism
alcohol, and, 2–012
burden of proof, 2–010—2–011
cause, 2–009
drugs, and, 2–012
evidence, 2–007—2–008
introduction, 2–006
self-induced, 2–012
standard of proof, 2–010—2–011
battery
consent, 7–071
generally, 7–069—7–073
omission to act, 2–020, 7–070
unlawful force, 7–072—7–073
bibliography, 2–051
blackmail, 9–033—9–036
burglary, 9–024—9–028
causation
condition of victim, 2–035
generally, 2–032—2–033
substantial cause, 2–034
supervening events, 2–036—2–050
'thin skull' cases, 2–035

causing death by dangerous driving, 7–059
causing grievous bodily harm
    generally, 7–090
    omission to act, 2–019
child sex offences, 7–136
conduct
    automatism, 2–007—2–012
    generally, 2–005—2–006
    state of affairs, 2–013—2–014
coincidence of actus reus and mens rea,
    2–077—2–079
conspiracy
    object of agreement, 6–033—6–038
    parties to agreement, 6–039—6–041
    rationale, 6–031
    requirement of agreement, 6–031—6–032
criminal damage, 10–003—10–006
damage to property
    blackmail, 9–033—9–036
    burglary, 9–024—9–028
    criminal damage, 10–003—10–006
    handling, 9–038—9–045
    omission to act, 2–022
    robbery, 9–020
    theft, 8–004—8–037
failure to act
    conclusion, 2–031
    generally, 2–015—2–016
    medical treatment, 2–028—2–030
    offences against the person, 2–017—2–021
    offences against property, 2–022
    person who is under duty to act,
        2–023—2–027
    statutory duty, 2–024
    supervening fault, 2–027
    voluntary assumption of duty, 2–026
generally, 2–004
grievous bodily harm
    causing, 2–019
    inflicting, 2–021
handling, 9–038—9–045
homicide
    causing death by dangerous driving, 7–059
    infanticide, 7–058
    manslaughter, 7–009—7–012
    murder, 7–009—7–012
    omission to act, 2–017—2–021
    suicide, 7–057
    voluntary manslaughter, 7–018
inchoate offences
    attempts, 6–003—6–007
    conspiracy, 6–031—6–041
    incitement, 6–019—6–020
incitement, 6–019—6–020
infanticide, 7–058
inflicting grievous bodily harm
    generally, 7–083—7–087
    omission to act, 2–021
introduction, 2–001—2–003

involuntary conduct
    burden of proof, 2–010—2–011
    cause, 2–009
    evidence, 2–007—2–008
    introduction, 2–006
    self-induced, 2–012
    standard of proof, 2–010—2–011
involuntary manslaughter, 7–037
manslaughter
    generally, 7–009—7–012
    human being, 7–012
    jurisdiction, 7–010
    involuntary manslaughter, 7–037
    omission to act, 2–018
    reasonable creature in rerum natura,
        7–012
    unlawful killing, 7–011
M'naghten Rules, 2–009
meaning, 2–004
murder
    generally, 7–009—7–012
    human being, 7–012
    jurisdiction, 7–010
    omission to act, 2–018
    reasonable creature in rerum natura,
        7–012
    unlawful killing, 7–011
not guilty pleas, 2–001
offences against the person
    assault, 7–063—7–066
    battery, 7–069—7–073
    manslaughter, 7–009—7–012
    murder, 7–009—7–012
    omission to act, 2–017—2–021
    unlawful wounding, 7–083—7–087
    voluntary manslaughter, 7–018
    wounding with intent, 7–090
offences against property
    blackmail, 9–033—9–036
    burglary, 9–024—9–028
    criminal damage, 10–003—10–006
    handling, 9–038—9–045
    omission to act, 2–022
    robbery, 9–020
    theft, 8–004—8–037
omission to act
    conclusion, 2–031
    generally, 2–015—2–016
    medical treatment, 2–028—2–030
    offences against the person, 2–017—2–021
    offences against property, 2–022
    person who is under duty to act,
        2–023—2–027
    statutory duty, 2–024
    supervening fault, 2–027
    voluntary assumption of duty, 2–026
rape, 7–120—7–128
reading materials, 2–051
robbery, 9–020

secondary parties
  commission of actus reus, 4–035
  generally, 4–034
  introduction, 4–005
  joint trial of principal and secondary
      party, 4–038—4–040
  no principal offender, 4–036
  previous acquittal of principal offender,
      4–037
sexual assault, 7–133
sexual offences
  assault by penetration, 7–132
  child sex offences, 7–136
  child under 13, against, 7–135
  rape, 7–120—7–128
  sexual assault, 7–133
state of affairs offences, 2–013—2–014
status offences, 2–013—2–014
strict liability, and, 3–001
suicide, 7–057
theft
  appropriates, 8–004—8–019
  belonging to another, 8–028—8–037
  property, 8–020—8–027
unlawful wounding
  generally, 7–083—7–087
  omission to act, 2–021
voluntary conduct
  automatism, 2–007—2–012
  generally, 2–005—2–006
  state of affairs, 2–013—2–014
voluntary manslaughter, 7–018
wounding with intent
  generally, 7–090
  omission to act, 2–019
Advertising rewards
  generally, 9–056
Age
  criminal responsibility, 5–098—5–100
Aggravated burglary
  generally, 9–030—9–031
Aggravated criminal damage
  generally, 10–008—10–010
Agreements
  conspiracy
    general requirement, 6–031—6–032
    introduction, 6–029
    object, 6–033—6–038
    parties, 6–039—6–041
Aiding and abetting
  And see **Secondary parties**
  attempts, 6–002
  generally, 4–008
  joint enterprise, and, 4–027—4–028
  mental element, 4–012—4–013
  omission, 4–011
  presence, 4–010
  relevant conduct, 4–009 —4–011

Alcohol
  automatism, 2–012
  intoxication, 5–041
"Allowing"
  meaning, 3–005
"Alter ego doctrine"
  corporate liability, 4–061—4–062
Alternative verdicts
  offences against the person, 7–094
"Appropriates"
  And see **Theft**
  attempted theft, 8–011
  bona fide purchaser, 8–019
  case precedents, 8–010
  civil law, and, 8–012
  company as victim, 8–014
  dealings, 8–018
  deception, 8–011
  Gallasso decision, 8–013
  generally, 8–004—8–008
  gifts, 8–016—8–017
  Gomez decision, 8–009
  jurisdictional issues, 8–015
  keeping, 8–018
  omissions, 8–018
Arson
  generally, 10–012
Assault
  actual bodily harm
    actus reus, 7–076
    bodily harm, 7–078—7–079
    introduction, 7–076
    mens rea, 7–080
    occasioning actual bodily harm, 7–077
  actus reus
    generally, 7–063—7–066
    omission to act, 2–020
  apprehension of application of immediate
      force, 7–067
  hostility, 7–075
  introduction, 7–062
  mens rea, 7–074—7–075
  racially aggravated offences, 7–097
  religiously aggravated offences, 7–097
  sexual offences
    assault by penetration, 7–132
    sexual assault, 7–133
  unlawful force, 7–068
Assault by penetration
  child under 13, on, 7–135
  generally, 7–132
Assistance
  See **Encouraging or assisting crime**
Assisting police
  secondary parties, 4–047
Attempts
  accomplices, 6–002
  actus reus
    generally, 6–003—6–007

'last act' test, 6–007
  preparatory acts, 6–005
  reform proposals, 6–007
aiding and abetting, 6–002
bibliography, 6–020
conspiracy, 6–002
counselling and procuring, 6–002
duress, 5–080
general principles, 6–002
impossibility
  examples, 6–014—6–018
  generally, 6–013
  introduction, 6–002
indictment, 6–001
intention, 6–008
involuntary manslaughter, 6–002
'last act' test
  generally, 6–007
  introduction, 6–004
mens rea, 6–008—6–011
mode of trial, 6–002
murder, 5–080
preparatory acts
  generally, 6–019
  introduction, 6–005
restrictions on scope, 6–002
sentencing, 6–002
specific intent crimes, 6–012
statutory provision, 6–002
theft, 8–011
Automatism
alcohol, 2–012
burden of proof, 2–010—2–011
cause, 2–009
drugs, 2–012
evidence, 2–007—2–008
insanity, and, 5–010—5–012
intoxication, and, 5–037—5–039
introduction, 2–006
self-induced
  generally, 2–012
  intoxication, 5–037—5–039
standard of proof, 2–010—2–011
Basic intent
intoxication, 5–028—5–034
wounding with intent, 7–092
Battery
actus reus
  generally, 7–069—7–073
  omission to act, 2–020
consent, 7–071
hostility, 7–075
introduction, 7–062
mens rea, 7–074—7–075
omissions, 7–070
racially aggravated offences, 7–097
religiously aggravated offences, 7–097
unlawful force, 7–072—7–073

"Belonging to another"
And see **Theft**
abandonment, 8–031
basic provision, 8–029—8–031
bribes, 8–037
constructive trusts, 8–037
criminal damage, 10–003—10–006
equitable interests, 8–031
extended meaning, 8–032—8–037
fraud, 8–030
introduction, 8–028
mistake, 8–035—8–036
proceeds of dealings, 8–033
secret profits, 8–037
Blackmail
accompanied by menaces, 9–034
actus reus, 9–033—9–036
demand, 9–033
intent to cause loss to another, 9–035
introduction, 9–032
unwarranted demand, 9–036
view to gain for maker or another, 9–035
"Blameworthiness"
mens rea, 2–052
Blasphemy
strict liability, 3–003
Bolam test
omissions, 2–028
Bona fide purchaser
See **Theft**
Boxing
offences against the person, 7–109
Bribes
theft, 8–037
Burden of proof
automatism, 2–010—2–011
generally, 1–010
Burglary
actus reus, 9–024—9–028
aggravated offence, 9–030—9–031
aggravated trespass, 9–023
building, 9–027
dwelling, 9–023
entry, 9–024—9–025
generally, 9–023
mens rea, 9–029
part of a building, 9–028
trespasser, 9–026
Caldwell recklessness
See **Mens rea**
Causation
condition of victim, 2–035
de minimis, 2–034
generally, 2–032—2–033
substantial cause, 2–034
supervening events
  administration of drugs, 2–043—2–045
  conduct by victim, 2–049
  fright and flight cases, 2–037—2–038

introduction, 2–036
medical treatment cases, 2–046—2–048
psychological makeup of victim,
  2–049—2–050
subsequent events, 2–039
third party conduct, 2–040—2–042
'thin skull' cases, 2–035
"Cause"
meaning, 3–006
Causing children to engage in sexual activity
generally, 7–136
Causing children to watch sexual acts
generally, 7–136
Causing death by dangerous driving
generally, 7–059
Causing grievous bodily harm
See **Wounding with intent**
Causing sexual activity without consent
child under 13, on, 7–135
generally, 7–134
Child sex offences
generally, 7–136
Children
conspiracy, 6–041
doli incapax, 5–098
infant of 10 years or more, 5–098—5–099
infant under 10 years, 5–097
offences against the person, 7–002
sexual offences, 7–135—7–136
Choses in action
theft, 8–022
Common assault
assault
  actual bodily harm, 7–076—7–080
  actus reus, 7–063—7–066
  apprehension of application of immediate
    force, 7–067
  hostility, 7–075
  mens rea, 7–074—7–075
  unlawful force, 7–068
battery
  actus reus, 7–069—7–073
  consent, 7–071
  hostility, 7–075
  mens rea, 7–074—7–075
  omissions, 7–070
  unlawful force, 7–072—7–073
introduction, 7–062
racially aggravated offences, 7–097
religiously aggravated offences, 7–097
Common law
generally, 1–005
Companies
And see **Corporate liability**
generally, 4–059—4–069
theft, 8–014
Company officers
corporate liability, 4–061—4–062

Compensation
offences against property, 9–058
Complicity
actus reus
  commission of actus reus, 4–035
  introduction, 4–034
  joint trial of principal and secondary
    party, 4–038—4–040
  no principal offender, 4–036
  previous acquittal of principal offender,
    4–037
aiding and abetting
  generally, 4–008
  mental element, 4–012—4–013
  omission, 4–011
  presence, 4–010
  relevant conduct, 4–009 —4–011
assistance after commission of crime, 4–047
background, 4–001
counselling and procuring
  generally, 4–008
  mental element, 4–012—4–013
  omission, 4–011
  presence, 4–010
  relevant conduct, 4–009 —4–011
Cunningham recklessness, 4–007
failure to act, 4–011
introduction, 4–005
knowledge of type of crime, 4–006—4–007
mens rea, 4–005
'no-questions-asked' case, 4–006
omissions, 4–011
presence, 4–010
recklessness, 4–007
reform proposals, 4–046
repentance before commission of crime,
  4–042—4–045
Condition of victim
See **Causation**
"Conditional intention"
conspiracy, 6–049
theft, 8–050—8–051
Conduct
actus reus
  automatism, 2–007—2–012
    generally, 2–005—2–006
    state of affairs, 2–013—2–014
  automatism
  alcohol, and, 2–012
  burden of proof, 2–010—2–011
  cause. 2–009
  drugs, and, 2–012
  evidence, 2–007—2–008
  introduction, 2–006
  self-induced, 2–012
  standard of proof, 2–010—2–011
conspiracy
  active participation, 6–047—6–048
  generally, 6–045

intervening events, 2–049
state of affairs, 2–013—2–014

Conjoined twins
offences against the person, 7–004

Consent
battery, 7–071
boxing, 7–109
exceptions to general rule, 7–107—7–112
football, 7–110
horseplay, 7–112
introduction, 7–098
limits of defence, 7–099—7–106
meaning, 7–113
medical treatment, 7–111
rape, 7–121—7–128
reform proposals, 7–116
rough horseplay, 7–112
rugby, 7–110
sporting activities, 7–108—7–110

Conspiracy
acquittal of co-conspirator, 6–042
active participation, 6–047—6–048
actus reus
acquittal of co-conspirator, 6–042
rationale, 6–031
object of agreement, 6–033—6–038
parties to agreement, 6–039—6–041
requirement of agreement, 6–031—6–032
agreement
general requirement, 6–031—6–032
introduction, 6–029
object, 6–033—6–038
parties, 6–039—6–041
attempts, 6–002
children, 6–041
commit criminal offence, to, 6–033
commit murder abroad, to, 6–033
conditional intention, 6–049
corrupting public morals, 6–034
course of conduct
active participation, 6–047—6–048
generally, 6–045
defraud, to
'defraud', 6–035—6–036
mens rea, 6–037
reform proposals, 6–038
doli incapax, 6–041
generally, 6–029—6–030
husband and wife, 6–040
impossibility, 6–050
intention
conditional intention, 6–049
each conspirator, by, 6–046
mens rea
active participation, 6–047—6–048
conditional intention, 6–049
course of conduct, 6–045
intention on part of each conspirator, 6–046

recklessness, 6–043—6–044
minors, 6–041
negligence, 6–043—6–044
object of agreement
commit criminal offence, to, 6–033
commit murder abroad, to, 6–033
corrupt public morals, to, 6–034
defraud, to, 6–035—6–038
introduction, 6–033
outrage public decency, to, 6–034
outraging public decency, 6–034
parties to agreement
husband and wife, 6–040
introduction, 6–039
one of parties is exempt, 6–041
rationale, 6–031
recklessness, 6–043—6–044
strict liability, 6–043—6–044
territorial jurisdiction, 6–051

Conspiracy to defraud
'defraud', 6–035—6–036
mens rea, 6–037
reform proposals, 6–038

Constructive knowledge
mens rea, 2–076

Constructive manslaughter
See **Unlawful act manslaughter**

Constructive trusts
theft, 8–037

Corporate killing
See **Corporate manslaughter**

Corporate liability
alter ago doctrine, 4–061—4–062
bibliography, 4–070
excluded crimes, 4–064
general principles, 4–059
"hands and brains", 4–061
identification doctrine
generally, 4–061—4–062
reforms, 4–066—4–067
manslaughter
generally, 4–066—4–067
penalties, 4–068
member liability, 4–063
penalties, 4–064—4–065
shareholder liability, 4–063
summary, 4–069
vicarious liability, 4–060

Corporate manslaughter
generally, 4–066—4–067
penalties, 4–068

Corpses
See **Human remains**

Corrupting public morals
See **Against public morals**

Counselling and procuring
And see **Secondary parties**
attempts, 6–002
generally, 4–008

mental element, 4–012—4–013
omission, 4–011
presence, 4–010
relevant conduct, 4–009 —4–011
Course of conduct
active participation, 6–047—6–048
generally, 6–045
Courts
structure, 1–005—1–008
Crime prevention
self-defence, 5–046
Criminal damage
actus reus, 10–003—10–006
aggravated offence, 10–008—10–010
arson, 10–012
basic offence, 10–002
bibliography, 10–019
damage, 10–004
defence, 10–015—10–018
destruction, 10–004
introduction, 10–001
lawful excuse, 10–015—10–018
mens rea, 10–007
omission to act, 2–022
possession with intent, 10–014
property belonging to another, 10–005
threats to commit, 10–001
without lawful excuse, 10–006
Criminal evidence
automatism, 2–007—2–008
Criminal law
classification of offences, 1–005—1–008
introduction, 1–001
proof
burden of proof, 1–010
introduction, 1–009
standard of proof, 1–011
purposes, 1–002—1–004
Criminal libel
strict liability, 3–003
Criminal offences
classification, 1–005—1–008
either way offences, 1–006
indictable offences, 1–006
summary offences, 1–006
"Culpability"
mens rea, 2–052
Cunningham **recklessness**
See **Involuntary manslaughter**
See **Mens rea**
See **Secondary parties**
Damage
criminal damage, 10–004
Damage to property
actus reus, 10–003—10–006
aggravated offence, 10–008—10–010
arson, 10–012
basic offence, 10–002
bibliography, 10–019

damage, 10–004
defence, 10–015—10–018
destruction, 10–004
introduction, 10–001
lawful excuse, 10–015—10–018
mens rea, 10–007
omission to act, 2–022
possession with intent, 10–014
property belonging to another, 10–005
threats to commit, 10–001
without lawful excuse, 10–006
Dangerous dogs
strict liability, 3–018—3–019
De minimis
causation, 2–034
Dealings
See **Theft**
"Defect of reason"
insanity, 5–008
Defence of property
generally, 5–051
Defences
abnormality of mind
cause, 5–017—5–019
effect, 5–020
introduction, 5–015
procedural note, 5–021
suffering, 5–016
criminal damage, 10–015—10–018
defect of reason, 5–008
defence of others
duty to retreat, 5–048
generally, 5–047
imminence of violence, 5–049—5–050
defence of property, 5–051
diminished responsibility
bibliography, 5–026
cause of abnormality of mind,
5–017—5–019
conclusions, 5–023—5–025
EC law, and, 5–023—5–025
effect of abnormality of mind, 5–020
generally, 5–015
hospital orders, and, 5–022
intoxication, and, 5–040
procedural note, 5–021
suffering from abnormality of mind, 5–016
disability, 5–001
disease of the mind, 5–009
duress
ambit, 5–072—5–081
apposite test, 5–087—5–088
attempted murder, 5–080
background, 5–071
bibliography, 5–096
circumstances, 5–093—5–095
constituents, 5–082—5–091
murder, 5–072—5–079
nature of threat, 5–082—5–086

other criminal offences, 5–081
reform proposals, 5–089—5–091
voluntary joining of criminal gang, 5–092
duress of circumstances, 5–093—5–095
entrapment
bibliography, 5–103
generally, 5–100—5–102
fitness to plead, 5–001—5–004
hospital orders
generally, 5–022
introduction, 5–003
infancy
children of 10 years or more,
5–098—5–099
children under 10 years, 5–097
doli incapax, 5–098
insanity
automatism, 5–010—5–012
bibliography, 5–026
conclusions, 5–023—5–025
current position, 5–013—5–014
defect of reason, 5–008
disease of the mind, 5–009
EC law, and, 5–023—5–025
generally, 5–006—5–007
intoxication, and, 5–040
introduction, 5–001—5–004
M'naghten Rules, 5–006—5–007
meaning, 5–006—5–007
scope, 5–005
intoxication
bibliography, 5–043
diminished responsibility, and, 5–040
drinking, and, 5–041
generally, 5–027
insanity, and, 5–040
involuntary intoxication, 5–035—5–036
non-harmful drugs, 5–037—5–039
reform proposals, 5–042
self-induced automatism, 5–037—5–039
voluntary intoxication, 5–028—5–034
lawful excuse, 10–015—10–018
necessity
bibliography, 5–070
duress of circumstances, 5–093—5–095
general defence, as, 5–069
introduction, 5–062
killing of another, 5–063—5–064
medical treatment, 5–065—5–067
statutory restrictions, 5–068
schizophrenia, 5–001
self-defence
bibliography, 5–061
defence of others, and, 5–047—5–050
defence of property, 5–051
excessive force, 5–052—5–059
introduction, 5–044
prevention of crime, 5–046
summary, 5–060

use of force, 5–045
strict liability, 3–026
superior orders, 5–104—5–105
unfitness to plead, 5–001—5–004
use of force, 5–045
Delegation
vicarious liability, 4–054—4–055
Destruction of property
criminal damage, 10–004
Deterrence
purpose of criminal law, 1–004
Diminished responsibility
abnormality of mind
cause, 5–017—5–019
effect, 5–020
introduction, 5–015
suffering, 5–016
bibliography, 5–026
conclusions, 5–023—5–025
EC law, and, 5–023—5–025
generally, 5–015
hospital orders, and, 5–022
intoxication, and, 5–040
manslaughter, 7–018
procedural note, 5–021
Direct intent
See **Mens rea**
Directors
corporate liability, 4–061—4–062
"Disease of the mind"
insanity, 5–009
Dishonesty
And see **Theft**
belief in consent, 8–041
belief in legal right, 8–040
belief that owner cannot be traced, 8–042
handling, 9–049
meaning, 8–039
other cases, 8–043—8–045
Doli incapax
conspiracy, 6–041
generally, 5–098—5–100
offences against the person, 7–002
Drugs
automatism, 2–012
intervening events, 2–043—2–045
intoxication, 5–037—5–039
joint responsibility for administration,
2–043—2–045
strict liability, 3–016
unlawful act manslaughter, 7–042—7–043
Duress
ambit, 5–072—5–081
apposite test, 5–087—5–088
attempted murder, 5–080
background, 5–071
bibliography, 5–096
circumstances, 5–093—5–095
constituents, 5–082—5–086

murder
 comparison with necessity, 5–076
 conclusions, 5–078—5–079
 executive discretion, 5–075
 heroism, 5–073
 introduction, 5–072
 Law Commission report, 5–077
 sanctity of human life, 5–073
 terrorism, 5–074
 nature of threat
  generally, 5–082
  immediacy, 5–085—5–086
  recipient, 5–083
  specificity, 5–084
 necessity, 5–093—5–095
 objective approach, 5–087—5–088
 other criminal offences, 5–081
 reform proposals, 5–089—5–091
 threat
  generally, 5–082
  immediacy, 5–085—5–086
  recipient, 5–083
  specificity, 5–084
 voluntary joining of criminal gang, 5–092
Duty of care
 gross negligence manslaughter,
  7–051—7–052
Egg shell skull
 causation, 2–035
Either way offences
 generally, 1–006
Electricity
 abstraction, 9–054
 theft, 8–021
Employers
 And see **Vicarious liability**
 generally, 4–050—4–057
"Encourage"
 secondary parties, 4–008
Encouraging or assisting crime
 background, 6–021—6–024
 defences, 6–027
 elements, 6–025
 jurisdiction, 6–028
 mental element, 6–026—6–027
 strict liability offences, 6–026
 territorial application, 6–028
 types of offence, 6–024—6–025
 Tyrrell principle, 6–028
Engaging in sexual activity in presence of
 children
 generally, 7–136
Entrapment
 bibliography, 5–103
 generally, 5–100—5–102
Environmental law
 strict liability, 3–014—3–015
Equitable interests
 theft, 8–031

Evidence
 See **Criminal evidence**
Evidential burden
 See also **Burden of proof**
 See also **Standard of proof**
 automatism, 2–010—2–011
Ex turpi causa
 gross negligence manslaughter,
  7–051—7–052
Excessive force
 See **Reasonable force**
Failure to act
 conclusion, 2–031
 generally, 2–015—2–016
 medical treatment, 2–028—2–030
 offences against the person
  assault, 2–017
  battery, 2–017
  causing grievous bodily harm, 2–019
  inflicting grievous bodily harm, 2–021
  manslaughter, 2–018
  murder, 2–018
  wounding, 2–019
 offences against property, 2–022
 persons under duty to act
  duty arising from status, 2–025
  duty imposed by statute, 2–024
  introduction, 2–023
  spouses, 2–025
  supervening fault, 2–027
  voluntary assumption of duty, 2–026
 secondary parties, 4–011
 statutory duty, 2–024
 supervening fault, 2–027
 voluntary assumption of duty, 2–026
False accounting
 generally, 9–055
Fitness to plead
 generally, 5–001—5–004
Flight and fright cases
 See **Intervening events**
Foetus
 offences against the person, 7–004
"Following orders"
 defence, 5–104—5–105
Food sales
 strict liability, 3–014
Football
 offences against the person, 7–110
Fraud
 See also **Deception**
 abuse of position, by, 9–010
 ancillary offences, 9–013—9–014
 conspiracy to defraud
  'defraud', 6–035—6–036
  mens rea, 6–037
  reform proposals, 6–038
 failing to disclose information, 9–008—9–009
 false representation, by, 9–005—9–007

generally, 9–004
introduction, 9–001—9–003
obtaining services dishonestly, 9–011—9–012
rape, 7–127—7–128
theft, 8–030
Gas
theft, 8–021
Gifts
theft, 8–016—8–017
Going equipped to steal
generally, 9–057
Grievous bodily harm
causing
actus reus, 7–090
basic intent, 7–092
caused grievous bodily harm, 7–092
introduction, 7–081
maliciously wounded, 7–092
mens rea, 7–091—7–093
omission to act, 2–019
ulterior intent, 7–093
inflicting
actus reus, 7–083—7–087
generally, 7–082
introduction, 7–081
mens rea, 7–088—7–089
omission to act, 2–021
racially aggravated offences, 7–097
religiously aggravated offences, 7–097
unlawful, 7–087
omission to act
causing, 2–019
inflicting, 2–021
Gross negligence manslaughter
See **Manslaughter by gross negligence**
Handling
actus reus, 9–038—9–045
arranged to receive, 9–042
arranges retention, etc, 9–043—9–044
assists retention, etc, 9–043—9–044
believing goods to be stolen, 9–047
dishonesty, 9–049
introduction, 9–037
knowing goods to be stolen, 9–047—9–048
mens rea, 9–046—9–050
methods, 9–041—9–045
otherwise than in course of the stealing,
    9–045
proof, 9–050
received, 9–042
retention, removal, disposal or realisation,
    9–043—9–044
stolen goods, 9–038—9–040
summary, 9–051
undertakes retention, etc, 9–043—9–044
"Heroism"
duress, 5–073

"Horseplay"
offences against the person, 7–112
Hospital orders
See **also Diminished responsibility**
generally, 5–022
introduction, 5–003
"Human being"
murder, 7–012
Human remains
offences against the person, 7–005
theft, 8–025
Human rights
generally, 1–005
gross negligence manslaughter, 7–053
Husband and wife
See **Spouses**
"Identification doctrine"
corporate liability, 4–061—4–062
Impossibility
attempts
examples, 6–014—6–018
generally, 6–013
introduction, 6–002
conspiracy, 6–050
Inchoate offences
attempts
actus reus, 6–003—6–007
bibliography, 6–020
general principles, 6–002
impossibility, 6–013—6–018
mens rea, 6–008—6–011
preparatory acts, 6–019
specific intent crimes, 6–012
attempting the impossible
examples, 6–014—6–018
generally, 6–013
introduction, 6–002
bibliography, 6–052
conspiracy
acquittal of co-conspirator, 6–042
active participation, 6–047—6–048
actus reus, 6–031—6–042
agreement, 6–031—6–041
commit criminal offence, to, 6–033
commit murder abroad, to, 6–033
conditional intention, 6–049
corrupt public morals, to, 6–034
course of conduct, 6–045
defraud, to, 6–035—6–038
generally, 6–029—6–030
husband and wife, 6–040
impossibility, 6–050
intention on part of each conspirator,
    6–046
mens rea, 6–043—6–049
object of agreement, 6–033—6–038
outrage public decency, to, 6–034
parties to agreement, 6–039—6–041
rationale, 6–031

recklessness, 6–043—6–044
territorial jurisdiction, 6–051
conspiracy to defraud
'defraud', 6–035—6–036
mens rea, 6–037
reform proposals, 6–038
encouragement or assistance
background, 6–021—6–024
defences, 6–027
elements, 6–025
jurisdiction, 6–028
mental element, 6–026—6–027
strict liability offences, 6–026
territorial application, 6–028
types of offence, 6–024—6–025
Tyrrell principle, 6–028
incitement, 6–021—6–024
introduction, 6–001

Incitement
generally, 6–018—6–024

Indictable offences
generally, 1–006

Indictments
inchoate offences, 6–001

Infanticide
generally, 7–058

Infants
See **Minors**

Inflicting grievous bodily harm
See **Unlawful wounding**

Insanity
automatism, 5–010—5–012
bibliography, 5–026
conclusions, 5–023—5–025
current position, 5–013—5–014
defect of reason, 5–008
disease of the mind, 5–009
EC law, and, 5–023—5–025
generally, 5–006—5–007
introduction, 5–001—5–004
M'naghten Rules, 5–006—5–007
meaning, 5–006—5–007
scope, 5–005

Intangible property
theft, 8–022

Intellectual property
theft, 8–023

Intention
attempts, 6–008
conditional
conspiracy, 6–049
theft, 8–050—8–051
conspiracy
conditional intention, 6–049
each conspirator, by, 6–046
direct intent, 2–055—2–058
generally, 2–055—2–061
introduction, 2–054
oblique intent, 2–057

rape, 7–129
theft
conditional intention, 8–050—8–051
permanently deprive, 8–046—8–049

Intoxication
bibliography, 5–043
diminished responsibility, and, 5–040
drinking, and, 5–041
generally, 5–027
insanity, and, 5–040
involuntary intoxication, 5–035—5–036
non-harmful drugs, 5–037—5–039
reform proposals, 5–042
self-induced automatism, 5–037—5–039
voluntary intoxication, 5–028—5–034

Involuntary conduct
attempts, 6–002
burden of proof, 2–010—2–011
cause, 2–009
evidence, 2–007—2–008
introduction, 2–006
self-induced, 2–012
standard of proof, 2–010—2–011

Involuntary intoxication
generally, 5–035—5–036

Involuntary manslaughter
actus reus, 7–037
constructive manslaughter, 7–038
Cunningham recklessness, 7–037
felony murder rule, 7–038
gross negligence manslaughter
duty of care, 7–051—7–052
ex turpi causa, 7–051—7–052
generally, 7–048—7–050
human rights, 7–053
introduction, 7–037
mens rea, 7–037
other categories, 7–054
recklessness, 7–054
reform proposals, 7–055
unlawful act manslaughter
administration of drugs, 7–042—7–043
aimed at particular victim, 7–046
cause of death, 7–047
dangerousness of act, 7–044—7–045
introduction, 7–038
mens rea, 7–038
unlawfulness of act, 7–039—7–041

Joint enterprise
aiding and abetting, and, 4–027—4–028
example, 4–029—4–032
manslaughter, 4–024—4–026
murder
general principles, 4–015—4–016
proof, 4–017
recklessness, 4–019—4–020
remoteness, 4–018
nature of, 4–014
reform proposals, 4–033

unforeseen consequences
  general principles, 4–022—4–023
  manslaughter, 4–024—4–026
Joint responsibility
  administration of drugs, 2–043—2–045
Jurisdiction
  conspiracy, 6–051
  murder, 7–010
"Keeping"
  theft, 8–018
"Killing"
  murder, 7–015
"Knowingly"
  meaning, 3–009
Knowledge
  actual, 2–074
  constructive, 2–076
  generally, 2–073
  recklessness, and, 2–075
  secondary parties, 4–006—4–007
Land
  See **Theft**
"Laser pointers"
  offences against the person, 7–095
Last act test
  See **Attempts**
"Lawful excuse"
  criminal damage, 10–015—10–018
Licensees
  vicarious liability
    delegation principle, 4–054—4–055
    generally, 4–053
Machinery
  making off without payment, 9–015—9–018
Making unwarranted demands with menaces
  See **Blackmail**
Malice
  mens rea, 2–065
Malicious damage
  generally, 10–001
  "Maliciously"
    meaning, 3–010
Manslaughter
  actus reus
    generally, 7–009—7–012
    human being, 7–012
    introduction, 7–018
    involuntary manslaughter, 7–037
    jurisdiction, 7–010
    omission to act, 2–018
    reasonable creature in rerum natura,
      7–012
    unlawful killing, 7–011
  companies
    generally, 4–064—4–065
    reforms, 4–066
  constructive manslaughter, 7–038
  corporate liability
    generally, 4–066—4–067

  penalties, 4–068
diminished responsibility, 7–018
gross negligence manslaughter
  duty of care, 7–051—7–052
  ex turpi causa, 7–051—7–052
  generally, 7–048—7–050
  human rights, 7–053
introduction, 7–018
involuntary manslaughter
  actus reus, 7–037
  constructive manslaughter, 7–038—7–047
  Cunningham recklessness, 7–037
  felony murder rule, 7–038
  gross negligence manslaughter,
    7–048—7–053
  introduction, 7–037
  mens rea, 7–037
  other categories, 7–054
  reform proposals, 7–055
  unlawful act manslaughter, 7–038—7–047
joint enterprise, 4–024—4–026
necessity, 5–063—5–064
omissions, 2–018
provocation
  bibliography, 7–036
  cooling-off, 7–021—7–022
  introduction, 7–018
  nature, 7–019—7–023
  objective question, 7–026—7–027
  reform proposals, 7–035
  role of judge and jury, 7–023
  self-control, 7–027—7–034
  self-induced, 7–024
  test, 7–025—7–035
recklessness manslaughter, 7–054
reform proposals
  involuntary manslaughter, 7–055
  provocation, 7–035
suicide pact, 7–018
unlawful act manslaughter
  administration of drugs, 7–042—7–043
  aimed at particular victim, 7–046
  cause of death, 7–047
  dangerousness of act, 7–044—7–045
  introduction, 7–038
  mens rea, 7–038
  unlawfulness of act, 7–039—7–041
voluntary manslaughter, 7–018
Manslaughter by gross negligence
  duty of care, 7–051—7–052
  ex turpi causa, 7–051—7–052
  generally, 7–048—7–050
  human rights, 7–053
M'naghten rules
  actus reus, 2–009
  insanity, 5–006—5–007
Medical treatment
  intervening events, 2–046—2–048
  necessity, 5–065—5–067

offences against the person, 7–111
omissions, 2–028—2–030
Mens rea
  actual bodily harm, 7–080
  actual knowledge, 2–074
  assault, 7–074—7–075
  attempts, 6–008—6–011
  battery, 7–074—7–075
  constructive knowledge, 2–076
  bibliography, 2–086
  blameworthiness, 2–052
  Caldwell recklessness, 2–067—2–068
  coincidence of actus reus and mens rea,
    2–077—2–079
  conspiracy
    active participation, 6–047—6–048
    conditional intention, 6–049
    course of conduct, 6–045
    intention on part of each conspirator,
      6–046
    recklessness, 6–043—6–044
  constructive knowledge, 2–076
  criminal damage, 10–007
  culpability, 2–052
  Cunningham recklessness, 2–066
  direct intent, 2–055—2–058
  elements
    intention, 2–055—2–061
    introduction, 2–054
    knowledge, 2–073—2–076
    negligence, 2–063—2–064
    recklessness, 2–065—2–072
  encouragement or assistance
    background, 6–021—6–024
    defences, 6–027
    elements, 6–025
    jurisdiction, 6–028
    mental element, 6–026—6–027
    strict liability offences, 6–026
    territorial application, 6–028
    types of offence, 6–024—6–025
    Tyrrell principle, 6–028
  generally, 2–001—2–003
  handling, 9–046—9–050
  inchoate offences
    attempts, 6–008—6–011
    conspiracy, 6–043—6–049
    encouragement or assistance,
      6–021—6–028
    incitement, 6–021—6–024
  incitement, 6–021—6–024
  intention
    direct intent, 2–055—2–058
    generally, 2–055—2–061
    introduction, 2–054
    oblique intent, 2–057
  introduction, 2–052—2–053
  involuntary manslaughter, 7–037
  knowledge

    actual, 2–074
    constructive, 2–076
    generally, 2–073
    recklessness, and, 2–075
  malice, 2–065
  mistake
    generally, 2–082—2–083
    lawfulness, and, 2–084—2–085
    overview, 2–054
  motive, 2–052
  murder
    generally, 7–014
    introduction, 7–013
    killing of a human being, 7–015
    other external elements, 7–016
    overview, 2–053
  negligence, 2–063—2–064
  oblique intent, 2–057
  rape, 7–129—7–131
  recklessness
    Caldwell, 2–067—2–068
    Cunningham, 2–066
    generally, 2–065
    knowledge, and, 2–075
    reasonableness test, 2–069—2–072
  secondary parties, 4–005
  strict liability, and, 3–001
  theft
    dishonesty, 8–039—8–045
    intention to permanently deprive,
      8–046—8–049
    introduction, 8–038
  transferred malice, 2–080—2–081
  unlawful act manslaughter, 7–038
  unlawful wounding, 7–088—7–089
  wounding with intent, 7–091—7–093
Minors
  children of 10 years or more, 5–098—5–099
  children under 10 years, 5–097
  conspiracy, 6–041
  doli incapax, 5–098
Mistake
  mens rea
    generally, 2–082—2–083
    lawfulness, and, 2–084—2–085
    overview, 2–054
  self-defence, 5–053
  theft, 8–035—8–036
Mistake of fact
  self-defence, 5–053
Mode of trial
  attempts, 6–002
Motive
  mens rea, 2–052
Murder
  actus reus
    generally, 7–009—7–012
    human being, 7–012
    jurisdiction, 7–010

omission to act, 2–018
reasonable creature in rerum natura,
    7–012
unlawful killing, 7–011
attempts, 5–080
duress
    comparison with necessity, 5–076
    conclusions, 5–078—5–079
    executive discretion, 5–075
    heroism, 5–073
    introduction, 5–072
    Law Commission report, 5–077
    sanctity of human life, 5–073
    terrorism, 5–074
human being, 7–012
introduction, 7–007
joint enterprise
    general principles, 4–015—4–016
    proof, 4–017
    recklessness, 4–019—4–020
    remoteness, 4–018
jurisdiction, 7–010
killing of a human being, 7–015
mens rea
    generally, 7–014
    introduction, 7–013
    killing of a human being, 7–015
    other external elements, 7–016
    overview, 2–053
necessity, 5–063—5–064
    omissions to act, 2–018
    penalties, 7–008
    reasonable creature in rerum natura,
        7–012
    reform proposals, 7–017
    self-defence, 5–056—5–058
    sentencing, 7–008
    unlawful killing, 7–011
Necessity
    bibliography, 5–070
    duress of circumstances, 5–093—5–095
    general defence, as, 5–069
    introduction, 5–062
    killing of another, 5–063—5–064
    medical treatment, 5–065—5–067
    statutory restrictions, 5–068
Negligence
    conspiracy, 6–043—6–044
    mens rea, 2–063—2–064
Not guilty pleas
    actus reus, 2–001
Novus actus interveniens
    See Intervening events
    Oblique intent
    See Mens rea
Obtaining services dishonestly
    generally, 9–011—9–012
Offences against property
    abstraction of electricity, 9–054

actus reus
    blackmail, 9–033—9–036
    burglary, 9–024—9–028
    criminal damage, 10–003—10–006
    handling, 9–038—9–040
    omission to act, 2–022
    robbery, 9–020
    theft, 8–004—8–037
advertising rewards, 9–056
aggravated burglary, 9–030—9–031
aggravated criminal damage,
    10–008—10–010
aggravated trespass, 9–023
arson, 10–012
bibliography, 9–059
blackmail
    accompanied by menaces, 9–034
    actus reus, 9–033—9–036
    demand, 9–033
    intent to cause loss to another, 9–035
    introduction, 9–032
    unwarranted demand, 9–036
    view to gain for maker or another, 9–035
burglary
    actus reus, 9–024—9–028
    aggravated offence, 9–030—9–031
    aggravated trespass, 9–023
    building, 9–027
    dwelling, 9–023
    entry, 9–024—9–025
    generally, 9–023
    mens rea, 9–029
    part of a building, 9–028
    trespasser, 9–026
compensation, 9–058
criminal damage
    actus reus, 10–003—10–006
    aggravated offence, 10–008—10–010
    arson, 10–012
    basic offence, 10–002
    bibliography, 10–019
    damage, 10–004
    defence, 10–015—10–018
    destruction, 10–004
    introduction, 10–001
    lawful excuse, 10–015—10–018
    mens rea, 10–007
    possession with intent, 10–014
    property belonging to another, 10–005
    threats to commit, 10–001
    without lawful excuse, 10–006
false accounting, 9–055
fraud
    abuse of position, by, 9–010
    ancillary offences, 9–013—9–014
    failing to disclose information,
        9–008—9–009
    false representation, by, 9–005—9–007
    generally, 9–004

introduction, 9–001—9–003
going equipped to steal, 9–057
handling
    actus reus, 9–038—9–045
    arranged to receive, 9–042
    arranges retention, etc, 9–043—9–044
    assists retention, etc, 9–043—9–044
    believing goods to be stolen, 9–047
    dishonesty, 9–049
    introduction, 9–037
    knowing goods to be stolen, 9–047—9–048
    mens rea, 9–046—9–050
    methods, 9–041—9–045
    otherwise than in course of the stealing,
      9–045
    proof, 9–050
    received, 9–042
    retention, removal, disposal or realisation,
      9–043—9–044
    stolen goods, 9–038—9–040
    summary, 9–051
    undertakes retention, etc, 9–043—9–044
legislative framework, 8–001—8–002
making off without payment, 9–015—9–018
making unwarranted demands with menaces
    accompanied by menaces, 9–034
    demand, 9–033
    intent to cause loss to another, 9–035
    introduction, 9–032
    unwarranted demand, 9–036
    view to gain for maker or another, 9–035
malicious damage, 10–001
obtaining services dishonestly, 9–011—9–012
omission to act, 2–022
ownership, 8–001
"possession", 8–001
possession with intent to damage, 10–014
procuring execution of valuable security by
    deception, 9–055
removing articles from public place, 9–053
restitution, 9–058
robbery
    actus reus, 9–020
    force, 9–020—9–021
    generally, 9–020—9–021
    summary, 9–022
stealing, 8–001
taking motor vehicles without consent, 9–053
temporary deprivation, 9–053
theft
    And see **Theft**
    actus reus, 8–004—8–037
    appropriates, 8–004—8–019
    belonging to another, 8–028—8–037
    bibliography, 8–052
    conditional intention, 8–050—8–051
    definition, 8–003
    dishonesty, 8–039—8–045

    intention to permanently deprive,
      8–046—8–049
    introduction, 8–003
    legislative framework, 8–001—8–002
    mens rea, 8–038—8–049
    property, 8–020—8–027
threatening to commit criminal damage,
    10–013
TWOCing, 9–053
Offences against public morals
conspiracy, 6–034
Offences against the person
actual bodily harm
    actus reus, 7–076
    bodily harm, 7–078—7–079
    introduction, 7–076
    mens rea, 7–080
    occasioning actual bodily harm, 7–077
    racially aggravated offences, 7–097
    religiously aggravated offences, 7–097
actus reus
    assault, 7–063—7–066
    battery, 7–069—7–073
    manslaughter, 7–009—7–012
    murder, 7–009—7–012
    omission to act, 2–017—2–021
    unlawful wounding, 7–083—7–087
    voluntary manslaughter, 7–018
    wounding with intent, 7–090
alternative verdicts, 7–094
assault
    actual bodily harm, 7–076—7–080
    actus reus, 7–063—7–066
    apprehension of application of immediate
      force, 7–067
    hostility, 7–075
    introduction, 7–062
    mens rea, 7–074—7–075
    racially aggravated offences, 7–097
    religiously aggravated offences, 7–097
    unlawful force, 7–068
battery
    actus reus, 7–069—7–073
    consent, 7–071
    hostility, 7–075
    introduction, 7–062
    mens rea, 7–074—7–075
    omissions, 7–070
    racially aggravated offences, 7–097
    religiously aggravated offences, 7–097
    unlawful force, 7–072—7–073
bibliography, 7–117
causing death by dangerous driving, 7–059
children, 7–002
common assault
    assault, 7–063—7–068
    battery, 7–069—7–075
    introduction, 7–062
    racially aggravated offences, 7–097

religiously aggravated offences, 7–097
conjoined twins, 7–004
consent
    boxing, 7–109
    exceptions to general rule, 7–107—7–112
    football, 7–110
    horseplay, 7–112
    introduction, 7–098
    limits of defence, 7–099—7–106
    meaning, 7–113
    medical treatment, 7–111
    reform proposals, 7–116
    rough horseplay, 7–112
    rugby, 7–110
    sporting activities, 7–108—7–110
corpses, 7–005
doli incapax, 7–002
fatal offences
    bibliography, 7–060
    causing death by dangerous driving, 7–059
    infanticide, 7–058
    introduction, 7–006
    manslaughter, 7–018—7–055
    murder, 7–007—7–016
    suicide, 7–057
foetus, 7–004
gross negligence manslaughter
    duty of care, 7–051—7–052
    ex turpi causa, 7–051—7–052
    generally, 7–048—7–050
    human rights, 7–053
hierarchy, 7–096
homicide
    bibliography, 7–060
    causing death by dangerous driving, 7–059
    infanticide, 7–058
    introduction, 7–006
    manslaughter, 7–018—7–055
    murder, 7–007—7–016
    suicide, 7–057
horseplay, 7–112
infanticide, 7–058
introduction, 7–001
involuntary manslaughter
    actus reus, 7–037
    constructive manslaughter, 7–038—7–047
    Cunningham recklessness, 7–037
    felony murder rule, 7–038
    gross negligence manslaughter,
        7–048—7–053
    introduction, 7–037
    mens rea, 7–037
    other categories, 7–054
    reform proposals, 7–055
    unlawful act manslaughter, 7–038—7–047
laser pointers, 7–095
manslaughter
    actus reus, 7–009—7–012
    categories, 7–018

    diminished responsibility, 7–018
    generally, 7–018
    gross negligence manslaughter,
        7–048—7–053
    human being, 7–012
    introduction, 7–007
    involuntary manslaughter, 7–037—7–055
    jurisdiction, 7–010
    mens rea, 7–013
    omission to act, 2–018
    penalties, 7–008
    provocation, 7–019—7–036
    reasonable creature in rerum natura,
        7–012
    sentencing, 7–008
    suicide pact, 7–018
    unlawful act manslaughter, 7–038—7–047
    unlawful killing, 7–011
    voluntary manslaughter, 7–018
medical treatment, 7–111
murder
    actus reus, 7–009—7–012
    human being, 7–012
    introduction, 7–007
    jurisdiction, 7–010
    killing of a human being, 7–015
    mens rea, 7–013—7–016
    omission to act, 2–018
    penalties, 7–008
    reasonable creature in rerum natura,
        7–012
    reform proposals, 7–017
    sentencing, 7–008
    unlawful killing, 7–011
non-fatal offences
    actual bodily harm, 7–076—7–080
    common assault, 7–062—7–075
    general framework, 7–061
    reform proposals, 7–114—7–115
    wounding, 7–081—7–093
omission to act
    assault, 2–017
    battery, 2–017
    causing grievous bodily harm, 2–019
    inflicting grievous bodily harm, 2–021
    manslaughter, 2–018
    murder, 2–018
    wounding, 2–019
parties to offence, 7–002
provocation
    bibliography, 7–036
    cooling-off, 7–021—7–022
    introduction, 7–018
    nature, 7–019—7–023
    objective question, 7–026—7–027
    reform proposals, 7–035
    role of judge and jury, 7–023
    self-control, 7–027—7–034
    self-induced, 7–024

test, 7–025—7–035
racially aggravated offences, 7–097
reform proposals
    consent, 7–116
    involuntary manslaughter, 7–055
    murder, 7–017
    non-fatal offences, 7–114—7–115
    voluntary manslaughter, 7–035
religiously aggravated offences, 7–097
self-defence, 7–006
sexual offences
    assault by penetration, 7–132
    bibliography, 7–137
    causing a person to engage in sexual
        activity without consent, 7–134
    child sex offences, 7–136
    children, against, 7–135
    introduction, 7–118
    rape, 7–119—7–131
    sexual assault, 7–133
suicide, 7–057
types, 7–001
unborn child, 7–004
unlawful act manslaughter
    administration of drugs, 7–042—7–043
    aimed at particular victim, 7–046
    cause of death, 7–047
    dangerousness of act, 7–044—7–045
    introduction, 7–038
    mens rea, 7–038
    unlawfulness of act, 7–039—7–041
unlawful homicide, 7–006
unlawful wounding
    actus reus, 7–083—7–087
    generally, 7–082
    introduction, 7–081
    mens rea, 7–088—7–089
    unlawful, 7–087
victims
    corpses, 7–005
    introduction, 7–003
    unborn child, 7–004
voluntary manslaughter
    actus reus, 7–018
    bibliography, 7–036
    cooling-off, 7–021—7–022
    diminished responsibility, 7–018
    introduction, 7–018
    mens rea, 7–018
    nature of provocation, 7–019—7–023
    objective question, 7–026—7–027
    reform proposals, 7–035
    role of judge and jury, 7–023
    self-control, 7–027—7–034
    self-induced provocation, 7–024
    suicide pact, 7–018
    test for provocation, 7–025—7–035
wounding
    introduction, 7–081

section 18, under, 7–090—7–093
section 20, under, 7–082—7–089
unlawful wounding, 7–082—7–089
wounding with intent, 7–090—7–093
wounding with intent
    actus reus, 7–090
    basic intent, 7–092
    caused grievous bodily harm, 7–092
    introduction, 7–081
    maliciously wounded, 7–092
    mens rea, 7–091—7–093
    ulterior intent, 7–093
Offenders
accessories
    And see **Secondary parties**
    generally, 4–001
actus reus
    commission of actus reus, 4–035
    introduction, 4–034
    joint trial of principal and secondary
        party, 4–038—4–040
    no principal offender, 4–036
    previous acquittal of principal offender,
        4–037
bibliography, 4–048
classification, 4–001
companies
    And see **Corporate liability**
    generally, 4–059—4–069
employers
    And see **Vicarious liability**
    generally, 4–050—4–057
introduction, 4–001—4–002
joint enterprise
    distinguished from accessoryship,
        4–027—4–028
    example, 4–029—4–032
    murder, and, 4–015—4–020
    nature of, 4–014
    reform proposals, 4–033
    unforeseen consequences, 4–022—4–026
perpetrators, 4–003—4–004
principals, 4–003—4–004
secondary parties
    actus reus, 4–005
    aiding and abeting, 4–008—4–013
    assistance after commission of crime,
        4–047
    background, 4–001
    counselling and procuring, 4–008—4–013
    introduction, 4–005
    knowledge of type of crime, 4–006—4–007
    mens rea, 4–005
    reform proposals, 4–046
    repentance before commission of crime,
        4–042—4–045
victims, 4–041

Omissions
conclusion, 2–031
generally, 2–015—2–016
medical treatment, 2–028—2–030
offences against the person
    assault, 2–017
    battery, 2–017
    causing grievous bodily harm, 2–019
    inflicting grievous bodily harm, 2–021
    manslaughter, 2–018
    murder, 2–018
    wounding, 2–019
offences against property, 2–022
person who is under duty to act
    duty arising from status, 2–025
    duty imposed by statute, 2–024
    introduction, 2–023
    spouses, 2–025
    supervening fault, 2–027
    voluntary assumption of duty, 2–026
    secondary parties, 4–011
statutory duty, 2–024
supervening fault, 2–027
voluntary assumption of duty, 2–026
Outraging public decency
conspiracy, 6–034
strict liability, 3–003
Ownership
generally, 8–001
Parliamentary sovereignty
generally, 1–005
"Participation"
conspiracy, 6–047—6–048
Parties
accessories
    And see **Secondary parties**
    generally, 4–001
actus reus
    commission of actus reus, 4–035
    introduction, 4–034
    joint trial of principal and secondary
        party, 4–038—4–040
    no principal offender, 4–036
    previous acquittal of principal offender,
        4–037
bibliography, 4–048
classification, 4–001
companies
    And see **Corporate liability**
    generally, 4–059—4–069
conspiracy
    husband and wife, 6–040
    introduction, 6–039
    one of parties is exempt, 6–041
employers
    And see **Vicarious liability**
    generally, 4–050—4–057
introduction, 4–001—4–002
joint enterprise

distinguished from accessoryship,
    4–027—4–028
example, 4–029—4–032
murder, and, 4–015—4–020
nature of, 4–014
reform proposals, 4–033
unforeseen consequences, 4–022—4–026
offences against the person, 7–002
perpetrators, 4–003—4–004
principal offenders, 4–003—4–004
secondary parties
    actus reus, 4–005
    aiding and abetting, 4–008—4–013
    assistance after commission of crime,
        4–047
    background, 4–001
    counselling and procuring, 4–008—4–013
    introduction, 4–005
    knowledge of type of crime, 4–006—4–007
    mens rea, 4–005
    reform proposals, 4–046
    repentance before commission of crime,
        4–042—4–045
    victims, 4–041
Penalties
See also **Sentencing**
corporate liability, 4–064—4–065
corporate manslaughter, 4–068
murder, 7–008
strict liability, 3–020
Penetration
assault, 7–132
rape, 7–120
"Permitting"
meaning, 3–005
Perpetrators
See **Principal offenders**
Plants
theft, 8–026
"Possess"
meaning, 3–008
Possession
offences against property, 8–001
strict liability, 3–007
Possession with intent to damage
criminal damage, 10–014
Preparatory acts
See **Attempts**
Presence
secondary parties, 4–010
Prevention of crime
See **Crime prevention**
Principal offenders
generally, 4–003—4–004
Proceeds of sale
theft, 8–033
Procuring
generally, 4–008
mental element, 4–012—4–013

omission, 4–011
presence, 4–010
relevant conduct, 4–009—4–011
Procuring execution of valuable security by
deception
generally, 9–055
Proof
burden of proof, 1–010
excessive force, 5–059
handling, 9–050
introduction, 1–009
standard of proof, 1–011
Property
And see **Theft**
choses in action, 8–022
criminal damage, 10–005
deceased's property, 8–024
electricity, 8–021
gas, 8–021
generally, 8–020—8–024
human remains, 8–025
intangible property, 8–022
intellectual property, 8–023
land, 8–025
plants, 8–026
water, 8–021
wild creatures, 8–027
wild plants, 8–026
Provocation
And see **Manslaughter**
bibliography, 7–036
cooling-off, 7–021—7–022
introduction, 7–018
nature, 7–019—7–023
objective question, 7–026—7–027
reform proposals, 7–035
role of judge and jury, 7–023
self-control, 7–027—7–034
self-induced, 7–024
test, 7–025—7–035
Public nuisance
strict liability, 3–003
Public safety
strict liability, 3–018—3–019
Punishment
purpose of criminal law, 1–004
Purchasers without notice
theft, 8–019
Quasi-crimes
See **Regulatory offences**
Racially aggravated offences
offences against the person, 7–097
Rape
actus reus, 7–120—7–128
child under 13, of, 7–135
fraud, 7–127—7–128
generally, 7–119
intention, 7–129

lack of consent, 7–121—7–128
mens rea, 7–129—7–131
no reasonable belief that victim is
consenting, 7–130—7–131
penetration, 7–120
"Reasonable creature in rerum natura"
murder, 7–012
Reasonable force
assault, 7–068
battery, 7–072—7–073
generally, 5–052
mistake of fact, 5–053
murder, 5–056—5–058
objective approach, 5–053—5–055
proof, 5–059
Rebuttable presumptions
strict liability, 3–003
Recklessness
Caldwell, 2–067—2–068
conspiracy, 6–043—6–044
Cunningham
generally, 2–066
secondary parties, 4–007
generally, 2–065
involuntary manslaughter, 7–054
knowledge, 2–075
involuntary manslaughter, 7–054
joint enterprise, 4–019—4–020
reasonableness test, 2–069—2–072
secondary parties, 4–007
Regulatory offences
dangerous dogs, 3–018—3–019
drugs, 3–016
environmental law, 3–014—3–015
generally, 3–011—3–013
public safety, 3–018—3–019
road traffic, 3–017
sale of food and drink, 3–014
Religiously aggravated offences
offences against the person, 7–097
Remoteness
joint enterprise, 4–018
Removing articles from public place
generally, 9–053
"Repentance"
secondary parties, 4–042—4–045
Restitution
generally, 9–058
Road traffic offences
strict liability, 3–017
Robbery
actus reus, 9–020
force, 9–020—9–021
generally, 9–020—9–021
summary, 9–022
Rugby
offences against the person, 7–110

Schizophrenia
  insanity, 5–001
Secondary parties
  actus reus
    commission of, 4–035
    introduction, 4–034
    joint trial of principal and secondary
        party, 4–038—4–040
    no principal offender, 4–036
    previous acquittal of principal offender,
        4–037
  aiding and abetting
    generally, 4–008
    mental element, 4–012—4–013
    omission, 4–011
    presence, 4–010
    relevant conduct, 4–009 —4–011
  assistance after commission of crime, 4–047
  background, 4–001
  counselling and procuring
    generally, 4–008
    mental element, 4–012—4–013
    omission, 4–011
    presence, 4–010
    relevant conduct, 4–009—4–011
  Cunningham recklessness, 4–007
  failure to act, 4–011
  introduction, 4–005
  knowledge of type of crime, 4–006—4–007
  mens rea, 4–005
  'no-questions-asked' case, 4–006
  omissions, 4–011
  presence, 4–010
  recklessness, 4–007
  reform proposals, 4–046
  repentance before commission of crime,
    4–042—4–045
Secret profits
  theft, 8–037
Self-control
  See **Provocation**
Self-defence
  bibliography, 5–061
  defence of others
    duty to retreat, 5–048
    generally, 5–047
    imminence of violence, 5–049—5–050
  defence of property, 5–051
  excessive force
    generally, 5–052
    mistake of fact, 5–053
    murder, 5–056—5–058
    objective approach, 5–053—5–055
    proof, 5–059
  introduction, 5–044
  manslaughter, 7–006
  murder, 7–006
  prevention of crime, 5–046
  summary, 5–060

  use of force, 5–045
Self-induced automatism
  See **Automatism**
Sentencing
  attempts, 6–002
  murder, 7–008
  theft, 8–003
Sexual activity with children
  generally, 7–136
Sexual assault
  child under 13, on, 7–135
  generally, 7–133
Sexual offences
  assault by penetration
    child under 13, on, 7–135
    generally, 7–132
  bibliography, 7–137
  causing children to engage in sexual activity,
    7–136
  causing children to watch sexual acts, 7–136
  causing sexual activity without consent
    child under 13, on, 7–135
    generally, 7–134
  child sex offences, 7–136
  child under 13, against, 7–135
  engaging in sexual activity in presence of
    children, 7–136
  introduction, 7–118
  rape
    actus reus, 7–120—7–128
    child under 13, on, 7–135
    fraud, 7–127—7–128
    generally, 7–119
    intention, 7–129
    lack of consent, 7–121—7–128
    mens rea, 7–129—7–131
    no reasonable belief that victim is
        consenting, 7–130—7–131
    penetration, 7–120
  reforms, 7–118
  sexual activity with children, 7–136
  sexual assault
    child under 13, on, 7–135
    generally, 7–133
Shareholders
  corporate liability, 4–063
Specific intent
  attempts, 6–012
  intoxication, 5–028—5–034
Sports
  offences against the person, 7–108—7–110
Spouses
  conspiracy, 6–040
Standard of proof
  automatism, 2–010—2–011
  generally, 1–011
"State of affairs offences"
  actus reus, 2–013—2–014

"Status offences"
actus reus, 2–013—2–014
strict liability, 3–001
Statutes
generally, 1–005
Statutory duties
omissions, 2–024
Statutory interpretation
strict liability, 3–003
Stealing
See **Theft**
Strict liability
background, 3–002
bibliography, 3–029
blasphemous libel, 3–003
conspiracy, 6–043—6–044
criminal libel, 3–003
defences, 3–026
developments in law
B (A Minor) v DPP decision, 3–022
Barnfather and other decisions,
3–024—3–025
introduction, 3–021
R v K decision, 3–023
identification of crimes
allowing, 3–005
cause, 3–006
generally, 3–004
introduction, 3–003
knowingly, 3–009
maliciously, 3–010
permitting, 3–005
possess, 3–008
possession, 3–007
wilfully, 3–010
introduction, 3–001
modern principles
B (A Minor) v DPP decision, 3–022
Barnfather and other decisions,
3–024—3–025
introduction, 3–021
R v K decision, 3–023
nature of, 3–003
omissions, and, 2–024
outraging public decency, 3–003
penalties, 3–020
public nuisance, 3–003
purpose, 3–027—3–028
quasi crimes
dangerous dogs, 3–018—3–019
drugs, 3–016
environment laws, 3–014—3–015
generally, 3–011—3–013
public safety, 3–018—3–019
road traffic, 3–017
sale of food and drink, 3–014
rebuttable presumptions, 3–003
status offences, 3–001
statutory interpretation, and, 3–003

vicarious liability, and, 4–052
"Substantial cause"
causation, 2–034
Suicide
generally, 7–057
Summary offences
generally, 1–006
"Superior orders"
defence, 5–104—5–105
Supervening events
See **Intervening events**
Taking vehicles without consent
generally, 9–053
Telegraphic transfers
See **Electronic funds transfer**
Territorial jurisdiction
See **Jurisdiction**
Terrorism
duress, 5–074
Theft
abandonment, 8–031
actus reus
appropriates, 8–004—8–019
belonging to another, 8–028—8–037
property, 8–020—8–027
appropriates
attempted theft, 8–011
bona fide purchaser, 8–019
case precedents, 8–010
civil law, and, 8–012
company as victim, 8–014
dealings, 8–018
deception, 8–011
Gallasso decision, 8–013
generally, 8–004—8–008
gifts, 8–016—8–017
Gomez decision, 8–009
jurisdictional issues, 8–015
keeping, 8–018
omissions, 8–018
attempted theft, 8–011
belonging to another
abandonment, 8–031
basic provision, 8–029—8–031
bribes, 8–037
constructive trusts, 8–037
equitable interests, 8–031
extended meaning, 8–032—8–037
fraud, 8–030
introduction, 8–028
mistake, 8–035—8–036
proceeds of dealings, 8–033
secret profits, 8–037
bibliography, 8–052
bona fide purchaser, 8–019
bribes, 8–037
choses in action, 8–022
company as victim, 8–014

conditional intention, 8–050—8–051
constructive trusts, 8–037
dealings, 8–018
deceased's property, 8–024
definition, 8–003
dishonesty
    belief in consent, 8–041
    belief in legal right, 8–040
    belief that owner cannot be traced, 8–042
    meaning, 8–039
    other cases, 8–043—8–045
electricity, 8–021
equitable interests, 8–031
fraud, 8–030
gas, 8–021
gifts, 8–016—8–017
human remains, 8–025
intangible property, 8–022
intellectual property, 8–023
intention
    conditional intention, 8–050—8–051
    permanently deprive, 8–046—8–049
introduction, 8–003
keeping, 8–018
land, 8–025
legislative framework, 8–001—8–002
mens rea
    dishonesty, 8–039—8–045
    intention to permanently deprive,
        8–046—8–049
    introduction, 8–038
mistake, 8–035—8–036
plants, 8–026
proceeds of dealings, 8–033
property
    choses in action, 8–022
    deceased's property, 8–024
    electricity, 8–021
    gas, 8–021
    generally, 8–020—8–024
    human remains, 8–025
    intangible property, 8–022
    intellectual property, 8–023
    land, 8–025
    plants, 8–026
    water, 8–021
    wild creatures, 8–027
    wild plants, 8–026
secret profits, 8–037
sentencing, 8–003
water, 8–021
wild creatures, 8–027
wild plants, 8–026
Thin skull cases
    See **Egg shell skull**
Third party acts
    intervening events, 2–040—2–042

Threatening to commit criminal damage
    generally, 10–013
Threats
    generally, 5–082
    immediacy, 5–085—5–086
    recipient, 5–083
    specificity, 5–084
Transferred malice
    mens rea, 2–080—2–081
TWOC
    See **Taking vehicles without consent**
Unborn children
    offences against the person, 7–004
Unfitness to plead
    See **Fitness to plead**
Unforeseen consequences
    See **Joint enterprise**
Unlawful act manslaughter
    administration of drugs, 7–042—7–043
    aimed at particular victim, 7–046
    cause of death, 7–047
    dangerousness of act, 7–044—7–045
    introduction, 7–038
    mens rea, 7–038
    unlawfulness of act, 7–039—7–041
Unlawful force
    See **Reasonable force**
Unlawful killing
    murder, 7–011
Unlawful wounding
    actus reus, 7–083—7–087
    generally, 7–082
    introduction, 7–081
    mens rea, 7–088—7–089
    omission to act, 2–021
    racially aggravated offences, 7–097
    religiously aggravated offences, 7–097
    unlawful, 7–087
Use of force
    assault, 7–068
    battery, 7–072—7–073
    excessive force
        assault, 7–068
        battery, 7–072—7–073
        generally, 5–052
        mistake of fact, 5–053
        murder, 5–056—5–058
        objective approach, 5–053—5–055
        proof, 5–059
    robbery, 9–020—9–021
    self-defence, 5–045
Vicarious liability
    companies, 4–060
    conclusion, 4–058
    employers, 4–050
    express liability, 4–051
    implied liability, 4–052
    inapplicability, 4–056
    introduction, 4–050

licensee cases
  delegation principle, 4–054—4–055
  generally, 4–053
rationale, 4–050
statutory liability, 4–051
strict liability, 4–052
summary, 4–057

Victims
offences against the person
  corpses, 7–005
  introduction, 7–003
  unborn child, 7–004
  parties, as, 4–041

"Voluntary assumption of duty"
omissions, 2–026

Voluntary conduct
See **Conduct**

Voluntary intoxication
generally, 5–028—5–034

Voluntary manslaughter
See **Manslaughter**

Water
theft, 8–021

Wildlife
theft, 8–027

Wild plants
See **Theft**

"Wilfully"
meaning, 3–010

Wounding
omission to act
  s.18 offence, 2–019
  s 20 offence, 2–021
s.18 offence
  actus reus, 7–090
  basic intent, 7–092
  caused grievous bodily harm, 7–092
  introduction, 7–081
  maliciously wounded, 7–092
  mens rea, 7–091—7–093
  ulterior intent, 7–093
s.20 offence
  actus reus, 7–083—7–087
  generally, 7–082
  introduction, 7–081
  mens rea, 7–088—7–089
  racially aggravated offences, 7–097
  religiously aggravated offences, 7–097
  unlawful, 7–087

Wounding with intent
actus reus, 7–090
basic intent, 7–092
caused grievous bodily harm, 7–092
introduction, 7–081
maliciously wounded, 7–092
mens rea, 7–091—7–093
omission to act, 2–019
ulterior intent, 7–093